THE OXFORD

SPANISH
DICTIONARY

Also available

THE OXFORD FRENCH DICTIONARY
THE OXFORD GERMAN DICTIONARY
THE OXFORD ITALIAN DICTIONARY
THE OXFORD RUSSIAN DICTIONARY

THE OXFORD SPANISH DICTIONARY

Spanish–English
English–Spanish

Español–Inglés
Inglés–Español

Christine Lea

BERKLEY BOOKS, NEW YORK

THE OXFORD SPANISH DICTIONARY

A Berkley Book / published in mass market paperback by arrangement with Oxford University Press, Inc.

PRINTING HISTORY
Oxford University Press edition published 1994
Berkley edition / August 1997

Copyright © 1993, 1997 by Oxford University Press.
First published in 1993 as *The Oxford Spanish Minidictionary*.
First published in 1994 as *The Oxford Paperback Spanish Dictionary*.
Oxford is a registered trademark of Oxford University Press.
All rights reserved. No part of this publication may be reproduced,
stored in a retrieval system, or transmitted, in any form or by any means,
electronic, mechanical, photocopying, recording, or otherwise,
without the prior permission of Oxford University Press.
For information, contact: Oxford University Press, 198 Madison Avenue,
New York, New York 10016.

The Putnam Berkley World Wide Web site address is
http://www.berkley.com

ISBN: 0-425-16009-2

BERKLEY®
Berkley Books are published by The Berkley Publishing Group,
200 Madison Avenue, New York, New York 10016.
BERKLEY and the "B" design
are trademarks belonging to Berkley Publishing Corporation.

PRINTED IN THE UNITED STATES OF AMERICA

10 9 8 7 6

Contents · Índice

Preface

This dictionary has been written with speakers of both English and Spanish in mind and contains the most useful words and expressions of the English and Spanish languages of today. Wide coverage of culinary and automotive terms has been included to help the tourist.

Common abbreviations, names of countries, and other useful geographical names are included.

English pronunciation is given by means of the International Phonetic Alphabet. It is shown for all headwords and for those derived words whose pronunciation is not easily deduced from that of a headword. The rules for pronunciation of Spanish are given on page x.

I should like to thank particularly Mary-Carmen Beaven, whose comments have been invaluable. I would also like to acknowledge the help given me unwittingly by Dr M. Janes and Mrs J. Andrews, whose French and Italian Minidictionaries have served as models for the present work.

C.A.L.

Prefacio

Este diccionario de Oxford se escribió tanto para los hablantes de español como para los hablantes de inglés y contiene las palabras y frases más corrientes de ambas lenguas de hoy. Se incluyen muchos términos culinarios y de automovilismo que pueden servir al turista.

Las abreviaturas más corrientes, los nombres de países, y otros términos geográficos figuran en este diccionario.

La pronunciación inglesa sigue el Alfabeto Fonético Internacional. Se incluye para cada palabra clave y todas las derivadas cuya pronunciación no es fácil de deducir a partir de la palabra clave. Las reglas de la pronunciación española se encuentran en la página x.

Quisiera agradecer la ayuda de Mary-Carmen Beaven, cuyas observaciones me han sido muy valiosas. También quiero expresar mi agradecimiento al Dr. M. Janes y a la Sra. J. Andrews, cuyos minidiccionarios de francés y de italiano me han servido de modelo para el presente.

C.A.L.

Introduction

The swung dash (~) is used to replace a headword or that part of a headword preceding the vertical bar (|). In both English and Spanish only irregular plurals are given. Normally Spanish nouns and adjectives ending in an unstressed vowel form the plural by adding *s* (e.g. *libro, libros*). Nouns and adjectives ending in a stressed vowel or a consonant add *es* (e.g. *rubí, rubíes; pared, paredes*). An accent on the final syllable is not required when *es* is added (e.g. *nación, naciones*). Final *z* becomes *ces* (e.g. *vez, veces*). Spanish nouns and adjectives ending in *o* form the feminine by changing the final *o* to *a* (e.g. *hermano, hermana*). Most Spanish nouns and adjectives ending in anything other than final *o* do not have a separate feminine form with the exception of those denoting nationality etc; these add *a* to the masculine singular form (e.g. *español, española*). An accent on the final syllable is then not required (e.g. *inglés, inglesa*). Adjectives ending in *án*, *ón*, or *or* behave like those denoting nationality with the following exceptions: *inferior, mayor, mejor, menor, peor, superior*, where the feminine has the same form as the masculine. Spanish verb tables will be found in the appendix.

The Spanish alphabet

In Spanish *ch*, *ll* and *ñ* are considered separate letters and in the Spanish–English section, therefore, they will be found after *cu*, *lu* and *ny* respectively.

Introducción

Con el propósito de facilitar la consulta, las cabezas de artículo, los compuestos y los derivados aparecen en azul. La tilde (~) se emplea para sustituir la palabra cabeza de artículo o aquella parte de tal palabra que precede a la barra vertical (|). Tanto en inglés como en español se dan los plurales solamente si son irregulares. Para formar el plural regular en inglés se añade la letra *s* al sustantivo singular, pero se añade *es* cuando se trata de una palabra que termina en *ch*, *sh*, *s*, *ss*, *us*, *x*, o *z* (p.ej. *sash*, *sashes*). En el caso de una palabra que termine en *y* precedida por una consonante, la *y* se transforma en *ies* (p.ej. *baby*, *babies*). Para formar el tiempo pasado y el participio pasado se añade *ed* al infinitivo de los verbos regulares ingleses (p.ej. *last*, *lasted*). En el caso de los verbos ingleses que terminan en *e* muda se añade sólo la *d* (p.ej. *move*, *moved*). En el caso de los verbos ingleses que terminan en *y*- hay que cambiar la *y* por *ied* (p.ej. *carry*, *carried*). Los verbos irregulares se encuentran en el diccionario por orden alfabético remitidos al infinitivo, y también en la lista del apéndice.

Pronunciation of Spanish

Vowels

a	is between pronunciation of *a* in English *cat* and *arm*
e	is like *e* in English *bed*
i	is like *ee* in English *see* but a little shorter
o	is like *o* in English *bought* but a little longer
u	is like *oo* in English *too*
y	when a vowel is as Spanish **i**

Consonants

b
  (1) in initial position or after nasal consonant is like English *b*
  (2) in other positions is between English *b* and English *v*

c
  (1) before **e** or **i** is like *th* in English *thin*
  (2) in other positions is like *c* in English *cat*

ch   is like *ch* in English *chip*

d
  (1) in initial position, after nasal consonants and after **l** is like English *d*
  (2) in other positions is like *th* in English *this*

f   is like English *f*

g
  (1) before **e** or **i** is like *ch* in Scottish *loch*
  (2) in initial position is like *g* in English *get*
  (3) in other positions is like (2) but a little softer

h   is silent in Spanish but see also **ch**

j   is like *ch* in Scottish *loch*

k   is like English *k*

l   is like English *l* but see also **ll**

ll   is like *lli* in English *million*

m   is like English *m*

n   is like English *n*

ñ   is like *ni* in English *opinion*

p   is like English *p*

q   is like English *k*

r   is rolled or trilled

s   is like *s* in English *sit*

t   is like English *t*

v
  (1) in initial position or after nasal consonant is like English *b*
  (2) in other positions is between English *b* and English *v*

w   is like Spanish **b** or **v**
x   is like English *x*
y   is like English *y*
z   is like *th* in English *thin*

Pronunciación Inglesa

Símbolos fonéticos

Vocales y diptongos

iː	see	ə	ago
ɪ	sit	eɪ	page
e	ten	əʊ	home
æ	hat	aɪ	five
ɑː	ah	aɪə	fire
ɒ	got	aʊ	now
ɔː	saw	aʊə	flour
ʊ	put	ɔɪ	join
uː	too	ɪə	near
ʌ	cup	eə	hair
ɜː	fur	ʊə	poor

Consonantes

p	pen	s	so
b	bad	z	zoo
t	tea	ʃ	she
d	dip	ʒ	measure
k	cat	h	how
g	got	m	man
tʃ	chin	n	no
dʒ	June	ŋ	sing
f	fall	l	leg
v	voice	r	red
θ	thin	j	yes
ð	then	w	wet

Abbreviations · Abreviaturas

adjective	*a*	adjetivo
abbreviation	*abbr/abrev*	abreviatura
administration	*admin*	administración
adverb	*adv*	adverbio
American	*Amer*	americano
anatomy	*anat*	anatomía
archaeology	*archaeol*	arqueología
architecture	*archit/arquit*	arquitectura
definite article	*art def*	artículo definido
indefinite article	*art indef*	artículo indefinido
astrology	*astr*	astrología
automobile	*auto*	automóvil
auxiliary	*aux*	auxiliar
aviation	*aviat/aviac*	aviación
biology	*biol*	biología
botany	*bot*	botánica
commerce	*com*	comercio
computing	*comput*	informática
conjunction	*conj*	conjunción
cooking	*culin*	cocina
electricity	*elec*	electricidad
school	*escol*	enseñanza
Spain	*Esp*	España
feminine	*f*	femenino
familiar	*fam*	familiar
figurative	*fig*	figurado
philosophy	*fil*	filosofía
photography	*foto*	fotografía
geography	*geog*	geografía
geology	*geol*	geología
grammar	*gram*	gramática
humorous	*hum*	humorístico
interjection	*int*	interjección
interrogative	*inter*	interrogativo
invariable	*invar*	invariable
legal, law	*jurid*	jurídico
Latin American	*LAm*	latinoamericano
language	*lang*	lengua(je)
masculine	*m*	masculino
mathematics	*mat(h)*	matemáticas
mechanics	*mec*	mecánica
medicine	*med*	medicina
military	*mil*	militar
music	*mus*	música
mythology	*myth*	mitología
noun	*n*	nombre

nautical	*naut*	náutica
oneself	*o.s.*	uno mismo, se
proprietary term	*P*	marca registrada
pejorative	*pej*	peyorativo
philosophy	*phil*	filosofía
photography	*photo*	fotografía
plural	*pl*	plural
politics	*pol*	política
possessive	*poss*	posesivo
past participle	*pp*	participio pasado
prefix	*pref*	prefijo
preposition	*prep*	preposición
present participle	*pres p*	participio de presente
pronoun	*pron*	pronombre
psychology	*psych*	psicología
past tense	*pt*	tiempo pasado
railroad	*rail*	ferrocarril
relative	*rel*	relativo
religion	*relig*	religión
school	*schol*	enseñanza
singular	*sing*	singular
slang	*sl*	argot
someone	*s.o.*	alguien
something	*sth*	algo
technical	*tec*	técnico
television	*TV*	televisión
university	*univ*	universidad
auxiliary verb	*v aux*	verbo auxiliar
verb	*vb*	verbo
intransitive verb	*vi*	verbo intransitivo
pronominal verb	*vpr*	verbo pronominal
transitive verb	*vt*	verbo transitivo
transitive & intransitive verb	*vti*	verbo transitivo e intransitivo

Proprietary terms

This dictionary includes some words which have, or are asserted to have, proprietary status as trademarks. Their inclusion does not imply that they have acquired for legal purposes a non-proprietary or general significance, nor any other judgment concerning their legal status. In cases where the editorial staff have some evidence that a word has proprietary status this is indicated in the entry for that word by the symbol ®, but no judgment concerning the legal status of such words is made or implied thereby.

Marcas registradas

Este diccionario incluye algunas palabras que son o pretenden ser marcas registradas. No debe atribuirse ningún valor jurídico ni a la presencia ni a la ausencia de tal designación.

A

a *prep* in, at; (*dirección*) to; (*tiempo*) at; (*hasta*) to, until; (*fecha*) on; (*más tarde*) later; (*medio*) by; (*precio*) for, at. **~ 5 km** 5 km away. **¿~ cuántos estamos?** what's the date? **~l día siguiente** the next day. **~ la francesa** in the French fashion. **~ las 2** at 2 o'clock. **~ los 25 años** (*edad*) at the age of 25; (*después de*) after 25 years. **~ no ser por** but for. **~ que** I bet. **~ 28 de febrero** on the 28th of February

ábaco *m* abacus

abad *m* abbot

abadejo *m* (*pez*) cod

abad|esa *f* abbess. **~ía** *f* abbey

abajo *adv* (down) below; (*dirección*) down(wards); (*en casa*) downstairs. ● *int* down with. **calle ~** down the street. **el ~ firmante** the undersigned. **escaleras ~** downstairs. **la parte de ~** the bottom part. **los de ~** those at the bottom. **más ~** below.

abalanzarse [10] *vpr* rush towards

abalorio *m* glass bead

abanderado *m* standard-bearer

abandon|ado *adj* abandoned; (*descuidado*) neglected; (*personas*) untidy. **~ar** *vt* leave ‹*un lugar*›; abandon ‹*personas, cosas*›. ● *vi* give up. **~arse** *vpr* give in; (*descuidarse*) let o.s. go. **~o** *m* abandonment; (*estado*) abandon

abani|car [7] *vt* fan. **~co** *m* fan. **~queo** *m* fanning

abarata|miento *m* reduction in price. **~r** *vt* reduce. **~rse** *vpr* (*precios*) come down

abarca *f* sandal

abarcar [7] *vt* put one's arms around, embrace; (*comprender*) embrace; (*LAm, acaparar*) monopolize

abarquillar *vt* warp. **~se** *vpr* warp

abarrotar *vt* overfill, pack full

abarrotes *mpl* (*LAm*) groceries

abast|ecer [11] *vt* supply. **~ecimiento** *m* supply; (*acción*) supplying. **~o** *m* supply. **dar ~o a** a supply

abati|do *a* depressed. **~miento** *m* depression. **~r** *vt* knock down, demolish; (*fig, humillar*) humiliate. **~rse** *vpr* swoop (*sobre* on); (*ponerse abatido*) get depressed

abdica|ción *f* abdication. **~r** [7] *vt* give up. ● *vi* abdicate

abdom|en *m* abdomen. **~inal** *a* abdominal

abec|é *m* (*fam*) alphabet, ABC. **~edario** *m* alphabet

abedul *m* birch (tree)

abej|a *f* bee. **~arrón** *m* bumble-bee. **~ón** *m* drone. **~orro** *m* bumble-bee; (*insecto coleóptero*) cockchafer

aberración *f* aberration

abertura *f* opening

abet|al *m* fir wood. **~o** *m* fir (tree)

abierto *pp véase* **abrir**. ● *a* open

abigarra|do *a* multi-coloured; (*fig, mezclado*) mixed. **~miento** *m* variegation

abigeato *m* (*Mex*) rustling

abism|al *a* abysmal; (*profundo*) deep. **~ar** *vt* throw into an abyss; (*fig, abatir*) humble. **~arse** *vpr* be absorbed (*en* in), be lost (*en* in). **~o** *m* abyss; (*fig, diferencia*) world of difference

abizcochado *a* spongy

abjura|ción *f* abjuration. **~r** *vt* forswear. ● *vi.* **~r de** forswear

ablanda|miento *m* softening. **~r** *vt* soften. **~rse** *vpr* soften

ablución *f* ablution

abnega|ción *f* self-sacrifice. **~do** *a* self-sacrificing

aboba|do *a* silly. **~miento** *m* silliness

aboca|do *a* ‹*vino*› medium. **~r** [7] *vt* pour out

abocetar *vt* sketch

abocinado *a* trumpet-shaped

abochornar *vt* suffocate; (*fig, avergonzar*) embarrass. ~**se** *vpr* feel embarrassed; (*plantas*) wilt

abofetear *vt* slap

aboga|cía *f* legal profession. ~**do** *m* lawyer; (*notario*) solicitor; (*en el tribunal*) barrister, attorney (*Amer*). ~**r** [12] *vi* plead

abolengo *m* ancestry

aboli|ción *f* abolition. ~**cionismo** *m* abolitionism. ~**cionista** *m & f* abolitionist. ~**r** [24] *vt* abolish

abolsado *a* baggy

abolla|dura *f* dent. ~**r** *vt* dent

bomba|do *a* convex; (*Arg, borracho*) drunk. ~**r** *vt* make convex. ~**rse** *vpr* (*LAm, corromperse*) start to rot, go bad

abomina|ble *a* abominable. ~**ción** *f* abomination. ~**r** *vt* detest. ● *vi*. ~**r de** detest

abona|ble *a* payable. ~**do** *a* paid. ● *m* subscriber

abonanzar *vi* (*tormenta*) abate; (*tiempo*) improve

abon|ar *vt* pay; (*en agricultura*) fertilize. ~**aré** *m* promissory note. ~**arse** *vpr* subscribe. ~**o** *m* payment; (*estiércol*) fertilizer; (*a un periódico*) subscription

aborda|ble *a* reasonable; (*persona*) approachable. ~**je** *m* boarding. ~**r** *vt* tackle (*un asunto*); approach (*una persona*); (*naut*) come alongside

aborigen *a & m* native

aborrascarse [7] *vpr* get stormy

aborrec|er [11] *vt* hate; (*exasperar*) annoy. ~**ible** *a* loathsome. ~**ido** *a* hated. ~**imiento** *m* hatred

aborregado *a* (*cielo*) mackerel

abort|ar *vi* have a miscarriage. ~**ivo** *a* abortive. ~**o** *m* miscarriage; (*voluntario*) abortion; (*fig, monstruo*) abortion. **hacerse** ~**ar** have an abortion

abotaga|miento *m* swelling. ~**rse** [12] *vpr* swell up

abotonar *vt* button (up)

aboveda|do *a* vaulted. ~**r** *vt* vault

abra *f* cove

abracadabra *m* abracadabra

abrasa|dor *a* burning. ~**r** *vt* burn; (*fig, consumir*) consume. ~**rse** *vpr* burn

abrasi|ón *f* abrasion; (*geología*) erosion. ~**vo** *a* abrasive

abraz|adera *f* bracket. ~**ar** *vt* [10] embrace; (*encerrar*) enclose. ~**arse**

vpr embrace. ~**o** *m* hug. **un fuerte** ~**o de** (*en una carta*) with best wishes from

abrecartas *m* paper-knife

ábrego *m* south wind

abrelatas *m invar* tin opener (*Brit*), can opener

abreva|dero *m* watering place. ~**r** *vt* water (*animales*). ~**rse** *vpr* (*animales*) drink

abrevia|ción *f* abbreviation; (*texto abreviado*) abridged text. ~**do** *a* brief; (*texto*) abridged. ~**r** *vt* abbreviate; abridge (*texto*); cut short (*viaje etc*). ● *vi* be brief. ~**tura** *f* abbreviation

abrig|ada *f* shelter. ~**adero** *m* shelter. ~**ado** *a* (*lugar*) sheltered; (*personas*) well wrapped up. ~**ar** [12] *vt* shelter; cherish (*esperanza*); harbour (*duda, sospecha*). ~**arse** *vpr* (take) shelter; (*con ropa*) wrap up. ~**o** *m* (over)coat; (*lugar*) shelter

abril *m* April. ~**eño** *a* April

abrillantar *vt* polish

abrir [*pp* **abierto**] *vt/i* open. ~**se** *vpr* open; (*extenderse*) open out; (*el tiempo*) clear

abrocha|dor *m* buttonhook. ~**r** *vt* do up; (*con botones*) button up

abrojo *m* thistle

abroncar [7] *vt* (*fam*) tell off; (*abuchear*) boo; (*avergonzar*) shame. ~**se** *vpr* be ashamed; (*enfadarse*) get annoyed

abroquelarse *vpr* shield o.s.

abruma|dor *a* overwhelming. ~**r** *vt* overwhelm

abrupto *a* steep; (*áspero*) harsh

abrutado *a* brutish

absceso *m* abscess

absentismo *m* absenteeism

ábside *m* apse

absintio *m* absinthe

absolu|ción *f* (*relig*) absolution; (*jurid*) acquittal

absolut|amente *adv* absolutely, completely. ~**ismo** *m* absolutism. ~**ista** *a & m & f* absolutist. ~**o** *a* absolute. ~**orio** *a* of acquittal. **en** ~**o** (*de manera absoluta*) absolutely; (*con sentido negativo*) (not) at all

absolver [2, *pp* **absuelto**] *vt* (*relig*) absolve; (*jurid*) acquit

absor|bente *a* absorbent; (*fig, interesante*) absorbing. ~**ber** *vt* absorb. ~**ción** *f* absorption. ~**to** *a* absorbed

abstemio *a* teetotal. ● *m* teetotaller

absten|ción f abstention. **~erse** [40] vpr abstain, refrain (**de** from)

abstinen|cia f abstinence. **~te** a abstinent

abstra|cción f abstraction. **~cto** a abstract. **~er** [41] vt abstract. **~erse** vpr be lost in thought. **~ído** a absent-minded

abstruso a abstruse

absuelto a (relig) absolved; (jurid) acquitted

absurdo a absurd. ● m absurd thing

abuche|ar vt boo. **~o** m booing

abuel|a f grandmother. **~o** m grandfather. **~os** mpl grandparents

ab|ulia f lack of willpower. **~úlico** a weak-willed

abulta|do a bulky. **~miento** m bulkiness. **~r** vt enlarge; (hinchar) swell; (fig, exagerar) exaggerate. ● vi be bulky

abunda|ncia f abundance. **~nte** a abundant, plentiful. **~r** vi be plentiful. **nadar en la ~ncia** be rolling in money

aburguesa|miento m conversion to a middle-class way of life. **~rse** vpr become middle-class

aburri|do a (con estar) bored; (con ser) boring. **~miento** m boredom; (cosa pesada) bore. **~r** vt bore. **~rse** vpr be bored, get bored

abus|ar vi take advantage. **~ar de la bebida** drink too much. **~ivo** a excessive. **~o** m abuse. **~ón** a (fam) selfish

abyec|ción f wretchedness. **~to** a abject

acá adv here; (hasta ahora) until now. **~ y allá** here and there. **de ~ para allá** to and fro. **de ayer ~** since yesterday

acaba|do a finished; (perfecto) perfect; (agotado) worn out. ● m finish. **~miento** m finishing; (fin) end. **~r** vt/i finish. **~rse** vpr finish; (agotarse) run out; (morirse) die. **~r con** put an end to. **~r de** (+ infinitivo) have just (+ pp). **~ de llegar** he has just arrived. **~r por** (+ infinitivo) end up (+ gerundio). **¡se acabó!** that's it!

acabóse m. **ser el ~** be the end, be the limit

acacia f acacia

acad|emia f academy. **~émico** a academic

acaec|er [11] vi happen. **~imiento** m occurrence

acalora|damente adv heatedly. **~do** a heated. **~miento** m heat. **~r** vt warm up; (fig, excitar) excite. **~rse** vpr get hot; (fig, excitarse) get excited

acallar vt silence

acampanado a bell-shaped

acampar vi camp

acanala|do a grooved. **~dura** f groove. **~r** vt groove

acantilado a steep. ● m cliff

acanto m acanthus

acapara|r vt hoard; (monopolizar) monopolize. **~miento** m hoarding; (monopolio) monopolizing

acaracolado a spiral

acaricia|dor a caressing. **~r** vt caress; (rozar) brush; ⟨proyectos etc⟩ have in mind

ácaro m mite

acarre|ar vt transport; ⟨desgracias etc⟩ cause. **~o** m transport

acartona|do a ⟨persona⟩ wizened. **~rse** vpr (ponerse rígido) go stiff; ⟨persona⟩ become wizened

acaso adv maybe, perhaps. ● m chance. **~ llueva mañana** perhaps it will rain tomorrow. **al ~** at random. **por si ~** in case

acata|miento m respect (**a** for). **~r** vt respect

acatarrarse vpr catch a cold, get a cold

acaudalado a well off

acaudillar vt lead

acceder vi agree; (tener acceso) have access

acces|ibilidad f accessibility. **~ible** a accessible; ⟨persona⟩ approachable. **~o** m access, entry; (med, ataque) attack; (llegada) approach

accesorio a & m accessory

accidentado a ⟨terreno⟩ uneven; (agitado) troubled; ⟨persona⟩ injured

accident|al a accidental. **~arse** vpr have an accident. **~e** m accident

acci|ón f (incl jurid) action; (hecho) deed. **~onar** vt work. ● vi gesticulate. **~onista** m & f shareholder

acebo m holly (tree)

acebuche m wild olive tree

acecinar vt cure ⟨carne⟩. **~se** vpr become wizened

acech|ar vt spy on; (aguardar) lie in wait for. **~o** m spying. **al ~o** on the look-out

acedera *f* sorrel

acedía *f* (*pez*) plaice; (*acidez*) heartburn

aceit|ar *vt* oil; (*culin*) add oil to. **~e** *m* oil; (*de oliva*) olive oil. **~era** *f* oil bottle; (*para engrasar*) oilcan. **~ero** *a* oil. **~oso** *a* oily

aceitun|a *f* olive. **~ado** *a* olive. **~o** *m* olive tree

acelera|ción *f* acceleration. **~damente** *adv* quickly. **~dor** *m* accelerator. **~r** *vt* accelerate; (*fig*) speed up, quicken

acelga *f* chard

ac|émila *f* mule; (*como insulto*) ass (*fam*). **~emilero** *m* muleteer

acendra|do *a* pure. **~r** *vt* purify; refine (*metales*)

acensuar *vt* tax

acent|o *m* accent; (*énfasis*) stress. **~uación** *f* accentuation. **~uar** [21] *vt* stress; (*fig*) emphasize. **~uarse** *vpr* become noticeable

aceña *f* water-mill

acepción *f* meaning, sense

acepta|ble *a* acceptable. **~ción** *f* acceptance; (*aprobación*) approval. **~r** *vt* accept

acequia *f* irrigation channel

acera *f* pavement (*Brit*), sidewalk (*Amer*)

acerado *a* steel; (*fig, mordaz*) sharp

acerca de *prep* about

acerca|miento *m* approach; (*fig*) reconciliation. **~r** [7] *vt* bring near. **~rse** *vpr* approach

acería *f* steelworks

acerico *m* pincushion

acero *m* steel. **~ inoxidable** stainless steel

acérrimo *a* (*fig*) staunch

acert|ado *a* right, correct; (*apropiado*) appropriate. **~ar** [1] *vt* hit (*el blanco*); (*adivinar*) get right, guess. ● *vi* get right. **~ar a** a happen to. **~ar con** hit on. **~ijo** *m* riddle

acervo *m* pile; (*bienes*) common property

acetato *m* acetate

acético *a* acetic

acetileno *m* acetylene

acetona *f* acetone

aciago *a* unlucky

aciano *m* cornflower

ac|íbar *m* aloes; (*planta*) aloe; (*fig, amargura*) bitterness. **~ibarar** *vt* add aloes to; (*fig, amargar*) embitter

acicala|do *a* dressed up, overdressed. **~r** *vt* dress up. **~rse** *vpr* get dressed up

acicate *m* spur

acid|ez *f* acidity. **~ificar** [7] *vt* acidify. **~ificarse** *vpr* acidify

ácido *a* sour. ● *m* acid

acierto *m* success; (*idea*) good idea; (*habilidad*) skill

aclama|ción *f* acclaim; (*aplausos*) applause. **~r** *vt* acclaim; (*aplaudir*) applaud

aclara|ción *f* explanation. **~r** *vt* lighten (*colores*); (*explicar*) clarify; (*enjuagar*) rinse. ● *vi* (*el tiempo*) brighten up. **~rse** *vpr* become clear. **~torio** *a* explanatory

aclimata|ción *f* acclimatization, acclimation (*Amer*). **~r** *vt* acclimatize, acclimate (*Amer*). **~rse** *vpr* become acclimatized, become acclimated (*Amer*)

acné *m* acne

acobardar *vt* intimidate. **~se** *vpr* get frightened

acocil *m* (*Mex*) freshwater shrimp

acod|ado *a* bent. **~ar** *vt* (*doblar*) bend; (*agricultura*) layer. **~arse** *vpr* lean on (*en* on). **~o** *m* layer

acog|edor *a* welcoming; (*ambiente*) friendly. **~er** [14] *vt* welcome; (*proteger*) shelter; (*recibir*) receive. **~erse** *vpr* take refuge. **~ida** *f* welcome; (*refugio*) refuge

acogollar *vi* bud. **~se** *vpr* bud

acolcha|do *a* quilted. **~r** *vt* quilt, pad

acólito *m* acolyte; (*monaguillo*) altar boy

acomet|edor *a* aggressive; (*emprendedor*) enterprising. **~er** *vt* attack; (*emprender*) undertake; (*llenar*) fill. **~ida** *f* attack. **~ividad** *f* aggression; (*iniciativa*) enterprise

acomod|able *a* adaptable. **~adizo** *a* accommodating. **~ado** *a* well off. **~ador** *m* usher. **~adora** *f* usherette. **~amiento** *m* suitability. **~ar** *vt* arrange; (*adaptar*) adjust. ● *vi* be suitable. **~arse** *vpr* settle down; (*adaptarse*) conform. **~aticio** *a* accommodating. **~o** *m* position

acompaña|do *a* accompanied; (*concurrido*) busy. **~miento** *m* accompaniment. **~nta** *f* companion. **~nte** *m* companion; (*mus*) accompanist. **~r** *vt* accompany; (*adjuntar*) enclose. **~rse** *vpr* (*mus*) accompany o.s.

acompasa|do *a* rhythmic. **~r** *vt* keep in time; (*fig, ajustar*) adjust

acondiciona|do *a* equipped. **~miento** *m* conditioning. **~r** *vt* fit out; (*preparar*) prepare

acongojar *vt* distress. **~se** *vpr* get upset

acónito *m* aconite

aconseja|ble *a* advisable. **~do** *a* advised. **~r** *vt* advise. **~rse** *vpr* take advice. **~rse con** consult

aconsonantar *vt/i* rhyme

acontec|er [11] *vi* happen. **~imiento** *m* event

acopi|ar *vt* collect. **~o** *m* store

acopla|do *a* coordinated. **~miento** *m* coupling; (*elec*) connection. **~r** *vt* fit; (*elec*) connect; (*rail*) couple

acoquina|miento *m* intimidation. **~r** *vt* intimidate. **~rse** *vpr* be intimidated

acoraza|do *a* armour-plated. ● *m* battleship. **~r** [10] *vt* armour

acorazonado *a* heart-shaped

acorcha|do *a* spongy. **~rse** *vpr* go spongy; (*parte del cuerpo*) go to sleep

acord|ado *a* agreed. **~ar** [2] *vt* agree (upon); (*decidir*) decide; (*recordar*) remind. **~e** *a* in agreement; (*mus*) harmonious. ● *m* chord

acorde|ón *m* accordion. **~onista** *m & f* accordionist

acordona|do *a* ‹*lugar*› cordoned off. **~miento** *m* cordoning off. **~r** *vt* tie, lace; (*rodear*) surround, cordon off

acorrala|miento *m* (*de animales*) rounding up; (*de personas*) cornering. **~r** *vt* round up ‹*animales*›; corner ‹*personas*›

acorta|miento *m* shortening. **~r** *vt* shorten; (*fig*) cut down

acos|ar *vt* hound; (*fig*) pester. **~o** *m* pursuit; (*fig*) pestering

acostar [2] *vt* put to bed; (*naut*) bring alongside. ● *vi* (*naut*) reach land. **~se** *vpr* go to bed; (*echarse*) lie down; (*Mex, parir*) give birth

acostumbra|do *a* (*habitual*) usual. **~do** *a* used to, accustomed to. **~r** *vt* get used. **me ha acostumbrado a levantarme de noche** he's got me used to getting up at night. ● *vi*. **~r (a)** be accustomed to. **acostumbro comer a la una** I usually have lunch at one o'clock. **~rse** *vpr* become accustomed, get used

acota|ción *f* (*nota*) marginal note; (*en el teatro*) stage direction; (*cota*) elevation mark. **~do** *a* enclosed. **~r** *vt* mark out ‹*terreno*›; (*anotar*) annotate

ácrata *a* anarchistic. ● *m & f* anarchist

acre *m* acre. ● *a* ‹*olor*› pungent; ‹*sabor*› sharp, bitter

acrecenta|miento *m* increase. **~r** [1] *vt* increase. **~rse** *vpr* increase

acrec|er [11] *vt* increase. **~imiento** *m* increase

acredita|do *a* reputable; (*pol*) accredited. **~r** *vt* prove; accredit ‹*representante diplomático*›; (*garantizar*) guarantee; (*autorizar*) authorize. **~rse** *vpr* make one's name

acreedor *a* worthy (**a** of). ● *m* creditor

acribillar *vt* (*a balazos*) riddle (**a** with); (*a picotazos*) cover (**a** with); (*fig, a preguntas etc*) pester (**a** with)

acrimonia *f* (*de sabor*) sharpness; (*de olor*) pungency; (*fig*) bitterness

acrisola|do *a* pure; (*fig*) proven. **~r** *vt* purify; (*confirmar*) prove

acritud *f* (*de sabor*) sharpness; (*de olor*) pungency; (*fig*) bitterness

acr|obacia *f* acrobatics. **~obacias aéreas** aerobatics. **~óbata** *m & f* acrobat. **~obático** *a* acrobatic. **~obatismo** *m* acrobatics

acrónimo *m* acronym

acróstico *a & m* acrostic

acta *f* minutes; (*certificado*) certificate

actinia *f* sea anemone

actitud *f* posture, position; (*fig*) attitude, position

activ|ación *f* speed-up. **~amente** *adv* actively. **~ar** *vt* activate; (*acelerar*) speed up. **~idad** *f* activity. **~o** *a* active. ● *m* assets

acto *m* act; (*ceremonia*) ceremony. **en el ~** immediately

act|or *m* actor. **~riz** *f* actress

actuación *f* action; (*conducta*) behaviour; (*theat*) performance

actual *a* present; ‹*asunto*› topical. **~idad** *f* present. **~idades** *fpl* current affairs. **~ización** *f* modernization. **~izar** [10] *vt* modernize. **~mente** *adv* now, at the present time. **en la ~idad** nowadays

actuar [21] *vt* work. ● *vi* act. **~ como, ~ de** act as

actuario *m* clerk of the court. ～ **(de seguros)** actuary
acuarel|a *f* watercolour. ～**ista** *m & f* watercolourist
acuario *m* aquarium. **A～** Aquarius
acuartela|do *a* quartered. ～**miento** *m* quartering. ～**r** *vt* quarter, billet; (*mantener en cuartel*) confine to barracks
acuático *a* aquatic
acuci|ador pressing. ～**ar** *vt* urge on; (*dar prisa a*) hasten. ～**oso** *a* keen
acuclillarse *vpr* crouch down, squat down
acuchilla|do *a* slashed; ⟨*persona*⟩ stabbed. ～**r** *vt* slash; stab ⟨*persona*⟩; (*alisar*) smooth
acudir *vi*. ～ **a** go to, attend; keep ⟨*una cita*⟩; (*en auxilio*) go to help
acueducto *m* aqueduct
acuerdo *m* agreement. ● *vb véase* **acordar**. **¡de ～!** OK! **de ～ con** in accordance with. **estar de ～** agree. **ponerse de ～** agree
acuesto *vb véase* **acostar**
acuidad *f* acuity, sharpness
acumula|ción *f* accumulation. ～**dor** *a* accumulative. ● *m* accumulator. ～**r** *vt* accumulate. ～**rse** *vpr* accumulate
acunar *vt* rock
acuña|ción *f* minting, coining. ～**r** *vt* mint, coin
acuos|idad *f* wateriness. ～**o** *a* watery
acupuntura *f* acupuncture
acurrucarse [7] *vpr* curl up
acusa|ción *f* accusation. ～**do** *a* accused; (*destacado*) marked. ● *m* accused. ～**dor** *a* accusing. ● *m* accuser. ～**r** *vt* accuse; (*mostrar*) show; (*denunciar*) denounce. ～**rse** *vpr* confess; (*notarse*) become marked. ～**torio** *a* accusatory
acuse *m*. ～ **de recibo** acknowledgement of receipt
acus|ica *m & f* (*fam*) telltale. ～**ón** *a & m* telltale
acústic|a *f* acoustics. ～**o** *a* acoustic
achacar [7] *vt* attribute
achacoso *a* sickly
achaflanar *vt* bevel
achantar *vt* (*fam*) intimidate. ～**se** *vpr* hide; (*fig*) back down
achaparrado *a* stocky
achaque *m* ailment
achares *mpl* (*fam*). **dar ～** make jealous

achata|miento *m* flattening. ～**r** *vt* flatten
achica|do *a* childish. ～**r** [7] *vt* make smaller; (*fig, empequeñecer, fam*) belittle; (*naut*) bale out. ～**rse** *vpr* become smaller; (*humillarse*) be humiliated
achicopalado *a* (*Mex*) depressed
achicoria *f* chicory
achicharra|dero *m* inferno. ～**nte** *a* sweltering. ～**r** *vt* burn; (*fig*) pester. ～**rse** *vpr* burn
achispa|do *a* tipsy. ～**rse** *vpr* get tipsy
achocolatado *a* (chocolate-)brown
achuch|ado *a* (*fam*) hard. ～**ar** *vt* jostle, push. ～**ón** *m* shove, push
achulado *a* cocky
adagio *m* adage, proverb; (*mus*) adagio
adalid *m* leader
adamascado *a* damask
adapta|ble *a* adaptable. ～**ción** *f* adaptation. ～**dor** *m* adapter. ～**r** *vt* adapt; (*ajustar*) fit. ～**rse** *vpr* adapt o.s.
adecentar *vt* clean up. ～**se** *vpr* tidy o.s. up
adecua|ción *f* suitability. ～**damente** *adv* suitably. ～**do** *a* suitable. ～**r** *vt* adapt, make suitable
adelant|ado *a* advanced; ⟨*niño*⟩ precocious; ⟨*reloj*⟩ fast. ～**amiento** *m* advance(ment); (*auto*) overtaking. ～**ar** *vt* advance, move forward; (*acelerar*) speed up; put forward ⟨*reloj*⟩; (*auto*) overtake. ● *vi* advance, go forward; ⟨*reloj*⟩ gain, be fast. ～**arse** *vpr* advance, move forward; ⟨*reloj*⟩ gain; (*auto*) overtake. ～**e** *adv* forward. ● *int* come in!; *¡siga!*) carry on! ～**o** *m* advance; (*progreso*) progress. **más ～e** (*lugar*) further on; (*tiempo*) later on. **pagar por ～ado** pay in advance.
adelfa *f* oleander
adelgaza|dor *a* slimming. ～**miento** *m* slimming. ～**r** [10] *vt* make thin. ● *vi* lose weight; (*adrede*) slim. ～**rse** *vpr* lose weight; (*adrede*) slim
ademán *m* gesture. **ademanes** *mpl* (*modales*) manners. **en ～ de** as if to
además *adv* besides; (*también*) also. ～ **de** besides
adentr|arse *vpr*. ～ **en** penetrate into; study thoroughly ⟨*tema etc*⟩. ～**o** *adv* in(side). **mar ～o** out at sea. **tierra ～o** inland
adepto *m* supporter

aderez|ar [10] *vt* flavour ‹*bebidas*›; (*condimentar*) season; dress ‹*ensalada*›. **∼o** *m* flavouring; (*con condimentos*) seasoning; (*para ensalada*) dressing

adeud|ar *vt* owe. **∼o** *m* debit

adhe|rencia *f* adhesion; (*fig*) adherence. **∼rente** *a* adherent. **∼rir** [4] *vt* stick on. ● *vi* stick. **∼rirse** *vpr* stick; (*fig*) follow. **∼sión** *f* adhesion; (*fig*) support. **∼sivo** *a* & *m* adhesive

adici|ón *f* addition. **∼onal** *a* additional. **∼onar** *vt* add

adicto *a* devoted. ● *m* follower

adiestra|do *a* trained. **∼miento** *m* training. **∼r** *vt* train. **∼rse** *vpr* practise

adinerado *a* wealthy

adiós *int* goodbye!; (*al cruzarse con alguien*) hello!

adit|amento *m* addition; (*accesorio*) accessory. **∼ivo** *m* additive

adivin|ación *f* divination; (*por conjeturas*) guessing. **∼ador** *m* fortune-teller. **∼anza** *f* riddle. **∼ar** *vt* foretell; (*acertar*) guess. **∼o** *m* fortune-teller

adjetivo *a* adjectival. ● *m* adjective

adjudica|ción *f* award.. **∼r** [7] *vt* award. **∼rse** *vpr* appropriate. **∼tario** *m* winner of an award

adjunt|ar *vt* enclose. **∼o** *a* enclosed; (*auxiliar*) assistant. ● *m* assistant

adminículo *m* thing, gadget

administra|ción *f* administration; (*gestión*) management. **∼dor** *m* administrator; (*gerente*) manager. **∼dora** *f* administrator; manageress. **∼r** *vt* administer. **∼tivo** *a* administrative

admira|ble *a* admirable. **∼ción** *f* admiration. **∼dor** *m* admirer. **∼r** *vt* admire; (*asombrar*) astonish. **∼rse** *vpr* be astonished. **∼tivo** *a* admiring

admi|sibilidad *f* admissibility. **∼sible** *a* acceptable. **∼sión** *f* admission; (*aceptación*) acceptance. **∼tir** *vt* admit; (*aceptar*) accept

adobar *vt* (*culin*) pickle; (*fig*) twist

adobe *m* sun-dried brick. **∼ra** *f* mould for making (sun-dried) bricks

adobo *m* pickle

adocena|do *a* common. **∼rse** *vpr* become common

adoctrinamiento *m* indoctrination

adolecer [11] *vi* be ill. **∼ de** suffer with

adolescen|cia *f* adolescent. **∼te** *a* & *m* & *f* adolescent

adonde *conj* where

adónde *adv* where?

adop|ción *f* adoption. **∼tar** *vt* adopt. **∼tivo** *a* adoptive; ‹*patria*› of adoption

adoqu|ín *m* paving stone; (*imbécil*) idiot. **∼inado** *m* paving. **∼inar** *vt* pave

adora|ble *a* adorable. **∼ción** *f* adoration. **∼dor** *a* adoring. ● *n* worshipper. **∼r** *vt* adore

adormec|edor *a* soporific; ‹*droga*› sedative. **∼er** [11] *vt* send to sleep; (*fig, calmar*) calm, soothe. **∼erse** *vpr* fall asleep; (*un miembro*) go to sleep. **∼ido** *a* sleepy; ‹*un miembro*› numb. **∼imiento** *m* sleepiness; (*de un miembro*) numbness

adormidera *f* opium poppy

adormilarse *vpr* doze

adorn|ar *vt* adorn (**con, de** with). **∼o** *m* decoration

adosar *vt* lean (**a** against)

adqui|rido *a* acquired. **∼rir** [4] *vt* acquire; (*comprar*) buy. **∼sición** *f* acquisition; (*compra*) purchase. **∼sitivo** *a* acquisitive. **poder** *m* **∼sitivo** purchasing power

adrede *adv* on purpose

adrenalina *f* adrenalin

adscribir [*pp* **adscrito**] *vt* appoint

aduan|a *f* customs. **∼ero** *a* customs. ● *m* customs officer

aducir [47] *vt* allege

adueñarse *vpr* take possession

adul|ación *f* flattery. **∼ador** *a* flattering. ● *m* flatterer. **∼ar** *vt* flatter

ad|ulteración *f* adulteration. **∼ulterar** *vt* adulterate. ● *vi* commit adultery. **∼ulterino** *a* adulterous. **∼ulterio** *m* adultery. **∼últera** *f* adulteress. **∼últero** *a* adulterous. ● *m* adulterer

adulto *a* & *m* adult, grown-up

adusto *a* severe, harsh

advenedizo *a* & *m* upstart

advenimiento *m* advent, arrival; (*subida al trono*) accession

adventicio *a* accidental

adverbi|al *a* adverbial. **∼o** *m* adverb

advers|ario *m* adversary. **∼idad** *f* adversity. **∼o** *a* adverse, unfavourable

advert|encia *f* warning; (*prólogo*) foreword. **∼ido** *a* informed. **∼ir** [4] *vt* warn; (*notar*) notice

adviento *m* Advent
advocación *f* dedication
adyacente *a* adjacent
aéreo *a* air; *(photo)* aerial; *(ferro-carril)* overhead; *(fig)* flimsy
aeróbica *f* aerobics
aerodeslizador *m* hovercraft
aerodinámic|a *f* aerodynamics. **~o** *a* aerodynamic
aeródromo *m* aerodrome, airdrome *(Amer)*
aero|espacial *a* aerospace. **~faro** *m* beacon. **~lito** *m* meteorite. **~nauta** *m* & *f* aeronaut. **~náutica** *f* aeronautics. **~náutico** *a* aeronautical. **~nave** *f* airship. **~puerto** *m* airport. **~sol** *m* aerosol
afab|ilidad *f* affability. **~le** *a* affable
afamado *a* famous
af|án *m* hard work; *(deseo)* desire. **~anar** *vt (fam)* pinch. **~anarse** *vpr* strive (**en, por** to). **~anoso** *a* laborious
afea|miento *m* disfigurement. **~r** *vt* disfigure, make ugly; *(censurar)* censure
afección *f* disease
afecta|ción *f* affectation. **~do** *a* affected. **~r** *vt* affect
afect|ísimo *a* affectionate. **~ísimo amigo** *(en cartas)* my dear friend. **~ividad** *f* emotional nature. **~ivo** *a* sensitive. **~o** *m (cariño)* affection. ● *a.* **~o a** attached to. **~uosidad** *f* affection. **~uoso** *a* affectionate. **con un ~uoso saludo** *(en cartas)* with kind regards. **suyo ~ísimo** *(en cartas)* yours sincerely
afeita|do *m* shave. **~dora** *f* electric razor. **~r** *vt* shave. **~rse** *vpr* (have a) shave
afelpado *a* velvety
afemina|do *a* effeminate. ● *m* effeminate person. **~miento** *m* effeminacy. **~rse** *vpr* become effeminate
aferrar [1] *vt* grasp
afgano *a* & *m* Afghan
afianza|miento *m (reforzar)* strengthening; *(garantía)* guarantee. **~rse** [10] *vpr* become established
afici|ón *f* liking; *(conjunto de aficionados)* fans. **~onado** *a* keen (**a** on), fond (**a** of). ● *m* fan. **~onar** *vt* make fond. **~onarse** *vpr* take a liking to. **por ~ón** as a hobby

afila|do *a* sharp. **~dor** *m* knifegrinder. **~dura** *f* sharpening. **~r** *vt* sharpen. **~rse** *vpr* get sharp; *(ponerse flaco)* grow thin
afilia|ción *f* affiliation. **~do** *a* affiliated. **~rse** *vpr* become a member (**a** of)
afiligranado *a* filigreed; *(fig)* delicate
afín *a* similar; *(próximo)* adjacent; *(personas)* related
afina|ción *f* refining; *(auto, mus)* tuning. **~do** *a* finished; *(mus)* in tune. **~r** *vt* refine; *(afilar)* sharpen; *(acabar)* finish; *(auto, mus)* tune. ● *vi* be in tune. **~rse** *vpr* become more refined
afincarse [7] *vpr* settle
afinidad *f* affinity; *(parentesco)* relationship
afirma|ción *f* affirmation. **~r** *vt* make firm; *(asentir)* affirm. **~rse** *vpr* steady o.s.; *(confirmar)* confirm. **~tivo** *a* affirmative
aflic|ción *f* affliction. **~tivo** *a* distressing
afligi|do *a* distressed. ● *m* afflicted. **~r** [14] *vt* distress. **~rse** *vpr* grieve
afloja|miento *m* loosening. **~r** *vt* loosen; *(relajar)* ease. ● *vi* let up
aflora|miento *m* outcrop. **~r** *vi* appear on the surface
aflu|encia *f* flow. **~ente** *a* flowing. ● *m* tributary. **~ir** [17] *vi* flow (**a** into)
af|onía *f* hoarseness. **~ónico** *a* hoarse
aforismo *m* aphorism
aforo *m* capacity
afortunado *a* fortunate, lucky
afrancesado *a* francophile
afrent|a *f* insult; *(vergüenza)* disgrace. **~ar** *vt* insult. **~oso** *a* insulting
África *f* Africa. **~ del Sur** South Africa
africano *a* & *m* African
afrodisíaco *a* & *m*, **afrodisiaco** *a* & *m* aphrodisiac
afrontar *vt* bring face to face; *(enfrentar)* face, confront
afuera *adv* out(side). **¡~!** out of the way! **~s** *fpl* outskirts
agachar *vt* lower. **~se** *vpr* bend over
agalla *f (de los peces)* gill. **~s** *fpl (fig)* guts
agarrada *f* row
agarrader|a *f (LAm)* handle. **~o** *m* handle. **tener ~as** *(LAm)*, **tener ~os** have influence

agarr|ado a (fig, fam) mean. ~**ador** a (Arg) ⟨bebida⟩ strong. ~**ar** vt grasp; (esp LAm) take, catch. ● vi ⟨plantas⟩ take root. ~**arse** vpr hold on; (reñirse, fam) fight. ~**ón** m tug; (LAm, riña) row

agarrota|miento m tightening; (auto) seizing up. ~**r** vt tie tightly; ⟨el frío⟩ stiffen; garotte ⟨un reo⟩. ~**rse** vpr go stiff; (auto) seize up

agasaj|ado m guest of honour. ~**ar** vt look after well. ~**o** m good treatment

ágata f agate

agavilla|dora f (máquina) binder. ~**r** vt bind

agazaparse vpr hide

agencia f agency. ~ **de viajes** travel agency. ~ **inmobiliaria** estate agency (Brit), real estate agency (Amer). ~**r** vt find. ~**rse** vpr find (out) for o.s.

agenda f notebook

agente m agent; (de policía) policeman. ~ **de aduanas** customs officer. ~ **de bolsa** stockbroker

ágil a agile

agilidad f agility

agita|ción f waving; (de un líquido) stirring; (intranquilidad) agitation. ~**do** a ⟨el mar⟩ rough; (fig) agitated. ~**dor** m (pol) agitator

agitanado a gypsy-like

agitar vt wave; shake ⟨botellas etc⟩; stir ⟨líquidos⟩; (fig) stir up. ~**se** vpr wave; ⟨el mar⟩ get rough; (fig) get excited

aglomera|ción f agglomeration; (de tráfico) traffic jam. ~**r** vt amass. ~**rse** vpr form a crowd

agn|osticismo m agnosticism. ~**óstico** a & m agnostic

agobi|ador a ⟨trabajo⟩ exhausting; ⟨calor⟩ oppressive. ~**ante** a ⟨trabajo⟩ exhausting; ⟨calor⟩ oppressive. ~**ar** vt weigh down; (fig, abrumar) overwhelm. ~**o** m weight; (cansancio) exhaustion; (opresión) oppression

agolpa|miento m (de gente) crowd; (de cosas) pile. ~**rse** vpr crowd together

agon|ía f death throes; (fig) agony. ~**izante** a dying; ⟨luz⟩ failing. ~**izar** [10] vi be dying

agor|ar [16] vt prophesy. ~**ero** a of ill omen. ● m soothsayer

agostar vt wither

agosto m August. **hacer su ~** feather one's nest

agota|do a exhausted; ⟨libro⟩ out of print. ~**dor** a exhausting. ~**miento** m exhaustion. ~**r** vt exhaust. ~**rse** vpr be exhausted; ⟨libro⟩ go out of print

agracia|do a attractive; (que tiene suerte) lucky. ~**r** make attractive

agrada|ble a pleasant, nice. ~**r** vi please. **esto me ~** I like this

agradec|er [11] vt thank ⟨persona⟩; be grateful for ⟨cosa⟩. ~**ido** a grateful. ~**imiento** m gratitude. **¡muy ~ido!** thanks a lot!

agrado m pleasure; (amabilidad) friendliness

agrandar vt enlarge; (fig) exaggerate. ~**se** vpr get bigger

agrario a agrarian, land; ⟨política⟩ agricultural

agrava|miento m worsening. ~**nte** a aggravating. ● f additional problem. ~**r** vt aggravate; (aumentar el peso) make heavier. ~**rse** vpr get worse

agravi|ar vt offend; (perjudicar) wrong. ~**arse** vpr be offended. ~**o** m offence

agraz m. **en ~** prematurely

agredir [24] vt attack. ~ **de palabra** insult

agrega|do m aggregate; (funcionario diplomático) attaché. ~**r** [12] vt add; (unir) join; appoint ⟨persona⟩

agremiar vt form into a union. ~**se** vpr form a union

agres|ión f aggression; (ataque) attack. ~**ividad** f aggressiveness. ~**ivo** a aggressive. ~**or** m aggressor

agreste a country

agria|do a (fig) embittered. ~**r** [regular, o raramente 20] vt sour. ~**rse** vpr turn sour; (fig) become embittered

agr|ícola a agricultural. ~**icultor** a agricultural. ● m farmer. ~**icultura** f agriculture, farming

agridulce a bitter-sweet; (culin) sweet-and-sour

agriera f (LAm) heartburn

agrietar vt crack. ~**se** vpr crack; ⟨piel⟩ chap

agrimens|or m surveyor. ~**ura** f surveying

agrio a sour; (fig) sharp. ~**s** mpl citrus fruits

agronomía f agronomy

agropecuario a farming

agrupa|ción f group; (acción) grouping. ~r vt group. ~rse vpr form a group

agua f water; (lluvia) rain; (marea) tide; (vertiente del tejado) slope. ~ abajo downstream. ~ arriba upstream. ~ bendita holy water. ~ caliente hot water. estar entre dos ~s sit on the fence. hacer ~ (naut) leak. nadar entre dos ~s sit on the fence

aguacate m avocado pear; (árbol) avocado pear tree

aguacero m downpour, heavy shower

agua corriente running water

aguachinarse vpr (Mex) ⟨cultivos⟩ be flooded

aguada f watering place; (naut) drinking water; (acuarela) watercolour

agua de colonia eau-de-Cologne

aguad|o a watery. ~ucho m refreshment kiosk

agua: ~dulce fresh water. ~fiestas m & f invar spoil-sport, wet blanket. ~ fría cold water. ~fuerte m etching

aguaje m spring tide

agua: ~mala f, ~mar m jellyfish

aguamarina f aquamarine

agua: ~miel f mead. ~ mineral con gas fizzy mineral water. ~ mineral sin gas still mineral water. ~nieve f sleet

aguanoso a watery; ⟨tierra⟩ waterlogged

aguant|able a bearable. ~aderas fpl patience. ~ar vt put up with, bear; (sostener) support. ● vi hold out. ~arse vpr restrain o.s. ~e m patience; (resistencia) endurance

agua: ~pié m watery wine. ~ potable** drinking water. ~r [15] vt water down. ~ salada salt water.

aguardar vt wait for. ● vi wait

agua: ~rdiente m (cheap) brandy. ~rrás m turpentine, turps (fam). ~turma f Jerusalem artichoke. ~zal m puddle

agud|eza f sharpness; (fig, perspicacia) insight; (fig, ingenio) wit. ~izar [10] vt sharpen. ~izarse vpr ⟨enfermedad⟩ get worse. ~o a sharp; ⟨ángulo, enfermedad⟩ acute; ⟨voz⟩ high-pitched

agüero m omen. ser de buen ~ augur well

aguij|ada f goad. ~ar vt (incl fig) goad. ~ón m point of a goad. ~onazo m prick. ~onear vt goad

águila f eagle; (persona perspicaz) astute person

aguileña f columbine

aguil|eño a aquiline. ~ucho m eaglet

aguinaldo m Christmas box

aguja f needle; (del reloj) hand; (arquit) steeple. ~s fpl (rail) points

agujer|ear vt make holes in. ~o m hole

agujetas fpl stiffness. tener ~ be stiff

agujón m hairpin

agusanado a full of maggots

agutí m (LAm) guinea pig

aguza|do a sharp. ~miento m sharpening. ~r [10] vt sharpen

ah int ah!, oh!

aherrojar vt (fig) oppress

ahí adv there. de ~ que so that. por ~ over there; (aproximadamente) thereabouts

ahija|da f god-daughter, godchild. ~do m godson, godchild. ~r vt adopt

ahínco m enthusiasm; (empeño) insistence

ahíto a full up

ahog|ado a (en el agua) drowned; (asfixiado) suffocated. ~ar [12] vt (en el agua) drown; (asfixiar) suffocate; put out ⟨fuego⟩. ~arse vpr (en el agua) drown; (asfixiarse) suffocate. ~o m breathlessness; (fig, angustia) distress; (apuro) financial trouble

ahondar vt deepen. ● vi go deep. ~ en (fig) examine in depth. ~se vpr get deeper

ahora adv now; (hace muy poco) just now; (dentro de poco) very soon. ~ bien but. ~ mismo right now. de ~ en adelante from now on, in future. por ~ for the time being

ahorca|dura f hanging. ~r [7] vt hang. ~rse vpr hang o.s.

ahorita adv (fam) now. ~ mismo right now

ahorquillar vt shape like a fork

ahorr|ador a thrifty. ~ar vt save. ~arse vpr save o.s. ~o m saving; (cantidad ahorrada) savings. ~os mpl savings

ahuecar [7] vt hollow; fluff up ⟨colchón⟩; deepen ⟨la voz⟩; (marcharse, fam) clear off (fam)

ahuizote m (Mex) bore

ahulado *m* (*LAm*) oilskin

ahuma|do *a* (*culin*) smoked; (*de colores*) smoky. ~**r** *vt* (*culin*) smoke; (*llenar de humo*) fill with smoke. ● *vi* smoke. ~**rse** *vpr* become smoky; ‹*comida*› acquire a smoky taste; (*emborracharse, fam*) get drunk

ahusa|do *a* tapering. ~**rse** *vpr* taper

ahuyentar *vt* drive away; banish ‹*pensamientos etc*›

airado *a* annoyed

aire *m* air; (*viento*) breeze; (*corriente*) draught; (*aspecto*) appearance; (*mus*) tune, air. ~**ación** *f* ventilation. ~**acondicionado** air-conditioned. ~**ar** *vt* air; (*ventilar*) ventilate; (*fig, publicar*) make public. ~**arse** *vpr*. **salir para** ~**arse** go out for some fresh air. **al** ~ **libre** in the open air. **darse** ~**s** give o.s. airs

airón *m* heron

airos|amente *adv* gracefully. ~**o** *a* draughty; (*fig*) elegant

aisla|do *a* isolated; (*elec*) insulated. ~**dor** *a* (*elec*) insulating. ● *m* (*elec*) insulator. ~**miento** *m* isolation; (*elec*) insulation. ~**nte** *a* insulating. ~**r** [23] *vt* isolate; (*elec*) insulate

ajajá *int* good! splendid!

ajar *vt* crumple; (*estropear*) spoil

ajedre|cista *m* & *f* chess-player. ~**z** *m* chess. ~**zado** *a* chequered, checked

ajenjo *m* absinthe

ajeno *a* (*de otro*) someone else's; (*de otros*) other people's; (*extraño*) alien

ajetre|arse *vpr* be busy. ~**o** *m* bustle

ají *m* (*LAm*) chilli; (*salsa*) chilli sauce

aj|iaceite *m* garlic sauce. ~**ilimójili** *m* piquant garlic sauce. ~**illo** *m* garlic. **al** ~**illo** cooked with garlic. ~**o** *m* garlic. ~**o-a-rriero** *m* cod in garlic sauce

ajorca *f* bracelet

ajuar *m* furnishings; (*de novia*) trousseau

ajuma|do *a* (*fam*) drunk. ~**rse** *vpr* (*fam*) get drunk

ajust|ado *a* right; ‹*vestido*› tight. ~**ador** *m* fitter. ~**amiento** *m* fitting; (*adaptación*) adjustment; (*acuerdo*) agreement; (*de una cuenta*) settlement. ~**ar** *vt* fit; (*adaptar*) adapt; (*acordar*) agree; settle ‹*una cuenta*›; (*apretar*) tighten. ● *vi* fit. ~**arse** *vpr* fit; (*adaptarse*) adapt o.s.; (*acordarse*) come to an agreement. ~**e** *m* fitting; (*adaptación*) adjustment; (*acuerdo*)

agreement; (*de una cuenta*) settlement

ajusticiar *vt* execute

al = **a** + **el**

ala *f* wing; (*de sombrero*) brim; (*deportes*) winger

alaba|ncioso *a* boastful. ~**nza** *f* praise. ~**r** *vt* praise. ~**rse** *vpr* boast

alabastro *m* alabaster

álabe *m* (*paleta*) paddle; (*diente*) cog

alabe|ar *vt* warp. ~**arse** *vpr* warp. ~**o** *m* warping

alacena *f* cupboard (*Brit*), closet (*Amer*)

alacrán *m* scorpion

alacridad *f* alacrity

alado *a* winged

alambi|cado *a* distilled; (*fig*) subtle. ~**camiento** *m* distillation; (*fig*) subtlety. ~**car** [7] *vt* distil. ~**que** *m* still

alambr|ada *f* wire fence; (*de alambre de espinas*) barbed wire fence. ~**ar** *vt* fence. ~**e** *m* wire. ~**e de espinas** barbed wire. ~**era** *f* fireguard

alameda *f* avenue; (*plantío de álamos*) poplar grove

álamo *m* poplar. ~ **temblón** aspen

alano *m* mastiff

alarde *m* show. ~**ar** *vi* boast

alarga|dera *f* extension. ~**do** *a* long. ~**dor** *m* extension. ~**miento** *m* lengthening. ~**r** [12] *vt* lengthen; stretch out ‹*mano etc*›; (*dar*) give, pass. ~**rse** *vpr* lengthen, get longer

alarido *m* shriek

alarm|a *f* alarm. ~**ante** *a* alarming. ~**ar** *vt* alarm, frighten. ~**arse** *vpr* be alarmed. ~**ista** *m* & *f* alarmist

alba *f* dawn

albacea *m* executor. ● *f* executrix

albacora (*culin*) tuna(-fish)

albahaca *f* basil

albanés *a* & *m* Albanian

Albania *f* Albania

albañal *m* sewer, drain

albañil *m* bricklayer. ~**ería** *f* (*arte*) bricklaying

albarán *m* delivery note

albarda *f* packsaddle; (*Mex*) saddle. ~**r** *vt* saddle

albaricoque *m* apricot. ~**ro** *m* apricot tree

albatros *m* albatross

albedrío *m* will. **libre** ~ free will

albéitar *m* veterinary surgeon (*Brit*), veterinarian (*Amer*), vet (*fam*)

alberca *f* tank, reservoir

alberg|ar [12] *vt* (*alojar*) put up; ‹*viviendas*› house; (*dar asilo*) shelter. ∼**arse** *vpr* stay; (*refugiarse*) shelter. ∼**ue** *m* accommodation; (*refugio*) shelter. ∼**ue de juventud** youth hostel

albóndiga *f* meatball, rissole

albor *m* dawn. ∼**ada** *f* dawn; (*mus*) dawn song. ∼**ear** *vi* dawn

albornoz *m* (*de los moros*) burnous; (*para el baño*) bathrobe

alborot|adizo *a* excitable. ∼**ado** *a* excited; (*aturdido*) hasty. ∼**ador** *a* rowdy. ● *m* trouble-maker. ∼**ar** *vt* disturb, upset. ● *vi* make a racket. ∼**arse** *vpr* get excited; ‹*el mar*› get rough. ∼**o** *m* row, uproar

alboroz|ado *a* overjoyed. ∼**ar** [10] *vt* make laugh; (*regocijar*) make happy. ∼**arse** *vpr* be overjoyed. ∼**o** *m* joy

albufera *f* lagoon

álbum *m* (*pl* ∼**es** *o* ∼**s**) album

alcachofa *f* artichoke

alcald|e *m* mayor. ∼**esa** *f* mayoress. ∼**ía** *f* mayoralty; (*oficina*) mayor's office

álcali *m* alkali

alcalino *a* alkaline

alcance *m* reach; (*de arma, telescopio etc*) range; (*déficit*) deficit

alcancía *f* money-box

alcantarilla *f* sewer; (*boca*) drain

alcanzar [10] *vt* (*llegar a*) catch up; (*coger*) reach; catch ‹*un autobús*›; ‹*bala etc*› strike, hit. ● *vi* reach; (*ser suficiente*) be enough. ∼ **a** manage

alcaparra *f* caper

alcaucil *m* artichoke

alcayata *f* hook

alcazaba *f* fortress

alcázar *m* fortress

alcoba *f* bedroom

alcoh|ol *m* alcohol. ∼**ol desnaturalizado** methylated spirits, meths (*fam*). ∼**ólico** *a* & *m* alcoholic. ∼**olímetro** *m* breathalyser (*Brit*). ∼**olismo** *m* alcoholism. ∼**olizarse** [10] *vpr* become an alcoholic

Alcorán *m* Koran

alcornoque *m* cork-oak; (*persona torpe*) idiot

alcuza *f* (*olive*) oil bottle

aldaba *f* door-knocker. ∼**da** *f* knock at the door

alde|a *f* village. ∼**ano** *a* village; (*campesino*) rustic, country. ∼**huela** *f* hamlet

alea|ción *f* alloy. ∼**r** *vt* alloy

aleatorio *a* uncertain

alecciona|dor *a* instructive. ∼**miento** *m* instruction. ∼**r** *vt* instruct

aledaños *mpl* outskirts

alega|ción *f* allegation; (*Arg, Mex, disputa*) argument. ∼**r** [12] *vt* claim; (*jurid*) allege. ● *vi* (*LAm*) argue. ∼**to** *m* plea

aleg|oría *f* allegory. ∼**órico** *a* allegorical

alegr|ar *vt* make happy; (*avivar*) brighten up. ∼**arse** *vpr* be happy; (*emborracharse*) get merry. ∼**e** *a* happy; (*achispado*) merry, tight. ∼**emente** *adv* happily. ∼**ía** *f* happiness. ∼**ón** *m* sudden joy, great happiness

aleja|do *a* distant. ∼**miento** *m* removal; (*entre personas*) estrangement; (*distancia*) distance. ∼**r** *vt* remove; (*ahuyentar*) get rid of; (*fig, apartar*) separate. ∼**rse** *vpr* move away

alela|do *a* stupid. ∼**r** *vt* stupefy. ∼**rse** *vpr* be stupefied

aleluya *m* & *f* alleluia

alemán *a* & *m* German

Alemania *f* Germany. ∼ **Occidental** (*historia*) West Germany. ∼ **Oriental** (*historia*) East Germany

alenta|dor *a* encouraging. ∼**r** [1] *vt* encourage. ● *vi* breathe

alerce *m* larch

al|ergia *f* allergy. ∼**érgico** *a* allergic

alero *m* (*del tejado*) eaves

alerón *m* aileron

alerta *adv* alert, on the alert. ¡∼! look out! ∼**r** *vt* alert

aleta *f* wing; (*de pez*) fin

aletarga|do *a* lethargic. ∼**miento** *m* lethargy. ∼**r** [12] *vt* make lethargic. ∼**rse** *vpr* become lethargic

alet|azo *m* (*de un ave*) flap of the wings; (*de un pez*) flick of the fin. ∼**ear** *vi* flap its wings, flutter. ∼**eo** *m* flapping (of the wings)

aleve *a* treacherous

alevín *m* young fish

alevos|ía *f* treachery. ∼**o** *a* treacherous

alfab|ético *a* alphabetical. ∼**etizar** [10] *vt* alphabetize; teach to read and write ‹*a uno*›. ∼**eto** *m* alphabet. ∼**eto Morse** Morse code

alfalfa *f* lucerne (*Brit*), alfalfa (*Amer*)

alfar *m* pottery. ∼**ería** *f* pottery. ∼**ero** *m* potter

alféizar *m* window-sill

alferecía f epilepsy

alférez m second lieutenant

alfil m (en ajedrez) bishop

alfile|r m pin. **~razo** m pinprick. **~tero** m pin-case

alfombr|a f (grande) carpet; (pequeña) rug, mat. **~ar** vt carpet. **~illa** f rug, mat; (med) German measles

alforja f saddle-bag

algas fpl seaweed

algarabía f (fig, fam) gibberish, non-sense

algarada f uproar

algarrob|a f carob bean. **~o** m carob tree

algazara f uproar

álgebra f algebra

algebraico a algebraic

álgido a (fig) decisive

algo pron something; (en frases interrogativas) anything. ● adv rather. **¿~ más?** is there anything else? **¿quieres tomar ~?** (de beber) would you like a drink?; (de comer) would you like something to eat?

algod|ón m cotton. **~ón de azúcar** candy floss (Brit), cotton candy (Amer). **~onero** a cotton. ● m cotton plant. **~ón hidrófilo** cotton wool

alguacil m bailiff

alguien pron someone, somebody; (en frases interrogativas) anyone, anybody

alguno a (delante de nombres masculinos en singular **algún**) some; (en frases interrogativas) any; (pospuesto al nombre en frases negativas) at all. **no tiene idea alguna** he hasn't any idea at all. ● pron one; (en plural) some; (alguien) someone. **alguna que otra vez** from time to time. **algunas veces, alguna vez** sometimes

alhaja f piece of jewellery; (fig) treasure. **~r** vt deck with jewels; (amueblar) furnish

alharaca f fuss

alhelí m wallflower

alheña f privet

alhucema f lavender

alia|do a allied. ● m ally. **~nza** f alliance; (anillo) wedding ring. **~r** [20] vt combine. **~rse** vpr be combined; (formar una alianza) form an alliance

alias adv & m alias

alicaído a (fig, débil) weak; (fig, abatido) depressed

alicates mpl pliers

aliciente m incentive; (de un lugar) attraction

alien|ado a mentally ill. **~ista** m & f psychiatrist

aliento m breath; (ánimo) courage

aligera|miento m lightening; (alivio) alleviation. **~r** vt make lighter; (aliviar) alleviate, ease; (apresurar) quicken

alij|ar vt (descargar) unload; smuggle ⟨contrabando⟩. **~o** m unloading; (contrabando) contraband

alimaña f vicious animal

aliment|ación f food; (acción) feeding. **~ar** vt feed; (nutrir) nourish. ● vi be nourishing. **~arse** vpr feed (con, de on). **~icio** a nourishing. **~o** m food. **~os** mpl (jurid) alimony. **productos** mpl **~icios** foodstuffs

alimón. al ~ adv jointly

alinea|ción f alignment; (en deportes) line-up. **~r** vt align, line up

aliñ|ar vt (culin) season. **~o** m seasoning

alioli m garlic sauce

alisar vt smooth

alisios apl. **vientos** mpl **~** trade winds

aliso m alder (tree)

alista|miento m enrolment. **~r** vt put on a list; (mil) enlist. **~rse** vpr enrol; (mil) enlist

aliteración f alliteration

alivi|ador a comforting. **~ar** vt lighten; relieve ⟨dolor, etc⟩; (hurtar, fam) steal, pinch (fam). **~arse** vpr ⟨dolor⟩ diminish; ⟨persona⟩ get better. **~o** m relief

aljibe m tank

alma f soul; (habitante) inhabitant

almac|én m warehouse; (LAm, tienda) grocer's shop; (de un arma) magazine. **~enes** mpl department store. **~enaje** m storage; (derechos) storage charges. **~enamiento** m storage; (mercancías almacenadas) stock. **~enar** vt store; stock up with ⟨provisiones⟩. **~enero** m (Arg) shop-keeper. **~enista** m & f shopkeeper

almádena f sledge-hammer

almanaque m almanac

almeja f clam

almendr|a f almond. **~ado** a almond-shaped. **~o** m almond tree

almiar m haystack

alm|íbar m syrup. **~ibarado** a syrupy. **~ibarar** vt cover in syrup

almid|ón *m* starch. **~onado** *a* starched; (*fig, estirado*) starchy

alminar *m* minaret

almirant|azgo *m* admiralty. **~e** *m* admiral

almirez *m* mortar

almizcle *m* musk

almohad|a *f* cushion; (*de la cama*) pillow; (*funda*) pillowcase. **~illa** *f* small cushion; (*acerico*) pincushion. **~ón** *m* large pillow, bolster. **consultar con la ~a** sleep on it

almorranas *fpl* haemorrhoids, piles

alm|orzar [2 & 10] *vt* (*a mediodía*) have for lunch; (*desayunar*) have for breakfast. **●** *vi* (*a mediodía*) have lunch; (*desayunar*) have breakfast. **~uerzo** *m* (*a mediodía*) lunch; (*desayuno*) breakfast

alocado *a* scatter-brained

alocución *f* address, speech

aloja|r *m* (Mex) lodger, guest. **~miento** *m* accommodation. **~r** *vt* put up. **~rse** *vpr* stay

alondra *f* lark

alpaca *f* alpaca

alpargat|a *f* canvas shoe, espadrille. **~ería** *f* shoe shop

Alpes *mpl* Alps

alpin|ismo *m* mountaineering, climbing. **~ista** *m & f* mountaineer, climber. **~o** *a* Alpine

alpiste *m* birdseed

alquil|ar *vt* (*tomar en alquiler*) hire ⟨*vehículo*⟩, rent ⟨*piso, casa*⟩; (*dar en alquiler*) hire (out) ⟨*vehículo*⟩, rent (out) ⟨*piso, casa*⟩. **~arse** *vpr* (*casa*) be let; ⟨*vehículo*⟩ be on hire. **se alquila** to let (*Brit*), for rent (*Amer*). **~er** *m* (*acción de alquilar un piso etc*) renting; (*acción de alquilar un vehículo*) hiring; (*precio por el que se alquila un piso etc*) rent; (*precio por el que se alquila un vehículo*) hire charge. **de ~er** for hire

alquimi|a *f* alchemy. **~sta** *m* alchemist

alquitara *f* still. **~r** *vt* distil

alquitr|án *m* tar. **~anar** *vt* tar

alrededor *adv* around. **~ de** around; (*con números*) about. **~es** *mpl* surroundings; (*de una ciudad*) outskirts

alta *f* discharge

altamente *adv* highly

altaner|ía *f* (*orgullo*) pride. **~o** *a* proud, haughty

altar *m* altar

altavoz *m* loudspeaker

altera|bilidad *f* changeability. **~ble** *a* changeable. **~ción** *f* change, alteration. **~do** *a* changed, altered; (*perturbado*) disturbed. **~r** *vt* change, alter; (*perturbar*) disturb; (*enfadar*) anger, irritate. **~rse** *vpr* change, alter; (*agitarse*) get upset; (*enfadarse*) get angry; (*comida*) go off

alterca|do *m* argument. **~r** [7] *vi* argue

altern|ado *a* alternate. **~ador** *m* alternator. **~ante** *a* alternating. **~ar** *vt/i* alternate. **~arse** *vpr* take turns. **~ativa** *f* alternative. **~ativo** *a* alternating. **~o** *a* alternate

alteza *f* height. **A~** (*título*) Highness

altibajos *mpl* (*de terreno*) unevenness; (*fig*) ups and downs

altiplanicie *f* high plateau

altísimo *a* very high. **●** *m*. **el A~** the Almighty

altisonante *a*, **altísono** *a* pompous

altitud *f* height; (*aviat, geog*) altitude

altiv|ez *f* arrogance. **~o** *a* arrogant

alto *a* high; ⟨*persona*⟩ tall; ⟨*voz*⟩ loud; (*fig, elevado*) lofty; (*mus*) ⟨*nota*⟩ high(-pitched); (*mus*) ⟨*voz, instrumento*⟩ alto; ⟨*horas*⟩ early. **tiene 3 metros de ~** it is 3 metres high. **●** *adv* high; (*de sonidos*) loud(ly). **●** *m* height; (*de un edificio*) high floor; (*viola*) viola; (*voz*) alto; (*parada*) stop. **●** *int* halt!, stop! **en lo ~ de** on the top of

altoparlante *m* (*esp LAm*) loudspeaker

altruis|mo *m* altruism. **~ta** *a* altruistic. **●** *m & f* altruist

altura *f* height; (*altitud*) altitude; (*de agua*) depth; (*fig, cielo*) sky. **a estas ~s** at this stage. **tiene 3 metros de ~** it is 3 metres high

alubia *f* French bean

alucinación *f* hallucination

alud *m* avalanche

aludi|do *a* in question. **darse por ~do** take it personally. **no darse por ~do** turn a deaf ear. **~r** *vi* mention

alumbra|do *a* lit; (*achispado, fam*) tipsy. **●** *m* lighting. **~miento** *m* lighting; (*parto*) childbirth. **~r** *vt* light. **●** *vi* give birth. **~rse** *vpr* (*emborracharse*) get tipsy

aluminio *m* aluminium (*Brit*), aluminum (*Amer*)

alumno *m* pupil; (*univ*) student

aluniza|je m landing on the moon. ~**r** [10] vi land on the moon

alusi|ón f allusion. ~**vo** a allusive

alverja f vetch; (LAm, guisante) pea

alza f rise. ~**cuello** m clerical collar, dog-collar (fam). ~**da** f (de caballo) height; (jurid) appeal. ~**do** a raised; (persona) fraudulently bankrupt; (Mex, soberbio) vain; (precio) fixed. ~**miento** m raising; (aumento) rise, increase; (pol) revolt. ~**r** [10] vt raise, lift (up); raise (precios). ~**rse** vpr rise; (ponerse en pie) stand up; (pol) revolt; (quebrar) go fraudulently bankrupt; (apelar) appeal

allá adv there. ¡~ él! that's his business. ~ **fuera** out there. ~ **por el 1970** around about 1970. **el más** ~ the beyond. **más** ~ further on. **más** ~ **de** beyond. **por** ~ over there

allana|miento m levelling; (de obstáculos) removal. ~**miento de morada** burglary. ~**r** vt level; remove (obstáculos); (fig) iron out (dificultades etc); burgle (una casa). ~**rse** vpr level off; (hundirse) fall down; (ceder) submit (**a** to)

allega|do a close. ● m relation. ~**r** [12] vt collect

allí adv there; (tiempo) then. ~ **donde** wherever. ~ **fuera** out there. **por** ~ over there

ama f lady of the house. ~ **de casa** housewife. ~ **de cría** wet-nurse. ~ **de llaves** housekeeper

amab|ilidad f kindness. ~**le** a kind; (simpático) nice

amado a dear. ~**r** m lover

amaestra|do a trained; (en circo) performing. ~**miento** m training. ~**r** vt train

amag|ar [12] vt (amenazar) threaten; (mostrar intención de) show signs of. ● vi threaten; (algo bueno) be in the offing. ~**o** m threat; (señal) sign; (med) symptom

amalgama f amalgam. ~**r** vt amalgamate

amamantar vt breast-feed

amancebarse vpr live together

amanecer m dawn. ● vi dawn; (persona) wake up. **al** ~ at dawn, at daybreak

amanera|do a affected. ~**miento** m affectation. ~**rse** vpr become affected

amanezca f (Mex) dawn

amansa|dor m tamer. ~**miento** m taming. ~**r** vt tame; break in (un caballo); soothe (dolor etc). ~**rse** vpr calm down

amante a fond. ● m & f lover

amañ|ar vt arrange. ~**o** m scheme

amapola f poppy

amar vt love

amara|je m landing on the sea; (de astronave) splash-down. ~**r** vt land on the sea; (astronave) splash down

amarg|ado a embittered. ~**ar** [12] vt make bitter; embitter (persona). ~**arse** vpr get bitter. ~**o** a bitter. ● m bitterness. ~**ura** f bitterness

amariconado a effeminate

amarill|ear vi go yellow. ~**ento** a yellowish; (tez) sallow. ~**ez** f yellow; (de una persona) paleness. ~**o** a & m yellow

amarra f mooring rope. ~**s** fpl (fig, fam) influence. ~**do** a (LAm) mean. ~**r** vt moor; (atar) tie. ● vi (empollar, fam) study hard, swot (fam)

amartillar vt cock (arma de fuego)

amas|ar vt knead; (fig, tramar, fam) concoct, cook up (fam). ~**ijo** m dough; (acción) kneading; (fig, mezcla, fam) hotchpotch

amate m (Mex) fig tree

amateur a & m & f amateur

amatista f amethyst

amazona f Amazon; (mujer varonil) mannish woman; (que monta a caballo) horsewoman

Amazonas m. **el río** ~ the Amazon

ambages mpl circumlocutions. **sin** ~ in plain language

ámbar m amber

ambarino a amber

ambici|ón f ambition. ~**onar** vt strive after. ~**onar ser** have an ambition to be. ~**oso** a ambitious. ● m ambitious person

ambidextro a ambidextrous. ● m ambidextrous person

ambient|ar vt give an atmosphere to. ~**arse** vpr adapt o.s. ~**e** m atmosphere; (medio) environment

ambig|uamente adv ambiguously. ~**üedad** f ambiguity. ~**uo** a ambiguous; (fig, afeminado, fam) effeminate

ámbito m ambit

ambos a & pron both. ~ **a dos** both (of them)

ambulancia f ambulance; (hospital móvil) field hospital

ambulante *a* travelling

ambulatorio *m* out-patients' department

amedrentar *vt* frighten, scare. **~se** *vpr* be frightened

amén *m* amen. ● *int* amen! **en un decir ~** in an instant

amenaza *f* threat. **~dor** *a*, **~nte** *a* threatening. **~r** [10] *vt* threaten

amen|idad *f* pleasantness. **~izar** [10] *vt* brighten up. **~o** *a* pleasant

América *f* America. **~ Central** Central America. **~ del Norte** North America. **~ del Sur** South America. **~ Latina** Latin America

american|a *f* jacket. **~ismo** *m* Americanism. **~ista** *m & f* Americanist. **~o** *a* American

amerindio *a & m & f* Amerindian, American Indian

ameriza|je *m* landing on the sea; (*de astronave*) splash-down. **~r** [10] *vt* land on the sea; (*astronave*) splash down

ametralla|dora *f* machine-gun. **~r** *vt* machine-gun

amianto *m* asbestos

amig|a *f* friend; (*novia*) girl-friend; (*amante*) lover. **~able** *a* friendly. **~ablemente** *adv* amicably. **~rse** [12] *vpr* live together

am|ígdala *f* tonsil. **~igdalitis** *f* tonsillitis

amigo *a* friendly. ● *m* friend; (*novio*) boy-friend; (*amante*) lover. **ser ~ de** be fond of. **ser muy ~s** be good friends

amilanar *vt* frighten, scare. **~se** *vpr* be frightened

aminorar *vt* lessen; slow down (*velocidad*)

amist|ad *f* friendship. **~ades** *mpl* friends. **~osamente** *adv* amicably. **~oso** *a* friendly

amnesia *f* amnesia

amnist|ía *f* amnesty. **~iar** [20] *vt* grant an amnesty to

amo *m* master; (*dueño*) owner; (*jefe*) boss; (*cabeza de familia*) head of the family

amodorra|miento *m* sleepiness. **~rse** *vpr* get sleepy

amojonar *vt* mark out

amola|dor *m* knife-grinder. **~r** [2] *vt* sharpen; (*molestar, fam*) annoy

amoldar *vt* mould; (*acomodar*) fit

amonedar *vt* coin, mint

amonesta|ción *f* rebuke, reprimand; (*de una boda*) banns. **~r** *vt* rebuke, reprimand; (*anunciar la boda*) publish the banns

amoniaco *m*, **amoníaco** *m* ammonia

amontillado *m* Amontillado, pale dry sherry

amontona|damente *adv* in a heap. **~miento** *m* piling up. **~r** *vt* pile up; (*fig, acumular*) accumulate. **~rse** *vpr* pile up; (*gente*) crowd together; (*amancebarse, fam*) live together

amor *m* love. **~es** *mpl* (*relaciones amorosas*) love affairs. **con mil ~es**, **de mil ~es** with (the greatest of) pleasure. **hacer el ~** make love. **por (el) ~ de Dios** for God's sake

amorata|do *a* purple; (*de frío*) blue. **~rse** *vpr* go black and blue

amorcillo *m* Cupid

amordazar [10] *vt* gag; (*fig*) silence

amorfo *a* amorphous, shapeless

amor: ~ío *m* affair. **~oso** *a* loving; (*cartas*) love

amortajar *vt* shroud

amortigua|dor *a* deadening. ● *m* (*auto*) shock absorber. **~miento** *m* deadening; (*de la luz*) dimming. **~r** [15] *vt* deaden (*ruido*); dim (*luz*); cushion (*golpe*); tone down (*color*)

amortiza|ble *a* redeemable. **~ción** *f* (*de una deuda*) repayment; (*recuperación*) redemption. **~r** [10] *vt* repay (*una deuda*)

amoscarse [7] *vpr* (*fam*) get cross, get irritated

amostazarse [10] *vpr* get cross

amotina|do *a & m* insurgent, rebellious. **~miento** *m* riot; (*mil*) mutiny. **~r** *vt* incite to riot. **~rse** *vpr* rebel; (*mil*) mutiny

ampar|ar *vt* help; (*proteger*) protect. **~arse** *vpr* seek protection; (*de la lluvia*) shelter. **~o** *m* protection; (*de la lluvia*) shelter. **al ~o de** under the protection of

amperio *m* ampere, amp (fam)

amplia|ción *f* extension; (*photo*) enlargement. **~r** [20] *vt* enlarge, extend; (*photo*) enlarge

amplifica|ción *f* amplification. **~dor** *m* amplifier. **~r** [7] *vt* amplify

ampli|o *a* wide; (*espacioso*) spacious; (*ropa*) loose-fitting. **~tud** *f* extent; (*espaciosidad*) spaciousness; (*espacio*) space

ampolla *f* (*med*) blister; (*frasco*) flask; (*de medicamento*) ampoule, phial

ampuloso *a* pompous

amputa|ción *f* amputation; (*fig*) deletion. ~**r** *vt* amputate; (*fig*) delete

amueblar *vt* furnish

amuinar *vt* (*Mex*) annoy

amuralla|do *a* walled. ~**r** *vt* build a wall around

anacardo *m* (*fruto*) cashew nut

anaconda *f* anaconda

anacr|ónico *a* anachronistic. ~**o-nismo** *m* anachronism

ánade *m* & *f* duck

anagrama *m* anagram

anales *mpl* annals

analfabet|ismo *m* illiteracy. ~**o** *a* & *m* illiterate

analgésico *a* & *m* analgesic, painkiller

an|álisis *m* *invar* analysis. ~**álisis de sangre** blood test. ~**alista** *m* & *f* analyst. ~**alítico** *a* analytical. ~**ali-zar** [10] *vt* analyze

an|alogía *f* analogy. ~**álogo** *a* analogous

ananás *m* pineapple

anaquel *m* shelf

anaranjado *a* orange

an|arquía *f* anarchy. ~**árquico** *a* anarchic. ~**arquismo** *m* anarchism. ~**arquista** *a* anarchistic. ● *m* & *f* anarchist

anatema *m* anathema

anat|omía *f* anatomy. ~**ómico** *a* anatomical

anca *f* haunch; (*parte superior*) rump; (*nalgas, fam*) bottom. ~**s** *fpl* **de rana** frogs' legs

ancestral *a* ancestral

anciano *a* elderly, old. ● *m* elderly man, old man; (*relig*) elder. **los** ~**s** old people

ancla *f* anchor. ~**dero** *m* anchorage. ~**r** *vi* anchor, drop anchor. **echar** ~**s** anchor. **levar** ~**s** weigh anchor

áncora *f* anchor; (*fig*) refuge

ancho *a* wide; (*ropa*) loose-fitting; (*fig*) relieved; (*demasiado grande*) too big; (*ufano*) smug. ● *m* width; (*rail*) gauge. **a mis anchas, a sus anchas etc** comfortable, relaxed. **quedarse tan** ~ behave as if nothing has happened. **tiene 3 metros de** ~ it is 3 metres wide

anchoa *f* anchovy

anchura *f* width; (*medida*) measurement

andaderas *fpl* baby-walker

andad|or *a* good at walking. ● *m* baby-walker. ~**ura** *f* walking; (*manera de andar*) walk

Andalucía *f* Andalusia

andaluz *a* & *m* Andalusian

andamio *m* platform. ~**s** *mpl* scaffolding

andar [25] *vt* (*recorrer*) cover, go. ● *vi* walk; (*máquina*) go, work; (*estar*) be; (*moverse*) move. ● *m* walk. **¡anda!** go on! come on! ~ *vi* (*itinerante*) wandering. ~ **por** be about. ~**se** *vpr* (*marcharse*) go away

andén *m* platform; (*de un muelle*) quayside; (*LAm, acera*) pavement (*Brit*), sidewalk (*Amer*)

Andes *mpl* Andes

andino *a* Andean

Andorra *f* Andorra

andrajo *m* rag. ~**so** *a* ragged

andurriales *mpl* (*fam*) out-of-the-way place

anduve *vb véase* **andar**

anécdota *f* anecdote

anega|dizo *a* subject to flooding. ~**r** [12] *vt* flood. ~**rse** *vpr* be flooded, flood

anejo *a* attached. ● *m* annexe; (*de libro etc*) appendix

an|emia *f* anaemia. ~**émico** *a* anaemic

anest|esia *f* anaesthesia. ~**ésico** *a* & *m* anaesthetic. ~**esista** *m* & *f* anaesthetist

anex|ión *f* annexation. ~**ionar** *vt* annex. ~**o** *a* attached. ● *m* annexe

anfibio *a* amphibious. ● *m* amphibian

anfiteatro *m* amphitheatre; (*en un teatro*) upper circle

anfitri|ón *m* host. ~**ona** *f* hostess

ángel *m* angel; (*encanto*) charm

angelical *a*, **angélico** *a* angelic

angina *f*. ~ **de pecho** angina (pectoris). **tener** ~**s** have tonsillitis

anglicano *a* & *m* Anglican

anglicismo *m* Anglicism

anglófilo *a* & *m* Anglophile

anglo|hispánico *a* Anglo-Spanish. ~**sajón** *a* & *m* Anglo-Saxon

angosto *a* narrow

anguila *f* eel

angula *f* elver, baby eel

angular *a* angular

ángulo *m* angle; (*rincón, esquina*) corner; (*curva*) bend

anguloso *a* angular

angusti|a *f* anguish. **∼ar** *vt* distress; (*inquietar*) worry. **∼arse** *vpr* get distressed; (*inquietarse*) get worried. **∼oso** *a* anguished; (*que causa angustia*) distressing

anhel|ante *a* panting; (*deseoso*) longing. **∼ar** *vt* (+ *nombre*) long for; (+ *verbo*) long to. ● *vi* pant. **∼o** *m* (*fig*) yearning. **∼oso** *a* panting; (*fig*) eager

anidar *vi* nest

anill|a *f* ring. **∼o** *m* ring. **∼o de boda** wedding ring

ánima *f* soul

anima|ción *f* (*de personas*) life; (*de cosas*) liveliness; (*bullicio*) bustle; (*en el cine*) animation. **∼do** *a* lively; (*sitio etc*) busy. **∼dor** *m* compère, host

animadversión *f* ill will

animal *a* animal; (*fig, torpe, fam*) stupid. ● *m* animal; (*fig, idiota, fam*) idiot; (*fig, bruto, fam*) brute

animar *vt* give life to; (*dar ánimo*) encourage; (*dar vivacidad*) liven up. **∼se** *vpr* (*decidirse*) decide; (*ponerse alegre*) cheer up. **¿te animas a venir al cine?** do you fancy coming to the cinema?

ánimo *m* soul; (*mente*) mind; (*valor*) courage; (*intención*) intention. **¡∼!** come on!, cheer up! **dar ∼s** encourage

animosidad *f* animosity

animoso *a* brave; (*resuelto*) determined

aniquila|ción *f* annihilation. **∼miento** *m* annihilation. **∼r** *vt* annihilate; (*acabar con*) ruin. **∼rse** *vpr* deteriorate

anís *m* aniseed; (*licor*) anisette

aniversario *m* anniversary

ano *m* anus

anoche *adv* last night, yesterday evening

anochecer [11] *vi* get dark; (*persona*) be at dusk. **anochecí en Madrid** I was in Madrid at dusk. ● *m* nightfall, dusk. **al ∼** at nightfall

anodino *a* indifferent

an|omalía *f* anomaly. **∼ómalo** *a* anomalous

an|onimato *m* anonymity. **∼ónimo** *a* anonymous; (*sociedad*) limited. ● *m* anonymity; (*carta*) anonymous letter

anormal *a* abnormal; (*fam*) stupid, silly. **∼idad** *f* abnormality

anota|ción *f* noting; (*acción de poner notas*) annotation; (*nota*) note. **∼r** *vt* (*poner nota*) annotate; (*apuntar*) make a note of

anquilosa|miento *m* paralysis. **∼r** *vt* paralyze. **∼rse** *vpr* become paralyzed

ansi|a *f* anxiety, worry; (*anhelo*) yearning. **∼ar** [20 *o regular*] *vt* long for. **∼edad** *f* anxiety. **∼oso** *a* anxious; (*deseoso*) eager

antag|ónico *a* antagonistic. **∼onismo** *m* antagonism. **∼onista** *m & f* antagonist

antaño *adv* in days gone by

antártico *a & m* Antarctic

ante *prep* in front of, before; (*en comparación con*) compared with; (*frente a peligro, enemigo*) in the face of; (*en vista de*) in view of. ● *m* (*piel*) suede. **∼anoche** *adv* the night before last. **∼ayer** *adv* the day before yesterday. **∼brazo** *m* forearm

ante... *pref* ante...

antece|dente *a* previous. ● *m* antecedent. **∼dentes** *mpl* history, background. **∼dentes penales** criminal record. **∼der** *vt* precede. **∼sor** *m* predecessor; (*antepasado*) ancestor

antedicho *a* aforesaid

antelación *f* advance. **con ∼** in advance

antemano *adv.* **de ∼** beforehand

antena *f* antenna; (*radio, TV*) aerial

anteojeras *fpl* blinkers

anteojo *m* telescope. **∼s** *mpl* (*gemelos*) opera glasses; (*prismáticos*) binoculars; (*LAm, gafas*) glasses, spectacles

ante: ∼pasados *mpl* forebears, ancestors. **∼pecho** *m* rail; (*de ventana*) sill. **∼poner** [34] *vt* put in front (**a** of); (*fig*) put before, prefer. **∼proyecto** *m* preliminary sketch; (*fig*) blueprint. **∼puesto** *a* put before

anterior *a* previous; (*delantero*) front, fore. **∼idad** *f.* **con ∼idad** previously. **∼mente** *adv* previously

antes *adv* before; (*antiguamente*) in days gone by; (*mejor*) rather; (*primero*) first. **∼ de** before. **∼ de ayer** the day before yesterday. **∼ de que** + *subj* before. **∼ de que llegue** before he arrives. **cuanto ∼, lo ∼ posible** as soon as possible

antesala *f* anteroom; (*sala de espera*) waiting-room. **hacer ∼** wait (to be received)

anti... *pref* anti...

anti: ~**aéreo** *a* anti-aircraft. ~**bió-tico** *a & m* antibiotic. ~**ciclón** *m* anticyclone

anticip|ación *f* anticipation. **con** ~**ación** in advance. **con media hora de** ~**ación** half an hour early. ~**a-damente** *adv* in advance. ~**ado** *a*. **por** ~**ado** in advance. ~**ar** *vt* bring forward; advance ‹*dinero*›. ~**arse** *vpr* be early. ~**o** *m* (*dinero*) advance; (*fig*) foretaste

anti: ~**concepcional** *a & m* contraceptive. ~**conceptivo** *a & m* contraceptive. ~**congelante** *m* antifreeze

anticua|do *a* old-fashioned. ~**rio** *m* antique dealer. ~**rse** *vpr* go out of date

anticuerpo *m* antibody

antídoto *m* antidote

anti: ~**estético** *a* ugly. ~**faz** *m* mask. ~**gás** *a invar*. **careta** ~**gás** gas mask

antig|ualla *f* old relic. ~**uamente** *adv* formerly; (*hace mucho tiempo*) long ago. ~**üedad** *f* antiquity; (*objeto*) antique; (*en un empleo*) length of service. ~**uo** *a* old, ancient. **chapado a la** ~**ua** old-fashioned

antílope *m* antelope

Antillas *fpl* West Indies

antinatural *a* unnatural

antip|atía *f* dislike; (*cualidad de antipático*) unpleasantness. ~**ático** *a* unpleasant, unfriendly

anti: ~**semita** *m & f* anti-Semite. ~**semítico** *a* anti-Semitic. ~**se-mitismo** *m* anti-Semitism. ~**sép-tico** *a & m* antiseptic. ~**social** *a* antisocial

antítesis *f invar* antithesis

antoj|adizo *a* capricious. ~**arse** *vpr* fancy. **se le** ~**a un caramelo** he fancies a sweet. ~**o** *m* whim; (*de embarazada*) craving

antología *f* anthology

antorcha *f* torch

antro *m* cavern; (*fig*) dump, hole. ~ **de perversión** den of iniquity

antropófago *m* cannibal

antrop|ología *f* anthropology. ~**ó-logo** *m & f* anthropologist

anua|l *a* annual. ~**lidad** *f* annuity. ~**lmente** *adv* yearly. ~**rio** *m* yearbook

anudar *vt* tie, knot; (*fig, iniciar*) begin; (*fig, continuar*) resume. ~**se**

vpr get into knots. ~**se la voz** get a lump in one's throat

anula|ción *f* annulment, cancellation. ~**r** *vt* annul, cancel. ● *a* ‹*dedo*› ring. ● *m* ring finger

Anunciación *f* Annunciation

anunci|ante *m & f* advertiser. ~**ar** *vt* announce; advertise ‹*producto comercial*›; (*presagiar*) be a sign of. ~**arse** *vpr* promise to be. ~**o** *m* announcement; (*para vender algo*) advertisement, advert (*fam*); (*cartel*) poster

anzuelo *m* (fish)hook; (*fig*) bait. **tragar el** ~ be taken in, fall for it

añadi|do *a* added. ~**dura** *f* addition. ~**r** *vt* add. **por** ~**dura** besides

añejo *a* ‹*vino*› mature; ‹*jamón etc*› cured

añicos *mpl* bits. **hacer** ~ (*romper*) smash (to pieces); (*dejar cansado*) wear out

añil *m* indigo

año *m* year. ~ **bisiesto** leap year. ~ **nuevo** new year. **al** ~ per year, a year. **¿cuántos** ~**s tiene?** tiene 5 ~**s** how old is he? he's 5 (years old). **el** ~ **pasado** last year. **el** ~ **que viene** next year. **entrado en** ~**s** elderly. **los** ~**s 60** the sixties

añora|nza *f* nostalgia. ~**r** *vt* miss. ● *vi* pine

apabullar *vt* crush; (*fig*) intimidate

apacentar [1] *vt* graze. ~**se** *vpr* graze

apacib|ilidad *f* gentleness; (*calma*) peacefulness. ~**le** *a* gentle; ‹*tiempo*› mild

apacigua|dor *a* pacifying. ~**mien-to** *m* appeasement. ~**r** [15] *vt* pacify; (*calmar*) calm; relieve ‹*dolor etc*›. ~**rse** *vpr* calm down

apadrina|miento *m* sponsorship. ~**r** *vt* sponsor; be godfather to ‹*a un niño*›; (*en una boda*) be best man for

apaga|dizo *a* slow to burn. ~**do** *a* extinguished; ‹*color*› dull; (*aparato eléctrico*) off; ‹*persona*› lifeless; ‹*sonido*› muffled. ~**r** [12] *vt* put out ‹*fuego, incendio*›; turn off, switch off ‹*aparato eléctrico*›; quench ‹*sed*›; muffle ‹*sonido*›. ~**rse** *vpr* ‹*fuego*› go out; ‹*luz*› go out; ‹*sonido*› die away; (*fig*) pass away

apagón *m* blackout

apalabrar *vt* make a verbal agreement; (*contratar*) engage. ~**se** *vpr* come to a verbal agreement

apalanca|miento *m* leverage. **~r** [7] *vt* (*levantar*) lever up; (*abrir*) lever open

apalea|miento *m* (*de grano*) winnowing; (*de alfombras, frutos, personas*) beating. **~r** *vt* winnow ⟨*grano*⟩; beat ⟨*alfombras, frutos, personas*⟩; (*fig*) be rolling in ⟨*dinero*⟩

apantallado *a* (*Mex*) stupid

apañ|ado *a* handy. **~ar** *vt* (*arreglar*) fix; (*remendar*) mend; (*agarrar*) grasp, take hold of. **~arse** *vpr* get along, manage. ¡**estoy ~ado!** that's all I need!

aparador *m* sideboard

aparato *m* apparatus; (*máquina*) machine; (*teléfono*) telephone; (*radio, TV*) set; (*ostentación*) show, pomp. **~samente** *adv* ostentatiously; (*impresionante*) spectacularly. **~sidad** *f* ostentation. **~so** *a* showy, ostentatious; ⟨*caída*⟩ spectacular

aparca|miento *m* car park (*Brit*), parking lot (*Amer*). **~r** [7] *vt/i* park

aparea|miento *m* pairing off. **~r** *vt* pair off; mate ⟨*animales*⟩. **~rse** *vpr* match; ⟨*animales*⟩ mate

aparecer [11] *vi* appear. **~se** *vpr* appear

aparej|ado *a* ready; (*adecuado*) fitting. **llevar ~ado, traer ~ado** mean, entail. **~o** *m* preparation; (*avíos*) equipment

aparent|ar *vt* (*afectar*) feign; (*parecer*) look. ● *vi* show off. **~a 20 años** she looks like she's 20. **~e** *a* apparent; (*adecuado, fam*) suitable

apari|ción *f* appearance; (*visión*) apparition. **~encia** *f* appearance; (*fig*) show. **cubrir las ~encias** keep up appearances

apartad|ero *m* lay-by; (*rail*) siding. **~o** *a* separated; (*aislado*) isolated. ● *m* (*de un texto*) section. **~o** (**de correos**) post-office box, PO box

apartamento *m* flat (*Brit*), apartment

apart|amiento *m* separation; (*LAm, piso*) flat (*Brit*), apartment; (*aislamiento*) seclusion. **~ar** *vt* separate; (*quitar*) remove. **~arse** *vpr* leave; abandon ⟨*creencia*⟩; (*quitarse de en medio*) get out of the way; (*aislarse*) cut o.s. off. **~e** *adv* apart; (*por separado*) separately; (*además*) besides. ● *m* aside; (*párrafo*) new paragraph. **~e de** apart from. **dejar**

~e leave aside. **eso ~e** apart from that

apasiona|do *a* passionate; (*entusiasta*) enthusiastic; (*falto de objetividad*) biassed. ● *m* lover (**de** of). **~miento** *m* passion. **~r** *vt* excite. **~rse** *vpr* get excited (**de, por** about), be mad (**de, por** about); (*ser parcial*) become biassed

ap|atía *f* apathy. **~ático** *a* apathetic

apea|dero *m* (*rail*) halt. **~r** *vt* fell ⟨*árbol*⟩; (*disuadir*) dissuade; overcome ⟨*dificultad*⟩; sort out ⟨*problema*⟩. **~rse** *vpr* (*de un vehículo*) get off

apechugar [12] *vi* push (with one's chest). **~ con** put up with

apedrear *vt* stone

apeg|ado *a* attached. **~o** *m* (*fam*) affection. **tener ~o a** be fond of

apela|ción *f* appeal. **~r** appeal; (*recurrir*) resort (**a** to)

apelmazar [10] *vt* compress

apellid|ar *vt* call. **~arse** *vpr* be called. **¿cómo te apellidas?** what's your surname? **~o** *m* surname

apenar *vt* pain. **~se** *vpr* grieve

apenas *adv* hardly, scarcely; (*enseguida que*) as soon as. **~ si** (*fam*) hardly

ap|éndice *m* (*med*) appendix; (*fig*) appendage; (*de un libro*) appendix. **~endicitis** *f* appendicitis

apercibi|miento *m* warning. **~r** *vt* warn (**de** of, about); (*amenazar*) threaten. **~rse** *vpr* prepare; (*percatarse*) provide o.s. (**de** with)

apergaminado *a* ⟨*piel*⟩ wrinkled

aperitivo *m* (*bebida*) aperitif; (*comida*) appetizer

aperos *mpl* agricultural equipment

apertura *f* opening

apesadumbrar *vt* upset. **~se** *vpr* be upset

apestar *vt* stink out; (*fastidiar*) pester. ● *vi* stink (**a** of)

apet|ecer [11] *vt* long for; (*interesar*) appeal to. **¿te ~ece una copa?** do you fancy a drink? do you feel like a drink?. ● *vi* be welcome. **~ecible** *a* attractive. **~ito** *m* appetite; (*fig*) desire. **~itoso** *a* tempting

apiadarse *vpr* feel sorry (**de** for)

ápice *m* (*nada, en frases negativas*) anything. **no ceder un ~** not give an inch

apicult|or *m* bee-keeper. **~ura** *f* bee-keeping

apilar *vt* pile up

apiñar *vt* pack in. **~se** *vpr* ⟨*personas*⟩ crowd together; ⟨*cosas*⟩ be packed tight

apio *m* celery

apisonadora *f* steamroller

aplacar [7] *vt* placate; relieve ⟨*dolor*⟩

aplanar *vt* smooth. **~se** *vpr* become smooth; ⟨*persona*⟩ lose heart

aplasta|nte *a* overwhelming. **~r** *vt* crush. **~rse** *vpr* flatten o.s.

aplatanarse *vpr* become lethargic

aplau|dir *vt* clap, applaud; (*fig*) applaud. **~so** *m* applause; (*fig*) praise

aplaza|miento *m* postponement. **~r** [10] *vt* postpone; defer ⟨*pago*⟩

aplebeyarse *vpr* lower o.s.

aplica|ble *a* applicable. **~ción** *f* application. **~do** *a* ⟨*persona*⟩ diligent. **~r** [7] *vt* apply; (*fijar*) attach. **~rse** *vpr* apply o.s.

aplom|ado *a* self-confident; (*vertical*) vertical. **~o** *m* (self-) confidence, aplomb; (*verticalidad*) verticality

apocado *a* timid

Apocalipsis *f* Apocalypse

apocalíptico *a* apocalyptic

apoca|miento *m* diffidence. **~r** [7] *vt* belittle ⟨*persona*⟩. **~rse** *vpr* feel small

apodar *vt* nickname

apodera|do *m* representative. **~r** *vt* authorize. **~rse** *vpr* seize

apodo *m* nickname

apogeo *m* (*fig*) height

apolilla|do *a* moth-eaten. **~rse** *vpr* get moth-eaten

apolítico *a* non-political

apología *f* defence

apoltronarse *vpr* get lazy

apoplejía *f* stroke

apoquinar *vt/i* (*fam*) fork out

aporrear *vt* hit, thump; beat up ⟨*persona*⟩

aporta|ción *f* contribution. **~r** *vt* contribute

aposent|ar *vt* put up, lodge. **~o** *m* room, lodgings

apósito *m* dressing

aposta *adv* on purpose

apostar¹ [2] *vt/i* bet

apostar² *vt* station. **~se** *vpr* station o.s.

apostilla *f* note. **~r** *vt* add notes to

apóstol *m* apostle

apóstrofo *m* apostrophe

apoy|ar *vt* lean (**en** against); (*descansar*) rest; (*asentar*) base; (*reforzar*) support. **~arse** *vpr* lean, rest. **~o** *m* support

apreci|able *a* appreciable; (*digno de estima*) worthy. **~ación** *f* appreciation; (*valoración*) appraisal. **~ar** *vt* value; (*estimar*) appreciate. **~ativo** *a* appreciative. **~o** *m* appraisal; (*fig*) esteem

aprehensión *f* capture

apremi|ante *a* urgent, pressing. **~ar** *vt* urge; (*obligar*) compel; (*dar prisa a*) hurry up. ● *vi* be urgent. **~o** *m* urgency; (*obligación*) obligation

aprender *vt/i* learn. **~se** *vpr* learn (by heart)

aprendiz *m* apprentice. **~aje** *m* apprenticeship

aprensi|ón *f* apprehension; (*miedo*) fear. **~vo** *a* apprehensive, fearful

apresa|dor *m* captor. **~miento** *m* capture. **~r** *vt* seize; (*prender*) capture

aprestar *vt* prepare. **~se** *vpr* prepare

apresura|damente *adv* hurriedly, in a hurry. **~do** *a* in a hurry; (*hecho con prisa*) hurried. **~miento** *m* hurry. **~r** *vt* hurry. **~rse** *vpr* hurry

apret|ado *a* tight; (*difícil*) difficult; (*tacaño*) stingy, mean. **~ar** [1] *vt* tighten; press ⟨*botón*⟩; squeeze ⟨*persona*⟩; (*comprimir*) press down. ● *vi* be too tight. **~arse** *vpr* crowd together. **~ón** *m* squeeze. **~ón de manos** handshake

aprieto *m* difficulty. **verse en un ~** be in a tight spot

aprisa *adv* quickly

aprisionar *vt* imprison

aproba|ción *f* approval. **~r** [2] *vt* approve (of); pass ⟨*examen*⟩. ● *vi* pass

apropia|do *a* appropriate. **~rse** *vpr*. **~rse de** appropriate, take

aprovecha|ble *a* usable. **~do** *a* (*aplicado*) diligent; (*ingenioso*) resourceful; (*egoísta*) selfish; (*económico*) thrifty. **~miento** *m* advantage; (*uso*) use. **~r** *vt* take advantage of; (*utilizar*) make use of. ● *vi* be useful. **~rse** *vpr* make the most of it. **~rse de** take advantage of. **¡que aproveche!** enjoy your meal!

aprovisionar *vt* supply (**con, de** with)

aproxima|ción f approximation; (*proximidad*) closeness; (*en la lotería*) consolation prize. **~damente** adv roughly, approximately. **~do** a approximate, rough. **~r** vt bring near; (*fig*) bring together ⟨*personas*⟩. **~rse** vpr come closer, approach

apt|itud f suitability; (*capacidad*) ability. **~o** a (*capaz*) capable; (*adecuado*) suitable

apuesta f bet

apuesto m smart. ● vb véase **apostar**[1]

apunta|ción f note. **~do** a sharp. **~dor** m prompter

apuntalar vt shore up

apunt|amiento m aiming; (*nota*) note. **~ar** vt aim ⟨*arma*⟩; (*señalar*) point at; (*anotar*) make a note of, note down; (*sacar punta*) sharpen; (*en el teatro*) prompt. **~arse** vpr put one's name down; score ⟨*triunfo, tanto etc*⟩. **~e** m note; (*bosquejo*) sketch. **tomar ~s** take notes

apuñalar vt stab

apur|adamente adv with difficulty. **~ado** a difficult; (*sin dinero*) hard up; (*agotado*) exhausted; (*exacto*) precise, carefully done. **~ar** vt exhaust; (*acabar*) finish; drain ⟨*vaso etc*⟩; (*fastidiar*) annoy; (*causar vergüenza*) embarrass. **~arse** vpr worry; (*esp LAm, apresurarse*) hurry up. **~o** m tight spot, difficult situation; (*vergüenza*) embarrassment; (*estrechez*) hardship, want; (*esp LAm, prisa*) hurry

aquejar vt trouble

aquel a (f **aquella**, mpl **aquellos**, fpl **aquellas**) that; (*en plural*) those; (*primero de dos*) former

aquél pron (f **aquélla**, mpl **aquéllos**, fpl **aquéllas**) that one; (*en plural*) those; (*primero de dos*) the former

aquello pron that; (*asunto*) that business

aquí adv here. **de ~** from here. **de ~ a 15 días** in a fortnight's time. **de ~ para allí** to and fro. **de ~ que** so that. **hasta ~** until now. **por ~** around here

aquiescencia f acquiescence

aquietar vt calm (down)

aquí: ~ fuera out here. **~ mismo** right here

árabe a & m & f Arab; (*lengua*) Arabic

Arabia f Arabia. **~ saudita, ~ saudí** Saudi Arabia

arábigo a Arabic

arado m plough. **~r** m ploughman

Aragón m Aragon

aragonés a & m Aragonese

arancel m tariff. **~ario** a tariff

arandela f washer

araña f spider; (*lámpara*) chandelier

arañar vt scratch

arar vt plough

arbitra|je m arbitration; (*en deportes*) refereeing. **~r** vt/i arbitrate; (*en fútbol etc*) referee; (*en tenis etc*) umpire

arbitr|ariedad f arbitrariness. **~ario** a arbitrary. **~io** m (*free*) will; (*jurid*) decision, judgement

árbitro m arbitrator; (*en fútbol etc*) referee; (*en tenis etc*) umpire

árbol m tree; (*eje*) axle; (*palo*) mast

arbol|ado m trees. **~adura** f rigging. **~eda** f wood

árbol: ~ genealógico family tree. **~ de navidad** Christmas tree

arbusto m bush

arca f (*caja*) chest. **~ de Noé** Noah's ark

arcada f arcade; (*de un puente*) arches; (*náuseas*) retching

arca|ico a archaic. **~ísmo** m archaism

arcángel m archangel

arcano m mystery. ● a mysterious, secret

arce m maple (tree)

arcén m (*de autopista*) hard shoulder; (*de carretera*) verge

arcilla f clay

arco m arch; (*de curva*) arc; (*arma, mus*) bow. **~ iris** m rainbow

archipiélago m archipelago

archiv|ador m filing cabinet. **~ar** vt file (away). **~o** m file; (*de documentos históricos*) archives

arder vt/i burn; (*fig, de ira*) seethe. **~se** vpr burn (up). **estar que arde** be very tense. **y va que arde** and that's enough

ardid m trick, scheme

ardiente a burning. **~mente** adv passionately

ardilla f squirrel

ardor m heat; (*fig*) ardour. **~ de estómago** m heartburn. **~oso** a burning

arduo a arduous

área f area

arena f sand; (en deportes) arena; (en los toros) (bull)ring. **~l** m sandy area

arenga f harangue. **~r** [12] vt harangue

aren|isca f sandstone. **~isco** a, **~oso** a sandy

arenque m herring. **~ ahumado** kipper

argamasa f mortar

Argel m Algiers. **~ia** f Algeria

argelino a & m Algerian

argentado a silver-plated

Argentina f. **la ~** Argentina

argentin|ismo m Argentinism. **~o** a silvery; (de la Argentina) Argentinian, Argentine. ● m Argentinian

argolla f ring

argot m slang

argucia f sophism

argüir [19] vt (deducir) deduce; (probar) prove, show; (argumentar) argue; (echar en cara) reproach. ● vi argue

argument|ación f argument. **~ador** a argumentative. **~ar** vt/i argue. **~o** m argument; (de libro, película etc) story, plot; (resumen) synopsis

aria f aria

aridez f aridity, dryness

árido a arid, dry. ● m. **~s** mpl dry goods

Aries m Aries

arisco a ⟨persona⟩ unsociable; ⟨animal⟩ vicious

arist|ocracia f aristocracy. **~ócrata** m & f aristocrat. **~ocrático** a aristocratic

aritmética f arithmetic

arma f arm, weapon; (sección) section. **~da** f navy; (flota) fleet. **~ de fuego** firearm. **~do** a armed (de with). **~dura** f armour; (de gafas etc) frame; (tec) framework. **~mento** m arms, armaments; (acción de armar) armament. **~r** vt arm (de with); (montar) put together. **~r un lío** kick up a fuss. **La A~da Invencible** the Armada

armario m cupboard; (para ropa) wardrobe. **~ ropero** wardrobe

armatoste m monstrosity, hulk (fam)

armazón m & f frame(work)

armer|ía f gunsmith's shop; (museo) war museum. **~o** m gunsmith

armiño m ermine

armisticio m armistice

armonía f harmony

armónica f harmonica, mouth organ

armoni|oso a harmonious. **~zación** f harmonizing. **~zar** [10] vt harmonize. ● vi harmonize; ⟨personas⟩ get on well (con with); ⟨colores⟩ go well (con with)

arnés m armour. **arneses** mpl harness

aro m ring, hoop; (Arg, pendiente) earring

arom|a m aroma; (de vino) bouquet. **~ático** a aromatic. **~atizar** [10] vt perfume; (culin) flavour

arpa f harp

arpado a serrated

arpía f harpy; (fig) hag

arpillera f sackcloth, sacking

arpista m & f harpist

arp|ón m harpoon. **~onar** vt, **~onear** vt harpoon

arque|ar vt arch, bend. **~arse** vpr arch, bend. **~o** m arching, bending

arque|ología f archaeology. **~ológico** a archaeological. **~ólogo** m archaeologist

arquería f arcade

arquero m archer; (com) cashier

arqueta f chest

arquetipo m archetype; (prototipo) prototype

arquitect|o m architect. **~ónico** a architectural. **~ura** f architecture

arrabal m suburb; (LAm, tugurio) slum. **~es** mpl outskirts. **~ero** a suburban; (de modales groseros) common

arracima|do a in a bunch; (apiñado) bunched together. **~rse** vpr bunch together

arraiga|damente adv firmly. **~r** [12] vi take root. **~rse** vpr take root; (fig) settle

arran|cada f sudden start. **~car** [7] vt pull up ⟨planta⟩; extract ⟨diente⟩; (arrebatar) snatch; (auto) start. ● vi start. **~carse** vpr start. **~que** m sudden start; (auto) start; (de emoción) outburst

arras fpl security

arrasa|dor a overwhelming, devastating. **~r** vt level, smooth; raze to the ground ⟨edificio etc⟩; (llenar) fill to the brim. ● vi ⟨el cielo⟩ clear. **~rse** vpr ⟨el cielo⟩ clear; ⟨los ojos⟩ fill with tears; (triunfar) triumph

arrastr|ado *a* (*penoso*) wretched. **~ar** *vt* pull; (*rozar contra el suelo*) drag (along); give rise to ‹*consecuencias*›. ● *vi* trail on the ground. **~arse** *vpr* crawl; (*humillarse*) grovel. **~e** *m* dragging; (*transporte*) haulage. **estar para el ~e** (*fam*) have had it, be worn out. **ir ~ado** be hard up

arrayán *m* myrtle

arre *int* gee up! **~ar** *vt* urge on; give ‹*golpe*›

arrebañar *vt* scrape together; scrape clean ‹*plato etc*›

arrebat|ado *a* enraged; (*irreflexivo*) impetuous; ‹*cara*› flushed. **~ar** *vt* snatch (away); ‹*el viento*› blow away; (*fig*) win (over); captivate ‹*corazón etc*›. **~arse** *vpr* get carried away. **~o** *m* (*de cólera etc*) fit; (*éxtasis*) extasy

arrebol *m* red glow

arreciar *vi* get worse, increase

arrecife *m* reef

arregl|ado *a* neat; (*bien vestido*) well-dressed; (*moderado*) moderate. **~ar** *vt* arrange; (*poner en orden*) tidy up; sort out ‹*asunto, problema etc*›; (*reparar*) mend. **~arse** *vpr* (*ponerse bien*) improve; (*prepararse*) get ready; (*apañarse*) manage, make do; (*ponerse de acuerdo*) come to an agreement. **~árselas** manage, get by. **~o** *m* (*incl mus*) arrangement; (*acción de reparar*) repair; (*acuerdo*) agreement; (*orden*) order. **con ~o a** according to

arrellanarse *vpr* lounge, sit back

arremangar [12] *vt* roll up ‹*mangas*›; tuck up ‹*falda*›. **~se** *vpr* roll up one's sleeves

arremet|er *vt/i* attack. **~ida** *f* attack

arremolinarse *vpr* mill about

arrenda|dor *m* (*que da en alquiler*) landlord; (*que toma en alquiler*) tenant. **~miento** *m* renting; (*contrato*) lease; (*precio*) rent. **~r** [1] *vt* (*dar casa en alquiler*) let; (*dar cosa en alquiler*) hire out; (*tomar en alquiler*) rent. **~tario** *m* tenant

arreos *mpl* harness

arrepenti|miento *m* repentance, regret. **~rse** [4] *vpr*. **~rse de** be sorry, regret; repent ‹*pecados*›

arrest|ar *vt* arrest, detain; (*encarcelar*) imprison. **~o** *m* arrest; (*encarcelamiento*) imprisonment

arriar [20] *vt* lower ‹*bandera, vela*›; (*aflojar*) loosen; (*inundar*) flood. **~se** *vpr* be flooded

arriba *adv* (up) above; (*dirección*) up(wards); (*en casa*) upstairs. ● *int* up with; (*¡levántate!*) up you get!; (*¡ánimo!*) come on! **¡~ España!** long live Spain! **~ mencionado** aforementioned. **calle ~** up the street. **de ~ abajo** from top to bottom. **de 100 pesetas para ~** more than 100 pesetas. **escaleras ~** upstairs. **la parte de ~** the top part. **los de ~** those at the top. **más ~** above

arribar *vi* ‹*barco*› reach port; (*esp LAm, llegar*) arrive

arribista *m & f* self-seeking person, arriviste

arribo *m* (*esp LAm*) arrival

arriero *m* muleteer

arriesga|do *a* risky. **~r** [12] *vt* risk; (*aventurar*) venture. **~rse** *vpr* take a risk

arrim|ar *vt* bring close(r); (*apartar*) move out of the way ‹*cosa*›; (*apartar*) push aside ‹*persona*›. **~arse** *vpr* come closer, approach; (*apoyarse*) lean (**a** on). **~o** *m* support. **al ~o de** with the support of

arrincona|do *a* forgotten. **~rse** *vt* put in a corner; (*perseguir*) corner; (*arrumbar*) put aside; (*apartar a uno*) leave out, ignore. **~rse** *vpr* become a recluse

arriscado *a* ‹*terreno*› uneven

arrobar *vt* entrance. **~se** *vpr* be enraptured

arrocero *a* rice

arrodillarse *vpr* kneel (down)

arrogan|cia *f* arrogance; (*orgullo*) pride. **~te** *a* arrogant; (*orgulloso*) proud

arrogarse [12] *vpr* assume

arroj|ado *a* brave. **~ar** *vt* throw; (*dejar caer*) drop; (*emitir*) give off, throw out; (*producir*) produce. ● *vi* (*esp LAm, vomitar*) be sick. **~arse** *vpr* throw o.s. **~o** *m* courage

arrolla|dor *a* overwhelming. **~r** *vt* roll (up); (*atropellar*) run over; ‹*ejército*› crush; ‹*agua*› sweep away; (*tratar sin respeto*) have no respect for

arropar *vt* wrap up; (*en la cama*) tuck up; (*fig, amparar*) protect. **~se** *vpr* wrap (o.s.) up

arroy|o *m* stream; (*de una calle*) gutter; (*fig, de lágrimas*) flood; (*fig, de sangre*) pool. **poner en el ~o** throw into the street. **~uelo** *m* small stream

arroz *m* rice. ~**al** *m* rice field. ~ **con leche** rice pudding

arruga *f* (*en la piel*) wrinkle, line; (*en tela*) crease. ~**r** [12] *vt* wrinkle; crumple ‹*papel*›; crease ‹*tela*›. ~**rse** *vpr* ‹*la piel*› wrinkle, get wrinkled; ‹*tela*› crease, get creased

arruinar *vt* ruin; (*destruir*) destroy. ~**se** ‹*persona*› be ruined; ‹*edificio*› fall into ruins

arrullar *vt* lull to sleep. ● *vi* ‹*palomas*› coo. ~**se** *vpr* bill and coo

arrumaco *m* caress; (*zalamería*) flattery

arrumbar *vt* put aside

arsenal *m* (*astillero*) shipyard; (*de armas*) arsenal; (*fig*) store

arsénico *m* arsenic

arte *m* en singular, *f* en plural art; (*habilidad*) skill; (*astucia*) cunning. **bellas** ~**s** fine arts. **con** ~ skilfully. **malas** ~**s** trickery. **por amor al** ~ for nothing, for love

artefacto *m* device

arter|amente *adv* artfully. ~**ía** *f* cunning

arteria *f* artery; (*fig, calle*) main road

artero *a* cunning

artesan|al *a* craft. ~**ía** *f* handicrafts. ~**o** *m* artisan, craftsman. **objeto** *m* **de** ~**ía** hand-made article

ártico *a & m* Arctic

articula|ción *f* joint; (*pronunciación*) articulation. ~**damente** *adv* articulately. ~**do** *a* articulated; ‹*lenguaje*› articulate. ~**r** *vt* articulate

articulista *m & f* columnist

artículo *m* article. ~**s** *mpl* (*géneros*) goods. ~ **de exportación** export commodity. ~ **de fondo** editorial, leader

artificial *a* artificial

artificiero *m* bomb-disposal expert

artificio *m* (*habilidad*) skill; (*dispositivo*) device; (*engaño*) trick. ~**so** *a* clever; (*astuto*) artful

artilugio *m* gadget

artiller|ía *f* artillery. ~**o** *m* artilleryman, gunner

artimaña *f* trap

art|ista *m & f* artist; (*en espectáculos*) artiste. ~**ísticamente** *adv* artistically. ~**ístico** *a* artistic

artr|ítico *a* arthritic. ~**itis** *f* arthritis

arveja *f* vetch; (*LAm, guisante*) pea

arzobispo *m* archbishop

as *m* ace

asa *f* handle

asad|o *a* roast(ed). ● *m* roast (meat), joint. ~**o a la parrilla** grilled. ~**o al horno** (*sin grasa*) baked; (*con grasa*) roast. ~**or** *m* spit. ~**ura** *f* offal

asalariado *a* salaried. ● *m* employee

asalt|ante *m* attacker; (*de un banco*) robber. ~**ar** *vt* storm ‹*fortaleza*›; attack ‹*persona*›; raid ‹*banco etc*›; (*fig*) ‹*duda*› assail; (*fig*) ‹*idea etc*› cross one's mind. ~**o** *m* attack; (*en boxeo*) round

asamble|a *f* assembly; (*reunión*) meeting; (*congreso*) conference. ~**ísta** *m & f* member of an assembly

asapán *m* (*Mex*) flying squirrel

asar *vt* roast; (*fig, acosar*) pester (**a** with). ~**se** *vpr* be very hot. ~ **a la parrilla** grill. ~ **al horno** (*sin grasa*) bake; (*con grasa*) roast

asbesto *m* asbestos

ascendencia *f* descent

ascend|ente *a* ascending. ~**er** [1] *vt* promote. ● *vi* go up, ascend; ‹*cuenta etc*› come to, amount to; (*ser ascendido*) be promoted. ~**iente** *m & f* ancestor; (*influencia*) influence

ascens|ión *f* ascent; (*de grado*) promotion. ~**ional** *a* upward. ~**o** *m* ascent; (*de grado*) promotion. **día** *m* **de la A**~**ión** Ascension Day

ascensor *m* lift (*Brit*), elevator (*Amer*). ~**ista** *m & f* lift attendant (*Brit*), elevator operator (*Amer*)

asc|eta *m & f* ascetic. ~**ético** *a* ascetic

asco *m* disgust. **dar** ~ be disgusting; (*fig, causar enfado*) be infuriating. **estar hecho un** ~ be disgusting. **hacer** ~**s de algo** turn up one's nose at sth. **me da** ~ **el ajo** I can't stand garlic. **¡qué** ~**!** how disgusting! **ser un** ~ be a disgrace

ascua *f* ember. **estar en** ~**s** be on tenterhooks

asea|damente *adv* cleanly. ~**do** *a* clean; (*arreglado*) neat. ~**r** *vt* (*lavar*) wash; (*limpiar*) clean; (*arreglar*) tidy up

asedi|ar *vt* besiege; (*fig*) pester. ~**o** *m* siege

asegura|do *a & m* insured. ~**dor** *m* insurer. ~**r** *vt* secure, make safe; (*decir*) assure; (*concertar un seguro*) insure; (*preservar*) safeguard. ~**rse** *vpr* make sure

asemejarse *vpr* be alike

asenta|da *f*. **de una** ~**da** at a sitting. ~**do** *a* situated; (*arraigado*) established. ~**r** [1] *vt* place; (*asegurar*) settle; (*anotar*) note down. ● *vi* be suitable. ~**rse** *vpr* settle; (*estar situado*) be situated

asenti|miento *m* consent. ~**r** [4] *vi* agree (**a** to). ~**r con la cabeza** nod

aseo *m* cleanliness. ~**s** *mpl* toilets

asequible *a* obtainable; (*precio*) reasonable; (*persona*) approachable

asesin|ar *vt* murder; (*pol*) assassinate. ~**ato** *m* murder; (*pol*) assassination. ~**o** *m* murderer; (*pol*) assassin

asesor *m* adviser, consultant. ~**a-miento** *m* advice. ~**ar** *vt* advise. ~**arse** *vpr*. ~**arse con/de** consult. ~**ía** *f* consultancy; (*oficina*) consultant's office

asestar *vt* aim (*arma*); strike (*golpe etc*); (*disparar*) fire

asevera|ción *f* assertion. ~**r** *vt* assert

asfalt|ado *a* asphalt. ~**ar** *vt* asphalt. ~**o** *m* asphalt

asfixia *f* suffocation. ~**nte** *a* suffocating. ~**r** *vt* suffocate. ~**rse** *vpr* suffocate

así *adv* so; (*de esta manera*) like this, like that. ● *a* such. ~ ~, ~ **asá**, ~ **asado** so-so. ~ **como** just as. ~... **como** both... and. ~ **pues** so. ~ **que** so; (*enseguida*) as soon as. ~ **sea** so be it. ~ **y todo** even so. **aun** ~ even so. **¿no es** ~**?** isn't that right? **y** ~ **(sucesivamente)** and so on

Asia *f* Asia

asiático *a* & *m* Asian

asidero *m* handle; (*fig, pretexto*) excuse

asidu|amente *adv* regularly. ~**idad** *f* regularity. ~**o** *a* & *m* regular

asiento *m* seat; (*situación*) site. ~ **delantero** front seat. ~ **trasero** back seat. **tome Vd** ~ please take a seat

asigna|ción *f* assignment; (*sueldo*) salary. ~**r** *vt* assign; allot (*porción, tiempo etc*)

asignatura *f* subject. ~ **pendiente** (*escol*) failed subject; (*fig*) matter still to be resolved

asil|ado *m* inmate. ~**ado político** refugee. ~**o** *m* asylum; (*fig*) shelter; (*de ancianos etc*) home. ~**o de huérfanos** orphanage. **pedir** ~**o político** ask for political asylum

asimétrico *a* asymmetrical

asimila|ción *f* assimilation. ~**r** *vt* assimilate. ~**rse** *vpr* be assimilated. ~**rse a** resemble

asimismo *adv* in the same way, likewise

asir [45] *vt* grasp. ~**se** *vpr* grab hold (**a, de** of)

asist|encia *f* attendance; (*gente*) people (present); (*en un teatro etc*) audience; (*ayuda*) assistance. ~**encia médica** medical care. ~**enta** *f* assistant; (*mujer de la limpieza*) charwoman. ~**ente** *m* assistant. ~**ente social** social worker. ~**ido** *a* assisted. ~**ir** *vt* assist, help; (*un médico*) treat. ● *vi*. ~**ir a** attend, be present at

asm|a *f* asthma. ~**ático** *a* & *m* asthmatic

asn|ada *f* (*fig*) silly thing. ~**o** *m* donkey; (*fig*) ass

asocia|ción *f* association; (*com*) partnership. ~**do** *a* associated; (*miembro etc*) associate. ● *m* associate. ~**r** *vt* associate; (*com*) take into partnership. ~**rse** *vpr* associate; (*com*) become a partner

asolador *a* destructive

asolar[1] *vt* destroy. ~**se** *vpr* be destroyed

asolar[2] *vt* dry up (*plantas*)

asoma|da *f* brief appearance. ~**r** *vt* show. ● *vi* appear, show. ~**rse** *vpr* (*persona*) lean out (**a, por** of); (*cosa*) appear

asombr|adizo *a* easily frightened. ~**ar** *vt* (*pasmar*) amaze; (*sorprender*) surprise. ~**arse** *vpr* be amazed; (*sorprenderse*) be surprised. ~**o** *m* amazement, surprise. ~**osamente** *adv* amazingly. ~**oso** *a* amazing, astonishing

asomo *m* sign. **ni por** ~ by no means

asonada *f* mob; (*motín*) riot

aspa *f* cross, X-shape; (*de molino*) (windmill) sail. ~**do** *a* X-shaped

aspaviento *m* show, fuss. ~**s** *mpl* gestures. **hacer** ~**s** make a big fuss

aspecto *m* look, appearance; (*fig*) aspect

aspereza *f* roughness; (*de sabor etc*) sourness

áspero *a* rough; (*sabor etc*) bitter

aspersión *f* sprinkling

aspiración *f* breath; (*deseo*) ambition

aspirador *a* suction. ~**a** *f* vacuum cleaner

aspira|nte *m* candidate. ~**r** *vt* breathe in; (*máquina*) suck up. ● *vi* breathe in; (*máquina*) suck. ~**r a** aspire to

aspirina *f* aspirin

asquear *vt* sicken. ● *vi* be sickening. ～**se** *vpr* be disgusted

asqueros|amente *adv* disgustingly. ～**idad** *f* filthiness. ～**o** *a* disgusting

asta *f* spear; (*de la bandera*) flagpole; (*mango*) handle; (*cuerno*) horn. **a media** ～ at half-mast. ～**do** *a* horned

asterisco *m* asterisk

astilla *f* splinter. ～**s** *fpl* firewood. ～**r** *vt* splinter. **hacer** ～**s** smash. **hacerse** ～**s** shatter

astillero *m* shipyard

astringente *a* & *m* astringent

astro *m* star

astr|ología *f* astrology. ～**ólogo** *m* astrologer

astrona|uta *m* & *f* astronaut. ～**ve** *f* spaceship

astr|onomía *f* astronomy. ～**onómico** *a* astronomical. ～**ónomo** *m* astronomer

astu|cia *f* cleverness; (*ardid*) cunning. ～**to** *a* astute; (*taimado*) cunning

asturiano *a* & *m* Asturian

Asturias *fpl* Asturias

asueto *m* time off, holiday

asumir *vt* assume

asunción *f* assumption. **A**～ Assumption

asunto *m* subject; (*cuestión*) matter; (*de una novela*) plot; (*negocio*) business. ～**s** *mpl* **exteriores** foreign affairs. **el** ～ **es que** the fact is that

asusta|dizo *a* easily frightened. ～**r** *vt* frighten. ～**rse** *vpr* be frightened

ataca|nte *m* & *f* attacker. ～**r** [7] *vt* attack

atad|ero *m* rope; (*cierre*) fastening; (*gancho*) hook. ～**ijo** *m* bundle. ～**o** *a* tied; (*fig*) timid. ● *m* bundle. ～**ura** *f* tying; (*cuerda*) string

ataj|ar *vi* take a short cut. ～**o** *m* short cut; (*grupo*) bunch. **echar por el** ～**o** take the easy way out

atalaya *f* watch-tower; (*fig*) vantage point

atañer [22] *vt* concern

ataque *m* attack; (*med*) fit, attack. ～ **al corazón** heart attack. ～ **de nervios** hysterics

atar *vt* tie (up). ～**se** *vpr* get tied up

atardecer [11] *vi* get dark. ● *m* dusk. **al** ～ at dusk

atarea|do *a* busy. ～**rse** *vpr* work hard

atasc|adero *m* (*fig*) stumbling block. ～**ar** [7] *vt* block; (*fig*) hinder. ～**arse** *vpr* get stuck; ⟨*tubo etc*⟩ block. ～**o** *m* obstruction; (*auto*) traffic jam

ataúd *m* coffin

atav|iar [20] *vt* dress up. ～**iarse** *vpr* dress up, get dressed up. ～**ío** *m* dress, attire

atemorizar [10] *vt* frighten. ～**se** *vpr* be frightened

Atenas *fpl* Athens

atenazar [10] *vt* (*fig*) torture; ⟨*duda, miedo*⟩ grip

atención *f* attention; (*cortesía*) courtesy, kindness; (*interés*) interest. ¡～! look out! ～ a beware of. **llamar la** ～ attract attention, catch the eye. **prestar** ～ pay attention

atender [1] *vt* attend to; heed ⟨*consejo etc*⟩; (*cuidar*) look after. ● *vi* pay attention

atenerse [40] *vpr* abide (**a** by)

atentado *m* offence; (*ataque*) attack. ～ **contra la vida de uno** attempt on s.o.'s life

atentamente *adv* attentively; (*con cortesía*) politely; (*con amabilidad*) kindly. **le saluda** ～ (*en cartas*) yours faithfully

atentar *vi* commit an offence. ～ **contra la vida de uno** make an attempt on s.o.'s life

atento *a* attentive; (*cortés*) polite; (*amable*) kind

atenua|nte *a* extenuating. ● *f* extenuating circumstance. ～**r** [21] *vt* attenuate; (*hacer menor*) diminish, lessen. ～**rse** *vpr* weaken

ateo *a* atheistic. ● *m* atheist

aterciopelado *a* velvety

aterido *a* frozen (stiff), numb (with cold)

aterra|dor *a* terrifying. ～**r** *vt* terrify. ～**rse** *vpr* be terrified

aterriza|je *m* landing. ～**je forzoso** emergency landing. ～**r** [10] *vt* land

aterrorizar [10] *vt* terrify

atesorar *vt* hoard

atesta|do *a* packed, full up. ● *m* sworn statement. ～**r** *vt* fill up, pack; (*jurid*) testify

atestiguar [15] *vt* testify to; (*fig*) prove

atiborrar *vt* fill, stuff. ～**se** *vpr* stuff o.s.

ático *m* attic

atilda|do *a* elegant, neat. ～**r** *vt* put a tilde over; (*arreglar*) tidy up. ～**rse** *vpr* smarten o.s. up

atina|damente adv rightly. ~**do** a right; (juicioso) wise, sensible. ~**r** vt/i hit upon; (acertar) guess right

atípico a exceptional

atiplado a high-pitched

atirantar vt tighten

atisb|ar vt spy on; (vislumbrar) make out. ~**o** m spying; (indicio) hint, sign

atizar [10] vt poke; give ⟨golpe⟩; (fig) stir up; arouse, excite ⟨pasión etc⟩

atlántico a Atlantic. **el (océano) A~** the Atlantic (Ocean)

atlas m atlas

atl|eta m & f athlete. ~**ético** a athletic. ~**etismo** m athletics

atm|ósfera f atmosphere. ~**osférico** a atmospheric

atolondra|do a scatter-brained; (aturdido) bewildered. ~**miento** m bewilderment; (irreflexión) thoughtlessness. ~**r** vt bewilder; (pasmar) stun. ~**rse** vpr be bewildered

atolladero m bog; (fig) tight corner

at|ómico a atomic. ~**omizador** m atomizer. ~**omizar** [10] vt atomize

átomo m atom

atónito m amazed

atonta|do a bewildered; (tonto) stupid. ~**r** vt stun. ~**rse** vpr get confused

atormenta|dor a tormenting. ● m tormentor. ~**r** vt torture. ~**rse** vpr worry, torment o.s.

atornillar vt screw on

atosigar [12] vt pester

atracadero m quay

atracador m bandit

atracar [7] vt (amarrar) tie up; (arrimar) bring alongside; rob ⟨banco, persona⟩. ● vi ⟨barco⟩ tie up; ⟨astronave⟩ dock. ~**se** vpr stuff o.s. (**de** with)

atracci|ón f attraction. ~**ones** fpl entertainment, amusements

atrac|o m hold-up, robbery. ~**ón** m. **darse un ~ón** stuff o.s.

atractivo a attractive. ● m attraction; (encanto) charm

atraer [41] vt attract

atragantarse vpr choke (**con** on). **la historia se me atraganta** I can't stand history

atranc|ar [7] vt bolt ⟨puerta⟩; block up ⟨tubo etc⟩. ~**arse** vpr get stuck; ⟨tubo⟩ get blocked. ~**o** m difficulty

atrapar vt trap; (fig) land ⟨empleo etc⟩; catch ⟨resfriado⟩

atrás adv behind; (dirección) back(wards); (tiempo) previously, before. ● int back! **dar un paso ~** step backwards. **hacia ~, para ~** backwards

atras|ado a behind; ⟨reloj⟩ slow; (con deudas) in arrears; ⟨país⟩ backward. **llegar ~ado** arrive late. ~**ar** vt slow down; (retrasar) put back; (demorar) delay, postpone. ● vi ⟨reloj⟩ be slow. ~**arse** vpr be late; ⟨reloj⟩ be slow; (quedarse atrás) be behind. ~**o** m delay; (de un reloj) slowness; (de un país) backwardness. ~**os** mpl arrears

atravesa|do a lying across; (bizco) cross-eyed; (fig, malo) wicked. ~**r** [1] vt cross; (traspasar) go through; (poner transversalmente) lay across. ~**rse** vpr lie across; (en la garganta) get stuck, stick; (entrometerse) interfere

atrayente a attractive

atrev|erse vpr dare. ~**erse con** tackle. ~**ido** a daring, bold; (insolente) insolent. ~**imiento** m daring, boldness; (descaro) insolence

atribución f attribution. **atribuciones** fpl authority

atribuir [17] vt attribute; confer ⟨función⟩. ~**se** vpr take the credit for

atribular vt afflict. ~**se** vpr be distressed

atribut|ivo a attributive. ~**o** m attribute; (símbolo) symbol

atril m lectern; (mus) music stand

atrincherar vt fortify with trenches. ~**se** vpr entrench (o.s.)

atrocidad f atrocity. **decir ~es** make silly remarks. **¡qué ~!** how terrible!

atrochar vi take a short cut

atrojarse vpr (Mex) be cornered

atrona|dor a deafening. ~**r** [2] vt deafen

atropell|adamente adv hurriedly. ~**ado** a hasty. ~**ar** vt knock down, run over; (empujar) push aside; (maltratar) bully; (fig) outrage, insult. ~**arse** vpr rush. ~**o** m (auto) accident; (fig) outrage

atroz a atrocious; (fam) huge. ~**mente** adv atrociously, awfully

atuendo m dress, attire

atufar vt choke; (fig) irritate. ~**se** vpr be overcome; (enfadarse) get cross

atún m tuna (fish)

aturdi|do a bewildered; (irreflexivo) thoughtless. ~**r** vt bewilder, stun;

⟨*ruido*⟩ deafen. **~rse** *vpr* be stunned; (*intentar olvidar*) try to forget
atur(r)ullar *vt* bewilder
atusar *vt* smooth; trim ⟨*pelo*⟩
auda|cia *f* boldness, audacity. **~z** *a* bold
audib|ilidad *f* audibility. **~le** *a* audible
audición *f* hearing; (*concierto*) concert
audiencia *f* audience; (*tribunal*) court
auditor *m* judge-advocate; (*de cuentas*) auditor
auditorio *m* audience; (*sala*) auditorium
auge *m* peak; (*com*) boom
augur|ar *vt* predict; ⟨*cosas*⟩ augur. **~io** *m* omen. **~ios** *mpl*. **con nuestros ~ios para** with our best wishes for
augusto *a* august
aula *f* class-room; (*univ*) lecture room
aulaga *f* gorse
aull|ar [23] *vi* howl. **~ido** *m* howl
aument|ar *vt* increase; put up ⟨*precios*⟩; magnify ⟨*imagen*⟩; step up ⟨*producción, voltaje*⟩. ● *vi* increase. **~arse** *vpr* increase. **~ativo** *a & m* augmentative. **~o** *m* increase; (*de sueldo*) rise
aun *adv* even. **~ así** even so. **~ cuando** although. **más ~** even more. **ni ~** not even
aún *adv* still, yet. **~ no ha llegado** it still hasn't arrived, it hasn't arrived yet
aunar [23] *vt* join. **~se** *vpr* join together
aunque *conj* although, (even) though
aúpa *int* up! **de ~** wonderful
aureola *f* halo
auricular *m* (*de teléfono*) receiver. **~es** *mpl* headphones
aurora *f* dawn
ausen|cia *f* absence. **~tarse** *vpr* leave. **~te** *a* absent. ● *m & f* absentee; (*jurid*) missing person. **en ~ de** in the absence of
auspicio *m* omen. **bajo los ~s de** sponsored by
auster|idad *f* austerity. **~o** *a* austere
austral *a* southern. ● *m* (*unidad monetaria argentina*) austral
Australia *m* Australia
australiano *a & m* Australian
Austria *f* Austria

austriaco, **austríaco** *a & m* Austrian
aut|enticar [7] authenticate. **~enticidad** *f* authenticity. **~éntico** *a* authentic
auto *m* sentence; (*auto, fam*) car. **~s** *mpl* proceedings
auto... *pref* auto...
auto|ayuda *f* self-help. **~biografía** *f* autobiography. **~biográfico** *a* autobiographical. **~bombo** *m* self-glorification
autobús *m* bus. **en ~** by bus
autocar *m* coach (*Brit*), (long-distance) bus (*Amer*)
aut|ocracia *f* autocracy. **~ócrata** *m & f* autocrat. **~ocrático** *a* autocratic
autóctono *a* autochthonous
auto: **~determinación** *f* self-determination. **~defensa** *f* self-defence. **~didacto** *a* self-taught. ● *m* autodidact. **~escuela** *f* driving school. **~giro** *m* autogiro
autógrafo *m* autograph
automación *f* automation
autómata *m* robot
autom|ático *a* automatic. ● *m* press-stud. **~atización** *f* automation. **~atizar** [10] *vt* automate
automotor *a* (*f* **automotriz**) self-propelled. ● *m* diesel train
autom|óvil *a* self-propelled. ● *m* car. **~ovilismo** *m* motoring. **~ovilista** *m & f* driver, motorist
aut|onomía *f* autonomy. **~onómico** *a*, **~ónomo** *a* autonomous
autopista *f* motorway (*Brit*), freeway (*Amer*)
autopsia *f* autopsy
autor *m* author. **~a** *f* author(ess)
autori|dad *f* authority. **~tario** *a* authoritarian. **~tarismo** *m* authoritarianism
autoriza|ción *f* authorization. **~damente** *adv* officially. **~do** *a* authorized, offical; ⟨*opinión etc*⟩ authoritative. **~r** [10] *vt* authorize
auto: **~rretrato** *m* self-portrait. **~servicio** *m* self-service restaurant. **~stop** *m* hitch-hiking. **hacer ~stop** hitch-hike
autosuficien|cia *f* self-sufficiency. **~te** *a* self-sufficient
autovía *f* dual carriageway
auxili|ar *a* assistant; ⟨*servicios*⟩ auxiliary. ● *m* assistant. ● *vt* help. **~o** *m* help. **¡~o!** help! **~os espirituales** last rites. **en ~o de** in aid of. **pedir**

~o shout for help. **primeros** ~os first aid

Av. *abrev* (*Avenida*) Ave, Avenue

aval *m* guarantee

avalancha *f* avalanche

avalar *vt* guarantee

avalorar *vt* enhance; (*fig*) encourage

avance *m* advance; (*en el cine*) trailer; (*balance*) balance; (*de noticias*) early news bulletin. ~ **informativo** publicity hand-out

avante *adv* (*esp LAm*) forward

avanza|do *a* advanced. ~**r** [10] *vt* move forward. ● *vi* advance

avar|icia *f* avarice. ~**icioso** *a*, ~**iento** *a* greedy; (*tacaño*) miserly. ~**o** *a* miserly. ● *m* miser

avasalla|dor *a* overwhelming. ~**r** *vt* dominate

Avda. *abrev* (*Avenida*) Ave, Avenue

ave *f* bird. ~ **de paso** (*incl fig*) bird of passage. ~ **de presa**, ~ **de rapiña** bird of prey

avecinarse *vpr* approach

avecindarse *vpr* settle

avejentarse *vpr* age

avellan|a *f* hazel-nut. ~**o** *m* hazel (tree)

avemaría *f* Hail Mary. **al** ~ at dusk

avena *f* oats

avenar *vt* drain

avenida *f* (*calle*) avenue; (*de río*) flood

avenir [53] *vt* reconcile. ~**se** *vpr* come to an agreement

aventaja|do *a* outstanding. ~**r** *vt* surpass

aventar [1] *vt* fan; winnow ‹*grano etc*›; ‹*viento*› blow away

aventur|a *f* adventure; (*riesgo*) risk. ~**a amorosa** love affair. ~**ado** *a* risky. ~**ar** *vt* risk. ~**arse** *vpr* dare. ~**a sentimental** love affair. ~**ero** *a* adventurous. ● *m* adventurer

avergonza|do *a* ashamed; (*embarazado*) embarrassed. ~**r** [10 & 16] *vt* shame; (*embarazar*) embarrass. ~**rse** *vpr* be ashamed; (*embarazarse*) be embarrassed

aver|ía *f* (*auto*) breakdown; (*daño*) damage. ~**iado** *a* broken down; ‹*fruta*› damaged, spoilt. ~**iar** [20] *vt* damage. ~**iarse** *vpr* get damaged; ‹*coche*› break down

averigua|ble *a* verifiable. ~**ción** *f* verification; (*investigación*) investigation; (*Mex, disputa*) argument. ~**dor** *m* investigator. ~**r**

[15] *vt* verify; (*enterarse de*) find out; (*investigar*) investigate. ● *vi* (*Mex*) quarrel

aversión *f* aversion (**a, hacia, por** for)

avestruz *m* ostrich

aviación *f* aviation; (*mil*) air force

aviado *a* (*Arg*) well off. **estar** ~ be in a mess

aviador *m* (*aviat*) member of the crew; (*piloto*) pilot; (*Arg, prestamista*) money-lender; (*Arg, de minas*) mining speculator

aviar [20] *vt* get ready, prepare; (*arreglar*) tidy; (*reparar*) repair; (*LAm, prestar dinero*) lend money; (*dar prisa*) hurry up. ~**se** *vpr* get ready. **¡aviate!** hurry up!

av|ícola *a* poultry. ~**icultor** *m* poultry farmer. ~**icultura** *f* poultry farming

avidez *f* eagerness, greed

ávido *a* eager, greedy

avieso *a* (*maligno*) wicked

avinagra|do *a* sour. ~**r** *vt* sour; (*fig*) embitter. ~**rse** *vpr* go sour; (*fig*) become embittered

avío *m* preparation. ~**s** *mpl* provisions; (*utensilios*) equipment

avi|ón *m* aeroplane (*Brit*), airplane (*Amer*). ~**oneta** *f* light aircraft

avis|ado *a* wise. ~**ar** *vt* warn; (*informar*) notify, inform; call ‹*médico etc*›. ~**o** *m* warning; (*anuncio*) notice. **estar sobre** ~**o** be on the alert. **mal** ~**ado** ill-advised. **sin previo** ~**o** without notice

avisp|a *f* wasp. ~**ado** *a* sharp. ~**ero** *m* wasps' nest; (*fig*) mess. ~**ón** *m* hornet

avistar *vt* catch sight of

avitualla|miento *m* supplying. ~**r** *vt* provision

avivar *vt* stoke up ‹*fuego*›; brighten up ‹*color*›; arouse ‹*interés, pasión*›; intensify ‹*dolor*›. ~**se** *vpr* revive; (*animarse*) cheer up

axila *f* axilla, armpit

axiom|a *m* axiom. ~**ático** *a* axiomatic

ay *int* (*de dolor*) ouch!; (*de susto*) oh!; (*de pena*) oh dear! ~ **de** poor. **¡~ de ti!** poor you!

aya *f* governess, child's nurse

ayer *adv* yesterday. ● *m* past. **antes de** ~ the day before yesterday. ~ **por la mañana** yesterday morning. ~ **(por la) noche** last night

ayo *m* tutor

ayote *m* (*Mex*) pumpkin

ayuda *f* help, aid. ∼ **de cámara** valet. ∼**nta** *f*, ∼**nte** *m* assistant; (*mil*) adjutant. ∼**nte técnico sanitario (ATS)** nurse. ∼**r** *vt* help

ayun|ar *vi* fast. ∼**as** *fpl*. **estar en** ∼**as** have had no breakfast; (*fig, fam*) be in the dark. ∼**o** *m* fasting

ayuntamiento *m* town council, city council; (*edificio*) town hall

azabache *m* jet

azad|a *f* hoe. ∼**ón** *m* (large) hoe

azafata *f* air hostess

azafrán *m* saffron

azahar *m* orange blossom

azar *m* chance; (*desgracia*) misfortune. **al** ∼ at random. **por** ∼ by chance

azararse *vpr* go wrong; (*fig*) get flustered

azaros|amente *adv* hazardously. ∼**o** *a* hazardous, risky; ⟨*persona*⟩ unlucky

azoga|do *a* restless. ∼**rse** [12] *vpr* be restless

azolve *m* (*Mex*) obstruction

azora|do *a* flustered, excited, alarmed. ∼**miento** *m* confusion, embarrassment. ∼**r** *vt* embarrass; (*aturdir*) alarm. ∼**rse** *vpr* get flustered, be alarmed

Azores *fpl* Azores

azot|aina *f* beating. ∼**ar** *vt* whip, beat. ∼**e** *m* whip; (*golpe*) smack; (*fig, calamidad*) calamity

azotea *f* flat roof. **estar mal de la** ∼ be mad

azteca *a & m & f* Aztec

az|úcar *m & f* sugar. ∼**ucarado** *a* sweet. ∼**ucarar** *vt* sweeten. ∼**ucarero** *m* sugar bowl

azucena *f* (white) lily

azufre *m* sulphur

azul *a & m* blue. ∼**ado** *a* bluish. ∼ **de lavar** (washing) blue. ∼ **marino** navy blue

azulejo *m* tile

azuzar *vt* urge on, incite

B

bab|a *f* spittle. ∼**ear** *vi* drool, slobber; ⟨*niño*⟩ dribble. **caerse la** ∼**a** be delighted

babel *f* bedlam

babe|o *m* drooling; (*de un niño*) dribbling. ∼**ro** *m* bib

Babia *f*. **estar en** ∼ have one's head in the clouds

babieca *a* stupid. ● *m & f* simpleton

babor *m* port. **a** ∼ to port, on the port side

babosa *f* slug

babosada *f* (*Mex*) silly remark

babos|ear *vt* slobber over; ⟨*niño*⟩ dribble over. ∼**eo** *m* drooling; (*de niño*) dribbling. ∼**o** *a* slimy; (*LAm, tonto*) silly

babucha *f* slipper

babuino *m* baboon

baca *f* luggage rack

bacaladilla *f* small cod

bacalao *m* cod

bacon *m* bacon

bacteria *f* bacterium

bache *m* hole; (*fig*) bad patch

bachillerato *m* school-leaving examination

badaj|azo *m* stroke (of a bell). ∼**o** *m* clapper; (*persona*) chatterbox

bagaje *m* baggage; (*animal*) beast of burden; (*fig*) knowledge

bagatela *f* trifle

Bahamas *fpl* Bahamas

bahía *f* bay

bail|able *a* dance. ∼**ador** *a* dancing. ● *m* dancer. ∼**aor** *m* Flamenco dancer. ∼**ar** *vt/i* dance. ∼**arín** dancer. ∼**arina** *f* dancer; (*de baile clásico*) ballerina. ∼**e** *m* dance. ∼**e de etiqueta** ball. **ir a** ∼**ar** go dancing

baja *f* drop, fall; (*mil*) casualty. ∼ **por maternidad** maternity leave. ∼**da** *f* slope; (*acto de bajar*) descent. ∼**mar** *m* low tide. ∼**r** *vt* lower; (*llevar abajo*) get down; bow ⟨*la cabeza*⟩. ∼**r la escalera** go downstairs. ● *vi* go down; ⟨*temperatura, precio*⟩ fall. ∼**rse** *vpr* bend down. ∼**r(se) de** get out of ⟨*coche*⟩; get off ⟨*autobús, caballo, tren, bicicleta*⟩. **dar(se) de** ∼ take sick leave

bajeza *f* vile deed

bajío *m* sandbank

bajo *a* low; (*de estatura*) short, small; ⟨*cabeza, ojos*⟩ lowered; (*humilde*) humble, low; (*vil*) vile, low; ⟨*color*⟩ pale; ⟨*voz*⟩ low; (*mus*) deep. ● *m* lowland; (*bajío*) sandbank; (*mus*) bass. ● *adv* quietly; ⟨*volar*⟩ low. ● *prep* under; (*temperatura*) below. ∼ **la lluvia** in the rain. **los** ∼**s fondos** the low district. **por lo** ∼ under one's breath; (*fig*) in secret

bajón *m* drop; (*de salud*) decline; (*com*) slump

bala *f* bullet; (*de algodón etc*) bale. **~ perdida** stray bullet. **como una ~** like a shot

balada *f* ballad

baladí *a* trivial

baladrón *a* boastful

baladron|ada *f* boast. **~ear** *vi* boast

balan|ce *m* swinging; (*de una cuenta*) balance; (*documento*) balance sheet. **~cear** *vt* balance. ● *vi* hesitate. **~cearse** *vpr* swing; (*vacilar*) hesitate. **~ceo** *m* swinging. **~za** *f* scales; (*com*) balance

balar *vi* bleat

balaustrada *f* balustrade, railing(s); (*de escalera*) banisters

balay *m* (*LAm*) wicker basket

balazo *m* (*disparo*) shot; (*herida*) bullet wound

balboa *f* (*unidad monetaria panameña*) balboa

balbuc|ear *vt/i* stammer; (*niño*) babble. **~eo** *m* stammering; (*de niño*) babbling. **~iente** *a* stammering; (*niño*) babbling. **~ir** [24] *vt/i* stammer; (*niño*) babble

balc|ón *m* balcony. **~onada** *f* row of balconies. **~onaje** *m* row of balconies

balda *f* shelf

baldado *a* disabled, crippled; (*rendido*) shattered. ● *m* disabled person, cripple

baldaquín *m*, **baldaquino** *m* canopy

baldar *vt* cripple

balde *m* bucket. **de ~** free (of charge). **en ~** in vain. **~ar** *vt* wash down

baldío *a* ⟨*terreno*⟩ waste; (*fig*) useless

baldosa *f* (*floor*) tile; (*losa*) flagstone

balduque *m* (*incl fig*) red tape

balear *a* Balearic. ● *m* native of the Balearic Islands. **las Islas** *fpl* **B~es** the Balearics, the Balearic Islands

baleo *m* (*LAm, tiroteo*) shooting; (*Mex, abanico*) fan

balido *m* bleat; (*varios sonidos*) bleating

bal|ín *m* small bullet. **~ines** *mpl* shot

balística *f* ballistics

baliza *f* (*naut*) buoy; (*aviac*) beacon

balneario *m* spa; (*con playa*) seaside resort. ● *a.* **estación** *f* **balnearia** spa; (*con playa*) seaside resort

balompié *m* football (*Brit*), soccer

bal|ón *m* ball, football. **~oncesto** *m* basketball. **~onmano** *m* handball. **~onvolea** *m* volleyball

balotaje *m* (*LAm*) voting

balsa *f* (*de agua*) pool; (*plataforma flotante*) raft

bálsamo *m* balsam; (*fig*) balm

balsón *m* (*Mex*) stagnant water

baluarte *m* (*incl fig*) bastion

balumba *f* mass, mountain

ballena *f* whale

ballesta *f* crossbow

ballet /ba'le/ (*pl* **ballets** /ba'le/) *m* ballet

bambole|ar *vi* sway; ⟨*mesa etc*⟩ wobble. **~arse** *vpr* sway; ⟨*mesa etc*⟩ wobble. **~o** *m* swaying; (*de mesa etc*) wobbling

bambú *m* (*pl* **bambúes**) bamboo

banal *a* banal. **~idad** *f* banality

banan|a *f* (*esp LAm*) banana. **~o** *m* (*LAm*) banana tree

banast|a *f* large basket. **~o** *m* large round basket

banc|a *f* banking; (*en juegos*) bank; (*LAm, asiento*) bench. **~ario** *a* bank, banking. **~arrota** *f* bankruptcy. **~o** *m* (*asiento*) bench; (*com*) bank; (*bajío*) sandbank. **hacer ~arrota, ir a la ~arrota** go bankrupt

banda *f* (*incl mus, radio*) band; (*grupo*) gang, group; (*lado*) side. **~da** *f* (*de aves*) flock; (*de peces*) shoal. **~ de sonido, ~ sonora** sound-track

bandeja *f* tray; (*LAm, plato*) serving dish. **servir algo en ~ a uno** hand sth to s.o. on a plate

bandera *f* flag; (*estandarte*) banner, standard

banderill|a *f* banderilla. **~ear** *vt* stick the banderillas in. **~ero** *m* banderillero

banderín *m* pennant, small flag, banner

bandido *m* bandit

bando *m* edict, proclamation; (*partido*) faction. **~s** *mpl* banns. **pasarse al otro** go over to the other side

bandolero *m* bandit

bandolina *f* mandolin

bandoneón *m* large accordion

banjo *m* banjo

banquero *m* banker

banqueta *f* stool; (*LAm, acera*) pavement (*Brit*), sidewalk (*Amer*)

banquete *m* banquet; (*de boda*) wedding reception. **~ar** *vt/i* banquet

banquillo *m* bench; (*jurid*) dock; (*taburete*) footstool

bañ|ado *m* (*LAm*) swamp. **~ador** *m* (*de mujer*) swimming costume; (*de hombre*) swimming trunks. **~ar** *vt* bathe, immerse; bath ⟨*niño*⟩; (*culin, recubrir*) coat. **~arse** *vpr* go swimming, have a swim; (*en casa*) have a bath. **~era** *f* bath, bath-tub. **~ero** *m* life-guard. **~ista** *m & f* bather. **~o** *m* bath; (*en piscina, mar etc*) swim; (*bañera*) bath, bath-tub; (*capa*) coat(ing)

baptisterio *m* baptistery; (*pila*) font

baquet|a *f* (*de fusil*) ramrod; (*de tambor*) drumstick. **~ear** *vt* bother. **~eo** *m* nuisance, bore

bar *m* bar

barahúnda *f* uproar

baraja *f* pack of cards. **~r** *vt* shuffle; juggle, massage ⟨*cifras etc*⟩. • *vi* argue (**con** with); (*enemistarse*) fall out (**con** with). **~s** *fpl* argument. **jugar a la ~** play cards. **jugar a dos ~s, jugar con dos ~s** be deceitful, indulge in double-dealing

baranda *f*, **barandal** *m*, **barandilla** *f* handrail; (*de escalera*) banisters

barat|a *f* (*Mex*) sale. **~ija** *f* trinket. **~illo** *m* junk shop; (*géneros*) cheap goods. **~o** *a* cheap. • *m* sale. • *adv* cheap(ly). **~ura** *f* cheapness

baraúnda *f* uproar

barba *f* chin; (*pelo*) beard. **~do** *a* bearded

barbacoa *f* barbecue; (*Mex, carne*) barbecued meat

bárbaramente *adv* savagely; (*fig*) tremendously

barbari|dad *f* barbarity; (*fig*) outrage; (*mucho, fam*) awful lot (*fam*). **¡qué ~dad!** how awful! **~e** *f* barbarity; (*fig*) ignorance. **~smo** *m* barbarism

bárbaro *a* barbaric, cruel; (*bruto*) uncouth; (*estupendo, fam*) terrific (*fam*). • *m* barbarian. **¡qué ~!** how marvellous!

barbear *vt* (*afeitar*) shave; (*Mex, lisonjear*) fawn on

barbecho *m* fallow

barber|ía *f* barber's (shop). **~o** *m* barber; (*Mex, adulador*) flatterer

barbi|lampiño *a* beardless; (*fig*) inexperienced, green. **~lindo** *m* dandy

barbilla *f* chin

barbitúrico *m* barbiturate

barbo *m* barbel. **~ de mar** red mullet

barbot|ar *vt/i* mumble. **~ear** *vt/i* mumble. **~eo** *m* mumbling

barbudo *a* bearded

barbullar *vi* jabber

barca *f* (small) boat. **~ de pasaje** ferry. **~je** *m* fare. **~za** *f* barge

Barcelona *f* Barcelona

barcelonés *a* of Barcelona, from Barcelona. • *m* native of Barcelona

barco *m* boat; (*navío*) ship. **~ cisterna** tanker. **~ de vapor** steamer. **~ de vela** sailing boat. **ir en ~** go by boat

bario *m* barium

barítono *m* baritone

barman *m* (*pl* **barmans**) barman

barniz *m* varnish; (*para loza etc*) glaze; (*fig*) veneer. **~ar** [10] *vt* varnish; glaze ⟨*loza etc*⟩

bar|ométrico *a* barometric. **~ómetro** *m* barometer

bar|ón *m* baron. **~onesa** *f* baroness

barquero *m* boatman

barra *f* bar; (*pan*) French bread; (*de oro o plata*) ingot; (*palanca*) lever. **~ de labios** lipstick. **no pararse en ~s** stop at nothing

barrabasada *f* mischief, prank

barraca *f* hut; (*vivienda pobre*) shack, shanty

barranco *m* ravine, gully; (*despeñadero*) cliff, precipice

barre|dera *f* road-sweeper. **~dura** *f* rubbish. **~minas** *m invar* minesweeper

barren|a *f* drill, bit. **~ar** *vt* drill. **~o** *m* large (mechanical) drill. **entrar en ~a** ⟨*avión*⟩ go into a spin

barrer *vt* sweep; (*quitar*) sweep aside

barrera *f* barrier. **~ del sonido** sound barrier

barriada *f* district

barrica *f* barrel

barricada *f* barricade

barrido *m* sweeping

barrig|a *f* (pot-)belly. **~ón** *a*, **~udo** *a* pot-bellied

barril *m* barrel. **~ete** *m* keg, small barrel

barrio *m* district, area. **~bajero** *a* vulgar, common. **~s bajos** poor quarter, poor area. **el otro ~** (*fig, fam*) the other world

barro *m* mud; (*arcilla*) clay; (*arcilla cocida*) earthenware

barroco *a* Baroque. • *m* Baroque style

barrote *m* heavy bar

barrunt|ar *vt* sense, have a feeling. **~e** *m*, **~o** *m* sign; (*presentimiento*) feeling

bartola *f*. **tenderse a la ~**, **tumbarse a la ~** take it easy

bártulos *mpl* things. **liar los ~** pack one's bags

barullo *m* uproar; (*confusión*) confusion. **a ~ galore**

basa *f*, **basamento** *m* base; (*fig*) basis

basar *vt* base. **~se** *vpr*. **~se en** be based on

basc|a *f* crowd. **~as** *fpl* nausea. **~osidad** *f* filth. **la ~a** the gang

báscula *f* scales

bascular *vi* tilt

base *f* base; (*fig*) basis, foundation. **a ~ de** thanks to; (*mediante*) by means of; (*en una receta*) as the basic ingredient(s). **a ~ de bien** very well. **partiendo de la ~ de**, **tomando como ~** on the basis of

básico *a* basic

basílica *f* basilica

basilisco *m* basilisk. **hecho un ~** furious

basta *f* tack, tacking stitch

bastante *a* enough; (*varios*) quite a few, quite a lot of. ● *adv* rather, fairly; (*mucho tiempo*) long enough; (*suficiente*) enough; (*Mex, muy*) very

bastar *vi* be enough. **¡basta!** that's enough! **basta decir que** suffice it to say that. **basta y sobra** that's more than enough

bastardilla *f* italics. **poner en ~** italicize

bastardo *m* bastard; (*fig, vil*) mean, base

bastidor *m* frame; (*auto*) chassis. **~es** *mpl* (*en el teatro*) wings. **entre ~es** behind the scenes

bastión *f* (*incl fig*) bastion

basto *a* coarse. **~s** *mpl* (*naipes*) clubs

bast|ón *m* walking stick. **empuñar el ~ón** take command. **~onazo** *m* blow with a stick

basur|a *f* rubbish, garbage (*Amer*); (*en la calle*) litter. **~ero** *m* dustman (*Brit*), garbage collector (*Amer*); (*sitio*) rubbish dump; (*recipiente*) dustbin (*Brit*), garbage can (*Amer*). **cubo** *m* **de la ~a** dustbin (*Brit*), garbage can (*Amer*)

bata *f* dressing-gown; (*de médico etc*) white coat. **~ de cola** Flamenco dress

batall|a *f* battle. **~a campal** pitched battle. **~ador** *a* fighting. ● *m* fighter. **~ar** *vi* battle, fight. **~ón** *m* battalion. ● *a*. **cuestión** *f* **batallona** vexed question. **de ~a** everyday

batata *f* sweet potato

bate *m* bat. **~ador** *m* batter; (*cricket*) batsman

batería *f* battery; (*mus*) percussion. **~ de cocina** kitchen utensils, pots and pans

batido *a* beaten; (*nata*) whipped. ● *m* batter; (*bebida*) milk shake. **~ra** *f* beater. **~ra eléctrica** mixer

batín *m* dressing-gown

batir *vt* beat; (*martillar*) hammer; mint (*monedas*); whip (*nata*); (*derribar*) knock down. **~ el récord** break the record. **~ palmas** clap. **~se** *vpr* fight

batuta *f* baton. **llevar la ~** be in command, be the boss

baúl *m* trunk; (*LAm, auto*) boot (*Brit*), trunk (*Amer*)

bauti|smal *a* baptismal. **~smo** *m* baptism, christening. **~sta** *a & m & f* Baptist. **~zar** [10] *vt* baptize, christen

baya *f* berry

bayeta *f* (floor-)cloth

bayoneta *f* bayonet. **~zo** *m* (*golpe*) bayonet thrust; (*herida*) bayonet wound

baza *f* (*naipes*) trick; (*fig*) advantage. **meter ~** interfere

bazar *m* bazaar

bazofia *f* leftovers; (*basura*) rubbish

beat|itud *f* (*fig*) bliss. **~o** *a* blessed; (*de religiosidad afectada*) sanctimonious

bebé *m* baby

beb|edero *m* drinking trough; (*sitio*) watering place. **~edizo** *a* drinkable. ● *m* potion; (*veneno*) poison. **~edor** *a* drinking. ● *m* héavy drinker. **~er** *vt/i* drink. **dar de ~er a uno** give s.o. a drink. **~ida** *f* drink. **~ido** *a* tipsy, drunk

beca *f* grant, scholarship. **~rio** *m* scholarship holder, scholar

becerro *m* calf

befa *f* jeer, taunt. **~r** *vt* scoff at. **~rse** *vpr*. **~rse de** scoff at. **hacer ~ de** scoff at

beige /beis, bes/ *a & m* beige

béisbol *m* baseball

beldad *f* beauty

belén *m* crib, nativity scene; (*barullo*) confusion

belga *a & m & f* Belgian

Bélgica *f* Belgium

bélico *a*, **belicoso** *a* warlike

beligerante *a* belligerent

bella|co *a* wicked. ● *m* rogue. ~**quear** *vi* cheat. ~**quería** *f* dirty trick

bell|eza *f* beauty. ~**o** *a* beautiful. ~**as artes** *fpl* fine arts

bellota *f* acorn

bemol *m* flat. **tener (muchos)** ~**es** be difficult

bencina *f* (*Arg, gasolina*) petrol (*Brit*), gasoline (*Amer*)

bend|ecir [46 *pero imperativo* **bendice**, *futuro, condicional y pp regulares*] *vt* bless. ~**ición** *f* blessing. ~**ito** *a* blessed, holy; (*que tiene suerte*) lucky; (*feliz*) happy

benefactor *m* benefactor. ~**a** *f* benefactress

benefic|encia *f* (*organización pública*) charity. ~**iar** *vt* benefit. ~**iarse** *vpr* benefit. ~**iario** *m* beneficiary; (*de un cheque etc*) payee. ~**io** *m* benefit; (*ventaja*) advantage; (*ganancia*) profit, gain. ~**ioso** *a* beneficial, advantageous

benéfico *a* beneficial; (*de beneficencia*) charitable

benemérito *a* worthy

beneplácito *m* approval

ben|evolencia *f* benevolence. ~**évolo** *a* benevolent

bengala *f* flare. **luz** *f* **de B** ~ flare

benign|idad *f* kindness; (*falta de gravedad*) mildness. ~**o** *a* kind; (*moderado*) gentle, mild; ‹*tumor*› benign

beodo *a* drunk

berberecho *m* cockle

berenjena *f* aubergine (*Brit*), eggplant. ~**l** *m* (*fig*) mess

bermejo *a* red

berr|ear *vi* ‹*animales*› low, bellow; ‹*niño*› howl; (*cantar mal*) screech. ~**ido** *m* bellow; (*de niño*) howl; (*de cantante*) screech

berrinche *m* temper; (*de un niño*) tantrum

berro *m* watercress

berza *f* cabbage

besamel(a) *f* white sauce

bes|ar *vt* kiss; (*rozar*) brush against. ~**arse** *vpr* kiss (each other); (*tocarse*) touch each other. ~**o** *m* kiss

bestia *f* beast; (*bruto*) brute; (*idiota*) idiot. ~ **de carga** beast of burden. ~**l** *a* bestial, animal; (*fig, fam*) terrific. ~**lidad** *f* bestiality; (*acción brutal*) horrid thing

besugo *m* sea-bream. **ser un** ~ be stupid

besuquear *vt* cover with kisses

betún *m* bitumen; (*para el calzado*) shoe polish

biberón *m* feeding-bottle

Biblia *f* Bible

bíblico *a* biblical

bibliografía *f* bibliography

biblioteca *f* library; (*librería*) bookcase. ~ **de consulta** reference library. ~ **de préstamo** lending library. ~**rio** *m* librarian

bicarbonato *m* bicarbonate. ~ **sódico** bicarbonate of soda

bici *f* (*fam*) bicycle, bike (*fam*). ~**cleta** *f* bicycle. **ir en** ~**cleta** go by bicycle, cycle. **montar en** ~**cleta** ride a bicycle

bicolor *a* two-colour

bicultural *a* bicultural

bicho *m* (*animal*) small animal, creature; (*insecto*) insect. ~ **raro** odd sort. **cualquier** ~ **viviente, todo** ~ **viviente** everyone

bidé *m*, **bidet** *m* bidet

bidón *m* drum, can

bien *adv* (**mejor**) well; (*muy*) very, quite; (*correctamente*) right; (*de buena gana*) willingly. ● *m* good; (*efectos*) property; (*provecho*) advantage, benefit. **¡~!** fine!, OK!, good! **~... (o)** ~ either... or. ~ **que** although. **¡está** ~! fine! alright! **más** ~ rather. **¡muy** ~! good! **no** ~ as soon as. **¡qué** ~! marvellous!, great! (*fam*). **si** ~ although

bienal *a* biennial

bien: ~aventurado *a* fortunate. ~**estar** *m* well-being. ~**hablado** *a* well-spoken. ~**hechor** *m* benefactor. ~**hechora** *f* benefactress. ~**intencionado** *a* well-meaning

bienio *m* two years, two year-period

bien: ~quistar *vt* reconcile. ~**quistarse** *vpr* become reconciled. ~**quisto** *a* well-liked

bienvenid|a *f* welcome. ~**o** *a* welcome. **¡~o!** welcome! **dar la** ~**a a uno** welcome s.o.

bife *m* (*Arg*), **biftek** *m* steak

bifurca|ción *f* fork, junction. ~**rse** [7] *vpr* fork

bi|gamia *f* bigamy. **~ígamo** *a* bigamous. ● *m & f* bigamist

bigot|e *m* moustache. **~udo** *a* with a big moustache

bikini *m* bikini; (*culin*) toasted cheese and ham sandwich

bilingüe *a* bilingual

billar *m* billiards

billete *m* ticket; (*de banco*) note (*Brit*), bill (*Amer*). **~ de banco** banknote. **~ de ida y vuelta** return ticket (*Brit*), round-trip ticket (*Amer*). **~ sencillo** single ticket (Brit), one-way ticket (*Amer*). **~ro** *m*, **~ra** *f* wallet, billfold (*Amer*)

billón *m* billion (*Brit*), trillion (*Amer*)

bimbalete *m* (*Mex*) swing

bi|mensual *a* fortnightly, twice-monthly. **~mestral** *a* two-monthly. **~motor** *a* twin-engined. ● *m* twin-engined plane

binocular *a* binocular. **~es** *mpl* binoculars

biodegradable *a* biodegradable

bi|ografía *f* biography. **~ográfico** *a* biographical. **~ógrafo** *m* biographer

bi|ología *f* biology. **~ológico** *a* biological. **~ólogo** *m* biologist

biombo *m* folding screen

biopsia *f* biopsy

bioquímic|a *f* biochemistry; (*persona*) biochemist. **~o** *m* biochemist

bípedo *m* biped

biplano *m* biplane

biquini *m* bikini

birlar *vt* (*fam*) steal, pinch (*fam*)

birlibirloque *m*. **por arte de ~** (as if) by magic

Birmania *f* Burma

birmano *a & m* Burmese

biromen *m* (*Arg*) ball-point pen

bis *m* encore. ● *adv* twice. ¡**~!** encore! **vivo en el 3 ~** I live at 3A

bisabuel|a *f* great-grandmother. **~o** *m* great-grandfather. **~os** *mpl* great-grandparents

bisagra *f* hinge

bisar *vt* encore

bisbise|ar *vt* whisper. **~o** *m* whisper(ing)

bisemanal *a* twice-weekly

bisiesto *a* leap. **año** *m* **~** leap year

bisniet|a *f* great-granddaughter. **~o** *m* great-grandson. **~os** *mpl* great-grandchildren

bisonte *m* bison

bisté *m*, **bistec** *m* steak

bisturí *m* scalpel

bisutería *f* imitation jewellery, costume jewellery

bizco *a* cross-eyed. **quedarse ~** be dumbfounded

bizcocho *m* sponge (cake); (*Mex, galleta*) biscuit

bizquear *vi* squint

blanc|a *f* white woman; (*mus*) minim. **~o** *a* white; ⟨*tez*⟩ fair. ● *m* white; (*persona*) white man; (*intervalo*) interval; (*espacio*) blank; (*objetivo*) target. **~o de huevo** white of egg, egg-white. **dar en el ~o** hit the mark. **dejar en ~o** leave blank. **pasar la noche en ~o** have a sleepless night. **~o y negro** black and white. **~ura** *f* whiteness. **~uzco** *a* whitish

blandir [24] *vt* brandish

bland|o *a* soft; ⟨*carácter*⟩ weak; (*cobarde*) cowardly; ⟨*palabras*⟩ gentle, tender. **~ura** *f* softness. **~uzco** *a* softish

blanque|ar *vt* whiten; white-wash ⟨*paredes*⟩; bleach ⟨*tela*⟩. ● *vi* turn white; (*presentarse blanco*) look white. **~cino** *a* whitish. **~o** *m* whitening

blasfem|ador *a* blasphemous. ● *m* blasphemer. **~ar** *vi* blaspheme. **~ia** *f* blasphemy. **~o** *a* blasphemous. ● *m* blasphemer

blas|ón *m* coat of arms; (*fig,*) honour, glory. **~onar** *vt* emblazon. ● *vi* boast (**de** of, about)

bledo *m* nothing. **me importa un ~, no se me da un ~** I couldn't care less

blinda|je *m* armour. **~r** *vt* armour

bloc *m* (*pl* **blocs**) pad

bloque *m* block; (*pol*) bloc. **~ar** *vt* block; (*mil*) blockade; (*com*) freeze. **~o** *m* blockade; (*com*) freezing. **en ~** en bloc

blusa *f* blouse

boato *m* show, ostentation

bob|ada *f* silly thing. **~alicón** *a* stupid. **~ería** *f* silly thing. **decir ~adas** talk nonsense

bobina *f* bobbin, reel; (*foto*) spool; (*elec*) coil

bobo *a* silly, stupid. ● *m* idiot, fool

boca *f* mouth; (*fig, entrada*) entrance; (*de cañón*) muzzle; (*agujero*) hole. **~ abajo** face down. **~ arriba** face up. **a ~ de jarro** point-blank. **con la ~ abierta** dumbfounded

bocacalle f junction. **la primera ~ a la derecha** the first turning on the right

bocad|illo m sandwich; (*comida ligera, fam*) snack. **~o** m mouthful; (*mordisco*) bite; (*de caballo*) bit

boca: ~jarro. a ~jarro point-blank. **~manga** f cuff

bocanada f puff; (*de vino etc*) mouthful

bocaza f invar, **bocazas** f invar bigmouth

boceto m outline, sketch

bocina f horn. **~zo** m toot, blast. **tocar la ~** sound one's horn

bock m beer mug

bocha f bowl. **~s** fpl bowls

bochinche m uproar

bochorno m sultry weather; (*fig, vergüenza*) embarrassment. **~so** a oppressive; (*fig*) embarrassing. **¡qué ~!** how embarrassing!

boda f marriage; (*ceremonia*) wedding

bodeg|a f cellar; (*de vino*) wine cellar; (*almacén*) warehouse; (*de un barco*) hold. **~ón** m cheap restaurant; (*pintura*) still life

bodoque m pellet; (*tonto, fam*) thickhead

bofes mpl lights. **echar los ~** slog away

bofet|ada f slap; (*fig*) blow. **dar una ~ada a uno** slap s.o. in the face. **darse de ~adas** clash. **~ón** m punch

boga m & f rower; (*hombre*) oarsman; (*mujer*) oarswoman; (*moda*) fashion. **estar en ~** be in fashion, be in vogue. **~da** f stroke (of the oar). **~dor** rower, oarsman. **~r** [12] vt row. **~vante** m (*crustáceo*) lobster

Bogotá f Bogotá

bogotano a from Bogotá. ● m native of Bogotá

bohemio a & m Bohemian

bohío m (*LAm*) hut

boicot m (*pl* **boicots**) boycott. **~ear** vt boycott. **~eo** m boycott. **hacer el ~** boycott

boina f beret

boîte /bwat/ m night-club

bola f ball; (*canica*) marble; (*naipes*) slam; (*betún*) shoe polish; (*mentira*) fib; (*Mex, reunión desordenada*) rowdy party. **~ del mundo** (*fam*) globe. **contar ~s** tell fibs. **dejar que**

ruede la ~ let things take their course. **meter ~s** tell fibs

bolas fpl (*LAm*) bolas

boleada f (*Mex*) polishing of shoes

boleadoras (*LAm*) fpl bolas

bolera f bowling alley

bolero m (*baile, chaquetilla*) bolero; (*fig, mentiroso, fam*) liar; (*Mex, limpiabotas*) bootblack

boletín m bulletin; (*publicación periódica*) journal; (*escolar*) report. **~ de noticias** news bulletin. **~ de precios** price list. **~ informativo** news bulletin. **~ meteorológico** weather forecast

boleto m (*esp LAm*) ticket

boli m (*fam*) Biro (P), ball-point pen

boliche m (*juego*) bowls; (*bolera*) bowling alley

bolígrafo m Biro (P), ball-point pen

bolillo m bobbin; (*Mex, panecillo*) (bread) roll

bolívar m (*unidad monetaria venezolana*) bolívar

Bolivia f Bolivia

boliviano a Bolivian. ● m Bolivian; (*unidad monetaria de Bolivia*) boliviano

bolo m skittle

bolsa f bag; (*monedero*) purse; (*LAm, bolsillo*) pocket; (*com*) stock exchange; (*cavidad*) cavity. **~ de agua caliente** hot-water bottle

bolsillo m pocket; (*monedero*) purse. **de ~** pocket

bolsista m & f stockbroker

bolso m (*de mujer*) handbag

boll|ería f baker's shop. **~ero** m baker. **~o** m roll; (*con azúcar*) bun; (*abolladura*) dent; (*chichón*) lump; (*fig, jaleo, fam*) fuss

bomba f bomb; (*máquina*) pump; (*noticia*) bombshell. **~ de aceite** (*auto*) oil pump. **~ de agua** (*auto*) water pump. **~ de incendios** fire-engine. **pasarlo ~** have a marvellous time

bombach|as fpl (*LAm*) knickers, pants. **~o** m (*esp Mex*) baggy trousers, baggy pants (*Amer*)

bombarde|ar vt bombard; (*mil*) bomb. **~o** m bombardment; (*mil*) bombing. **~ro** m (*avión*) bomber

bombazo m explosion

bombear vt pump; (*mil*) bomb

bombero m fireman. **cuerpo** m **de ~s** fire brigade (*Brit*), fire department (*Amer*)

bombilla _f_ (light) bulb; (_LAm, para mate_) pipe for drinking maté; (_Mex, cucharón_) ladle

bombín _m_ pump; (_sombrero, fam_) bowler (hat) (_Brit_), derby (_Amer_)

bombo _m_ (_tambor_) bass drum. **a ~ y platillos** with a lot of fuss

bomb|ón _m_ chocolate. **ser un ~ón** be a peach. **~ona** _f_ container. **~onera** _f_ chocolate box

bonachón _a_ easygoing; (_bueno_) good-natured

bonaerense _a_ from Buenos Aires. ● _m_ native of Buenos Aires

bonanza _f_ (_naut_) fair weather; (_prosperidad_) prosperity. **ir en ~** (_naut_) have fair weather; (_fig_) go well

bondad _f_ goodness; (_amabilidad_) kindness. **tenga la ~ de** would you be kind enough to. **~osamente** _adv_ kindly. **~oso** _a_ kind

bongo _m_ (_LAm_) canoe

boniato _m_ sweet potato

bonito _a_ nice; (_mono_) pretty. **¡muy ~!**, **¡qué ~!** that's nice!, very nice!. ● _m_ bonito

bono _m_ voucher; (_título_) bond. **~ del Tesoro** government bond

boñiga _f_ dung

boqueada _f_ gasp. **dar las ~s** be dying

boquerón _m_ anchovy

boquete _m_ hole; (_brecha_) breach

boquiabierto _a_ open-mouthed; (_fig_) amazed, dumbfounded. **quedarse ~** be amazed

boquilla _f_ mouthpiece; (_para cigarrillos_) cigarette-holder; (_filtro de cigarillo_) tip

borboll|ar _vi_ bubble. **~ón** _m_ bubble. **hablar a ~ones** gabble. **salir a ~ones** gush out

borbot|ar _vt_ bubble. **~ón** _m_ bubble. **hablar a ~ones** gabble. **salir a ~ones** gush out

bordado _a_ embroidered. ● _m_ embroidery. **quedar ~, salir ~** come out very well

bordante _m_ (_Mex_) lodger

bordar _vt_ embroider; (_fig, fam_) do very well

bord|e _m_ edge; (_de carretera_) side; (_de plato etc_) rim; (_de un vestido_) hem. **~ear** _vt_ go round the edge of; (_fig_) border on. **~illo** _m_ kerb. **al ~e de** on the edge of; (_fig_) on the brink of

bordo _m_ board. **a ~** on board

borinqueño _a_ & _m_ Puerto Rican

borla _f_ tassel

borra _f_ flock; (_pelusa_) fluff; (_sedimento_) sediment

borrach|era _f_ drunkenness. **~ín** _m_ drunkard. **~o** _a_ drunk. ● _m_ drunkard; (_temporalmente_) drunk. **estar ~o** be drunk. **ni ~o** never in a million years. **ser ~o** be a drunkard

borrador _m_ rough copy; (_libro_) rough notebook

borradura _f_ crossing-out

borrajear _vt/i_ scribble

borrar _vt_ rub out; (_tachar_) cross out

borrasc|a _f_ storm. **~oso** _a_ stormy

borreg|o _m_ year-old lamb; (_fig_) simpleton; (_Mex, noticia falsa_) hoax. **~uil** _a_ meek

borric|ada _f_ silly thing. **~o** _m_ donkey; (_fig, fam_) ass

borrón _m_ smudge; (_fig, imperfección_) blemish; (_de una pintura_) sketch. **~ y cuenta nueva** let's forget about it!

borroso _a_ blurred; (_fig_) vague

bos|caje _m_ thicket. **~coso** _a_ wooded. **~que** _m_ wood, forest. **~quecillo** _m_ copse

bosquej|ar _vt_ sketch. **~o** _m_ sketch

bosta _f_ dung

bostez|ar [10] _vi_ yawn. **~o** _m_ yawn

bota _f_ boot; (_recipiente_) leather wine bottle

botadero _m_ (_Mex_) ford

botánic|a _f_ botany. **~o** _a_ botanical. ● _m_ botanist

botar _vt_ launch. ● _vi_ bounce. **estar que bota** be hopping mad

botarat|ada _f_ silly thing. **~e** _m_ idiot

bote _m_ bounce; (_golpe_) blow; (_salto_) jump; (_sacudida_) jolt; (_lata_) tin, can; (_vasija_) jar; (_en un bar_) jar for tips; (_barca_) boat. **~ salvavidas** lifeboat. **de ~ en ~** packed

botell|a _f_ bottle. **~ita** _f_ small bottle

botica _f_ chemist's (shop) (_Brit_), drugstore (_Amer_). **~rio** _m_ chemist (_Brit_), druggist (_Amer_)

botija _f_, **botijo** _m_ earthenware jug

botín _m_ half boot; (_despojos_) booty; (_LAm, calcetín_) sock

botiquín _m_ medicine chest; (_de primeros auxilios_) first aid kit

bot|ón _m_ button; (_yema_) bud. **~onadura** _f_ buttons. **~ón de oro** buttercup. **~ones** _m invar_ bellboy (_Brit_), bellhop (_Amer_)

botulismo _m_ botulism

boutique /buˈtik/ _m_ boutique

bóveda _f_ vault

boxe|ador m boxer. ~ar vi box. ~o m boxing

boya f buoy; (corcho) float. ~nte a buoyant

bozal m (de perro etc) muzzle; (de caballo) halter

bracear vi wave one's arms; (nadar) swim, crawl

bracero m labourer. **de** ~ (fam) arm in arm

braga f underpants, knickers; (cuerda) rope. ~dura f crotch. ~s fpl knickers, pants. ~zas m invar (fam) henpecked man

bragueta f flies

braille /breil/ m Braille

bram|ar vi roar; (vaca) moo; (viento) howl. ~ido m roar

branquia f gill

bras|a f hot coal. **a la** ~**a** grilled. ~**ero** m brazier; (LAm, hogar) hearth

Brasil m. **el** ~ Brazil

brasile|ño a & m Brazilian. ~**ro** a & m (LAm) Brazilian

bravata f boast

bravío a wild; (persona) coarse, uncouth

brav|o a brave; (animales) wild; (mar) rough. ¡~! int well done! bravo! ~**ura** f ferocity; (valor) courage

braz|a f fathom. **nadar a** ~**a** do the breast-stroke. ~**ada** f waving of the arms; (en natación) stroke; (cantidad) armful. ~**ado** m armful. ~**al** m arm-band. ~**alete** m bracelet; (brazal) arm-band. ~**o** m arm; (de animales) foreleg; (rama) branch. ~**o derecho** right-hand man. **a** ~**o** by hand. **del** ~**o** arm in arm

brea f tar, pitch

brear vt ill-treat

brécol m broccoli

brecha f gap; (mil) breach; (med) gash. **estar en la** ~ be in the thick of it

brega f struggle. ~**r** [12] vi struggle; (trabajar mucho) work hard, slog away. **andar a la** ~ work hard

breña f, **breñal** m scrub

Bretaña f Brittany. **Gran** ~ Great Britain

breve a short. ~**dad** f shortness. **en** ~ soon, shortly. **en** ~**s momentos** soon

brez|al m moor. ~**o** m heather

brib|ón m rogue, rascal. ~**onada** f, ~**onería** f dirty trick

brida f bridle. **a toda** ~ at full speed

bridge /britʃ/ m bridge

brigada f squad; (mil) brigade. **general de** ~ brigadier (Brit), brigadier-general (Amer)

brill|ante a brilliant. ● m diamond. ~**antez** f brilliance. ~**ar** vi shine; (centellear) sparkle. ~**o** m shine; (brillantez) brilliance; (centelleo) sparkle. **dar** ~**o, sacar** ~**o** polish

brinc|ar [7] vi jump up and down. ~**o** m jump. **dar un** ~**o** jump. **estar que brinca** be hopping mad. **pegar un** ~**o** jump

brind|ar vt offer. ● vi. ~**ar por** toast, drink a toast to. ~**is** m toast

br|ío m energy; (decisión) determination. ~**ioso** a spirited; (garboso) elegant

brisa f breeze

británico a British. ● m Briton, British person

brocado m brocade

bróculi m broccoli

brocha f paintbrush; (para afeitarse) shaving-brush

broche m clasp, fastener; (joya) brooch; (Arg, sujetapapeles) paperclip

brocheta f skewer

brom|a f joke. ~**a pesada** practical joke. ~**ear** vi joke. ~**ista** a fun-loving. ● m & f joker. **de** ~**a, en** ~**a** in fun. **ni de** ~**a** never in a million years

bronca f row; (represión) telling-off

bronce m bronze. ~**ado** a bronze; (por el sol) tanned, sunburnt. ~**ar** vt tan (piel). ~**arse** vpr get a suntan

bronco a rough

bronquitis f bronchitis

broqueta f skewer

brot|ar vi (plantas) bud, sprout; (med) break out; (líquido) gush forth; (lágrimas) well up. ~**e** m bud, shoot; (med) outbreak; (de líquido) gushing; (de lágrimas) welling-up

bruces mpl. **de** ~ face down(wards). **caer de** ~ fall flat on one's face

bruj|a f witch. ● a (Mex) penniless. ~**ear** vi practise witchcraft. ~**ería** f witchcraft. ~**o** m wizard, magician; (LAm) medicine man

brújula f compass

brum|a f mist; (fig) confusion. ~**oso** a misty, foggy

bruñi|do m polish. ~**r** [22] vt polish

brusco a (*repentino*) sudden; ⟨*persona*⟩ brusque
Bruselas *fpl* Brussels
brusquedad *f* abruptness
brut|al a brutal. **~alidad** *f* brutality; (*estupidez*) stupidity. **~o** a (*estúpido*) stupid; (*tosco*) rough, uncouth; ⟨*peso, sueldo*⟩ gross
bucal a oral
buce|ar *vi* dive; (*fig*) explore. **~o** *m* diving
bucle *m* curl
budín *m* pudding
budis|mo *m* Buddhism. **~ta** *m & f* Buddhist
buen *véase* **bueno**
buenamente *adv* easily; (*voluntariamente*) willingly
buenaventura *f* good luck; (*adivinación*) fortune. **decir la ~ a uno**, **echar la ~ a uno** tell s.o.'s fortune
bueno a (*delante de nombre masculino en singular* **buen**) good; (*apropiado*) fit; (*amable*) kind; ⟨*tiempo*⟩ fine. ● *int* well!; (*de acuerdo*) OK!, very well! **¡buena la has hecho!** you've gone and done it now! **¡buenas noches!** good night! **¡buenas tardes!** (*antes del atardecer*) good afternoon!; (*después del atardecer*) good evening! **¡~s días!** good morning! **estar de buenas** be in a good mood. **por las buenas** willingly
Buenos Aires *m* Buenos Aires
buey *m* ox
búfalo *m* buffalo
bufanda *f* scarf
bufar *vi* snort. **estar que bufa** be hopping mad
bufete *m* (*mesa*) writing-desk; (*despacho*) lawyer's office
bufido *m* snort; (*de ira*) outburst
buf|o a comic. **~ón** a comical. ● *m* buffoon. **~onada** *f* joke
bugle *m* bugle
buharda *f*, **buhardilla** *f* attic; (*ventana*) dormer window
búho *m* owl
buhoner|ía *f* pedlar's wares. **~o** *m* pedlar
buitre *m* vulture
bujía *f* candle; (*auto*) spark(ing)plug
bula *f* bull
bulbo *m* bulb
bulevar *m* avenue, boulevard
Bulgaria *f* Bulgaria
búlgaro a & *m* Bulgarian
bulo *m* hoax

bulto *m* (*volumen*) volume; (*tamaño*) size; (*forma*) shape; (*paquete*) package; (*protuberancia*) lump. **a ~** roughly
bulla *f* uproar; (*muchedumbre*) crowd
bullicio *m* hubbub; (*movimiento*) bustle. **~so** a bustling; (*ruidoso*) noisy
bullir [22] *vt* stir, move. ● *vi* boil; (*burbujear*) bubble; (*fig*) bustle
buñuelo *m* doughnut; (*fig*) mess
BUP *abrev* (*Bachillerato Unificado Polivalente*) secondary school education
buque *m* ship, boat
burbuj|a *f* bubble. **~ear** *vi* bubble; ⟨*vino*⟩ sparkle. **~eo** *m* bubbling
burdel *m* brothel
burdo a rough, coarse; (*excusa*) clumsy
burgu|és a middle-class, bourgeois. ● *m* middle-class person. **~esía** *f* middle class, bourgeoisie
burla *f* taunt; (*broma*) joke; (*engaño*) trick. **~dor** a mocking. ● *m* seducer. **~r** *vt* trick, deceive; (*seducir*) seduce. **~rse** *vpr*. **~rse de** mock, make fun of
burlesco a funny
burlón a mocking
bur|ocracia *f* civil service. **~ócrata** *m & f* civil servant. **~ocrático** a bureaucratic
burro *m* donkey; (*fig*) ass
bursátil a stock-exchange
bus *m* (*fam*) bus
busca *f* search. **a la ~ de** in search of. **en ~ de** in search of
busca: **~pié** *m* feeler. **~pleitos** *m* *invar* (*LAm*) trouble-maker
buscar [7] *vt* look for. ● *vi* look. **buscársela** ask for it. **ir a ~ a uno** fetch s.o.
buscarruidos *m* *invar* troublemaker
buscona *f* prostitute
busilis *m* snag
búsqueda *f* search
busto *m* bust
butaca *f* armchair; (*en el teatro etc*) seat
butano *m* butane
buzo *m* diver
buzón *m* postbox (*Brit*), mailbox (*Amer*)

C

C/ *abrev* (*Calle*) St, Street, Rd, Road

cabal *a* exact; (*completo*) complete. **no estar en sus ∼es** not be in one's right mind

cabalga|dura *f* mount, horse. **∼r** [12] *vt* ride. ● *vi* ride, go riding. **∼ta** *f* ride; (*desfile*) procession

cabalmente *adv* completely; (*exactamente*) exactly

caballa *f* mackerel

caballada *f* (*LAm*) stupid thing

caballeresco *a* gentlemanly. **literatura** *f* **caballeresca** books of chivalry

caballer|ía *f* mount, horse. **∼iza** *f* stable. **∼izo** *m* groom

caballero *m* gentleman; (*de orden de caballería*) knight; (*tratamiento*) sir. **∼samente** *adv* like a gentleman. **∼so** *a* gentlemanly

caballete *m* (*del tejado*) ridge; (*de la nariz*) bridge; (*de pintor*) easel

caballito *m* pony. **∼ del diablo** dragonfly. **∼ de mar** sea-horse. **los ∼s** (*tiovivo*) merry-go-round

caballo *m* horse; (*del ajedrez*) knight; (*de la baraja española*) queen. **∼ de vapor** horsepower. **a ∼** on horseback

cabaña *f* hut

cabaret /kaba're/ *m* (*pl* **cabarets** /kaba're/) night-club

cabece|ar *vi* nod; (*para negar*) shake one's head. **∼o** *m* nodding, nod; (*acción de negar*) shake of the head

cabecera *f* (*de la cama, de la mesa*) head; (*en un impreso*) heading

cabecilla *m* leader

cabell|o *m* hair. **∼os** *mpl* hair. **∼udo** *a* hairy

caber [28] *vi* fit (**en** into). **los libros no caben en la caja** the books won't fit into the box. **no cabe duda** there's no doubt

cabestr|illo *m* sling. **∼o** *m* halter

cabeza *f* head; (*fig, inteligencia*) intelligence. **∼da** *f* butt; (*golpe recibido*) blow; (*saludo, al dormirse*) nod. **∼zo** *m* butt; (*en fútbol*) header. **andar de ∼** have a lot to do. **dar una ∼da** nod off

cabida *f* capacity; (*extensión*) area. **dar ∼ a** leave room for, leave space for

cabina *f* (*de avión*) cabin, cockpit; (*electoral*) booth; (*de camión*) cab. **∼ telefónica** telephone box (*Brit*), telephone booth (*Amer*)

cabizbajo *a* crestfallen

cable *m* cable

cabo *m* end; (*trozo*) bit; (*mil*) corporal; (*mango*) handle; (*geog*) cape; (*naut*) rope. **al ∼** eventually. **al ∼ de una hora** after an hour. **de ∼ a rabo** from beginning to end. **llevar(se) a ∼** carry out

cabr|a *f* goat. **∼a montesa** *f* mountain goat. **∼iola** *f* jump, skip. **∼itilla** *f* kid. **∼ito** *m* kid

cabrón *m* cuckold

cabuya *f* (*LAm*) pita, agave

cacahuate *m* (*Mex*), **cacahuete** *m* peanut

cacao *m* (*planta y semillas*) cacao; (*polvo*) cocoa; (*fig*) confusion

cacare|ar *vt* boast about. ● *vi* (*gallo*) crow; (*gallina*) cluck. **∼o** *m* (*incl fig*) crowing; (*de gallina*) clucking

cacería *f* hunt

cacerola *f* casserole, saucepan

caciqu|e *m* cacique, Indian chief; (*pol*) cacique, local political boss. **∼il** *a* despotic. **∼ismo** *m* caciquism, despotism

caco *m* pickpocket, thief

cacof|onía *f* cacophony. **∼ónico** *a* cacophonous

cacto *m* cactus

cacumen *m* acumen

cacharro *m* earthenware pot; (*para flores*) vase; (*coche estropeado*) wreck; (*cosa inútil*) piece of junk; (*chisme*) thing. **∼s** *mpl* pots and pans

cachear *vt* frisk

cachemir *m*, **cachemira** *f* cashmere

cacheo *m* frisking

cachetada *f* (*LAm*), **cachete** *m* slap

cachimba *f* pipe

cachiporra *f* club, truncheon. **∼zo** *m* blow with a club

cachivache *m* thing, piece of junk

cacho *m* bit, piece; (*LAm, cuerno*) horn; (*miga*) crumb

cachondeo *m* (*fam*) joking, joke

cachorro *m* (*perrito*) puppy; (*de otros animales*) young

cada *a invar* each, every. **∼ uno** each one, everyone. **uno de ∼ cinco** one in five

cadalso *m* scaffold

cadáver *m* corpse. **ingresar ∼** be dead on arrival

cadena *f* chain; (*TV*) channel. **∼ de fabricación** production line. **∼ de montañas** mountain range. **∼ perpetua** life imprisonment

cadencia *f* cadence, rhythm

cadera f hip

cadete m cadet

caduc|ar [7] vi expire. **∼idad** f. **fecha** f de **∼idad** sell-by date. **∼o** a decrepit

cae|dizo a unsteady. **∼r** [29] vi fall. **∼rse** vpr fall (over). **dejar ∼r** drop. **estar al ∼r** be about to happen. **este vestido no me ∼ bien** this dress doesn't suit me. **hacer ∼r** knock over. **Juan me ∼ bien** I get on well with Juan. **su cumpleaños cayó en martes** his birthday fell on a Tuesday

café m coffee; (cafetería) café. ● a. **color ∼** coffee-coloured. **∼ con leche** white coffee. **∼ cortado** coffee with a little milk. **∼ (solo)** black coffee

cafe|ína f caffeine. **∼tal** m coffee plantation. **∼tera** f coffee-pot. **∼tería** f café. **∼tero** a coffee

caíd|a f fall; (disminución) drop; (pendiente) slope. **∼o** a fallen; (abatido) dejected. ● m fallen

caigo vb véase **caer**

caimán m cayman, alligator

caj|a f box; (grande) case; (de caudales) safe; (donde se efectúan los pagos) cash desk; (en supermercado) check-out. **∼a de ahorros** savings bank. **∼a de caudales, ∼a fuerte** safe. **∼a postal de ahorros** post office savings bank. **∼a registradora** till. **∼ero** m cashier. **∼etilla** f packet. **∼ita** f small box. **∼ón** m large box; (de mueble) drawer; (puesto de mercado) stall. **ser de ∼ón** be a matter of course

cal m lime

cala f cove

calaba|cín m marrow; (fig, idiota, fam) idiot. **∼za** f pumpkin; (fig, idiota, fam) idiot

calabozo m prison; (celda) cell

calado a soaked. ● m (naut) draught. **estar ∼ hasta los huesos** be soaked to the skin

calamar m squid

calambre m cramp

calami|dad f calamity, disaster. **∼toso** a calamitous, disastrous

calar vt soak; (penetrar) pierce; (fig, penetrar) see through; sample ⟨fruta⟩. **∼se** vpr get soaked; (zapatos) leak; (auto) stall

calavera f skull

calcar [7] vt trace; (fig) copy

calceta f. **hacer ∼** knit

calcetín m sock

calcinar vt burn

calcio m calcium

calco m tracing. **∼manía** f transfer. **papel** m **de ∼** tracing-paper

calcula|dor a calculating. **∼dora** f calculator. **∼dora de bolsillo** pocket calculator. **∼r** vt calculate; (suponer) reckon, think

cálculo m calculation; (fig) reckoning

caldea|miento m heating. **∼r** vt heat, warm. **∼rse** vpr get hot

calder|a f boiler; (Arg, para café) coffee-pot; (Arg, para té) teapot. **∼eta** f small boiler

calderilla f small change, coppers

calder|o m small boiler. **∼ón** m large boiler

caldo m stock; (sopa) soup, broth. **poner a ∼ a uno** give s.o. a dressing-down

calefacción f heating. **∼ central** central heating

caleidoscopio m kaleidoscope

calendario m calendar

caléndula f marigold

calenta|dor m heater. **∼miento** m heating; (en deportes) warm-up. **∼r** [1] vt heat, warm. **∼rse** vpr get hot, warm up

calentur|a f fever, (high) temperature. **∼iento** a feverish

calibr|ar vt calibrate; (fig) measure. **∼e** m calibre; (diámetro) diameter; (fig) importance

calidad f quality; (función) capacity. **en ∼ de** as

cálido a warm

calidoscopio m kaleidoscope

caliente a hot, warm; (fig, enfadado) angry

califica|ción f qualification; (evaluación) assessment; (nota) mark. **∼r** [7] vt qualify; (evaluar) assess; mark ⟨examen etc⟩. **∼r de** describe as, label. **∼tivo** a qualifying. ● m epithet

caliz|a f limestone. **∼o** a lime

calm|a f calm. **¡∼a!** calm down! **∼ante** a & m sedative. **∼ar** vt calm, soothe. ● vi ⟨viento⟩ abate. **∼arse** vpr calm down; ⟨viento⟩ abate. **∼oso** a calm; (flemático, fam) phlegmatic. **en ∼a** calm. **perder la ∼a** lose one's composure

calor *m* heat, warmth. **hace** ∼ it's hot. **tener** ∼ be hot
caloría *f* calorie
calorífero *m* heater
calumni|a *f* calumny; (*oral*) slander; (*escrita*) libel. ∼**ar** *vt* slander; (*por escrito*) libel. ∼**oso** *a* slanderous; ‹*cosa escrita*› libellous
caluros|amente *adv* warmly. ∼**o** *a* warm
calv|a *f* bald patch. ∼**ero** *m* clearing. ∼**icie** *f* baldness. ∼**o** *a* bald; ‹*terreno*› barren
calza *f* (*fam*) stocking; (*cuña*) wedge
calzada *f* road
calza|do *a* wearing shoes. ● *m* footwear, shoe. ∼**dor** *m* shoehorn. ∼**r** [10] *vt* put shoes on; (*llevar*) wear. ● *vi* wear shoes. ∼**rse** *vpr* put on. **¿qué número calza Vd?** what size shoe do you take?
calz|ón *m* shorts; (*ropa interior*) knickers, pants. ∼**ones** *mpl* shorts. ∼**oncillos** *mpl* underpants
calla|do *a* quiet. ∼**r** *vt* silence; keep ‹*secreto*›; hush up ‹*asunto*›. ● *vi* be quiet, keep quiet, shut up (*fam*). ∼**rse** *vpr* be quiet, keep quiet, shut up (*fam*). **¡cállate!** be quiet! shut up! (*fam*)
calle *f* street, road; (*en deportes, en autopista*) lane. ∼ **de dirección única** one-way street. ∼ **mayor** high street, main street. **abrir** ∼ make way
callej|a *f* narrow street. ∼**ear** *vi* wander about the streets. ∼**ero** *a* street. ● *m* street plan. ∼**ón** *m* alley. ∼**uela** *f* back street, side street. ∼**ón sin salida** cul-de-sac
call|ista *m* & *f* chiropodist. ∼**o** *m* corn, callus. ∼**os** *mpl* tripe. ∼**oso** *a* hard, rough
cama *f* bed. ∼ **de matrimonio** double bed. ∼ **individual** single bed. **caer en la** ∼ fall ill. **guardar** ∼ be confined to bed
camada *f* litter; (*fig, de ladrones*) gang
camafeo *m* cameo
camaleón *m* chameleon
cámara *f* room; (*de reyes*) royal chamber; (*fotográfica*) camera; (*de armas, pol*) chamber. ∼ **fotográfica** camera. **a** ∼ **lenta** in slow motion
camarada *f* colleague; (*amigo*) companion

camarer|a *f* chambermaid; (*de restaurante etc*) waitress; (*en casa*) maid. ∼**o** *m* waiter
camarín *m* dressing-room; (*naut*) cabin
camarón *m* shrimp
camarote *m* cabin
cambi|able *a* changeable; (*com etc*) exchangeable. ∼**ante** *a* variable. ∼**ar** *vt* change; (*trocar*) exchange. ● *vi* change. ∼**ar de idea** change one's mind. ∼**arse** *vpr* change. ∼**o** *m* change; (*com*) exchange rate; (*moneda menuda*) (small) change. ∼**sta** *m* & *f* money-changer. **en** ∼**o** on the other hand
camelia *f* camellia
camello *m* camel
camilla *f* stretcher; (*sofá*) couch
camina|nte *m* traveller. ∼**r** *vt* cover. ● *vi* travel; (*andar*) walk; ‹*río, astros etc*› move. ∼**ta** *f* long walk
camino *m* road; (*sendero*) path, track; (*dirección, medio*) way. ∼ **de** towards, on the way to. **abrir** ∼ make way. **a medio** ∼, **a la mitad del** ∼ half-way. **de** ∼ on the way. **ponerse en** ∼ set out
cami|ón *m* lorry; (*Mex, autobús*) bus. ∼**onero** *m* lorry-driver. ∼**oneta** *f* van
camis|a *f* shirt; (*de un fruto*) skin. ∼**a de dormir** nightdress. ∼**a de fuerza** strait-jacket. ∼**ería** *f* shirt shop. ∼**eta** *f* T-shirt; (*ropa interior*) vest. ∼**ón** *m* nightdress
camorra *f* (*fam*) row. **buscar** ∼ look for trouble, pick a quarrel
camote *m* (*LAm*) sweet potato
campamento *m* camp
campan|a *f* bell. ∼**ada** *f* stroke of a bell; (*de reloj*) striking. ∼**a de fuerza** tower, belfry. ∼**eo** *m* peal of bells. ∼**illa** *f* bell. ∼**udo** *a* bell-shaped; ‹*estilo*› bombastic
campaña *f* countryside; (*mil, pol*) campaign. **de** ∼ (*mil*) field
campe|ón *a* & *m* champion. ∼**onato** *m* championship
campes|ino *a* country. ● *m* peasant. ∼**tre** *a* country
camping /'kampin/ *m* (*pl* **campings** /'kampin/) camping; (*lugar*) campsite. **hacer** ∼ go camping
campiña *f* countryside
campo *m* country; (*agricultura, fig*) field; (*de tenis*) court; (*de fútbol*)

pitch; (*de golf*) course. **~santo** *m* cemetery

camufla|do *a* camouflaged. **~je** *m* camouflage. **~r** *vt* camouflage

cana *f* grey hair, white hair. **echar una ~ al aire** have a fling. **peinar~s** be getting old

Canadá *m*. **el ~** Canada

canadiense *a & m* Canadian

canal *m* (*incl TV*) channel; (*artificial*) canal; (*del tejado*) gutter. **~ de la Mancha** English Channel. **~ de Panamá** Panama Canal. **~ón** *m* (*horizontal*) gutter; (*vertical*) drainpipe

canalla *f* rabble. ● *m* (*fig, fam*) swine. **~da** *f* dirty trick

canapé *m* sofa, couch; (*culin*) canapé

Canarias *fpl*. **(las islas) ~** the Canary Islands, the Canaries

canario *a* of the Canary Islands. ● *m* native of the Canary Islands; (*pájaro*) canary

canast|a *f* (large) basket. **~illa** *f* small basket; (*para un bebé*) layette. **~illo** *m* small basket. **~o** *m* (large) basket

cancela *f* gate

cancela|ción *f* cancellation. **~r** *vt* cancel; write off ⟨*deuda*⟩; (*fig*) forget

cáncer *m* cancer. **C~** Cancer

canciller *m* chancellor; (*LAm, ministro de asuntos exteriores*) Minister of Foreign Affairs

canci|ón *f* song. **~ón de cuna** lullaby. **~onero** *m* song-book. **¡siempre la misma ~ón!** always the same old story!

cancha *f* (*de fútbol*) pitch, ground; (*de tenis*) court

candado *m* padlock

candel|a *f* candle. **~ero** *m* candlestick. **~illa** *f* candle

candente *a* (*rojo*) red-hot; (*blanco*) white-hot; (*fig*) burning

candidato *m* candidate

candidez *f* innocence; (*ingenuidad*) naïvety

cándido *a* naïve

candil *m* oil-lamp; (*Mex, araña*) chandelier. **~ejas** *fpl* footlights

candinga *m* (*Mex*) devil

candor *m* innocence; (*ingenuidad*) naïvety. **~oso** *a* innocent; (*ingenuo*) naïve

canela *f* cinnamon. **ser ~** be beautiful

cangrejo *m* crab. **~ de río** crayfish

canguro *m* kangaroo; (*persona*) baby-sitter

can|íbal *a & m* cannibal. **~ibalismo** *m* cannibalism

canica *f* marble

canijo *m* weak

canino *a* canine. ● *m* canine (tooth)

canje *m* exchange. **~ar** *vt* exchange

cano *a* grey-haired

canoa *f* canoe; (*con motor*) motor boat

canon *m* canon

can|ónigo *m* canon. **~onizar** [10] *vt* canonize

canoso *a* grey-haired

cansa|do *a* tired. **~ncio** *m* tiredness. **~r** *vt* tire; (*aburrir*) bore. ● *vi* be tiring; (*aburrir*) get boring. **~rse** *vpr* get tired

cantábrico *a* Cantabrian. **el mar ~** the Bay of Biscay

cantidad *f* quantity; (*número*) number; (*de dinero*) sum. **una ~ de** lots of

cantilena *f*, **cantinela** *f* song

cantimplora *f* water-bottle

cantina *f* canteen; (*rail*) buffet

canta|nte *a* singing. ● *m* singer; (*en óperas*) opera singer. **~or** *m* Flamenco singer. **~r** *vt/i* sing. ● *m* singing; (*canción*) song; (*poema*) poem. **~rlas claras** speak frankly

cántar|a *f* pitcher. **~o** *m* pitcher. **llover a ~os** pour down

cante *m* folk song. **~ flamenco**, **~ jondo** Flamenco singing

cantera *f* quarry

canto *m* singing; (*canción*) song; (*borde*) edge; (*de un cuchillo*) blunt edge; (*esquina*) corner; (*piedra*) pebble. **~ rodado** boulder. **de ~** on edge

cantonés *a* Cantonese

cantor *a* singing. ● *m* singer

canturre|ar *vt/i* hum. **~o** *m* humming

canuto *m* tube

caña *f* stalk, stem; (*planta*) reed; (*vaso*) glass; (*de la pierna*) shin. **~ de azúcar** sugar-cane. **~ de pescar** fishing-rod

cañada *f* ravine; (*camino*) track

cáñamo *m* hemp. **~ índio** cannabis

cañ|ería *f* pipe; (*tubería*) piping. **~o** *m* pipe, tube; (*de fuente*) jet. **~ón** *m* pipe, tube; (*de órgano*) pipe; (*de chimenea*) flue; (*arma de fuego*) cannon; (*desfiladero*) canyon. **~onazo** *m* gunshot. **~onera** *f* gunboat

caoba *f* mahogany

ca|os *m* chaos. **~ótico** *a* chaotic

capa *f* cloak; (*de pintura*) coat; (*culin*) coating; (*geol*) stratum, layer

capacidad *f* capacity; (*fig*) ability

capacitar *vt* qualify, enable; (*instruir*) train

caparazón *m* shell

capataz *m* foreman

capaz *a* capable, able; (*espacioso*) roomy. **~ para** which holds, with a capacity of

capazo *m* large basket

capcioso *a* sly, insidious

capellán *m* chaplain

caperuza *f* hood; (*de pluma*) cap

capilla *f* chapel; (*mus*) choir

capita *f* small cloak, cape

capital *a* capital, very important. ● *m* (*dinero*) capital. ● *f* (*ciudad*) capital; (*LAm, letra*) capital (letter). **~ de provincia** county town

capitali|smo *m* capitalism. **~sta** *a* & *m* & *f* capitalist. **~zar** [10] *vt* capitalize

capit|án *m* captain. **~anear** *vt* lead, command; (*un equipo*) captain

capitel *m* (*arquit*) capital

capitulaci|ón *f* surrender; (*acuerdo*) agreement. **~ones** *fpl* marriage contract

capítulo *m* chapter. **~s matrimoniales** marriage contract

capó *m* bonnet (*Brit*), hood (*Amer*)

capón *m* (*pollo*) capon

caporal *m* chief, leader

capota *f* (*de mujer*) bonnet; (*auto*) folding top, sliding roof

capote *m* cape

Capricornio *m* Capricorn

capricho *m* whim. **~so** *a* capricious, whimsical. **a ~** capriciously

cápsula *f* capsule

captar *vt* harness ‹*agua*›; grasp ‹*sentido*›; hold ‹*atención*›; win ‹*confianza*›; (*radio*) pick up

captura *f* capture. **~r** *vt* capture

capucha *f* hood

capullo *m* bud; (*de insecto*) cocoon

caqui *m* khaki

cara *f* face; (*de una moneda*) obverse; (*de un objeto*) side; (*aspecto*) look, appearance; (*descaro*) cheek. **~ a** towards; (*frente a*) facing. **~ a ~** face to face. **~ o cruz** heads or tails. **dar la ~** face up to. **hacer ~ a** face. **no volver la ~ atrás** not look back. **tener ~ de** look, seem to be. **tener ~ para** have the face to. **tener mala ~** look ill. **volver la ~** look the other way

carabela *f* caravel, small light ship

carabina *f* rifle; (*fig, señora, fam*) chaperone

Caracas *m* Caracas

caracol *m* snail; (*de pelo*) curl. **¡~es!** Good Heavens! **escalera** *f* **de ~** spiral staircase

carácter *m* (*pl* **caracteres**) character. **con ~ de, por su ~ de** as

característic|a *f* characteristic; (*LAm, teléfonos*) dialling code. **~o** *a* characteristic, typical

caracteriza|do *a* characterized; (*prestigioso*) distinguished. **~r** [10] *vt* characterize

cara: ~ dura cheek, nerve. **~dura** *m* & *f* cheeky person, rotter (*fam*)

caramba *int* good heavens!, goodness me!

carámbano *m* icicle

caramelo *m* sweet (*Brit*), candy (*Amer*); (*azúcar fundido*) caramel

carancho *m* (*Arg*) vulture

carapacho *m* shell

caraqueño *a* from Caracas. ● *m* native of Caracas

carátula *f* mask; (*fig, teatro*) theatre; (*Mex, esfera del reloj*) face

caravana *f* caravan; (*fig, grupo*) group; (*auto*) long line, traffic jam

caray *int* (*fam*) good heavens!, goodness me!

carb|ón *m* coal; (*papel*) carbon (paper); (*para dibujar*) charcoal. **~oncillo** *m* charcoal. **~onero** *a* coal. ● *m* coal-merchant. **~onizar** [10] *vt* (*fig*) burn (to a cinder). **~ono** *m* carbon

carburador *m* carburettor

carcajada *f* burst of laughter. **reírse a ~s** roar with laughter. **soltar una ~** burst out laughing

cárcel *m* prison, jail; (*en carpintería*) clamp

carcel|ario *a* prison. **~ero** *a* prison. ● *m* prison officer

carcom|a *f* woodworm. **~er** *vt* eat away; (*fig*) undermine. **~erse** *vpr* be eaten away; (*fig*) waste away

cardenal *m* cardinal; (*contusión*) bruise

cárdeno *a* purple

cardiaco, cardíaco, *a* cardiac, heart. ● *m* heart patient

cardinal *a* cardinal

cardiólogo m cardiologist, heart specialist

cardo m thistle

carear vt bring face to face ‹personas›; compare ‹cosas›

carecer [11] vi. ~ **de** lack. ~ **de sentido** not to make sense

caren|cia f lack. ~**te** a lacking

carero a expensive

carestía f (precio elevado) high price; (escasez) shortage

careta f mask

carey m tortoiseshell

carga f load; (fig) burden; (acción) loading; (de barco) cargo; (obligación) obligation. ~**do** a loaded; (fig) burdened; ‹tiempo› heavy; ‹hilo› live; ‹pila› charged. ~**mento** m load; (acción) loading; (de un barco) cargo. ~**nte** a demanding. ~**r** [12] vt load; (fig) burden; (mil, elec) charge; fill ‹pluma etc›; (fig, molestar, fam) annoy. ● vi load. ~**r con** pick up. ~**rse** vpr (llenarse) fill; ‹cielo› become overcast; (enfadarse, fam) get cross. **llevar la ~ de algo** be responsible for sth

cargo m load; (fig) burden; (puesto) post; (acusación) accusation, charge; (responsabilidad) charge. **a ~ de** in the charge of. **hacerse ~ de** take responsibility for. **tener a su ~** be in charge of

carguero m (Arg) beast of burden; (naut) cargo ship

cari m (LAm) grey

cariacontecido a crestfallen

caria|do a decayed. ~**rse** vpr decay

caribe a Caribbean. **el mar** m **C~** the Caribbean (Sea)

caricatura f caricature

caricia f caress

caridad f charity. **¡por ~!** for goodness sake!

caries f invar (dental) decay

carilampiño a clean-shaven

cariño m affection; (caricia) caress. ~ **mío** my darling. ~**samente** adv tenderly, lovingly; (en carta) with love from. ~**so** a affectionate. **con mucho ~** (en carta) with love from. **tener ~ a** be fond of. **tomar ~ a** take a liking to. **un ~** (en carta) with love from

carism|a m charisma. ~**ático** a charismatic

caritativo a charitable

cariz m look

carlinga f cockpit

carmesí a & m crimson

carmín m (de labios) lipstick; (color) red

carnal a carnal; ‹pariente› blood, full. **primo ~** first cousin

carnaval m carnival. ~**esco** a carnival. **martes** m **de ~** Shrove Tuesday

carne f (incl de frutos) flesh; (para comer) meat. ~ **de cerdo** pork. ~ **de cordero** lamb. ~ **de gallina** gooseflesh. ~ **picada** mince. ~ **de ternera** veal. ~ **de vaca** beef. **me pone la ~ de gallina** it gives me the creeps. **ser de ~ y hueso** be only human

carné m card; (cuaderno) notebook. ~ **de conducir** driving licence (Brit), driver's license (Amer). ~ **de identidad** identity card.

carnero m sheep; (culin) lamb

carnet /kar'ne/ m card; (cuaderno) notebook. ~ **de conducir** driving licence (Brit), driver's license (Amer). ~ **de identidad** identity card

carnicer|ía f butcher's (shop); (fig) massacre. ~**o** a carnivorous; (fig, cruel) cruel, savage. ● m butcher; (animal) carnivore

carnívoro a carnivorous. ● m carnivore

carnoso a fleshy

caro a dear. ● adv dear, dearly. **costar ~ a uno** cost s.o. dear

carpa f carp; (tienda) tent

carpeta f file, folder. ~**zo** m. **dar ~zo a** shelve, put on one side

carpinter|ía f carpentry. ~**o** m carpinter, joiner

carraspe|ar vi clear one's throat. ~**ra** f. **tener ~ra** have a frog in one's throat

carrera f run; (prisa) rush; (concurso) race; (recorrido, estudios) course; (profesión) profession, career

carreta f cart. ~**da** f cart-load

carrete m reel; (película) 35mm film

carretera f road. ~ **de circunvalación** bypass, ring road. ~ **nacional** A road (Brit), highway (Amer). ~ **secundaria** B road (Brit), secondary road (Amer)

carret|illa f trolley; (de una rueda) wheelbarrow; (de bebé) baby-walker. ~**ón** m small cart

carril m rut; (rail) rail; (de autopista etc) lane

carrillo *m* cheek; (*polea*) pulley

carrizo *m* reed

carro *m* cart; (*LAm, coche*) car. **~ de asalto**, **~ de combate** tank

carrocería *f* (*auto*) bodywork; (*taller*) car repairer's

carroña *f* carrion

carroza *f* coach, carriage; (*en desfile de fiesta*) float

carruaje *m* carriage

carrusel *m* merry-go-round

carta *f* letter; (*documento*) document; (*lista de platos*) menu; (*lista de vinos*) list; (*geog*) map; (*naipe*) card. **~ blanca** free hand. **~ de crédito** credit card

cartearse *vpr* correspond

cartel *m* poster; (*de escuela etc*) wall-chart. **~era** *f* hoarding; (*en periódico*) entertainments. **~ito** *m* notice. **de ~** celebrated. **tener ~** be a hit, be successful

cartera *f* wallet; (*de colegial*) satchel; (*para documentos*) briefcase

cartería *f* sorting office

carterista *m* pickpocket

cartero *m* postman, mailman (*Amer*)

cartílago *m* cartilage

cartilla *f* first reading book. **~ de ahorros** savings book. **leerle la ~ a uno** tell s.o. off

cartón *m* cardboard

cartucho *m* cartridge

cartulina *f* thin cardboard

casa *f* house; (*hogar*) home; (*empresa*) firm; (*edificio*) building. **~ de correos** post office. **~ de huéspedes** boarding-house. **~ de socorro** first aid post. **amigo** *m* **de la ~** family friend. **ir a ~** go home. **salir de ~** go out

casad|a *f* married woman. **~o a** married. ● *m* married man. **los recién ~os** the newly-weds

casamentero *m* matchmaker

casa|miento *m* marriage; (*ceremonia*) wedding. ● *vi* marry. **~rse** *vpr* get married

cascabel *m* small bell. **~eo** *m* jingling

cascada *f* waterfall

cascado *a* broken; (*voz*) harsh

cascanueces *m invar* nutcrackers

cascar [7] *vt* break; crack (*frutos secos*); (*pegar*) beat. ● *vi* (*fig, fam*) chatter, natter (*fam*). **~se** *vpr* crack

cáscara *f* (*de huevo, frutos secos*) shell; (*de naranja*) peel; (*de plátano*) skin

casco *m* helmet; (*de cerámica etc*) piece, fragment; (*cabeza*) head; (*de barco*) hull; (*envase*) empty bottle; (*de caballo*) hoof; (*de una ciudad*) part, area

cascote *m* rubble

caserío *m* country house; (*conjunto de casas*) hamlet

casero *a* home-made; (*doméstico*) domestic, household; (*amante del hogar*) home-loving; (*reunión*) family. ● *m* owner; (*vigilante*) caretaker

caseta *f* small house, cottage. **~ de baño** bathing hut

caset(t)e *m & f* cassette

casi *adv* almost, nearly; (*en frases negativas*) hardly. **~ ~** very nearly. **~ nada** hardly any. **¡~ nada!** is that all! **~ nunca** hardly ever

casilla *f* small house; (*cabaña*) hut; (*de mercado*) stall; (*en ajedrez etc*) square; (*departamento de casillero*) pigeon-hole

casillero *m* pigeon-holes

casimir *m* cashmere

casino *m* casino; (*sociedad*) club

caso *m* case; (*atención*) notice. **~ perdido** hopeless case. **~ urgente** emergency. **darse el ~ (de) que** happen. **el ~ es que** the fact is that. **en ~ de** in the event of. **en cualquier ~** in any case, whatever happens. **en ese ~** in that case. **en todo ~** in any case. **en último ~** as a last resort. **hacer ~ de** take notice of. **poner por ~** suppose

caspa *f* dandruff

cáspita *int* good heavens!, goodness me!

casquivano *a* scatter-brained

cassette *m & f* cassette

casta *f* (*de animal*) breed; (*de persona*) descent

castaña *f* chestnut

castañet|a *f* click of the fingers. **~ear** *vi* (*dientes*) chatter

castaño *a* chestnut, brown. ● *m* chestnut (tree)

castañuela *f* castanet

castellano *a* Castilian. ● *m* (*persona*) Castilian; (*lengua*) Castilian, Spanish. **~parlante** *a* Castilian-speaking, Spanish-speaking. **¿habla Vd ~?** do you speak Spanish?

castidad *f* chastity

castig|ar [12] *vt* punish; (*en deportes*) penalize. **~o** *m* punishment; (*en deportes*) penalty

Castilla f Castille. ~ **la Nueva** New Castille. ~ **la Vieja** Old Castille

castillo m castle

cast|izo a true; ‹lengua› pure. ~**o** a pure

castor m beaver

castra|ción f castration. ~**r** vt castrate

castrense m military

casual a chance, accidental. ~**idad** f chance, coincidence. ~**mente** adv by chance. **dar la** ~**idad** happen. **de** ~**idad, por** ~**idad** by chance. **¡qué** ~**idad!** what a coincidence!

cataclismo m cataclysm

catador m taster; (fig) connoisseur

catalán a & m Catalan

catalejo m telescope

catalizador m catalyst

cat|alogar [12] vt catalogue; (fig) classify. ~**álogo** m catalogue

Cataluña f Catalonia

catamarán m catamaran

cataplúm int crash! bang!

catapulta f catapult

catar vt taste, try

catarata f waterfall, falls; (med) cataract

catarro m cold

cat|ástrofe m catastrophe. ~**astrófico** a catastrophic

catecismo m catechism

catedral f cathedral

catedrático m professor; (de instituto) teacher, head of department

categ|oría f category; (clase) class. ~**órico** a categorical. **de** ~**oría** important. **de primera** ~**oría** first-class

catinga f (LAm) bad smell

catita f (Arg) parrot

catoche m (Mex) bad mood

cat|olicismo m catholicism. ~**ólico** a (Roman) Catholic. ● m (Roman) Catholic

catorce a & m fourteen

cauce m river bed; (fig, artificial) channel

caución f caution; (jurid) guarantee

caucho m rubber

caudal m (de río) flow; (riqueza) wealth. ~**oso** a (río) large

caudillo m leader, caudillo

causa f cause; (motivo) reason; (jurid) lawsuit. ~**r** vt cause. **a** ~ **de, por** ~ **de** because of

cáustico a caustic

cautel|a f caution. ~**arse** vpr guard against. ~**osamente** adv warily, cautiously. ~**oso** a cautious, wary

cauterizar [10] vt cauterize; (fig) apply drastic measures to

cautiv|ar vt capture; (fig, fascinar) captivate. ~**erio** m, ~**idad** f captivity. ~**o** a & m captive

cauto a cautious

cavar vt/i dig

caverna f cave, cavern

caviar m caviare

cavidad f cavity

cavil|ar vi ponder, consider. ~**oso** a worried

cayado m (de pastor) crook; (de obispo) crozier

caza f hunting; (una expedición) hunt; (animales) game. ● m fighter. ~**dor** m hunter. ~**dora** f jacket. ~ **mayor** big game hunting. ~ **menor** small game hunting. ~**r** [10] vt hunt; (fig) track down; (obtener) catch, get. **andar a (la)** ~ **de** be in search of. **dar** ~ chase, go after

cazo m saucepan; (cucharón) ladle. ~**leta** f (small) saucepan

cazuela f casserole

cebada f barley

ceb|ar vt fatten (up); (con trampa) bait; prime ‹arma de fuego›. ~**o** m bait; (de arma de fuego) charge

ceboll|a f onion. ~**ana** f chive. ~**eta** f spring onion. ~**ino** m chive

cebra f zebra

cece|ar vi lisp. ~**o** m lisp

cedazo m sieve

ceder vt give up. ● vi give in; (disminuir) ease off; (fallar) give way, collapse. **ceda el paso** give way

cedilla f cedilla

cedro m cedar

cédula f document; (ficha) index card

CE(E) abrev (Comunidad (Económica) Europea) E(E)C, European (Economic) Community

cefalea f severe headache

ceg|ador a blinding. ~**ar** [1 & 12] vt blind; (tapar) block up. ~**arse** vpr be blinded (**de** by). ~**ato** a short-sighted. ~**uera** f blindness

ceja f eyebrow

cejar vi move back; (fig) give way

celada f ambush; (fig) trap

cela|dor m (de niños) monitor; (de cárcel) prison warder; (de museo etc) attendant. ~**r** vt watch

celda f cell

celebra|ción *f* celebration. **~r** *vt* celebrate; (*alabar*) praise. **~rse** *vpr* take place

célebre *a* famous; (*fig, gracioso*) funny

celebridad *f* fame; (*persona*) celebrity

celeridad *f* speed

celest|e *a* heavenly. **~ial** *a* heavenly. **azul ~e** sky-blue

celibato *m* celibacy

célibe *a* celibate

celo *m* zeal. **~s** *mpl* jealousy. **dar ~s** make jealous. **papel** *m* **~** adhesive tape, Sellotape (P). **tener ~s** be jealous

celofán *m* cellophane

celoso *a* enthusiastic; (*que tiene celos*) jealous

celta *a* Celtic. ● *m & f* Celt

céltico *a* Celtic

célula *f* cell

celular *a* cellular

celuloide *m* celluloid

celulosa *f* cellulose

cellisca *f* sleetstorm

cementerio *m* cemetery

cemento *m* cement; (*hormigón*) concrete; (*LAm, cola*) glue

cena *f* dinner; (*comida ligera*) supper. **~duría** *f* (*Mex*) restaurant

cenag|al *m* marsh, bog; (*fig*) tight spot. **~oso** *a* muddy

cenar *vt* have for dinner; (*en cena ligera*) have for supper. ● *vi* have dinner; (*tomar cena ligera*) have supper

cenicero *m* ashtray

cenit *m* zenith

ceniz|a *f* ash. **~o** *a* ashen. ● *m* jinx

censo *m* census. **~ electoral** electoral roll

censura *f* censure; (*de prensa etc*) censorship. **~r** *vt* censure; censor (*prensa etc*)

centavo *a & m* hundredth; (*moneda*) centavo

centell|a *f* flash; (*chispa*) spark. **~ar** *vi*, **~ear** *vi* sparkle. **~eo** *m* sparkle, sparkling

centena *f* hundred. **~r** *m* hundred. **a ~res** by the hundred

centenario *a* centenary; ⟨*persona*⟩ centenarian. ● *m* centenary; (*persona*) centenarian

centeno *m* rye

centésim|a *f* hundredth. **~o** *a* hundredth; (*moneda*) centésimo

cent|ígrado *a* centigrade, Celsius. **~igramo** *m* centigram. **~ilitro** *m* centilitre. **~ímetro** *m* centimetre

céntimo *a* hundredth. ● *m* cent

centinela *f* sentry

centolla *f*, **centollo** *m* spider crab

central *a* central. ● *f* head office. **~ de correos** general post office. **~ eléctrica** power station. **~ nuclear** nuclear power station. **~ telefónica** telephone exchange. **~ismo** *m* centralism. **~ita** *f* switchboard

centraliza|ción *f* centralization. **~r** [10] *vt* centralize

centrar *vt* centre

céntrico *a* central

centrífugo *a* centrifugal

centro *m* centre. **~ comercial** shopping centre

Centroamérica *f* Central America

centroamericano *a & m* Central American

centuplicar [7] *vt* increase a hundredfold

ceñi|do *a* tight. **~r** [5 & 22] *vt* surround, encircle; ⟨*vestido*⟩ be a tight fit. **~rse** *vpr* limit o.s. (**a** to)

ceñ|o *m* frown. **~udo** *a* frowning. **fruncir el ~o** frown

cepill|ar *vt* brush; (*en carpintería*) plane. **~o** *m* brush; (*en carpintería*) plane. **~o de dientes** toothbrush

cera *f* wax

cerámic|a *f* ceramics; (*materia*) pottery; (*objeto*) piece of pottery. **~o** *a* ceramic

cerca *f* fence. ● *adv* near, close. **~s** *mpl* foreground. **~ de** *prep* near; (*con números, con tiempo*) nearly. **de ~** from close up, closely

cercado *m* enclosure

cercan|ía *f* nearness, proximity. **~ías** *fpl* outskirts. **tren** *m* **de ~ías** local train. **~o** *a* near, close. **C~o Oriente** *m* Near East

cercar [7] *vt* fence in, enclose; ⟨*gente*⟩ surround, crowd round; (*asediar*) besiege

cerciorar *vt* convince. **~se** *vpr* make sure, find out

cerco *m* (*grupo*) circle; (*cercado*) enclosure; (*asedio*) siege

Cerdeña *f* Sardinia

cerdo *m* pig; (*carne*) pork

cereal *m* cereal

cerebr|al *a* cerebral. **~o** *m* brain; (*fig, inteligencia*) intelligence, brains

ceremoni|a *f* ceremony. **~al** *a* ceremonial. **~oso** *a* ceremonious, stiff

céreo *a* wax

cerez|a *f* cherry. **~o** cherry tree

cerill|a *f* match. **~o** *m* (*Mex*) match

cern|er [1] *vt* sieve. **~erse** *vpr* hover; (*fig, amenazar*) hang over. **~idor** *m* sieve

cero *m* nought, zero; (*fútbol*) nil (*Brit*), zero (*Amer*); (*tenis*) love; (*persona*) nonentity. **partir de ~** start from scratch

cerquillo *m* (*LAm, flequillo*) fringe

cerquita *adv* very near

cerra|do *a* shut, closed; (*espacio*) shut in, enclosed; (*cielo*) overcast; (*curva*) sharp. **~dura** *f* lock; (*acción de cerrar*) shutting, closing. **~jero** *m* locksmith. **~r** [1] *vt* shut, close; (*con llave*) lock; (*con cerrojo*) bolt; (*cercar*) enclose; turn off (*grifo*); block up (*agujero etc*). ● *vi* shut, close. **~rse** *vpr* shut, close; (*herida*) heal. **~r con llave** lock

cerro *m* hill. **irse por los ~s de Úbeda** ramble on

cerrojo *m* bolt. **echar el ~** bolt

certamen *m* competition, contest

certero *a* accurate

certeza *f*, **certidumbre** *f* certainty

certifica|do *a* (*carta etc*) registered. ● *m* certificate; (*carta*) registered letter. **~r** [7] *vt* certify; register (*carta etc*)

certitud *f* certainty

cervato *m* fawn

cerve|cería *f* beerhouse, bar; (*fábrica*) brewery. **~za** *f* beer. **~za de barril** draught beer. **~za de botella** bottled beer

cesa|ción *f* cessation, suspension. **~nte** *a* out of work. **~r** *vt* stop. ● *vi* stop, cease; (*dejar un empleo*) give up. **sin ~r** incessantly

cesáreo *a* Caesarian. **operación** *f* **cesárea** Caesarian section

cese *m* cessation; (*de un empleo*) dismissal

césped *m* grass, lawn

cest|a *f* basket. **~ada** *f* basketful. **~o** *m* basket. **~o de los papeles** wastepaper basket

cetro *m* sceptre; (*fig*) power

cianuro *m* cyanide

ciática *f* sciatica

cibernética *f* cybernetics

cicatriz *f* scar. **~ación** *f* healing. **~ar** [10] *vt/i* heal. **~arse** *vpr* heal

ciclamino *m* cyclamen

cíclico *a* cyclic(al)

ciclis|mo *m* cycling. **~ta** *m* & *f* cyclist

ciclo *m* cycle; (*LAm, curso*) course

ciclomotor *m* moped

ciclón *m* cyclone

ciclostilo *m* cyclostyle, duplicating machine

ciego *a* blind. ● *m* blind man, blind person. **a ciegas** in the dark

cielo *m* sky; (*relig*) heaven; (*persona*) darling. **¡~s!** good heavens!, goodness me!

ciempiés *m invar* centipede

cien *a* a hundred. **~ por ~** (*fam*) completely, one hundred per cent. **me pone a ~** it drives me mad

ciénaga *f* bog, swamp

ciencia *f* science; (*fig*) knowledge. **~s** *fpl* (*univ etc*) science. **~s empresariales** business studies. **saber a ~ cierta** know for a fact, know for certain

cieno *m* mud

científico *a* scientific. ● *m* scientist

ciento *a* & *m* (*delante de nombres, y numerales a los que multiplica* **cien**) a hundred, one hundred. **por ~** per cent

cierne *m* blossoming. **en ~** in blossom; (*fig*) in its infancy

cierre *m* fastener; (*acción de cerrar*) shutting, closing. **~ de cremallera** zip, zipper (*Amer*)

cierro *vb véase* **cerrar**

cierto *a* certain; (*verdad*) true. **estar en lo ~** be right. **lo ~ es que** the fact is that. **no es ~** that's not true. **¿no es ~?** right? **por ~** certainly, by the way. **si bien es ~ que** although

ciervo *m* deer

cifra *f* figure, number; (*cantidad*) sum. **~do** *a* coded. **~r** *vt* code; (*resumir*) summarize. **en ~** code, in code

cigala *f* (Norway) lobster

cigarra *f* cicada

cigarr|illo *m* cigarette. **~o** *m* (*cigarillo*) cigarette; (*puro*) cigar

cigüeña *f* stork

cil|índrico *a* cylindrical. **~indro** *m* cylinder; (*Mex, organillo*) barrel organ

cima *f* top; (*fig*) summit

címbalo *m* cymbal

cimbrear *vt* shake. **~se** *vpr* sway

:imentar [1] *vt* lay the foundations of; (*fig, reforzar*) strengthen
:imer|a *f* crest. **~o** *a* highest
:imiento *m* foundations; (*fig*) source. **desde los ~s** from the very beginning
:inc *m* zinc
:incel *m* chisel. **~ar** *vt* chisel
:inco *a & m* five
:incuent|a *a & m* fifty; (*quincuagésimo*) fiftieth. **~ón** *a* about fifty
:ine *m* cinema. **~matografiar** [20] *vt* film
:inético *a* kinetic
cínico *a* cynical; (*desvergonzado*) shameless. ● *m* cynic
cinismo *m* cynicism; (*desvergüenza*) shamelessness
:inta *f* band; (*adorno de pelo etc*) ribbon; (*película*) film; (*magnética*) tape; (*de máquina de escribir etc*) ribbon. **~ aisladora, ~ aislante** insulating tape. **~ magnetofónica** magnetic tape. **~ métrica** tape measure
cintur|a *f* waist. **~ón** *m* belt. **~ón de seguridad** safety belt. **~ón salvavidas** lifebelt
ciprés *m* cypress (tree)
circo *m* circus
circuito *m* circuit; (*viaje*) tour. **~ cerrado** closed circuit. **corto ~** short circuit
circula|ción *f* circulation; (*vehículos*) traffic. **~r** *a* circular. ● *vt* circulate. ● *vi* circulate; (*líquidos*) flow; (*conducir*) drive; (*autobús etc*) run
círculo *m* circle. **~ vicioso** vicious circle. **en ~** in a circle
circunci|dar *vt* circumcise. **~sión** *f* circumcision
circunda|nte *a* surrounding. **~r** *vt* surround
circunferencia *f* circumference
circunflejo *m* circumflex
circunscri|bir [*pp* **circunscrito**] *vt* confine. **~pción** *f* (*distrito*) district. **~pción electoral** constituency
circunspecto *a* wary, circumspect
circunstan|cia *f* circumstance. **~te** *a* surrounding. ● *m* bystander. **los ~tes** those present
circunvalación *f.* **carretera** *f* **de ~** bypass, ring road
cirio *m* candle
ciruela *f* plum. **~ claudia** greengage. **~ damascena** damson
ciru|gía *f* surgery. **~jano** *m* surgeon
cisne *m* swan

cisterna *f* tank, cistern
cita *f* appointment; (*entre chico y chica*) date; (*referencia*) quotation. **~ción** *f* quotation; (*jurid*) summons. **~do** *a* aforementioned. **~r** *vt* make an appointment with; (*mencionar*) quote; (*jurid*) summons. **~rse** *vpr* arrange to meet
cítara *f* zither
ciudad *f* town; (*grande*) city. **~anía** *f* citizenship; (*habitantes*) citizens. **~ano** *a* civic ● *m* citizen, inhabitant; (*habitante de ciudad*) city dweller
cívico *a* civic
civil *a* civil. ● *m* civil guard. **~idad** *f* politeness
civiliza|ción *f* civilization. **~r** [10] *vt* civilize. **~rse** *vpr* become civilized
civismo *m* community spirit
cizaña *f* (*fig*) discord
clam|ar *vi* cry out, clamour. **~or** *m* cry; (*griterío*) noise, clamour; (*protesta*) outcry. **~oroso** *a* noisy
clandestin|idad *f* secrecy. **~o** *a* clandestine, secret
clara *f* (*de huevo*) egg white
claraboya *f* skylight
clarear *vi* dawn; (*aclarar*) brighten up. **~se** *vpr* be transparent
clarete *m* rosé
claridad *f* clarity; (*luz*) light
clarifica|ción *f* clarification. **~r** [7] *vt* clarify
clarín *m* bugle
clarinet|e *m* clarinet; (*músico*) clarinettist. **~ista** *m & f* clarinettist
clarividen|cia *f* clairvoyance; (*fig*) far-sightedness. **~te** *a* clairvoyant; (*fig*) far-sighted
claro *a* (*con mucha luz*) bright; (*transparente, evidente*) clear; (*colores*) light; (*líquido*) thin. ● *m* (*en bosque etc*) clearing; (*espacio*) gap. ● *adv* clearly. ● *int* of course! **~ de luna** moonlight. **¡~ que sí!** yes of course! **¡~ que no!** of course not!
clase *f* class; (*aula*) classroom. **~ media** middle class. **~ obrera** working class. **~ social** social class. **dar ~s** teach. **toda ~ de** all sorts of
clásico *a* classical; (*fig*) classic. ● *m* classic
clasifica|ción *f* classification; (*deportes*) league. **~r** [7] *vt* classify; (*seleccionar*) sort
claudia *f* greengage

claudicar [7] (ceder) give in; (cojear) limp

claustro m cloister; (univ) staff

claustrof|obia f claustrophobia. ~**óbico** a claustrophobic

cláusula f clause

clausura f closure; (ceremonia) closing ceremony. ~**r** vt close

clava|do a fixed; (con clavo) nailed. ~**r** vt knock in (clavo); (introducir a mano) stick; (fijar) fix; (juntar) nail together. **es ~do a su padre** he's the spitting image of his father

clave f key; (mus) clef; (clavicémbalo) harpsichord

clavel m carnation

clavicémbalo m harpsichord

clavícula f collar bone, clavicle

clavija f peg; (elec) plug

clavo m nail; (culin) clove

claxon m (pl **claxons** /'klakson/) horn

clemen|cia f clemency, mercy. ~**te** a clement, merciful

clementina f tangerine

cleptómano m kleptomaniac

cler|ecía f priesthood. ~**ical** a clerical

clérigo m priest

clero m clergy

cliché m cliché; (foto) negative

cliente m & f client, customer; (de médico) patient. ~**la** f clientele, customers; (de médico) patients, practice

clim|a m climate. ~**ático** a climatic. ~**atizado** a air-conditioned. ~**atológico** a climatological

clínic|a f clinic. ~**o** a clinical. ● m clinician

clip m (pl **clips**) clip

clo m cluck. **hacer ~** cluck

cloaca f drain, sewer

cloque|ar vi cluck. ~**o** m clucking

cloro m chlorine

club m (pl **clubs** o **clubes**) club

coacci|ón f coercion, compulsion. ~**onar** vt coerce, compel

coagular vt coagulate; clot (sangre); curdle (leche). ~**se** vpr coagulate; (sangre) clot; (leche) curdle

coalición f coalition

coartada f alibi

coartar vt hinder; restrict (libertad etc)

cobard|e a cowardly. ● m coward. ~**ía** f cowardice

cobaya f, **cobayo** m guinea pig

cobert|era f (tapadera) lid. ~**izo** m lean-to, shelter. ~**or** m bedspread, (manta) blanket. ~**ura** f covering

cobij|a f (LAm, ropa de cama) bedclothes; (Mex, manta) blanket. ~**ar** vt shelter. ~**arse** vpr shelter, take shelter. ~**o** m shelter

cobra f cobra

cobra|dor m conductor. ~**dora** f conductress. ~**r** vt collect; (ganar) earn; charge (precio); cash (cheque); (recuperar) recover. ● vi be paid. ~**rse** vpr recover

cobre m copper; (mus) brass (instruments)

cobro m collection; (de cheque) cashing; (pago) payment. **ponerse en ~** go into hiding. **presentar al ~** cash

cocada f (LAm) sweet coconut

cocaína f cocaine

cocción f cooking; (tec) baking, firing

cocear vt/i kick

coc|er [2 & 9] vt/i cook; (hervir) boil; (en horno) bake. ~**ido** a cooked. ● m stew

cociente m quotient. ~ **intelectual** intelligence quotient, IQ

cocin|a f kitchen; (arte de cocinar) cookery, cuisine; (aparato) cooker. ~**a de gas** gas cooker. ~**a eléctrica** electric cooker. ~**ar** vt/i cook. ~**ero** m cook

coco m coconut; (árbol) coconut palm; (cabeza) head; (duende) bogeyman. **comerse el ~** think hard

cocodrilo m crocodile

cocotero m coconut palm

cóctel m (pl **cóctels** o **cócteles**) cocktail; (reunión) cocktail party

coche m car (Brit), motor car (Brit), automobile (Amer); (de tren) coach, carriage. ~**-cama** sleeper. ~ **fúnebre** hearse. ~**ra** f garage; (de autobuses) depot. ~ **restaurante** dining-car. ~**s de choque** dodgems

cochin|ada f dirty thing. ~**o** a dirty, filthy. ● m pig

cod|azo m nudge (with one's elbow); (Mex, aviso secreto) tip-off. ~**ear** vt/i elbow, nudge

codici|a f greed. ~**ado** a coveted, sought after. ~**ar** vt covet. ~**oso** a greedy (**de** for)

código m code. ~ **de la circulación** Highway Code

codo m elbow; (dobladura) bend. **hablar por los ~s** talk too much. **hasta los ~s** up to one's neck

odorniz m quail

oeducación f coeducation

oerción f coercion

oetáneo a & m contemporary

oexist|encia f coexistence. ~**ir** vi coexist

ofradía f brotherhood

ofre m chest

oger [14] vt (España) take; catch ⟨tren, autobús, pelota, catarro⟩; (agarrar) take hold of; (del suelo) pick up; pick ⟨frutos etc⟩. ● vi (caber) fit. ~**se** vpr trap, catch

ogollo m (de lechuga etc) heart; (fig, lo mejor) cream; (fig, núcleo) centre

ogote m back of the neck

ohech|ar vt bribe. ~**o** m bribery

oherente a coherent

ohesión f cohesion

ohete m rocket; (Mex, pistola) pistol

ohibi|ción f inhibition. ~**r** vt restrict; inhibit ⟨persona⟩. ~**rse** vpr feel inhibited; (contenerse) restrain o.s.

oincid|encia f coincidence. ~**ente** a coincidental. ~**ir** vt coincide. **dar la** ~**encia** happen

oje|ar vt limp; ⟨mueble⟩ wobble. ~**ra** f lameness

oj|ín m cushion. ~**inete** m small cushion. ~**inete de bolas** ball bearing

ojo a lame; ⟨mueble⟩ wobbly. ● m lame person

ol f cabbage. ~**es de Bruselas** Brussel sprouts

ola f tail; (fila) queue; (para pegar) glue. **a la** ~ at the end. **hacer** ~ queue (up). **tener** ~, **traer** ~ have serious consequences

olabora|ción f collaboration. ~**dor** m collaborator. ~**r** vi collaborate

olada f washing. **hacer la** ~ do the washing

olador m strainer

olapso m collapse; (fig) stoppage

olar [2] vt strain ⟨líquidos⟩; (lavar) wash; pass ⟨moneda falsa etc⟩. ● vi ⟨líquido⟩ seep through; (fig) be believed, wash (fam). ~**se** vpr slip; (no hacer caso de la cola) jump the queue; (en fiesta) gatecrash; (meter la pata) put one's foot in it

olch|a f bedspread. ~**ón** m mattress. ~**oneta** f mattress

olear vi wag its tail; ⟨asunto⟩ not be resolved. **vivito y coleando** alive and kicking

colecci|ón f collection; (fig, gran número de) a lot of. ~**onar** vt collect. ~**onista** m & f collector

colecta f collection

colectiv|idad f community. ~**o** a collective. ● m (Arg) minibus

colector m (en las alcantarillas) main sewer

colega m & f colleague

colegi|al m schoolboy. ~**ala** f schoolgirl. ~**o** m private school; (de ciertas profesiones) college. ~**o mayor** hall of residence

colegir [5 & 14] vt gather

cólera f cholera; (ira) anger, fury. **descargar su** ~ vent one's anger. **montar en** ~ fly into a rage

colérico a furious, irate

colesterol m cholesterol

coleta f pigtail

colga|nte a hanging. ● m pendant. ~**r** [2 & 12] vt hang; hang out ⟨colada⟩; hang up ⟨abrigo etc⟩. ● vi hang; (teléfono) hang up, ring off. ~**rse** vpr hang o.s. **dejar a uno** ~**do** let s.o. down

cólico m colic

coliflor m cauliflower

colilla f cigarette end

colina f hill

colinda|nte a adjacent. ~**r** vt border (con on)

colisión f collision, crash; (fig) clash

colmar vt fill to overflowing; (fig) fulfill. ~ **a uno de amabilidad** overwhelm s.o. with kindness

colmena f beehive, hive

colmillo m eye tooth, canine (tooth); (de elefante) tusk; (de otros animales) fang

colmo m height. **ser el** ~ be the limit, be the last straw

coloca|ción f positioning; (empleo) job, position. ~**r** [7] vt put, place; (buscar empleo) find work for. ~**rse** vpr find a job

Colombia f Colombia

colombiano a & m Colombian

colon m colon

colón m (unidad monetaria de Costa Rica y El Salvador) colón

Colonia f Cologne

coloni|a f colony; (agua de colonia) eau-de-Cologne; (LAm, barrio) suburb. ~**a de verano** holiday camp. ~**al** a colonial. ~**ales** mpl imported foodstuffs; (comestibles en general) groceries. ~**alista** m & f colonialist.

~zación f colonization. **~zar** [10] colonize

coloqui|al a colloquial. **~o** m conversation; (*congreso*) conference

color m colour. **~ado** a (*rojo*) red. **~ante** m colouring. **~ar** vt colour. **~ear** vt/i colour. **~ete** m rouge. **~ido** m colour. **de ~** colour. **en ~** (*fotos, película*) colour

colosal a colossal; (*fig, magnífico, fam*) terrific

columna f column; (*fig, apoyo*) support

columpi|ar vt swing. **~arse** vpr swing. **~o** m swing

collar m necklace; (*de perro etc*) collar

coma f comma. ● m (*med*) coma

comadre f midwife; (*madrina*) godmother; (*vecina*) neighbour. **~ar** vi gossip

comadreja f weasel

comadrona f midwife

comand|ancia f command. **~ante** m commander. **~o** m command; (*soldado*) commando

comarca f area, region

comba f bend; (*juguete*) skipping-rope. **~r** vt bend. **~rse** vpr bend. **saltar a la ~** skip

combat|e m fight; (*fig*) struggle. **~iente** m fighter. **~ir** vt/i fight

combina|ción f combination; (*bebida*) cocktail; (*arreglo*) plan, scheme; (*prenda*) slip. **~r** vt combine; (*arreglar*) arrange; (*armonizar*) match, go well with. **~rse** vpr combine; (*ponerse de acuerdo*) agree (**para** to)

combustible m fuel

comedia f comedy; (*cualquier obra de teatro*) play. **hacer la ~** pretend

comedi|do a reserved. **~rse** [5] vpr be restrained

comedor m dining-room; (*restaurante*) restaurant; (*persona*) glutton. **ser buen ~** have a good appetite

comensal m companion at table, fellow diner

comentar vt comment on; (*anotar*) annotate. **~io** m commentary; (*observación*) comment; (*fam*) gossip. **~ista** m & f commentator

comenzar [1 & 10] vt/i begin, start

comer vt eat; (*a mediodía*) have for lunch; (*corroer*) eat away; (*en ajedrez*) take. ● vi eat; (*a mediodía*) have lunch. **~se** vpr eat (up). **dar de ~ a** feed

comerci|al a commercial. **~ante** m trader; (*de tienda*) shopkeeper. **~ar** vt trade (**con, en** in); (*con otra persona*) do business. **~o** m commerce; (*actividad*) trade; (*tienda*) shop; (*negocio*) business

comestible a edible. **~s** mpl food. **tienda de ~s** grocer's (shop) (*Brit*) grocery (*Amer*)

cometa m comet. ● f kite

comet|er vt commit; make (*falta*). **~ido** m task

comezón m itch

comicastro m poor actor, ham (*fam*)

comicios mpl elections

cómico a comic(al). ● m comic actor; (*cualquier actor*) actor

comida f food; (*a mediodía*) lunch. **hacer la ~** prepare the meals

comidilla f topic of conversation. **ser la ~ del pueblo** be the talk of the town

comienzo m beginning, start. **a ~s de** at the beginning of

comil|ón a greedy. **~ona** f feast

comillas fpl inverted commas

comino m cumin. **(no) me importa un ~** I couldn't care less

comisar|ía f police station. **~io** m commissioner; (*deportes*) steward. **~io de policía** police superintendent

comisión f assignment; (*comité*) commission, committee; (*com*) commission

comisura f corner. **~ de los labios** corner of the mouth

comité m committee

como prep like, as. ● conj as; (*en cuanto*) as soon as. **~ quieras** as you like. **~ sabes** as you know. **~ si** as if

cómo adv how? **¿~?** I beg your pardon? **¿~ está Vd?** how are you? **¡~ no!** (*esp LAm*) of course! **¿~ son?** what are they like? **¿~ te llamas?** what's your name? **¡y ~!** and how!

cómoda f chest of drawers

comodidad f comfort. **a su ~** at your convenience

cómodo a comfortable; (*útil*) handy

comoquiera conj. **~ que** since. **~ que sea** however it may be

compacto a compact; (*denso*) dense; (*líneas etc*) close

compadecer [11] vt feel sorry for. **~se** vpr. **~se de** feel sorry for

compadre m godfather; (*amigo*) friend

compañ|ero *m* companion; (*de trabajo*) colleague; (*amigo*) friend. ~**ía** *f* company. **en** ~**ía de** with

compara|ble *a* comparable. ~**ción** *f* comparison. ~**r** *vt* compare. ~**tivo** *a* & *m* comparative. **en** ~**ción con** in comparison with, compared with

comparecer [11] *vi* appear

comparsa *f* group; (*en el teatro*) extra

compartimiento *m* compartment

compartir *vt* share

compás *m* (*instrumento*) (pair of) compasses; (*ritmo*) rhythm; (*división*) bar (*Brit*), measure (*Amer*); (*naut*) compass. **a** ~ in time

compasi|ón *f* compassion, pity. **tener** ~**ón de** feel sorry for. ~**vo** *a* compassionate

compatib|ilidad *f* compatibility. ~**le** *a* compatible

compatriota *m* & *f* compatriot

compeler *vt* compel, force

compendi|ar *vt* summarize. ~**o** *m* summary

compenetración *f* mutual understanding

compensa|ción *f* compensation. ~**ción por despido** redundancy payment. ~**r** *vt* compensate

competen|cia *f* competition; (*capacidad*) competence; (*terreno*) field, scope. ~**te** *a* competent; (*apropiado*) appropriate, suitable

competi|ción *f* competition. ~**dor** *m* competitor. ~**r** [5] *vi* compete

compilar *vt* compile

compinche *m* accomplice; (*amigo, fam*) friend, mate (*fam*)

complac|encia *f* pleasure; (*indulgencia*) indulgence. ~**er** [32] *vt* please; (*prestar servicio*) help. ~**erse** *vpr* have pleasure, be pleased. ~**iente** *a* helpful; (*marido*) complaisant

complej|idad *f* complexity. ~**o** *a* & *m* complex

complement|ario *a* complementary. ~**o** *m* complement; (*gram*) object, complement

complet|ar *vt* complete. ~**o** *a* complete; (*lleno*) full; (*perfecto*) perfect

complexión *f* disposition; (*constitución*) constitution

complica|ción *f* complication. ~**r** [7] *vt* complicate; involve (*persona*). ~**rse** *vpr* become complicated

cómplice *m* accomplice

complot *m* (*pl* **complots**) plot

compon|ente *a* component. ● *m* component; (*culin*) ingredient; (*miembro*) member. ~**er** [34] *vt* make up; (*mus, literatura etc*) write, compose; (*reparar*) mend; (*culin*) prepare; (*arreglar*) restore; settle ⟨*estómago*⟩; reconcile ⟨*diferencias*⟩. ~**erse** *vpr* be made up; (*arreglarse*) get ready. ~**érselas** manage

comporta|miento *m* behaviour. ~**r** *vt* involve. ~**rse** *vpr* behave. ~**rse como es debido** behave properly. ~**rse mal** misbehave

composi|ción *f* composition. ~**tor** *m* composer

compostelano *a* from Santiago de Compostela. ● *m* native of Santiago de Compostela

compostura *f* composition; (*arreglo*) repair; (*culin*) condiment; (*comedimiento*) composure

compota *f* stewed fruit

compra *f* purchase. ~ **a plazos** hire purchase. ~**dor** *m* buyer; (*en una tienda*) customer. ~**r** *vt* buy. ~**venta** *f* dealing. **hacer la** ~, **ir a la** ~, **ir de** ~**s** do the shopping, go shopping. **negocio** *m* **de** ~**venta** second-hand shop

compren|der *vt* understand; (*incluir*) include. ~**sible** *a* understandable. ~**sión** *f* understanding. ~**sivo** *a* understanding; (*que incluye*) comprehensive

compresa *f* compress; (*de mujer*) sanitary towel

compr|esión *f* compression. ~**imido** *a* compressed. ● *m* pill, tablet. ~**imir** *vt* compress; keep back ⟨*lágrimas*⟩; (*fig*) restrain

comproba|nte *m* (*recibo*) receipt. ~**r** *vt* check; (*confirmar*) confirm

comprometer *vt* compromise; (*arriesgar*) endanger. ~**erse** *vpr* compromise o.s.; (*obligarse*) agree to. ~**ido** *a* ⟨*situación*⟩ awkward, embarrassing

compromiso *m* obligation; (*apuro*) predicament; (*cita*) appointment; (*acuerdo*) agreement. **sin** ~ without obligation

compuesto *a* compound; ⟨*persona*⟩ smart. ● *m* compound

compungido *a* sad, sorry

computador *m*, **computadora** *f* computer

computar *vt* calculate

cómputo *m* calculation

comulgar [12] *vi* take Communion
común *a* common. ● *m* community.
en ~ in common. **por lo ~** generally
comunal *a* municipal, communal
comunica|ción *f* communication.
~do *m* communiqué. **~do a la
prensa** press release. **~r** [7] *vt/i* communicate; pass on ⟨*enfermedad,
información*⟩. **~rse** *vpr* communicate; ⟨*enfermedad*⟩ spread.
~tivo *a* communicative. **está ~ndo**
(*al teléfono*) it's engaged, the line's
engaged
comunidad *f* community. **~ de vecinos** residents' association. **C~
(Económica) Europea** European
(Economic) Community. **en ~** together
comunión *f* communion; (*relig*)
(Holy) Communion
comunis|mo *m* communism. **~ta** *a
& m & f* communist
comúnmente *adv* generally,
usually
con *prep* with; (*a pesar de*) in spite of;
(+ *infinitivo*) by. **~ decir la verdad**
by telling the truth. **~ que** so. **~ tal
que** as long as
conato *m* attempt
concatenación *f* chain, linking
cóncavo *a* concave
concebir [5] *vt/i* conceive
conceder *vt* concede, grant; award
⟨*premio*⟩; ⟨*admitir*⟩ admit
concej|al *m* councillor. **~o** *m* town
council
concentra|ción *f* concentration.
~do *m* concentrated. **~r** *vt* concentrate. **~rse** *vpr* concentrate
concep|ción *f* conception. **~to** *m*
concept; (*opinión*) opinion. **bajo
ningún ~to** in no way. **en mi ~to** in
my view. **por ningún ~to** in no way
concerniente *a* concerning. **en lo ~
a** with regard to
concertar [1] *vt* (*mus*) harmonize;
(*coordinar*) coordinate; (*poner de
acuerdo*) agree. ● *vi* be in tune; (*fig*)
agree. **~se** *vpr* agree
concertina *f* concertina
concesión *f* concession
conciencia *f* conscience; (*conocimiento*) consciousness. **~ción** *f*
awareness. **~ limpia** clear conscience. **~ sucia** guilty conscience.
a ~ de que fully aware that. **en ~**
honestly. **tener ~ de** be aware of. **tomar ~ de** become aware of

concienzudo *a* conscientious
concierto *m* concert; (*acuerdo*)
agreement; (*mus, composición*) concerto
concilia|ble *a* reconcilable. **~ción** *f*
reconciliation. **~r** *vt* reconcile. **~r el
sueño** get to sleep. **~rse** *vpr* gain
concilio *m* council
conciso *m* concise
conciudadano *m* fellow citizen
conclu|ir [17] *vt* finish; (*deducir*) conclude. ● *vi* finish, end. **~irse** *vpr*
finish, end. **~sión** *f* conclusion.
~yente *a* conclusive
concord|ancia *f* agreement. **~ar** [2]
vt reconcile. ● *vi* agree. **~e** *a* in
agreement. **~ia** *f* harmony
concret|amente *adv* specifically, to
be exact. **~ar** *vt* make specific. **~ar-
se** *vpr* become definite; (*limitarse*)
confine o.s. **~o** *a* concrete; (*determinado*) specific, particular. ● *m*
(*LAm, hormigón*) concrete. **en ~o**
definite; (*concretamente*) to be exact;
(*en resumen*) in short
concurr|encia *f* coincidence; (*reu-
nión*) crowd, audience. **~ido** *a*
crowded, busy. **~ir** *vi* meet; (*asistir*)
attend; (*coincidir*) coincide; (*contribuir*) contribute; (*en concurso*)
compete
concurs|ante *m & f* competitor, contestant. **~ar** *vi* compete, take part.
~o *m* competition; (*concurrencia*)
crowd; (*ayuda*) help
concha *f* shell; (*carey*) tortoiseshell
condado *m* county
conde *m* earl, count
condena *f* sentence. **~ción** *f* condemnation. **~do** *m* convict. **~r** *vt*
condemn; (*jurid*) convict
condensa|ción *f* condensation. **~r**
vt condense. **~rse** *vpr* condense
condesa *f* countess
condescende|ncia *f* condescension;
(*tolerancia*) indulgence. **~r** [1] *vi*
agree; (*dignarse*) condescend
condici|ón *f* condition; (*naturaleza*)
nature. **~onado** *a*, **~onal** *a* conditional. **~onar** *vt* condition. **a ~ón
de (que)** on the condition that
condiment|ar *vt* season. **~o** *m* condiment
condolencia *f* condolence
condominio *m* joint ownership
condón *m* condom
condonar *vt* (*perdonar*) reprieve;
cancel ⟨*deuda*⟩

conducir [47] *vt* drive ⟨*vehículo*⟩; carry ⟨*electricidad, gas, agua etc*⟩. ● *vi* drive; (*fig, llevar*) lead. **~se** *vpr* behave. **¿a qué conduce?** what's the point?

conducta *f* behaviour

conducto *m* pipe, tube; (*anat*) duct. **por ~ de** through

conductor *m* driver; (*jefe*) leader; (*elec*) conductor

conduzco *vb véase* **conducir**

conectar *vt/i* connect; (*enchufar*) plug in

conejo *m* rabbit

conexión *f* connection

confabularse *vpr* plot

confecci|ón *f* making; (*prenda*) ready-made garment. **~ones** *fpl* clothing, clothes. **~onado** *a* ready-made. **~onar** *vt* make

confederación *f* confederation

conferencia *f* conference; (*al teléfono*) long-distance call; (*univ etc*) lecture. **~ cumbre**, **~ en la cima**, **~ en la cumbre** summit conference. **~nte** *m & f* lecturer

conferir [4] *vt* confer; award ⟨*premio*⟩

confes|ar [1] *vt/i* confess. **~arse** *vpr* confess. **~ión** *f* confession. **~ional** *a* confessional. **~ionario** *m* confessional. **~or** *m* confessor

confeti *m* confetti

confia|do *a* trusting; (*seguro de sí mismo*) confident. **~nza** *f* trust; (*en sí mismo*) confidence; (*intimidad*) familiarity. **~r** [20] *vt* entrust. ● *vi* trust. **~rse** *vpr* put one's trust in

confiden|cia *f* confidence, secret. **~cial** *a* confidential. **~te** *m & f* close friend; (*de policía*) informer

configuración *f* configuration, shape

conf|ín *m* border. **~inar** *vt* confine; (*desterrar*) banish. ● *vi* border (**con** on). **~ines** *mpl* outermost parts

confirma|ción *f* confirmation. **~r** *vt* confirm

confiscar [7] *vt* confiscate

confit|ería *f* sweet-shop (*Brit*), candy store (*Amer*). **~ura** *f* jam

conflagración *f* conflagration

conflicto *m* conflict

confluencia *f* confluence

conforma|ción *f* conformation, shape. **~r** *vt* (*acomodar*) adjust. ● *vi* agree. **~rse** *vpr* conform

conform|e *a* in agreement; (*contento*) happy, satisfied; (*según*) according (**con** to). ● *conj* as. ● *int* OK!

~e a in accordance with, according to. **~idad** *f* agreement; (*tolerancia*) resignation. **~ista** *m & f* conformist

conforta|ble *a* comfortable. **~nte** *a* comforting. **~r** *vt* comfort

confronta|ción *f* confrontation; (*comparación*) comparison. **~r** *vt* confront; (*comparar*) compare

confu|ndir *vt* blur; (*equivocar*) mistake, confuse; (*perder*) lose; (*mezclar*) mix up, confuse. **~ndirse** *vpr* become confused; (*equivocarse*) make a mistake. **~sión** *f* confusion; (*vergüenza*) embarrassment. **~so** *a* confused; (*avergonzado*) embarrassed

congela|do *a* frozen. **~dor** *m* freezer. **~r** *vt* freeze

congeniar *vi* get on

congesti|ón *f* congestion. **~onado** *a* congested. **~onar** *vt* congest. **~onarse** *vpr* become congested

congoja *f* distress

congraciar *vt* win over. **~se** *vpr* ingratiate o.s.

congratular *vt* congratulate

congrega|ción *f* gathering; (*relig*) congregation. **~rse** [12] *vpr* gather, assemble

congres|ista *m & f* delegate, member of a congress. **~o** *m* congress, conference. **C~o de los Diputados** House of Commons

cónico *a* conical

conífer|a *f* conifer. **~o** *a* coniferous

conjetura *f* conjecture, guess. **~r** *vt* conjecture, guess

conjuga|ción *f* conjugation. **~r** [12] *vt* conjugate

conjunción *f* conjunction

conjunto *a* joint. ● *m* collection; (*mus*) band; (*ropa*) suit, outfit. **en ~** altogether

conjura *f*, **conjuración** *f* conspiracy

conjurar *vt* plot, conspire

conmemora|ción *f* commemoration. **~r** *vt* commemorate. **~tivo** *a* commemorative

conmigo *pron* with me

conminar *vt* threaten; (*avisar*) warn

conmiseración *f* commiseration

conmo|ción *f* shock; (*tumulto*) upheaval; (*terremoto*) earthquake. **~cionar** *vt* shock. **~ cerebral** concussion. **~ver** [2] *vt* shake; (*emocionar*) move

conmuta|dor *m* switch. **~r** *vt* exchange

connivencia *f* connivance

connota|ción *f* connotation. **~r** *vt* connote

cono *m* cone

conoc|edor *a* & *m* expert. **~er** [11] *vt* know; (*por primera vez*) meet; (*reconocer*) recognize, know. **~erse** *vpr* know o.s.; (*dos personas*) know each other; (*notarse*) be obvious. **dar a ~er** make known. **darse a ~er** make o.s. known. **~ido** *a* well-known. ● *m* acquaintance. **~imiento** *m* knowledge; (*sentido*) consciousness; (*conocido*) acquaintance. **perder el ~imiento** faint. **se ~e que** apparently. **tener ~imiento de** know about

conozco *vb véase* **conocer**

conque *conj* so

conquense *a* from Cuenca. ● *m* native of Cuenca

conquista *f* conquest. **~dor** *a* conquering. ● *m* conqueror; (*de América*) conquistador; (*fig*) lady-killer. **~r** *vt* conquer, win

consabido *a* well-known

consagra|ción *f* consecration. **~r** *vt* consecrate; (*fig*) devote. **~rse** *vpr* devote o.s.

consanguíneo *m* blood relation

consciente *a* conscious

consecución *f* acquisition; (*de un deseo*) realization

consecuen|cia *f* consequence; (*firmeza*) consistency. **~te** *a* consistent. **a ~cia de** as a result of. **en ~cia, por ~cia** consequently

consecutivo *a* consecutive

conseguir [5 & 13] *vt* get, obtain; (*lograr*) manage; achieve ‹*objetivo*›

conseja *f* story, fable

consej|ero *m* adviser; (*miembro de consejo*) member. **~o** *m* advice; (*pol*) council. **~o de ministros** cabinet

consenso *m* assent, consent

consenti|do *a* ‹*niño*› spoilt. **~miento** *m* consent. **~r** [4] *vt* allow. ● *vi* consent. **~rse** *vpr* break

conserje *m* porter, caretaker. **~ría** *f* porter's office

conserva *f* preserves; (*mermelada*) jam, preserve; (*en lata*) tinned food. **~ción** *f* conservation; (*de alimentos*) preservation; (*de edificio*) maintenance. **en ~** preserved

conservador *a* & *m* (*pol*) conservative

conservar *vt* keep; preserve ‹*alimentos*›. **~se** *vpr* keep; ‹*costumbre etc*› survive

conservatorio *m* conservatory

considera|ble *a* considerable. **~ción** *f* consideration; (*respeto*) respect. **~do** *a* considered; (*amable*) considerate; (*respetado*) respected. **~r** *vt* consider; (*respetar*) respect. **de ~ción** considerable. **de su ~ción** (*en cartas*) yours faithfully. **tomar en ~ción** take into consideration

consigna *f* order; (*rail*) left luggage office (*Brit*), baggage room (*Amer*); (*eslogan*) slogan

consigo *pron* (*él*) with him; (*ella*) with her; (*Ud, Uds*) with you; (*uno mismo*) with o.s.

consiguiente *a* consequent. **por ~** consequently

consist|encia *f* consistency. **~ente** *a* consisting (**en** of); (*firme*) solid. **~ir** *vi* consist (**en** of); (*deberse*) be due (**en** to)

consola|ción *f* consolation. **~r** [2] *vt* console, comfort

consolidar *vt* consolidate. **~se** *vpr* consolidate

consomé *m* clear soup, consommé

consonan|cia *f* consonance. **~te** *a* consonant. ● *f* consonant

consorcio *m* consortium

consorte *m* & *f* consort

conspicuo *a* eminent; (*visible*) visible

conspira|ción *f* conspiracy. **~dor** *m* conspirator. **~r** *vi* conspire

constan|cia *f* constancy. **~te** *a* constant

constar *vi* be clear; (*figurar*) appear, figure; (*componerse*) consist. **hacer ~** point out. **me consta que** I'm sure that. **que conste que** believe me

constatar *vt* check; (*confirmar*) confirm

constelación *f* constellation

consternación *f* consternation

constipa|do *m* cold. ● *a.* **estar ~do** have a cold. **~rse** *vpr* catch a cold

constitu|ción *f* constitution; (*establecimiento*) setting up. **~cional** *a* constitutional. **~ir** [17] *vt* constitute; (*formar*) form; (*crear*) set up, establish. **~irse** *vpr* set o.s. up (**en** as); (*presentarse*) appear. **~tivo** *a*, **~yente** *a* constituent

constreñir [5 & 22] *vt* force, oblige; (*restringir*) restrain

constricción *f* constriction

constru|cción *f* construction. **~ctor** *m* builder. **~ir** [17] *vt* construct; build ‹*edificio*›

consuelo *m* consolation, comfort

consuetudinario *a* customary

cónsul *m* consul

consula|do *m* consulate. ~**r** *a* consular

consult|a *f* consultation. ~**ar** *vt* consult. ~**orio** *m* surgery. ~**orio sentimental** problem page. **horas** *fpl* **de** ~**a** surgery hours. **obra** *f* **de** ~**a** reference book

consumar *vt* complete; commit ‹*crimen*›; consummate ‹*matrimonio*›

consum|ición *f* consumption; (*bebida*) drink; (*comida*) food. ~**ido** *a* ‹*persona*› skinny, wasted; ‹*frutas*› shrivelled. ~**idor** *m* consumer. ~**ir** *vt* consume. ~**irse** *vpr* ‹*persona*› waste away; ‹*cosa*› wear out; (*quedarse seco*) dry up. ~**ismo** *m* consumerism. ~**o** *m* consumption

contab|ilidad *f* book-keeping; (*profesión*) accountancy. ~**le** *m* & *f* accountant

contacto *m* contact. **ponerse en** ~ **con** get in touch with

contado *a* counted. ~**s** *apl* few. ~**r** *m* meter; (*LAm, contable*) accountant. **al** ~ cash

contagi|ar *vt* infect ‹*persona*›; pass on ‹*enfermedd*›; (*fig*) contaminate. ~**o** *m* infection. ~**oso** *a* infectious

contamina|ción *f* contamination, pollution. ~**r** *vt* contaminate, pollute

contante *a*. **dinero** *m* ~ cash

contar [2] *vt* count; tell ‹*relato*›. ● *vi* count. ~ **con** rely on, count on. ~**se** *vpr* be included (**entre** among); (*decirse*) be said

contempla|ción *f* contemplation. ~**r** *vt* look at; (*fig*) contemplate. **sin** ~**ciones** unceremoniously

contemporáneo *a* & *m* contemporary

contend|er [1] *vi* compete. ~**iente** *m* & *f* competitor

conten|er [40] *vt* contain; (*restringir*) restrain. ~**erse** *vpr* restrain o.s. ~**ido** *a* contained. ● *m* contents

content|ar *vt* please. ~**arse** *vpr*. ~**arse de** be satisfied with, be pleased with. ~**o** *a* (*alegre*) happy; (*satisfecho*) pleased

contesta|ción *f* answer. ~**dor** *m*. ~ **automático** answering machine. ~**r** *vt/i* answer; (*replicar*) answer back

contexto *m* context

contienda *f* struggle

contigo *pron* with you

contiguo *a* adjacent

continen|cia *f* continence. ~**tal** *a* continental. ~**te** *m* continent

contingen|cia *f* contingency. ~**te** *a* contingent. ● *m* contingent; (*cuota*) quota

continu|ación *f* continuation. ~**ar** [21] *vt* continue, resume. ● *vi* continue. ~**ará** (*en revista, TV etc*) to be continued. ~**idad** *f* continuity. ~**o** *a* continuous; (*muy frecuente*) continual. **a** ~**ación** immediately after. **corriente** *f* ~**a** direct current

contorno *m* outline; (*geog*) contour. ~**s** *mpl* surrounding area

contorsión *f* contortion

contra *adv* & *prep* against. ● *m* cons. **en** ~ against

contraalmirante *m* rear-admiral

contraata|car [7] *vt/i* counterattack. ~**que** *m* counter-attack

contrabajo *m* double-bass; (*persona*) double-bass player

contrabalancear *vt* counterbalance

contraband|ista *m* & *f* smuggler. ~**o** *m* contraband

contracción *f* contraction

contrachapado *m* plywood

contrad|ecir [46] *vt* contradict. ~**icción** *f* contradiction. ~**ictorio** *a* contradictory

contraer [41] *vt* contract. ~ **matrimonio** marry. ~**se** *vpr* contract; (*limitarse*) limit o.s.

contrafuerte *m* buttress

contragolpe *m* backlash

contrahecho *a* fake; ‹*moneda*› counterfeit; ‹*persona*› hunchbacked

contraindicación *f* contraindication

contralto *m* alto. ● *f* contralto

contramano. **a** ~ in the wrong direction

contrapartida *f* compensation

contrapelo. **a** ~ the wrong way

contrapes|ar *vt* counterbalance. ~**o** *m* counterbalance

contraponer [34] oppose; (*comparar*) compare

contraproducente *a* counter-productive

contrari|ar [20] *vt* oppose; (*molestar*) annoy. ~**edad** *f* obstacle; (*disgusto*) annoyance. ~**o** *a* contrary; ‹*dirección*› opposite; ‹*persona*› opposed. **al** ~**o** on the contrary. **al** ~**o de** contrary to. **de lo** ~**o** otherwise. **en** ~**o**

against. **llevar la ~a** contradict. **por el ~o** on the contrary

contrarrestar *vt* counteract

contrasentido *m* contradiction

contraseña *f* secret mark; (*palabra*) password

contrast|ar *vt* check, verify. ● *vi* contrast. **~e** *m* contrast; (*en oro, plata etc*) hallmark

contratar *vt* sign a contract for; engage ‹*empleados*›

contratiempo *m* setback; (*accidente*) accident

contrat|ista *m & f* contractor. **~o** *m* contract

contraven|ción *f* contravention. **~ir** [53] *vi*. **~ir a** contravene

contraventana *f* shutter

contribu|ción *f* contribution; (*tributo*) tax. **~ir** [17] *vt/i* contribute. **~yente** *m & f* contributor; (*que paga impuestos*) taxpayer

contrincante *m* rival, opponent

contrito *a* contrite

control *m* control; (*inspección*) check. **~ar** *vt* control; (*examinar*) check

controversia *f* controversy

contundente *a* ‹*arma*› blunt; ‹*argumento etc*› convincing

conturbar *vt* perturb

contusión *f* bruise

convalec|encia *f* convalescence. **~er** [11] *vi* convalesce. **~iente** *a & m & f* convalescent

convalidar *vt* confirm; recognize ‹*título*›

convenc|er [9] *vt* convince. **~imiento** *m* conviction

convenci|ón *f* convention. **~onal** *a* conventional

conveni|encia *f* convenience; (*aptitud*) suitability. **~encias (sociales)** conventions. **~ente** *a* suitable; (*aconsejable*) advisable; (*provechoso*) useful, advantageous. **~o** *m* agreement. **~r** [53] *vt* agree. ● *vi* agree; (*ser conveniente*) be convenient for, suit; (*ser aconsejable*) be advisable

convento *m* (*de monjes*) monastery; (*de monjas*) convent

convergente *a* converging

converger [14] *vi*, **convergir** [14] *vi* converge

conversa|ción *f* conversation. **~r** *vi* converse, talk

conver|sión *f* conversion. **~so** *a* converted. ● *m* convert. **~tible** *a* convertible. **~tir** [4] *vt* convert. **~tirse** *vpr* be converted

convexo *a* convex

convic|ción *f* conviction. **~to** *a* convicted

convida|do *m* guest. **~r** *vt* invite. **te convido a un helado** I'll treat you to an ice-cream

convincente *a* convincing

convite *m* invitation; (*banquete*) banquet

conviv|encia *f* coexistence. **~ir** *vi* live together

convocar [7] *vt* convene ‹*reunión*›; summon ‹*personas*›

convoy *m* convoy; (*rail*) train; (*vinagrera*) cruet

convulsión *f* convulsion; (*fig*) upheaval

conyugal *a* conjugal; (*vida*) married

cónyuge *m* spouse. **~s** *mpl* (married) couple

coñac *m* (*pl* **coñacs**) brandy

coopera|ción *f* co-operation. **~r** *vi* co-operate. **~tiva** *f* co-operative. **~tivo** *a* co-operative

coord|enada *f* coordinate. **~inación** *f* co-ordination. **~inar** *vt* co-ordinate

copa *f* glass; (*deportes, fig*) cup. **~s** *fpl* (*naipes*) hearts. **tomar una ~** have a drink

copia *f* copy. **~ en limpio** fair copy. **~r** *vt* copy. **sacar una ~** make a copy

copioso *a* copious; ‹*lluvia, nevada etc*› heavy

copla *f* verse; (*canción*) song

copo *m* flake. **~ de nieve** snowflake. **~s de maíz** cornflakes

coquet|a *f* flirt; (*mueble*) dressing-table. **~ear** *vi* flirt. **~eo** *m* flirtation. **~o** *a* flirtatious

coraje *m* courage; (*rabia*) anger. **dar ~** make mad, make furious

coral *a* choral. ● *m* (*materia, animal*) coral

Corán *m* Koran

coraza *f* (*naut*) armour-plating; (*de tortuga*) shell

coraz|ón *m* heart; (*persona*) darling. **~onada** *f* hunch; (*impulso*) impulse. **sin ~ón** heartless. **tener buen ~ón** be good-hearted

corbata *f* tie, necktie (*esp Amer*). **~ de lazo** bow tie

corcova f hump. **~do** a hunchbacked
corchea f quaver
corchete m fastener, hook and eye; (*gancho*) hook; (*paréntesis*) square bracket
corcho m cork
cordel m cord, thin rope
cordero m lamb
cordial a cordial, friendly. ● m tonic. **~idad** f cordiality, warmth
cordillera f mountain range
córdoba m (*unidad monetaria de Nicaragua*) córdoba
Córdoba f Cordova
cordón m string; (*de zapatos*) lace; (*cable*) flex; (*fig*) cordon. **~ umbilical** umbilical cord
corear vt chant
coreografía f choreography
corista m & f member of the chorus. ● f (*bailarina*) chorus girl
cornet|a f bugle. **~in** m cornet
Cornualles m Cornwall
cornucopia f cornucopia
cornudo a horned. ● m cuckold
coro m chorus; (*relig*) choir
corona f crown; (*de flores*) wreath, garland. **~ción** f coronation. **~r** vt crown
coronel m colonel
coronilla f crown. **estar hasta la ~** be fed up
corporación f corporation
corporal a corporal
corpulento a stout
corpúsculo m corpuscle
corral m pen. **aves** fpl **de ~** poultry
correa f strap; (*de perro*) lead; (*cinturón*) belt
correc|ción f correction; (*reprensión*) rebuke; (*cortesía*) good manners. **~to a** correct; (*cortés*) polite
corre|dizo a running. **nudo ~dizo** slip knot. **puerta** f **~diza** sliding door. **~dor** m runner; (*pasillo*) corridor; (*agente*) agent, broker. **~dor automovilista** racing driver
corregir [5 & 14] vt correct; (*reprender*) rebuke
correlaci|ón f correlation. **~onar** vt correlate
correo m courier; (*correos*) post, mail; (*tren*) mail train. **~s** mpl post office. **echar al ~** post
correr vt run; (*viajar*) travel; draw (*cortinas*). ● vi run; (*agua, electricidad etc*) flow; (*tiempo*) pass. **~se**

vpr (*apartarse*) move along; (*pasarse*) go too far; (*colores*) run. **~se una juerga** have a ball
correspond|encia f correspondence. **~er** vi correspond; (*ser adecuado*) be fitting; (*contestar*) reply; (*pertenecer*) belong; (*incumbir*) fall to. **~erse** vpr (*amarse*) love one another. **~iente** a corresponding
corresponsal m correspondent
corrid|a f run. **~a de toros** bullfight. **~o** a (*peso*) good; (*continuo*) continuous; (*avergonzado*) embarrassed. **de ~a** from memory
corriente a (*agua*) running; (*monedas, publicación, cuenta, año etc*) current; (*ordinario*) ordinary. ● f current; (*de aire*) draught; (*fig*) tendency. ● m current month. **al ~** (*al día*) up-to-date; (*enterado*) aware
corr|illo m small group, circle. **~o** m circle
corroborar vt corroborate
corroer [24 & 37] vt corrode; (*geol*) erode; (*fig*) eat away. **~se** vpr corrode
corromper vt rot (*madera*); turn bad (*alimentos*); (*fig*) corrupt. ● vi (*fam*) stink. **~se** vpr (*madera*) rot; (*alimentos*) go bad; (*fig*) be corrupted
corrosi|ón f corrosion. **~vo** a corrosive
corrupción f (*de madera etc*) rot; (*soborno*) bribery; (*fig*) corruption
corsé m corset
cortacésped m invar lawn-mower
cortad|o a cut; (*leche*) sour; (*avergonzado*) embarrassed; (*confuso*) confused. ● m coffee with a little milk. **~ura** f cut
corta|nte a sharp; (*viento*) biting; (*frío*) bitter. **~r** vt cut; (*recortar*) cut out; (*aislar, detener*) cut off; (*interrumpir*) cut in. ● vi cut. **~rse** vpr cut o.s.; (*leche etc*) curdle; (*al teléfono*) cut off; (*fig*) be embarrassed, become tongue-tied. **~rse el pelo** have one's hair cut. **~rse las uñas** cut one's nails
cortauñas m invar nail-clippers
corte m cutting; (*de instrumento cortante*) cutting edge; (*de corriente*) cut; (*de prendas de vestir*) cut; (*de tela*) length. ● f court. **~ de luz** power cut. **~ y confección** dressmaking. **hacer la ~** court. **las C~s** the Spanish parliament

cortej|ar vt court. **~o** m (de rey etc) entourage. **~o fúnebre** cortège, funeral procession. **~o nupcial** wedding procession

cortés a polite

cortesan|a f courtesan. **~o** m courtier

cortesía f courtesy

corteza f bark; (de naranja etc) peel, rind; (de pan) crust

cortijo m farm; (casa) farmhouse

cortina f curtain

corto a short; (escaso) scanty; (apocado) shy. **~circuito** m short circuit. **~ de alcances** dim, thick. **~ de oído** hard of hearing. **~ de vista** short-sighted. **a la corta o a la larga** sooner or later. **quedarse ~** fall short; (miscalcular) under-estimate

Coruña f. **La ~** Corunna

corvo a bent

cosa f thing; (asunto) business; (idea) idea. **~ de** about. **como si tal ~** just like that; (como si no hubiera pasado nada) as if nothing had happened. **decirle a uno cuatro ~s** tell s.o. a thing or two. **lo que son las ~s** much to my surprise

cosaco a & m Cossack

cosech|a f harvest; (de vino) vintage. **~ar** vt harvest. **~ero** m harvester

coser vt/i sew. **~se** vpr stick to s.o. **eso es ~ y cantar** it's as easy as pie

cosmético a & m cosmetic

cósmico a cosmic

cosmonauta m & f cosmonaut

cosmopolita a & m & f cosmopolitan

cosmos m cosmos

cosquillas fpl ticklishness. **buscar a uno las ~** provoke s.o. **hacer ~** tickle. **tener ~** be ticklish

costa f coast. **a ~ de** at the expense of. **a toda ~** at any cost

costado m side

costal m sack

costar [2] vt/i cost. **~ caro** be expensive. **cueste lo que cueste** at any cost

Costa Rica f Costa Rica

costarricense a & m, **costarriqueño** a & m Costa Rican

coste m cost. **~ar** vt pay for; (naut) sail along the coast

costero a coastal

costilla f rib; (chuleta) chop

costo m cost. **~so** a expensive

costumbre f custom, habit. **de ~** a usual. ● adv usually

costur|a f sewing; (línea) seam; (confección) dressmaking. **~era** f dressmaker. **~ero** m sewing box

cotejar vt compare

cotidiano a daily

cotille|ar vt gossip. **~o** m gossip

cotiza|ción f quotation, price. **~r** [10] vt (en la bolsa) quote. ● vi pay one's subscription. **~rse** vpr fetch; (en la bolsa) stand at; (fig) be valued

coto m enclosure; (de caza) preserve. **~ de caza** game preserve

cotorr|a f parrot; (urraca) magpie; (fig) chatterbox. **~ear** vi chatter

coyuntura f joint; (oportunidad) opportunity; (situación) situation; (circunstancia) occasion, juncture

coz f kick

cráneo m skull

cráter m crater

crea|ción f creation. **~dor** a creative. ● m creator. **~r** vt create

crec|er [11] vi grow; (aumentar) increase. **~ida** f (de río) flood. **~ido** a (persona) grown-up; (número) large, considerable; (plantas) fully-grown. **~iente** a growing; (luna) crescent. **~imiento** m growth

credencial a credential. **~es** fpl credentials

credibilidad f credibility

crédito m credit. **digno de ~** reliable, trustworthy

credo m creed. **en un ~** in a flash

crédulo a credulous

cre|encia f belief. **~er** [18] believe; (pensar) think. **~o que no** I don't think so, I think not. **~o que sí** I think so. ● vi believe. **~erse** vpr consider o.s. **no me lo ~o** I don't believe it. **~íble** a credible. **¡ya lo ~o!** I should think so!

crema f cream; (culin) custard. **~ bronceadora** sun-tan cream

cremación f cremation; (de basura) incineration

cremallera f zip, zipper (Amer)

crematorio m crematorium; (de basura) incinerator

crepitar vi crackle

crepúsculo m twilight

crescendo m crescendo

cresp|o a frizzy. **~ón** m crêpe

cresta f crest; (tupé) toupee; (geog) ridge

Creta f Crete

cretino m cretin

creyente *m* believer

cría *f* breeding; (*animal*) baby animal

cria|da *f* maid, servant. ~**dero** *m* nursery. ~**do** *a* brought up. ● *m* servant. ~**dor** *m* breeder. ~**nza** *f* breeding. ~**r** [20] *vt* suckle; grow (*plantas*); breed (*animales*); (*educar*) bring up. ~**rse** *vpr* grow up

criatura *f* creature; (*niño*) baby

crim|en *m* crime. ~**inal** *a* & *m* & *f* criminal

crin *m* mane; (*relleno*) horsehair

crinolina *f* crinoline

crío *m* child

criollo *a* & *m* Creole

cripta *f* crypt

crisantemo *m* chrysanthemum

crisis *f* crisis

crisol *m* melting-pot

crispar *vt* twitch; (*irritar, fam*) annoy. ~ **los nervios a uno** get on s.o.'s nerves

cristal *m* crystal; (*vidrio*) glass; (*de una ventana*) pane of glass. ~ **de aumento** magnifying glass. ~**ino** *a* crystalline; (*fig*) crystal-clear. ~**izar** [10] crystallize. **limpiar los ~es** clean the windows

cristian|amente *adv* in a Christian way. ~**dad** *f* Christianity. ~**ismo** *m* Christianity. ~**o** *a* & *m* Christian

Cristo *m* Christ

cristo *m* crucifix

criterio *m* criterion; (*opinión*) opinion

cr|ítica *f* criticism; (*reseña*) review. ~**iticar** [7] *vt* criticize. ~**ítico** *a* critical. ● *m* critic

croar *vi* croak

crom|ado *a* chromium-plated. ~**o** *m* chromium, chrome

cromosoma *m* chromosome

crónic|a *f* chronicle; (*de periódico*) news. ~**o** *a* chronic

cronista *m* & *f* reporter

cronol|ogía *f* chronology. ~**ógico** *a* chronological

cron|ometraje *m* timing. ~**ometrar** *vt* time. ~**ómetro** *m* chronometer; (*en deportes*) stopwatch

croquet /'kroket/ *m* croquet

croqueta *f* croquette

cruce *m* crossing; (*de calles, de carreteras*) crossroads; (*de peatones*) (pedestrian) crossing

crucial *a* cross-shaped; (*fig*) crucial

crucifi|car [7] *vt* crucify. ~**jo** *m* crucifix. ~**xión** *f* crucifiction

crucigrama *m* crossword (puzzle)

crudo *a* raw; (*fig*) crude. **petróleo** *m* ~ crude oil

cruel *a* cruel. ~**dad** *f* cruelty

cruji|do *m* (*de seda, de hojas secas etc*) rustle; (*de muebles etc*) creak. ~**r** *vi* (*seda, hojas secas etc*) rustle; (*muebles etc*) creak

cruz *f* cross; (*de moneda*) tails. ~ **gamada** swastika. **la C~ Roja** the Red Cross

cruzada *f* crusade

cruzar [10] *vt* cross; (*poner de un lado a otro*) lay across. ~**se** *vpr* cross; (*pasar en la calle*) pass

cuaderno *m* exercise book; (*para apuntes*) notebook

cuadra *f* (*caballeriza*) stable; (*LAm, manzana*) block

cuadrado *a* & *m* square

cuadragésimo *a* fortieth

cuadr|ar *vt* square. ● *vi* suit; (*estar de acuerdo*) agree. ~**arse** *vpr* (*mil*) stand to attention; (*fig*) dig one's heels in. ~**ilátero** *a* quadrilateral. ● *m* quadrilateral; (*boxeo*) ring

cuadrilla *f* group; (*pandilla*) gang

cuadro *m* square; (*pintura*) painting; (*de obra de teatro, escena*) scene; (*de jardín*) bed; (*de números*) table; (*de mando etc*) panel; (*conjunto del personal*) staff. ~ **de distribución** switchboard. **a ~s, de ~s** check. **en ~** in a square. **¡qué ~!**, **¡vaya un ~!** what a sight!

cuadrúpedo *m* quadruped

cuádruple *a* & *m* quadruple

cuajar *vt* thicken; clot (*sangre*); curdle (*leche*); (*llenar*) fill up. ● *vi* (*nieve*) settle; (*fig, fam*) work out. **cuajado de** full of. ~**se** *vpr* coagulate; (*sangre*) clot; (*leche*) curdle. ~**ón** *m* clot

cual *pron*. **el ~, la ~** etc (*animales y cosas*) that, which; (*personas, sujeto*) who, that; (*personas, objeto*) whom. ● *adv* as, like. ● *a* such as. ~ **si** as if. ~**... tal** like... like. **cada ~** everyone. **por lo ~** because of which

cuál *pron* which

cualidad *f* quality; (*propiedad*) property

cualquiera *a* (*delante de nombres* **cualquier**, *pl* **cualesquiera**) any. ● *pron* (*pl* **cualesquiera**) anyone, anybody; (*cosas*) whatever, which-ever. **un** ~ a nobody

cuando *adv* when. ● *conj* when; (*aunque*) even if. ~ **más** at the most. ~ **menos** at the least. ~ **no** if not. **aun** ~ even if. **de** ~ **en** ~ from time to time

cuándo *adv* & *conj* when. ¿**de** ~ **acá**?, ¿**desde** ~? since when?

cuant|ía *f* quantity; (*extensión*) extent. ~**ioso** *a* abundant

cuanto *a* as much... as, as many... as. ● *pron* as much as, as many as. ● *adv* as much as. ~ **más, mejor** the more the merrier. **en** ~ as soon as. **en** ~ **a** as for. **por** ~ since. **unos** ~**s** a few, some

cuánto *a* (*interrogativo*) how much?; (*interrogativo en plural*) how many?; (*exclamativo*) what a lot of! ● *pron* how much?; (*en plural*) how many? ● *adv* how much. ¿~ **tiempo?** how long? ¡~ **tiempo sin verte!** it's been a long time! ¿**a** ~? how much? ¿**a** ~**s estamos?** what's the date today? **un Sr. no sé** ~**s** Mr So-and-So

cuáquero *m* Quaker

cuarent|a *a* & *m* forty; (*cuadragésimo*) fortieth. ~**ena** *f* (about) forty; (*med*) quarantine. ~**ón** *a* about forty

cuaresma *f* Lent

cuarta *f* (*palmo*) span

cuartear *vt* quarter, divide into four; (*zigzaguear*) zigzag. ~**se** *vpr* crack

cuartel *m* (*mil*) barracks. ~ **general** headquarters. **no dar** ~ show no mercy

cuarteto *m* quartet

cuarto *a* fourth. ● *m* quarter; (*habitación*) room. ~ **de baño** bathroom. ~ **de estar** living room. ~ **de hora** quarter of an hour. **estar sin un** ~ be broke. **menos** ~ (a) quarter to. **y** ~ (a) quarter past

cuarzo *m* quartz

cuatro *a* & *m* four. ~**cientos** *a* & *m* four hundred

Cuba *f* Cuba

cuba: ~**libre** *m* rum and Coke (P). ~**no** *a* & *m* Cuban

cúbico *a* cubic

cubículo *m* cubicle

cubiert|a *f* cover, covering; (*de la cama*) bedspread; (*techo*) roof; (*neumático*) tyre; (*naut*) deck. ~**o** *a* covered; (*cielo*) overcast. ● *m* place

setting, cutlery; (*comida*) meal. **a** ~**o** under cover. **a** ~**o de** safe from

cubis|mo *m* cubism. ~**ta** *a* & *m* & *f* cubist

cubil *m* den, lair. ~**ete** *m* bowl; (*molde*) mould; (*para echar los dados*) cup

cubo *m* bucket; (*en geometría y matemáticas*) cube

cubrecama *m* bedspread

cubrir *vt* [*pp* **cubierto**] cover; ‹*sonido*› drown; fill ‹*vacante*›. ~**se** *vpr* cover o.s.; (*ponerse el sombrero*) put on one's hat; ‹*el cielo*› cloud over, become overcast

cucaracha *f* cockroach

cuclillas. en ~ *adv* squatting

cuclillo *m* cuckoo

cuco *a* shrewd; (*mono*) pretty, nice. ● *m* cuckoo; (*insecto*) grub

cucurucho *m* cornet

cuchar|a *f* spoon. ~**ada** *f* spoonful. ~**adita** *f* teaspoonful. ~**illa** *f*, ~**ita** *f* teaspoon. ~**ón** *m* ladle

cuchiche|ar *vi* whisper. ~**o** *m* whispering

cuchill|a *f* large knife; (*de carnicero*) cleaver; (*hoja de afeitar*) razor blade. ~**ada** *f* slash; (*herida*) knife wound. ~**o** *m* knife

cuchitril *m* pigsty; (*fig*) hovel

cuello *m* neck; (*de camisa*) collar. **cortar el** ~ **a uno** cut s.o.'s throat

cuenc|a *f* hollow; (*del ojo*) (eye) socket; (*geog*) basin. ~**o** *m* hollow; (*vasija*) bowl

cuenta *f* count; (*acción de contar*) counting; (*factura*) bill; (*en banco, relato*) account; (*asunto*) affair; (*de collar etc*) bead. ~ **corriente** current account, checking account (*Amer*). **ajustar las** ~**s** settle accounts. **caer en la** ~ **de que** realize that. **darse** ~ **de** realize. **en resumidas** ~**s** in short. **por mi** ~ for myself. **tener en** ~, **tomar en** ~ bear in mind

cuentakilómetros *m invar* milometer

cuent|ista *m* & *f* story-writer; (*de mentiras*) fibber. ~**o** *m* story; (*mentira*) fib, tall story. ● *vb véase* **contar**

cuerda *f* rope; (*más fina*) string; (*mus*) string. ~ **floja** tightrope. **dar** ~ **a** wind up ‹*un reloj*›

cuerdo *a* ‹*persona*› sane; ‹*acción*› sensible

cuern|a *f* horns. ~**o** *m* horn

cuero *m* leather; (*piel*) skin; (*del grifo*) washer. ~ **cabelludo** scalp. **en ~s (vivos)** stark naked

cuerpo *m* body

cuervo *m* crow

cuesta *f* slope, hill. ~ **abajo** downhill. ~ **arriba** uphill. **a ~s** on one's back

cuesti|ón *f* matter; (*altercado*) quarrel; (*dificultad*) trouble. ~**onario** *m* questionnaire

cueva *f* cave; (*sótano*) cellar

cuida|do *m* care; (*preocupación*) worry; (*asunto*) affair. ¡~**do!** (be) careful! ~**doso** *a* careful. ~**dosamente** *adv* carefully. ~**r** *vt* look after. ● *vi*. ~**r de** look after. ~**rse** *vpr* look after o.s. ~**rse de** be careful to. **tener** ~**do** be careful

culata *f* (*de arma de fuego*) butt; (*auto*) cylinder head. ~**zo** *m* recoil

culebra *f* snake

culebrón *m* (*LAm*) soap opera

culinario *a* culinary

culmina|ción *f* culmination. ~**r** *vi* culminate

culo *m* (*fam*) bottom. **ir de** ~ go downhill

culpa *f* fault; (*jurid*) guilt. ~**bilidad** *f* guilt. ~**ble** *a* guilty. ● *m* culprit. ~**r** *vt* blame (**de** for). **echar la** ~ blame. **por** ~ **de** because of. **tener la** ~ **de** be to blame for

cultiv|ar *vt* farm; grow ⟨*plantas*⟩; (*fig*) cultivate. ~**o** *m* farming; (*de plantas*) growing

cult|o *a* ⟨*tierra etc*⟩ cultivated; ⟨*persona*⟩ educated. ● *m* cult; (*homenaje*) worship. ~**ura** *f* culture. ~**ural** *a* cultural

culturismo *m* body-building

cumbre *f* summit; (*fig*) height

cumpleaños *m invar* birthday

cumplido *a* perfect; (*grande*) large; (*cortés*) polite. ● *m* compliment. ~**r** *a* reliable. **de** ~ courtesy. **por** ~ out of politeness

cumplim|entar *vt* carry out; (*saludar*) pay a courtesy call to; (*felicitar*) congratulate. ~**iento** *m* carrying out, execution

cumplir *vt* carry out; observe ⟨*ley*⟩; serve ⟨*condena*⟩; reach ⟨*años*⟩; keep ⟨*promesa*⟩. ● *vi* do one's duty. ~**se** *vpr* expire; (*realizarse*) be fulfilled. **hoy cumple 3 años** he's 3 (years old) today. **por** ~ as a mere formality

cumulativo *a* cumulative

cúmulo *m* pile, heap

cuna *f* cradle; (*fig, nacimiento*) birthplace

cundir *vi* spread; (*rendir*) go a long way

cuneta *f* gutter

cuña *f* wedge

cuñad|a *f* sister-in-law. ~**o** *m* brother-in-law

cuño *m* stamp. **de nuevo** ~ new

cuota *f* quota; (*de sociedad etc*) subscription, fees

cupe *vb véase* **caber**

cupé *m* coupé

Cupido *m* Cupid

cupo *m* cuota

cupón *m* coupon

cúpula *f* dome

cura *f* cure; (*tratamiento*) treatment. ● *m* priest. ~**ble** *a* curable. ~**ción** *f* healing. ~**ndero** *m* faith-healer. ~**r** *vt* (*incl culin*) cure; dress ⟨*herida*⟩; (*tratar*) treat; (*fig*) remedy; tan ⟨*pieles*⟩. ● *vi* ⟨*persona*⟩ get better; ⟨*herida*⟩ heal; (*fig*) be cured. ~**rse** *vpr* get better

curios|ear *vi* pry; (*mirar*) browse. ~**idad** *f* curiosity; (*limpieza*) cleanliness. ~**o** *a* curious; (*raro*) odd, unusual; (*limpio*) clean

curriculum vitae *m* curriculum vitae

cursar *vt* send; (*estudiar*) study

cursi *a* pretentious, showy. ● *m* affected person

cursillo *m* short course

cursiva *f* italics

curso *m* course; (*univ etc*) year. **en** ~ under way; (*año etc*) current

curtir *vt* tan; (*fig*) harden. ~**se** *vpr* become tanned; (*fig*) become hardened

curv|a *f* curve; (*de carretera*) bend. ~**o** *a* curved

cúspide *f* peak

custodi|a *f* care, safe-keeping. ~**ar** *vt* take care of. ~**o** *a* & *m* guardian

cutáneo *a* skin. **enfermedad** *f* **cutánea** skin disease

cutícula *f* cuticle

cutis *m* skin, complexion

cuyo *pron* (*de persona*) whose, of whom; (*de cosa*) whose, of which. **en** ~ **caso** in which case

CH

chabacano *a* common; ⟨*chiste etc*⟩ vulgar. ● *m* (*Mex, albaricoque*) apricot

chabola f shack. **~s** fpl shanty town

chacal m jackal

chacota f fun. **echar a ~** make fun of

chacra f (LAm) farm

cháchara f chatter

chacharear vt (Mex) sell. ● vi chatter

chafar vt crush. **quedar chafado** be nonplussed

chal m shawl

chalado a (fam) crazy

chalé m house (with a garden), villa

chaleco m waistcoat, vest (Amer). **~ salvavidas** life-jacket

chalequear vt (Arg, Mex) trick

chalet m (pl **chalets**) house (with a garden), villa

chalón m (LAm) shawl

chalote m shallot

chalupa f boat

chamac|a f (esp Mex) girl. **~o** m (esp Mex) boy

chamagoso a (Mex) filthy

chamarr|a f sheepskin jacket. **~o** m (LAm) coarse blanket

chamba f (fam) fluke; (Mex, empleo) job. **por ~** by fluke

champán m, **champaña** m champagne

champiñón m mushroom

champú m (pl **champúes** o **champús**) shampoo

chamuscar [7] vt scorch; (Mex, vender) sell cheaply

chance m (esp LAm) chance

chanclo m clog; (de caucho) rubber overshoe

chancho m (LAm) pig

chanchullo m swindle, fiddle (fam)

chandal m tracksuit

chanquete m whitebait

chantaj|e m blackmail. **~ista** m & f blackmailer

chanza f joke

chapa f plate, sheet; (de madera) plywood; (de botella) metal top. **~do** a plated. **~do a la antigua** oldfashioned. **~do de oro** gold-plated

chaparrón m downpour. **llover a chaparrones** pour (down), rain cats and dogs

chapotear vi splash

chapuce|ar vt botch; (Mex, engañar) deceive. **~ro** a (persona) careless; (cosas) shoddy. ● m careless worker

chapurrar vt, **chapurrear** vt speak badly, speak a little; mix (licores)

chapuza f botched job, mess; (de poca importancia) odd job

chaqueta f jacket. **cambiar la ~** change sides

chaquetero m turncoat

charada f charade

charc|a f pond, pool. **~o** m puddle, pool. **cruzar el ~o** cross the water; (ir a América) cross the Atlantic

charla f chat; (conferencia) talk. **~dor** a talkative. **~r** vi (fam) chat

charlatán a talkative. ● m chatterbox; (curandero) charlatan

charol m varnish; (cuero) patent leather

chárter a charter

chascar [7] vt crack ⟨látigo⟩; click ⟨lengua⟩; snap ⟨dedos⟩. ● vi ⟨látigo⟩ crack; (con la lengua) click one's tongue; ⟨los dedos⟩ snap

chascarrillo m joke, funny story

chasco m disappointment; (broma) joke; (engaño) trick

chasis m (auto) chassis

chasqu|ear vt crack ⟨látigo⟩; click ⟨lengua⟩; snap ⟨dedos⟩. ● vi ⟨látigo⟩ crack; (con la lengua) click one's tongue; ⟨los dedos⟩ snap. **~ido** m crack; (de la lengua) click; (de los dedos) snap

chatarra f scrap iron; (fig) scrap

chato a ⟨nariz⟩ snub; ⟨persona⟩ snub-nosed; ⟨objetos⟩ flat. ● m wine glass; (niño, mujer, fam) dear, darling; (hombre, fam) mate (fam)

chaval m (fam) boy, lad. **~a** f girl, lass

che int (Arg) listen!, hey!

checo a & m Czech. **la república** f **Checa** the Czech Republic

checoslovaco a & m (history) Czechoslovak

Checoslovaquia f (history) Czechoslovakia

chelín m shilling

chelo a (Mex, rubio) fair

cheque m cheque. **~ de viaje** traveller's cheque. **~ra** f cheque-book

chica f girl; (criada) maid, servant

chicano a & m Chicano, Mexican-American

chicle m chewing-gum

chico a (fam) small. ● m boy. **~s** mpl children

chicoleo m compliment

chicoria f chicory

chicharra f cicada; (fig) chatterbox

chicharrón m (de cerdo) crackling; (fig) sunburnt person

chichón m bump, lump

chifla|do a (fam) crazy, daft. **~r** vt (fam) drive crazy. **~rse** vpr be mad (**por** about). **le chifla el chocolate** he's mad about chocolate. **le tiene chiflada esa chica** he's crazy about that girl

Chile m Chile

chile m chilli

chileno a & m Chilean

chill|ar vi scream, shriek; ⟨gato⟩ howl; ⟨ratón⟩ squeak; ⟨cerdo⟩ squeal. **~ido** m scream, screech; (de gato etc) howl. **~ón** a noisy; ⟨colores⟩ loud; ⟨sonido⟩ shrill

chimenea f chimney; ⟨hogar⟩ fireplace

chimpancé m chimpanzee

China f China

chinch|ar vt (fam) annoy, pester. **~e** m drawing-pin (Brit), thumbtack (Amer); ⟨insecto⟩ bedbug, (fig) nuisance. **~eta** f drawing-pin (Brit), thumbtack (Amer)

chinela f slipper

chino a & m Chinese

Chipre m Cyprus

chipriota a & m & f Cypriot

chiquillo a childish. ● m child, kid (fam)

chiquito a small, tiny. ● m child, kid (fam)

chiribita f spark. **estar que echa ~s** be furious

chirimoya f custard apple

chiripa f fluke. **por ~** by fluke

chirivía f parsnip

chirri|ar vi creak; ⟨pájaro⟩ chirp. **~do** m creaking; (al freír) sizzling; (de pájaros) chirping

chis int sh!, hush!; (para llamar a uno, fam) hey!, psst!

chism|e m gadget, thingumajig (fam); ⟨chismorreo⟩ piece of gossip. **~es** mpl things, bits and pieces. **~orreo** m gossip. **~oso** a gossipy. ● m gossip

chispa f spark; ⟨gota⟩ drop; ⟨gracia⟩ wit; (fig) sparkle. **estar que echa ~(s)** be furious

chispea|nte a sparkling. **~r** vi spark; (lloviznar) drizzle; (fig) sparkle

chisporrotear vt throw out sparks; ⟨fuego⟩ crackle; ⟨aceite⟩ sizzle

chistar vi speak. **sin ~** without saying a word

chiste m joke, funny story. **hacer ~ de** make fun of. **tener ~** be funny

chistera f (fam) top hat, topper (fam)

chistoso a funny

chiva|r vi inform ⟨policía⟩; ⟨niño⟩ tell. **~tazo** m tip-off. **~to** m informer; ⟨niño⟩ telltale

chivo m kid, young goat

choca|nte a surprising; ⟨persona⟩ odd. **~r** [7] vt clink ⟨vasos⟩; shake ⟨la mano⟩. ● vi collide, hit. **~r con**, **~r contra** crash into. **lo ~nte es que** the surprising thing is that

chocolate m chocolate. **tableta** f **de ~** bar of chocolate

choch|ear vi be senile. **~o** a senile; (fig) soft

chófer m chauffeur; ⟨conductor⟩ driver

cholo a & m (LAm) half-breed

chopo m poplar

choque m collision; (fig) clash; ⟨eléctrico⟩ shock; ⟨auto, rail etc⟩ crash, accident; ⟨sacudida⟩ jolt

chorizo m salami

chorr|ear vi gush forth; (fig) be dripping. **~o** m jet, stream; ⟨caudal pequeño⟩ trickle; (fig) stream. **a ~os** (fig) in abundance. **hablar a ~os** jabber

chovinis|mo m chauvinism. **~ta** a chauvinistic. ● m & f chauvinist

choza f hut

chubas|co m squall, heavy shower; (fig) bad patch. **~quero** m raincoat, anorak

chuchería f trinket; (culin) sweet

chufa f tiger nut

chuleta f chop

chulo a insolent; ⟨vistoso⟩ showy. ● m ruffian; ⟨rufián⟩ pimp

chumbo m prickly pear; (fam) bump. **higo** m **~** prickly pear

chup|ada f suck; ⟨al cigarro etc⟩ puff. **~ado** a skinny; ⟨fácil, fam⟩ very easy. **~ar** vt suck, lick; puff at ⟨cigarro etc⟩; ⟨absorber⟩ absorb. **~arse** vpr lose weight. **~ete** m dummy (Brit), pacifier (Amer)

churro m fritter; (fam) mess. **me salió un ~** I made a mess of it

chusco a funny

chusma f riff-raff

chutar vi shoot. **¡va que chuta!** it's going well!

D

dactilógrafo m typist

dado m dice. ● a given; ⟨hora⟩ gone. **~ que** since, given that

dalia f dahlia

daltoniano a colour-blind

dama f lady; (*en la corte*) lady-in-waiting. **~s** fpl draughts (*Brit*), checkers (*Amer*)

damasco m damask

danés a Danish. ● m Dane; (*idioma*) Danish

danza f dance; (*acción*) dancing; (*enredo*) affair. **~r** [10] vt/i dance

dañ|ado a damaged. **~ar** vt damage; harm ⟨*persona*⟩. **~ino** a harmful. **~o** m damage; (*a una persona*) harm. **~oso** a harmful. **~os y perjuicios** damages. **hacer ~o a** harm; hurt ⟨*persona*⟩. **hacerse ~o** hurt o.s.

dar [26] vt give; (*producir*) yield; strike ⟨*la hora*⟩. ● vi give. **da igual** it doesn't matter. **¡dale!** go on! **da lo mismo** it doesn't matter. **~ a** ⟨*ventana*⟩ look on to; ⟨*edificio*⟩ face. **~ a luz** give birth. **~ con** meet ⟨*persona*⟩; find ⟨*cosa*⟩; **~ de cabeza** fall flat on one's face. **~ por** assume; (+ *infinitivo*) decide. **~se** vpr give o.s. up; (*suceder*) happen. **dárselas de** make o.s. out to be. **~se por** consider o.s. **¿qué más da?** it doesn't matter!

dardo m dart

dársena f dock

datar vt date. ● vi. **~ de** date from

dátil m date

dato m fact. **~s** mpl data, information

de prep of; (*procedencia*) from; (*suposición*) if. **~ día** by day. **~ dos en dos** two by two. **~ haberlo sabido** if I (you, he etc) had known. **~ niño** as a child. **el libro ~ mi amigo** my friend's book. **las 2 ~ la madrugada** 2 (o'clock) in the morning. **un puente ~ hierro** an iron bridge. **soy ~ Loughborough** I'm from Loughborough

deambular vi stroll

debajo adv underneath. **~ de** underneath, under. **el de ~** the one underneath. **por ~** underneath. **por ~ de** below

debat|e m debate. **~ir** vt debate

deber vt owe. ● vi have to, must. ● m duty. **~es** mpl homework. **~se** vpr. **~se a** be due to. **debo marcharme** I must go, I have to go

debido a due; (*correcto*) proper. **~ a** due to. **como es ~** as is proper. **con el respeto ~** with due respect

débil a weak; ⟨*ruido*⟩ faint; ⟨*luz*⟩ dim

debili|dad f weakness. **~tar** vt weaken. **~tarse** vpr weaken, get weak

débito m debit; (*deuda*) debt

debutar vi make one's debut

década f decade

deca|dencia f decline. **~dente** a decadent. **~er** [29] vi decline; (*debilitarse*) weaken. **~ído** a depressed. **~imiento** m decline, weakening

decano m dean; (*miembro más antiguo*) senior member

decantar vt decant ⟨*vino etc*⟩

decapitar vt behead

decena f ten; (*aproximadamente*) about ten

decencia f decency, honesty

decenio m decade

decente a ⟨*persona*⟩ respectable, honest; ⟨*cosas*⟩ modest; (*limpio*) clean, tidy

decepci|ón f disappointment. **~onar** vt disappoint

decibelio m decibel

decidi|do a decided; ⟨*persona*⟩ determined, resolute. **~r** vt decide; settle ⟨*cuestión etc*⟩. ● vi decide. **~rse** vpr make up one's mind

decimal a & m decimal

décimo a & m tenth. ● m (*de lotería*) tenth part of a lottery ticket

decimo: ~ctavo a & m eighteenth. **~cuarto** a & m fourteenth. **~nono** a & m, **~noveno** a & m nineteenth. **~quinto** a & m fifteenth. **~séptimo** a & m seventeenth. **~sexto** a & m sixteenth. **~tercero** a & m, **~tercio** a & m thirteenth

decir [46] vt say; (*contar*) tell. ● m saying. **~se** vpr be said. **~ que no** say no. **~ que sí** say yes. **dicho de otro modo** in other words. **dicho y hecho** no sooner said than done. **¿dígame?** can I help you? **¡dígame!** (*al teléfono*) hello! **digamos** let's say. **es ~** that is to say. **mejor dicho** rather. **¡no me digas!** you don't say!, really! **por así ~, por ~lo así** so to speak, as it were. **querer ~** mean. **se dice que** it is said that, they say that

decisi|ón f decision. **~vo** a decisive

declamar vt declaim

declara|ción f statement. **~ción de renta** income tax return. **~r** vt/i declare. **~rse** vpr declare o.s.; (*epidemia etc*) break out

declina|ción f (*gram*) declension. **~r** vt/i decline; ⟨*salud*⟩ deteriorate

declive *m* slope; (*fig*) decline. **en ~** sloping

decolorar *vt* discolour, fade. **~se** *vpr* become discoloured, fade

decora|ción *f* decoration. **~do** *m* (*en el teatro*) set. **~dor** *m* decorator. **~r** *vt* decorate. **~tivo** *a* decorative

decoro *m* decorum; (*respeto*) respect. **~so** *a* proper; (*modesto*) modest; ⟨*profesión*⟩ honourable

decrecer [11] *vi* decrease, diminish; ⟨*aguas*⟩ subside

decrépito *a* decrepit

decret|ar *vt* decree. **~o** *m* decree

dedal *m* thimble

dedica|ción *f* dedication. **~r** [7] *vt* dedicate; devote ⟨*tiempo*⟩. **~toria** *f* dedication, inscription

ded|il *m* finger-stall. **~illo** *m*. **al ~illo** at one's fingertips. **~o** *m* finger; (*del pie*) toe. **~o anular** ring finger. **~ corazón** middle finger. **~o gordo** thumb. **~o índice** index finger. **~o meñique** little finger. **~o pulgar** thumb

deduc|ción *f* deduction. **~ir** [47] *vt* deduce; (*descontar*) deduct

defect|o *m* fault, defect. **~uoso** *a* defective

defen|der [1] *vt* defend. **~sa** *f* defence. **~sivo** *a* defensive. **~sor** *m* defender. **abogado** *m* **~sor** defence counsel

deferen|cia *f* deference. **~te** *a* deferential

deficien|cia *f* deficiency. **~cia mental** mental handicap. **~te** *a* deficient; (*imperfecto*) defective. **~te mental** mentally handicapped

déficit *m invar* deficit

defini|ción *f* definition. **~do** *a* defined. **~r** *vt* define; (*aclarar*) clarify. **~tivo** *a* definitive. **en ~tiva** (*en resumen*) in short

deflación *f* deflation

deform|ación *f* deformation; (*TV etc*) distortion. **~ar** *vt* deform; (*TV etc*) distort. **~arse** *vpr* go out of shape. **~e** *a* deformed; (*feo*) ugly

defraudar *vt* cheat; (*decepcionar*) disappoint; evade ⟨*impuestos etc*⟩

defunción *f* death

degenera|ción *f* degeneration; (*moral*) degeneracy. **~do** *a* degenerate. **~r** *vi* degenerate

deglutir *vt/i* swallow

degollar [16] *vt* cut s.o.'s throat; (*fig, arruinar*) ruin

degradar *vt* degrade. **~se** *vpr* lower o.s.

degusta|ción *f* tasting. **~r** *vt* taste

dehesa *f* pasture

dei|dad *f* deity. **~ficar** [7] *vt* deify

deja|ción *f* surrender. **~dez** *f* abandon; (*pereza*) laziness. **~do** *a* negligent. **~r** *vt* leave; (*abandonar*) abandon; (*prestar*) lend; (*permitir*) let. **~r aparte, ~r a un lado** leave aside. **~r de** stop. **no ~r de** not fail to

dejo *m* aftertaste; (*tonillo*) accent

del = **de** + **el**

delantal *m* apron

delante *adv* in front; (*enfrente*) opposite. **~ de** in front of. **de ~** front

delanter|a *f* front; (*de teatro etc*) front row; (*ventaja*) advantage. **coger la ~a** get ahead. **~o** *a* front. forward. **llevar la ~a** be ahead ● *m*

delat|ar *vt* denounce. **~or** *m* informer

delega|ción *f* delegation; (*sucursal*) branch. **~do** *m* delegate; (*com*) agent, representative. **~r** [12] *vt* delegate

deleit|ar *vt* delight. **~e** *m* delight

deletéreo *a* deleterious

deletre|ar *vt* spell (out). **~o** *m* spelling

deleznable *a* brittle, crumbly; (*argumento etc*) weak

delfín *m* dolphin

delgad|ez *f* thinness. **~o** *a* thin; (*esbelto*) slim. **~ucho** *a* skinny

delibera|ción *f* deliberation. **~r** *vt* discuss, decide. ● *vi* deliberate

delicad|eza *f* delicacy; (*fragilidad*) frailty; (*tacto*) tact. **~o** *a* delicate; (*sensible* sensitive; (*discreto*) tactful, discreet. **falta de ~eza** tactlessness

delici|a *f* delight. **~oso** *a* delightful; ⟨*sabor etc*⟩ delicious; (*gracioso, fam*) funny

delimitar *vt* delimit

delincuen|cia *f* delinquency. **~te** *a* & *m* delinquent

delinea|nte *m* draughtsman. **~r** *vt* outline; (*dibujar*) draw

delinquir [8] *vi* commit an offence

delir|ante *a* delirious. **~ar** *vi* be delirious; (*fig*) talk nonsense. **~io** *m* delirium; (*fig*) frenzy

delito *m* crime, offence

delta *f* delta

demacrado *a* emaciated

demagogo *m* demagogue

demanda f. **en ~ de** asking for; (en busca de) in search of. **~nte** m & f (jurid) plaintiff. **~r** vt (jurid) bring an action against

demarca|ción f demarcation. **~r** [7] vt demarcate

demás a rest of the, other. ● pron rest, others. **lo ~** the rest. **por ~** useless; (muy) very. **por lo ~** otherwise

demasía f excess; (abuso) outrage; (atrevimiento) insolence. **en ~** too much

demasiado a too much; (en plural) too many. ● adv too much; (con adjetivo) too

demen|cia f madness. **~te** a demented, mad

dem|ocracia f democracy. **~ócrata** m & f democrat. **~ocrático** a democratic

demol|er [2] vt demolish. **~ición** f demolition

demonio m devil, demon. **¡~s!** hell! **¿cómo ~s?** how the hell? **¡qué ~s!** what the hell!

demora f delay. **~r** vt delay. ● vi stay on. **~rse** vpr be a long time

demostra|ción f demonstration, show. **~r** [2] vt demonstrate; (mostrar) show; (probar) prove. **~tivo** a demonstrative

denegar [1 & 12] vt refuse

deng|oso a affected, finicky. **~ue** m affectation

denigrar vt denigrate

denomina|ción f denomination. **~do** a called. **~dor** m denominator. **~r** vt name

denotar vt denote

dens|idad f density. **~o** a dense, thick

denta|dura f teeth. **~dura postiza** denture, false teeth. **~l** a dental

dentera f. **dar ~ a uno** set s.o.'s teeth on edge; (dar envidia) make s.o. green with envy

dentífrico m toothpaste

dentista m & f dentist

dentro adv inside; (de un edificio) indoors. **~ de** in. **~ de poco** soon. **por ~** inside

denuncia f report; (acusación) accusation. **~r** vt report (a crime); (periódico etc) denounce; (indicar) indicate

departamento m department; (Arg, piso) flat (Brit), apartment (Amer)

dependencia f dependence; (sección) section; (sucursal) branch

depender vi depend (**de** on)

dependient|a f shop assistant. **~e** a dependent (**de** on). ● m employee; (de oficina) clerk; (de tienda) shop assistant

depila|ción f depilation. **~r** vt depilate. **~torio** a depilatory

deplora|ble a deplorable. **~r** vt deplore, regret

deponer [34] vt remove from office. ● vi give evidence

deporta|ción f deportation. **~r** vt deport

deport|e m sport. **~ista** m sportsman. ● f sportswoman. **~ivo** a sports. ● m sports car. **hacer ~e** take part in sports

deposición f deposition; (de un empleo) removal from office

dep|ositador m depositor. **~ositante** m & f depositor. **~ositar** vt deposit; (poner) put, place. **~ósito** m deposit; (conjunto de cosas) store; (almacén) warehouse; (mil) depot; (de líquidos) tank

deprava|ción f depravity. **~do** a depraved. **~r** vt deprave. **~rse** vpr become depraved

deprecia|ción f depreciation. **~r** vt depreciate. **~rse** vpr depreciate

depresión f depression

deprim|ente a depressing. **~ido** a depressed. **~ir** vt depress. **~irse** vpr get depressed

depura|ción f purification; (pol) purging. **~r** vt purify; (pol) purge

derech|a f (mano) right hand; (lado) right. **~ista** a right-wing. ● m & f right-winger. **~o** a right; (vertical) upright; (recto) straight. ● adv straight. ● m right; (ley) law; (lado) right side. **~os** mpl dues. **~os de autor** royalties. **a la ~a** on the right; (hacia el lado derecho) to the right. **todo ~o** straight on

deriva f drift. **a la ~** drifting, adrift

deriva|ción f derivation; (cambio) diversion. **~do** a derived. ● m derivative, by-product. **~r** vt derive; (cambiar la dirección de) divert. ● vi. **~r de** derive from, be derived from. **~rse** vpr be derived

derram|amiento m spilling. **~amiento de sangre** bloodshed. **~ar**

vt spill; (*verter*) pour; shed ⟨*lágrimas*⟩. **~arse** *vpr* spill. **~e** *m* spilling; (*pérdida*) leakage; (*cantidad perdida*) spillage; (*med*) discharge; (*med, de sangre*) haemorrhage

derretir [5] *vt* melt. **~se** *vpr* melt; (*enamorarse*) fall in love (**por** with)

derriba|do *a* fallen down. **~r** *vt* knock down; bring down, overthrow ⟨*gobierno etc*⟩. **~rse** *vpr* fall down

derrocar [7] *vt* bring down, overthrow ⟨*gobierno etc*⟩

derroch|ar *vt* squander. **~e** *m* waste

derrot|a *f* defeat; (*rumbo*) course. **~ar** *vt* defeat. **~ado** *a* defeated; ⟨*vestido*⟩ shabby. **~ero** *m* course

derrumba|miento *m* collapse. **~r** *vt* (*derribar*) knock down. **~rse** *vpr* collapse

desaborido *a* tasteless; ⟨*persona*⟩ dull

desabotonar *vt* unbutton, undo. ● *vi* bloom. **~se** *vpr* come undone

desabrido *a* tasteless; ⟨*tiempo*⟩ unpleasant; ⟨*persona*⟩ surly

desabrochar *vt* undo. **~se** *vpr* come undone

desacat|ar *vt* have no respect for. **~o** *m* disrespect

desac|ertado *a* ill-advised; (*erróneo*) wrong. **~ertar** [1] *vt* be wrong. **~ierto** *m* mistake

desaconseja|ble *a* inadvisable. **~do** *a* unwise, ill-advised. **~r** *vt* advise against, dissuade

desacorde *a* discordant

desacostumbra|do *a* unusual. **~r** *vt* give up

desacreditar *vt* discredit

desactivar *vt* defuse

desacuerdo *m* disagreement

desafiar [20] *vt* challenge; (*afrontar*) defy

desafilado *a* blunt

desafina|do *a* out of tune. **~r** *vi* be out of tune. **~rse** *vpr* go out of tune

desafío *m* challenge; (*combate*) duel

desaforado *a* ⟨*comportamiento*⟩ outrageous; (*desmedido*) excessive; ⟨*sonido*⟩ loud; (*enorme*) huge

desafortunad|amente *adv* unfortunately. **~o** *a* unfortunate

desagrada|ble *a* unpleasant. **~r** *vt* displease. **~ vi** be unpleasant. **me ~ el sabor** I don't like the taste

desagradecido *a* ungrateful

desagrado *m* displeasure. **con ~** unwillingly

desagravi|ar *vt* make amends to. **~o** *m* amends; (*expiación*) atonement

desagregar [12] *vt* break up. **~se** *vpr* disintegrate

desagüe *m* drain; (*acción*) drainage. **tubo** *m* **de ~** drain-pipe

desaguisado *a* illegal. ● *m* offence; (*fam*) disaster

desahog|ado *a* roomy; (*adinerado*) well-off; (*fig, descarado, fam*) impudent. **~ar** [12] *vt* relieve; vent ⟨*ira*⟩. **~arse** *vpr* (*desfogarse*) let off steam. **~o** *m* comfort; (*alivio*) relief

desahuci|ar *vt* deprive of hope; give up hope for ⟨*enfermo*⟩; evict ⟨*inquilino*⟩. **~o** *m* eviction

desair|ado *a* humiliating; ⟨*persona*⟩ humiliated, spurned. **~ar** *vt* snub ⟨*persona*⟩; disregard ⟨*cosa*⟩. **~e** *m* rebuff

desajuste *m* maladjustment; (*avería*) breakdown

desal|entador *a* disheartening. **~entar** [1] *vt* (*fig*) discourage. **~iento** *m* discouragement

desaliño *m* untidiness, scruffiness

desalmado *a* wicked

desalojar *vt* eject ⟨*persona*⟩; evacuate ⟨*sitio*⟩. ● *vi* move (house)

desampar|ado *a* helpless; (*abandonado*) abandoned. **~ar** *vt* abandon. **~o** *m* helplessness; (*abandono*) abandonment

desangelado *a* insipid, dull

desangrar *vt* bleed. **~se** *vpr* bleed

desanima|do *a* down-hearted. **~r** *vt* discourage. **~rse** *vpr* lose heart

desánimo *m* discouragement

desanudar *vt* untie

desapacible *a* unpleasant; ⟨*sonido*⟩ harsh

desapar|ecer [11] *vi* disappear; ⟨*efecto*⟩ wear off. **~ecido** *a* disappeared. ● *m* missing person. **~ecidos** *mpl* missing. **~ición** *f* disappearance

desapasionado *a* dispassionate

desapego *m* indifference

desapercibido *a* unnoticed

desaplicado *a* lazy

desaprensi|ón *f* unscrupulousness. **~vo** *a* unscrupulous

desaproba|ción *f* disapproval. **~r** [2] *vt* disapprove of; (*rechazar*) reject.

desaprovecha|do *a* wasted; ⟨*alumno*⟩ lazy. **~r** *vt* waste

desarm|ar vt disarm; (desmontar) take to pieces. ~**e** m disarmament

desarraig|ado a rootless. ~**ar** [12] vt uproot; (fig, erradicar) wipe out. ~**o** m uprooting; (fig) eradication

desarregl|ado a untidy; (desordenado) disorderly. ~**ar** vt mess up; (deshacer el orden) make untidy. ~**o** m disorder; (de persona) untidiness

desarroll|ado a (well-) developed. ~**ar** vt develop; (desenrollar) unroll, unfold. ~**arse** vpr (incl foto) develop; (desenrollarse) unroll; (suceso) take place. ~**o** m development

desarrugar [12] vt smooth out

desarticular vt dislocate (hueso); (fig) break up

desaseado a dirty; (desordenado) untidy

desasirse [45] vpr let go (**de** of)

desasos|egar [1 & 12] vt disturb. ~**e-garse** vpr get uneasy. ~**iego** m anxiety; (intranquilidad) restlessness

desastr|ado a scruffy. ~**e** m disaster. ~**oso** a disastrous

desata|do a untied; (fig) wild. ~**r** vt untie; (fig, soltar) unleash. ~**rse** vpr come undone

desatascar [7] vt pull out of the mud; unblock (tubo etc)

desaten|ción f inattention; (descortesía) discourtesy. ~**der** [1] vt not pay attention to; neglect (deber etc). ~**to** a inattentive; (descortés) discourteous

desatin|ado a silly. ~**o** m silliness; (error) mistake

desatornillar vt unscrew

desatracar [7] vt/i cast off

desautorizar [10] vt declare unauthorized; (desmentir) deny

desavenencia f disagreement

desayun|ar vt have for breakfast. ● vi have breakfast. ~**o** m breakfast

desazón m (fig) anxiety

desbandarse vpr (mil) disband; (dispersarse) disperse

desbarajust|ar vt throw into confusion. ~**e** m confusion

desbaratar vt spoil

desbloquear vt unfreeze

desbocado a (vasija etc) chipped; (caballo) runaway; (persona) foul-mouthed

desborda|nte a overflowing. ~**r** vt go beyond; (exceder) exceed. ● vi overflow. ~**rse** vpr overflow

descabalgar [12] vi dismount

descabellado a crazy

descabezar [10] vt behead

descafeinado a decaffeinated. ● m decaffeinated coffee

descalabr|ar vt injure in the head; (fig) damage. ~**o** m disaster

descalificar [7] vt disqualify; (desacreditar) discredit

descalz|ar [10] vt take off (zapato). ~**o** a barefoot

descaminar vt misdirect; (fig) lead astray

descamisado a shirtless; (fig) shabby

descampado a open. ● m open ground

descans|ado a rested; (trabajo) easy. ~**apiés** m footrest. ~**ar** vt/i rest. ~**illo** m landing. ~**o** m rest; (descansillo) landing; (en deportes) half-time; (en el teatro etc) interval

descapotable a convertible

descarado a insolent, cheeky; (sin vergüenza) shameless

descarg|a f unloading; (mil, elec) discharge. ~**ar** [12] vt unload; (mil, elec) discharge, shock; deal (golpe etc). ● vi flow into. ~**o** m unloading; (recibo) receipt; (jurid) evidence

descarnado a scrawny, lean; (fig) bare

descaro m insolence, cheek; (cinismo) nerve, effrontery

descarriar [20] vt misdirect; (fig) lead astray. ~**se** vpr go the wrong way; (res) stray; (fig) go astray

descarrila|miento m derailment. ~**r** vi be derailed. ~**se** vpr be derailed

descartar vt discard; (rechazar) reject. ~**se** vpr discard

descascarar vt shell

descen|dencia f descent; (personas) descendants. ~**dente** a descending. ~**der** [1] vt lower, get down; go down (escalera etc). ● vi go down; (provenir) be descended (**de** from). ~**diente** m & f descendent. ~**so** m descent; (de temperatura, fiebre etc) fall, drop

descentralizar [10] vt decentralize

descifrar vt decipher; decode (clave)

descolgar [2 & 12] vt take down; pick up (el teléfono). ~**se** vpr let o.s. down; (fig, fam) turn up

descolorar vt discolour, fade

descolori|do a discoloured, faded; ⟨persona⟩ pale. **~r** vt discolour, fade

descomedido a rude; ⟨excesivo⟩ excessive, extreme

descomp|ás m disproportion. **~asado** a disproportionate

descomp|oner [34] vt break down; decompose ⟨substancia⟩; distort ⟨rasgos⟩; ⟨estropear⟩ break; ⟨desarreglar⟩ disturb, spoil. **~onerse** vpr decompose; ⟨persona⟩ lose one's temper. **~osición** f decomposition; ⟨med⟩ diarrhoea. **~ostura** f breaking; ⟨de un motor⟩ breakdown; ⟨desorden⟩ disorder. **~uesto** a broken; ⟨podrido⟩ decomposed; ⟨encolerizado⟩ angry. **estar ~uesto** have diarrhoea

descomunal a ⟨fam⟩ enormous

desconc|ertante a disconcerting. **~ertar** [1] vt disconcert; ⟨dejar perplejo⟩ puzzle. **~ertarse** vpr be put out, be disconcerted; ⟨mecanismo⟩ break down. **~ierto** m confusion

desconectar vt disconnect

desconfia|do a distrustful. **~nza** f distrust, suspicion. **~r** [20] vi. **~r de** not trust; ⟨no creer⟩ doubt

descongelar vt defrost; ⟨com⟩ unfreeze

desconoc|er [11] vt not know, not recognize. **~ido** a unknown; ⟨cambiado⟩ unrecognizable. ● m stranger. **~imiento** m ignorance

desconsidera|ción f lack of consideration. **~do** a inconsiderate

descons|olado a distressed. **~olar** [2] vt distress. **~olarse** vpr despair. **~uelo** m distress; ⟨tristeza⟩ sadness

desconta|do a. **dar por ~do** take for granted. **por ~do** of course. **~r** [2] vt discount

descontent|adizo a hard to please. **~ar** vt displease. **~o** a unhappy (**de** about), discontented (**de** with). ● m discontent

descontrolado a uncontrolled

descorazonar vt discourage. **~se** vpr lose heart

descorchar vt uncork

descorrer vt draw ⟨cortina⟩. **~ el cerrojo** unbolt the door

descort|és a rude, discourteous. **~esía** f rudeness

descos|er vt unpick. **~erse** vpr come undone. **~ido** a unstitched; ⟨fig⟩ disjointed. **como un ~ido** a lot

descoyuntar vt dislocate

descrédito m disrepute. **ir en ~ de** damage the reputation of

descreído a unbelieving

descremar vt skim

descri|bir [pp **descrito**] vt describe. **~pción** f description. **~ptivo** a descriptive

descuartizar [10] vt cut up

descubierto a discovered; ⟨no cubierto⟩ uncovered; ⟨expuesto⟩ exposed; ⟨cielo⟩ clear; ⟨sin sombrero⟩ bareheaded. ● m overdraft; ⟨déficit⟩ deficit. **poner al ~** expose

descubri|miento m discovery. **~r** [pp **descubierto**] vt discover; ⟨quitar lo que cubre⟩ uncover; ⟨revelar⟩ reveal; unveil ⟨estatua⟩. **~rse** vpr be discovered; ⟨cielo⟩ clear; ⟨quitarse el sombrero⟩ take off one's hat

descuento m discount

descuid|ado a careless; ⟨aspecto etc⟩ untidy; ⟨desprevenido⟩ unprepared. **~ar** vt neglect. ● vi not worry. **~arse** vpr be careless; ⟨no preocuparse⟩ not worry. ¡**~a**! don't worry! **~o** m carelessness; ⟨negligencia⟩ negligence. **al ~o** nonchalantly. **estar ~ado** not worry, rest assured

desde prep ⟨lugar etc⟩ from; ⟨tiempo⟩ since, from. **~ hace poco** for a short time. **~ hace un mes** for a month. **~ luego** of course. **~ Madrid hasta Barcelona** from Madrid to Barcelona. **~ niño** since childhood

desdecir [46, pero imperativo **desdice**, futuro y condicional regulares] vi. **~ de** be unworthy of; ⟨no armonizar⟩ not match. **~se** vpr. be take back ⟨palabras etc⟩; go back on ⟨promesa⟩

desd|én m scorn. **~eñable** a contemptible. **~eñar** vt scorn. **~eñoso** a scornful

desdicha f misfortune. **~do** a unfortunate. **por ~** unfortunately

desdoblar vt straighten; ⟨desplegar⟩ unfold

desea|ble a desirable. **~r** vt want; wish ⟨algo a uno⟩. **de ~r** desirable. **le deseo un buen viaje** I hope you have a good journey. **¿qué desea Vd?** can I help you?

desecar [7] vt dry up

desech|ar vt throw out. **~o** m rubbish

desembalar vt unpack

desembarazar [10] *vt* clear. ~**se** *vpr* free o.s.

desembarca|dero *m* landing stage. ~**r** [7] *vt* unload. ● *vi* disembark

desemboca|dura *f* (*de río*) mouth; (*de calle*) opening. ~**r** [7] *vi.* ~**r en** ⟨*río*⟩ flow into; ⟨*calle*⟩ join; (*fig*) lead to, end in

desembols|ar *vt* pay. ~**o** *m* payment

desembragar [12] *vi* declutch

desembrollar *vt* unravel

desembuchar *vt* tell, reveal a secret

desemejan|te *a* unlike, dissimilar. ~**za** *f* dissimilarity

desempapelar *vt* unwrap

desempaquetar *vt* unpack, unwrap

desempat|ar *vi* break a tie. ~**e** *m* tie-breaker

desempeñ|ar *vt* redeem; play ⟨*papel*⟩; hold ⟨*cargo*⟩; perform, carry out ⟨*deber etc*⟩. ~**arse** *vpr* get out of debt. ~**o** *m* redemption; (*de un papel, de un cargo*) performance

desemple|ado *a* unemployed. ● *m* unemployed person. ~**o** *m* unemployment. **los** ~**ados** *mpl* the unemployed

desempolvar *vt* dust; (*fig*) unearth

desencadenar *vt* unchain; (*fig*) unleash. ~**se** *vpr* break loose; ⟨*guerra etc*⟩ break out

desencajar *vt* dislocate; (*desconectar*) disconnect. ~**se** *vpr* become distorted

desencant|ar *vt* disillusion. ~**o** *m* disillusionment

desenchufar *vt* unplug

desenfad|ado *a* uninhibited. ~**ar** *vt* calm down. ~**arse** *vpr* calm down. ~**o** *m* openness; (*desenvoltura*) assurance

desenfocado *a* out of focus

desenfren|ado *a* unrestrained. ~**arse** *vpr* rage. ~**o** *m* licentiousness

desenganchar *vt* unhook

desengañ|ar *vt* disillusion. ~**arse** *vpr* be disillusioned; (*darse cuenta*) realize. ~**o** *m* disillusionment, disappointment

desengrasar *vt* remove the grease from. ● *vi* lose weight

desenla|ce *m* outcome. ~**zar** [10] *vt* undo; solve ⟨*problema*⟩

desenmarañar *vt* unravel

desenmascarar *vt* unmask

desenojar *vt* calm down. ~**se** *vpr* calm down

desenred|ar *vt* unravel. ~**arse** *vpr* extricate o.s. ~**o** *m* denouement

desenrollar *vt* unroll, unwind

desenroscar [7] *vt* unscrew

desentenderse [1] *vpr* want nothing to do with; (*afectar ignorancia*) pretend not to know. **hacerse el desentendido** (*fingir no oír*) pretend not to hear

desenterrar [1] *vt* exhume; (*fig*) unearth

desenton|ar *vi* be out of tune; ⟨*colores*⟩ clash. ~**o** *m* rudeness

desentrañar *vt* work out

desenvoltura *f* ease; (*falta de timidez*) confidence; (*descaro*) insolence

desenvolver [2, *pp* **desenvuelto**] *vt* unwrap; expound ⟨*idea etc*⟩. ~**se** *vpr* act with confidence

deseo *m* wish, desire. ~**so** *a* desirous. **arder en** ~**s de** long for. **buen** ~ good intentions. **estar** ~**so de** be eager to

desequilibr|ado *a* unbalanced. ~**io** *m* imbalance

des|erción *f* desertion; (*pol*) defection. ~**ertar** *vt* desert. ~**értico** *a* desert-like. ~**ertor** *m* deserter

desespera|ción *f* despair. ~**do** *a* desperate. ~**nte** *a* infuriating. ~**r** *vt* drive to despair. ● *vi* despair (**de** of). ~**rse** *vpr* despair

desestimar *vt* (*rechazar*) reject

desfachat|ado *a* brazen, impudent. ~**ez** *f* impudence

desfalc|ar [7] *vt* embezzle. ~**o** *m* embezzlement

desfallec|er [11] *vt* weaken. ● *vi* get weak; (*desmayarse*) faint. ~**imiento** *m* weakness

desfas|ado *a* ⟨*persona*⟩ out of place, out of step; ⟨*máquina etc*⟩ out of phase. ~**e** *m* jet-lag. **estar** ~**ado** have jet-lag

desfavor|able *a* unfavourable. ~**ecer** [11] *vt* ⟨*ropa*⟩ not suit

desfigurar *vt* disfigure; (*desdibujar*) blur; (*fig*) distort

desfiladero *m* pass

desfil|ar *vi* march (past). ~**e** *m* procession, parade. ~**e de modelos** fashion show

desfogar [12] *vt* vent (**en, con** on). ~**se** *vpr* let off steam

desgajar *vt* tear off; (*fig*) uproot ⟨*persona*⟩. ~**se** *vpr* come off

desgana f (falta de apetito) lack of appetite; (med) weakness, faintness; (fig) unwillingness

desgarr|ador a heart-rending. ~ar vt tear; (fig) break ‹corazón›. ~o m tear, rip; (descaro) insolence. ~ón m tear

desgast|ar vt wear away; wear out ‹ropa›. ~arse vpr wear away; ‹ropa› be worn out; ‹persona› wear o.s. out. ~e m wear

desgracia f misfortune; (accidente) accident; (mala suerte) bad luck. ~damente adv unfortunately. ~do a unlucky; (pobre) poor; (desagradable) unpleasant. ● m unfortunate person, poor devil (fam). ~r vt spoil. **caer en ~** fall from favour. **estar en ~** be unfortunate. **por ~** unfortunately. **¡qué ~!** what a shame!

desgranar vt shell ‹guisantes etc›

desgreñado a ruffled, dishevelled

desgua|ce m scrapyard. ~zar [10] vt scrap

deshabitado a uninhabited

deshabituarse [21] vpr get out of the habit

deshacer [31] vt undo; strip ‹cama›; unpack ‹maleta›; (desmontar) take to pieces; break ‹trato›; (derretir) melt; (en agua) dissolve; (destruir) destroy; (estropear) spoil; (derrotar) defeat. ~se vpr come undone; (descomponerse) fall to pieces; (derretirse) melt. ~se de algo get rid of sth. ~se en lágrimas burst into tears. ~se por hacer algo go out of one's way to do sth

deshelar [1] vt thaw. ~se vpr thaw

desheredar vt disinherit

deshidratar vt dehydrate. ~se vpr become dehydrated

deshielo m thaw

deshilachado a frayed

deshincha|do a ‹neumático› flat. ~vt deflate. ~rse vpr go down

deshollina|dor m (chimney-)sweep. ~r vt sweep ‹chimenea›

deshon|esto a dishonest; (obsceno) indecent. ~or m, ~ra f disgrace. ~rar vt dishonour

deshora f. **a ~** (a hora desacostumbrada) at an unusual time; (a hora inoportuna) at an inconvenient time; (a hora avanzada) very late

deshuesar vt bone ‹carne›; stone ‹fruta›

desidia f laziness

desierto a deserted. ● m desert

designa|ción f designation. ~r vt designate; (fijar) fix

desigual a unequal; ‹terreno› uneven; (distinto) different. ~dad f inequality

desilusi|ón f disappointment; (pérdida de ilusiones) disillusionment. ~onar vt disappoint; (quitar las ilusiones) disillusion. ~onarse vpr become disillusioned

desinfecta|nte m disinfectant. ~r vt disinfect

desinfestar vt decontaminate

desinflar vt deflate. ~se vpr go down

desinhibido a uninhibited

desintegra|ción f disintegration. ~r vt disintegrate. ~rse vpr disintegrate

desinter|és m impartiality; (generosidad) generosity. ~esado a impartial; (liberal) generous

desistir vi. **~ de** give up

desleal a disloyal. ~tad f disloyalty

desleír [51] vt thin down, dilute

deslenguado a foul-mouthed

desligar [12] vt untie; (separar) separate; (fig, librar) free. ~se vpr break away; (de un compromiso) free o.s.

deslizar [10] vt slide, slip. ~se vpr slide, slip; ‹tiempo› slide by, pass; (fluir) flow

deslucido a tarnished; (gastado) worn out; (fig) undistinguished

deslumbrar vt dazzle

deslustrar vt tarnish

desmadr|ado a unruly. ~arse vpr get out of control. ~e m excess

desmán m outrage

desmandarse vpr get out of control

desmantelar vt dismantle; (despojar) strip

desmañado a clumsy

desmaquillador m make-up remover

desmay|ado a unconscious. ~ar vi lose heart. ~arse vpr faint. ~o m faint; (estado) unconsciousness; (fig) depression

desmedido a excessive

desmedrarse vpr waste away

desmejorarse vpr deteriorate

desmelenado a dishevelled

desmembrar vt (fig) divide up

desmemoriado *a* forgetful

desmentir [4] *vt* deny. **~se** *vpr* contradict o.s.; (*desdecirse*) go back on one's word

desmenuzar [10] *vt* crumble; chop ⟨*carne etc*⟩

desmerecer [11] *vt* be unworthy of. ● *vi* deteriorate

desmesurado *a* excessive; (*enorme*) enormous

desmigajar *vt*, **desmigar** [12] *vt* crumble

desmonta|ble *a* collapsible. **~r** *vt* (*quitar*) remove; (*desarmar*) take to pieces; (*derribar*) knock down; (*allanar*) level. ● *vi* dismount

desmoralizar [10] *vt* demoralize

desmoronar *vt* wear away; (*fig*) make inroads into. **~se** *vpr* crumble

desmovilizar [10] *vt/i* demobilize

desnatar *vt* skim

desnivel *m* unevenness; (*fig*) difference, inequality

desnud|ar *vt* strip; undress, strip ⟨*persona*⟩. **~arse** *vpr* get undressed. **~ez** *f* nudity. **~o** *a* naked; (*fig*) bare. ● *m* nude

desnutri|ción *f* malnutrition. **~do** *a* undernourished

desobed|ecer [11] *vt* disobey. **~iencia** *f* disobedience. **~iente** *a* disobedient

desocupa|do *a* ⟨*asiento etc*⟩ vacant, free; (*sin trabajo*) unemployed; (*ocioso*) idle. **~r** *vt* vacate

desodorante *m* deodorant

desoír [50] *vt* take no notice of

desola|ción *f* desolation; (*fig*) distress. **~do** *a* desolate; ⟨*persona*⟩ sorry, sad. **~r** *vt* ruin; (*desconsolar*) distress

desollar *vt* skin; (*fig, criticar*) criticize; (*fig, hacer pagar demasiado, fam*) fleece

desorbitante *a* excessive

desorden *m* disorder, untidiness; (*confusión*) confusion. **~ado** *a* untidy. **~ar** *vt* disarrange, make a mess of

desorganizar [10] *vt* disorganize; (*trastornar*) disturb

desorienta|do *a* confused. **~r** *vt* disorientate. **~rse** *vpr* lose one's bearings

desovar *vi* ⟨*pez*⟩ spawn; ⟨*insecto*⟩ lay eggs

despabila|do *a* wide awake; (*listo*) quick. **~r** *vt* (*despertar*) wake up; (*avivar*) brighten up. **~rse** *vpr* wake up; (*avivarse*) brighten up. **¡despabílate!** get a move on!

despacio *adv* slowly. ● *int* easy does it! **~to** *adv* slowly

despach|ar *vt* finish; (*tratar con*) deal with; (*vender*) sell; (*enviar*) send; (*despedir*) send away; issue ⟨*billete*⟩. ● *vi* hurry up. **~arse** *vpr* get rid; (*terminar*) finish. **~o** *m* dispatch; (*oficina*) office; (*venta*) sale; (*del teatro*) box office

despampanante *a* stunning

desparejado *a* odd

desparpajo *m* confidence; (*descaro*) impudence

desparramar *vt* scatter; spill ⟨*líquidos*⟩; squander ⟨*fortuna*⟩

despavorido *a* terrified

despectivo *a* disparaging; ⟨*sentido etc*⟩ pejorative

despecho *m* spite. **a ~ de** in spite of. **por ~** out of spite

despedazar [10] *vt* tear to pieces

despedi|da *f* goodbye, farewell. **~da de soltero** stag-party. **~r** [5] *vt* say goodbye, see off; dismiss ⟨*empleado*⟩; evict ⟨*inquilino*⟩; (*arrojar*) throw; give off ⟨*olor etc*⟩. **~rse** *vpr*. **~rse de** say goodbye to

despeg|ado *a* cold, indifferent. **~ar** [12] *vt* unstick. ● *vi* ⟨*avión*⟩ take off. **~o** *m* indifference. **~ue** *m* take-off

despeinar *vt* ruffle the hair of

despeja|do *a* clear; ⟨*persona*⟩ wide awake. **~r** *vt* clear; (*aclarar*) clarify. ● *vi* clear. **~rse** *vpr* (*aclararse*) become clear; ⟨*cielo*⟩ clear; ⟨*tiempo*⟩ clear up; ⟨*persona*⟩ liven up

despellejar *vt* skin

despensa *f* pantry, larder

despeñadero *m* cliff

desperdici|ar *vt* waste. **~o** *m* waste. **~os** *mpl* rubbish. **no tener ~o** be good all the way through

desperezarse [10] *vpr* stretch

desperfecto *m* flaw

desperta|dor *m* alarm clock. **~r** [1] *vt* wake up; (*fig*) awaken. **~rse** *vpr* wake up

despiadado *a* merciless

despido *m* dismissal

despierto *a* awake; (*listo*) bright

despilfarr|ar *vt* waste. **~o** *m* squandering; (*gasto innecesario*) extravagance

despista|do *a* (*con estar*) confused; (*con ser*) absent-minded. **~r** *vt* throw

off the scent; (fig) mislead. ~rse vpr
go wrong; (fig) get confused
despiste m swerve; (error) mistake;
(confusión) muddle
desplaza|do a out of place.
~miento m displacement; (de
opinión etc) swing, shift. ~r [10] vt
displace. ~rse vpr travel
despl|egar [1 & 12] vt open out;
spread ⟨alas⟩; (fig) show. ~iegue m
opening; (fig) show
desplomarse vpr lean; (caerse) collapse
desplumar vt pluck; (fig, fam) fleece
despobla|do m deserted area. ~r [2]
vt depopulate
despoj|ar vt deprive ⟨persona⟩; strip
⟨cosa⟩. ~o m plundering; (botín)
booty. ~os mpl left-overs; (de res)
offal; (de ave) giblets
desposado a & m newly-wed
déspota m & f despot
despreci|able a despicable; ⟨can-
tidad⟩ negligible. ~ar vt despise;
(rechazar) scorn. ~o m contempt
desprend|er vt remove; give off
⟨olor⟩. ~erse vpr fall off; (fig) part
with; (deducirse) follow. ~imiento
m loosening; (generosidad) gener-
osity
despreocupa|ción f carelessness.
~do a unconcerned; (descuidado)
careless. ~rse vpr not worry
desprestigiar vt discredit
desprevenido a unprepared. **coger
a uno** ~ catch s.o. unawares
desproporci|ón f disproportion.
~onado a disproportionate
despropósito m irrelevant remark
desprovisto a. ~ de lacking, without
después adv after, afterwards; (más
tarde) later; (a continuación) then. ~
de after. ~ **de comer** after eating. ~
de todo after all. ~ **que** after. **poco**
~ soon after. **una semana** ~ a week
later
desquiciar vt (fig) disturb
desquit|ar vt compensate. ~arse
vpr make up for; (vengarse) take revenge. ~e m compensation; (venganza) revenge
destaca|do a outstanding. ~r [7] vt
emphasize. ● vi stand out. ~rse vpr
stand out
destajo m piece-work. **hablar a** ~
talk nineteen to the dozen

destap|ar vt uncover; open ⟨botella⟩.
~arse vpr reveal one's true self. ~e
m (fig) permissiveness
destartalado a ⟨habitación⟩ untidy;
⟨casa⟩ rambling
destell|ar vi sparkle. ~o m sparkle;
(de estrella) twinkle; (fig) glimmer
destemplado a out of tune; (agrio)
harsh; ⟨tiempo⟩ unsettled; ⟨persona⟩
out of sorts
desteñir [5 & 22] vt fade; (manchar)
discolour. ● vi fade. ~se vpr fade;
⟨color⟩ run
desterra|do m exile. ~r [1] vt banish
destetar vt wean
destiempo m. **a** ~ at the wrong moment
destierro m exile
destil|ación f distillation. ~ar vt
distil. ~ería f distillery
destin|ar vt destine; (nombrar) ap-
point. ~atario m addressee. ~o m
(uso) use, function; (lugar) destination; (empleo) position; (suerte)
destiny. **con** ~ **a** going to, bound
for. **dar** ~o **a** find a use for
destitu|ción f dismissal. ~ir [17] vt
dismiss
destornilla|dor m screwdriver. ~r
vt unscrew
destreza f skill
destripar vt rip open
destroz|ar [10] vt ruin; (fig) shatter.
~o m destruction. **causar** ~os,
hacer ~os ruin
destru|cción f destruction. ~ctivo a
destructive. ~ir [17] vt destroy; de-
molish ⟨edificio⟩
desunir vt separate
desus|ado a old-fashioned; (insólito)
unusual. ~o m disuse. **caer en** ~o
become obsolete
desvaído a pale; (borroso) blurred;
⟨persona⟩ dull
desvalido a needy, destitute
desvalijar vt rob; burgle ⟨casa⟩
desvalorizar [10] vt devalue
desván m loft
desvanec|er [11] vt make disappear;
tone down ⟨colores⟩; (borrar) blur;
(fig) dispel. ~erse vpr disappear;
(desmayarse) faint. ~imiento m
(med) fainting fit
desvariar [20] vi be delirious; (fig)
talk nonsense
desvel|ar vt keep awake. ~arse vpr
stay awake, have a sleepless night.
~o m insomnia, sleeplessness

desvencijar *vt* break; (*agotar*) exhaust

desventaja *f* disadvantage

desventura *f* misfortune. **~do** *a* unfortunate

desverg|onzado *a* impudent, cheeky. **~üenza** *f* impudence, cheek

desvestirse [5] *vpr* undress

desv|iación *f* deviation; (*auto*) diversion. **~iar** [20] *vt* deflect, turn aside. **~iarse** *vpr* be deflected; (*del camino*) make a detour; (*del tema*) stray. **~ío** *m* diversion; (*frialdad*) indifference

desvivirse *vpr* long (*por* for); (*afanarse*) strive, do one's utmost

detall|ar *vt* relate in detail. **~e** *m* detail; (*fig*) gesture. **~ista** *m & f* retailer. **al ~e** in detail; (*al por menor*) retail. **con todo ~e** in great detail. **en ~es** in detail. **¡qué ~e!** how thoughtful!

detect *vt* detect. **~ive** *m* detective

deten|ción *f* stopping; (*jurid*) arrest; (*en la cárcel*) detention. **~er** [40] *vt* stop; (*jurid*) arrest; (*encarcelar*) detain; (*retrasar*) delay. **~erse** *vpr* stop; (*entretenerse*) spend a lot of time. **~idamente** *adv* carefully. **~ido** *a* (*jurid*) under arrest; (*minucioso*) detailed. ● *m* prisoner

detergente *a & m* detergent

deterior|ar *vt* damage, spoil. **~arse** *vpr* deteriorate. **~o** *m* damage

determina|ción *f* determination; (*decisión*) decison. **~nte** *a* decisive. **~r** *vt* determine; (*decidir*) decide; (*fijar*) fix. **tomar una ~ción** make a decision

detestar *vt* detest

detonar *vi* explode

detrás *adv* behind; (*en la parte posterior*) on the back. **~ de** behind. **por ~** on the back; (*detrás de*) behind

detrimento *m* detriment. **en ~ de** to the detriment of

detrito *m* debris

deud|a *f* debt. **~or** *m* debtor

devalua|ción *f* devaluation. **~r** [21] *vt* devalue

devanar *vt* wind

devasta|dor *a* devastating. **~r** *vt* devastate

devoción *f* devotion

devol|ución *f* return; (*com*) repayment, refund. **~ver** [5] (*pp* **devuelto**) *vt* return; (*com*) repay, refund; restore (*edificio etc*). ● *vi* be sick

devorar *vt* devour

devoto *a* devout; (*amigo etc*) devoted. ● *m* enthusiast

di *vb véase* **dar**

día *m* day. **~ de fiesta** (public) holiday. **~ del santo** saint's day. **~ festivo** (public) holiday. **~ hábil, ~ laborable** working day. **al ~** up to date. **al ~ siguiente** (on) the following day. **¡buenos ~s!** good morning! **dar los buenos ~s** say good morning. **de ~** by day. **el ~ de hoy** today. **el ~ de mañana** tomorrow. **en pleno ~** in broad daylight. **en su ~** in due course. **todo el santo ~** all day long. **un ~ de estos** one of these days. **un ~ sí y otro no** every other day. **vivir al ~** live from hand to mouth

diab|etes *f* diabetes. **~ético** *a* diabetic

diab|lo *m* devil. **~lura** *f* mischief. **~ólico** *a* diabolical

diácono *m* deacon

diadema *f* diadem

diáfano *a* diaphanous

diafragma *m* diaphragm

diagn|osis *f* diagnosis. **~osticar** [7] *vt* diagnose. **~óstico** *a* diagnostic

diagonal *a & f* diagonal

diagrama *m* diagram

dialecto *m* dialect

diálisis *f* dialysis

di|alogar [12] *vi* talk. **~álogo** *m* dialogue

diamante *m* diamond

diámetro *m* diameter

diana *f* reveille; (*blanco*) bull's-eye

diapasón *m* (*para afinar*) tuning fork

diapositiva *f* slide, transparency

diari|amente *adv* every day. **~o** *a* daily. ● *m* newspaper; (*libro*) diary. **a ~o** daily. **~o hablado** (*en la radio*) news bulletin. **de ~o** everyday, ordinary

diarrea *f* diarrhoea

diatriba *f* diatribe

dibuj|ar *vt* draw. **~o** *m* drawing. **~os animados** cartoon (film)

diccionario *m* dictionary

diciembre *m* December

dictado *m* dictation

dictad|or *m* dictator. **~ura** *f* dictatorship

dictamen *m* opinion; (*informe*) report

dictar *vt* dictate; pronounce ⟨*sentencia etc*⟩

dich|a *f* happiness. ~**o** *a* said; (*susodicho*) aforementioned. ● *m* saying. ~**oso** *a* happy; (*afortunado*) fortunate. ~**o y hecho** no sooner said than done. **mejor** ~**o** rather. **por** ~**a** fortunately.

didáctico *a* didactic

dieci|nueve *a & m* nineteen. ~**ocho** *a & m* eighteen. ~**séis** *a & m* sixteen. ~**siete** *a & m* seventeen.

diente *m* tooth; (*de tenedor*) prong; (*de ajo*) clove. ~ **de león** dandelion. **hablar entre** ~**s** mumble

diesel /'disel/ *a* diesel

diestr|a *f* right hand. ~**o** *a* (*derecho*) right; (*hábil*) skillful

dieta *f* diet

diez *a & m* ten

diezmar *vt* decimate

difama|ción *f* (*con palabras*) slander; (*por escrito*) libel. ~**r** *vt* (*hablando*) slander; (*por escrito*) libel

diferen|cia *f* difference; (*desacuerdo*) disagreement. ~**ciar** *vt* differentiate between. ● *vi* differ. ~**ciarse** *vpr* differ. ~**te** *a* different

difer|ido *a* (*TV etc*) recorded. ~**ir** [4] *vt* postpone, defer. ● *vi* differ

dif|ícil *a* difficult. ~**icultad** *f* difficulty; (*problema*) problem. ~**icultar** *vt* make difficult

difteria *f* diphtheria

difundir *vt* spread; (*TV etc*) broadcast. ~**se** *vpr* spread

difunto *a* late, deceased. ● *m* deceased

difusión *f* spreading

dige|rir [4] *vt* digest. ~**stión** *f* digestion. ~**stivo** *a* digestive

digital *a* digital; (*de los dedos*) finger

dignarse *vpr* deign. **dígnese Vd** be so kind as

dign|atario *m* dignitary. ~**idad** *f* dignity; (*empleo*) office. ~**o** *a* worthy; (*apropiado*) appropriate

digo *vb véase* **decir**

digresión *f* digression

dije *vb véase* **decir**

dila|ción *f* delay. ~**tación** *f* dilation, expansion. ~**tado** *a* extensive; ⟨*tiempo*⟩ long. ~**tar** *vt* expand; (*med*) dilate; (*prolongar*) prolong. ~**tarse** *vpr* expand; (*med*) dilate; (*extenderse*) extend. **sin** ~**ción** immediately

dilema *m* dilemma

diligen|cia *f* diligence; (*gestión*) job; (*historia*) stagecoach. ~**te** *a* diligent

dilucidar *vt* explain; solve ⟨*misterio*⟩

diluir [17] *vt* dilute

diluvio *m* flood

dimensión *f* dimension; (*tamaño*) size

diminut|ivo *a & m* diminutive. ~**o** *a* minute

dimi|sión *f* resignation. ~**tir** *vt/i* resign

Dinamarca *f* Denmark

dinamarqués *a* Danish. ● *m* Dane

din|ámica *f* dynamics. ~**ámico** *a* dynamic. ~**amismo** *m* dynamism

dinamita *f* dynamite

dínamo *m*, **dinamo** *m* dynamo

dinastía *f* dynasty

dineral *m* fortune

dinero *m* money. ~ **efectivo** cash. ~ **suelto** change

dinosaurio *m* dinosaur

diócesis *f* diocese

dios *m* god. ~**a** *f* goddess. **¡D**~ **mío!** good heavens! **¡gracias a D**~**!** thank God! **¡válgame D**~**!** bless my soul!

diploma *m* diploma

diplomacia *f* diplomacy

diplomado *a* qualified

diplomático *a* diplomatic. ● *m* diplomat

diptongo *m* diphthong

diputa|ción *f* delegation. ~**ción provincial** county council. ~**do** *m* delegate; (*pol, en España*) member of the Cortes; (*pol, en Inglaterra*) Member of Parliament; (*pol, en Estados Unidos*) congressman

dique *m* dike

direc|ción *f* direction; (*señas*) address; (*los que dirigen*) management; (*pol*) leadership. ~**ción prohibida** no entry. ~**ción única** one-way. ~**ta** *f* (*auto*) top gear. ~**tiva** *f* directive, guideline. ~**tivo** *m* executive. ~**to** *a* direct; ⟨*línea*⟩ straight; ⟨*tren*⟩ through. ~**tor** *m* director; (*mus*) conductor; (*de escuela etc*) headmaster; (*de periódico*) editor; (*gerente*) manager. ~**tora** *f* (*de escuela etc*) headmistress. **en** ~**to** (*TV etc*) live. **llevar la** ~**ción de** direct

dirig|ente *a* ruling. ● *m & f* leader; (*de empresa*) manager. ~**ible** *a & m* dirigible. ~**ir** [14] *vt* direct; (*mus*) conduct; run ⟨*empresa etc*⟩; address

⟨*carta etc*⟩. **~irse** *vpr* make one's way; (*hablar*) address

discernir [1] *vt* distinguish

disciplina *f* discipline. **~r** *vt* discipline. **~rio** *a* disciplinary

discípulo *m* disciple; (*alumno*) pupil

disco *m* disc; (*mus*) record; (*deportes*) discus; (*de teléfono*) dial; (*auto*) lights; (*rail*) signal

disconforme *a* not in agreement

discontinuo *a* discontinuous

discord|ante *a* discordant. **~e** *a* discordant. **~ia** *f* discord

discoteca *f* discothèque, disco (*fam*); (*colección de discos*) record library

discreción *f* discretion

discrepa|ncia *f* discrepancy; (*desacuerdo*) disagreement. **~r** *vi* differ

discreto *a* discreet; (*moderado*) moderate; (*color*) subdued

discrimina|ción *f* discrimination. **~r** *vt* (*distinguir*) discriminate between; (*tratar injustamente*) discriminate against

disculpa *f* apology; (*excusa*) excuse. **~r** *vt* excuse, forgive. **~rse** *vpr* apologize. **dar ~s** make excuses. **pedir ~s** apologize *vt*

discurrir *vt* think up. ● *vi* think (**en** about); ⟨*tiempo*⟩ pass

discurs|ante *m* speaker. **~ar** *vi* speak (**sobre** about). **~o** *m* speech

discusión *f* discussion; (*riña*) argument. **eso no admite ~** there can be no argument about that

discuti|ble *a* debatable. **~r** *vt* discuss; (*argumentar*) argue about; (*contradecir*) contradict. ● *vi* discuss; (*argumentar*) argue

disec|ar [7] *vt* dissect; stuff ⟨*animal muerto*⟩. **~ción** *f* dissection

disemina|ción *f* dissemination. **~r** *vt* disseminate, spread

disentería *f* dysentery

disenti|miento *m* dissent, disagreement. **~r** [4] *vi* disagree (**de** with) (**en** on)

diseñ|ador *m* designer. **~ar** *vt* design. **~o** *m* design; (*fig*) sketch

disertación *f* dissertation

disfraz *m* disguise; (*vestido*) fancy dress. **~ar** [10] *vt* disguise. **~arse** *vpr*. **~arse de** disguise o.s. as

disfrutar *vt* enjoy. ● *vi* enjoy o.s. **~ de** enjoy

disgregar [12] *vt* disintegrate

disgust|ar *vt* displease; (*molestar*) annoy. **~arse** *vpr* get annoyed, get

upset; ⟨*dos personas*⟩ fall out. **~o** *m* annoyance; (*problema*) trouble; (*repugnancia*) disgust; (*riña*) quarrel; (*dolor*) sorrow, grief

disiden|cia *f* disagreement, dissent. **~te** *a & m & f* dissident

disímil *a* (*LAm*) dissimilar

disimular *vt* conceal. ● *vi* pretend

disipa|ción *f* dissipation; (*de dinero*) squandering. **~r** *vt* dissipate; (*derrochar*) squander

diskette *m* floppy disk

dislocarse [7] *vpr* dislocate

disminu|ción *f* decrease. **~ir** [17] *vi* diminish

disociar *vt* dissociate

disolver [2, *pp* **disuelto**] *vt* dissolve. **~se** *vpr* dissolve

disonante *a* dissonant

dispar *a* different

disparar *vt* fire. ● *vi* shoot (**contra** at)

disparat|ado *a* absurd. **~ar** *vi* talk nonsense. **~e** *m* silly thing; (*error*) mistake. **decir ~es** talk nonsense. **¡qué ~e!** how ridiculous! **un ~e** (*mucho, fam*) a lot, an awful lot (*fam*)

disparidad *f* disparity

disparo *m* (*acción*) firing; (*tiro*) shot

dispensar *vt* distribute; (*disculpar*) excuse. **¡Vd dispense!** forgive me

dispers|ar *vt* scatter, disperse. **~arse** *vpr* scatter, disperse. **~ión** *f* dispersion. **~o** *a* scattered

dispon|er [34] *vt* arrange; (*preparar*) prepare. ● *vi.* **~er de** have; (*vender etc*) dispose of. **~erse** *vpr* get ready. **~ibilidad** *f* availability. **~ible** *a* available

disposición *f* arrangement; (*aptitud*) talent; (*disponibilidad*) disposal; (*jurid*) order, decree. **~ de ánimo** frame of mind. **a la ~** at the disposal of. **a su ~** at your service

dispositivo *m* device

dispuesto *a* ready; (*hábil*) clever; (*inclinado*) disposed; (*servicial*) helpful

disputa *f* dispute. **~r** *vt* dispute. ● *vi.* **~r por** argue about; (*competir para*) compete for. **sin ~** undoubtedly

distan|cia *f* distance. **~ciar** *vt* space out; (*en deportes*) outdistance. **~ciarse** *vpr* ⟨*dos personas*⟩ fall out. **~te** *a* distant. **a ~cia** from a distance. **guardar las ~cias** keep one's distance

distar *vi* be away; (*fig*) be far. **dista 5 kilómetros** it's 5 kilometres away

distin|ción f distinction. ~**guido** a distinguished; (*en cartas*) Honoured. ~**guir** [13] vt/i distinguish. ~**guirse** vpr distinguish o.s.; (*diferenciarse*) differ; (*verse*) be visible. ~**tivo** a distinctive. ● m badge. ~**to** a different; (*claro*) distinct

distorsión f distortion; (*med*) sprain

distra|cción f amusement; (*descuido*) absent-mindedness, inattention. ~**er** [41] vt distract; (*divertir*) amuse, embezzle ⟨*fondos*⟩. ● vi be entertaining. ~**erse** vpr amuse o.s.; (*descuidarse*) not pay attention. ~**ído** a amusing; (*desatento*) absent-minded

distribu|ción f distribution. ~**idor** m distributor, agent. ~**idor automático** vending machine. ~**ir** [17] vt distribute

distrito m district

disturbio m disturbance

disuadir vt dissuade

diurético a & m diuretic

diurno a daytime

divagar [12] vi (*al hablar*) digress

diván m settee, sofa

diverg|encia f divergence. ~**ente** a divergent. ~**ir** [14] vi diverge

diversidad f diversity

diversificar [7] vt diversify

diversión f amusement, entertainment; (*pasatiempo*) pastime

diverso a different

diverti|do a amusing; (*que tiene gracia*) funny; (*agradable*) enjoyable. ~**r** [4] vt amuse, entertain. ~**rse** vpr enjoy o.s.

dividir vt divide; (*repartir*) share out

divin|idad f divinity. ~**o** a divine

divisa f emblem. ~**s** fpl foreign exchange

divisar vt make out

divis|ión f division. ~**or** m divisor. ~**orio** a dividing

divorci|ado a divorced. ● m divorcee. ~**ar** vt divorce. ~**arse** vpr get divorced. ~**o** m divorce

divulgar [12] vt divulge; (*propagar*) spread. ~**se** vpr become known

do m C; (*solfa*) doh

dobl|adillo m hem; (*de pantalón*) turn-up (*Brit*), cuff (*Amer*). ~**ado** a double; (*plegado*) folded; ⟨*película*⟩ dubbed. ~**ar** vt double; (*plegar*) fold; (*torcer*) bend; turn ⟨*esquina*⟩; dub ⟨*película*⟩. ● vi turn; ⟨*campana*⟩ toll. ~**arse** vpr double; (*encorvarse*) bend; (*ceder*) give in. ~**e** a double. ● m

double; (*pliegue*) fold. ~**egar** [12] vt (*fig*) force to give in. ~**egarse** vpr give in. **el** ~**e** twice as much

doce a & m twelve. ~**na** f dozen. ~**no** a twelfth

docente a teaching. ● m & f teacher

dócil a obedient

doct|o a learned. ~**or** m doctor. ~**orado** m doctorate. ~**rina** f doctrine

document|ación f documentation, papers. ~**al** a & m documentary. ~**ar** vt document. ~**arse** vpr gather information. ~**o** m document. **D~o Nacional de Identidad** national identity card

dogm|a m dogma. ~**ático** a dogmatic

dólar m dollar

dol|er [2] vi hurt, ache; (*fig*) grieve. **me duele la cabeza** my head hurts. **le duele el estómago** he has a pain in his stomach. ~**erse** vpr regret; (*quejarse*) complain. ~**or** m pain; (*sordo*) ache; (*fig*) sorrow. ~**oroso** a painful. ~**or de cabeza** headache. ~**or de muelas** toothache

domar vt tame; break in ⟨*caballo*⟩

dom|esticar [7] vt domesticate. ~**éstico** a domestic. ● m servant

domicilio m home. **a** ~ at home. **servicio a** ~ home delivery service

domina|ción f domination. ~**nte** a dominant; ⟨*persona*⟩ domineering. ~**r** vt dominate; (*contener*) control; (*conocer*) have a good knowledge of. ● vi dominate; (*destacarse*) stand out. ~**rse** vpr control o.s.

domin|go m Sunday. ~**guero** a Sunday. ~**ical** a Sunday

dominio m authority; (*territorio*) domain; (*fig*) good knowledge

dominó m (*juego*) dominoes

don m talent, gift; (*en un sobre*) Mr. ~ **Pedro** Pedro. **tener** ~ **de lenguas** have a gift for languages. **tener** ~ **de gentes** have a way with people

donación f donation

donaire m grace, charm

dona|nte m (*de sangre*) donor. ~**r** vt donate

doncella f (*criada*) maid

donde adv where

dónde adv where? **¿hasta** ~? how far? **¿por** ~? whereabouts?; (*¿por qué camino?*) which way? **¿a** ~ **vas?** where are you going? **¿de** ~ **eres?** where are you from?

dondequiera adv anywhere; (en todas partes) everywhere. ~ que wherever. por ~ everywhere

doña f (en un sobre) Mrs. ~ María María

dora|do a golden; (cubierto de oro) gilt. ~dura f gilding. ~r vt gilt; (culin) brown

dormi|lón m sleepyhead. ● a lazy. ~r [6] vt send to sleep. ● vi sleep. ~rse vpr go to sleep. ~tar vi doze. ~torio m bedroom. ~r la siesta have an afternoon nap, have a siesta. echarse a dormir go to bed

dors|al a back. ● m (en deportes) number. ~o m back

dos a & m two. ~cientos a & m two hundred. cada ~ por tres every five minutes. de ~ en ~ in twos, in pairs. en un ~ por tres in no time. los dos, las dos both (of them)

dosi|ficar [7] vt dose; (fig) measure out. ~s f dose

dot|ado a gifted. ~ar vt give a dowry; (proveer) endow (de with). ~e m dowry

doy vb véase **dar**

dragar [12] vt dredge

drago m dragon tree

dragón m dragon

dram|a m drama; (obra de teatro) play. ~ático a dramatic. ~atizar [10] vt dramatize. ~aturgo m playwright

drástico a drastic

droga f drug. ~dicto m drug addict. ~do a drugged. ● m drug addict. ~r [12] vt drug. ~rse vpr take drugs. ~ta m & f (fam) drug addict

droguería f hardware shop (Brit), hardware store (Amer)

dromedario m dromedary

ducha f shower. ~rse vpr have a shower

dud|a f doubt. ~ar vt/i doubt. ~oso a doubtful; (sospechoso) dubious. poner en ~a question. sin ~a (alguna) without a doubt

duelo m duel; (luto) mourning

duende m imp

dueñ|a f owner, proprietress; (de una pensión) landlady. ~o m owner, proprietor; (de una pensión) landlord

duermo vb véase **dormir**

dul|ce a sweet; (agua) fresh; (suave) soft, gentle. ● m sweet. ~zura f sweetness; (fig) gentleness

duna f dune

dúo m duet, duo

duodécimo a & m twelfth

duplica|do a in duplicate. ● m duplicate. ~r [7] vt duplicate. ~rse vpr double

duque m duke. ~sa f duchess

dura|ción f duration, length. ~dero a lasting

durante prep during, in; (medida de tiempo) for. ~ todo el año all year round

durar vi last

durazno m (LAm, fruta) peach

dureza f hardness, toughness; (med) hard patch

durmiente a sleeping

duro a hard; (culin) tough; (fig) harsh. ● adv hard. ● m five-peseta coin. ser ~ de oído be hard of hearing

E

e conj and

ebanista m & f cabinet-maker

ébano m ebony

ebri|edad f drunkenness. ~o a drunk

ebullición f boiling

eccema m eczema

eclesiástico a ecclesiastical. ● m clergyman

eclipse m eclipse

eco m echo. hacer(se) ~ echo

ecolog|ía f ecology. ~ista m & f ecologist

economato m cooperative store

econ|omía f economy; (ciencia) economics. ~ómicamente adv economically. ~ómico a economic(al); (no caro) inexpensive. ~omista m & f economist. ~omizar [10] vt/i economize

ecuación f equation

ecuador m equator. el E~ Ecuador

ecuánime a level-headed; (imparcial) impartial

ecuanimidad f equanimity

ecuatoriano a & m Ecuadorian

ecuestre a equestrian

echar vt throw; post ‹carta›; give off ‹olor›; pour ‹líquido›; sprout ‹hojas etc›; (despedir) throw out; dismiss ‹empleado›; (poner) put on; put out ‹raíces›; show ‹película›. ~se vpr throw o.s.; (tumbarse) lie down. ~ a start. ~ a perder spoil. ~ de menos

miss. **~se atrás** (*fig*) back down.
echárselas de feign

edad *f* age. **~ avanzada** old age. **E~ de Piedra** Stone Age. **E~ Media** Middle Ages. **¿qué ~ tiene?** how old is he?

edición *f* edition; (*publicación*) publication

edicto *m* edict

edific|ación *f* building. **~ante** *a* edifying. **~ar** [7] *vt* build; (*fig*) edify. **~io** *m* building; (*fig*) structure

Edimburgo *m* Edinburgh

edit|ar *vt* publish. **~or** *a* publishing. **●** *m* publisher. **~orial** *a* editorial. **●** *m* leading article. **●** *f* publishing house

edredón *m* eiderdown

educa|ción *f* upbringing; (*modales*) (good) manners; (*enseñanza*) education. **~do** *a* polite. **~dor** *m* teacher. **~r** [7] *vt* bring up; (*enseñar*) educate. **~tivo** *a* educational. **bien ~do** polite. **falta de ~ción** rudeness, bad manners. **mal ~do** rude

edulcorante *m* sweetener

EE.UU. *abrev* (*Estados Unidos*) USA, United States (of America)

efect|ivamente *adv* really; (*por supuesto*) indeed. **~ivo** *a* effective; (*auténtico*) real; (*empleo*) permanent. **●** *m* cash. **~o** *m* effect; (*impresión*) impression. **~os** *mpl* belongings; (*com*) goods. **~uar** [21] *vt* carry out, effect; make (*viaje, compras etc*). **en ~o** in fact; (*por supuesto*) indeed

efervescente *a* effervescent; (*bebidas*) fizzy

efica|cia *f* effectiveness; (*de persona*) efficiency. **~z** *a* effective; (*persona*) efficient

eficien|cia *f* efficiency. **~te** *a* efficient

efigie *f* effigy

efímero *a* ephemeral

efluvio *m* outflow

efusi|ón *n* effusion. **~vo** *a* effusive; (*gracias*) warm

Egeo *m*. **mar ~** Aegean Sea

égida *f* aegis

egipcio *a & m* Egyptian

Egipto *m* Egypt

ego|céntrico *a* egocentric. **●** *m* egocentric person. **~ísmo** *m* selfishness. **~ísta** *a* selfish. **●** *m* selfish person

egregio *a* eminent

egresar *vi* (*LAm*) leave; (*univ*) graduate

eje *m* axis; (*tec*) axle

ejecu|ción *f* execution; (*mus etc*) performance. **~tante** *m & f* executor; (*mus etc*) performer. **~tar** *vt* carry out; (*mus etc*) perform; (*matar*) execute

ejecutivo *m* director, manager

ejempl|ar *a* exemplary. **●** *m* (*ejemplo*) example, specimen; (*libro*) copy; (*revista*) issue, number. **~ificar** [7] *vt* exemplify. **~o** *m* example. **dar ~o** set an example. **por ~o** for example. **sin ~** unprecedented

ejerc|er [9] *vt* exercise; practise (*profesión*); exert (*influencia*). **●** *vi* practise. **~icio** *m* exercise; (*de una profesión*) practice. **~itar** *vt* exercise. **~itarse** *vpr* exercise. **hacer ~icios** take exercise

ejército *m* army

el *art def m* (*pl* **los**) the. **●** *pron* (*pl* **los**) the one. **~ de Antonio** Antonio's. **~ que** whoever, the one

él *pron* (*persona*) he; (*persona con prep*) him; (*cosa*) it. **el libro de ~** his book

elabora|ción *f* processing; (*fabricación*) manufacture. **~r** *vt* process; manufacture (*producto*); (*producir*) produce

el|asticidad *f* elasticity. **~ástico** *a & m* elastic

elec|ción *f* choice; (*de político etc*) election. **~ciones** *fpl* (*pol*) election. **~tor** *m* voter. **~torado** *m* electorate. **~toral** *a* electoral

electrici|dad *f* electricity. **~sta** *m & f* electrician

eléctrico *a* electric; (*de la electricidad*) electrical

electrificar [7] *vt*, **electrizar** [10] *vt* electrify

electrocutar *vt* electrocute

electrodo *m* electrode

electrodoméstico *a* electrical household. **~s** *mpl* electrical household appliances

electrólisis *f* electrolysis

electrón *m* electron

electrónic|a *f* electronics. **~o** *a* electronic

elefante *m* elephant

elegan|cia *f* elegance. **~te** *a* elegant

elegía *f* elegy

elegi|ble *a* eligible. **~do** *a* chosen. **~r** [5 & 14] *vt* choose; (*por votación*) elect

element|al *a* elementary. **~o** *m* element; (*persona*) person, bloke (*fam*). **~os** *mpl* (*nociones*) basic principles

elenco *m* (*en el teatro*) cast

eleva|ción *f* elevation; (*de precios*) rise, increase; (*acción*) raising. **~dor** *m* (*LAm*) lift. **~r** *vt* raise; (*promover*) promote

elimina|ción *f* elimination. **~r** *vt* eliminate. **~toria** *f* preliminary heat

el|ipse *f* ellipse. **~íptico** *a* elliptical

élite /e'lit, e'lite/ *f* elite

elixir *m* elixir

elocución *f* elocution

elocuen|cia *f* eloquence. **~te** *a* eloquent

elogi|ar *vt* praise. **~o** *m* praise

elote *m* (*Mex*) corn on the cob

eludir *vt* avoid, elude

ella *pron* (*persona*) she; (*persona con prep*) her; (*cosa*) it. **~s** *pron pl* they; (*con prep*) them. **el libro de ~** her book. **el libro de ~s** their book

ello *pron* it

ellos *pron pl* they; (*con prep*) them. **el libro de ~** their book

emaciado *a* emaciated

emana|ción *f* emanation. **~r** *vi* emanate (**de** from); (*originarse*) originate (**de** from, in)

emancipa|ción *f* emancipation. **~do** *a* emancipated. **~r** *vt* emancipate. **~rse** *vpr* become emancipated

embadurnar *vt* smear

embajad|a *f* embassy. **~or** *m* ambassador

embalar *vt* pack

embaldosar *vt* tile

embalsamar *vt* embalm

embalse *m* dam; (*pantano*) reservoir

embaraz|ada *a* pregnant. **●** *f* pregnant woman. **~ar** [10] *vt* hinder. **~o** *m* hindrance; (*de mujer*) pregnancy. **~oso** *a* awkward, embarrassing

embar|cación *f* boat. **~cadero** *m* jetty, pier. **~car** [7] *vt* embark ⟨*personas*⟩; ship ⟨*mercancías*⟩. **~carse** *vpr* embark. **~carse en** (*fig*) embark upon

embargo *m* embargo; (*jurid*) seizure. **sin ~** however

embarque *m* loading

embarullar *vt* muddle

embaucar [7] *vt* deceive

embeber *vt* absorb; (*empapar*) soak. **●** *vi* shrink. **~se** *vpr* be absorbed

embelesar *vt* delight. **~se** *vpr* be delighted

embellecer [11] *vt* embellish

embesti|da *f* attack. **~r** [5] *vt/i* attack

emblema *m* emblem

embobar *vt* amaze

embobecer [11] *vt* make silly. **~se** *vpr* get silly

embocadura *f* (*de un río*) mouth

emboquillado *a* tipped

embolsar *vt* pocket

emborrachar *vt* get drunk. **~se** *vpr* get drunk

emborrascarse [7] *vpr* get stormy

emborronar *vt* blot

embosca|da *f* ambush. **~rse** [7] *vpr* lie in wait

embotar *vt* blunt; (*fig*) dull

embotella|miento *m* (*de vehículos*) traffic jam. **~r** *vt* bottle

embrague *m* clutch

embriag|ar [12] *vt* get drunk; (*fig*) intoxicate; (*fig, enajenar*) enrapture. **~arse** *vpr* get drunk. **~uez** *f* drunkenness; (*fig*) intoxication

embrión *m* embryo

embroll|ar *vt* mix up; involve ⟨*personas*⟩. **~arse** *vpr* get into a muddle; (*en un asunto*) get involved. **~o** *m* tangle; (*fig*) muddle. **~ón** *m* troublemaker

embromar *vt* make fun of; (*engañar*) fool

embruja|do *a* bewitched; ⟨*casa etc*⟩ haunted. **~r** *vt* bewitch

embrutecer [11] *vt* brutalize

embuchar *vt* wolf ⟨*comida*⟩

embudo *m* funnel

embuste *m* lie. **~ro** *a* deceitful. **●** *m* liar

embuti|do *m* (*culin*) sausage. **~r** *vt* stuff

emergencia *f* emergency; (*acción de emerger*) emergence. **en caso de ~** in case of emergency

emerger [14] *vi* appear, emerge; ⟨*submarino*⟩ surface

emigra|ción *f* emigration. **~nte** *m* & *f* emigrant. **~r** *vi* emigrate

eminen|cia *f* eminence. **~te** *a* eminent

emisario *m* emissary

emis|ión *f* emission; (*de dinero*) issue; (*TV etc*) broadcast. **~or** *a* issuing; (*TV etc*) broadcasting. **~ora** *f* radio station

emitir vt emit; let out ‹grito›; (TV etc) broadcast; (expresar) express; (poner en circulación) issue

emoci|ón f emotion; (excitación) excitement. ~**onado** a moved. ~**o-nante** a exciting; (conmovedor) moving. ~**onar** vt excite; (conmover) move. ~**onarse** vpr get excited; (conmoverse) be moved. **¡qué** ~**ón!** how exciting!

emotivo a emotional; (conmovedor) moving

empacar [7] vt (LAm) pack

empacho m indigestion; (vergüenza) embarrassment

empadronar vt register. ~**se** vpr register

empalagoso a sickly; (demasiado amable) ingratiating; (demasiado sentimental) mawkish

empalizada f fence

empalm|ar vt connect, join. ● vi meet. ~**e** m junction; (de trenes) connection

empanad|a f (savoury) pie. ~**illa** f (small) pie. ~**o** a fried in breadcrumbs

empanizado a (Mex) fried in breadcrumbs

empantanar vt flood. ~**se** vpr become flooded; (fig) get bogged down

empañar vt mist; dull ‹metales etc›; (fig) tarnish. ~**se** vpr ‹cristales› steam up

empapar vt soak; (absorber) soak up. ~**se** vpr be soaked

empapela|do m wallpaper. ~**r** vt paper; (envolver) wrap (in paper)

empaquetar vt package; pack together ‹personas›

emparedado m sandwich

emparejar vt match; (nivelar) make level. ~**se** vpr pair off

empast|ar vt fill ‹muela›. ~**e** m filling

empat|ar vi draw. ~**e** m draw

empedernido a inveterate; (insensible) hard

empedrar [1] vt pave

empeine m instep

empeñ|ado a in debt; (decidido) determined; (acalorado) heated. ~**ar** vt pawn; pledge ‹palabras›; (principiar) start. ~**arse** vpr (endeudarse) get into debt; (meterse) get involved; (estar decidido a) insist (**en** on). ~**o** m pledge; (resolución) determination. **casa de** ~**s** pawnshop

empeorar vt make worse. ● vi get worse. ~**se** vpr get worse

empequeñecer [11] vt dwarf; (fig) belittle

empera|dor m emperor. ~**triz** f empress

empezar [1 & 10] vt/i start, begin. **para** ~ to begin with

empina|do a upright; ‹cuesta› steep. ~**r** vt raise. ~**rse** vpr ‹persona› stand on tiptoe; ‹animal› rear

empírico a empirical

emplasto m plaster

emplaza|miento m (jurid) summons; (lugar) site. ~**r** [10] vt summon; (situar) site

emple|ado m employee. ~**ar** vt use; employ ‹persona›; spend ‹tiempo›. ~**arse** vpr be used; ‹persona› be employed. ~**o** m use; (trabajo) employment; (puesto) job

empobrecer [11] vt impoverish. ~**se** vpr become poor

empolvar vt powder

empoll|ar vt incubate ‹huevos›; (estudiar, fam) swot up (Brit), grind away at (Amer). ● vi ‹ave› sit; (estudiante) swot (Brit), grind away (Amer). ~**ón** m swot

emponzoñar vt poison

emporio m emporium; (LAm, almacén) department store

empotra|do a built-in, fitted. ~**r** vt fit

emprendedor a enterprising

emprender vt undertake; set out on ‹viaje etc›. ~**la con uno** pick a fight with s.o.

empresa f undertaking; (com) company, firm. ~**rio** m impresario; (com) contractor

empréstito m loan

empuj|ar vt push; press ‹botón›. ~**e** m push, shove; (fig) drive. ~**ón** m push, shove

empuñar vt grasp; take up ‹pluma, espada›

emular vt emulate

emulsión f emulsion

en prep in; (sobre) on; (dentro) inside, in; (con dirección) into; (medio de transporte) by. ~ **casa** at home. ~ **coche** by car. ~ **10 días** in 10 days. **de pueblo** ~ **pueblo** from town to town

enagua f petticoat

enajena|ción f alienation; (éxtasis) rapture. ~**r** vt alienate; (volver loco) drive mad; (*fig, extasiar*) enrapture. **~ción mental** insanity

enamora|do *a* in love. ● *m* lover. **~r** *vt* win the love of. **~rse** *vpr* fall in love (**de** with)

enan|ito *m* dwarf. **~o** *a & m* dwarf

enardecer [11] *vt* inflame. **~se** *vpr* get excited (**por** about)

encabeza|miento *m* heading; (*de periódico*) headline. **~r** [10] *vt* introduce ⟨*escrito*⟩; (*poner título a*) entitle; head ⟨*una lista*⟩; lead ⟨*revolución etc*⟩; (*empadronar*) register

encadenar *vt* chain; (*fig*) tie down

encaj|ar *vt* fit; fit together ⟨*varias piezas*⟩. ● *vi* fit; (*estar de acuerdo*) tally. **~arse** *vpr* squeeze into. **~e** *m* lace; (*acción de encajar*) fitting

encajonar *vt* box; (*en sitio estrecho*) squeeze in

encalar *vt* whitewash

encallar *vt* run aground; (*fig*) get bogged down

encaminar *vt* direct. **~se** *vpr* make one's way

encandilar *vt* (*pasmar*) bewilder; (*estimular*) stimulate

encanecer [11] *vi* go grey

encant|ado *a* enchanted; (*hechizado*) bewitched; ⟨*casa etc*⟩ haunted. **~ador** *a* charming. ● *m* magician. **~amiento** *m* magic. **~ar** *vt* bewitch; (*fig*) charm, delight. **~o** *m* magic; (*fig*) delight. **¡~ado!** pleased to meet you! **me ~a la leche** I love milk

encapotado *a* ⟨*cielo*⟩ overcast

encapricharse *vpr*. **~ con** take a fancy to

encarar *vt* face. **~se** *vpr*. **~se con** face

encarcelar *vt* imprison

encarecer [11] *vt* put up the price of; (*alabar*) praise. ● *vi* go up

encarg|ado *a* in charge. ● *m* manager, attendant, person in charge. **~ar** [12] *vt* entrust; (*pedir*) order. **~arse** *vpr* take charge (**de** of). **~o** *m* job; (*com*) order; (*recado*) errand. **hecho de ~o** made to measure

encariñarse *vpr*. **~ con** take to, become fond of

encarna|ción *f* incarnation. **~do** *a* incarnate; (*rojo*) red. ● *m* red

encarnizado *a* bitter

encarpetar *vt* file; (*LAm, dar carpetazo*) shelve

encarrilar *vt* put back on the rails; (*fig*) direct, put on the right road

encasillar *vt* pigeonhole

encastillarse *vpr*. **~ en** (*fig*) stick to

encauzar [10] *vt* channel

encend|edor *m* lighter. **~er** [1] *vt* light; (*pegar fuego a*) set fire to; switch on, turn on ⟨*aparato eléctrico*⟩; (*fig*) arouse. **~erse** *vpr* light; (*prender fuego*) catch fire; (*excitarse*) get excited; (*ruborizarse*) blush. **~ido** *a* lit; ⟨*aparato eléctrico*⟩ on; (*rojo*) bright red. ● *m* (*auto*) ignition

encera|do *a* waxed. ● *m* (*pizarra*) blackboard. **~r** *vt* wax

encerr|ar [1] *vt* shut in; (*con llave*) lock up; (*fig, contener*) contain. **~ona** *f* trap

encía *f* gum

encíclica *f* encyclical

enciclop|edia *f* encyclopaedia. **~édico** *a* encyclopaedic

encierro *m* confinement; (*cárcel*) prison

encima *adv* on top; (*arriba*) above. **~ de** on, on top of; (*sobre*) over; (*además de*) besides, as well as. **por ~** on top; (*a la ligera*) superficially. **por ~ de todo** above all

encina *f* holm oak

encinta *a* pregnant

enclave *m* enclave

enclenque *a* weak; (*enfermizo*) sickly

encog|er [14] *vt* shrink; (*contraer*) contract. **~erse** *vpr* shrink. **~erse de hombros** shrug one's shoulders. **~ido** *a* shrunk; (*fig, tímido*) timid

encolar *vt* glue; (*pegar*) stick

encolerizar [10] *vt* make angry. **~se** *vpr* get angry, lose one's temper

encomendar [1] *vt* entrust

encomi|ar *vt* praise. **~o** *m* praise

encono *m* bitterness, ill will

encontra|do *a* contrary, conflicting. **~r** [2] *vt* find; (*tropezar con*) meet. **~rse** *vpr* meet; (*hallarse*) be. **no ~rse** feel uncomfortable

encorvar *vt* bend, curve. **~se** *vpr* stoop

encrespado *a* ⟨*pelo*⟩ curly; ⟨*mar*⟩ rough

encrucijada *f* crossroads

encuaderna|ción *f* binding. **~dor** *m* bookbinder. **~r** *vt* bind

encuadrar *vt* frame

encub|ierto *a* hidden. **~rir** [*pp* **encubierto**] *vt* hide, conceal; shelter ⟨*delincuente*⟩

encuentro m meeting; (colisión) crash; (en deportes) match; (mil) skirmish

encuesta f survey; (investigación) inquiry

encumbra|do a eminent. ~r vt (fig, elevar) exalt. ~rse vpr rise

encurtidos mpl pickles

encharcar [7] vt flood. ~se vpr be flooded

enchuf|ado a switched on. ~ar vt plug in; fit together ‹tubos etc›. ~e m socket; (clavija) plug; (de tubos etc) joint; (fig, empleo, fam) cushy job; (influencia, fam) influence. **tener** ~e have friends in the right places

endeble a weak

endemoniado a possessed; (malo) wicked

enderezar [10] vt straighten out; (poner vertical) put upright (again); (fig, arreglar) put right, sort out; (dirigir) direct. ~se vpr straighten out

endeudarse vpr get into debt

endiablado a possessed; (malo) wicked

endomingarse [12] vpr dress up

endosar vt endorse ‹cheque etc›; (fig, fam) lumber

endrogarse [12] vpr (Mex) get into debt

endulzar [10] vt sweeten; (fig) soften

endurecer [11] vt harden. ~se vpr harden; (fig) become hardened

enema m enema

enemi|go a hostile. ● m enemy. ~stad f enmity. ~star vt make an enemy of. ~starse vpr fall out (con with)

en|ergía f energy. ~érgico a ‹persona› lively; ‹decisión› forceful

energúmeno m madman

enero m January

enervar vt enervate

enésimo a nth, umpteenth (fam)

enfad|adizo a irritable. ~ado a cross, angry. ~ar vt make cross, anger; (molestar) annoy. ~arse vpr get cross. ~o m anger; (molestia) annoyance

énfasis m invar emphasis, stress. **poner** ~ stress, emphasize

enfático a emphatic

enferm|ar vi fall ill. ~edad f illness. ~era f nurse. ~ería f sick bay. ~ero m (male) nurse. ~izo a sickly. ~o a ill. ● m patient

enflaquecer [11] vt make thin. ● vi lose weight

enfo|car [7] vt shine on; focus ‹lente etc›; (fig) consider. ~que m focus; (fig) point of view

enfrascarse [7] vpr (fig) be absorbed

enfrentar vt face, confront; (poner frente a frente) bring face to face. ~se vpr. ~se con confront; (en deportes) meet

enfrente adv opposite. ~ **de** opposite. **de** ~ opposite

enfria|miento m cooling; (catarro) cold. ~r [20] vt cool (down); (fig) cool down. ~rse vpr go cold; (fig) cool off

enfurecer [11] vt infuriate. ~se vpr lose one's temper; ‹mar› get rough

enfurruñarse vpr sulk

engalanar vt adorn. ~se vpr dress up

enganchar vt hook; hang up ‹ropa›. ~se vpr (mil) enlist

engañ|ar vt deceive, trick; (ser infiel) be unfaithful. ~arse vpr be wrong, be mistaken; (no admitir la verdad) deceive o.s. ~o m deceit, trickery; (error) mistake. ~oso a deceptive; ‹persona› deceitful

engarzar [10] vt string ‹cuentas›; set ‹joyas›; (fig) link

engatusar vt (fam) coax

engendr|ar vt breed; (fig) produce. ~o m (monstruo) monster; (fig) brainchild

englobar vt include

engomar vt glue

engordar vt fatten. ● vi get fatter, put on weight

engorro m nuisance

engranaje m (auto) gear

engrandecer [11] vt (enaltecer) exalt, raise

engrasar vt grease; (con aceite) oil; (ensuciar) make greasy

engreído a arrogant

engrosar [2] vt swell. ● vi ‹persona› get fatter; ‹río› swell

engullir [22] vt gulp down

enharinar vt sprinkle with flour

enhebrar vt thread

enhorabuena f congratulations. **dar la** ~ congratulate

enigm|a m enigma. ~ático a enigmatic

enjabonar vt soap; (fig, fam) butter up

enjalbegar [12] vt whitewash

enjambre m swarm

enjaular *vt* put in a cage

enjuag|ar [12] *vt* rinse (out). **~a-torio** *m* mouthwash. **~ue** *m* rinsing; *(para la boca)* mouthwash

enjugar [12] *vt* dry; *(limpiar)* wipe; cancel *‹deuda›*

enjuiciar *vt* pass judgement on

enjuto *a* *‹persona›* skinny

enlace *m* connection; *(matrimonial)* wedding

enlatar *vt* tin, can

enlazar [10] *vt* tie together; *(fig)* relate, connect

enlodar *vt*, **enlodazar** [10] *vt* cover in mud

enloquecer [11] *vt* drive mad. ● *vi* go mad. **~se** *vpr* go mad

enlosar *vt* *(con losas)* pave; *(con baldosas)* tile

enlucir [11] *vt* plaster

enluta|do *a* in mourning. **~r** *vt* dress in mourning; *(fig)* sadden

enmarañar *vt* tangle (up), entangle; *(confundir)* confuse. **~se** *vpr* get into a tangle; *(confundirse)* get confused

enmarcar [7] *vt* frame

enmascarar *vt* mask. **~se de** masquerade as

enm|endar *vt* correct. **~endarse** *vpr* mend one's way. **~ienda** *f* correction; *(de ley etc)* amendment

enmohecerse [11] *vpr* *(con óxido)* go rusty; *(con hongos)* go mouldy

enmudecer [11] *vi* be dumbstruck; *(callar)* say nothing

ennegrecer [11] *vt* blacken

ennoblecer [11] *vt* ennoble; *(fig)* add style to

enoj|adizo *a* irritable. **~ado** *a* angry, cross. **~ar** *vt* make cross, anger; *(molestar)* annoy. **~arse** *vpr* get cross. **~o** *m* anger; *(molestia)* annoyance. **~oso** *a* annoying

enorgullecerse [11] *vpr* be proud

enorm|e *a* enormous; *(malo)* wicked. **~emente** *adv* enormously. **~idad** *f* immensity; *(atrocidad)* enormity. **me gusta una ~idad** I like it enormously

enrabiar *vt* infuriate

enraizar [10 & 20] *vi* take root

enrarecido *a* rarefied

enrasar *vt* make level

enred|adera *f* creeper. **~adero** *a* climbing. **~ar** *vt* tangle (up), entangle; *(confundir)* confuse; *(comprometer a uno)* involve, implicate; *(sembrar la discordia)* cause trouble between. ● *vi* get up to mischief. **~ar con** fiddle with, play with. **~arse** *vpr* get into a tangle; *(confundirse)* get confused; *‹persona›* get involved. **~o** *m* tangle; *(fig)* muddle, mess

enrejado *m* bars

enrevesado *a* complicated

enriquecer [11] *vt* make rich; *(fig)* enrich. **~se** *vpr* get rich

enrojecer [11] *vt* turn red, redden. **~se** *vpr* *‹persona›* go red, blush

enrolar *vt* enlist

enrollar *vt* roll (up); wind *‹hilo etc›*

enroscar [7] *vt* coil; *(atornillar)* screw in

ensalad|a *f* salad. **~era** *f* salad bowl. **~illa** *f* Russian salad. **armar una ~a** make a mess

ensalzar [10] *vt* praise; *(enaltecer)* exalt

ensambladura *f*, **ensamblaje** *m* *(acción)* assembling; *(efecto)* joint

ensamblar *vt* join

ensanch|ar *vt* widen; *(agrandar)* enlarge. **~arse** *vpr* get wider. **~e** *m* widening; *(de ciudad)* new district

ensangrentar [1] *vt* stain with blood

ensañarse *vpr*. **~ con** treat cruelly

ensartar *vt* string *‹cuentas etc›*

ensay|ar *vt* test; rehearse *‹obra de teatro etc›*. **~arse** *vpr* rehearse. **~o** *m* test, trial; *(composición literaria)* essay

ensenada *f* inlet, cove

enseña|nza *f* education; *(acción de enseñar)* teaching. **~nza media** secondary education. **~r** *vt* teach; *(mostrar)* show

enseñorearse *vpr* take over

enseres *mpl* equipment

ensillar *vt* saddle

ensimismarse *vpr* be lost in thought

ensoberbecerse [11] *vpr* become conceited

ensombrecer [11] *vt* darken

ensordecer [11] *vt* deafen. ● *vi* go deaf

ensortijar *vt* curl *‹pelo etc›*

ensuciar *vt* dirty. **~se** *vpr* get dirty

ensueño *m* dream

entablar *vt* *(empezar)* start

entablillar *vt* put in a splint

entalegar [12] *vt* put into a bag; *(fig)* hoard

entallar *vt* fit *‹un vestido›*. ● *vi* fit

entarimado *m* parquet

ente *m* entity, being; *(persona rara, fam)* odd person; *(com)* firm, company

entend|er [1] vt understand; (opinar) believe, think; (querer decir) mean. ● vi understand. **~erse** vpr make o.s. understood; (comprenderse) be understood. **~er de** know all about. **~erse con** get on with. **~ido** a understood; (enterado) well-informed. ● interj agreed!, OK! (fam). **~imiento** m understanding. **a mi ~er** in my opinion. **dar a ~er** hint. **no darse por ~ido** pretend not to understand, turn a deaf ear

entenebrecer [11] vt darken. **~se** vpr get dark

enterado a well-informed; (que sabe) aware. **no darse por ~** pretend not to understand, turn a deaf ear

enteramente adv entirely, completely

enterar vt inform. **~se** vpr. **~se de** find out about, hear of. **¡entérate!** listen! **¿te enteras?** do you understand?

entereza f (carácter) strength of character

enternecer [11] vt (fig) move, touch. **~se** vpr be moved, be touched

entero a entire, whole; (firme) firm. **por ~** entirely, completely

enterra|dor m gravedigger. **~r** [1] vt bury

entibiar vt cool. **~se** vpr cool down; (fig) cool off

entidad f entity; (organización) organization; (com) company

entierro m burial; (ceremonia) funeral

entona|ción f intonation; (fig) arrogance. **~r** vt intone. ● vi (mus) be in tune; (colores) match. **~rse** vpr (fortalecerse) tone o.s. up; (engreírse) be arrogant

entonces adv then. **en aquel ~, por aquel ~** at that time, then

entontecer [11] vt make silly. **~se** vpr get silly

entornar vt half close; leave ajar (puerta)

entorpecer [11] vt (frío etc) numb; (dificultar) hinder

entra|da f entrance; (acceso) admission, entry; (billete) ticket; (de datos, tec) input. **~do** a. **~do en años** elderly. **ya ~da la noche** late at night. **~nte** a next, coming. **dar ~da a** (admitir) admit. **de ~da** right away.

entraña f (fig) heart. **~s** fpl entrails; (fig) heart. **~ble** a (cariño etc) deep; (amigo) close. **~r** vt involve

entrar vt put; (traer) bring. ● vi go in, enter; (venir) come in, enter; (empezar) start, begin. **no ~ ni salir en** have nothing to do with

entre prep (de dos personas o cosas) between; (más de dos) among(st)

entreab|ierto a half-open. **~rir** [pp entreabierto] vt half open

entreacto m interval

entrecano a (pelo) greying; (persona) who is going grey

entrecejo m forehead. **arrugar el ~, fruncir el ~** to frown

entrecerrar [1] vt (Amer) half close

entrecortado a (voz) faltering; (respiración) laboured

entrecruzar [10] vt intertwine

entrega f handing over; (de mercancías etc) delivery; (de novela etc) instalment; (dedicación) commitment. **~r** [12] vt hand over, deliver, give. **~rse** vpr surrender, give o.s. up; (dedicarse) devote o.s. (a to)

entrelazar [10] vt intertwine

entremés m hors-d'oeuvre; (en el teatro) short comedy

entremet|er vt insert. **~erse** vpr interfere. **~ido** a interfering

entremezclar vt mix

entrena|dor m trainer. **~miento** m training. **~r** vt train. **~rse** vpr train

entrepierna f crotch

entresacar [7] vt pick out

entresuelo m mezzanine

entretanto adv meanwhile

entretejer vt interweave

entreten|er [40] vt entertain, amuse; (detener) delay, keep; (mantener) keep alive, keep going. **~erse** vpr amuse o.s.; (tardar) delay, linger. **~ido** a entertaining. **~imiento** m entertainment; (mantenimiento) upkeep

entrever [43] vt make out, glimpse

entrevista f interview; (reunión) meeting. **~rse** vpr have an interview

entristecer [11] vt sadden, make sad. **~se** vpr be sad

entromet|erse vpr interfere. **~ido** a interfering

entroncar [7] vi be related

entruchada f, **entruchado** m (fam) plot

entumec|erse [11] vpr go numb. **~ido** a numb

enturbiar *vt* cloud

entusi|asmar *vt* fill with enthusiasm; (*gustar mucho*) delight. **~asmarse** *vpr.* **~asmarse con** get enthusiastic about; (*ser aficionado a*) be mad about, love. **~asmo** *m* enthusiasm. **~asta** *a* enthusiastic. ● *m* & *f* enthusiast. **~ástico** *a* enthusiastic

enumera|ción *f* count, reckoning. **~r** *vt* enumerate

enuncia|ción *f* enunciation. **~r** *vt* enunciate

envainar *vt* sheathe

envalentonar *vt* encourage. **~se** *vpr* be brave, pluck up courage

envanecer [11] *vt* make conceited. **~se** *vpr* be conceited

envas|ado *a* tinned. ● *m* packaging. **~ar** *vt* package; (*en latas*) tin, can; (*en botellas*) bottle. **~e** *m* packing; (*lata*) tin, can; (*botella*) bottle

envejec|er [11] *vt* make old. ● *vi* get old, grow old. **~erse** *vpr* get old, grow old. **~ido** *a* aged, old

envenenar *vt* poison

envergadura *f* (*alcance*) scope

envés *m* wrong side

envia|do *a* sent. ● *m* representative; (*de la prensa*) correspondent. **~r** *vt* send

enviciar *vt* corrupt

envidi|a *f* envy; (*celos*) jealousy. **~able** *a* enviable. **~ar** *vt* envy, be envious of. **~oso** *a* envious. **tener ~a a** envy

envilecer [11] *vt* degrade

envío *m* sending, dispatch; (*de mercancías*) consignment; (*de dinero*) remittance. **~ contra reembolso** cash on delivery. **gastos** *mpl* **de ~** postage and packing (costs)

enviudar *vi* ⟨*mujer*⟩ become a widow, be widowed; ⟨*hombre*⟩ become a widower, be widowed

env|oltura *f* wrapping. **~olver** [2, *pp* **envuelto**] *vt* wrap; (*cubrir*) cover; (*fig, acorralar*) corner; (*fig, enredar*) involve; (*mil*) surround. **~olvimiento** *m* involvement. **~uelto** *a* wrapped (up)

enyesar *vt* plaster; (*med*) put in plaster

enzima *f* enzyme

épica *f* epic

epicentro *m* epicentre

épico *a* epic

epid|emia *f* epidemic. **~émico** *a* epidemic

epil|epsia *f* epilepsy. **~éptico** *a* epileptic

epílogo *m* epilogue

episodio *m* episode

epístola *f* epistle

epitafio *m* epitaph

epíteto *m* epithet

epítome *m* epitome

época *f* age; (*período*) period. **hacer ~** make history, be epoch-making

equidad *f* equity

equilátero *a* equilateral

equilibr|ar *vt* balance. **~io** *m* balance; (*de balanza*) equilibrium. **~ista** *m* & *f* tightrope walker

equino *a* horse, equine

equinoccio *m* equinox

equipaje *m* luggage (*esp Brit*), baggage (*esp Amer*); (*de barco*) crew

equipar *vt* equip; (*de ropa*) fit out

equiparar *vt* make equal; (*comparar*) compare

equipo *m* equipment; (*en deportes*) team

equitación *f* riding

equivale|ncia *f* equivalence. **~nte** *a* equivalent. **~r** [42] *vi* be equivalent; (*significar*) mean

equivoca|ción *f* mistake, error. **~do** *a* wrong. **~r** [7] *vt* mistake. **~rse** *vpr* be mistaken, be wrong, make a mistake. **~rse de** be wrong about. **~rse de número** dial the wrong number. **si no me equivoco** if I'm not mistaken

equívoco *a* equivocal; (*sospechoso*) suspicious. ● *m* ambiguity; (*juego de palabras*) pun; (*doble sentido*) double meaning

era *f* era. ● *vb véase* **ser**

erario *m* treasury

erección *f* erection; (*fig*) establishment

eremita *m* hermit

eres *vb véase* **ser**

erguir [48] *vt* raise. **~ la cabeza** hold one's head high. **~se** *vpr* straighten up

erigir [14] *vt* erect. **~se** *vpr* set o.s. up (**en** as)

eriza|do *a* prickly. **~rse** [10] *vpr* stand on end

erizo *m* hedgehog; (*de mar*) sea urchin. **~ de mar, ~ marino** sea urchin

ermita *f* hermitage. **~ño** *m* hermit

erosi|ón *f* erosion. **~onar** *vt* erode

er|ótico *a* erotic. **~otismo** *m* eroticism

errar [1, la **i** inicial se escribe **y**] *vt* miss. ● *vi* wander; (*equivocarse*) make a mistake, be wrong

errata *f* misprint

erróneo *a* erroneous, wrong

error *m* error, mistake. **estar en un ~** be wrong, be mistaken

eructar *vi* belch

erudi|ción *f* learning, erudition. **~to** *a* learned

erupción *f* eruption; (*med*) rash

es *vb véase* **ser**

esa *a véase* **ese**

ésa *pron véase* **ése**

esbelto *a* slender, slim

esboz|ar [10] *vt* sketch, outline. **~o** *m* sketch, outline

escabeche *m* pickle. **en ~** pickled

escabroso *a* ⟨*terreno*⟩ rough; ⟨*asunto*⟩ difficult; (*atrevido*) crude

escabullirse [22] *vpr* slip away

escafandra *f*, **escafandro** *m* diving-suit

escala *f* scale; (*escalera de mano*) ladder; (*de avión*) stopover. **~da** *f* climbing; (*pol*) escalation. **~r** *vt* scale; break into ⟨*una casa*⟩. ● *vi* (*pol*) escalate. **hacer ~ en** stop at. **vuelo sin ~s** non-stop flight

escaldar *vt* scald

escalera *f* staircase, stairs; (*de mano*) ladder. **~ de caracol** spiral staircase. **~ de incendios** fire escape. **~ mecánica** escalator. **~ plegable** step-ladder

escalfa|do *a* poached. **~r** *vt* poach

escalinata *f* flight of steps

escalofrío *m* shiver

escal|ón *m* step; (*de escalera interior*) stair; (*de escala*) rung. **~onar** *vt* spread out

escalope *m* escalope

escam|a *f* scale; (*de jabón*) flake; (*fig*) suspicion. **~oso** *a* scaly

escamotear *vt* make disappear; (*robar*) steal, pinch (*fam*); disregard ⟨*dificultad*⟩

escampar *vi* stop raining

esc|andalizar [10] *vt* scandalize, shock. **~andalizarse** *vpr* be shocked. **~ándalo** *m* scandal; (*alboroto*) uproar. **~andaloso** *a* scandalous; (*alborotador*) noisy

Escandinavia *f* Scandinavia

escandinavo *a & m* Scandinavian

escaño *m* bench; (*pol*) seat

escapa|da *f* escape; (*visita*) flying visit. **~do** *a* in a hurry. **~r** *vi* escape. **~rse** *vpr* escape; ⟨*líquido, gas*⟩ leak. **dejar ~r** let out

escaparate *m* (shop) window. **ir de ~s** go window-shopping

escapatoria *f* (*fig, fam*) way out

escape *m* (*de gas, de líquido*) leak; (*fuga*) escape; (*auto*) exhaust

escarabajo *m* beetle

escaramuza *f* skirmish

escarbar *vt* scratch; pick ⟨*dientes, herida etc*⟩; (*fig, escudriñar*) delve (**en** into)

escarcha *f* frost. **~do** *a* ⟨*fruta*⟩ crystallized

escarlat|a *a invar* scarlet. **~ina** *f* scarlet fever

escarm|entar [1] *vt* punish severely. ● *vi* learn one's lesson. **~iento** *m* punishment; (*lección*) lesson

escarn|ecer [11] *vt* mock. **~io** *m* ridicule

escarola *f* endive

escarpa *f* slope. **~do** *a* steep

escas|ear *vi* be scarce. **~ez** *f* scarcity, shortage; (*pobreza*) poverty. **~o** *a* scarce; (*poco*) little; (*insuficiente*) short; (*muy justo*) barely

escatimar *vt* be sparing with

escayola *f* plaster. **~r** *vt* put in plaster

escena *f* scene; (*escenario*) stage. **~rio** *m* stage; (*en el cine*) scenario; (*fig*) scene

escénico *a* scenic

escenografía *f* scenery

esc|epticismo *m* scepticism. **~éptico** *a* sceptical. ● *m* sceptic

esclarecer [11] *vt* (*fig*) throw light on, clarify

esclavina *f* cape

esclav|itud *f* slavery. **~izar** [10] *vt* enslave. **~o** *m* slave

esclerosis *f* sclerosis

esclusa *f* lock

escoba *f* broom

escocer [2 & 9] *vt* hurt. ● *vi* sting

escocés *a* Scottish. ● *m* Scotsman

Escocia *f* Scotland

escog|er [14] *vt* choose, select. **~ido** *a* chosen; (*de buena calidad*) choice

escolar *a* school. ● *m* schoolboy. ● *f* schoolgirl. **~idad** *f* schooling

escolta *f* escort

escombros *mpl* rubble

escond|er vt hide. **~erse** vpr hide. **~idas. a ~idas** secretly. **~ite** m hiding place; (juego) hide-and-seek. **~rijo** m hiding place

escopeta f shotgun. **~zo** m shot

escoplo m chisel

escoria f slag; (fig) dregs

Escorpión m Scorpio

escorpión m scorpion

escot|ado a low-cut. **~adura** f low neckline. **~ar** vt cut out. ● vi pay one's share. **~e** m low neckline. **ir a ~e, pagar a ~e** share the expenses

escozor m pain

escri|bano m clerk. **~biente** m clerk. **~bir** [pp **escrito**] vt/i write. **~bir a máquina** type. **~birse** vpr write to each other; (deletrearse) be spelt. **~to** a written. ● m writing; (documento) document. **~tor** m writer. **~torio** m desk; (oficina) office. **~tura** f (hand)writing; (documento) document; (jurid) deed. **¿cómo se escribe...?** how do you spell...? **poner por ~to** put into writing

escr|úpulo m scruple; (escrupulosidad) care, scrupulousness. **~upuloso** a scrupulous

escrut|ar vt scrutinize; count (votos). **~inio** m count. **hacer el ~inio** count the votes

escuadr|a f (instrumento) square; (mil) squad; (naut) fleet. **~ón** m squadron

escuálido a skinny; (sucio) squalid

escuchar vt listen to. ● vi listen

escudilla f bowl

escudo m shield. **~ de armas** coat of arms

escudriñar vt examine

escuela f school. **~ normal** teachers' training college

escueto a simple

escuincle m (Mex, perro) stray dog; (Mex, muchacho, fam) child, kid (fam)

escul|pir vt sculpture. **~tor** m sculptor. **~tora** f sculptress. **~tura** f sculpture; (en madera) carving

escupir vt/i spit

escurr|eplatos m invar plate-rack. **~idizo** a slippery. **~ir** vt drain; wring out (ropa). ● vi drip; (ser resbaladizo) be slippery. **~irse** vpr slip

ese a (f **esa**, mpl **esos**, fpl **esas**) that; (en plural) those

ése pron (f **ésa**, mpl **ésos**, fpl **ésas**) that one; (en plural) those; (primero de dos) the former. **ni por ésas** on no account

esencia f essence. **~l** a essential. **lo ~l** the main thing

esf|era f sphere; (de reloj) face. **~érico** a spherical

esfinge f sphinx

esf|orzarse [2 & 10] vpr make an effort. **~uerzo** m effort

esfumarse vpr fade away; (persona) vanish

esgrim|a f fencing. **~ir** vt brandish; (fig) use

esguince m swerve; (med) sprain

eslab|ón m link. **~onar** vt link (together)

eslavo a Slav, Slavonic

eslogan m slogan

esmalt|ar vt enamel; varnish (uñas); (fig) adorn. **~e** m enamel. **~e de uñas, ~e para las uñas** nail varnish (Brit), nail polish (Amer)

esmerado a careful

esmeralda f emerald

esmerarse vpr take care (en over)

esmeril m emery

esmero m care

esmoquin m dinner jacket, tuxedo (Amer)

esnob a invar snobbish. ● m & f (pl **esnobs**) snob. **~ismo** m snobbery

esnórkel m snorkel

eso pron that. **¡~ es!** that's it! **~ mismo** exactly. **¡~ no!** certainly not! **¡~ sí!** of course. **a ~ de** about. **en ~** at that moment. **¿no es ~?** isn't that right? **por ~** therefore. **y ~ que** although

esos a pl véase **ese**

ésos pron pl véase **ése**

espabila|do a bright. **~r** vt snuff (vela); (avivar) brighten up; (despertar) wake up. **~rse** vpr wake up; (apresurarse) hurry up

espaci|al a space. **~ar** vt space out. **~o** m space. **~oso** a spacious

espada f sword. **~s** fpl (en naipes) spades

espagueti m spaghetti

espald|a f back. **~illa** f shoulder-blade. **a ~a de uno** behind s.o.'s back. **a las ~as** on one's back. **tener las ~as anchas** be broad-shouldered. **volver la ~a a uno**, **volver las ~a a uno** give s.o. the cold shoulder

espant|ada f stampede. **∼adizo** a timid, timorous. **∼ajo** m, **∼apájaros** m invar scarecrow. **∼ar** vt frighten; (ahuyentar) frighten away. **∼arse** vpr be frightened; (ahuyentarse) be frightened away. **∼o** m terror; (horror) horror. **∼oso** a frightening; (muy grande) terrible. **¡qué ∼ajo!** what a sight!

España f Spain

español a Spanish. ● m (persona) Spaniard; (lengua) Spanish. **los ∼es** the Spanish. **∼izado** a Hispanicized

esparadrapo m sticking-plaster, plaster (Brit)

esparci|do a scattered; (fig) widespread. **∼r** [9] vt scatter; (difundir) spread. **∼rse** vpr be scattered; (difundirse) spread; (divertirse) enjoy o.s.

espárrago m asparagus

esparto m esparto (grass)

espasm|o m spasm. **∼ódico** a spasmodic

espátula f spatula; (en pintura) palette knife

especia f spice

especial a special. **∼idad** f speciality (Brit), specialty (Amer). **∼ista** a & m & f specialist. **∼ización** f specialization. **∼izar** [10] vt specialize. **∼izarse** vpr specialize. **∼mente** adv especially. **en ∼** especially

especie f kind, sort; (en biología) species; (noticia) piece of news. **en ∼** in kind

especifica|ción f specification. **∼r** [7] vt specify

específico a specific

espect|áculo m sight; (diversión) entertainment, show. **∼ador** m & f spectator. **∼acular** a spectacular

espectro m spectre; (en física) spectrum

especula|ción f speculation. **∼dor** m speculator. **∼r** vi speculate. **∼tivo** a speculative

espej|ismo m mirage. **∼o** m mirror. **∼o retrovisor** (auto) rear-view mirror

espeleólogo m potholer

espeluznante a horrifying

espera f wait. **sala** f **de ∼** waiting room

espera|nza f hope. **∼r** vt hope; (aguardar) wait for; (creer) expect. ● vi hope; (aguardar) wait. **∼r en uno** trust in s.o. **en ∼ de** awaiting. **espero**

que no I hope not. **espero que sí** I hope so

esperma f sperm

esperpento m fright; (disparate) nonsense

espes|ar vt thicken. **∼arse** vpr thicken. **∼o** a thick; (pasta etc) stiff. **∼or** m, **∼ura** f thickness; (bot) thicket

espetón m spit

esp|ía f spy. **∼iar** [20] vt spy on. ● vi spy

espiga f (de trigo etc) ear

espina f thorn; (de pez) bone; (dorsal) spine; (astilla) splinter; (fig, dificultad) difficulty. **∼ dorsal** spine

espinaca f spinach

espinazo m spine

espinilla f shin; (med) blackhead

espino m hawthorn. **∼ artificial** barbed wire. **∼so** a thorny; (pez) bony; (fig) difficult

espionaje m espionage

espiral a & f spiral

espirar vt/i breathe out

esp|iritismo m spiritualism. **∼iritoso** a spirited. **∼iritista** m & f spiritualist. **∼íritu** m spirit; (mente) mind; (inteligencia) intelligence. **∼iritual** a spiritual. **∼iritualismo** m spiritualism

espita f tap, faucet (Amer)

espl|éndido a splendid; (persona) generous. **∼endor** m splendour

espliego m lavender

espolear vt (fig) spur on

espoleta f fuse

espolvorear vt sprinkle

esponj|a f sponge; (tejido) towelling. **∼oso** a spongy. **pasar la ∼a** forget about it

espont|aneidad f spontaneity. **∼áneo** a spontaneous

esporádico a sporadic

espos|a f wife. **∼as** fpl handcuffs. **∼ar** vt handcuff. **∼o** m husband. **los ∼os** the couple

espuela f spur; (fig) incentive. **dar de ∼s** spur on

espum|a f foam; (en bebidas) froth; (de jabón) lather. **∼ar** vt skim. ● vi foam; (bebidas) froth; (jabón) lather. **∼oso** a (vino) sparkling. **echar ∼a** foam, froth

esqueleto m skeleton

esquem|a m outline. **∼ático** a sketchy

esqu|í *m* (*pl* **esquís**) ski; (*el deporte*) skiing. **∼iador** *m* skier. **∼iar** [20] *vi* ski

esquilar *vt* shear

esquimal *a & m* Eskimo

esquina *f* corner

esquirol *m* blackleg

esquiv|ar *vt* avoid. **∼o** *a* aloof

esquizofrénico *a & m* schizophrenic

esta *a véase* **este**

ésta *pron véase* **éste**

estab|ilidad *f* stability. **∼ilizador** *m* stabilizer. **∼ilizar** [10] *vt* stabilize. **∼le** *a* stable

establec|er [11] *vt* establish. **∼erse** *vpr* settle; (*com*) start a business. **∼i-miento** *m* establishment

establo *m* cowshed

estaca *f* stake; (*para apalear*) stick. **∼da** *f* (*cerca*) fence

estación *f* station; (*del año*) season; (*de vacaciones*) resort. **∼ de servicio** service station

estaciona|miento *m* parking. **∼r** *vt* station; (*auto*) park. **∼rio** *a* stationary

estadio *m* stadium; (*fase*) stage

estadista *m* statesman. ● *f* stateswoman

estadístic|a *f* statistics. **∼o** *a* statistical

estado *m* state. **∼ civil** marital status. **∼ de ánimo** frame of mind. **∼ de cuenta** bank statement. **∼ mayor** (*mil*) staff. **en buen ∼** in good condition. **en ∼ (interesante)** pregnant

Estados Unidos *mpl* United States

estadounidense *a* American, United States. ● *m & f* American

estafa *f* swindle. **∼r** *vt* swindle

estafeta *f* (*oficina de correos*) (sub-) post office

estala|ctita *f* stalactite. **∼gmita** *f* stalagmite

estall|ar *vi* explode; ⟨olas⟩ break; ⟨guerra, epidemia etc⟩ break out; (*fig*) burst. **∼ar en llanto** burst into tears. **∼ar de risa** burst out laughing. **∼ido** *m* explosion; (*de guerra, epidemia etc*) outbreak; (*de risa etc*) outburst

estamp|a *f* print; (*aspecto*) appearance. **∼ado** *a* printed. ● *m* printing; (*tela*) cotton print. **∼ar** *vt* stamp; (*imprimir*) print. **dar a la ∼a** (*imprimir*) print; (*publicar*) publish. **la viva ∼a** the image

estampía. de ∼ía suddenly

estampido *m* explosion

estampilla *f* stamp; (*Mex*) (postage) stamp

estanca|do *a* stagnant. **∼miento** *m* stagnation. **∼r** [7] *vt* stem; (*com*) turn into a monopoly

estanci|a *f* stay; (*Arg, finca*) ranch, farm; (*cuarto*) room. **∼ero** *m* (*Arg*) farmer

estanco *a* watertight. ● *m* tobacconist's (shop)

estandarte *m* standard, banner

estanque *m* lake; (*depósito de agua*) reservoir

estanquero *m* tobacconist

estante *m* shelf. **∼ría** *f* shelves; (*para libros*) bookcase

estañ|o *m* tin. **∼adura** *f* tin-plating

estar [27] *vi* be; (*quedarse*) stay; (*estar en casa*) be in. **¿estamos?** alright? **estamos a 29 de noviembre** it's the 29th of November. **∼ para** be about to. **∼ por** remain to be; (*con ganas de*) be tempted to; (*ser partidario de*) be in favour of. **∼se** *vpr* stay. **¿cómo está Vd?, ¿cómo estás?** how are you?

estarcir [9] *vt* stencil

estatal *a* state

estático *a* static; (*pasmado*) dumbfounded

estatua *f* statue

estatura *f* height

estatut|ario *a* statutory. **∼o** *m* statute

este *m* east; (*viento*) east wind. ● *a* (*f* **esta**, *mpl* **estos**, *fpl* **estas**) this; (*en plural*) these. ● *int* (*LAm*) well, er

éste *pron* (*f* **ésta**, *mpl* **éstos**, *fpl* **éstas**) this one, (*en plural*) these; (*segundo de dos*) the latter

estela *f* wake; (*arquit*) carved stone

estera *f* mat; (*tejido*) matting

est|éreo *a* stereo. **∼ereofónico** *a* stereo, stereophonic

esterilla *f* mat

estereotip|ado *a* stereotyped. **∼o** *m* stereotype

est|éril *a* sterile; ⟨mujer⟩ infertile; ⟨terreno⟩ barren. **∼erilidad** *f* sterility; (*de mujer*) infertility; (*de terreno*) barrenness

esterlina *a* sterling. **libra** *f* **∼** pound sterling

estético *a* aesthetic

estevado *a* bow-legged

estiércol *m* dung; (*abono*) manure

estigma m stigma. ∼s mpl (relig) stigmata

estilarse vpr be used

estil|ista m & f stylist. ∼izar [10] vt stylize. ∼o m style. **por el** ∼o of that sort

estilográfica f fountain pen

estima f esteem. ∼do a esteemed. ∼do señor (en cartas) Dear Sir. ∼r vt esteem; have great respect for ⟨persona⟩; (valorar) value; (juzgar) think

est|imulante a stimulating. ● m stimulant. ∼imular vt stimulate; (incitar) incite. ∼ímulo m stimulus

estipular vt stipulate

estir|ado a stretched; ⟨persona⟩ haughty. ∼ar vt stretch; (fig) stretch out. ∼ón m pull, tug; (crecimiento) sudden growth

estirpe m stock

estival a summer

esto pron neutro this; (este asunto) this business. **en** ∼ at this point. **en** ∼ **de** in this business of. **por** ∼ therefore

estofa f class. **de baja** ∼ ⟨gente⟩ low-class

estofa|do a stewed. ● m stew. ∼r vt stew

estoic|ismo m stoicism. ∼o a stoical. ● m stoic

estómago m stomach. **dolor** m **de** ∼ stomach-ache

estorb|ar vt hinder, obstruct; (molestar) bother, annoy. ● vi be in the way. ∼o m hindrance; (molestia) nuisance

estornino m starling

estornud|ar vi sneeze. ∼o m sneeze

estos a mpl véase **este**

éstos pron mpl véase **éste**

estoy vb véase **estar**

estrabismo m squint

estrado m stage; (mus) bandstand

estrafalario a outlandish

estrag|ar [12] vt devastate. ∼o m devastation. **hacer** ∼os devastate

estragón m tarragon

estrambótico a outlandish

estrangula|ción f strangulation. ∼dor m strangler; (auto) choke. ∼miento m blockage; (auto) bottleneck. ∼r vt strangle

estraperlo m black market. **comprar algo de** ∼ buy sth on the black market

estratagema f stratagem

estrateg|a m & f strategist. ∼ia f strategy

estratégic|amente adv strategically. ∼o a strategic

estrato m stratum

estratosfera f stratosphere

estrech|ar vt make narrower; take in ⟨vestido⟩; (apretar) squeeze; hug ⟨persona⟩. ∼ar la mano a uno shake hands with s.o. ∼arse vpr become narrower; (apretarse) squeeze up. ∼ez f narrowness; (apuro) tight spot; (falta de dinero) want. ∼o a narrow; ⟨vestido etc⟩ tight; (fig, íntimo) close. ● m straits. ∼o de miras, de miras ∼as narrow-minded

estregar [1 & 12] vt rub

estrella f star. ∼ de mar, ∼mar m starfish

estrellar vt smash; fry ⟨huevos⟩. ∼se vpr smash; (fracasar) fail. ∼se contra crash into

estremec|er [11] vt shake. ∼erse vpr tremble (de with). ∼imiento m shaking

estren|ar vt use for the first time; wear for the first time ⟨vestido etc⟩; show for the first time ⟨película⟩. ∼arse vpr make one's début; ⟨película⟩ have its première; ⟨obra de teatro⟩ open. ∼o m first use; (de película) première; (de obra de teatro) first night

estreñi|do a constipated. ∼miento m constipation

estr|épito m din. ∼epitoso a noisy; (fig) resounding

estreptomicina f streptomycin

estrés m stress

estría f groove

estribar vt rest (en on); (consistir) lie (en in)

estribillo m refrain; (muletilla) catchphrase

estribo m stirrup; (de vehículo) step; (contrafuerte) buttress. **perder los** ∼s lose one's temper

estribor m starboard

estricto a strict

estridente a strident, raucous

estrofa f strophe

estropajo m scourer. ∼so a ⟨carne etc⟩ tough; ⟨persona⟩ slovenly

estropear vt spoil; (romper) break. ∼se vpr be damaged; ⟨fruta etc⟩ go bad; (fracasar) fail

estructura f structure. ∼l a structural

estruendo *m* din; (*de mucha gente*) uproar. **~so** *a* deafening

estrujar *vt* squeeze; (*fig*) drain

estuario *m* estuary

estuco *m* stucco

estuche *m* case

estudi|ante *m & f* student. **~antil** *a* student. **~ar** *vt* study. **~o** *m* study; (*de artista*) studio. **~oso** *a* studious

estufa *f* heater; (*LAm*) cooker

estupefac|ción *f* astonishment. **~iente** *a* astonishing. ● *m* narcotic. **~to** *a* astonished

estupendo *a* marvellous; (*hermoso*) beautiful

est|upidez *f* stupidity; (*acto*) stupid thing. **~úpido** *a* stupid

estupor *m* amazement

esturión *m* sturgeon

estuve *vb véase* **estar**

etapa *f* stage. **hacer ~ en** break the journey at. **por ~s** in stages

etc *abrev* (*etcétera*) etc

etcétera *adv* et cetera

éter *m* ether

etéreo *a* ethereal

etern|amente *adv* eternally. **~idad** *f* eternity. **~izar** [10] *vt* drag out. **~izarse** *vpr* be interminable. **~o** *a* eternal

étic|a *f* ethics. **~o** *a* ethical

etimología *f* etymology

etiqueta *f* ticket, tag; (*ceremonial*) etiquette. **de ~** formal

étnico *a* ethnic

eucalipto *m* eucalyptus

eufemismo *m* euphemism

euforia *f* euphoria

Europa *f* Europe

europe|o *a & m* European. **~izar** [10] *vt* Europeanize

eutanasia *f* euthanasia

evacua|ción *f* evacuation. **~r** [21 *o regular*] *vt* evacuate

evadir *vt* avoid. **~se** *vpr* escape

evaluar [21] *vt* evaluate

evang|élico *a* evangelical. **~elio** *m* gospel. **~elista** *m & f* evangelist

evapora|ción *f* evaporation. **~r** *vi* evaporate. **~rse** *vpr* evaporate; (*fig*) disappear

evasi|ón *f* evasion; (*fuga*) escape. **~vo** *a* evasive

evento *m* event. **a todo ~** at all events

eventual *a* possible. **~idad** *f* eventuality

eviden|cia *f* evidence. **~ciar** *vt* show. **~ciarse** *vpr* be obvious. **~te** *a* obvious. **~temente** *adv* obviously. **poner en ~cia** show; (*fig*) make a fool of

evitar *vt* avoid; (*ahorrar*) spare

evocar [7] *vt* evoke

evolución *f* evolution. **~onado** *a* fully-developed. **~onar** *vi* evolve; (*mil*) manoeuvre

ex *pref* ex-, former

exacerbar *vt* exacerbate

exact|amente *adv* exactly. **~itud** *f* exactness. **~o** *a* exact; (*preciso*) accurate; (*puntual*) punctual. **¡~!** exactly!. **con ~itud** exactly

exagera|ción *f* exaggeration. **~do** *a* exaggerated. **~r** *vt/i* exaggerate

exalta|do *a* exalted; (*fanático*) fanatical. **~r** *vt* exalt. **~rse** *vpr* get excited

exam|en *m* examination; (*escol, univ*) exam(ination). **~inador** *m* examiner. **~inar** *vt* examine. **~inarse** *vpr* take an exam

exánime *a* lifeless

exaspera|ción *f* exasperation. **~r** *vt* exasperate. **~rse** *vpr* get exasperated

excava|ción *f* excavation. **~dora** *f* digger. **~r** *vt* excavate

excede|ncia *f* leave of absence. **~nte** *a & m* surplus. **~r** *vi* exceed. **~rse** *vpr* go too far. **~rse a sí mismo** excel o.s.

excelen|cia *f* excellence; (*tratamiento*) Excellency. **~te** *a* excellent

exc|entricidad *f* eccentricity. **~éntrico** *a & m* eccentric

excepci|ón *f* exception. **~onal** *a* exceptional. **a ~ón de, con ~ón de** except (for)

except|o *prep* except (for). **~uar** [21] *vt* except

exces|ivo *a* excessive. **~o** *m* excess. **~o de equipaje** excess luggage (*esp Brit*), excess baggage (*esp Amer*)

excita|ble *a* excitable. **~ción** *f* excitement. **~nte** *a* exciting. ● *m* stimulant. **~r** *vt* excite; (*incitar*) incite. **~rse** *vpr* get excited

exclama|ción *f* exclamation. **~r** *vi* exclaim

exclu|ir [17] *vt* exclude. **~sión** *f* exclusion. **~siva** *f* sole right; (*en la prensa*) exclusive (story). **~sive**

adv exclusive; (*exclusivamente*) exclusively. ~**sivo** *a* exclusive

excomu|lgar [12] *vt* excommunicate. ~**nión** *f* excommunication

excremento *m* excrement

exculpar *vt* exonerate; (*jurid*) acquit

excursi|ón *f* excursion, trip. ~**onista** *m* & *f* day-tripper. **ir de** ~**ón** go on an excursion

excusa *f* excuse; (*disculpa*) apology. ~**r** *vt* excuse. **presentar sus** ~**s** apologize

execra|ble *a* loathsome. ~**r** *vt* loathe

exento *a* exempt; (*libre*) free

exequias *fpl* funeral rites

exhala|ción *f* shooting star. ~**r** *vt* exhale, breath out; give off ‹*olor etc*›. ~**rse** *vpr* hurry. **como una** ~**ción** at top speed

exhaust|ivo *a* exhaustive. ~**o** *a* exhausted

exhibi|ción *f* exhibition. ~**cionista** *m* & *f* exhibitionist. ~**r** *vt* exhibit

exhortar *vt* exhort (**a** to)

exhumar *vt* exhume; (*fig*) dig up

exig|encia *f* demand. ~**ente** *a* demanding. ~**ir** [14] *vt* demand. **tener muchas** ~**encias** be very demanding

exiguo *a* meagre

exil|(i)ado *a* exiled. ● *m* exile. ~**(i)arse** *vpr* go into exile. ~**io** *m* exile

eximio *a* distinguished

eximir *vt* exempt; (*liberar*) free

existencia *f* existence. ~**s** *fpl* stock

existencial *a* existential. ~**ismo** *m* existentialism

exist|ente *a* existing. ~**ir** *vi* exist

éxito *m* success. **no tener** ~ fail. **tener** ~ be successful

exitoso *a* successful

éxodo *m* exodus

exonerar *vt* (*de un empleo*) dismiss; (*de un honor etc*) strip

exorbitante *a* exorbitant

exorci|smo *m* exorcism. ~**zar** [10] *vt* exorcise

exótico *a* exotic

expan|dir *vt* expand; (*fig*) spread. ~**dirse** *vpr* expand. ~**sión** *f* expansion. ~**sivo** *a* expansive

expatria|do *a* & *m* expatriate. ~**r** *vt* banish. ~**rse** *vpr* emigrate; (*exiliarse*) go into exile

expectativa *f*. **estar a la** ~ be on the lookout

expedición *f* dispatch; (*cosa expedida*) shipment; (*mil, científico etc*) expedition

expediente *m* expedient; (*jurid*) proceedings; (*documentos*) record, file

expedi|r [5] *vt* dispatch, send; issue ‹*documento*›. ~**to** *a* clear

expeler *vt* expel

expende|dor *m* dealer. ~**dor automático** vending machine. ~**duría** *f* shop; (*de billetes*) ticket office. ~**r** *vt* sell

expensas *fpl*. **a** ~ **de** at the expense of. **a mis** ~ at my expense

experiencia *f* experience

experiment|al *a* experimental. ~**ar** *vt* test, experiment with; (*sentir*) experience. ~**o** *m* experiment

experto *a* & *m* expert

expiar [20] *vt* atone for

expirar *vi* expire; (*morir*) die

explana|da *f* levelled area; (*paseo*) esplanade. ~**r** *vt* level

explayar *vt* extend. ~**se** *vpr* spread out, extend; (*hablar*) be long-winded; (*confiarse*) confide (**a** in)

expletivo *m* expletive

explica|ción *f* explanation. ~**r** [7] *vt* explain. ~**rse** *vpr* understand; (*hacerse comprender*) explain o.s. **no me lo explico** I can't understand it

explícito *a* explicit

explora|ción *f* exploration. ~**dor** *m* explorer; (*muchacho*) boy scout. ~**r** *vt* explore. ~**torio** *a* exploratory

explosi|ón *f* explosion; (*fig*) outburst. ~**onar** *vt* blow up. ~**vo** *a* & *m* explosive

explota|ción *f* working; (*abuso*) exploitation. ~**r** *vt* work ‹*mina*›; farm ‹*tierra*›; (*abusar*) exploit. ● *vi* explode

expone|nte *m* exponent. ~**r** [34] *vt* expose; display ‹*mercancías*›; (*explicar*) expound; exhibit ‹*cuadros etc*›; (*arriesgar*) risk. ● *vi* hold an exhibition. ~**rse** *vpr* run the risk (**a** of)

exporta|ción *f* export. ~**dor** *m* exporter. ~**r** *vt* export

exposición *f* exposure; (*de cuadros etc*) exhibition; (*en escaparate etc*) display; (*explicación*) exposition, explanation

expresamente *adv* specifically

expres|ar *vt* express. ~**arse** *vpr* express o.s. ~**ión** *f* expression. ~**ivo** *a* expressive; (*cariñoso*) affectionate

expreso *a* express. ● *m* express messenger; (*tren*) express

exprimi|dor *m* squeezer. ∼**r** *vt* squeeze; (*explotar*) exploit
expropiar *vt* expropriate
expuesto *a* on display; ⟨*lugar etc*⟩ exposed; (*peligroso*) dangerous. **estar** ∼**a** be liable to
expuls|ar *vt* expel; throw out ⟨*persona*⟩; send off ⟨*jugador*⟩. ∼**ión** *f* expulsion
expurgar [12] *vt* expurgate
exquisit|o *a* exquisite. ∼**amente** *adv* exquisitely
extasiar [20] *vt* enrapture
éxtasis *m invar* ecstasy
extático *a* ecstatic
extend|er [1] *vt* spread (out); draw up ⟨*documento*⟩. ∼**erse** *vpr* spread; ⟨*paisaje etc*⟩ extend, stretch; (*tenderse*) stretch out. ∼**ido** *a* spread out; (*generalizado*) widespread; ⟨*brazos*⟩ outstretched
extens|amente *adv* widely; (*detalladamente*) in full. ∼**ión** *f* extension; (*amplitud*) expanse; (*mus*) range. ∼**o** *a* extensive
extenuar [21] *vt* exhaust
exterior *a* external, exterior; (*del extranjero*) foreign; ⟨*aspecto etc*⟩ outward. ● *m* exterior; (*países extranjeros*) abroad. ∼**izar** [10] *vt* show
extermin|ación *f* extermination. ∼**ar** *vt* exterminate. ∼**io** *m* extermination
externo *a* external; ⟨*signo etc*⟩ outward. ● *m* day pupil
extin|ción *f* extinction. ∼**guir** [13] *vt* extinguish. ∼**guirse** *vpr* die out; ⟨*fuego*⟩ go out. ∼**to** *a* extinguished; ⟨*raza etc*⟩ extinct. ∼**tor** *m* fire extinguisher
extirpa|r *vt* uproot; extract ⟨*muela etc*⟩; remove ⟨*tumor*⟩. ∼**ción** *f* (*fig*) eradication
extorsi|ón *f* (*fig*) inconvenience. ∼**onar** *vt* inconvenience
extra *a invar* extra; (*de buena calidad*) good-quality; ⟨*huevos*⟩ large. **paga** *f* ∼ bonus
extrac|ción *f* extraction; (*de lotería*) draw. ∼**to** *m* extract
extradición *f* extradition
extraer [41] *vt* extract
extranjero *a* foreign. ● *m* foreigner; (*países*) foreign countries. **del** ∼ from abroad. **en el** ∼, **por el** ∼ abroad

extrañ|ar *vt* surprise; (*encontrar extraño*) find strange; (*LAm, echar de menos*) miss; (*desterrar*) banish. ∼**arse** *vpr* be surprised (**de** at); ⟨*2 personas*⟩ grow apart. ∼**eza** *f* strangeness; (*asombro*) surprise. ∼**o** *a* strange. ● *m* stranger
extraoficial *a* unofficial
extraordinario *a* extraordinary. ● *m* (*correo*) special delivery; (*plato*) extra dish; (*de periódico etc*) special edition. **horas** *fpl* **extraordinarias** overtime
extrarradio *m* suburbs
extrasensible *a* extra-sensory
extraterrestre *a* extraterrestrial. ● *m* alien
extravagan|cia *f* oddness, eccentricity. ∼**te** *a* odd, eccentric
extravertido *a* & *m* extrovert
extrav|iado *a* lost; ⟨*lugar*⟩ isolated. ∼**iar** [20] *vt* lose. ∼**iarse** *vpr* get lost; ⟨*objetos*⟩ be missing. ∼**io** *m* loss
extremar *vt* overdo. ∼**se** *vpr* make every effort
extremeño *a* from Extremadura. ● *m* person from Extremadura
extrem|idad *f* extremity. ∼**idades** *fpl* extremities. ∼**ista** *a* & *m* & *f* extremist. ∼**o** *a* extreme. ● *m* end; (*colmo*) extreme. **en** ∼**o** extremely. **en último** ∼**o** as a last resort
extrovertido *a* & *m* extrovert
exuberan|cia *f* exuberance. ∼**te** *a* exuberant
exulta|ción *f* exultation. ∼**r** *vi* exult
eyacular *vt*/*i* ejaculate

F

fa *m* F; (*solfa*) fah
fabada *f* Asturian stew
fábrica *f* factory. **marca** *f* **de** ∼ trade mark
fabrica|ción *f* manufacture. ∼**ción en serie** mass production. ∼**nte** *m* & *f* manufacturer. ∼**r** [7] *vt* manufacture; (*inventar*) fabricate
fábula *f* fable; (*mentira*) story, lie; (*chisme*) gossip
fabuloso *a* fabulous
facci|ón *f* faction. ∼**ones** *fpl* (*de la cara*) features
faceta *f* facet
fácil *a* easy; (*probable*) likely; ⟨*persona*⟩ easygoing

facili|dad f ease; (*disposición*) aptitude. **~dades** fpl facilities. **~tar** vt facilitate; (*proporcionar*) provide

fácilmente adv easily

facistol m lectern

facón m (*Arg*) gaucho knife

facsímil(e) m facsimile

factible a feasible

factor m factor

factoría f agency; (*esp LAm, fábrica*) factory

factura f bill, invoice; (*hechura*) manufacture. **~r** vt (*hacer la factura*) invoice; (*cobrar*) charge; (*en ferrocarril*) register (*Brit*), check (*Amer*)

faculta|d f faculty; (*capacidad*) ability; (*poder*) power. **~tivo** a optional

facha f (*aspecto, fam*) look

fachada f façade; (*fig, apariencia*) show

faena f job. **~s domésticas** housework

fagot m bassoon; (*músico*) bassoonist

faisán m pheasant

faja f (*de tierra*) strip; (*corsé*) corset; (*mil etc*) sash

fajo m bundle; (*de billetes*) wad

falang|e f (*política española*) Falange. **~ista** m & f Falangist

falda f skirt; (*de montaña*) side

fálico a phallic

fals|ear vt falsify, distort. **~edad** f falseness; (*mentira*) lie, falsehood. **~ificación** f forgery. **~ificador** m forger. **~ificar** [7] vt forge. **~o** a false; (*equivocado*) wrong; (*falsificado*) fake

falt|a f lack; (*ausencia*) absence; (*escasez*) shortage; (*defecto*) fault, defect; (*culpa*) fault; (*error*) mistake; (*en fútbol etc*) foul; (*en tenis*) fault. **~ar** vi be lacking; (*estar ausente*) be absent. **~o** a lacking (**de** in). **a ~a de** for lack of. **echar en ~a** miss. **hacer ~a** be necessary. **me hace ~a** I need. **¡no ~aba más!** don't mention it! (*naturalmente*) of course! **sacar ~as** find fault

falla f (*incl geol*) fault. **~r** vi fail; (*romperse*) break, give way; (*motor, tiro etc*) miss. **sin ~r** without fail

fallec|er [11] vi die. **~ido** a late. ● m deceased

fallido a vain; (*fracasado*) unsuccessful

fallo m failure; (*defecto*) fault; (*jurid*) sentence

fama f fame; (*reputación*) reputation. **de mala ~** of ill repute. **tener ~ de** have the reputation of

famélico a starving

familia f family. **~ numerosa** large family. **~r** a familiar; (*de la familia*) family; (*sin ceremonia*) informal. **~ridad** f familiarity. **~rizarse** [10] vpr become familiar (**con** with)

famoso a famous

fanático a fanatical. ● m fanatic

fanfarr|ón a boastful. ● m braggart. **~onada** f boasting; (*dicho*) boast. **~onear** vi show off

fango m mud. **~so** a muddy

fantas|ear vi daydream; (*imaginar*) fantasize. **~ía** f fantasy. **de ~** fancy

fantasma m ghost

fantástico a fantastic

fantoche m puppet

faringe f pharynx

fardo m bundle

farfullar vi jabber, gabble

farmac|éutico a pharmaceutical. ● m chemist (*Brit*), pharmacist, druggist (*Amer*). **~ia** f (*ciencia*) pharmacy; (*tienda*) chemist's (shop) (*Brit*), pharmacy, drugstore (*Amer*)

faro m lighthouse; (*aviac*) beacon; (*auto*) headlight

farol m lantern; (*de la calle*) street lamp. **~a** f street lamp. **~ita** f small street lamp

farsa f farce

fas adv. **por ~ o por nefas** rightly or wrongly

fascículo m instalment

fascina|ción f fascination. **~r** vt fascinate

fascis|mo m fascism. **~ta** a & m & f fascist

fase f phase

fastidi|ar vt annoy; (*estropear*) spoil. **~arse** vpr (*aguantarse*) put up with it; (*hacerse daño*) hurt o.s. **~o** m nuisance; (*aburrimiento*) boredom. **~oso** a annoying. **¡para que te ~es!** so there! **¡qué ~o!** what a nuisance!

fatal a fateful; (*mortal*) fatal; (*pésimo, fam*) terrible. **~idad** f fate; (*desgracia*) misfortune. **~ista** m & f fatalist

fatig|a f fatigue. **~as** fpl troubles. **~ar** [12] vt tire. **~arse** vpr get tired. **~oso** a tiring

fatuo a fatuous

fauna f fauna

fausto *a* lucky

favor *m* favour. **~able** *a* favourable. **a ~ de, en ~ de** in favour of. **haga el ~ de** would you be so kind as to, please. **por ~** please

favorec|edor *a* flattering. **~er** [11] *vt* favour; ⟨*vestido, peinado etc*⟩ suit. **~ido** *a* favoured

favorit|ismo *m* favouritism. **~o** *a* & *m* favourite

faz *f* face

fe *f* faith. **dar ~ de** certify. **de buena ~** in good faith

fealdad *f* ugliness

febrero *m* February

febril *a* feverish

fecund|ación *f* fertilization. **~ación artificial** artificial insemination. **~ar** *vt* fertilize. **~o** *a* fertile; (*fig*) prolific

fecha *f* date. **~r** *vt* date. **a estas ~s** now; (*todavía*) still. **hasta la ~** so far. **poner la ~** date

fechoría *f* misdeed

federa|ción *f* federation. **~l** *a* federal

feísimo *a* hideous

felici|dad *f* happiness. **~dades** *fpl* best wishes; (*congratulaciones*) congratulations. **~tación** *f* congratulation. **~tar** *vt* congratulate. **~tarse** *vpr* be glad

feligr|és *m* parishioner. **~esía** *f* parish

felino *a* & *m* feline

feliz *a* happy; (*afortunado*) lucky. **¡Felices Pascuas!** Happy Christmas! **¡F~ Año Nuevo!** Happy New Year!

felpudo *a* plush. **●** *m* doormat

femeni|l *a* feminine. **~no** *a* feminine; (*biol, bot*) female. **●** *m* feminine. **feminidad** *f* femininity. **feminista** *a* & *m* & *f* feminist

fen|omenal *a* phenomenal. **~ómeno** *m* phenomenon; (*monstruo*) freak

feo *a* ugly; (*desagradable*) nasty; (*malo*) bad

féretro *m* coffin

feria *f* fair; (*verbena*) carnival; (*descanso*) holiday; (*Mex, cambio*) change. **~do** *a*. **día ~do** holiday

ferment|ación *f* fermentation. **~ar** *vt/i* ferment. **~o** *m* ferment

fero|cidad *f* ferocity. **~z** *a* fierce; (*persona*) savage

férreo *a* iron. **vía férrea** railway (*Brit*), railroad (*Amer*)

ferret|ía *f* ironmonger's (shop) (*Brit*), hardware store (*Amer*). **~o** *m* ironmonger (*Brit*), hardware dealer (*Amer*)

ferro|bús *m* local train. **~carril** *m* railway (*Brit*), railroad (*Amer*). **~viario** *a* rail. **●** *m* railwayman (*Brit*), railroad worker (*Amer*)

fértil *a* fertile

fertili|dad *f* fertility. **~zante** *m* fertilizer. **~zar** [10] *vt* fertilize

férvido *a* fervent

ferv|iente *a* fervent. **~or** *m* fervour

festej|ar *vt* celebrate; entertain ⟨*persona*⟩; court ⟨*novia etc*⟩; (*Mex, golpear*) beat. **~o** *m* entertainment; (*celebración*) celebration

festiv|al *m* festival. **~idad** *f* festivity. **~o** *a* festive; (*humorístico*) humorous. **día ~o** feast day, holiday

festonear *vt* festoon

fétido *a* stinking

feto *m* foetus

feudal *a* feudal

fiado *m*. **al ~** on credit. **~r** *m* fastener; (*jurid*) guarantor

fiambre *m* cold meat

fianza *f* (*dinero*) deposit; (*objeto*) surety. **bajo ~** on bail. **dar ~** pay a deposit

fiar [20] *vt* guarantee; (*vender*) sell on credit; (*confiar*) confide. **●** *vi* trust. **~se** *vpr*. **~se de** trust

fiasco *m* fiasco

fibra *f* fibre; (*fig*) energy. **~ de vidrio** fibreglass

fic|ción *f* fiction. **~ticio** *a* fictitious; (*falso*) false

fich|a *f* token; (*tarjeta*) index card; (*en los juegos*) counter. **~ar** *vt* file. **~ero** *m* card index. **estar ~ado** have a (police) record

fidedigno *a* reliable

fidelidad *f* faithfulness. **alta ~** hi-fi (*fam*), high fidelity

fideos *mpl* noodles

fiebre *f* fever. **~ del heno** hay fever. **tener ~** have a temperature

fiel *a* faithful; ⟨*memoria, relato etc*⟩ reliable. **●** *m* believer; (*de balanza*) needle. **los ~es** the faithful

fieltro *m* felt

fier|a *f* wild animal; (*persona*) brute. **~o** *a* fierce; (*cruel*) cruel. **estar hecho una ~a** be furious

fierro *m* (*LAm*) iron

fiesta *f* party; (*día festivo*) holiday. **~s** *fpl* celebrations. **~ nacional**

figura 101 **flato**

bank holiday (*Brit*), national holiday

figura *f* figure; (*forma*) shape; (*en obra de teatro*) character; (*en naipes*) court-card. **~r** *vt* feign; (*representar*) represent. ● *vi* figure; (*ser importante*) be important. **~rse** *vpr* imagine. **¡figúrate!** just imagine! **~tivo** *a* figurative

fij|ación *f* fixing. **~ar** *vt* fix; stick ‹*sello*›; post ‹*cartel*›. **~arse** *vpr* settle; (*fig, poner atención*) notice. **¡fíjate!** just imagine! **~o** *a* fixed; (*firme*) stable; ‹*persona*› settled. **de ~o** certainly

fila *f* line; (*de soldados etc*) file; (*en el teatro, cine etc*) row; (*cola*) queue. **ponerse en ~** line up

filamento *m* filament

fil|antropía *f* philanthropy. **~antrópico** *a* philanthropic. **~ántropo** *m* philanthropist

filarmónico *a* philharmonic

filat|elia *f* stamp collecting, philately. **~élico** *a* philatelic. ● *m* stamp collector, philatelist

filete *m* fillet

filfa *f* (*fam*) hoax

filial *a* filial. ● *f* subsidiary

filigrana *f* filigree (work); (*en papel*) watermark

Filipinas *fpl*. **las (islas) ~** the Philippines

filipino *a* Philippine, Filipino

filmar *vt* film

filo *m* edge; (*de hoja*) cutting edge; (*Mex, hambre*) hunger. **al ~ de las doce** at exactly twelve o'clock. **dar ~ a, sacar ~ a** sharpen

filología *f* philology

filón *m* vein; (*fig*) gold-mine

fil|osofía *f* philosophy. **~osófico** *a* philosophical. **~ósofo** *m* philosopher

filtr|ar *vt* filter. **~arse** *vpr* filter; ‹*dinero*› disappear. **~o** *m* filter; (*bebida*) philtre

fin *m* end; (*objetivo*) aim. **~ de semana** weekend. **a ~ de** in order to. **a ~ de cuentas** all things considered. **a ~ de que** in order that. **a ~es de** at the end of. **al ~** finally. **al ~ y al cabo** after all. **dar ~ a** end. **en ~** in short. **poner ~ a** end. **por ~** finally. **sin ~** endless

final *a* final, last. ● *m* end. ● *f* final. **~idad** *f* aim. **~ista** *m & f* finalist. **~izar** [10] *vt/i* end. **~mente** *adv* finally

financi|ar *vt* finance. **~ero** *a* financial. ● *m* financier

finca *f* property; (*tierras*) estate; (*LAm, granja*) farm

finés *a* Finnish. ● *m* Finn; (*lengua*) Finnish

fingi|do *a* false. **~r** [14] *vt* feign; (*simular*) simulate. ● *vi* pretend. **~rse** *vpr* pretend to be

finito *a* finite

finlandés *a* Finnish. ● *m* (*persona*) Finn; (*lengua*) Finnish

Finlandia *f* Finland

fin|o *a* fine; (*delgado*) slender; (*astuto*) shrewd; ‹*sentido*› keen; (*cortés*) polite; ‹*jerez*› dry. **~ura** *f* fineness; (*astucia*) shrewdness; (*de sentido*) keenness; (*cortesía*) politeness

fiordo *m* fiord

firma *f* signature; (*empresa*) firm

firmamento *m* firmament

firmar *vt* sign

firme *a* firm; (*estable*) stable, steady; ‹*persona*› steadfast. ● *m* (*pavimento*) (road) surface. ● *adv* hard. **~za** *f* firmness. **de ~** hard. **en ~** firm, definite

fisc|al *a* fiscal. ● *m & f* public prosecutor. **~o** *m* treasury

fisg|ar [12] *vt* pry into ‹*asunto*›; spy on ‹*persona*›. ● *vi* pry. **~ón** *a* prying. ● *m* busybody

físic|a *f* physics. **~o** *a* physical. ● *m* physique; (*persona*) physicist

fisi|ología *f* physiology. **~ológico** *a* physiological. **~ólogo** *m* physiologist

fisioterap|euta *m & f* physiotherapist. **~ia** *f* physiotherapy. **~ista** *m & f* (*fam*) physiotherapist

fisonom|ía *f* physiognomy, face. **~ista** *m & f*. **ser buen ~ista** be good at remembering faces

fisura *f* (*Med*) fracture

fláccido *a* flabby

flaco *a* thin, skinny; (*débil*) weak

flagelo *m* scourge

flagrante *a* flagrant. **en ~** redhanded

flamante *a* splendid; (*nuevo*) brand-new

flamenco *a* flamenco; (*de Flandes*) Flemish. ● *m* (*música etc*) flamenco

flan *m* crème caramel

flaqueza *f* thinness; (*debilidad*) weakness

flash *m* flash

flato *m*, **flatulencia** *f* flatulence

flaut|a f flute. ● m & f (músico) flautist, flutist (Amer). **~ín** m piccolo. **~ista** m & f flautist, flutist (Amer)

fleco m fringe

flecha f arrow

flem|a f phlegm. **~ático** a phlegmatic

flequillo m fringe

fletar vt charter

flexib|ilidad f flexibility. **~le** a flexible. ● m flex, cable

flirte|ar vi flirt. **~o** m flirting

floj|ear vi ease up. **~o** a loose; (poco fuerte) weak; ‹viento› light; (perezoso) lazy

flor f flower; (fig) cream. **~a** f flora. **~al** a floral. **~ecer** [11] vi flower, bloom; (fig) flourish. **~eciente** a (fig) flourishing. **~ero** m flower vase. **~ido** a flowery; (selecto) select; ‹lenguaje› florid. **~ista** m & f florist

flota f fleet

flot|ador m float. **~ar** vi float. **~e** m. **a ~e** afloat

flotilla f flotilla

fluctua|ción f fluctuation. **~r** [21] vi fluctuate

flu|idez f fluidity; (fig) fluency. **~ido** a fluid; (fig) fluent. ● m fluid. **~ir** [17] vi flow. **~jo** m flow. **~o y reflujo** ebb and flow

fluorescente a fluorescent

fluoruro m fluoride

fluvial a river

fobia f phobia

foca f seal

foc|al a focal. **~o** m focus; (lámpara) floodlight; (LAm, bombilla) light bulb

fogón m (cocina) cooker

fogoso a spirited

folio m leaf

folkl|ore m folklore. **~órico** a folk

follaje m foliage

follet|ín m newspaper serial. **~o** m pamphlet

follón m (lío) mess; (alboroto) row

fomentar vt foment, stir up

fonda f (pensión) boarding-house

fondo m bottom; (parte más lejana) bottom, end; (de escenario, pintura etc) background; (profundidad) depth. **~s** mpl funds, money. **a ~** thoroughly. **en el ~** deep down

fonético a f phonetics. **~o** a phonetic

fono m (LAm, del teléfono) earpiece

fontaner|ía plumbing. **~o** m plumber

footing /'futin/ m jogging

forastero a alien. ● m stranger

forceje|ar vi struggle. **~o** m struggle

fórceps m invar forceps

forense a forensic

forjar vt forge

forma f form, shape; (horma) mould; (modo) way; (de zapatero) last. **~s** fpl conventions. **~ción** f formation; (educación) training. **dar ~ a** shape; (expresar) formulate. **de ~ que** so (that). **de todas ~s** anyway. **estar en ~** be in good form. **guardar ~s** keep up appearances

formal a formal; (de fiar) reliable; (serio) serious. **~idad** f formality; (fiabilidad) reliability; (seriedad) seriousness

formar vt form; (hacer) make; (enseñar) train. **~se** vpr form; (desarrollarse) develop

formato m format

formidable a formidable; (muy grande) enormous; (muy bueno, fam) marvellous

fórmula f formula; (receta) recipe

formular vt formulate; make ‹queja etc›; (expresar) express

fornido a well-built

forraje m fodder. **~ar** vt/i forage

forr|ar vt (en el interior) line; (en el exterior) cover. **~o** m lining; (cubierta) cover. **~o del freno** brake lining

fortale|cer [11] vt strengthen. **~za** f strength; (mil) fortress; (fuerza moral) fortitude

fortificar [7] vt fortify

fortuito a fortuitous. **encuentro** m **~** chance meeting

fortuna f fortune; (suerte) luck. **por ~** fortunately

forz|ado a hard. **~ar** [2 & 10] vt force. **~osamente** adv necessarily. **~oso** a inevitable; (necesario) necessary

fosa f grave

fosfato m phosphate

fósforo m phosphorus; (cerilla) match

fósil a & m fossil

fosilizarse [10] vpr fossilize

foso m ditch

foto f photo, photograph. **sacar ~s** take photographs

fotocopia f photocopy. **~dora** f photocopier. **~r** vt photocopy

fotogénico a photogenic

fot|ografía f photography; (foto) photograph. **~ografiar** [20] vt photograph. **~ográfico** a photographic. **~ógrafo** m photographer. **sacar ~ografías** take photographs

foyer m foyer

frac m (pl **fraques** o **fracs**) tails

fracas|ar vi fail. **~o** m failure

fracción f fraction; (pol) faction

fractura f fracture. **~r** vt fracture, break. **~rse** vpr fracture, break

fragan|cia f fragrance. **~te** a fragrant

fragata f frigate

fr|ágil a fragile; (débil) weak. **~agilidad** f fragility; (debilidad) weakness

fragment|ario a fragmentary. **~o** m fragment

fragor m din

fragoso a rough

fragua f forge. **~r** [15] vt forge; (fig) concoct. ● vi harden

fraile m friar; (monje) monk

frambuesa f raspberry

francés a French. ● m (persona) Frenchman; (lengua) French

Francia f France

franco a frank; (com) free. ● m (moneda) franc

francotirador m sniper

franela f flannel

franja f border; (fleco) fringe

franque|ar vt clear; stamp (carta); overcome (obstáculo). **~o** m stamping; (cantidad) postage

franqueza f frankness; (familiaridad) familiarity

franquis|mo m General Franco's regime; (política) Franco's policy. **~ta** a pro-Franco

frasco m small bottle

frase f phrase; (oración) sentence. **~ hecha** set phrase

fratern|al a fraternal. **~idad** f fraternity

fraud|e m fraud. **~ulento** a fraudulent

fray m brother, friar

frecuen|cia f frequency. **~tar** vt frequent. **~te** a frequent. **con ~cia** frequently

frega|dero m sink. **~r** [1 & 12] vt scrub; wash up (los platos); mop (el suelo); (LAm, fig, molestar, fam) annoy

freír [51, pp **frito**] vt fry; (fig, molestar, fam) annoy. **~se** vpr fry; (persona) be very hot, be boiling (fam)

frenar vt brake; (fig) check

fren|esí m frenzy. **~ético** a frenzied

freno m (de caballería) bit; (auto) brake; (fig) check

frente m front. ● f forehead. **~ a** opposite; (en contra de) opposed to. **~ por ~** opposite; (en un choque) head-on. **al ~** at the head; (hacia delante) forward. **arrugar la ~** frown. **de ~** forward. **hacer ~ a** face (cosa); stand up to (persona)

fresa f strawberry

fresc|a f fresh air. **~o** a (frío) cool; (nuevo) fresh; (descarado) cheeky. ● m fresh air; (frescor) coolness; (mural) fresco; (persona) impudent person. **~or** m coolness. **~ura** f freshness; (frío) coolness; (descaro) cheek. **al ~o** in the open air. **hacer ~o** be cool. **tomar el ~o** get some fresh air

fresno m ash (tree)

friable a friable

frialdad f coldness; (fig) indifference

fricci|ón f rubbing; (fig, tec) friction; (masaje) massage. **~onar** vt rub

frigidez f coldness; (fig) frigidity

frígido a frigid

frigorífico m refrigerator, fridge (fam)

frijol m bean. **~es refritos** (Mex) purée of black beans

frío a & m cold. **coger ~** catch cold. **hacer ~** be cold

frisar vi. **~ en** be getting on for, be about

frito a fried; (exasperado) exasperated. **me tiene ~** I'm sick of him

fr|ivolidad f frivolity. **~ívolo** a frivolous

fronda f foliage

fronter|a f frontier; (fig) limit. **~izo** a frontier. **~o** a opposite

frontón m pelota court

frotar vt rub; strike (cerilla)

fructífero a fruitful

frugal a frugal

fruncir [9] vt gather (tela); wrinkle (piel)

fruslería f trifle

frustra|ción f frustration. **~r** vt frustrate. **~rse** vpr (fracasar) fail. **quedar ~do** be disappointed

frut|a f fruit. **~ería** f fruit shop. **~ero** a fruit. ● m fruiterer; (recipiente) fruit bowl. **~icultura** f fruit-growing. **~illa** *f* (*LAm*) strawberry. **~o** *m* fruit

fucsia *f* fuchsia

fuego *m* fire. **~s artificiales** fireworks. **a ~ lento** on a low heat. **tener ~** have a light

fuente *f* fountain; (*manantial*) spring; (*plato*) serving dish; (*fig*) source

fuera *adv* out; (*al exterior*) outside; (*en otra parte*) away; (*en el extranjero*) abroad. ● *vb véase* **ir** *y* **ser**. **~ de** outside; (*excepto*) except for, besides. **por ~** on the outside

fuerte *a* strong; (*color*) bright; (*sonido*) loud; (*dolor*) severe; (*duro*) hard; (*grande*) large; (*lluvia, nevada*) heavy. ● *m* fort; (*fig*) strong point. ● *adv* hard; (*con hablar etc*) loudly; (*mucho*) a lot

fuerza *f* strength; (*poder*) power; (*en física*) force; (*mil*) forces. **~ de voluntad** will-power. **a ~ de** by dint of, by means of. **a la ~** by necessity. **por ~** by force; (*por necesidad*) by necessity. **tener ~s para** have the strength to

fuese *vb véase* **ir** *y* **ser**

fug|a *f* flight, escape; (*de gas etc*) leak; (*mus*) fugue. **~arse** [12] *vpr* flee, escape. **~az** *a* fleeting. **~itivo** *a* & *m* fugitive. **ponerse en ~a** take to flight

fui *vb véase* **ir** *y* **ser**

fulano *m* so-and-so. **~, mengano y zutano** Tom, Dick and Harry

fulgor *m* brilliance; (*fig*) splendour

fulminar *vt* strike by lightning; (*fig, mirar*) look daggers at

fuma|dor *a* smoking. ● *m* smoker. **~r** *vt/i* smoke. **~rse** *vpr* smoke; (*fig, gastar*) squander. **~rada** *f* puff of smoke. **~r en pipa** smoke a pipe. **prohibido ~r** no smoking

funámbulo *m* tightrope walker

funci|ón *f* function; (*de un cargo etc*) duties; (*de teatro*) show, performance. **~onal** *a* functional. **~onar** *vi* work, function. **~onario** *m* civil servant. **no ~ona** out of order

funda *f* cover. **~ de almohada** pillowcase

funda|ción *f* foundation. **~mental** *a* fundamental. **~mentar** *vt* lay the foundations of; (*fig*) base. **~mento** *m* foundation. **~r** *vt* found; (*fig*) base. **~rse** *vpr* be based

fundi|ción *f* melting; (*de metales*) smelting; (*taller*) foundry. **~r** *vt* melt; smelt (*metales*); cast (*objeto*); blend (*colores*); (*fusionar*) merge. **~rse** *vpr* melt; (*unirse*) merge

fúnebre *a* funeral; (*sombrío*) gloomy

funeral *a* funeral. ● *m* funeral. **~es** *mpl* funeral

funicular *a* & *m* funicular

furg|ón *m* van. **~oneta** *f* van

fur|ia *f* fury; (*violencia*) violence. **~ibundo** *a* furious. **~ioso** *a* furious. **~or** *m* fury

furtivo *a* furtive

furúnculo *m* boil

fuselaje *m* fuselage

fusible *m* fuse

fusil *m* gun. **~ar** *vt* shoot

fusión *f* melting; (*unión*) fusion; (*com*) merger

fútbol *m* football

futbolista *m* footballer

fútil *a* futile

futur|ista *a* futuristic. ● *m* & *f* futurist. **~o** *a* & *m* future

G

gabán *m* overcoat

garbardina *f* raincoat; (*tela*) gabardine

gabinete *m* (*pol*) cabinet; (*en museo etc*) room; (*de dentista, médico etc*) consulting room

gacela *f* gazelle

gaceta *f* gazette

gachas *fpl* porridge

gacho *a* drooping

gaélico *a* Gaelic

gafa *f* hook. **~s** *fpl* glasses, spectacles. **~s de sol** sun-glasses

gaf|ar *vt* hook; (*fam*) bring bad luck to. **~e** *m* jinx

gaita *f* bagpipes

gajo *m* (*de naranja, nuez etc*) segment

gala|s *fpl* finery, best clothes. **estar de ~** be dressed up. **hacer ~ de** show off

galán *m* (*en el teatro*) male lead; (*enamorado*) lover

galante *a* gallant. **~ar** *vt* court. **~ría** *f* gallantry

galápago *m* turtle

galardón *m* reward

galaxia *f* galaxy

galeón *m* galleon

galera *f* galley

galería f gallery
Gales m Wales. **país de** ~ Wales
gal|és a Welsh. ● m Welshman; (*lengua*) Welsh. ~**esa** f Welshwoman
galgo m greyhound
Galicia f Galicia
galimatías m invar (*fam*) gibberish
galón m gallon; (*cinta*) braid; (*mil*) stripe
galop|ar vi gallop. ~**e** m gallop
galvanizar [10] vt galvanize
gallard|ía f elegance. ~**o** a elegant
gallego a & m Galician
galleta f biscuit (*Brit*), cookie (*Amer*)
gall|ina f hen, chicken; (*fig, fam*) coward. ~**o** m cock
gama f scale; (*fig*) range
gamba f prawn (*Brit*), shrimp (*Amer*)
gamberro m hooligan
gamuza f (*piel*) chamois leather
gana f wish, desire; (*apetito*) appetite. **de buena** ~ willingly. **de mala** ~ reluctantly. **no me da la** ~ I don't feel like it. **tener** ~**s de** (+ *infinitivo*) feel like (+ *gerundio*)
ganad|ería f cattle raising; (*ganado*) livestock. ~**o** m livestock. ~**o de cerda** pigs. ~**o lanar** sheep. ~**o vacuno** cattle
ganar vt earn; (*en concurso, juego etc*) win; (*alcanzar*) reach; (*aventajar*) beat. ● vi (*vencer*) win; (*mejorar*) improve. ~**se la vida** earn a living. **salir ganando** come out better off
ganch|illo m crochet. ~**o** m hook. ~**oso** a, ~**udo** a hooked. **echar el** ~**o a** hook. **hacer** ~**illo** crochet. **tener** ~**o** be very attractive
gandul a & m & f good-for-nothing
ganga f bargain; (*buena situación*) easy job, cushy job (*fam*)
gangrena f gangrene
gans|ada f silly thing. ~**o** m goose
gañi|do m yelping. ~**r** [22] vi yelp
garabat|ear vt/i (*garrapatear*) scribble. ~**o** m (*garrapato*) scribble
garaj|e m garage. ~**ista** m & f garage attendant
garant|e m & f guarantor. ~**ía** f guarantee. ~**ir** [24] vt (*esp LAm*), ~**izar** [10] vt guarantee
garapiñado a. **almendras** fpl **garapiñadas** sugared almonds
garbanzo m chick-pea
garbo m poise; (*de escrito*) style. ~**so** a elegant
garfio m hook

garganta f throat; (*desfiladero*) gorge; (*de botella*) neck
gárgaras fpl. **hacer** ~ gargle
gargarismo m gargle
gárgola f gargoyle
garita f hut; (*de centinela*) sentry box
garito m gambling den
garra f (*de animal*) claw; (*de ave*) talon
garrafa f carafe
garrapata f tick
garrapat|ear vi scribble. ~**o** m scribble
garrote m club, cudgel; (*tormento*) garrotte
gárrulo a garrulous
garúa f (*LAm*) drizzle
garza f heron
gas m gas. **con** ~ fizzy. **sin** ~ still
gasa f gauze
gaseosa f lemonade
gasfitero m (*Arg*) plumber
gas|óleo m diesel. ~**olina** f petrol (*Brit*), gasoline (*Amer*), gas (*Amer*). ~**olinera** f petrol station (*Brit*), gas station (*Amer*); (*lancha*) motor boat. ~**ómetro** m gasometer
gast|ado a spent; (*vestido etc*) worn out. ~**ador** m spendthrift. ~**ar** vt spend; (*consumir*) use; (*malgastar*) waste; wear (*vestido etc*); crack (*broma*). ● vi spend. ~**arse** vpr wear out. ~**o** m expense; (*acción de gastar*) spending
gástrico a gastric
gastronomía f gastronomy
gat|a f cat. **a** ~**as** on all fours. ~**ear** vi crawl
gatillo m trigger; (*de dentista*) (dental) forceps
gat|ito m kitten. ~**o** m cat. **dar** ~**o por liebre** take s.o. in
gaucho a & m Gaucho
gaveta f drawer
gavilla f sheaf; (*de personas*) band, gang
gaviota f seagull
gazpacho m gazpacho, cold soup
géiser m geyser
gelatina f gelatine; (*jalea*) jelly
gelignita f gelignite
gema f gem
gemelo m twin. ~**s** mpl (*anteojos*) binoculars; (*de camisa*) cuff-links. **G**~**s** Gemini
gemido m groan
Géminis mpl Gemini

gemir [5] *vi* groan; ⟨*animal*⟩ whine, howl

gen *m*, **gene** *m* gene

geneal|ogía *f* genealogy. **∼ógico** *a* genealogical. **árbol** *m* **∼ógico** family tree

generación *f* generation

general *a* general; (*corriente*) common. ● *m* general. **∼ísimo** *m* generalissimo, supreme commander. **∼ización** *f* generalization. **∼izar** [10] *vt/i* generalize. **∼mente** *adv* generally. **en ∼** in general. **por lo ∼** generally

generar *vt* generate

género *m* type, sort; (*biol*) genus; (*gram*) gender; (*producto*) product. **∼s de punto** knitwear. **∼ humano** mankind

generos|idad *f* generosity. **∼o** *a* generous; ⟨*vino*⟩ full-bodied

génesis *m* genesis

genétic|a *f* genetics. **∼o** *a* genetic

genial *a* brilliant; (*agradable*) pleasant

genio *m* temper; (*carácter*) nature; (*talento, persona*) genius

genital *a* genital. **∼es** *mpl* genitals

gente *f* people; (*nación*) nation; (*familia, fam*) family; (*Mex, persona*) person

gentil *a* charming; (*pagano*) pagan. **∼eza** *f* elegance; (*encanto*) charm; (*amabilidad*) kindness

gentío *m* crowd

genuflexión *f* genuflection

genuino *a* genuine

ge|ografía *f* geography. **∼ográfico** *a* geographical. **∼ógrafo** *m* geographer

ge|ología *f* geology. **∼ólogo** *m* geologist

geom|etría *f* geometry. **∼étrico** *a* geometrical

geranio *m* geranium

geren|cia *f* management. **∼te** *m* manager

geriatría *f* geriatrics

germánico *a & m* Germanic

germen *m* germ

germicida *f* germicide

germinar *vi* germinate

gestación *f* gestation

gesticul|ación *f* gesticulation. **∼r** *vi* gesticulate; (*hacer muecas*) grimace

gesti|ón *f* step; (*administración*) management. **∼onar** *vt* take steps to arrange; (*dirigir*) manage

gesto *m* expression; (*ademán*) gesture; (*mueca*) grimace

Gibraltar *m* Gibraltar

gibraltareño *a & m* Gibraltarian

gigante *a* gigantic. ● *m* giant. **∼sco** *a* gigantic

gimn|asia *f* gymnastics. **∼asio** *m* gymnasium, gym (*fam*). **∼asta** *m & f* gymnast. **∼ástica** *f* gymnastics

gimotear *vi* whine

ginebra *f* gin

Ginebra *f* Geneva

ginec|ología *f* gynaecology. **∼ólogo** *m* gynaecologist

gira *f* excursion; (*a varios sitios*) tour

girar *vt* spin; (*por giro postal*) transfer. ● *vi* rotate, go round; ⟨*camino etc*⟩ turn

girasol *m* sunflower

gir|atorio *a* revolving. **∼o** *m* turn; (*com*) draft; (*locución*) expression. **∼o postal** postal order

giroscopio *m* gyroscope

gis *m* chalk

gitano *a & m* gypsy

glacia|l *a* icy. **∼r** *m* glacier

gladiador *m* gladiator

glándula *f* gland

glasear *vt* glaze; (*culin*) ice

glicerina *f* glycerine

glicina *f* wisteria

glob|al *a* global; (*fig*) overall. **∼o** *m* globe; (*aeróstato, juguete*) balloon

glóbulo *m* globule; (*med*) corpuscle

gloria *f* glory. **∼rse** *vpr* boast (**de** about)

glorieta *f* bower; (*auto*) roundabout (*Brit*), (traffic) circle (*Amer*)

glorificar [7] *vt* glorify

glorioso *a* glorious

glosario *m* glossary

glot|ón *a* gluttonous. ● *m* glutton. **∼onería** *f* gluttony

glucosa *f* glucose

gnomo /'nomo/ *m* gnome

gob|ernación *f* government. **∼ernador** *a* governing. ● *m* governor. **∼ernante** *a* governing. **∼ernar** [1] *vt* govern; (*dirigir*) manage, direct. **∼ierno** *m* government; (*dirección*) management, direction. **∼ierno de la casa** housekeeping. **Ministerio** *m* **de la G∼ernación** Home Office (*Brit*), Department of the Interior (*Amer*)

goce *m* enjoyment

gol *m* goal

golf *m* golf

golfo *m* gulf; (*niño*) urchin; (*holgazán*) layabout

golondrina *f* swallow

golos|ina *f* titbit; (*dulce*) sweet. ~o *a* fond of sweets

golpe *m* blow; (*puñetazo*) punch; (*choque*) bump; (*de emoción*) shock; (*acceso*) fit; (*en fútbol*) shot; (*en golf, en tenis, de remo*) stroke. ~ar *vt* hit; (*dar varios golpes*) beat; (*con mucho ruido*) bang; (*con el puño*) punch. ● *vi* knock. ~ **de estado** coup d'etat. ~ **de fortuna** stroke of luck. ~ **de mano** raid. ~ **de vista** glance. ~ **militar** military coup. **de** ~ suddenly. **de un** ~ at one go

gom|a *f* rubber; (*para pegar*) glue; (*anillo*) rubber band; (*elástico*) elastic. ~**a de borrar** rubber. ~**a de pegar** glue. ~**a espuma** foam rubber. ~**ita** *f* rubber band

gongo *m* gong

gord|a *f* (*Mex*) thick tortilla. ~**iflón** *m* (*fam*), ~**inflón** *m* (*fam*) fatty. ~o *a* ⟨*persona*⟩ fat; ⟨*carne*⟩ fatty; (*grande*) large, big. ● *m* first prize. ~**ura** *f* fatness; (*grasa*) fat

gorila *f* gorilla

gorje|ar *vi* chirp. ~o *m* chirping

gorra *f* cap

gorrión *m* sparrow

gorro *m* cap; (*de niño*) bonnet

got|a *f* drop; (*med*) gout. ~**ear** *vi* drip. ~**eo** *m* dripping. ~**era** *f* leak. **ni** ~a nothing

gótico *a* Gothic

gozar [10] *vt* enjoy. ● *vi*. ~ **de** enjoy. ~**se** *vpr* enjoy

gozne *m* hinge

gozo *m* pleasure; (*alegría*) joy. ~**so** *a* delighted

graba|ción *f* recording. ~**do** *m* engraving, print; (*en libro*) illustration. ~**r** *vt* engrave; record ⟨*discos etc*⟩

gracejo *m* wit

graci|a *f* grace; (*favor*) favour; (*humor*) wit. ~**as** *fpl* thanks. **¡**~**as!** thank you!, thanks! ~**oso** *a* funny. ● *m* fool, comic character. **dar las** ~**as** thank. **hacer** ~a amuse; (*gustar*) please. **¡muchas** ~**as!** thank you very much! **tener** ~**a** be funny

grad|a *f* step; (*línea*) row; (*de anfiteatro*) tier. ~**ación** *f* gradation. ~o *m* degree; (*escol*) year (*Brit*), grade (*Amer*); (*voluntad*) willingness

gradua|ción *f* graduation; (*de alcohol*) proof. ~**do** *m* graduate. ~**l** *a* gradual. ~**r** [21] *vt* graduate; (*medir*) measure; (*univ*) confer a degree on. ~**rse** *vpr* graduate

gráfic|a *f* graph. ~o *a* graphic. ● *m* graph

grajo *m* rook

gram|ática *f* grammar. ~**atical** *a* grammatical

gramo *m* gram, gramme (*Brit*)

gramófono *m* record-player, gramophone (*Brit*), phonograph (*Amer*)

gran *a* véase **grande**

grana *f* (*color*) scarlet

granada *f* pomegranate; (*mil*) grenade

granate *m* garnet

Gran Bretaña *f* Great Britain

grande *a* (*delante de nombre en singular* **gran**) big, large; (*alto*) tall; (*fig*) great. ● *m* grandee. ~**za** *f* greatness

grandioso *a* magnificent

granel *m*. **a** ~ in bulk; (*suelto*) loose; (*fig*) in abundance

granero *m* barn

granito *m* granite; (*grano*) small grain

graniz|ado *m* iced drink. ~**ar** [10] *vi* hail. ~o *m* hail

granj|a *f* farm. ~**ero** *m* farmer

grano *m* grain; (*semilla*) seed; (*de café*) bean; (*med*) spot. ~**s** *mpl* cereals

granuja *m & f* rogue

gránulo *m* granule

grapa *f* staple

gras|a *f* grease; (*culin*) fat. ~**iento** *a* greasy

gratifica|ción *f* (*propina*) tip; (*de sueldo*) bonus. ~**r** [7] *vt* (*dar propina*) tip

gratis *adv* free

gratitud *f* gratitude

grato *a* pleasant; (*bienvenido*) welcome

gratuito *a* free; (*fig*) uncalled for

grava *f* gravel

grava|men *m* obligation. ~**r** *vt* tax; (*cargar*) burden

grave *a* serious; (*pesado*) heavy; ⟨*sonido*⟩ low; ⟨*acento*⟩ grave. ~**dad** *f* gravity

gravilla *f* gravel

gravita|ción *f* gravitation. ~**r** *vi* gravitate; (*apoyarse*) rest (**sobre** on); (*fig, pesar*) weigh (**sobre** on)

gravoso *a* onerous; (*costoso*) expensive

graznar *vi* ⟨*cuervo*⟩ caw; ⟨*pato*⟩ quack

Grecia *f* Greece

gregario *a* gregarious

greguería *f* uproar

gremio *m* union

greñ|a *f* mop of hair. **~udo** *a* unkempt

gresca *f* uproar; (*riña*) quarrel

griego *a* & *m* Greek

grieta *f* crack

grifo *m* tap, faucet (*Amer*); (*animal fantástico*) griffin

grilletes *mpl* shackles

grillo *m* cricket; (*bot*) shoot. **~s** *mpl* shackles

grima *f*. **dar** **~** annoy

gringo *m* (*LAm*) Yankee (*fam*), American

gripe *f* flu (*fam*), influenza

gris *a* grey. ● *m* grey; (*policía, fam*) policeman

grit|ar *vt* shout (for); (*como protesta*) boo. ● *vi* shout. **~ería** *f*, **~erío** *m* uproar. **~o** *m* shout; (*de dolor, sorpresa*) cry; (*chillido*) scream. **dar ~s** shout

grosella *f* redcurrant. **~ negra** blackcurrant

groser|ía *f* coarseness; (*palabras etc*) coarse remark. **~o** *a* coarse; (*descortés*) rude

grosor *m* thickness

grotesco *a* grotesque

grúa *f* crane

grues|a *f* gross. **~o** *a* thick; ⟨*persona*⟩ fat, stout. ● *m* thickness; (*fig*) main body

grulla *f* crane

grumo *m* clot; (*de leche*) curd

gruñ|ido *m* grunt; (*fig*) grumble. **~r** [22] *vi* grunt; ⟨*perro*⟩ growl; (*refunfuñar*) grumble

grupa *f* hindquarters

grupo *m* group

gruta *f* grotto

guacamole *m* (*Mex*) avocado purée

guadaña *f* scythe

guagua *f* trifle; (*esp LAm, autobús, fam*) bus

guante *m* glove

guapo *a* good-looking; ⟨*chica*⟩ pretty; (*elegante*) smart

guarapo *m* (*LAm*) sugar cane liquor

guarda *m* & *f* guard; (*de parque etc*) keeper. ● *f* protection. **~barros** *m invar* mudguard. **~bosque** *m* gamekeeper. **~costas** *m invar* coastguard

vessel. **~dor** *a* careful. ● *m* keeper. **~espaldas** *m invar* bodyguard. **~meta** *m invar* goalkeeper. **~r** *vt* keep; (*vigilar*) guard; (*proteger*) protect; (*reservar*) save, keep. **~rse** *vpr* be on one's guard. **~rse de** (+ *infinitivo*) avoid (+ *gerundio*). **~rropa** *m* wardrobe; (*en local público*) cloakroom. **~vallas** *m invar* (*LAm*) goalkeeper

guardería *f* nursery

guardia *f* guard; (*custodia*) care. ● *f* guard. **G~ Civil** Civil Guard. **~ municipal** policeman. **~ de tráfico** traffic policeman. **estar de ~** be on duty. **estar en ~** be on one's guard. **montar la ~** mount guard

guardián *m* guardian; (*de parque etc*) keeper; (*de edificio*) caretaker

guardilla *f* attic

guar|ecer [11] (*albergar*) give shelter to. **~ecerse** *vpr* take shelter. **~ida** *f* den, lair; (*de personas*) hideout

guarn|ecer [11] *vt* provide; (*adornar*) decorate; (*culin*) garnish. **~ición** *m* decoration; (*de caballo*) harness; (*culin*) garnish; (*mil*) garrison; (*de piedra preciosa*) setting

guarro *m* pig

guasa *f* joke; (*ironía*) irony

guaso *a* (*Arg*) coarse

guasón *a* humorous. ● *m* joker

Guatemala *f* Guatemala

guatemalteco *a* from Guatemala. ● *m* person from Guatemala

guateque *m* party

guayaba *f* guava; (*dulce*) guava jelly

guayabera *f* (*Mex*) shirt

gubernamental *a*, **gubernativo** *a* governmental

güero *a* (*Mex*) fair

guerr|a *f* war; (*método*) warfare. **~a civil** civil war. **~ear** *vi* wage war. **~ero** *a* war; (*belicoso*) fighting. ● *m* warrior. **~illa** *f* band of guerillas. **~illero** *m* guerilla. **dar ~a** annoy

guía *m* & *f* guide. ● *f* guidebook; (*de teléfonos*) directory; (*de ferrocarriles*) timetable

guiar [20] *vt* guide; (*llevar*) lead; (*auto*) drive. **~se** *vpr* be guided (**por** by)

guij|arro *m* pebble. **~o** *m* gravel

guillotina *f* guillotine

guind|a *f* morello cherry. **~illa** *f* chilli

guiñapo *m* rag; (*fig, persona*) reprobate

guiñ|ar *vt/i* wink. **~o** *m* wink. **hacer**
~os wink

gui|ón *m* hyphen, dash; (*de película
etc*) script. **~onista** *m & f* script-
writer

guirnalda *f* garland

güiro *m* (*LAm*) gourd

guisa *f* manner, way. **a ~ de** as. **de
tal ~** in such a way

guisado *m* stew

guisante *m* pea. **~ de olor** sweet pea

guis|ar *vt/i* cook. **~o** *m* dish

güisqui *m* whisky

guitarr|a *f* guitar. **~ista** *m & f* gui-
tarist

gula *f* gluttony

gusano *m* worm; (*larva de mosca*)
maggot

gustar *vt* taste. ● *vi* please. **¿te
gusta?** do you like it? **me gusta el
vino** I like wine

gusto *m* taste; (*placer*) pleasure. **~so**
a tasty; (*agradable*) pleasant. **a ~**
comfortable. **a mi ~** to my liking.
buen ~ (good) taste. **con mucho ~**
with pleasure. **dar ~** please. **mucho
~** pleased to meet you

gutural *a* guttural

H

ha *vb* véase **haber**

haba *f* broad bean; (*de café etc*) bean

Habana *f.* **la ~** Havana

haban|era *f* habanera, Cuban dance.
~ero *a* from Havana. ● *m* person
from Havana. **~o** *m* (*puro*) Havana

haber *v aux* [30] have. ● *v impersonal*
(*presente s & pl* **hay**, *imperfecto s & pl*
había, *pretérito s & pl* **hubo**) be. **hay
5 bancos en la plaza** there are 5
banks in the square. **hay que
hacerlo** it must be done, you have to
do it. **he aquí** here is, here are. **no
hay de qué** don't mention it, not at
all. **¿qué hay?** (*¿qué pasa?*) what's
the matter?; (*¿qué tal?*) how are you?

habichuela *f* bean

hábil *a* skilful; (*listo*) clever; (*adecuado*) suitable

habilidad *f* skill; (*astucia*) cleverness

habilita|ción *f* qualification. **~r** *vt*
qualify

habita|ble *a* habitable. **~ción** *f*
room; (*casa etc*) dwelling; (*cuarto de*

dormir) bedroom; (*en biología*) habitat. **~ción de matrimonio,** **~ción
doble** double room. **~ción individual,** **~ción sencilla** single room.
~do *a* inhabited. **~nte** *m* inhabitant. **~r** *vt* live in. ● *vi* live

hábito *m* habit

habitual *a* usual, habitual; (*cliente*)
regular. **~mente** *adv* usually

habituar [21] *vt* accustom. **~se** *vpr.*
~se a get used to

habla *f* speech; (*idioma*) language;
(*dialecto*) dialect. **al ~** (*al teléfono*)
speaking. **ponerse al ~ con** get in
touch with. **~dor** *a* talkative. ● *m*
chatterbox. **~duría** *f* rumour.
~durías *fpl* gossip. **~nte** *a* speaking. ● *m & f* speaker. **~r** *vt* speak.
● *vi* speak, talk (**con** to). **~rse** *vpr*
speak. **¡ni ~r!** out of the question! **se
~ español** Spanish spoken

hacedor *m* creator, maker

hacendado *m* landowner; (*LAm*)
farmer

hacendoso *a* hard-working

hacer [31] *vt* do; (*fabricar, producir
etc*) make; (*en matemáticas*) make,
be. ● *v impersonal* (*con expresiones
meteorológicas*) be; (*con determinado
periodo de tiempo*) ago. **~se** *vpr* become; (*acostumbrarse*) get used (**a**
to); (*estar hecho*) be made. **~ de** act
as. **~se a la mar** put to sea. **~se el
sordo** pretend to be deaf. **hace buen
tiempo** it's fine weather. **hace calor**
it's hot. **hace frío** it's cold. **hace
poco** recently. **hace 7 años** 7 years
ago. **hace sol** it's sunny. **hace viento**
it's windy. **¿qué le vamos a ~?** what
are we going to do?

hacia *prep* towards; (*cerca de*) near;
(*con tiempo*) at about. **~ abajo** down-
(wards). **~ arriba** up(wards). **~ las
dos** at about two o'clock

hacienda *f* country estate; (*en LAm*)
ranch; (*LAm, ganado*) livestock; (*pú-
blica*) treasury. **Ministerio** *m* **de H~**
Ministry of Finance; (*en Gran
Bretaña*) Exchequer; (*en Estados
Unidos*) Treasury. **ministro** *m* **de H~**
Minister of Finance; (*en Gran
Bretaña*) Chancellor of the Ex-
chequer; (*en Estados Unidos*) Sec-
retary of the Treasury

hacinar *vt* stack

hacha *f* axe; (*antorcha*) torch

hachís *m* hashish

hada f fairy. **cuento** m **de** ~s fairy tale

hado m fate

hago vb véase **hacer**

Haití m Haiti

halag|ar [12] vt flatter. ~**üeño** a flattering

halcón m falcon

hálito m breath

halo m halo

hall /xol/ m hall

halla|r vt find; (descubrir) discover. ~**rse** vpr be. ~**zgo** m discovery

hamaca f hammock; (asiento) deckchair

hambr|e f hunger; (de muchos) famine. ~**iento** a starving. **tener** ~**e** be hungry

Hamburgo m Hamburg

hamburguesa f hamburger

hamp|a f underworld. ~**ón** m thug

handicap /'xandikap/ m handicap

hangar m hangar

haragán a lazy, idle. ● m layabout

harap|iento a in rags. ~**o** m rag

harina f flour

harpa f harp

hart|ar vt satisfy; (fastidiar) annoy. ~**arse** vpr (comer) eat one's fill; (cansarse) get fed up (**de** with). ~**azgo** m surfeit. ~**o** a full; (cansado) tired; (fastidiado) fed up (**de** with). ● adv enough; (muy) very. ~**ura** f surfeit; (abundancia) plenty; (de deseo) satisfaction

hasta prep as far as; (con tiempo) until, till; (Mex) not until. ● adv even. ¡~ **la vista!** goodbye!, see you! (fam). ¡~ **luego!** see you later! ¡~ **mañana!** see you tomorrow! ¡~ **pronto!** see you soon!

hast|iar [20] vt annoy; (cansar) weary, tire; (aburrir) bore. ~**iarse** vpr get fed up (**de** with). ~**ío** m weariness; (aburrimiento) boredom; (asco) disgust

hat|illo m bundle (of belongings); (ganado) small flock. ~**o** m belongings; (ganado) flock, herd

haya f beech (tree). ● vb véase **haber**

Haya f. **la** ~ the Hague

haz m bundle; (de trigo) sheaf; (de rayos) beam

hazaña f exploit

hazmerreír m laughing-stock

he vb véase **haber**

hebdomadario a weekly

hebilla f buckle

hebra f thread; (fibra) fibre

hebreo a Hebrew; (actualmente) Jewish. ● m Hebrew; (actualmente) Jew; (lengua) Hebrew

hecatombe f (fig) disaster

hechi|cera f witch. ~**cería** f witchcraft. ~**cero** a magic. ● m wizard. ~**zar** [10] vt cast a spell on; (fig) fascinate. ~**zo** m witchcraft; (un acto de brujería) spell; (fig) fascination

hech|o pp de **hacer**. ● a mature; (terminado) finished; (vestidos etc) ready-made; (culin) done. ● m fact; (acto) deed; (cuestión) matter; (suceso) event. ~**ura** f making; (forma) form; (del cuerpo) build; (calidad de fabricación) workmanship. **de** ~**o** in fact

hed|er [1] vi stink. ~**iondez** f stench. ~**iondo** a stinking, smelly. ~**or** m stench

hela|da f freeze; (escarcha) frost. ~**dera** f (LAm) refrigerator, fridge (Brit, fam). ~**dería** f ice-cream shop. ~**do** a frozen; (muy frío) very cold. ● m ice-cream. ~**dora** f freezer. ~**r** [1] vt freeze. ~**rse** vpr freeze

helecho m fern

hélice f spiral; (propulsor) propeller

heli|cóptero m helicopter. ~**puerto** m heliport

hembra f female; (mujer) woman

hemisferio m hemisphere

hemorragia f haemorrhage

hemorroides fpl haemorrhoids, piles

henchir [5] vt fill. ~**se** vpr stuff o.s.

hend|er [1] vt split. ~**idura** f crack, split; (geol) fissure

heno m hay

heráldica f heraldry

herb|áceo a herbaceous. ~**olario** m herbalist. ~**oso** a grassy

hered|ad f country estate. ~**ar** vt/i inherit. ~**era** f heiress. ~**ero** m heir. ~**itario** a hereditary

herej|e m heretic. ~**ía** f heresy

herencia f inheritance; (fig) heritage

heri|da f injury. ~**do** a injured, wounded. ● m injured person. ~**r** [4] vt injure, wound; (fig) hurt. ~**rse** vpr hurt o.s. **los** ~**dos** the injured; (cantidad) the number of injured

herman|a f sister. ~**a política** sister-in-law. ~**astra** f stepsister. ~**astro** m stepbrother. ~**dad** f brotherhood. ~**o** m brother. ~**o**

político brother-in-law. **~os gemelos** twins

hermético a hermetic; (fig) watertight

hermos|o a beautiful; (espléndido) splendid; ‹hombre› handsome. **~ura** f beauty

hernia f hernia

héroe m hero

hero|ico a heroic; (droga) heroin. **~ína** f heroine; **~ismo** m heroism

herr|adura f horseshoe. **~amienta** f tool. **~ería** f smithy. **~ero** m blacksmith. **~umbre** f rust

herv|idero m (manantial) spring; (fig) hotbed; (multitud) throng. **~ir** [4] vt/i boil. **~or** m boiling; (fig) ardour

heterogéneo a heterogeneous

heterosexual a & m & f heterosexual

hex|agonal a hexagonal. **~ágono** m hexagon

hiato m hiatus

hiberna|ción f hibernation. **~r** vi hibernate

hibisco m hibiscus

híbrido a & m hybrid

hice vb véase **hacer**

hidalgo m nobleman

hidrata|nte a moisturizing. **~r** vt hydrate; ‹crema etc› moisturize. **crema** f **~nte** moisturizing cream

hidráulico a hydraulic

hidroavión m seaplane

hidroeléctrico a hydroelectric

hidrófilo a absorbent

hidr|ofobia f rabies. **~ófobo** a rabid

hidrógeno m hydrogen

hidroplano m seaplane

hiedra f ivy

hiel f (fig) bitterness

hielo m ice; (escarcha) frost; (fig) coldness

hiena f hyena; (fig) brute

hierba f grass; (culin, med) herb. **~buena** f mint. **mala ~** weed; (gente) bad people, evil people

hierro m iron

hígado m liver

higi|ene f hygiene. **~énico** a hygienic

hig|o m fig. **~uera** f fig tree

hij|a f daughter. **~a política** daughter-in-law. **~astra** f stepdaughter. **~astro** m stepson. **~o** m son. **~o**

político son-in-law. **~os** mpl sons; (chicos y chicas) children

hilar vt spin. **~ delgado** split hairs

hilaridad f laughter, hilarity

hilera f row; (mil) file

hilo m thread; (elec) wire; (de líquido) trickle; (lino) linen

hilv|án m tacking. **~anar** vt tack; (fig, bosquejar) outline

himno m hymn. **~ nacional** anthem

hincapié m. **hacer ~ en** stress, insist on

hincar [7] vt drive in. **~se** vpr sink into. **~se de rodillas** kneel down

hincha f (fam) grudge; (aficionado, fam) fan

hincha|do a inflated; (med) swollen; ‹persona› arrogant. **~r** vt inflate, blow up. **~rse** vpr swell up; (fig, comer mucho, fam) gorge o.s. **~zón** f swelling; (fig) arrogance

hindi m Hindi

hindú a Hindu

hiniesta f (bot) broom

hinojo m fennel

hiper... pref hyper...

hiper|mercado m hypermarket. **~sensible** a hypersensitive. **~tensión** f high blood pressure

hípico a horse

hipn|osis f hypnosis. **~ótico** a hypnotic. **~otismo** m hypnotism. **~otizador** m hypnotist. **~otizar** [10] vt hypnotize

hipo m hiccup. **tener ~** have hiccups

hipocondríaco a & m hypochondriac

hip|ocresía f hypocrisy. **~ócrita** a hypocritical. ● m & f hypocrite

hipodérmico a hypodermic

hipódromo m racecourse

hipopótamo m hippopotamus

hipoteca f mortgage. **~r** [7] vt mortgage

hip|ótesis f invar hypothesis. **~otético** a hypothetical

hiriente a offensive, wounding

hirsuto a shaggy

hirviente a boiling

hispánico a Hispanic

hispano... pref Spanish

Hispanoamérica f Spanish America

hispano|americano a Spanish American. **~hablante** a, **~parlante** a Spanish-speaking

hist|eria f hysteria. **~érico** a hysterical. **~erismo** m hysteria

hist|oria f history; (cuento) story. **~oriador** m historian. **~órico** a historical. **~orieta** f tale; (con dibujos) strip cartoon. **pasar a la ∼oria** go down in history

hito *m* milestone

hizo *vb véase* **hacer**

hocico *m* snout; (*fig, de enfado*) grimace

hockey *m* hockey. **∼ sobre hielo** ice hockey

hogar *m* hearth; (*fig*) home. **∼eño** *a* home; (*persona*) home-loving

hogaza *f* large loaf

hoguera *f* bonfire

hoja *f* leaf; (*de papel, metal etc*) sheet; (*de cuchillo, espada etc*) blade. **∼ de afeitar** razor blade. **∼lata** *f* tin. **∼latería** *f* tinware. **∼latero** *m* tinsmith

hojaldre *m* puff pastry, flaky pastry

hojear *vt* leaf through; (*leer superficialmente*) glance through

hola *int* hello!

Holanda *f* Holland

holand|és *a* Dutch. ● *m* Dutchman; (*lengua*) Dutch. **∼esa** *f* Dutchwoman

holg|ado *a* loose; (*fig*) comfortable. **∼ar** [2 & 12] *vt* (*no trabajar*) not work, have a day off; (*sobrar*) be unnecessary. **∼azán** *a* lazy. ● *m* idler. **∼ura** *f* looseness; (*fig*) comfort; (*en mecánica*) play. **huelga decir que** needless to say

holocausto *m* holocaust

hollín *m* soot

hombre *m* man; (*especie humana*) man(kind). ● *int* Good Heavens!; (*de duda*) well. **∼ de estado** statesman. **∼ de negocios** businessman. **∼ rana** frogman. **el ∼ de la calle** the man in the street

hombr|era *f* epaulette; (*almohadilla*) shoulder pad. **∼o** *m* shoulder

hombruno *a* masculine

homenaje *m* homage; (*fig*) tribute. **rendir ∼ a** pay tribute to

home|ópata *m* homoeopath. **∼opatía** *f* homoeopathy. **∼opático** *a* homoeopathic

homicid|a *a* murderous. ● *m & f* murderer. **∼io** *m* murder

homogéneo *a* homogeneous

homosexual *a & m & f* homosexual. **∼idad** *f* homosexuality

hond|o *a* deep. **∼onada** *f* hollow. **∼ura** *f* depth

Honduras *fpl* Honduras

hondureño *a & m* Honduran

honest|idad *f* decency. **∼o** *a* proper

hongo *m* fungus; (*culin*) mushroom; (*venenoso*) toadstool

hon|or *m* honour. **∼orable** *a* honourable. **∼orario** *a* honorary. **∼orarios** *mpl* fees. **∼ra** *f* honour; (*buena fama*) good name. **∼radez** *f* honesty. **∼rado** *a* honest. **∼rar** *vt* honour. **∼rarse** *vpr* be honoured

hora *f* hour; (*momento determinado, momento oportuno*) time. **∼ avanzada** late hour. **∼ punta** rush hour. **∼s** *fpl* **de trabajo** working hours. **∼s** *fpl* **extraordinarias** overtime. **a estas ∼s** now. **¿a qué ∼?** at what time? when? **de ∼ en ∼** hourly. **de última ∼** last-minute. **en buena ∼** at the right time. **media ∼** half an hour. **¿qué ∼ es?** what time is it? **¿tiene Vd ∼?** can you tell me the time?

horario *a* time; (*cada hora*) hourly. ● *m* timetable. **a ∼** (*LAm*) on time

horca *f* gallows

horcajadas *fpl*. **a ∼** astride

horchata *f* tiger-nut milk

horda *f* horde

horizont|al *a & f* horizontal. **∼e** *m* horizon

horma *f* mould; (*para fabricar calzado*) last; (*para conservar forma del calzado*) shoe-tree

hormiga *f* ant

hormigón *m* concrete

hormigue|ar *vt* tingle; (*bullir*) swarm. **me ∼a la mano** I've got pins and needles in my hand. **∼o** *m* tingling; (*fig*) anxiety

hormiguero *m* anthill; (*de gente*) swarm

hormona *f* hormone

horn|ada *f* batch. **∼ero** *m* baker. **∼illo** *m* cooker. **∼o** *m* oven; (*para ladrillos, cerámica etc*) kiln; (*tec*) furnace

horóscopo *m* horoscope

horquilla *f* pitchfork; (*para el pelo*) hairpin

horr|endo *a* awful. **∼ible** *a* horrible. **∼ipilante** *a* terrifying. **∼or** *m* horror; (*atrocidad*) atrocity. **∼orizar** [10] *vt* horrify. **∼orizarse** *vpr* be horrified. **∼oroso** *a* horrifying. **¡qué ∼or!** how awful!

hort|aliza *f* vegetable. **∼elano** *m* market gardener. **∼icultura** *f* horticulture

hosco *a* surly; (*lugar*) gloomy

hospeda|je *m* lodging. **~r** *vt* put up. **~rse** *vpr* lodge

hospital *m* hospital

hospital|ario *m* hospitable. **~idad** *f* hospitality

hostal *m* boarding-house

hostería *f* inn

hostia *f* (*relig*) host; (*golpe, fam*) punch

hostigar [12] *vt* whip; (*fig, excitar*) urge; (*fig, molestar*) pester

hostil *a* hostile. **~idad** *f* hostility

hotel *m* hotel. **~ero** *a* hotel. ● *m* hotelier

hoy *adv* today. **~ (en) día** nowadays. **~ mismo** this very day. **~ por ~** for the time being. **de ~ en adelante** from now on

hoy|a *f* hole; (*sepultura*) grave. **~o** *m* hole; (*sepultura*) grave. **~uelo** *m* dimple

hoz *f* sickle; (*desfiladero*) pass

hube *vb véase* **haber**

hucha *f* money box

hueco *a* hollow; (*vacío*) empty; (*esponjoso*) spongy; (*resonante*) resonant. ● *m* hollow

huelg|a *f* strike. **~a de brazos caídos** sit-down strike. **~a de celo** work-to-rule. **~a de hambre** hunger strike. **~uista** *m & f* striker. **declarar la ~a, declararse en ~a** come out on strike

huelo *vb véase* **oler**

huella *f* footprint; (*de animal, vehículo etc*) track. **~ dactilar, ~ digital** fingerprint

huérfano *a* orphaned. ● *m* orphan. **~ de** without

huero *a* empty

huert|a *f* market garden (*Brit*), truck farm (*Amer*); (*terreno de regadío*) irrigated plain. **~o** *m* vegetable garden; (*de árboles frutales*) orchard

huesa *f* grave

hueso *m* bone; (*de fruta*) stone. **~so** *a* bony

huésped *m* guest; (*que paga*) lodger; (*animal*) host

huesudo *a* bony

huev|a *f* roe. **~era** *f* eggcup. **~o** *m* egg. **~o duro** hard-boiled egg. **~o escalfado** poached egg. **~o estrellado, ~o frito** fried egg. **~o pasado por agua** boiled egg. **~os revueltos** scrambled eggs

hui|da *f* flight, escape. **~dizo** *a* (*tímido*) shy; (*fugaz*) fleeting. **~r** [17] *vt/i* flee, run away; (*evitar*) avoid

huipil *m* (*Mex*) embroidered smock

huitlacoche *m* (*Mex*) edible black fungus

hule *m* oilcloth, oilskin

human|idad *f* mankind; (*fig*) humanity. **~idades** *fpl* humanities. **~ismo** *m* humanism. **~ista** *m & f* humanist. **~itario** *a* humanitarian. **~o** *a* human; (*benévolo*) humane. ● *m* human (being)

hum|areda *f* cloud of smoke. **~ear** *vi* smoke; (*echar vapor*) steam

humed|ad *f* dampness (*en meteorología*) humidity. **~ecer** [11] *vt* moisten. **~ecerse** *vpr* become moist

húmedo *a* damp; (*clima*) humid; (*mojado*) wet

humi|ldad *f* humility. **~lde** *a* humble. **~llación** *f* humiliation. **~llar** *vt* humiliate. **~llarse** *vpr* humble o.s.

humo *m* smoke; (*vapor*) steam; (*gas nocivo*) fumes. **~s** *mpl* conceit

humor *m* mood, temper; (*gracia*) humour. **~ismo** *m* humour. **~ista** *m & f* humorist. **~ístico** *a* humorous. **estar de mal ~** be in a bad mood

hundi|do *a* sunken. **~miento** *m* sinking. **~r** *vt* sink; destroy (*edificio*). **~rse** *vpr* sink; (*edificio*) collapse

húngaro *a & m* Hungarian

Hungría *f* Hungary

huracán *m* hurricane

huraño *a* unsociable

hurg|ar [12] *vt* poke; (*fig*) stir up. **~ón** *m* poker

hurón *m* ferret. ● *a* unsociable

hurra *int* hurray!

hurraca *f* magpie

hurtadillas *fpl* **a ~** stealthily

hurt|ar *vt* steal. **~o** *m* theft; (*cosa robada*) stolen object

husmear *vt* sniff out; (*fig*) pry into

huyo *vb véase* **huir**

I

Iberia *f* Iberia

ibérico *a* Iberian

ibero *a & m* Iberian

íbice *m* ibex, mountain goat

Ibiza *f* Ibiza

iceberg /iθ'ber/ *m* iceberg

icono *m* icon

ictericia *f* jaundice

ida f outward journey; (*salida*) departure. **de ~ y vuelta** return (*Brit*), round-trip (*Amer*)

idea f idea; (*opinión*) opinion. **cambiar de ~** change one's mind. **no tener la más remota ~, no tener la menor ~** not have the slightest idea, not have a clue (*fam*)

ideal a ideal; (*imaginario*) imaginary. ● m ideal. **~ista** m & f idealist. **~izar** [10] vt idealize

idear vt think up, conceive; (*inventar*) invent

ídem pron & adv the same

idéntico a identical

identi|dad f identity. **~ficación** f identification. **~ficar** [7] vt identify. **~ficarse** vpr. **~ficarse con** identify with

ideol|ogía f ideology. **~ógico** a ideological

idílico a idyllic

idilio m idyll

idioma m language. **~ático** a idiomatic

idiosincrasia f idiosyncrasy

idiot|a a idiotic. ● m & f idiot. **~ez** f idiocy

idiotismo m idiom

idolatrar vt worship; (*fig*) idolize

ídolo m idol

idóneo a suitable (**para** for)

iglesia f church

iglú m igloo

ignición f ignition

ignomini|a f ignominy, disgrace. **~oso** a ignominious

ignora|ncia f ignorance. **~nte** a ignorant. ● m ignoramus. **~r** vt not know, be unaware of

igual a equal; (*mismo*) the same; (*similar*) like; (*llano*) even; (*liso*) smooth. ● adv easily. ● m equal. **~ que** (the same) as. **al ~ que** the same as. **da ~, es ~** it doesn't matter

igual|ar vt make equal; (*ser igual*) equal; (*allanar*) level. **~arse** vpr be equal. **~dad** f equality. **~mente** adv equally; (*también*) also, likewise; (*respuesta de cortesía*) the same to you

ijada f flank

ilegal a illegal

ilegible a illegible

ilegítimo a illegitimate

ileso a unhurt

ilícito a illicit

ilimitado a unlimited

ilógico a illogical

ilumina|ción f illumination; (*alumbrado*) lighting; (*fig*) enlightenment. **~r** vt light (up); (*fig*) enlighten. **~rse** vpr light up

ilusi|ón f illusion; (*sueño*) dream; (*alegría*) joy. **~onado** a excited. **~onar** vt give false hope. **~onarse** vpr have false hopes. **hacerse ~ones** build up one's hopes. **me hace ~ón** I'm thrilled; I'm looking forward to (*algo en el futuro*)

ilusionis|mo m conjuring. **~ta** m & f conjurer

iluso a easily deceived. ● m dreamer. **~rio** a illusory

ilustra|ción f learning; (*dibujo*) illustration. **~do** a learned; (*con dibujos*) illustrated. **~r** vt explain; (*instruir*) instruct; (*añadir dibujos etc*) illustrate. **~rse** vpr acquire knowledge. **~tivo** a illustrative

ilustre a illustrious

imagen f image; (*TV etc*) picture

imagina|ble a imaginable. **~ción** f imagination. **~r** vt imagine. **~rse** vpr imagine. **~rio** m imaginary. **~tivo** a imaginative

imán m magnet

imantar vt magnetize

imbécil a stupid. ● m & f imbecile, idiot

imborrable a indelible; (*recuerdo etc*) unforgettable

imbuir [17] vt imbue (**de** with)

imita|ción f imitation. **~r** vt imitate

impacien|cia f impatience. **~tarse** vpr lose one's patience. **~te** a impatient; (*intranquilo*) anxious

impacto m impact

impar a odd

imparcial a impartial. **~idad** f impartiality

impartir vt impart

impasible a impassive

impávido a fearless; (*impasible*) impassive

impecable a impeccable

impedi|do a disabled. **~menta** f (*esp mil*) baggage. **~mento** m hindrance. **~r** [5] vt prevent; (*obstruir*) hinder

impeler vt drive

impenetrable a impenetrable

impenitente a unrepentant

impensa|ble a unthinkable. **~do** a unexpected

imperar vi reign

imperativo *a* imperative; ⟨persona⟩ imperious

imperceptible *a* imperceptible

imperdible *m* safety pin

imperdonable *a* unforgivable

imperfec|ción *f* imperfection. **∼to** *a* imperfect

imperial *a* imperial. ● *f* upper deck. **∼ismo** *m* imperialism

imperio *m* empire; (*poder*) rule; (*fig*) pride. **∼so** *a* imperious

impermeable *a* waterproof. ● *m* raincoat

impersonal *a* impersonal

impertérrito *a* undaunted

impertinen|cia *f* impertinence. **∼te** *a* impertinent

imperturbable *a* imperturbable

ímpetu *m* impetus; (*impulso*) impulse; (*impetuosidad*) impetuosity

impetuos|idad *f* impetuosity; (*violencia*) violence. **∼o** *a* impetuous; (*violento*) violent

impío *a* ungodly; ⟨acción⟩ irreverent

implacable *a* implacable

implantar *vt* introduce

implica|ción *f* implication. **∼r** [7] *vt* implicate; (*significar*) imply

implícito *a* implicit

implora|ción *f* entreaty. **∼r** *vt* implore

imponderable *a* imponderable; (*inapreciable*) invaluable

impon|ente *a* imposing; (*fam*) terrific. **∼er** [34] *vt* impose; (*requerir*) demand; deposit ⟨dinero⟩. **∼erse** *vpr* be imposed; (*hacerse obedecer*) assert o.s.; (*hacerse respetar*) command respect. **∼ible** *a* taxable

impopular *a* unpopular. **∼idad** *f* unpopularity

importa|ción *f* import; (*artículo*) import. **∼dor** *a* importing. ● *m* importer

importa|ncia *f* importance; (*tamaño*) size. **∼nte** *a* important; (*en cantidad*) considerable. **∼r** *vt* import; (*valer*) cost. ● *vi* be important, matter. **¡le importa...?** would you mind...? **no ∼** it doesn't matter

importe *m* price; (*total*) amount

importun|ar *vt* bother. **∼o** *a* troublesome; (*inoportuno*) inopportune

imposib|ilidad *f* impossibility. **∼le** *a* impossible. **hacer lo ∼le** do all one can

imposición *f* imposition; (*impuesto*) tax

impostor *m & f* impostor

impotable *a* undrinkable

impoten|cia *f* impotence. **∼te** *a* powerless, impotent

impracticable *a* impracticable; (*intransitable*) unpassable

impreca|ción *f* curse. **∼r** [7] *vt* curse

imprecis|ión *f* vagueness. **∼o** *a* imprecise

impregnar *vt* impregnate; (*empapar*) soak; (*fig*) cover

imprenta *f* printing; (*taller*) printing house, printer's

imprescindible *a* indispensable, essential

impresi|ón *f* impression; (*acción de imprimir*) printing; (*tirada*) edition; (*huella*) imprint. **∼onable** *a* impressionable. **∼onante** *a* impressive; (*espantoso*) frightening. **∼onar** *vt* impress; (*conmover*) move; (*foto*) expose. **∼onarse** *vpr* be impressed; (*conmover*) be moved

impresionis|mo *m* impressionism. **∼ta** *a & m & f* impressionist

impreso *a* printed. ● *m* printed paper, printed matter. **∼ra** *f* printer

imprevis|ible *a* unforeseeable. **∼to** *a* unforeseen

imprimir [*pp* **impreso**] *vt* impress; print ⟨libro etc⟩

improbab|ilidad *f* improbability. **∼le** *a* unlikely, improbable

improcedente *a* unsuitable

improductivo *a* unproductive

improperio *m* insult. **∼s** *mpl* abuse

impropio *a* improper

improvis|ación *f* improvisation. **∼adamente** *adv* suddenly. **∼ado** *a* improvised. **∼ar** *vt* improvise. **∼o** *a*. **de ∼o** suddenly

impruden|cia *f* imprudence. **∼te** *a* imprudent

impuden|cia *f* impudence. **∼te** *a* impudent

imp|údico *a* immodest; (*desvergonzado*) shameless. **∼udor** *m* immodesty; (*desvergüenza*) shamelessness

impuesto *a* imposed. ● *m* tax. **∼ sobre el valor añadido** VAT, value added tax

impugnar *vt* contest; (*refutar*) refute

impulsar *vt* impel

impuls|ividad *f* impulsiveness. **∼ivo** *a* impulsive. **∼o** *m* impulse

impun|e *a* unpunished. **~idad** *f* impunity

impur|eza *f* impurity. **~o** *a* impure

imputa|ción *f* charge. **~r** *vt* attribute; ⟨*acusar*⟩ charge

inacabable *a* interminable

inaccesible *a* inaccessible

inaceptable *a* unacceptable

inacostumbrado *a* unaccustomed

inactiv|idad *f* inactivity. **~o** *a* inactive

inadaptado *a* maladjusted

inadecuado *a* inadequate; ⟨*inapropiado*⟩ unsuitable

inadmisible *a* inadmissible; ⟨*intolerable*⟩ intolerable

inadvert|ido *a* unnoticed. **~encia** *f* inadvertence

inagotable *a* inexhaustible

inaguantable *a* unbearable; ⟨*persona*⟩ insufferable

inaltera|ble unchangeable; ⟨*color*⟩ fast; ⟨*carácter*⟩ calm. **~do** *a* unchanged

inanimado *a* inanimate

inaplicable *a* inapplicable

inapreciable *a* imperceptible

inapropiado *a* inappropriate

inarticulado *a* inarticulate

inasequible *a* out of reach

inaudito *a* unheard-of

inaugura|ción *f* inauguration. **~l** *a* inaugural. **~r** *vt* inaugurate

inca *a* Incan. ● *m & f* Inca. **~ico** *a* Incan

incalculable *a* incalculable

incandescen|cia *f* incandescence. **~te** *a* incandescent

incansable *a* tireless

incapa|cidad *f* incapacity. **~citar** *vt* incapacitate. **~z** *a* incapable

incauto *a* unwary; ⟨*fácil de engañar*⟩ gullible

incendi|ar *vt* set fire to. **~arse** *vpr* catch fire. **~ario** *a* incendiary. ● *m* arsonist. **~o** *m* fire

incentivo *m* incentive

incertidumbre *f* uncertainty

incesante *a* incessant

incest|o *m* incest. **~uoso** *a* incestuous

inciden|cia *f* incidence; ⟨*incidente*⟩ incident. **~tal** *a* incidental. **~te** *m* incident

incidir *vi* fall; ⟨*influir*⟩ influence

incienso *m* incense

incierto *a* uncertain

incinera|ción *f* incineration; ⟨*de cadáveres*⟩ cremation. **~dor** *m* incinerator. **~r** *vt* incinerate; cremate ⟨*cadáver*⟩

incipiente *a* incipient

incisión *f* incision

incisivo *a* incisive. ● *m* incisor

incitar *vt* incite

incivil *a* rude

inclemen|cia *f* harshness. **~te** *a* harsh

inclina|ción *f* slope; ⟨*de la cabeza*⟩ nod; ⟨*fig*⟩ inclination. **~r** *vt* incline. **~rse** *vpr* lean; ⟨*encorvarse*⟩ stoop; ⟨*en saludo*⟩ bow; ⟨*fig*⟩ be inclined. **~rse a** ⟨*parecerse*⟩ resemble

inclu|ido *a* included; ⟨*precio*⟩ inclusive; ⟨*en cartas*⟩ enclosed. **~ir** [17] *vt* include; ⟨*en cartas*⟩ enclose. **~sión** *f* inclusion. **~sive** *adv* inclusive. **hasta el lunes ~sive** up to and including Monday. **~so** *a* included; ⟨*en cartas*⟩ enclosed. ● *adv* including; ⟨*hasta*⟩ even

incógnito *a* unknown. **de ~** incognito

incoheren|cia *f* incoherence. **~te** *a* incoherent

incoloro *a* colourless

incólume *a* unharmed

incomestible *a*, **incomible** *a* uneatable, inedible

incomodar *vt* inconvenience; ⟨*molestar*⟩ bother. **~se** *vpr* trouble o.s.; ⟨*enfadarse*⟩ get angry

incómodo *a* uncomfortable; ⟨*inoportuno*⟩ inconvenient

incomparable *a* imcomparable

incompatib|ilidad *f* incompatibility. **~le** *a* incompatible

incompeten|cia *f* incompetence. **~te** *a* incompetent

incompleto *a* incomplete

incompren|dido *a* misunderstood. **~sible** *a* incomprehensible. **~sión** *f* incomprehension

incomunicado *a* isolated; ⟨*preso*⟩ in solitary confinement

inconcebible *a* inconceivable

inconciliable *a* irreconcilable

inconcluso *a* unfinished

incondicional *a* unconditional

inconfundible *a* unmistakable

incongruente *a* incongruous

inconmensurable *a* ⟨*fam*⟩ enormous

inconscien|cia *f* unconsciousness; ⟨*irreflexión*⟩ recklessness. **~te** *a* unconscious; ⟨*irreflexivo*⟩ reckless

inconsecuente *a* inconsistent
inconsiderado *a* inconsiderate
inconsistente *a* insubstantial
inconsolable *a* unconsolable
inconstan|cia *f* inconstancy. ~**te** *a* changeable; ⟨*persona*⟩ fickle
incontable *a* countless
incontaminado *a* uncontaminated
incontenible *a* irrepressible
incontestable *a* indisputable
incontinen|cia *f* incontinence. ~**te** *a* incontinent
inconvenien|cia *f* disadvantage. ~**te** *a* inconvenient; (*inapropiado*) inappropriate; (*incorrecto*) improper. ● *m* difficulty; (*desventaja*) drawback
incorpora|ción *f* incorporation. ~**r** *vt* incorporate; (*culin*) mix. ~**rse** *vpr* sit up; join ⟨*sociedad, regimiento etc*⟩
incorrecto *a* incorrect; ⟨*acción*⟩ improper; (*descortés*) discourteous
incorregible *a* incorrigible
incorruptible *a* incorruptible
incrédulo *a* incredulous
increíble *a* incredible
increment|ar *vt* increase. ~**o** *m* increase
incriminar *vt* incriminate
incrustar *vt* encrust
incuba|ción *f* incubation. ~**dora** *f* incubator. ~**r** *vt* incubate; (*fig*) hatch
incuestionable *a* unquestionable
inculcar [7] *vt* inculcate
inculpar *vt* accuse; (*culpar*) blame
inculto *a* uncultivated; ⟨*persona*⟩ uneducated
incumplimiento *m* non-fulfilment; (*de un contrato*) breach
incurable *a* incurable
incurrir *vi*. ~ **en** incur; fall into ⟨*error*⟩; commit ⟨*crimen*⟩
incursión *f* raid
indaga|ción *f* investigation. ~**r** [12] *vt* investigate
indebido *a* undue
indecen|cia *f* indecency. ~**te** *a* indecent
indecible *a* inexpressible
indecis|ión *f* indecision. ~**o** *a* undecided
indefenso *a* defenceless
indefini|ble *a* indefinable. ~**do** *a* indefinite
indeleble *a* indelible
indelicad|eza *f* indelicacy. ~**o** *a* indelicate; (*falto de escrúpulo*) unscrupulous

indemn|e *a* undamaged; ⟨*persona*⟩ unhurt. ~**idad** *f* indemnity. ~**izar** [10] *vt* indemnify, compensate
independ|encia *f* independence. ~**iente** *a* independent
independizarse [10] *vpr* become independent
indescifrable *a* indecipherable, incomprehensible
indescriptible *a* indescribable
indeseable *a* undesirable
indestructible *a* indestructible
indetermina|ble *a* indeterminable. ~**do** *a* indeterminate
India *f*. **la** ~ India. **las** ~**s** *fpl* the Indies
indica|ción *f* indication; (*sugerencia*) suggestion. ~**ciones** *fpl* directions. ~**dor** *m* indicator; (*tec*) gauge. ~**r** [7] *vt* show, indicate; (*apuntar*) point at; (*hacer saber*) point out; (*aconsejar*) advise. ~**tivo** *a* indicative. ● *m* indicative; (*al teléfono*) dialling code
índice *m* indication; (*dedo*) index finger; (*de libro*) index; (*catálogo*) catalogue; (*aguja*) pointer
indicio *m* indication, sign; (*vestigio*) trace
indiferen|cia *f* indifference. ~**te** *a* indifferent. **me es** ~**te** it's all the same to me
indígena *a* indigenous. ● *m* & *f* native
indigen|cia *f* poverty. ~**te** *a* needy
indigest|ión *f* indigestion. ~**o** *a* undigested; (*difícil de digerir*) indigestible
indign|ación *f* indignation. ~**ado** *a* indignant. ~**ar** *vt* make indignant. ~**arse** *vpr* be indignant. ~**o** *a* unworthy; (*despreciable*) contemptible
indio *a* & *m* Indian
indirect|a *f* hint. ~**o** *a* indirect
indisciplina *f* lack of discipline. ~**do** *a* undisciplined
indiscre|ción *f* indiscretion. ~**to** *a* indiscreet
indiscutible *a* unquestionable
indisoluble *a* indissoluble
indispensable *a* indispensable
indisp|oner [34] *vt* (*enemistar*) set against. ~**onerse** *vpr* fall out; (*ponerse enfermo*) fall ill. ~**osición** *f* indisposition. ~**uesto** *a* indisposed
indistinto *a* indistinct
individu|al *a* individual; ⟨*cama*⟩ single. ~**alidad** *f* individuality. ~**a-lista** *m* & *f* individualist. ~**alizar** [10]

vt individualize. ~**o** *a* & *m* individual

índole *f* nature; (*clase*) type

indolen|cia *f* indolence. ~**te** *a* indolent

indoloro *a* painless

indomable *a* untameable

indómito *a* indomitable

Indonesia *f* Indonesia

inducir [47] *vt* induce; (*deducir*) infer

indudable *a* undoubted. ~**mente** *adv* undoubtedly

indulgen|cia *f* indulgence. ~**te** *a* indulgent

indult|ar *vt* pardon; exempt (*de un pago etc*). ~**o** *m* pardon

industria *f* industry. ~**l** *a* industrial. ● *m* industrialist. ~**lización** *f* industrialization. ~**lizar** [10] *vt* industrialize

industriarse *vpr* do one's best

industrioso *a* industrious

inédito *a* unpublished; (*fig*) unknown

ineducado *a* impolite

inefable *a* inexpressible

ineficaz *a* ineffective

ineficiente *a* inefficient

inelegible *a* ineligible

ineludible *a* inescapable, unavoidable

inept|itud *f* ineptitude. ~**o** *a* inept

inequívoco *a* unequivocal

iner|cia *f* inertia

inerme *a* unarmed; (*fig*) defenceless

inerte *a* inert

inesperado *a* unexpected

inestable *a* unstable

inestimable *a* inestimable

inevitable *a* inevitable

inexacto *a* inaccurate; (*incorrecto*) incorrect; (*falso*) untrue

inexistente *a* non-existent

inexorable *a* inexorable

inexper|iencia *f* inexperience. ~**to** *a* inexperienced

inexplicable *a* inexplicable

infalible *a* infallible

infam|ar *vt* defame. ~**atorio** *a* defamatory. ~**e** *a* infamous; (*fig, muy malo, fam*) awful. ~**ia** *f* infamy

infancia *f* infancy

infant|a *f* infanta, princess. ~**e** *m* infante, prince; (*mil*) infantryman. ~**ería** *f* infantry. ~**il** *a* (*de niño*) child's; (*como un niño*) infantile

infarto *m* coronary (thrombosis)

infatigable *a* untiring

infatua|ción *f* conceit. ~**rse** *vpr* get conceited

infausto *a* unlucky

infec|ción *f* infection. ~**cioso** *a* infectious. ~**tar** *vt* infect. ~**tarse** *vpr* become infected. ~**to** *a* infected; (*fam*) disgusting

infecundo *a* infertile

infeli|cidad *f* unhappiness. ~**z** *a* unhappy

inferior *a* inferior. ● *m* & *f* inferior. ~**idad** *f* lower; (*calidad*) inferiority

inferir [4] *vt* infer; (*causar*) cause

infernal *a* infernal, hellish

infestar *vt* infest; (*fig*) inundate

infi|delidad *f* unfaithfulness. ~**el** *a* unfaithful

infierno *m* hell

infiltra|ción *f* infiltration. ~**rse** *vpr* infiltrate

ínfimo *a* lowest

infini|dad *f* infinity. ~**tivo** *m* infinitive. ~**to** *a* infinite. ● *m* infinite; (*en matemáticas*) infinity. **una** ~**dad de** countless

inflación *f* inflation; (*fig*) conceit

inflama|ble *a* (in)flammable. ~**ción** *f* inflammation. ~**r** *vt* set on fire; (*fig, med*) inflame. ~**rse** *vpr* catch fire; (*med*) become inflamed

inflar *vt* inflate; (*fig, exagerar*) exaggerate

inflexi|ble *a* inflexible. ~**ón** *f* inflexion

infligir [14] *vt* inflict

influ|encia *f* influence. ~**enza** *f* flu (*fam*), influenza. ~**ir** [17] *vt/i* influence. ~**jo** *m* influence. ~**yente** *a* influential

informa|ción *f* information. ~**ciones** *fpl* (*noticias*) news; (*de teléfonos*) directory enquiries. ~**dor** *m* informant

informal *a* informal; (*incorrecto*) incorrect

inform|ante *m* & *f* informant. ~**ar** *vt/i* inform. ~**arse** *vpr* find out. ~**ática** *f* information technology. ~**ativo** *a* informative

informe *a* shapeless. ● *m* report; (*información*) information

infortun|ado *a* unfortunate. ~**io** *m* misfortune

infracción *f* infringement

infraestructura *f* infrastructure

infranqueable *a* impassable; (*fig*) insuperable

infrarrojo *a* infrared

infrecuente *a* infrequent

infringir [14] *vt* infringe

infructuoso *a* fruitless

infundado *a* unfounded

infu|ndir *vt* instil. **~sión** *f* infusion

ingeniar *vt* invent

ingenier|ía *f* engineering. **~o** *m* engineer

ingenio *m* ingenuity; (*agudeza*) wit; (*LAm, de azúcar*) refinery. **~so** *a* ingenious

ingenu|idad *f* ingenuousness. **~o** *a* ingenuous

ingerir [4] *vt* swallow

Inglaterra *f* England

ingle *f* groin

ingl|és *a* English. ● *m* Englishman; (*lengua*) English. **~esa** *f* Englishwoman

ingrat|itud *f* ingratitude. **~o** *a* ungrateful; (*desagradable*) thankless

ingrediente *m* ingredient

ingres|ar *vt* deposit. ● *vi*. **~ar en** come in, enter; join (*sociedad*). **~o** *m* entry; (*en sociedad, hospital etc*) admission. **~os** *mpl* income

inh|ábil *a* unskillful; (*no apto*) unfit. **~abilidad** *f* unskillfulness

inhabitable *a* uninhabitable

inhala|ción *f* inhalation. **~dor** *m* inhaler. **~r** *vt* inhale

inherente *a* inherent

inhibi|ción *f* inhibition. **~r** *vt* inhibit

inhospitalario *a*, **inhóspito** *a* inhospitable

inhumano *a* inhuman

inicia|ción *f* beginning. **~l** *a & f* initial. **~r** *vt* initiate; (*comenzar*) begin, start. **~tiva** *f* initiative

inicio *m* beginning

inicuo *a* iniquitous

inigualado *a* unequalled

ininterrumpido *a* continuous

injer|encia *f* interference. **~ir** [4] *vt* insert. **~irse** *vpr* interfere

injert|ar *vt* graft. **~to** *m* graft

injuri|a *f* insult; (*ofensa*) offence. **~ar** *vt* insult. **~oso** *a* offensive

injust|icia *f* injustice. **~o** *a* unjust

inmaculado *a* immaculate

inmaduro *a* unripe; (*persona*) immature

inmediaciones *fpl* neighbourhood

inmediat|amente *adv* immediately. **~o** *a* immediate; (*contiguo*) next

inmejorable *a* excellent

inmemorable *a* immemorial

inmens|idad *f* immensity. **~o** *a* immense

inmerecido *a* undeserved

inmersión *f* immersion

inmigra|ción *f* immigration. **~nte** *a & m* immigrant. **~r** *vt* immigrate

inminen|cia *f* imminence. **~te** *a* imminent

inmiscuirse [17] *vpr* interfere

inmobiliario *a* property

inmoderado *a* immoderate

inmodesto *a* immodest

inmolar *vt* sacrifice

inmoral *a* immoral. **~idad** *f* immorality

inmortal *a* immortal. **~izar** [10] *vt* immortalize

inmóvil *a* immobile

inmueble *a*. **bienes ~s** property

inmund|icia *f* filth. **~icias** *fpl* rubbish. **~o** *a* filthy

inmun|e *a* immune. **~idad** *f* immunity. **~ización** *f* immunization. **~izar** [10] *vt* immunize

inmuta|ble *a* unchangeable. **~rse** *vpr* turn pale

innato *a* innate

innecesario *a* unnecessary

innegable *a* undeniable

innoble *a* ignoble

innova|ción *f* innovation. **~r** *vt/i* innovate

innumerable *a* innumerable

inocen|cia *f* innocence. **~tada** *f* practical joke. **~te** *a* innocent. **~tón** *a* naïve

inocuo *a* innocuous

inodoro *a* odourless. ● *m* toilet

inofensivo *a* inoffensive

inolvidable *a* unforgettable

inoperable *a* inoperable

inopinado *a* unexpected

inoportuno *a* untimely; (*incómodo*) inconvenient

inorgánico *a* inorganic

inoxidable *a* stainless

inquebrantable *a* unbreakable

inquiet|ar *vt* worry. **~arse** *vpr* get worried. **~o** *a* worried; (*agitado*) restless. **~ud** *f* anxiety

inquilino *m* tenant

inquirir [4] *vt* enquire into, investigate

insaciable *a* insatiable

insalubre *a* unhealthy

insanable *a* incurable

insatisfecho *a* unsatisfied; (*descontento*) dissatisfied

inscri|bir [*pp* **inscrito**] *vt* inscribe; (*en registro etc*) enrol, register. **~birse** *vpr* register. **~pción** *f* inscription; (*registro*) registration

insect|icida *m* insecticide. **~o** *m* insect

insegur|idad *f* insecurity. **~o** *a* insecure; (*dudoso*) uncertain

insemina|ción *f* insemination. **~r** *vt* inseminate

insensato *a* senseless

insensible *a* insensitive; (*med*) insensible; (*imperceptible*) imperceptible

inseparable *a* inseparable

insertar *vt* insert

insidi|a *f* trap. **~oso** *a* insidious

insigne *a* famous

insignia *f* badge; (*bandera*) flag

insignificante *a* insignificant

insincero *a* insincere

insinua|ción *f* insinuation. **~nte** *a* insinuating. **~r** [21] *vt* insinuate. **~rse** *vpr* ingratiate o.s. **~rse en** creep into

insípido *a* insipid

insist|encia *f* insistence. **~ente** *a* insistent. **~ir** *vi* insist; (*hacer hincapié*) stress

insolación *f* sunstroke

insolen|cia *f* rudeness, insolence. **~te** *a* rude, insolent

insólito *a* unusual

insoluble *a* insoluble

insolven|cia *f* insolvency. **~te** *a & m & f* insolvent

insomn|e *a* sleepless. **~io** *m* insomnia

insondable *a* unfathomable

insoportable *a* unbearable

insospechado *a* unexpected

insostenible *a* untenable

inspec|ción *f* inspection. **~cionar** *vt* inspect. **~tor** *m* inspector

inspira|ción *f* inspiration. **~r** *vt* inspire. **~rse** *vpr* be inspired

instala|ción *f* installation. **~r** *vt* install. **~rse** *vpr* settle

instancia *f* request

instant|ánea *f* snapshot. **~áneo** *a* instantaneous; (*café etc*) instant. **~e** *m* instant. **a cada ~e** constantly. **al ~e** immediately

instar *vt* urge

instaura|ción *f* establishment. **~r** *vt* establish

instiga|ción *f* instigation. **~dor** *m* instigator. **~r** [12] *vt* instigate; (*incitar*) incite

instint|ivo *a* instinctive. **~o** *m* instinct

institu|ción *f* institution. **~cional** *a* institutional. **~ir** [17] *vt* establish. **~to** *m* institute; (*escol*) (secondary) school. **~triz** *f* governess

instru|cción *f* instruction. **~ctivo** *a* instructive. **~ctor** *m* instructor. **~ir** [17] *vt* instruct; (*enseñar*) teach

instrument|ación *f* instrumentation. **~al** *a* instrumental. **~o** *m* instrument; (*herramienta*) tool

insubordina|ción *f* insubordination. **~r** *vt* stir up. **~rse** *vpr* rebel

insuficien|cia *f* insufficiency; (*inadecuación*) inadequacy. **~te** *a* insufficient

insufrible *a* insufferable

insular *a* insular

insulina *f* insulin

insulso *a* tasteless; (*fig*) insipid

insult|ar *vt* insult. **~o** *m* insult

insuperable *a* insuperable; (*excelente*) excellent

insurgente *a* insurgent

insurrec|ción *f* insurrection. **~to** *a* insurgent

intacto *a* intact

intachable *a* irreproachable

intangible *a* intangible

integra|ción *f* integration. **~l** *a* integral; (*completo*) complete; ⟨pan⟩ wholemeal (*Brit*), wholewheat (*Amer*). **~r** *vt* make up

integridad *f* integrity; (*entereza*) wholeness

íntegro *a* complete; (*fig*) upright

intelect|o *m* intellect. **~ual** *a & m & f* intellectual

inteligen|cia *f* intelligence. **~te** *a* intelligent

inteligible *a* intelligible

intemperancia *f* intemperance

intemperie *f* bad weather. **a la ~** in the open

intempestivo *a* untimely

intenci|ón *f* intention. **~onado** *a* deliberate. **~onal** *a* intentional. **bien ~onado** well-meaning. **mal ~onado** malicious. **segunda ~ón** duplicity

intens|idad *f* intensity. **~ificar** [7] *vt* intensify. **~ivo** *a* intensive. **~o** *a* intense

intent|ar *vt* try. **~o** *m* intent; *(tentativa)* attempt. **de~o** intentionally

intercalar *vt* insert

intercambio *m* exchange

interceder *vt* intercede

interceptar *vt* intercept

intercesión *f* intercession

interdicto *m* ban

inter|és *m* interest; *(egoísmo)* self-interest. **~esado** *a* interested; *(parcial)* biassed; *(egoísta)* selfish. **~esante** *a* interesting. **~esar** *vt* interest; *(afectar)* concern. ● *vi* be of interest. **~esarse** *vpr* take an interest *(por* in)

interfer|encia *f* interference. **~ir** [4] *vi* interfere

interino *a* temporary; *(persona)* acting. ● *m* stand-in; *(médico)* locum

interior *a* interior. ● *m* inside. **Ministerio** *m* **del I~** Home Office *(Brit)*, Department of the Interior *(Amer)*

interjección *f* interjection

interlocutor *m* speaker

interludio *m* interlude

intermediario *a & m* intermediary

intermedio *a* intermediate. ● *m* interval

interminable *a* interminable

intermitente *a* intermittent. ● *m* indicator

internacional *a* international

intern|ado *m* *(escol)* boarding-school. **~ar** *vt* intern; *(en manicomio)* commit. **~arse** *vpr* penetrate. **~o** *a* internal; *(escol)* boarding. ● *m* *(escol)* boarder

interpelar *vt* appeal

interponer [34] *vt* interpose. **~se** *vpr* intervene

int|erpretación *f* interpretation. **~erpretar** *vt* interpret. **~érprete** *m* interpreter; *(mus)* performer

interroga|ción *f* question; *(acción)* interrogation; *(signo)* question mark. **~r** [12] *vt* question. **~tivo** *a* interrogative

interru|mpir *vt* interrupt; *(suspender)* stop. **~pción** *f* interruption. **~ptor** *m* switch

intersección *f* intersection

interurbano *a* inter-city; *(conferencia)* long-distance

intervalo *m* interval; *(espacio)* space. **a ~s** at intervals

interven|ir [53] *vt* control; *(med)* operate on. ● *vi* intervene; *(participar)* take part. **~tor** *m* inspector; *(com)* auditor

intestino *m* intestine

intim|ar *vi* become friendly. **~idad** *f* intimacy

intimidar *vt* intimidate

íntimo *a* intimate. ● *m* close friend

intitular *vt* entitle

intolera|ble *a* intolerable. **~nte** *a* intolerant

intoxicar [7] *vt* poison

intranquil|izar [10] *vt* worry. **~o** *a* worried

intransigente *a* intransigent

intransitable *a* impassable

intransitivo *a* intransitive

intratable *a* intractable

intrépido *a* intrepid

intriga *f* intrigue. **~nte** *a* intriguing. **~r** [12] *vt/i* intrigue

intrincado *a* intricate

intrínseco *a* intrinsic

introduc|ción *f* introduction. **~ir** [47] *vt* introduce; *(meter)* insert. **~irse** *vpr* get into; *(entrometerse)* interfere

intromisión *f* interference

introvertido *a & m* introvert

intrus|ión *f* intrusion. **~o** *a* intrusive. ● *m* intruder

intui|ción *f* intuition. **~r** [17] *vt* sense. **~tivo** *a* intuitive

inunda|ción *f* flooding. **~r** *vt* flood

inusitado *a* unusual

in|útil *a* useless; *(vano)* futile. **~utilidad** *f* uselessness

invadir *vt* invade

inv|alidez *f* invalidity; *(med)* disability. **~álido** *a & m* invalid

invaria|ble *a* invariable. **~do** *a* unchanged

invas|ión *f* invasion. **~or** *a* invading. ● *m* invader

invectiva *f* invective

invencible *a* invincible

inven|ción *f* invention. **~tar** *vt* invent

inventario *m* inventory

invent|iva *f* inventiveness. **~ivo** *a* inventive. **~or** *m* inventor

invernadero *m* greenhouse

invernal *a* winter

inverosímil *a* improbable

inversión *f* inversion; *(com)* investment

inverso *a* inverse; *(contrario)* opposite. **a la inversa** the other way round

invertebrado *a & m* invertebrate

inverti|do a inverted; (*homosexual*) homosexual. ● m homosexual. ~r [4] vt reverse; (*volcar*) turn upside down; (*com*) invest; spend ‹*tiempo*›

investidura f investiture

investiga|ción f investigation; (*univ*) research. ~**dor** m investigator. ~r [12] vt investigate

investir [5] vt invest

inveterado a inveterate

invicto a unbeaten

invierno m winter

inviolable a inviolate

invisib|ilidad f invisibility. ~**le** a invisible

invita|ción f invitation. ~**do** m guest. ~r vt invite. **te invito a una copa** I'll buy you a drink

invoca|ción f invocation. ~r [7] vt invoke

involuntario a involuntary

invulnerable a invulnerable

inyec|ción f injection. ~**tar** vt inject

ion m ion

ir [49] vi go; ‹*ropa*› (*convenir*) suit. ● m going. ~**se** vpr go away. ~ **a hacer** be going to do. ~ **a pie** walk. ~ **de paseo** go for a walk. ~ **en coche** go by car. **no me va ni me viene** it's all the same to me. **no vaya a ser que** in case. **¡qué va!** nonsense! **va mejorando** it's gradually getting better. **¡vamos!**, **¡vámonos!** come on! let's go! **¡vaya!** fancy that! **¡vete a saber!** who knows? **¡ya voy!** I'm coming!

ira f anger. ~**cundo** a irascible

Irak m Iraq

Irán m Iran

iraní a & m & f Iranian

iraquí a & m & f Iraqi

iris m (*anat*) iris; (*arco iris*) rainbow

Irlanda f Ireland

irland|és a Irish. ● m Irishman; (*lengua*) Irish. ~**esa** f Irishwoman

ir|onía f irony. ~**ónico** a ironic

irracional a irrational

irradiar vt/i radiate

irrazonable a unreasonable

irreal a unreal. ~**idad** f unreality

irrealizable a unattainable

irreconciliable a irreconcilable

irreconocible a unrecognizable

irrecuperable a irretrievable

irreducible a irreducible

irreflexión f impetuosity

irrefutable a irrefutable

irregular a irregular. ~**idad** f irregularity

irreparable a irreparable

irreprimible a irrepressible

irreprochable a irreproachable

irresistible a irresistible

irresoluto a irresolute

irrespetuoso a disrespectful

irresponsable a irresponsible

irrevocable a irrevocable

irriga|ción f irrigation. ~r [12] vt irrigate

irrisorio a derisive; (*insignificante*) ridiculous

irrita|ble a irritable. ~**ción** f irritation. ~r vt irritate. ~**rse** vpr get annoyed

irrumpir vi burst (**en** in)

irrupción f irruption

isla f island. **las I~s Británicas** the British Isles

Islam m Islam

islámico a Islamic

islandés a Icelandic. ● m Icelander; (*lengua*) Icelandic

Islandia f Iceland

isleño a island. ● m islander

Israel m Israel

israelí a & m Israeli

istmo /'ismo/ m isthmus

Italia f Italy

italiano a & m Italian

itinerario a itinerary

IVA abrev (*impuesto sobre el valor añadido*) VAT, value added tax

izar [10] vt hoist

izquierd|a f left(-hand); (*pol*) left (-wing). ~**ista** m & f leftist. ~**o** a left. **a la ~a** on the left; (*con movimiento*) to the left

J

ja int ha!

jabalí m wild boar

jabalina f javelin

jab|ón m soap. ~**onar** vt soap. ~**onoso** a soapy

jaca f pony

jacinto m hyacinth

jacta|ncia f boastfulness; (*acción*) boasting. ~**rse** vpr boast

jadea|nte a panting. ~r vi pant

jaez m harness

jaguar m jaguar

jalea f jelly

jaleo m row, uproar. **armar un ~** kick up a fuss

jalón *m* (*LAm, tirón*) pull; (*Mex, trago*) drink

Jamaica *f* Jamaica

jamás *adv* never; (*en frases afirmativas*) ever

jamelgo *m* nag

jamón *m* ham. ~ **de York** boiled ham. ~ **serrano** cured ham

Japón *m*. **el** ~ Japan

japonés *a & m* Japanese

jaque *m* check. ~ **mate** checkmate

jaqueca *f* migraine. **dar** ~ bother

jarabe *m* syrup

jardín *m* garden. ~ **de la infancia** kindergarten, nursery school

jardiner|ía *f* gardening. ~**o** *m* gardener

jarocho *a* (*Mex*) from Veracruz

jarr|a *f* jug. ~**o** *m* jug. **echar un** ~**o de agua fría a** throw cold water on. **en** ~**as** with hands on hips

jaula *f* cage

jauría *f* pack of hounds

jazmín *m* jasmine

jef|a *f* boss. ~**atura** *f* leadership; (*sede*) headquarters. ~**e** *m* boss; (*pol etc*) leader. ~**e de camareros** head waiter. ~**e de estación** stationmaster. ~**e de ventas** sales manager

jengibre *m* ginger

jeque *m* sheikh

jer|arquía *f* hierarchy. ~**árquico** *a* hierarchical

jerez *m* sherry. **al** ~ with sherry

jerga *f* coarse cloth; (*argot*) jargon

jerigonza *f* jargon; (*galimatías*) gibberish

jeringa *f* syringe; (*LAm, molestia*) nuisance. ~**r** [12] *vt* (*fig, molestar, fam*) annoy

jeroglífico *m* hieroglyph(ic)

jersey *m* (*pl* **jerseys**) jersey

Jerusalén *m* Jerusalem

Jesucristo *m* Jesus Christ. **antes de** ~ BC, before Christ

jesuita *a & m & f* Jesuit

Jesús *m* Jesus. ● *int* good heavens!; (*al estornudar*) bless you!

jícara *f* small cup

jilguero *m* goldfinch

jinete *m* rider, horseman

jipijapa *f* straw hat

jirafa *f* giraffe

jirón *m* shred, tatter

jitomate *m* (*Mex*) tomato

jocoso *a* funny, humorous

jorna|da *f* working day; (*viaje*) journey; (*etapa*) stage. ~**l** *m* day's wage; (*trabajo*) day's work. ~**lero** *m* day labourer

joroba *f* hump. ~**do** *a* hunchbacked. ● *m* hunchback. ~**r** *vt* annoy

jota *f* letter J; (*danza*) jota, popular dance; (*fig*) iota. **ni** ~ nothing

joven (*pl* **jóvenes**) *a* young. ● *m* young man, youth. ● *f* young woman, girl

jovial *a* jovial

joy|a *f* jewel. ~**as** *fpl* jewellery. ~**ería** *f* jeweller's (shop). ~**ero** *m* jeweller; (*estuche*) jewellery box

juanete *m* bunion

jubil|ación *f* retirement. ~**ado** *a* retired. ~**ar** *vt* pension off. ~**arse** *vpr* retire. ~**eo** *m* jubilee

júbilo *m* joy

jubiloso *a* jubilant

judaísmo *m* Judaism

judía *f* Jewish woman; (*alubia*) bean. ~ **blanca** haricot bean. ~ **escarlata** runner bean. ~ **verde** French bean

judicial *a* judicial

judío *a* Jewish. ● *m* Jewish man

judo *m* judo

juego *m* game; (*de niños, tec*) play; (*de azar*) gambling; (*conjunto*) set. ● *vb* *véase* **jugar. estar en** ~ be at stake. **estar fuera de** ~ be offside. **hacer** ~ match

juerga *f* spree

jueves *m* Thursday

juez *m* judge. ~ **de instrucción** examining magistrate. ~ **de línea** linesman

juga|dor *m* player; (*en juegos de azar*) gambler. ~**r** [3] *vt* play. ● *vi* play; (*a juegos de azar*) gamble; (*apostar*) bet. ~**rse** *vpr* risk. ~**r al fútbol** play football

juglar *m* minstrel

jugo *m* juice; (*de carne*) gravy; (*fig*) substance. ~**so** *a* juicy; (*fig*) substantial

juguet|e *m* toy. ~**ear** *vi* play. ~**ón** *a* playful

juicio *m* judgement; (*opinión*) opinion; (*razón*) reason. ~**so** *a* wise. **a mi** ~ in my opinion

juliana *f* vegetable soup

julio *m* July

junco *m* rush, reed

jungla *f* jungle

junio *m* June

junt|a *f* meeting; (*consejo*) board, committee; (*pol*) junta; (*tec*) joint. ~**ar** *vt* join; (*reunir*) collect. ~**arse**

vpr join; ⟨*gente*⟩ meet. **~o** *a* joined; (*en plural*) together. **~o a** next to. **~ura** *f* joint. **por ~o** all together

jura|do *a* sworn. ● *m* jury; (*miembro de jurado*) juror. **~mento** *m* oath. **~r** *vt/i* swear. **~r en falso** commit perjury. **jurárselas a uno** have it in for s.o. **prestar ~mento** take the oath

jurel *m* (type of) mackerel

jurídico *a* legal

juris|dicción *f* jurisdiction. **~prudencia** *f* jurisprudence

justamente *a* exactly; (*con justicia*) fairly

justicia *f* justice

justifica|ción *f* justification. **~r** [7] *vt* justify

justo *a* fair, just; (*exacto*) exact; ⟨*ropa*⟩ tight. ● *adv* just. **~ a tiempo** just in time

juven|il *a* youthful. **~tud** *f* youth; (*gente joven*) young people

juzga|do *m* (*tribunal*) court. **~r** [12] *vt* judge. **a ~r por** judging by

K

kilo *m*, **kilogramo** *m* kilo, kilogram

kil|ometraje *m* distance in kilometres, mileage. **~ométrico** *a* (*fam*) endless. **~ómetro** *m* kilometre. **~ómetro cuadrado** square kilometre

kilovatio *m* kilowatt

kiosco *m* kiosk

L

la *m* A; (*solfa*) lah. ● *art def f* the. ● *pron* (*ella*) her; (*Vd*) you; (*ello*) it. **~ de** the one. **~ de Vd** your one, yours. **~ que** whoever, the one

laberinto *m* labyrinth, maze

labia *f* glibness

labio *m* lip

labor *f* work; (*tarea*) job. **~able** *a* working. **~ar** *vi* work. **~es** *fpl de aguja* needlework. **~es** *fpl de ganchillo* crochet. **~es** *fpl de punto* knitting. **~es** *fpl domésticas* housework

laboratorio *m* laboratory

laborioso *a* laborious

laborista *a* Labour. ● *m & f* member of the Labour Party

labra|do *a* worked; ⟨*madera*⟩ carved; ⟨*metal*⟩ wrought; ⟨*tierra*⟩ ploughed. **~dor** *m* farmer; (*obrero*) labourer. **~nza** *f* farming. **~r** *vt* work; carve ⟨*madera*⟩; cut ⟨*piedra*⟩; till ⟨*la tierra*⟩; (*fig, causar*) cause

labriego *m* peasant

laca *f* lacquer

lacayo *m* lackey

lacerar *vt* lacerate

lacero *m* lassoer; (*cazador*) poacher

lacio *a* straight; (*flojo*) limp

lacón *m* shoulder of pork

lacónico *a* laconic

lacra *f* scar

lacr|ar *vt* seal. **~e** *m* sealing wax

lactante *a* breast-fed

lácteo *a* milky. **productos** *mpl* **~s** dairy products

ladear *vt/i* tilt. **~se** *vpr* lean

ladera *f* slope

ladino *a* astute

lado *m* side. **al ~** near. **al ~ de** at the side of, beside. **los de al ~** the next door neighbours. **por otro ~** on the other hand. **por todos ~s** on all sides. **por un ~** on the one hand

ladr|ar *vi* bark. **~ido** *m* bark

ladrillo *m* brick; (*de chocolate*) block

ladrón *a* thieving. ● *m* thief

lagart|ija *f* (small) lizard. **~o** *m* lizard

lago *m* lake

lágrima *f* tear

lagrimoso *a* tearful

laguna *f* small lake; (*fig, omisión*) gap

laico *a* lay

lamé *m* lamé

lamedura *f* lick

lament|able *a* lamentable, pitiful. **~ar** *vt* be sorry about. **~arse** *vpr* lament; (*quejarse*) complain. **~o** *m* moan

lamer *vt* lick; ⟨*olas etc*⟩ lap

lámina *f* sheet; (*foto*) plate; (*dibujo*) picture

lamina|do *a* laminated. **~r** *vt* laminate

lámpara *f* lamp; (*bombilla*) bulb; (*lamparón*) grease stain. **~ de pie** standard lamp

lamparón *m* grease stain

lampiño *a* clean-shaven, beardless

lana *f* wool. **~r** *a*. **ganado** *m* **~r** sheep. **de ~** wool(len)

lanceta *f* lancet

lancha *f* boat. **~ motora** *f* motor boat. **~ salvavidas** lifeboat

lanero *a* wool(len)

langost|a *f* (*crustáceo marino*) lobster; (*insecto*) locust. **~ino** *m* prawn

languide|cer [11] *vi* languish. **~z** *f* languor

lánguido *a* languid; (*decaído*) listless

lanilla *f* nap; (*tela fina*) flannel

lanudo *a* woolly

lanza *f* lance, spear

lanza|llamas *m invar* flame-thrower. **~miento** *m* throw; (*acción de lanzar*) throwing; (*de proyectil, de producto*) launch. **~r** [10] *vt* throw; (*de un avión*) drop; launch (*proyectil, producto*). **~rse** *vpr* fling o.s.

lapicero *m* (propelling) pencil

lápida *f* memorial tablet. **~ sepulcral** tombstone

lapidar *vt* stone

lápiz *m* pencil; (*grafito*) lead. **~ de labios** lipstick

Laponia *f* Lapland

lapso *m* lapse

larg|a *f*. **a la ~a** in the long run. **dar ~as** put off. **~ar** [12] *vt* slacken; (*dar, fam*) give; (*fam*) deal ‹*bofetada etc*›. **~arse** *vpr* (*fam*) go away, clear off (*fam*). **~o** *a* long; (*demasiado*) too long. **• m** length. **¡~o!** go away! **~ueza** *f* generosity. **a lo ~o** lengthwise. **a lo ~o de** along. **tener 100 metros de ~o** be 100 metres long

laring|e *f* larynx. **~itis** *f* laryngitis

larva *f* larva

las *art def fpl* the. **• pron** them. **~ de** those, the ones. **~ de Vd** your ones, yours. **~ que** whoever, the ones

lascivo *a* lascivious

láser *m* laser

lástima *f* pity; (*queja*) complaint. **dar ~** be pitiful. **ella me da ~** I feel sorry for her. **¡qué ~!** what a pity!

lastim|ado *a* hurt. **~ar** *vt* hurt. **~arse** *vpr* hurt o.s. **~ero** *a* doleful. **~oso** *a* pitiful

lastre *m* ballast

lata *f* tinplate; (*envase*) tin (*esp Brit*), can; (*molestia, fam*) nuisance. **dar la ~** be a nuisance. **¡qué ~!** what a nuisance!

latente *a* latent

lateral *a* side, lateral

latido *m* beating; (*cada golpe*) beat

latifundio *m* large estate

latigazo *m* (*golpe*) lash; (*chasquido*) crack

látigo *m* whip

latín *m* Latin. **saber ~** (*fam*) not be stupid

latino *a* Latin. **L~américa** *f* Latin America. **~americano** *a & m* Latin American

latir *vi* beat; ‹*herida*› throb

latitud *f* latitude

latón *m* brass

latoso *a* annoying; (*pesado*) boring

laucha *f* (*Arg*) mouse

laúd *m* lute

laudable *a* laudable

laureado *a* honoured; (*premiado*) prize-winning

laurel *m* laurel; (*culin*) bay

lava *f* lava

lava|ble *a* washable. **~bo** *m* wash-basin; (*retrete*) toilet. **~dero** *m* sink, wash-basin. **~do** *m* washing. **~do de cerebro** brainwashing. **~do en seco** dry-cleaning. **~dora** *f* washing machine. **~ndería** *f* laundry. **~ndería automática** launderette, laundromat (*esp Amer*). **~parabrisas** *m invar* windscreen washer (*Brit*), windshield washer (*Amer*). **~platos** *m & f invar* dishwasher; (*Mex, fregadero*) sink. **~r** *vt* wash. **~r en seco** dry-clean. **~rse** *vpr* have a wash. **~rse las manos** (*incl fig*) wash one's hands. **~tiva** *f* enema. **~vajillas** *m & f invar* dishwasher

lax|ante *a & m* laxative. **~o** *a* loose

laz|ada *f* bow. **~o** *m* knot; (*lazada*) bow; (*fig, vínculo*) tie; (*cuerda con nudo corredizo*) lasso; (*trampa*) trap

le *pron* (*acusativo, él*) him; (*acusativo, Vd*) you; (*dativo, él*) (to) him; (*dativo, ella*) (to) her; (*dativo, ello*) (to) it; (*dativo, Vd*) (to) you

leal *a* loyal; (*fiel*) faithful. **~tad** *f* loyalty; (*fidelidad*) faithfulness

lebrel *m* greyhound

lección *f* lesson; (*univ*) lecture

lect|or *m* reader; (*univ*) language assistant. **~ura** *f* reading

leche *f* milk; (*golpe*) bash. **~ condensada** condensed milk. **~ desnatada** skimmed milk. **~ en polvo** powdered milk. **~ra** *f* (*vasija*) milk jug. **~ría** *f* dairy. **~ro** *a* milk, dairy. **• m** milkman. **~ sin desnatar** whole milk. **tener mala ~** be spiteful

lecho *m* bed

lechoso *a* milky

lechuga *f* lettuce

lechuza *f* fowl

leer [18] *vt/i* read

legación f legation

legado m legacy; (*enviado*) legate

legajo m bundle, file

legal a legal. **~idad** f legality. **~izar** [10] vt legalize; (*certificar*) authenticate. **~mente** adv legally

legar [12] vt bequeath

legendario a legendary

legible a legible

legi|ón f legion. **~onario** m legionary

legisla|ción f legislation. **~dor** m legislator. **~r** vi legislate. **~tura** f legislature

leg|itimidad f legitimacy. **~ítimo** a legitimate; (*verdadero*) real

lego a lay; (*ignorante*) ignorant. ● m layman

legua f league

legumbre f vegetable

lejan|ía f distance. **~o** a distant

lejía f bleach

lejos adv far. **~ de** far from. **a lo ~** in the distance. **desde ~** from a distance, from afar

lelo a stupid

lema m motto

lencería f linen; (*de mujer*) lingerie

lengua f tongue; (*idioma*) language. **irse de la ~** talk too much. **morderse la ~** hold one's tongue. **tener mala ~** have a vicious tongue

lenguado m sole

lenguaje m language

lengüeta f (*de zapato*) tongue

lengüetada f, **lengüetazo** m lick

lente f lens. **~s** mpl glasses. **~s de contacto** contact lenses

lentej|a f lentil. **~uela** f sequin

lentilla f contact lens

lent|itud f slowness. **~o** a slow

leñ|a f firewood. **~ador** m woodcutter. **~o** m log

Leo m Leo

le|ón m lion. **León** Leo. **~ona** f lioness

leopardo m leopard

leotardo m thick tights

lepr|a f leprosy. **~oso** m leper

lerdo a dim; (*torpe*) clumsy

les pron (*acusativo*) them; (*acusativo, Vds*) you; (*dativo*) (to) them; (*dativo, Vds*) (to) you

lesbia(na) f lesbian

lesbiano a, **lesbio** a lesbian

lesi|ón f wound. **~onado** a injured. **~onar** vt injure; (*dañar*) damage

letal a lethal

letanía f litany

let|árgico a lethargic. **~argo** m lethargy

letr|a f letter; (*escritura*) handwriting; (*de una canción*) words, lyrics. **~a de cambio** bill of exchange. **~a de imprenta** print. **~ado** a learned. **~ero** m notice; (*cartel*) poster

letrina f latrine

leucemia f leukaemia

levadizo a. **puente ~** drawbridge

levadura f yeast. **~ en polvo** baking powder

levanta|miento m lifting; (*sublevación*) uprising. **~r** vt raise, lift; (*construir*) build; (*recoger*) pick up; (*separar*) take off. **~rse** vpr get up; (*ponerse de pie*) stand up; (*erguirse, sublevarse*) rise up

levante m east; (*viento*) east wind. **L~** Levant

levar vt weigh (*ancla*). ● vi set sail

leve a light; (*enfermedad etc*) slight; (*de poca importancia*) trivial. **~dad** f lightness; (*fig*) slightness

léxico m vocabulary

lexicografía f lexicography

ley f law; (*parlamentaria*) act. **plata** f **de ~** sterling silver

leyenda f legend

liar [20] vt tie; (*envolver*) wrap up; roll (*cigarillo*); (*fig, confundir*) confuse; (*fig, enredar*) involve. **~se** vpr get involved

libanés a & m Lebanese

Líbano m. **el ~** Lebanon

libel|ista m & f satirist. **~o** m satire

libélula f dragonfly

libera|ción f liberation. **~dor** a liberating. ● m liberator

liberal a & m & f liberal. **~idad** f liberality. **~mente** adv liberally

liber|ar vt free. **~tad** f freedom. **~tad de cultos** freedom of worship. **~tad de imprenta** freedom of the press. **~tad provisional** bail. **~tar** vt free. **en ~tad** free

libertino m libertine

Libia f Libya

libido m libido

libio a & m Libyan

libra f pound. **~ esterlina** pound sterling

Libra f Libra

libra|dor m (*com*) drawer. **~r** vt free; (*de un peligro*) rescue. **~rse** vpr free o.s. **~rse de** get rid of

libre a free; ⟨aire⟩ open; (en natación) freestyle. ~ **de impuestos** tax-free. ● m (Mex) taxi
librea f livery
libr|ería f bookshop (Brit), bookstore (Amer); (mueble) bookcase. ~**ero** m bookseller. ~**eta** f notebook. ~**o** m book. ~**o de a bordo** logbook. ~**o de bolsillo** paperback. ~**o de ejercicios** exercise book. ~**o de reclamaciones** complaints book
licencia f permission; (documento) licence. ~**do** m graduate. ~ **para manejar** (LAm) driving licence. ~**r** vt (mil) discharge; (echar) dismiss. ~**tura** f degree
licencioso a licentious
liceo m (esp LAm) (secondary) school
licita|dor m bidder. ~**r** vt bid for
lícito a legal; (permisible) permissible
licor m liquid; (alcohólico) liqueur
licua|dora f liquidizer. ~**r** [21] liquefy
lid f fight. **en buena** ~ by fair means
líder m leader
liderato m, **liderazgo** m leadership
lidia f bullfighting; (lucha) fight; (LAm, molestia) nuisance. ~**r** vt/i fight
liebre f hare
lienzo m linen; (del pintor) canvas; (muro, pared) wall
liga f garter; (alianza) league; (mezcla) mixture. ~**dura** f bond; (mus) slur; (med) ligature. ~**mento** m ligament. ~**r** [12] vt tie; (fig) join; (mus) slur. ● vi mix. ~**r con** (fig) pick up. ~**rse** vpr commit o.s.
liger|eza f lightness; (agilidad) agility; (rapidez) swiftness; (de carácter) fickleness. ~**o** a light; (rápido) quick; (ágil) agile; (superficial) superficial; (de poca importancia) slight. ● adv quickly. **a la** ~**a** lightly, superficially
liguero m suspender belt
lija f dogfish; (papel de lija) sandpaper. ~**r** vt sand
lila f lilac
Lima f Lima
lima f file; (fruta) lime. ~**duras** fpl filings. ~**r** vt file (down)
limbo m limbo
limita|ción f limitation. ~**do** a limited. ~**r** vt limit. ~**r con** border on. ~**tivo** a limiting
límite m limit. ~ **de velocidad** speed limit

limítrofe a bordering
limo m mud
lim|ón m lemon. ~**onada** f lemonade
limosn|a f alms. ~**ear** vi beg. **pedir** ~**a** beg
limpia f cleaning. ~**botas** m invar bootblack. ~**parabrisas** m invar windscreen wiper (Brit), windshield wiper (Amer). ~**pipas** m invar pipecleaner. ~**r** vt clean; (enjugar) wipe
limpi|eza f cleanliness; (acción de limpiar) cleaning. ~**eza en seco** dry-cleaning. ~**o** a clean; ⟨cielo⟩ clear; (fig, honrado) honest. ● adv fairly. **en** ~**o** (com) net. **jugar** ~**o** play fair
linaje m lineage; (fig, clase) kind
lince m lynx
linchar vt lynch
lind|ante a bordering (con on). ~**ar** vi border (con on). ~**e** f boundary. ~**ero** m border
lindo a pretty, lovely. **de lo** ~ (fam) a lot
línea f line. **en** ~**s generales** in broad outline. **guardar la** ~ watch one's figure
lingote m ingot
lingü|ista m & f linguist. ~**ística** f linguistics. ~**ístico** a linguistic
lino m flax; (tela) linen
linóleo m, **linóleum** m lino, linoleum
linterna f lantern; (de bolsillo) torch, flashlight (Amer)
lío m bundle; (jaleo) fuss; (embrollo) muddle; (amorío) affair
liquen m lichen
liquida|ción f liquidation; (venta especial) (clearance) sale. ~**r** vt liquify; (com) liquidate; settle ⟨cuenta⟩
líquido a liquid; (com) net. ● m liquid
lira f lyre; (moneda italiana) lira
líric|a f lyric poetry. ~**o** a lyric(al)
lirio m iris. ~ **de los valles** lily of the valley
lirón m dormouse; (fig) sleepyhead. **dormir como un** ~ sleep like a log
Lisboa f Lisbon
lisia|do a disabled. ~**r** vt disable; (herir) injure
liso a smooth; ⟨pelo⟩ straight; ⟨tierra⟩ flat; (sencillo) plain
lisonj|a f flattery. ~**eador** a flattering. ● m flatterer. ~**ear** vt flatter. ~**ero** a flattering
lista f stripe; (enumeración) list; (de platos) menu. ~ **de correos** poste

restante. **~do** *a* striped. **a ~s** striped

listo *a* clever; (*preparado*) ready

listón *m* ribbon; (*de madera*) strip

lisura *f* smoothness

litera *f* (*en barco*) berth; (*en tren*) sleeper; (*en habitación*) bunk bed

literal *a* literal

litera|rio *a* literary. **~tura** *f* literature

litig|ar [12] *vi* dispute; (*jurid*) litigate. **~io** *m* dispute; (*jurid*) litigation

litografía *f* (*arte*) lithography; (*cuadro*) lithograph

litoral *a* coastal. ● *m* coast

litro *m* litre

lituano *a* & *m* Lithuanian

liturgia *f* liturgy

liviano *a* fickle, inconstant

lívido *a* livid

lizo *m* warp thread

lo *art def neutro*. **~ importante** what is important, the important thing. ● *pron* (*él*) him; (*ello*) it. **~ que** what(ever), that which

loa *f* praise. **~ble** *a* praiseworthy. **~r** *vt* praise

lobo *m* wolf

lóbrego *a* gloomy

lóbulo *m* lobe

local *a* local. ● *m* premises; (*lugar*) place. **~idad** *f* locality; (*de un espectáculo*) seat; (*entrada*) ticket. **~izar** [10] *vt* localize; (*encontrar*) find, locate

loción *f* lotion

loco *a* mad; (*fig*) foolish. ● *m* lunatic. **~ de alegría** mad with joy. **estar ~ por** be crazy about. **volverse ~** go mad

locomo|ción *f* locomotion. **~tora** *f* locomotive

locuaz *a* talkative

locución *f* expression

locura *f* madness; (*acto*) crazy thing. **con ~** madly

locutor *m* announcer

locutorio *m* (*de teléfono*) telephone booth

lod|azal *m* quagmire. **~o** *m* mud

logaritmo *m* logarithm, log

lógic|a *f* logic. **~o** *a* logical

logística *f* logistics

logr|ar *vt* get; win (*premio*). **~ hacer** manage to do. **~o** *m* achievement; (*de premio*) winning; (*éxito*) success

loma *f* small hill

lombriz *f* worm

lomo *m* back; (*de libro*) spine; (*doblez*) fold. **~ de cerdo** loin of pork

lona *f* canvas

loncha *f* slice; (*de tocino*) rasher

londinense *a* from London. ● *m* Londoner

Londres *m* London

loneta *f* thin canvas

longánimo *a* magnanimous

longaniza *f* sausage

longev|idad *f* longevity. **~o** *a* long-lived

longitud *f* length; (*geog*) longitude

lonja *f* slice; (*de tocino*) rasher; (*com*) market

lord *m* (*pl* **lores**) lord

loro *m* parrot

los *art def mpl* the. ● *pron* them. **~ de Antonio** Antonio's. **~ que** whoever, the ones

losa *f* slab; (*baldosa*) flagstone. **~ sepulcral** tombstone

lote *m* share

lotería *f* lottery

loto *m* lotus

loza *f* crockery

lozano *a* fresh; ⟨*vegetación*⟩ lush; ⟨*persona*⟩ lively

lubri(fi)ca|nte *a* lubricating. ● *m* lubricant. **~r** [7] *vt* lubricate

lucero *m* (*estrella*) bright star; (*planeta*) Venus

lucid|ez *f* lucidity. **~o** *a* splendid

lúcido *a* lucid

luciérnaga *f* glow-worm

lucimiento *m* brilliance

lucir [11] *vt* (*fig*) show off. ● *vi* shine; ⟨*lámpara*⟩ give off light; ⟨*joya*⟩ sparkle. **~se** *vpr* (*fig*) shine, excel

lucr|ativo *a* lucrative. **~o** *m* gain

lucha *f* fight. **~dor** *m* fighter. **~r** *vi* fight

luego *adv* then; (*más tarde*) later. ● *conj* therefore. **~ que** as soon as. **desde ~** of course

lugar *m* place. **~ común** cliché. **~eño** *a* village. **dar ~ a** give rise to. **en ~ de** instead of. **en primer ~** in the first place. **hacer ~** make room. **tener ~** take place

lugarteniente *m* deputy

lúgubre *a* gloomy

lujo *m* luxury. **~so** *a* luxurious. **de ~** de luxe

lujuria *f* lust

lumbago *m* lumbago

lumbre *f* fire; (*luz*) light. **¿tienes ~?** have you got a light?

luminoso a luminous; (*fig*) brilliant

luna f moon; (*de escaparate*) window; (*espejo*) mirror. ~ **de miel** honeymoon. ~**r** a lunar. ● m mole. **claro de** ~ moonlight. **estar en la** ~ be miles away

lunes m Monday. **cada** ~ **y cada martes** day in, day out

lupa f magnifying glass

lúpulo m hop

lustr|abotas m invar (*LAm*) bootblack. ~**ar** vt shine, polish. ~**e** m shine; (*fig, esplendor*) splendour. ~**oso** a shining. **dar** ~**e** a, **sacar** ~**e** a polish

luto m mourning. **estar de** ~ be in mourning

luxación f dislocation

Luxemburgo m Luxemburg

luz f light; (*electricidad*) electricity. **luces** fpl intelligence. ~ **antiniebla** (*auto*) fog light. **a la** ~ **de** in the light of. **a todas luces** obviously. **dar a** ~ give birth. **hacer la** ~ **sobre** shed light on. **sacar a la** ~ bring to light

enough. ~**rse** vpr come near; (*ir*) go (round). ~**r a** (*conseguir*) manage to. ~**r a saber** find out. ~**r a ser** become

llen|ar vt fill (up); (*rellenar*) fill in. ~**o** a full. ● m (*en el teatro etc*) full house. **de** ~ completely

lleva|dero a tolerable. ~**r** vt carry; (*inducir, conducir*) lead; (*acompañar*) take; wear ‹ropa›; (*traer*) bring. ~**rse** vpr run off with ‹cosa›. ~**rse bien** get on well together. ¿**cuánto tiempo** ~**s aquí?** how long have you been here? **llevo 3 años estudiando inglés** I've been studying English for 3 years

llor|ar vi cry; ‹ojos› water. ~**iquear** vi whine. ~**iqueo** m whining. ~**o** m crying. ~**ón** a whining. ● m crybaby. ~**oso** a tearful

llov|er [2] vi rain. ~**izna** f drizzle. ~**iznar** vi drizzle

llueve vb véase **llover**

lluvi|a f rain; (*fig*) shower. ~**oso** a rainy; ‹clima› wet

LL

llaga f wound; (*úlcera*) ulcer

llama f flame; (*animal*) llama

llamada f call; (*golpe*) knock; (*señal*) sign

llama|do a known as. ~**miento** m call. ~**r** vt call; (*por teléfono*) ring (up). ● vi call; (*golpear en la puerta*) knock; (*tocar el timbre*) ring. ~**rse** vpr be called. ~**r por teléfono** ring (up), telephone. ¿**cómo te** ~**s?** what's your name?

llamarada f blaze; (*fig*) blush; (*fig, de pasión etc*) outburst

llamativo a loud, gaudy

llamear vi blaze

llan|eza f simplicity. ~**o** a flat, level; ‹persona› natural; (*sencillo*) plain. ● m plain

llanta f (*auto*) (wheel) rim; (*LAm, neumático*) tyre

llanto m weeping

llanura f plain

llave f key; (*para tuercas*) spanner; (*grifo*) tap (*Brit*), faucet (*Amer*); (*elec*) switch. ~ **inglesa** monkey wrench. ~**ro** m key-ring. **cerrar con** ~ lock. **echar la** ~ lock up

llega|da f arrival. ~**r** [12] vi arrive, come; (*alcanzar*) reach; (*bastar*) be

M

maca f defect; (*en fruta*) bruise

macabro a macabre

macaco a (*LAm*) ugly. ● m macaque (monkey)

macadam m, **macadán** m Tarmac (*P*)

macanudo a (*fam*) great

macarrón m macaroon. ~**es** mpl macaroni

macerar vt macerate

maceta f mallet; (*tiesto*) flowerpot

macilento a wan

macizo a solid. ● m mass; (*de plantas*) bed

macrobiótico a macrobiotic

mácula f stain

macuto m knapsack

mach /mak/ m. (**número de**) ~ Mach (number)

machac|ar [7] vt crush. ● vi go on (**en** about). ~**ón** a boring. ● m bore

machamartillo. a ~ adv firmly

machaqueo m crushing

machet|azo m blow with a machete; (*herida*) wound from a machete. ~**e** m machete

mach|ista m male chauvinist. ~**o** a male; (*varonil*) macho

machón m buttress

machucar [7] vt crush; (*estropear*) damage

madeja f skein

madera m (vino) Madeira. ● f wood; (naturaleza) nature. **~ble** a yielding timber. **~je** m, **~men** m woodwork

madero m log; (de construcción) timber

madona f Madonna

madr|astra f stepmother. **~e** f mother. **~eperla** f mother-of-pearl. **~eselva** f honeysuckle

madrigal m madrigal

madriguera f den; (de liebre) burrow

madrileño a of Madrid. ● m person from Madrid

madrina f godmother; (en una boda) chief bridesmaid

madroño m strawberry-tree

madrug|ada f dawn. **~ador** a who gets up early. ● m early riser. **~ar** [12] vi get up early. **~ón** m. **darse un ~ón** get up very early

madur|ación f maturing; (de fruta) ripening. **~ar** vt/i mature; (fruta) ripen. **~ez** f maturity; (de fruta) ripeness. **~o** a mature; (fruta) ripe

maestr|a f teacher. **~ía** f skill. **~o** m master. **~a, ~o (de escuela)** school-teacher

mafia f Mafia

magdalena f madeleine, small sponge cake

magia f magic

mágico a magic; (maravilloso) magical

magín m (fam) imagination

magisterio m teaching (profession); (conjunto de maestros) teachers

magistrado m magistrate; (juez) judge

magistral a teaching; (bien hecho) masterly; (lenguaje) pedantic

magistratura f magistracy

magn|animidad f magnanimity. **~ánimo** a magnanimous

magnate m magnate

magnesia f magnesia. **~ efervescente** milk of magnesia

magnético a magnetic

magneti|smo m magnetism. **~zar** [10] vt magnetize

magnetofón m, **magnetófono** m tape recorder

magnificencia f magnificence

magnífico a magnificent

magnitud f magnitude

magnolia f magnolia

mago m magician. **los (tres) reyes ~s** the Magi

magr|a f slice of ham. **~o** a lean; (tierra) poor; (persona) thin

magulla|dura f bruise. **~r** vt bruise

mahometano a & m Muhammadan

maíz m maize, corn (Amer)

majada f sheepfold; (estiércol) manure; (LAm) flock of sheep

majader|ía f silly thing. **~o** m idiot; (mano del mortero) pestle. ● a stupid

majador m crusher

majagranzas m idiot

majar vt crush; (molestar) bother

majest|ad f majesty. **~uoso** a majestic

majo a nice

mal adv badly; (poco) poorly; (difícilmente) hardly; (equivocadamente) wrongly. ● a see **malo**. ● m evil; (daño) harm; (enfermedad) illness. **~ que bien** somehow (or other). **de ~ en peor** worse and worse. **hacer ~ en** be wrong to. **¡menos ~!** thank goodness!

malabar a. **juegos ~es** juggling. **~ismo** m juggling. **~ista** m & f juggler

malaconsejado a ill-advised

malacostumbrado a with bad habits

malagueño a of Málaga. ● m person from Málaga

malamente adv badly; (fam) hardly enough

malandanza f misfortune

malapata m & f nuisance

malaria f malaria

Malasia f Malaysia

malasombra m & f clumsy person

malavenido a incompatible

malaventura f misfortune. **~do** a unfortunate

malayo a Malay(an)

malbaratar vt sell off cheap; (malgastar) squander

malcarado a ugly

malcasado a unhappily married; (infiel) unfaithful

malcomer vi eat poorly

malcriad|eza f (LAm) bad manners. **~o** a (niño) spoilt

maldad f evil; (acción) wicked thing

maldecir [46 pero imperativo **maldice**, futuro y condicional regulares, pp **maldecido** o **maldito**] vt curse. ● vi speak ill (de of); (quejarse) complain (de about)

maldici|ente a backbiting; (que blasfema) foul-mouthed. **~ón** f curse

maldit|a f tongue. **¡~a sea!** damn it! **~o** a damned. ● m (*en el teatro*) extra

maleab|ilidad f malleability. **~le** a malleable

malea|nte a wicked. ● m vagrant. **~r** vt damage; (*pervertir*) corrupt. **~rse** vpr be spoilt; (*pervertirse*) be corrupted

malecón m breakwater; (*rail*) embankment; (*para atracar*) jetty

maledicencia f slander

maleficio m curse

maléfico a evil

malestar m indisposition; (*fig*) uneasiness

malet|a f (suit)case; (*auto*) boot, trunk (*Amer*); (*LAm, lío de ropa*) bundle; (*LAm, de bicicleta*) saddle-bag. **hacer la ~a** pack one's bags. ● m & f (*fam*) bungler. **~ero** m porter; (*auto*) boot, trunk (*Amer*). **~ín** m small case

malevolencia f malevolence

malévolo a malevolent

maleza f weeds; (*matorral*) undergrowth

malgasta|dor a wasteful. ● m spendthrift. **~r** vt waste

malgeniado a (*LAm*) bad-tempered

malhablado a foul-mouthed

malhadado a unfortunate

malhechor m criminal

malhumorado a bad-tempered

malici|a f malice. **~arse** vpr suspect. **~as** fpl (*fam*) suspicions. **~oso** a malicious

malign|idad f malice; (*med*) malignancy. **~o** a malignant; (*persona*) malicious

malintencionado a malicious

malmandado a disobedient

malmirado a (*con estar*) disliked; (*con ser*) inconsiderate

malo a (*delante de nombre masculino en singular* **mal**) bad; (*enfermo*) ill. **~ de** difficult. **estar de malas** be out of luck; (*malhumorado*) be in a bad mood. **lo ~ es que** the trouble is that. **ponerse a malas con uno** fall out with s.o. **por las malas** by force

malogr|ar vt waste; (*estropear*) spoil. **~arse** vpr fall through. **~o** m failure

maloliente a smelly

malparto m miscarriage

malpensado a nasty, malicious

malquerencia f dislike

malquist|ar vt set against. **~arse** vpr fall out. **~o** a disliked

malsano a unhealthy; (*enfermizo*) sickly

malsonante a ill-sounding; (*grosero*) offensive

malta f malt; (*cerveza*) beer

maltés a & m Maltese

maltratar vt ill-treat

maltrecho a battered

malucho a (*fam*) poorly

malva f mallow. **(color de) ~** a invar mauve

malvado a wicked

malvavisco m marshmallow

malvender vt sell off cheap

malversa|ción f embezzlement. **~dor** a embezzling. ● m embezzler. **~r** vt embezzle

Malvinas fpl. **las islas ~** the Falkland Islands

malla f mesh. **cota de ~** coat of mail

mallo m mallet

Mallor|ca f Majorca. **~quín** a & m Majorcan

mama f teat; (*de mujer*) breast

mamá f mum(my)

mama|da f sucking. **~r** vt suck; (*fig*) grow up with; (*engullir*) gobble

mamario a mammary

mamarrach|adas fpl nonsense. **~o** m clown; (*cosa ridícula*) (ridiculous) sight

mameluco a Brazilian half-breed; (*necio*) idiot

mamífero a mammalian. ● m mammal

mamola f. **hacer la ~** chuck (under the chin); (*fig*) make fun of

mamotreto m notebook; (*libro voluminoso*) big book

mampara f screen

mamporro m blow

mampostería f masonry

mamut m mammoth

maná f manna

manada f herd; (*de lobos*) pack. **en ~** in crowds

manager /'manaʒer/ m manager

mana|ntial m spring; (*fig*) source. **~r** vi flow; (*fig*) abound. ● vt run with

manaza f big hand; (*sucia*) dirty hand. **ser un ~s** be clumsy

manceb|a f concubine. **~ía** f brothel. **~o** m youth; (*soltero*) bachelor

mancera f plough handle

mancilla f stain. **~r** vt stain

manco a (*de una mano*) one-handed; (*de las dos manos*) handless; (*de un* *brazo)* one-armed; *(de los dos brazos)* armless

mancomún *adv.* **de** ~ jointly

mancomún|adamente *adv* jointly. **~ar** *vt* unite; *(jurid)* make jointly liable. **~arse** *vpr* unite. **~idad** *f* union

mancha *f* stain

Mancha *f.* **la** ~ la Mancha (region of Spain). **el canal de la** ~ the English Channel

mancha|do *a* dirty; *(animal)* spotted. **~r** *vt* stain. **~rse** *vpr* get dirty

manchego *a* of la Mancha. ● *m* person from la Mancha

manchón *m* large stain

manda *f* legacy

manda|dero *m* messenger. **~miento** *m* order; *(relig)* commandment. **~r** *vt* order; *(enviar)* send; *(gobernar)* rule. ● *vi* be in command. **¿mande?** *(esp LAm)* pardon?

mandarín *m* mandarin

mandarin|a *f* *(naranja)* mandarin; *(lengua)* Mandarin. **~o** *m* mandarin tree

mandat|ario *m* attorney. **~o** *m* order; *(jurid)* power of attorney

mandíbula *f* jaw

mandil *m* apron

mandioca *f* cassava

mando *m* command; *(pol)* term of office. ~ **a distancia** remote control. **los** ~**s** the leaders

mandolina *f* mandolin

mandón *a* bossy

manducar [7] *vt* *(fam)* stuff oneself with

manecilla *f* needle; *(de reloj)* hand

manej|able *a* manageable. **~ar** *vt* handle; *(fig)* manage; *(LAm, conducir)* drive. **~arse** *vpr* behave. **~o** *m* handling; *(intriga)* intrigue

manera *f* way. **~s** *fpl* manners. **de** ~ **que** so (that). **de ninguna** ~ not at all. **de otra** ~ otherwise. **de todas** ~**s** anyway

manga *f* sleeve; *(tubo de goma)* hose(pipe); *(red)* net; *(para colar)* filter

mangante *m* beggar; *(fam)* scrounger

mangle *m* mangrove

mango *m* handle; *(fruta)* mango

mangonear *vt* boss about. ● *vi* *(entrometerse)* interfere

manguera *f* hose(pipe)

manguito *m* muff

manía *f* mania; *(antipatía)* dislike

maniaco *a*, **maníaco** *a* maniac(al). ● *m* maniac

maniatar *vt* tie s.o.'s hands

maniático *a* maniac(al); *(fig)* crazy

manicomio *m* lunatic asylum

manicura *f* manicure; *(mujer)* manicurist

manido *a* stale; *(carne)* high

manifesta|ción *f* manifestation; *(pol)* demonstration. **~nte** *m* demonstrator. **~r** [1] *vi* manifest; *(pol)* state. **~rse** *vpr* show; *(pol)* demonstrate

manifiesto *a* clear; *(error)* obvious; *(verdad)* manifest. ● *m* manifesto

manilargo *a* light-fingered

manilla *f* bracelet; *(de hierro)* handcuffs

manillar *m* handlebar(s)

maniobra *f* manoeuvring; *(rail)* shunting; *(fig)* manoeuvre. **~r** *vt* operate; *(rail)* shunt. ● *vi* manoeuvre. **~s** *fpl* *(mil)* manoeuvres

manipula|ción *f* manipulation. **~r** *vt* manipulate

maniquí *m* dummy. ● *f* model

manirroto *a* extravagant. ● *m* spendthrift

manita *f* little hand

manivela *f* crank

manjar *m* *(special)* dish

mano *f* hand; *(de animales)* front foot; *(de perros, gatos)* front paw. ~ **de obra** work force. **¡**~**s arriba!** hands up! **a** ~ by hand; *(próximo)* handy. **de segunda** ~ second hand. **echar una** ~ lend a hand. **tener buena** ~ **para** be good at

manojo *m* bunch

manose|ar *vt* handle; *(fig)* overwork. **~o** *m* handling

manotada *f*, **manotazo** *m* slap

manote|ar *vi* gesticulate. **~o** *m* gesticulation

mansalva. **a** ~ *adv* without risk

mansarda *f* attic

mansedumbre *f* gentleness; *(de animal)* tameness

mansión *f* stately home

manso *a* gentle; *(animal)* tame

manta *f* blanket. ~ **eléctrica** electric blanket. **a** ~ **(de Dios)** a lot

mantec|a *f* fat; *(LAm)* butter. **~ado** *m* bun; *(helado)* ice-cream. **~oso** *a* greasy

mantel *m* tablecloth; *(del altar)* altar cloth. **~ería** *f* table linen

manten|er [40] *vt* support; (*conservar*) keep; (*sostener*) maintain. **~erse** *vpr* remain. **~ de/con** live off. **~imiento** *m* maintenance

mantequ|era *f* butter churn. **~ería** *f* dairy. **~illa** *f* butter

mantilla *f* mantilla

manto *m* cloak

mantón *m* shawl

manual *a & m* manual

manubrio *m* crank

manufactura *f* manufacture; (*fábrica*) factory

manuscrito *a* handwritten. ● *m* manuscript

manutención *f* maintenance

manzana *f* apple. **~r** *m* (*apple*) orchard

manzanilla *f* camomile tea; (*vino*) manzanilla, pale dry sherry

manzano *m* apple tree

maña *f* skill. **~s** *fpl* cunning

mañan|a *f* morning; (*el día siguiente*) tomorrow. ● *m* future. ● *adv* tomorrow. **~ero** *a* who gets up early. ● *m* early riser. **~a por la ~a** tomorrow morning. **pasado ~a** the day after tomorrow. **por la ~a** in the morning

mañoso *a* clever; (*astuto*) crafty

mapa *m* map. **~mundi** *m* map of the world

mapache *m* racoon

mapurite *m* skunk

maqueta *f* scale model

maquiavélico *a* machiavellian

maquilla|je *m* make-up. **~r** *vt* make up. **~rse** *vpr* make up

máquina *f* machine; (*rail*) engine. **~ de escribir** typewriter. **~ fotográfica** camera

maquin|ación *f* machination. **~al** *a* mechanical. **~aria** *f* machinery. **~ista** *m & f* operator; (*rail*) engine driver

mar *m & f* sea. **alta ~** high seas. **la ~ de** (*fam*) lots of

maraña *f* thicket; (*enredo*) tangle; (*embrollo*) muddle

maravedí *m* (*pl* **maravedís, maravedises**) maravedi, old Spanish coin

maravill|a *f* wonder. **~ar** *vt* astonish. **~arse** *vpr* be astonished (**con** at). **~oso** *a* marvellous, wonderful. **a ~a, a las mil ~as** marvellously. **contar/decir ~as de** speak wonderfully of. **hacer ~as** work wonders

marbete *m* label

marca *f* mark; (*de fábrica*) trademark; (*deportes*) record. **~do** *a* marked. **~dor** *m* marker; (*deportes*) scoreboard. **~r** [7] *vt* mark; (*señalar*) show; (*anotar*) note down; score ‹*un gol*›; dial ‹*número de teléfono*›. ● *vi* score. **de ~** brand name; (*fig*) excellent. **de ~ mayor** (*fam*) first-class

marcial *a* martial

marciano *a & m* Martian

marco *m* frame; (*moneda alemana*) mark; (*deportes*) goal-posts

marcha *f* (*incl mus*) march; (*auto*) gear; (*curso*) course. **a toda ~** at full speed. **dar/hacer ~ atrás** put into reverse. **poner en ~** start; (*fig*) set in motion

marchante *m* (*f* **marchanta**) dealer; (*LAm, parroquiano*) client

marchar *vi* go; (*funcionar*) work, go. **~se** *vpr* go away, leave

marchit|ar *vt* wither. **~arse** *vpr* wither. **~o** *a* withered

marea *f* tide. **~do** *a* sick; (*en el mar*) seasick; (*aturdido*) dizzy; (*borracho*) drunk. **~r** *vt* sail, navigate; (*baquetear*) annoy. **~rse** *vpr* feel sick; (*en un barco*) be seasick; (*estar aturdido*) feel dizzy; (*irse la cabeza*) feel faint; (*emborracharse*) get slightly drunk

marejada *f* swell; (*fig*) wave

maremagno *m* (*de cosas*) sea; (*de gente*) (noisy) crowd

mareo *m* sickness; (*en el mar*) seasickness; (*aturdimiento*) dizziness; (*fig, molestia*) nuisance

marfil *m* ivory. **~eño** *a* ivory. **torre** **de ~** ivory tower

margarina *f* margarine

margarita *f* pearl; (*bot*) daisy

marg|en *m* margin; (*borde*) edge, border; (*de un río*) bank; (*de un camino*) side; (*nota marginal*) marginal note. **~inado** *a* on the edge. ● *m* outcast. **~inal** *a* marginal. **~inar** *vt* (*excluir*) exclude; (*dejar márgenes*) leave margins; (*poner notas*) write notes in the margin. **al ~en** (*fig*) outside

mariachi (*Mex*) *m* (*música popular de Jalisco*) Mariachi; (*conjunto popular*) Mariachi band

mariano *a* Marian

marica *f* (*hombre afeminado*) sissy; (*urraca*) magpie

maricón *m* homosexual, queer (*sl*)

marid|aje *m* married life; (*fig*) harmony. **~o** *m* husband

mariguana *f*, **marihuana** *f* marijuana

marimacho *m* mannish woman

marimandona *f* bossy woman

marimba *f* (type of) drum; (*LAm, especie de xilofón*) marimba

marimorena *f* (*fam*) row

marin|a *f* coast; (*cuadro*) seascape; (*conjunto de barcos*) navy; (*arte de navegar*) seamanship. **~era** *f* seamanship; (*conjunto de marineros*) crew. **~ero** *a* marine; ‹*barco*› seaworthy. ● *m* sailor. **~o** *a* marine. **~a de guerra** navy. **~a mercante** merchant navy. **a la ~era** in tomato and garlic sauce. **azul ~o** navy blue

marioneta *f* puppet. **~s** *fpl* puppet show

maripos|a *f* butterfly. **~ear** *vi* be fickle; (*galantear*) flirt. **~ón** *m* flirt. **~a nocturna** moth

mariquita *f* ladybird, ladybug (*Amer*)

marisabidilla *f* know-all

mariscador *m* shell-fisher

mariscal *m* marshal

maris|co *m* seafood, shellfish. **~quero** *m* (*persona que pesca mariscos*) seafood fisherman; (*persona que vende mariscos*) seafood seller

marital *a* marital

marítimo *a* maritime; ‹*ciudad etc*› coastal, seaside

maritornes *f* uncouth servant

marmit|a *f* pot. **~ón** *m* kitchen boy

mármol *m* marble

marmol|era *f* marblework, marbles. **~ista** *m* & *f* marble worker

marmóreo *a* marble

marmota *f* marmot

maroma *f* rope; (*LAm, función de volatines*) tightrope walking

marqu|és *m* marquess. **~esa** *f* marchioness. **~esina** *f* glass canopy

marquetería *f* marquetry

marrajo *a* ‹*toro*› vicious; ‹*persona*› cunning. ● *m* shark

marran|a *f* sow. **~ada** *f* filthy thing; (*cochinada*) dirty trick. **~o** *a* filthy. ● *m* hog

marrar *vt* (*errar*) miss; (*fallar*) fail

marrón *a* & *m* brown

marroquí *a* & *m* & *f* Moroccan. ● *m* (*tafilete*) morocco

marrubio *m* (*bot*) horehound

Marruecos *m* Morocco

marruller|ía *f* cajolery. **~o** *a* cajoling. ● *m* cajoler

marsopa *f* porpoise

marsupial *a* & *m* marsupial

marta *f* marten

martajar *vt* (*Mex*) grind ‹*maíz*›

Marte *m* Mars

martes *m* Tuesday

martill|ada *f* blow with a hammer. **~ar** *vt* hammer. **~azo** *m* blow with a hammer. **~ear** *vt* hammer. **~eo** *m* hammering. **~o** *m* hammer

martín *m* **pescador** kingfisher

martinete *m* (*macillo del piano*) hammer; (*mazo*) drop hammer

martingala *f* (*ardid*) trick

mártir *m* & *f* martyr

martir|io *m* martyrdom. **~izar** [10] *vt* martyr; (*fig*) torment, torture. **~ologio** *m* martyrology

marxis|mo *m* Marxism. **~ta** *a* & *m* & *f* Marxist

marzo *m* March

más *adv* & *a* (*comparativo*) more; (*superlativo*) most. **~ caro** dearer. **~ curioso** more curious. **el ~ caro** the dearest; (*de dos*) the dearer. **el ~ curioso** the most curious; (*de dos*) the more curious. ● *conj* and, plus. ● *m* plus (sign). **~ bien** rather. **~ de** (*cantidad indeterminada*) more than. **~ o menos** more or less. **~ que** more than. **~ y ~** more and more. **a lo ~** at (the) most. **de ~** too many. **es ~** moreover. **no ~** no more

masa *f* dough; (*cantidad*) mass; (*física*) mass. **en ~** en masse

masacre *f* massacre

masaj|e *m* massage. **~ista** *m* masseur. ● *f* masseuse

masca|da *f* (*LAm*) plug of tobacco. **~dura** *f* chewing. **~r** [7] *vt* chew

máscara *f* mask; (*persona*) masked figure/person

mascar|ada *f* masquerade. **~illa** *f* mask. **~ón** *m* (large) mask

mascota *f* mascot

masculin|idad *f* masculinity. **~o** *a* masculine; ‹*sexo*› male. ● *m* masculine

mascullar [3] *vt* mumble

masilla *f* putty

masivo *a* massive, large-scale

mas|ón *m* (free)mason. **~onería** *f* (free)masonry. **~ónico** *a* masonic

masoquis|mo *m* masochism. **~ta** *a* masochistic. ● *m* & *f* masochist

mastate *m* (*Mex*) loincloth

mastelero *m* topmast

mastica|ción *f* chewing. **~r** [7] *vt* chew; (*fig*) chew over

mástil *m* mast; (*palo*) pole; (*en instrumentos de cuerda*) neck

mastín *m* mastiff

mastitis *f* mastitis

mastodonte *m* mastodon

mastoides *a* & *f* mastoid

mastuerzo *m* cress

masturba|ción *f* masturbation. **~rse** *vpr* masturbate

mata *f* grove; (*arbusto*) bush

matad|ero *m* slaughterhouse. **~or** *a* killing. ● *m* killer; (*torero*) matador

matadura *f* sore

matamoscas *m invar* fly swatter

mata|nza *f* killing. **~r** *vt* kill (*personas*); slaughter (*reses*). **~rife** *m* butcher. **~rse** *vpr* commit suicide; (*en un accidente*) be killed. **estar a ~r con uno** be deadly enemies with s.o.

matarratas *m invar* cheap liquor

matasanos *m invar* quack

matasellos *m invar* postmark

match *m* match

mate *a* matt, dull; ‹*sonido*› dull. ● *m* (*ajedrez*) (check)mate; (*LAm, bebida*) maté

matemátic|as *fpl* mathematics, maths (*fam*), math (*Amer, fam*). **~o** *a* mathematical. ● *m* mathematician

materia *f* matter; (*material*) material. **~ prima** raw material. **en ~ de** on the question of

material *a* & *m* material. **~idad** *f* material nature. **~ismo** *m* materialism. **~ista** *a* materialistic. ● *m* & *f* materialist. **~izar** [10] *vt* materialize. **~izarse** *vpr* materialize. **~mente** *adv* materially; (*absolutamente*) absolutely

matern|al *a* maternal; (*como de madre*) motherly. **~idad** *f* motherhood; (*casa de maternidad*) maternity home. **~o** *a* motherly; ‹*lengua*› mother

matin|al *a* morning. **~ée** *m* matinée

matiz *m* shade. **~ación** *f* combination of colours. **~ar** [10] *vt* blend ‹*colores*›; (*introducir variedad*) vary; (*teñir*) tinge (**de** with)

matojo *m* bush

mat|ón *m* bully. **~onismo** *m* bullying

matorral *m* scrub; (*conjunto de matas*) thicket

matra|ca *f* rattle. **~quear** *vt* rattle; (*dar matraca*) pester. **dar ~ca** pester. **ser un(a) ~ca** be a nuisance

matraz *m* flask

matriarca|do *m* matriarchy. **~l** *a* matriarchal

matr|ícula *f* (*lista*) register, list; (*acto de matricularse*) registration; (*auto*) registration number. **~icular** *vt* register. **~icularse** *vpr* enrol, register

matrimoni|al *a* matrimonial. **~o** *m* marriage; (*pareja*) married couple

matritense *a* from Madrid

matriz *f* matrix; (*anat*) womb, uterus

matrona *f* matron; (*partera*) midwife

Matusalén *m* Methuselah. **más viejo que ~** as old as Methuselah

matute *m* smuggling. **~ro** *m* smuggler

matutino *a* morning

maula *f* piece of junk

maull|ar *vi* miaow. **~ido** *m* miaow

mauritano *a* & *m* Mauritanian

mausoleo *m* mausoleum

maxilar *a* maxillary. **hueso ~** jaw(bone)

máxima *f* maxim

máxime *adv* especially

máximo *a* maximum; (*más alto*) highest. ● *m* maximum

maya *f* daisy; (*persona*) Maya Indian

mayestático *a* majestic

mayo *m* May; (*palo*) maypole

mayólica *f* majolica

mayonesa *f* mayonnaise

mayor *a* (*más grande, comparativo*) bigger; (*más grande, superlativo*) biggest; (*de edad, comparativo*) older; (*de edad, superlativo*) oldest; (*adulto*) grown-up; (*principal*) main, major; (*mus*) major. ● *m* & *f* boss; (*adulto*) adult. **~al** *m* foreman; (*pastor*) head shepherd. **~azgo** *m* entailed estate. **al por ~** wholesale

mayordomo *m* butler

mayor|ía *f* majority. **~ista** *m* & *f* wholesaler. **~mente** *adv* especially

mayúscul|a *f* capital (letter). **~o** *a* capital; (*fig, grande*) big

maza *f* mace

mazacote *m* hard mass

mazapán *m* marzipan

mazmorra *f* dungeon

mazo *m* mallet; (*manojo*) bunch

mazorca *f*. **~ de maíz** corn on the cob

me *pron* (*acusativo*) me; (*dativo*) (to) me; (*reflexivo*) (to) myself

meandro *m* meander

mecánic|a *f* mechanics. **~o** *a* mechanical. ● *m* mechanic

mecani|smo *m* mechanism. **~zación** *f* mechanization. **~zar** [10] *vt* mechanize

mecanograf|ía *f* typing. **~iado** *a* typed, typewritten. **~iar** [20] *vt* type

mecanógrafo *m* typist

mecate *m* (*LAm*) (*pita*) rope

mecedora *f* rocking chair

mecenazgo *m* patronage

mecer [9] *vt* rock; swing ‹*columpio*›. **~se** *vpr* rock; (*en un columpio*) swing

mecha *f* (*de vela*) wick; (*de mina*) fuse

mechar *vt* stuff, lard

mechero *m* (cigarette) lighter

mechón *m* (*de pelo*) lock

medall|a *f* medal. **~ón** *m* medallion; (*relicario*) locket

media *f* stocking; (*promedio*) average

mediación *f* mediation

mediado *a* half full; ‹*trabajo etc*› halfway through. **a ~s de marzo** in the middle of March

mediador *m* mediator

medialuna *f* croissant

median|amente *adv* fairly. **~era** *f* party wall. **~ero** *a* ‹*muro*› party. **~a** *f* average circumstances. **~o** *a* average, medium; (*mediocre*) mediocre

medianoche *f* midnight; (*culin*) small sandwich

mediante *prep* through, by means of

mediar *vi* mediate; (*llegar a la mitad*) be halfway (**en** through)

mediatizar [10] *vt* annex

medic|ación *f* medication. **~amento** *m* medicine. **~ina** *f* medicine. **~inal** *a* medicinal. **~inar** *vt* administer medicine

medición *f* measurement

médico *a* medical. ● *m* doctor. **~ de cabecera** GP, general practitioner

medid|a *f* measurement; (*unidad*) measure; (*disposición*) measure, step; (*prudencia*) moderation. **~or** *m* (*LAm*) meter. **a la ~a** made to measure. **a ~a que** as. **en cierta ~a** to a certain point

mediero *m* share-cropper

medieval *a* medieval. **~ista** *m* & *f* medievalist

medio *a* half (a); (*mediano*) average. **~ litro** half a litre. ● *m* middle; (*manera*) means; (*en deportes*)

half(-back). **en ~** in the middle (**de** of). **por ~ de** through

mediocr|e *a* (*mediano*) average; (*de escaso mérito*) mediocre. **~idad** *f* mediocrity

mediodía *m* midday, noon; (*sur*) south

medioevo *m* Middle Ages

Medio Oriente *m* Middle East

medir [5] *vt* medir; weigh up ‹*palabras etc*›. ● *vi* measure, be. **~se** *vpr* (*moderarse*) be moderate

medita|bundo *a* thoughtful. **~ción** *f* meditation. **~r** *vt* think about. ● *vi* meditate

Mediterráneo *m* Mediterranean

mediterráneo *a* Mediterranean

médium *m* & *f* medium

medrar *vi* thrive

medroso *a* (*con estar*) frightened; (*con ser*) fearful

médula *f* marrow

medusa *f* jellyfish

mefítico *a* noxious

mega... *pref* mega...

megáfono *m* megaphone

megal|ítico *a* megalithic. **~ito** *m* megalith

megal|omanía *f* megalomania. **~ómano** *m* megalomaniac

mejicano *a* & *m* Mexican

Méjico *m* Mexico

mejido *a* ‹*huevo*› beaten

mejilla *f* cheek

mejillón *m* mussel

mejor *a* & *adv* (*comparativo*) better; (*superlativo*) best. **~a** *f* improvement. **~able** *a* improvable. **~amiento** *m* improvement. **~ dicho** rather. **a lo ~** perhaps. **tanto ~** so much the better

mejorana *f* marjoram

mejorar *vt* improve, better. ● *vi* get better

mejunje *m* mixture

melanc|olía *f* melancholy. **~ólico** *a* melancholic

melaza *f* molasses, treacle (*Amer*)

melen|a *f* long hair; (*de león*) mane. **~udo** *a* long-haired

melifluo *a* mellifluous

melillense *a* of/from Melilla. ● *m* person from Melilla

melindr|e *m* (*mazapán*) sugared marzipan cake; (*masa frita con miel*) honey fritter. **~oso** *a* affected

melocot|ón *m* peach. **~onero** *m* peach tree

mel|odía _f_ melody. **~ódico** _a_ melodic. **~odioso** _a_ melodious

melodram|a _m_ melodrama. **~áticamente** _adv_ melodramatically. **~ático** _a_ melodramatic

melómano _m_ music lover

mel|ón _m_ melon; _(bobo)_ fool. **~onada** _f_ something stupid

meloncillo _m_ _(animal)_ mongoose

melos|idad _f_ sweetness. **~o** _a_ sweet

mella _f_ notch. **~do** _a_ jagged. **~r** _vt_ notch

mellizo _a & m_ twin

membran|a _f_ membrane. **~oso** _a_ membranous

membrete _m_ letterhead

membrill|ero _m_ quince tree. **~o** _m_ quince

membrudo _a_ burly

memez _f_ something silly

memo _a_ stupid. ● _m_ idiot

memorable _a_ memorable

memorando _m_, **memorándum** _m_ notebook; _(nota)_ memorandum

memoria _f_ memory; _(informe)_ report; _(tesis)_ thesis. **~s** _fpl_ _(recuerdos personales)_ memoirs. **de ~** from memory

memorial _m_ memorial. **~ista** _m_ amanuensis

memor|ión _m_ good memory. **~ista** _a_ having a good memory. **~ístico** _a_ memory

mena _f_ ore

menaje _m_ furnishings

menci|ón _f_ mention. **~onado** _a_ aforementioned. **~onar** _vt_ mention

menda|cidad _f_ mendacity. **~z** _a_ lying

mendi|cante _a & m_ mendicant. **~cidad** _f_ begging. **~gar** [12] _vt_ beg (for). ● _vi_ beg. **~go-m** _m_ beggar

mendrugo _m_ _(pan)_ hard crust; _(zoquete)_ blockhead

mene|ar _vt_ move, shake. **~arse** _vpr_ move, shake. **~o** _m_ movement, shake

menester _m_ need. **~oso** _a_ needy. **ser ~** be necessary

menestra _f_ stew

menestral _m_ artesan

mengano _m_ so-and-so

mengua _f_ decrease; _(falta)_ lack; _(descrédito)_ discredit. **~do** _a_ miserable; _(falto de carácter)_ spineless. **~nte** _a_ decreasing; ‹_luna_› waning; ‹_marea_› ebb. ● _f_ _(del mar)_ ebb tide;

(de un río) low water. **~r** [15] _vt/i_ decrease, diminish

meningitis _f_ meningitis

menisco _m_ meniscus

menjurje _m_ mixture

menopausia _f_ menopause

menor _a_ _(más pequeño, comparativo)_ smaller; _(más pequeño, superlativo)_ smallest; _(más joven, comparativo)_ younger; _(más joven, superlativo)_; _(mus)_ minor. ● _m & f_ _(menor de edad)_ minor. **al por ~** retail

Menorca _f_ Minorca

menorquín _a & m_ Minorcan

menos _a_ _(comparativo)_ less; _(comparativo, con plural)_ fewer; _(superlativo)_ least; _(superlativo, con plural)_ fewest. ● _adv_ _(comparativo)_ less; _(superlativo)_ least. ● _prep_ except. **~cabar** _vt_ lessen; _(fig, estropear)_ damage. **~cabo** _m_ lessening. **~preciable** _a_ contemptible. **~preciar** _vt_ despise. **~precio** _m_ contempt. **a ~ que** unless. **al ~** at least. **ni mucho ~** far from it. **por lo ~** at least

mensaje _m_ message. **~ro** _m_ messenger

menso _a_ _(Mex)_ stupid

menstru|ación _f_ menstruation. **~al** _a_ menstrual. **~ar** [21] _vi_ menstruate. **~o** _m_ menstruation

mensual _a_ monthly. **~idad** _f_ monthly pay

ménsula _f_ bracket

mensurable _a_ measurable

menta _f_ mint

mental _a_ mental. **~idad** _f_ mentality. **~mente** _adv_ mentally

mentar [1] _vt_ mention, name

mente _f_ mind

mentecato _a_ stupid. ● _m_ idiot

mentir [4] _vi_ lie. **~a** _f_ lie. **~oso** _a_ lying. ● _m_ liar. **de ~ijillas** for a joke

mentís _m_ _invar_ denial

mentol _m_ menthol

mentor _m_ mentor

menú _m_ menu

menudear _vi_ happen frequently

menudencia _f_ trifle

menudeo _m_ retail trade

menudillos _mpl_ giblets

menudo _a_ tiny; ‹_lluvia_› fine; _(insignificante)_ insignificant. **~s** _mpl_ giblets. **a ~** often

meñique _a_ ‹_dedo_› little. ● _m_ little finger

meollo _m_ brain; _(médula)_ marrow; _(parte blanda)_ soft part; _(fig, inteligencia)_ brains

meramente *adv* merely

mercachifle *m* hawker; (*fig*) profiteer

mercader *m* (*LAm*) merchant

mercado *m* market. **M~ Común** Common Market. **~ negro** black market

mercan|cía *f* article. **~cías** *fpl* goods, merchandise. **~te** *a* & *m* merchant. **~til** *a* mercantile, commercial. **~tilismo** *m* mercantilism

mercar [7] *vt* buy

merced *f* favour. **su/vuestra ~** your honour

mercenario *a* & *m* mercenary

mercer|ía *f* haberdashery, notions (*Amer*). **~o** *m* haberdasher

mercurial *a* mercurial

Mercurio *m* Mercury

mercurio *m* mercury

merec|edor *a* deserving. **~er** [11] *vt* deserve. ● *vi* be deserving. **~idamente** *adv* deservedly. **~ido** *a* well deserved. **~imiento** *m* (*mérito*) merit

merend|ar [1] vt have as an afternoon snack. ● *vi* have an afternoon snack. **~ero** *m* snack bar; (*lugar*) picnic area

merengue *m* meringue

meretriz *f* prostitute

mergo *m* cormorant

meridian|a *f* (*diván*) couch. **~o** *a* midday; (*fig*) dazzling. ● *m* meridian

meridional *a* southern. ● *m* southerner

merienda *f* afternoon snack

merino *a* merino

mérito *m* merit; (*valor*) worth

meritorio *a* meritorious. ● *m* unpaid trainee

merlo *m* black wrasse

merluza *f* hake

merma *f* decrease. **~r** *vt/i* decrease, reduce

mermelada *f* jam

mero *a* mere; (*Mex, verdadero*) real. ● *adv* (*Mex, precisamente*) exactly; (*Mex, verdaderamente*) really. ● *m* grouper

merode|ador *a* marauding. ● *m* marauder. **~ar** *vi* maraud. **~o** *m* marauding

merovingio *a* & *m* Merovingian

mes *m* month; (*mensualidad*) monthly pay

mesa *f* table; (*para escribir o estudiar*) desk. **poner la ~** lay the table

mesana *f* (*palo*) mizen-mast

mesarse *vpr* tear at one's hair

mesenterio *m* mesentery

meseta *f* plateau; (*descansillo*) landing

mesiánico *a* Messianic

Mesías *m* Messiah

mesilla *f* small table. **~ de noche** bedside table

mesón *m* inn

mesoner|a *f* landlady. **~o** *m* landlord

mestiz|aje *m* crossbreeding. **~o** *a* (*persona*) half-caste; (*animal*) crossbred. ● *m* (*persona*) half-caste; (*animal*) cross-breed

mesura *f* moderation. **~do** *a* moderate

meta *f* goal; (*de una carrera*) finish

metabolismo *m* metabolism

metacarpiano *m* metacarpal

metafísic|a *f* metaphysics. **~o** *a* metaphysical

met|áfora *f* metaphor. **~afórico** *a* metaphorical

met|al *m* metal; (*instrumentos de latón*) brass; (*de la voz*) timbre. **~álico** *a* (*objeto*) metal; (*sonido*) metallic. **~alizarse** [10] *vpr* (*fig*) become mercenary

metal|urgia *f* metallurgy. **~úrgico** *a* metallurgical

metam|órfico *a* metamorphic. **~orfosear** *vt* transform. **~orfosis** *f* metamorphosis

metano *m* methane

metatarsiano *m* metatarsal

metátesis *f invar* metathesis

metedura *f*. **~ de pata** blunder

mete|órico *a* meteoric. **~orito** *m* meteorite. **~oro** *m* meteor. **~orología** *f* meteorology. **~orológico** *a* meteorological. **~orólogo** *m* meteorologist

meter *vt* put, place; (*ingresar*) deposit; score (*un gol*); (*enredar*) involve; (*causar*) make. **~se** *vpr* get; (*entrometerse*) meddle. **~se con uno** pick a quarrel with s.o.

meticulos|idad *f* meticulousness. **~o** *a* meticulous

metido *m* reprimand. ● *a*. **~ en años** getting on. **estar muy ~ con uno** be well in with s.o.

metilo *m* methyl

metódico *a* methodical

metodis|mo *m* Methodism. **~ta** *a* & *m* & *f* Methodist

método *m* method

metodología *f* methodology

metomentodo *m* busybody

metraje *m* length. **de largo** ~ ⟨*película*⟩ feature

metrall|a *f* shrapnel. ~**eta** *f* submachine gun

métric|a *f* metrics. ~**o** *a* metric; ⟨*verso*⟩ metrical

metro *m* metre; (*tren*) underground, subway (*Amer*). ~ **cuadrado** square metre

metrónomo *m* metronome

metr|ópoli *f* metropolis. ~**opolitano** *a* metropolitan. ● *m* metropolitan; (*tren*) underground, subway (*Amer*)

mexicano *a* & *m* (*LAm*) Mexican

México *m* (*LAm*) Mexico. ~ **D. F.** Mexico City

mezcal *m* (*Mex*) (type of) brandy

mezc|la *f* (*acción*) mixing; (*substancia*) mixture; (*argamasa*) mortar. ~**lador** *m* mixer. ~**lar** *vt* mix; shuffle ⟨*los naipes*⟩. ~**larse** *vpr* mix; (*intervenir*) interfere. ~**olanza** *f* mixture

mezquin|dad *f* meanness. ~**o** *a* mean; (*escaso*) meagre. ● *m* mean person

mezquita *f* mosque

mi *a* my. ● *m* (*mus*) E; (*solfa*) mi

mí *pron* me

miaja *f* crumb

miasma *m* miasma

miau *m* miaow

mica *f* (*silicato*) mica; (*Mex, embriaguez*) drunkenness

mico *m* (long-tailed) monkey

micro... *pref* micro...

microbio *m* microbe

micro: ~**biología** *f* microbiology. ~**cosmo** *m* microcosm. ~**film(e)** *m* microfilm

micrófono *m* microphone

micrómetro *m* micrometer

microonda *f* microwave. **horno de** ~**s** microwave oven

microordenador *m* microcomputer

microsc|ópico *a* microscopic. ~**opio** *m* microscope

micro: ~**surco** *m* long-playing record. ~**taxi** *m* minicab

miedo *m* fear. ~**so** *a* fearful. **dar** ~ frighten. **morirse de** ~ be scared to death. **tener** ~ be frightened

miel *f* honey

mielga *f* lucerne, alfalfa (*Amer*)

miembro *m* limb; (*persona*) member

mientras *conj* while. ● *adv* meanwhile. ~ **que** whereas. ~ **tanto** in the meantime

miércoles *m* Wednesday. ~ **de ceniza** Ash Wednesday

mierda *f* (*vulgar*) shit

mies *f* corn, grain (*Amer*)

miga *f* crumb; (*fig, meollo*) essence. ~**jas** *fpl* crumbs. ~**r** [12] *vt* crumble

migra|ción *f* migration. ~**torio** *a* migratory

mijo *m* millet

mil *a* & *m* a/one thousand. ~**es de** thousands of. ~ **novecientos noventa y dos** nineteen ninety-two. ~ **pesetas** a thousand pesetas

milagro *m* miracle. ~**so** *a* miraculous

milano *m* kite

mildeu *m*, **mildiu** *m* mildew

milen|ario *a* millenial. ~**io** *m* millennium

milenrama *f* milfoil

milésimo *a* & *m* thousandth

mili *f* (*fam*) military service

milicia *f* soldiering; (*gente armada*) militia

mili|gramo *m* milligram. ~**litro** *m* millilitre

milímetro *m* millimetre

militante *a* militant

militar *a* military. ● *m* soldier. ~**ismo** *m* militarism. ~**ista** *a* militaristic. ● *m* & *f* militarist. ~**izar** [10] *vt* militarize

milonga *f* (*Arg, canción*) popular song; (*Arg, baile*) popular dance

milord *m*. **vivir como un** ~ live like a lord

milpies *m invar* woodlouse

milla *f* mile

millar *m* thousand. **a** ~**es** by the thousand

mill|ón *m* million. ~**onada** *f* fortune. ~**onario** *m* millionaire. ~**onésimo** *a* & *m* millionth. **un** ~**n de libros** a million books

mimar *vt* spoil

mimbre *m* & *f* wicker. ~**arse** *vpr* sway. ~**ra** *f* osier. ~**ral** *m* osier-bed

mimetismo *m* mimicry

mímic|a *f* mime. ~**o** *a* mimic

mimo *m* mime; (*a un niño*) spoiling; (*caricia*) caress

mimosa *f* mimosa

mina *f* mine. ~**r** *vt* mine; (*fig*) undermine

minarete m minaret

mineral m mineral; (*mena*) ore. ~**ogía** f mineralogy. ~**ogista** m & f mineralogist

miner|ía f mining. ~**o** a mining. ● m miner

mini... pref mini...

miniar vt paint in miniature

miniatura f miniature

minifundio m smallholding

minimizar [10] vt minimize

mínim|o a & m minimum. ~**um** m minimum

minino m (*fam*) cat, puss (*fam*)

minio m red lead

minist|erial a ministerial. ~**erio** m ministry. ~**ro** m minister

minor|ación f diminution. ~**a** f minority. ~**idad** f minority. ~**ista** m & f retailer

minuci|a f trifle. ~**osidad** f thoroughness. ~**oso** a thorough; (*con muchos detalles*) detailed

minué m minuet

minúscul|a f small letter, lower case letter. ~**o** a tiny

minuta f draft; (*menú*) menu

minut|ero m minute hand. ~**o** m minute

mío a & pron mine. **un amigo** ~ a friend of mine

miop|e a short-sighted. ● m & f short-sighted person. ~**ía** f short-sightedness

mira f sight; (*fig, intención*) aim. ~**da** f look. ~**do** a thought of; (*comedido*) considerate; (*cirunspecto*) circumspect. ~**dor** m windowed balcony; (*lugar*) viewpoint. ~**miento** m consideration. ~**r** vt look at; (*observar*) watch; (*considerar*) consider. ~**r fijamente a** stare at. ● vi look; ⟨*edificio etc*⟩ face. ~**rse** vpr ⟨*personas*⟩ look at each other. **a la** ~ on the lookout. **con** ~**s a** with a view to. **echar una** ~**da a** glance at

mirilla f peephole

miriñaque m crinoline

mirlo m blackbird

mirón a nosey. ● m nosey-parker; (*espectador*) onlooker

mirra f myrrh

mirto m myrtle

misa f mass

misal m missal

mis|antropía f misanthropy. ~**antrópico** a misanthropic. ~**ántropo** m misanthropist

miscelánea f miscellany; (*Mex, tienda*) corner shop

miser|able a very poor; (*lastimoso*) miserable; (*tacaño*) mean. ~**ia** f extreme poverty; (*suciedad*) squalor

misericordi|a f pity; (*piedad*) mercy. ~**oso** a merciful

mísero a very poor; (*lastimoso*) miserable; (*tacaño*) mean

misil m missile

misi|ón f mission. ~**onal** a missionary. ~**onero** m missionary

misiva f missive

mism|amente adv just. ~**ísimo** a very same. ~**o** a same; (*después de pronombre personal*) myself, yourself, himself, herself, itself, ourselves, yourselves, themselves; (*enfático*) very. ● adv right. **ahora** ~ right now. **aquí** ~ right here

mis|oginia f misogyny. ~**ógino** m misogynist

misterio m mystery. ~**so** a mysterious

místic|a f mysticism. ~**o** a mystical

mistifica|ción f falsification; (*engaño*) trick. ~**r** [7] vt falsify; (*engañar*) deceive

mitad f half; (*centro*) middle

mítico a mythical

mitiga|ción f mitigation. ~**r** [12] vt mitigate; quench ⟨*sed*⟩; relieve ⟨*dolor etc*⟩

mitin m meeting

mito m myth. ~**logía** f mythology. ~**lógico** a mythological

mitón m mitten

mitote m (*LAm*) Indian dance

mitra f mitre. ~**do** m prelate

mixteca f (*Mex*) southern Mexico

mixt|o a mixed. ● m passenger and goods train; (*cerilla*) match. ~**ura** f mixture

mnemotécnic|a f mnemonics. ~**o** a mnemonic

moaré m moiré

mobiliario m furniture

moblaje m furniture

moca m mocha

moce|dad f youth. ~**ro** m young people. ~**tón** m strapping lad

moción f motion

moco m mucus

mochales a invar. **estar** ~ be round the bend

mochila f rucksack

mocho a blunt. ● m butt end

mochuelo m little owl

moda f fashion. **~l** a modal. **~les** mpl manners. **~lidad** f kind. **de ~** in fashion

model|ado m modelling. **~ador** m modeller. **~ar** vt model; (fig, configurar) form. **~o** m model

modera|ción f moderation. **~do** a moderate. **~r** vt moderate; reduce ⟨velocidad⟩. **~rse** vpr control oneself

modern|amente adv recently. **~idad** f modernity. **~ismo** m modernism. **~ista** m & f modernist. **~izar** [10] vt modernize. **~o** a modern

modest|ia f modesty. **~o** a modest

modicidad f reasonableness

módico a moderate

modifica|ción f modification. **~r** [7] vt modify

modismo m idiom

modist|a f dressmaker. **~o** m & f designer

modo m manner, way; (gram) mood; (mus) mode. **~ de ser** character. **de ~ que** so that. **de ningún ~** certainly not. **de todos ~s** anyhow

modorr|a f drowsiness. **~o** a drowsy

modoso a well-behaved

modula|ción f modulation. **~dor** m modulator. **~r** vt modulate

módulo m module

mofa f mockery. **~rse** vpr. **~rse de** make fun of

mofeta f skunk

moflet|e m chubby cheek. **~udo** a with chubby cheeks

mogol m Mongol. **el Gran M~** the Great Mogul

moh|ín m grimace. **~ino** a sulky. **hacer un ~ín** pull a face

moho m mould; (óxido) rust. **~so** a mouldy; ⟨metales⟩ rusty

moisés m Moses basket

mojado a damp, wet

mojama f salted tuna

mojar vt wet; (empapar) soak; (humedecer) moisten, dampen. ● vi. **~ en** get involved in

mojicón m blow in the face; (bizcocho) sponge cake

mojiganga f masked ball; (en el teatro) farce

mojigat|ería f hypocrisy. **~o** m hypocrite

mojón m boundary post; (señal) signpost

molar m molar

mold|e m mould; (aguja) knitting needle. **~ear** vt mould, shape; (fig) form. **~ura** f moulding

mole f mass, bulk. ● m (Mex, guisado) (Mexican) stew with chili sauce

mol|écula f molecule. **~ecular** a molecular

mole|dor a grinding. ● m grinder; (persona) bore. **~r** [2] grind; (hacer polvo) pulverize

molest|ar vt annoy; (incomodar) bother. **¿le ~a que fume?** do you mind if I smoke? **no ~ar** do not disturb. ● vi be a nuisance. **~arse** vpr bother; (ofenderse) take offence. **~ia** f bother, nuisance; (inconveniente) inconvenience; (incomodidad) discomfort. **~o** a annoying; (inconveniente) inconvenient; (ofendido) offended

molicie f softness; (excesiva comodidad) easy life

molido a ground; (fig, muy cansado) worn out

molienda f grinding

molin|ero m miller. **~ete** m toy windmill. **~illo** m mill; (juguete) toy windmill. **~o** m (water) mill. **~o de viento** windmill

molusco m mollusc

mollar a soft

molleja f gizzard

mollera f (de la cabeza) crown; (fig, sesera) brains

moment|áneamente adv momentarily; (por el momento) right now. **~áneo** a momentary. **~o** m moment; (mecánica) momentum

momi|a f mummy. **~ficación** f mummification. **~ficar** [7] vt mummify. **~ficarse** vpr become mummified

momio a lean. ● m bargain; (trabajo) cushy job

monaca|l a monastic. **~to** m monasticism

monada f beautiful thing; (de un niño) charming way; (acción tonta) silliness

monaguillo m altar boy

mon|arca m & f monarch. **~arquía** f monarchy. **~árquico** a monarchic(al). **~arquismo** m monarchism

mon|asterio m monastery. **~ástico** a monastic

monda f pruning; (peladura) peel

mond|adientes m invar toothpick. **~adura** f pruning; (peladura) peel.

~**ar** vt peel ⟨fruta etc⟩; dredge ⟨un río⟩. ~**o** a (sin pelo) bald; (sin dinero) broke; (sencillo) plain

mondongo m innards

moned|a f coin; (de un país) currency. ~**ero** m minter; (porta-monedas) purse

monetario a monetary

mongol a & m Mongolian

mongolismo m Down's syndrome

monigote m weak character; (muñeca) rag doll; (dibujo) doodle

monises mpl money, dough (fam)

monitor m monitor

monj|a f nun. ~**e** m monk. ~**il** a nun's; (como de monja) like a nun

mono m monkey; (sobretodo) overalls. ● a pretty

mono... pref mono...

monocromo a & m monochrome

monóculo m monocle

mon|ogamia f monogamy. ~**ó-gamo** a monogamous

monografía f monograph

monograma m monogram

monol|ítico a monolithic. ~**ito** m monolith

mon|ologar [12] vi soliloquize. ~**ólogo** m monologue

monoman|ía f monomania. ~**iaco** m monomaniac

monoplano m monoplane

monopoli|o m monopoly. ~**zar** [10] vt monopolize

monos|ilábico a monosyllabic. ~**í-labo** m monosyllable

monoteís|mo m monotheism. ~**ta** a monotheistic. ● m & f monotheist

mon|otonía f monotony. ~**ótono** a monotonous

monseñor m monsignor

monserga f boring talk

monstruo m monster. ~**sidad** f monstrosity. ~**so** a monstrous

monta f mounting; (valor) value

montacargas m invar service lift

monta|do a mounted. ~**dor** m fitter. ~**je** m assembly; (cine) montage; (teatro) staging, production

montañ|a f mountain. ~**ero** m mountaineer. ~**és** a mountain. ● m highlander. ~**ismo** m mountaineering. ~**oso** a mountainous. ~**a rusa** big dipper

montaplatos m invar service lift

montar vt ride; (subirse) get on; (ensamblar) assemble; cock ⟨arma⟩; set up ⟨una casa, un negocio⟩. ● vi

ride; (subirse a) mount. ~ **a caballo** ride a horse

montaraz a ⟨animales⟩ wild; ⟨personas⟩ mountain

monte m (montaña) mountain; (terreno inculto) scrub; (bosque) forest. ~ **de piedad** pawn-shop. **ingeniero** m **de** ~**s** forestry expert

montepío m charitable fund for dependents

monter|a f cloth cap. ~**o** m hunter

montés a wild

Montevideo m Montevideo

montevideano a & m Montevidean

montículo m hillock

montón m heap, pile. **a montones** in abundance, lots of

montuoso a hilly

montura f mount; (silla) saddle

monument|al a monumental; (fig, muy grande) enormous. ~**o** m monument

monzón m & f monsoon

moñ|a f hair ribbon. ~**o** m bun

moque|o m runny nose. ~**ro** m handkerchief

moqueta f fitted carpet

moquillo m distemper

mora f mulberry; (zarzamora) blackberry

morada f dwelling

morado a purple

morador m inhabitant

moral m mulberry tree. ● f morals. ● a moral. ~**eja** f moral. ~**idad** f morality. ~**ista** m & f moralist. ~**izador** a moralizing. ● m moralist. ~**izar** [10] vt moralize

morapio m (fam) cheap red wine

morar vi live

moratoria f moratorium

morbidez f softness

mórbido a soft; (malsano) morbid

morbo m illness. ~**sidad** f morbidity. ~**so** a unhealthy

morcilla f black pudding

morda|cidad f bite. ~**z** a biting

mordaza f gag

mordazmente adv bitingly

morde|dura f bite. ~**r** [2] vt bite; (fig, quitar porciones a) eat into; (denigrar) gossip about. ● vi bite

mordis|car [7] vt nibble (at). ● vi nibble. ~**co** m bite. ~**quear** vt nibble (at)

morelense a (Mex) from Morelos. ● m & f person from Morelos

morena _f_ (_geol_) moraine

moreno _a_ dark; (_de pelo obscuro_) dark-haired; (_de raza negra_) negro

morera _f_ mulberry tree

morería _f_ Moorish lands; (_barrio_) Moorish quarter

moretón _m_ bruise

morfema _m_ morpheme

morfin|a _f_ morphine. ~**ómano** _a_ morphine. ● _m_ morphine addict

morfol|ogía _f_ morphology. ~**ógico** _a_ morphological

moribundo _a_ moribund

morillo _m_ andiron

morir [6] (_pp_ **muerto**) _vi_ die; (_fig, extinguirse_) die away; (_fig, terminar_) end. ~**se** _vpr_ die. ~**se de hambre** starve to death; (_fig_) be starving. **se muere por una flauta** she's dying to have a flute

moris|co _a_ Moorish. ● _m_ Moor. ~**ma** _f_ Moors

morm|ón _m_ & _f_ Mormon. ~**ónico** _a_ Mormon. ~**onismo** _m_ Mormonism

moro _a_ Moorish. ● _m_ Moor

moros|idad _f_ dilatoriness. ~**o** _a_ dilatory

morrada _f_ butt; (_puñetazo_) punch

morral _m_ (_mochila_) rucksack; (_del cazador_) gamebag; (_para caballos_) nosebag

morralla _f_ rubbish

morrillo _m_ nape of the neck

morriña _f_ homesickness

morro _m_ snout

morrocotudo _a_ (_esp Mex_) (_fam_) terrific (_fam_)

morsa _f_ walrus

mortaja _f_ shroud

mortal _a_ & _m_ & _f_ mortal. ~**idad** _f_ mortality. ~**mente** _adv_ mortally

mortandad _f_ death toll

mortecino _a_ failing; (_color_) faded

mortero _m_ mortar

mortífero _a_ deadly

mortifica|ción _f_ mortification. ~**r** [7] _vt_ (_med_) damage; (_atormentar_) plague; (_humillar_) humiliate. ~**rse** _vpr_ (_Mex_) feel embarassed

mortuorio _a_ death

morueco _m_ ram

moruno _a_ Moorish

mosaico _a_ of Moses, Mosaic. ● _m_ mosaic

mosca _f_ fly. ~**rda** _f_ blowfly. ~**rdón** _m_ botfly; (_mosca de cuerpo azul_) bluebottle

moscatel _a_ muscatel

moscón _m_ botfly; (_mosca de cuerpo azul_) bluebottle

moscovita _a_ & _m_ & _f_ Muscovite

Moscú _m_ Moscow

mosque|arse _vpr_ get cross. ~**o** _m_ resentment

mosquete _m_ musket. ~**ro** _m_ musketeer

mosquit|ero _m_ mosquito net. ~**o** _m_ mosquito; (_mosca pequeña_) fly, gnat

mostacho _m_ moustache

mostachón _m_ macaroon

mostaza _f_ mustard

mosto _m_ must

mostrador _m_ counter

mostrar [2] _vt_ show. ~**se** _vpr_ (show oneself to) be. **se mostró muy amable** he was very kind

mostrenco _a_ ownerless; (_animal_) stray; (_torpe_) thick; (_gordo_) fat

mota _f_ spot, speck

mote _m_ nickname; (_lema_) motto

motea|do _a_ speckled. ~**r** _vt_ speckle

motejar _vt_ call

motel _m_ motel

motete _m_ motet

motín _m_ riot; (_rebelión_) uprising; (_de tropas_) mutiny

motiv|ación _f_ motivation. ~**ar** _vt_ motivate; (_explicar_) explain. ~**o** _m_ reason. **con** ~**o de** because of

motocicl|eta _f_ motor cycle, motor bike (_fam_). ~**ista** _m_ & _f_ motorcyclist

motón _m_ pulley

motonave _f_ motor boat

motor _a_ motor. ● _m_ motor, engine. ~**a** _f_ motor boat. ~ **de arranque** starter motor

motoris|mo _m_ motorcycling. ~**ta** _m_ & _f_ motorist; (_de una moto_) motorcyclist

motorizar [10] _vt_ motorize

motriz _a_ & _f_ motive, driving

move|dizo _a_ movable; (_poco firme_) unstable; (_persona_) fickle. ~**r** [2] _vt_ move; shake (_la cabeza_); (_provocar_) cause. ~**rse** _vpr_ move; (_darse prisa_) hurry up. **arenas** _fpl_ ~**dizas** quicksand

movi|ble _a_ movable. ~**do** _a_ moved; (_foto_) blurred; (_inquieto_) fidgety

móvil _a_ movable. ● _m_ motive

movili|dad _f_ mobility. ~**zación** _f_ mobilization. ~**zar** [10] _vt_ mobilize

movimiento _m_ movement, motion; (_agitación_) bustle

moza _f_ girl; (_sirvienta_) servant, maid. ~**lbete** _m_ young lad

mozárabe *a* Mozarabic. ● *m* & *f* Mozarab

moz|o *m* boy, lad. ∼**uela** *f* young girl. ∼**uelo** *m* young boy/lad

muaré *m* moiré

mucam|a *f* (*Arg*) servant. ∼**o** *m* (*Arg*) servant

mucos|idad *f* mucus. ∼**o** *a* mucous

muchach|a *f* girl; (*sirvienta*) servant, maid. ∼**o** *m* boy, lad; (*criado*) servant

muchedumbre *f* crowd

muchísimo *a* very much. ● *adv* a lot

mucho *a* much (*pl* many), a lot of. ● *pron* a lot; (*personas*) many (people). ● *adv* a lot, very much; (*de tiempo*) long, a long time. **ni** ∼ **menos** by no means. **por** ∼ **que** however much

muda *f* change of clothing; (*de animales*) moult. ∼**ble** *a* changeable; ⟨*personas*⟩ fickle. ∼**nza** *f* change; (*de casa*) removal. ∼**r** *vt/i* change. ∼**rse** (*de ropa*) change one's clothes; (*de casa*) move (house)

mudéjar *a* & *m* & *f* Mudéjar

mud|ez *f* dumbness. ∼**o** *a* dumb; (*callado*) silent

mueble *a* movable. ● *m* piece of furniture

mueca *f* grimace, face. **hacer una** ∼ pull a face

muela *f* (*diente*) tooth; (*diente molar*) molar; (*piedra de afilar*) grindstone; (*piedra de molino*) millstone

muelle *a* soft. ● *m* spring; (*naut*) wharf; (*malecón*) jetty

muérdago *m* mistletoe

muero *vb véase* **morir**

muert|e *f* death; (*homicidio*) murder. ∼**o** *a* dead; (*matado, fam*) killed; ⟨*colores*⟩ pale. ● *m* dead person; (*cadáver*) body, corpse

muesca *f* nick; (*ranura*) slot

muestra *f* sample; (*prueba*) proof; (*modelo*) model; (*seal*) sign. ∼**rio** *m* collection of samples

muestro *vb véase* **mostrar**

muevo *vb véase* **mover**

mugi|do *m* moo. ∼**r** [14] *vi* moo; (*fig*) roar

mugr|e *m* dirt. ∼**iento** *a* dirty, filthy

mugrón *m* sucker

muguete *m* lily of the valley

mujer *f* woman; (*esposa*) wife. ● *int* my dear! ∼**iego** *a* ⟨*hombre*⟩ fond of the women. ∼**il** *a* womanly. ∼**io** *m* (crowd of) women. ∼**zuela** *f* prostitute

mújol *m* mullet

mula *f* mule; (*Mex*) unsaleable goods. ∼**da** *f* drove of mules

mulato *a* & *m* mulatto

mulero *m* muleteer

mulet|a *f* crutch; (*fig*) support; (*toreo*) stick with a red flag

mulo *m* mule

multa *f* fine. ∼**r** *vt* fine

multi... *pref* multi...

multicolor *a* multicolour(ed)

multicopista *m* copying machine

multiforme *a* multiform

multilateral *a* multilateral

multilingüe *a* multilingual

multimillonario *m* multimillionaire

múltiple *a* multiple

multiplic|ación *f* multiplication. ∼**ar** [7] *vt* multiply. ∼**arse** *vpr* multiply; (*fig*) go out of one's way. ∼**idad** *f* multiplicity

múltiplo *a* & *m* multiple

multitud *f* multitude, crowd. ∼**inario** *a* multitudinous

mulli|do *a* soft. ● *m* stuffing. ∼**r** [22] *vt* soften

mund|ano *a* wordly; (*de la sociedad elegante*) society. ● *m* socialite. ∼**ial** *a* world-wide. **la segunda guerra** ∼**ial** the Second World War. ∼**illo** *m* world, circles. ∼**o** *m* world. ∼**ología** *f* worldly wisdom. **todo el** ∼**o** everybody

munición *f* ammunition; (*provisiones*) supplies

municip|al *a* municipal. ∼**alidad** *f* municipality. ∼**io** *m* municipality; (*ayuntamiento*) town council

mun|ificencia *f* munificence. ∼**ífico** *a* munificent

muñe|ca *f* (*anat*) wrist; (*juguete*) doll; (*maniquí*) dummy. ∼**co** *m* boy doll. ∼**quera** *f* wristband

muñón *m* stump

mura|l *a* mural, wall. ● *m* mural. ∼**lla** *f* (city) wall. ∼**r** *vt* wall

murciélago *m* bat

murga *f* street band; (*lata*) bore, nuisance. **dar la** ∼ bother, be a pain (*fam*)

murmullo *m* (*de personas*) whisper(ing), murmur(ing); (*del agua*) rippling; (*del viento*) sighing, rustle

murmura|ción *f* gossip. ∼**dor** *a* gossiping. ● *m* gossip. ∼**r** *vi* murmur; (*hablar en voz baja*) whisper; (*quejarse en voz baja*) mutter; (*criticar*) gossip

muro m wall

murri|a f depression. **~o** a depressed

mus m card game

musa f muse

musaraña f shrew

muscula|r a muscular. **~tura** f muscles

músculo m muscle

musculoso a muscular

muselina f muslin

museo m museum. **~ de arte** art gallery

musgaño m shrew

musgo m moss. **~so** a mossy

música f music

musical a & m musical

músico a musical. ● m musician

music|ología f musicology. **~ólogo** m musicologist

musitar vt/i mumble

muslímico a Muslim

muslo m thigh

mustela a weasel

musti|arse vpr wither, wilt. **~o** a ⟨plantas⟩ withered; ⟨cosas⟩ faded; ⟨personas⟩ gloomy; (Mex, hipócrita) hypocritical

musulmán a & m Muslim

muta|bilidad f mutability. **~ción** f change; (en biología) mutation

mutila|ción f mutilation. **~do** a crippled. ● m cripple. **~r** vt mutilate; cripple, maim ⟨persona⟩

mutis m (en el teatro) exit. **~mo** m silence

mutu|alidad f mutuality; (asociación) friendly society. **~amente** adv mutually. **~o** a mutual

muy adv very; (demasiado) too

N

nab|a f swede. **~o** m turnip

nácar m mother-of-pearl

nac|er [11] vi be born; ⟨huevo⟩ hatch; ⟨planta⟩ sprout. **~ido** a born. **~iente** a ⟨sol⟩ rising. **~imiento** m birth; (de río) source; (belén) crib. **dar ~imiento a** give rise to. **lugar de ~imiento** place of birth. **recien ~ido** newborn. **volver a ~er** have a narrow escape

naci|ón f nation. **~onal** a national. **~onalidad** f nationality. **~onalismo** m nationalism. **~onalista** m & f nationalist. **~onalizar** [10] vt

nationalize. **~onalizarse** vpr become naturalized

nada pron nothing, not anything. ● adv not at all. **¡~ de eso!** nothing of the sort! **antes de ~** first of all. **¡de ~!** (después de 'gracias') don't mention it! **para ~** (not) at all. **por ~ del mundo** not for anything in the world

nada|dor m swimmer. **~r** vi swim

nadería f trifle

nadie pron no one, nobody

nado adv. **a ~** swimming

nafta f (LAm, gasolina) petrol, (Brit), gas (Amer)

nailon m nylon

naipe m (playing) card. **juegos** mpl **de ~s** card games

nalga f buttock. **~s** fpl bottom

nana f lullaby

Nápoles m Naples

naranj|a f orange. **~ada** f orangeade. **~al** m orange grove. **~o** m orange tree

narcótico a & m narcotic

nariz f nose; (orificio de la nariz) nostril. **¡narices!** rubbish!

narra|ción f narration. **~dor** m narrator. **~r** vt tell. **~tivo** a narrative

nasal a nasal

nata f cream

natación f swimming

natal a birth; ⟨pueblo etc⟩ home. **~idad** f birth rate

natillas fpl custard

natividad f nativity

nativo a & m native

nato a born

natural a natural. ● m native. **~eza** f nature; (nacionalidad) nationality; (ciudadanía) naturalization. **~eza muerta** still life. **~idad** f naturalness. **~ista** m & f naturalist. **~izar** [10] vt naturalize. **~izarse** vpr become naturalized. **~mente** adv naturally. ● int of course!

naufrag|ar [12] vi ⟨barco⟩ sink; ⟨persona⟩ be shipwrecked; (fig) fail. **~io** m shipwreck

náufrago a shipwrecked. ● m shipwrecked person

náusea f nausea. **dar ~s a uno** make s.o. feel sick. **sentir ~s** feel sick

nauseabundo a sickening

náutico a nautical

navaja f penknife; (de afeitar) razor. **~zo** m slash

naval a naval

Navarra f Navarre
nave f ship; (de iglesia) nave. ~ **espacial** spaceship. **quemar las** ~**s** burn one's boats
navega|ble a navigable; ‹barco› seaworthy. ~**ción** f navigation. ~**nte** m & f navigator. ~**r** [12] vi sail; ‹avión› fly
Navid|ad f Christmas. ~**eño** a Christmas. **en** ~**ades** at Christmas. **¡feliz** ~**ad!** Happy Christmas! **por** ~**ad** at Christmas
navío m ship
nazi a & m & f Nazi
neblina f mist
nebuloso a misty; (fig) vague
necedad f foolishness. **decir** ~**es** talk nonsense. **hacer una** ~ do sth stupid
necesari|amente adv necessarily. ~**o** a necessary
necesi|dad f necessity; (pobreza) poverty. ~**dades** fpl hardships. **por** ~**dad** (out) of necessity. ~**tado** a in need (**de** of); (pobre) needy. ~**tar** vt need. ● vi. ~**tar de** need
necio a silly. ● m idiot
necrología f obituary column
néctar m nectar
nectarina f nectarine
nefasto a unfortunate, ominous
nega|ción f negation; (desmentimiento) denial; (gram) negative. ~**do** a incompetent. ~**r** [1 & 12] vt deny; (rehusar) refuse. ~**rse** vpr. ~**rse a** refuse. ~**tiva** f negative; (acción) denial; (acción de rehusar) refusal. ~**tivo** a & m negative
negligen|cia f negligence. ~**te** a negligent
negoci|able a negotiable. ~**ación** f negotiation. ~**ante** m & f dealer. ~**ar** vt/i negotiate. ~**ar en** trade in. ~**o** m business; (com, trato) deal. ~**os** mpl business. **hombre** m **de** ~**os** businessman
negr|a f Negress; (mus) crotchet. ~**o** a black; ‹persona› Negro. ● m (color) black; (persona) Negro. ~**ura** f blackness. ~**uzco** a blackish
nene m & f baby, child
nenúfar m water lily
neo... pref neo...
neocelandés a from New Zealand. ● m New Zealander
neolítico a Neolithic
neón m neon
nepotismo m nepotism

nervio m nerve; (tendón) sinew; (bot) vein. ~**sidad** f, ~**sismo** m nervousness; (impaciencia) impatience. ~**so** a nervous; (de temperamento) highly-strung. **crispar los** ~**s a uno** (fam) get on s.o.'s nerves. **ponerse** ~**so** get excited
neto a clear; ‹verdad› simple; (com) net
neumático a pneumatic. ● m tyre
neumonía f pneumonia
neuralgia f neuralgia
neur|ología f neurology. ~**ólogo** m neurologist
neur|osis f neurosis. ~**ótico** a neurotic
neutr|al a neutral. ~**alidad** f neutrality. ~**alizar** [10] vt neutralize. ~**o** a neutral; (gram) neuter
neutrón m neutron
neva|da f snowfall. ~**r** [1] vi snow. ~**sca** f blizzard
nevera f fridge (Brit, fam), refrigerator
nevisca f light snowfall. ~**r** [7] vi snow lightly
nexo m link
ni conj nor, neither; (ni siquiera) not even. ~**...** ~ neither... nor. ~ **que** as if. ~ **siquiera** not even
Nicaragua f Nicaragua
nicaragüense a & m & f Nicaraguan
nicotina f nicotine
nicho m niche
nido m nest; (de ladrones) den; (escondrijo) hiding-place
niebla f fog; (neblina) mist. **hay** ~ it's foggy
niet|a f granddaughter. ~**o** m grandson. ~**os** mpl grandchildren
nieve f snow; (LAm, helado) icecream
Nigeria f Nigeria. ~**no** a Nigerian
niki m T-shirt
nilón m nylon
nimbo m halo
nimi|edad f triviality. ~**o** a insignificant
ninfa f nymph
ninfea f water lily
ningún véase **ninguno**
ninguno a (delante de nombre masculino en singular **ningún**) no, not any. ● pron none; (persona) no-one, nobody; (de dos) neither. **de ninguna manera, de ningún modo** by no means. **en ninguna parte** nowhere

niñ|a *f* (little) girl. **~ada** *f* childish thing. **~era** *f* nanny. **~ería** *f* childish thing. **~ez** *f* childhood. **~o** *a* childish. ● *m* (little) boy. **de ~o** as a child. **desde ~o** from childhood

níquel *m* nickel

níspero *m* medlar

nitidez *f* clearness

nítido *a* clear; *(foto)* sharp

nitrato *m* nitrate

nítrico *a* nitric

nitrógeno *m* nitrogen

nivel *m* level; *(fig)* standard. **~ar** *vt* level. **~arse** *vpr* become level. **~ de vida** standard of living

no *adv* not; *(como respuesta)* no. **¿~?** isn't it? **~ más** only. **¡a que ~!** I bet you don't! **¡cómo ~!** of course! **Felipe ~ tiene hijos** Felipe has no children. **¡que ~!** certainly not!

nob|iliario *a* noble. **~le** *a & m & f* noble. **~leza** *f* nobility

noción *f* notion. **nociones** *fpl* rudiments

nocivo *a* harmful

nocturno *a* nocturnal; *(clase)* evening; *(tren etc)* night. ● *m* nocturne

noche *f* night. **~ vieja** New Year's Eve. **de ~** at night. **hacer ~** spend the night. **media ~** midnight. **por la ~** at night

Nochebuena *f* Christmas Eve

nodo *m* *(Esp, película)* newsreel

nodriza *f* nanny

nódulo *m* nodule

nogal *m* walnut(-tree)

nómada *a* nomadic. ● *m & f* nomad

nombr|adía *f* fame. **~ado** *a* famous; *(susodicho)* aforementioned. **~amiento** *m* appointment. **~ar** *vt* appoint; *(citar)* mention. **~e** *m* name; *(gram)* noun; *(fama)* renown. **~e de pila** Christian name. **en ~e de** in the name of. **no tener ~e** be unspeakable. **poner de ~e** call

nomeolvides *m invar* forget-me-not

nómina *f* payroll

nomina|l *a* nominal. **~tivo** *a & m* nominative. **~tivo a** *(cheque etc)* made out to

non *a* odd. ● *m* odd number

nonada *f* trifle

nono *a* ninth

nordeste *a* *(región)* north-eastern; *(viento)* north-easterly. ● *m* north-east

nórdico *a* northern. ● *m* northerner

noria *f* water-wheel; *(en una feria)* ferris wheel

norma *f* rule

normal *a* normal. ● *f* teachers' training college. **~idad** normality *(Brit)*, normalcy *(Amer)*. **~izar** [10] *vt* normalize. **~mente** *adv* normally, usually

Normandía *f* Normandy

noroeste *a* *(región)* north-western; *(viento)* north-westerly. ● *m* north-west

norte *m* north; *(viento)* north wind; *(fig, meta)* aim

Norteamérica *f* (North) America

norteamericano *a & m* (North) American

norteño *a* northern. ● *m* northerner

Noruega *f* Norway

noruego *a & m* Norwegian

nos *pron* *(acusativo)* us; *(dativo)* (to) us; *(reflexivo)* (to) ourselves; *(recíproco)* (to) each other

nosotros *pron* we; *(con prep)* us

nost|algia *f* nostalgia; *(de casa, de patria)* homesickness. **~álgico** *a* nostalgic

nota *f* note; *(de examen etc)* mark. **~ble** *a* notable. **~ción** *f* notation. **~r** *vt* notice; *(apuntar)* note down. **de mala ~** notorious. **de ~** famous. **digno de ~** notable. **es de ~r** it should be noted. **hacerse ~r** stand out

notario *m* notary

notici|a *f* (piece of) news. **~as** *fpl* news. **~ario** *m* news. **~ero** *a* news. **atrasado de ~as** behind the times. **tener ~as de** hear from

notifica|ción *f* notification. **~r** [7] *vt* notify

notori|edad *f* notoriety. **~o** *a* well-known; *(evidente)* obvious

novato *m* novice

novecientos *a & m* nine hundred

noved|ad *f* newness; *(noticia)* news; *(cambio)* change; *(moda)* latest fashion. **~oso** *a* *(LAm)* novel. **sin ~ad** no news

novel|a *f* novel. **~ista** *m & f* novelist

noveno *a* ninth

novent|a *a & m* ninety; *(nonagésimo)* ninetieth. **~ón** *a & m* ninety-year-old

novia *f* girlfriend; *(prometida)* fiancée; *(en boda)* bride. **~zgo** *m* engagement

novicio *m* novice

noviembre *m* November

novilunio *m* new moon
novill|a *f* heifer. **~o** *m* bullock. **hacer ~os** play truant
novio *m* boyfriend; (*prometido*) fiancé; (*en boda*) bridegroom. **los ~s** the bride and groom
novísimo *a* very new
nub|arrón *m* large dark cloud. **~e** *f* cloud; (*de insectos etc*) swarm. **~lado** *a* cloudy, overcast. **●** *m* cloud. **~lar** *vt* cloud. **~larse** *vpr* become cloudy. **~loso** *a* cloudy
nuca *f* back of the neck
nuclear *a* nuclear
núcleo *m* nucleus
nudillo *m* knuckle
nudis|mo *m* nudism. **~ta** *m & f* nudist
nudo *m* knot; (*de asunto etc*) crux. **~so** *a* knotty. **tener un ~ en la garganta** have a lump in one's throat
nuera *f* daughter-in-law
nuestro *a* our; (*pospuesto al sustantivo*) of ours. **●** *pron* ours. **~ coche** our car. **un coche ~** a car of ours
nueva *f* (piece of) news. **~s** *fpl* news. **~mente** *adv* newly; (*de nuevo*) again
Nueva York *f* New York
Nueva Zelanda *f*, **Nueva Zelandia** *f* (*LAm*) New Zealand
nueve *a & m* nine
nuevo *a* new. **de ~** again
nuez *f* nut; (*del nogal*) walnut; (*anat*) Adam's apple. **~ de Adán** Adam's apple. **~ moscada** nutmeg
nul|idad *f* incompetence; (*persona, fam*) nonentity. **~o** *a* useless; (*jurid*) null and void
num|eración *f* numbering. **~eral** *a & m* numeral. **~erar** *vt* number. **~érico** *a* numerical
número *m* number; (*arábigo, romano*) numeral; (*de zapatos etc*) size. **sin ~** countless
numeroso *a* numerous
nunca *adv* never, not ever. **~ (ja)más** never again. **casi ~** hardly ever. **más que ~** more than ever
nupcia|l *a* nuptial. **~s** *fpl* wedding. **banquete ~l** wedding breakfast
nutria *f* otter
nutri|ción *f* nutrition. **~do** *a* nourished, fed; (*fig*) large; (*aplausos*) loud; (*fuego*) heavy. **~r** *vt* nourish, feed; (*fig*) feed. **~tivo** *a* nutritious. **valor** *m* **~tivo** nutritional value
nylon *m* nylon

Ñ

ña *f* (*LAm, fam*) Mrs
ñacanina *f* (*Arg*) poisonous snake
ñame *m* yam
ñapindá *m* (*Arg*) mimosa
ñato *adj* (*LAm*) snub-nosed
ño *m* (*LAm, fam*) Mr
ñoñ|ería *f*, **~ez** *f* insipidity. **~o** *a* insipid; (*tímido*) bashful; (*quisquilloso*) prudish
ñu *m* gnu

O

o *conj* or. **~ bien** rather. **~... ~** either... or. **~ sea** in other words
oasis *m invar* oasis
obcecar [7] *vt* blind
obed|ecer [11] *vt/i* obey. **~iencia** *f* obedience. **~iente** *a* obedient
obelisco *m* obelisk
obertura *f* overture
obes|idad *f* obesity. **~o** *a* obese
obispo *m* bishop
obje|ción *f* objection. **~tar** *vt/i* object
objetiv|idad *f* objectivity. **~o** *a* objective. **●** *m* objective; (*foto etc*) lens
objeto *m* object
objetor *m* objector. **~ de conciencia** conscientious objector
oblicuo *a* oblique; (*mirada*) sidelong
obliga|ción *f* obligation; (*com*) bond. **~do** *a* obliged; (*forzoso*) obligatory; **~r** [12] *vt* force, oblige. **~rse** *vpr*. **~rse a** undertake to. **~torio** *a* obligatory
oboe *m* oboe; (*músico*) oboist
obra *f* work; (*de teatro*) play; (*construcción*) building. **~ maestra** masterpiece. **en ~s** under construction. **por ~ de** thanks to. **~r** *vt* do; (*construir*) build
obrero *a* labour; (*clase*) working. **●** *m* workman; (*en fábrica*) worker
obscen|idad *f* obscenity. **~o** *a* obscene
obscu... *véase* **oscu...**
obsequi|ar *vt* lavish attention on. **~ar con** give, present with. **~o** *m* gift, present; (*agasajo*) attention. **~oso** *a* obliging. **en ~o de** in honour of

observa|ción f observation; (*objeción*) objection. **~dor** m observer. **~ncia** f observance. **~nte** a observant. **~r** vt observe; (*notar*) notice. **~rse** vpr be noted. **~torio** m observatory. **hacer una ~ción** make a remark

obses|ión f obsession. **~ionar** vt obsess. **~ivo** a obsessive. **~o** a obsessed

obst|aculizar [10] vt hinder. **~áculo** m obstacle

obstante. no ~ adv however, nevertheless. ● prep in spite of

obstar vi. **~ para** prevent

obstétrico a obstetric

obstina|ción f obstinacy. **~do** a obstinate. **~rse** vpr be obstinate. **~rse en** (+ *infinitivo*) persist in (+ *gerundio*)

obstru|cción f obstruction. **~ir** [17] vt obstruct

obtener [40] vt get, obtain

obtura|dor m (*foto*) shutter. **~r** vt plug; fill ⟨*muela etc*⟩

obtuso a obtuse

obviar vt remove

obvio a obvious

oca f goose

ocasi|ón f occasion; (*oportunidad*) opportunity; (*motivo*) cause. **~onal** a chance. **~onar** vt cause. **aprovechar la ~ón** take the opportunity. **con ~ón de** on the occasion of. **de ~ón** bargain; (*usado*) secondhand. **en ~ones** sometimes. **perder una ~ón** miss a chance

ocaso m sunset; (*fig*) decline

occident|al a western. ● m & f westerner. **~e** m west

océano m ocean

ocio m idleness; (*tiempo libre*) leisure time. **~sidad** f idleness. **~so** a idle; (*inútil*) pointless

oclusión f occlusion

octano m octane. **índice** m **de ~** octane number, octane rating

octav|a f octave. **~o** a & m eighth

octogenario a & m octogenarian, eighty-year-old

oct|ogonal a octagonal. **~ógono** m octagon

octubre m October

oculista m & f oculist, optician

ocular a eye

ocult|ar vt hide. **~arse** vpr hide. **~o** a hidden; (*secreto*) secret

ocupa|ción f occupation. **~do** a occupied; (*persona*) busy. **~nte** m occupant. **~r** vt occupy. **~rse** vpr look after

ocurr|encia f occurrence, event; (*idea*) idea; (*que tiene gracia*) witty remark. **~ir** vi happen. **~irse** vpr occur. **¿qué ~e?** what's the matter? **se me ~e que** it occurs to me that

ochent|a a & m eighty. **~ón** a & m eighty-year-old

ocho a & m eight. **~cientos** a & m eight hundred

oda f ode

odi|ar vt hate. **~o** m hatred. **~oso** a hateful

odisea f odyssey

oeste m west; (*viento*) west wind

ofen|der vt offend; (*insultar*) insult. **~derse** vpr take offence. **~sa** f offence. **~siva** f offensive. **~sivo** a offensive

oferta f offer; (*en subasta*) bid; (*regalo*) gift. **~s de empleo** situations vacant. **en ~** on (special) offer

oficial a official. ● m skilled worker; (*funcionario*) civil servant; (*mil*) officer. **~a** f skilled (woman) worker

oficin|a f office. **~a de colocación** employment office. **~a de Estado** government office. **~a de turismo** tourist office. **~ista** m & f office worker. **horas** fpl **de ~a** business hours

oficio m job; (*profesión*) profession; (*puesto*) post. **~so** a (*no oficial*) unofficial

ofrec|er [11] vt offer; give ⟨*fiesta, banquete etc*⟩; (*prometer*) promise. **~erse** vpr (*persona*) volunteer; (*cosa*) occur. **~imiento** m offer

ofrenda f offering. **~r** vt offer

ofusca|ción f blindness; (*confusión*) confusion. **~r** [7] vt blind; (*confundir*) confuse. **~rse** vpr be dazzled

ogro m ogre

oí|ble a audible. **~da** f hearing. **~do** m hearing; (*anat*) ear. **al ~do** in one's ear. **de ~das** by hearsay. **de ~do** by ear. **duro de ~do** hard of hearing

oigo vb véase **oír**

oír [50] vt hear. **~ misa** go to mass. **¡oiga!** listen!; (*al teléfono*) hello!

ojal m buttonhole

ojalá int I hope so! ● conj if only

ojea|da f glance. **~r** vt eye; (*para inspeccionar*) see; (*ahuyentar*) scare

away. **dar una ～da a, echar una
～da a** glance at
ojeras *fpl* (*del ojo*) bags
ojeriza *f* ill will. **tener ～ a** have a
grudge against
ojete *m* eyelet
ojo *m* eye; (*de cerradura*) keyhole; (*de
un puente*) span. **¡～!** careful!
ola *f* wave
olé *int* bravo!
olea|da *f* wave. **～je** *m* swell
óleo *m* oil; (*cuadro*) oil painting
oleoducto *m* oil pipeline
oler [2, *las formas que empezarían
por* **ue** *se escriben* **hue**] *vt* smell;
(*curiosear*) pry into; (*descubrir*) discover. ● *vi* smell (**a** of)
olfat|ear *vt* smell, sniff; (*fig*) sniff
out. **～o** *m* (sense of) smell; (*fig*) in-
tuition
olimpiada *f*, **olimpíada** *f* Olympic
games, Olympics
olímpico *a* ⟨*juegos*⟩ Olympic
oliv|a *f* olive; (*olivo*) olive tree. **～ar** *m*
olive grove. **～o** *m* olive tree
olmo *m* elm (tree)
olor *m* smell. **～oso** *a* sweet-smelling
olvid|adizo *a* forgetful. **～ar** *vt*
forget. **～arse** *vpr* forget; (*estar olvidado*) be forgotten. **～o** *m* oblivion;
(*acción de olvidar*) forgetfulness. **se
me ～ó** I forgot
olla *f* pot, casserole; (*guisado*) stew.
～ a/de presión, ～ exprés pressure
cooker. **～ podrida** Spanish stew
ombligo *m* navel
ominoso *a* awful, abominable
omi|sión *f* omission; (*olvido*) for-
getfulness. **～tir** *vt* omit
ómnibus *a* omnibus
omnipotente *a* omnipotent
omóplato *m*, **omoplato** *m* shoulder
blade
once *a & m* eleven
ond|a *f* wave. **～a corta** short wave.
～a larga long wave. **～ear** *vi* wave;
⟨*agua*⟩ ripple; (*del pelo*) wave. **～ular** *vi*
wave. **longitud** *f* **de ～a** wavelength
oneroso *a* onerous
ónice *m* onyx
onomástico *a*. **día ～, fiesta
onomástica** name-day
ONU *abrev* (*Organización de las Naciones Unidas*) UN, United Nations
onza *f* ounce
opa *a* (*LAm*) stupid
opaco *a* opaque; (*fig*) dull

ópalo *m* opal
opción *f* option
ópera *f* opera
opera|ción *f* operation; (*com*) trans-
action. **～dor** *m* operator; (*cirujano*)
surgeon; (*TV*) cameraman. **～r** *vt*
operate on; work ⟨*milagro etc*⟩. ● *vi*
operate; (*com*) deal. **～rse** *vpr* occur;
(*med*) have an operation. **～torio** *a*
operative
opereta *f* operetta
opin|ar *vi* think. **～ión** *f* opinion. **la
～ión pública** public opinion
opio *m* opium
opone|nte *a* opposing. ● *m & f*
opponent. **～r** *vt* oppose; offer ⟨*resistencia*⟩; raise ⟨*objeción*⟩. **～rse** *vpr*
be opposed; ⟨*dos personas*⟩ oppose
each other
oporto *m* port (wine)
oportun|idad *f* opportunity; (*cua-
lidad de oportuno*) timeliness. **～ista**
m & f opportunist. **～o** *a* opportune;
(*apropiado*) suitable
oposi|ción *f* opposition. **～ciones** *fpl*
competition, public examination.
～tor *m* candidate
opres|ión *f* oppression; (*ahogo*)
difficulty in breathing. **～ivo** *a*
oppressive. **～o** *a* oppressed. **～or** *m*
oppressor
oprimir *vt* squeeze; press ⟨*botón etc*⟩;
⟨*ropa*⟩ be too tight for; (*fig*) oppress
oprobio *m* disgrace
optar *vi* choose. **～ por** opt for
óptic|a *f* optics; (*tienda*) optician's
(shop). **～o** *a* optic(al). ● *m* optician
optimis|mo *m* optimism. **～ta** *a*
optimistic. ● *m & f* optimist
opuesto *a* opposite; (*enemigo*)
opposed
opulen|cia *f* opulence. **～to** *a* opu-
lent
oración *f* prayer; (*discurso*) speech;
(*gram*) sentence
oráculo *m* oracle
orador *m* speaker
oral *a* oral
orar *vi* pray
oratori|a *f* oratory. **～o** *a* oratorical.
● *m* (*mus*) oratorio
orbe *m* orb
órbita *f* orbit
orden *m & f* order; (*Mex, porción*)
portion. **～ado** *a* tidy. **～ del día**
agenda. **órdenes** *fpl* **sagradas** Holy
Orders. **a sus órdenes** (*esp Mex*) can

I help you? **en** ~ in order. **por** ~ in turn

ordenador *m* computer

ordena|nza *f* order. ● *m* (*mil*) orderly. ~**r** *vt* put in order; (*mandar*) order; (*relig*) ordain

ordeñar *vt* milk

ordinal *a* & *m* ordinal

ordinario *a* ordinary; (*grosero*) common

orear *vt* air

orégano *m* oregano

oreja *f* ear

orfanato *m* orphanage

orfebre *m* goldsmith, silversmith

orfeón *m* choral society

orgánico *a* organic

organigrama *m* flow chart

organillo *m* barrel-organ

organismo *m* organism

organista *m* & *f* organist

organiza|ción *f* organization. ~**dor** *m* organizer. ~**r** [10] *vt* organize. ~**rse** *vpr* get organized

órgano *m* organ

orgasmo *m* orgasm

orgía *f* orgy

orgullo *m* pride. ~**so** *a* proud

orientación *f* direction

oriental *a* & *m* & *f* oriental

orientar *vt* position. ~**se** *vpr* point; ⟨*persona*⟩ find one's bearings

oriente *m* east. **O**~ **Medio** Middle East

orificio *m* hole

orig|en *m* origin. ~**inal** *a* original; (*excéntrico*) odd. ~**inalidad** *f* originality. ~**inar** *vt* give rise to. ~**inario** *a* original; (*nativo*) native. **dar** ~**en a** give rise to. **ser** ~**inario de** come from

orilla *f* (*del mar*) shore; (*de río*) bank; (*borde*) edge

orín *m* rust

orina *f* urine. ~**l** *m* chamber-pot. ~**r** *vi* urinate

oriundo *a*. ~ **de** ⟨*persona*⟩ (originating) from; ⟨*animal etc*⟩ native to

orla *f* border

ornamental *a* ornamental

ornitología *f* ornithology

oro *m* gold. ~**s** *mpl* Spanish card suit. ~ **de ley** 9 carat gold. **hacerse de** ~ make a fortune. **prometer el** ~ **y el moro** promise the moon

oropel *m* tinsel

orquesta *f* orchestra. ~**l** *a* orchestral. ~**r** *vt* orchestrate

orquídea *f* orchid

ortiga *f* nettle

ortodox|ia *f* orthodoxy. ~**o** *a* orthodox

ortografía *f* spelling

ortop|edia *f* orthopaedics. ~**édico** *a* orthopaedic

oruga *f* caterpillar

orzuelo *m* sty

os *pron* (*acusativo*) you; (*dativo*) (to) you; (*reflexivo*) (to) yourselves; (*recíproco*) (to) each other

osad|ía *f* boldness. ~**o** *a* bold

oscila|ción *f* swinging; (*de precios*) fluctuation; (*tec*) oscillation. ~**r** *vi* swing; ⟨*precio*⟩ fluctuate; (*tec*) oscillate; (*fig, vacilar*) hesitate

oscur|ecer [11] *vi* darken; (*fig*) obscure. ~**ecerse** *vpr* grow dark; (*nublarse*) cloud over. ~**idad** *f* darkness; (*fig*) obscurity. ~**o** *a* dark; (*fig*) obscure. **a** ~**as** in the dark

óseo *a* bony

oso *m* bear. ~ **de felpa**, ~ **de peluche** teddy bear

ostensible *a* obvious

ostent|ación *f* ostentation. ~**ar** *vt* show off; (*mostrar*) show. ~**oso** *a* ostentatious

osteoartritis *f* osteoarthritis

oste|ópata *m* & *f* osteopath. ~**opatía** *f* osteopathy

ostión *m* (*esp Mex*) oyster

ostra *f* oyster

ostracismo *m* ostracism

Otan *abrev* (*Organización del Tratado del Atlántico Norte*) NATO, North Atlantic Treaty Organization

otear *vt* observe; (*escudriñar*) scan, survey

otitis *f* inflammation of the ear

otoño *m* autumn (*Brit*), fall (*Amer*)

otorga|miento *m* granting; (*documento*) authorization. ~**r** [12] *vt* give; (*jurid*) draw up

otorrinolaringólogo *m* ear, nose and throat specialist

otro *a* other; (*uno más*) another. ● *pron* another (one); (*en plural*) others; (*otra persona*) someone else. **el** ~ the other. **el uno al** ~ one another, each other

ovación *f* ovation

oval *a* oval

óvalo *m* oval

ovario *m* ovary

oveja *f* sheep; (*hembra*) ewe

overol *m* (*LAm*) overalls

ovino *a* sheep

ovillo *m* ball. **hacerse un ~** curl up

OVNI *abrev* (*objeto volante no identificado*) UFO, unidentified flying object

ovulación *f* ovulation

oxida|ción *f* rusting. **~r** *vi* rust. **~rse** *vpr* go rusty

óxido *m* oxide

oxígeno *m* oxygen

oye *vb véase* **oír**

oyente *a* listening. ● *m & f* listener

ozono *m* ozone

P

pabellón *m* bell tent; (*edificio*) building; (*de instrumento*) bell; (*bandera*) flag

pabilo *m* wick

paceño *a* from La Paz. ● *m* person from La Paz

pacer [11] *vi* graze

pacien|cia *f* patience. **~te** *a & m & f* patient

pacificar [7] *vt* pacify; reconcile ⟨*dos personas*⟩. **~se** *vpr* calm down

pacífico *a* peaceful. **el (Océano m) P~** the Pacific (Ocean)

pacifis|mo *m* pacifism. **~ta** *a & m & f* pacifist

pact|ar *vi* agree, make a pact. **~o** *m* pact, agreement

pachucho *a* ⟨*fruta*⟩ overripe; ⟨*persona*⟩ poorly

padec|er [11] *vt/i* suffer (**de** from); (*soportar*) bear. **~imiento** *m* suffering; (*enfermedad*) ailment

padrastro *m* stepfather

padre *a* (*fam*) great. ● *m* father. **~s** *mpl* parents

padrino *m* godfather; (*en boda*) best man

padrón *m* census

paella *f* paella

paga *f* pay, wages. **~ble** *a*, **~dero** *a* payable

pagano *a & m* pagan

pagar [12] *vt* pay; pay for ⟨*compras*⟩. ● *vi* pay. **~é** *m* IOU

página *f* page

pago *m* payment

pagoda *f* pagoda

país *m* country; (*región*) region. **~natal** native land. **el P~ Vasco** the Basque Country. **los P~es Bajos** the Low Countries

paisa|je *m* countryside. **~no** *a* of the same country. ● *m* compatriot

paja *f* straw; (*fig*) nonsense

pajarera *f* aviary

pájaro *m* bird. **~ carpintero** woodpecker

paje *m* page

Pakistán *m*. **el ~** Pakistan

pala *f* shovel; (*laya*) spade; (*en deportes*) bat; (*de tenis*) racquet

palabr|a *f* word; (*habla*) speech. **~ota** *f* swear-word. **decir ~otas** swear. **pedir la ~** ask to speak. **soltar ~otas** swear. **tomar la ~a** (begin to) speak

palacio *m* palace; (*casa grande*) mansion

paladar *m* palate

paladino *a* clear; (*público*) public

palanca *f* lever; (*fig*) influence. **~ de cambio (de velocidades)** gear lever (*Brit*), gear shift (*Amer*)

palangana *f* wash-basin

palco *m* (*en el teatro*) box

Palestina *f* Palestine

palestino *a & m* Palestinian

palestra *f* (*fig*) arena

paleta *f* (*de pintor*) palette; (*de albañil*) trowel

paleto *m* yokel

paliativo *a & m* palliative

palide|cer [11] *vi* turn pale. **~z** *f* paleness

pálido *a* pale

palillo *m* small stick; (*de dientes*) toothpick

palique *m*. **estar de ~** be chatting

paliza *f* beating

palizada *f* fence; (*recinto*) enclosure

palma *f* (*de la mano*) palm; (*árbol*) palm (tree); (*de dátiles*) date palm. **~s** *fpl* applause. **~da** *f* slap. **~das** *fpl* applause. **dar ~(da)s** clap. **tocar las ~s** clap

palmera *f* date palm

palmo *m* span; (*fig, pequeña cantidad*) small amount. **~ a ~** inch by inch

palmote|ar *vi* clap, applaud. **~o** *m* clapping, applause

palo *m* stick; (*del teléfono etc*) pole; (*mango*) handle; (*de golf*) club; (*golpe*) blow; (*de naipes*) suit; (*mástil*) mast

paloma *f* pigeon, dove

palomitas *fpl* popcorn

palpa|ble *a* palpable. **~r** *vt* feel

palpita|ción f palpitation. **~nte** a throbbing. **~r** vi throb; (latir) beat

palta f (LAm) avocado pear

pal|údico a marshy; (de paludismo) malarial. **~udismo** m malaria

pamp|a f pampas. **~ear** vi (LAm) travel across the pampas. **~ero** a of the pampas

pan m bread; (barra) loaf. **~ integral** wholemeal bread (Brit), wholewheat bread (Amer). **~ tostado** toast. **~ rallado** breadcrumbs. **ganarse el ~** earn one's living

pana f corduroy

panacea f panacea

panader|ía f bakery; (tienda) baker's (shop). **~o** m baker

panal m honeycomb

Panamá f Panama

panameño a & m Panamanian

pancarta f placard

panda m panda; (pandilla) gang

pander|eta f (small) tambourine. **~o** m tambourine

pandilla f gang

panecillo m (bread) roll

panel m panel

panfleto m pamphlet

pánico m panic

panor|ama m panorama. **~ámico** a panoramic

panqué m (LAm) pancake

pantaletas fpl (LAm) underpants, knickers

pantal|ón m trousers. **~ones** mpl trousers. **~ón corto** shorts. **~ón tejano, ~ón vaquero** jeans

pantalla f screen; (de lámpara) (lamp)shade

pantano m marsh; (embalse) reservoir. **~so** a boggy

pantera f panther

pantomima f pantomime

pantorrilla f calf

pantufla f slipper

panucho m (Mex) stuffed tortilla

panz|a f belly. **~ada** f (hartazgo, fam) bellyful; (golpe, fam) blow in the belly. **~udo** a fat, pot-bellied

pañal m nappy (Brit), diaper (Amer)

pañ|ería f draper's (shop). **~o** m material; (de lana) woollen cloth; (trapo) cloth. **~o de cocina** dishcloth; (para secar) tea towel. **~o higiénico** sanitary towel. **en ~os menores** in one's underclothes

pañuelo m handkerchief; (de cabeza) scarf

papa m pope. **●** f (esp LAm) potato. **~s francesas** (LAm) chips

papá m dad(dy). **~s** mpl parents. **P~ Noel** Father Christmas

papada f (de persona) double chin

papado m papacy

papagayo m parrot

papal a papal

papanatas m invar simpleton

paparrucha f (tontería) silly thing

papaya f pawpaw

papel m paper; (en el teatro etc) role. **~ carbón** carbon paper. **~ celofán** celophane paper. **~ de calcar** carbon paper. **~ de embalar, ~ de envolver** wrapping paper. **~ de plata** silver paper. **~ de seda** tissue paper. **~era** f waste-paper basket. **~ería** f stationer's (shop). **~eta** f ticket; (para votar) paper. **~ higiénico** toilet paper. **~ pintado** wallpaper. **~ secante** blotting paper. **blanco como el ~** as white as a sheet. **desempeñar un ~, hacer un ~** play a role

paperas fpl mumps

paquebote m packet (boat)

paquete m packet; (paquebote) packet (boat); (Mex, asunto difícil) difficult job. **~ postal** parcel

paquistaní a & m Pakistani

par a equal; (número) even. **●** m couple; (dos cosas iguales) pair; (igual) equal; (título) peer. **a la ~** at the same time; (monedas) at par. **al ~ que** at the same time. **a ~es** two by two. **de ~ en ~** wide open. **sin ~** without equal

para prep for; (hacia) towards; (antes del infinitivo) (in order) to. **~ con** to(wards). **¿~ qué?** why? **~ que** so that

parabienes mpl congratulations

parábola f (narración) parable

parabrisas m invar windscreen (Brit), windshield (Amer)

paraca f (LAm) strong wind (from the Pacific)

paraca|ídas m invar parachute. **~idista** m & f parachutist; (mil) paratrooper

parachoques m invar bumper (Brit), fender (Amer); (rail) buffer

parad|a f (acción) stopping; (sitio) stop; (de taxis) rank; (mil) parade. **~ero** m whereabouts; (alojamiento) lodging. **~o** a stationary; (obrero) unemployed; (lento) slow. **dejar ~o**

confuse. **tener mal ～ero** come to a sticky end

paradoja f paradox

parador m state-owned hotel

parafina f paraffin

par|afrasear vt paraphrase. **～áfrasis** f invar paraphrase

paraguas m invar umbrella

Paraguay m Paraguay

paraguayo a & m Paraguayan

paraíso m paradise; (en el teatro) gallery

paralel|a f parallel (line). **～as** fpl parallel bars. **～o** a & m parallel

par|álisis f invar paralysis. **～alítico** a paralytic. **～alizar** [10] vt paralyse

paramilitar a paramilitary

páramo m barren plain

parang|ón m comparison. **～onar** vt compare

paraninfo m hall

paranoi|a f paranoia. **～co** a paranoiac

parapeto m parapet; (fig) barricade

parapléjico a & m paraplegic

parar vt/i stop. **～se** vpr stop. **sin ～** continuously

pararrayos m invar lightning conductor

parásito a parasitic. ● m parasite

parasol m parasol

parcela f plot. **～r** vt divide into plots

parcial a partial. **～idad** f prejudice; (pol) faction. **a tiempo ～** part-time

parco a sparing, frugal

parche m patch

pardo a brown

parear vt pair off

parec|er m opinion; (aspecto) appearance. ● vi [11] seem; (asemejarse) look like; (aparecer) appear. **～erse** vpr resemble, look like. **～ido** a similar. ● m similarity. **al ～er** apparently. **a mi ～er** in my opinion. **bien ～ido** good-looking. **me ～e** I think. **¿qué te parece?** what do you think? **según ～e** apparently

pared f wall. **～ón** m thick wall; (de ruinas) standing wall. **～ por medio** next door. **llevar al ～ón** shoot

parej|a f pair; (hombre y mujer) couple; (la otra persona) partner. **～o** a alike, the same; (liso) smooth

parente|la f relations. **～sco** m relationship

paréntesis m invar parenthesis; (signo ortográfico) bracket. **entre ～** (fig) by the way

paria m & f outcast

paridad f equality

pariente m & f relation, relative

parihuela f, **parihuelas** fpl stretcher

parir vt give birth to. ● vi have a baby, give birth

París m Paris

parisiense a & m & f, **parisino** a & m Parisian

parking /'parkin/ m car park (Brit), parking lot (Amer)

parlament|ar vi discuss. **～ario** a parliamentary. ● m member of parliament (Brit), congressman (Amer). **～o** m parliament

parlanchín a talkative. ● m chatterbox

parmesano a Parmesan

paro m stoppage; (desempleo) unemployment; (pájaro) tit

parodia f parody. **～r** vt parody

parpadear vi blink; ⟨luz⟩ flicker; ⟨estrella⟩ twinkle

párpado m eyelid

parque m park. **～ de atracciones** funfair. **～ infantil** children's playground. **～ zoológico** zoo, zoological gardens

parqué m parquet

parquedad f frugality; (moderación) moderation

parra f grapevine

párrafo m paragraph

parrilla f grill; (LAm, auto) radiator grill. **～da** f grill. **a la ～** grilled

párroco m parish priest

parroquia f parish; (iglesia) parish church. **～no** m parishioner; (cliente) customer

parsimoni|a f thrift. **～oso** a thrifty

parte m message; (informe) report. ● f part; (porción) share; (lado) side; (jurid) party. **dar ～** report. **de mi ～** for me. **de ～ de** from. **¿de ～ de quién?** (al teléfono) who's speaking? **en cualquier ～** anywhere. **en gran ～** largely. **en ～** partly. **en todas ～s** everywhere. **la mayor ～** the majority. **ninguna ～** nowhere. **por otra ～** on the other hand. **por todas ～s** everywhere

partera f midwife

partición f sharing out

participa|ción f participation; (noticia) notice; (de lotería) lottery ticket. **～nte** a participating. ● m & f participant. **～r** vt notify. ● vi take part

participio *m* participle

partícula *f* particle

particular *a* particular; ‹*clase*› private. ● *m* matter. ~**idad** *f* peculiarity. ~**izar** [10] *vt* distinguish; ‹*detallar*› give details about. **en ~** in particular. **nada de ~** nothing special

partida *f* departure; (*en registro*) entry; (*documento*) certificate; (*juego*) game; (*de gente*) group. **mala ~** dirty trick

partidario *a & m* partisan. ~ **de** keen on

parti|do *a* divided. ● *m* (*pol*) party; (*encuentro*) match; (*equipo*) team. ~**r** *vt* divide; (*romper*) break; (*repartir*) share; crack ‹*nueces*›. ● *vi* leave; (*empezar*) start. ~**rse** *vpr* (*romperse*) break; (*dividirse*) split. **a ~r de** (starting) from

partitura *f* (*mus*) score

parto *m* birth; (*fig*) creation. **estar de ~** be in labour

párvulo *m*. **colegio de ~s** nursery school

pasa *f* raisin. ~ **de Corinto** currant. ~ **de Esmirna** sultana

pasa|ble *a* passable. ~**da** *f* passing; (*de puntos*) row. ~**dero** *a* passable. ~**dizo** *m* passage. ~**do** *a* past; ‹*día, mes etc*› last; (*anticuado*) old-fashioned; ‹*comida*› bad, off. ~**do mañana** the day after tomorrow. ~**dor** *m* bolt; (*de pelo*) hair-slide; (*culin*) strainer. **de ~da** in passing. **el lunes ~do** last Monday

pasaje *m* passage; (*naut*) crossing; (*viajeros*) passengers. ~**ro** *a* passing. ● *m* passenger

pasamano(s) *m* handrail; (*barandilla de escalera*) banister(s)

pasamontañas *m invar* Balaclava (helmet)

pasaporte *m* passport

pasar *vt* pass; (*poner*) put; (*filtrar*) strain; spend ‹*tiempo*›; (*tragar*) swallow; show ‹*película*›; (*tolerar*) tolerate, overlook; give ‹*mensaje, enfermedad*›. ● *vi* pass; (*suceder*) happen; (*ir*) go; (*venir*) come; ‹*tiempo*› go by. ~ **de** have no interest in. ~**se** *vpr* pass; (*terminarse*) be over; ‹*flores*› wither; ‹*comida*› go bad; spend ‹*tiempo*›; (*excederse*) go too far. ~**lo bien** have a good time. ~ **por alto** leave out. **como si no hubiese pasado nada** as if nothing had

happened. **lo que pasa es que** the fact is that. **pase lo que pase** whatever happens. **¡pase Vd!** come in!, go in! **¡que lo pases bien!** have a good time! **¿qué pasa?** what's the matter?, what's happening?

pasarela *f* footbridge; (*naut*) gangway

pasatiempo *m* hobby, pastime

pascua *f* (*fiesta de los hebreos*) Passover; (*de Resurrección*) Easter; (*Navidad*) Christmas. ~**s** *fpl* Christmas. **hacer la ~ a uno** mess things up for s.o. **¡y santas ~s!** and that's all!

pase *m* pass

pase|ante *m & f* passer-by. ~**ar** *vt* take for a walk; (*exhibir*) show off. ● *vi* go for a walk; (*en coche etc*) go for a ride. ~**arse** *vpr* go for a walk; (*en coche etc*) go for a ride. ~**o** *m* walk; (*en coche etc*) ride; (*calle*) avenue. ~**o marítimo** promenade. **dar un ~o** for a walk. **¡vete a ~o!** (*fam*) go away!, get lost! (*fam*)

pasillo *m* passage

pasión *f* passion

pasiv|idad *f* passiveness. ~**o** *a* passive

pasm|ar *vt* astonish. ~**arse** *vpr* be astonished. ~**o** *m* astonishment. ~**oso** *a* astonishing

paso *a* ‹*fruta*› dried ● *m* step; (*acción de pasar*) passing; (*huella*) footprint; (*manera de andar*) walk; (*camino*) way through; (*entre montañas*) pass; (*estrecho*) strait(s). ~ **a nivel** level crossing (*Brit*), grade crossing (*Amer*). ~ **de cebra** Zebra crossing. ~ **de peatones** pedestrian crossing. ~ **elevado** flyover. **a cada ~** at every turn. **a dos ~s** very near. **al ~ que** at the same time as. **a ~ lento** slowly. **ceda el ~** give way. **de ~** in passing. **de ~ por** on the way through. **prohibido el ~** no entry

pasodoble *m* (*baile*) pasodoble

pasota *m & f* drop-out

pasta *f* paste; (*masa*) dough; (*dinero, fam*) money. ~**s** *fpl* pasta; (*pasteles*) pastries. ~ **de dientes**, ~ **dentífrica** toothpaste

pastar *vt/i* graze

pastel *m* cake; (*empanada*) pie; (*lápiz*) pastel. ~**ería** *f* cakes; (*tienda*) cake shop, confectioner's

paste(u)rizar [10] *vt* pasteurize

pastiche *m* pastiche

pastilla *f* pastille; (*de jabón*) bar; (*de chocolate*) piece

pastinaca f parsnip

pasto m pasture; (*hierba*) grass; (*Mex, césped*) lawn. **~r** m shepherd; (*relig*) minister. **~ral** a pastoral

pata f leg; (*pie*) paw, foot. **~s arriba** upside down. **a cuatro ~s** on all fours. **meter la ~** put one's foot in it. **tener mala ~** have bad luck

pataca f Jerusalem artichoke

pata|da f kick. **~lear** vt stamp; (*niño pequeño*) kick

pataplum int crash!

patata f potato. **~s fritas** chips (*Brit*), French fries (*Amer*). **~s fritas (a la inglesa)** (potato) crisps (*Brit*), potato chips (*Amer*)

patent|ar vt patent. **~e** a obvious. ● f licence. **~e de invención** patent

patern|al a paternal; (*cariño etc*) fatherly. **~idad** f paternity. **~o** a paternal; (*cariño etc*) fatherly

patético a moving

patillas fpl sideburns

patín m skate; (*juguete*) scooter

pátina f patina

patina|dero m skating rink. **~dor** m skater. **~je** m skating. **~r** vi skate; (*deslizarse*) slide. **~zo** m skid; (*fig, fam*) blunder

patio m patio. **~ de butacas** stalls (*Brit*), orchestra (*Amer*)

pato m duck

patol|ogía f pathology. **~ógico** a pathological

patoso a clumsy

patraña f hoax

patria f native land

patriarca m patriarch

patrimonio m inheritance; (*fig*) heritage

patri|ota a patriotic. ● m & f patriot. **~ótico** a patriotic. **~otismo** m patriotism

patrocin|ar vt sponsor. **~io** m sponsorship

patr|ón m patron; (*jefe*) boss; (*de pensión etc*) landlord; (*modelo*) pattern. **~onato** m patronage; (*fundación*) trust, foundation

patrulla f patrol; (*fig, cuadrilla*) group. **~r** vt/i patrol

paulatinamente adv slowly

pausa f pause. **~do** a slow

pauta f guideline

paviment|ar vt pave. **~o** m pavement

pavo m turkey. **~ real** peacock

pavor m terror. **~oso** a terrifying

payas|ada f buffoonery. **~o** m clown

paz f peace. **La P~** La Paz

peaje m toll

peatón m pedestrian

pebet|a f (*LAm*) little girl. **~e** m little boy

peca f freckle

peca|do m sin; (*defecto*) fault. **~dor** m sinner. **~minoso** a sinful. **~r** [7] vi sin

pecoso a freckled

pectoral a pectoral; (*para la tos*) cough

peculiar a peculiar, particular. **~idad** f peculiarity

pech|era f front. **~ero** m bib. **~o** m chest; (*de mujer*) breast; (*fig, corazón*) heart. **~uga** f breast. **dar el ~o** breast-feed (*a un niño*); (*afrontar*) confront. **tomar a ~o** take to heart

pedagogo m teacher

pedal m pedal. **~ear** vi pedal

pedante a pedantic

pedazo m piece, bit. **a ~s** in pieces. **hacer ~s** break to pieces. **hacerse ~s** fall to pieces

pedernal m flint

pedestal m pedestal

pedestre a pedestrian

pediatra m & f paediatrician

pedicuro m chiropodist

pedi|do m order. **~r** [5] vt ask (for); (*com, en restaurante*) order. ● vi ask. **~r prestado** borrow

pegadizo a sticky; (*mus*) catchy

pegajoso a sticky

pega|r [12] vt stick (on); (*coser*) sew on; give (*enfermedad etc*); (*juntar*) join; (*golpear*) hit; (*dar*) give. ● vi stick. **~rse** vpr stick; (*pelearse*) hit each other. **~r fuego a** set fire to. **~tina** f sticker

pein|ado m hairstyle. **~ar** vt comb. **~arse** vpr comb one's hair. **~e** m comb. **~eta** f ornamental comb

p.ej. abrev (*por ejemplo*) e.g., for example

pela|do a (*fruta*) peeled; (*cabeza*) bald; (*número*) exactly; (*terreno*) barren. ● m bare patch. **~dura** f (*acción*) peeling; (*mondadura*) peelings

pela|je m (*de animal*) fur; (*fig, aspecto*) appearance. **~mbre** m (*de animal*) fur; (*de persona*) thick hair

pelar vt cut the hair; (*mondar*) peel; (*quitar el pellejo*) skin

peldaño *m* step; (*de escalera de mano*) rung

pelea *f* fight; (*discusión*) quarrel. **~r** *vi* fight. **~rse** *vpr* fight

peletería *f* fur shop

peliagudo *a* difficult, tricky

pelícano *m*, **pelicano** *m* pelican

película *f* film (*esp Brit*), movie (*Amer*). **~ de dibujos (animados)** cartoon (film). **~ en colores** colour film

peligro *m* danger; (*riesgo*) risk. **~so** *a* dangerous. **poner en ~** endanger

pelirrojo *a* red-haired

pelma *m & f*, **pelmazo** *m* bore, nuisance

pel|o *m* hair; (*de barba o bigote*) whisker. **~ón** *a* bald; (*rapado*) with very short hair. **no tener ~os en la lengua** be outspoken. **tomar el ~o a uno** pull s.o.'s leg

pelota *f* ball; (*juego vasco*) pelota. **~ vasca** pelota. **en ~(s)** naked

pelotera *f* squabble

pelotilla *f*. **hacer la ~ a** ingratiate o.s. with

peluca *f* wig

peludo *a* hairy

peluquer|ía *f* (*de mujer*) hairdresser's; (*de hombre*) barber's. **~o** *m* (*de mujer*) hairdresser; (*de hombre*) barber

pelusa *f* down; (*celos, fam*) jealousy

pelvis *f* pelvis

pella *f* lump

pelleja *f*, **pellejo** *m* skin

pellizc|ar [7] *vt* pinch. **~o** *m* pinch

pena *f* sadness; (*dificultad*) difficulty. **~ de muerte** death penalty. **a duras ~s** with difficulty. **da ~ que** it's a pity that. **me da ~ que** I'm sorry that. **merecer la ~** be worthwhile. **¡qué ~!** what a pity! **valer la ~** be worthwhile

penacho *m* tuft; (*fig*) plume

penal *a* penal; (*criminal*) criminal. ● *m* prison. **~idad** *f* suffering; (*jurid*) penalty. **~izar** [10] *vt* penalize

penalty *m* penalty

penar *vt* punish. ● *vi* suffer. **~ por** long for

pend|er *vi* hang. **~iente** *a* hanging; (*terreno*) sloping; (*cuenta*) outstanding; (*fig*) (*asunto etc*) pending. ● *m* earring. ● *f* slope

pendón *m* banner

péndulo *a* hanging. ● *m* pendulum

pene *m* penis

penetra|nte *a* penetrating; (*sonido*) piercing; (*herida*) deep. **~r** *vt* penetrate; (*fig*) pierce; (*entender*) understand. ● *vi* penetrate; (*entrar*) go into

penicilina *f* penicillin

pen|ínsula *f* peninsula. **península Ibérica** Iberian Peninsula. **~insular** *a* peninsular

penique *m* penny

peniten|cia *f* penitence; (*castigo*) penance. **~te** *a & m & f* penitent

penoso *a* painful; (*difícil*) difficult

pensa|do *a* thought. **~dor** *m* thinker. **~miento** *m* thought. **~r** [1] *vt* think; (*considerar*) consider. ● *vi* think. **~r en** think about. **~tivo** *a* thoughtful. **bien ~do** all things considered. **cuando menos se piensa** when least expected. **menos ~do** least expected. **¡ni ~rlo!** certainly not! **pienso que sí** I think so

pensi|ón *f* pension; (*casa de huéspedes*) guest-house. **~ón completa** full board. **~onista** *m & f* pensioner; (*huésped*) lodger; (*escol*) boarder

pentágono *m* pentagon

pentagrama *m* stave

Pentecostés *m* Whitsun; (*fiesta judía*) Pentecost

penúltimo *a & m* penultimate, last but one

penumbra *f* half-light

penuria *f* shortage

peñ|a *f* rock; (*de amigos*) group; (*club*) club. **~ón** *m* rock. **el peñón de Gibraltar** The Rock (of Gibraltar)

peón *m* labourer; (*en ajedrez*) pawn; (*en damas*) piece; (*juguete*) (spinning) top

peonía *f* peony

peonza *f* (spinning) top

peor *a* (*comparativo*) worse; (*superlativo*) worst. ● *adv* worse. **~ que ~** worse and worse. **lo ~** the worst thing. **tanto ~** so much the worse

pepin|illo *m* gherkin. **~o** *m* cucumber. **(no) me importa un ~o** I couldn't care less

pepita *f* pip

pepitoria *f* fricassee

pequeñ|ez *f* smallness; (*minucia*) trifle. **~ito** *a* very small, tiny. **~o** *a* small, little. **de ~o** as a child. **en ~o** in miniature

pequinés *m* (*perro*) Pekinese

pera *f* (*fruta*) pear. **~l** *m* pear (tree)

percance *m* setback

percatarse *vpr*. **~ de** notice

perc|epción f perception. **~eptible** a perceptible. **~eptivo** a perceptive. **~ibir** vt perceive; earn ‹dinero›
percusión f percussion
percutir vt tap
percha f hanger; ‹de aves› perch. **de ~** off the peg
perde|dor a losing. ● m loser. **~r** [1] vt lose; ‹malgastar› waste; miss ‹tren etc›. ● vi lose; ‹tela› fade. **~rse** vpr get lost; ‹desparecer› disappear; ‹desperdiciarse› be wasted; ‹estropearse› be spoilt. **echar(se) a ~r** spoil
pérdida f loss; ‹de líquido› leak; ‹de tiempo› waste
perdido a lost
perdiz f partridge
perd|ón m pardon, forgiveness. ● int sorry! **~onar** vt excuse, forgive; ‹jurid› pardon. **¡~one (Vd)!** sorry! **pedir ~ón** apologize
perdura|ble a lasting. **~r** vi last
perece|dero a perishable. **~r** [11] vi perish
peregrin|ación f pilgrimage. **~ar** vi go on a pilgrimage; ‹fig, fam› travel. **~o** a strange. ● m pilgrim
perejil m parsley
perengano m so-and-so
perenne a everlasting; ‹bot› perennial
perentorio a peremptory
perez|a f laziness. **~oso** a lazy
perfec|ción f perfection. **~cionamiento** m perfection; ‹mejora› improvement. **~cionar** vt perfect; ‹mejorar› improve. **~cionista** m & f perfectionist. **~tamente** adv perfectly. ● int of course! **~to** a perfect; ‹completo› complete. **a la ~ción** perfectly, to perfection
perfidia f treachery
pérfido a treacherous
perfil m profile; ‹contorno› outline; **~es** mpl ‹fig, rasgos› features. **~ado** a ‹bien terminado› well-finished. **~ar** vt draw in profile; ‹fig› put the finishing touches to
perfora|ción f perforation. **~do** m perforation. **~dora** f punch. **~r** vt pierce, perforate; punch ‹papel, tarjeta etc›
perfum|ar vt perfume. **~arse** vpr put perfume on. **~e** m perfume, scent. **~ería** f perfumery
pergamino m parchment
pericia f expertise

pericón m popular Argentinian dance
perif|eria f ‹de población› outskirts. **~érico** a peripheral
perilla f ‹barba› goatee
perímetro m perimeter
periódico a periodic(al). ● m newspaper
periodis|mo m journalism. **~ta** m & f journalist
período m, **periodo** m period
periquito m budgerigar
periscopio m periscope
perito a & m expert
perju|dicar [7] vt harm; ‹desfavorecer› not suit. **~dicial** a harmful. **~icio** m harm. **en ~icio de** to the detriment of
perjur|ar vi perjure o.s. **~io** m perjury
perla f pearl. **de ~s** adv very well. ● a excellent
permane|cer [11] vi remain. **~ncia** f permanence; ‹estancia› stay. **~nte** a permanent. ● f perm
permeable a permeable
permi|sible a permissible. **~sivo** a permissive. **~so** m permission; ‹documento› licence; ‹mil etc› leave. **~so de conducción, ~so de conducir** driving licence (Brit), driver's license (Amer). **~tir** vt allow, permit. **~tirse** vpr be allowed. **con ~so** excuse me. **¿me ~te?** may I?
permutación f exchange; ‹math› permutation
pernicioso a pernicious; ‹persona› wicked
pernio m hinge
perno m bolt
pero conj but. ● m fault; ‹objeción› objection
perogrullada f platitude
perol m pan
peronista m & f follower of Juan Perón
perorar vi make a speech
perpendicular a & f perpendicular
perpetrar vt perpetrate
perpetu|ar [21] vt perpetuate. **~o** a perpetual
perplej|idad f perplexity. **~o** a perplexed
perr|a f ‹animal› bitch; ‹moneda› coin, penny (Brit), cent (Amer); ‹rabieta› tantrum. **~era** f kennel. **~ería** f ‹mala jugada› dirty trick; ‹palabra› harsh word. **~o** a awful

● *m* dog. **~o corredor** hound. **~o de aguas** spaniel. **~o del hortelano** dog in the manger. **~o galgo** greyhound. **de ~os** awful. **estar sin una ~a** be broke

persa *a & m & f* Persian

perse|cución *f* pursuit; (*tormento*) persecution. **~guir** [5 & 13] *vt* pursue; (*atormentar*) persecute

persevera|ncia *f* perseverance. **~nte** *a* persevering. **~r** *vi* persevere

persiana *f* (Venetian) blind

persist|encia *f* persistence. **~ente** *a* persistent. **~ir** *vi* persist

person|a *f* person. **~as** *fpl* people. **~aje** *m* (*persona importante*) important person; (*de obra literaria*) character. **~al** *a* personal; (*para una persona*) single. ● *m* staff. **~alidad** *f* personality. **~arse** *vpr* appear in person. **~ificar** [7] *vt* personify. **~ificación** *f* personification

perspectiva *f* perspective

perspica|cia *f* shrewdness; (*de vista*) keen eye-sight. **~z** *a* shrewd; (*vista*) keen

persua|dir *vt* persuade. **~sión** *f* persuasion. **~sivo** *a* persuasive

pertenecer [11] *vi* belong

pertinaz *a* persistent

pertinente *a* relevant

perturba|ción *f* disturbance. **~r** *vt* perturb

Perú *m*. **el ~** Peru

peruano *a & m* Peruvian

perver|sión *f* perversion. **~so** *a* perverse. ● *m* pervert. **~tir** [4] *vt* pervert

pervivir *vi* live on

pesa *f* weight. **~dez** *f* weight; (*de cabeza etc*) heaviness; (*lentitud*) sluggishness; (*cualidad de fastidioso*) tediousness; (*cosa fastidiosa*) bore, nuisance

pesadilla *f* nightmare

pesad|o *a* heavy; (*lento*) slow; (*duro*) hard; (*aburrido*) boring, tedious. **~umbre** *f* (*pena*) sorrow

pésame *m* sympathy, condolences

pesar *vt/i* weigh. ● *m* sorrow; (*remordimiento*) regret. **a ~ de (que)** in spite of. **me pesa que** I'm sorry that. **pese a (que)** in spite of

pesario *m* pessary

pesca *f* fishing; (*peces*) fish; (*pescado*) catch. **~da** *f* hake. **~dería** *f* fish shop. **~dilla** *f* whiting. **~do** *m* fish. **~dor** *a* fishing. ● *m* fisherman. **~r**

[7] *vt* catch. ● *vi* fish. **ir de ~** go fishing

pescuezo *m* neck

pesebre *m* manger

pesero *m* (*Mex*) minibus taxi

peseta *f* peseta; (*Mex*) twenty-five centavos

pesimis|mo *m* pessimism. **~ta** *a* pessimistic. ● *m & f* pessimist

pésimo *a* very bad, awful

peso *m* weight; (*moneda*) peso. **~ bruto** gross weight. **~ neto** net weight. **a ~** by weight. **de ~** influential

pesquero *a* fishing

pesquisa *f* inquiry

pestañ|a *f* eyelash. **~ear** *vi* blink. **sin ~ear** without batting an eyelid

pest|e *f* plague; (*hedor*) stench. **~icida** *m* pesticide. **~ilencia** *f* pestilence; (*hedor*) stench

pestillo *m* bolt

pestiño *m* pancake with honey

petaca *f* tobacco case; (*LAm, maleta*) suitcase

pétalo *m* petal

petardo *m* firework

petición *f* request; (*escrito*) petition. **a ~ de** at the request of

petirrojo *m* robin

petrificar [7] *vt* petrify

petr|óleo *m* oil. **~olero** *a* oil. ● *m* oil tanker. **~olífero** *a* oil-bearing

petulante *a* arrogant

peyorativo *a* pejorative

pez *f* fish; (*substancia negruzca*) pitch. **~ espada** swordfish

pezón *m* nipple; (*bot*) stalk

pezuña *f* hoof

piada *f* chirp

piadoso *a* compassionate; (*devoto*) devout

pian|ista *m & f* pianist. **~o** *m* piano. **~o de cola** grand piano

piar [20] *vi* chirp

pib|a *f* (*LAm*) little girl. **~e** *m* (*LAm*) little boy

picad|illo *m* mince; (*guiso*) stew. **~o** *a* perforated; (*carne*) minced; (*ofendido*) offended; (*mar*) choppy; (*diente*) bad. **~ura** *f* bite, sting; (*de polilla*) moth hole

picante *a* hot; (*palabras etc*) cutting

picaporte *m* door-handle; (*aldaba*) knocker

picar [7] *vt* prick, pierce; (*ave*) peck; (*insecto, pez*) bite; (*avispa*) sting; (*comer poco*) pick at; mince (*carne*).

● *vi* prick; ⟨*ave*⟩ peck; ⟨*insecto, pez*⟩ bite; ⟨*sol*⟩ scorch; ⟨*sabor fuerte*⟩ be hot. ～ **alto** aim high

picard|ear *vt* corrupt. ～**ía** *f* wickedness; (*travesura*) naughty thing

picaresco *a* roguish; ⟨*literatura*⟩ picaresque

pícaro *a* villainous; ⟨*niño*⟩ mischievous. ● *m* rogue

picatoste *m* toast; (*frito*) fried bread

picazón *f* itch

pico *m* beak; (*punta*) corner; (*herramienta*) pickaxe; (*cima*) peak. ～**tear** *vt* peck; (*comer, fam*) pick at. **y** ～ (*con tiempo*) a little after; (*con cantidad*) a little more than

picudo *a* pointed

pich|ona *f* (*fig*) darling; ～**ón** *m* pigeon

pido *vb véase* **pedir**

pie *m* foot; (*bot, de vaso*) stem. ～ **cuadrado** square foot. **a cuatro** ～**s** on all fours. **al** ～ **de la letra** literally. **a** ～ **on** foot. **a** ～(**s**) **juntillas** (*fig*) firmly. **buscarle tres** ～**s al gato** split hairs. **de** ～ standing (up). **de** ～**s a cabeza** from head to foot. **en** ～ standing (up). **ponerse de/en** ～ stand up

piedad *f* pity; (*relig*) piety

piedra *f* stone; (*de mechero*) flint; (*granizo*) hailstone

piel *f* skin; (*cuero*) leather. **artículos de** ～ leather goods

pienso *vb véase* **pensar**

pierdo *vb véase* **perder**

pierna *f* leg. **estirar las** ～**s** stretch one's legs

pieza *f* piece; (*parte*) part; (*obra teatral*) play; (*moneda*) coin; (*habitación*) room. ～ **de recambio** spare part

pífano *m* fife

pigment|ación *f* pigmentation. ～**o** *m* pigment

pigmeo *a* & *m* pygmy

pijama *m* pyjamas

pila *f* (*montón*) pile; (*recipiente*) basin; (*eléctrica*) battery. ～ **bautismal** font

píldora *f* pill

pilot|ar *vt* pilot. ～**o** *m* pilot

pilla|je *m* pillage. ～**r** *vt* pillage; (*alcanzar, agarrar*) catch; (*atropellar*) run over

pillo *a* wicked. ● *m* rogue

pim|entero *m* (*vasija*) pepper-pot. ～**entón** *m* paprika, cayenne pepper.

～**ienta** *f* pepper. ～**iento** *m* pepper. **grano** *m* **de** ～**ienta** peppercorn

pináculo *m* pinnacle

pinar *m* pine forest

pincel *m* paintbrush. ～**ada** *f* brushstroke. **la última** ～**ada** (*fig*) the finishing touch

pinch|ar *vt* pierce, prick; puncture ⟨*neumático*⟩; (*fig, incitar*) push; (*med, fam*) give an injection to. ～**azo** *m* prick; (*en neumático*) puncture. ～**itos** *mpl* kebab(s); (*tapas*) savoury snacks. ～**o** *m* point

ping|ajo *m* rag. ～**o** *m* rag

ping-pong *m* table tennis, pingpong

pingüino *m* penguin

pino *m* pine (tree)

pint|a *f* spot; (*fig, aspecto*) appearance. ～**ada** *f* graffiti. ～**ar** *vt* paint. ～**arse** *vpr* put on make-up. ～**or** *m* painter. ～**or de brocha gorda** painter and decorator. ～**oresco** *a* picturesque. ～**ura** *f* painting. **no** ～**a nada** (*fig*) it doesn't count. **tener** ～**a de** look like

pinza *f* (clothes-)peg (*Brit*), (clothes-) pin (*Amer*); (*de cangrejo etc*) claw. ～**s** *fpl* tweezers

pinzón *m* chaffinch

piñ|a *f* pine cone; (*ananás*) pineapple; (*fig, grupo*) group. ～**ón** *m* (*semilla*) pine nut

pío *a* pious; ⟨*caballo*⟩ piebald. ● *m* chirp. **no decir (ni)** ～ not say a word

piocha *f* pickaxe

piojo *m* louse

pionero *m* pioneer

pipa *f* pipe; (*semilla*) seed; (*de girasol*) sunflower seed

pipián *m* (*LAm*) stew

pique *m* resentment; (*rivalidad*) rivalry. **irse a** ～ sink

piqueta *f* pickaxe

piquete *m* picket

piragua *f* canoe

pirámide *f* pyramid

pirata *m* & *f* pirate

Pirineos *mpl* Pyrenees

piropo *m* (*fam*) compliment

piruet|a *f* pirouette. ～**ear** *vi* pirouette

pirulí *m* lollipop

pisa|da *f* footstep; (*huella*) footprint. ～**papeles** *m invar* paperweight. ～**r** *vt* tread on; (*apretar*) press; (*fig*) walk over. ● *vi* tread. **no** ～**r el césped** keep off the grass

piscina *f* swimming pool; (*para peces*) fish-pond

Piscis *m* Pisces

piso *m* floor; (*vivienda*) flat (*Brit*), apartment (*Amer*); (*de zapato*) sole

pisotear *vt* trample (on)

pista *f* track; (*fig, indicio*) clue. **~ de aterrizaje** runway. **~ de baile** dance floor. **~ de hielo** skating-rink. **~ de tenis** tennis court

pistacho *m* pistachio (nut)

pisto *m* fried vegetables

pistol|a *f* pistol. **~era** *f* holster. **~ero** *m* gunman

pistón *m* piston

pit|ar *vt* whistle at. ● *vi* blow a whistle; (*auto*) sound one's horn. **~ido** *m* whistle

pitill|era *f* cigarette case. **~o** *m* cigarette

pito *m* whistle; (*auto*) horn

pitón *m* python

pitorr|arse *vpr*. **~arse de** make fun of. **~o** *m* teasing

pitorro *m* spout

pivote *m* pivot

pizarr|a *f* slate; (*encerrado*) blackboard. **~ón** *m* (*LAm*) blackboard

pizca *f* (*fam*) tiny piece; (*de sal*) pinch. **ni ~** not at all

pizz|a *f* pizza. **~ería** *f* pizzeria

placa *f* plate; (*conmemorativa*) plaque; (*distintivo*) badge

pláceme *m* congratulations

place|ntero *a* pleasant. **~r** [32] *vt* please. **me ~** I like. ● *m* pleasure

plácido *a* placid

plaga *f* plague; (*fig, calamidad*) disaster; (*fig, abundancia*) glut. **~r** [12] *vt* fill

plagi|ar *vt* plagiarize. **~o** *m* plagiarism

plan *m* plan; (*med*) course of treatment. **a todo ~** on a grand scale. **en ~ de** as

plana *f* (*llanura*) plain; (*página*) page. **en primera ~** on the front page

plancha *f* iron; (*lámina*) sheet. **~do** *m* ironing. **~r** *vt/i* iron. **a la ~** grilled. **tirarse una ~** put one's foot in it

planeador *m* glider

planear *vt* plan. ● *vi* glide

planeta *m* planet. **~rio** *a* planetary. ● *m* planetarium

planicie *f* plain

planifica|ción *f* planning. **~r** [7] *vt* plan

planilla *f* (*LAm*) list

plano *a* flat. ● *m* plane; (*de ciudad*) plan. **primer ~** foreground; (*foto*) close-up

planta *f* (*anat*) sole; (*bot, fábrica*) plant; (*plano*) ground plan; (*piso*) floor. **~ baja** ground floor (*Brit*), first floor (*Amer*)

planta|ción *f* plantation. **~do** *a* planted. **~r** *vt* plant; deal (*golpe*). **~rse en la calle** throw out. **~rse** *vpr* stand; (*fig*) stand firm. **bien ~do** good-looking

plantear *vt* (*exponer*) expound; (*causar*) create; raise (*cuestión*)

plantilla *f* insole; (*modelo*) pattern; (*personal*) personnel

plaqué *m* plate

plasma *m* plasma

plástico *a & m* plastic

plata *f* silver; (*fig, dinero, fam*) money. **~ de ley** sterling silver. **~ alemana** nickel silver

plataforma *f* platform

plátano *m* plane (tree); (*fruta*) banana; (*platanero*) banana tree

platea *f* stalls (*Brit*), orchestra (*Amer*)

plateado *a* silver-plated; (*color de plata*) silver

pl|ática *f* chat, talk. **~aticar** [7] *vi* chat, talk

platija *f* plaice

platillo *m* saucer; (*mus*) cymbal. **~ volante** flying saucer

platino *m* platinum. **~s** *mpl* (*auto*) points

plato *m* plate; (*comida*) dish; (*parte de una comida*) course

platónico *a* platonic

plausible *a* plausible; (*loable*) praiseworthy

playa *f* beach; (*fig*) seaside

plaza *f* square; (*mercado*) market; (*sitio*) place; (*empleo*) job. **~ de toros** bullring

plazco *vb* *véase* **placer**

plazo *m* period; (*pago*) instalment; (*fecha*) date. **comprar a ~s** buy on hire purchase (*Brit*), buy on the installment plan (*Amer*)

plazuela *f* little square

pleamar *f* high tide

plebe *f* common people. **~yo** *a & m* plebeian

plebiscito *m* plebiscite

plectro m plectrum

plega|ble a pliable; ⟨silla etc⟩ folding. **~r** [1 & 12] vt fold. **~rse** vpr bend; (fig) give way

pleito m (court) case; (fig) dispute

plenilunio m full moon

plen|itud f fullness; (fig) height. **~o** a full. **en ~o día** in broad daylight. **en ~o verano** at the height of the summer

pleuresía f pleuresy

plieg|o m sheet. **~ue** m fold; (en ropa) pleat

plinto m plinth

plisar vt pleat

plom|ero m (esp LAm) plumber. **~o** m lead; (elec) fuse. **de ~o** lead

pluma f feather; (para escribir) pen. **~ estilográfica** fountain pen. **~je** m plumage

plúmbeo a leaden

plum|ero m feather duster; (para plumas, lápices etc) pencil-case. **~ón** m down

plural a & m plural. **~idad** f plurality; (mayoría) majority. **en ~** in the plural

pluriempleo m having more than one job

plus m bonus

pluscuamperfecto m pluperfect

plusvalía f appreciation

plut|ocracia f plutocracy. **~ócrata** m & f plutocrat. **~ocrático** a plutocratic

plutonio m plutonium

pluvial a rain

pobla|ción f population; (ciudad) city, town; (pueblo) village. **~do** a populated. ● m village. **~r** [2] vt populate; (habitar) inhabit. **~rse** vpr get crowded

pobre a poor. ● m & f poor person; (fig) poor thing. **¡~cito!** poor (little) thing! **¡~ de mí!** poor (old) me! **~za** f poverty

pocilga f pigsty

poción f potion

poco a not much, little; (en plural) few; (unos) a few. ● m (a) little. ● adv little, not much; (con adjetivo) not very; (poco tiempo) not long. **~ a ~** little by little, gradually. **a ~ de** soon after. **dentro de ~** soon. **hace ~** not long ago. **poca cosa** nothing much. **por ~** (fam) nearly

podar vt prune

poder [33] vi be able. **no pudo venir** he couldn't come. **¿puedo hacer algo?** can I do anything? **¿puedo pasar?** may I come in? ● m power. **~es** mpl **públicos** authorities. **~oso** a powerful. **en el ~** in power. **no ~ con** not be able to cope with; (no aguantar) not be able to stand. **no ~ más** be exhausted; (estar harto de algo) not be able to manage any more. **no ~ menos que** not be able to help. **puede que** it is possible that. **puede ser** it is possible. **¿se puede ...?** may I ...?

podrido a rotten

po|ema m poem. **~esía** f poetry; (poema) poem. **~eta** m poet. **~ético** a poetic

polaco a Polish. ● m Pole; (lengua) Polish

polar a polar. **estrella ~** polestar

polarizar [10] vt polarize

polca f polka

polea f pulley

pol|émica f controversy. **~émico** a polemic(al). **~emizar** [10] vi argue

polen m pollen

policía f police (force); (persona) policewoman. ● m policeman. **~co** a police; ⟨novela etc⟩ detective

policlínica f clinic, hospital

policromo, polícromo a polychrome

polideportivo m sports centre

poliéster m polyester

poliestireno m polystyrene

polietileno m polythene

pol|igamia f polygamy. **~ígamo** a polygamous

políglota m & f polyglot

polígono m polygon

polilla f moth

polio(mielitis) f polio(myelitis)

pólipo m polyp

politécnic|a f polytechnic. **~o** a polytechnic

polític|a f politics. **~o** a political; ⟨pariente⟩ -in-law. ● m politician. **padre ~o** father-in-law

póliza f document; (de seguros) policy

polo m pole; (helado) ice lolly (Brit); (juego) polo. **~ helado** ice lolly (Brit). **~ norte** North Pole

Polonia f Poland

poltrona f armchair

polución f (contaminación) pollution

polv|areda f cloud of dust; (fig, escándalo) scandal. **~era** f compact.

~o *m* powder; (*suciedad*) dust. ~os *mpl* powder. **en** ~o powdered. **estar hecho** ~o be exhausted. **quitar el** ~o dust

pólvora *f* gunpowder; (*fuegos artificiales*) fireworks

polvor|iento *a* dusty. ~ón *m* Spanish Christmas shortcake

poll|ada *f* brood. ~era *f* (*para niños*) baby-walker; (*LAm, falda*) skirt. ~ería *f* poultry shop. ~o *m* chicken; (*gallo joven*) chick

pomada *f* ointment

pomelo *m* grapefruit

pómez *a*. **piedra** *f* ~ pumice stone

pomp|a *f* bubble; (*esplendor*) pomp. ~as fúnebres funeral. ~oso *a* pompous; (*espléndido*) splendid

pómulo *m* cheek; (*hueso*) cheekbone

poncha|do *a* (*Mex*) punctured, flat. ~r *vt* (*Mex*) puncture

ponche *m* punch

poncho *m* poncho

ponderar *vt* (*alabar*) speak highly of

poner [34] *vt* put; put on ⟨*ropa, obra de teatro, TV etc*⟩; (*suponer*) suppose; lay ⟨*la mesa, un huevo*⟩; (*hacer*) make; (*contribuir*) contribute; give ⟨*nombre*⟩; show ⟨*película, interés*⟩; open ⟨*una tienda*⟩; equip ⟨*una casa*⟩. ● *vi* lay. ~se *vpr* put o.s.; (*volverse*) get; put on ⟨*ropa*⟩; ⟨*sol*⟩ set. ~ **con** (*al teléfono*) put through to. ~ **en claro** clarify. ~ **por escrito** put into writing. ~ **una multa** fine. ~se **a** start to. ~se **a mal con uno** fall out with s.o. **pongamos** let's suppose

pongo *vb véase* **poner**

poniente *m* west; (*viento*) west wind

pont|ificado *m* pontificate. ~ifical *a* pontifical. ~ificar [7] *vi* pontificate. ~ifice *m* pontiff

pontón *m* pontoon

popa *f* stern

popelín *m* poplin

popul|acho *m* masses. ~ar *a* popular; ⟨*lenguaje*⟩ colloquial. ~aridad *f* popularity. ~arizar [10] *vt* popularize. ~oso *a* populous

póquer *m* poker

poquito *m* a little bit. ● *adv* a little

por *prep* for; (*para*) (in order) to; (*a través de*) through; (*a causa de*) because of; (*como agente*) by; (*en matemática*) times; (*como función*) as; (*en lugar de*) instead of. ~ **la calle** along the street. ~ **mí** as for me, for my part. ~ **si** in case. ~ **todo el país**

throughout the country. **50 kilómetros** ~ **hora** 50 kilometres per hour

porcelana *f* china

porcentaje *m* percentage

porcino *a* pig. ● *m* small pig

porción *f* portion; (*de chocolate*) piece

pordiosero *m* beggar

porf|ía *f* persistence; (*disputa*) dispute. ~iado *a* persistent. ~iar [20] *vi* insist. **a** ~ía in competition

pormenor *m* detail

pornogr|afía *f* pornography. ~áfico *a* pornographic

poro *m* pore. ~so *a* porous

poroto *m* (*LAm, judía*) bean

porque *conj* because; (*para que*) so that

porqué *m* reason

porquería *f* filth; (*basura*) rubbish; (*grosería*) dirty trick

porra *f* club; (*culin*) fritter

porrón *m* wine jug (with a long spout)

portaaviones *m invar* aircraft-carrier

portada *f* façade; (*de libro*) title page

portador *m* bearer

porta|equipaje(s) *m invar* boot (*Brit*), trunk (*Amer*); (*encima del coche*) roof-rack. ~estandarte *m* standard-bearer

portal *m* hall; (*puerta principal*) main entrance; (*soportal*) porch

porta|lámparas *m invar* socket. ~ligas *m invar* suspender belt. ~monedas *m invar* purse

portarse *vpr* behave

portátil *a* portable

portavoz *m* megaphone; (*fig, persona*) spokesman

portazgo *m* toll

portazo *m* bang. **dar un** ~ slam the door

porte *m* transport; (*precio*) carriage. ~ador *m* carrier

portento *m* marvel

porteño *a* (*de Buenos Aires*) from Buenos Aires. ● *m* person from Buenos Aires

porter|ía *f* caretaker's lodge, porter's lodge; (*en deportes*) goal. ~o *m* caretaker, porter; (*en deportes*) goalkeeper. ~o **automático** intercom (*fam*)

portezuela *f* small door; (*auto*) door

pórtico *m* portico

portill|a f gate; (*en barco*) porthole. **~o** m opening

portorriqueño a Puerto Rican

Portugal m Portugal

portugués a & m Portuguese

porvenir m future

posada f guest house; (*mesón*) inn

posaderas fpl (*fam*) bottom

posar vt put. ● vi ⟨*pájaro*⟩ perch; ⟨*modelo*⟩ sit. **~se** vpr settle

posdata f postscript

pose|edor m owner. **~er** [18] vt have, own; (*saber*) know well. **~ído** a possessed. **~sión** f possession. **~sionar** vt. **~sionar de** hand over. **~sionarse** vpr. **~sionarse de** take possession of. **~sivo** a possessive

posfechar vt postdate

posguerra f post-war years

posib|ilidad f possibility. **~le** a possible. **de ser ~le** if possible. **en lo ~le** as far as possible. **hacer todo lo ~le para** do everything possible to. **si es ~le** if possible

posición f position

positivo a positive

poso m sediment

posponer [34] vt put after; (*diferir*) postpone

posta f. **a ~** on purpose

postal a postal. ● f postcard

poste m pole

postergar [12] vt pass over; (*diferir*) postpone

posteri|dad f posterity. **~or** a back; (*ulterior*) later. **~ormente** adv later

postigo m door; (*contraventana*) shutter

postizo a false, artificial. ● m hairpiece

postra|do a prostrate. **~r** vt prostrate. **~rse** vpr prostrate o.s.

postre m dessert, sweet (*Brit*). **de ~** for dessert

postular vt postulate; collect ⟨*dinero*⟩

póstumo a posthumous

postura f position, stance

potable a drinkable; ⟨*agua*⟩ drinking

potaje m vegetable stew

potasio m potassium

pote m jar

poten|cia f power. **~cial** a & m potential. **~te** a powerful. **en ~cia** potential

potingue m (*fam*) concoction

potr|a f filly. **~o** m colt; (*en gimnasia*) horse. **tener ~a** be lucky

pozo m well; (*hoyo seco*) pit; (*de mina*) shaft

pozole m (*Mex*) stew

práctica f practice; (*destreza*) skill. **en la ~** in practice. **poner en ~** put into practice

practica|ble a practicable. **~nte** m & f nurse. **~r** [7] vt practise; play ⟨*deportes*⟩; (*ejecutar*) carry out

práctico a practical; (*diestro*) skilled. ● m practitioner

prad|era f meadow; (*terreno grande*) prairie. **~o** m meadow

pragmático a pragmatic

preámbulo m preamble

precario a precarious

precaución f precaution; (*cautela*) caution. **con ~** cautiously

precaver vt guard against

prece|dencia f precedence; (*prioridad*) priority. **~nte** a preceding. ● m precedent. **~r** vt/i precede

precepto m precept. **~r** m tutor

precia|do a valuable; (*estimado*) esteemed. **~rse** vpr boast

precinto m seal

precio m price. **~ de venta al público** retail price. **al ~ de** at the cost of. **no tener ~** be priceless. **¿qué ~ tiene?** how much is it?

precios|idad f value; (*cosa preciosa*) beautiful thing. **~o** a precious; (*bonito*) beautiful. **¡es una ~idad!** it's beautiful!

precipicio m precipice

precipita|ción f precipitation. **~damente** adv hastily. **~do** a hasty. **~r** vt hurl; (*acelerar*) accelerate; (*apresurar*) hasten. **~rse** vpr throw o.s.; (*correr*) rush; (*actuar sin reflexionar*) act rashly

precis|amente a exactly. **~ar** vt require; (*determinar*) determine. **~ión** f precision; (*necesidad*) need. **~o** a precise; (*necesario*) necessary

preconcebido a preconceived

precoz a early; (*niño*) precocious

precursor m forerunner

predecesor m predecessor

predecir [46]; o [46, *pero imperativo* **predice**, *futuro y condicional regulares*] vt foretell

predestina|ción f predestination. **~r** vt predestine

prédica f sermon

predicamento m influence

predicar [7] vt/i preach

predicción f prediction; (del tiempo) forecast

predilec|ción f predilection. **~to** a favourite

predisponer [34] vt predispose

predomin|ante a predominant. **~ar** vt dominate. ● vi predominate. **~io** m predominance

preeminente a pre-eminent

prefabricado a prefabricated

prefacio m preface

prefect|o m prefect. **~ura** f prefecture

prefer|encia f preference. **~ente** a preferential. **~ible** a preferable. **~ido** a favourite. **~ir** [4] vt prefer. **de ~encia** preferably

prefigurar vt foreshadow

prefij|ar vt fix beforehand; (gram) prefix. **~o** m prefix; (telefónico) dialling code

preg|ón m announcement. **~onar** vt announce

pregunta f question. **~r** vt/i ask. **~rse** vpr wonder. **hacer ~s** ask questions

prehistórico a prehistoric

preju|icio m prejudice. **~zgar** [12] vt prejudge

prelado m prelate

preliminar a & m preliminary

preludio m prelude

premarital a, **prematrimonial** a premarital

prematuro a premature

premedita|ción f premeditation. **~r** vt premeditate

premi|ar vt give a prize to; (recompensar) reward. **~o** m prize; (recompensa) reward; (com) premium. **~o gordo** first prize

premonición f premonition

premura f urgency; (falta) lack

prenatal a antenatal

prenda f pledge; (de vestir) article of clothing, garment; (de cama etc) linen. **~s** fpl (cualidades) talents; (juego) forfeits. **~r** vt captivate. **~rse** vpr be captivated (de by); (enamorarse) fall in love (de with)

prender vt capture; (sujetar) fasten. ● vi catch; (arraigar) take root. **~se** vpr (encenderse) catch fire

prensa f press. **~r** vt press

preñado a pregnant; (fig) full

preocupa|ción f worry. **~do** a worried. **~r** vt worry. **~rse** vpr worry.

~rse de look after. **¡no te preocupes!** don't worry!

prepara|ción f preparation. **~do** a prepared. ● m preparation. **~r** vt prepare. **~rse** vpr get ready. **~tivo** a preparatory. ● m preparation. **~torio** a preparatory

preponderancia f preponderance

preposición f preposition

prepotente a powerful; (fig) presumptuous

prerrogativa f prerogative

presa f (acción) capture; (cosa) catch; (embalse) dam

presagi|ar vt presage. **~o** m omen; (premonición) premonition

présbita a long-sighted

presb|iteriano a & m Presbyterian. **~iterio** m presbytery. **~ítero** m priest

prescindir vi. **~ de** do without; (deshacerse de) dispense with

prescri|bir (pp **prescrito**) vt prescribe. **~pción** f prescription

presencia f presence; (aspecto) appearance. **~r** vt be present at; (ver) witness. **en ~ de** in the presence of

presenta|ble a presentable. **~ción** f presentation; (aspecto) appearance; (de una persona a otra) introduction. **~dor** m presenter. **~r** vt present; (ofrecer) offer; (hacer conocer) introduce; show (película). **~rse** vpr present o.s.; (hacer conocer) introduce o.s.; (aparecer) turn up

presente a present; (este) this. ● m present. **los ~s** those present. **tener ~** remember

presenti|miento m presentiment; (de algo malo) foreboding. **~r** [4] vt have a presentiment of

preserva|ción f preservation. **~r** vt preserve. **~tivo** m condom

presiden|cia f presidency; (de asamblea) chairmanship. **~cial** a presidential. **~ta** f (woman) president. **~te** m president; (de asamblea) chairman. **~te del gobierno** leader of the government, prime minister

presidi|ario m convict. **~o** m prison

presidir vt preside over

presilla f fastener

presi|ón f pressure. **~onar** vt press; (fig) put pressure on. **a ~ón** under pressure. **hacer ~ón** press

preso a under arrest; (fig) stricken. ● m prisoner

presta|do *a* (*a uno*) lent; (*de uno*) borrowed. **~mista** *f* & *m* moneylender. **pedir ~do** borrow

préstamo *m* loan; (*acción de pedir prestado*) borrowing

prestar *vt* lend; give ⟨*ayuda etc*⟩; pay ⟨*atención*⟩. ● *vi* lend

prestidigita|ción *f* conjuring. **~dor** *m* magician

prestigio *m* prestige. **~so** *a* prestigious

presu|mido *a* presumptuous. **~mir** *vt* presume. ● *vi* be conceited. **~nción** *f* presumption. **~nto** *a* presumed. **~ntuoso** *a* presumptuous

presup|oner [34] *vt* presuppose. **~uesto** *m* budget

presuroso *a* quick

preten|cioso *a* pretentious. **~der** *vt* try to; (*afirmar*) claim; (*solicitar*) apply for; (*cortejar*) court. **~dido** *a* so-called. **~diente** *m* pretender; (*a una mujer*) suitor. **~sión** *f* pretension; (*aspiración*) aspiration

pretérito *m* preterite, past

pretexto *m* pretext. **a ~ de** on the pretext of

prevalec|er [11] *vi* prevail. **~iente** *a* prevalent

prevalerse [42] *vpr* take advantage

preven|ción *f* prevention; (*prejuicio*) prejudice. **~ido** *a* ready; (*precavido*) cautious. **~ir** [53] *vt* prepare; (*proveer*) provide; (*precaver*) prevent; (*advertir*) warn. **~tivo** *a* preventive

prever [43] *vt* foresee; (*prepararse*) plan

previo *a* previous

previs|ible *a* predictable. **~ión** *f* forecast; (*prudencia*) prudence. **~ión de tiempo** weather forecast. **~to** *a* foreseen

prima *f* (*pariente*) cousin; (*cantidad*) bonus

primario *a* primary

primate *m* primate; (*fig, persona*) important person

primavera *f* spring. **~l** *a* spring

primer *a* véase **primero**

primer|a *f* (*auto*) first (gear); (*en tren etc*) first class. **~o** *a* (*delante de nombre masculino en singular* **primer**) first; (*principal*) main; (*anterior*) former; (*mejor*) best. ● *n* (the) first. ● *adv* first. **~a enseñanza** primary education. **a ~os de** at the beginning of. **de ~a** first-class

primitivo *a* primitive

primo *m* cousin; (*fam*) fool. **hacer el ~** be taken for a ride

primogénito *a* & *m* first-born, eldest

primor *m* delicacy; (*cosa*) beautiful thing

primordial *a* basic

princesa *f* princess

principado *m* principality

principal *a* principal. ● *m* (*jefe*) head, boss (*fam*)

príncipe *m* prince

principi|ante *m* & *f* beginner. **~ar** *vt/i* begin, start. **~o** *m* beginning; (*moral, idea*) principle; (*origen*) origin. **al ~o** at first. **a ~o(s) de** at the beginning of. **dar ~o a** a start. **desde el ~o** from the outset. **en ~o** in principle. **~os** *mpl* (*nociones*) rudiments

pring|oso *a* greasy. **~ue** *m* dripping; (*mancha*) grease mark

prior *m* prior. **~ato** *m* priory

prioridad *f* priority

prisa *f* hurry, haste. **a ~** quickly. **a toda ~** (*fam*) as quickly as possible. **correr ~** be urgent. **darse ~** hurry (up). **de ~** quickly. **tener ~** be in a hurry

prisi|ón *f* prison; (*encarcelamiento*) imprisonment. **~onero** *m* prisoner

prism|a *m* prism. **~áticos** *mpl* binoculars

priva|ción *f* deprivation. **~do** *a* (*particular*) private. **~r** *vt* deprive (**de** of); (*prohibir*) prevent (**de** from). ● *vi* be popular. **~tivo** *a* exclusive (**de** to)

privilegi|ado *a* privileged; (*muy bueno*) exceptional. **~o** *m* privilege

pro *prep* for. ● *m* advantage. ● *pref* pro-. **el ~ y el contra** the pros and cons. **en ~ de** on behalf of. **los ~s y los contras** the pros and cons

proa *f* bows

probab|ilidad *f* probability. **~le** *a* probable, likely. **~lemente** *adv* probably

proba|dor *m* fitting-room. **~r** [2] *vt* try; try on ⟨*ropa*⟩; (*demostrar*) prove. ● *vi* try. **~rse** *vpr* try on

probeta *f* test-tube

problem|a *m* problem. **~ático** *a* problematic

procaz *a* insolent

proced|encia *f* origin. **~ente** *a* (*razonable*) reasonable. **~ente de** (coming) from. **~er** *m* conduct. ● *vi* proceed. **~er contra** start legal proceedings against. **~er de** come from.

~**imiento** *m* procedure; (*sistema*) process; (*jurid*) proceedings

procesador *m*. ~ **de textos** word processor

procesal *a*. **costas** ~**es** legal costs

procesamiento *m* processing. ~ **de textos** word-processing

procesar *vt* prosecute

procesión *f* procession

proceso *m* process; (*jurid*) trial; (*transcurso*) course

proclama *f* proclamation. ~**ción** *f* proclamation. ~**r** *vt* proclaim

procrea|ción *f* procreation. ~**r** *vt* procreate

procura|dor *m* attorney, solicitor. ~**r** *vt* try; (*obtener*) get; (*dar*) give

prodigar [12] *vt* lavish. ~**se** *vpr* do one's best

prodigio *m* prodigy; (*milagro*) miracle. ~**ioso** *a* prodigious

pródigo *a* prodigal

produc|ción *f* production. ~**ir** [47] *vt* produce; (*causar*) cause. ~**irse** *vpr* (*aparecer*) appear; (*suceder*) happen. ~**tivo** *a* productive. ~**to** *m* product. ~**tor** *m* producer. ~**to derivado** by-product. ~**tos agrícolas** farm produce. ~**tos de belleza** cosmetics. ~**tos de consumo** consumer goods

proeza *f* exploit

profan|ación *f* desecration. ~**ar** *vt* desecrate. ~**o** *a* profane

profecía *f* prophecy

proferir [4] *vt* utter; hurl (*insultos etc*)

profes|ar *vt* profess; practise (*profesión*). ~**ión** *f* profession. ~**ional** *a* professional. ~**or** *m* teacher; (*en universidad etc*) lecturer. ~**orado** *m* teaching profession; (*conjunto de profesores*) staff

prof|eta *m* prophet. ~**ético** *a* prophetic. ~**etizar** [10] *vt/i* prophesize

prófugo *a* & *m* fugitive

profund|idad *f* depth. ~**o** *a* deep; (*fig*) profound

profus|ión *f* profusion. ~**o** *a* profuse. **con** ~**ión** profusely

progenie *f* progeny

programa *m* programme; (*de ordenador*) program; (*de estudios*) curriculum. ~**ción** *f* programming; (*TV etc*) programmes; (*en periódico*) TV guide. ~**r** *vt* programme; program (*ordenador*). ~**dor** *m* computer programmer

progres|ar *vi* (make) progress. ~**ión** *f* progression. ~**ista** *a* progressive. ~**ivo** *a* progressive. ~**o** *m* progress. **hacer** ~**os** make progress

prohibi|ción *f* prohibition. ~**do** *a* forbidden. ~**r** *vt* forbid. ~**tivo** *a* prohibitive

prójimo *m* fellow man

prole *f* offspring

proletari|ado *m* proletariat. ~**o** *a* & *m* proletarian

prol|iferación *f* proliferation. ~**iferar** *vi* proliferate. ~**ífico** *a* prolific

prolijo *a* long-winded, extensive

prólogo *m* prologue

prolongar [12] *vt* prolong; (*alargar*) lengthen. ~**se** *vpr* go on

promedio *m* average

prome|sa *f* promise. ~**ter** *vt/i* promise. ~**terse** *vpr* (*novios*) get engaged. ~**térselas muy felices** have high hopes. ~**tida** *f* fiancée. ~**tido** *a* promised; (*novios*) engaged. ● *m* fiancé

prominen|cia *f* prominence. ~**te** *a* prominent

promiscu|idad *f* promiscuity. ~**o** *a* promiscuous

promoción *f* promotion

promontorio *m* promontory

promo|tor *m* promoter. ~**ver** [2] *vt* promote; (*causar*) cause

promulgar [12] *vt* promulgate

pronombre *m* pronoun

pron|osticar [7] *vt* predict. ~**óstico** *m* prediction; (*del tiempo*) forecast; (*med*) prognosis

pront|itud *f* quickness. ~**o** *a* quick; (*preparado*) ready. ● *adv* quickly; (*dentro de poco*) soon; (*temprano*) early. ● *m* urge. **al** ~**o** at first. **de** ~**o** suddenly. **por lo** ~**o** for the time being; (*al menos*) anyway. **tan** ~**o como** as soon as

pronuncia|ción *f* pronunciation. ~**miento** *m* revolt. ~**r** *vt* pronounce; deliver (*discurso*). ~**rse** *vpr* be pronounced; (*declararse*) declare o.s.; (*sublevarse*) rise up

propagación *f* propagation

propaganda *f* propaganda; (*anuncios*) advertising

propagar [12] *vt/i* propagate. ~**se** *vpr* spread

propano *m* propane

propasarse *vpr* go too far

propens|ión *f* inclination. ~**o** *a* inclined

propiamente *adv* exactly
propici|ar *vt* (*provocar*) cause, bring about. **~o** *a* favourable
propie|dad *f* property; (*posesión*) possession. **~tario** *m* owner
propina *f* tip
propio *a* own; (*característico*) typical; (*natural*) natural; (*apropiado*) proper. **de ~** on purpose. **el médico ~** the doctor himself
proponer [34] *vt* propose. **~se** *vpr* propose
proporci|ón *f* proportion. **~onado** *a* proportioned. **~onal** *a* proportional. **~onar** *vt* proportion; (*facilitar*) provide
proposición *f* proposition
propósito *m* intention. **a ~** (*adrede*) on purpose; (*de paso*) incidentally. **a ~ de** with regard to. **de ~** on purpose
propuesta *f* proposal
propuls|ar *vt* propel; (*fig*) promote. **~ión** *f* propulsion. **~ión a chorro** jet propulsion
prórroga *f* extension
prorrogar [12] *vt* extend
prorrumpir *vi* burst out
prosa *f* prose. **~ico** *a* prosaic
proscri|bir (*pp* proscrito) *vt* banish; (*prohibido*) ban. **~to** *a* banned. ● *m* exile; (*persona*) outlaw
prosecución *f* continuation
proseguir [5 & 13] *vt/i* continue
prospección *f* prospecting
prospecto *m* prospectus
prosper|ar *vi* prosper. **~idad** *f* prosperity; (*éxito*) success
próspero *a* prosperous. **¡P~ Año Nuevo!** Happy New Year!
prostit|ución *f* prostitution. **~uta** *f* prostitute
protagonista *m & f* protagonist
prote|cción *f* protection. **~ctor** *a* protective. ● *m* protector; (*patrocinador*) patron. **~ger** [14] *vt* protect. **~gida** *f* protegée. **~gido** *a* protected. ● *m* protegé
proteína *f* protein
protesta *f* protest; (*declaración*) protestation
protestante *a & m & f* (*relig*) Protestant
protestar *vt/i* protest
protocolo *m* protocol
protuberan|cia *f* protuberance. **~te** *a* protuberant

provecho *m* benefit. **¡buen ~!** enjoy your meal! **de ~** useful. **en ~ de** to the benefit of. **sacar ~ de** benefit from
proveer [18] (*pp* proveído *y* provisto) *vt* supply, provide
provenir [53] *vi* come (**de** from)
proverbi|al *a* proverbial. **~o** *m* proverb
providencia *f* providence. **~l** *a* providential
provincia *f* province. **~l** *a*, **~no** *a* provincial
provisi|ón *f* provision; (*medida*) measure. **~onal** *a* provisional
provisto *a* provided (**de** with)
provoca|ción *f* provocation. **~r** [7] *vt* provoke; (*causar*) cause. **~tivo** *a* provocative
próximamente *adv* soon
proximidad *f* proximity
próximo *a* next; (*cerca*) near
proyec|ción *f* projection. **~tar** *vt* hurl; cast ‹*luz*›; show ‹*película*›. **~til** *m* missile. **~to** *m* plan. **~to de ley** bill. **~tor** *m* projector. **en ~to** planned
pruden|cia *f* prudence. **~nte** *a* prudent, sensible
prueba *f* proof; (*examen*) test; (*de ropa*) fitting. **a ~** on trial. **a ~ de** proof against. **a ~ de agua** waterproof. **en ~ de** in proof of. **poner a ~** test
pruebo *vb véase* **probar**
psicoan|álisis *f* psychoanalysis. **~alista** *m & f* psychoanalyst. **~alizar** [10] *vt* psychoanalyse
psicodélico *a* psychedelic
psic|ología *f* psychology. **~ológico** *a* psychological. **~ólogo** *m* psychologist
psicópata *m & f* psychopath
psicosis *f* psychosis
psique *f* psyche
psiqui|atra *m & f* psychiatrist. **~atría** *f* psychiatry. **~átrico** *a* psychiatric
psíquico *a* psychic
ptas, pts *abrev* (*pesetas*) pesetas
púa *f* sharp point; (*bot*) thorn; (*de erizo*) quill; (*de peine*) tooth; (*mus*) plectrum
pubertad *f* puberty
publica|ción *f* publication. **~r** [7] *vt* publish; (*anunciar*) announce
publici|dad *f* publicity; (*com*) advertising. **~tario** *a* advertising

público *a* public. ● *m* public; (*de espectáculo etc*) audience. **dar al ~** publish

puchero *m* cooking pot; (*guisado*) stew. **hacer ~s** (*fig, fam*) pout

pude *vb véase* **poder**

púdico *a* modest

pudiente *a* rich

pudín *m* pudding

pudor *m* modesty. **~oso** *a* modest

pudrir (*pp* **podrido**) *vt* rot; (*fig, molestar*) annoy. **~se** *vpr* rot

puebl|ecito *m* small village. **~o** *m* town; (*aldea*) village; (*nación*) nation, people

puedo *vb véase* **poder**

puente *m* bridge; (*fig, fam*) long weekend. **~ colgante** suspension bridge. **~ levadizo** drawbridge. **hacer ~** (*fam*) have a long weekend

puerco *a* filthy; (*grosero*) coarse. ● *m* pig. **~ espín** porcupine

pueril *a* childish

puerro *m* leek

puerta *f* door; (*en deportes*) goal; (*de ciudad*) gate. **~ principal** main entrance. **a ~ cerrada** behind closed doors

puerto *m* port; (*fig, refugio*) refuge; (*entre montañas*) pass. **~ franco** free port

Puerto Rico *m* Puerto Rico

puertorriqueño *a & m* Puerto Rican

pues *adv* (*entonces*) then; (*bueno*) well. ● *conj* since

puest|a *f* setting; (*en juegos*) bet. **~a de sol** sunset. **~a en escena** staging. **~a en marcha** starting. **~o** *a* put; (*vestido*) dressed. ● *m* place; (*empleo*) position, job; (*en mercado etc*) stall. ● *conj*. **~o que** since. **~o de socorro** first aid post

pugna *f* fight. **~r** *vt* fight

puja *f* effort; (*en subasta*) bid. **~r** *vt* struggle; (*en subasta*) bid

pulcro *a* neat

pulga *f* flea; (*de juego*) tiddly-wink. **tener malas ~s** be bad-tempered

pulga|da *f* inch. **~r** *m* thumb; (*del pie*) big toe

puli|do *a* neat. **~mentar** *vt* polish. **~mento** *m* polishing; (*substancia*) polish. **~r** *vt* polish; (*suavizar*) smooth

pulm|ón *m* lung. **~onar** *a* pulmonary. **~onía** *f* pneumonia

pulpa *f* pulp

pulpería *f* (*LAm*) grocer's shop (*Brit*), grocery store (*Amer*)

púlpito *m* pulpit

pulpo *m* octopus

pulque *m* (*Mex*) pulque, alcoholic Mexican drink

pulsa|ción *f* pulsation. **~dor** *a* pulsating. ● *m* button. **~r** *vt* (*mus*) play

pulsera *f* bracelet; (*de reloj*) strap

pulso *m* pulse; (*muñeca*) wrist; (*firmeza*) steady hand; (*fuerza*) strength; (*fig, tacto*) tact. **tomar el ~ a uno** take s.o.'s pulse

pulular *vi* teem with

pulveriza|dor *m* (*de perfume*) atomizer. **~r** [10] *vt* pulverize; atomize ‹*líquido*›

pulla *f* cutting remark

pum *int* bang!

puma *m* puma

puna *f* puna, high plateau

punitivo *a* punitive

punta *f* point; (*extremo*) tip; (*clavo*) (small) nail. **estar de ~** be in a bad mood. **estar de ~ con uno** be at odds with s.o. **ponerse de ~ con uno** fall out with s.o. **sacar ~ a** sharpen; (*fig*) find fault with

puntada *f* stitch

puntal *m* prop, support

puntapié *m* kick

puntear *vt* mark; (*mus*) pluck

puntera *f* toe

puntería *f* aim; (*destreza*) markmanship

puntiagudo *a* sharp, pointed

puntilla *f* (*encaje*) lace. **de ~s** on tiptoe

punto *m* point; (*señal*) dot; (*de examen*) mark; (*lugar*) spot, place; (*de taxis*) stand; (*momento*) moment; (*punto final*) full stop (*Brit*), period (*Amer*); (*puntada*) stitch; (*de tela*) mesh. **~ de admiración** exclamation mark. **~ de arranque** starting point. **~ de exclamación** exclamation mark. **~ de interrogación** question mark. **~ de vista** point of view. **~ final** full stop. **~ muerto** (*auto*) neutral (gear). **~ y aparte** full stop, new paragraph (*Brit*), period, new paragraph (*Amer*). **~ y coma** semicolon. **a ~** on time; (*listo*) ready. **a ~ de** on the point of. **de ~** knitted. **dos ~s** colon. **en ~** exactly. **hacer ~** knit. **hasta cierto ~** to a certain extent

puntuación f punctuation; (en deportes, acción) scoring; (en deportes, número de puntos) score

puntual a punctual; (exacto) accurate. ∼**idad** f punctuality; (exactitud) accuracy

puntuar [21] vt punctuate. ● vi score

punza|da f prick; (dolor) pain; (fig) pang. ∼**nte** a sharp. ∼**r** [10] vt prick

puñado m handful. **a** ∼**s** by the handful

puñal m dagger. ∼**ada** f stab

puñ|etazo m punch. ∼**o** m fist; (de ropa) cuff; (mango) handle. **de su** ∼**o (y letra)** in his own handwriting

pupa f spot; (en los labios) cold sore. **hacer** ∼ hurt. **hacerse** ∼ hurt o.s.

pupila f pupil

pupitre m desk

puquío m (Arg) spring

puré m purée; (sopa) thick soup. ∼ **de patatas** mashed potatoes

pureza f purity

purga f purge. ∼**r** [12] vt purge. ∼**torio** m purgatory

purifica|ción f purification. ∼**r** [7] vt purify

purista m & f purist

puritano a puritanical. ● m puritan

puro a pure; (cielo) clear; (fig) simple. ● m cigar. **de** ∼ so. **de pura casualidad** by sheer chance

púrpura f purple

purpúreo a purple

pus m pus

puse vb véase **poner**

pusilánime a cowardly

pústula f spot

puta f whore

putrefacción f putrefaction

pútrido a rotten, putrid

Q

que pron rel (personas, sujeto) who; (personas, complemento) whom; (cosas) which, that. ● conj that. **¡**∼ **tengan Vds buen viaje!** have a good journey! **¡**∼ **venga!** let him come! ∼ **venga o no venga** whether he comes or not. **a** ∼ I bet. **creo** ∼ **tiene razón** I think (that) he is right. **de** ∼ from which. **yo** ∼ **tú** if I were you

qué a (con sustantivo) what; (con a o adv) how. ● pron what. **¡**∼ **bonito!**

how nice. **¿en** ∼ **piensas?** what are you thinking about?

quebra|da f gorge; (paso) pass. ∼**dizo** a fragile. ∼**do** a broken; (com) bankrupt. ● m (math) fraction. ∼**dura** f fracture; (hondonada) gorge. ∼**ntar** vt break; (debilitar) weaken. ∼**nto** m (pérdida) loss; (daño) damage. ∼**r** [1] vt break. ● vi break; (com) go bankrupt. ∼**rse** vpr break

quechua a & m & f Quechuan

queda f curfew

quedar vi stay, remain; (estar) be; (faltar, sobrar) be left. ∼ **bien** come off well. ∼**se** vpr stay. ∼ **con** arrange to meet. ∼ **en** agree to. ∼ **en nada** come to nothing. ∼ **por** (+ infinitivo) remain to be (+ pp)

quehacer m job. ∼**es domésticos** household chores

quej|a f complaint; (de dolor) moan. ∼**arse** vpr complain (de about); (gemir) moan. ∼**ido** m moan. ∼**oso** a complaining

quema|do a burnt; (fig, fam) bitter. ∼**dor** m burner. ∼**dura** f burn. ∼**r** vt burn; (prender fuego a) set fire to. ● vi burn. ∼**rse** vpr burn o.s.; (consumirse) burn up; (con el sol) get sunburnt. ∼**rropa** adv. **a** ∼**rropa** pointblank

quena f Indian flute

quepo vb véase **caber**

queque m (Mex) cake

querella f (riña) quarrel, dispute; (juríd) charge

quer|er [35] vt want; (amar) love; (necesitar) need. ∼**er decir** mean. ∼**ido** a dear; (amado) loved. ● m darling; (amante) lover. **como quiera que** since; (de cualquier modo) however. **cuando quiera que** whenever. **donde quiera** wherever. **¿quieres darme ese libro?** would you pass me that book? **quiere llover** it's trying to rain. **¿quieres un helado?** would you like an ice-cream? **quisiera ir a la playa** I'd like to go to the beach. **sin** ∼**er** without meaning to

queroseno m kerosene

querubín m cherub

ques|adilla f cheesecake; (Mex, empanadilla) pie. ∼**o** m cheese. ∼**o de bola** Edam cheese

quiá int never!, surely not!

quicio m frame. **sacar de** ∼ **a uno** infuriate s.o.

quiebra f break; (fig) collapse; (com) bankruptcy
quiebro m dodge
quien pron rel (sujeto) who; (complemento) whom
quién pron interrogativo (sujeto) who; (tras preposición) whom. ¿de ~? whose. ¿de ~ son estos libros? whose are these books?
quienquiera pron whoever
quiero vb véase **querer**
quiet|o a still; (inmóvil) motionless; ⟨carácter etc⟩ calm. ~ud f stillness
quijada f jaw
quilate m carat
quilla f keel
quimera f (fig) illusion
químic|a f chemistry. ~o a chemical. ● m chemist
quincalla f hardware; (de adorno) trinket
quince a & m fifteen. ~ días a fortnight. ~na f fortnight. ~nal a fortnightly
quincuagésimo a fiftieth
quiniela f pools coupon. ~s fpl (football) pools
quinientos a & m five hundred
quinino m quinine
quinqué m oil-lamp; (fig, fam) shrewdness
quinquenio m (period of) five years
quinta f (casa) villa
quintaesencia f quintessence
quintal m a hundred kilograms
quinteto m quintet
quinto a & m fifth
quiosco m kiosk; (en jardín) summerhouse; (en parque etc) bandstand
quirúrgico a surgical
quise vb véase **querer**
quisque pron. cada ~ (fam) (absolutely) everybody
quisquill|a f trifle; (camarón) shrimp. ~oso a irritable; (chinchorrero) fussy
quita|manchas m invar stain remover. ~nieves m invar snow plough. ~r vt remove, take away; take off ⟨ropa⟩; (robar) steal. ~ndo (a excepción de, fam) apart from. ~rse vpr be removed; take off ⟨ropa⟩. ~rse de (no hacerlo más) stop. ~rse de en medio get out of the way. ~sol m invar sunshade
Quito m Quito

quizá(s) adv perhaps
quórum m quorum

R

rábano m radish. ~ picante horse-radish. me importa un ~ I couldn't care less
rabi|a f rabies; (fig) rage. ~ar vi (de dolor) be in great pain; (estar enfadado) be furious; (fig, tener ganas, fam) long. ~ar por algo long for sth. ~ar por hacer algo long to do sth. ~eta f tantrum. dar ~a infuriate
rabino m Rabbi
rabioso a rabid; (furioso) furious; ⟨dolor etc⟩ violent
rabo m tail
racial a racial
racimo m bunch
raciocinio m reason; (razonamiento) reasoning
ración f share, ration; (de comida) portion
racional a rational. ~izar [10] vt rationalize
racionar vt (limitar) ration; (repartir) ration out
racis|mo m racism. ~ta a racist
racha f gust of wind; (fig) spate
radar m radar
radiación f radiation
radiactiv|idad f radioactivity. ~o a radioactive
radiador m radiator
radial a radial
radiante a radiant
radical a & m & f radical
radicar [7] vi (estar) be. ~ en (fig) lie in
radio m radius; (de rueda) spoke; (elemento metálico) radium. ● f radio
radioactiv|idad f radioactivity. ~o a radioactive
radio|difusión f broadcasting. ~emisora f radio station. ~escucha m & f listener
radiografía f radiography
radi|ología f radiology. ~ólogo m radiologist
radioterapia f radiotherapy
radioyente m & f listener
raer [36] vt scrape off
ráfaga f (de viento) gust; (de luz) flash; (de ametralladora) burst
rafia f raffia
raído a threadbare

raigambre f roots; (fig) tradition

raíz f root. **a ~ de** immediately after. **echar raíces** (fig) settle

raja f split; (culin) slice. **~r** vt split. **~rse** vpr split; (fig) back out

rajatabla. a ~ vigorously

ralea f sort

ralo a sparse

ralla|dor m grater. **~r** vt grate

rama f branch. **~je** m branches. **~l** m branch. **en ~** raw

rambla f gully; (avenida) avenue

ramera f prostitute

ramifica|ción f ramification. **~rse** [7] vpr branch out

ramilla f twig

ramillete m bunch

ramo m branch; (de flores) bouquet

rampa f ramp, slope

ramplón a vulgar

rana f frog. **ancas** fpl **de ~** frogs' legs. **no ser ~** not be stupid

rancio a rancid; (vino) old; (fig) ancient

ranch|ero m cook; (LAm, jefe de rancho) farmer. **~o** m (LAm) ranch, farm

rango m rank

ranúnculo m buttercup

ranura f groove; (para moneda) slot

rapar vt shave; crop (pelo)

rapaz a rapacious; (ave) of prey. ● m bird of prey

rapidez f speed

rápido a fast, quick. ● adv quickly. ● m (tren) express. **~s** mpl rapids

rapiña f robbery. **ave** f **de ~** bird of prey

rapsodia f rhapsody

rapt|ar vt kidnap. **~o** m kidnapping; (de ira etc) fit; (éxtasis) ecstasy

raqueta f racquet

raramente adv seldom, rarely

rarefacción f rarefaction

rar|eza f rarity; (cosa rara) oddity. **~o** a rare; (extraño) odd. **es ~o que** it is strange that. **¡qué ~o!** how strange!

ras m. **a ~ de** level with

rasar vt level; (rozar) graze

rasca|cielos m invar skyscraper. **~dura** f scratch. **~r** [7] vt scratch; (raspar) scrape

rasgar [12] vt tear

rasgo m stroke. **~s** mpl (facciones) features

rasguear vt strum; (fig, escribir) write

rasguñ|ar vt scratch. **~o** m scratch

raso a (llano) flat; (liso) smooth; (cielo) clear; (cucharada etc) level; (vuelo etc) low. ● m satin. **al ~** in the open air. **soldado** m **~** private

raspa f (de pescado) backbone

raspa|dura f scratch; (acción) scratching. **~r** vt scratch; (rozar) scrape

rastr|a f rake. **a ~as** dragging. **~ear** vt track. **~eo** m dragging. **~ero** a creeping; (vuelo) low. **~illar** vt rake. **~illo** m rake. **~o** m rake; (huella) track; (señal) sign. **el R~o** the flea market in Madrid. **ni ~o** not a trace

rata f rat

rate|ar vt steal. **~ría** f pilfering. **~ro** m petty thief

ratifica|ción f ratification. **~r** [7] vt ratify

rato m moment, short time. **~s libres** spare time. **a ~s** at times. **hace un ~** a moment ago. **¡hasta otro ~!** (fam) see you soon! **pasar mal ~** have a rough time

rat|ón m mouse. **~onera** f mouse-trap; (madriguera) mouse hole

raud|al m torrent; (fig) floods. **~o** a swift

raya f line; (lista) stripe; (de pelo) parting. **~r** vt rule. ● vi border (con on). **a ~s** striped. **pasar de la ~** go too far

rayo m ray; (descarga eléctrica) lightning. **~s X** X-rays

raza f race; (de animal) breed. **de ~** (caballo) thoroughbred; (perro) pedigree

raz|ón f reason. **a ~ón de** at the rate of. **perder la ~ón** go out of one's mind. **tener ~ón** be right. **~onable** a reasonable. **~onamiento** m reasoning. **~onar** vt reason out. ● vi reason

re m D; (solfa) re

reac|ción f reaction. **~cionario** a & m reactionary. **~ción en cadena** chain reaction. **~tor** m reactor; (avión) jet

real a real; (de rey etc) royal. ● m real, old Spanish coin

realce m relief; (fig) splendour

realidad f reality; (verdad) truth. **en ~** in fact

realis|mo m realism. **~ta** a realistic. ● m & f realist; (monárquico) royalist

realiza|ción f fulfilment. **~r** [10] vt carry out; make (viaje); achieve

⟨meta⟩; ⟨vender⟩ sell. **~rse** vpr ⟨plan etc⟩ be carried out; ⟨sueño, predicción etc⟩ come true; ⟨persona⟩ fulfil o.s.

realzar [10] vt ⟨fig⟩ enhance

reanima|ción f revival. **~r** vt revive. **~rse** vpr revive

reanudar vt resume; renew ⟨amistad⟩

reaparecer [11] vi reappear

rearm|ar vt rearm. **~e** m rearmament

reavivar vt revive

rebaja f reduction. **~do** a ⟨precio⟩ reduced. **~r** vt lower. **en ~s** in the sale

rebanada f slice

rebaño m herd; ⟨de ovejas⟩ flock

rebasar vt exceed; ⟨dejar atrás⟩ leave behind

rebatir vt refute

rebel|arse vpr rebel. **~de** a rebellious. ● m rebel. **~día** f rebelliousness. **~ión** f rebellion

reblandecer [11] vt soften

rebosa|nte a overflowing. **~r** vi overflow; ⟨abundar⟩ abound

rebot|ar vt bounce; ⟨rechazar⟩ repel. ● vi bounce; ⟨bala⟩ ricochet. **~e** m bounce, rebound. **de ~e** on the rebound

rebozar [10] vt wrap up; ⟨culin⟩ coat in batter

rebullir [22] vi stir

rebusca|do a affected. **~r** [7] vt search thoroughly

rebuznar vi bray

recabar vt claim

recado m errand; ⟨mensaje⟩ message. **dejar ~** leave a message

reca|er [29] vi fall back; ⟨med⟩ relapse; ⟨fig⟩ fall. **~ída** f relapse

recalcar [7] vt squeeze; ⟨fig⟩ stress

recalcitrante a recalcitrant

recalentar [1] vt ⟨de nuevo⟩ reheat; ⟨demasiado⟩ overheat

recamar vt embroider

recámara f small room; ⟨de arma de fuego⟩ chamber; ⟨LAm, dormitorio⟩ bedroom

recambio m change; ⟨de pluma etc⟩ refill. **~s** mpl spare parts. **de ~** spare

recapitula|ción f summing up. **~r** vt sum up

recarg|ar [12] vt overload; ⟨aumentar⟩ increase; recharge ⟨batería⟩. **~o** m increase

recat|ado a modest. **~ar** vt hide. **~arse** vpr hide o.s. away; ⟨actuar

discretamente⟩ act discreetly. **~o** m prudence; ⟨modestia⟩ modesty. **sin ~arse, sin ~o** openly

recauda|ción f ⟨cantidad⟩ takings. **~dor** m tax collector. **~r** vt collect

recel|ar vt/i suspect. **~o** m distrust; ⟨temor⟩ fear. **~oso** a suspicious

recepci|ón f reception. **~onista** m & f receptionist

receptáculo m receptacle

recept|ivo a receptive. **~or** m receiver

recesión f recession

receta f recipe; ⟨med⟩ prescription

recib|imiento m ⟨acogida⟩ welcome. **~ir** vt receive; ⟨acoger⟩ welcome. ● vi entertain. **~irse** vpr graduate. **~o** m receipt. **acusar ~o** acknowledge receipt

reci|én adv recently; ⟨casado, nacido etc⟩ newly. **~ente** a recent; ⟨culin⟩ fresh

recinto m enclosure

recio a strong; ⟨voz⟩ loud. ● adv hard; ⟨en voz alta⟩ loudly

recipiente m ⟨persona⟩ recipient; ⟨cosa⟩ receptacle

recíproco a reciprocal. **a la recíproca** vice versa

recita|l m recital; ⟨de poesías⟩ reading. **~r** vt recite

reclama|ción f claim; ⟨queja⟩ complaint. **~r** vt claim. ● vi appeal

reclinar vi lean. **~se** vpr lean

reclu|ir [17] vt shut away. **~sión** f seclusion; ⟨cárcel⟩ prison. **~so** m prisoner

recluta m recruit. ● f recruitment. **~miento** m recruitment; ⟨conjunto de reclutas⟩ recruits. **~r** vt recruit

recobrar vt recover. **~se** vpr recover

recodo m bend

recog|er [14] vt collect; pick up ⟨cosa caída⟩; ⟨cosechar⟩ harvest; ⟨dar asilo⟩ shelter. **~erse** vpr withdraw; ⟨ir a casa⟩ go home; ⟨acostarse⟩ go to bed. **~ida** f collection; ⟨cosecha⟩ harvest. **~ido** a withdrawn; ⟨pequeño⟩ small

recolección f harvest

recomenda|ción f recommendation. **~r** [1] vt recommend; ⟨encomendar⟩ entrust

recomenzar [1 & 10] vt/i start again

recompensa f reward. **~r** vt reward

recomponer [34] vt mend

reconcilia|ción f reconciliation. **~r** vt reconcile. **~rse** vpr be reconciled

recóndito a hidden

reconoc|er [11] *vt* recognize; (*admitir*) acknowledge; (*examinar*) examine. **~imiento** *m* recognition; (*admisión*) acknowledgement; (*agradecimiento*) gratitude; (*examen*) examination

reconozco *vb véase* **reconocer**

reconquista *f* reconquest. **~r** *vt* reconquer; (*fig*) win back

reconsiderar *vt* reconsider

reconstitu|ir [17] *vt* reconstitute. **~yente** *m* tonic

reconstru|cción *f* reconstruction. **~ir** [17] *vt* reconstruct

récord /'rekor/ *m* record. **batir un ~** break a record

recordar [2] *vt* remember; (*hacer acordar*) remind; (*LAm, despertar*) wake up. ● *vi* remember. **que yo recuerde** as far as I remember. **si mal no recuerdo** if I remember rightly

recorr|er *vt* tour ‹*país*›; (*pasar por*) travel through; cover ‹*distancia*›; (*registrar*) look over. **~ido** *m* journey; (*itinerario*) route

recort|ado *a* jagged. **~ar** *vt* cut (out). **~e** *m* cutting (out); (*de periódico etc*) cutting

recoser *vt* mend

recostar [2] *vt* lean. **~se** *vpr* lie back

recoveco *m* bend; (*rincón*) nook

recre|ación *f* recreation. **~ar** *vt* re-create; (*divertir*) entertain. **~arse** *vpr* amuse o.s. **~ativo** *a* recreational. **~o** *m* recreation; (*escol*) break

recrimina|ción *f* recrimination. **~r** *vt* reproach

recrudecer [11] *vi* increase, worsen, get worse

recta *f* straight line

rect|angular *a* rectangular; ‹*triángulo*› right-angled. **~ángulo** *a* rectangular; ‹*triángulo*› right-angled. ● *m* rectangle

rectifica|ción *f* rectification. **~r** *vt* rectify

rect|itud *f* straightness; (*fig*) honesty. **~o** *a* straight; (*fig, justo*) fair; (*fig, honrado*) honest. ● *m* rectum. **todo ~o** straight on

rector *a* governing. ● *m* rector

recuadro *m* (*en periódico*) box

recubrir [*pp* **recubierto**] *vt* cover

recuerdo *m* memory; (*regalo*) souvenir. ● *vb véase* **recordar**. **~s** *mpl* (*saludos*) regards

recupera|ción *f* recovery. **~r** *vt* recover. **~rse** *vpr* recover. **~r el tiempo perdido** make up for lost time

recur|rir *vi*. **~rir a** resort to ‹*cosa*›; turn to ‹*persona*›. **~so** *m* resort; (*medio*) resource; (*jurid*) appeal. **~sos** *mpl* resources

recusar *vt* refuse

rechaz|ar [10] *vt* repel; reflect ‹*luz*›; (*no aceptar*) refuse; (*negar*) deny. **~o** *m*. **de ~o** on the rebound; (*fig*) consequently

rechifla *f* booing; (*burla*) derision

rechinar *vi* squeak; ‹*madera etc*› creak; ‹*dientes*› grind

rechistar *vt* murmur. **sin ~** without saying a word

rechoncho *a* stout

red *f* network; (*malla*) net; (*para equipaje*) luggage rack; (*fig, engaño*) trap

redac|ción *f* editing; (*conjunto de redactores*) editorial staff; (*oficina*) editorial office; (*escol, univ*) essay. **~tar** *vt* write. **~tor** *m* writer; (*de periódico*) editor

redada *f* casting; (*de policía*) raid

redecilla *f* small net; (*para el pelo*) hairnet

rededor *m*. **al ~**, **en ~** around

reden|ción *f* redemption. **~tor** *a* redeeming

redil *f* sheepfold

redimir *vt* redeem

rédito *m* interest

redoblar *vt* redouble; (*doblar*) bend back

redoma *f* flask

redomado *a* sly

redond|a *f* (*de imprenta*) roman (type); (*mus*) semibreve (*Brit*), whole note (*Amer*). **~amente** *adv* (*categóricamente*) flatly. **~ear** *vt* round off. **~el** *m* circle; (*de plaza de toros*) arena. **~o** *a* round; (*completo*) complete. ● *m* circle. **a la ~a** around. **en ~o** round; (*categóricamente*) flatly

reduc|ción *f* reduction. **~ido** *a* reduced; (*limitado*) limited; (*pequeño*) small; ‹*precio*› low. **~ir** [47] *vt* reduce. **~irse** *vpr* be reduced; (*fig*) amount

reduje *vb véase* **reducir**

redundan|cia *f* redundancy. **~te** *a* redundant

reduplicar [7] *vt* (*aumentar*) redouble

reduzco *vb véase* **reducir**

reedificar [7] *vt* reconstruct

reembols|ar *vt* reimburse. **~o** *m* repayment. **contra ~o** cash on delivery

reemplaz|ar [10] *vt* replace. **~o** *m* replacement

reemprender *vt* start again

reenviar [20] *vt*, **reexpedir** [5] *vt* forward

referencia *f* reference; (*información*) report. **con ~ a** with reference to. **hacer ~ a** refer to

referéndum *m* (*pl* **referéndums**) referendum

referir [4] *vt* tell; (*remitir*) refer. **~se** *vpr* refer. **por lo que se refiere a** as regards

refiero *vb véase* **referir**

refilón. de ~ obliquely

refin|amiento *m* refinement. **~ar** *vt* refine. **~ería** *f* refinery

reflector *m* reflector; (*proyector*) searchlight

reflej|ar *vt* reflect. **~o** *a* reflected; (*med*) reflex. ● *m* reflection; (*med*) reflex; (*en el pelo*) highlights

reflexi|ón *f* reflection. **~onar** *vi* reflect. **~vo** *a* ‹*persona*› thoughtful; (*gram*) reflexive. **con ~ón** on reflection. **sin ~ón** without thinking

reflujo *m* ebb

reforma *f* reform. **~s** *fpl* (*reparaciones*) repairs. **~r** *vt* reform. **~rse** *vpr* reform

reforzar [2 & 10] *vt* reinforce

refrac|ción *f* refraction. **~tar** *vt* refract. **~tario** *a* heat-resistant

refrán *m* saying

refregar [1 & 12] *vt* rub

refrenar *vt* rein in ‹*caballo*›; (*fig*) restrain

refrendar *vt* endorse

refresc|ar [7] *vt* refresh; (*enfriar*) cool. ● *vi* get cooler. **~arse** *vpr* refresh o.s.; (*salir*) go out for a walk. **~o** *m* cold drink. **~os** *mpl* refreshments

refrigera|ción *f* refrigeration; (*aire acondicionado*) air-conditioning. **~r** *vt* refrigerate. **~dor** *m*, **~dora** *f* refrigerator

refuerzo *m* reinforcement

refugi|ado *m* refugee. **~arse** *vpr* take refuge. **~o** *m* refuge, shelter

refulgir [14] *vi* shine

refundir *vt* (*fig*) revise, rehash

refunfuñar *vi* grumble

refutar *vt* refute

regadera *f* watering-can; (*Mex, ducha*) shower

regala|damente *adv* very well. **~do** *a* as a present, free; (*cómodo*) comfortable. **~r** *vt* give; (*agasajar*) treat very well. **~rse** *vpr* indulge o.s.

regaliz *m* liquorice

regalo *m* present, gift; (*placer*) joy; (*comodidad*) comfort

regañ|adientes. a ~adientes reluctantly. **~ar** *vt* scold. ● *vi* moan; (*dos personas*) quarrel. **~o** *m* (*reprensión*) scolding

regar [1 & 12] *vt* water

regata *f* regatta

regate *m* dodge; (*en deportes*) dribbling. **~ar** *vt* haggle over; (*economizar*) economize on. ● *vi* haggle; (*en deportes*) dribble. **~o** *m* haggling; (*en deportes*) dribbling

regazo *m* lap

regencia *f* regency

regenerar *vt* regenerate

regente *m & f* regent; (*director*) manager

régimen *m* (*pl* **regímenes**) rule; (*pol*) regime; (*med*) diet. **~ alimenticio** diet

regimiento *m* regiment

regio *a* royal

regi|ón *f* region. **~onal** *a* regional

regir [5 & 14] *vt* rule; govern ‹*país*›; run ‹*colegio, empresa*›. ● *vi* apply, be in force

registr|ado *a* registered. **~ador** *m* recorder; (*persona*) registrar. **~ar** *vt* register; (*grabar*) record; (*examinar*) search. **~arse** *vpr* register; (*darse*) be reported. **~o** *m* (*acción de registrar*) registration; (*libro*) register; (*cosa anotada*) entry; (*inspección*) search. **~o civil** (*oficina*) register office

regla *f* ruler; (*norma*) rule; (*menstruación*) period, menstruation. **~mentación** *f* regulation. **~mentar** *vt* regulate. **~mentario** *a* obligatory. **~mento** *m* regulations. **en ~** in order. **por ~ general** as a rule

regocij|ar *vt* delight. **~arse** *vpr* be delighted. **~o** *m* delight. **~os** *mpl* festivities

regode|arse *vpr* be delighted. **~o** *m* delight

regordete *a* chubby

regres|ar *vi* return. **~ión** *f* regression. **~ivo** *a* backward. **~o** *m* return

reguer|a f irrigation ditch. **~o** m irrigation ditch; (*señal*) trail

regula|dor m control. **~r** a regular; (*mediano*) average; (*no bueno*) so-so. ● vt regulate; (*controlar*) control. **~ridad** f regularity. **con ~ridad** regularly. **por lo ~r** as a rule

rehabilita|ción f rehabilitation; (*en un empleo etc*) reinstatement. **~r** vt rehabilitate; (*al empleo etc*) reinstate

rehacer [31] vt redo; (*repetir*) repeat; (*reparar*) repair. **~se** vpr recover

rehén m hostage

rehogar [12] vt sauté

rehuir [17] vt avoid

rehusar vt/i refuse

reimpr|esión f reprinting. **~imir** (*pp* **reimpreso**) vt reprint

reina f queen. **~do** m reign. **~nte** a ruling; (*fig*) prevailing. **~r** vi reign; (*fig*) prevail

reincidir vi relapse, repeat an offence

reino m kingdom. **R~ Unido** United Kingdom

reinstaurar vt restore

reintegr|ar vt reinstate (*persona*); refund (*cantidad*). **~arse** vpr return. **~o** m refund

reír [51] vi laugh. **~se** vpr laugh. **~se de** laugh at. **echarse a ~** burst out laughing

reivindica|ción f claim. **~r** [7] vt claim; (*restaurar*) restore

rej|a f grille, grating. **~illa** f grille, grating; (*red*) luggage rack; (*de mimbre*) wickerwork. **entre ~as** behind bars

rejuvenecer [11] vt/i rejuvenate. **~se** vpr be rejuvenated

relaci|ón f relation(ship); (*relato*) tale; (*lista*) list. **~onado** a concerning. **~onar** vt relate (**con** to). **~onarse** vpr be connected. **bien ~onado** well-connected. **con ~ón a, en ~ón a** in relation to. **hacer ~ón a** refer to

relaja|ción f relaxation; (*aflojamiento*) slackening. **~do** a loose. **~r** vt relax; (*aflojar*) slacken. **~rse** vpr relax

relamerse vpr lick one's lips

relamido a overdressed

rel|ámpago m (flash of) lightning. **~ampaguear** vi thunder; (*fig*) sparkle

relatar vt tell, relate

relativ|idad f relativity. **~o** a relative. **en lo ~o a** in relation to

relato m tale; (*informe*) report

relegar [12] vt relegate. **~ al olvido** forget about

relev|ante a outstanding. **~ar** vt relieve; (*substituir*) replace. **~o** m relief. **carrera** f **de ~os** relay race

relieve m relief; (*fig*) importance. **de ~** important. **poner de ~** emphasize

religi|ón f religion. **~osa** f nun. **~oso** a religious. ● m monk

relinch|ar vi neigh. **~o** m neigh

reliquia f relic

reloj m clock; (*de bolsillo o pulsera*) watch. **~ de caja** grandfather clock. **~ de pulsera** wrist-watch. **~ de sol** sundial. **~ despertador** alarm clock. **~ería** f watchmaker's (shop). **~ero** m watchmaker

reluci|ente a shining. **~r** [11] vi shine; (*destellar*) sparkle

relumbrar vi shine

rellano m landing

rellen|ar vt refill; (*culin*) stuff; fill in (*formulario*). **~o** a full up; (*culin*) stuffed. ● m filling; (*culin*) stuffing

remach|ar vt rivet; (*fig*) drive home. **~e** m rivet

remangar [12] vt roll up

remanso m pool; (*fig*) haven

remar vi row

remat|ado a (*total*) complete; (*niño*) very naughty. **~ar** vt finish off; (*agotar*) use up; (*com*) sell off cheap. **~e** m end; (*fig*) finishing touch. **de ~e** completely

remedar vt imitate

remedi|ar vt remedy; (*ayudar*) help; (*poner fin a*) put a stop to; (*fig, resolver*) solve. **~o** m remedy; (*fig*) solution. **como último ~o** as a last resort. **no hay más ~o** there's no other way. **no tener más ~o** have no choice

remedo m imitation

rem|endar [1] vt repair. **~iendo** m patch; (*fig, mejora*) improvement

remilg|ado a fussy; (*afectado*) affected. **~o** m fussiness; (*afectación*) affectation

reminiscencia f reminiscence

remirar vt look again at

remisión f sending; (*referencia*) reference; (*perdón*) forgiveness

remiso a remiss

remit|e m sender's name and address. **~ente** m sender. **~ir** vt send; (*referir*) refer. ● vi diminish

remo *m* oar

remoj|ar *vt* soak; (*fig, fam*) celebrate. ~o *m* soaking. **poner a** ~o soak

remolacha *f* beetroot. ~ **azucarera** sugar beet

remolcar [7] *vt* tow

remolino *m* swirl; (*de aire etc*) whirl; (*de gente*) throng

remolque *m* towing; (*cabo*) towrope; (*vehículo*) trailer. **a** ~ on tow. **dar** ~ **a** tow

remontar *vt* mend. ~**se** *vpr* soar; (*con tiempo*) go back to

rémora *f* (*fig*) hindrance

remord|er [2] *vi* (*fig*) worry. ~**imiento** *m* remorse. **tener** ~**imientos** feel remorse

remoto *a* remote

remover [2] *vt* move; stir (*líquido*); turn over (*tierra*); (*quitar*) remove; (*fig, activar*) revive

remozar [10] *vt* rejuvenate (*persona*); renovate (*edificio etc*)

remunera|ción *f* remuneration. ~**r** *vt* remunerate

renac|er [11] *vi* be reborn; (*fig*) revive. ~**imiento** *m* rebirth. **R**~ Renaissance

renacuajo *m* tadpole; (*fig*) tiddler

rencilla *f* quarrel

rencor *m* bitterness. ~**oso** *a* (*estar*) resentful; (*ser*) spiteful. **guardar** ~ **a** have a grudge against

rendi|ción *f* surrender. ~**do** *a* submissive; (*agotado*) exhausted

rendija *f* crack

rendi|miento *m* efficiency; (*com*) yield. ~**r** [5] *vt* yield; (*vencer*) defeat; (*agotar*) exhaust; pay (*homenaje*). ● *vi* pay; (*producir*) produce. ~**rse** *vpr* surrender

renega|do *a & m* renegade. ~**r** [1 & 12] *vt* deny. ● *vi* grumble. ~**r de** renounce (*fe etc*); disown (*personas*)

RENFE *abrev* (*Red Nacional de los Ferrocarriles Españoles*) Spanish National Railways

renglón *m* line; (*com*) item. **a** ~ **seguido** straight away

reno *m* reindeer

renombr|ado *a* renowned. ~**e** *m* renown

renova|ción *f* renewal; (*de edificio*) renovation; (*de cuarto*) decorating. ~**r** *vt* renew; renovate (*edificio*); decorate (*cuarto*)

rent|a *f* income; (*alquiler*) rent; (*deuda*) national debt. ~**able** *a* profitable. ~**ar** *vt* produce, yield; (*LAm, alquilar*) rent, hire. ~**a vitalicia** (life) annuity. ~**ista** *m & f* person of independent means

renuncia *f* renunciation. ~**r** *vi.* ~**r a** renounce, give up

reñi|do *a* hard-fought. ~**r** [5 & 22] *vt* tell off. ● *vi* quarrel. **estar** ~**do con** be incompatible with (*cosas*); be on bad terms with (*personas*)

reo *m & f* culprit; (*jurid*) accused. ~ **de Estado** person accused of treason. ~ **de muerte** prisoner sentenced to death

reojo *adv.* **mirar de** ~ look out of the corner of one's eye at; (*fig*) look askance at

reorganizar [10] *vt* reorganize

repanchigarse [12] *vpr*, **repantigarse** [12] *vpr* sprawl out

repar|ación *f* repair; (*acción*) repairing; (*fig, compensación*) reparation. ~**ar** *vt* repair; (*fig*) make amends for; (*notar*) notice. ● *vi.* ~**ar en** notice; (*hacer caso de*) pay attention to. ~**o** *m* fault; (*objeción*) objection. **poner** ~**os** raise objections

repart|ición *f* division. ~**idor** *m* delivery man. ~**imiento** *m* distribution. ~**ir** *vt* distribute, share out; deliver (*cartas, leche etc*); hand out (*folleto, premio*). ~**o** *m* distribution; (*de cartas, leche etc*) delivery; (*actores*) cast

repas|ar *vt* go over; check (*cuenta*); revise (*texto*); (*leer a la ligera*) glance through; (*coser*) mend. ● *vi* go back. ~**o** *m* revision; (*de ropa*) mending. **dar un** ~**o** look through

repatria|ción *f* repatriation. ~**r** *vt* repatriate

repecho *m* steep slope

repele|nte *a* repulsive. ~**r** *vt* repel

repensar [1] *vt* reconsider

repent|e *adv.* **de** ~ suddenly. ~**ino** *a* sudden

repercu|sión *f* repercussion. ~**tir** *vi* reverberate; (*fig*) have repercussions (**en** on)

repertorio *m* repertoire; (*lista*) index

repeti|ción *f* repetition; (*mus*) repeat. ~**damente** *adv* repeatedly. ~**r** [5] *vt* repeat; (*imitar*) copy; ● *vi.* ~**r de** have a second helping of. **¡que se repita!** encore!

repi|car [7] *vt* ring (*campanas*). ~**que** *m* peal

repisa f shelf. **~ de chimenea** mantlepiece

repito vb véase **repetir**

replegarse [1 & 12] vpr withdraw

repleto a full up

réplica a answer; (copia) replica

replicar [7] vi answer

repliegue m crease; (mil) withdrawal

repollo m cabbage

reponer [34] vt replace; revive ⟨obra de teatro⟩; (contestar) reply. **~se** vpr recover

report|aje m report. **~ero** m reporter

repos|ado a quiet; (sin prisa) unhurried. **~ar** vi rest. **~arse** vpr settle. **~o** m rest

repost|ar vt replenish; refuel ⟨avión⟩; fill up ⟨coche etc⟩. **~ería** f cake shop

repren|der vt reprimand. **~sible** a reprehensible

represalia f reprisal. **tomar ~s** retaliate

representa|ción f representation; (en el teatro) performance. **en ~ción de** representing. **~nte** m representative; (actor) actor. • f representative; (actriz) actress. **~r** vt represent; perform ⟨obra de teatro⟩; play ⟨papel⟩; (aparentar) look. **~rse** vpr imagine. **~tivo** a representative

represi|ón f repression. **~vo** a repressive

reprimenda f reprimand

reprimir vt supress. **~se** vpr stop o.s.

reprobar [2] vt condemn; reproach ⟨persona⟩

réprobo a & m reprobate

reproch|ar vt reproach. **~e** m reproach

reproduc|ción f reproduction. **~ir** [47] vt reproduce. **~tor** a reproductive

reptil m reptile

rep|ública f republic. **~ublicano** a & m republican

repudiar vt repudiate

repuesto m store; (auto) spare (part). **de ~** in reserve

repugna|ncia f disgust. **~nte** a repugnant. **~r** vt disgust

repujar vt emboss

repuls|a f rebuff. **~ión** f repulsion. **~ivo** a repulsive

reputa|ción f reputation. **~do** a reputable. **~r** vt consider

requebrar [1] vt flatter

requemar vt scorch; (culin) burn; tan ⟨piel⟩

requeri|miento m request; (jurid) summons. **~r** [4] vt need; (pedir) ask

requesón m cottage cheese

requete... pref extremely

requiebro m compliment

réquiem m (pl **réquiems**) m requiem

requis|a f inspection; (mil) requisition. **~ar** vt requisition. **~ito** m requirement

res f animal. **~ lanar** sheep. **~ vacuna** (vaca) cow; (toro) bull; (buey) ox. **carne de ~** (Mex) beef

resabido a well-known; ⟨persona⟩ pedantic

resabio m (unpleasant) after-taste; (vicio) bad habit

resaca f undercurrent; (después de beber alcohol) hangover

resaltar vi stand out. **hacer ~** emphasize

resarcir [9] vt repay; (compensar) compensate. **~se** vpr make up for

resbal|adizo a slippery. **~ar** vi slip; (auto) skid; ⟨líquido⟩ trickle. **~arse** vpr slip; (auto) skid; ⟨líquido⟩ trickle. **~ón** m slip; (de vehículo) skid

rescat|ar vt ransom; (recuperar) recapture; (fig) recover. **~e** m ransom; (recuperación) recapture; (salvamento) rescue

rescindir vt cancel

rescoldo m embers

resecar [7] vt dry up; (med) remove. **~se** vpr dry up

resenti|do a resentful. **~miento** m resentment. **~rse** vpr feel the effects; (debilitarse) be weakened; (ofenderse) take offence (**de** at)

reseña f account; (en periódico) report, review. **~r** vt describe; (en periódico) report on, review

resero m (Arg) herdsman

reserva f reservation; (provisión) reserve(s). **~ción** f reservation. **~do** a reserved. **~r** vt reserve; (guardar) keep, save. **~rse** vpr save o.s. **a ~ de** except for. **a ~ de que** unless. **de ~** in reserve

resfria|do m cold; (enfriamiento) chill. **~r** vt. **~r a uno** give s.o. a cold. **~rse** vpr catch a cold; (fig) cool off

resguard|ar vt protect. **~arse** vpr protect o.s.; (fig) take care. **~o** m protection; (garantía) guarantee; (recibo) receipt

resid|encia f residence; (*univ*) hall of residence, dormitory (*Amer*); (*de ancianos etc*) home. **~encial** a residential. **~ente** a & m & f resident. **~ir** vi reside; (*fig*) lie

residu|al a residual. **~o** m remainder. **~os** mpl waste

resigna|ción f resignation. **~damente** adv with resignation. **~r** vt resign. **~rse** vpr resign o.s. (**a**, **con** to)

resina f resin

resist|encia f resistence. **~ente** a resistent. **~ir** vt resist; (*soportar*) bear. ● vi resist. **oponer ~encia** a resist

resma f ream

resobado a trite

resol|ución f resolution; (*solución*) solution; (*decisión*) decision. **~ver** [2] (*pp* **resuelto**) resolve; solve (*problema etc*). **~verse** vpr be solved; (*resultar bien*) work out; (*decidirse*) make up one's mind

resollar [2] vi breathe heavily. **sin ~** without saying a word

resona|ncia f resonance. **~nte** a resonant; (*fig*) resounding. **~r** [2] vi resound. **tener ~ncia** cause a stir

resopl|ar vi puff; (*por enfado*) snort; (*por cansancio*) pant. **~ido** m heavy breathing; (*de enfado*) snort; (*de cansancio*) panting

resorte m spring. **tocar (todos los) ~s** (*fig*) pull strings

respald|ar vt back; (*escribir*) endorse. **~arse** vpr lean back. **~o** m back

respect|ar vi concern. **~ivo** a respective. **~o** m respect. **al ~o** on the matter. **(con) ~o** a as regards. **en/ por lo que ~a** as regards

respet|able a respectable. ● m audience. **~ar** vt respect. **~o** m respect. **~uoso** a respectful. **de ~o** best. **faltar al ~o** a be disrespectful to. **hacerse ~ar** command respect

respingo m start

respir|ación f breathing; (*med*) respiration; (*ventilación*) ventilation. **~ador** a respiratory. **~ar** vi breathe; (*fig*) breathe a sigh of relief. **no ~ar** (*no hablar*) not say a word. **~o** m breathing; (*fig*) rest

respland|ecer [11] vi shine. **~eciente** a shining. **~or** m brilliance; (*de llamas*) glow

responder vi answer; (*replicar*) answer back; (*fig*) reply, respond. **~ de** answer for

responsab|ilidad f responsibility. **~le** a responsible. **hacerse ~le de** assume responsibilty for

respuesta f reply, answer

resquebra|dura f crack. **~jar** vt crack. **~jarse** vpr crack

resquemor m (*fig*) uneasiness

resquicio m crack; (*fig*) possibility

resta f subtraction

restablecer [11] vt restore. **~se** vpr recover

restallar vi crack

restante a remaining. **lo ~** the rest

restar vt take away; (*substraer*) subtract. ● vi be left

restaura|ción f restoration. **~nte** m restaurant. **~r** vt restore

restitu|ción f restitution. **~ir** [17] vt return; (*restaurar*) restore

resto m rest, remainder; (*en matemática*) remainder. **~s** mpl remains; (*de comida*) leftovers

restorán m restaurant

restregar [1 & 12] vt rub

restri|cción f restriction. **~ngir** [14] vt restrict, limit

resucitar vt resuscitate; (*fig*) revive. ● vi return to life

resuelto a resolute

resuello m breath; (*respiración*) breathing

resulta|do m result. **~r** vi result; (*salir*) turn out; (*ser*) be; (*ocurrir*) happen; (*costar*) come to

resum|en m summary. **~ir** vt summarize; (*recapitular*) sum up; (*abreviar*) abridge. **en ~en** in short

resur|gir [14] vi reappear; (*fig*) revive. **~gimiento** m resurgence. **~rección** f resurrection

retaguardia f (*mil*) rearguard

retahíla f string

retal m remnant

retama f, **retamo** m (*LAm*) broom

retar vt challenge

retardar vt slow down; (*demorar*) delay

retazo m remnant; (*fig*) piece, bit

retemblar [1] vi shake

rete... *pref* extremely

reten|ción f retention. **~er** [40] vt keep; (*en la memoria*) retain; (*no dar*) withhold

reticencia f insinuation; (*reserva*) reticence, reluctance

retina f retina

retintín m ringing. **con ~** (*fig*) sarcastically

retir|ada *f* withdrawal. ~**ado** *a* secluded; ⟨*jubilado*⟩ retired. ~**ar** *vt* move away; ⟨*quitar*⟩ remove; withdraw ⟨*dinero*⟩; ⟨*jubilar*⟩ pension off. ~**arse** *vpr* draw back; ⟨*mil*⟩ withdraw; ⟨*jubilarse*⟩ retire; ⟨*acostarse*⟩ go to bed. ~**o** *m* retirement; ⟨*pensión*⟩ pension; ⟨*lugar apartado*⟩ retreat

reto *m* challenge

retocar [7] *vt* retouch

retoño *m* shoot

retoque *m* ⟨*acción*⟩ retouching; ⟨*efecto*⟩ finishing touch

retorc|er [2 & 9] *vt* twist; wring ⟨*ropa*⟩. ~**erse** *vpr* get twisted up; ⟨*de dolor*⟩ writhe. ~**imiento** *m* twisting; ⟨*de ropa*⟩ wringing

retóric|a *f* rhetoric; ⟨*grandilocuencia*⟩ grandiloquence. ~**o** *m* rhetorical

retorn|ar *vt/i* return. ~**o** *m* return

retortijón *m* twist; ⟨*de tripas*⟩ stomach cramp

retoz|ar [10] *vi* romp, frolic. ~**ón** *a* playful

retractar *vt* retract. ~**se** *vpr* retract

retra|er [41] *vt* retract. ~**erse** *vpr* withdraw. ~**ido** *a* retiring

retransmitir *vt* relay

retras|ado *a* behind; ⟨*reloj*⟩ slow; ⟨*poco desarrollado*⟩ backward; ⟨*anticuado*⟩ old-fashioned; ⟨*med*⟩ mentally retarded. ~**ar** *vt* delay; put back ⟨*reloj*⟩; ⟨*retardar*⟩ slow down. ● *vi* fall behind; ⟨*reloj*⟩ be slow. ~**arse** *vpr* be behind; ⟨*reloj*⟩ be slow. ~**o** *m* delay; ⟨*poco desarrollo*⟩ backwardness; ⟨*reloj*⟩ slowness. ~**os** *mpl* arrears. **con 5 minutos de ~o** 5 minutes late. **traer ~o** be late

retrat|ar *vt* paint a portrait of; ⟨*foto*⟩ photograph; ⟨*fig*⟩ portray. ~**ista** *m* & *f* portrait painter. ~**o** *m* portrait; ⟨*fig, descripción*⟩ description. **ser el vivo ~o de** be the living image of

retreparse *vpr* lean back

retreta *f* retreat

retrete *m* toilet

retribu|ción *f* payment. ~**ir** [17] *vt* pay

retroce|der *vi* move back; ⟨*fig*⟩ back down. ~**so** *m* backward movement; ⟨*de arma de fuego*⟩ recoil; ⟨*med*⟩ relapse

retrógrado *a* & *m* ⟨*pol*⟩ reactionary

retropropulsión *f* jet propulsion

retrospectivo *a* retrospective

retrovisor *m* rear-view mirror

retumbar *vt* echo; ⟨*trueno etc*⟩ boom

reuma *m*, **reúma** *m* rheumatism

reum|ático *a* rheumatic. ~**atismo** *m* rheumatism

reuni|ón *f* meeting; ⟨*entre amigos*⟩ reunion. ~**r** [23] *vt* join together; ⟨*recoger*⟩ gather (together). ~**rse** *vpr* join together; ⟨*personas*⟩ meet

rev|álida *f* final exam. ~**alidar** *vt* confirm; ⟨*escol*⟩ take an exam in

revancha *f* revenge. **tomar la ~** get one's own back

revela|ción *f* revelation. ~**do** *m* developing. ~**dor** *a* revealing. ~**r** *vt* reveal; ⟨*foto*⟩ develop

revent|ar [1] *vi* burst; ⟨*tener ganas*⟩ be dying to. ~**arse** *vpr* burst. ~**ón** *m* burst; ⟨*auto*⟩ puncture

reverbera|ción *f* ⟨*de luz*⟩ reflection; ⟨*de sonido*⟩ reverberation. ~**r** *vi* ⟨*luz*⟩ be reflected; ⟨*sonido*⟩ reverberate

reveren|cia *f* reverence; ⟨*muestra de respeto*⟩ bow; ⟨*muestra de respeto de mujer*⟩ curtsy. ~**ciar** *vt* revere. ~**do** *a* respected; ⟨*relig*⟩ reverend. ~**te** *a* reverent

revers|ible *a* reversible. ~**o** *m* reverse

revertir [4] *vi* revert

revés *m* wrong side; ⟨*desgracia*⟩ misfortune; ⟨*en deportes*⟩ backhand. **al ~** the other way round; ⟨*con lo de arriba abajo*⟩ upside down; ⟨*con lo de dentro fuera*⟩ inside out

revesti|miento *m* coating. ~**r** [5] *vt* cover; put on ⟨*ropa*⟩; ⟨*fig*⟩ take on

revis|ar *vt* check; overhaul ⟨*mecanismo*⟩; service ⟨*coche etc*⟩. ~**ión** *f* check(ing); ⟨*inspección*⟩ inspection; ⟨*de coche etc*⟩ service. ~**or** *m* inspector

revist|a *f* magazine; ⟨*inspección*⟩ inspection; ⟨*artículo*⟩ review; ⟨*espectáculo*⟩ revue. ~**ero** *m* critic; ⟨*mueble*⟩ magazine rack. **pasar ~a a** inspect

revivir *vi* come to life again

revocar [7] *vt* revoke; whitewash ⟨*pared*⟩

revolcar [2 & 7] *vt* knock over. ~**se** *vpr* roll

revolotear *vi* flutter

revoltijo *m*, **revoltillo** *m* mess. ~ **de huevos** scrambled eggs

revoltoso *a* rebellious; ⟨*niño*⟩ naughty

revoluci|ón f revolution. **~onar** vt revolutionize. **~onario** a & m revolutionary

revolver [2, pp **revuelto**] vt mix; stir ⟨líquido⟩; (desordenar) mess up; (pol) stir up. **~se** vpr turn round. **~se contra** turn on

revólver m revolver

revoque m (con cal) whitewashing

revuelo m fluttering; (fig) stir

revuelt|a f turn; (de calle etc) bend; (motín) revolt; (conmoción) disturbance. **~o** a mixed up; ⟨líquido⟩ cloudy; (mar) rough; ⟨tiempo⟩ unsettled; ⟨huevos⟩ scrambled

rey m king. **~es** mpl king and queen

reyerta f quarrel

rezagarse [12] vpr fall behind

rez|ar [10] vt say. ● vi pray; (decir) say. **~o** m praying; (oración) prayer

rezongar [12] vi grumble

rezumar vt/i ooze

ría f estuary

riachuelo m stream

riada f flood

ribera f bank

ribete m border; (fig) embellishment

ricino m. **aceite de ~** castor oil

rico a rich; (culin, fam) delicious. ● m rich person

rid|ículo a ridiculous. **~iculizar** [10] vt ridicule

riego m watering; (irrigación) irrigation

riel m rail

rienda f rein

riesgo m risk. **a ~ de** at the risk of. **correr (el) ~ de** run the risk of

rifa f raffle. **~r** vt raffle. **~rse** vpr (fam) quarrel over

rifle m rifle

rigidez f rigidity; (fig) inflexibility

rígido a rigid; (fig) inflexible

rig|or m strictness; (exactitud) exactness; (de clima) severity. **~uroso** a rigorous. **de ~or** compulsory. **en ~or** strictly speaking

rima f rhyme. **~r** vt/i rhyme

rimbombante a resounding; ⟨lenguaje⟩ pompous; (fig, ostentoso) showy

rimel m mascara

rincón m corner

rinoceronte m rhinoceros

riña f quarrel; (pelea) fight

riñ|ón m kidney. **~onada** f loin; (guiso) kidney stew

río m river; (fig) stream. ● vb véase **reír**. **~ abajo** downstream. **~ arriba** upstream

rioja m Rioja wine

riqueza f wealth; (fig) richness. **~s** fpl riches

riquísimo a delicious

risa f laugh. **desternillarse de ~** split one's sides laughing. **la ~** laughter

risco m cliff

ris|ible a laughable. **~otada** f guffaw

ristra f string

risueño a smiling; (fig) happy

rítmico a rhythmic(al)

ritmo m rhythm; (fig) rate

rit|o m rite; (fig) ritual. **~ual** a & m ritual. **de ~ual** customary

rival a & m & f rival. **~idad** f rivalry. **~izar** [10] vi rival

riz|ado a curly. **~ar** [10] vt curl; ripple ⟨agua⟩. **~o** m curl; (en agua) ripple. **~oso** a curly

róbalo m bass

robar vt steal ⟨cosa⟩; rob ⟨persona⟩; (raptar) kidnap

roble m oak (tree)

roblón m rivet

robo m theft; (fig, estafa) robbery

robot m (pl **robots**) m robot

robust|ez f strength. **~o** a strong

roca f rock

roce m rubbing; (toque ligero) touch; (señal) mark; (fig, entre personas) contact

rociar [20] vt spray

rocín m nag

rocío m dew

rodaballo m turbot

rodado m (Arg, vehículo) vehicle

rodaja f disc; (culin) slice

roda|je m (de película) shooting; (de coche) running in. **~r** [2] vt shoot ⟨película⟩; run in ⟨coche⟩; (recorrer) travel. ● vi roll; ⟨coche⟩ run; (hacer una película) shoot

rode|ar vt surround. **~arse** vpr surround o.s. (**de** with). **~o** m long way round; (de ganado) round-up. **andar con ~os** beat about the bush. **sin ~os** plainly

rodill|a f knee. **~era** f knee-pad. **de ~as** kneeling

rodillo m roller; (culin) rolling-pin

rododendro m rhododendron

rodrigón m stake

roe|dor m rodent. **~r** [37] vt gnaw

rogar [2 & 12] *vt/i* ask; (*relig*) pray. **se ruega a los Sres pasajeros...** passengers are requested.... **se ruega no fumar** please do not smoke

roj|ete *m* rouge. ~**ez** *f* redness. ~**izo** *a* reddish. ~**o** *a* & *m* red. **ponerse** ~**o** blush

roll|izo *a* round; (*persona*) plump. ~**o** *m* roll; (*de cuerda*) coil; (*culin, rodillo*) rolling-pin; (*fig, pesadez, fam*) bore

romance *a* Romance. ● *m* Romance language; (*poema*) romance. **hablar en** ~ speak plainly

rom|ánico *a* Romanesque; (*lengua*) Romance. ~**ano** *a* & *m* Roman. **a la** ~**ana** (*culin*) (deep-)fried in batter

rom|anticismo *m* romanticism. ~**ántico** *a* romantic

romería *f* pilgrimage

romero *m* rosemary

romo *a* blunt; (*nariz*) snub; (*fig, torpe*) dull

rompe|cabezas *m invar* puzzle; (*con tacos de madera*) jigsaw (puzzle). ~**nueces** *m invar* nutcrackers. ~**olas** *m invar* breakwater

romp|er (*pp* **roto**) *vt* break; break off (*relaciones etc*). ● *vi* break; (*sol*) break through. ~**erse** *vpr* break. ~**er a** burst out. ~**imiento** *m* (*de relaciones etc*) breaking off

ron *m* rum

ronc|ar [7] *vi* snore. ~**o** *a* hoarse

roncha *f* lump; (*culin*) slice

ronda *f* round; (*patrulla*) patrol; (*carretera*) ring road. ~**lla** *f* group of serenaders; (*invención*) story. ~**r** *vt/i* patrol

rondón *adv.* **de** ~ unannounced

ronquedad *f*, **ronquera** *f* hoarseness

ronquido *m* snore

ronronear *vi* purr

ronzal *m* halter

roñ|a *f* (*suciedad*) grime. ~**oso** *a* dirty; (*oxidado*) rusty; (*tacaño*) mean

rop|a *f* clothes, clothing. ~**a blanca** linen; (*ropa interior*) underwear. ~**a de cama** bedclothes. ~**a hecha** ready-made clothes. ~**a interior** underwear. ~**aje** *m* robes; (*excesivo*) heavy clothing. ~**ero** *m* wardrobe

ros|a *a invar* pink. ● *f* rose; (*color*) pink. ~**áceo** *a* pink. ~**ado** *a* rosy. ● *m* (*vino*) rosé. ~**al** *m* rose-bush

rosario *m* rosary; (*fig*) series

rosbif *m* roast beef

rosc|a *f* coil; (*de tornillo*) thread; (*de pan*) roll. ~**o** *m* roll

rosetón *m* rosette

rosquilla *f* doughnut; (*oruga*) grub

rostro *m* face

rota|ción *f* rotation. ~**tivo** *a* rotary

roto *a* broken

rótula *f* kneecap

rotulador *m* felt-tip pen

rótulo *m* sign; (*etiqueta*) label

rotundo *a* emphatic

rotura *f* break

roturar *vt* plough

roza *f* groove. ~**dura** *f* scratch

rozagante *a* showy

rozar [10] *vt* rub against; (*ligeramente*) brush against; (*ensuciar*) dirty; (*fig*) touch on. ~**se** *vpr* rub; (*con otras personas*) mix

Rte. *abrev* (*Remite(nte)*) sender

rúa *f* (small) street

rubéola *f* German measles

rubí *m* ruby

rubicundo *a* ruddy

rubio *a* (*pelo*) fair; (*persona*) fair-haired; (*tabaco*) Virginian

rubor *m* blush; (*fig*) shame. ~**izado** *a* blushing; (*fig*) ashamed. ~**izar** [10] *vt* make blush. ~**izarse** *vpr* blush

rúbrica *f* red mark; (*de firma*) flourish; (*título*) heading

rudeza *f* roughness

rudiment|al *a* rudimentary. ~**os** *mpl* rudiments

rudo *a* rough; (*sencillo*) simple

rueda *f* wheel; (*de mueble*) castor; (*de personas*) ring; (*culin*) slice. ~ **de prensa** press conference

ruedo *m* edge; (*redondel*) arena

ruego *m* request; (*súplica*) entreaty. ● *vb véase* **rogar**

rufi|án *m* pimp; (*granuja*) villain. ~**anesco** *a* roguish

rugby *m* Rugby

rugi|do *m* roar. ~**r** [14] *vi* roar

ruibarbo *m* rhubarb

ruido *m* noise; (*alboroto*) din; (*escándalo*) commotion. ~**so** *a* noisy; (*fig*) sensational

ruin *a* despicable; (*tacaño*) mean

ruina *f* ruin; (*colapso*) collapse

ruindad *f* meanness

ruinoso *a* ruinous

ruiseñor *m* nightingale

ruleta *f* roulette

rulo *m* (*culin*) rolling-pin; (*del pelo*) curler

Rumania *f* Romania

rumano *a & m* Romanian
rumba *f* rumba
rumbo *m* direction; (*fig*) course; (*fig, generosidad*) lavishness. **~so** *a* lavish. **con ~ a** in the direction of. **hacer ~ a** head for
rumia|nte *a & m* ruminant. **~r** *vt* chew; (*fig*) chew over. ● *vi* ruminate
rumor *m* rumour; (*ruido*) murmur. **~earse** *vpr* be rumoured. **~oso** *a* murmuring
runrún *m* rumour; (*ruido*) murmur. **~unearse** *vpr* be rumoured
ruptura *f* break; (*de relaciones etc*) breaking off
rural *a* rural
Rusia *f* Russia
ruso *a & m* Russian
rústico *a* rural; (*de carácter*) coarse. **en rústica** paperback
ruta *f* route; (*camino*) road; (*fig*) course
rutilante *a* shining
rutina *f* routine. **~rio** *a* routine

S

S.A. *abrev* (*Sociedad Anónima*) Ltd, Limited, plc, Public Limited Company
sábado *m* Saturday
sabana *f* (*esp LAm*) savannah
sábana *f* sheet
sabandija *f* bug
sabañón *m* chilblain
sabático *a* sabbatical
sab|elotodo *m & f invar* ´know-all (*fam*). **~er** [38] *vt* know; (*ser capaz de*) be able to, know how to; (*enterarse de*) learn. ● *vi*. **~er a** taste of. **~er** *m* knowledge. **~ido** *a* well-known. **~iduría** *f* wisdom; (*conocimientos*) knowledge. **a ~er si** I wonder if. **¡haberlo ~ido!** if only I'd known! **hacer ~er** let know. **no sé cuántos** what's-his-name. **para que lo sepas** let me tell you. **¡qué sé yo!** how should I know? **que yo sepa** as far as I know. **¿~es nadar?** can you swim? **un no sé qué** a certain sth. **¡yo qué sé!** how should I know?
sabiendas *adv*. **a ~** knowingly; (*a propósito*) on purpose
sabio *a* learned; (*prudente*) wise
sabor *m* taste, flavour; (*fig*) flavour. **~ear** *vt* taste; (*fig*) savour

sabot|aje *m* sabotage. **~eador** *m* saboteur. **~ear** *vt* sabotage
sabroso *a* tasty; (*fig, substancioso*) meaty
sabueso *m* (*perro*) bloodhound; (*fig, detective*) detective
saca|corchos *m invar* corkscrew. **~puntas** *m invar* pencil-sharpener
sacar [7] *vt* take out; put out ⟨*parte del cuerpo*⟩; (*quitar*) remove; take ⟨*foto*⟩; win ⟨*premio*⟩; get ⟨*billete, entrada etc*⟩; withdraw ⟨*dinero*⟩; reach ⟨*solución*⟩; draw ⟨*conclusión*⟩; make ⟨*copia*⟩. **~ adelante** bring up ⟨*niño*⟩; carry on ⟨*negocio*⟩
sacarina *f* saccharin
sacerdo|cio *m* priesthood. **~tal** *a* priestly. **~te** *m* priest
saciar *vt* satisfy
saco *m* bag; (*anat*) sac; (*LAm, chaqueta*) jacket; (*de mentiras*) pack. **~ de dormir** sleeping-bag
sacramento *m* sacrament
sacrific|ar [7] *vt* sacrifice. **~arse** *vpr* sacrifice o.s. **~io** *m* sacrifice
sacr|ilegio *m* sacrilege. **~ílego** *a* sacrilegious
sacro *a* sacred, holy. **~santo** *a* sacrosanct
sacudi|da *f* shake; (*movimiento brusco*) jolt, jerk; (*fig*) shock. **~da eléctrica** electric shock. **~r** *vt* shake; (*golpear*) beat; (*ahuyentar*) chase away. **~rse** *vpr* shake off; (*fig*) get rid of
sádico *a* sadistic. ● *m* sadist
sadismo *m* sadism
saeta *f* arrow; (*de reloj*) hand
safari *m* safari
sagaz *a* shrewd
Sagitario *m* Sagittarius
sagrado *a* sacred, holy. ● *m* sanctuary
Sahara *m*, **Sáhara** /'saxara/ *m* Sahara
sainete *m* short comedy
sal *f* salt
sala *f* room; (*en teatro*) house. **~ de espectáculos** concert hall, auditorium. **~ de espera** waiting-room. **~ de estar** living-room. **~ de fiestas** nightclub
sala|do *a* salty; ⟨*agua del mar*⟩ salt; (*vivo*) lively; (*encantador*) cute; (*fig*) witty. **~r** *vt* salt
salario *m* wages
salazón *f* (*carne*) salted meat; (*pescado*) salted fish

salchich|a f (pork) sausage. **~ón** m salami

sald|ar vt pay ⟨cuenta⟩; ⟨vender⟩ sell off; (fig) settle. **~o** m balance; ⟨venta⟩ sale; ⟨lo que queda⟩ remnant

salero m salt-cellar

salgo vb véase **salir**

sali|da f departure; ⟨puerta⟩ exit, way out; ⟨de gas, de líquido⟩ leak; ⟨de astro⟩ rising; ⟨com, posibilidad de venta⟩ opening; ⟨chiste⟩ witty remark; (fig) way out. **~da de emergencia** emergency exit. **~ente** a projecting; (fig) outstanding. **~r** [52] vi leave; ⟨de casa etc⟩ go out; ⟨revista etc⟩ be published; ⟨resultar⟩ turn out; ⟨astro⟩ rise; ⟨aparecer⟩ appear. **~rse** vpr leave; ⟨recipiente, líquido etc⟩ leak. **~r adelante** get by. **~rse con la suya** get one's own way

saliva f saliva

salmo m psalm

salm|ón m salmon. **~onete** m red mullet

salmuera f brine

salón m lounge, sitting-room. **~ de actos** assembly hall. **~ de fiestas** dancehall

salpica|dero m ⟨auto⟩ dashboard. **~dura** f splash; ⟨acción⟩ splashing. **~r** [7] vt splash; (fig) sprinkle

sals|a f sauce; ⟨para carne asada⟩ gravy; (fig) spice. **~a verde** parsley sauce. **~era** f sauce-boat

salt|amontes m invar grasshopper. **~ar** vt jump (over); (fig) miss out. ● vi jump; ⟨romperse⟩ break; ⟨líquido⟩ spurt out; ⟨desprenderse⟩ come off; ⟨pelota⟩ bounce; ⟨estallar⟩ explode. **~eador** m highwayman. **~ear** vt rob; ⟨culin⟩ sauté. ● vi skip through

saltimbanqui m acrobat

salt|o m jump; ⟨al agua⟩ dive. **~o de agua** waterfall. **~ón** a ⟨ojos⟩ bulging. ● m grasshopper. **a ~os** by jumping; (fig) by leaps and bounds. **de un ~o** with one jump

salud f health; (fig) welfare. ● int cheers! **~able** a healthy

salud|ar vt greet, say hello to; (mil) salute. **~o** m greeting; (mil) salute. **~os** mpl best wishes. **le ~a atentamente** ⟨en cartas⟩ yours faithfully

salva f salvo; ⟨de aplausos⟩ thunders

salvación f salvation

salvado m bran

Salvador m. **El ~** El Salvador

salvaguardia f safeguard

salvaje a ⟨planta, animal⟩ wild; ⟨primitivo⟩ savage. ● m & f savage

salvamanteles m invar table-mat

salva|mento m rescue. **~r** vt save, rescue; ⟨atravesar⟩ cross; ⟨recorrer⟩ travel; (fig) overcome. **~rse** vpr save o.s. **~vidas** m invar lifebelt. **chaleco** m **~vidas** life-jacket

salvia f sage

salvo a safe. ● adv & prep except (for). **~ que** unless. **~conducto** m safe-conduct. **a ~** out of danger. **poner a ~** put in a safe place

samba f samba

San a Saint, St. **~ Miguel** St Michael

sana|r vt cure. ● vi recover. **~torio** m sanatorium

sanci|ón f sanction. **~onar** vt sanction

sancocho m ⟨LAm⟩ stew

sandalia f sandal

sándalo m sandalwood

sandía f water melon

sandwich /'sambitʃ/ m ⟨pl **sandwichs**, **sandwiches**⟩ sandwich

sanear vt drain

sangr|ante a bleeding; (fig) flagrant. **~ar** vt/i bleed. **~e** f blood. **a ~e fría** in cold blood

sangría f ⟨bebida⟩ sangria

sangriento a bloody

sangu|ijuela f leech. **~íneo** a blood

san|idad f health. **~itario** a sanitary. **~o** a healthy; ⟨seguro⟩ sound. **~o y salvo** safe and sound. **cortar por lo ~o** settle things once and for all

santiamén m. **en un ~** in an instant

sant|idad f sanctity. **~ificar** [7] vt sanctify. **~iguar** [15] vt make the sign of the cross over. **~iguarse** vpr cross o.s. **~o** a holy; ⟨delante de nombre⟩ Saint, St. ● m saint; ⟨día⟩ saint's day, name day. **~uario** m sanctuary. **~urrón** a sanctimonious, hypocritical

sañ|a f fury; ⟨crueldad⟩ cruelty. **~oso** a, **~udo** a furious

sapo m toad; ⟨bicho, fam⟩ small animal, creature

saque m ⟨en tenis⟩ service; ⟨en fútbol⟩ throw-in; ⟨inicial en fútbol⟩ kick-off

saque|ar vt loot. **~o** m looting

sarampión m measles

sarape m ⟨Mex⟩ blanket

sarc|asmo m sarcasm. **~ástico** a sarcastic

sardana f Catalonian dance

sardina f sardine

sardo a & m Sardinian

sardónico a sardonic

sargento m sergeant

sarmiento m vine shoot

sarpullido m rash

sarta f string

sartén f frying-pan (Brit), fry-pan (Amer)

sastre m tailor. **~ría** f tailoring; (tienda) tailor's (shop)

Satanás m Satan

satánico a satanic

satélite m satellite

satinado a shiny

sátira f satire

satírico a satirical. ● m satirist

satisf|acción f satisfaction. **~acer** [31] vt satisfy; (pagar) pay; (gustar) please; meet (gastos, requisitos). **~acerse** vpr satisfy o.s.; (vengarse) take revenge. **~actorio** a satisfactory. **~echo** a satisfied. **~echo de sí mismo** smug

satura|ción f saturation. **~r** vt saturate

Saturno m Saturn

sauce m willow. **~ llorón** weeping willow

saúco m elder

savia f sap

sauna f sauna

saxofón m, **saxófono** m saxophone

saz|ón f ripeness; (culin) seasoning. **~onado** a ripe; (culin) seasoned. **~onar** vt ripen; (culin) season. **en ~ón** in season

se pron (él) him; (ella) her; (Vd) you; (reflexivo, él) himself; (reflexivo, ella) herself; (reflexivo, ello) itself; (reflexivo, uno) oneself; (reflexivo, Vd) yourself; (reflexivo, ellos, ellas) themselves; (reflexivo, Vds) yourselves; (recíproco) (to) each other. **~ dice** people say, they say, it is said (que that). **~ habla español** Spanish spoken

sé vb véase **saber** y **ser**

sea vb véase **ser**

sebo m tallow; (culin) suet

seca|dor m drier; (de pelo) hair-drier. **~nte** a drying. ● m blotting-paper. **~r** [7] vt dry. **~rse** vpr dry; (río etc) dry up; (persona) dry o.s.

sección f section

seco a dry; (frutos, flores) dried; (flaco) thin; (respuesta) curt; (escueto) plain. **a secas** just. **en ~** (bruscamente) suddenly. **lavar en ~** dry-clean

secre|ción f secretion. **~tar** vt secrete

secretar|ía f secretariat. **~io** m secretary

secreto a & m secret

secta f sect. **~rio** a sectarian

sector m sector

secuela f consequence

secuencia f sequence

secuestr|ar vt confiscate; kidnap (persona); hijack (avión). **~o** m seizure; (de persona) kidnapping; (de avión) hijack(ing)

secular a secular

secundar vt second, help. **~io** a secondary

sed f thirst. ● vb véase **ser**. **tener ~** be thirsty. **tener ~ de** (fig) be hungry for

seda f silk

sedante a & m, **sedativo** a & m sedative

sede f seat; (relig) see

sedentario a sedentary

sedici|ón f sedition. **~oso** a seditious

sediento a thirsty

sediment|ar vi deposit. **~arse** vpr settle. **~o** m sediment

seduc|ción f seduction. **~ir** [47] vt seduce; (atraer) attract. **~tor** a seductive. ● m seducer

sega|dor m harvester. **~dora** f harvester, mower. **~r** [1 & 12] vt reap

seglar a secular. ● m layman

segmento m segment

segoviano m person from Segovia

segrega|ción f segregation. **~r** [12] vt segregate

segui|da f. **en ~da** immediately. **~do** a continuous; (en plural) consecutive. ● adv straight; (después) after. **todo ~do** straight ahead. **~dor** a following. ● m follower. **~r** [5 & 13] vt follow (continuar) continue

según prep according to. ● adv it depends; (a medida que) as

segundo a second. ● m second; (culin) second course

segur|amente adv certainly; (muy probablemente) surely. **~idad** f safety; (certeza) certainty; (aplomo) confidence. ~**idad en sí mismo** self-confidence. ~**idad social** social security. ~**o** *a* safe; (*cierto*) certain, sure; (*firme*) secure; (*de fiar*) reliable. ● *adv* for certain. ● *m* insurance; (*dispositivo de seguridad*) safety device. ~**o de sí mismo** self-confident. ~**o de terceros** third-party insurance

seis *a & m* six. ~**cientos** *a & m* six hundred

seísmo *m* earthquake

selec|ción *f* selection. ~**cionar** *vt* select, choose. ~**tivo** *a* selective. ~**to** *a* selected; (*fig*) choice

selva *f* forest; (*jungla*) jungle

sell|ar *vt* stamp; (*cerrar*) seal. ~**o** *m* stamp; (*en documento oficial*) seal; (*fig, distintivo*) hallmark

semáforo *m* semaphore; (*auto*) traffic lights; (*rail*) signal

semana *f* week. ~**l** *a* weekly. ~**rio** *a & m* weekly. **S~ Santa** Holy Week

semántic|a *f* semantics. ~**o** *a* semantic

semblante *m* face; (*fig*) look

sembrar [1] *vt* sow; (*fig*) scatter

semeja|nte *a* similar; (*tal*) such. ● *m* fellow man; (*cosa*) equal. ~**nza** *f* similarity. ~**r** *vi* seem. ~**rse** *vpr* look alike. **a ~nza de** like. **tener ~nza con** resemble

semen *m* semen. ~**tal** *a* stud. ● *m* stud animal

semestr|al *a* half-yearly. ~**e** *m* six months

semibreve *m* semibreve (*Brit*), whole note (*Amer*)

semic|ircular *a* semicircular. ~**írculo** *m* semicircle

semicorchea *f* semiquaver (*Brit*), sixteenth note (*Amer*)

semifinal *f* semifinal

semill|a *f* seed. ~**ero** *m* nursery; (*fig*) hotbed

seminario *m* (*univ*) seminar; (*relig*) seminary

sem|ita *a* Semitic. ● *m* Semite. ~**ítico** *a* Semitic

sémola *f* semolina

senado *m* senate; (*fig*) assembly. ~**r** *m* senator

sencill|ez *f* simplicity. ~**o** *a* simple; (*uno solo*) single

senda *f*, **sendero** *m* path

sendos *a pl* each

seno *m* bosom. ~ **materno** womb

sensaci|ón *f* sensation. ~**onal** *a* sensational

sensat|ez *f* good sense. ~**o** *a* sensible

sensi|bilidad *f* sensibility. ~**ble** *a* sensitive; (*notable*) notable; (*lamentable*) lamentable. ~**tivo** *a* ⟨*órgano*⟩ sense

sensual *a* sensual. ~**idad** *f* sensuality

senta|do *a* sitting (down). **dar algo por ~do** take something for granted. ~**r** [1] *vt* place; (*establecer*) establish. ● *vi* suit; (*de medidas*) fit; ⟨*comida*⟩ agree with. ~**rse** *vpr* sit (down); ⟨*sedimento*⟩ settle

sentencia *f* saying; (*jurid*) sentence. ~**r** *vt* sentence

sentido *a* deeply felt; (*sincero*) sincere; (*sensible*) sensitive. ● *m* sense; (*dirección*) direction. ~ **común** common sense. ~ **del humor** sense of humour. ~ **único** one-way. **doble** ~ double meaning. **no tener** ~ not make sense. **perder el** ~ faint. **sin** ~ unconscious; ⟨*cosa*⟩ senseless

sentim|ental *a* sentimental. ~**iento** *m* feeling; (*sentido*) sense; (*pesar*) regret

sentir [4] *vt* feel; (*oír*) hear; (*lamentar*) be sorry for. ● *vi* feel; (*lamentarse*) be sorry. ● *m* (*opinión*) opinion. ~**se** *vpr* feel. **lo siento** I'm sorry

seña *f* sign. ~**s** *fpl* (*dirección*) address; (*descripción*) description

señal *f* sign; (*rail etc*) signal; (*telefónico*) tone; (*com*) deposit. ~**ado** *a* notable. ~**ar** *vt* signal; (*poner señales en*) mark; (*apuntar*) point out; ⟨*manecilla, aguja*⟩ point to; (*determinar*) fix. ~**arse** *vpr* stand out. **dar ~es de** show signs of. **en ~ de** as a token of

señero *a* alone; (*sin par*) unique

señor *m* man; (*caballero*) gentleman; (*delante de nombre propio*) Mr; (*tratamiento directo*) sir. ~**a** *f* lady, woman; (*delante de nombre propio*) Mrs; (*esposa*) wife; (*tratamiento directo*) madam. ~**ial** *a* ⟨*casa*⟩ stately. ~**ita** *f* young lady; (*delante de nombre propio*) Miss; (*tratamiento directo*) miss. ~**ito** *m* young gentleman. **el ~ alcalde** the mayor. **el ~** Mr. **muy ~ mío** Dear Sir. **¡no ~!** certainly not! **ser ~ de** be master of, control

señuelo *m* lure

sepa *vb véase* **saber**

separa|ción f separation. **~do** a separate. **~r** vt separate; (apartar) move away; (de empleo) dismiss. **~rse** vpr separate; (amigos) part. **~tista** a & m & f separatist. **por ~do** separately

septentrional a north(ern)

séptico a septic

septiembre m September

séptimo a seventh

sepulcro m sepulchre

sepult|ar vt bury. **~ura** f burial; (tumba) grave. **~urero** m gravedigger

sequedad f dryness. **~ía** f drought

séquito m entourage; (fig) aftermath

ser [39] vi be. **●** m being. **~** de be made of; (provenir de) come from; (pertenecer a) belong to. **~ humano** human being. **a no ~ que** unless. **¡así sea!** so be it! **es más** what is more. **lo que sea** anything. **no sea que, no vaya a ~ que** in case. **o sea** in other words. **sea lo que fuere** be that as it may. **sea... sea** either... or. **siendo así que** since. **soy yo** it's me

seren|ar vt calm down. **~arse** vpr calm down; (tiempo) clear up. **~ata** f serenade. **~idad** f serenity. **~o** a (cielo) clear; (tiempo) fine; (fig) calm. **●** m night watchman. **al ~o** in the open

seri|al m serial. **~e** f series. **fuera de ~e** (fig, extraordinario) special. **producción** f **en ~** mass production

seri|edad f seriousness. **~o** a serious; (confiable) reliable. **en ~o** seriously. **poco ~o** frivolous

sermón m sermon

serp|enteante a winding. **~entear** vi wind. **~iente** f snake. **~iente de cascabel** rattlesnake

serrano a mountain; (jamón) cured

serr|ar [1] vt saw. **~ín** m sawdust. **~ucho** m (hand)saw

servi|cial a helpful. **~cio** m service; (conjunto) set; (aseo) toilet. **~cio a domicilio** delivery service. **~dor** m servant. **~dumbre** f servitude; (criados) servants, staff. **~l** a servile. **su (seguro) ~dor** (en cartas) yours faithfully

servilleta f serviette, (table) napkin

servir [5] vt serve; (ayudar) help; (en restaurante) wait on. **●** vi serve; (ser útil) be of use. **~se** vpr help o.s. **~se de** use. **no ~ de nada** be useless. **para ~le** at your service. **sírvase sentarse** please sit down

sesear vi pronounce the Spanish c as an s

sesent|a a & m sixty. **~ón** a & m sixty-year-old

seseo m pronunciation of the Spanish c as an s

sesg|ado a slanting. **~o** m slant; (fig, rumbo) turn

sesión f session; (en el cine) showing; (en el teatro) performance

ses|o m brain; (fig) brains. **~udo** a inteligent; (sensato) sensible

seta f mushroom

sete|cientos a & m seven hundred. **~nta** a & m seventy. **~ntón** a & m seventy-year-old

setiembre m September

seto m fence; (de plantas) hedge. **~ vivo** hedge

seudo... pref pseudo...

seudónimo m pseudonym

sever|idad f severity. **~o** a severe; (disciplina, profesor etc) strict

Sevilla f Seville

sevillan|as fpl popular dance from Seville. **~o** m person from Seville

sexo m sex

sext|eto m sextet. **~o** a sixth

sexual a sexual. **~idad** f sexuality

si m (mus) B; (solfa) te. **●** conj if; (dubitativo) whether. **~ no** or else. **por ~ (acaso)** in case

sí pron reflexivo (él) himself; (ella) herself; (ello) itself; (uno) oneself; (Vd) yourself; (ellos, ellas) themselves; (Vds) yourselves; (recíproco) each other

sí adv yes. **●** m consent

Siamés a & m Siamese

Sicilia f Sicily

sida m Aids

siderurgia f iron and steel industry

sidra f cider

siega f harvesting; (época) harvest time

siembra f sowing; (época) sowing time

siempre adv always. **~ que** if. **como ~** as usual. **de ~** (acostumbrado) usual. **lo de ~** the same old story. **para ~** for ever

sien f temple

siento vb véase **sentar** y **sentir**

sierra f saw; (cordillera) mountain range

siervo m slave

siesta f siesta

siete a & m seven

sífilis *f* syphilis

sifón *m* U-bend; (*de soda*) syphon

sigilo *m* secrecy

sigla *f* initials, abbreviation

siglo *m* century; (*época*) time, age; (*fig, mucho tiempo, fam*) ages; (*fig, mundo*) world

significa|ción *f* meaning; (*importancia*) significance. **~do** *a* (*conocido*) well-known. ● *m* meaning. **~r** [7] *vt* mean; (*expresar*) express. **~rse** *vpr* stand out. **~tivo** *a* significant

signo *m* sign. **~ de admiración** exclamation mark. **~ de interrogación** question mark

sigo *vb véase* **seguir**

siguiente *a* following, next. **lo ~** the following

sílaba *f* syllable

silb|ar *vt/i* whistle. **~ato** *m*, **~ido** *m* whistle

silenci|ador *m* silencer. **~ar** *vt* hush up. **~o** *m* silence. **~oso** *a* silent

sílfide *f* sylph

silicio *m* silicon

silo *m* silo

silueta *f* silhouette; (*dibujo*) outline

silvestre *a* wild

sill|a *f* chair; (*de montar*) saddle; (*relig*) see. **~a de ruedas** wheelchair. **~ín** *m* saddle. **~ón** *m* armchair

simb|ólico *a* symbolic(al). **~olismo** *m* symbolism. **~olizar** [10] *vt* symbolize

símbolo *m* symbol

sim|etría *f* symmetry. **~étrico** *a* symmetric(al)

simiente *f* seed

similar *a* similar

simp|atía *f* liking; (*cariño*) affection; (*fig, amigo*) friend. **~ático** *a* nice, likeable; (*amable*) kind. **~atizante** *m & f* sympathizer. **~atizar** [10] *vi* get on (well together). **me es ~ático** I like

simpl|e *a* simple; (*mero*) mere. **~eza** *f* simplicity; (*tontería*) stupid thing; (*insignificancia*) trifle. **~icidad** *f* simplicity. **~ificar** [7] *vt* simplify. **~ón** *m* simpleton

simposio *m* symposium

simula|ción *f* simulation. **~r** *vt* feign

simultáneo *a* simultaneous

sin *prep* without. **~ que** without

sinagoga *f* synagogue

sincer|idad *f* sincerity. **~o** *a* sincere

síncopa *f* (*mus*) syncopation

sincopar *vt* syncopate

sincronizar [10] *vt* synchronize

sindica|l *a* (trade-)union. **~lista** *m & f* trade-unionist. **~to** *m* trade union

síndrome *m* syndrome

sinfín *m* endless number

sinf|onía *f* symphony. **~ónico** *a* symphonic

singular *a* singular; (*excepcional*) exceptional. **~izar** [10] *vt* single out. **~izarse** *vpr* stand out

siniestro *a* sinister; (*desgraciado*) unlucky. ● *m* disaster

sinnúmero *m* endless number

sino *m* fate. ● *conj* but; (*salvo*) except

sínodo *m* synod

sinónimo *a* synonymous. ● *m* synonym

sinrazón *f* wrong

sintaxis *f* syntax

síntesis *f invar* synthesis

sint|ético *a* synthetic. **~etizar** [10] *vt* synthesize; (*resumir*) summarize

síntoma *f* sympton

sintomático *a* symptomatic

sinton|ía *f* (*en la radio*) signature tune. **~izar** [10] *vt* (*con la radio*) tune (in)

sinuoso *a* winding

sinvergüenza *m & f* scoundrel

sionis|mo *m* Zionism. **~ta** *m & f* Zionist

siquiera *conj* even if. ● *adv* at least. **ni ~** not even

sirena *f* siren

Siria *f* Syria

sirio *a & m* Syrian

siroco *m* sirocco

sirvienta *f*, **sirviente** *m* servant

sirvo *vb véase* **servir**

sise|ar *vt/i* hiss. **~o** *m* hissing

sísmico *a* seismic

sismo *m* earthquake

sistem|a *m* system. **~ático** *a* systematic. **por ~a** anywhere

sitiar *vt* besiege; (*fig*) surround

sitio *m* place; (*espacio*) space; (*mil*) siege. **en cualquier ~** anywhere

situa|ción *f* position. **~r** [21] *vt* situate; (*poner*) put; (*depositar*) deposit. **~rse** *vpr* be successful, establish o.s.

slip /es'lip/ *m* (*pl* **slips** /es'lip/) underpants, briefs

slogan /es'logan/ *m* (*pl* **slogans** /es'logan/) slogan

smoking /es'mokin/ *m* (*pl* **smokings** /es'mokin/) dinner jacket (*Brit*), tuxedo (*Amer*)

sobaco *m* armpit

sobar vt handle; knead ‹masa›

soberan|ía f sovereignty. **~o** a sovereign; (fig) supreme. ● m sovereign

soberbi|a f pride; (altanería) arrogance. **~o** a proud; (altivo) arrogant

soborn|ar vt bribe. **~o** m bribe

sobra f surplus. **~s** fpl leftovers. **~do** a more than enough. **~nte** a surplus. **~r** vi be left over; (estorbar) be in the way. **de ~** more than enough

sobrasada f Majorcan sausage

sobre prep on; (encima de) on top of; (más o menos) about; (por encima de) above; (sin tocar) over; (además de) on top of. ● m envelope. **~cargar** [12] vt overload. **~coger** [14] vt startle. **~cogerse** vpr be startled. **~cubierta** f dust cover. **~dicho** a aforementioned. **~entender** [1] vt understand, infer. **~entendido** a implicit. **~humano** a superhuman. **~llevar** vt bear. **~mesa** f. **de ~mesa** after-dinner. **~natural** a supernatural. **~nombre** m nickname. **~pasar** vt exceed. **~poner** [34] vt superimpose; (fig, anteponer) put before. **~ponerse** vpr overcome. **~pujar** vt surpass. **~saliente** a (fig) outstanding. ● m excellent mark. **~salir** [52] vi stick out; (fig) stand out. **~saltar** vt startle. **~salto** m fright. **~sueldo** m bonus. **~todo** m overall; (abrigo) overcoat. **~ todo** above all, especially. **~venir** [53] vi happen. **~viviente** a surviving. ● m & f survivor. **~vivir** vi survive. **~volar** vt fly over

sobriedad f restraint

sobrin|a f niece. **~o** m nephew

sobrio a moderate, sober

socarr|ón a sarcastic; (taimado) sly. **~onería** f sarcasm

socavar vt undermine

soci|able a sociable. **~al** a social. **~aldemocracia** f social democracy. **~aldemócrata** m & f social democrat. **~alismo** m socialism. **~alista** a & m & f socialist. **~alizar** [10] vt nationalize. **~edad** f society; (com) company. **~edad anónima** limited company. **~o** m member; (com) partner. **~ología** f sociology. **~ólogo** m sociologist

socorr|er vt help. **~o** m help

soda f (bebida) soda (water)

sodio m sodium

sofá m sofa, settee

sofistica|ción f sophistication. **~do** a sophisticated. **~r** [7] vt adulterate

sofoca|ción f suffocation. **~nte** a (fig) stifling. **~r** [7] vt suffocate; (fig) stifle. **~rse** vpr suffocate; (ruborizarse) blush

soga f rope

soja f soya (bean)

sojuzgar [12] vt subdue

sol m sun; (luz solar) sunlight; (mus) G; (solfa) soh. **al ~** in the sun. **día** m **de ~** sunny day. **hace ~, hay ~** it is sunny. **tomar el ~** sunbathe

solamente adv only

solapa f lapel; (de bolsillo etc) flap. **~do** a sly. **~r** vt/i overlap

solar a solar. ● m plot

solariego a ‹casa› ancestral

solaz m relaxation

soldado m soldier. **~ raso** private

solda|dor m welder; (utensilio) soldering iron. **~r** [2] vt weld, solder

solea|do a sunny. **~r** vt put in the sun

soledad f solitude; (aislamiento) loneliness

solemn|e a solemn. **~idad** f solemnity; (ceremonia) ceremony

soler [2] vi be in the habit of. **suele despertarse a las 6** he usually wakes up at 6 o'clock

sol|icitar vt request; apply for ‹empleo›; attract ‹atención›. **~ícito** a solicitous. **~icitud** f (atención) concern; (petición) request; (para un puesto) application

solidaridad f solidarity

solid|ez f solidity; (de color) fastness. **~ificar** [7] vt solidify. **~ificarse** vpr solidify

sólido a solid; ‹color› fast; (robusto) strong. ● m solid

soliloquio m soliloquy

solista m & f soloist

solitario a solitary; (aislado) lonely. ● m recluse; (juego, diamante) solitaire

solo a (sin compañía) alone; (aislado) lonely; (único) only; (mus) solo; ‹café› black. ● m solo; (juego) solitaire. **a solas** alone

sólo adv only. **~ que** only. **aunque ~ sea** even if it is only. **con ~ que** if; (con tal que) as long as. **no ~... sino también** not only... but also... **tan ~** only

solomillo m sirloin

solsticio m solstice

soltar [2] *vt* let go of; (*dejar caer*) drop; (*dejar salir, decir*) let out; give (*golpe etc*). ∼**se** *vpr* come undone; (*librarse*) break loose

solter|a *f* single woman. ∼**o** *a* single. ● *m* bachelor. **apellido** *m* **de** ∼**a** maiden name

soltura *f* looseness; (*agilidad*) agility; (*en hablar*) ease, fluency

solu|ble *a* soluble. ∼**ción** *f* solution. ∼**cionar** *vt* solve; settle (*huelga, asunto*)

solvent|ar *vt* resolve; settle (*deuda*). ∼**e** *a* & *m* solvent

sollo *m* sturgeon

solloz|ar [10] *vi* sob. ∼**o** *m* sob

sombr|a *f* shade; (*imagen oscura*) shadow. ∼**eado** *a* shady. **a la** ∼**a** in the shade

sombrero *m* hat. ∼ **hongo** bowler hat

sombrío *a* sombre

somero *a* shallow

someter *vt* subdue; subject (*persona*); (*presentar*) submit. ∼**se** *vpr* give in

somn|oliento *a* sleepy. ∼**ífero** *m* sleeping-pill

somos *vb véase* **ser**

son *m* sound. ● *vb véase* **ser**

sonámbulo *m* sleepwalker

sonar [2] *vt* blow; ring (*timbre*). ● *vi* sound; (*timbre, teléfono etc*) ring; (*reloj*) strike; (*pronunciarse*) be pronounced; (*mus*) play; (*fig, ser conocido*) be familiar. ∼**se** *vpr* blow one's nose. ∼ **a** sound like

sonata *f* sonata

sonde|ar *vt* sound; (*fig*) sound out. ∼**o** *m* sounding; (*fig*) poll

soneto *m* sonnet

sónico *a* sonic

sonido *m* sound

sonoro *a* sonorous; (*ruidoso*) loud

sonr|eír [51] *vi* smile. ∼**eírse** *vpr* smile. ∼**iente** *a* smiling. ∼**isa** *f* smile

sonroj|ar *vt* make blush. ∼**arse** *vpr* blush. ∼**o** *m* blush

sonrosado *a* rosy, pink

sonsacar [7] *vt* wheedle out

soñ|ado *a* dream. ∼**ador** *m* dreamer. ∼**ar** [2] *vi* dream (**con** of). ¡**ni** ∼**arlo!** not likely! (**que**) **ni** ∼**ado** marvellous

sopa *f* soup

sopesar *vt* (*fig*) weigh up

sopl|ar *vt* blow; blow out (*vela*); blow off (*polvo*); (*inflar*) blow up. ● *vi* blow. ∼**ete** *m* blowlamp. ∼**o** *m* puff; (*fig, momento*) moment

soporífero *a* soporific. ● *m* sleeping-pill

soport|al *m* porch. ∼**ales** *mpl* arcade. ∼**ar** *vt* support; (*fig*) bear. ∼**e** *m* support

soprano *f* soprano

sor *f* sister

sorb|er *vt* suck; sip (*bebida*); (*absorber*) absorb. ∼**ete** *m* sorbet, waterice. ∼**o** *m* swallow; (*pequeña cantidad*) sip

sord|amente *adv* silently, dully. ∼**era** *f* deafness

sórdido *a* squalid; (*tacaño*) mean

sordo *a* deaf; (*silencioso*) quiet. ● *m* deaf person. ∼**mudo** *a* deaf and dumb. **a la sorda**, **a sordas** on the quiet. **hacerse el** ∼ turn a deaf ear

sorna *f* sarcasm. **con** ∼ sarcastically

soroche *m* (*LAm*) mountain sickness

sorpre|ndente *a* surprising. ∼**nder** *vt* surprise; (*coger desprevenido*) catch. ∼**sa** *f* surprise

sorte|ar *vt* draw lots for; (*rifar*) raffle; (*fig*) avoid. ● *vi* draw lots; (*con moneda*) toss up. ∼**o** *m* draw; (*rifa*) raffle; (*fig*) avoidance

sortija *f* ring; (*de pelo*) ringlet

sortilegio *m* witchcraft; (*fig*) spell

sos|egado *a* calm. ∼**egar** [1 & 12] *vt* calm. ● *vi* rest. ∼**iego** *m* calmness. **con** ∼**iego** calmly

soslayo. al ∼, **de** ∼ sideways

soso *a* tasteless; (*fig*) dull

sospech|a *f* suspicion. ∼**ar** *vt/i* suspect. ∼**oso** *a* suspicious. ● *m* suspect

sost|én *m* support; (*prenda femenina*) bra (*fam*), brassière. ∼**ener** [40] *vt* support; (*sujetar*) hold; (*mantener*) maintain; (*alimentar*) sustain. ∼**enerse** *vpr* support o.s.; (*continuar*) remain. ∼**enido** *a* sustained; (*mus*) sharp. ● *m* (*mus*) sharp

sota *f* (*de naipes*) jack

sótano *m* basement

sotavento *m* lee

soto *m* grove; (*matorral*) thicket

soviético *a* (*historia*) Soviet

soy *vb véase* **ser**

Sr *abrev* (*Señor*) Mr. ∼ **a** *abrev* (*Señora*) Mrs. ∼**ta** *abrev* (*Señorita*) Miss

su *a* (*de él*) his; (*de ella*) her; (*de ello*) its; (*de uno*) one's; (*de Vd*) your; (*de ellos, de ellas*) their; (*de Vds*) your

suav|e *a* smooth; (*fig*) gentle; ⟨*color, sonido*⟩ soft. **~idad** *f* smoothness, softness. **~izar** [10] *vt* smooth, soften

subalimentado *a* underfed

subalterno *a* secondary; ⟨*persona*⟩ auxiliary

subarrendar [1] *vt* sublet

subasta *f* auction; (*oferta*) tender. **~** *vt* auction

sub|campeón *m* runner-up. **~consciencia** *f* subconscious. **~consciente** *a* & *m* subconscious. **~continente** *m* subcontinent. **~desarrollado** *a* under-developed. **~director** *m* assistant manager

súbdito *m* subject

sub|dividir *vt* subdivide. **~estimar** *vt* underestimate. **~gerente** *m* & *f* assistant manager

subi|da *f* ascent; (*aumento*) rise; (*pendiente*) slope. **~do** *a* ⟨*precio*⟩ high; ⟨*color*⟩ bright; ⟨*color*⟩ strong. **~r** *vt* go up; (*poner*) put; (*llevar*) take up; (*aumentar*) increase. **●** *vi* go up. **~r a** get into ⟨*coche*⟩; get on ⟨*autobús, avión, barco, tren*⟩; (*aumentar*) increase. **~rse** *vpr* climb up. **~rse a** get on ⟨*tren etc*⟩

súbito *a* sudden. **●** *adv* suddenly. **de ~** suddenly

subjetivo *m* subjective

subjuntivo *a* & *m* subjunctive

subleva|ción *f* uprising. **~r** *vt* incite to rebellion. **~rse** *vpr* rebel

sublim|ar *vt* sublimate. **~e** *a* sublime

submarino *a* underwater. **●** *m* submarine

subordinado *a* & *m* subordinate

subrayar *vt* underline

subrepticio *a* surreptitious

subsanar *vt* remedy; overcome ⟨*dificultad*⟩

subscri|bir *vt* (*pp* **subscrito**) sign. **~birse** *vpr* subscribe. **~pción** *f* subscription

subsidi|ario *a* subsidiary. **~o** *m* subsidy. **~o de paro** unemployment benefit

subsiguiente *a* subsequent

subsist|encia *f* subsistence. **~ir** *vi* subsist; (*perdurar*) survive

substanci|a *f* substance. **~al** *a* important. **~oso** *a* substantial

substantivo *m* noun

substitu|ción *f* substitution. **~ir** [17] *vt/i* substitute. **~to** *a* & *m* substitute

substraer [41] *vt* take away

subterfugio *m* subterfuge

subterráneo *a* underground. **●** *m* (*bodega*) cellar; (*conducto*) underground passage

subtítulo *m* subtitle

suburb|ano *a* suburban. **●** *m* suburban train. **~io** *m* suburb; (*en barrio pobre*) slum

subvenci|ón *f* grant. **~onar** *vt* subsidize

subver|sión *f* subversion. **~sivo** *a* subversive. **~tir** [4] *vt* subvert

subyugar [12] *vt* subjugate; (*fig*) subdue

succión *f* suction

suce|der *vi* happen; (*seguir*) follow; (*substituir*) succeed. **~dido** *m* event. **lo ~dido** what happened. **~sión** *f* succession. **~sivo** *a* successive; (*consecutivo*) consecutive. **~so** *m* event; (*incidente*) incident. **~sor** *m* successor. **en lo ~sivo** in future. **lo que ~de es que** the trouble is that. **¿qué ~de?** what's the matter?

suciedad *f* dirt; (*estado*) dirtiness

sucinto *a* concise; (*prenda*) scanty

sucio *a* dirty; (*vil*) mean; ⟨*conciencia*⟩ guilty. **en ~** in rough

sucre *m* (*unidad monetaria del Ecuador*) sucre

suculento *a* succulent

sucumbir *vi* succumb

sucursal *f* branch (office)

Sudáfrica *m* & *f* South Africa

sudafricano *a* & *m* South African

Sudamérica *f* South America

sudamericano *a* & *m* South American

sudar *vt* work hard for. **●** *vi* sweat

sud|este *m* south-east; (*viento*) south-east wind. **~oeste** *m* south-west; (*viento*) south-west wind

sudor *m* sweat

Suecia *f* Sweden

sueco *a* Swedish. **●** *m* (*persona*) Swede; (*lengua*) Swedish. **hacerse el ~** pretend not to hear

suegr|a *f* mother-in-law. **~o** *m* father-in-law. **mis ~os** my in-laws

suela *f* sole

sueldo *m* salary

suelo *m* ground; (*dentro de edificio*) floor; (*tierra*) land. **●** *vb véase* **soler**

suelto *a* loose; (*libre*) free; (*sin pareja*) odd; ⟨*lenguaje*⟩ fluent. **●** *m* (*en periódico*) item; (*dinero*) change

sueño *m* sleep; (*ilusión*) dream. **tener ~** be sleepy

suero *m* serum; *(de leche)* whey

suerte *f* luck; *(destino)* fate; *(azar)* chance. **de otra ~** otherwise. **de ~ que so. echar ~s** draw lots. **por ~** fortunately. **tener ~** be lucky

suéter *m* jersey

suficien|cia *f* sufficiency; *(presunción)* smugness; *(aptitud)* suitability. **~te** *a* sufficient; *(presumido)* smug. **~temente** *adv* enough

sufijo *m* suffix

sufragio *m* *(voto)* vote

sufri|do *a* ‹persona› long-suffering; ‹tela› hard-wearing. **~miento** *m* suffering. **~r** *vt* suffer; *(experimentar)* undergo; *(soportar)* bear. ● *vi* suffer

suge|rencia *f* suggestion. **~rir** [4] *vt* suggest. **~stión** *f* suggestion. **~stionable** *a* impressionable. **~stionar** *vt* influence. **~stivo** *a* *(estimulante)* stimulating; *(atractivo)* attractive

suicid|a *a* suicidal. ● *m & f* suicide; *(fig)* maniac. **~arse** *vpr* commit suicide. **~io** *m* suicide

Suiza *f* Switzerland

suizo *a* Swiss. ● *m* Swiss; *(bollo)* bun

suje|ción *f* subjection. **~tador** *m* fastener; *(de pelo, papeles etc)* clip; *(prenda femenina)* bra *(fam)*, brassière. **~tapapeles** *m invar* paper-clip. **~tar** *vt* fasten; *(agarrar)* hold; *(fig)* restrain. **~tarse** *vr* subject o.s.; *(ajustarse)* conform. **~to** *a* fastened; *(susceptible)* subject. ● *m* individual

sulfamida *f* sulpha (drug)

sulfúrico *a* sulphuric

sult|án *m* sultan. **~ana** *f* sultana

suma *f* sum; *(total)* total. **en ~** in short. **~mente** *adv* extremely. **~r** *vt* add (up); *(fig)* gather. ● *vi* add up. **~rse** *vpr*. **~rse a** join in

sumario *a* brief. ● *m* summary; *(jurid)* indictment

sumergi|ble *m* submarine. ● *a* submersible. **~r** [14] *vt* submerge

sumidero *m* drain

suministr|ar *vt* supply. **~o** *m* supply; *(acción)* supplying

sumir *vt* sink; *(fig)* plunge

sumis|ión *f* submission. **~o** *a* submissive

sumo *a* greatest; *(supremo)* supreme. **a lo ~** at the most

suntuoso *a* sumptuous

supe *vb véase* **saber**

superar *vt* surpass; *(vencer)* overcome; *(dejar atrás)* get past. **~se** *vpr* excel o.s.

superchería *f* swindle

superestructura *f* superstructure

superfici|al *a* superficial. **~e** *f* surface; *(extensión)* area. **de ~e** surface

superfluo *a* superfluous

superhombre *m* superman

superintendente *m* superintendent

superior *a* superior; *(más alto)* higher; *(mejor)* better; *(piso)* upper. ● *m* superior. **~idad** *f* superiority

superlativo *a & m* superlative

supermercado *m* supermarket

supersónico *a* supersonic

superstici|ón *f* superstition. **~oso** *a* superstitious

supervis|ión *f* supervision. **~or** *m* supervisor

superviviente *a* surviving. ● *m & f* survivor

suplantar *vt* supplant

suplement|ario *a* supplementary. **~o** *m* supplement

suplente *a & m & f* substitute

súplica *f* entreaty; *(petición)* request

suplicar [7] *vt* beg

suplicio *m* torture

suplir *vt* make up for; *(reemplazar)* replace

supo|ner [34] *vt* suppose; *(significar)* mean; *(costar)* cost. **~sición** *f* supposition

supositorio *m* suppository

suprem|acía *f* supremacy. **~o** *a* supreme; ‹momento etc› critical

supr|esión *f* suppression. **~imir** *vt* suppress; *(omitir)* omit

supuesto *a* supposed. ● *m* assumption. **~ que** if. **¡por ~!** of course!

sur *m* south; *(viento)* south wind

surc|ar [7] *vt* plough. **~o** *m* furrow; *(de rueda)* rut; *(en la piel)* wrinkle

surgir [14] *vi* spring up; *(elevarse)* loom up; *(aparecer)* appear; ‹dificultad, oportunidad› arise, crop up

surrealis|mo *m* surrealism. **~ta** *a & m & f* surrealist

surti|do *a* well-stocked; *(variado)* assorted. ● *m* assortment, selection. **~dor** *m* *(de gasolina)* petrol pump *(Brit)*, gas pump *(Amer)*. **~r** *vt* supply; have ‹efecto›. **~rse** *vpr* provide o.s. **(de** with)

susceptib|ilidad *f* susceptibility; *(sensibilidad)* sensitivity. **~le** *a* susceptible; *(sensible)* sensitive

suscitar *vt* provoke; arouse ⟨*curiosidad, interés, sospechas*⟩

suscr... *véase* **subscr...**

susodicho *a* aforementioned

suspen|der *vt* hang (up); (*interrumpir*) suspend; (*univ etc*) fail. **~derse** *vpr* stop. **~sión** *f* suspension. **~so** *a* hanging; (*pasmado*) amazed; (*univ etc*) failed. ● *m* fail. **en ~so** pending

suspicaz *a* suspicious

suspir|ar *vi* sigh. **~o** *m* sigh

sust... *véase* **subst...**

sustent|ación *f* support. **~ar** *vt* support; (*alimentar*) sustain; (*mantener*) maintain. **~o** *m* support; (*alimento*) sustenance

susto *m* fright. **caerse del ~** be frightened to death

susurr|ar *vi* ⟨*persona*⟩ whisper; ⟨*agua*⟩ murmur; ⟨*hojas*⟩ rustle. **~o** *m* (*de persona*) whisper; (*de agua*) murmur; (*de hojas*) rustle

sutil *a* fine; (*fig*) subtle. **~eza** *f* fineness; (*fig*) subtlety

suyo *a* & *pron* (*de él*) his; (*de ella*) hers; (*de ello*) its; (*de uno*) one's; (*de Vd*) yours; (*de ellos, de ellas*) theirs; (*de Vds*) yours. **un amigo ~** a friend of his, a friend of theirs, etc

T

taba *f* (*anat*) ankle-bone; (*juego*) jacks

tabac|alera *f* (state) tobacconist. **~alero** *a* tobacco. **~o** *m* tobacco; (*cigarillos*) cigarettes; (*rapé*) snuff

tabalear *vi* drum (with one's fingers)

Tabasco *m* Tabasco (**P**)

tabern|a *f* bar. **~ero** *m* barman; (*dueño*) landlord

tabernáculo *m* tabernacle

tabique *m* (thin) wall

tabl|a *f* plank; (*de piedra etc*) slab; (*estante*) shelf; (*de vestido*) pleat; (*lista*) list; (*índice*) index; (*en matemática etc*) table. **~ado** *m* platform; (*en el teatro*) stage. **~ao** *m* place where flamenco shows are held. **~as reales** backgammon. **~ero** *m* board. **~ero de mandos** dashboard. **hacer ~a rasa de** disregard

tableta *f* tablet; (*de chocolate*) bar

tabl|illa *f* small board. **~ón** *m* plank. **~ón de anuncios** notice board (*esp Brit*), bulletin board (*Amer*)

tabú *m* taboo

tabular *vt* tabulate

taburete *m* stool

tacaño *a* mean

tacita *f* small cup

tácito *a* tacit

taciturno *a* taciturn; (*triste*) miserable

taco *m* plug; (*LAm*, *tacón*) heel; (*de billar*) cue; (*de billetes*) book; (*fig, lío, fam*) mess; (*Mex, culin*) filled tortilla

tacógrafo *m* tachograph

tacón *m* heel

táctic|a *f* tactics. **~o** *a* tactical

táctil *a* tactile

tacto *m* touch; (*fig*) tact

tacuara *f* (*Arg*) bamboo

tacurú *m* (small) ant

tacha *f* fault; (*clavo*) tack. **poner ~s a** find fault with. **sin ~** flawless

tachar *vt* (*borrar*) rub out; (*con raya*) cross out. **~ de** accuse of

tafia *f* (*LAm*) rum

tafilete *m* morocco

tahúr *m* card-sharp

Tailandia *f* Thailand

tailandés *a* & *m* Thai

taimado *a* sly

taj|ada *f* slice. **~ante** *a* sharp. **~o** *m* slash; (*fig, trabajo, fam*) job; (*culin*) chopping block. **sacar ~ada** profit

Tajo *m* Tagus

tal *a* such; (*ante sustantivo en singular*) such a. ● *pron* (*persona*) someone; (*cosa*) such a thing. ● *adv* so; (*de tal manera*) in such a way. **~ como** the way. **~ cual** (*tal como*) the way; (*regular*) fair. **~ para cual** (*fam*) two of a kind. **con ~ que** as long as. **¿qué ~?** how are you? **un ~** a certain

taladr|ar *vt* drill. **~o** *m* drill; (*agujero*) drill hole

talante *m* mood. **de buen ~** willingly

talar *vt* fell; (*fig*) destroy

talco *m* talcum powder

talcualillo *a* (*fam*) so so

talega *f*, **talego** *m* sack

talento *m* talent

TALGO *m* high-speed train

talismán *m* talisman

tall|ón *m* heel; (*recibo*) counterfoil; (*cheque*) cheque. **~onario** *m* receipt book; (*de cheques*) cheque book

talla *f* carving; (*grabado*) engraving; (*de piedra preciosa*) cutting; (*estatura*) height; (*medida*) size; (*palo*) measuring stick; (*Arg, charla*) gossip. **~do** *a* carved. ● *m* carving. **~dor** *m* engraver

tallarín *m* noodle

talle *m* waist; (*figura*) figure; (*medida*) size

taller *m* workshop; (*de pintor etc*) studio

tallo *m* stem, stalk

tamal *m* (*LAm*) tamale

tamaño *a* (*tan grande*) so big a; (*tan pequeño*) so small a. ● *m* size. **de ~ natural** life-size

tambalearse *vpr* (*persona*) stagger; (*cosa*) wobble

también *adv* also, too

tambor *m* drum. **~ del freno** brake drum. **~ilear** *vi* drum

Támesis *m* Thames

tamiz *m* sieve. **~ar** [10] *vt* sieve

tampoco *adv* nor, neither, not either

tampón *m* tampon; (*para entintar*) ink-pad

tan *adv* so. **tan... ~** as... as

tanda *f* group; (*capa*) layer; (*de obreros*) shift

tangente *a* & *f* tangent

Tánger *m* Tangier

tangible *a* tangible

tango *m* tango

tanque *m* tank; (*camión, barco*) tanker

tante|ar *vt* estimate; (*ensayar*) test; (*fig*) weigh up. ● *vi* score. **~o** *m* estimate; (*prueba*) test; (*en deportes*) score

tanto *a* (*en singular*) so much; (*en plural*) so many; (*comparación en singular*) as much; (*comparación en plural*) as many. ● *pron* so much; (*en plural*) so many. ● *adv* so much; (*tiempo*) so long. ● *m* certain amount; (*punto*) point; (*gol*) goal. **~ como** as well as; (*cantidad*) as much as. **~ más... cuanto que** all the more... because. **~ si... como si** whether... or. a **~s de** sometime in. **en ~, entre ~** meanwhile. **en ~ que** while. **~ meanwhile. estar al ~ de** be up to date with. **hasta ~ que** until. **no es para ~** it's not as bad as all that. **otro ~** the same; (*el doble*) as much again. **por (lo) ~** so. **un ~** *adv* somewhat

tañer [22] *vt* play

tapa *f* lid; (*de botella*) top; (*de libro*) cover. **~s** *fpl* savoury snacks

tapacubos *m invar* hub-cap

tapa|dera *f* cover, lid; (*fig*) cover. **~r** *vt* cover; (*abrigar*) wrap up; (*obturar*) plug; put the top on (*botella*)

taparrabo(s) *m invar* loincloth; (*bañador*) swimming-trunks

tapete *m* (*de mesa*) table cover; (*alfombra*) rug

tapia *f* wall. **~r** *vt* enclose

tapicería *f* tapestry; (*de muebles*) upholstery

tapioca *f* tapioca

tapiz *m* tapestry. **~ar** [10] *vt* hang with tapestries; upholster (*muebles*)

tap|ón *m* stopper; (*corcho*) cork; (*med*) tampon; (*tec*) plug. **~onazo** *m* pop

taqu|igrafía *f* shorthand. **~ígrafo** *m* shorthand writer

taquill|a *f* ticket office; (*archivador*) filing cabinet; (*fig, dinero*) takings. **~ero** *m* clerk, ticket seller. ● *a* box-office

tara *f* (*peso*) tare; (*defecto*) defect

taracea *f* marquetry

tarántula *f* tarantula

tararear *vt/i* hum

tarda|nza *f* delay. **~r** *vi* take; (*mucho tiempo*) take a long time. **a más ~r** at the latest. **sin ~r** without delay

tard|e *adv* late. ● *f* (*antes del atardecer*) afternoon; (*después del atardecer*) evening. **~e o temprano** sooner or later. **~ío** *a* late. **de ~e en ~e** from time to time. **por la ~e** in the afternoon

tardo *a* (*torpe*) slow

tarea *f* task, job

tarifa *f* rate, tariff

tarima *f* platform

tarjeta *f* card. **~ de crédito** credit card. **~ postal** postcard

tarro *m* jar

tarta *f* cake; (*torta*) tart. **~ helada** ice-cream gateau

tartamud|ear *vi* stammer. **~o** *a* stammering. ● *m* stammerer. **es ~o** he stammers

tártaro *m* tartar

tarugo *m* chunk

tasa *f* valuation; (*precio*) fixed price; (*índice*) rate. **~r** *vt* fix a price for; (*limitar*) ration; (*evaluar*) value

tasca *f* bar

tatarabuel|a *f* great-great-grandmother. **~o** *m* great-great-grandfather

tatua|je *m* (*acción*) tattooing; (*dibujo*) tattoo. **~r** [21] *vt* tattoo

taurino a bullfighting
Tauro m Taurus
tauromaquia f bullfighting
tax|i m taxi. **~ímetro** m taxi meter. **~ista** m & f taxi-driver
tayuyá m (Arg) water melon
taz|a f cup. **~ón** m bowl
te pron (acusativo) you; (dativo) (to) you; (reflexivo) (to) yourself
té m tea. **dar el ~** bore
tea f torch
teatr|al a theatre; (exagerado) theatrical. **~alizar** [10] vt dramatize. **~o** m theatre; (literatura) drama. **obra** f **~al** play
tebeo m comic
teca f teak
tecla f key. **~do** m keyboard. **tocar la ~, tocar una ~** pull strings
técnica f technique
tecn|icismo m technicality
técnico a technical. ● m technician
tecnol|ogía f technology. **~ógico** a technological
tecolote m (Mex) owl
tecomate m (Mex) earthenware cup
tech|ado m roof. **~ar** vt roof. **~o** m (interior) ceiling; (exterior) roof. **~umbre** f roofing. **bajo ~ado** indoors
teja f tile. **~do** m roof. **a toca ~** cash
teje|dor m weaver. **~r** vt weave; (hacer punto) knit
tejemaneje m (fam) fuss; (intriga) scheming
tejido m material; (anat, fig) tissue. **~s** mpl textiles
tejón m badger
tela f material; (de araña) web; (en líquido) skin
telar m loom. **~es** mpl textile mill
telaraña f spider's web, cobweb
tele f (fam) television
tele|comunicación f telecommunication. **~diario** m television news. **~dirigido** a remote-controlled. **~férico** m cable-car; (tren) cable-railway
tel|efonear vt/i telephone. **~efónico** a telephone. **~efonista** m & f telephonist. **~éfono** m telephone. **al ~éfono** on the phone
tel|egrafía f telegraphy. **~egrafiar** [20] vt telegraph. **~egráfico** a telegraphic. **~égrafo** m telegraph
telegrama m telegram
telenovela f television soap opera
teleobjetivo m telephoto lens

telep|atía f telepathy. **~ático** a telepathic
telesc|ópico a telescopic. **~opio** m telescope
telesilla m ski-lift, chair-lift
telespectador m viewer
telesquí m ski-lift
televi|dente m & f viewer. **~sar** vt televise. **~sión** f television. **~sor** m television (set)
télex m telex
telón m curtain. **~ de acero** (historia) Iron Curtain
tema m subject; (mus) theme
tembl|ar [1] vi shake; (de miedo) tremble; (de frío) shiver; (fig) shudder. **~or** m shaking; (de miedo) trembling; (de frío) shivering. **~or de tierra** earthquake. **~oroso** a trembling
temer vt be afraid (of). ● vi be afraid. **~se** vpr be afraid
temerario a reckless
tem|eroso a frightened. **~ible** a fearsome. **~or** m fear
témpano m floe
temperamento m temperament
temperatura f temperature
temperie f weather
tempest|ad f storm. **~uoso** a stormy. **levantar ~ades** (fig) cause a storm
templ|ado a moderate; (tibio) warm; ‹clima, tiempo› mild; (valiente) courageous; (listo) bright. **~anza** f moderation; (de clima o tiempo) mildness. **~ar** vt temper; (calentar) warm; (mus) tune. **~e** m tempering; (temperatura) temperature; (humor) mood
templ|ete m niche; (pabellón) pavilion. **~o** m temple
tempora|da f time; (época) season. **~l** a temporary. ● m (tempestad) storm; (período de lluvia) rainy spell
tempran|ero a ‹frutos› early. **~o** a & adv early. **ser ~ero** be an early riser
tena|cidad f tenacity
tenacillas fpl tongs
tenaz a tenacious
tenaza f, **tenazas** fpl pliers; (para arrancar clavos) pincers; (para el fuego, culin) tongs
tende|ncia f tendency. **~nte** a. **~nte a** aimed at. **~r** [1] vt spread (out); hang out ‹ropa a secar›; (colocar) lay. ● vi have a tendency (a to). **~rse** vpr stretch out

tender|ete *m* stall. **∼o** *m* shop-keeper

tendido *a* spread out; ⟨*ropa*⟩ hung out; ⟨*persona*⟩ stretched out. ● *m* (*en plaza de toros*) front rows. **∼s** *mpl* (*ropa lavada*) washing

tendón *m* tendon

tenebroso *a* gloomy; (*turbio*) shady

tenedor *m* fork; (*poseedor*) holder

tener [40] *vt* have (got); (*agarrar*) hold; be ⟨*años, calor, celos, cuidado, frío, ganas, hambre, miedo, razón, sed etc*⟩. **¡ahí tienes!** there you are! **tengo calor** I'm hot. **tiene 3 años** he's 3 (years old). **∼se** *vpr* stand up; (*considerarse*) consider o.s., think o.s. **∼ al corriente, ∼ al día** keep up to date. **∼ 2 cm de largo** be 2 cms long. **∼ a uno por** consider s.o. **∼ que** have (got) to. **tenemos que comprar pan** we've got to buy some bread. **¡ahí tienes!** there you are! **no ∼ nada que ver con** have nothing to do with. **¿qué tienes?** what's the matter (with you)? **¡tenga!** here you are!

tengo *vb véase* **tener**

teniente *m* lieutenant. **∼ de alcalde** deputy mayor

tenis *m* tennis. **∼ta** *m & f* tennis player

tenor *m* sense; (*mus*) tenor. **a este ∼** in this fashion

tens|ión *f* tension; (*presión*) pressure; (*arterial*) blood pressure; (*elec*) voltage; (*de persona*) tenseness. **∼o** *a* tense

tentación *f* temptation

tentáculo *m* tentacle

tenta|dor *a* tempting. **∼r** [1] *vt* feel; (*seducir*) tempt

tentativa *f* attempt

tenue *a* thin; ⟨*luz, voz*⟩ faint

teñi|do *m* dye. **∼r** [5 & 22] *vt* dye; (*fig*) tinge (**de** with). **∼rse** *vpr* dye one's hair

te|ología *f* theology. **∼ológico** *a* theological. **∼ólogo** *m* theologian

teorema *m* theorem

te|oría *f* theory. **∼órico** *a* theoretical

tepache *m* (*Mex*) (alcoholic) drink

tequila *f* tequila

TER *m* high-speed train

terap|éutico *a* therapeutic. **∼ia** *f* therapy

tercer *a véase* **tercero**. **∼a** *f* (*auto*) third (gear). **∼o** *a* (*delante de nombre*

masculino en singular **tercer**) third. ● *m* third party

terceto *m* trio

terciar *vi* mediate. **∼ en** join in. **∼se** *vpr* occur

tercio *m* third

terciopelo *m* velvet

terco *a* obstinate

tergiversar *vt* distort

termal *a* thermal. **∼s** *fpl* thermal baths

termes *m invar* termite

térmico *a* thermal

termina|ción *f* ending; (*conclusión*) conclusion. **∼l** *a & m* terminal. **∼nte** *a* categorical. **∼r** *vt* finish, end. **∼rse** *vpr* come to an end. **∼r por** end up

término *m* end; (*palabra*) term; (*plazo*) period. **∼ medio** average. **∼ municipal** municipal district. **dar ∼ a** finish off. **en último ∼** as a last resort. **estar en buenos ∼s con** be on good terms with. **llevar a ∼** carry out. **poner ∼ a** put an end to. **primer ∼** foreground

terminología *f* terminology

termita *f* termite

termo *m* Thermos flask (P), flask

termómetro *m* thermometer

termo|nuclear *a* thermonuclear. **∼sifón** *m* boiler. **∼stato** *m* thermostat

terner|a *f* (*carne*) veal. **∼o** *m* calf

ternura *f* tenderness

terquedad *f* stubbornness

terracota *f* terracotta

terrado *m* flat roof

terraplén *m* embankment

terrateniente *m & f* landowner

terraza *f* terrace; (*terrado*) flat roof

terremoto *m* earthquake

terre|no *a* earthly. ● *m* land; (*solar*) plot; (*fig*) field. **∼stre** *a* earthly; (*mil*) ground

terr|ible *a* terrible. **∼iblemente** *adv* awfully. **∼ífico** *a* terrifying

territori|al *a* territorial. **∼o** *m* territory

terrón *m* (*de tierra*) clod; (*culin*) lump

terror *m* terror. **∼ífico** *a* terrifying. **∼ismo** *m* terrorism. **∼ista** *m & f* terrorist

terr|oso *a* earthy; (*color*) brown. **∼uño** *m* land; (*patria*) native land

terso *a* polished; (*piel*) smooth

tertulia *f* social gathering, get-together (*fam*). **∼r** *vi* (*LAm*) get together. **estar de** ~ chat. **hacer** ~ get together

tesi|na f dissertation. ~**s** f invar thesis; (opinión) theory

tesón m perseverance

tesor|ería f treasury. ~**ero** m treasurer. ~**o** m treasure; (tesorería) treasury; (libro) thesaurus

testa f (fam) head. ~**ferro** m figurehead

testa|mento m will. **T~mento** (relig) Testament. ~**r** vi make a will

testarudo a stubborn

testículo m testicle

testi|ficar [7] vt/i testify. ~**go** m witness. ~**go de vista**, ~**go ocular**, ~**go presencial** eyewitness. ~**monio** m testimony

teta f nipple; (de biberón) teat

tétanos m tetanus

tetera f (para el té) teapot; (Mex, biberón) feeding-bottle

tetilla f nipple; (de biberón) teat

tétrico a gloomy

textil a & m textile

text|o m text. ~**ual** a textual

textura f texture

teyú m (Arg) iguana

tez f complexion

ti pron you

tía f aunt; (fam) woman

tiara f tiara

tibio a lukewarm. **ponerle** ~ **a uno** insult s.o.

tiburón m shark

tic m tic

tiempo m time; (atmosférico) weather; (mus) tempo; (gram) tense; (en deportes) half. **a su** ~ in due course. **a** ~ in time. **¿cuánto** ~? how long? **hace buen** ~ the weather is fine. **hace** ~ some time ago. **mucho** ~ a long time. **perder el** ~ waste time. **¿qué** ~ **hace?** what is the weather like?

tienda f shop; (de campaña) tent. ~ **de comestibles**, ~ **de ultramarinos** grocer's (shop) (Brit), grocery store (Amer)

tiene vb véase **tener**

tienta. a ~**s** gropingly. **andar a** ~**s** grope one's way

tiento m touch; (de ciego) blind person's stick; (fig) tact

tierno a tender; (joven) young

tierra f land; (planeta, elec) earth; (suelo) ground; (geol) soil, earth. **caer**

por ~ (fig) crumble. **por** ~ overland, by land

tieso a stiff; (firme) firm; (engreído) conceited; (orgulloso) proud

tiesto m flowerpot

tifoideo a typhoid

tifón m typhoon

tifus m typhus; (fiebre tifoidea) typhoid (fever); (en el teatro) people with complimentary tickets

tigre m tiger

tijera f, **tijeras** fpl scissors; (de jardín) shears

tijeret|a f (insecto) earwig; (bot) tendril. ~**ear** vt snip

tila f lime(-tree); (infusión) lime tea

tild|ar vt. ~**ar de** (fig) call. ~**e** m tilde

tilín m tinkle. **hacer** ~ appeal

tilingo a (Arg, Mex) silly

tilma f (Mex) poncho

tilo m lime(-tree)

timar vt swindle

timbal m drum; (culin) timbale, meat pie

timbiriche m (Mex) (alcoholic) drink

timbr|ar vt stamp. ~**e** m (sello) stamp; (elec) bell; (sonido) timbre. **tocar el** ~**e** ring the bell

timidez f shyness

tímido a shy

timo m swindle

timón m rudder; (fig) helm

tímpano m kettledrum; (anat) eardrum. ~**s** mpl (mus) timpani

tina f tub. ~**ja** f large earthenware jar

tinglado m (fig) intrigue

tinieblas fpl darkness; (fig) confusion

tino f (habilidad) skill; (moderación) moderation; (tacto) tact

tint|a f ink. ~**e** m dyeing; (color) dye; (fig) tinge. ~**ero** m ink-well. **de buena** ~**a** on good authority

tint|ín m tinkle; (de vasos) chink, clink. ~**inear** vi tinkle; ⟨vasos⟩ chink, clink

tinto a ⟨vino⟩ red

tintorería f dyeing; (tienda) dry cleaner's

tintura f dyeing; (color) dye; (noción superficial) smattering

tío m uncle; (fam) man. ~**s** mpl uncle and aunt

tiovivo m merry-go-round

típico a typical

tipo m type; (persona, fam) person; (figura de mujer) figure; (figura de hombre) build; (com) rate

tip|ografía *f* typography. **~o-gráfico** *a* typographic(al). **~ógrafo** *m* printer

típula *f* crane-fly, daddy-long-legs

tique *m*, **tíquet** *m* ticket

tiquete *m* (*LAm*) ticket

tira *f* strip. **la ~ de** lots of

tirabuzón *m* corkscrew; (*de pelo*) ringlet

tirad|a *f* distance; (*serie*) series; (*de libros etc*) edition. **~o** *a* (*barato*) very cheap; (*fácil, fam*) very easy. **~or** *m* (*asa*) handle; (*juguete*) catapult (*Brit*), slingshot (*Amer*). **de una ~a** at one go

tiran|ía *f* tyranny. **~izar** [10] *vt* tyrannize. **~o** *a* tyrannical. ● *m* tyrant

tirante *a* tight; (*fig*) tense; (*relaciones*) strained. ● *m* shoulder strap. **~s** *mpl* braces (*esp Brit*), suspenders (*Amer*)

tirar *vt* throw; (*desechar*) throw away; (*derribar*) knock over; give (*golpe, coz etc*); (*imprimir*) print. ● *vi* (*disparar*) shoot. **~se** *vpr* throw o.s.; (*tumbarse*) lie down. **~a** tend to (be); (*parecerse a*) resemble. **~ de** pull; (*atraer*) attract. **a todo ~** at the most. **ir tirando** get by

tirita *f* sticking-plaster, plaster (*Brit*)

tirit|ar *vi* shiver. **~ón** *m* shiver

tiro *m* throw; (*disparo*) shot; (*alcance*) range. **~ a gol** shot at goal. **a ~** within range. **errar el ~** miss. **pegarse un ~** shoot o.s.

tiroides *m* thyroid (gland)

tirón *m* tug. **de un ~** in one go

tirote|ar *vt* shoot at. **~o** *m* shooting

tisana *f* herb tea

tisis *f* tuberculosis

tisú *m* (*pl* **tisus**) tissue

títere *m* puppet. **~ de guante** glove puppet. **~s** *mpl* puppet show

titilar *vi* quiver; (*estrella*) twinkle

titiritero *m* puppeteer; (*acróbata*) acrobat; (*malabarista*) juggler

titube|ante *a* shaky; (*fig*) hesistant. **~ar** *vi* stagger; (*cosa*) be unstable; (*fig*) hesitate. **~o** *m* hesitation

titula|do *a* (*libro*) entitled; (*persona*) qualified. **~r** *m* headline; (*persona*) holder. ● *vt* call. **~rse** *vpr* be called

título *m* title; (*persona*) titled person; (*académico*) qualification; (*univ*) degree; (*de periódico etc*) headline; (*derecho*) right. **a ~ de** as, by way of

tiza *f* chalk

tiz|nar *vt* dirty. **~ne** *m* soot. **~ón** *m* half-burnt stick; (*fig*) stain

toall|a *f* towel. **~ero** *m* towel-rail

tobillo *m* ankle

tobogán *m* slide; (*para la nieve*) toboggan

tocadiscos *m invar* record-player

toca|do *a* (*con sombrero*) wearing. ● *m* hat. **~dor** *m* dressing-table. **~dor de señoras** ladies' room. **~nte** *a* touching. **~r** [7] *vt* touch; (*mus*) play; ring (*timbre*); (*mencionar*) touch on; (*barco*) stop at. ● *vi* knock; (*corresponder a uno*) be one's turn. **~rse** *vpr* touch each other; (*cubrir la cabeza*) cover one's head. **en lo que ~a, en lo ~nte a** as for. **estar ~do (de la cabeza)** be mad. **te ~ a ti** it's your turn

tocateja. a ~ cash

tocayo *m* namesake

tocino *m* bacon

tocólogo *m* obstetrician

todavía *adv* still, yet. **~ no** not yet

todo *a* all; (*entero*) the whole; (*cada*) every. ● *adv* completely, all. ● *m* whole. ● *pron* everything, all; (*en plural*) everyone. **~ el día** all day. **~ el mundo** everyone. **~ el que** anyone who. **~ incluido** all in. **~ lo contrario** quite the opposite. **~ lo que** anything which. **~s los días** every day. **~s los dos** both (of them). **~s los tres** all three. **ante ~** above all. **a ~ esto** meanwhile. **con ~** still, however. **del ~** completely. **en ~ el mundo** anywhere. **estar en ~** be on the ball. **es ~ uno** it's all the same. **nosotros ~s** all of us. **sobre ~** above all

toldo *m* sunshade

tolera|ncia *f* tolerance. **~nte** *a* tolerant. **~r** *vt* tolerate

tolondro *m* (*chichón*) lump

toma *f* taking; (*med*) dose; (*de agua*) outlet; (*elec*) socket; (*elec, clavija*) plug. ● *int* well!, fancy that! **~ de corriente** power point. **~dura** *f*. **~dura de pelo** hoax. **~r** *vt* take; catch (*autobús, tren etc*); (*beber*) drink, have; (*comer*) eat, have. ● *vi* take; (*dirigirse*) go. **~rse** *vpr* take; (*beber*) drink, have; (*comer*) eat, have. **~r a bien** take well. **~r a mal** take badly. **~r en serio** take seriously. **~rla con uno** pick on s.o. **~r nota** take note. **~r por** take for. **~ y**

daca give and take. **¿qué va a ~r?** what would you like?

tomate m tomato

tomavistas m invar cine-camera

tómbola f tombola

tomillo m thyme

tomo m volume

ton. sin ~ ni son without rhyme or reason

tonada f, **tonadilla** f tune

tonel m barrel. **~ada** f ton. **~aje** m tonnage

tónic|a f tonic water; (*mus*) tonic. **~o** a tonic; (*sílaba*) stressed. ● m tonic

tonificar [7] vt invigorate

tono m tone; (*mus, modo*) key; (*color*) shade

tont|ería f silliness; (*cosa*) silly thing; (*dicho*) silly remark. **~o** a silly. ● m fool, idiot; (*payaso*) clown. **dejarse de ~erías** stop wasting time. **hacer el ~o** act the fool. **hacerse el ~o** feign ignorance

topacio m topaz

topar vt (*animal*) butt; (*persona*) bump into; (*fig*) run into. ● vi. **~ con** run into

tope a maximum. ● m end; (*de tren*) buffer. **hasta los ~s** crammed full. **ir a ~** go flat out

tópico a topical. ● m cliché

topo m mole

topogr|afía f topography. **~áfico** a topographical

toque m touch; (*sonido*) sound; (*de campana*) peal; (*de reloj*) stroke; (*fig*) crux. **~ de queda** curfew. **~tear** vt keep fingering, fiddle with. **dar el último ~** put the finishing touches

toquilla f shawl

tórax m thorax

torbellino m whirlwind; (*de polvo*) cloud of dust; (*fig*) whirl

torcer [2 & 9] vt twist; (*doblar*) bend; wring out (*ropa*). ● vi turn. **~se** vpr twist; (*fig, desviarse*) go astray; (*fig, frustrarse*) go wrong

tordo a dapple grey. ● m thrush

tore|ar vt fight; (*evitar*) dodge; (*entretener*) put off. ● vi fight (bulls). **~o** m bullfighting. **~ro** m bullfighter

torment|a f storm. **~o** m torture. **~oso** a stormy

tornado m tornado

tornar vt return

tornasolado a irridescent

torneo m tournament

tornillo m screw

torniquete m (*entrada*) turnstile

torno m lathe; (*de alfarero*) wheel. **en ~ a** around

toro m bull. **~s** mpl bullfighting. **ir a los ~s** go to a bullfight

toronja f grapefruit

torpe a clumsy; (*estúpido*) stupid

torped|ero m torpedo-boat. **~o** m torpedo

torpeza f clumsiness; (*de inteligencia*) slowness

torpor m torpor

torrado m toasted chick-pea

torre f tower; (*en ajedrez*) castle, rook

torrefac|ción f roasting. **~to** a roasted

torren|cial a torrential. **~te** m torrent; (*circulatorio*) bloodstream; (*fig*) flood

tórrido a torrid

torrija f French toast

torsión f twisting

torso m torso

torta f tart; (*bollo, fam*) cake; (*golpe*) slap, punch; (*Mex, bocadillo*) sandwich. **~zo** m slap, punch. **no entender ni ~** not understand a word of it. **pegarse un ~zo** have a bad accident

tortícolis f stiff neck

tortilla f omelette; (*Mex, de maiz*) tortilla, maize cake. **~ francesa** plain omelette

tórtola f turtle-dove

tortuga f tortoise; (*de mar*) turtle

tortuoso a winding; (*fig*) devious

tortura f torture. **~r** vt torture

torvo a grim

tos f cough. **~ ferina** whooping cough

tosco a crude; (*persona*) coarse

toser vi cough

tósigo m poison

tosquedad f crudeness; (*de persona*) coarseness

tost|ada f toast. **~ado** a (*pan*) toasted; (*café*) roasted; (*persona*) tanned; (*marrón*) brown. **~ar** vt toast (*pan*); roast (*café*); tan (*piel*). **~ón** m (*pan*) crouton; (*lata*) bore

total a total. ● adv after all. ● m total; (*totalidad*) whole. **~idad** f whole. **~itario** a totalitarian. **~izar** [10] vt total. **~ que** so, to cut a long story short

tóxico a toxic

toxicómano m drug addict

toxina f toxin

tozudo a stubborn

traba f bond; (fig, obstáculo) obstacle. **poner** ~**s a** hinder

trabaj|ador a hard-working. ● m worker. ~**ar** vt work (**de** as); knead (masa); (estudiar) work at; (actor) act. ● vi work. ~**o** m work. ~**os** mpl hardships. ~**os forzados** hard labour. ~**oso** a hard. **costar** ~**o** be difficult. ¿**en qué** ~**as?** what work do you do?

trabalenguas m invar tongue-twister

traba|r vt (sujetar) fasten; (unir) join; (empezar) start; (culin) thicken. ~**rse** vpr get tangled up. **trabársele la lengua** get tongue-tied. ~**zón** f joining; (fig) connection

trabucar [7] vt mix up

trácala f (Mex) trick

tracción f traction

tractor m tractor

tradici|ón f tradition. ~**onal** a traditional. ~**onalista** m & f traditionalist

traduc|ción f translation. ~**ir** [47] vt translate (**al** into). ~**tor** m translator

traer [41] vt bring; (llevar) carry; (atraer) attract. **traérselas** be difficult

trafica|nte m & f dealer. ~**r** [7] vi deal

tráfico m traffic; (com) trade

traga|deras fpl (fam) throat. **tener buenas** ~**deras** (ser crédulo) swallow anything; (ser tolerante) be easy-going. ~**luz** m skylight. ~**perras** f invar slot-machine. ~**r** [12] vt swallow; (comer mucho) devour; (absorber) absorb; (fig) swallow up. **no (poder)** ~**r** not be able to stand. ~**rse** vpr swallow; (fig) swallow up

tragedia f tragedy

trágico a tragic. ● m tragedian

trag|o m swallow, gulp; (pequeña porción) sip; (fig, disgusto) blow. ~**ón** a greedy. ● m glutton. **echar(se) un** ~**o** have a drink

trai|ción f treachery; (pol) treason. ~**cionar** vt betray. ~**cionero** a treacherous. ~**dor** a treacherous. ● m traitor

traigo vb véase **traer**

traje m dress; (de hombre) suit. ● vb véase **traer**. ~ **de baño** swimming-costume. ~ **de ceremonia**, ~ **de etiqueta**, ~ **de noche** evening dress

traj|ín m (transporte) haulage; (jaleo, fam) bustle. ~**inar** vt transport. ● vi bustle about

trama f weft; (fig) link; (fig, argumento) plot. ~**r** vt weave; (fig) plot

tramitar vt negotiate

trámite m step. ~**s** mpl procedure. **en** ~ in hand

tramo m (parte) section; (de escalera) flight

tramp|a f trap; (puerta) trapdoor; (fig) trick. ~**illa** f trapdoor. **hacer** ~**a** cheat

trampolín m trampoline; (fig, de piscina) springboard

tramposo a cheating. ● m cheat

tranca f stick; (de puerta) bar

trance m moment; (hipnótico etc) trance. **a todo** ~ at all costs

tranco m stride

tranquil|idad f (peace and) quiet; (de espíritu) peace of mind. ~**izar** [10] vt reassure. ~**o** a quiet; (conciencia) clear; (mar) calm; (despreocupado) thoughtless. **estáte** ~**o** don't worry

trans... pref (véase también **tras...**) trans...

transacción f transaction; (acuerdo) compromise

transatlántico a transatlantic. ● m (ocean) liner

transbord|ador m ferry. ~**ar** vt transfer. ~**arse** vpr change. ~**o** m transfer. **hacer** ~**o** change (**en** at)

transcri|bir (pp **transcrito**) vt transcribe. ~**pción** f transcription

transcur|rir vi pass. ~**so** m course

transeúnte a temporary. ● m & f passer-by

transfer|encia f transfer. ~**ir** [4] vt transfer

transfigurar vt transfigure

transforma|ción f transformation. ~**dor** m transformer. ~**r** vt transform

transfusión f transfusion. **hacer una** ~ give a blood transfusion

transgre|dir vt transgress. ~**sión** f transgression

transición f transition

transido a overcome

transigir [14] vi give in, compromise

transistor m transistor; (radio) radio

transita|ble a passable. ~**r** vi go

transitivo a transitive

tránsito m transit; (tráfico) traffic

transitorio a transitory

translúcido *a* translucent

transmi|sión *f* transmission; (*radio, TV*) broadcast. **~sor** *m* transmitter. **~sora** *f* broadcasting station. **~tir** *vt* transmit; (*radio, TV*) broadcast; (*fig*) pass on

transparen|cia *f* transparency. **~tar** *vt* show. **~te** *a* transparent

transpira|ción *f* perspiration. **~r** *vi* transpire; (*sudar*) sweat

transponer [34] *vt* move. ● *vi* disappear round ‹esquina etc›; disappear behind ‹montaña etc›. **~se** *vpr* disappear

transport|ar *vt* transport. **~e** *m* transport. **empresa** *f* **de ~es** removals company

transversal *a* transverse; ‹calle› side

tranvía *m* tram

trapacería *f* swindle

trapear *vt* (*LAm*) mop

trapecio *m* trapeze; (*math*) trapezium

trapiche *m* (*para azúcar*) mill; (*para aceitunas*) press

trapicheo *m* fiddle

trapisonda *f* (*jaleo, fam*) row; (*enredo, fam*) plot

trapo *m* rag; (*para limpiar*) cloth. **~s** *mpl* (*fam*) clothes. **a todo ~** out of control

tráquea *f* windpipe, trachea

traquete|ar *vt* bang, rattle. **~o** *m* banging, rattle

tras *prep* after; (*detrás*) behind; (*encima de*) as well as

tras... *pref* (*véase también* **trans...**) trans...

trascende|ncia *f* importance. **~ntal** *a* transcendental; (*importante*) important. **~r** [1] *vi* (*oler*) smell (**a** of); (*saberse*) become known; (*extenderse*) spread

trasegar [1 & 12] *vt* move around

trasero *a* back, rear. ● *m* (*anat*) bottom

trasgo *m* goblin

traslad|ar *vt* move; (*aplazar*) postpone; (*traducir*) translate; (*copiar*) copy. **~o** *m* transfer; (*copia*) copy; (*mudanza*) removal. **dar ~o** send a copy

trasl|úcido *a* translucent. **~ucirse** [11] *vpr* be translucent; (*dejarse ver*) show through; (*fig, revelarse*) be revealed. **~uz** *m*. **al ~uz** against the light

trasmano *m*. **a ~** out of reach; (*fig*) out of the way

trasnochar *vt* (*acostarse tarde*) go to bed late; (*no acostarse*) stay up all night; (*no dormir*) be unable to sleep; (*pernoctar*) spend the night

traspas|ar *vt* pierce; (*transferir*) transfer; (*pasar el límite*) go beyond. **~o** *m* transfer. **se ~a** for sale

traspié *m* trip; (*fig*) slip. **dar un ~** stumble; (*fig*) slip up

trasplant|ar *vt* transplant. **~e** *m* transplanting; (*med*) transplant

trastada *f* stupid thing; (*jugada*) dirty trick, practical joke

traste *m* fret. **dar al ~ con** ruin. **ir al ~** fall through

trastero *m* storeroom

trastienda *f* back room; (*fig*) shrewdness

trasto *m* piece of furniture; (*cosa inútil*) piece of junk; (*persona*) useless person, dead loss (*fam*)

trastorn|ado *a* mad. **~ar** *vt* upset; (*volver loco*) drive mad; (*fig, gustar mucho, fam*) delight. **~arse** *vpr* get upset; (*volverse loco*) go mad. **~o** *m* (*incl med*) upset; (*pol*) disturbance; (*fig*) confusion

trastrocar [2 & 7] *vt* change round

trat|able *a* friendly. **~ado** *m* treatise; (*acuerdo*) treaty. **~amiento** *m* treatment; (*título*) title. **~ante** *m & f* dealer. **~ar** *vt* (*incl med*) treat; deal with ‹asunto etc›; (*com*) deal; (*manejar*) handle; (*de tú, de Vd*) address (**de** as); (*llamar*) call. ● *vi* deal (with). **~ar con** have to do with; know ‹persona›; (*com*) deal in. **~ar de** be about; (*intentar*) try. **~o** *m* treatment; (*acuerdo*) agreement; (*título*) title; (*relación*) relationship. **¡~o hecho!** agreed! **~os** *mpl* dealings. **¿de qué se ~a?** what's it about?

traum|a *m* trauma. **~ático** *a* traumatic

través *m* (*inclinación*) slant. **a ~ de** through; (*de un lado a otro*) across. **de ~** across; (*de lado*) sideways. **mirar de ~** look askance at

travesaño *m* crosspiece

travesía *f* crossing; (*calle*) side-street

trav|esura *f* prank. **~ieso** *a* ‹niño› mischievous, naughty

trayecto *m* road; (*tramo*) stretch; (*ruta*) route; (*viaje*) journey. **~ria** *f* trajectory; (*fig*) course

traz|a *f* plan; (*aspecto*) look, appearance; (*habilidad*) skill. **~ado** *a*. **bien ~ado** good-looking. **mal ~ado** unattractive. ● *m* plan. **~ar** [10] *vt* draw; (*bosquejar*) sketch. **~o** *m* line

trébol *m* clover. **~es** *mpl* (*en naipes*) clubs

trece *a* & *m* thirteen

trecho *m* stretch; (*distancia*) distance; (*tiempo*) while. **a ~s** in places. **de ~ en ~** at intervals

tregua *f* truce; (*fig*) respite

treinta *a* & *m* thirty

tremendo *a* terrible; (*extraordinario*) terrific

trementina *f* turpentine

tren *m* train; (*equipaje*) luggage. **~ de aterrizaje** landing gear. **~ de vida** lifestyle

tren|cilla *f* braid. **~za** *f* braid; (*de pelo*) plait. **~zar** [10] *vt* plait

trepa|dor *a* climbing. **~r** *vt/i* climb

tres *a* & *m* three. **~cientos** *a* & *m* three hundred. **~illo** *m* three-piece suite; (*mus*) triplet

treta *f* trick

tri|angular *a* triangular. **~ángulo** *m* triangle

trib|al *a* tribal. **~u** *f* tribe

tribulación *f* tribulation

tribuna *f* platform; (*de espectadores*) stand

tribunal *m* court; (*de examen etc*) board; (*fig*) tribunal

tribut|ar *vt* pay. **~o** *m* tribute; (*impuesto*) tax

triciclo *m* tricycle

tricolor *a* three-coloured

tricornio *a* three-cornered. ● *m* three-cornered hat

tricotar *vt/i* knit

tridimensional *a* three-dimensional

tridente *m* trident

trigésimo *a* thirtieth

trig|al *m* wheat field. **~o** *m* wheat

trigonometría *f* trigonometry

trigueño *a* olive-skinned; ⟨*pelo*⟩ dark blonde

trilogía *f* trilogy

trilla|do *a* (*fig, manoseado*) trite; (*fig, conocido*) well-known. **~r** *vt* thresh

trimestr|al *a* quarterly. **~e** *m* quarter; (*escol, univ*) term

trin|ar *vi* warble. **estar que trina** be furious

trinchar *vt* carve

trinchera *f* ditch; (*mil*) trench; (*rail*) cutting; (*abrigo*) trench coat

trineo *m* sledge

trinidad *f* trinity

Trinidad *f* Trinidad

trino *m* warble

trío *m* trio

tripa *f* intestine; (*culin*) tripe; (*fig, vientre*) tummy, belly. **~s** *fpl* (*de máquina etc*) parts, workings. **me duele la ~** I've got tummy-ache. **revolver las ~s** turn one's stomach

tripicallos *mpl* tripe

tripl|e *a* triple. ● *m*. **el ~e (de)** three times as much (as). **~icado** *a*. **por ~icado** in triplicate. **~icar** [7] *vt* treble

trípode *m* tripod

tríptico *m* triptych

tripula|ción *f* crew. **~nte** *m* & *f* member of the crew. **~r** *vt* man

triquitraque *m* (*ruido*) clatter

tris *m* crack; (*de papel etc*) ripping noise. **estar en un ~** be on the point of

triste *a* sad; ⟨*paisaje, tiempo etc*⟩ gloomy; (*fig, insignificante*) miserable. **~za** *f* sadness

tritón *m* newt

triturar *vt* crush

triunf|al *a* triumphal. **~ante** *a* triumphant. **~ar** *vi* triumph (**de, sobre** over). **~o** *m* triumph

triunvirato *m* triumvirate

trivial *a* trivial

triza *f* piece. **hacer algo ~s** smash sth to pieces

trocar [2 & 7] *vt* (ex)change

trocear *vt* cut up, chop

trocito *m* small piece

trocha *f* narrow path; (*atajo*) short cut

trofeo *m* trophy

tromba *f* waterspout. **~ de agua** heavy downpour

trombón *m* trombone; (*músico*) trombonist

trombosis *f invar* thrombosis

trompa *f* horn; (*de orquesta*) French horn; (*de elefante*) trunk; (*hocico*) snout; (*juguete*) (spinning) top; (*anat*) tube. ● *m* horn player. **coger una ~** (*fam*) get drunk

trompada *f*, **trompazo** *m* bump

trompet|a *f* trumpet; (*músico*) trumpeter, trumpet player; (*clarín*) bugle. **~illa** *f* ear-trumpet

trompicar [7] *vi* trip

trompo *m* (*juguete*) (spinning) top

trona|da *f* thunder storm. **~r** *vt* (*Mex*) shoot. ● *vi* thunder

tronco *m* trunk. **dormir como un ~** sleep like a log

tronchar *vt* bring down; (*fig*) cut short. **~se de risa** laugh a lot

trono *m* throne

trop|a *f* troops. **~el** *m* mob. **ser de ~a** be in the army

tropero *m* (*Arg, vaquero*) cowboy

tropez|ar [1 & 10] *vi* trip; (*fig*) slip up. **~ar con** run into. **~ón** *m* stumble; (*fig*) slip

tropical *a* tropical

trópico *a* tropical. ● *m* tropic

tropiezo *m* slip; (*desgracia*) mishap

trot|ar *vi* trot. **~e** *m* trot; (*fig*) toing and froing. **al ~e** trotting; (*de prisa*) in a rush. **de mucho ~e** hard-wearing

trozo *m* piece, bit. **a ~s** in bits

truco *m* knack; (*ardid*) trick. **coger el ~** get the knack

trucha *f* trout

trueno *m* thunder; (*estampido*) bang

trueque *m* exchange. **aun a ~ de** even at the expense of

trufa *f* truffle. **~r** *vt* stuff with truffles

truhán *m* rogue; (*gracioso*) jester

truncar [7] *vt* truncate; (*fig*) cut short

tu *a* your

tú *pron* you

tuba *f* tuba

tubérculo *m* tuber

tuberculosis *f* tuberculosis

tub|ería *f* pipes; (*oleoducto etc*) pipeline. **~o** *m* tube. **~o de ensayo** test tube. **~o de escape** (*auto*) exhaust (pipe). **~ular** *a* tubular

tuerca *f* nut

tuerto *a* one-eyed, blind in one eye. ● *m* one-eyed person

tuétano *m* marrow; (*fig*) heart. **hasta los ~s** completely

tufo *m* fumes; (*olor*) bad smell

tugurio *m* hovel, slum

tul *m* tulle

tulipán *m* tulip

tulli|do *a* paralysed. **~r** [22] *vt* cripple

tumba *f* grave, tomb

tumb|ar *vt* knock down, knock over; (*fig, en examen, fam*) fail; (*pasmar, fam*) overwhelm. **~arse** *vpr* lie down. **~o** *m* jolt. **dar un ~o** tumble. **~ona** *f* settee; (*sillón*) armchair; (*de lona*) deckchair

tumefacción *f* swelling

tumido *a* swollen

tumor *m* tumour

tumulto *m* turmoil; (*pol*) riot

tuna *f* prickly pear; (*de estudiantes*) student band

tunante *m* & *f* rogue

túnel *m* tunnel

Túnez *m* (*ciudad*) Tunis; (*país*) Tunisia

túnica *f* tunic

Tunicia *f* Tunisia

tupé *m* toupee; (*fig*) nerve

tupido *a* thick

turba *f* peat; (*muchedumbre*) mob

turba|ción *f* disturbance, upset; (*confusión*) confusion. **~do** *a* upset

turbante *m* turban

turbar *vt* upset; (*molestar*) disturb. **~se** *vpr* be upset

turbina *f* turbine

turbi|o *a* cloudy; ⟨*vista*⟩ blurred; ⟨*asunto etc*⟩ unclear. **~ón** *m* squall

turbulen|cia *f* turbulence; (*disturbio*) disturbance. **~te** *a* turbulent; ⟨*persona*⟩ restless

turco *a* Turkish. ● *m* Turk; (*lengua*) Turkish

tur|ismo *m* tourism; (*coche*) car. **~ista** *m* & *f* tourist. **~ístico** *a* tourist. **oficina** *f* **de ~ismo** tourist office

turn|arse *vpr* take turns (**para** to). **~o** *m* turn; (*de trabajo*) shift. **por ~o** in turn

turquesa *f* turquoise

Turquía *f* Turkey

turrón *m* nougat

turulato *a* (*fam*) stunned

tutear *vt* address as *tú*. **~se** *vpr* be on familiar terms

tutela *f* (*jurid*) guardianship; (*fig*) protection

tuteo *m* use of the familiar *tú*

tutor *m* guardian; (*escol*) form master

tuve *vb véase* **tener**

tuyo *a* & *pron* yours. **un amigo ~** a friend of yours

U

u *conj* or

ubicuidad *f* ubiquity

ubre *f* udder

ucraniano *a* & *m* Ukranian

Ud *abrev* (*Usted*) you

uf *int* phew!; (*de repugnancia*) ugh!

ufan|arse *vpr* be proud (**con, de** of); (*jactarse*) boast (**con, de** about). **~o** *a* proud

ujier *m* usher

úlcera *f* ulcer

ulterior *a* later; ‹*lugar*› further. **~mente** *adv* later, subsequently

últimamente *adv* (*recientemente*) recently; (*al final*) finally; (*en último caso*) as a last resort

ultim|ar *vt* complete. **~átum** *m* ultimatum

último *a* last; (*más reciente*) latest; (*más lejano*) furthest; (*más alto*) top; (*más bajo*) bottom; (*fig, extremo*) extreme. **estar en las últimas** be on one's last legs; (*sin dinero*) be down to one's last penny. **por ~** finally. **ser lo ~** (*muy bueno*) be marvellous; (*muy malo*) be awful. **vestido a la última** dressed in the latest fashion

ultra *a* ultra, extreme

ultraj|ante *a* outrageous. **~e** *m* outrage

ultramar *m* overseas countries. **de ~, en ~** overseas

ultramarino *a* overseas. **~s** *mpl* groceries. **tienda de ~s** grocer's (shop) (*Brit*), grocery store (*Amer*)

ultranza. a ~ (*con decisión*) decisively; (*extremo*) extreme

ultra|sónico *a* ultrasonic. **~violeta** *a invar* ultraviolet

ulular *vi* howl; (*búho*) hoot

umbilical *a* umbilical

umbral *m* threshold

umbrío *a*, **umbroso** *a* shady

un *art indef m* (*pl* **unos**) a. **● a** one. **~os** *a pl* some

una *art indef* f a. **la ~** one o'clock

un|ánime *a* unanimous. **~animidad** *f* unanimity

undécimo *a* eleventh

ung|ir [14] *vt* anoint. **~üento** *m* ointment

únic|amente *adv* only. **~o** *a* only; (*fig, incomparable*) unique

unicornio *m* unicorn

unid|ad *f* unit; (*cualidad*) unity. **~o** *a* united

unifica|ción *f* unification. **~r** [7] *vt* unite, unify

uniform|ar *vt* standardize; (*poner uniforme a*) put into uniform. **~e** *a & m* uniform. **~idad** *f* uniformity

uni|génito *a* only. **~lateral** *a* unilateral

uni|ón *f* union; (*cualidad*) unity; (*tec*) joint. **~r** *vt* join; mix ‹*líquidos*›. **~rse** *vpr* join together

unísono *m* unison. **al ~** in unison

unitario *a* unitary

universal *a* universal

universi|dad *f* university. **U~dad a Distancia** Open University. **~tario** *a* university

universo *m* universe

uno *a* one; (*en plural*) some. **● pron** one; (*alguien*) someone, somebody. **● m** one. **~ a otro** each other. **~ y otro** both. **(los) ~s... (los) otros** some... others

untar *vt* grease; (*med*) rub; (*fig, sobornar, fam*) bribe

uña *f* nail; (*de animal*) claw; (*casco*) hoof

upa *int* up!

uranio *m* uranium

Urano *m* Uranus

urban|idad *f* politeness. **~ismo** *m* town planning. **~ístico** *a* urban. **~ización** *f* development. **~izar** [10] *vt* civilize; develop ‹*terreno*›. **~o** *a* urban

urbe *f* big city

urdimbre *f* warp

urdir *vt* (*fig*) plot

urg|encia *f* urgency; (*emergencia*) emergency; (*necesidad*) urgent need. **~ente** *a* urgent. **~ir** [14] *vi* be urgent. **carta** *f* **~ente** express letter

urinario *m* urinal

urna *f* urn; (*pol*) ballot box

urraca *f* magpie

URSS *abrev* (*historia*) (*Unión de Repúblicas Socialistas Soviéticas*) USSR, Union of Soviet Socialist Republics

Uruguay *m*. **el ~** Uruguay

uruguayo *a & m* Uruguayan

us|ado *a* used; ‹*ropa etc*› worn. **~anza** *f* usage, custom. **~ar** *vt* use; (*llevar*) wear. **~o** *m* use; (*costumbre*) usage, custom. **al ~o** (*de moda*) in fashion; (*a la manera de*) in the style of. **de ~o externo** for external use

usted *pron* you

usual *a* usual

usuario *a* user

usur|a *f* usury. **~ero** *m* usurer

usurpar *vt* usurp

usuta *f* (*Arg*) sandal

utensilio *m* tool; (*de cocina*) utensil. **~s** *mpl* equipment

útero *m* womb

útil *a* useful. **~es** *mpl* implements

utili|dad *f* usefulness. **~tario** *a* utilitarian; ⟨*coche*⟩ utility. **~zación** *f* use, utilization. **~zar** [10] *vt* use, utilize

uva *f* grape. **~ pasa** raisin. **mala ~** bad mood

V

vaca *f* cow; ⟨*carne*⟩ beef

vacaciones *fpl* holiday(s). **estar de ~** be on holiday. **ir de ~** go on holiday

vaca|nte *a* vacant. **●** *f* vacancy. **~r** [7] *vi* fall vacant

vaci|ar [20] *vt* empty; (*ahuecar*) hollow out; (*en molde*) cast; (*afilar*) sharpen. **~edad** *f* emptiness; (*tontería*) silly thing, frivolity

vacila|ción *f* hesitation. **~nte** *a* unsteady; (*fig*) hesitant. **~r** *vi* sway; (*dudar*) hesitate; (*fam*) tease

vacío *a* empty; (*vanidoso*) vain. **●** *m* empty space; (*estado*) emptiness; (*en física*) vacuum; (*fig*) void

vacuidad *f* emptiness; (*tontería*) silly thing, frivolity

vacuna *f* vaccine. **~ción** *f* vaccination. **~r** *vt* vaccinate

vacuno *a* bovine

vacuo *a* empty

vade *m* folder

vad|ear *vt* ford. **~o** *m* ford

vaga|bundear *vi* wander. **~bundo** *a* vagrant; ⟨*perro*⟩ stray. **●** *m* tramp. **~r** [12] *vi* wander (about)

vagina *f* vagina

vago *a* vague; (*holgazán*) idle; ⟨*foto*⟩ blurred. **●** *m* idler

vag|ón *m* carriage; (*de mercancías*) truck, wagon. **~ón restaurante** dining-car. **~oneta** *f* truck

vahído *m* dizzy spell

vaho *m* breath; (*vapor*) steam. **~s** *mpl* inhalation

vaina *f* sheath; (*bot*) pod

vainilla *f* vanilla

vaivén *m* swaying; (*de tráfico*) coming and going; (*fig, de suerte*) change. **vaivenes** *mpl* (*fig*) ups and downs

vajilla *f* dishes, crockery. **lavar la ~** wash up

vale *m* voucher; (*pagaré*) IOU. **~dero** *a* valid

valenciano *a* from Valencia

valent|ía *f* courage; (*acción*) brave deed. **~ón** *m* braggart

valer [42] *vt* be worth; (*costar*) cost; (*fig, significar*) mean. **●** *vi* be worth; (*costar*) cost; (*servir*) be of use; (*ser valedero*) be valid; (*estar permitido*) be allowed. **●** *m* worth. **~ la pena** worthwhile, be worth it. **¿cuánto vale?** how much is it?. **no ~ para nada** be useless. **¡vale!** all right!, OK! (*fam*). **¿vale?** all right?, OK? (*fam*)

valeroso *a* courageous

valgo *vb* *véase* **valer**

valía *f* worth

validez *f* validity. **dar ~ a** validate

válido *a* valid

valiente *a* brave; (*valentón*) boastful; (*en sentido irónico*) fine. **●** *m* brave person; (*valentón*) braggart

valija *f* case; (*de correos*) mailbag. **~ diplomática** diplomatic bag

val|ioso *a* valuable. **~or** *m* value, worth; (*descaro, fam*) nerve. **~ores** *mpl* securities. **~oración** *f* valuation. **~orar** *vt* value. **conceder ~or a** attach importance to. **objetos** *mpl* **de ~or** valuables. **sin ~or** worthless

vals *m* *invar* waltz

válvula *f* valve

valla *f* fence; (*fig*) barrier

valle *m* valley

vampiro *m* vampire

vanagloriarse [20 *o regular*] *vpr* boast

vanamente *adv* uselessly, in vain

vandalismo *m* vandalism

vándalo *m* vandal

vanguardia *f* vanguard. **de ~** (*en arte, música etc*) avant-garde

vanid|ad *f* vanity. **~oso** *a* vain

vano *a* vain; (*inútil*) useless. **en ~** in vain

vapor *m* steam; (*gas*) vapour; (*naut*) steamer. **~izador** *m* spray. **~izar** [10] vaporize. **al ~** (*culin*) steamed

vaquer|ía *f* dairy. **~o** *m* cow-herd, cowboy. **~os** *mpl* jeans

vara *f* stick; (*de autoridad*) staff; (*medida*) yard

varar *vi* run aground

varia|ble *a* & *f* variable. **~ción** *f* variation. **~nte** *f* version. **~ntes** *fpl* hors d'oeuvres. **~r** [20] *vt* change; (*dar variedad a*) vary. **●** *vi* vary; (*cambiar*) change

varice *f* varicose vein

varicela f chickenpox
varicoso a having varicose veins
variedad f variety
varilla f stick; (de metal) rod
vario a varied; (en plural) several
varita f wand
variz f varicose vein
var|ón a male. ● m man; (niño) boy.
~**onil** a manly
vasc|o a & m Basque. ~**ongado** a
Basque. ~**uence** a & m Basque. **las**
V~**ongadas** the Basque provinces
vasectomía f vasectomy
vaselina f Vaseline (P), petroleum
jelly
vasija f pot, container
vaso m glass; (anat) vessel
vástago m shoot; (descendiente) des-
cendant; (varilla) rod
vasto a vast
Vaticano m Vatican
vaticin|ar vt prophesy. ~**io** m proph-
esy
vatio m watt
vaya vb véase **ir**
Vd abrev (Usted) you
vecin|dad f neighbourhood, vicin-
ity; (vecinos) neighbours. ~**dario** m
inhabitants, neighbourhood. ~**o** a
neighbouring; (de al lado) next-door.
● m neighbour
veda|do m preserve. ~**do de caza**
game preserve. ~**r** vt prohibit
vega f fertile plain
vegeta|ción f vegetation. ~**l** a
vegetable. ● m plant, vegetable. ~**r**
vi grow; (persona) vegetate. ~**riano**
a & m vegetarian
vehemente a vehement
vehículo m vehicle
veinte a & m twenty. ~**na** f score
veinti|cinco a & m twenty-five. ~**cu-**
atro a & m twenty-four. ~**dós** a & m
twenty-two. ~**nueve** a & m twenty-
nine; ~**ocho** a & m twenty-eight.
~**séis** a & m twenty-six. ~**siete** a
& m twenty-seven. ~**trés** a & m
twenty-three. ~**ún** a twenty-one.
~**uno** a & m (delante de nombre masculino **veintún**) twenty-one
vejar vt humiliate; (molestar) vex
vejez f old age
vejiga f bladder; (med) blister
vela f (naut) sail; (de cera) candle;
(falta de sueño) sleeplessness;
(vigilia) vigil. **pasar la noche en** ~
have a sleepless night
velada f evening party

vela|do a veiled; (foto) blurred. ~**r**
vt watch over; (encubrir) veil; (foto)
blur. ● vi stay awake, not sleep. ~**r**
por look after. ~**rse** vpr (foto) blur
velero m sailing-ship
veleta f weather vane
velo m veil
veloc|idad f speed; (auto etc) gear.
~**ímetro** m speedometer. ~**ista** m &
f sprinter. **a toda** ~**idad** at full speed
velódromo m cycle-track
veloz a fast, quick
vell|o m down. ~**ón** m fleece. ~**udo**
a hairy
vena f vein; (en madera) grain. **estar**
de/en ~ be in the mood
venado m deer; (culin) venison
vencedor a winning. ● m winner
vencejo m (pájaro) swift
venc|er [9] vt beat; (superar) over-
come. ● vi win; (plazo) expire.
~**erse** vpr collapse; (persona) control o.s. ~**ido** a beaten; (com, atrasado) in arrears. **darse por** ~**ido**
give up. **los** ~**idos** mpl (en deportes
etc) the losers
venda f bandage. ~**je** m dressing. ~**r**
vt bandage
vendaval m gale
vende|dor a selling. ● m seller,
salesman. ~**dor ambulante** pedlar.
~**r** vt sell. ~**rse** vpr sell. ~**rse caro**
play hard to get. **se** ~ for sale
vendimia f grape harvest; (de vino)
vintage, year
Venecia f Venice
veneciano a Venetian
veneno m poison; (fig, malevolencia)
spite. ~**so** a poisonous
venera f scallop shell
venera|ble a venerable. ~**ción** f
reverence. ~**r** vt revere
venéreo a venereal
venero m (yacimiento) seam; (de
agua) spring; (fig) source
venezolano a & m Venezuelan
Venezuela f Venezuela
venga|nza f revenge. ~**r** [12] vt
avenge. ~**rse** vpr take revenge (**de**,
por for) (**de**, **en** on). ~**tivo** a vindictive
vengo vb véase **venir**
venia f (permiso) permission
venial a venial
veni|da f arrival; (vuelta) return.
~**dero** a coming. ~**r** [53] vi come;
(estar, ser) be. ~**r a para** come to. ~**r**

bien suit. **la semana que viene** next week. **¡venga!** come on!

venta f sale; (*posada*) inn. **en ~** for sale

ventaj|a f advantage. **~oso** a advantageous

ventan|a f window; (*de la nariz*) nostril. **~illa** f window

ventarrón m (*fam*) strong wind

ventear vt (*olfatear*) sniff

ventero m innkeeper

ventila|ción f ventilation. **~dor** m fan. **~r** vt air

vent|isca f blizzard. **~olera** f gust of wind. **~osa** f sucker. **~osidad** f wind, flatulence. **~oso** a windy

ventrílocuo m ventriloquist

ventrudo a pot-bellied

ventur|a f happiness; (*suerte*) luck. **~oso** a happy, lucky. **a la ~a** at random. **echar la buena ~a a uno** tell s.o.'s fortune. **por ~a** by chance; (*afortunadamente*) fortunately

Venus f Venus

ver [43] vt see; watch ‹*televisión*›. ● vi see. **~se** vpr see o.s.; (*encontrarse*) find o.s.; ‹*dos personas*› meet. **a mi (modo de) ~** in my view. **a ~** let's see. **de buen ~** good-looking. **dejarse ~** show. **¡habráse visto!** did you ever! **no poder ~** not be able to stand. **no tener nada que ~ con** have nothing to do with. **¡para que veas!** so there! **vamos a ~** let's see. **ya lo veo** that's obvious. **ya ~ás** you'll see. **ya ~emos** we'll see

vera f edge; (*de río*) bank

veracruzano a from Veracruz

veran|eante m & f tourist, holidaymaker. **~ear** vi spend one's holiday. **~eo** m (summer) holiday. **~iego** a summer. **~o** m summer. **casa** f **de ~eo** summer-holiday home. **ir de ~eo** go on holiday. **lugar** m **de ~eo** holiday resort

veras fpl. **de ~** really

veraz a truthful

verbal a verbal

verbena f (*bot*) verbena; (*fiesta*) fair; (*baile*) dance

verbo m verb. **~so** a verbose

verdad f truth. **¿~?** isn't it?, aren't they?, won't it? etc. **~eramente** adv really. **~ero** a true; (*fig*) real. **a decir ~** to tell the truth. **de ~** really. **la pura ~** the plain truth. **si bien es ~ que** although

verd|e a green; ‹*fruta etc*› unripe; ‹*chiste etc*› dirty, blue. ● m green; (*hierba*) grass. **~or** m greenness

verdugo m executioner; (*fig*) tyrant

verdu|lería f greengrocer's (shop). **~lero** m greengrocer. **~ra** f (green) vegetable(s)

vereda f path; (*LAm*, *acera*) pavement (*Brit*), sidewalk (*Amer*)

veredicto m verdict

vergel m large garden; (*huerto*) orchard

verg|onzoso a shameful; (*tímido*) shy. **~üenza** f shame; (*timidez*) shyness. **¡es una ~üenza!** it's a disgrace! **me da ~üenza** I'm ashamed; (*tímido*) I'm shy about. **tener ~üenza** be ashamed; (*tímido*) be shy

verídico a true

verifica|ción f verification. **~r** [7] vt check. **~rse** vpr take place; (*resultar verdad*) come true

verja f grating; (*cerca*) railings; (*puerta*) iron gate

vermú m, **vermut** m vermouth

vernáculo a vernacular

verosímil a likely; ‹*relato etc*› credible

verraco m boar

verruga f wart

versado a versed

versar vi turn. **~ sobre** be about

versátil a versatile; (*fig*) fickle

versión f version; (*traducción*) translation

verso m verse; (*línea*) line

vértebra f vertebra

verte|dero m rubbish tip; (*desaguadero*) drain. **~dor** m drain. **~r** [1] vt pour; (*derramar*) spill. ● vi flow

vertical a & f vertical

vértice f vertex

vertiente f slope

vertiginoso a dizzy

vértigo m dizziness; (*med*) vertigo. **de ~** (*fam*) amazing

vesania f rage; (*med*) insanity

vesícula f blister. **~ biliar** gallbladder

vespertino a evening

vestíbulo m hall; (*de hotel, teatro etc*) foyer

vestido m (*de mujer*) dress; (*ropa*) clothes

vestigio m trace. **~s** mpl remains

vest|imenta f clothing. **~ir** [5] vt (*ponerse*) put on; (*llevar*) wear; dress ‹*niño etc*›. ● vi dress; (*llevar*)

wear. **~irse** *vpr* get dressed; (*llevar*)
wear. **~uario** *m* wardrobe; (*cuarto*)
dressing-room
Vesuvio *m* Vesuvius
vetar *vt* veto
veterano *a* veteran
veterinari|a *f* veterinary science.
~o *a* veterinary. ● *m* vet (*fam*), veterinary surgeon (*Brit*), veterinarian
(*Amer*)
veto *m* veto. **poner el ~ a** veto
vetusto *a* ancient
vez *f* time; (*turno*) turn. **a la ~** at the
same time; (*de una vez*) in one go. **alguna que otra ~** from time to time.
alguna ~ sometimes; (*en preguntas*)
ever. **algunas veces** sometimes. **a su
~** in (his) turn. **a veces** sometimes.
cada ~ más more and more. **de una
~** in one go. **de una ~ para siempre**
once and for all. **de ~ en cuando**
from time to time. **dos veces** twice. **2
veces 4** 2 times 4. **en ~ de** instead
of. **érase una ~, había una ~** once
upon a time. **muchas veces** often.
otra ~ again. **pocas veces, rara ~**
rarely. **repetidas veces** again and
again. **tal ~** perhaps. **una ~ (que)**
once
vía *f* road; (*rail*) line; (*anat*) tract; (*fig*)
way. ● *prep* via. **~ aérea** by air. **~ de
comunicación** *f* means of com-
munication. **~ férrea** railway (*Brit*),
railroad (*Amer*). **~ rápida** fast lane.
estar en ~s de be in the process of
viab|ilidad *f* viability. **~le** *a* viable
viaducto *m* viaduct
viaj|ante *m & f* commercial trav-
eller. **~ar** *vi* travel. **~e** *m* journey;
(*corto*) trip. **~e de novios** honeymoon. **~ero** *m* traveller; (*pasajero*) passenger. **¡buen ~e!** have a
good journey!
víbora *f* viper
vibra|ción *f* vibration. **~nte** *a*
vibrant. **~r** *vt/i* vibrate
vicario *m* vicar
vice... *pref* vice-...
viceversa *adv* vice versa
vici|ado *a* corrupt; (*aire*) stale. **~ar**
vt corrupt; (*estropear*) spoil. **~o** *m*
vice; (*mala costumbre*) bad habit.
~oso *a* dissolute; (*círculo*) vicious
vicisitud *f* vicissitude
víctima *f* victim; (*de un accidente*)
casualty
victori|a *f* victory. **~oso** *a* victorious
vid *f* vine

vida *f* life; (*duración*) lifetime. **¡~
mía!** my darling! **de por ~** for life.
en mi ~ never (in my life). **en ~ de**
during the lifetime of. **estar en ~** be
alive
vídeo *m* video recorder
video|cinta *f* videotape. **~juego** *m*
video game
vidriar *vt* glaze
vidri|era *f* stained glass window;
(*puerta*) glass door; (*LAm, escaparate*) shop window. **~ería** *f* glass
works. **~ero** *m* glazier. **~o** *m* glass.
~oso *a* glassy
vieira *f* scallop
viejo *a* old. ● *m* old person
Viena *f* Vienna
viene *vb véase* **venir**
viento *m* wind. **hacer ~** be windy
vientre *f* belly; (*matriz*) womb; (*intestino*) bowels. **llevar un niño en el ~**
be pregnant
viernes *m* Friday. **V~ Santo** Good
Friday
viga *f* beam; (*de metal*) girder
vigen|cia *f* validity. **~te** *a* valid; (*ley*)
in force. **entrar en ~cia** come into
force
vigésimo *a* twentieth
vigía *f* (*torre*) watch-tower; (*persona*)
lookout
vigil|ancia *f* vigilance. **~ante** *a*
vigilant. ● *m* watchman, supervisor.
~ar *vt* keep an eye on. ● *vi* be vigilant; (*vigía etc*) keep watch. **~ia** *f*
vigil; (*relig*) fasting
vigor *m* vigour; (*vigencia*) force.
~oso *a* vigorous. **entrar en ~** come
into force
vil *a* vile. **~eza** *f* vileness; (*acción*)
vile deed
vilipendiar *vt* abuse
vilo. en ~ in the air
villa *f* town; (*casa*) villa. **la V~**
Madrid
villancico *m* (Christmas) carol
villano *a* rustic; (*grosero*) coarse
vinagre *m* vinegar. **~ra** *f* vinegar
bottle. **~ras** *fpl* cruet. **~ta** *f* vinaigrette (sauce)
vincular *vt* bind
vínculo *m* bond
vindicar [7] *vt* avenge; (*justificar*)
vindicate
vine *vb véase* **venir**
vinicult|or *m* wine-grower. **~ura** *f*
wine growing

vino *m* wine. ~ **de Jerez** sherry. ~ **de la casa** house wine. ~ **de mesa** table wine

viña *f*, **viñedo** *m* vineyard

viola *f* viola; (*músico*) viola player

violación *f* violation; (*de una mujer*) rape

violado *a & m* violet

violar *vt* violate; break ⟨*ley*⟩; rape ⟨*mujer*⟩

violen|cia *f* violence; (*fuerza*) force; (*embarazo*) embarrassment. ~**tar** *vt* force; break into ⟨*casa etc*⟩. ~**tarse** *vpr* force o.s. ~**to** *a* violent; (*fig*) awkward. **hacer** ~**cia a** force

violeta *a invar & f* violet

viol|ín *m* violin; (*músico*) violinist. ~**inista** *m & f* violinist. ~**ón** *m* double bass; (*músico*) double-bass player. ~**onc(h)elista** *m & f* cellist. ~**onc(h)elo** *m* cello

vira|je *m* turn. ~**r** *vt* turn. ● *vi* turn; (*fig*) change direction

virg|en *a & f* virgin. ~**inal** *a* virginal. ~**inidad** *f* virginity

Virgo *m* Virgo

viril *a* virile. ~**idad** *f* virility

virtual *a* virtual

virtud *f* virtue; (*capacidad*) ability. **en** ~ **de** by virtue of

virtuoso *a* virtuous. ● *m* virtuoso

viruela *f* smallpox. **picado de** ~**s** pock-marked

virulé. a la ~ (*fam*) crooked; (*estropeado*) damaged

virulento *a* virulent

virus *m invar* virus

visa|do *m* visa. ~**r** *vt* endorse

vísceras *fpl* entrails

viscos|a *f* viscose. ~**o** *a* viscous

visera *f* visor; (*de gorra*) peak

visib|ilidad *f* visibility. ~**le** *a* visible

visig|odo *a* Visigothic. ● *m* Visigoth. ~**ótico** *a* Visigothic

visillo *m* (*cortina*) net curtain

visi|ón *f* vision; (*vista*) sight. ~**onario** *a & m* visionary

visita *f* visit; (*persona*) visitor. ~ **de cumplido** courtesy call. ~**nte** *m & f* visitor. ~**r** *vt* visit. **tener** ~ have visitors

vislumbr|ar *vt* glimpse. ~**e** *f* glimpse; (*resplandor, fig*) glimmer

viso *m* sheen; (*aspecto*) appearance

visón *m* mink

visor *m* viewfinder

víspera *f* day before, eve

vista *f* sight, vision; (*aspecto, mirada*) look; (*panorama*) view. **apartar la** ~ look away; (*fig*) turn a blind eye. **a primera** ~, **a simple** ~ at first sight. **clavar la** ~ **en** stare at. **con** ~**s a** with a view to. **en** ~ **de** in view of, considering. **estar a la** ~ be obvious. **hacer la** ~ **gorda** turn a blind eye. **perder de** ~ lose sight of. **tener a la** ~ have in front of one. **volver la** ~ **atrás** look back

vistazo *m* glance. **dar/echar un** ~ **a** glance at

visto *a* seen; (*corriente*) common; (*considerado*) considered. ● *vb véase* **vestir.** ~ **bueno** passed. ~ **que** since. **bien** ~ acceptable. **está** ~ **que** it's obvious that. **lo nunca** ~ an unheard-of thing. **mal** ~ unacceptable. **por lo** ~ apparently

vistoso *a* colourful, bright

visual *a* visual. ● *f* glance. **echar una** ~ **a** have a look at

vital *a* vital. ~**icio** *a* life. ● *m* (*life*) annuity. ~**idad** *f* vitality

vitamina *f* vitamin

viticult|or *m* wine-grower. ~**ura** *f* wine growing

vitorear *vt* cheer

vítreo *a* vitreous

vitrina *f* showcase

vituper|ar *vt* censure. ~**io** *m* censure. ~**ios** *mpl* abuse

viud|a *f* widow. ~**ez** *f* widowhood. ~**o** *a* widowed. ● *m* widower

viva *m* cheer

vivacidad *f* liveliness

vivamente *adv* vividly; (*sinceramente*) sincerely

vivaz *a* (*bot*) perennial; (*vivo*) lively

víveres *mpl* supplies

vivero *m* nursery; (*fig*) hotbed

viveza *f* vividness; (*de inteligencia*) sharpness; (*de carácter*) liveliness

vivido *a* true

vívido *a* vivid

vivienda *f* housing; (*casa*) house; (*piso*) flat

viviente *a* living

vivificar [7] *vt* (*animar*) enliven

vivir *vt* live through. ● *vi* live. ● *m* life. ~ **de** live on. **de mal** ~ dissolute. **¡viva!** hurray! **¡viva el rey!** long live the king!

vivisección *f* vivisection

vivo *a* alive; (*viviente*) living; ⟨*color*⟩ bright; (*listo*) clever; (*fig*) lively. **a lo** ~, **al** ~ vividly

Vizcaya *f* Biscay

vizconde *m* viscount. **∼sa** *f* viscountess

vocab|lo *m* word. **∼ulario** *m* vocabulary

vocación *f* vocation

vocal *a* vocal. ● *f* vowel. ● *m* & *f* member. **∼ista** *m* & *f* vocalist

voce|ar *vt* call ⟨*mercancías*⟩; (*fig*) proclaim. ● *vi* shout. **∼río** *m* shouting

vociferar *vi* shout

vodka *m* & *f* vodka

vola|da *f* flight. **∼dor** *a* flying. ● *m* rocket. **∼ndas. en ∼ndas** in the air; (*fig, rápidamente*) very quickly. **∼nte** *a* flying. ● *m* (*auto*) steering-wheel; (*nota*) note; (*rehilete*) shuttlecock; (*tec*) flywheel. **∼r** [2] *vt* blow up. ● *vi* fly; (*desaparecer, fam*) disappear

volátil *a* volatile

volcán *m* volcano. **∼ico** *a* volcanic

vol|car [2 & 7] *vt* knock over; (*adrede*) empty out. ● *vi* overturn. **∼carse** *vpr* fall over; (*vehículo*) overturn; (*fig*) do one's utmost. **∼carse en** throw o.s. into

vol(e)ibol *m* volleyball

volquete *m* tipper, dump truck

voltaje *m* voltage

volte|ar *vt* turn over; (*en el aire*) toss; ring ⟨*campanas*⟩. **∼reta** *f* somersault

voltio *m* volt

voluble *a* (*fig*) fickle

volum|en *m* volume; (*importancia*) importance. **∼inoso** *a* voluminous

voluntad *f* will; (*fuerza de voluntad*) will-power; (*deseo*) wish; (*intención*) intention. **buena ∼** goodwill. **mala ∼** ill will

voluntario *a* voluntary. ● *m* volunteer. **∼so** *a* willing; (*obstinado*) wilful

voluptuoso *a* voluptuous

volver [2, *pp* **vuelto**] *vt* turn; (*de arriba a abajo*) turn over; (*devolver*) restore. ● *vi* return; (*fig*) revert. **∼se** *vpr* turn round; (*regresar*) return; (*hacerse*) become. **∼ a hacer algo** do sth again. **∼ en sí** come round

vomit|ar *vt* bring up. ● *vi* be sick, vomit. **∼ivo** *m* emetic. ● *a* disgusting

vómito *m* vomit; (*acción*) vomiting

vorágine *f* maelstrom

voraz *a* voracious

vos *pron* (*LAm*) you

vosotros *pron* you; (*reflexivo*) yourselves. **el libro de ∼** your book

vot|ación *f* voting; (*voto*) vote. **∼ante** *m* & *f* voter. **∼ar** *vt* vote for.

● *vi* vote. **∼o** *m* vote; (*relig*) vow; (*maldición*) curse. **hacer ∼os por** hope for

voy *vb véase* **ir**

voz *f* voice; (*grito*) shout; (*rumor*) rumour; (*palabra*) word. **∼ pública** public opinion. **aclarar la ∼** clear one's throat. **a media ∼** softly. **a una ∼** unanimously. **dar voces** shout. **en ∼ alta** loudly

vuelco *m* upset. **el corazón me dio un ∼** my heart missed a beat

vuelo *m* flight; (*acción*) flying; (*de ropa*) flare. **al ∼** in flight; (*fig*) in passing

vuelta *f* turn; (*curva*) bend; (*paseo*) walk; (*revolución*) revolution; (*regreso*) return; (*dinero*) change. **a la ∼** on one's return; (*de página*) over the page. **a la ∼ de la esquina** round the corner. **dar la ∼ al mundo** go round the world. **dar una ∼** go for a walk. **estar de ∼** be back. **¡hasta la ∼!** see you soon!

vuelvo *vb véase* **volver**

vuestro *a* your. ● *pron* yours. **un amigo ∼** a friend of yours

vulg|ar *a* vulgar; ⟨*persona*⟩ common. **∼aridad** *f* ordinariness; (*trivialidad*) triviality; (*grosería*) vulgarity. **∼arizar** [10] *vt* popularize. **∼o** *m* common people

vulnerab|ilidad *f* vulnerability. **∼le** *a* vulnerable

W

wáter *m* toilet

whisky /'wiski/ *m* whisky

X

xenofobia *f* xenophobia

xilófono *m* xylophone

Y

y *conj* and

ya *adv* already; (*ahora*) now; (*luego*) later; (*en seguida*) immediately; (*pronto*) soon. ● *int* of course! **∼ no** no longer. **∼ que** since. **¡∼, ∼!** oh yes!, all right!

yacaré *m* (*LAm*) alligator

yac|er [44] *vi* lie. **∼imiento** *m* deposit; (*de petróleo*) oilfield

yanqui m & f American, Yank(ee)

yate m yacht

yegua f mare

yeísmo m pronunciation of the Spanish ll like the Spanish y

yelmo m helmet

yema f (bot) bud; (de huevo) yolk; (golosina) sweet. ~ **del dedo** fingertip

yergo vb véase **erguir**

yermo a uninhabited; (no cultivable) barren. ● m wasteland

yerno m son-in-law

yerro m mistake. ● vb véase **errar**

yerto a stiff

yeso m gypsum; (arquit) plaster. ~ **mate** plaster of Paris

yo pron I. ● m ego. ~ **mismo** I myself. **soy** ~ it's me

yodo m iodine

yoga m yoga

yogur m yog(h)urt

York. de ~ (jamón) cooked

yuca f yucca

Yucatán m Yucatán

yugo m yoke

Yugoslavia f Yugoslavia

yugoslavo a & m Yugoslav

yunque m anvil

yunta f yoke

yuxtaponer [34] vt juxtapose

yuyo m (Arg) weed

Z

zafarse vpr escape; get out of (obligación etc)

zafarrancho m (confusión) mess; (riña) quarrel

zafio a coarse

zafiro m sapphire

zaga f rear. **no ir en** ~ not be inferior

zaguán m hall

zaherir [4] vt hurt one's feelings

zahorí m clairvoyant; (de agua) water diviner

zaino a (caballo) chestnut; (vaca) black

zalamer|ía f flattery. ~**o** a flattering. ● m flatterer

zamarra f (piel) sheepskin; (prenda) sheepskin jacket

zamarrear vt shake

zamba f (esp LAm) South American dance; (samba) samba

zambulli|da f dive. ~**r** [22] vt plunge. ~**rse** vpr dive

zamparse vpr fall; (comer) gobble up

zanahoria f carrot

zancad|a f stride. ~**illa** f trip. **echar la** ~**illa a uno, poner la** ~**illa a uno** trip s.o. up

zanc|o m stilt. ~**udo** a long-legged. ● m (LAm) mosquito

zanganear vi idle

zángano m drone; (persona) idler

zangolotear vt fiddle with. ● vi rattle; (persona) fidget

zanja f ditch. ~**r** vt (fig) settle

zapapico m pickaxe

zapat|ear vt/i tap with one's feet. ~**ería** f shoe shop; (arte) shoemaking. ~**ero** m shoemaker; (el que remienda zapatos) cobbler. ~**illa** f slipper. ~**illas deportivas** trainers. ~**o** m shoe

zaragata f turmoil

Zaragoza f Saragossa

zarand|a f sieve. ~**ear** vt sieve; (sacudir) shake

zarcillo m earring

zarpa f claw, paw

zarpar vi weigh anchor

zarza f bramble. ~**mora** f blackberry

zarzuela f musical, operetta

zascandil m scatterbrain

zenit m zenith

zigzag m zigzag. ~**uear** vi zigzag

zinc m zinc

zipizape m (fam) row

zócalo m skirting-board; (pedestal) plinth

zodíaco m, **zodíaco** m zodiac

zona f zone; (área) area

zoo m zoo. ~**logía** f zoology. ~**lógico** a zoological

zoólogo m zoologist

zopenco a stupid. ● m idiot

zoquete m (de madera) block; (persona) blockhead

zorr|a f fox; (hembra) vixen. ~**o** m fox

zozobra f (fig) anxiety. ~**r** vi be shipwrecked; (fig) be ruined

zueco m clog

zulú a & m Zulu

zumb|ar vt (fam) give (golpe etc). ● vi buzz. ~**ido** m buzzing

zumo m juice

zurci|do m darning. ~**r** [9] vt darn

zurdo a left-handed; (mano) left

zurrar vt (fig, dar golpes, fam) beat up

zurriago m whip

zutano m so-and-so

ENGLISH–SPANISH
INGLÉS–ESPAÑOL

A

a /ə, eɪ/ *indef art* (*before vowel* **an**) un *m*; una *f*

aback /ə'bæk/ *adv.* **be taken ~** quedar desconcertado

abacus /'æbəkəs/ *n* ábaco *m*

abandon /ə'bændən/ *vt* abandonar. ● *n* abandono *m*, desenfado *m*. **~ed** *a* abandonado; ⟨*behaviour*⟩ perdido. **~ment** *n* abandono *m*

abase /ə'beɪs/ *vt* degradar. **~ment** *n* degradación *f*

abashed /ə'bæʃt/ *a* confuso

abate /ə'beɪt/ *vt* disminuir. ● *vi* disminuir; ⟨*storm etc*⟩ calmarse. **~ment** *n* disminución *f*

abattoir /'æbətwɑ:(r)/ *n* matadero *m*

abbess /'æbɪs/ *n* abadesa *f*

abbey /'æbɪ/ *n* abadía *f*

abbot /'æbət/ *n* abad *m*

abbreviat|e /ə'bri:vɪeɪt/ *vt* abreviar. **~ion** /-'eɪʃn/ *n* abreviatura *f*, (*act*) abreviación *f*

ABC /'eɪbi:'si:/ *n* abecé *m*, abecedario *m*

abdicat|e /'æbdɪkeɪt/ *vt/i* abdicar. **~ion** /-'eɪʃn/ *n* abdicación *f*

abdom|en /'æbdəmən/ *n* abdomen *m*. **~inal** /-'dɒmnl/ *a* abdominal

abduct /æb'dʌkt/ *vt* secuestrar. **~ion** /-ʃn/ *n* secuestro *m*. **~or** *n* secuestrador *m*

aberration /æbə'reɪʃn/ *n* aberración *f*

abet /ə'bet/ *vt* (*pt* **abetted**) (*jurid*) ser cómplice de

abeyance /ə'beɪəns/ *n.* **in ~** en suspenso

abhor /əb'hɔ:(r)/ *vt* (*pt* **abhorred**) aborrecer. **~rence** /-'hɒrəns/ *n* aborrecimiento *m*; (*thing*) abominación *f*. **~rent** /-'hɒrənt/ *a* aborrecible

abide /ə'baɪd/ *vt* (*pt* **abided**) soportar. ● *vi* (*old use, pt* **abode**) morar. **~ by** atenerse a; cumplir ⟨*promise*⟩

abiding /ə'baɪdɪŋ/ *a* duradero, permanente

ability /ə'bɪlətɪ/ *n* capacidad *f*, (*cleverness*) habilidad *f*

abject /'æbdʒekt/ *a* (*wretched*) miserable; (*vile*) abyecto

ablaze /ə'bleɪz/ *a* en llamas

able /'eɪbl/ *a* (**-er, -est**) capaz. **be ~** poder; (*know how to*) saber

ablutions /ə'blu:ʃnz/ *npl* ablución *f*

ably /'eɪblɪ/ *adv* hábilmente

abnormal /æb'nɔ:ml/ *a* anormal. **~ity** /-'mælətɪ/ *n* anormalidad *f*

aboard /ə'bɔ:d/ *adv* a bordo. ● *prep* a bordo de

abode /ə'bəʊd/ *see* **abide**. ● *n* (*old use*) domicilio *m*

abolish /ə'bɒlɪʃ/ *vt* suprimir, abolir

abolition /æbə'lɪʃn/ *n* supresión *f*, abolición *f*

abominable /ə'bɒmɪnəbl/ *a* abominable

abominat|e /ə'bɒmɪneɪt/ *vt* abominar. **~ion** /-'neɪʃn/ *n* abominación *f*

aborigin|al /æbə'rɪdʒənl/ *a & n* aborigen (*m & f*), indígena (*m & f*). **~es** /-i:z/ *npl* aborígenes *mpl*

abort /ə'bɔ:t/ *vt* hacer abortar. ● *vi* abortar. **~ion** /-ʃn/ *n* aborto *m* provocado; (*fig*) aborto *m*. **~ionist** *n* abortista *m & f*. **~ive** *a* abortivo; (*fig*) fracasado

abound /ə'baʊnd/ *vi* abundar (**in** de, en)

about /ə'baʊt/ *adv* (*approximately*) alrededor de; (*here and there*) por todas partes; (*in existence*) por aquí. **~ here** por aquí. **be ~ to** estar a punto de. **be up and ~** estar levantado. ● *prep* sobre; (*around*) alrededor de; (*somewhere in*) en. **talk ~** hablar de. **~-face** *n* (*fig*) cambio *m* rotundo. **~-turn** *n* (*fig*) cambio *m* rotundo

above /ə'bʌv/ *adv* arriba. ● *prep* encima de; (*more than*) más de. **~ all** sobre todo. **~-board** *a* honrado.

● *adv* abiertamente. **~-mentioned** *a* susodicho

abrasi|on /əˈbreɪʒn/ *n* abrasión *f.* **~ve** /əˈbreɪsɪv/ *a & n* abrasivo (*m*); (*fig*) agresivo, brusco

abreast /əˈbrest/ *adv* de frente. **keep ~ of** mantenerse al corriente de

abridge /əˈbrɪdʒ/ *vt* abreviar. **~ment** *n* abreviación *f*; (*abstract*) resumen *m*

abroad /əˈbrɔːd/ *adv* (*be*) en el extranjero; (*go*) al extranjero; (*far and wide*) por todas partes

abrupt /əˈbrʌpt/ *a* brusco. **~ly** *adv* (*suddenly*) repentinamente; (*curtly*) bruscamente. **~ness** *n* brusquedad *f*

abscess /ˈæbsɪs/ *n* absceso *m*

abscond /əbˈskɒnd/ *vi* fugarse

absen|ce /ˈæbsəns/ *n* ausencia *f*; (*lack*) falta *f.* **~t** /ˈæbsənt/ *a* ausente. /æbˈsent/ *vr.* **~ o.s.** ausentarse. **~tly** *adv* distraídamente. **~t-minded** *a* distraído. **~t-mindedness** *n* distracción *f*, despiste *m*

absentee /æbsənˈtiː/ *n* ausente *m & f.* **~ism** *n* absentismo *m*

absinthe /ˈæbsɪnθ/ *n* ajenjo *m*

absolute /ˈæbsəluːt/ *a* absoluto. **~ly** *adv* absolutamente

absolution /æbsəˈluːʃn/ *n* absolución *f*

absolve /əbˈzɒlv/ *vt* (*from sin*) absolver; (*from obligation*) liberar

absor|b /əbˈzɔːb/ *vt* absorber. **~bent** *a* absorbente. **~ption** *n* absorción *f*

abstain /əbˈsteɪn/ *vi* abstenerse (**from** de)

abstemious /əbˈstiːmɪəs/ *a* abstemio

abstention /əbˈstenʃn/ *n* abstención *f*

abstinen|ce /ˈæbstɪnəns/ *n* abstinencia *f.* **~t** *a* abundante

abstract /ˈæbstrækt/ *a* abstracto. ● *n* (*quality*) abstracto *m*; (*summary*) resumen *m.* /əbˈstrækt/ *vt* extraer; (*summarize*) resumir. **~ion** /-ʃn/ *n* abstracción *f*

abstruse /əbˈstruːs/ *a* abstruso

absurd /əbˈsɜːd/ *a* absurdo. **~ity** *n* absurdo *m*, disparate *m*

abundan|ce /əˈbʌndəns/ *n* abundancia *f.* **~t** *a* abundante

abuse /əˈbjuːz/ *vt* (*misuse*) abusar de; (*ill-treat*) maltratar; (*insult*) insultar. /əˈbjuːs/ *n* abuso *m*; (*insults*) insultos *mpl*

abusive /əˈbjuːsɪv/ *a* injurioso

abut /əˈbʌt/ *vi* (*pt* **abutted**) confinar (**on** con)

abysmal /əˈbɪzməl/ *a* abismal; (*bad, fam*) pésimo; (*fig*) profundo

abyss /əˈbɪs/ *n* abismo *m*

acacia /əˈkeɪʃə/ *n* acacia *f*

academic /ækəˈdemɪk/ *a* académico; (*pej*) teórico. ● *n* universitario *m*, catedrático *m.* **~ian** /-dəˈmɪʃn/ *n* académico *m*

academy /əˈkædəmɪ/ *n* academia *f.* **~ of music** conservatorio *m*

accede /əkˈsiːd/ *vi.* **~ to** acceder a ⟨*request*⟩; tomar posesión de ⟨*office*⟩. **~ to the throne** subir al trono

accelerat|e /əkˈseləreɪt/ *vt* acelerar. **~ion** /-ˈreɪʃn/ *n* aceleración *f.* **~or** *n* acelerador *m*

accent /ˈæksənt/ *n* acento *m.* /ækˈsent/ *vt* acentuar

accentuate /əkˈsentʃʊeɪt/ *vt* acentuar

accept /əkˈsept/ *vt* aceptar. **~able** *a* aceptable. **~ance** *n* aceptación *f*; (*approval*) aprobación *f*

access /ˈækses/ *n* acceso *m.* **~ibility** /-ɪˈbɪlətɪ/ *n* accesibilidad *f.* **~ible** /əkˈsesəbl/ *a* accesible; ⟨*person*⟩ tratable

accession /ækˈseʃn/ *n* (*to power, throne etc*) ascenso *m*; (*thing added*) adquisición *f*

accessory /əkˈsesərɪ/ *a* accesorio. ● *n* accesorio *m*, complemento *m*; (*jurid*) cómplice *m & f*

accident /ˈæksɪdənt/ *n* accidente *m*; (*chance*) casualidad *f.* **by ~** por accidente, por descuido, sin querer; (*by chance*) por casualidad. **~al** /-ˈdentl/ *a* accidental, fortuito. **~ally** /-ˈdentəlɪ/ *adv* por accidente, por descuido, sin querer; (*by chance*) por casualidad

acclaim /əˈkleɪm/ *vt* aclamar. ● *n* aclamación *f*

acclimatiz|ation /əklaɪmətaɪˈzeɪʃn/ *n* aclimatación *f.* **~e** /əˈklaɪmətaɪz/ *vt* aclimatar. ● *vi* aclimatarse

accolade /ˈækəleɪd/ *n* (*of knight*) acolada *f*; (*praise*) encomio *m*

accommodat|e /əˈkɒmədeɪt/ *vt* (*give hospitality to*) alojar; (*adapt*) acomodar; (*supply*) proveer; (*oblige*) complacer. **~ing** *a* complaciente. **~ion** /-ˈdeɪʃn/ *n* alojamiento *m*; (*rooms*) habitaciones *fpl*

accompan|iment /əˈkʌmpənɪmənt/ *n* acompañamiento *m.* **~ist** *n* acompañante *m & f.* ~**y** /əˈkʌmpənɪ/ *vt* acompañar

accomplice /əˈkʌmplɪs/ *n* cómplice *m & f*

accomplish /əˈkʌmplɪʃ/ *vt* (*complete*) acabar; (*achieve*) realizar; (*carry out*) llevar a cabo. ~**ed** *a* consumado. ~**ment** *n* realización *f*; (*ability*) talento *m*; (*thing achieved*) triunfo *m*, logro *m*

accord /əˈkɔːd/ *vi* concordar. ● *vt* conceder. ● *n* acuerdo *m*; (*harmony*) armonía *f*. **of one's own** ~ espontáneamente. ~**ance** *n*. **in** ~**ance with** de acuerdo con

according /əˈkɔːdɪŋ/ *adv*. ~ **to** según. ~**ly** *adv* en conformidad; (*therefore*) por consiguiente

accordion /əˈkɔːdɪən/ *n* acordeón *m*

accost /əˈkɒst/ *vt* abordar

account /əˈkaʊnt/ *n* cuenta *f*; (*description*) relato *m*; (*importance*) importancia *f*. **on** ~ **of** a causa de. **no** ~ de ninguna manera. **on this** ~ por eso. **take** ~ **of** tener en cuenta. ● *vt* considerar. ~ **for** dar cuenta de, explicar

accountab|ility /əkaʊntəˈbɪlətɪ/ *n* responsabilidad *f*. ~**le** *a* responsable (**for** de)

accountan|cy /əˈkaʊntənsɪ/ *n* contabilidad *f*. ~**t** *n* contable *m & f*

accoutrements /əˈkuːtrəmənts/ *npl* equipo *m*

accredited /əˈkredɪtɪd/ *a* acreditado; (*authorized*) autorizado

accrue /əˈkruː/ *vi* acumularse

accumulat|e /əˈkjuːmjʊleɪt/ *vt* acumular. ● *vi* acumularse. ~**ion** /-ˈleɪʃn/ *n* acumulación *f*. ~**or** *n* (*elec*) acumulador *m*

accura|cy /ˈækjərəsɪ/ *n* exactitud *f*, precisión *f*. ~**te** *a* exacto, preciso

accus|ation /ækjuːˈzeɪʃn/ *n* acusación *f*. ~**e** *vt* acusar

accustom /əˈkʌstəm/ *vt* acostumbrar. ~**ed** *a* acostumbrado. **get** ~**ed (to)** acostumbrarse (a)

ace /eɪs/ *n* as *m*

acetate /ˈæsɪteɪt/ *n* acetato *m*

ache /eɪk/ *n* dolor *m*. ● *vi* doler. **my leg** ~**s** me duele la pierna

achieve /əˈtʃiːv/ *vt* realizar; lograr (*success*). ~**ment** *n* realización *f*; (*feat*) éxito *m*; (*thing achieved*) proeza *f*, logro *m*

acid /ˈæsɪd/ *a & n* ácido (*m*). ~**ity** /əˈsɪdətɪ/ *n* acidez *f*

acknowledge /əkˈnɒlɪdʒ/ *vt* reconocer. ~ **receipt of** acusar recibo de. ~**ment** *n* reconocimiento *m*; (*com*) acuse *m* de recibo

acme /ˈækmɪ/ *n* cima *f*

acne /ˈæknɪ/ *n* acné *m*

acorn /ˈeɪkɔːn/ *n* bellota *f*

acoustic /əˈkuːstɪk/ *a* acústico. ~**s** *npl* acústica *f*

acquaint /əˈkweɪnt/ *vt*. ~ **s.o. with** poner a uno al corriente de. **be** ~**ed with** conocer (*person*); saber (*fact*). ~**ance** *n* conocimiento *m*; (*person*) conocido *m*

acquiesce /ækwɪˈes/ *vi* consentir (**in** en). ~**nce** *n* aquiescencia *f*, consentimiento *m*

acqui|re /əˈkwaɪə(r)/ *vt* adquirir; aprender (*language*). ~**re a taste for** tomar gusto a. ~**sition** /ækwɪˈzɪʃn/ *n* adquisición *f*. ~**sitive** /-ˈkwɪzətɪv/ *a* codicioso

acquit /əˈkwɪt/ *vt* (*pt* **acquitted**) absolver; ~ **o.s. well** defenderse bien, tener éxito. ~**tal** *n* absolución *f*

acre /ˈeɪkə(r)/ *n* acre *m*. ~**age** *n* superficie *f* (en acres)

acrid /ˈækrɪd/ *a* acre

acrimon|ious /ækrɪˈməʊnɪəs/ *a* cáustico, mordaz. ~**y** /ˈækrɪmənɪ/ *n* acrimonia *f*, acritud *f*

acrobat /ˈækrəbæt/ *n* acróbata *m & f*. ~**ic** /-ˈbætɪk/ *a* acrobático. ~**ics** /-ˈbætɪks/ *npl* acrobacia *f*

acronym /ˈækrənɪm/ *n* acrónimo *m*, siglas *fpl*

across /əˈkrɒs/ *adv & prep* (*side to side*) de un lado al otro; (*on other side*) del otro lado de; (*crosswise*) a través. **go** *or* **walk** ~ atravesar

act /ækt/ *n* acto *m*; (*action*) acción *f*; (*in variety show*) número *m*; (*decree*) decreto *m*. ● *vt* hacer (*part, role*). ● *vi* actuar; (*pretend*) fingir; (*function*) funcionar. ~ **as** actuar de. ~ **for** representar. ~**ing** *a* interino. ● *n* (*of play*) representación *f*; (*by actor*) interpretación *f*; (*profession*) profesión *f* de actor

action /ˈækʃn/ *n* acción *f*; (*jurid*) demanda *f*; (*plot*) argumento *m*. **out of** ~ (*on sign*) no funciona. **put out of** ~ inutilizar. **take** ~ tomar medidas

activate /ˈæktɪveɪt/ *vt* activar

activ|e /ˈæktɪv/ *a* activo; (*energetic*) enérgico; (*volcano*) en actividad. ~**ity** /-ˈtɪvətɪ/ *n* actividad *f*

act|or /'æktə(r)/ n actor m. **~ress** n actriz f

actual /'æktʃʊəl/ a verdadero. **~ity** /-'ælətɪ/ n realidad f. **~ly** adv en realidad, efectivamente; (even) incluso

actuary /'æktʃʊərɪ/ n actuario m

actuate /'æktjʊeɪt/ vt accionar, impulsar

acumen /'ækjʊmen/ n perspicacia f

acupunctur|e /'ækjʊpʌŋktʃə(r)/ n acupuntura f. **~ist** n acupunturista m & f

acute /ə'kjuːt/ a agudo. **~ly** adv agudamente. **~ness** n agudeza f

ad /æd/ n (fam) anuncio m

AD /eɪ'diː/ abbr (Anno Domini) d.J.C.

adamant /'ædəmənt/ a inflexible

Adam's apple /'ædəmz'æpl/ n nuez f (de Adán)

adapt /ə'dæpt/ vt adaptar. ● vi adaptarse

adaptab|ility /ədæptə'bɪlɪtɪ/ n adaptabilidad f. **~le** /ə'dæptəbl/ a adaptable

adaptation /ædæp'teɪʃn/ n adaptación f; (of book etc) versión f

adaptor /ə'dæptə(r)/ n (elec) adaptador m

add /æd/ vt añadir. ● vi sumar. **~ up** sumar; (fig) tener sentido. **~ up to** equivaler a

adder /'ædə(r)/ n víbora f

addict /'ædɪkt/ n adicto m; (fig) entusiasta m & f. **~ed** /ə'dɪktɪd/ a. **~ed to** adicto a; (fig) fanático de. **~ion** /-ʃn/ n (med) dependencia f; (fig) afición f. **~ive** a que crea dependencia

adding machine /'ædɪŋməʃiːn/ n máquina f de sumar, sumadora f

addition /ə'dɪʃn/ n suma f. **in ~** además. **~al** /-ʃənl/ a suplementario

additive /'ædɪtɪv/ a & n aditivo (m)

address /ə'dres/ n señas fpl, dirección f; (speech) discurso m. ● vt poner la dirección; (speak to) dirigirse a. **~ee** /ædre'siː/ n destinatario m

adenoids /'ædɪnɔɪdz/ npl vegetaciones fpl adenoideas

adept /'ædept/ a & n experto (m)

adequa|cy /'ædɪkwəsɪ/ n suficiencia f. **~te** a suficiente, adecuado. **~tely** adv suficientemente, adecuadamente

adhere /əd'hɪə(r)/ vi adherirse (to a); observar (rule). **~nce** /-rəns/ n adhesión f; (to rules) observancia f

adhesion /əd'hiːʒn/ n adherencia f

adhesive /əd'hiːsɪv/ a & n adhesivo (m)

ad infinitum /ædɪnfɪ'naɪtəm/ adv hasta el infinito

adjacent /ə'dʒeɪsnt/ a contiguo

adjective /'ædʒɪktɪv/ n adjetivo m

adjoin /ə'dʒɔɪn/ vt lindar con. **~ing** a contiguo

adjourn /ə'dʒɜːn/ vt aplazar; suspender (meeting etc). ● vi suspenderse. **~ to** trasladarse a

adjudicate /ə'dʒuːdɪkeɪt/ vt juzgar. ● vi actuar como juez

adjust /ə'dʒʌst/ vt ajustar (machine); (arrange) arreglar. ● vi. **~ (to)** adaptarse (a). **~able** a ajustable. **~ment** n adaptación f; (tec) ajuste m

ad lib /æd'lɪb/ a improvisado. ● vi (pt -libbed) (fam) improvisar

administer /əd'mɪnɪstə(r)/ vt administrar, dar, proporcionar

administrat|ion /ədmɪnɪ'streɪʃn/ n administración f. **~or** n administrador m

admirable /'ædmərəbl/ a admirable

admiral /'ædmərəl/ n almirante m

admiration /ædmə'reɪʃn/ n admiración f

admire /əd'maɪə(r)/ vt admirar. **~r** /-'maɪərə(r)/ n admirador m; (suitor) enamorado m

admissible /əd'mɪsəbl/ a admisible

admission /əd'mɪʃn/ n admisión f; (entry) entrada f

admit /əd'mɪt/ vt (pt admitted) dejar entrar; (acknowledge) admitir, reconocer. **~ to** confesar. **be ~ted** (to hospital etc) ingresar. **~tance** n entrada f. **~tedly** adv es verdad que

admoni|sh /əd'mɒnɪʃ/ vt reprender; (advise) aconsejar. **~tion** /-'nɪʃn/ n reprensión f

ado /ə'duː/ n alboroto m; (trouble) dificultad f. **without more ~** en seguida, sin más

adolescen|ce /ædə'lesns/ n adolescencia f. **~t** a & n adolescente (m & f)

adopt /ə'dɒpt/ vt adoptar. **~ed** a (child) adoptivo. **~ion** /-ʃn/ n adopción f. **~ive** a adoptivo

ador|able /ə'dɔːrəbl/ a adorable. **~ation** /ædə'reɪʃn/ n adoración f. **~e** /ə'dɔː(r)/ vt adorar

adorn /ə'dɔːn/ vt adornar. **~ment** n adorno m

adrenalin /ə'drenəlɪn/ n adrenalina f

adrift /ə'drɪft/ *a & adv* a la deriva

adroit /ə'drɔɪt/ *a* diestro

adulation /ædju'leɪʃn/ *n* adulación *f*

adult /'ædʌlt/ *a & n* adulto (*m*)

adulterat|ion /ədʌltə'reɪʃn/ *n* adulteración *f*. **~e** /ə'dʌltəreɪt/ *vt* adulterar

adulter|er /ə'dʌltərə(r)/ *n* adúltero *m*. **~ess** *n* adúltera *f*. **~ous** *a* adúltero. **~y** *n* adulterio *m*

advance /əd'vɑːns/ *vt* adelantar. ● *vi* adelantarse. ● *n* adelanto *m*. **in ~** con anticipación, por adelantado. **~d** *a* avanzado; ⟨studies⟩ superior. **~ment** *n* adelanto *m*; (*in job*) promoción *f*

advantage /əd'vɑːntɪdʒ/ *n* ventaja *f*. **take ~ of** aprovecharse de; abusar de ⟨person⟩. **~ous** /ædvən'teɪdʒəs/ *a* ventajoso

advent /'ædvənt/ *n* venida *f*. **A~** *n* adviento *m*

adventur|e /əd'ventʃə(r)/ *n* aventura *f*. **~er** *n* aventurero *m*. **~ous** *a* ⟨persona⟩ aventurero; ⟨cosa⟩ arriesgado; (*fig, bold*) llamativo

adverb /'ædvɜːb/ *n* adverbio *m*

adversary /'ædvəsəri/ *n* adversario *m*

advers|e /'ædvɜːs/ *a* adverso, contrario, desfavorable. **~ity** /əd'vɜːsəti/ *n* infortunio *m*

advert /'ædvɜːt/ *n* (*fam*) anuncio *m*. **~ise** /'ædvətaɪz/ *vt* anunciar. ● *vi* hacer publicidad; (*seek, sell*) poner un anuncio. **~isement** /əd'vɜːtɪsmənt/ *n* anuncio *m*. **~iser** /-ə(r)/ *n* anunciante *m & f*

advice /əd'vaɪs/ *n* consejo *m*; (*report*) informe *m*

advis|able /əd'vaɪzəbl/ *a* aconsejable. **~e** *vt* aconsejar; (*inform*) avisar. **~e against** aconsejar en contra de. **~er** *n* consejero *m*; (*consultant*) asesor *m*. **~ory** *a* consultivo

advocate /'ædvəkət/ *n* defensor *m*; (*jurid*) abogado *m*. /'ædvəkeɪt/ *vt* recomendar

aegis /'iːdʒɪs/ *n* égida *f*. **under the ~ of** bajo la tutela de, patrocinado por

aeon /'iːən/ *n* eternidad *f*

aerial /'eərɪəl/ *a* aéreo. ● *n* antena *f*

aerobatics /eərə'bætɪks/ *npl* acrobacia *f* aérea

aerobics /eə'rɒbɪks/ *npl* aeróbica *f*

aerodrome /'eərədrəʊm/ *n* aeródromo *m*

aerodynamic /eərəʊdaɪ'næmɪk/ *a* aerodinámico

aeroplane /'eərəpleɪn/ *n* avión *m*

aerosol /'eərəsɒl/ *n* aerosol *m*

aesthetic /iːs'θetɪk/ *a* estético

afar /ə'fɑː(r)/ *adv* lejos

affable /'æfəbl/ *a* afable

affair /ə'feə(r)/ *n* asunto *m*. **(love) ~** aventura *f*, amorío *m*. **~s** *npl* (*business*) negocios *mpl*

affect /ə'fekt/ *vt* afectar; (*pretend*) fingir

affect|ation /æfek'teɪʃn/ *n* afectación *f*. **~ed** *a* afectado, amanerado

affection /ə'fekʃn/ *n* cariño *m*; (*disease*) afección *f*. **~ate** /-ʃənət/ *a* cariñoso

affiliat|e /ə'fɪlɪeɪt/ *vt* afiliar. **~ion** /-'eɪʃn/ *n* afiliación *f*

affinity /ə'fɪnəti/ *n* afinidad *f*

affirm /ə'fɜːm/ *vt* afirmar. **~ation** /æfə'meɪʃn/ *n* afirmación *f*

affirmative /ə'fɜːmətɪv/ *a* afirmativo. ● *n* respuesta *f* afirmativa

affix /ə'fɪks/ *vt* sujetar; añadir ⟨signature⟩; pegar ⟨stamp⟩

afflict /ə'flɪkt/ *vt* afligir. **~ion** /-ʃn/ *n* aflicción *f*, pena *f*

affluen|ce /'æfluəns/ *n* riqueza *f*. **~t** *a* rico. ● *n* (*geog*) afluente *m*

afford /ə'fɔːd/ *vt* permitirse; (*provide*) dar

affray /ə'freɪ/ *n* reyerta *f*

affront /ə'frʌnt/ *n* afrenta *f*, ofensa *f*. ● *vt* afrentar, ofender

afield /ə'fiːld/ *adv*. **far ~** muy lejos

aflame /ə'fleɪm/ *adv & a* en llamas

afloat /ə'fləʊt/ *adv* a flote

afoot /ə'fʊt/ *adv*. **sth is ~** se está tramando algo

aforesaid /ə'fɔːsed/ *a* susodicho

afraid /ə'freɪd/ *a*. **be ~** tener miedo (**of** a); (*be sorry*) sentir, lamentar

afresh /ə'freʃ/ *adv* de nuevo

Africa /'æfrɪkə/ *n* África *f*. **~n** *a & n* africano (*m*)

after /'ɑːftə(r)/ *adv* después; (*behind*) detrás. ● *prep* después de; (*behind*) detrás de. **be ~** (*seek*) buscar, andar en busca de. ● *conj* después de que. ● *a* posterior

afterbirth /'ɑːftəbɜːθ/ *n* placenta *f*

after-effect /'ɑːftərɪfekt/ *n* consecuencia *f*, efecto *m* secundario

aftermath /'ɑːftəmæθ/ *n* secuelas *fpl*

afternoon /ɑːftə'nuːn/ *n* tarde *f*

aftershave /ˈɑːftəʃeɪv/ n loción f para después del afeitado

afterthought /ˈɑːftəθɔːt/ n ocurrencia f tardía

afterwards /ˈɑːftəwədz/ adv después

again /əˈgen/ adv otra vez; (besides) además. ~ **and** ~ una y otra vez

against /əˈgenst/ prep contra, en contra de

age /eɪdʒ/ n edad f. **of** ~ mayor de edad. **under** ~ menor de edad. ● vt/i (pres p **ageing**) envejecer. ~**d** /ˈeɪdʒd/ a de ... años. ~**d 10** de 10 años, que tiene 10 años. ~**d** /ˈeɪdʒɪd/ a viejo, anciano. ~**less** a siempre joven; (eternal) eterno, inmemorial. ~**s** (fam) siglos mpl

agency /ˈeɪdʒənsɪ/ n agencia f, organismo m, oficina f; (means) mediación f

agenda /əˈdʒendə/ npl orden m del día

agent /ˈeɪdʒənt/ n agente m & f; (representative) representante m & f

agglomeration /əglɒməˈreɪʃn/ n aglomeración f

aggravat|e /ˈægrəveɪt/ vt agravar; (irritate, fam) irritar. ~**ion** /-ˈveɪʃn/ n agravación f; (irritation, fam) irritación f

aggregate /ˈægrɪgət/ a total. ● n conjunto m. /ˈægrɪgeɪt/ vt agregar. ● vi ascender a

aggress|ion /əˈgreʃn/ n agresión f. ~**ive** a agresivo. ~**iveness** n agresividad f. ~**or** n agresor m

aggrieved /əˈgriːvd/ a apenado, ofendido

aghast /əˈgɑːst/ a horrorizado

agil|e /ˈædʒaɪl/ a ágil. ~**ity** /əˈdʒɪlətɪ/ n agilidad f

agitat|e /ˈædʒɪteɪt/ vt agitar. ~**ion** /-ˈteɪʃn/ n agitación f, excitación f. ~**or** n agitador m

agnostic /ægˈnɒstɪk/ a & n agnóstico (m). ~**ism** /-sɪzəm/ n agnosticismo m

ago /əˈgəʊ/ adv hace. **a long time** ~ hace mucho tiempo. **3 days** ~ hace 3 días

agog /əˈgɒg/ a ansioso

agon|ize /ˈægənaɪz/ vi atormentarse. ~**izing** a atroz, angustioso, doloroso. ~**y** n dolor m (agudo); (mental) angustia f

agree /əˈgriː/ vt acordar. ● vi estar de acuerdo; (of figures) concordar; (get on) entenderse. ~ **with** (of food etc) sentar bien a. ~**able** /əˈgriːəbl/ a agradable. **be** ~**able** (willing) estar de acuerdo. ~**d** a (time, place) convenido. ~**ment** /əˈgriːmənt/ n acuerdo m. **in** ~**ment** de acuerdo

agricultur|al /ægrɪˈkʌltʃərəl/ a agrícola. ~**e** /ˈægrɪkʌltʃə(r)/ n agricultura f

aground /əˈgraʊnd/ adv. **run** ~ (of ship) varar, encallar

ahead /əˈhed/ adv delante; (of time) antes de. **be** ~ ir delante

aid /eɪd/ vt ayudar. ● n ayuda f. **in** ~ **of** a beneficio de

aide /eɪd/ n (Amer) ayudante m & f

AIDS /eɪdz/ n (med) SIDA m

ail /eɪl/ vt afligir. ~**ing** a enfermo. ~**ment** n enfermedad f

aim /eɪm/ vt apuntar; (fig) dirigir. ● vi apuntar; (fig) pretender. ● n puntería f; (fig) propósito m. ~**less** a, ~**lessly** adv sin objeto, sin rumbo

air /eə(r)/ n aire m. **be on the** ~ estar en el aire. **put on** ~**s** darse aires. ● vt airear. ● a (base etc) aéreo. ~**borne** a en el aire; (mil) aerotransportado. ~-**conditioned** a climatizado, con aire acondicionado. ~**craft** /ˈeəkrɑːft/ n (pl invar) avión m. ~**field** /ˈeəfiːld/ n aeródromo m. **A**~ **Force** fuerzas fpl aéreas. ~**gun** /ˈeəgʌn/ n escopeta f de aire comprimido. ~**lift** /ˈeəlɪft/ n puente m aéreo. ~**line** /ˈeəlaɪn/ n línea f aérea. ~**lock** /ˈeəlɒk/ n (in pipe) burbuja f de aire; (chamber) esclusa f de aire. ~ **mail** n correo m aéreo. ~**man** /ˈeəmən/ n (pl -**men**) n aviador m. ~**port** /ˈeəpɔːt/ n aeropuerto m. ~**tight** /ˈeətaɪt/ a hermético. ~**worthy** /ˈeəwɜːðɪ/ a en condiciones de vuelo. ~**y** /ˈeərɪ/ a (-ier, -iest) aireado; (manner) ligero

aisle /aɪl/ n nave f lateral; (gangway) pasillo m

ajar /əˈdʒɑː(r)/ adv & a entreabierto

akin /əˈkɪn/ a semejante (**a** to)

alabaster /ˈæləbɑːstə(r)/ n alabastro m

alacrity /əˈlækrətɪ/ n prontitud f

alarm /əˈlɑːm/ n alarma f; (clock) despertador m. ● vt asustar. ~**ist** n alarmista m & f

alas /əˈlæs/ int ¡ay!, ¡ay de mí!

albatross /ˈælbətrɒs/ n albatros m

albino /ælˈbiːnəʊ/ a & n albino (m)

album /ˈælbəm/ n álbum m

alchem|ist /ˈælkəmɪst/ n alquimista m & f. **~y** n alquimia f

alcohol /ˈælkəhɒl/ n alcohol m. **~ic** /-ˈhɒlɪk/ a & n alcohólico (m). **~ism** n alcoholismo m

alcove /ˈælkəʊv/ n nicho m

ale /eɪl/ n cerveza f

alert /əˈlɜːt/ a vivo; (watchful) vigilante. ● n alerta f. **on the ~** alerta. ● vt avisar. **~ness** n vigilancia f

algebra /ˈældʒɪbrə/ n álgebra f

Algeria /ælˈdʒɪərɪə/ n Argelia f. **~n** a & n argelino (m)

alias /ˈeɪlɪəs/ n (pl -ases) alias m invar. ● adv alias

alibi /ˈælɪbaɪ/ (pl -is) coartada f

alien /ˈeɪlɪən/ n extranjero m. ● a ajeno

alienat|e /ˈeɪlɪəneɪt/ vt enajenar. **~ion** /-ˈneɪʃn/ n enajenación f

alight¹ /əˈlaɪt/ vi bajar; ⟨bird⟩ posarse

alight² /əˈlaɪt/ a ardiendo; ⟨light⟩ encendido

align /əˈlaɪn/ vt alinear. **~ment** n alineación f

alike /əˈlaɪk/ a parecido, semejante. **look** or **be ~** parecerse. ● adv de la misma manera

alimony /ˈælɪmənɪ/ n pensión f alimenticia

alive /əˈlaɪv/ a vivo. **~ to** sensible a. **~ with** lleno de

alkali /ˈælkəlaɪ/ n (pl -is) álcali m. **~ne** a alcalino

all /ɔːl/ a & pron todo. **~ but one** todos excepto uno. **~ of it** todo. ● adv completamente. **~ but** casi. **~ in** (fam) rendido. **~ of a sudden** de pronto. **~ over** (finished) acabado; (everywhere) por todas partes. **~ right!** ¡vale! **be ~ for** estar a favor de. **not at ~** de ninguna manera; (after thanks!) ¡no hay de qué!

allay /əˈleɪ/ vt aliviar ⟨pain⟩; aquietar ⟨fears etc⟩

all-clear /ɔːlˈklɪə(r)/ n fin m de (la) alarma

allegation /ælɪˈɡeɪʃn/ n alegato m

allege /əˈledʒ/ vt alegar. **~dly** /-ɪdlɪ/ adv según se dice, supuestamente

allegiance /əˈliːdʒəns/ n lealtad f

allegor|ical /ælɪˈɡɒrɪkl/ a alegórico. **~y** /ˈælɪɡərɪ/ n alegoría f

allerg|ic /əˈlɜːdʒɪk/ a alérgico. **~y** /ˈælədʒɪ/ n alergia f

alleviat|e /əˈliːvɪeɪt/ vt aliviar. **~ion** /-ˈeɪʃn/ n alivio m

alley /ˈælɪ/ (pl -eys) n callejuela f; (for bowling) bolera f

alliance /əˈlaɪəns/ n alianza f

allied /ˈælaɪd/ a aliado

alligator /ˈælɪɡeɪtə(r)/ n caimán m

allocat|e /ˈæləkeɪt/ vt asignar; (share out) repartir. **~ion** /-ˈkeɪʃn/ n asignación f; (share) ración f; (distribution) reparto m

allot /əˈlɒt/ vt (pt allotted) asignar. **~ment** n asignación f; (share) ración f; (land) parcela f

all-out /ɔːlˈaʊt/ a máximo

allow /əˈlaʊ/ vt permitir; (grant) conceder; (reckon on) prever; (agree) admitir. **~ for** tener en cuenta. **~ance** /əˈlaʊəns/ n concesión f; (pension) pensión f; (com) rebaja f. **make ~ances for** ser indulgente con; (take into account) tener en cuenta

alloy /ˈælɔɪ/ n aleación f. /əˈlɔɪ/ vt alear

all-round /ɔːlˈraʊnd/ a completo

allude /əˈluːd/ vi aludir

allure /əˈlʊə(r)/ vt atraer. ● n atractivo m

allusion /əˈluːʒn/ n alusión f

ally /ˈælaɪ/ n aliado m. /əˈlaɪ/ vt aliarse

almanac /ˈɔːlmənæk/ n almanaque m

almighty /ɔːlˈmaɪtɪ/ a todopoderoso; (big, fam) enorme. ● n. **the A~** el Todopoderoso m

almond /ˈɑːmənd/ n almendra f; (tree) almendro (m)

almost /ˈɔːlməʊst/ adv casi

alms /ɑːmz/ n limosna f

alone /əˈləʊn/ a solo. ● adv sólo, solamente

along /əˈlɒŋ/ prep por, a lo largo de. ● adv. **~ with** junto con. **all ~** todo el tiempo. **come ~** venga

alongside /əlɒŋˈsaɪd/ adv (naut) al costado. ● prep al lado de

aloof /əˈluːf/ adv apartado. ● a reservado. **~ness** n reserva f

aloud /əˈlaʊd/ adv en voz alta

alphabet /ˈælfəbet/ n alfabeto m. **~ical** /-ˈbetɪkl/ a alfabético

alpine /ˈælpaɪn/ a alpino

Alps /ælps/ npl. **the ~** los Alpes mpl

already /ɔːlˈredɪ/ adv ya

Alsatian /ælˈseɪʃn/ n (geog) alsaciano m; (dog) pastor m alemán

also /'ɔːlsəʊ/ *adv* también; (*moreover*) además

altar /'ɔːltə(r)/ *n* altar *m*

alter /'ɔːltə(r)/ *vt* cambiar. ● *vi* cambiarse. ~**ation** /-'reɪʃn/ *n* modificación *f*; (*to garment*) arreglo *m*

alternate /ɔːl'tɜːnət/ *a* alterno. /'ɔːltəneɪt/ *vt/i* alternar. ~**ly** *adv* alternativamente

alternative /ɔːl'tɜːnətɪv/ *a* alternativo. ● *n* alternativa *f*. ~**ly** *adv* en cambio, por otra parte

although /ɔːl'ðəʊ/ *conj* aunque

altitude /'æltɪtjuːd/ *n* altitud *f*

altogether /ɔːltə'geðə(r)/ *adv* completamente; (*on the whole*) en total

altruis|m /'æltruːɪzəm/ *n* altruismo *m*. ~**t** /'æltruːɪst/ *n* altruista *m* & *f*. ~**tic** /-'ɪstɪk/ *a* altruista

aluminium /æljʊ'mɪnɪəm/ *n* aluminio *m*

always /'ɔːlweɪz/ *adv* siempre

am /æm/ *see* **be**

a.m. /'eɪem/ *abbr* (*ante meridiem*) de la mañana

amalgamate /ə'mælgəmeɪt/ *vt* amalgamar. ● *vi* amalgamarse

amass /ə'mæs/ *vt* amontonar

amateur /'æmətə(r)/ *n* aficionado *m*. ● *a* no profesional; (*in sports*) amateur. ~**ish** *a* (*pej*) torpe, chapucero

amaz|e /ə'meɪz/ *vt* asombrar. ~**ed** *a* asombrado, estupefacto. **be** ~**ed at** quedarse asombrado de, asombrarse de. ~**ement** *n* asombro *m*. ~**ingly** *adv* extraordinariamente

ambassador /æm'bæsədə(r)/ *n* embajador *m*

amber /'æmbə(r)/ *n* ámbar *m*; (*auto*) luz *f* amarilla

ambidextrous /æmbɪ'dekstrəs/ *a* ambidextro

ambience /'æmbɪəns/ *n* ambiente *m*

ambigu|ity /æmbɪ'gjuːətɪ/ *n* ambigüedad *f*. ~**ous** /æm'bɪgjʊəs/ *a* ambiguo

ambit /'æmbɪt/ *n* ámbito *m*

ambiti|on /æm'bɪʃn/ *n* ambición *f*. ~**ous** *a* ambicioso

ambivalen|ce /æm'bɪvələns/ *n* ambivalencia *f*. ~**t** *a* ambivalente

amble /'æmbl/ *vi* andar despacio, andar sin prisa

ambulance /'æmbjʊləns/ *n* ambulancia *f*

ambush /'æmbʊʃ/ *n* emboscada *f*. ● *vt* tender una emboscada a

amen /ɑː'men/ *int* amén

amenable /ə'miːnəbl/ *a*. ~ **to** (*responsive*) sensible a, flexible a

amend /ə'mend/ *vt* enmendar. ~**ment** *n* enmienda *f*. ~**s** *npl.* **make** ~**s** reparar

amenities /ə'miːnətɪz/ *npl* atractivos *mpl*, comodidades *fpl*, instalaciones *fpl*

America /ə'merɪkə/ *n* América; (*North America*) Estados *mpl* Unidos. ~**n** *a* & *n* americano (*m*); (*North American*) estadounidense (*m* & *f*). ~**nism** *n* americanismo *m*. ~**nize** *vt* americanizar

amethyst /'æmɪθɪst/ *n* amatista *f*

amiable /'eɪmɪəbl/ *a* simpático

amicabl|e /'æmɪkəbl/ *a* amistoso. ~**y** *adv* amistosamente

amid(st) /ə'mɪd(st)/ *prep* entre, en medio de

amiss /ə'mɪs/ *a* malo. ● *adv* mal. **sth** ~ algo que no va bien. **take sth** ~ llevar algo a mal

ammonia /ə'məʊnɪə/ *n* amoníaco *m*, amoniaco *m*

ammunition /æmjʊ'nɪʃn/ *n* municiones *fpl*

amnesia /æm'niːzɪə/ *n* amnesia *f*

amnesty /'æmnəstɪ/ *n* amnistía *f*

amok /ə'mɒk/ *adv.* **run** ~ volverse loco

among(st) /ə'mʌŋ(st)/ *prep* entre

amoral /eɪ'mɒrəl/ *a* amoral

amorous /'æmərəs/ *a* amoroso

amorphous /ə'mɔːfəs/ *a* amorfo

amount /ə'maʊnt/ *n* cantidad *f*; (*total*) total *m*, suma *f*. ● *vi.* ~ **to** sumar; (*fig*) equivaler a, significar

amp(ere) /'amp(eə(r))/ *n* amperio *m*

amphibi|an /æm'fɪbɪən/ *n* anfibio *m*. ~**ous** *a* anfibio

amphitheatre /'æmfɪθɪətə(r)/ *n* anfiteatro *m*

ampl|e /'æmpl/ *a* (**-er, -est**) amplio; (*enough*) suficiente; (*plentiful*) abundante. ~**y** *adv* ampliamente, bastante

amplif|ier /'æmplɪfaɪə(r)/ *n* amplificador *m*. ~**y** *vt* amplificar

amputat|e /'æmpjʊteɪt/ *vt* amputar. ~**ion** /-'teɪʃn/ *n* amputación *f*

amus|e /ə'mjuːz/ *vt* divertir. ~**ement** *n* diversión *f*. ~**ing** *a* divertido

an /ən, æn/ *see* **a**

anachronism /ə'nækrənɪzəm/ *n* anacronismo *m*

anaemi|a /ə'niːmɪə/ *n* anemia *f*. ~**c** *a* anémico

anaesthe|sia /ænɪs'θiːzɪə/ n anestesia f. **~tic** /ænɪs'θetɪk/ n anestésico m. **~tist** /ə'niːsθɪtɪst/ n anestesista m & f

anagram /'ænəgræm/ n anagrama m

analogy /ə'nælədʒɪ/ n analogía f

analys|e /'ænəlaɪz/ vt analizar. **~is** /ə'næləsɪs/ n (pl -yses /-siːz/) n análisis m. **~t** /'ænəlɪst/ n analista m & f

analytic(al) /ænə'lɪtɪk(əl)/ a analítico

anarch|ist /'ænəkɪst/ n anarquista m & f. **~y** n anarquía f

anathema /ə'næθəmə/ n anatema f

anatom|ical /ænə'tɒmɪkl/ a anatómico. **~y** /ə'nætəmɪ/ n anatomía f

ancest|or /'ænsestə(r)/ n antepasado m. **~ral** /-'sestrəl/ a ancestral. **~ry** /'ænsestrɪ/ n ascendencia f

anchor /'æŋkə(r)/ n ancla f. ● vt anclar; (fig) sujetar. ● vi anclar

anchovy /'æntʃəvɪ/ n (fresh) boquerón m; (tinned) anchoa f

ancient /'eɪnʃənt/ a antiguo, viejo

ancillary /æn'sɪlərɪ/ a auxiliar

and /ənd, ænd/ conj y; (before i- and hi-) e. **go ~ see him** vete a verle. **more ~ more** siempre más, cada vez más. **try ~ come** ven si puedes, trata de venir

Andalusia /ændə'luːzjə/ f Andalucía f

anecdote /'ænɪkdəʊt/ n anécdota f

anew /ə'njuː/ adv de nuevo

angel /'eɪndʒl/ n ángel m. **~ic** /æn'dʒelɪk/ a angélico

anger /'æŋgə(r)/ n ira f. ● vt enojar

angle¹ /'æŋgl/ n ángulo m; (fig) punto m de vista

angle² /'æŋgl/ vi pescar con caña. **~ for** (fig) buscar. **~r** /-ə(r)/ n pescador m

Anglican /'æŋglɪkən/ a & n anglicano (m)

Anglo-... /'æŋgləʊ/ pref anglo...

Anglo-Saxon /'æŋgləʊ'sæksn/ a & n anglosajón (m)

angr|ily /'æŋgrɪlɪ/ adv con enojo. **~y** /'æŋgrɪ/ a (-ier, -iest) enojado. **get ~y** enfadarse

anguish /'æŋgwɪʃ/ n angustia f

angular /'æŋgjʊlə(r)/ a angular; ⟨face⟩ anguloso

animal /'ænɪməl/ a & n animal (m)

animat|e /'ænɪmət/ a vivo. /'ænɪmeɪt/ vt animar. **~ion** /-'meɪʃn/ n animación f

animosity /ænɪ'mɒsətɪ/ n animosidad f

aniseed /'ænɪsiːd/ n anís m

ankle /'æŋkl/ n tobillo m. **~ sock** escarpín m, calcetín m

annals /'ænlz/ npl anales mpl

annex /ə'neks/ vt anexionar. **~ation** /ænek'seɪʃn/ n anexión f

annexe /'æneks/ n anexo m, dependencia f

annihilat|e /ə'naɪəleɪt/ vt aniquilar. **~ion** /-'leɪʃn/ n aniquilación f

anniversary /ænɪ'vɜːsərɪ/ n aniversario m

annotat|e /'ænəteɪt/ vt anotar. **~ion** /-'teɪʃn/ n anotación f

announce /ə'naʊns/ vt anunciar, comunicar. **~ment** n anuncio m, aviso m, declaración f. **~r** /-ə(r)/ n (radio, TV) locutor m

annoy /ə'nɔɪ/ vt molestar. **~ance** n disgusto m. **~ed** a enfadado. **~ing** a molesto

annual /'ænjʊəl/ a anual. ● n anuario m. **~ly** adv cada año

annuity /ə'njuːətɪ/ n anualidad f. **life ~** renta f vitalicia

annul /ə'nʌl/ vt (pt annulled) anular. **~ment** n anulación f

anoint /ə'nɔɪnt/ vt ungir

anomal|ous /ə'nɒmələs/ a anómalo. **~y** n anomalía f

anon /ə'nɒn/ adv (old use) dentro de poco

anonymous /ə'nɒnɪməs/ a anónimo

anorak /'ænəræk/ n anorac m

another /ə'nʌðə(r)/ a & pron otro (m). **~ 10 minutes** 10 minutos más. **in ~ way** de otra manera. **one ~** unos a otros

answer /'ɑːnsə(r)/ n respuesta f; (solution) solución f. ● vt contestar a; escuchar, oír ⟨prayer⟩. **~ the door** abrir la puerta. ● vi contestar. **~ back** replicar. **~ for** ser responsable de. **~able** a responsable. **~ing-machine** n contestador m automático

ant /ænt/ n hormiga f

antagoni|sm /æn'tægənɪzəm/ n antagonismo m. **~stic** /-'nɪstɪk/ a antagónico, opuesto. **~ze** /æn'tægənaɪz/ vt provocar la enemistad de

Antarctic /æn'tɑːktɪk/ a antártico. ● n Antártico m

ante-... /'ænti/ *pref* ante...

antecedent /ænti'si:dnt/ *n* antecedente *m*

antelope /'æntiləup/ *n* antílope *m*

antenatal /'æntineitl/ *a* prenatal

antenna /æn'tenə/ *n* antena *f*

anthem /'ænθəm/ *n* himno *m*

anthill /'ænthil/ *n* hormiguero *m*

anthology /æn'θɒlədʒi/ *n* antología *f*

anthropolog|ist /ænθrə'pɒlədʒist/ *n* antropólogo *m*. **~y** *n* antropología *f*

anti-... /'ænti/ *pref* anti... **~aircraft** *a* antiaéreo

antibiotic /æntibai'ɒtik/ *a & n* antibiótico (*m*)

antibody /'æntibɒdi/ *n* anticuerpo *m*

antic /'æntik/ *n* payasada *f*, travesura *f*

anticipat|e /æn'tisipeit/ *vt* anticiparse a; (*foresee*) prever; (*forestall*) prevenir. **~ion** /-'peiʃn/ *n* anticipación *f*; (*expectation*) esperanza *f*

anticlimax /ænti'klaimæks/ *n* decepción *f*

anticlockwise /ænti'klɒkwaiz/ *adv & a* en sentido contrario al de las agujas del reloj, hacia la izquierda

anticyclone /ænti'saikləun/ *n* anticiclón *m*

antidote /'æntidəut/ *m* antídoto *m*

antifreeze /'æntifri:z/ *n* anticongelante *m*

antipathy /æn'tipəθi/ *n* antipatía *f*

antiquarian /ænti'kweəriən/ *a & n* anticuario (*m*)

antiquated /'æntikweitid/ *a* anticuado

antique /æn'ti:k/ *a* antiguo. ● *n* antigüedad *f*. **~ dealer** anticuario *m*. **~ shop** tienda *f* de antigüedades

antiquity /æn'tikwəti/ *n* antigüedad *f*

anti-Semitic /æntisi'mitik/ *a* antisemítico

antiseptic /ænti'septik/ *a & n* antiséptico (*m*)

antisocial /ænti'səuʃl/ *a* antisocial

antithesis /æn'tiθəsis/ *n* (*pl* **-eses** /-si:z/) antítesis *f*

antler /'æntlər/ *n* cornamenta *f*

anus /'einəs/ *n* ano *m*

anvil /'ænvil/ *n* yunque *m*

anxiety /æŋ'zaiəti/ *n* ansiedad *f*; (*worry*) inquietud *f*; (*eagerness*) anhelo *m*

anxious /'æŋkʃəs/ *a* inquieto; (*eager*) deseoso. **~ly** *adv* con inquietud; (*eagerly*) con impaciencia

any /'eni/ *a* algún *m*; (*negative*) ningún *m*; (*whatever*) cualquier; (*every*) todo. **at ~ moment** en cualquier momento. **have you ~ wine?** ¿tienes vino? ● *pron* alguno; (*negative*) ninguno. **have we ~?** ¿tenemos algunos? **not ~** ninguno. ● *adv* (*a little*) un poco, algo. **is it ~ better?** ¿está algo mejor? **it isn't ~ good** no sirve para nada

anybody /'enibɒdi/ *pron* alguien; (*after negative*) nadie. **~ can do it** cualquiera sabe hacerlo, cualquiera puede hacerlo

anyhow /'enihau/ *adv* de todas formas; (*in spite of all*) a pesar de todo; (*badly*) de cualquier modo

anyone /'eniwʌn/ *pron* alguien; (*after negative*) nadie

anything /'eniθiŋ/ *pron* algo; (*whatever*) cualquier cosa; (*after negative*) nada. **~ but** todo menos

anyway /'eniwei/ *adv* de todas formas

anywhere /'eniweə(r)/ *adv* en cualquier parte; (*after negative*) en ningún sitio; (*everywhere*) en todas partes. **~ else** en cualquier otro lugar. **~ you go** dondequiera que vayas

apace /ə'peis/ *adv* rápidamente

apart /ə'pɑ:t/ *adv* aparte; (*separated*) apartado, separado. **~ from** aparte de. **come ~** romperse. **take ~** desmontar

apartheid /ə'pɑ:theit/ *n* segregación *f* racial, apartheid *m*

apartment /ə'pɑ:tmənt/ *n* (*Amer*) apartamento *m*

apath|etic /æpə'θetik/ *a* apático, indiferente. **~y** /'æpəθi/ *n* apatía *f*

ape /eip/ *n* mono *m*. ● *vt* imitar

aperient /ə'piəriənt/ *a & n* laxante (*m*)

aperitif /ə'perətif/ *n* aperitivo *m*

aperture /'æpətʃuə(r)/ *n* abertura *f*

apex /'eipeks/ *n* ápice *m*

aphorism /'æfərizəm/ *n* aforismo *m*

aphrodisiac /æfrə'diziæk/ *a & n* afrodisíaco (*m*), afrodisiaco (*m*)

apiece /ə'pi:s/ *adv* cada uno

aplomb /ə'plɒm/ *n* aplomo *m*

apolog|etic /əpɒlə'dʒetik/ *a* lleno de disculpas. **be ~etic** disculparse. **~ize** /ə'pɒlədʒaiz/ *vi* disculparse

(for de). ~y /ə'pɒlədʒɪ/ *n* disculpa *f*; (*poor specimen*) birria *f*

apople|ctic /æpə'plektɪk/ *a* apoplético. ~**xy** /'æpəpleksɪ/ *n* apoplejía *f*

apostle /ə'pɒsl/ *n* apóstol *m*

apostrophe /ə'pɒstrəfɪ/ *n* (*punctuation mark*) apóstrofo *m*

appal /ə'pɔːl/ *vt* (*pt* **appalled**) horrorizar. ~**ling** *a* espantoso

apparatus /æpə'reɪtəs/ *n* aparato *m*

apparel /ə'pærəl/ *n* ropa *f*, indumentaria *f*

apparent /ə'pærənt/ *a* aparente; (*clear*) evidente. ~**ly** *adv* por lo visto

apparition /æpə'rɪʃn/ *n* aparición *f*

appeal /ə'piːl/ *vi* apelar; (*attract*) atraer. ● *n* llamamiento *m*; (*attraction*) atractivo *m*; (*jurid*) apelación *f*. ~**ing** *a* atrayente

appear /ə'pɪə(r)/ *vi* aparecer; (*arrive*) llegar; (*seem*) parecer; (*on stage*) actuar. ~**ance** *n* aparición *f*; (*aspect*) aspecto *m*

appease /ə'piːz/ *vt* aplacar; (*pacify*) apaciguar

append /ə'pend/ *vt* adjuntar. ~**age** /ə'pendɪdʒ/ *n* añadidura *f*

appendicitis /əpendɪ'saɪtɪs/ *n* apendicitis *f*

appendix /ə'pendɪks/ *n* (*pl* **-ices** /-siːz/) (*of book*) apéndice *m*. (*pl* **-ixes**) (*anat*) apéndice *m*

appertain /æpə'teɪn/ *vi* relacionarse (**to** con)

appetite /'æpɪtaɪt/ *n* apetito *m*

appetiz|er /'æpɪtaɪzə(r)/ *n* aperitivo *m*. ~**ing** *a* apetitoso

applau|d /ə'plɔːd/ *vt/i* aplaudir. ~**se** *n* aplausos *mpl*

apple /'æpl/ *n* manzana *f*. ~**-tree** *n* manzano *m*

appliance /ə'plaɪəns/ *n* aparato *m*. **electrical** ~ electrodoméstico *m*

applicable /'æplɪkəbl/ *a* aplicable; (*relevant*) pertinente

applicant /'æplɪkənt/ *n* candidato *m*, solicitante *m* & *f*

application /æplɪ'keɪʃn/ *n* aplicación *f*, (*request*) solicitud *f*. ~ **form** formulario *m* (de solicitud)

appl|ied /ə'plaɪd/ *a* aplicado. ~**y** /ə'plaɪ/ *vt* aplicar. ● *vi* aplicarse; (*ask*) dirigirse. ~**y for** solicitar ⟨*job etc*⟩

appoint /ə'pɔɪnt/ *vt* nombrar; (*fix*) señalar. ~**ment** *n* cita *f*; (*job*) empleo *m*

apportion /ə'pɔːʃn/ *vt* repartir

apposite /'æpəzɪt/ *a* apropiado

apprais|al /ə'preɪzl/ *n* evaluación *f*. ~**e** *vt* evaluar

appreciable /ə'priːʃəbl/ *a* sensible; (*considerable*) considerable

appreciat|e /ə'priːʃɪeɪt/ *vt* apreciar; (*understand*) comprender; (*be grateful for*) agradecer. ● *vi* (*increase value*) aumentar en valor. ~**ion** /-'eɪʃn/ *n* aprecio *m*; (*gratitude*) agradecimiento *m*. ~**ive** /ə'priːʃɪətɪv/ *a* (*grateful*) agradecido

apprehen|d /æprɪ'hend/ *vt* detener; (*understand*) comprender. ~**sion** /-ʃn/ *n* detención *f*; (*fear*) recelo *m*

apprehensive /æprɪ'hensɪv/ *a* aprensivo

apprentice /ə'prentɪs/ *n* aprendiz *m*. ● *vt* poner de aprendiz. ~**ship** *n* aprendizaje *m*

approach /ə'prəʊtʃ/ *vt* acercarse a. ● *vi* acercarse. ● *n* acercamiento *m*; (*to problem*) enfoque *m*; (*access*) acceso *m*. **make** ~**es to** dirigirse a. ~**able** *a* accesible

approbation /æprə'beɪʃn/ *n* aprobación *f*

appropriate /ə'prəʊprɪət/ *a* apropiado. /ə'prəʊprɪeɪt/ *vt* apropiarse de. ~**ly** *adv* apropiadamente

approval /ə'pruːvl/ *n* aprobación *f*. **on** ~ a prueba

approv|e /ə'pruːv/ *vt/i* aprobar. ~**ingly** *adv* con aprobación

approximat|e /ə'prɒksɪmət/ *a* aproximado. /ə'prɒksɪmeɪt/ *vt* aproximarse a. ~**ely** *adv* aproximadamente. ~**ion** /-'meɪʃn/ *n* aproximación *f*

apricot /'eɪprɪkɒt/ *n* albaricoque *m*, chabacano *m* (*Mex*). ~**-tree** *n* albaricoquero *m*, chabacano *m* (*Mex*)

April /'eɪprəl/ *n* abril *m*. ~ **fool!** ¡inocentón!

apron /'eɪprən/ *n* delantal *m*

apropos /'æprəpəʊ/ *adv* a propósito

apse /æps/ *n* ábside *m*

apt /æpt/ *a* apropiado; ⟨*pupil*⟩ listo. **be** ~ **to** tener tendencia a

aptitude /'æptɪtjuːd/ *n* aptitud *f*

aptly /'æptlɪ/ *adv* acertadamente

aqualung /'ækwəlʌŋ/ *n* pulmón *m* acuático

aquarium /ə'kweərɪəm/ *n* (*pl* **-ums**) acuario *m*

Aquarius /ə'kweərɪəs/ *n* Acuario *m*

aquatic /ə'kwætɪk/ *a* acuático

aqueduct /ˈækwɪdʌkt/ *n* acueducto *m*

aquiline /ˈækwɪlaɪn/ *a* aquilino

Arab /ˈærəb/ *a & n* árabe *m*. **~ian** /əˈreɪbɪən/ *a* árabe. **~ic** /ˈærəbɪk/ *a & n* árabe (*m*). **~ic numerals** números *mpl* arábigos

arable /ˈærəbl/ *a* cultivable

arbiter /ˈɑːbɪtə(r)/ *n* árbitro *m*

arbitrary /ˈɑːbɪtrərɪ/ *a* arbitrario

arbitrat|e /ˈɑːbɪtreɪt/ *vi* arbitrar. **~ion** /-ˈtreɪʃn/ *n* arbitraje *m*. **~or** *n* árbitro *m*

arc /ɑːk/ *n* arco *m*

arcade /ɑːˈkeɪd/ *n* arcada *f*; (*around square*) soportales *mpl*; (*shops*) galería *f*. **amusement ~** galería *f* de atracciones

arcane /ɑːˈkeɪn/ *a* misterioso

arch¹ /ɑːtʃ/ *n* arco *m*. ● *vt* arquear. ● *vi* arquearse

arch² /ɑːtʃ/ *a* malicioso

archaeolog|ical /ɑːkɪəˈlɒdʒɪkl/ *a* arqueológico. **~ist** /ɑːkɪˈɒlədʒɪst/ *n* arqueólogo *m*. **~y** /ɑːkɪˈɒlədʒɪ/ *n* arqueología *f*

archaic /ɑːˈkeɪɪk/ *a* arcaico

archbishop /ɑːtʃˈbɪʃəp/ *n* arzobispo *m*

arch-enemy /ɑːtʃˈenəmɪ/ *n* enemigo *m* jurado

archer /ˈɑːtʃə(r)/ *n* arquero *m*. **~y** *n* tiro *m* al arco

archetype /ˈɑːkɪtaɪp/ *n* arquetipo *m*

archipelago /ɑːkɪˈpeləgəʊ/ *n* (*pl* -**os**) archipiélago *m*

architect /ˈɑːkɪtekt/ *n* arquitecto *m*. **~ure** /ˈɑːkɪtektʃə(r)/ *n* arquitectura *f*. **~ural** /-ˈtektʃərəl/ *a* arquitectónico

archiv|es /ˈɑːkaɪvz/ *npl* archivo *m*. **~ist** /-ɪvɪst/ *n* archivero *m*

archway /ˈɑːtʃweɪ/ *n* arco *m*

Arctic /ˈɑːktɪk/ *a* ártico. ● *n* Ártico *m*

arctic /ˈɑːktɪk/ *a* glacial

ardent /ˈɑːdənt/ *a* ardiente, fervoroso, apasionado. **~ly** *adv* ardientemente

ardour /ˈɑːdə(r)/ *n* ardor *m*, fervor *m*, pasión *f*

arduous /ˈɑːdjʊəs/ *a* arduo

are /ɑː(r)/ *see* **be**

area /ˈeərɪə/ *n* (*surface*) superficie *f*; (*region*) zona *f*; (*fig*) campo *m*

arena /əˈriːnə/ *n* arena *f*; (*in circus*) pista *f*; (*in bullring*) ruedo *m*

aren't /ɑːnt/ = **are not**

Argentin|a /ɑːdʒənˈtiːnə/ *n* Argentina *f*. **~ian** /-ˈtɪnɪən/ *a & n* argentino (*m*)

arguable /ˈɑːgjʊəbl/ *a* discutible

argue /ˈɑːgjuː/ *vi* discutir; (*reason*) razonar

argument /ˈɑːgjʊmənt/ *n* disputa *f*; (*reasoning*) argumento *m*. **~ative** /-ˈmentətɪv/ *a* discutidor

arid /ˈærɪd/ *a* árido

Aries /ˈeəriːz/ *n* Aries *m*

arise /əˈraɪz/ *vi* (*pt* **arose**, *pp* **arisen**) levantarse; (*fig*) surgir. **~ from** resultar de

aristocra|cy /ærɪˈstɒkrəsɪ/ *n* aristocracia *f*. **~t** /ˈærɪstəkræt/ *n* aristócrata *m & f*. **~tic** /-ˈkrætɪk/ *a* aristocrático

arithmetic /əˈrɪθmətɪk/ *n* aritmética *f*

ark /ɑːk/ *n* (*relig*) arca *f*

arm¹ /ɑːm/ *n* brazo *m*. **~ in ~** cogidos del brazo

arm² /ɑːm/ *n*. **~s** *npl* armas *fpl*. ● *vt* armar

armada /ɑːˈmɑːdə/ *n* armada *f*

armament /ˈɑːməmənt/ *n* armamento *m*

armchair /ˈɑːmtʃeə(r)/ *n* sillón *m*

armed robbery /ɑːmdˈrɒbərɪ/ *n* robo *m* a mano armada

armful /ˈɑːmfʊl/ *n* brazada *f*

armistice /ˈɑːmɪstɪs/ *n* armisticio *m*

armlet /ˈɑːmlɪt/ *n* brazalete *m*

armour /ˈɑːmə(r)/ *n* armadura *f*. **~ed** /*a* blindado

armoury /ˈɑːmərɪ/ *n* arsenal *m*

armpit /ˈɑːmpɪt/ *n* sobaco *m*, axila *f*

army /ˈɑːmɪ/ *n* ejército *m*

aroma /əˈrəʊmə/ *n* aroma *m*. **~tic** /ærəˈmætɪk/ *a* aromático

arose /əˈrəʊz/ *see* **arise**

around /əˈraʊnd/ *adv* alrededor; (*near*) cerca. **all ~** por todas partes. ● *prep* alrededor de; (*with time*) a eso de

arouse /əˈraʊz/ *vt* despertar

arpeggio /ɑːˈpedʒɪəʊ/ *n* arpegio *m*

arrange /əˈreɪndʒ/ *vt* arreglar; (*fix*) fijar. **~ment** *n* arreglo *m*; (*agreement*) acuerdo *m*; (*pl*, *plans*) preparativos *mpl*

array /əˈreɪ/ *vt* (*dress*) ataviar; (*mil*) formar. ● *n* atavío *m*; (*mil*) orden *m*; (*fig*) colección *f*, conjunto *m*

arrears /əˈrɪəz/ *npl* atrasos *mpl*. **in ~** atrasado en pagos

arrest /ə'rest/ *vt* detener; llamar ⟨*attention*⟩. ● *n* detención *f*. **under ~** detenido

arriv|al /ə'raɪvl/ *n* llegada *f*. **new ~al** recién llegado *m*. **~e** /ə'raɪv/ *vi* llegar

arrogan|ce /'ærəgəns/ *n* arrogancia *f*. **~t** *a* arrogante. **~tly** *adv* con arrogancia

arrow /'ærəʊ/ *n* flecha *f*

arsenal /'ɑːsənl/ *n* arsenal *m*

arsenic /'ɑːsnɪk/ *n* arsénico *m*

arson /'ɑːsn/ *n* incendio *m* provocado. **~ist** *n* incendiario *m*

ash /æʃ/ *n* ceniza *f*

ash² /æʃ/ *n.* ~(-tree) fresno *m*

art¹ /ɑːt/ *n* arte *m*. **A~s** *npl* (*Univ*) Filosofía y Letras *fpl*. **fine ~s** bellas artes *fpl*

art² /ɑːt/ (*old use, with thou*) = **are**

artefact /'ɑːtɪfækt/ *n* artefacto *m*

arterial /ɑː'tɪərɪəl/ *a* arterial. **~ road** *n* carretera *f* nacional

artery /'ɑːtərɪ/ *n* arteria *f*

artesian /ɑː'tiːzjən/ *a.* **~ well** pozo *m* artesiano

artful /'ɑːtfʊl/ *a* astuto. **~ness** *n* astucia *f*

art gallery /'ɪtgælərɪ/ *n* museo *m* de pinturas, pinacoteca *f*, galería *f* de arte

arthriti|c /ɑː'θrɪtɪk/ *a* artrítico. **~s** /ɑː'θraɪtɪs/ *n* artritis *f*

artichoke /'ɑːtɪtʃəʊk/ *n* alcachofa *f*. **Jerusalem ~** pataca *f*

article /'ɑːtɪkl/ *n* artículo *m*. **~ of clothing** prenda *f* de vestir. **leading ~** artículo de fondo

articulat|e /ɑː'tɪkjʊlət/ *a* articulado; ⟨*person*⟩ elocuente. /ɑː'tɪkjʊleɪt/ *vt/i* articular. **~ed lorry** *n* camión *m* con remolque. **~ion** /-'leɪʃn/ *n* articulación *f*

artifice /'ɑːtɪfɪs/ *n* artificio *m*

artificial /ɑːtɪ'fɪʃl/ *a* artificial; ⟨*hair etc*⟩ postizo

artillery /ɑː'tɪlərɪ/ *n* artillería *f*

artisan /'ɑːtɪzæn/ *n* artesano *m*

artist /'ɑːtɪst/ *n* artista *m & f*

artiste /ɑː'tiːst/ *n* (*in theatre*) artista *m & f*

artist|ic /ɑː'tɪstɪk/ *a* artístico. **~ry** *n* arte *m*, habilidad *f*

artless /'ɑːtlɪs/ *a* ingenuo

arty /'ɑːtɪ/ *a* (*fam*) que se las da de artista

as /æz, əz/ *adv & conj* como; (*since*) ya que; (*while*) mientras. **~ big ~** tan grande como. **~ far ~** (*distance*) hasta; (*qualitative*) en cuanto a. **~**

far ~ I know que yo sepa. **~ if** como si. **~ long ~** mientras. **~ much ~** tanto como. **~ soon ~** tan pronto como. **~ well** también

asbestos /æz'bestɒs/ *n* amianto *m*, asbesto *m*

ascen|d /ə'send/ *vt/i* subir. **~t** /ə'sent/ *n* subida *f*

ascertain /æsə'teɪn/ *vt* averiguar

ascetic /ə'setɪk/ *a* ascético. ● *n* asceta *m & f*

ascribe /ə'skraɪb/ *vt* atribuir

ash¹ /æʃ/ *n* ceniza *f*

ashamed /ə'ʃeɪmd/ *a* avergonzado. **be ~** avergonzarse

ashen /'æʃn/ *a* ceniciento

ashore /ə'ʃɔː(r)/ *adv* a tierra. **go ~** desembarcar

ash: ~tray /'æʃtreɪ/ *n* cenicero *m*. **A~ Wednesday** *n* Miércoles *m* de Ceniza

Asia /'eɪʃə/ *n* Asia *f*. **~n** *a & n* asiático (*m*). **~tic** /-ɪ'ætɪk/ *a* asiático

aside /ə'saɪd/ *adv* a un lado. ● *n* (*in theatre*) aparte *m*

asinine /'æsɪnaɪn/ *a* estúpido

ask /ɑːsk/ *vt* pedir; preguntar ⟨*question*⟩; (*invite*) invitar. **~ about** enterarse de. **~ after** pedir noticias de. **~ for help** pedir ayuda. **~ for trouble** buscarse problemas. **~ s.o. in** invitar a uno a pasar

askance /ə'skæns/ *adv.* **look ~ at** mirar de soslayo

askew /ə'skjuː/ *adv & a* ladeado

asleep /ə'sliːp/ *adv & a* dormido. **fall ~** dormirse, quedar dormido

asparagus /ə'spærəgəs/ *n* espárrago *m*

aspect /'æspekt/ *n* aspecto *m*; (*of house etc*) orientación *f*

aspersions /ə'spɜːʃnz/ *npl.* **cast ~ on** difamar

asphalt /'æsfælt/ *n* asfalto *m*. ● *vt* asfaltar

asphyxia /æs'fɪksɪə/ *n* asfixia *f*. **~te** /əs'fɪksɪeɪt/ *vt* asfixiar. **~tion** /-'eɪʃn/ *n* asfixia *f*

aspic /'æspɪk/ *n* gelatina *f*

aspir|ation /æspə'reɪʃn/ *n* aspiración *f*. **~e** /əs'paɪə(r)/ *vi* aspirar

aspirin /'æsprɪn/ *n* aspirina *f*

ass /æs/ *n* asno *m*; (*fig, fam*) imbécil *m*

assail /ə'seɪl/ *vt* asaltar. **~ant** *n* asaltador *m*

assassin /əˈsæsɪn/ n asesino m.
~ate /əˈsæsɪneɪt/ vt asesinar.
~ation /-ˈeɪʃn/ n asesinato m

assault /əˈsɔːlt/ n (mil) ataque m;
(jurid) atentado m. ● vt asaltar

assemblage /əˈsemblɪdʒ/ n (of
things) colección f; (of people)
reunión f; (mec) montaje m

assemble /əˈsembl/ vt reunir; (mec)
montar. ● vi reunirse

assembly /əˈsemblɪ/ n reunión f;
(pol-etc) asamblea f. ~ **line** n línea f
de montaje

assent /əˈsent/ n asentimiento m.
● vi asentir

assert /əˈsɜːt/ vt afirmar; hacer valer
⟨one's rights⟩. **~ion** /-ʃn/ n afirmación f. **~ive** a positivo, firme

assess /əˈses/ vt valorar; (determine)
determinar; fijar ⟨tax etc⟩. **~ment** n
valoración f

asset /ˈæset/ n (advantage) ventaja f;
(pl, com) bienes mpl

assiduous /əˈsɪdjʊəs/ a asiduo

assign /əˈsaɪn/ vt asignar; (appoint)
nombrar

assignation /æsɪgˈneɪʃn/ n asignación f; (meeting) cita f

assignment /əˈsaɪnmənt/ n asignación f, misión f; (task) tarea f

assimilat|e /əˈsɪmɪleɪt/ vt asimilar.
● vi asimilarse. **~ion** /-ˈeɪʃn/ n
asimilación f

assist /əˈsɪst/ vt/i ayudar. **~ance** n
ayuda f. **~ant** /əˈsɪstənt/ n ayudante
m & f; (shop) dependienta f, dependiente m. ● a auxiliar, adjunto

associat|e /əˈsəʊʃɪeɪt/ vt asociar.
● vi asociarse. /əˈsəʊʃɪət/ a aso-
ciado. ● n colega m & f; (com) socio
m. **~ion** /-ˈeɪʃn/ n asociación f. **A~
ion football** n fútbol m

assort|ed /əˈsɔːtɪd/ a surtido.
~ment n surtido m

assume /əˈsjuːm/ vt suponer; tomar
⟨power, attitude⟩; asumir ⟨role, bur-
den⟩

assumption /əˈsʌmpʃn/ n suposición f. **the A~** la Asunción f

assur|ance /əˈʃʊərəns/ n seguridad
f; (insurance) seguro m. **~e**
/əˈʃʊə(r)/ vt asegurar. **~ed** a seguro.
~edly /-rɪdlɪ/ adv seguramente

asterisk /ˈæstərɪsk/ n asterisco m

astern /əˈstɜːn/ adv a popa

asthma /ˈæsmə/ n asma f. **~tic**
/-ˈmætɪk/ a & n asmático (m)

astonish /əˈstɒnɪʃ/ vt asombrar.
~ing a asombroso. **~ment** n asombro m

astound /əˈstaʊnd/ vt asombrar

astray /əˈstreɪ/ adv & a. **go ~** ex-
traviarse. **lead ~** llevar por mal
camino

astride /əˈstraɪd/ adv a horcajadas.
● prep a horcajadas sobre

astringent /əˈstrɪndʒənt/ a astringente; (fig) austero. ● n astringente m

astrolog|er /əˈstrɒlədʒə(r)/ n as-
trólogo m. **~y** n astrología f

astronaut /ˈæstrənɔːt/ n astronauta
m & f

astronom|er /əˈstrɒnəmə(r)/ n as-
trónomo m. **~ical** /æstrəˈnɒmɪkl/ a
astronómico. **~y** /əˈstrɒnəmɪ/ n
astronomía f

astute /əˈstjuːt/ a astuto. **~ness** n
astucia f

asunder /əˈsʌndə(r)/ adv en pedazos; (in two) en dos

asylum /əˈsaɪləm/ n asilo m. **lunatic
~** manicomio m

at /ət, æt/ prep a. **~ home** en casa. **~
night** por la noche. **~ Robert's** en
casa de Roberto. **~ once** en seguida;
(simultaneously) a la vez. **~ sea** en el
mar. **~ the station** en la estación. **~
times** a veces. **not ~ all** nada; (after
thanks) ¡de nada!

ate /et/ see **eat**

atheis|m /ˈeɪθɪɪzəm/ n ateísmo m. **~t**
/ˈeɪθɪɪst/ n ateo m

athlet|e /ˈæθliːt/ n atleta m & f. **~ic**
/-ˈletɪk/ a atlético. **~ics** /-ˈletɪks/ npl
atletismo m

Atlantic /ətˈlæntɪk/ a & n atlántico
(m). ● n. **~ (Ocean)** (Océano m) Atlántico m

atlas /ˈætləs/ n atlas m

atmospher|e /ˈætməsfɪə(r)/ n atmós-
fera f; (fig) ambiente m. **~ic** /-ˈferɪk/
a atmosférico. **~ics** /-ˈferɪks/ npl
parásitos mpl

atom /ˈætəm/ n átomo m. **~ic**
/əˈtɒmɪk/ a atómico

atomize /ˈætəmaɪz/ vt atomizar. **~r**
/ˈætəmaɪzə(r)/ n atomizador m

atone /əˈtəʊn/ vi. **~ for** expiar.
~ment n expiación f

atroci|ous /əˈtrəʊʃəs/ a atroz. **~ty**
/əˈtrɒsətɪ/ n atrocidad f

atrophy /ˈætrəfɪ/ n atrofia f

attach /əˈtætʃ/ vt sujetar; adjuntar
⟨document etc⟩. **be ~ed to** (be fond
of) tener cariño a

attaché /ə'tæʃeɪ/ n agregado m. **~ case** maletín m

attachment /ə'tætʃmənt/ n (affection) cariño m; (tool) accesorio m

attack /ə'tæk/ n ataque m. ● vt/i atacar. **~er** n agresor m

attain /ə'teɪn/ vt conseguir. **~able** a alcanzable. **~ment** n logro m. **~ments** npl conocimientos mpl, talento m

attempt /ə'tempt/ vt intentar. ● n tentativa f; (attack) atentado m

attend /ə'tend/ vt asistir a; (escort) acompañar. ● vi prestar atención. **~ to** (look after) ocuparse de. **~ance** n asistencia f; (people present) concurrencia f. **~ant** /ə'tendənt/ a concomitante. ● n encargado m; (servant) sirviente m

attention /ə'tenʃn/ n atención f. **~!** (mil) ¡firmes! **pay ~** prestar atención

attentive /ə'tentɪv/ a atento. **~ness** n atención f

attenuate /ə'tenjʊeɪt/ vt atenuar

attest /ə'test/ vt atestiguar. ● vi dar testimonio. **~ation** /æte'steɪʃn/ n testimonio m

attic /'ætɪk/ n desván m

attire /ə'taɪə(r)/ n atavío m. ● vt vestir

attitude /'ætɪtjuːd/ n postura f

attorney /ə'tɜːnɪ/ n (pl **-eys**) apoderado m; (Amer) abogado m

attract /ə'trækt/ vt atraer. **~ion** /-ʃn/ n atracción f; (charm) atractivo m

attractive /ə'træktɪv/ a atractivo; (interesting) atrayente. **~ness** n atractivo m

attribute /ə'trɪbjuːt/ vt atribuir. /'ætrɪbjuːt/ n atributo m

attrition /ə'trɪʃn/ n desgaste m

aubergine /'əʊbəʒiːn/ n berenjena f

auburn /'ɔːbən/ a castaño

auction /'ɔːkʃn/ n subasta f. ● vt subastar. **~eer** /-ə'nɪə(r)/ n subastador m

audacious /ɔː'deɪʃəs/ a audaz. **~ty** /-æsətɪ/ n audacia f

audible /'ɔːdəbl/ a audible

audience /'ɔːdɪəns/ n (interview) audiencia f; (teatro, radio) público m

audio-visual /ɔːdɪəʊ'vɪʒʊəl/ a audio-visual

audit /'ɔːdɪt/ n revisión f de cuentas. ● vt revisar

audition /ɔː'dɪʃn/ n audición f. ● vt dar audición a

auditor /'ɔːdɪtə(r)/ n interventor m de cuentas

auditorium /ɔːdɪ'tɔːrɪəm/ n sala f, auditorio m

augment /ɔːg'ment/ vt aumentar

augur /'ɔːgə(r)/ vt augurar. **it ~s well** es de buen agüero

august /ɔː'gʌst/ a augusto

August /'ɔːgəst/ n agosto m

aunt /ɑːnt/ n tía f

au pair /əʊ'peə(r)/ n chica f au pair

aura /'ɔːrə/ n atmósfera f, halo m

auspices /'ɔːspɪsɪz/ npl auspicios mpl

auspicious /ɔː'spɪʃəs/ a propicio

auster|e /ɔː'stɪə(r)/ a austero. **~ity** /-erətɪ/ n austeridad f

Australia /ɒ'streɪlɪə/ n Australia f. **~n** a & n australiano (m)

Austria /'ɒstrɪə/ n Austria f. **~n** a & n austriaco (m)

authentic /ɔː'θentɪk/ a auténtico. **~ate** /ɔː'θentɪkeɪt/ vt autenticar. **~ity** /-ən'tɪsətɪ/ n autenticidad f

author /'ɔːθə(r)/ n autor m. **~ess** n autora f

authoritarian /ɔːθɒrɪ'teərɪən/ a autoritario

authoritative /ɔː'θɒrɪtətɪv/ a autorizado; (manner) autoritario

authority /ɔː'θɒrətɪ/ n autoridad f; (permission) autorización f

authoriz|ation /ɔːθəraɪ'zeɪʃn/ n autorización f. **~e** /'ɔːθəraɪz/ vt autorizar

authorship /'ɔːθəʃɪp/ n profesión f de autor; (origin) paternidad f literaria

autistic /ɔː'tɪstɪk/ a autista

autobiography /ɔːtəʊbaɪ'ɒgrəfɪ/ n autobiografía f

autocra|cy /ɔː'tɒkrəsɪ/ n autocracia f. **~t** /'ɔːtəkræt/ n autócrata m & f. **~tic** /-'krætɪk/ a autocrático

autograph /'ɔːtəgrɑːf/ n autógrafo m. ● vt firmar

automat|e /'ɔːtəmeɪt/ vt automatizar. **~ic** /ɔːtə'mætɪk/ a automático. **~ion** /-'meɪʃn/ n automatización f. **~on** /ɔː'tɒmətən/ n autómata m

automobile /'ɔːtəməbiːl/ n (Amer) coche m, automóvil m

autonom|ous /ɔː'tɒnəməs/ a autónomo. **~y** n autonomía f

autopsy /'ɔːtɒpsɪ/ n autopsia f

autumn /'ɔːtəm/ n otoño m. **~al** /-'tʌmnəl/ a de otoño, otoñal

auxiliary /ɔːgˈzɪlɪərɪ/ *a* auxiliar. ● *n* asistente *m*; (*verb*) verbo *m* auxiliar; (*pl, troops*) tropas *fpl* auxiliares

avail /əˈveɪl/ *vt/i* servir. ~ **o.s. of** aprovecharse de. ● *n* ventaja *f*. **to no** ~ inútil

availab|ility /əveɪləˈbɪlətɪ/ *n* disponibilidad *f*. ~**le** /əˈveɪləbl/ *a* disponible

avalanche /ˈævəlɑːnʃ/ *n* avalancha *f*

avaric|e /ˈævərɪs/ *n* avaricia *f*. ~**ious** /-ˈrɪʃəs/ *a* avaro

avenge /əˈvendʒ/ *vt* vengar

avenue /ˈævənjuː/ *n* avenida *f*; (*fig*) vía *f*

average /ˈævərɪdʒ/ *n* promedio *m*. **on** ~ por término medio. ● *a* medio. ● *vt* calcular el promedio de. ● *vi* alcanzar un promedio de

avers|e /əˈvɜːs/ *a* enemigo (**to** de). **be** ~**e to** sentir repugnancia por, no gustarle. ~**ion** /-ʃn/ *n* repugnancia *f*

avert /əˈvɜːt/ *vt* (*turn away*) apartar; (*ward off*) desviar

aviary /ˈeɪvɪərɪ/ *n* pajarera *f*

aviation /eɪvɪˈeɪʃn/ *n* aviación *f*

aviator /ˈeɪvɪeɪtə(r)/ *n* (*old use*) aviador *m*

avid /ˈævɪd/ *a* ávido. ~**ity** /-ˈvɪdətɪ/ *n* avidez *f*

avocado /ævəˈkɑːdəʊ/ *n* (*pl* -**os**) aguacate *m*

avoid /əˈvɔɪd/ *vt* evitar. ~**able** *a* evitable. ~**ance** *n* el evitar *m*

avuncular /əˈvʌŋkjʊlə(r)/ *a* de tío

await /əˈweɪt/ *vt* esperar

awake /əˈweɪk/ *vt/i* (*pt* **awoke**, *pp* **awoken**) despertar. ● *a* despierto. **wide** ~ completamente despierto; (*fig*) despabilado. ~**n** /əˈweɪkən/ *vt/i* despertar. ~**ning** *n* el despertar *m*

award /əˈwɔːd/ *vt* otorgar; (*jurid*) adjudicar. ● *n* premio *m*; (*jurid*) adjudicación *f*; (*scholarship*) beca *f*

aware /əˈweə(r)/ *a* consciente. **are you** ~ **that?** ¿te das cuenta de que? ~**ness** *n* conciencia *f*

awash /əˈwɒʃ/ *a* inundado

away /əˈweɪ/ *adv* (*absent*) fuera; (*far*) lejos; (*persistently*) sin parar. ● *a & n*. ~ (**match**) partido *m* fuera de casa

awe /ɔː/ *n* temor *m*. ~**some** *a* imponente. ~**struck** *a* atemorizado

awful /ˈɔːfʊl/ *a* terrible, malísimo. ~**ly** *adv* terriblemente

awhile /əˈwaɪl/ *adv* un rato

awkward /ˈɔːkwəd/ *a* difícil; (*inconvenient*) inoportuno; (*clumsy*) desmañado; (*embarrassed*) incómodo. ~**ly** *adv* con dificultad; (*clumsily*) de manera torpe. ~**ness** *n* dificultad *f*; (*discomfort*) molestia *f*; (*clumsiness*) torpeza *f*

awning /ˈɔːnɪŋ/ *n* toldo *m*

awoke, **awoken** /əˈwəʊk, əˈwəʊkən/ *see* **awake**

awry /əˈraɪ/ *adv & a* ladeado. **go** ~ salir mal

axe /æks/ *n* hacha *f*. ● *vt* (*pres p* **axing**) cortar con hacha; (*fig*) recortar

axiom /ˈæksɪəm/ *n* axioma *m*

axis /ˈæksɪs/ *n* (*pl* **axes** /-iːz/) eje *m*

axle /ˈæksl/ *n* eje *m*

ay(e) /aɪ/ *adv & n* sí (*m*)

B

BA *abbr see* **bachelor**

babble /ˈbæbl/ *vi* balbucir; (*chatter*) parlotear; (*of stream*) murmullar. ● *n* balbuceo *m*; (*chatter*) parloteo *m*; (*of stream*) murmullo *m*

baboon /bəˈbuːn/ *n* mandril *m*

baby /ˈbeɪbɪ/ *n* niño *m*, bebé *m*; (*Amer, sl*) chica *f*. ~**ish** /ˈbeɪbɪʃ/ *a* infantil. ~**sit** *vi* cuidar a los niños, hacer de canguro. ~**sitter** *n* persona *f* que cuida a los niños, canguro *m*

bachelor /ˈbætʃələ(r)/ *n* soltero *m*. **B**~ **of Arts (BA)** licenciado *m* en filosofía y letras. **B**~ **of Science (BSc)** licenciado *m* en ciencias

back /bæk/ *n* espalda *f*; (*of car*) parte *f* trasera; (*of chair*) respaldo *m*; (*of cloth*) revés *m*; (*of house*) parte *f* de atrás; (*of animal, book*) lomo *m*; (*of hand, document*) dorso *m*; (*of football*) defensa *m & f*. ~ **of beyond** en el quinto pino. ● *a* trasero; (*taxes*) atrasado. ● *adv* atrás; (*returned*) de vuelta. ● *vt* apoyar; (*betting*) apostar a; dar marcha atrás a (*car*). ● *vi* retroceder; (*car*) dar marcha atrás. ~ **down** *vi* volverse atrás. ~ **out** *vi* retirarse. ~ **up** *vi* (*auto*) retroceder. ~**ache** /ˈbækeɪk/ *n* dolor *m* de espalda. ~**bencher** *n* (*pol*) diputado *m* sin poder ministerial. ~**biting** /ˈbækbaɪtɪŋ/ *n* maledicencia *f*. ~**bone** /ˈbækbəʊn/ *n* columna *f* vertebral; (*fig*) pilar *m*. ~**chat** /ˈbæktʃæt/ *n* impertinencias *fpl*.

~**date** /bæk'deɪt/ vt antedatar. ~**er** /'bækə(r)/ n partidario m; (com) financiador m. ~**fire** /bæk'faɪə(r)/ vi (auto) petardear; (fig) fallar, salir el tiro por la culata. ~**gammon** /bæk'gæmən/ n backgamon m. ~**ground** /'bækgraʊnd/ n fondo m; (environment) antecedentes mpl. ~**hand** /'bækhænd/ n (sport) revés m. ~**handed** a dado con el dorso de la mano; (fig) equívoco, ambiguo. ~**hander** n (sport) revés m; (fig) ataque m indirecto; (bribe, sl) soborno m. ~**ing** /'bækɪŋ/ n apoyo m. ~**lash** /'bæklæʃ/ n reacción f. ~**log** /'bæklɒg/ n atrasos mpl. ~**side** /bæk'saɪd/ n (fam) trasero m. ~**stage** /bæk'steɪdʒ/ a de bastidores. ● adv entre bastidores. ~**stroke** /'bækstrəʊk/ n (tennis etc) revés m; (swimming) braza f de espaldas. ~**up** n apoyo m. ~**ward** /'bækwəd/ a (step etc) hacia atrás; (retarded) atrasado. ~**wards** /'bækwədz/ adv hacia atrás; (fall) de espaldas; (back to front) al revés. **go ~wards and forwards** ir de acá para allá. ~**water** /'bækwɔːtə(r)/ n agua f estancada; (fig) lugar m apartado

bacon /'beɪkən/ n tocino m.

bacteria /bæk'tɪərɪə/ npl bacterias fpl. ~**l** a bacteriano

bad /bæd/ a (worse, worst) malo; (serious) grave; (harmful) nocivo; (language) indecente. **feel ~** sentirse mal

bade /beɪd/ see **bid**

badge /bædʒ/ n distintivo m, chapa f

badger /'bædʒə(r)/ n tejón m. ● vt acosar

bad: ~**ly** adv mal. **want ~ly** desear muchísimo. ~**ly off** mal de dinero. ~**mannered** a mal educado

badminton /'bædmɪntən/ n bádminton m

bad-tempered /bæd'tempəd/ a (always) de mal genio; (temporarily) de mal humor

baffle /'bæfl/ vt desconcertar

bag /bæg/ n bolsa f; (handbag) bolso m. ● vt (pt bagged) ensacar; (take) coger (not LAm), agarrar (LAm). ~**s** npl (luggage) equipaje m. ~**s of** (fam) montones de

baggage /'bægɪdʒ/ n equipaje m

baggy /'bægɪ/ a (clothes) holgado

bagpipes /'bægpaɪps/ npl gaita f

Bahamas /bə'hɑːməz/ npl. **the ~** las Bahamas fpl

bail[1] /beɪl/ n caución f, fianza f. ● vt poner en libertad bajo fianza. **~ s.o. out** obtener la libertad de uno bajo fianza

bail[2] /beɪl/ n (cricket) travesaño m

bail[3] /beɪl/ vt (naut) achicar

bailiff /'beɪlɪf/ n alguacil m; (estate) administrador m

bait /beɪt/ n cebo m. ● vt cebar; (torment) atormentar

bak|e /beɪk/ vt cocer al horno. ● vi cocerse. ~**er** n panadero m. ~**ery** /'beɪkərɪ/ n panadería f. ~**ing** n cocción f; (batch) hornada f. ~**ing-powder** n levadura f en polvo

balance /'bæləns/ n equilibrio m; (com) balance m; (sum) saldo m; (scales) balanza f; (remainder) resto m. ● vt equilibrar; (com) saldar; nivelar (budget). ● vi equilibrarse; (com) saldarse. ~**d** a equilibrado

balcony /'bælkənɪ/ n balcón m

bald /bɔːld/ a (-er, -est) calvo; (tyre) desgastado

balderdash /'bɔːldədæʃ/ n tonterías fpl

bald: ~**ly** adv escuetamente. ~**ness** n calvicie f

bale /beɪl/ n bala f, fardo m. ● vi. ~ **out** lanzarse en paracaídas

Balearic /bælɪ'ærɪk/ a. ~ **Islands** Islas fpl Baleares

baleful /'beɪlfʊl/ a funesto

balk /bɔːk/ vt frustrar. ● vi. ~ **(at)** resistirse (a)

ball[1] /bɔːl/ n bola f; (tennis etc) pelota f; (football etc) balón m; (of yarn) ovillo m

ball[2] /bɔːl/ (dance) baile m

ballad /'bæləd/ n balada f

ballast /'bæləst/ n lastre m

ball: ~**bearing** n cojinete m de bolas. ~**cock** n llave f de bola

ballerina /bælə'riːnə/ f bailarina f

ballet /'bæleɪ/ n ballet m

ballistic /bə'lɪstɪk/ a balístico. ~**s** n balística f

balloon /bə'luːn/ n globo m

balloonist /bə'luːnɪst/ n aeronauta m & f

ballot /'bælət/ n votación f. ~ **(-paper)** n papeleta f. ~**box** n urna f

ball-point /'bɔːlpɔɪnt/ n. ~ **(pen)** bolígrafo m

ballroom /'bɔːlruːm/ n salón m de baile

ballyhoo /'bælɪ'hu:/ n (publicity) publicidad f sensacionalista; (uproar) jaleo m

balm /bɑːm/ n bálsamo m. ∼y a (mild) suave; (sl) chiflado

baloney /bə'ləʊnɪ/ n (sl) tonterías fpl

balsam /'bɔːlsəm/ n bálsamo m

balustrade /bælə'streɪd/ n barandilla f

bamboo /bæm'buː/ n bambú m

bamboozle /bæm'buːzl/ vt engatusar

ban /bæn/ vt (pt banned) prohibir. ∼ from excluir de. ● n prohibición f

banal /bə'nɑːl/ a banal. ∼ity /-ælətɪ/ n banalidad f

banana /bə'nɑːnə/ n plátano m, banana f (LAm). ∼-tree plátano m, banano m

band¹ /bænd/ n banda f

band² /bænd/ n (mus) orquesta f; (military, brass) banda f. ● vi. ∼ together juntarse

bandage /'bændɪdʒ/ n venda f. ● vt vendar

b & b abbr (bed and breakfast) cama f y desayuno

bandit /'bændɪt/ n bandido m

bandstand /'bændstænd/ n quiosco m de música

bandwagon /'bændwægən/ n. jump on the ∼ (fig) subirse al carro

bandy¹ /'bændɪ/ a (-ier, -iest) patizambo

bandy² /'bændɪ/ vt. ∼ about repetir. be bandied about estar en boca de todos

bandy-legged /'bændɪlegd/ a patizambo

bane /beɪn/ n (fig) perdición f. ∼ful a funesto

bang /bæŋ/ n (noise) ruido m; (blow) golpe m; (of gun) estampido m; (of door) golpe m. ● vt/i golpear. ● adv exactamente. ● int ¡pum!

banger /'bæŋə(r)/ n petardo m; (culin, sl) salchicha f

bangle /'bæŋgl/ n brazalete m

banish /'bænɪʃ/ vt desterrar

banisters /'bænɪstəz/ npl barandilla f

banjo /'bændʒəʊ/ n (pl -os) banjo m

bank¹ /bæŋk/ n (of river) orilla f. ● vt cubrir (fire). ● vi (aviat) ladearse

bank² /bæŋk/ n banco m. ● vt depositar. ∼ on vt contar con. ∼ with

tener una cuenta con. ∼er n banquero m. ∼ holiday n día m festivo, fiesta f. ∼ing n (com) banca f. ∼note /'bæŋknəʊt/ n billete m de banco

bankrupt /'bæŋkrʌpt/ a & n quebrado (m). ● vt hacer quebrar. ∼cy n bancarrota f, quiebra f

banner /'bænə(r)/ n bandera f; (in demonstration) pancarta f

banns /bænz/ npl amonestaciones fpl

banquet /'bæŋkwɪt/ n banquete m

bantamweight /'bæntəmweɪt/ n peso m gallo

banter /'bæntə(r)/ n chanza f. ● vi chancearse

bap /bæp/ n panecillo m blando

baptism /'bæptɪzəm/ n bautismo m; (act) bautizo m

Baptist /'bæptɪst/ n bautista m & f

baptize /bæp'taɪz/ vt bautizar

bar /bɑː(r)/ n barra f; (on window) reja f; (of chocolate) tableta f; (of soap) pastilla f; (pub) bar m; (mus) compás m; (jurid) abogacía f; (fig) obstáculo m. ● vt (pt barred) atrancar (door); (exclude) excluir; (prohibit) prohibir. ● prep excepto

barbar|ian /bɑː'beərɪən/ a & n bárbaro (m). ∼ic /bɑː'bærɪk/ a bárbaro. ∼ity /-ətɪ/ n barbaridad f. ∼ous /'bɑːbərəs/ a bárbaro

barbecue /'bɑːbɪkjuː/ n barbacoa f. ● vt asar a la parilla

barbed /bɑːbd/ a. ∼ wire alambre m de espinas

barber /'bɑːbə(r)/ n peluquero m, barbero m

barbiturate /bɑː'bɪtjʊrət/ n barbitúrico m

bare /beə(r)/ a (-er, est) desnudo; (room) con pocos muebles; (mere) simple; (empty) vacío. ● vt desnudar; (uncover) descubrir. ∼ one's teeth mostrar los dientes. ∼back /'beəbæk/ adv a pelo. ∼faced /'beəfeɪst/ a descarado. ∼foot a descalzo. ∼headed /'beəhedɪd/ a descubierto. ∼ly adv apenas. ∼ness n desnudez f

bargain /'bɑːgɪn/ n (agreement) pacto m; (good buy) ganga f. ● vi negociar; (haggle) regatear. ∼ for esperar, contar con

barge /bɑːdʒ/ n barcaza f. ● vi. ∼ in irrumpir

baritone /'bærɪtəʊn/ n barítono m

barium /'beərɪəm/ n bario m

bark[1] /bɑːk/ n (of dog) ladrido m. ● vi ladrar

bark[2] /bɑːk/ (of tree) corteza f

barley /'bɑːlɪ/ n cebada f. ~**water** n hordiate m

bar: ~**maid** /'bɑːmeɪd/ n camarera f. ~**man** /'bɑːmən/ n (pl -**men**) camarero m

barmy /'bɑːmɪ/ a (sl) chiflado

barn /bɑːn/ n granero m

barometer /bə'rɒmɪtə(r)/ n barómetro m

baron /'bærən/ n barón m. ~**ess** n baronesa f

baroque /bə'rɒk/ a & n barroco (m)

barracks /'bærəks/ npl cuartel m

barrage /'bærɑːʒ/ n (mil) barrera f; (dam) presa f; (of questions) bombardeo m

barrel /'bærəl/ n tonel m; (of gun) cañón m. ~**organ** n organillo m

barren /'bærən/ a estéril. ~**ness** n esterilidad f, aridez f

barricade /bærɪ'keɪd/ n barricada f. ● vt cerrar con barricadas

barrier /'bærɪə(r)/ n barrera f

barring /'bɑːrɪŋ/ prep salvo

barrister /'bærɪstə(r)/ n abogado m

barrow /'bærəʊ/ n carro m; (wheelbarrow) carretilla f

barter /'bɑːtə(r)/ n trueque m. ● vt trocar

base /beɪs/ n base f. ● vt basar. ● a vil

baseball /'beɪsbɔːl/ n béisbol m

baseless /'beɪslɪs/ a infundado

basement /'beɪsmənt/ n sótano m

bash /bæʃ/ vt golpear. ● n golpe m. **have a** ~ (sl) probar

bashful /'bæʃfl/ a tímido

basic /'beɪsɪk/ a básico, fundamental. ~**ally** adv fundamentalmente

basil /'bæzl/ n albahaca f

basilica /bə'zɪlɪkə/ n basílica f

basin /'beɪsn/ n (for washing) palangana f; (for food) cuenco m; (geog) cuenca f

basis /'beɪsɪs/ n (pl **bases** /-siːz/) base f

bask /bɑːsk/ vi asolearse; (fig) gozar (**in** de)

basket /'bɑːskɪt/ n cesta f; (big) cesto m. ~**ball** /'bɑːskɪtbɔːl/ n baloncesto m

Basque /bɑːsk/ a & n vasco (m). ~ **Country** n País m Vasco. ~ **Provinces** npl Vascongadas fpl

bass[1] /beɪs/ a bajo. ● n (mus) bajo m

bass[2] /bæs/ n (marine fish) róbalo m; (freshwater fish) perca f

bassoon /bə'suːn/ n fagot m

bastard /'bɑːstəd/ a & n bastardo (m). **you** ~! (fam) ¡cabrón!

baste /beɪst/ vt (sew) hilvanar; (culin) lard(e)ar

bastion /'bæstɪən/ n baluarte m

bat[1] /bæt/ n bate m; (for table tennis) raqueta f. **off one's own** ~ por sí solo. ● vt (pt **batted**) golpear. ● vi batear

bat[2] /bæt/ n (mammal) murciélago m

bat[3] /bæt/ vt. **without** ~**ting an eyelid** sin pestañear

batch /bætʃ/ n (of people) grupo m; (of papers) lío m; (of goods) remesa f; (of bread) hornada f

bated /'beɪtɪd/ a. **with** ~ **breath** con aliento entrecortado

bath /bɑːθ/ n (pl -**s** /bɑːðz/) baño m; (tub) bañera f; (pl, swimming pool) piscina f. ● vt bañar. ● vi bañarse

bathe /beɪð/ vt bañar. ● vi bañarse. ● n baño m. ~**r** /-ə(r)/ n bañista m & f

bathing /'beɪðɪŋ/ n baños mpl. ~**costume** n traje m de baño

bathroom /'bɑːθrʊm/ n cuarto m de baño

batman /'bætmən/ n (pl -**men**) (mil) ordenanza f

baton /'bætən/ n (mil) bastón m; (mus) batuta f

batsman /'bætsmən/ n (pl -**men**) bateador m

battalion /bə'tælɪən/ n batallón m

batter[1] /'bætə(r)/ vt apalear

batter[2] /'bætə(r)/ n batido m para rebozar, albardilla f

batter: ~**ed** a ⟨car etc⟩ estropeado; ⟨wife etc⟩ golpeado. ~**ing** n (fam) bombardeo m

battery /'bætərɪ/ n (mil, auto) batería f; (of torch, radio) pila f

battle /'bætl/ n batalla f; (fig) lucha f. ● vi luchar. ~**axe** /'bætlæks/ n (woman, fam) arpía f. ~**field** /'bætlfiːld/ n campo m de batalla. ~**ments** /'bætlmənts/ npl almenas fpl. ~**ship** /'bætlʃɪp/ n acorazado m

batty /'bætɪ/ a (sl) chiflado

baulk /bɔːlk/ vt frustrar. ● vi. ~ (**at**) resistirse (a)

bawd|iness /'bɔːdɪnəs/ n obscenidad f. ~**y** /'bɔːdɪ/ a (-**ier**, -**iest**) obsceno, verde

bawl /bɔːl/ vt/i gritar

bay¹ /beɪ/ n (geog) bahía f
bay² /beɪ/ n (bot) laurel m
bay³ /beɪ/ n (of dog) ladrido m. **keep at** ~ mantener a raya. ● vi ladrar
bayonet /'beɪənet/ n bayoneta f
bay window /beɪ'wɪndəʊ/ n ventana f salediza
bazaar /bə'zɑː(r)/ n bazar m
BC /biː'siː/ abbr (before Christ) a. de C., antes de Cristo
be /biː/ vi (pres **am**, **are**, **is**; pt **was**, **were**; pp **been**) (position or temporary) estar; (permanent) ser. ~ **cold/hot, etc** tener frío/calor, etc. ~ **reading/singing, etc** (aux) leer/cantar, etc. ~ **that as it may** sea como fuere. **he is 30** (age) tiene 30 años. **he is to come** (must) tiene que venir. **how are you?** ¿cómo estás? **how much is it?** ¿cuánto vale?, ¿cuánto es? **have been to** haber estado en. **it is cold/hot, etc** (weather) hace frío/calor, etc
beach /biːtʃ/ n playa f
beachcomber /'biːtʃkəʊmə(r)/ n raquero m
beacon /'biːkən/ n faro m
bead /biːd/ n cuenta f; (of glass) abalorio m
beak /biːk/ n pico m
beaker /'biːkə(r)/ n jarra f, vaso m
beam /biːm/ n viga f; (of light) rayo m; (naut) bao m. ● vt emitir. ● vi irradiar; (smile) sonreír. ~**ends** npl. **be on one's** ~**ends** no tener más dinero. ~**ing** a radiante
bean /biːn/ n judía; (broad bean) haba f; (of coffee) grano m
beano /'biːnəʊ/ n (pl **-os**) (fam) juerga f
bear¹ /beə(r)/ vt (pt **bore**, pp **borne**) llevar; parir (niño); (endure) soportar. ~ **right** torcer a la derecha. ~ **in mind** tener en cuenta. ~ **with** tener paciencia con
bear² /beə(r)/ n oso m
bearable /'beərəbl/ a soportable
beard /bɪəd/ n barba f. ~**ed** a barbudo
bearer /'beərə(r)/ n portador m; (of passport) poseedor m
bearing /'beərɪŋ/ n comportamiento m; (relevance) relación f; (mec) cojinete m. **get one's** ~**s** orientarse
beast /biːst/ n bestia f; (person) bruto m. ~**ly** /'biːstlɪ/ a (-**ier**, -**iest**) bestial; (fam) horrible

beat /biːt/ vt (pt **beat**, pp **beaten**) golpear; (culin) batir; (defeat) derrotar; (better) sobrepasar; (baffle) dejar perplejo. ~ **a retreat** (mil) batirse en retirada. ~ **it** (sl) largarse. ● vi (heart) latir. ● n latido m; (mus) ritmo m; (of policeman) ronda f. ~ **up** dar una paliza a; (culin) batir. ~**er** n batidor m. ~**ing** n paliza f
beautician /bjuː'tɪʃn/ n esteticista m & f
beautiful /'bjuːtɪfl/ a hermoso. ~**ly** adv maravillosamente
beautify /'bjuːtɪfaɪ/ vt embellecer
beauty /'bjuːtɪ/ n belleza f. ~ **parlour** n salón m de belleza. ~ **spot** (on face) lunar m; (site) lugar m pintoresco
beaver /'biːvə(r)/ n castor m
became /bɪ'keɪm/ see **become**
because /bɪ'kɒz/ conj porque. ● adv. ~ **of** a causa de
beck /bek/ n. **be at the** ~ **and call of** estar a disposición de
beckon /'bekən/ vt/i. ~ **(to)** hacer señas (a)
become /bɪ'kʌm/ vt (pt **became**, pp **become**) (clothes) sentar bien. ● vi hacerse, llegar a ser, volverse, convertirse en. **what has** ~ **of her?** ¿qué es de ella?
becoming /bɪ'kʌmɪŋ/ a (clothes) favorecedor
bed /bed/ n cama f; (layer) estrato m; (of sea, river) fondo m; (of flowers) macizo m. ● vi (pt **bedded**). ~ **down** acostarse. ~ **and breakfast** (b & b) cama y desayuno. ~**bug** /'bedbʌg/ n chinche f. ~**clothes** /'bedkləʊðz/ npl, ~**ding** n ropa f de cama
bedevil /bɪ'devl/ vt (pt **bedevilled**) (torment) atormentar
bedlam /'bedləm/ n confusión f, manicomio m
bed: ~**pan** /'bedpæn/ n orinal m de cama. ~**post** /'bedpəʊst/ n columna f de la cama
bedraggled /bɪ'drægld/ a sucio
bed: ~**ridden** /'bedrɪdn/ a encamado. ~**room** /'bedrʊm/ n dormitorio m, habitación f. ~**side** /'bedsaɪd/ n cabecera f. ~**sitting-room** /bed'sɪtɪŋruːm/ n salón m con cama, estudio m. ~**spread** /'bedspred/ n colcha f. ~**time** /'bedtaɪm/ n hora f de acostarse
bee /biː/ n abeja f. **make a** ~**line for** ir en línea recta hacia

beech /biːtʃ/ n haya f

beef /biːf/ n carne f de vaca, carne f de res (LAm). ● vi (sl) quejarse. **~burger** /'biːfbɜːgə(r)/ n hamburguesa f

beefeater /'biːfiːtə(r)/ n alabardero m de la torre de Londres

beefsteak /'biːfsteɪk/ n filete m, bistec m, bife m (Arg)

beefy /'biːfɪ/ a (-ier, -iest) musculoso

beehive /'biːhaɪv/ n colmena f

been /biːn/ see **be**

beer /bɪə(r)/ n cerveza f

beet /biːt/ n remolacha f

beetle /'biːtl/ n escarabajo m

beetroot /'biːtruːt/ n invar remolacha f

befall /bɪ'fɔːl/ vt (pt **befell**, pp **befallen**) acontecer a. ● vi acontecer

befit /bɪ'fɪt/ vt (pt **befitted**) convenir a

before /bɪ'fɔː(r)/ prep (time) antes de; (place) delante de. **~ leaving** antes de marcharse. ● adv (place) delante; (time) antes. **a week ~** una semana antes. **the week ~** la semana anterior. ● conj (time) antes de que. **~ he leaves** antes de que se vaya. **~hand** /bɪ'fɔːhænd/ adv de antemano

befriend /bɪ'frend/ vt ofrecer amistad a

beg /beg/ vt/i (pt **begged**) mendigar; (entreat) suplicar; (ask) pedir. **~ s.o.'s pardon** pedir perdón a uno. **I ~ your pardon!** ¡perdone Vd! **I ~ your pardon?** ¿cómo? **it's going ~ging** no lo quiere nadie

began /bɪ'gæn/ see **begin**

beget /bɪ'get/ vt (pt **begot**, pp **begotten**, pres p **begetting**) engendrar

beggar /'begə(r)/ n mendigo m; (sl) individuo m, tío m (fam)

begin /bɪ'gɪn/ vt/i (pt **began**, pp **begun**, pres p **beginning**) comenzar, empezar. **~ner** n principiante m & f. **~ning** n principio m

begot, begotten /bɪ'gɒt, bɪ'gɒtn/ see **beget**

begrudge /bɪ'grʌdʒ/ vt envidiar; (give) dar de mala gana

beguile /bɪ'gaɪl/ vt engañar, seducir; (entertain) entretener

begun /bɪ'gʌn/ see **begin**

behalf /bɪ'hɑːf/ n. **on ~ of** de parte de, en nombre de

behave /bɪ'heɪv/ vi comportarse, portarse. **~ (o.s.)** portarse bien.

~iour /bɪ'heɪvjə(r)/ n comportamiento m

behead /bɪ'hed/ vt decapitar

beheld /bɪ'held/ see **behold**

behind /bɪ'haɪnd/ prep detrás de. ● adv detrás; (late) atrasado. ● n (fam) trasero m

behold /bɪ'həʊld/ vt (pt **beheld**) (old use) mirar, contemplar

beholden /bɪ'həʊldən/ a agradecido

being /'biːɪŋ/ n ser m. **come into ~** nacer

belated /bɪ'leɪtɪd/ a tardío

belch /beltʃ/ vi eructar. ● vt. **~ out** arrojar ‹smoke›

belfry /'belfrɪ/ n campanario m

Belgi|an /'beldʒən/ a & n belga (m & f). **~um** /'beldʒəm/ n Bélgica f

belie /bɪ'laɪ/ vt desmentir

belie|f /bɪ'liːf/ n (trust) fe f; (opinion) creencia f. **~ve** /bɪ'liːv/ vt/i creer. **make ~ve** fingir. **~ver** /-ə(r)/ n creyente m & f; (supporter) partidario m

belittle /bɪ'lɪtl/ vt empequeñecer; (fig) despreciar

bell /bel/ n campana f; (on door) timbre m

belligerent /bɪ'lɪdʒərənt/ a & n beligerante (m & f)

bellow /'beləʊ/ vt gritar. ● vi bramar

bellows /'beləʊz/ npl fuelle m

belly /'belɪ/ n vientre m. **~ful** /'belfʊl/ n panzada f. **have a ~ful of** (sl) estar harto de

belong /bɪ'lɒŋ/ vi pertenecer; (club) ser socio (**to** de)

belongings /bɪ'lɒŋɪŋz/ npl pertenencias fpl. **personal ~** efectos mpl personales

beloved /bɪ'lʌvɪd/ a & n querido (m)

below /bɪ'ləʊ/ prep debajo de; (fig) inferior a. ● adv abajo

belt /belt/ n cinturón m; (area) zona f. ● vt (fig) rodear; (sl) pegar

bemused /bɪ'mjuːzd/ a perplejo

bench /bentʃ/ n banco m. **the B~** (jurid) la magistratura f

bend /bend/ vt (pt & pp **bent**) doblar; torcer ‹arm, leg›. ● vi doblarse; ‹road› torcerse. ● n curva f. **~ down/over** inclinarse

beneath /bɪ'niːθ/ prep debajo de; (fig) inferior a. ● adv abajo

benediction /benɪ'dɪkʃn/ n bendición f

benefactor /'benɪfæktə(r)/ n bienhechor m, benefactor m

beneficial /benɪ'fɪʃl/ *a* provechoso

beneficiary /benɪ'fɪʃərɪ/ *a & n* beneficiario (*m*)

benefit /'benɪfɪt/ *n* provecho *m*, ventaja *f*; (*allowance*) subsidio *m*; (*financial gain*) beneficio *m*. ● *vt* (*pt* benefited, *pres p* benefiting) aprovechar. ● *vi* aprovecharse

benevolen|ce /bɪ'nevələns/ *n* benevolencia *f*. ~**t** *a* benévolo

benign /bɪ'naɪn/ *a* benigno

bent /bent/ *see* **bend**. ● *n* inclinación *f*. ● *a* encorvado; (*sl*) corrompido

bequeath /bɪ'kwiːð/ *vt* legar

bequest /bɪ'kwest/ *n* legado *m*

bereave|d /bɪ'riːvd/ *n*. **the ~d** la familia *f* del difunto. ~**ment** *n* pérdida *f*; (*mourning*) luto *m*

bereft /bɪ'reft/ *a*. ~ **of** privado de

beret /'bereɪ/ *n* boina *f*

Bermuda /bə'mjuːdə/ *n* Islas *fpl* Bermudas

berry /'berɪ/ *n* baya *f*

berserk /bə's3ːk/ *a*. **go ~** volverse loco, perder los estribos

berth /b3ːθ/ *n* litera *f*; (*anchorage*) amarradero *m*. **give a wide ~ to** evitar. ● *vi* atracar

beseech /bɪ'siːtʃ/ *vt* (*pt* besought) suplicar

beset /bɪ'set/ *vt* (*pt* beset, *pres p* besetting) acosar

beside /bɪ'saɪd/ *prep* al lado de. **be ~ o.s.** estar fuera de sí

besides /bɪ'saɪdz/ *prep* además de; (*except*) excepto. ● *adv* además

besiege /bɪ'siːdʒ/ *vt* asediar; (*fig*) acosar

besought /bɪ'sɔːt/ *see* **beseech**

bespoke /bɪ'spəʊk/ *a* ⟨*tailor*⟩ que confecciona a la medida

best /best/ *a* (el) mejor. **the ~ thing is to...** lo mejor es... ● *adv* (lo) mejor. **like ~** preferir. ● *n* lo mejor. **at ~** a lo más. **do one's ~** hacer todo lo posible. **make the ~ of** contentarse con. ~ **man** *n* padrino *m* (de boda)

bestow /bɪ'stəʊ/ *vt* conceder

bestseller /best'selə(r)/ *n* éxito *m* de librería, bestseller *m*

bet /bet/ *n* apuesta *f*. ● *vt/i* (*pt* bet *or* betted) apostar

betray /bɪ'treɪ/ *vt* traicionar. ~**al** *n* traición *f*

betroth|al /bɪ'trəʊðəl/ *n* esponsales *mpl*. ~**ed** *a* prometido

better /'betə(r)/ *a & adv* mejor. ~**off** en mejores condiciones; (*richer*) más rico. **get ~** mejorar. **all the ~** tanto mejor. **I'd ~** más vale que. **the ~ part of** la mayor parte de. **the sooner the ~** cuanto antes mejor. ● *vt* mejorar; (*beat*) sobrepasar. ● *n* superior *m*. **get the ~ of** vencer a. **one's ~s** sus superiores *mpl*

between /bɪ'twiːn/ *prep* entre. ● *adv* en medio

beverage /'bevərɪdʒ/ *n* bebida *f*

bevy /'bevɪ/ *n* grupo *m*

beware /bɪ'weə(r)/ *vi* tener cuidado. ● *int* ¡cuidado!

bewilder /bɪ'wɪldə(r)/ *vt* desconcertar. ~**ment** *n* aturdimiento *m*

bewitch /bɪ'wɪtʃ/ *vt* hechizar

beyond /bɪ'jɒnd/ *prep* más allá de; (*fig*) fuera de. ~ **doubt** sin lugar a duda. ~ **reason** irrazonable. ● *adv* más allá

bias /'baɪəs/ *n* predisposición *f*; (*prejudice*) prejuicio *m*; (*sewing*) sesgo *m*. ● *vt* (*pt* biased) influir en. ~**ed** *a* parcial

bib /bɪb/ *n* babero *m*

Bible /'baɪbl/ *n* Biblia *f*

biblical /'bɪblɪkl/ *a* bíblico

bibliography /bɪblɪ'ɒɡrəfɪ/ *n* bibliografía *f*

biceps /'baɪseps/ *n* bíceps *m*

bicker /'bɪkə(r)/ *vi* altercar

bicycle /'baɪsɪkl/ *n* bicicleta *f*. ● *vi* ir en bicicleta

bid /bɪd/ *n* (*offer*) oferta *f*; (*attempt*) tentativa *f*. ● *vi* hacer una oferta. ● *vt* (*pt* bid, *pres p* bidding) ofrecer; (*pt* bid, *pp* bidden, *pres p* bidding) mandar; dar ⟨*welcome, good-day etc*⟩. ~**der** *n* postor *m*. ~**ding** *n* (*at auction*) ofertas *fpl*; (*order*) mandato *m*

bide /baɪd/ *vt*. ~ **one's time** esperar el momento oportuno

biennial /baɪ'enɪəl/ *a* bienal. ● *n* (*event*) bienal *f*; (*bot*) planta *f* bienal

bifocals /baɪ'fəʊklz/ *npl* gafas *fpl* bifocales, anteojos *mpl* bifocales (LA*m*)

big /bɪɡ/ *a* (bigger, biggest) grande; (*generous, sl*) generoso. ● *adv*. **talk ~** fanfarronear

bigam|ist /'bɪɡəmɪst/ *n* bígamo *m*. ~**ous** *a* bígamo. ~**y** *n* bigamia *f*

big-headed /bɪg'hedɪd/ *a* engreído

bigot /'bɪɡət/ *n* fanático *m*. ~**ed** *a* fanático. ~**ry** *n* fanatismo *m*

bigwig /'bɪɡwɪɡ/ *n* (*fam*) pez *m* gordo

bike /baɪk/ n (fam) bicicleta f, bici f (fam)

bikini /bɪˈkiːnɪ/ n (pl **-is**) biquini m, bikini m

bilberry /ˈbɪlbərɪ/ n arándano m

bile /baɪl/ n bilis f

bilingual /baɪˈlɪŋgwəl/ a bilingüe

bilious /ˈbɪlɪəs/ a (med) bilioso

bill¹ /bɪl/ n cuenta f; (invoice) factura f; (notice) cartel m; (Amer, banknote) billete m; (pol) proyecto m de ley. ● vt pasar la factura; (in theatre) anunciar

bill² /bɪl/ n (of bird) pico m

billet /ˈbɪlɪt/ n (mil) alojamiento m. ● vt alojar

billiards /ˈbɪlɪədz/ n billar m

billion /ˈbɪlɪən/ n billón m; (Amer) mil millones mpl

billy-goat /ˈbɪlɪgəʊt/ n macho m cabrío

bin /bɪn/ n recipiente m; (for rubbish) cubo m; (for waste paper) papelera f

bind /baɪnd/ vt (pt **bound**) atar; encuadernar ⟨book⟩; (jurid) obligar. ● n (sl) lata f. **~ing** /ˈbaɪndɪŋ/ n (of books) encuadernación f; (braid) ribete m

binge /bɪndʒ/ n (sl) (of food) comilona f; (of drink) borrachera f. **go on a ~** ir de juerga

bingo /ˈbɪŋgəʊ/ n bingo m

binoculars /bɪˈnɒkjʊləz/ npl prismáticos mpl

biochemistry /baɪəʊˈkemɪstrɪ/ n bioquímica f

biograph|er /baɪˈɒgrəfə(r)/ n biógrafo m. **~y** n biografía f

biolog|ical /baɪəˈlɒdʒɪkl/ a biológico. **~ist** n biólogo m. **~y** /baɪˈɒlədʒɪ/ n biología f

biped /ˈbaɪped/ n bípedo m

birch /bɜːtʃ/ n (tree) abedul m; (whip) férula f

bird /bɜːd/ n ave f; (small) pájaro m; (fam) tipo m; (girl, sl) chica f

Biro /ˈbaɪərəʊ/ n (pl **-os**) (P) bolígrafo m, biromen m (Arg)

birth /bɜːθ/ n nacimiento m. **~-certificate** n partida f de nacimiento. **~-control** n control m de la natalidad. **~day** /ˈbɜːθdeɪ/ n cumpleaños m invar. **~mark** /ˈbɜːθmɑːk/ n marca f de nacimiento. **~-rate** n natalidad f. **~right** /ˈbɜːθraɪt/ n derechos mpl de nacimiento

biscuit /ˈbɪskɪt/ n galleta f

bisect /baɪˈsekt/ vt bisecar

bishop /ˈbɪʃəp/ n obispo m

bit¹ /bɪt/ n trozo m; (quantity) poco m

bit² /bɪt/ see **bite**

bit³ /bɪt/ n (of horse) bocado m; (mec) broca f

bitch /bɪtʃ/ n perra f; (woman, fam) mujer f maligna, bruja f (fam). ● vi (fam) quejarse (**about** de). **~y** a malintencionado

bit|e /baɪt/ vt/i (pt **bit**, pp **bitten**) morder. **~e one's nails** morderse las uñas. ● n mordisco m; (mouthful) bocado m; (of insect etc) picadura f. **~ing** /ˈbaɪtɪŋ/ a mordaz

bitter /ˈbɪtə(r)/ a amargo; (of weather) glacial. **to the ~ end** hasta el final. ● n cerveza f amarga. **~ly** adv amargamente. **it's ~ly cold** hace un frío glacial. **~ness** n amargor m; (resentment) amargura f

bizarre /bɪˈzɑː(r)/ a extraño

blab /blæb/ vi (pt **blabbed**) chismear

black /blæk/ a (**-er, -est**) negro. **~ and blue** amoratado. ● vt ennegrecer; limpiar ⟨shoes⟩. **~ out** desmayarse; (make dark) apagar las luces de

blackball /ˈblækbɔːl/ vt votar en contra de

blackberry /ˈblækbərɪ/ n zarzamora f

blackbird /ˈblækbɜːd/ n mirlo m

blackboard /ˈblækbɔːd/ n pizarra f

blackcurrant /blækˈkʌrənt/ n casis f

blacken /ˈblækən/ vt ennegrecer. ● vi ennegrecerse

blackguard /ˈblægɑːd/ n canalla f

blackleg /ˈblækleg/ n esquirol m

blacklist /ˈblæklɪst/ vt poner en la lista negra

blackmail /ˈblækmeɪl/ n chantaje m. ● vt chantajear. **~er** n chantajista m & f

black-out /ˈblækaʊt/ n apagón m; (med) desmayo m; (of news) censura f

blacksmith /ˈblæksmɪθ/ n herrero m

bladder /ˈblædə(r)/ n vejiga f

blade /bleɪd/ n hoja f; (razor-blade) cuchilla f. **~ of grass** brizna f de hierba

blame /bleɪm/ vt echar la culpa a. **be to ~** tener la culpa. ● n culpa f. **~less** a inocente

bland /blænd/ a (**-er, -est**) suave

blandishments /'blændɪʃmənts/ *npl* halagos *mpl*

blank /blæŋk/ *a* en blanco; ⟨cartridge⟩ sin bala; (fig) vacío. **~ verse** *n* verso *m* suelto. ● *n* blanco *m*

blanket /'blæŋkɪt/ *n* manta *f*; (fig) capa *f*. ● *vt* (pt **blanketed**) (fig) cubrir (**in**, **with** de)

blare /bleə(r)/ *vi* sonar muy fuerte. ● *n* estrépito *m*

blarney /'blɑːnɪ/ *n* coba *f*. ● *vt* dar coba

blasé /'blɑːzeɪ/ *a* hastiado

blasphem|e /blæs'fiːm/ *vt/i* blasfemar. **~er** *n* blasfemador *m*. **~ous** /'blæsfəməs/ *a* blasfemo. **~y** /'blæsfəmɪ/ *n* blasfemia *f*

blast /blɑːst/ *n* explosión *f*; (gust) ráfaga *f*; (sound) toque *m*. ● *vt* volar. **~ed** *a* maldito. **~-furnace** *n* alto horno *m*. **~-off** *n* (of missile) despegue *m*

blatant /'bleɪtnt/ *a* patente; (shameless) descarado

blaze /'bleɪz/ *n* llamarada *f*; (of light) resplandor *m*; (fig) arranque *m*. ● *vi* arder en llamas; (fig) brillar. **~ a trail** abrir un camino

blazer /'bleɪzə(r)/ *n* chaqueta *f*

bleach /bliːtʃ/ *n* lejía *f*; (for hair) decolorante *m*. ● *vt* blanquear; decolorar ⟨hair⟩. ● *vi* blanquearse

bleak /bliːk/ *a* (**-er**, **-est**) desolado; (fig) sombrío

bleary /'blɪərɪ/ *a* ⟨eyes⟩ nublado; (indistinct) indistinto

bleat /bliːt/ *n* balido *m*. ● *vi* balar

bleed /bliːd/ *vt/i* (pt **bled**) sangrar

bleep /bliːp/ *n* pitido *m*. **~er** *n* busca *m*, buscapersonas *m*

blemish /'blemɪʃ/ *n* tacha *f*

blend /blend/ *n* mezcla *f*. ● *vt* mezclar. ● *vi* combinarse

bless /bles/ *vt* bendecir. **~ you!** (on sneezing) ¡Jesús! **~ed** *a* bendito. **be ~ed with** estar dotado de. **~ing** *n* bendición *f*; (advantage) ventaja *f*

blew /bluː/ *see* **blow**¹

blight /blaɪt/ *n* añublo *m*, tizón *m*; (fig) plaga *f*. ● *vt* añublar, atizonar; (fig) destrozar

blighter /'blaɪtə(r)/ *n* (sl) tío *m* (fam), sinvergüenza *m*

blind /blaɪnd/ *a* ciego. **~ alley** *n* callejón *m* sin salida. ● *n* persiana *f*; (fig) pretexto *m*. ● *vt* cegar. **~fold** /'blaɪndfəʊld/ *a* & *adv* con los ojos vendados. ● *n* venda *f*. ● *vt* vendar

los ojos. **~ly** *adv* a ciegas. **~ness** *n* ceguera *f*

blink /blɪŋk/ *vi* parpadear; (of light) centellear

blinkers /'blɪŋkəz/ *npl* anteojeras *fpl*; (auto) intermitente *m*

bliss /blɪs/ *n* felicidad *f*. **~ful** *a* feliz. **~fully** *adv* felizmente; (completely) completamente

blister /'blɪstə(r)/ *n* ampolla *f*. ● *vi* formarse ampollas

blithe /blaɪð/ *a* alegre

blitz /blɪts/ *n* bombardeo *m* aéreo. ● *vt* bombardear

blizzard /'blɪzəd/ *n* ventisca *f*

bloated /'bləʊtɪd/ *a* hinchado (**with** de)

bloater /'bləʊtə(r)/ *n* arenque *m* ahumado

blob /blɒb/ *n* gota *f*; (stain) mancha *f*

bloc /blɒk/ *n* (pol) bloque *m*

block /blɒk/ *n* bloque *m*; (of wood) zoquete *m*; (of buildings) manzana *f*, cuadra *f* (LAm); (in pipe) obstrucción *f*. **in ~ letters** en letra de imprenta. **traffic ~** embotellamiento *m*. ● *vt* obstruir. **~ade** /blɒ'keɪd/ *n* bloqueo *m*. ● *vt* bloquear. **~age** *n* obstrucción *f*

blockhead /'blɒkhed/ *n* (fam) zopenco *m*

bloke /bləʊk/ *n* (fam) tío *m* (fam), tipo *m*

blond /blɒnd/ *a* & *n* rubio (*m*). **~e** *a* & *n* rubia (*f*)

blood /blʌd/ *n* sangre *f*. **~ count** *n* recuento *m* sanguíneo. **~-curdling** *a* horripilante

bloodhound /'blʌdhaʊnd/ *n* sabueso *m*

blood: **~ pressure** *n* tensión *f* arterial. **high ~ pressure** hipertensión *f*. **~shed** /'blʌdʃed/ *n* efusión *f* de sangre, derramamiento *m* de sangre, matanza *f*. **~shot** /'blʌdʃɒt/ *a* sanguinolento; ⟨eye⟩ inyectado de sangre. **~stream** /'blʌdstriːm/ *n* sangre *f*

bloodthirsty /'blʌdθɜːstɪ/ *a* sanguinario

bloody /'blʌdɪ/ *a* (**-ier**, **-iest**) sangriento; (stained) ensangrentado; (sl) maldito. **~-minded** *a* (fam) terco

bloom /bluːm/ *n* flor *f*. ● *vi* florecer

bloomer /'bluːmə(r)/ *n* (sl) metedura *f* de pata

blooming *a* floreciente; *(fam)* maldito

blossom /'blɒsəm/ *n* flor *f*. ● *vi* florecer. ~ **out (into)** *(fig)* llegar a ser

blot /blɒt/ *n* borrón *m*. ● *vt* (*pt* **blotted**) manchar; *(dry)* secar. ~ **out** oscurecer

blotch /blɒtʃ/ *n* mancha *f*. ~**y** *a* lleno de manchas

blotter /'blɒtə(r)/ *n*, **blotting-paper** /'blɒtɪŋpeɪpə(r)/ *n* papel *m* secante

blouse /blauz/ *n* blusa *f*

blow¹ /bləʊ/ *vt* (*pt* **blew**, *pp* **blown**) soplar; fundir *(fuse)*; tocar *(trumpet)*. ● *vi* soplar; *(fuse)* fundirse; *(sound)* sonar. ● *n* *(puff)* soplo *m*. ~ **down** *vt* derribar. ~ **out** apagar *(candle)*. ~ **over** pasar. ~ **up** *vt* inflar; *(explode)* volar; *(photo)* ampliar. ● *vi* *(explode)* estallar; *(burst)* reventar

blow² /bləʊ/ *n* (*incl fig*) golpe *m*

blow-dry /'bləʊdraɪ/ *vt* secar con secador

blowlamp /'bləʊlæmp/ *n* soplete *m*

blow: ~**out** *n* (*of tyre*) reventón *m*. ~**up** *n* *(photo)* ampliación *f*

blowzy /'blauzɪ/ *a* desaliñado

blubber /'blʌbə(r)/ *n* grasa *f* de ballena

bludgeon /'blʌdʒən/ *n* cachiporra *f*. ● *vt* aporrear

blue /blu:/ *a* (**-er**, **-est**) azul; *(joke)* verde. ● *n* azul *m*. **out of the** ~ totalmente inesperado. ~**s** *npl*. **have the** ~**s** tener tristeza

bluebell /'blu:bel/ *n* campanilla *f*

bluebottle /'blu:bɒtl/ *n* moscarda *f*

blueprint /'blu:prɪnt/ *n* ferroprusiato *m*; *(fig, plan)* anteproyecto *m*

bluff /blʌf/ *a* *(person)* brusco. ● *n* *(poker)* farol *m*. ● *vt* engañar. ● *vi* *(poker)* tirarse un farol

blunder /'blʌndə(r)/ *vi* cometer un error. ● *n* metedura *f* de pata

blunt /blʌnt/ *a* desafilado; *(person)* directo, abrupto. ● *vt* desafilar. ~**ly** *adv* francamente. ~**ness** *n* embotadura *f*; *(fig)* franqueza *f*, brusquedad *f*

blur /blɜ:(r)/ *n* impresión *f* indistinta. ● *vt* (*pt* **blurred**) hacer borroso

blurb /blɜ:b/ *n* resumen *m* publicitario

blurt /blɜ:t/ *vt*. ~ **out** dejar escapar

blush /blʌʃ/ *vi* ruborizarse. ● *n* sonrojo *m*

bluster /'blʌstə(r)/ *vi* *(weather)* bramar; *(person)* fanfarronear. ~**y** *a* tempestuoso

boar /bɔ:(r)/ *n* verraco *m*

board /bɔ:d/ *n* tabla *f*, tablero *m*; *(for notices)* tablón *m*; *(food)* pensión *f*; *(admin)* junta *f*. ~ **and lodging** casa y comida. **above** ~ correcto. **full** ~ pensión *f* completa. **go by the** ~ ser abandonado. ● *vt* alojar; *(naut)* embarcar en. ● *vi* alojarse (**with** en casa de); *(at school)* ser interno. ~**er** *n* huésped *m*; *(schol)* interno *m*. ~**inghouse** *n* casa *f* de huéspedes, pensión *f*. ~**ing-school** *n* internado *m*

boast /bəʊst/ *vt* enorgullecerse de. ● *vi* jactarse. ● *n* jactancia *f*. ~**er** *n* jactancioso *m*. ~**ful** *a* jactancioso

boat /bəʊt/ *n* barco *m*; *(large)* navío *m*; *(small)* barca *f*

boater /bəʊtə(r)/ *n* *(hat)* canotié *m*

boatswain /'bəʊsn/ *n* contramaestre *m*

bob¹ /bɒb/ *vi* (*pt* **bobbed**) menearse, subir y bajar. ~ **up** presentarse súbitamente

bob² /bɒb/ *n invar* (*sl*) chelín *m*

bobbin /'bɒbɪn/ *n* carrete *m*; *(in sewing machine)* canilla *f*

bobby /'bɒbɪ/ *n* *(fam)* policía *m*, poli *m* *(fam)*

bobsleigh /'bɒbsleɪ/ *n* bob(sleigh) *m*

bode /bəʊd/ *vi* presagiar. ~ **well/ill** ser de buen/mal agüero

bodice /'bɒdɪs/ *n* corpiño *m*

bodily /'bɒdɪlɪ/ *a* físico, corporal. ● *adv* físicamente; *(in person)* en persona

body /'bɒdɪ/ *n* cuerpo *m*. ~**guard** /'bɒdɪgɑ:d/ *n* guardaespaldas *m invar*. ~**work** *n* carrocería *f*

boffin /'bɒfɪn/ *n* *(sl)* científico *m*

bog /bɒg/ *n* ciénaga *f*. ● *vt* (*pt* **bogged**). **get** ~**ged down** empantanarse

bogey /'bəʊgɪ/ *n* duende *m*; *(nuisance)* pesadilla *f*

boggle /'bɒgl/ *vi* sobresaltarse. **the mind** ~**s** ¡no es posible!

bogus /'bəʊgəs/ *a* falso

bogy /'bəʊgɪ/ *n* duende *m*; *(nuisance)* pesadilla *f*

boil¹ /bɔɪl/ *vt/i* hervir. **be** ~**ing hot** estar ardiendo; *(weather)* hacer mucho calor. ~ **away** evaporarse. ~ **down to** reducirse a. ~ **over** rebosar

boil² /bɔɪl/ *n* furúnculo *m*

boiled /'bɔɪld/ *a* hervido; ⟨*egg*⟩ pasado por agua

boiler /'bɔɪlə(r)/ *n* caldera *f.* ~ **suit** *n* mono *m*

boisterous /'bɔɪstərəs/ *a* ruidoso, bullicioso

bold /bəʊld/ *a* (**-er, -est**) audaz. ~**ness** *n* audacia *f*

Bolivia /bə'lɪvɪə/ *n* Bolivia *f.* ~**n** *a* & *n* boliviano (*m*)

bollard /'bɒləd/ *n* (*naut*) noray *m*; (*Brit, auto*) poste *m*

bolster /'bəʊlstə(r)/ *n* cabezal *m.* ● *vt.* ~ **up** sostener

bolt /bəʊlt/ *n* cerrojo *m*; (*for nut*) perno *m*; (*lightning*) rayo *m*; (*leap*) fuga *f.* ● *vt* echar el cerrojo a ⟨*door*⟩; engullir ⟨*food*⟩. ● *vi* fugarse. ● *adv.* ~ **upright** rígido

bomb /bɒm/ *n* bomba *f.* ● *vt* bombardear. ~**ard** /bɒm'bɑːd/ *vt* bombardear

bombastic /bɒm'bæstɪk/ *a* ampuloso

bomb: ~**er** /'bɒmə(r)/ *n* bombardero *m.* ~**ing** *n* bombardeo *m.* ~**shell** *n* bomba *f*

bonanza /bə'nænzə/ *n* bonanza *f*

bond /bɒnd/ *n* (*agreement*) obligación *f*; (*link*) lazo *m*; (*com*) bono *m*

bondage /'bɒndɪdʒ/ *n* esclavitud *f*

bone /bəʊn/ *n* hueso *m*; (*of fish*) espina *f.* ● *vt* deshuesar. ~**dry** *a* completamente seco. ~ **idle** *a* holgazán

bonfire /'bɒnfaɪə(r)/ *n* hoguera *f*

bonnet /'bɒnɪt/ *n* gorra *f*; (*auto*) capó *m*, tapa *f* del motor (*Mex*)

bonny /'bɒnɪ/ *a* (**-ier, -iest**) bonito

bonus /'bəʊnəs/ *n* prima *f*; (*fig*) plus *m*

bony /'bəʊnɪ/ *a* (**-ier, -iest**) huesudo; ⟨*fish*⟩ lleno de espinas

boo /buː/ *int* ¡bu! ● *vt/i* abuchear

boob /buːb/ *n* (*mistake, sl*) metedura *f* de pata. ● *vi* (*sl*) meter la pata

booby /'buːbɪ/ *n* bobo *m.* ~ **trap** trampa *f*; (*mil*) trampa *f* explosiva

book /bʊk/ *n* libro *m*; (*of cheques etc*) talonario *m*; (*notebook*) libreta *f*; (*exercise book*) cuaderno *m*; (*pl, com*) cuentas *fpl.* ● *vt* (*enter*) registrar; (*reserve*) reservar. ● *vi* reservar. ~**able** *a* que se puede reservar. ~**case** /'bʊkkeɪs/ *n* estantería *f*, librería *f.* ~**ing-office** (*in theatre*) taquilla *f*; (*rail*) despacho *m* de billetes. ~**let** /'bʊklɪt/ *n* folleto *m*

bookkeeping /'bʊkkiːpɪŋ/ *n* contabilidad *f*

bookmaker /'bʊkmeɪkə(r)/ *n* corredor *m* de apuestas

book: ~**mark** /'bʊkmɑː(r)k/ *n* señal *f.* ~**seller** /'bʊkselə(r)/ *n* librero *m.* ~**shop** /'bʊkʃɒp/ *n* librería *f.* ~**stall** /'bʊkstɔːl/ *n* quiosco *m* de libros. ~**worm** /'bʊkwɜːm/ *n* (*fig*) ratón *m* de biblioteca

boom /buːm/ *vi* retumbar; (*fig*) prosperar. ● *n* estampido *m*; (*com*) auge *m*

boon /buːn/ *n* beneficio *m*

boor /bʊə(r)/ *n* patán *m.* ~**ish** *a* grosero

boost /buːst/ *vt* estimular; reforzar ⟨*morale*⟩; aumentar ⟨*price*⟩; (*publicize*) hacer publicidad por. ● *n* empuje *m.* ~**er** *n* (*med*) revacunación *f*

boot /buːt/ *n* bota *f*; (*auto*) maletero *m*, baúl *m* (*LAm*). **get the** ~ (*sl*) ser despedido

booth /buːð/ *n* cabina *f*; (*at fair*) puesto *m*

booty /'buːtɪ/ *n* botín *m*

booze /buːz/ *vi* (*fam*) beber mucho. ● *n* (*fam*) alcohol *m*; (*spree*) borrachera *f*

border /'bɔːdə(r)/ *n* borde *m*; (*frontier*) frontera *f*; (*in garden*) arriate *m.* ● *vi.* ~ **on** lindar con

borderline /'bɔːdəlaɪn/ *n* línea *f* divisoria. ~ **case** *n* caso *m* dudoso

bore[1] /bɔː(r)/ *vt* (*tec*) taladrar. ● *vi* taladrar

bore[2] /bɔː(r)/ *vt* (*annoy*) aburrir. ● *n* (*person*) pelmazo *m*; (*thing*) lata *f*

bore[3] /bɔː(r)/ *see* **bear**[1]

boredom /'bɔːdəm/ *n* aburrimiento *m*

boring /'bɔːrɪŋ/ *a* aburrido, pesado

born /bɔːn/ *a* nato. **be** ~ nacer

borne /bɔːn/ *see* **bear**[1]

borough /'bʌrə/ *n* municipio *m*

borrow /'bɒrəʊ/ *vt* pedir prestado

Borstal /'bɔːstl/ *n* reformatorio *m*

bosh /bɒʃ/ *int* & *n* (*sl*) tonterías (*fpl*)

bosom /'bʊzəm/ *n* seno *m.* ~ **friend** *n* amigo *m* íntimo

boss /bɒs/ *n* (*fam*) jefe *m.* ● *vt.* ~ (**about**) (*fam*) dar órdenes a. ~**y** /'bɒsɪ/ *a* mandón

botanical /bə'tænɪkl/ *a* botánico. ~**ist** /'bɒtənɪst/ *n* botánico *m.* ~**y** /'bɒtənɪ/ *n* botánica *f*

botch /bɒtʃ/ *vt* chapucear. ● *n* chapuza *f*

both /bəʊθ/ *a* & *pron* ambos (*mpl*), los dos (*mpl*). ● *adv* al mismo tiempo, a la vez

bother /'bɒðə(r)/ *vt* molestar; (*worry*) preocupar. **~ it!** *int* ¡caramba! • *vi* molestarse. **~ about** preocuparse de. **~ doing** tenerse la molestia de hacer. • *n* molestia *f*

bottle /'bɒtl/ *n* botella; (*for baby*) biberón *m*. • *vt* embotellar. **~ up** (*fig*) reprimir. **~neck** /'bɒtlnek/ *n* (*traffic jam*) embotellamiento *m*. **~opener** *n* destapador *m*, abrebotellas *m invar*; (*corkscrew*) sacacorchos *m invar*

bottom /'bɒtəm/ *n* fondo *m*; (*of hill*) pie *m*; (*buttocks*) trasero *m*. • *a* último, inferior. **~less** *a* sin fondo

bough /baʊ/ *n* rama *f*

bought /bɔ:t/ *see* **buy**

boulder /'bəʊldə(r)/ *n* canto *m*

boulevard /'bu:ləvɑ:d/ *n* bulevar *m*

bounc|e /baʊns/ *vt* hacer rebotar. • *vi* rebotar; ⟨*person*⟩ saltar; ⟨*cheque, sl*⟩ ser rechazado. • *n* rebote *m*. **~ing** /'baʊnsɪŋ/ *a* robusto

bound[1] /baʊnd/ *vi* saltar. • *n* salto *m*

bound[2] /baʊnd/ *n*. **out of ~s** zona *f* prohibida

bound[3] /baʊnd/ *a*. **be ~ for** dirigirse a

bound[4] /baʊnd/ *see* **bind**. **~ to** obligado a; (*certain*) seguro de

boundary /'baʊndərɪ/ *n* límite *m*

boundless /'baʊndləs/ *a* ilimitado

bountiful /'baʊntɪfl/ *a* abundante

bouquet /bʊ'keɪ/ *n* ramo *m*; (*perfume*) aroma *m*; (*of wine*) buqué *m*, nariz *f*

bout /baʊt/ *n* período *m*; (*med*) ataque *m*; (*sport*) encuentro *m*

bow[1] /bəʊ/ *n* (*weapon, mus*) arco *m*; (*knot*) lazo *m*

bow[2] /baʊ/ *n* reverencia *f*. • *vi* inclinarse. • *vt* inclinar

bow[3] /baʊ/ *n* (*naut*) proa *f*

bowels /'baʊəlz/ *npl* intestinos *mpl*; (*fig*) entrañas *fpl*

bowl[1] /bəʊl/ *n* cuenco *m*; (*for washing*) palangana *f*; (*of pipe*) cazoleta *f*

bowl[2] /bəʊl/ *n* (*ball*) bola *f*. • *vt* (*cricket*) arrojar. • *vi* (*cricket*) arrojar la pelota. **~ over** derribar

bow-legged /bəʊ'legɪd/ *a* estevado

bowler[1] /'bəʊlə(r)/ *n* (*cricket*) lanzador *m*

bowler[2] /'bəʊlə(r)/ *n*. **~ (hat)** hongo *m*, bombín *m*

bowling /'bəʊlɪŋ/ *n* bolos *mpl*

bow-tie /bəʊ'taɪ/ *n* corbata *f* de lazo, pajarita *f*

box[1] /bɒks/ *n* caja *f*; (*for jewels etc*) estuche *m*; (*in theatre*) palco *m*

box[2] /bɒks/ *vt* boxear contra. **~ s.o.'s ears** dar una manotada a uno. • *vi* boxear. **~er** *n* boxeador *m*. **~ing** *n* boxeo *m*

box: **B~ing Day** *n* el 26 de diciembre. **~-office** *n* taquilla *f*. **~-room** *n* trastero *m*

boy /bɔɪ/ *n* chico *m*, muchacho *m*; (*young*) niño *m*

boycott /'bɔɪkɒt/ *vt* boicotear. • *n* boicoteo *m*

boy: **~friend** *n* novio *m*. **~hood** *n* niñez *f*. **~ish** *a* de muchacho; (*childish*) infantil

bra /brɑ:/ *n* sostén *m*, sujetador *m*

brace /breɪs/ *n* abrazadera *f*; (*dental*) aparato *m*. • *vt* asegurar. **~ o.s.** prepararse. **~s** *npl* tirantes *mpl*

bracelet /'breɪslɪt/ *n* pulsera *f*

bracing /'breɪsɪŋ/ *a* vigorizante

bracken /'brækən/ *n* helecho *m*

bracket /'brækɪt/ *n* soporte *m*; (*group*) categoría *f*; (*typ*) paréntesis *m invar*. **square ~s** corchetes *mpl*. • *vt* poner entre paréntesis; (*join together*) agrupar

brag /bræg/ *vi* (*pt* **bragged**) jactarse (**about** de)

braid /breɪd/ *n* galón *m*; (*of hair*) trenza *f*

brain /breɪn/ *n* cerebro *m*. • *vt* romper la cabeza

brain-child /'breɪntʃaɪld/ *n* invento *m*

brain: **~ drain** (*fam*) fuga *f* de cerebros. **~less** *a* estúpido. **~s** *npl* (*fig*) inteligencia *f*

brainstorm /'breɪnstɔ:m/ *n* ataque *m* de locura; (*Amer, brainwave*) idea *f* genial

brainwash /'breɪnwɒʃ/ *vt* lavar el cerebro

brainwave /'breɪnweɪv/ *n* idea *f* genial

brainy /'breɪnɪ/ *a* (**-ier, -iest**) inteligente

braise /breɪz/ *vt* cocer a fuego lento

brake /breɪk/ *n* freno *m*. **disc ~** freno de disco. **hand ~** freno de mano. • *vt/i* frenar. **~ fluid** *n* líquido *m* de freno. **~ lining** *n* forro *m* del freno. **~ shoe** *n* zapata *f* del freno

bramble /'bræmbl/ *n* zarza *f*

bran /bræn/ *n* salvado *m*

branch /brɑ:ntʃ/ *n* rama *f*; (*of road*) bifurcación *f*; (*com*) sucursal *m*; (*fig*)

ramo *m*. ● *vi*. ~ **off** bifurcarse. ~
out ramificarse

brand /brænd/ *n* marca *f*; (*iron*)
hierro *m*. ● *vt* marcar; (*reputation*)
tildar de

brandish /'brændɪʃ/ *vt* blandir

brand-new /brænd'nju:/ *a* flamante

brandy /'brændɪ/ *n* coñac *m*

brash /bræʃ/ *a* descarado

brass /brɑ:s/ *n* latón *m*. **get down to**
~ **tacks** (*fig*) ir al grano. **top** ~ (*sl*)
peces *mpl* gordos. ~**y** *a* (-**ier**, -**iest**)
descarado

brassière /'bræsjeə(r)/ *n* sostén *m*,
sujetador *m*

brat /bræt/ *n* (*pej*) mocoso *m*

bravado /brə'vɑ:dəʊ/ *n* bravata *f*

brave /breɪv/ *a* (-**er**, -**est**) valiente.
● *n* (*Red Indian*) guerrero *m* indio.
● *vt* afrontar. ~**ry** /-ərɪ/ *n* valentía *f*,
valor *m*

brawl /brɔ:l/ *n* alboroto *m*. ● *vi*
pelearse

brawn /brɔ:n/ *n* músculo *m*;
(*strength*) fuerza *f* muscular. ~**y** *a*
musculoso

bray /breɪ/ *n* rebuzno *m*. ● *vi* rebuznar

brazen /'breɪzn/ *a* descarado

brazier /'breɪzɪə(r)/ *n* brasero *m*

Brazil /brə'zɪl/ *n* el Brasil *m*. ~**ian** *a*
& *n* brasileño (*m*)

breach /bri:tʃ/ *n* violación *f*; (*of contract*) incumplimiento *m*; (*gap*) brecha *f*. ● *vt* abrir una brecha en

bread /bred/ *n* pan *m*. **loaf of** ~ pan.
~**crumbs** /'bredkrʌmz/ *npl* migajas
fpl; (*culin*) pan rallado. ~**line** *n*. **on
the** ~**line** en la miseria

breadth /bredθ/ *n* anchura *f*

bread-winner /'bredwɪnə(r)/ *n*
sostén *m* de la familia, cabeza *f* de
familia

break /breɪk/ *vt* (*pt* **broke**, *pp*
broken) romper; quebrantar (*law*);
batir (*record*); comunicar (*news*); interrumpir (*journey*). ● *vi* romperse;
(*news*) divulgarse. ● *n* ruptura *f*;
(*interval*) intervalo *m*; (*chance, fam*)
oportunidad *f*; (*in weather*) cambio
m. ~ **away** escapar. ~ **down** *vt*
derribar; analizar (*figures*). ● *vi*
estropearse; (*auto*) averiarse; (*med*)
sufrir un colapso; (*cry*) deshacerse
en lágrimas. ~ **into** forzar (*house
etc*); (*start doing*) ponerse a. ~ **off**
interrumpirse. ~ **out** (*war, disease*)
estallar; (*run away*) escaparse. ~ **up**

romperse; (*schools*) terminar. ~**able**
a frágil. ~**age** *n* rotura *f*

breakdown /'breɪkdaʊn/ *n* (*tec*)
falla *f*; (*med*) colapso *m*, crisis *f* ner-
viosa; (*of figures*) análisis *f*

breaker /'breɪkə(r)/ *n* (*wave*) cachón
m

breakfast /'brekfəst/ *n* desayuno *m*

breakthrough /'breɪkθru:/ *n* adelanto *m*

breakwater /'breɪkwɔ:tə(r)/ *n* rom-
peolas *m invar*

breast /brest/ *n* pecho *m*; (*of chicken
etc*) pechuga *f*. ~**stroke** *n* braza *f* de
pecho

breath /breθ/ *n* aliento *m*, respiración *f*. **out of** ~ sin aliento. **under
one's** ~ a media voz. ~**alyser**
/'breθəlaɪzə(r)/ *n* alcoholímetro *m*

breath|e /bri:ð/ *vt/i* respirar. ~**er**
/'bri:ðə(r)/ *n* descanso *m*, pausa *f*.
~**ing** *n* respiración *f*

breathtaking /'breθteɪkɪŋ/ *a* impresionante

bred /bred/ *see* **breed**

breeches /'brɪtʃɪz/ *npl* calzones *mpl*

breed /bri:d/ *vt/i* (*pt* **bred**) repro-
ducirse; (*fig*) engendrar. ● *n* raza *f*.
~**er** *n* criador *m*. ~**ing** *n* cría *f*; (*manners*) educación *f*

breez|e /bri:z/ *n* brisa *f*. ~**y** *a* de mu-
cho viento; (*person*) despreocupado.
it is ~**y** hace viento

Breton /'bretən/ *a* & *n* bretón (*m*)

brew /bru:/ *vt* hacer. ● *vi* fermentar;
(*tea*) reposar; (*fig*) prepararse. ● *n*
infusión *f*. ~**er** *n* cervecero *m*. ~**ery**
n fábrica *f* de cerveza, cervecería *f*

bribe /braɪb/ *n* soborno *m*. ● *vt*
sobornar. ~**ry** /-ərɪ/ *n* soborno *m*

brick /brɪk/ *n* ladrillo *m*. ● *vt*. ~ **up**
tapar con ladrillos. ~**layer**
/'brɪkleɪə(r)/ *n* albañil *m*

bridal /braɪdl/ *a* nupcial

bride /braɪd/ *n* novia *f*. ~**groom**
/'braɪdgrʊm/ *n* novio *m*. ~**smaid**
/'braɪdzmeɪd/ *n* dama *f* de honor

bridge[1] /brɪdʒ/ *n* puente *m*; (*of nose*)
caballete *m*. ● *vt* tender un puente
sobre. ~ **a gap** llenar un vacío

bridge[2] /brɪdʒ/ *n* (*cards*) bridge *m*

bridle /'braɪdl/ *n* brida *f*. ● *vt*
embridar. ~**path** *n* camino *m* de
herradura

brief /bri:f/ *a* (-**er**, -**est**) breve. ● *n* (*jurid*) escrito *m*. ● *vt* dar instruc-
ciones a. ~**case** /'bri:fkeɪs/ *n* maletín *m*. ~**ly** *adv* brevemente. ~**s** *npl*

(*man's*) calzoncillos *mpl*; (*woman's*) bragas *fpl*

brigad|e /brɪ'geɪd/ *n* brigada *f*. **~ier** /-ə'dɪə(r)/ *n* general *m* de brigada

bright /braɪt/ *a* (-er, -est) brillante, claro; (*clever*) listo; (*cheerful*) alegre. **~en** /'braɪtn/ *vt* aclarar; hacer más alegre (*house etc*). ● *vi* (*weather*) aclararse; (*face*) animarse. **~ly** *adv* brillantemente. **~ness** *n* claridad *f*

brillian|ce /'brɪljəns/ *n* brillantez *f*, brillo *m*. **~t** *a* brillante

brim /brɪm/ *n* borde *m*; (*of hat*) ala *f*. ● *vi* (*pt* **brimmed**) **~ over** desbordarse

brine /braɪn/ *n* salmuera *f*

bring /brɪŋ/ *vt* (*pt* **brought**) traer (*thing*); conducir (*person, vehicle*). **~ about** causar. **~ back** devolver. **~ down** derribar; rebajar (*price*). **~ off** lograr. **~ on** causar. **~ out** sacar; lanzar (*product*); publicar (*book*). **~ round/to** hacer volver en sí (*unconscious person*). **~ up** (*med*) vomitar; educar (*children*); plantear (*question*)

brink /brɪŋk/ *n* borde *m*

brisk /brɪsk/ *a* (-er, -est) enérgico, vivo. **~ness** *n* energía *f*

bristl|e /'brɪsl/ *n* cerda *f*. ● *vi* erizarse. **~ing with** erizado de

Brit|ain /'brɪtən/ *n* Gran Bretaña *f*. **~ish** /'brɪtɪʃ/ *a* británico. **the ~ish** los británicos. **~on** /'brɪtən/ *n* británico *m*

Brittany /'brɪtənɪ/ *n* Bretaña *f*

brittle /'brɪtl/ *a* frágil, quebradizo

broach /brəʊtʃ/ *vt* abordar (*subject*); espitar (*cask*)

broad /brɔːd/ *a* (-er, -est) ancho. **in ~ daylight** en pleno día. **~ bean** *n* haba *f*

broadcast /'brɔːdkɑːst/ *n* emisión *f*. ● *vt* (*pt* **broadcast**) emitir. ● *vi* hablar por la radio. **~ing** *a* de radiodifusión. ● *n* radio-difusión *f*

broad: **~en** /'brɔːdn/ *vt* ensanchar. ● *vi* ensancharse. **~ly** *adv* en general. **~-minded** *a* de miras amplias, tolerante, liberal

brocade /brə'keɪd/ *n* brocado *m*

broccoli /'brɒkəlɪ/ *n invar* brécol *m*

brochure /'brəʊʃə(r)/ *n* folleto *m*

brogue /brəʊg/ *n* abarca *f*; (*accent*) acento *m* regional

broke /brəʊk/ *see* **break**. ● *a* (*sl*) sin blanca

broken /'brəʊkən/ *see* **break**. ● *a*. **~ English** inglés *m* chapurreado. **~-hearted** *a* con el corazón destrozado

broker /'brəʊkə(r)/ *n* corredor *m*

brolly /'brɒlɪ/ *n* (*fam*) paraguas *m invar*

bronchitis /brɒŋ'kaɪtɪs/ *n* bronquitis *f*

bronze /brɒnz/ *n* bronce *m*. ● *vt* broncear. ● *vi* broncearse

brooch /brəʊtʃ/ *n* broche *m*

brood /bruːd/ *n* cría *f*; (*joc*) prole *m*. ● *vi* empollar; (*fig*) meditar. **~y** *a* contemplativo

brook[1] /brʊk/ *n* arroyo *m*

brook[2] /brʊk/ *vt* soportar

broom /bruːm/ *n* hiniesta *f*; (*brush*) escoba *f*. **~stick** /'bruːmstɪk/ *n* palo *m* de escoba

broth /brɒθ/ *n* caldo *m*

brothel /'brɒθl/ *n* burdel *m*

brother /'brʌðə(r)/ *n* hermano *m*. **~hood** *n* fraternidad *f*, (*relig*) hermandad *f*. **~-in-law** *n* cuñado *m*. **~ly** *a* fraternal

brought /brɔːt/ *see* **bring**

brow /braʊ/ *n* frente *f*; (*of hill*) cima *f*

browbeat /'braʊbiːt/ *vt* (*pt* -beat, *pp* -beaten) intimidar

brown /braʊn/ *a* (-er, -est) marrón; (*skin*) moreno; (*hair*) castaño. ● *n* marrón *m*. ● *vt* poner moreno; (*culin*) dorar. ● *vi* ponerse moreno; (*culin*) dorarse. **be ~ed off** (*sl*) estar hasta la coronilla

Brownie /'braʊnɪ/ *n* niña *f* exploradora

browse /braʊz/ *vi* (*in a shop*) curiosear; (*animal*) pacer

bruise /bruːz/ *n* magulladura *f*. ● *vt* magullar; machucar (*fruit*). ● *vi* magullarse; (*fruit*) machacarse

brunch /brʌntʃ/ *n* (*fam*) desayuno *m* tardío

brunette /bruː'net/ *n* morena *f*

brunt /brʌnt/ *n*. **the ~ of** lo más fuerte de

brush /brʌʃ/ *n* cepillo *m*; (*large*) escoba; (*for decorating*) brocha *f*; (*artist's*) pincel; (*skirmish*) escaramuza *f*. ● *vt* cepillar. **~ against** rozar. **~ aside** rechazar. **~ off** (*rebuff*) desairar. **~ up (on)** refrescar

brusque /bruːsk/ *a* brusco. **~ly** *adv* bruscamente

Brussels /'brʌslz/ *n* Bruselas *f*. **~ sprout** col *m* de Bruselas

brutal /'bru:tl/ *a* brutal. ~**ity** /-'tælətɪ/ *n* brutalidad *f*

brute /bru:t/ *n* bestia *f*. ~ **force** fuerza *f* bruta

BSc *abbr see* **bachelor**

bubble /'bʌbl/ *n* burbuja *f*. ● *vi* burbujear. ~ **over** desbordarse

bubbly /'bʌblɪ/ *a* burbujeante. ● *n* (*fam*) champaña *m*, champán *m* (*fam*)

buck[1] /bʌk/ *a* macho. ● *n* (*deer*) ciervo *m*. ● *vi* (*of horse*) corcovear. ~ **up** (*hurry*, *sl*) darse prisa; (*cheer up*, *sl*) animarse

buck[2] /bʌk/ (*Amer*, *sl*) dólar *m*

buck[3] /bʌk/ *n*. **pass the** ~ **to s.o.** echarle a uno el muerto

bucket /'bʌkɪt/ *n* cubo *m*

buckle /'bʌkl/ *n* hebilla *f*. ● *vt* abrochar. ● *vi* torcerse. ~ **down to** dedicarse con empeño a

bud /bʌd/ *n* brote *m*. ● *vi* (*pt* **budded**) brotar.

Buddhis|m /'bʊdɪzəm/ *n* budismo *m*. ~**t** /'bʊdɪst/ *a & n* budista (*m & f*)

budding /'bʌdɪŋ/ *a* (*fig*) en ciernes

buddy /'bʌdɪ/ *n* (*fam*) compañero *m*, amigote *m* (*fam*)

budge /bʌdʒ/ *vt* mover. ● *vi* moverse

budgerigar /'bʌdʒərɪgɑ:(r)/ *n* periquito *m*

budget /'bʌdʒɪt/ *n* presupuesto *m*. ● *vi* (*pt* **budgeted**) presupuestar

buff /bʌf/ *n* (*colour*) color *m* de ante; (*fam*) aficionado *m*. ● *vt* pulir

buffalo /'bʌfələʊ/ *n* (*pl* **-oes** *or* **-o**) búfalo *m*

buffer /'bʌfə(r)/ *n* parachoques *m invar*. ~ **state** *n* estado *m* tapón

buffet /'bʊfeɪ/ *n* (*meal*, *counter*) bufé *m*. /'bʌfɪt/ *n* golpe *m*; (*slap*) bofetada *f*. ● *vt* (*pt* **buffeted**) golpear

buffoon /bə'fu:n/ *n* payaso *m*, bufón *m*

bug /bʌg/ *n* bicho *m*; (*germ*, *sl*) microbio *m*; (*device*, *sl*) micrófono *m* oculto. ● *vt* (*pt* **bugged**) ocultar un micrófono en; intervenir ⟨*telephone*⟩; (*Amer*, *sl*) molestar

bugbear /'bʌgbeə(r)/ *n* pesadilla *f*

buggy /'bʌgɪ/ *n*. **baby** ~ (*esp Amer*) cochecito *m* de niño

bugle /'bju:gl/ *n* corneta *f*

build /bɪld/ *vt/i* (*pt* **built**) construir. ~ **up** *vt* urbanizar; (*increase*) aumentar. ● *n* (*of person*) figura *f*, tipo *m*. ~**er** *n* constructor *m*. ~**up** *n* aumento *m*; (*of gas etc*) acumulación *f*; (*fig*) propaganda *f*

built /bɪlt/ *see* **build**. ~**in** *a* empotrado. ~**up area** *n* zona *f* urbanizada

bulb /bʌlb/ *n* bulbo *m*; (*elec*) bombilla *f*. ~**ous** *a* bulboso

Bulgaria /bʌl'geərɪə/ *n* Bulgaria *f*. ~**n** *a & n* búlgaro (*m*)

bulg|e /bʌldʒ/ *n* protuberancia *f*. ● *vi* pandearse; (*jut out*) sobresalir. ~**ing** *a* abultado; ⟨*eyes*⟩ saltón

bulk /bʌlk/ *n* bulto *m*, volumen *m*. **in** ~ a granel; (*loose*) suelto. **the** ~ **of** la mayor parte de. ~**y** *a* voluminoso

bull /bʊl/ *n* toro *m*

bulldog /'bʊldɒg/ *n* buldog *m*

bulldozer /'bʊldəʊzə(r)/ *n* oruga *f* aplanadora, bulldozer *m*

bullet /'bʊlɪt/ *n* bala *f*

bulletin /'bʊlətɪn/ *n* anuncio *m*; (*journal*) boletín *m*

bullet-proof /'bʊlɪtpru:f/ *a* a prueba de balas

bullfight /'bʊlfaɪt/ *n* corrida *f* (de toros). ~**er** *n* torero *m*

bullion /'bʊljən/ *n* (*gold*) oro *m* en barras; (*silver*) plata *f* en barras

bull: ~**ring** /'bʊlrɪŋ/ *n* plaza *f* de toros. ~**'s-eye** *n* centro *m* del blanco, diana *f*

bully /'bʊlɪ/ *n* matón *m*. ● *vt* intimidar. ~**ing** intimidación *f*

bum[1] /bʌm/ *n* (*bottom*, *sl*) trasero *m*

bum[2] /bʌm/ *n* (*Amer*, *sl*) holgazán *m*

bumble-bee /'bʌmblbi:/ *n* abejorro *m*

bump /bʌmp/ *vt* chocar contra. ● *vi* dar sacudidas. ● *n* choque *m*; (*swelling*) chichón *m*. ~ **into** chocar contra; (*meet*) encontrar

bumper /'bʌmpə(r)/ *n* parachoques *m invar*. ● *a* abundante. ~ **edition** *n* edición *f* especial

bumpkin /'bʌmpkɪn/ *n* patán *m*, paleto *m* (*fam*)

bumptious /'bʌmpʃəs/ *a* presuntuoso

bun /bʌn/ *n* bollo *m*; (*hair*) moño *m*

bunch /bʌntʃ/ *n* manojo *m*; (*of people*) grupo *m*; (*of bananas*, *grapes*) racimo *m*, (*of flowers*) ramo *m*

bundle /'bʌndl/ *n* bulto *m*; (*of papers*) legajo *m*; (*of nerves*) manojo *m*. ● *vt*. ~ **up** atar

bung /bʌŋ/ *n* tapón *m*. ● *vt* tapar; (*sl*) tirar

bungalow /'bʌŋgələʊ/ *n* casa *f* de un solo piso, chalé *m*, bungalow *m*

bungle /'bʌŋgl/ *vt* chapucear

bunion /'bʌnjən/ *n* juanete *m*

bunk /bʌŋk/ *n* litera *f*

bunker /'bʌŋkə(r)/ *n* carbonera *f*; (*golf*) obstáculo *m*; (*mil*) refugio *m*, búnker *m*

bunkum /'bʌŋkəm/ *n* tonterías *fpl*

bunny /'bʌnɪ/ *n* conejito *m*

buoy /bɔɪ/ *n* boya *f*. ● *vt.* ~ **up** hacer flotar; (*fig*) animar

buoyan|cy /'bɔɪənsɪ/ *n* flotabilidad *f*; (*fig*) optimismo *m*. ~**t** /'bɔɪənt/ *a* boyante; (*fig*) alegre

burden /'bɜːdn/ *n* carga *f*. ● *vt* cargar (**with** de). ~**some** *a* pesado

bureau /'bjʊərəʊ/ *n* (*pl* -**eaux** /-əʊz/) escritorio *m*; (*office*) oficina *f*

bureaucra|cy /bjʊə'rɒkrəsɪ/ *n* burocracia *f*. ~**t** /'bjʊərəkræt/ *n* burócrata *m* & *f*. ~**tic** /-'krætɪk/ *a* burocrático

burgeon /'bɜːdʒən/ *vi* brotar; (*fig*) crecer

burgl|ar /'bɜːglə(r)/ *n* ladrón *m*. ~**ary** *n* robo *m* con allanamiento de morada. ~**e** /'bɜːgl/ *vt* robar con allanamiento

Burgundy /'bɜːgəndɪ/ *n* Borgoña *f*; (*wine*) vino *m* de Borgoña

burial /'berɪəl/ *n* entierro *m*

burlesque /bɜː'lesk/ *n* burlesco *m*

burly /'bɜːlɪ/ *a* (-**ier**, -**iest**) corpulento

Burm|a /'bɜːmə/ Birmania *f*. ~**ese** /-'miːz/ *a* & *n* birmano (*m*)

burn /bɜːn/ *vt* (*pt* **burned** *or* **burnt**) quemar. ● *vi* quemarse. ~ **down** *vt* destruir con fuego. ● *n* quemadura *f*. ~**er** *n* quemador *m*. ~**ing** *a* ardiente; (*food*) que quema; (*question*) candente

burnish /'bɜːnɪʃ/ *vt* lustrar, pulir

burnt /bɜːnt/ *see* **burn**

burp /bɜːp/ *n* (*fam*) eructo *m*. ● *vi* (*fam*) eructar

burr /bɜː(r)/ *n* (*bot*) erizo *m*

burrow /'bʌrəʊ/ *n* madriguera *f*. ● *vt* excavar

bursar /'bɜːsə(r)/ *n* tesorero *m*. ~**y** /'bɜːsərɪ/ *n* beca *f*

burst /bɜːst/ *vt* (*pt* **burst**) reventar. ● *vi* reventarse; (*tyre*) pincharse. ● *n* reventón *m*; (*mil*) ráfaga *f*; (*fig*) explosión *f*. ~ **of laughter** carcajada *f*

bury /'berɪ/ *vt* enterrar; (*hide*) ocultar

bus /bʌs/ *n* (*pl* **buses**) autobús *m*, camión *m* (*Mex*). ● *vi* (*pt* **bussed**) ir en autobús

bush /bʊʃ/ *n* arbusto *m*; (*land*) monte *m*. ~**y** *a* espeso

busily /'bɪzɪlɪ/ *adv* afanosamente

business /'bɪznɪs/ *n* negocio *m*; (*com*) negocios *mpl*; (*profession*) ocupación *f*; (*fig*) asunto *m*. **mind one's own** ~ ocuparse de sus propios asuntos. ~**like** *a* práctico, serio. ~**man** *n* hombre *m* de negocios

busker /'bʌskə(r)/ *n* músico *m* ambulante

bus-stop /'bʌsstɒp/ *n* parada *f* de autobús

bust[1] /bʌst/ *n* busto *m*; (*chest*) pecho *m*

bust[2] /bʌst/ *vt* (*pt* **busted** *or* **bust**) (*sl*) romper. ● *vi* romperse. ● *a* roto. **go** ~ (*sl*) quebrar

bustle /'bʌsl/ *vi* apresurarse. ● *n* bullicio *m*

bust-up /'bʌstʌp/ *n* (*sl*) riña *f*

busy /'bɪzɪ/ *a* (-**ier**, -**iest**) ocupado; (*street*) concurrido. ● *vt.* ~ **o.s. with** ocuparse de

busybody /'bɪzɪbɒdɪ/ *n* entrometido *m*

but /bʌt/ *conj* pero; (*after negative*) sino. ● *prep* menos. ~ **for** si no fuera por. **last** ~ **one** penúltimo. ● *adv* solamente

butane /'bjuːteɪn/ *n* butano *m*

butcher /'bʊtʃə(r)/ *n* carnicero *m*. ● *vt* matar; (*fig*) hacer una carnicería con. ~**y** *n* carnicería *f*, matanza *f*

butler /'bʌtlə(r)/ *n* mayordomo *m*

butt /bʌt/ *n* (*of gun*) culata *f*; (*of cigarette*) colilla *f*; (*target*) blanco *m*. ● *vi* topar. ~ **in** interrumpir

butter /'bʌtə(r)/ *n* mantequilla *f*. ● *vt* untar con mantequilla. ~ **up** *vt* (*fam*) lisonjear, dar jabón a. ~**bean** *n* judía *f*

buttercup /'bʌtəkʌp/ *n* ranúnculo *m*

butter-fingers /'bʌtəfɪŋgəz/ *n* manazas *m invar*, torpe *m*

butterfly /'bʌtəflaɪ/ *n* mariposa *f*

buttock /'bʌtək/ *n* nalga *f*

button /'bʌtn/ *n* botón *m*. ● *vt* abotonar. ● *vi* abotonarse. ~**hole** /'bʌtnhəʊl/ *n* ojal *m*. ● *vt* (*fig*) detener

buttress /'bʌtrɪs/ *n* contrafuerte *m*. ● *vt* apoyar

buxom /'bʌksəm/ *a* (*woman*) rollizo

buy /baɪ/ *vt* (*pt* **bought**) comprar. ● *n* compra *f*. ~**er** *n* comprador *m*

buzz /bʌz/ *n* zumbido *m*; (*phone call, fam*) llamada *f*. ● *vi* zumbar. ~ **off** (*sl*) largarse. ~**er** *n* timbre *m*

by /baɪ/ *prep* por; (*near*) cerca de; (*before*) antes de; (*according to*) según. ~ **and large** en conjunto, en general. ~ **car** en coche. ~ **oneself** por sí solo

bye-bye /'baɪbaɪ/ *int* (*fam*) ¡adiós!

by-election /'baɪɪlekʃn/ *n* elección *f* parcial

bygone /'baɪgɒn/ *a* pasado

by-law /'baɪlɔː/ *n* reglamento *m* (local)

bypass /'baɪpɑːs/ *n* carretera *f* de circunvalación. ● *vt* evitar

by-product /'baɪprɒdʌkt/ *n* subproducto *m*

bystander /'baɪstændə(r)/ *n* espectador *m*

byword /'baɪwɜːd/ *n* sinónimo *m*. **be a ~ for** ser conocido por

C

cab /kæb/ *n* taxi *m*; (*of lorry, train*) cabina *f*

cabaret /'kæbəreɪ/ *n* espectáculo *m*

cabbage /'kæbɪdʒ/ *n* col *m*, repollo *m*

cabin /'kæbɪn/ *n* cabaña *f*; (*in ship*) camarote *m*; (*in plane*) cabina *f*

cabinet /'kæbɪnɪt/ *n* (*cupboard*) armario *m*; (*for display*) vitrina *f*. **C~** (*pol*) gabinete *m*. **~-maker** *n* ebanista *m & f*

cable /'keɪbl/ *n* cable *m*. ● *vt* cablegrafiar. ~ **railway** *n* funicular *m*

cache /kæʃ/ *n* (*place*) escondrijo *m*; (*things*) reservas *fpl* escondidas. ● *vt* ocultar

cackle /'kækl/ *n* (*of hen*) cacareo *m*; (*laugh*) risotada *f*. ● *vi* cacarear; (*laugh*) reírse a carcajadas

cacophon|ous /kə'kɒfənəs/ *a* cacofónico. ~**y** *n* cacofonía *f*

cactus /'kæktəs/ *n* (*pl* **-ti** /-taɪ/) cacto *m*

cad /kæd/ *n* sinvergüenza m. ~**dish** *a* desvergonzado

caddie /'kædɪ/ *n* (*golf*) portador *m* de palos

caddy /'kædɪ/ *n* cajita *f*

cadence /'keɪdəns/ *n* cadencia *f*

cadet /kə'det/ *n* cadete *m*

cadge /kædʒ/ *vt/i* gorronear. ~**r** /-ə(r)/ *n* gorrón *m*

Caesarean /sɪ'zeərɪən/ *a* cesáreo. ~ **section** *n* cesárea *f*

café /'kæfeɪ/ *n* cafetería *f*

cafeteria /kæfɪ'tɪərɪə/ *n* autoservicio *m*

caffeine /'kæfiːn/ *n* cafeína *f*

cage /keɪdʒ/ *n* jaula *f*. ● *vt* enjaular

cagey /'keɪdʒɪ/ *a* (*fam*) evasivo

Cairo /'kaɪərəʊ/ *n* el Cairo *m*

cajole /kə'dʒəʊl/ *vt* engatusar. ~**ry** *n* engatusamiento *m*

cake /keɪk/ *n* pastel *m*, tarta *f*; (*sponge*) bizcocho m. ~ **of soap** pastilla *f* de jabón. ~**d** *a* incrustado

calamit|ous /kə'læmɪtəs/ *a* desastroso. ~**y** /kə'læmətɪ/ *n* calamidad *f*

calcium /'kælsɪəm/ *n* calcio *m*

calculat|e /'kælkjʊleɪt/ *vt/i* calcular; (*Amer*) suponer. ~**ing** *a* calculador. ~**ion** /-'leɪʃn/ *n* cálculo *m*. ~**or** *n* calculadora *f*

calculus /'kælkjʊləs/ *n* (*pl* **-li**) cálculo *m*

calendar /'kælɪndə(r)/ *n* calendario *m*

calf¹ /kɑːf/ *n* (*pl* **calves**) ternero *m*

calf² /kɑːf/ *n* (*pl* **calves**) (*of leg*) pantorrilla *f*

calibre /'kælɪbə(r)/ *n* calibre *m*

calico /'kælɪkəʊ/ *n* calicó *m*

call /kɔːl/ *vt/i* llamar. ● *n* llamada *f*; (*shout*) grito *m*; (*visit*) visita *f*. **be on ~** estar de guardia. **long distance ~** conferencia *f*. ~ **back** *vt* hacer volver; (*on phone*) volver a llamar. ● *vi* volver; (*on phone*) volver a llamar. ~ **for** pedir; (*fetch*) ir a buscar. ~ **off** cancelar. ~ **on** visitar. ~ **out** dar voces. ~ **together** convocar. ~ **up** (*mil*) llamar al servicio militar; (*phone*) llamar. ~**box** *n* cabina *f* telefónica. ~**er** *n* visita *f*; (*phone*) el que llama *m*. ~**ing** *n* vocación *f*

callous /'kæləs/ *a* insensible, cruel. ~**ness** *n* crueldad *f*

callow /'kæləʊ/ *a* (**-er**, **-est**) inexperto

calm /kɑːm/ *a* (**-er**, **-est**) tranquilo; (*weather*) calmoso. ● *n* tranquilidad *f*, calma *f*. ● *vt* calmar. ● *vi* calmarse. ~**ness** *n* tranquilidad *f*, calma *f*

calorie /'kælərɪ/ *n* caloría *f*

camber /'kæmbə(r)/ *n* curvatura *f*

came /keɪm/ *see* **come**

camel /'kæml/ *n* camello *m*

camellia /kə'miːlɪə/ *n* camelia *f*

cameo /'kæmɪəʊ/ *n* (*pl* **-os**) camafeo *m*

camera /'kæmərə/ *n* máquina *f* (fotográfica); (*TV*) cámara *f*. ~**man** *n* (*pl* **-men**) operador *m*, cámara *m*

camouflage /'kæməflɑːʒ/ n camuflaje m. ● vt encubrir; (mil) camuflar

camp[1] /kæmp/ n campamento m. ● vi acamparse

camp[2] /kæmp/ a (affected) amanerado

campaign /kæm'peɪn/ n campaña f. ● vi hacer campaña

camp: ~**bed** n catre m de tijera. ~**er** n campista m & f; (vehicle) caravana f. ~**ing** n camping m. **go** ~**ing** hacer camping. ~**site** /'kæmpsaɪt/ n camping m

campus /'kæmpəs/ n (pl -puses) ciudad f universitaria

can[1] /kæn/ v aux (pt **could**) (be able to) poder; (know how to) saber. ~**not** (neg), ~'**t** (neg, fam). **I** ~'**t go** no puedo ir

can[2] /kæn/ n lata f. ● vt (pt **canned**) enlatar. ~**ned music** música f grabada

Canad|a /'kænədə/ n el Canadá m. ~**ian** /kə'neɪdɪən/ a & n canadiense (m & f)

canal /kə'næl/ n canal m

canary /kə'neərɪ/ n canario m

cancel /'kænsl/ vt/i (pt **cancelled**) anular; cancelar ‹contract etc›; suspender ‹appointment etc›; (delete) tachar. ~**lation** /-'leɪʃn/ n cancelación f

cancer /'kænsə(r)/ n cáncer m. **C**~ n (astr) Cáncer m. ~**ous** a canceroso

candid /'kændɪd/ a franco

candida|cy /'kændɪdəsɪ/ n candidatura f. ~**te** /'kændɪdeɪt/ n candidato m

candle /'kændl/ n vela f. ~**stick** /'kændlstɪk/ n candelero m

candour /'kændə(r)/ n franqueza f

candy /'kændɪ/ n (Amer) caramelo m. ~**floss** n algodón m de azúcar

cane /keɪn/ n caña f; (for baskets) mimbre m; (stick) bastón m. ● vt (strike) castigar con palmeta

canine /'keɪnaɪn/ a canino

canister /'kænɪstə(r)/ n bote m

cannabis /'kænəbɪs/ n cáñamo m índico, hachís m, mariguana f

cannibal /'kænɪbl/ n caníbal m. ~**ism** n canibalismo m

cannon /'kænən/ n invar cañón m. ~**shot** cañonazo m

cannot /'kænət/ see **can**[1]

canny /'kænɪ/ a astuto

canoe /kə'nuː/ n canoa f, piragua f. ● vi ir en canoa. ~**ist** n piragüista m & f

canon /'kænən/ n canon m; (person) canónigo m. ~**ize** /'kænənaɪz/ vt canonizar

can-opener /'kænəʊpnə(r)/ n abrelatas m invar

canopy /'kænəpɪ/ n dosel m; (of parachute) casquete m

cant /kænt/ n jerga f

can't /kɑːnt/ see **can**[1]

cantankerous /kæn'tæŋkərəs/ a malhumorado

canteen /kæn'tiːn/ n cantina f; (of cutlery) juego m; (flask) cantimplora f

canter /'kæntə(r)/ n medio galope m. ● vi ir a medio galope

canvas /'kænvəs/ n lona f; (artist's) lienzo m

canvass /'kænvəs/ vi hacer campaña, solicitar votos. ~**ing** n solicitación f (de votos)

canyon /'kænjən/ n cañón m

cap /kæp/ n gorra f; (lid) tapa f; (of cartridge) cápsula f; (academic) birrete m; (of pen) capuchón m; (mec) casquete m. ● vt (pt **capped**) tapar, poner cápsula a; (outdo) superar

capab|ility /keɪpə'bɪlətɪ/ n capacidad f. ~**le** /'keɪpəbl/ a capaz. ~**ly** adv competentemente

capacity /kə'pæsətɪ/ n capacidad f; (function) calidad f

cape[1] /keɪp/ n (cloak) capa f

cape[2] /keɪp/ n (geog) cabo m

caper[1] /'keɪpə(r)/ vi brincar. ● n salto m; (fig) travesura f

caper[2] /'keɪpə(r)/ n (culin) alcaparra f

capital /'kæpɪtl/ a capital. ~ **letter** n mayúscula f. ● n (town) capital f; (money) capital m

capitalis|m /'kæpɪtəlɪzəm/ n capitalismo m. ~**t** a & n capitalista (m & f)

capitalize /'kæpɪtəlaɪz/ vt capitalizar; (typ) escribir con mayúsculas. ~ **on** aprovechar

capitulat|e /kə'pɪtʃʊleɪt/ vi capitular. ~**ion** /-'leɪʃn/ n capitulación f

capon /'keɪpən/ n capón m

capricious /kə'prɪʃəs/ a caprichoso

Capricorn /'kæprɪkɔːn/ n Capricornio m

capsicum /'kæpsɪkəm/ n pimiento m

capsize /kæpˈsaɪz/ vt hacer zozobrar. ● vi zozobrar

capsule /ˈkæpsjuːl/ n cápsula f

captain /ˈkæptɪn/ n capitán m. ● vt capitanear

caption /ˈkæpʃn/ n (heading) título m; (of cartoon etc) leyenda f

captivate /ˈkæptɪveɪt/ vt encantar

captiv|e /ˈkæptɪv/ a & n cautivo (m). ~ity /-ˈtɪvətɪ/ n cautiverio m, cautividad f

capture /ˈkæptʃə(r)/ vt prender; llamar ‹attention›; (mil) tomar. ● n apresamiento m; (mil) toma f

car /kɑː(r)/ n coche m, carro m (LAm)

carafe /kəˈræf/ n jarro m, garrafa f

caramel /ˈkærəmel/ n azúcar m quemado; (sweet) caramelo m

carat /ˈkærət/ n quilate m

caravan /ˈkærəvæn/ n caravana f

carbohydrate /kɑːbəʊˈhaɪdreɪt/ n hidrato m de carbono

carbon /ˈkɑːbən/ n carbono m; (paper) carbón m. ~ **copy** copia f al carbón

carburettor /kɑːbjʊˈretə(r)/ n carburador m

carcass /ˈkɑːkəs/ n cadáver m, esqueleto m

card /kɑːd/ n tarjeta f; (for games) carta f; (membership) carnet m; (records) ficha f

cardboard /ˈkɑːdbɔːd/ n cartón m

cardiac /ˈkɑːdɪæk/ a cardíaco

cardigan /ˈkɑːdɪgən/ n chaqueta f de punto, rebeca f

cardinal /ˈkɑːdɪnəl/ a cardinal. ● n cardenal m

card-index /ˈkɑːdɪndeks/ n fichero m

care /keə(r)/ n cuidado m; (worry) preocupación f; (protection) cargo m. ~ **of** a cuidado de, en casa de. **take ~ of** cuidar de ‹person›; ocuparse de ‹matter›. ● vi interesarse. **I don't ~** me es igual. ~ **about** interesarse por. ~ **for** cuidar de; (like) querer

career /kəˈrɪə(r)/ n carrera f. ● vi correr a toda velocidad

carefree /ˈkeəfriː/ a despreocupado

careful /ˈkeəfʊl/ a cuidadoso; (cautious) prudente. ~**ly** adv con cuidado

careless /ˈkeəlɪs/ a negligente; (not worried) indiferente. ~**ly** adv descuidadamente. ~**ness** n descuido m

caress /kəˈres/ n caricia f. ● vt acariciar

caretaker /ˈkeəteɪkə(r)/ n vigilante m; (of flats etc) portero m

car-ferry /ˈkɑːferɪ/ n transbordador m de coches

cargo /ˈkɑːgəʊ/ n (pl -oes) carga f

Caribbean /kærɪˈbiːən/ a caribe. ~ **Sea** n mar m Caribe

caricature /ˈkærɪkətʃʊə(r)/ n caricatura f. ● vt caricaturizar

carnage /ˈkɑːnɪdʒ/ n carnicería f, matanza f

carnal /ˈkɑːnl/ a carnal

carnation /kɑːˈneɪʃn/ n clavel m

carnival /ˈkɑːnɪvl/ n carnaval m

carol /ˈkærəl/ n villancico m

carouse /kəˈraʊz/ vi correrse una juerga

carousel /kærəˈsel/ n tiovivo m

carp[1] /kɑːp/ n invar carpa f

carp[2] /kɑːp/ vi. ~ **at** quejarse de

car park /ˈkɑːpɑːk/ n aparcamiento m

carpent|er /ˈkɑːpɪntə(r)/ n carpintero m. ~**ry** n carpintería f

carpet /ˈkɑːpɪt/ n alfombra f. **be on the ~** (fam) recibir un rapapolvo; (under consideration) estar sobre el tapete. ● vt alfombrar. ~-**sweeper** n escoba f mecánica

carriage /ˈkærɪdʒ/ n coche m; (mec) carro m; (transport) transporte m; (cost, bearing) porte m

carriageway /ˈkærɪdʒweɪ/ n calzada f, carretera f

carrier /ˈkærɪə(r)/ n transportista m & f; (company) empresa f de transportes; (med) portador m. ~-**bag** bolsa f

carrot /ˈkærət/ n zanahoria f

carry /ˈkærɪ/ vt llevar; transportar ‹goods›; (involve) llevar consigo, implicar. ● vi ‹sounds› llegar, oírse. ~ **off** llevarse. ~ **on** continuar; (complain, fam) quejarse. ~ **out** realizar; cumplir ‹promise, threat›. ~-**cot** n capazo m

cart /kɑːt/ n carro m. ● vt acarrear; (carry, fam) llevar

cartilage /ˈkɑːtɪlɪdʒ/ n cartílago m

carton /ˈkɑːtən/ n caja f (de cartón)

cartoon /kɑːˈtuːn/ n caricatura f, chiste m; (strip) historieta f; (film) dibujos mpl animados. ~**ist** n caricaturista m & f

cartridge /ˈkɑːtrɪdʒ/ n cartucho m

carve /kɑːv/ vt tallar; trinchar ‹meat›

cascade /kæs'keɪd/ n cascada f. ● vi caer en cascadas

case /keɪs/ n caso m; (jurid) proceso m; (crate) cajón m; (box) caja f; (suitcase) maleta f. **in any ~** en todo caso. **in ~** he comes por si viene. **in ~ of** en caso de. **lower ~** caja f baja, minúscula f. **upper ~** caja f alta, mayúscula f

cash /kæʃ/ n dinero m efectivo. **pay (in) ~** pagar al contado. ● vt cobrar. **~ in (on)** aprovecharse de. **~ desk** n caja f

cashew /'kæʃuː/ n anacardo m

cashier /kæ'ʃɪə(r)/ n cajero m

cashmere /kæʃ'mɪə(r)/ n casimir m, cachemir m

casino /kə'siːnəʊ/ n (pl -os) casino m

cask /kɑːsk/ n barril m

casket /'kɑːskɪt/ n cajita f

casserole /'kæsərəʊl/ n cacerola f; (stew) cazuela f

cassette /kə'set/ n casete m

cast /kɑːst/ vt (pt cast) arrojar; fundir ‹metal›; dar ‹vote›; (in theatre) repartir. ● n lanzamiento m; (in play) reparto m; (mould) molde m

castanets /kæstə'nets/ npl castañuelas fpl

castaway /'kɑːstəweɪ/ n náufrago m

caste /kɑːst/ n casta f

cast: **~ iron** n hierro m fundido. **~ iron** a de hierro fundido; (fig) sólido

castle /'kɑːsl/ n castillo m; (chess) torre f

cast-offs /'kɑːstɒfs/ npl desechos mpl

castor /'kɑːstə(r)/ n ruedecilla f

castor oil /kɑːstər'ɔɪl/ n aceite m de ricino

castor sugar /kɑːstə'ʃʊgə(r)/ n azúcar m extrafino

castrat|e /kæ'streɪt/ vt castrar. **~ion** /-ʃn/ n castración f

casual /'kæʒʊəl/ a casual; ‹meeting› fortuito; ‹work› ocasional; ‹attitude› despreocupado; ‹clothes› informal, de sport. **~ly** adv de paso

casualt|y /'kæʒʊəltɪ/ n accidente m; (injured) víctima f, herido m; (dead) víctima f, muerto m. **~ies** npl (mil) bajas fpl

cat /kæt/ n gato m

cataclysm /'kætəklɪzəm/ n cataclismo m

catacomb /'kætəkuːm/ n catacumba f

catalogue /'kætəlɒg/ n catálogo m. ● vt catalogar

catalyst /'kætəlɪst/ n catalizador m

catamaran /kætəmə'ræn/ n catamarán m

catapult /'kætəpʌlt/ n catapulta f; (child's) tirador m, tirachinos m invar

cataract /'kætərækt/ n catarata f

catarrh /kə'tɑː(r)/ n catarro m

catastroph|e /kə'tæstrəfɪ/ n catástrofe m. **~ic** /kætə'strɒfɪk/ a catastrófico

catch /kætʃ/ vt (pt caught) coger (not LAm), agarrar; (grab) asir; tomar ‹train, bus›; (unawares) sorprender; (understand) comprender; contraer ‹disease›. **~ a cold** resfriarse. **~ sight of** avistar. **~ (get stuck)** engancharse; ‹fire› prenderse. ● n cogida f, (of fish) pesca f; (on door) pestillo m; (on window) cerradura f. **~ on** (fam) hacerse popular. **~ up** poner al día. **~ up with** alcanzar; ponerse al corriente de ‹news etc›

catching /'kætʃɪŋ/ a contagioso

catchment /'kætʃmənt/ n. **~ area** n zona f de captación

catch-phrase /'kætʃfreɪz/ n eslogan m

catchword /'kætʃwɜːd/ n eslogan m, consigna f

catchy /'kætʃɪ/ a pegadizo

catechism /'kætɪkɪzəm/ n catecismo m

categorical /kætɪ'gɒrɪkl/ a categórico

category /'kætɪgərɪ/ n categoría f

cater /'keɪtə(r)/ vi proveer comida a. **~ for** proveer a ‹needs›. **~er** n proveedor m

caterpillar /'kætəpɪlə(r)/ n oruga f

cathedral /kə'θiːdrəl/ n catedral f

catholic /'kæθəlɪk/ a universal. **C~** a & n católico (m). **C~ism** /kə'θɒlɪsɪzəm/ n catolicismo m

catnap /'kætnæp/ n sueñecito m

cat's eyes /'kætsaɪz/ npl catafotos mpl

cattle /'kætl/ npl ganado m (vacuno)

cat|ty /'kætɪ/ a malicioso. **~walk** /'kætwɔːk/ n pasarela f

caucus /'kɔːkəs/ n comité m electoral

caught /kɔːt/ see **catch**

cauldron /'kɔːldrən/ n caldera f

cauliflower /'kɒlɪflaʊə(r)/ n coliflor f

cause /kɔːz/ n causa f, motivo m. ● vt causar

causeway /'kɔːzweɪ/ n calzada f elevada, carretera f elevada

caustic /'kɔːstɪk/ a & n cáustico (m)

cauterize /'kɔːtəraɪz/ vt cauterizar

caution /'kɔːʃn/ n cautela f; (warning) advertencia f. ● vt advertir; (jurid) amonestar

cautious /'kɔːʃəs/ a cauteloso, prudente. **~ly** adv con precaución, cautelosamente

cavalcade /kævəl'keɪd/ n cabalgata f

cavalier /kævə'lɪə(r)/ a arrogante

cavalry /'kævəlrɪ/ n caballería f

cave /keɪv/ n cueva f. ● vi. **~ in** hundirse. **~-man** n (pl **-men**) troglodita m

cavern /'kævən/ n caverna f, cueva f

caviare /'kævɪɑː(r)/ n caviar m

caving /'keɪvɪŋ/ n espeleología f

cavity /'kævətɪ/ n cavidad f; (in tooth) caries f

cavort /kə'vɔːt/ vi brincar

cease /siːs/ vt/i cesar. ● n. **without ~** sin cesar. **~-fire** n tregua f, alto m el fuego. **~less** a incesante

cedar /'siːdə(r)/ n cedro m

cede /siːd/ vt ceder

cedilla /sɪ'dɪlə/ n cedilla f

ceiling /'siːlɪŋ/ n techo m

celebrat|e /'selɪbreɪt/ vt celebrar. ● vi divertirse. **~ed** /'selɪbreɪtɪd/ a célebre. **~ion** /-'breɪʃn/ n celebración f; (party) fiesta f

celebrity /sɪ'lebrətɪ/ n celebridad f

celery /'selərɪ/ n apio m

celestial /sɪ'lestjəl/ a celestial

celiba|cy /'selɪbəsɪ/ n celibato m. **~te** /'selɪbət/ a & n célibe (m & f)

cell /sel/ n celda f; (biol) célula f; (elec) pila f

cellar /'selə(r)/ n sótano m; (for wine) bodega f

cell|ist /'tʃelɪst/ n violonc(h)elo m & f, violonc(h)elista m & f. **~o** /'tʃeləʊ/ n (pl **-os**) violonc(h)elo m

Cellophane /'seləfeɪn/ n (P) celofán m (P)

cellular /'seljʊlə(r)/ a celular

celluloid /'seljʊlɔɪd/ n celuloide m

cellulose /'seljʊləʊs/ n celulosa f

Celt /kelt/ n celta m & f. **~ic** a céltico

cement /sɪ'ment/ n cemento m. ● vt cementar; (fig) consolidar

cemetery /'semətrɪ/ n cementerio m

cenotaph /'senətɑːf/ n cenotafio m

censor /'sensə(r)/ n censor m. ● vt censurar. **~ship** n censura f

censure /'senʃə(r)/ n censura f. ● vt censurar

census /'sensəs/ n censo m

cent /sent/ n centavo m

centenary /sen'tiːnərɪ/ n centenario m

centigrade /'sentɪgreɪd/ a centígrado

centilitre /'sentɪliːtə(r)/ n centilitro m

centimetre /'sentɪmiːtə(r)/ n centímetro m

centipede /'sentɪpiːd/ n ciempiés m invar

central /'sentrəl/ a central; (of town) céntrico. **~ heating** n calefacción f central. **~ize** vt centralizar. **~ly** adv (situated) en el centro

centre /'sentə(r)/ n centro m. ● vt (pt **centred**) vi concentrarse

centrifugal /sen'trɪfjʊgəl/ a centrífugo

century /'sentʃərɪ/ n siglo m

ceramic /sɪ'ræmɪk/ a cerámico. **~s** npl cerámica f

cereal /'sɪərɪəl/ n cereal m

cerebral /'serɪbrəl/ a cerebral

ceremon|ial /serɪ'məʊnɪəl/ a & n ceremonial (m). **~ious** /-'məʊnɪəs/ a ceremonioso. **~y** /'serɪmənɪ/ n ceremonia f

certain /'sɜːtn/ a cierto. **for ~** seguro. **make ~ of** asegurarse de. **~ly** adv desde luego. **~ty** n certeza f

certificate /sə'tɪfɪkət/ n certificado m; (of birth, death etc) partida f

certify /'sɜːtɪfaɪ/ vt certificar

cessation /se'seɪʃən/ n cesación f

cesspit /'sespɪt/ n, **cesspool** /'sespuːl/ n pozo m negro; (fam) sentina f

chafe /tʃeɪf/ vt rozar. ● vi rozarse; (fig) irritarse

chaff /tʃæf/ vt zumbarse de

chaffinch /'tʃæfɪntʃ/ n pinzón m

chagrin /'ʃægrɪn/ n disgusto m

chain /tʃeɪn/ n cadena f. ● vt encadenar. **~ reaction** n reacción f en cadena. **~-smoker** n fumador m que siempre tiene un cigarillo encendido. **~ store** n sucursal m

chair /tʃeə(r)/ n silla f; (univ) cátedra f. ● vt presidir. **~-lift** n telesilla m

chairman /'tʃeəmən/ n (pl **-men**) presidente m

chalet /'ʃæleɪ/ n chalé m

chalice /'tʃælɪs/ n cáliz m

chalk /tʃɔːk/ n creta f; (stick) tiza f.
~**y** a cretáceo

challeng|e /'tʃælɪndʒ/ n desafío m;
(fig) reto m. ● vt desafiar; (question)
poner en duda. ~**ing** a estimulante

chamber /'tʃeɪmbə(r)/ n (old use)
cámara f. ~**-maid** /'tʃeɪmbəmeɪd/ n
camarera f. ~**-pot** n orinal m. ~**s**
npl despacho m, bufete m

chameleon /kə'miːljən/ n camaleón
m

chamois /'ʃæmɪ/ n gamuza f

champagne /ʃæm'peɪn/ n champaña m, champán m (fam)

champion /'tʃæmpɪən/ n campeón
m. ● vt defender. ~**ship** n campeonato m

chance /tʃɑːns/ n casualidad f; (likelihood) probabilidad f; (opportunity)
oportunidad f; (risk) riesgo m. **by** ~
por casualidad. ● a fortuito. ● vt
arriesgar. ● vi suceder. ~ **upon** tropezar con

chancellor /'tʃɑːnsələ(r)/ n canciller
m; (univ) rector m. **C**~ **of the Exchequer** Ministro m de Hacienda

chancy /'tʃɑːnsɪ/ a arriesgado;
(uncertain) incierto

chandelier /ʃændə'lɪə(r)/ n araña f
(de luces)

change /tʃeɪndʒ/ vt cambiar; (substitute) reemplazar. ~ **one's mind**
cambiar de idea. ● vi cambiarse. ● n
cambio m; (small coins) suelto m. ~
of life menopausia f. ~**able** a cam-
biable; ⟨weather⟩ variable. ~**-over** n
cambio m

channel /'tʃænl/ n canal m; (fig) medio m. **the C**~ **Islands** npl las islas
fpl Anglonormandas. **the (English)
C**~ el canal de la Mancha. ● vt (pt
channelled) acanalar; (fig) encauzar

chant /tʃɑːnt/ n canto m. ● vt/i cantar; (fig) salmodiar

chao|s /'keɪɒs/ n caos m, desorden m.
~**tic** /-'ɒtɪk/ a caótico, desordenado

chap[1] /tʃæp/ n (crack) grieta f. ● vt
(pt **chapped**) agrietar. ● vi agrietarse

chap[2] /tʃæp/ n (fam) hombre m, tío m
(fam)

chapel /'tʃæpl/ n capilla f

chaperon /'ʃæpərəʊn/ n acompa-
ñanta f. ● vt acompañar

chaplain /'tʃæplɪn/ n capellán m

chapter /'tʃæptə(r)/ n capítulo m

char[1] /tʃɑː(r)/ vt (pt **charred**) car-
bonizar

char[2] /tʃɑː(r)/ n asistenta f

character /'kærəktə(r)/ n carácter
m; (in play) personaje m. **in** ~
característico

characteristic /kærəktə'rɪstɪk/ a
característico. ~**ally** adv típicamente

characterize /'kærəktəraɪz/ vt ca-
racterizar

charade /ʃə'rɑːd/ n charada f, farsa f

charcoal /'tʃɑːkəʊl/ n carbón m vegetal; (for drawing) carboncillo m

charge /tʃɑːdʒ/ n precio m; (elec, mil)
carga f; (jurid) acusación f; (task,
custody) encargo m; (responsibility)
responsabilidad f. **in** ~ **of** responsable de, encargado de. **take** ~ **of**
encargarse de. ● vt pedir; (elec, mil)
cargar; (jurid) acusar; (entrust) encargar. ● vi cargar; (money) cobrar.
~**able** a a cargo (de)

chariot /'tʃærɪət/ n carro m

charisma /kə'rɪzmə/ n carisma m.
~**tic** /-'mætɪk/ a carismático

charitable /'tʃærɪtəbl/ a caritativo

charity /'tʃærɪtɪ/ n caridad f; (society) institución f benéfica

charlatan /'ʃɑːlətən/ n charlatán m

charm /tʃɑːm/ n encanto m; (spell)
hechizo m; (on bracelet) dije m,
amuleto m. ● vt encantar. ~**ing** a
encantador

chart /tʃɑːt/ n (naut) carta f de
marear; (table) tabla f. ● vt poner en
una carta de marear

charter /'tʃɑːtə(r)/ n carta f. ● vt conceder carta a, estatuir; alquilar ⟨bus,
train⟩; fletar ⟨plane, ship⟩. ~**ed
accountant** n contador m titulado.
~ **flight** n vuelo m charter

charwoman /'tʃɑːwʊmən/ n (pl
-women) asistenta f

chary /'tʃeərɪ/ a cauteloso

chase /tʃeɪs/ vt perseguir. ● vi
correr. ● n persecución f. ~ **away**,
~ **off** ahuyentar

chasm /'kæzəm/ n abismo m

chassis /'ʃæsɪ/ n chasis m

chaste /tʃeɪst/ a casto

chastise /tʃæs'taɪz/ vt castigar

chastity /'tʃæstətɪ/ n castidad f

chat /tʃæt/ n charla f. **have a** ~
charlar. ● vi (pt **chatted**) charlar

chattels /'tʃætlz/ n bienes mpl muebles

chatter /'tʃætə(r)/ n charla f. ● vi
charlar. **his teeth are** ~**ing** le

castañetean los dientes. ∼**box**
/'tʃætəbɒks/ n parlanchín m
chatty a hablador; ⟨style⟩ familiar
chauffeur /'ʃəʊfə(r)/ n chófer m
chauvinis|m /'ʃəʊvɪnɪzəm/ n
patriotería f; ⟨male⟩ machismo m. ∼**t**
/'ʃəʊvɪnɪst/ n patriotero m; ⟨male⟩
machista m & f
cheap /tʃiːp/ a (-er, -est) barato;
⟨poor quality⟩ de baja calidad; ⟨rate⟩
económico. ∼**en** /'tʃiːpən/ vt
abaratar. ∼**(ly)** adv barato, a bajo
precio. ∼**ness** n baratura f
cheat /tʃiːt/ vt defraudar; ⟨deceive⟩
engañar. ● vi (at cards) hacer
trampas. ● n trampa f; ⟨person⟩
tramposo m
check¹ /tʃek/ vt comprobar; ⟨exam-
ine⟩ inspeccionar; ⟨curb⟩ detener;
⟨chess⟩ dar jaque a. ● vi comprobar.
● n comprobación f; ⟨of tickets⟩ control m; ⟨curb⟩ freno m; ⟨chess⟩ jaque
m; ⟨bill, Amer⟩ cuenta f. ∼ **in** regis-
trarse; ⟨at airport⟩ facturar el
equipaje. ∼ **out** pagar la cuenta y
marcharse. ∼ **up** comprobar. ∼ **up**
on investigar
check² /tʃek/ n ⟨pattern⟩ cuadro m.
∼**ed** a a cuadros
checkmate /'tʃekmeɪt/ n jaque m
mate. ● vt dar mate a
check-up /'tʃekʌp/ n examen m
cheek /tʃiːk/ n mejilla f; ⟨fig⟩ descaro
m. ∼**bone** n pómulo m. ∼**y** a
descarado
cheep /tʃiːp/ vi piar
cheer /tʃɪə(r)/ n alegría f; ⟨applause⟩
viva m. ● vt alegrar; ⟨applaud⟩
aplaudir. ● vi alegrarse; ⟨applaud⟩
aplaudir. ∼ **up!** ¡anímate! ∼**ful** a
alegre. ∼**fulness** n alegría f
cheerio /tʃɪərɪ'əʊ/ int ⟨fam⟩ ¡adiós!,
¡hasta luego!
cheer: ∼**less** /'tʃɪəlɪs/ a triste. ∼**s!**
¡salud!
cheese /tʃiːz/ n queso m
cheetah /'tʃiːtə/ n guepardo m
chef /ʃef/ n cocinero m
chemical /'kemɪkl/ a químico. ● n
producto m químico
chemist /'kemɪst/ n farmacéutico m;
⟨scientist⟩ químico m. ∼**ry** n química
f. ∼**'s (shop)** n farmacia f
cheque /tʃek/ n cheque m, talón m.
∼**-book** n talonario m
chequered /'tʃekəd/ a a cuadros;
⟨fig⟩ con altibajos

cherish /'tʃerɪʃ/ vt cuidar; ⟨love⟩
querer; abrigar ⟨hope⟩
cherry /'tʃerɪ/ n cereza f. ∼**-tree** n
cerezo m
cherub /'tʃerəb/ n (pl -im) ⟨angel⟩
querubín m
chess /tʃes/ n ajedrez m. ∼**-board** n
tablero m de ajedrez
chest /tʃest/ n pecho m; ⟨box⟩ cofre
m, cajón m. ∼ **of drawers** n cómoda
f
chestnut /'tʃesnʌt/ n castaña f. ∼
tree n castaño m
chew /tʃuː/ vt masticar; ⟨fig⟩ rumiar.
∼**ing-gum** n chicle m
chic /ʃiːk/ a elegante. ● n elegancia f
chick /tʃɪk/ n polluelo m. ∼**en**
/'tʃɪkɪn/ n pollo m. ● a (sl) cobarde.
● vi. ∼**en out** (sl) retirarse. ∼**en-**
pox n varicela f
chicory /'tʃɪkərɪ/ n (in coffee) achicoria f; (in salad) escarola f
chide /tʃaɪd/ vt (pt chided) reprender
chief /tʃiːf/ n jefe m. ● a principal.
∼**ly** adv principalmente
chilblain /'tʃɪlbleɪn/ n sabañón m
child /tʃaɪld/ n (pl children
/'tʃɪldrən/) niño m; ⟨offspring⟩ hijo
m. ∼**birth** /'tʃaɪldbɜːθ/ n parto m.
∼**hood** n niñez f. ∼**ish** a infantil.
∼**less** a sin hijos. ∼**like** a inocente,
infantil
Chile /'tʃɪlɪ/ n Chile m. ∼**an** a & n
chileno (m)
chill /tʃɪl/ n frío m; ⟨illness⟩ resfriado
m. ● a frío. ● vt enfriar; refrigerar
⟨food⟩
chilli /'tʃɪlɪ/ n (pl -ies) chile m
chilly /'tʃɪlɪ/ a frío
chime /tʃaɪm/ n carillón m. ● vt tocar ⟨bells⟩; dar ⟨hours⟩. ● vi repicar
chimney /'tʃɪmnɪ/ n (pl -eys) chimenea f. ∼**-pot** n cañón m de chimenea.
∼**-sweep** n deshollinador m
chimpanzee /tʃɪmpæn'ziː/ n chimpancé m
chin /tʃɪn/ n barbilla f
china /'tʃaɪnə/ n porcelana f
Chin|a /'tʃaɪnə/ n China f. ∼**ese**
/-'niːz/ a & n chino (m)
chink¹ /tʃɪŋk/ n ⟨crack⟩ grieta f
chink² /tʃɪŋk/ n ⟨sound⟩ tintín m. ● vt
hacer tintinear. ● vi tintinear
chip /tʃɪp/ n pedacito m; ⟨splinter⟩ astilla f; ⟨culin⟩ patata f frita; ⟨gamb-
ling⟩ ficha f. **have a ∼ on one's**
shoulder guardar rencor. ● vt (pt

chipped) desportillar. ● *vi* desportillarse. ~ **in** *(fam)* interrumpir; *(with money)* contribuir

chiropodist /kɪˈrɒpədɪst/ *n* callista *m & f*

chirp /tʃɜ:p/ *n* pío *m*. ● *vi* piar

chirpy /ˈtʃɜ:pɪ/ *a* alegre

chisel /ˈtʃɪzl/ *n* formón *m*. ● *vt* *(pt* **chiselled**) cincelar

chit /tʃɪt/ *n* vale *m*, nota *f*

chit-chat /ˈtʃɪttʃæt/ *n* cháchara *f*

chivalr|ous *a* /ˈʃɪvəlrəs/ *a* caballeroso. ~**y** /ˈʃɪvəlrɪ/ *n* caballerosidad *f*

chive /tʃaɪv/ *n* cebollino *m*

chlorine /ˈklɔ:ri:n/ *n* cloro *m*

chock /tʃɒk/ *n* calzo *m*. ~**-a-block** *a*, ~**full** *a* atestado

chocolate /ˈtʃɒklɪt/ *n* chocolate *m*; *(individual sweet)* bombón *m*

choice /tʃɔɪs/ *n* elección *f*; *(preference)* preferencia *f*. ● *a* escogido

choir /ˈkwaɪə(r)/ *n* coro *m*. ~**boy** /ˈkwaɪəbɔɪ/ *n* niño *m* de coro

choke /tʃəʊk/ *vt* sofocar. ● *vi* sofocarse. ● *n* *(auto)* estrangulador *m*, estárter *m*

cholera /ˈkɒlərə/ *n* cólera *m*

cholesterol /kəˈlestərɒl/ *n* colesterol *m*

choose /tʃu:z/ *vt/i* *(pt* **chose**, *pp* **chosen**) elegir. ~**y** /ˈtʃu:zɪ/ *a* *(fam)* exigente

chop /tʃɒp/ *vt* *(pt* **chopped**) cortar. ● *n* *(culin)* chuleta *f*. ~ **down** talar. ~ **off** cortar. ~**per** *n* hacha *f*; *(butcher's)* cuchilla *f*; *(sl)* helicóptero *m*

choppy /ˈtʃɒpɪ/ *a* picado

chopstick /ˈtʃɒpstɪk/ *n* palillo *m* (chino)

choral /ˈkɔ:rəl/ *a* coral

chord /kɔ:d/ *n* cuerda *f*; *(mus)* acorde *m*

chore /tʃɔ:(r)/ *n* tarea *f*, faena *f*. **household** ~**s** *npl* faenas *fpl* domésticas

choreographer /kɒrɪˈɒɡrəfə(r)/ *n* coreógrafo *m*

chorister /ˈkɒrɪstə(r)/ *n* *(singer)* corista *m & f*

chortle /ˈtʃɔ:tl/ *n* risita *f* alegre. ● *vi* reírse alegremente

chorus /ˈkɔ:rəs/ *n* coro *m*; *(of song)* estribillo *m*

chose, chosen /tʃəʊz, ˈtʃəʊzn/ *see* **choose**

Christ /kraɪst/ *n* Cristo *m*

christen /ˈkrɪsn/ *vt* bautizar. ~**ing** *n* bautizo *m*

Christian /ˈkrɪstjən/ *a & n* cristiano (*m*). ~ **name** *n* nombre *m* de pila

Christmas /ˈkrɪsməs/ *n* Navidad *f*; *(period)* Navidades *fpl*. ● *a* de Navidad, navideño. ~**-box** *n* aguinaldo *m*. ~ **day** *n* día *m* de Navidad. ~ **Eve** *n* Nochebuena *f*. **Father** ~ *n* Papá *m* Noel. **Happy** ~**!** ¡Felices Pascuas!

chrom|e /krəʊm/ *n* cromo *m*. ~**ium** /ˈkrəʊmɪəm/ *n* cromo *m*. ~**ium plating** *n* cromado *m*

chromosome /ˈkrəʊməsəʊm/ *n* cromosoma *m*

chronic /ˈkrɒnɪk/ *a* crónico; *(bad, fam)* terrible

chronicle /ˈkrɒnɪkl/ *n* crónica *f*. ● *vt* historiar

chronolog|ical /krɒnəˈlɒdʒɪkl/ *a* cronológico. ~**y** /krəˈnɒlədʒɪ/ *n* cronología *f*

chrysanthemum /krɪˈsænθəməm/ *n* crisantemo *m*

chubby /ˈtʃʌbɪ/ *a* (**-ier, -iest**) regordete; *(face)* mofletudo

chuck /tʃʌk/ *vt* *(fam)* arrojar. ~ **out** tirar

chuckle /ˈtʃʌkl/ *n* risa *f* ahogada. ● *vi* reírse entre dientes

chuffed /tʃʌft/ *a* *(sl)* contento

chug /tʃʌɡ/ *vi* *(pt* **chugged**) *(of motor)* traquetear

chum /tʃʌm/ *n* amigo *m*, compinche *m*. ~**my** *a*. be ~**my** *(2 people)* ser muy amigos. be ~**my with** ser muy amigo de

chump /tʃʌmp/ *n* *(sl)* tonto *m*. ~ **chop** *n* chuleta *f*

chunk /tʃʌŋk/ *n* trozo *m* grueso. ~**y** /ˈtʃʌŋkɪ/ *a* macizo

church /tʃɜ:tʃ/ *n* iglesia *f*. ~**yard** /ˈtʃɜ:tʃjɑ:d/ *n* cementerio *m*

churlish /ˈtʃɜ:lɪʃ/ *a* grosero

churn /ˈtʃɜ:n/ *n* *(for milk)* lechera *f*, cántara *f*; *(for butter)* mantequera *f*. ● *vt* agitar. ~ **out** producir en profusión

chute /ʃu:t/ *n* tobogán *m*

chutney /ˈtʃʌtnɪ/ *n* *(pl* **-eys**) condimento *m* agridulce

cider /ˈsaɪdə(r)/ *n* sidra *f*

cigar /sɪˈɡɑ:(r)/ *n* puro *m*

cigarette /sɪɡəˈret/ *n* cigarillo *m*. ~**holder** *n* boquilla *f*

cine-camera /ˈsɪnɪkæmərə/ *n* cámara *f*, tomavistas *m invar*

cinema /ˈsɪnəmə/ *n* cine *m*

cinnamon /'sɪnəmən/ *n* canela *f*

cipher /'saɪfə(r)/ *n* (*math, fig*) cero *m*; (*secret system*) cifra *f*

circle /'sɜːkl/ *n* círculo *m*; (*in theatre*) anfiteatro *m*. ● *vt* girar alrededor de. ● *vi* dar vueltas

circuit /'sɜːkɪt/ *n* circuito *m*; (*chain*) cadena *f*

circuitous /sɜːˈkjuːɪtəs/ *a* indirecto

circular /'sɜːkjʊlə(r)/ *a* & *n* circular (*f*)

circularize /'sɜːkjʊləraɪz/ *vt* enviar circulares a

circulat|e /'sɜːkjʊleɪt/ *vt* hacer circular. ● *vi* circular. ∼**ion** /-'leɪʃn/ *n* circulación *f*; (*of journals*) tirada *f*

circumcis|e /'sɜːkəmsaɪz/ *vt* circuncidar. ∼**ion** /-'sɪʒn/ *n* circuncisión *f*

circumference /sə'kʌmfərəns/ *n* circunferencia *f*

circumflex /'sɜːkəmfleks/ *a* & *n* circunflejo (*m*)

circumspect /'sɜːkəmspekt/ *a* circunspecto

circumstance /'sɜːkəmstəns/ *n* circunstancia *f*. ∼**s** (*means*) *npl* situación *f* económica

circus /'sɜːkəs/ *n* circo *m*

cistern /'sɪstən/ *n* depósito *m*; (*of WC*) cisterna *f*

citadel /'sɪtədl/ *n* ciudadela *f*

citation /saɪ'teɪʃn/ *n* citación *f*

cite /saɪt/ *vt* citar

citizen /'sɪtɪzn/ *n* ciudadano *m*; (*inhabitant*) habitante *m* & *f*. ∼**ship** *n* ciudadanía *f*

citrus /'sɪtrəs/ *n*. ∼ **fruits** cítricos *mpl*

city /'sɪtɪ/ *n* ciudad *f*; **the C**∼ el centro *m* financiero de Londres

civic /'sɪvɪk/ *a* cívico. ∼**s** *npl* cívica *f*

civil /'sɪvl/ *a* civil, cortés

civilian /sɪ'vɪlɪən/ *a* & *n* civil (*m* & *f*). ∼ **clothes** *npl* traje *m* de paisano

civility /sɪ'vɪlətɪ/ *n* cortesía *f*

civiliz|ation /sɪvɪlaɪ'zeɪʃn/ *n* civilización *f*. ∼**e** /'sɪvəlaɪz/ *vt* civilizar.

civil: ∼ **servant** *n* funcionario *m*. ∼ **service** *n* administración *f* pública

civvies /'sɪvɪz/ *npl*. **in** ∼ (*sl*) en traje *m* de paisano

clad /klæd/ *see* **clothe**

claim /kleɪm/ *vt* reclamar; (*assert*) pretender. ● *n* reclamación *f*; (*right*) derecho *m*; (*jurid*) demanda *f*. ∼**ant** *n* demandante *m* & *f*, (*to throne*) pretendiente *m*

clairvoyant /kleə'vɔɪənt/ *n* clarividente *m* & *f*

clam /klæm/ *n* almeja *f*

clamber /'klæmbə(r)/ *vi* trepar a gatas

clammy /'klæmɪ/ *a* (**-ier, -iest**) húmedo

clamour /'klæmə(r)/ *n* clamor *m*. ● *vi*. ∼ **for** pedir a voces

clamp /klæmp/ *n* abrazadera *f*; (*auto*) cepo *m*. ● *vt* sujetar con abrazadera. ∼ **down on** reprimir

clan /klæn/ *n* clan *m*

clandestine /klæn'destɪn/ *a* clandestino

clang /klæŋ/ *n* sonido *m* metálico

clanger /'klæŋə(r)/ *n* (*sl*) metedura *f* de pata

clap /klæp/ *vt* (*pt* **clapped**) aplaudir; batir ‹*hands*›. ● *vi* aplaudir. ● *n* palmada *f*; (*of thunder*) trueno *m*

claptrap /'klæptræp/ *n* charlatanería *f*, tonterías *fpl*

claret /'klærət/ *n* clarete *m*

clarif|ication /klærɪfɪ'keɪʃn/ *n* aclaración *f*. ∼**y** /'klærɪfaɪ/ *vt* aclarar. ● *vi* aclararse

clarinet /klærɪ'net/ *n* clarinete *m*

clarity /'klærətɪ/ *n* claridad *f*

clash /klæʃ/ *n* choque *m*; (*noise*) estruendo *m*; (*contrast*) contraste *m*; (*fig*) conflicto *m*. ● *vt* golpear. ● *vi* encontrarse; ‹*dates*› coincidir; ‹*opinions*› estar en desacuerdo; ‹*colours*› desentonar

clasp /klɑːsp/ *n* cierre *m*. ● *vt* agarrar; apretar ‹*hand*›; (*fasten*) abrochar

class /klɑːs/ *n* clase *f*. **evening** ∼ *n* clase nocturna. ● *vt* clasificar

classic /'klæsɪk/ *a* & *n* clásico (*m*). ∼**al** *a* clásico. ∼**s** *npl* estudios *mpl* clásicos

classif|ication /klæsɪfɪ'keɪʃn/ *n* clasificación *f*. ∼**y** /'klæsɪfaɪ/ *vt* clasificar

classroom /'klɑːsruːm/ *n* aula *f*

classy /'klɑːsɪ/ *a* (*sl*) elegante

clatter /'klætə(r)/ *n* estrépito *m*. ● *vi* hacer ruido

clause /klɔːz/ *n* cláusula *f*; (*gram*) oración *f*

claustrophobia /klɔːstrə'fəʊbɪə/ *n* claustrofobia *f*

claw /klɔː/ *n* garra *f*; (*of cat*) uña *f*; (*of crab*) pinza *f*; (*device*) garfio *m*. ● *vt* arañar

clay /kleɪ/ *n* arcilla *f*

clean /kli:n/ *a* (**-er, -est**) limpio; ⟨*stroke*⟩ neto. ● *adv* completamente. ● *vt* limpiar. ● *vi* hacer la limpieza. ∼ **up** hacer la limpieza. ∼**-cut** *a* bien definido. ∼**er** *n* mujer *f* de la limpieza. ∼**liness** /'klenlınıs/ *n* limpieza *f*

cleanse /klenz/ *vt* limpiar; (*fig*) purificar. ∼**ing cream** *n* crema *f* desmaquilladora

clear /klıə(r)/ *a* (**-er, -est**) claro; (*transparent*) transparente; (*without obstacles*) libre; ⟨*profit*⟩ neto; ⟨*sky*⟩ despejado. **keep** ∼ **of** evitar. ● *adv* claramente. ● *vt* despejar; liquidar ⟨*goods*⟩; (*jurid*) absolver; (*jump over*) saltar por encima de; quitar ⟨*table*⟩. ● *vi* ⟨*weather*⟩ despejarse; ⟨*fog*⟩ disolverse. ∼ **off** *vi* (*sl*), ∼ **out** *vi* (*sl*) largarse. ∼ **up** *vt* (*tidy*) poner en orden; aclarar ⟨*mystery*⟩; ● *vi* ⟨*weather*⟩ despejarse

clearance /'klıərəns/ *n* espacio *m* libre; (*removal of obstructions*) despeje *m*; (*authorization*) permiso *m*; (*by customs*) despacho *m*; (*by security*) acreditación *f*. ∼ **sale** *n* liquidación *f*

clearing /'klıərıŋ/ *n* claro *m*

clearly /'klıəlı/ *adv* evidentemente

clearway /'klıəweı/ *n* carretera *f* en la que no se permite parar

cleavage /'kli:vıdʒ/ *n* escote *m*; (*fig*) división *f*

cleave /kli:v/ *vt* (*pt* **cleaved, clove** *or* **cleft**; *pp* **cloven** *or* **cleft**) hender. ● *vi* henderse

clef /klef/ *n* (*mus*) clave *f*

cleft /kleft/ *see* **cleave**

clemen|cy /'klemənsı/ *n* clemencia *f*. ∼**t** *a* clemente

clench /klentʃ/ *vt* apretar

clergy /'klɜ:dʒı/ *n* clero *m*. ∼**man** *n* (*pl* **-men**) clérigo *m*

cleric /'klerık/ *n* clérigo *m*. ∼**al** *a* clerical; (*of clerks*) de oficina

clerk /klɑ:k/ *n* empleado *m*; (*jurid*) escribano *m*

clever /'klevə(r)/ *a* (**-er, -est**) listo; (*skilful*) hábil. ∼**ly** *adv* inteligentemente; (*with skill*) hábilmente. ∼**ness** *n* inteligencia *f*

cliché /'kli:ʃeı/ *n* tópico *m*, frase *f* hecha

click /klık/ *n* golpecito *m*. ● *vi* chascar; (*sl*) llevarse bien

client /'klaıənt/ *n* cliente *m & f*

clientele /kli:ən'tel/ *n* clientela *f*

cliff /klıf/ *n* acantilado *m*

climat|e /'klaımıt/ *n* clima *m*. ∼**ic** /-'mætık/ *a* climático

climax /'klaımæks/ *n* punto *m* culminante

climb /klaım/ *vt* subir ⟨*stairs*⟩; trepar ⟨*tree*⟩; escalar ⟨*mountain*⟩. ● *vi* subir. ● *n* subida *f*. ∼ **down** bajar; (*fig*) volverse atrás, rajarse. ∼**er** *n* (*sport*) alpinista *m & f*; (*plant*) trepadora *f*

clinch /klıntʃ/ *vt* cerrar ⟨*deal*⟩

cling /klıŋ/ *vi* (*pt* **clung**) agarrarse; (*stick*) pegarse

clinic /'klınık/ *n* clínica *f*. ∼**al** /'klınıkl/ *a* clínico

clink /klıŋk/ *n* sonido *m* metálico. ● *vt* hacer tintinear. ● *vi* tintinear

clinker /'klıŋkə(r)/ *n* escoria *f*

clip[1] /klıp/ *n* (*for paper*) sujetapapeles *m invar*; (*for hair*) horquilla *f*. ● *vt* (*pt* **clipped**) (*join*) sujetar

clip[2] /klıp/ *n* (*with scissors*) tijeretada *f*; (*blow, fam*) golpe *m*. ● *vt* (*pt* **clipped**) (*cut*) cortar; (*fam*) golpear. ∼**pers** /'klıpəz/ *npl* (*for hair*) maquinilla *f* para cortar el pelo; (*for nails*) cortauñas *m invar*. ∼**ping** *n* recorte *m*

clique /kli:k/ *n* pandilla *f*

cloak /kləʊk/ *n* capa *f*. ∼**room** /'kləʊkru:m/ *n* guardarropa *m*; (*toilet*) servicios *mpl*

clobber /'klɒbə(r)/ *n* (*sl*) trastos *mpl*. ● *vt* (*sl*) dar una paliza a

clock /klɒk/ *n* reloj *m*. **grandfather** ∼ reloj *m* de caja. ● *vi*. ∼ **in** fichar, registrar la llegada. ∼**wise** /'klɒkwaız/ *a & adv* en el sentido de las agujas del reloj, a la derecha. ∼**work** /'klɒkwɜ:k/ *n* mecanismo *m* de relojería. **like** ∼**work** con precisión

clod /klɒd/ *n* terrón *m*

clog /klɒg/ *n* zueco *m*. ● *vt* (*pt* **clogged**) atascar. ● *vi* atascarse

cloister /'klɔıstə(r)/ *n* claustro *m*

close[1] /kləʊs/ *a* (**-er, -est**) cercano; (*together*) apretado; ⟨*friend*⟩ íntimo; ⟨*weather*⟩ bochornoso; ⟨*link etc*⟩ estrecho; ⟨*game, battle*⟩ reñido. **have a** ∼ **shave** (*fig*) escaparse de milagro. ● *adv* cerca. ● *n* recinto *m*

close[2] /kləʊz/ *vt* cerrar. ● *vi* cerrarse; (*end*) terminar. ● *n* fin *m*. ∼**d shop** *n* empresa *f* que emplea solamente a miembros del sindicato

close: ~**ly** *adv* de cerca; (*with attention*) atentamente; (*exactly*) exactamente. ~**ness** *n* proximidad *f*; (*togetherness*) intimidad *f*

closet /'klɒzɪt/ *n* (*Amer*) armario *m*

close-up /'kləʊsʌp/ *n* (*cinema etc*) primer plano *m*

closure /'kləʊʒə(r)/ *n* cierre *m*

clot /klɒt/ *n* (*culin*) grumo *m*; (*med*) coágulo *m*; (*sl*) tonto *m*. ● *vi* (*pt* **clotted**) cuajarse

cloth /klɒθ/ *n* tela *f*; (*duster*) trapo *m*; (*table-cloth*) mantel *m*

cloth|e /kləʊð/ *vt* (*pt* **clothed** or **clad**) vestir. ~**es** /kləʊðz/ *npl*, ~**ing** *n* ropa *f*

cloud /klaʊd/ *n* nube *f*. ● *vi* nublarse. ~**burst** /'klaʊdbɜ:st/ *n* chaparrón *m*. ~**y** *a* (**-ier**, **-iest**) nublado; (*liquid*) turbio

clout /klaʊt/ *n* bofetada *f*. ● *vt* abofetear

clove¹ /kləʊv/ *n* clavo *m*

clove² /kləʊv/ *n*. ~ **of garlic** *n* diente *m* de ajo

clove³ /kləʊv/ *see* **cleave**

clover /'kləʊvə(r)/ *n* trébol *m*

clown /klaʊn/ *n* payaso *m*. ● *vi* hacer el payaso

cloy /klɔɪ/ *vt* empalagar

club /klʌb/ *n* club *m*; (*weapon*) porra *f*; (*at cards*) trébol *m*. ● *vt* (*pt* **clubbed**) aporrear. ● *vi*. ~ **together** reunirse, pagar a escote

cluck /klʌk/ *vi* cloquear

clue /klu:/ *n* pista *f*; (*in crosswords*) indicación *f*. **not to have a** ~ no tener la menor idea

clump /klʌmp/ *n* grupo *m*. ● *vt* agrupar. ● *vi* pisar fuertemente

clums|iness /'klʌmzɪnɪs/ *n* torpeza *f*. ~**y** /'klʌmzɪ/ *a* (**-ier**, **-iest**) torpe

clung /klʌŋ/ *see* **cling**

cluster /'klʌstə(r)/ *n* grupo *m*. ● *vi* agruparse

clutch /klʌtʃ/ *vt* agarrar. ● *n* (*auto*) embrague *m*

clutter /'klʌtə(r)/ *n* desorden *m*. ● *vt* llenar desordenadamente

coach /kəʊtʃ/ *n* autocar *m*; (*of train*) vagón *m*; (*horse-drawn*) coche *m*; (*sport*) entrenador *m*. ● *vt* dar clases particulares; (*sport*) entrenar

coagulate /kəʊ'ægjʊleɪt/ *vt* coagular. ● *vi* coagularse

coal /kəʊl/ *n* carbón *m*. ~**field** /'kəʊlfi:ld/ *n* yacimiento *m* de carbón

coalition /kəʊə'lɪʃn/ *n* coalición *f*

coarse /kɔ:s/ *a* (**-er**, **-est**) grosero; (*material*) basto. ~**ness** *n* grosería *f*; (*texture*) basteza *f*

coast /kəʊst/ *n* costa *f*. ● *vi* (*with cycle*) deslizarse cuesta abajo; (*with car*) ir en punto muerto. ~**al** *a* costero. ~**er** /'kəʊstə(r)/ *n* (*ship*) barco *m* de cabotaje; (*for glass*) posavasos *m invar*. ~**guard** /'kəʊstgɑ:d/ *n* guardacostas *m invar*. ~**line** /'kəʊstlam/ *n* litoral *m*

coat /kəʊt/ *n* abrigo *m*; (*jacket*) chaqueta *f*; (*of animal*) pelo *m*; (*of paint*) mano *f*. ● *vt* cubrir, revestir. ~**ing** *n* capa *f*. ~ **of arms** *n* escudo *m* de armas

coax /kəʊks/ *vt* engatusar

cob /kɒb/ *n* (*of corn*) mazorca *f*

cobble¹ /'kɒbl/ *n* guijarro *m*, adoquín *m*. ● *vt* empedrar con guijarros, adoquinar

cobble² /'kɒbl/ *vt* (*mend*) remendar. ~**r** /'kɒblə(r)/ *n* (*old use*) remendón *m*

cobweb /'kɒbweb/ *n* telaraña *f*

cocaine /kə'keɪn/ *n* cocaína *f*

cock /kɒk/ *n* gallo *m*; (*mec*) grifo *m*; (*of gun*) martillo *m*. ● *vt* amartillar (*gun*); aguzar (*ears*). ~**-and-bull story** *n* patraña *f*. ~**erel** /'kɒkərəl/ *n* gallo *m*. ~**-eyed** *a* (*sl*) torcido

cockle /'kɒkl/ *n* berberecho *m*

cockney /'kɒknɪ/ *a & n* (*pl* **-eys**) londinense (*m & f*) (del este de Londres)

cockpit /'kɒkpɪt/ *n* (*in aircraft*) cabina *f* del piloto

cockroach /'kɒkrəʊtʃ/ *n* cucaracha *f*

cocksure /kɒk'ʃʊə(r)/ *a* presuntuoso

cocktail /'kɒkteɪl/ *n* cóctel *m*. **fruit** ~ macedonia *f* de frutas

cock-up /'kɒkʌp/ *n* (*sl*) lío *m*

cocky /'kɒkɪ/ *a* (**-ier**, **-iest**) engreído

cocoa /'kəʊkəʊ/ *n* cacao *m*; (*drink*) chocolate *m*

coconut /'kəʊkənʌt/ *n* coco *m*

cocoon /kə'ku:n/ *n* capullo *m*

cod /kɒd/ *n* (*pl* **cod**) bacalao *m*, abadejo *m*

coddle /'kɒdl/ *vt* mimar; (*culin*) cocer a fuego lento

code /kəʊd/ *n* código *m*; (*secret*) cifra *f*

codify /'kəʊdɪfaɪ/ *vt* codificar

cod-liver oil /'kɒdlɪvə(r)ɔɪl/ *n* aceite *m* de hígado de bacalao

coeducational /kəʊedʒʊ'keɪʃənl/ *a* mixto

coerc|e /kəʊ'ɜːs/ vt obligar. ~ion /-ʃn/ n coacción f

coexist /kəʊɪg'zɪst/ vi coexistir. ~ence n coexistencia f

coffee /'kɒfɪ/ n café m. ~-mill n molinillo m de café. ~-pot n cafetera f

coffer /'kɒfə(r)/ n cofre m

coffin /'kɒfɪn/ n ataúd m

cog /kɒg/ n diente m; (fig) pieza f

cogent /'kəʊdʒənt/ a convincente

cohabit /kəʊ'hæbɪt/ vi cohabitar

coherent /kəʊ'hɪərənt/ a coherente

coil /kɔɪl/ vt enrollar. ● n rollo m; (one ring) vuelta f

coin /kɔɪn/ n moneda f. ● vt acuñar. ~age n sistema m monetario

coincide /kəʊɪn'saɪd/ vi coincidir

coinciden|ce /kəʊ'ɪnsɪdəns/ n casualidad f. ~tal /-'dentl/ a casual; (coinciding) coincidente

coke /kəʊk/ n (coal) coque m

colander /'kʌləndə(r)/ n colador m

cold /kəʊld/ a (-er, -est) frío. be ~ tener frío. it is ~ hace frío. ● n frío m; (med) resfriado m. have a ~ estar constipado. ~-blooded a insensible. ~ cream n crema f. ~ feet (fig) miéditis f. ~ness n frialdad f. ~-shoulder vt tratar con frialdad. ~ sore n herpes m labial. ~ storage n conservación f en frigorífico

coleslaw /'kəʊlslɔː/ n ensalada f de col

colic /'kɒlɪk/ n cólico m

collaborat|e /kə'læbəreɪt/ vi colaborar. ~ion /-'reɪʃn/ n colaboración f. ~or n colaborador m

collage /'kɒlɑːʒ/ n collage m

collaps|e /kə'læps/ vi derrumbarse; (med) sufrir un colapso. ● n derrumbamiento m; (med) colapso m. ~ible /kə'læpsəbl/ a plegable

collar /'kɒlə(r)/ n cuello m; (for animals) collar m. ● vt (fam) hurtar. ~-bone n clavícula f

colleague /'kɒliːg/ n colega m & f

collect /kə'lekt/ vt reunir; (hobby) coleccionar; (pick up) recoger; recaudar ⟨rent⟩. ● vi ⟨people⟩ reunirse; ⟨things⟩ acumularse. ~ed /kə'lektɪd/ a reunido; ⟨person⟩ tranquilo. ~ion /-ʃn/ n colección f; (in church) colecta f; (of post) recogida f. ~ive /kə'lektɪv/ a colectivo. ~or n coleccionista m & f; (of taxes) recaudador m

college /'kɒlɪdʒ/ n colegio m; (of art, music etc) escuela f; (univ) colegio m mayor

collide /kə'laɪd/ vi chocar

colliery /'kɒlɪərɪ/ n mina f de carbón

collision /kə'lɪʒn/ n choque m

colloquial /kə'ləʊkwɪəl/ a familiar. ~ism n expresión f familiar

collusion /kə'luːʒn/ n connivencia f

colon /'kəʊlən/ n (gram) dos puntos mpl; (med) colon m

colonel /'kɜːnl/ n coronel m

colon|ial /kə'ləʊnɪəl/ a colonial. ~ize /'kɒlənaɪz/ vt colonizar. ~y /'kɒlənɪ/ n colonia f

colossal /kə'lɒsl/ a colosal

colour /'kʌlə(r)/ n color m. off ~ (fig) indispuesto. ● a de color(es), en color(es). ● vt colorar; (dye) teñir. ● vi (blush) sonrojarse. ~ bar n barrera f racial. ~-blind a daltoniano. ~ed /'kʌləd/ a de color. ~ful a lleno de color; (fig) pintoresco. ~less a incoloro. ~s npl (flag) bandera f

colt /kəʊlt/ n potro m

column /'kɒləm/ n columna f. ~ist /'kɒləmnɪst/ n columnista m & f

coma /'kəʊmə/ n coma m

comb /kəʊm/ n peine m. ● vt peinar; (search) registrar

combat /'kɒmbæt/ n combate m. ● vt (pt combated) combatir. ~ant /-ətənt/ n combatiente m & f

combination /kɒmbɪ'neɪʃn/ n combinación f

combine /kəm'baɪn/ vt combinar. ● vi combinarse. /'kɒmbaɪn/ n asociación f. ~harvester n cosechadora f

combustion /kəm'bʌstʃən/ n combustión f

come /kʌm/ vi (pt came, pp come) venir; (occur) pasar. ~ about ocurrir. ~ across encontrarse con ⟨person⟩; encontrar ⟨object⟩. ~ apart deshacerse. ~ away marcharse. ~ back volver. ~ by obtener; (pass) pasar. ~ down bajar. ~ in entrar. ~ in for recibir. ~ into heredar ⟨money⟩. ~ off desprenderse; (succeed) tener éxito. ~ off it! (fam) ¡no me vengas con eso! ~ out salir; (result) resultar. ~ round (after fainting) volver en sí; (be converted) cambiar de idea. ~ to llegar a ⟨decision etc⟩. ~ up subir; (fig) salir. ~ up with proponer ⟨idea⟩

comeback /'kʌmbæk/ n retorno m; (retort) réplica f

comedian /kə'miːdɪən/ n cómico m

comedown /'kʌmdaʊn/ n revés m

comedy /'kɒmədɪ/ n comedia f

comely /'kʌmlɪ/ a (-ier, -iest) (old use) bonito

comet /'kɒmɪt/ n cometa m

comeuppance /kʌm'ʌpəns/ n (Amer) merecido m

comf|ort /'kʌmfət/ n bienestar m; (consolation) consuelo m. ● vt consolar. **~ortable** a cómodo; (wealthy) holgado. **~y** /'kʌmfɪ/ a (fam) cómodo

comic /'kɒmɪk/ a cómico. ● n cómico m; (periodical) tebeo m. **~al** a cómico. **~ strip** n historieta f

coming /'kʌmɪŋ/ n llegada f. ● a próximo; (week, month etc) que viene. **~ and going** ir y venir

comma /'kɒmə/ n coma f

command /kə'mɑːnd/ n orden f; (mastery) dominio m. ● vt mandar; (deserve) merecer

commandeer /kɒmən'dɪə(r)/ vt requisar

commander /kə'mɑːndə(r)/ n comandante m

commanding /kə'mɑːndɪŋ/ a imponente

commandment /kə'mɑːndmənt/ n mandamiento m

commando /kə'mɑːndəʊ/ n (pl -os) comando m

commemorat|e /kə'meməreɪt/ vt conmemorar. **~ion** /-'reɪʃn/ n conmemoración f. **~ive** /-ətɪv/ a conmemorativo

commence /kə'mens/ vt/i empezar. **~ment** n principio m

commend /kə'mend/ vt alabar; (entrust) encomendar. **~able** a loable. **~ation** /kɒmen'deɪʃn/ n elogio m

commensurate /kə'menʃərət/ a proporcionado

comment /'kɒment/ n observación f. ● vi hacer observaciones

commentary /'kɒməntrɪ/ n comentario m; (radio, TV) reportaje m

commentat|e /'kɒmənteɪt/ vi narrar. **~or** n (radio, TV) locutor m

commerc|e /'kɒmɜːs/ n comercio m. **~ial** /kə'mɜːʃl/ a comercial. ● n anuncio m. **~ialize** vt comercializar

commiserat|e /kə'mɪzəreɪt/ vt compadecer. ● vi compadecerse (with de). **~ion** /-'reɪʃn/ n conmiseración f

commission /kə'mɪʃn/ n comisión f. **out of ~** fuera de servicio. ● vt encargar; (mil) nombrar

commissionaire /kəmɪʃə'neə(r)/ n portero m

commissioner /kə'mɪʃənə(r)/ n comisario m; (of police) jefe m

commit /kə'mɪt/ vt (pt committed) cometer; (entrust) confiar. **~ o.s.** comprometerse. **~ to memory** aprender de memoria. **~ment** n compromiso m

committee /kə'mɪtɪ/ n comité m

commodity /kə'mɒdətɪ/ n producto m, artículo m

common /'kɒmən/ a (-er, -est) común; (usual) corriente; (vulgar) ordinario. ● n ejido m

commoner /'kɒmənə(r)/ n plebeyo m

common: **~ law** n derecho m consuetudinario. **~ly** adv comúnmente. **C~ Market** n Mercado m Común

commonplace /'kɒmənpleɪs/ a banal. ● n banalidad f

common: **~-room** n sala f común, salón m común. **~ sense** n sentido m común

Commonwealth /'kɒmənwelθ/ n. **the ~** la Mancomunidad f Británica

commotion /kə'məʊʃn/ n confusión f

communal /'kɒmjʊnl/ a comunal

commune¹ /'kɒmjuːn/ n comuna f

commune² /kə'mjuːn/ vi comunicarse

communicat|e /kə'mjuːnɪkeɪt/ vt comunicar. ● vi comunicarse. **~ion** /-'keɪʃn/ n comunicación f. **~ive** /-ətɪv/ a comunicativo

communion /kə'mjuːnɪən/ n comunión f

communiqué /kə'mjuːnɪkeɪ/ n comunicado m

communis|m /'kɒmjʊnɪsəm/ n comunismo m. **~t** /'kɒmjʊnɪst/ n comunista m & f

community /kə'mjuːnətɪ/ n comunidad f. **~ centre** n centro m social

commute /kə'mjuːt/ vi viajar diariamente. ● vt (jurid) conmutar. **~r** /-ə(r)/ n viajero m diario

compact /kəm'pækt/ a compacto. /'kɒmpækt/ n (for powder) polvera f. **~ disc** /'kɒm-/ n disco m compacto

companion /kəm'pænɪən/ n compañero m. **~ship** n compañerismo m

company /'kʌmpənɪ/ n compañía f; (guests, fam) visita f; (com) sociedad f

compar|able /'kɒmpərəbl/ a comparable. **~ative** /kəm'pærətɪv/ a

comparativo; (*fig*) relativo. ● *n*
(*gram*) comparativo *m*. ~**e**
/kəm'peə(r)/ *vt* comparar. ● *vi*
poderse comparar. ~**ison** /kəm-
'pærɪsn/ *n* comparación *f*

compartment /kəm'pɑːtmənt/ *n*
compartimiento *m*; (*on train*)
departamento *m*

compass /'kʌmpəs/ *n* brújula *f*. ~**es**
npl compás *m*

compassion /kəm'pæʃn/ *n* compasión *f*. ~**ate** *a* compasivo

compatib|ility /kəmpætə'bɪlətɪ/ *n*
compatibilidad *f*. ~**le** /kəm'pætəbl/ *a*
compatible

compatriot /kəm'pætrɪət/ *n* compatriota *m* & *f*

compel /kəm'pel/ *vt* (*pt* **compelled**)
obligar. ~**ling** *a* irresistible

compendium /kəm'pendɪəm/ *n*
compendio *m*

compensat|e /'kɒmpənseɪt/ *vt* com-
pensar; (*for loss*) indemnizar. ● *vi*
compensar. ~**ion** /-'seɪʃn/ *n*
compensación *f*; (*financial*) indem-
nización *f*

compère /'kɒmpeə(r)/ *n* pre-
sentador *m*. ● *vt* presentar

compete /kəm'piːt/ *vi* competir

competen|ce /'kɒmpətəns/ *n* com-
petencia *f*, aptitud *f*. ~**t** /'kɒmpɪtənt/
a competente, capaz

competit|ion /kɒmpə'tɪʃn/ *n* (*con-
test*) concurso *m*; (*com*) competencia
f. ~**ive** /kəm'petətɪv/ *a* competidor;
⟨*price*⟩ competitivo. ~**or** /kəm-
'petɪtə(r)/ *n* competidor *m*; (*in contest*)
concursante *m* & *f*

compile /kəm'paɪl/ *vt* compilar. ~**r**
/-ə(r)/ *n* recopilador *m*, compilador
m

complacen|cy /kəm'pleɪsənsɪ/ *n*
satisfacción *f* de sí mismo. ~**t**
/kəm'pleɪsnt/ *a* satisfecho de sí mismo

complain /kəm'pleɪn/ *vi*. ~ (**about**)
quejarse (de). ~ **of** (*med*) sufrir de.
~**t** /kəm'pleɪnt/ *n* queja *f*; (*med*) enfermedad *f*

complement /'kɒmplɪmənt/ *n* complemento *m*. ● *vt* complementar.
~**ary** /-'mentrɪ/ *a* complementario

complet|e /kəm'pliːt/ *a* completo;
(*finished*) acabado; (*downright*) total.
● *vt* acabar; llenar ⟨*a form*⟩. ~**ely**
adv completamente. ~**ion** /-ʃn/ *n*
conclusión *f*

complex /'kɒmpleks/ *a* complejo.
● *n* complejo *m*

complexion /kəm'plekʃn/ *n* tez *f*;
(*fig*) aspecto *m*

complexity /kəm'pleksətɪ/ *n* com-
plejidad *f*

complian|ce /kəm'plaɪəns/ *n* sumi-
sión *f*. **in** ~**ce with** de acuerdo con.
~**t** *a* sumiso

complicat|e /'kɒmplɪkeɪt/ *vt* com-
plicar. ~**ed** *a* complicado. ~**ion**
/-'keɪʃn/ *n* complicación *f*

complicity /kəm'plɪsətɪ/ *n* com-
plicidad *f*

compliment /'kɒmplɪmənt/ *n* cumplido *m*; (*amorous*) piropo *m*. ● *vt*
felicitar. ~**ary** /-'mentrɪ/ *a* hala-
gador; (*given free*) de favor. ~**s** *npl*
saludos *mpl*

comply /kəm'plaɪ/ *vi*. ~ **with** conformarse con

component /kəm'pəʊnənt/ *a* & *n*
componente (*m*)

compose /kəm'pəʊz/ *vt* componer.
~ **o.s.** tranquilizarse. ~**d** *a* sereno

compos|er /kəm'pəʊzə(r)/ *n* com-
positor *m*. ~**ition** /kɒmpə'zɪʃn/ *n*
composición *f*

compost /'kɒmpɒst/ *n* abono *m*

composure /kəm'pəʊʒə(r)/ *n* serenidad *f*

compound[1] /'kɒmpaʊnd/ *n* compuesto *m*. ● *a* compuesto; ⟨*fracture*⟩
complicado. /kəm'paʊnd/ *vt* componer; agravar ⟨*problem etc*⟩. ● *vi*
(*settle*) arreglarse

compound[2] /'kɒmpaʊnd/ *n* (*enclosure*) recinto *m*

comprehen|d /kɒmprɪ'hend/ *vt*
comprender. ~**sion** /kɒmprɪ'henʃn/
n comprensión *f*

comprehensive /kɒmprɪ'hensɪv/ *a*
extenso; (*insurance*) a todo riesgo. ~
school *n* instituto *m*

compress /'kɒmpres/ *n* (*med*) compresa *f*. /kəm'pres/ *vt* comprimir;
(*fig*) condensar. ~**ion** /-ʃn/ *n*
compresión *f*

comprise /kəm'praɪz/ *vt* comprender

compromise /'kɒmprəmaɪz/ *n*
acuerdo *m*, acomodo *m*, arreglo *m*.
● *vt* comprometer. ● *vi* llegar a un
acuerdo

compuls|ion /kəm'pʌlʃn/ *n*
obligación *f*, impulso *m*. ~**ive**
/kəm'pʌlsɪv/ *a* compulsivo. ~**ory**
/kəm'pʌlsərɪ/ *a* obligatorio

compunction /kəm'pʌŋkʃn/ *n* remordimiento *m*

computer /kəm'pju:tə(r)/ *n* ordenador *m*. **~ize** *vt* instalar ordenadores en. **be ~ized** tener ordenador

comrade /'kɒmreɪd/ *n* camarada *m* & *f*. **~ship** *n* camaradería *f*

con[1] /kɒn/ *vt* (*pt* **conned**) (*fam*) estafar. ● *n* (*fam*) estafa *f*

con[2] /kɒn/ *see* **pro and con**

concave /'kɒnkeɪv/ *a* cóncavo

conceal /kən'si:l/ *vt* ocultar. **~ment** *n* encubrimiento *m*

concede /kən'si:d/ *vt* conceder

conceit /kən'si:t/ *n* vanidad *f*. **~ed** *a* engreído

conceiv|able /kən'si:vəbl/ *a* concebible. **~ably** *adv*. **may ~ably** es concebible que. **~e** /kən'si:v/ *vt/i* concebir

concentrat|e /'kɒnsəntreɪt/ *vt* concentrar. ● *vi* concentrarse. **~ion** /-'treɪʃn/ *n* concentración *f*. **~ion camp** *n* campo *m* de concentración

concept /'kɒnsept/ *n* concepto *m*

conception /kən'sepʃn/ *n* concepción *f*

conceptual /kən'septʃʊəl/ *a* conceptual

concern /kən'sɜ:n/ *n* asunto *m*; (*worry*) preocupación *f*; (*com*) empresa *f*. ● *vt* tener que ver con; (*deal with*) tratar de. **as far as I'm ~ed** en cuanto a mí. **be ~ed about** preocuparse por. **~ing** *prep* acerca de

concert /'kɒnsət/ *n* concierto *m*. **in ~** de común acuerdo. **~ed** /kən'sɜ:tɪd/ *a* concertado

concertina /kɒnsə'ti:nə/ *n* concertina *f*

concerto /kən'tʃɜ:təʊ/ *n* (*pl* **-os**) concierto *m*

concession /kən'seʃn/ *n* concesión *f*

conciliat|e /kən'sɪlɪeɪt/ *vt* conciliar. **~ion** /-'eɪʃn/ *n* conciliación *f*

concise /kən'saɪs/ *a* conciso. **~ly** *adv* concisamente. **~ness** *n* concisión *f*

conclu|de /kən'klu:d/ *vt* concluir. ● *vi* concluirse. **~ding** *a* final. **~sion** *n* conclusión *f*

conclusive /kən'klu:sɪv/ *a* decisivo. **~ly** *adv* concluyentemente

concoct /kən'kɒkt/ *vt* confeccionar; (*fig*) inventar. **~ion** /-ʃn/ *n* mezcla *f*; (*drink*) brebaje *m*

concourse /'kɒnkɔ:s/ *n* (*rail*) vestíbulo *m*

concrete /'kɒnkri:t/ *n* hormigón *m*. ● *a* concreto. ● *vt* cubrir con hormigón

concur /kən'kɜ:(r)/ *vi* (*pt* **concurred**) estar de acuerdo

concussion /kən'kʌʃn/ *n* conmoción *f* cerebral

condemn /kən'dem/ *vt* condenar. **~ation** /kɒndem'neɪʃn/ *n* condenación *f*, condena *f*; (*censure*) censura *f*

condens|ation /kɒnden'seɪʃn/ *n* condensación *f*. **~e** /kən'dens/ *vt* condensar. ● *vi* condensarse

condescend /kɒndɪ'send/ *vi* dignarse (**to** a). **~ing** *a* superior

condiment /'kɒndɪmənt/ *n* condimento *m*

condition /kən'dɪʃn/ *n* condición *f*. **on ~ that** a condición de que. ● *vt* condicionar. **~al** *a* condicional. **~er** *n* acondicionador *m*; (*for hair*) suavizante *m*

condolences /kən'dəʊlənsɪz/ *npl* pésame *m*

condom /'kɒndɒm/ *n* condón *m*

condone /kən'dəʊn/ *vt* condonar

conducive /kən'dju:sɪv/ *a*. **be ~ to** ser favorable a

conduct /kən'dʌkt/ *vt* conducir; dirigir ⟨*orchestra*⟩. /'kɒndʌkt/ *n* conducta *f*. **~or** /kən'dʌktə(r)/ *n* director *m*; (*of bus*) cobrador *m*. **~ress** *n* cobradora *f*

cone /kəʊn/ *n* cono *m*; (*for ice-cream*) cucurucho *m*

confectioner /kən'fekʃənə(r)/ *n* pastelero *m*. **~y** *n* dulces *mpl*, golosinas *fpl*

confederation /kənfedə'reɪʃn/ *n* confederación *f*

confer /kən'fɜ:(r)/ *vt* (*pt* **conferred**) conferir. ● *vi* consultar

conference /'kɒnfərəns/ *n* congreso *m*

confess /kən'fes/ *vt* confesar. ● *vi* confesarse. **~ion** /-ʃn/ *n* confesión *f*. **~ional** *n* confes(i)onario *m*. **~or** *n* confesor *m*

confetti /kən'fetɪ/ *n* confeti *m*, confetis *mpl*

confide /kən'faɪd/ *vt/i* confiar

confiden|ce /'kɒnfɪdəns/ *n* confianza *f*; (*secret*) confidencia *f*. **~ce trick** *n* estafa *f*, timo *m*. **~t** /'kɒnfɪdənt/ *a* seguro

confidential /kɒnfɪ'denʃl/ *a* confidencial

confine /kən'faɪn/ *vt* confinar; (*limit*) limitar. **~ment** *n* (*imprisonment*) prisión *f*; (*med*) parto *m*

confines /'kɒnfaɪnz/ *npl* confines *mpl*

confirm /kən'fɜːm/ *vt* confirmar. **~ation** /kɒnfə'meɪʃn/ *n* confirmación *f*. **~ed** *a* inveterado

confiscat|e /'kɒnfɪskeɪt/ *vt* confiscar. **~ion** /-'keɪʃn/ *n* confiscación *f*

conflagration /kɒnflə'greɪʃn/ *n* conflagración *f*

conflict /'kɒnflɪkt/ *n* conflicto *m*. /kən'flɪkt/ *vi* chocar. **~ing** /kən-/ *a* contradictorio

conform /kən'fɔːm/ *vt* conformar. ● *vi* conformarse. **~ist** *n* conformista *m & f*

confound /kən'faʊnd/ *vt* confundir. **~ed** *a* (*fam*) maldito

confront /kən'frʌnt/ *vt* hacer frente a; (*face*) enfrentarse con. **~ation** /kɒnfrʌn'teɪʃn/ *n* confrontación *f*

confus|e /kən'fjuːz/ *vt* confundir. **~ing** *a* desconcertante. **~ion** /-ʒn/ *n* confusión *f*

congeal /kən'dʒiːl/ *vt* coagular. ● *vi* coagularse

congenial /kən'dʒiːnɪəl/ *a* simpático

congenital /kən'dʒenɪtl/ *a* congénito

congest|ed /kən'dʒestɪd/ *a* congestionado. **~ion** /-tʃən/ *n* congestión *f*

congratulat|e /kən'grætjʊleɪt/ *vt* felicitar. **~ions** /-'leɪʃnz/ *npl* felicitaciones *fpl*

congregat|e /'kɒŋgrɪgeɪt/ *vi* congregarse. **~ion** /-'geɪʃn/ *n* asamblea *f*; (*relig*) fieles *mpl*, feligreses *mpl*

congress /'kɒŋgres/ *n* congreso *m*. **C~** (*Amer*) el Congreso

conic(al) /'kɒnɪk(l)/ *a* cónico

conifer /'kɒnɪfə(r)/ *n* conífera *f*

conjecture /kən'dʒektʃə(r)/ *n* conjetura *f*. ● *vt* conjeturar. ● *vi* hacer conjeturas

conjugal /'kɒndʒʊgl/ *a* conyugal

conjugat|e /'kɒndʒʊgeɪt/ *vt* conjugar. **~ion** /-'geɪʃn/ *n* conjugación *f*

conjunction /kən'dʒʌŋkʃn/ *n* conjunción *f*

conjur|e /'kʌndʒə(r)/ *vi* hacer juegos de manos. ● *vt*. **~e up** evocar. **~or** *n* prestidigitador *m*

conk /kɒŋk/ *vi*. **~ out** (*sl*) fallar; (*person*) desmayarse

conker /'kɒŋkə(r)/ *n* (*fam*) castaña *f* de Indias

conman /'kɒnmæn/ *n* (*fam*) estafador *m*, timador *m*

connect /kə'nekt/ *vt* juntar; (*elec*) conectar. ● *vi* unirse; (*elec*) conectarse. **~ with** (*train*) enlazar con. **~ed** *a* unido; (*related*) relacionado. **be ~ed with** tener que ver con, estar emparentado con

connection /kə'nekʃn/ *n* unión *f*; (*rail*) enlace *m*; (*elec*, *mec*) conexión *f*; (*fig*) relación *f*. **in ~ with** a propósito de, con respecto a. **~s** *npl* relaciones *fpl*

conniv|ance /kə'naɪvəns/ *n* connivencia *f*. **~e** /kə'naɪv/ *vi*. **~e at** hacer la vista gorda a

connoisseur /kɒnə'sɜː(r)/ *n* experto *m*

connot|ation /kɒnə'teɪʃn/ *n* connotación *f*. **~e** /kə'nəʊt/ *vt* connotar; (*imply*) implicar

conquer /'kɒŋkə(r)/ *vt* conquistar; (*fig*) vencer. **~or** *n* conquistador *m*

conquest /'kɒŋkwest/ *n* conquista *f*

conscience /'kɒnʃəns/ *n* conciencia *f*

conscientious /kɒnʃɪ'enʃəs/ *a* concienzudo

conscious /'kɒnʃəs/ *a* consciente; (*deliberate*) intencional. **~ly** *adv* a sabiendas. **~ness** *n* consciencia *f*; (*med*) conocimiento *m*

conscript /'kɒnskrɪpt/ *n* recluta *m*. /kən'skrɪpt/ *vt* reclutar. **~ion** /kən'skrɪpʃn/ *n* reclutamiento *m*

consecrat|e /'kɒnsɪkreɪt/ *vt* consagrar. **~ion** /-'kreɪʃn/ *n* consagración *f*

consecutive /kən'sekjʊtɪv/ *a* sucesivo

consensus /kən'sensəs/ *n* consenso *m*

consent /kən'sent/ *vi* consentir. ● *n* consentimiento *m*

consequ|en|ce /'kɒnsɪkwəns/ *n* consecuencia *f*. **~t** /'kɒnsɪkwənt/ *a* consiguiente. **~tly** *adv* por consiguiente

conservation /kɒnsə'veɪʃn/ *n* conservación *f*, preservación *f*. **~ist** /kɒnsə'veɪʃənɪst/ *n* conservacionista *m & f*

conservative /kən'sɜːvətɪv/ *a* conservador; (*modest*) prudente, moderado. **C~** *a & n* conservador (*m*)

conservatory /kən'sɜ:vətrɪ/ n (*greenhouse*) invernadero m

conserve /kən'sɜ:v/ vt conservar

consider /kən'sɪdə(r)/ vt considerar; (*take into account*) tomar en cuenta. ~**able** /kən'sɪdərəbl/ a considerable. ~**ably** adv considerablemente

considerat|e /kən'sɪdərət/ a considerado. ~**ion** /-'reɪʃn/ n consideración f

considering /kən'sɪdərɪŋ/ prep en vista de

consign /kən'saɪn/ vt consignar; (*send*) enviar. ~**ment** n envío m

consist /kən'sɪst/ vi. ~ **of** consistir en

consistency /kən'sɪstənsɪ/ n consistencia f; (*fig*) coherencia f

consistent /kən'sɪstənt/ a coherente; (*unchanging*) constante. ~ **with** compatible con. ~**ly** adv constantemente

consolation /kɒnsə'leɪʃn/ n consuelo m

console /kən'səʊl/ vt consolar

consolidat|e /kən'sɒlɪdeɪt/ vt consolidar. ● vi consolidarse. ~**ion** /-'deɪʃn/ n consolidación f

consonant /'kɒnsənənt/ n consonante f

consort /'kɒnsɔ:t/ n consorte m & f. /kən'sɔ:t/ vi. ~ **with** asociarse con

consortium /kən'sɔ:tɪəm/ n (*pl* -**tia**) consorcio m

conspicuous /kən'spɪkjʊəs/ a (*easily seen*) visible; (*showy*) llamativo; (*noteworthy*) notable

conspir|acy /kən'spɪrəsɪ/ n complot m, conspiración f. ~**e** /kən'spaɪə(r)/ vi conspirar

constab|le /'kʌnstəbl/ n policía m, guardia m. ~**ulary** /kən'stæbjʊlərɪ/ n policía f

constant /'kɒnstənt/ a constante. ~**ly** adv constantemente

constellation /kɒnstə'leɪʃn/ n constelación f

consternation /kɒnstə'neɪʃn/ n consternación f

constipat|ed /'kɒnstɪpeɪtɪd/ a estreñido. ~**ion** /-'peɪʃn/ n estreñimiento m

constituen|cy /kən'stɪtjʊənsɪ/ n distrito m electoral. ~**t** /kən'stɪtjʊənt/ n componente m; (*pol*) elector m

constitut|e /'kɒnstɪtju:t/ vt constituir. ~**ion** /-'tju:ʃn/ n constitución f. ~**ional** /-'tju:ʃənl/ a constitucional. ● n paseo m

constrain /kən'streɪn/ vt forzar, obligar, constreñir. ~**t** /kən'streɪnt/ n fuerza f

constrict /kən'strɪkt/ vt apretar. ~**ion** /-ʃn/ n constricción f

construct /kən'strʌkt/ vt construir. ~**ion** /-ʃn/ n construcción f. ~**ive** /kən'strʌktɪv/ a constructivo

construe /kən'stru:/ vt interpretar; (*gram*) construir

consul /'kɒnsl/ n cónsul m. ~**ar** /-jʊlə(r)/ a consular. ~**ate** /-ət/ n consulado m

consult /kən'sʌlt/ vt/i consultar. ~**ant** /kən'sʌltənt/ n asesor m; (*med*) especialista m & f; (*tec*) consejero m técnico. ~**ation** /kɒnsəl'teɪʃn/ n consulta f

consume /kən'sju:m/ vt consumir; (*eat*) comer; (*drink*) beber. ~**r** /-ə(r)/ n consumidor m. ● a de consumo. ~**rism** /kən'sju:mərɪzəm/ n protección f del consumidor, consumismo m

consumption /kən'sʌmpʃn/ n consumo m; (*med*) tisis f

contact /'kɒntækt/ n contacto m. ● vt ponerse en contacto con

contagious /kən'teɪdʒəs/ a contagioso

contain /kən'teɪn/ vt contener. ~ **o.s.** contenerse. ~**er** n recipiente m; (*com*) contenedor m

contaminat|e /kən'tæmɪneɪt/ vt contaminar. ~**ion** /-'neɪʃn/ n contaminación f

contemplat|e /'kɒntəmpleɪt/ vt contemplar; (*consider*) considerar. ~**ion** /-'pleɪʃn/ n contemplación f

contemporary /kən'tempərərɪ/ a & n contemporáneo (m)

contempt /kən'tempt/ n desprecio m. ~**ible** a despreciable. ~**uous** /-tjʊəs/ a desdeñoso

contend /kən'tend/ vt sostener. ● vi contender. ~**er** n contendiente m & f

content¹ /kən'tent/ a satisfecho. ● vt contentar

content² /'kɒntent/ n contenido m

contented /kən'tentɪd/ a satisfecho

contention /kən'tenʃn/ n contienda f; (*opinion*) opinión f, argumento m

contentment /kən'tentmənt/ n contento m

contest /'kɒntest/ n (*competition*) concurso m; (*fight*) contienda f. /kən'test/ vt disputar. ~**ant** /n contendiente m & f, concursante m & f

context /'kɒntekst/ n contexto m

continent /'kɒntɪnənt/ n continente m. **the C**~ Europa f. ~**al** /-'nentl/ a continental

contingency /kən'tɪndʒənsɪ/ n contingencia f

contingent /kən'tɪndʒənt/ a & n contingente (m)

continu|al /kən'tɪnjʊəl/ a continuo. ~**ance** /kən'tɪnjʊəns/ n continuación f. ~**ation** /-ʊ'eɪʃn/ n continuación f. ~**e** /kən'tɪnju:/ vt/i continuar; (*resume*) seguir. ~**ed** a continuo. ~**ity** /kɒntɪ'nju:ətɪ/ n continuidad f. ~**ity girl** (*cinema, TV*) secretaria f de rodaje. ~**ous** /kən'tɪnjʊəs/ a continuo. ~**ously** adv continuamente

contort /kən'tɔ:t/ vt retorcer. ~**ion** /-ʃn/ n contorsión f. ~**ionist** /-ʃənɪst/ n contorsionista m & f

contour /'kɒntʊə(r)/ n contorno m. ~ **line** n curva f de nivel

contraband /'kɒntrəbænd/ n contrabando m

contracepti|on /kɒntrə'sepʃn/ n contracepción f. ~**ve** /kɒntrə'septɪv/ a & n anticonceptivo (m)

contract /'kɒntrækt/ n contrato m. /kən'trækt/ vt contraer. ● vi contraerse. ~**ion** /kən'trækʃn/ n contracción f. ~**or** /kən'træktə(r)/ n contratista m & f

contradict /kɒntrə'dɪkt/ vt contradecir. ~**ion** /-ʃn/ n contradicción f. ~**ory** a contradictorio

contraption /kən'træpʃn/ n (*fam*) artilugio m

contrary /'kɒntrərɪ/ a & n contrario (m). **on the** ~ al contrario. ● adv. ~ **to** contrariamente a. /kən'treərɪ/ a terco

contrast /'kɒntrɑːst/ n contraste m. /kən'trɑːst/ vt poner en contraste. ● vi contrastar. ~**ing** a contrastante

contraven|e /kɒntrə'vi:n/ vt contravenir. ~**tion** /-'venʃn/ n contravención f

contribut|e /kən'trɪbjuːt/ vt/i contribuir. ~**e to** escribir para ⟨*newspaper*⟩. ~**ion** /kɒntrɪ'bjuːʃn/ n contribución f; (*from salary*) cotización f. ~**or** n contribuyente m & f, (*to newspaper*) colaborador m

contrite /'kɒntraɪt/ a arrepentido, pesaroso

contriv|ance /kən'traɪvəns/ n invención f. ~**e** /kən'traɪv/ vt idear. ~**e to** conseguir

control /kən'trəʊl/ vt (*pt* **controlled**) controlar. ● n control m. ~**s** npl (*mec*) mandos mpl

controvers|ial /kɒntrə'vɜːʃl/ a polémico, discutible. ~**y** /'kɒntrəvɜːsɪ/ n controversia f

conundrum /kə'nʌndrəm/ n adivinanza f; (*problem*) enigma m

conurbation /kɒnɜː'beɪʃn/ n conurbación f

convalesce /kɒnvə'les/ vi convalecer. ~**nce** n convalecencia f. ~**nt** a & n convaleciente (m & f). ~**nt home** n casa f de convalecencia

convector /kən'vektə(r)/ n estufa f de convección

convene /kən'vi:n/ vt convocar. ● vi reunirse

convenien|ce /kən'vi:nɪəns/ n conveniencia f, comodidad f. **all modern** ~**ces** todas las comodidades. **at your** ~**ce** según le convenga. ~**ces** npl servicios mpl. ~**t** /kən'vi:nɪənt/ a cómodo; (*place*) bien situado; (*time*) oportuno. **be** ~**t** convenir. ~**tly** adv convenientemente

convent /'kɒnvənt/ n convento m

convention /kən'venʃn/ n convención f; (*meeting*) congreso m. ~**al** a convencional

converge /kən'vɜːdʒ/ vi convergir

conversant /kən'vɜːsənt/ a. ~ **with** versado en

conversation /kɒnvə'seɪʃn/ n conversación f. ~**al** a de la conversación. ~**alist** n hábil conversador m

converse¹ /kən'vɜːs/ vi conversar

converse² /'kɒnvɜːs/ a inverso. ● n lo contrario. ~**ly** adv a la inversa

conver|sion /kən'vɜːʃn/ n conversión f. ~**t** /kən'vɜːt/ vt convertir. /'kɒnvɜːt/ n converso m. ~**tible** /kən'vɜːtɪbl/ a convertible. ● n (*auto*) descapotable m

convex /'kɒnveks/ a convexo

convey /kən'veɪ/ vt llevar; transportar ⟨*goods*⟩; comunicar ⟨*idea, feeling*⟩. ~**ance** n transporte m. ~**or belt** n cinta f transportadora

convict /kənˈvɪkt/ vt condenar. /ˈkɒnvɪkt/ n presidiario m. **~ion** /kənˈvɪkʃn/ n condena f; (belief) creencia f

convinc|e /kənˈvɪns/ vt convencer. **~ing** a convincente

convivial /kənˈvɪvɪəl/ a alegre

convoke /kənˈvəʊk/ vt convocar

convoluted /ˈkɒnvəluːtɪd/ a enrollado; ⟨argument⟩ complicado

convoy /ˈkɒnvɔɪ/ n convoy m

convuls|e /kənˈvʌls/ vt convulsionar. **be ~ed with laughter** desternillarse de risa. **~ion** /-ʃn/ n convulsión f

coo /kuː/ vi arrullar

cook /kʊk/ vt cocinar; (alter, fam) falsificar. **~ up** (fam) inventar. ● n cocinero m

cooker /ˈkʊkə(r)/ n cocina f

cookery /ˈkʊkərɪ/ n cocina f

cookie /ˈkʊkɪ/ n (Amer) galleta f

cool /kuːl/ a (-er, -est) fresco; (calm) tranquilo; (unfriendly) frío. ● n fresco m; (sl) calma f. ● vt enfriar. ● vi enfriarse. **~ down** ⟨person⟩ calmarse. **~ly** adv tranquilamente. **~ness** n frescura f

coop /kuːp/ n gallinero m. ● vt. **~ up** encerrar

co-operat|e /kəʊˈɒpəreɪt/ vi cooperar. **~ion** /-ˈreɪʃn/ n cooperación f

cooperative /kəʊˈɒpərətɪv/ a cooperativo. ● n cooperativa f

co-opt /kəʊˈɒpt/ vt cooptar

co-ordinat|e /kəʊˈɔːdɪneɪt/ vt coordinar. **~ion** /-ˈneɪʃn/ n coordinación f

cop /kɒp/ vt (pt copped) (sl) prender. ● n (sl) policía m

cope /kəʊp/ vi (fam) arreglárselas. **~ with** enfrentarse con

copious /ˈkəʊpɪəs/ a abundante

copper[1] /ˈkɒpə(r)/ n cobre m; (coin) perra f. ● a de cobre

copper[2] /ˈkɒpə(r)/ n (sl) policía m

coppice /ˈkɒpɪs/ n, **copse** /kɒps/ n bosquecillo m

Coptic /ˈkɒptɪk/ a copto

copulat|e /ˈkɒpjʊleɪt/ vi copular. **~ion** /-ˈleɪʃn/ n cópula f

copy /ˈkɒpɪ/ n copia f; (typ) material m. ● vt copiar

copyright /ˈkɒpɪraɪt/ n derechos mpl de autor

copy-writer /ˈkɒpɪraɪtə(r)/ n redactor m de textos publicitarios

coral /ˈkɒrəl/ n coral m

cord /kɔːd/ n cuerda f; (fabric) pana f. **~s** npl pantalones mpl de pana

cordial /ˈkɔːdɪəl/ a & n cordial (m)

cordon /ˈkɔːdn/ n cordón m. ● vt. **~ off** acordonar

corduroy /ˈkɔːdərɔɪ/ n pana f

core /kɔː(r)/ n (of apple) corazón m; (fig) meollo m

cork /kɔːk/ n corcho m. ● vt taponar. **~screw** /ˈkɔːkskruː/ n sacacorchos m invar

corn[1] /kɔːn/ n (wheat) trigo m; (Amer) maíz m; (seed) grano m

corn[2] /kɔːn/ n (hard skin) callo m

corned /kɔːnd/ a. **~ beef** n carne f de vaca en lata

corner /ˈkɔːnə(r)/ n ángulo m; (inside) rincón m; (outside) esquina f; (football) saque m de esquina. ● vt arrinconar; (com) acaparar. **~stone** n piedra f angular

cornet /ˈkɔːnɪt/ n (mus) corneta f; (for ice-cream) cucurucho m

cornflakes /ˈkɔːnfleɪks/ npl copos mpl de maíz

cornflour /ˈkɔːnflaʊə(r)/ n harina f de maíz

cornice /ˈkɔːnɪs/ n cornisa f

cornucopia /ˌkɔːnjʊˈkəʊpɪə/ n cuerno m de la abundancia

Corn|ish /ˈkɔːnɪʃ/ a de Cornualles. **~wall** /ˈkɔːnwəl/ n Cornualles m

corny /ˈkɔːnɪ/ a (trite, fam) gastado; (mawkish) sentimental, sensiblero

corollary /kəˈrɒlərɪ/ n corolario m

coronary /ˈkɒrənərɪ/ n trombosis f coronaria

coronation /ˌkɒrəˈneɪʃn/ n coronación f

coroner /ˈkɒrənə(r)/ n juez m de primera instancia

corporal[1] /ˈkɔːpərəl/ n cabo m

corporal[2] /ˈkɔːpərəl/ a corporal

corporate /ˈkɔːpərət/ a corporativo

corporation /ˌkɔːpəˈreɪʃn/ n corporación f; (of town) ayuntamiento m

corps /kɔː(r)/ n (pl corps /kɔːz/) cuerpo m

corpse /kɔːps/ n cadáver m

corpulent /ˈkɔːpjʊlənt/ a gordo, corpulento

corpuscle /ˈkɔːpʌsl/ n glóbulo m

corral /kəˈrɑːl/ n (Amer) corral m

correct /kəˈrekt/ a correcto; ⟨time⟩ exacto. ● vt corregir. **~ion** /-ʃn/ n corrección f

correlat|e /'kɒrəleɪt/ vt poner en correlación. **~ion** /-'leɪʃn/ n correlación f

correspond /kɒrɪ'spɒnd/ vi corresponder; (write) escribirse. **~ence** n correspondencia f. **~ent** n corresponsal m & f

corridor /'kɒrɪdɔː(r)/ n pasillo m

corroborate /kə'rɒbəreɪt/ vt corroborar

corro|de /kə'rəʊd/ vt corroer. ● vi corroerse. **~sion** n corrosión f

corrugated /'kɒrəgeɪtɪd/ a ondulado. **~ iron** n hierro m ondulado

corrupt /kə'rʌpt/ a corrompido. ● vt corromper. **~ion** /-ʃn/ n corrupción f

corset /'kɔːsɪt/ n corsé m

Corsica /'kɔːsɪkə/ n Córcega f. **~n** a & n corso (m)

cortège /kɔː'teɪʒ/ n cortejo m

cos /kɒs/ n lechuga f romana

cosh /kɒʃ/ n cachiporra f. ● vt aporrear

cosiness /'kəʊzɪnɪs/ n comodidad f

cosmetic /kɒz'metɪk/ a & n cosmético (m)

cosmic /'kɒzmɪk/ a cósmico

cosmonaut /'kɒzmənɔːt/ n cosmonauta m & f

cosmopolitan /kɒzmə'pɒlɪtən/ a & n cosmopolita (m & f)

cosmos /'kɒzmɒs/ n cosmos m

Cossack /'kɒsæk/ a & n cosaco (m)

cosset /'kɒsɪt/ vt (pt cosseted) mimar

cost /kɒst/ vi (pt cost) costar, valer. ● vt (pt costed) calcular el coste de. ● n precio m. **at all ~s** cueste lo que cueste. **to one's ~** a sus expensas. **~s** npl (jurid) costas f pl

Costa Rica /kɒstə'riːkə/ n Costa f Rica. **~n** a & n costarricense (m & f), costarriqueño (m)

costly /'kɒstlɪ/ a (-ier, -iest) caro, costoso

costume /'kɒstjuːm/ n traje m

cosy /'kəʊzɪ/ a (-ier, -iest) cómodo; ⟨place⟩ acogedor. ● n cubierta f (de tetera)

cot /kɒt/ n cuna f

cottage /'kɒtɪdʒ/ n casita f de campo. **~ cheese** n requesón m. **~ industry** n industria f casera. **~ pie** n carne f picada con puré de patatas

cotton /'kɒtn/ n algodón m. ● vi. **~ on** (sl) comprender. **~ wool** n algodón hidrófilo

couch /kaʊtʃ/ n sofá m. ● vt expresar

couchette /kuː'ʃet/ n litera f

cough /kɒf/ vi toser. ● n tos f. **~ up** (sl) pagar. **~ mixture** n jarabe m para la tos

could /kʊd, kəd/ pt of **can**

couldn't /'kʊdnt/ = **could not**

council /'kaʊnsl/ n consejo m; (of town) ayuntamiento m. **~ house** n vivienda f protegida. **~lor** /'kaʊnsələ(r)/ n concejal m

counsel /'kaʊnsl/ n consejo m; (pl invar) (jurid) abogado m. **~lor** n consejero m

count¹ /kaʊnt/ n recuento m. ● vt/i contar

count² /kaʊnt/ n (nobleman) conde m

countdown /'kaʊntdaʊn/ n cuenta f atrás

countenance /'kaʊntɪnəns/ n semblante m. ● vt aprobar

counter /'kaʊntə(r)/ n (in shop etc) mostrador m; (token) ficha f. ● adv. **~ to** en contra de. ● a opuesto. ● vt oponerse a; parar ⟨blow⟩. ● vi contraatacar

counter... /'kaʊntə(r)/ pref contra...

counteract /kaʊntər'ækt/ vt contrarrestar

counter-attack /'kaʊntərətæk/ n contraataque m. ● vt/i contraatacar

counterbalance /'kaʊntəbæləns/ n contrapeso m. ● vt/i contrapesar

counterfeit /'kaʊntəfɪt/ a falsificado. ● n falsificación f. ● vt falsificar

counterfoil /'kaʊntəfɔɪl/ n talón m

counterpart /'kaʊntəpɑːt/ n equivalente m; (person) homólogo m

counter-productive /'kaʊntəprə'dʌktɪv/ a contraproducente

countersign /'kaʊntəsaɪn/ vt refrendar

countess /'kaʊntɪs/ n condesa f

countless /'kaʊntlɪs/ a innumerable

countrified /'kʌntrɪfaɪd/ a rústico

country /'kʌntrɪ/ n (native land) país m; (countryside) campo m. **~ folk** n gente f del campo. **go to the ~** ir al campo; (pol) convocar elecciones generales

countryman /'kʌntrɪmən/ n (pl -men) campesino m; (of one's own country) compatriota m

countryside /'kʌntrɪsaɪd/ n campo m

county /'kaʊntɪ/ n condado m, provincia f

coup /ku:/ n golpe m

coupé /ˈkuːpeɪ/ n cupé m

couple /ˈkʌpl/ n (of things) par m; (of people) pareja f; (married) matrimonio m. **a ~ of** un par de. ● vt unir; (tec) acoplar. ● vi copularse

coupon /ˈkuːpɒn/ n cupón m

courage /ˈkʌrɪdʒ/ n valor m. **~ous** /kəˈreɪdʒəs/ a valiente. **~ously** adv valientemente

courgette /kʊəˈʒet/ n calabacín m

courier /ˈkʊrɪə(r)/ n mensajero m; (for tourists) guía m & f

course /kɔːs/ n curso m; (behaviour) conducta f; (aviat, naut) rumbo m; (culin) plato m; (for golf) campo m. **in due ~** a su debido tiempo. **in the ~ of** en el transcurso de, durante. **of ~** desde luego, por supuesto

court /kɔːt/ n corte f; (tennis) pista f; (jurid) tribunal m. ● vt cortejar; buscar (danger)

courteous /ˈkɜːtɪəs/ a cortés

courtesan /kɔːtɪˈzæn/ n (old use) cortesana f

courtesy /ˈkɜːtəsɪ/ n cortesía f

court: **~ier** /ˈkɔːtɪə(r)/ n (old use) cortesano m. **~ martial** n (pl **courts martial**) consejo m de guerra. **~ martial** vt (pt **~-martialled**) juzgar en consejo de guerra. **~ship** /ˈkɔːtʃɪp/ n cortejo m

courtyard /ˈkɔːtjɑːd/ n patio m

cousin /ˈkʌzn/ n primo m. **first ~** primo carnal. **second ~** primo segundo

cove /kəʊv/ n cala f

covenant /ˈkʌvənənt/ n acuerdo m

Coventry /ˈkɒvntrɪ/ n. **send to ~** hacer el vacío

cover /ˈkʌvə(r)/ vt cubrir; (journalism) hacer un reportaje sobre. **~ up** cubrir; (fig) ocultar. ● n cubierta f; (shelter) abrigo m; (lid) tapa f; (for furniture) funda f; (pretext) pretexto m; (of magazine) portada f. **~age** /ˈkʌvərɪdʒ/ n reportaje m. **~ charge** n precio m del cubierto. **~ing** n cubierta f. **~ing letter** n carta f explicatoria, carta f adjunta

covet /ˈkʌvɪt/ vt codiciar

cow /kaʊ/ n vaca f

coward /ˈkaʊəd/ n cobarde m. **~ly** a cobarde. **~ice** /ˈkaʊədɪs/ n cobardía f

cowboy /ˈkaʊbɔɪ/ n vaquero m

cower /ˈkaʊə(r)/ vi encogerse, acobardarse

cowl /kaʊl/ n capucha f; (of chimney) sombrerete m

cowshed /ˈkaʊʃed/ n establo m

coxswain /ˈkɒksn/ n timonel m

coy /kɔɪ/ a (**-er, -est**) (falsamente) tímido, remilgado

crab[1] /kræb/ n cangrejo m

crab[2] /kræb/ vi (pt **crabbed**) quejarse

crab-apple /ˈkræbæpl/ n manzana f silvestre

crack /kræk/ n grieta f; (noise) crujido m; (of whip) chasquido m; (joke, sl) chiste m. ● a (fam) de primera. ● vt agrietar; chasquear (whip, fingers); cascar (nut); gastar (joke); resolver (problem). ● vi agrietarse. **get ~ing** (fam) darse prisa. **~ down on** (fam) tomar medidas enérgicas contra. **~ up** vi fallar; (person) volverse loco. **~ed** /krækt/ a (sl) chiflado

cracker /ˈkrækə(r)/ n petardo m; (culin) galleta f (soso); (culin, Amer) galleta f

crackers /ˈkrækəz/ a (sl) chiflado

crackl|e /ˈkrækl/ vi crepitar. ● n crepitación f, crujido m. **~ing** /ˈkræklɪŋ/ n crepitación f, crujido m; (of pork) chicharrón m

crackpot /ˈkrækpɒt/ n (sl) chiflado m

cradle /ˈkreɪdl/ n cuna f. ● vt acunar

craft /krɑːft/ n destreza f; (technique) arte f; (cunning) astucia f. ● n invar (boat) barco m

craftsman /ˈkrɑːftsmən/ n (pl **-men**) artesano m. **~ship** n artesanía f

crafty /ˈkrɑːftɪ/ a (**-ier, -iest**) astuto

crag /kræg/ n despeñadero m. **~gy** a peñascoso

cram /kræm/ vt (pt **crammed**) rellenar. **~ with** llenar de. ● vi (for exams) empollar. **~-full** a atestado

cramp /kræmp/ n calambre m

cramped /kræmpt/ a apretado

cranberry /ˈkrænbərɪ/ n arándano m

crane /kreɪn/ n grúa f; (bird) grulla f. ● vt estirar (neck)

crank[1] /kræŋk/ n manivela f

crank[2] /kræŋk/ n (person) excéntrico m. **~y** a excéntrico

cranny /ˈkrænɪ/ n grieta f

crash /kræʃ/ n accidente m; (noise) estruendo m; (collision) choque m; (com) quiebra f. ● vt estrellar. ● vi quebrar con estrépito; (*have accident*) tener un accidente; ⟨*car etc*⟩ chocar; (*fail*) fracasar. ∼ **course** *n* curso *m* intensivo. ∼**helmet** *n* casco *m* protector. ∼**land** *vi* hacer un aterrizaje de emergencia, hacer un aterrizaje forzoso

crass /kræs/ *a* craso, burdo

crate /kreɪt/ *n* cajón *m*. ● *vt* embalar

crater /'kreɪtə(r)/ *n* cráter *m*

cravat /krə'væt/ *n* corbata *f*, fular *m*

crav|e /kreɪv/ *vi*. ∼**e for** anhelar. ∼**ing** *n* ansia *f*

crawl /krɔːl/ *vi* andar a gatas; (*move slowly*) avanzar lentamente; (*drag o.s.*) arrastrarse. ● *n* (*swimming*) crol *m*. **at a** ∼ a paso lento. ∼ **to** humillarse ante. ∼ **with** hervir de

crayon /'kreɪən/ *n* lápiz *m* de color

craze /kreɪz/ *n* manía *f*

craz|iness /'kreɪzɪnɪs/ *n* locura *f*. ∼**y** /'kreɪzɪ/ *a* (**-ier, -iest**) loco. **be** ∼**y about** andar loco por. ∼**y paving** *n* enlosado *m* irregular

creak /kriːk/ *n* crujido *m*; (*of hinge*) chirrido *m*. ● *vi* crujir; ⟨*hinge*⟩ chirriar

cream /kriːm/ *n* crema *f*; (*fresh*) nata *f*. ● *a* (*colour*) color de crema. ● *vt* (*remove*) desnatar; (*beat*) batir. ∼ **cheese** *n* queso *m* de nata. ∼**y** *a* cremoso

crease /kriːs/ *n* pliegue *m*; (*crumple*) arruga *f*. ● *vt* plegar; (*wrinkle*) arrugar. ● *vi* arrugarse

creat|e /kriː'eɪt/ *vt* crear. ∼**ion** /-ʃn/ *n* creación *f*. ∼**ive** *a* creativo. ∼**or** *n* creador *m*

creature /'kriːtʃə(r)/ *n* criatura *f*, bicho *m*, animal *m*

crèche /kreɪʃ/ *n* guardería *f* infantil

credence /'kriːdns/ *n* creencia *f*, fe *f*

credentials /krɪ'denʃlz/ *npl* credenciales *mpl*

credib|ility /kredə'bɪlətɪ/ *n* credibilidad *f*. ∼**le** /'kredəbl/ *a* creíble

credit /'kredɪt/ *n* crédito *m*; (*honour*) honor *m*. **take the** ∼ **for** atribuirse el mérito de. ● *vt* (*pt* **credited**) acreditar; (*believe*) creer. ∼ **s.o. with** atribuir a uno. ∼**able** *a* loable. ∼ **card** *n* tarjeta *f* de crédito. ∼**or** *n* acreedor *m*

credulous /'kredjʊləs/ *a* crédulo

creed /kriːd/ *n* credo *m*

creek /kriːk/ *n* ensenada *f*. **up the** ∼ (*sl*) en apuros

creep /kriːp/ *vi* (*pt* **crept**) arrastrarse; ⟨*plant*⟩ trepar. ● *n* (*sl*) persona *f* desagradable. ∼**er** *n* enredadera *f*. ∼**s** /kriːps/ *npl*. **give s.o. the** ∼**s** dar repugnancia a uno

cremat|e /krɪ'meɪt/ *vt* incinerar. ∼**ion** /-ʃn/ *n* cremación *f*. ∼**orium** /kremə'tɔːrɪəm/ *n* (*pl* **-ia**) crematorio *m*

Creole /'kriːəʊl/ *a & n* criollo (*m*)

crêpe /kreɪp/ *n* crespón *m*

crept /krept/ *see* **creep**

crescendo /krɪ'ʃendəʊ/ *n* (*pl* **-os**) crescendo *m*

crescent /'kresnt/ *n* media luna *f*; (*street*) calle *f* en forma de media luna

cress /kres/ *n* berro *m*

crest /krest/ *n* cresta *f*; (*coat of arms*) blasón *m*

Crete /kriːt/ *n* Creta *f*

cretin /'kretɪn/ *n* cretino *m*

crevasse /krɪ'væs/ *n* grieta *f*

crevice /'krevɪs/ *n* grieta *f*

crew[1] /kruː/ *n* tripulación *f*; (*gang*) pandilla *f*

crew[2] /kruː/ *see* **crow**[2]

crew: ∼ **cut** *n* corte *m* al rape. ∼ **neck** *n* cuello *m* redondo

crib /krɪb/ *n* cuna *f*; (*relig*) belén *m*; (*plagiarism*) plagio *m*. ● *vt/i* (*pt* **cribbed**) plagiar

crick /krɪk/ *n* calambre *m*; (*in neck*) tortícolis *f*

cricket[1] /'krɪkɪt/ *n* criquet *m*

cricket[2] /'krɪkɪt/ *n* (*insect*) grillo *m*

cricketer /'krɪkɪtə(r)/ *n* jugador *m* de criquet

crim|e /kraɪm/ *n* crimen *m*; (*acts*) criminalidad *f*. ∼**inal** /'krɪmɪnl/ *a & n* criminal (*m*)

crimp /krɪmp/ *vt* rizar

crimson /'krɪmzn/ *a & n* carmesí (*m*)

cringe /krɪndʒ/ *vi* encogerse; (*fig*) humillarse

crinkle /'krɪŋkl/ *vt* arrugar. ● *vi* arrugarse. ● *n* arruga *f*

crinoline /'krɪnəlɪn/ *n* miriñaque *m*

cripple /'krɪpl/ *n* lisiado *m*, mutilado *m*. ● *vt* lisiar; (*fig*) paralizar

crisis /'kraɪsɪs/ *n* (*pl* **crises** /'kraɪsiːz/) crisis *f*

crisp /krɪsp/ *a* (**-er, -est**) (*culin*) crujiente; ⟨*air*⟩ vigorizador. ∼**s** *npl* patatas *fpl* fritas a la inglesa

criss-cross /'krɪskrɒs/ *a* entrecruzado. ● *vt* entrecruzar. ● *vi* entrecruzarse

criterion /kraɪ'tɪərɪən/ n (pl **-ia**) criterio m

critic /'krɪtɪk/ n crítico m

critical /'krɪtɪkl/ a crítico. **~ly** adv críticamente; (ill) gravemente

critici|sm /'krɪtɪsɪzəm/ n crítica f. **~ze** /'krɪtɪsaɪz/ vt/i criticar

croak /krəʊk/ n (of person) gruñido m; (of frog) canto m. ● vi gruñir; ⟨frog⟩ croar

crochet /'krəʊʃeɪ/ n croché m, ganchillo m. ● vt hacer ganchillo

crock¹ /krɒk/ n (person, fam) vejancón m; (old car) cacharro m

crock² /krɒk/ n vasija f de loza

crockery /'krɒkərɪ/ n loza f

crocodile /'krɒkədaɪl/ n cocodrilo m. **~ tears** npl lágrimas fpl de cocodrilo

crocus /'krəʊkəs/ n (pl **-es**) azafrán m

crony /'krəʊnɪ/ n amigote m

crook /krʊk/ n (fam) maleante m & f, estafador m, criminal m; (stick) cayado m; (of arm) pliegue m

crooked /'krʊkɪd/ a torcido; (winding) tortuoso; (dishonest) poco honrado

croon /kruːn/ vt/i canturrear

crop /krɒp/ n cosecha f; (fig) montón m. ● vt (pt **cropped**) vi cortar. **~ up** surgir

cropper /'krɒpər/ n. **come a ~** (fall, fam) caer; (fail, fam) fracasar

croquet /'krəʊkeɪ/ n croquet m

croquette /krə'ket/ n croqueta f

cross /krɒs/ n cruz f; (of animals) cruce m. ● vt/i cruzar; (oppose) contrariar. **~ off** tachar. **~ o.s.** santiguarse. **~ out** tachar. **~ s.o.'s mind** ocurrírsele a uno. ● a enfadado. **talk at ~ purposes** hablar sin entenderse

crossbar /'krɒsbɑː(r)/ n travesaño m

cross-examine /krɒsɪg'zæmɪn/ vt interrogar

cross-eyed /'krɒsaɪd/ a bizco

crossfire /'krɒsfaɪə(r)/ n fuego m cruzado

crossing /'krɒsɪŋ/ n (by boat) travesía f; (on road) paso m para peatones

crossly /'krɒslɪ/ adv con enfado

cross-reference /krɒs'refrəns/ n referencia f

crossroads /'krɒsrəʊdz/ n cruce m (de carreteras)

cross-section /krɒs'sekʃn/ n sección f transversal; (fig) muestra f representativa

crosswise /'krɒswaɪz/ adv al través

crossword /'krɒswɜːd/ n crucigrama m

crotch /krɒtʃ/ n entrepiernas fpl

crotchety /'krɒtʃɪtɪ/ a de mal genio

crouch /kraʊtʃ/ vi agacharse

crow¹ /krəʊ/ n cuervo m. **as the ~ flies** en línea recta

crow² /krəʊ/ vi (pt **crew**) cacarear

crowbar /'krəʊbɑː(r)/ n palanca f

crowd /kraʊd/ n muchedumbre f. ● vt amontonar; (fill) llenar. ● vi amontonarse; (gather) reunirse. **~ed** a atestado

crown /kraʊn/ n corona f; (of hill) cumbre f; (of head) coronilla f. ● vt coronar; poner una corona a ⟨tooth⟩. **C~ Court** n tribunal m regional. **C~ prince** n príncipe m heredero

crucial /'kruːʃl/ a crucial

crucifix /'kruːsɪfɪks/ n crucifijo m. **~ion** /-'fɪkʃn/ n crucifixión f

crucify /'kruːsɪfaɪ/ vt crucificar

crude /kruːd/ a (**-er**, **-est**) (raw) crudo; (rough) tosco; (vulgar) ordinario

cruel /kruəl/ a (**crueller**, **cruellest**) cruel. **~ty** n crueldad f

cruet /'kruːɪt/ n vinagreras fpl

cruise /kruːz/ n crucero m. ● vi hacer un crucero; (of car) circular lentamente. **~r** n crucero m

crumb /krʌm/ n migaja f

crumble /'krʌmbl/ vt desmenuzar. ● vi desmenuzarse; (collapse) derrumbarse

crummy /'krʌmɪ/ a (**-ier**, **-iest**) (sl) miserable

crumpet /'krʌmpɪt/ n bollo m blando

crumple /'krʌmpl/ vt arrugar; estrujar ⟨paper⟩. ● vi arrugarse

crunch /krʌntʃ/ vt hacer crujir; (bite) ronzar, morder, masticar. ● n crujido m; (fig) momento m decisivo

crusade /kruː'seɪd/ n cruzada f. **~r** /-ə(r)/ n cruzado m

crush /krʌʃ/ vt aplastar; arrugar ⟨clothes⟩; estrujar ⟨paper⟩. ● n (crowd) aglomeración f. **have a ~ on** (sl) estar perdido por. **orange ~** n naranjada f

crust /krʌst/ n corteza f. **~y** a ⟨bread⟩ de corteza dura; ⟨person⟩ malhumorado

crutch /krʌtʃ/ n muleta f; (anat) entrepiernas fpl

crux /krʌks/ n (pl **cruxes**) punto m más importante, quid m, busilis m

cry /kraɪ/ n grito m. **be a far ~ from** (fig) distar mucho de. ● vi llorar; (call out) gritar. **~ off** rajarse. **~baby** n llorón m

crypt /krɪpt/ n cripta f

cryptic /'krɪptɪk/ a enigmático

crystal /'krɪstl/ n cristal m. **~lize** vt cristalizar. ● vi cristalizarse

cub /kʌb/ n cachorro m. **C~ (Scout)** n niño m explorador

Cuba /'kju:bə/ n Cuba f. **~n** a & n cubano (m)

cubby-hole /'kʌbɪhəʊl/ n casilla f; (room) chiribitil m, cuchitril m

cub|e /kju:b/ n cubo m. **~ic** a cúbico

cubicle /'kju:bɪkl/ n cubículo m; (changing room) caseta f

cubis|m /'kju:bɪzm/ n cubismo m. **~t** a & n cubista (m & f)

cuckold /'kʌkəʊld/ n cornudo m

cuckoo /'kʊku:/ n cuco m, cuclillo m

cucumber /'kju:kʌmbə(r)/ n pepino m

cuddl|e /'kʌdl/ vt abrazar. ● vi abrazarse. ● n abrazo m. **~y** a mimoso

cudgel /'kʌdʒl/ n porra f. ● vt (pt **cudgelled**) aporrear

cue¹ /kju:/ n indicación f; (in theatre) pie m

cue² /kju:/ n (in billiards) taco m

cuff /kʌf/ n puño m; (blow) bofetada f. **speak off the ~** hablar de improviso. ● vt abofetear. **~-link** n gemelo m

cul-de-sac /'kʌldəsæk/ n callejón m sin salida

culinary /'kʌlɪnərɪ/ a culinario

cull /kʌl/ vt coger (flowers); entresacar (animals)

culminat|e /'kʌlmɪneɪt/ vi culminar. **~ion** /-'neɪʃn/ n culminación f

culottes /kʊ'lɒts/ npl falda f pantalón

culprit /'kʌlprɪt/ n culpable m

cult /kʌlt/ n culto m

cultivat|e /'kʌltɪveɪt/ vt cultivar. **~ion** /-'veɪʃn/ n cultivo m; (fig) cultura f

cultur|al /'kʌltʃərəl/ a cultural. **~e** /'kʌltʃə(r)/ n cultura f; (bot etc) cultivo m. **~ed** a cultivado; (person) culto

cumbersome /'kʌmbəsəm/ a incómodo; (heavy) pesado

cumulative /'kju:mjʊlətɪv/ a cumulativo

cunning /'kʌnɪŋ/ a astuto. ● n astucia f

cup /kʌp/ n taza f; (prize) copa f

cupboard /'kʌbəd/ n armario m

Cup Final /kʌp'faɪnl/ n final f del campeonato

cupful /'kʌpfʊl/ n taza f

cupidity /kju:'pɪdɪtɪ/ n codicia f

curable /'kjʊərəbl/ a curable

curate /'kjʊərət/ n coadjutor m

curator /kjʊə'reɪtə(r)/ n (of museum) conservador m

curb /kɜ:b/ n freno m. ● vt refrenar

curdle /'kɜ:dl/ vt cuajar. ● vi cuajarse; (milk) cortarse

curds /kɜ:dz/ npl cuajada f, requesón m

cure /kjʊə/ vt curar. ● n cura f

curfew /'kɜ:fju:/ n queda f; (signal) toque m de queda

curio /'kjʊərɪəʊ/ n (pl **-os**) curiosidad f

curio|us /'kjʊərɪəs/ a curioso. **~sity** /-'ɒsətɪ/ n curiosidad f

curl /kɜ:l/ vt rizar (hair). **~ o.s. up** acurrucarse. ● vi (hair) rizarse; (paper) arrollarse. ● n rizo m. **~er** /'kɜ:lə(r)/ n bigudí m, rulo m. **~y** /'kɜ:lɪ/ a (**-ier, -iest**) rizado

currant /'kʌrənt/ n pasa f de Corinto

currency /'kʌrənsɪ/ n moneda f; (acceptance) uso m (corriente)

current /'kʌrənt/ a & n corriente (f). **~ events** asuntos mpl de actualidad. **~ly** adv actualmente

curriculum /kə'rɪkjʊləm/ n (pl **-la**) programa m de estudios. **~ vitae** n curriculum m vitae

curry¹ /'kʌrɪ/ n curry m

curry² /'kʌrɪ/ vt. **~ favour with** congraciarse con

curse /kɜ:s/ n maldición f; (oath) palabrota f. ● vt maldecir. ● vi decir palabrotas

cursory /'kɜ:sərɪ/ a superficial

curt /kɜ:t/ a brusco

curtail /kɜ:'teɪl/ vt abreviar; reducir (expenses)

curtain /'kɜ:tn/ n cortina f; (in theatre) telón m

curtsy /'kɜ:tsɪ/ n reverencia f. ● vi hacer una reverencia

curve /kɜ:v/ n curva f. ● vt encurvar. ● vi encorvarse; (road) torcerse

cushion /'kʊʃn/ n cojín m. ● vt amortiguar ⟨a blow⟩; (fig) proteger

cushy /'kʊʃɪ/ a (-ier, -iest) (fam) fácil

custard /'kʌstəd/ n natillas fpl

custodian /kʌ'stəʊdɪən/ n custodio m

custody /'kʌstədɪ/ n custodia f. **be in ∼** (jurid) estar detenido

custom /'kʌstəm/ n costumbre f; (com) clientela f

customary /'kʌstəmərɪ/ a acostumbrado

customer /'kʌstəmə(r)/ n cliente m

customs /'kʌstəmz/ npl aduana f. **∼ officer** n aduanero m

cut /kʌt/ vt/i (pt **cut**, pres p **cutting**) cortar; reducir ⟨prices⟩. ● n corte m; (reduction) reducción f. **∼ across** atravesar. **∼ back, ∼ down** reducir. **∼ in** interrumpir. **∼ off** cortar; (phone) desconectar; (fig) aislar. **∼ out** recortar; (omit) suprimir. **∼ through** atravesar. **∼ up** cortar en pedazos. **be ∼ up about** (fig) afligirse por

cute /kjuːt/ a (-er, -est) (fam) listo; (Amer) mono

cuticle /'kjuːtɪkl/ n cutícula f

cutlery /'kʌtlərɪ/ n cubiertos mpl

cutlet /'kʌtlɪt/ n chuleta f

cut-price /'kʌtpraɪs/ a a precio reducido

cut-throat /'kʌtθrəʊt/ a despiadado

cutting /'kʌtɪŋ/ a cortante; ⟨remark⟩ mordaz. ● n (from newspaper) recorte m; (of plant) esqueje m

cyanide /'saɪənaɪd/ n cianuro m

cybernetics /saɪbə'netɪks/ n cibernética f

cyclamen /'sɪkləmən/ n ciclamen m

cycle /'saɪkl/ n ciclo m; (bicycle) bicicleta f. ● vi ir en bicicleta

cyclic(al) /'saɪklɪk(l)/ a cíclico

cycli|ng /'saɪklɪŋ/ n ciclismo m. **∼st** n ciclista m & f

cyclone /'saɪkləʊn/ n ciclón m

cylind|er /'sɪlɪndə(r)/ n cilindro m. **∼er head** (auto) n culata f. **∼rical** /-'lɪndrɪkl/ a cilíndrico

cymbal /'sɪmbl/ n címbalo m

cynic /'sɪnɪk/ n cínico m. **∼al** a cínico. **∼ism** /-sɪzəm/ n cinismo m

cypress /'saɪprəs/ n ciprés m

Cypr|iot /'sɪprɪət/ a & n chipriota (m & f). **∼us** /'saɪprəs/ n Chipre f

cyst /sɪst/ n quiste m

czar /zɑː(r)/ n zar m

Czech /tʃek/ a & n checo (m). **the ∼ Republic** n la república f Checa

Czechoslovak /tʃekəʊ'sləʊvæk/ a & n (history) checoslovaco (m). **∼ia** /-ə'vækɪə/ n (history) Checoslovaquia f

D

dab /dæb/ vt (pt **dabbed**) tocar ligeramente. ● n toque m suave. **a ∼ of** un poquito de

dabble /'dæbl/ vi. **∼ in** meterse (superficialmente) en. **∼r** /ə(r)/ n aficionado m

dad /dæd/ n (fam) papá m. **∼dy** n (children's use) papá m. **∼dy-long-legs** n típula f

daffodil /'dæfədɪl/ n narciso m

daft /dɑːft/ a (-er, -est) tonto

dagger /'dægə(r)/ n puñal m

dahlia /'deɪlɪə/ n dalia f

daily /'deɪlɪ/ a diario. ● adv diariamente, cada día. ● n diario m; (cleaner, fam) asistenta f

dainty /'deɪntɪ/ a (-ier, -iest) delicado

dairy /'deərɪ/ n vaquería f; (shop) lechería f. ● a lechero

dais /deɪːs/ n estrado m

daisy /'deɪzɪ/ n margarita f

dale /deɪl/ n valle m

dally /'dælɪ/ vi tardar; (waste time) perder el tiempo

dam /dæm/ n presa f. ● vt (pt **dammed**) embalsar

damag|e /'dæmɪdʒ/ n daño m; (pl, jurid) daños mpl y perjuicios mpl. ● vt (fig) dañar, estropear. **∼ing** a perjudicial

damask /'dæməsk/ n damasco m

dame /deɪm/ n (old use) dama f; (Amer, sl) chica f

damn /dæm/ vt condenar; (curse) maldecir. ● int ¡córcholis! ● a maldito. ● n. **I don't care a ∼** (no) me importa un comino. **∼ation** /-'neɪʃn/ n condenación f, perdición f

damp /dæmp/ n humedad f. ● a (-er, -est) húmedo. ● vt mojar; (fig) ahogar. **∼er** /'dæmpə(r)/ n apagador m, sordina f; (fig) aguafiestas m invar. **∼ness** n humedad f

damsel /'dæmzl/ n (old use) doncella f

dance /dɑːns/ vt/i bailar. ● n baile m. **∼hall** n salón m de baile. **∼r**

/-ə(r)/ *n* bailador *m*; (*professional*) bailarín *m*

dandelion /'dændɪlaɪən/ *n* diente *m* de león

dandruff /'dændrʌf/ *n* caspa *f*

dandy /'dændɪ/ *n* petimetre *m*

Dane /deɪn/ *n* danés *m*

danger /'deɪndʒə(r)/ *n* peligro *m*; (*risk*) riesgo *m*. **~ous** *a* peligroso

dangle /'dæŋgl/ *vt* balancear. ● *vi* suspender, colgar

Danish /'deɪnɪʃ/ *a* danés. ● *m* (*lang*) danés *m*

dank /dæŋk/ *a* (**-er, -est**) húmedo, malsano

dare /deə(r)/ *vt* desafiar. ● *vi* atreverse a. **I ~ say** probablemente. ● *n* desafío *m*

daredevil /'deədevl/ *n* atrevido *m*

daring /'deərɪŋ/ *a* atrevido

dark /dɑːk/ *a* (**-er, -est**) oscuro; (*gloomy*) sombrío; ⟨*skin, hair*⟩ moreno. ● *n* oscuridad *f*; (*nightfall*) atardecer. **in the ~** a oscuras. **~en** /'dɑːkən/ *vt* oscurecer. ● *vi* oscurecerse. **~ horse** *n* persona *f* de talentos desconocidos. **~ness** *n* oscuridad *f*. **~room** *n* cámara *f* oscura

darling /'dɑːlɪŋ/ *a* querido. ● *n* querido *m*

darn /dɑːn/ *vt* zurcir

dart /dɑːt/ *n* dardo *m*. ● *vi* lanzarse; (*run*) precipitarse. **~board** /'dɑːtbɔːd/ *n* blanco *m*. **~s** *npl* los dardos *mpl*

dash /dæʃ/ *vi* precipitarse. **~ off** marcharse apresuradamente. **~ out** salir corriendo. ● *vt* lanzar; (*break*) romper; defraudar ⟨*hopes*⟩. ● *n* carrera *f*; (*small amount*) poquito *m*; (*stroke*) raya *f*. **cut a ~** causar sensación

dashboard /'dæʃbɔːd/ *n* tablero *m* de mandos

dashing /'dæʃɪŋ/ *a* vivo; (*showy*) vistoso

data /'deɪtə/ *npl* datos *mpl*. **~ processing** *n* proceso *m* de datos

date[1] /deɪt/ *n* fecha *f*; (*fam*) cita *f*. **to ~** hasta la fecha. ● *vt* fechar; (*go out with, fam*) salir con. ● *vi* datar; (*be old-fashioned*) quedar anticuado

date[2] /deɪt/ *n* (*fruit*) dátil *m*

dated /'deɪtɪd/ *a* pasado de moda

daub /dɔːb/ *vt* embadurnar

daughter /'dɔːtə(r)/ *n* hija *f*. **~-in-law** *n* nuera *f*

daunt /dɔːnt/ *vt* intimidar

dauntless /'dɔːntlɪs/ *a* intrépido

dawdle /'dɔːdl/ *vi* andar despacio; (*waste time*) perder el tiempo. **~r** /-ə(r)/ *n* rezagado *m*

dawn /dɔːn/ *n* amanecer *m*. ● *vi* amanecer; (*fig*) nacer. **it ~ed on me that** caí en la cuenta de que, comprendí que

day /deɪ/ *n* día *m*; (*whole day*) jornada *f*; (*period*) época *f*. **~break** *n* amanecer *m*. **~dream** *n* ensueño *m*. ● *vi* soñar despierto. **~light** /'deɪlaɪt/ *n* luz *f* del día. **~time** /'deɪtaɪm/ *n* día *m*

daze /deɪz/ *vt* aturdir. ● *n* aturdimiento *m*. **in a ~** aturdido

dazzle /'dæzl/ *vt* deslumbrar

deacon /'diːkən/ *n* diácono *m*

dead /ded/ *a* muerto; (*numb*) entumecido. **~ centre** justo en medio. ● *adv* completamente. **~ beat** rendido. **~ on time** justo a tiempo. **~ slow** muy lento. **stop ~** parar en seco. ● *n* muertos *mpl*. **in the ~ of night** en plena noche. **the ~** los muertos *mpl*. **~en** /'dedn/ *vt* amortiguar ⟨*sound, blow*⟩; calmar ⟨*pain*⟩. **~ end** *n* callejón *m* sin salida. **~ heat** *n* empate *m*

deadline /'dedlaɪn/ *n* fecha *f* tope, fin *m* de plazo

deadlock /'dedlɒk/ *n* punto *m* muerto

deadly /'dedlɪ/ *a* (**-ier, -iest**) mortal; (*harmful*) nocivo; (*dreary*) aburrido

deadpan /'dedpæn/ *a* impasible

deaf /def/ *a* (**-er, -est**) sordo. **~-aid** *n* audífono *m*. **~en** /'defn/ *vt* ensordecer. **~ening** *a* ensordecedor. **~mute** *n* sordomudo *m*. **~ness** *n* sordera *f*

deal /diːl/ *n* (*transaction*) negocio *m*; (*agreement*) pacto *m*; (*of cards*) reparto *m*; (*treatment*) trato *m*; (*amount*) cantidad *f*. **a great ~** muchísimo. ● *vt* (*pt* **dealt**) distribuir; dar ⟨*a blow, cards*⟩. ● *vi*. **~ in** comerciar en. **~ with** tratar con ⟨*person*⟩; tratar de ⟨*subject etc*⟩; ocuparse de ⟨*problem etc*⟩. **~er** *n* comerciante *m*. **~ings** /'diːlɪŋz/ *npl* trato *m*

dean /diːn/ *n* deán *m*; (*univ*) decano *m*

dear /dɪə(r)/ *a* (**-er, -est**) querido; (*expensive*) caro. ● *n* querido *m*; (*child*) pequeño *m*. ● *adv* caro. ● *int* ¡Dios mío! **~ me!** ¡Dios mío! **~ly** *adv*

tiernamente; (*pay*) caro; (*very much*)
muchísimo

dearth /dɜːθ/ *n* escasez *f*

death /deθ/ *n* muerte *f*. ~ **duty** *n*
derechos *mpl* reales. ~**ly** *a* mortal;
‹*silence*› profundo. ● *adv* como la
muerte. ~**'s head** *n* calavera *f*. ~
trap *n* lugar *m* peligroso.

débâcle /deɪˈbɑːkl/ *n* fracaso *m*,
desastre *m*

debar /dɪˈbɑː(r)/ *vt* (*pt* **debarred**) excluir

debase /dɪˈbeɪs/ *vt* degradar

debat|able /dɪˈbeɪtəbl/ *a* discutible.
~**e** /dɪˈbeɪt/ *n* debate *m*. ● *vt* debatir,
discutir. ● *vi* discutir; (*consider*) considerar

debauch /dɪˈbɔːtʃ/ *vt* corromper.
~**ery** *n* libertinaje *m*

debilit|ate /dɪˈbɪlɪteɪt/ *vt* debilitar.
~**y** /dɪˈbɪlətɪ/ *n* debilidad *f*

debit /ˈdebɪt/ *n* debe *m*. ● *vt*. ~ **s.o.'s**
account cargar en cuenta a uno

debonair /debəˈneə(r)/ *a* alegre

debris /ˈdebriː/ *n* escombros *mpl*

debt /det/ *n* deuda *f*. **be in** ~ tener
deudas. ~**or** *n* deudor *m*

debutante /ˈdebjuːtɑːnt/ *n* (*old use*)
debutante *f*

decade /ˈdekeɪd/ *n* década *f*

decaden|ce /ˈdekədəns/ *n* deca-
dencia *f*. ~**t** /ˈdekədənt/ *a* deca-
dente

decant /dɪˈkænt/ *vt* decantar. ~**er**
/ə(r)/ *n* garrafa *f*

decapitate /dɪˈkæpɪteɪt/ *vt* decapitar

decay /dɪˈkeɪ/ *vi* decaer; ‹*tooth*› ca-
riarse. ● *n* decadencia *f*; (*of tooth*) caries *f*

deceased /dɪˈsiːst/ *a* difunto

deceit /dɪˈsiːt/ *n* engaño *m*. ~**ful** *a*
falso. ~**fully** *adv* falsamente

deceive /dɪˈsiːv/ *vt* engañar

December /dɪˈsembə(r)/ *n* diciembre *m*

decen|cy /ˈdiːsənsɪ/ *n* decencia *f*. ~**t**
/ˈdiːsnt/ *a* decente; (*good*, *fam*)
bueno; (*kind*, *fam*) amable. ~**tly** *adv*
decentemente

decentralize /diːˈsentrəlaɪz/ *vt* descentralizar

decepti|on /dɪˈsepʃn/ *n* engaño *m*.
~**ve** /dɪˈseptɪv/ *a* engañoso

decibel /ˈdesɪbel/ *n* decibel(io) *m*

decide /dɪˈsaɪd/ *vt/i* decidir. ~**d**
/-ɪd/ *a* resuelto; (*unquestionable*)

indudable. ~**dly** /-ɪdlɪ/ *adv* deci-
didamente; (*unquestionably*) indudablemente

decimal /ˈdesɪml/ *a* & *n* decimal (*f*).
~ **point** *n* coma *f* (decimal)

decimate /ˈdesɪmeɪt/ *vt* diezmar

decipher /dɪˈsaɪfə(r)/ *vt* descifrar

decision /dɪˈsɪʒn/ *n* decisión *f*

decisive /dɪˈsaɪsɪv/ *a* decisivo; ‹*manner*› decidido. ~**ly** *adv* de manera
decisiva

deck /dek/ *n* cubierta *f*; (*of cards*,
Amer) baraja *f*. ~ **top** ~ (*of bus*)
imperial *m*. ● *vt* adornar. ~**-chair** *n*
tumbona *f*

declaim /dɪˈkleɪm/ *vt* declamar

declar|ation /dekləˈreɪʃn/ *n* de-
claración *f*. ~**e** /dɪˈkleə(r)/ *vt* declarar

decline /dɪˈklaɪn/ *vt* rehusar; (*gram*)
declinar. ● *vi* disminuir; (*deteriorate*) deteriorarse; (*fall*) bajar. ● *n*
decadencia *f*; (*decrease*) disminución
f; (*fall*) baja *f*

decode /diːˈkəʊd/ *vt* descifrar

decompos|e /diːkəmˈpəʊz/ *vt* des-
componer. ● *vi* descomponerse. ~**i-
tion** /-ɒmpəˈzɪʃn/ *n* descomposición
f

décor /ˈdeɪkɔː(r)/ *n* decoración *f*

decorat|e /ˈdekəreɪt/ *vt* decorar; em-
papelar y pintar ‹*room*›. ~**ion**
/-ˈreɪʃn/ *n* (*act*) decoración *f*; (*ornament*) adorno *m*. ~**ive** /-ətɪv/ *a*
decorativo. ~**or** /ˈdekəreɪtə(r)/ *n*
pintor *m* decorador. **interior** ~**or**
decorador *m* de interiores

decorum /dɪˈkɔːrəm/ *n* decoro *m*

decoy /ˈdiːkɔɪ/ *n* señuelo *m*. /dɪˈkɔɪ/
vt atraer con señuelo

decrease /dɪˈkriːs/ *vt* disminuir. ● *vi*
disminuirse. /ˈdiːkriːs/ *n* disminución *f*

decree /dɪˈkriː/ *n* decreto *m*; (*jurid*)
sentencia *f*. ● *vt* (*pt* **decreed**)
decretar

decrepit /dɪˈkrepɪt/ *a* decrépito

decry /dɪˈkraɪ/ *vt* denigrar

dedicat|e /ˈdedɪkeɪt/ *vt* dedicar.
~**ion** /-ˈkeɪʃn/ *n* dedicación *f*; (*in
book*) dedicatoria *f*

deduce /dɪˈdjuːs/ *vt* deducir

deduct /dɪˈdʌkt/ *vt* deducir. ~**ion**
/-ʃn/ *n* deducción *f*

deed /diːd/ *n* hecho *m*; (*jurid*)
escritura *f*

deem /diːm/ *vt* juzgar, considerar

deep /diːp/ a (**-er**, **est**) adv profundo. **get into ~ waters** meterse en honduras. **go off the ~ end** enfadarse. ● adv profundamente. **be ~ in thought** estar absorto en sus pensamientos. **~en** /ˈdiːpən/ vt profundizar. ● vi hacerse más profundo. **~freeze** n congelador m. **~ly** adv profundamente

deer /dɪə(r)/ n invar ciervo m

deface /dɪˈfeɪs/ vt desfigurar

defamation /defəˈmeɪʃn/ n difamación f

default /dɪˈfɔːlt/ vi faltar. ● n. **by ~** en rebeldía. **in ~ of** en ausencia de

defeat /dɪˈfiːt/ vt vencer; (frustrate) frustrar. ● n derrota f; (of plan etc) fracaso m. **~ism** /dɪˈfiːtɪzm/ n derrotismo m. **~ist** /dɪˈfiːtɪst/ n derrotista m & f

defect /ˈdiːfekt/ n defecto m. /dɪˈfekt/ vi desertar. **~ to** pasar a. **~ion** /dɪˈfekʃn/ n deserción f. **~ive** /dɪˈfektɪv/ a defectuoso

defence /dɪˈfens/ n defensa f. **~less** a indefenso

defend /dɪˈfend/ vt defender. **~ant** n (jurid) acusado m

defensive /dɪˈfensɪv/ a defensivo. ● n defensiva f

defer /dɪˈfɜː(r)/ vt (pt **deferred**) aplazar

deferen|ce /ˈdefərəns/ n deferencia f. **~tial** /-ˈrenʃl/ a deferente

defian|ce /dɪˈfaɪəns/ n desafío m. **in ~ce of** a despecho de. **~t** a desafiante. **~tly** adv con tono retador

deficien|cy /dɪˈfɪʃənsɪ/ n falta f. **~t** /dɪˈfɪʃnt/ a deficiente. **be ~t in** carecer de

deficit /ˈdefɪsɪt/ n déficit m

defile /dɪˈfaɪl/ vt ensuciar; (fig) deshonrar

define /dɪˈfaɪn/ vt definir

definite /ˈdefɪnɪt/ a determinado; (clear) claro; (firm) categórico. **~ly** adv claramente; (certainly) seguramente

definition /defɪˈnɪʃn/ n definición f

definitive /dɪˈfɪnətɪv/ a definitivo

deflat|e /dɪˈfleɪt/ vt desinflar. ● vi desinflarse. **~ion** /-ʃn/ n (com) deflación f

deflect /dɪˈflekt/ vt desviar. ● vi desviarse

deform /dɪˈfɔːm/ vt deformar. **~ed** a deforme. **~ity** n deformidad f

defraud /dɪˈfrɔːd/ vt defraudar

defray /dɪˈfreɪ/ vt pagar

defrost /diːˈfrɒst/ vt descongelar

deft /deft/ a (**-er**, **-est**) hábil. **~ness** n destreza f

defunct /dɪˈfʌŋkt/ a difunto

defuse /diːˈfjuːz/ vt desactivar ‹bomb›; (fig) calmar

defy /dɪˈfaɪ/ vt desafiar; (resist) resistir

degenerate /dɪˈdʒenəreɪt/ vi degenerar. /dɪˈdʒenərət/ a & n degenerado (m)

degrad|ation /degrəˈdeɪʃn/ n degradación f. **~e** /dɪˈɡreɪd/ vt degradar

degree /dɪˈɡriː/ n grado m; (univ) licenciatura f; (rank) rango m. **to a certain ~** hasta cierto punto. **to a ~** (fam) sumamente

dehydrate /diːˈhaɪdreɪt/ vt deshidratar

de-ice /diːˈaɪs/ vt descongelar

deign /deɪn/ vi. **~ to** dignarse

deity /ˈdiːɪtɪ/ n deidad f

deject|ed /dɪˈdʒektɪd/ a desanimado. **~ion** /-ʃn/ n abatimiento m

delay /dɪˈleɪ/ vt retardar; (postpone) aplazar. ● vi demorarse. ● n demora f

delectable /dɪˈlektəbl/ a deleitable

delegat|e /ˈdelɪɡeɪt/ vt delegar. /ˈdelɪɡət/ n delegado m. **~ion** /-ˈɡeɪʃn/ n delegación f

delet|e /dɪˈliːt/ vt tachar. **~ion** /-ʃn/ n tachadura f

deliberat|e /dɪˈlɪbəreɪt/ vt/i deliberar. /dɪˈlɪbərət/ a intencionado; ‹steps etc› pausado. **~ely** adv a propósito. **~ion** /-ˈreɪʃn/ n deliberación f

delica|cy /ˈdelɪkəsɪ/ n delicadeza f; (food) manjar m; (sweet food) golosina f. **~te** /ˈdelɪkət/ a delicado

delicatessen /delɪkəˈtesn/ n charcutería f fina

delicious /dɪˈlɪʃəs/ a delicioso

delight /dɪˈlaɪt/ n placer m. ● vt encantar. ● vi deleitarse. **~ed** a encantado. **~ful** a delicioso

delineat|e /dɪˈlɪnɪeɪt/ vt delinear. **~ion** /-ˈeɪʃn/ n delineación f

delinquen|cy /dɪˈlɪŋkwənsɪ/ n delincuencia f. **~t** /dɪˈlɪŋkwənt/ a & n delincuente (m & f)

deliri|ous /dɪˈlɪrɪəs/ a delirante. **~um** n delirio m

deliver /dɪˈlɪvə(r)/ vt entregar; (utter) pronunciar; (aim) lanzar; (set free) librar; (med) asistir al parto de.

~ance n liberación f. **~y** n entrega f; (of post) reparto m; (med) parto m

delta /'deltə/ n (geog) delta m

delude /dɪ'luːd/ vt engañar. **~ o.s.** engañarse

deluge /'deljuːdʒ/ n diluvio m

delusion /dɪ'luːʒn/ n ilusión f

de luxe /dɪ'lʌks/ a de lujo

delve /delv/ vi cavar. **~ into** (investigate) investigar

demagogue /'deməgɒg/ n demagogo m

demand /dɪ'mɑːnd/ vt exigir. ● n petición f; (claim) reclamación f; (com) demanda f. **in ~** muy popular, muy solicitado. **on ~** a solicitud. **~ing** a exigente. **~s** npl exigencias fpl

demarcation /diːmɑːˈkeɪʃn/ n demarcación f

demean /dɪ'miːn/ vt. **~ o.s.** degradarse. **~our** /dɪ'miːnə(r)/ n conducta f

demented /dɪ'mentɪd/ a demente

demerara /demə'reərə/ n. **~ (sugar)** n azúcar m moreno

demise /dɪ'maɪz/ n fallecimiento m

demo /'deməʊ/ n (pl -os) (fam) manifestación f

demobilize /diː'məʊbəlaɪz/ vt desmovilizar

democra|cy /dɪ'mɒkrəsɪ/ n democracia f. **~t** /'deməkræt/ n demócrata m & f. **~tic** /-'krætɪk/ a democrático

demoli|sh /dɪ'mɒlɪʃ/ vt derribar. **~tion** /demə'lɪʃn/ n demolición f

demon /'diːmən/ n demonio m

demonstrat|e /'demənstreɪt/ vt demostrar. ● vi manifestarse, hacer una manifestación. **~ion** /-'streɪʃn/ n demostración f; (pol etc) manifestación f

demonstrative /dɪ'mɒnstrətɪv/ a demostrativo

demonstrator /'demənstreɪtə(r)/ n demostrador m: (pol etc) manifestante m & f

demoralize /dɪ'mɒrəlaɪz/ vt desmoralizar

demote /dɪ'məʊt/ vt degradar

demure /dɪ'mjʊə(r)/ a recatado

den /den/ n (of animal) guarida f, madriguera f

denial /dɪ'naɪəl/ n denegación f; (statement) desmentimiento m

denigrate /'denɪgreɪt/ vt denigrar

denim /'denɪm/ n dril m (de algodón azul grueso). **~s** npl pantalón m vaquero

Denmark /'denmɑːk/ n Dinamarca f

denomination /dɪnɒmɪ'neɪʃn/ n denominación f; (relig) secta f

denote /dɪ'nəʊt/ vt denotar

denounce /dɪ'naʊns/ vt denunciar

dens|e /dens/ a (-er, -est) espeso; (person) torpe. **~ely** adv densamente. **~ity** n densidad f

dent /dent/ n abolladura f. ● vt abollar

dental /'dentl/ a dental. **~ surgeon** n dentista m & f

dentist /'dentɪst/ n dentista m & f. **~ry** n odontología f

denture /'dentʃə(r)/ n dentadura f postiza

denude /dɪ'njuːd/ vt desnudar; (fig) despojar

denunciation /dɪnʌnsɪ'eɪʃn/ n denuncia f

deny /dɪ'naɪ/ vt negar; desmentir (rumour); (disown) renegar

deodorant /diː'əʊdərənt/ a & n desodorante (m)

depart /dɪ'pɑːt/ vi marcharse; (train etc) salir. **~ from** apartarse de

department /dɪ'pɑːtmənt/ n departamento m; (com) sección f. **~ store** n grandes almacenes mpl

departure /dɪ'pɑːtʃə(r)/ n partida f; (of train etc) salida f. **~ from** (fig) desviación f

depend /dɪ'pend/ vi depender. **~ on** depender de; (rely) contar con. **~able** a seguro. **~ant** /dɪ'pendənt/ n familiar m & f dependiente. **~ence** n dependencia f. **~ent** a dependiente. **be ~ent on** depender de

depict /dɪ'pɪkt/ vt pintar; (in words) describir

deplete /dɪ'pliːt/ vt agotar

deplor|able /dɪ'plɔːrəbl/ a lamentable. **~e** /dɪ'plɔː(r)/ vt lamentar

deploy /dɪ'plɔɪ/ vt desplegar. ● vi desplegarse

depopulate /diː'pɒpjʊleɪt/ vt despoblar

deport /dɪ'pɔːt/ vt deportar. **~ation** /diːpɔː'teɪʃn/ n deportación f

depose /dɪ'pəʊz/ vt deponer

deposit /dɪ'pɒzɪt/ vt (pt **deposited**) depositar. ● n depósito m. **~or** n depositante m & f

depot /'depəʊ/ n depósito m; (Amer) estación f

deprav|e /dɪ'preɪv/ vt depravar. **~ity** /-'prævətɪ/ n depravación f

deprecate /'deprɪkeɪt/ vt desaprobar

depreciat|e /dɪ'priːʃɪeɪt/ vt depreciar. ● vi depreciarse. **~ion** /-'eɪʃn/ n depreciación f

depress /dɪ'pres/ vt deprimir; (press down) apretar. **~ion** /-ʃn/ n depresión f

depriv|ation /deprɪ'veɪʃn/ n privación f. **~e** /dɪ'praɪv/ vt. **~ of** privar de

depth /depθ/ n profundidad f. **be out of one's ~** perder pie; (fig) meterse en honduras. **in the ~s of** en lo más hondo de

deputation /depjʊ'teɪʃn/ n diputación f

deputize /'depjʊtaɪz/ vi. **~ for** sustituir a

deputy /'depjʊtɪ/ n sustituto m. **~ chairman** n vicepresidente m

derail /dɪ'reɪl/ vt hacer descarrilar. **~ment** n descarrilamiento m

deranged /dɪ'reɪndʒd/ a ⟨mind⟩ trastornado

derelict /'derəlɪkt/ a abandonado

deri|de /dɪ'raɪd/ vt mofarse de. **~sion** /-'rɪʒn/ n mofa f. **~sive** a burlón; **~sory** /dɪ'raɪsərɪ/ a mofador; ⟨offer etc⟩ irrisorio

deriv|ation /derɪ'veɪʃn/ n derivación f. **~ative** /dɪ'rɪvətɪv/ a & n derivado (m). **~e** /dɪ'raɪv/ vt/i derivar

derogatory /dɪ'rɒgətrɪ/ a despectivo

derv /dɜːv/ n gasóleo m

descen|d /dɪ'send/ vt/i descender, bajar. **~dant** n descendiente m & f. **~t** /dɪ'sent/ n descenso m; (lineage) descendencia f

descri|be /dɪs'kraɪb/ vt describir. **~ption** /-'krɪpʃn/ n descripción f. **~ptive** /-'krɪptɪv/ a descriptivo

desecrat|e /'desɪkreɪt/ vt profanar. **~ion** /-'kreɪʃn/ n profanación f

desert[1] /dɪ'zɜːt/ vt abandonar. ● vi (mil) desertar

desert[2] /'dezət/ a & n desierto (m)

deserter /dɪ'zɜːtə(r)/ n desertor m

deserts /dɪ'zɜːts/ npl lo merecido. **get one's ~** llevarse su merecido

deserv|e /dɪ'zɜːv/ vt merecer. **~edly** adv merecidamente. **~ing** a ⟨person⟩ digno de; ⟨action⟩ meritorio

design /dɪ'zaɪn/ n diseño m; (plan) proyecto m; (pattern) modelo m; (aim) propósito m. **have ~s on** poner la mira en. ● vt diseñar; (plan) proyectar

designat|e /'dezɪgneɪt/ vt designar; (appoint) nombrar. **~ion** /-'neɪʃn/ n denominación f; (appointment) nombramiento m

designer /dɪ'zaɪnə(r)/ n diseñador m; (of clothing) modisto m; (in theatre) escenógrafo m

desirab|ility /dɪzaɪərə'bɪlətɪ/ n conveniencia f. **~le** /dɪ'zaɪərəbl/ a deseable

desire /dɪ'zaɪə(r)/ n deseo m. ● vt desear

desist /dɪ'zɪst/ vi desistir

desk /desk/ n escritorio m; (at school) pupitre m; (in hotel) recepción f; (com) caja f

desolat|e /'desələt/ a desolado; (uninhabited) deshabitado. **~ion** /-'leɪʃn/ n desolación f

despair /dɪ'speə(r)/ n desesperación f. ● vi. **~ of** desesperarse de

desperat|e /'despərət/ a desesperado; (dangerous) peligroso. **~ely** adv desesperadamente. **~ion** /-'reɪʃn/ n desesperación f

despicable /dɪ'spɪkəbl/ a despreciable

despise /dɪ'spaɪz/ vt despreciar

despite /dɪ'spaɪt/ prep a pesar de

desponden|cy /dɪ'spɒndənsɪ/ n abatimiento m. **~t** /dɪ'spɒndənt/ a desanimado

despot /'despɒt/ n déspota m

dessert /dɪ'zɜːt/ n postre m. **~spoon** n cuchara f de postre

destination /destɪ'neɪʃn/ n destino m

destine /'destɪn/ vt destinar

destiny /'destɪnɪ/ n destino m

destitute /'destɪtjuːt/ a indigente. **~ of** desprovisto de

destroy /dɪ'strɔɪ/ vt destruir

destroyer /dɪ'strɔɪə(r)/ n (naut) destructor m

destructi|on /dɪ'strʌkʃn/ n destrucción f. **~ve** a destructivo

desultory /'desəltrɪ/ a irregular

detach /dɪ'tætʃ/ vt separar. **~able** a separable. **~ed** a separado. **~ed house** n chalet m. **~ment** /dɪ'tætʃmənt/ n separación f; (mil) destacamento m; (fig) indiferencia f

detail /'di:teɪl/ n detalle m. ● vt detallar; (mil) destacar. ~ed a detallado

detain /dɪ'teɪn/ vt detener; (delay) retener. ~ee /di:teɪ'ni:/ n detenido m

detect /dɪ'tekt/ vt percibir; (discover) descubrir. ~ion /-ʃn/ n descubrimiento m, detección f. ~or n detector m

detective /dɪ'tektɪv/ n detective m. ~ story n novela f policíaca

detention /dɪ'tenʃn/ n detención f

deter /dɪ'tɜ:(r)/ vt (pt deterred) disuadir; (prevent) impedir

detergent /dɪ'tɜ:dʒənt/ a & n detergente (m)

deteriorat|e /dɪ'tɪərɪəreɪt/ vi deteriorarse. ~ion /-'reɪʃn/ n deterioro m

determination /dɪtɜ:mɪ'neɪʃn/ n determinación f

determine /dɪ'tɜ:mɪn/ vt determinar; (decide) decidir. ~d a determinado; (resolute) resuelto

deterrent /dɪ'terənt/ n fuerza f de disuasión

detest /dɪ'test/ vt aborrecer. ~able a odioso

detonat|e /'detəneɪt/ vt hacer detonar. ● vi detonar. ~ion /-'neɪʃn/ n detonación f. ~or n detonador m

detour /'di:tʊə(r)/ n desviación f

detract /dɪ'trækt/ vi. ~ from (lessen) disminuir

detriment /'detrɪmənt/ n perjuicio m. ~al /-'mentl/ a perjudicial

devalu|ation /di:vælju:'eɪʃn/ n desvalorización f. ~e /di:'vælju:/ vt desvalorizar

devastat|e /'devəsteɪt/ vt devastar. ~ing a devastador; (fig) arrollador

develop /dɪ'veləp/ vt desarrollar; contraer ⟨illness⟩; urbanizar ⟨land⟩. ● vi desarrollarse; (show) aparecerse. ~er n (foto) revelador m. ~ing country n país m en vías de desarrollo. ~ment n desarrollo m. (new) ~ment novedad f

deviant /'di:vɪənt/ a desviado

deviat|e /'di:vɪeɪt/ vi desviarse. ~ion /-'eɪʃn/ n desviación f

device /dɪ'vaɪs/ n dispositivo m; (scheme) estratagema f

devil /'devl/ n diablo m. ~ish a diabólico

devious /'di:vɪəs/ a tortuoso

devise /dɪ'vaɪz/ vt idear

devoid /dɪ'vɔɪd/ a. ~ of desprovisto de

devolution /di:və'lu:ʃn/ n descentralización f; (of power) delegación f

devot|e /dɪ'vəʊt/ vt dedicar. ~ed a leal. ~edly adv con devoción f. ~ee /devə'ti:/ n partidario m. ~ion /-ʃn/ n dedicación f. ~ions npl (relig) oraciones fpl

devour /dɪ'vaʊə(r)/ vt devorar

devout /dɪ'vaʊt/ a devoto

dew /dju:/ n rocío m

dext|erity /dek'sterətɪ/ n destreza f. ~(e)rous /'dekstrəs/ a diestro

diabet|es /daɪə'bi:ti:z/ n diabetes f. ~ic /-'betɪk/ a & n diabético (m)

diabolical /daɪə'bɒlɪkl/ a diabólico

diadem /'daɪədem/ n diadema f

diagnos|e /'daɪəgnəʊz/ vt diagnosticar. ~is /daɪəg'nəʊsɪs/ n (pl -oses /-siz/) diagnóstico m

diagonal /daɪ'ægənl/ a & n diagonal (f)

diagram /'daɪəgræm/ n diagrama m

dial /'daɪəl/ n cuadrante m; (on phone) disco m. ● vt (pt dialled) marcar

dialect /'daɪəlekt/ n dialecto m

dial: ~ling code n prefijo m. ~ling tone n señal f para marcar

dialogue /'daɪəlɒg/ n diálogo m

diameter /daɪ'æmɪtə(r)/ n diámetro m

diamond /'daɪəmənd/ n diamante m; (shape) rombo m. ~s npl (cards) diamantes mpl

diaper /'daɪəpə(r)/ n (Amer) pañal m

diaphanous /daɪ'æfənəs/ a diáfano

diaphragm /'daɪəfræm/ n diafragma m

diarrhoea /daɪə'rɪə/ n diarrea f

diary /'daɪərɪ/ n diario m; (book) agenda f

diatribe /'daɪətraɪb/ n diatriba f

dice /daɪs/ n invar dado m. ● vt (culin) cortar en cubitos

dicey /'daɪsɪ/ a (sl) arriesgado

dictat|e /dɪk'teɪt/ vt/i dictar. ~es /'dɪkteɪts/ npl dictados mpl. ~ion /dɪk'teɪʃn/ n dictado m

dictator /dɪk'teɪtə(r)/ n dictador m. ~ship n dictadura f

diction /'dɪkʃn/ n dicción f

dictionary /'dɪkʃənərɪ/ n diccionario m

did /dɪd/ see **do**

didactic /daɪ'dæktɪk/ a didáctico

diddle /'dɪdl/ vt (sl) estafar

didn't /'dɪdnt/ = **did not**

die[1] /daɪ/ *vi* (*pres p* **dying**) morir. **be dying to** morirse por. **~ down** disminuir. **~ out** extinguirse

die[2] /daɪ/ *n* (*tec*) cuño *m*

die-hard /'daɪhɑːd/ *n* intransigente *m & f*

diesel /'diːzl/ *n* (*fuel*) gasóleo *m*. **~ engine** *n* motor *m* diesel

diet /'daɪət/ *n* alimentación *f*; (*restricted*) régimen *m*. ● *vi* estar a régimen. **~etic** /daɪə'tetɪk/ *a* dietético. **~itian** *n* dietético *m*

differ /'dɪfə(r)/ *vi* ser distinto; (*disagree*) no estar de acuerdo. **~ence** /'dɪfrəns/ *n* diferencia *f*; (*disagreement*) desacuerdo *m*. **~ent** /'dɪfrənt/ *a* distinto, diferente

differentia|l /dɪfə'renʃl/ *a & n* diferencial (*f*). **~te** /dɪfə'renʃɪeɪt/ *vt* diferenciar. ● *vi* diferenciarse

differently /'dɪfrəntlɪ/ *adv* de otra manera

difficult /'dɪfɪkəlt/ *a* difícil. **~y** *n* dificultad *f*

diffiden|ce /'dɪfɪdəns/ *n* falta *f* de confianza. **~t** /'dɪfɪdənt/ *a* que falta confianza

diffus|e /dɪ'fjuːs/ *a* difuso. /dɪ'fjuːz/ *vt* difundir. ● *vi* difundirse. **~ion** /-ʒn/ *n* difusión *f*

dig /dɪg/ *n* (*poke*) empujón *m*; (*poke with elbow*) codazo *m*; (*remark*) indirecta *f*; (*archaeol*) excavación *f*. ● *vt* (*pt* **dug**, *pres p* **digging**) cavar; (*thrust*) empujar. ● *vi* cavar. **~ out** extraer. **~ up** desenterrar. **~s** *npl* (*fam*) alojamiento *m*

digest /'daɪdʒest/ *n* resumen *m*. ● *vt* digerir. **~ible** *a* digerible. **~ion** /-ʃn/ *n* digestión *f*. **~ive** *a* digestivo

digger /'dɪgə(r)/ *n* (*mec*) excavadora *f*

digit /'dɪdʒɪt/ *n* cifra *f*; (*finger*) dedo *m*. **~al** /'dɪdʒɪtl/ *a* digital

dignif|ied /'dɪgnɪfaɪd/ *a* solemne. **~y** /'dɪgnɪfaɪ/ *vt* dignificar

dignitary /'dɪgnɪtərɪ/ *n* dignatario *m*

dignity /'dɪgnətɪ/ *n* dignidad *f*

digress /daɪ'gres/ *vi* divagar. **~ from** apartarse de. **~ion** /-ʃn/ *n* digresión *f*

dike /daɪk/ *n* dique *m*

dilapidated /dɪ'læpɪdeɪtɪd/ *a* ruinoso

dilat|e /daɪ'leɪt/ *vt* dilatar. ● *vi* dilatarse. **~ion** /-ʃn/ *n* dilatación *f*

dilatory /'dɪlətərɪ/ *a* dilatorio, lento

dilemma /daɪ'lemə/ *n* dilema *m*

diligen|ce /'dɪlɪdʒəns/ *n* diligencia *f*. **~t** /'dɪlɪdʒənt/ *a* diligente

dilly-dally /'dɪlɪdælɪ/ *vi* (*fam*) perder el tiempo

dilute /daɪ'ljuːt/ *vt* diluir

dim /dɪm/ *a* (**dimmer, dimmest**) (*weak*) débil; (*dark*) oscuro; (*stupid, fam*) torpe. ● *vt* (*pt* **dimmed**) amortiguar. ● *vi* apagarse. **~ the headlights** bajar los faros

dime /daɪm/ *n* (*Amer*) moneda *f* de diez centavos

dimension /daɪ'menʃn/ *n* dimensión *f*

diminish /dɪ'mɪnɪʃ/ *vt/i* disminuir

diminutive /dɪ'mɪnjʊtɪv/ *a* diminuto. ● *n* diminutivo *m*

dimness /'dɪmnɪs/ *n* debilidad *f*; (*of room etc*) oscuridad *f*

dimple /'dɪmpl/ *n* hoyuelo *m*

din /dɪn/ *n* jaleo *m*

dine /daɪn/ *vi* cenar. **~r** /-ə(r)/ *n* comensal *m & f*; (*rail*) coche *m* restaurante

dinghy /'dɪŋgɪ/ *n* (*inflatable*) bote *m* neumático

ding|iness /'dɪndʒɪnɪs/ *n* suciedad *f*. **~y** /'dɪndʒɪ/ *a* (**-ier, -iest**) miserable, sucio

dining-room /'daɪnɪŋruːm/ *n* comedor *m*

dinner /'dɪnə(r)/ *n* cena *f*. **~-jacket** *n* esmoquin *m*. **~ party** *n* cena *f*

dinosaur /'daɪnəsɔː(r)/ *n* dinosaurio *m*

dint /dɪnt/ *n*. **by ~ of** a fuerza de

diocese /'daɪəsɪs/ *n* diócesis *f*

dip /dɪp/ *vt* (*pt* **dipped**) sumergir. ● *vi* bajar. **~ into** hojear ‹*book*›. ● *n* (*slope*) inclinación *f*; (*in sea*) baño *m*

diphtheria /dɪf'θɪərɪə/ *n* difteria *f*

diphthong /'dɪfθɒŋ/ *n* diptongo *m*

diploma /dɪ'pləʊmə/ *n* diploma *m*

diplomacy /dɪ'pləʊməsɪ/ *n* diplomacia *f*

diplomat /'dɪpləmæt/ *n* diplomático *m*. **~ic** /-'mætɪk/ *a* diplomático

dipstick /'dɪpstɪk/ *n* (*auto*) varilla *f* del nivel de aceite

dire /daɪə(r)/ *a* (**-er, -est**) terrible; ‹*need, poverty*› extremo

direct /dɪ'rekt/ *a* directo. ● *adv* directamente. ● *vt* dirigir; (*show the way*) indicar

direction /dɪ'rekʃn/ *n* dirección *f*. **~s** *npl* instrucciones *fpl*

directly /dɪ'rektlɪ/ *adv* directamente; (*at once*) en seguida. ● *conj* (*fam*) en cuanto

director /dɪˈrektə(r)/ n director m

directory /dɪˈrektərɪ/ n guía f

dirge /dɜːdʒ/ n canto m fúnebre

dirt /dɜːt/ n suciedad f. **~-track** (sport) pista f de ceniza. **~y** /ˈdɜːtɪ/ a (-ier, -iest) sucio. **~y trick** n mala jugada f. **~y word** n palabrota f. ● vt ensuciar

disability /dɪsəˈbɪlətɪ/ n invalidez f

disable /dɪsˈeɪbl/ vt incapacitar. **~d** a minusválido

disabuse /dɪsəˈbjuːz/ vt desengañar

disadvantage /dɪsədˈvɑːntɪdʒ/ n desventaja f. **~d** a desventajado

disagree /dɪsəˈgriː/ vi no estar de acuerdo; (food, climate) sentar mal a. **~able** /dɪsəˈgriːəbl/ a desagradable. **~ment** n desacuerdo m; (quarrel) riña f

disappear /dɪsəˈpɪə(r)/ vi desaparecer. **~ance** n desaparición f

disappoint /dɪsəˈpɔɪnt/ vt desilusionar, decepcionar. **~ment** n desilusión f, decepción f

disapprov|al /dɪsəˈpruːvl/ n desaprobación f. **~e** /dɪsəˈpruːv/ vi. **~ of** desaprobar

disarm /dɪsˈɑːm/ vt/i desarmar. **~ament** n desarme m

disarray /dɪsəˈreɪ/ n desorden m

disast|er /dɪˈzɑːstə(r)/ n desastre m. **~rous** a catastrófico

disband /dɪsˈbænd/ vt disolver. ● vi disolverse

disbelief /dɪsbɪˈliːf/ n incredulidad f

disc /dɪsk/ n disco m

discard /dɪsˈkɑːd/ vt descartar; abandonar (beliefs etc)

discern /dɪˈsɜːn/ vt percibir. **~ible** a perceptible. **~ing** a perspicaz

discharge /dɪsˈtʃɑːdʒ/ vt descargar; cumplir (duty); (dismiss) despedir; poner en libertad (prisoner); (mil) licenciar. /ˈdɪstʃɑːdʒ/ n descarga f; (med) secreción f; (mil) licenciamiento m; (dismissal) despedida f

disciple /dɪˈsaɪpl/ n discípulo m

disciplin|arian /dɪsɪplɪˈneərɪən/ n ordenancista m & f. **~ary** a disciplinario. **~e** /ˈdɪsɪplɪn/ n disciplina f. ● vt disciplinar; (punish) castigar

disc jockey /ˈdɪskdʒɒkɪ/ n (on radio) pinchadiscos m & f invar

disclaim /dɪsˈkleɪm/ vt desconocer. **~er** n renuncia f

disclos|e /dɪsˈkləʊz/ vt revelar. **~ure** /-ʒə(r)/ n revelación f

disco /ˈdɪskəʊ/ n (pl -os) (fam) discoteca f

discolo|ur /dɪsˈkʌlə(r)/ vt decolorar. ● vi decolorarse. **~ration** /-ˈreɪʃn/ n decoloración f

discomfort /dɪsˈkʌmfət/ n malestar m; (lack of comfort) incomodidad f

disconcert /dɪskənˈsɜːt/ vt desconcertar

disconnect /dɪskəˈnekt/ vt separar; (elec) desconectar

disconsolate /dɪsˈkɒnsələt/ a desconsolado

discontent /dɪskənˈtent/ n descontento m. **~ed** a descontento

discontinue /dɪskənˈtɪnjuː/ vt interrumpir

discord /ˈdɪskɔːd/ n discordia f; (mus) disonancia f. **~ant** /-ˈskɔːdənt/ a discorde; (mus) disonante

discothèque /ˈdɪskətek/ n discoteca f

discount /ˈdɪskaʊnt/ n descuento m. /dɪsˈkaʊnt/ vt hacer caso omiso de; (com) descontar

discourage /dɪsˈkʌrɪdʒ/ vt desanimar; (dissuade) disuadir

discourse /ˈdɪskɔːs/ n discurso m

discourteous /dɪsˈkɜːtɪəs/ a descortés

discover /dɪsˈkʌvə(r)/ vt descubrir. **~y** n descubrimiento m

discredit /dɪsˈkredɪt/ vt (pt discredited) desacreditar. ● n descrédito m

discreet /dɪsˈkriːt/ a discreto. **~ly** adv discretamente

discrepancy /dɪˈskrepənsɪ/ n discrepancia f

discretion /dɪˈskreʃn/ n discreción f

discriminat|e /dɪsˈkrɪmɪneɪt/ vt/i discriminar. **~e between** distinguir entre. **~ing** a perspicaz. **~ion** /-ˈneɪʃn/ n discernimiento m; (bias) discriminación f

discus /ˈdɪskəs/ n disco m

discuss /dɪˈskʌs/ vt discutir. **~ion** /-ʃn/ n discusión f

disdain /dɪsˈdeɪn/ n desdén m. ● vt desdeñar. **~ful** a desdeñoso

disease /dɪˈziːz/ n enfermedad f. **~d** a enfermo

disembark /dɪsɪmˈbɑːk/ vt/i desembarcar

disembodied /dɪsɪmˈbɒdɪd/ a incorpóreo

disenchant /dɪsɪn'tʃɑːnt/ vt desencantar. **~ment** n desencanto m

disengage /dɪsɪn'geɪdʒ/ vt soltar. **~ the clutch** desembragar. **~ment** n soltura f

disentangle /dɪsɪn'tæŋgl/ vt desenredar

disfavour /dɪs'feɪvə(r)/ n desaprobación f. **fall into ~** ⟨person⟩ caer en desgracia; ⟨custom, word⟩ caer en desuso

disfigure /dɪs'fɪgə(r)/ vt desfigurar

disgorge /dɪs'gɔːdʒ/ vt arrojar; ⟨river⟩ descargar; (fig) restituir

disgrace /dɪs'greɪs/ n deshonra f; ⟨disfavour⟩ desgracia f. ● vt deshonrar. **~ful** a vergonzoso

disgruntled /dɪs'grʌntld/ a descontento

disguise /dɪs'gaɪz/ vt disfrazar. ● n disfraz m. **in ~** disfrazado

disgust /dɪs'gʌst/ n repugnancia f, asco m. ● vt repugnar, dar asco. **~ing** a repugnante, asqueroso

dish /dɪʃ/ n plato m. ● vt. **~ out** (fam) distribuir. **~ up** servir. **~cloth** /'dɪʃklɒθ/ n bayeta f

dishearten /dɪs'hɑːtn/ vt desanimar

dishevelled /dɪ'ʃevld/ a desaliñado; ⟨hair⟩ despeinado

dishonest /dɪs'ɒnɪst/ a ⟨person⟩ poco honrado; ⟨means⟩ fraudulento. **~y** n falta f de honradez

dishonour /dɪs'ɒnə(r)/ n deshonra f. ● vt deshonrar. **~able** a deshonroso. **~ably** adv deshonrosamente

dishwasher /'dɪʃwɒʃə(r)/ n lavaplatos m & f

disillusion /dɪsɪ'luːʒn/ vt desilusionar. **~ment** n desilusión f

disincentive /dɪsɪn'sentɪv/ n freno m

disinclined /dɪsɪn'klaɪnd/ a poco dispuesto

disinfect /dɪsɪn'fekt/ vt desinfectar. **~ant** n desinfectante m

disinherit /dɪsɪn'herɪt/ vt desheredar

disintegrate /dɪs'ɪntɪgreɪt/ vt desintegrar. ● vi desintegrarse

disinterested /dɪs'ɪntrəstɪd/ a desinteresado

disjointed /dɪs'dʒɔɪntɪd/ a inconexo

disk /dɪsk/ n disco m

dislike /dɪs'laɪk/ n aversión f. ● vt tener aversión a

dislocat|e /'dɪsləkeɪt/ vt dislocar(se) ⟨limb⟩. **~ion** n -'keɪʃn/ n dislocación f

dislodge /dɪs'lɒdʒ/ vt sacar; (oust) desalojar

disloyal /dɪs'lɔɪəl/ a desleal. **~ty** n deslealtad f

dismal /'dɪzməl/ a triste; (bad) fatal

dismantle /dɪs'mæntl/ vt desarmar

dismay /dɪs'meɪ/ n consternación f. ● vt consternar

dismiss /dɪs'mɪs/ vt despedir; (reject) rechazar. **~al** n despedida f; (of idea) abandono m

dismount /dɪs'maʊnt/ vi apearse

disobedien|ce /dɪsə'biːdɪəns/ n desobediencia f. **~t** /dɪsə'biːdɪənt/ a desobediente

disobey /dɪsə'beɪ/ vt/i desobedecer

disorder /dɪs'ɔːdə(r)/ n desorden m; (ailment) trastorno m. **~ly** a desordenado

disorganize /dɪs'ɔːgənaɪz/ vt desorganizar

disorientate /dɪs'ɔːrɪənteɪt/ vt desorientar

disown /dɪs'əʊn/ vt repudiar

disparaging /dɪs'pærɪdʒɪŋ/ a despreciativo. **~ly** adv con desprecio

disparity /dɪs'pærətɪ/ n disparidad f

dispassionate /dɪs'pæʃənət/ a desapasionado

dispatch /dɪs'pætʃ/ vt enviar. ● n envío m; (report) despacho m. **~rider** n correo m

dispel /dɪs'pel/ vt (pt dispelled) disipar

dispensable /dɪs'pensəbl/ a prescindible

dispensary /dɪs'pensərɪ/ n farmacia f

dispensation /dɪspen'seɪʃn/ n distribución f; (relig) dispensa f

dispense /dɪs'pens/ vt distribuir; (med) preparar; (relig) dispensar; administrar ⟨justice⟩. **~ with** prescindir de. **~r** /-ə(r)/ n (mec) distribuidor m automático; (med) farmacéutico m

dispers|al /dɪ'spɜːsl/ n dispersión f. **~e** /dɪ'spɜːs/ vt dispersar. ● vi dispersarse

dispirited /dɪs'pɪrɪtɪd/ a desanimado

displace /dɪs'pleɪs/ vt desplazar

display /dɪs'pleɪ/ vt mostrar; exhibir ⟨goods⟩; manifestar ⟨feelings⟩. ● n exposición f; (of feelings) manifestación f; (pej) ostentación f

displeas|e /dɪs'pliːz/ vt desagradar. **be ~ed with** estar disgustado con. **~ure** /-'pleʒə(r)/ n desagrado m

dispos|able /dɪsˈpəʊzəbl/ *a* desechable. **~al** *n* (*of waste*) eliminación *f*. **at s.o.'s ~al** a la disposición de uno. **~e** /dɪsˈpəʊz/ *vt* disponer. **be well ~ed towards** estar bien dispuesto hacia. ● *vi*. **~e of** deshacerse de

disposition /dɪspəˈzɪʃn/ *n* disposición *f*

disproportionate /dɪsprəˈpɔːʃənət/ *a* desproporcionado

disprove /dɪsˈpruːv/ *vt* refutar

dispute /dɪsˈpjuːt/ *vt* disputar. ● *n* disputa *f*. **in ~** disputado

disqualif|ication /dɪskwɒlɪfɪˈkeɪʃn/ *n* descalificación *f*. **~y** /dɪsˈkwɒlɪfaɪ/ *vt* incapacitar; (*sport*) descalificar

disquiet /dɪsˈkwaɪət/ *n* inquietud *f*

disregard /dɪsrɪˈgɑːd/ *vt* no hacer caso de. ● *n* indiferencia *f* (**for** a)

disrepair /dɪsrɪˈpeə(r)/ *n* mal estado *m*

disreputable /dɪsˈrepjʊtəbl/ *a* de mala fama

disrepute /dɪsrɪˈpjuːt/ *n* descrédito *m*

disrespect /dɪsrɪsˈpekt/ *n* falta *f* de respeto

disrobe /dɪsˈrəʊb/ *vt* desvestir. ● *vi* desvestirse

disrupt /dɪsˈrʌpt/ *vt* interrumpir; trastornar (*plans*). **~ion** /-ʃn/ *n* interrupción *f*; (*disorder*) desorganización *f*. **~ive** *a* desbaratador

dissatisfaction /dɪsætɪsˈfækʃn/ *n* descontento *m*

dissatisfied /dɪˈsætɪsfaɪd/ *a* descontento

dissect /dɪˈsekt/ *vt* disecar. **~ion** /-ʃn/ *n* disección *f*

disseminat|e /dɪˈsemɪneɪt/ *vt* diseminar. **~ion** /-ˈneɪʃn/ *n* diseminación *f*

dissent /dɪˈsent/ *vi* disentir. ● *n* disentimiento *m*

dissertation /dɪsəˈteɪʃn/ *n* disertación *f*; (*univ*) tesis *f*

disservice /dɪsˈsɜːvɪs/ *n* mal servicio *m*

dissident /ˈdɪsɪdənt/ *a & n* disidente (*m & f*)

dissimilar /dɪˈsɪmɪlə(r)/ *a* distinto

dissipate /ˈdɪsɪpeɪt/ *vt* disipar; (*fig*) desvanecer. **~d** *a* disoluto

dissociate /dɪˈsəʊʃɪeɪt/ *vt* disociar

dissolut|e /ˈdɪsəluːt/ *a* disoluto. **~ion** /dɪsəˈluːʃn/ *n* disolución *f*

dissolve /dɪˈzɒlv/ *vt* disolver. ● *vi* disolverse

dissuade /dɪˈsweɪd/ *vt* disuadir

distan|ce /ˈdɪstəns/ *n* distancia *f*. **from a ~ce** desde lejos. **in the ~ce** a lo lejos. **~t** /ˈdɪstənt/ *a* lejano; (*aloof*) frío

distaste /dɪsˈteɪst/ *n* aversión *f*. **~ful** *a* desagradable

distemper[1] /dɪˈstempə(r)/ *n* (*paint*) temple *m*. ● *vt* pintar al temple

distemper[2] /dɪˈstempə(r)/ *n* (*of dogs*) moquillo *m*

distend /dɪsˈtend/ *vt* dilatar. ● *vi* dilatarse

distil /dɪsˈtɪl/ *vt* (*pt* **distilled**) destilar. **~lation** /-ˈleɪʃn/ *n* destilación *f*. **~lery** /dɪsˈtɪlərɪ/ *n* destilería *f*

distinct /dɪsˈtɪŋkt/ *a* distinto; (*clear*) claro; (*marked*) marcado. **~ion** /-ʃn/ *n* distinción *f*; (*in exam*) sobresaliente *m*. **~ive** *a* distintivo. **~ly** *adv* claramente

distinguish /dɪsˈtɪŋgwɪʃ/ *vt/i* distinguir. **~ed** *a* distinguido

distort /dɪsˈtɔːt/ *vt* torcer. **~ion** /-ʃn/ *n* deformación *f*

distract /dɪsˈtrækt/ *vt* distraer. **~ed** *a* aturdido. **~ing** *a* molesto. **~ion** /-ʃn/ *n* distracción *f*; (*confusion*) aturdimiento *m*

distraught /dɪsˈtrɔːt/ *a* aturdido

distress /dɪsˈtres/ *n* angustia *f*; (*poverty*) miseria *f*; (*danger*) peligro *m*. ● *vt* afligir. **~ing** *a* penoso

distribut|e /dɪsˈtrɪbjuːt/ *vt* distribuir. **~ion** /-ˈbjuːʃn/ *n* distribución *f*. **~or** *n* distribuidor *m*; (*auto*) distribuidor *m* de encendido

district /ˈdɪstrɪkt/ *n* distrito *m*; (*of town*) barrio *m*

distrust /dɪsˈtrʌst/ *n* desconfianza *f*. ● *vt* desconfiar de

disturb /dɪsˈtɜːb/ *vt* molestar; (*perturb*) inquietar; (*move*) desordenar; (*interrupt*) interrumpir. **~ance** *n* disturbio *m*; (*tumult*) alboroto *m*. **~ed** *a* trastornado. **~ing** *a* inquietante

disused /dɪsˈjuːzd/ *a* fuera de uso

ditch /dɪtʃ/ *n* zanja *f*; (*for irrigation*) acequia *f*. ● *vt* (*sl*) abandonar

dither /ˈdɪðə(r)/ *vi* vacilar

ditto /ˈdɪtəʊ/ *adv* ídem

divan /dɪˈvæn/ *n* diván *m*

dive /daɪv/ vi tirarse de cabeza; (*rush*) meterse (precipitadamente); (*underwater*) bucear. ● n salto m; (*of plane*) picado m; (*place, fam*) taberna f. ~r n saltador m; (*underwater*) buzo m

diverge /daɪˈvɜːdʒ/ vi divergir. ~nt /daɪˈvɜːdʒənt/ a divergente

divers|e /daɪˈvɜːs/ a diverso. ~ify /daɪˈvɜːsɪfaɪ/ vt diversificar. ~ity /daɪˈvɜːsətɪ/ n diversidad f

diver|sion /daɪˈvɜːʃn/ n desvío m; (*distraction*) diversión f. ~t /daɪˈvɜːt/ vt desviar; (*entertain*) divertir

divest /daɪˈvest/ vt. ~ of despojar de

divide /dɪˈvaɪd/ vt dividir. ● vi dividirse

dividend /ˈdɪvɪdend/ n dividendo m

divine /dɪˈvaɪn/ a divino

diving-board /ˈdaɪvɪŋbɔːd/ n trampolín m

diving-suit /ˈdaɪvɪŋsuːt/ n escafandra f

divinity /dɪˈvɪnɪtɪ/ n divinidad f

division /dɪˈvɪʒn/ n división f

divorce /dɪˈvɔːs/ n divorcio m. ● vt divorciarse de; (*judge*) divorciar. ● vi divorciarse. ~e /dɪvɔːˈsiː/ n divorciado m

divulge /daɪˈvʌldʒ/ vt divulgar

DIY abbr see **do-it-yourself**

dizz|iness /ˈdɪzɪnɪs/ n vértigo m. ~y /ˈdɪzɪ/ a (-ier, -iest) mareado; (*speed*) vertiginoso. **be** or **feel** ~**y** marearse

do /duː/ vt (3 sing pres **does**, pt **did**, pp **done**) hacer; (*swindle, sl*) engañar. ● vi hacer; (*fare*) ir; (*be suitable*) convenir; (*be enough*) bastar. ● n (pl **dos** or **do's**) (*fam*) fiesta f. ● v aux. ~ **you speak Spanish? Yes I** ~ ¿habla Vd español? Sí. **doesn't he?**, **don't you?** ¿verdad? ~ **in** (*emphatic*) ¡pase Vd! ~ **away with** abolir. ~ **in** (*exhaust, fam*) agotar; (*kill, sl*) matar. ~ **out** (*clean*) limpiar. ~ **up** abotonar (*coat etc*); renovar (*house*). ~ **with** tener que ver con; (*need*) necesitar. ~ **without** prescindir de. ~**ne in** (*fam*) arruinado. ~**ne in** (*fam*) agotado. **well** ~**ne** (*culin*) bien hecho. **well** ~**ne!** ¡muy bien!

docile /ˈdəʊsaɪl/ a dócil

dock[1] /dɒk/ n dique m. ● vt poner en dique. ● vi atracar al muelle

dock[2] /dɒk/ n (*jurid*) banquillo m de los acusados

dock: ~**er** n estibador m. ~**yard** /ˈdɒkjɑːd/ n astillero m

doctor /ˈdɒktə(r)/ n médico m, doctor m; (*univ*) doctor m. ● vt castrar (*cat*); (*fig*) adulterar

doctorate /ˈdɒktərət/ n doctorado m

doctrine /ˈdɒktrɪn/ n doctrina f

document /ˈdɒkjʊmənt/ n documento m. ~**ary** /-ˈmentrɪ/ a & n documental (m)

doddering /ˈdɒdərɪŋ/ a chocho

dodge /dɒdʒ/ vt esquivar. ● vi esquivarse. ● n regate m; (*fam*) truco m

dodgems /ˈdɒdʒəmz/ npl autos mpl de choque

dodgy /ˈdɒdʒɪ/ a (-ier, -iest) (*awkward*) difícil

does /dʌz/ see **do**

doesn't /ˈdʌznt/ = **does not**

dog /dɒg/ n perro m. ● vt (pt **dogged**) perseguir. ~**collar** n (*relig, fam*) alzacuello m. ~**eared** a (*book*) sobado

dogged /ˈdɒgɪd/ a obstinado

doghouse /ˈdɒghaʊs/ n (*Amer*) perrera f. **in the** ~ (*sl*) en desgracia

dogma /ˈdɒgmə/ n dogma m. ~**tic** /-ˈmætɪk/ a dogmático

dogsbody /ˈdɒgzbɒdɪ/ n (*fam*) burro m de carga

doh /dəʊ/ n (*mus, first note of any musical scale*) do m

doily /ˈdɔɪlɪ/ n tapete m

doings /ˈduːɪŋz/ npl (*fam*) actividades fpl

do-it-yourself /duːɪtjɔːˈself/ (*abbr* **DIY**) n bricolaje m. ~ **enthusiast** n manitas m

doldrums /ˈdɒldrəmz/ npl. **be in the** ~ estar abatido

dole /dəʊl/ vt. ~ **out** distribuir. ● n (*fam*) subsidio m de paro. **on the** ~ (*fam*) parado

doleful /ˈdəʊlfl/ a triste

doll /dɒl/ n muñeca f. ● vt. ~ **up** (*fam*) emperejilar

dollar /ˈdɒlə(r)/ n dólar m

dollop /ˈdɒləp/ n (*fam*) masa f

dolphin /ˈdɒlfɪn/ n delfín m

domain /dəʊˈmeɪn/ n dominio m; (*fig*) campo m

dome /dəʊm/ n cúpula f. ~**d** a abovedado

domestic /dəˈmestɪk/ a doméstico; (*trade, flights, etc*) nacional

domesticated a (*animal*) domesticado

domesticity /dɒmeˈstɪsətɪ/ n
domesticidad f
domestic: ~ **science** n economía f
doméstica. ~ **servant** n doméstico m.
dominant /ˈdɒmɪnənt/ a dominante
dominat|e /ˈdɒmɪneɪt/ vt/i domi-
nar. ~**ion** /-ˈneɪʃn/ n dominación f
domineer /dɒmɪˈnɪə(r)/ vi tiranizar
Dominican Republic /dəmɪnɪkən
rɪˈpʌblɪk/ n República f Dominicana
dominion /dəˈmɪnjən/ n dominio m
domino /ˈdɒmɪnəʊ/ n (pl ~es) ficha
f de dominó. ~**es** npl (game) dominó
m
don[1] /dɒn/ n profesor m
don[2] /dɒn/ vt (pt **donned**) ponerse
donat|e /dəʊˈneɪt/ vt donar. ~**ion**
/-ʃn/ n donativo m
done /dʌn/ n see **do**
donkey /ˈdɒŋkɪ/ n burro m. ~**-work**
n trabajo m penoso
donor /ˈdəʊnə(r)/ n donante m & f
don't /dəʊnt/ = **do not**
doodle /ˈduːdl/ vi garrapatear
doom /duːm/ n destino m; (death)
muerte f. ● vt. be ~**ed to** ser con-
denado a
doomsday /ˈduːmzdeɪ/ n día m del
juicio final
door /dɔː(r)/ n puerta f. ~**man** /ˈdɔː
mən/ n (pl **-men**) portero m. ~**mat**
/ˈdɔːmæt/ n felpudo m. ~**step** /ˈdɔː
step/ n peldaño m. ~**way** /ˈdɔːweɪ/ n
entrada f
dope /dəʊp/ n (fam) droga f; (idiot,
sl) imbécil m. ● vt (fam) drogar. ~**y** a
(sl) torpe
dormant /ˈdɔːmənt/ a inactivo
dormer /ˈdɔːmə(r)/ n. ~ (**window**)
buhardilla f
dormitory /ˈdɔːmɪtrɪ/ n dormitorio
m
dormouse /ˈdɔːmaʊs/ n (pl **-mice**)
lirón m
dos|age /ˈdəʊsɪdʒ/ n dosis f. ~**e**
/dəʊs/ n dosis f
doss /dɒs/ vi (sl) dormir. ~**-house** n
refugio m
dot /dɒt/ n punto m. **on the** ~ en
punto. ● vt (pt **dotted**) salpicar. be
~**ted with** estar salpicado de
dote /dəʊt/ vi. ~ **on** adorar
dotted line /dɒtɪdˈlaɪn/ n línea f de
puntos
dotty /ˈdɒtɪ/ a (**-ier**, **-iest**) (fam)
chiflado
double /ˈdʌbl/ a doble. ● adv doble,
dos veces. ● n doble m; (person) doble

m & f. **at the** ~ corriendo. ● vt
doblar; redoblar (efforts etc). ● vi
doblarse. ~**bass** n contrabajo m. ~
bed n cama f de matrimonio. ~
breasted a cruzado. ~ **chin** n
papada f. ~**cross** vt traicionar. ~
dealing n doblez m & f. ~**decker** n
autobús m de dos pisos. ~ **Dutch** n
galimatías m. ~**jointed** a con arti-
culaciones dobles. ~**s** npl (tennis)
doble m
doubt /daʊt/ n duda f. ● vt dudar;
(distrust) dudar de, desconfiar de.
~**ful** a dudoso. ~**less** adv sin duda
doubly /ˈdʌblɪ/ adv doblemente
dough /dəʊ/ n masa f; (money, sl)
dinero m, pasta f (sl)
doughnut /ˈdəʊnʌt/ n buñuelo m
douse /daʊs/ vt mojar; apagar (fire)
dove /dʌv/ n paloma f
dowager /ˈdaʊədʒə(r)/ n viuda f
(con bienes o título del marido)
dowdy /ˈdaʊdɪ/ a (**-ier**, **-iest**) poco
atractivo
down[1] /daʊn/ adv abajo. ~ **with**
abajo. **come** ~ bajar. **go** ~ bajar;
(sun) ponerse. ● prep abajo. ● a (sad)
triste. ● vt derribar; (drink, fam)
beber
down[2] /daʊn/ n (feathers) plumón m
down-and-out /ˈdaʊnəndaʊt/ n
vagabundo m
downcast /ˈdaʊnkɑːst/ a abatido
downfall /ˈdaʊnfɔːl/ n caída f; (fig)
perdición f
downgrade /daʊnˈgreɪd/ vt degradar
down-hearted /daʊnˈhɑːtɪd/ a abatido
downhill /daʊnˈhɪl/ adv cuesta
abajo
down payment /ˈdaʊnpeɪmənt/ n
depósito m
downpour /ˈdaʊnpɔː(r)/ n aguacero
m
downright /ˈdaʊnraɪt/ a completo;
(honest) franco. ● adv completamente
downs /daʊnz/ npl colinas fpl
downstairs /daʊnˈsteəz/ adv abajo.
/ˈdaʊnsteəz/ a de abajo
downstream /ˈdaʊnstriːm/ adv río
abajo
down-to-earth /daʊntʊˈɜːθ/ a práctico
downtrodden /ˈdaʊntrɒdn/ a opri-
mido

down: ~ **under** en las antípodas; (in Australia) en Australia. ~**ward** /'daʊnwəd/ a & adv, ~**wards** adv hacia abajo

dowry /'daʊərɪ/ n dote f

doze /dəʊz/ vi dormitar. ~ **off** dormirse, dar una cabezada. ● n sueño m ligero

dozen /'dʌzn/ n docena f. ~**s of** (fam) miles de, muchos

Dr abbr (Doctor) Dr, Doctor m. ~ **Broadley** (el) Doctor Broadley

drab /dræb/ a monótono

draft /drɑːft/ n borrador m; (outline) bosquejo m; (com) letra f de cambio; (Amer, mil) reclutamiento m; (Amer, of air) corriente f de aire. ● vt bosquejar; (mil) destacar; (Amer, conscript) reclutar

drag /dræg/ vt (pt **dragged**) arrastrar; rastrear ⟨river⟩. ● vi arrastrarse por el suelo. ● n (fam) lata f. **in** ~ (man, sl) vestido de mujer

dragon /'drægən/ n dragón m

dragon-fly /'drægənflaɪ/ n libélula f

drain /dreɪn/ vt desaguar; apurar ⟨tank, glass⟩; (fig) agotar. ● vi escurrirse. ● n desaguadero m. **be a** ~ **on** agotar. ~**ing-board** n escurridero m

drama /'drɑːmə/ n drama m; (art) arte m teatral. ~**tic** /drə'mætɪk/ a dramático. ~**tist** /'dræmətɪst/ n dramaturgo m. ~**tize** /'dræmətaɪz/ vt adaptar al teatro; (fig) dramatizar

drank /dræŋk/ see **drink**

drape /dreɪp/ vt cubrir; (hang) colgar. ~**s** npl (Amer) cortinas fpl

drastic /'dræstɪk/ a drástico

draught /drɑːft/ n corriente f de aire. ~ **beer** n cerveza f de barril. ~**s** n pl (game) juego m de damas

draughtsman /'drɑːftsmən/ n (pl -men) diseñador m

draughty /'drɑːftɪ/ a lleno de corrientes de aire

draw /drɔː/ vt (pt **drew**, pp **drawn**) tirar; (attract) atraer; dibujar ⟨picture⟩; trazar ⟨line⟩; retirar ⟨money⟩. ~ **the line at** trazar el límite. ● vi (sport) empatar; dibujar ⟨pictures⟩; (in lottery) sortear. ● n (sport) empate m; (in lottery) sorteo m. ~ **in** ⟨days⟩ acortarse. ~ **out** sacar ⟨money⟩. ~ **up** pararse; redactar ⟨document⟩; acercar ⟨chair⟩

drawback /'drɔːbæk/ n desventaja f

drawbridge /'drɔːbrɪdʒ/ n puente m levadizo

drawer /drɔː(r)/ n cajón m. ~**s** /drɔːz/ npl calzoncillos mpl; (women's) bragas fpl

drawing /'drɔːɪŋ/ n dibujo m. ~**-pin** n chinche m, chincheta f

drawing-room /'drɔːɪŋruːm/ n salón m

drawl /drɔːl/ n habla f lenta

drawn /drɔːn/ see **draw**. ● a ⟨face⟩ ojeroso

dread /dred/ n terror m. ● vt temer. ~**ful** /'dredfl/ a terrible. ~**fully** adv terriblemente

dream /driːm/ n sueño m. ● vt/i (pt **dreamed** or **dreamt**) soñar. ● a ideal. ~ **up** idear. ~**er** n soñador m. ~**y** a soñador

drear|iness /'drɪərɪnɪs/ n tristeza f; (monotony) monotonía f. ~**y** /'drɪərɪ/ a (-ier, -iest) triste; (boring) monótono

dredge[1] /dredʒ/ n draga f. ● vt dragar

dredge[2] /dredʒ/ n (culin) espolvorear

dredger[1] /'dredʒə(r)/ n draga f

dredger[2] /'dredʒə(r)/ n (for sugar) espolvoreador m

dregs /dregz/ npl heces fpl; (fig) hez f

drench /drentʃ/ vt empapar

dress /dres/ n vestido m; (clothing) ropa f. ● vt vestir; (decorate) adornar; (med) vendar; (culin) aderezar, aliñar. ● vi vestirse. ~ **circle** n primer palco m

dresser[1] /'dresə(r)/ n (furniture) aparador m

dresser[2] /'dresə(r)/ n (in theatre) camarero m

dressing /'dresɪŋ/ n (sauce) aliño m; (bandage) vendaje m. ~**-case** n neceser m. ~**-down** n rapapolvo m, reprensión f. ~**-gown** n bata f. ~**-room** n tocador m; (in theatre) camarín m. ~**-table** n tocador m

dressmak|er /'dresmeɪkə(r)/ n modista m & f. ~**ing** n costura f

dress rehearsal /'dresrɪhɜːsl/ n ensayo m general

dressy /'dresɪ/ a (-ier, -iest) elegante

drew /druː/ see **draw**

dribble /'drɪbl/ vi gotear; ⟨baby⟩ babear; (in football) regatear

dribs and drabs /drɪbzn'dræbz/ npl. **in** ~ poco a poco, en cantidades pequeñas

drie|d /draɪd/ a ⟨food⟩ seco; ⟨fruit⟩ paso. ~**r** /'draɪə(r)/ n secador m

drift /drɪft/ vi ir a la deriva; ⟨snow⟩ amontonarse. ● n (movement) dirección f; (of snow) montón m; (meaning) significado m. ~**er** n persona f sin rumbo. ~**wood** /'drɪftwʊd/ n madera f flotante

drill /drɪl/ n (tool) taladro m; (training) ejercicio m; (fig) lo normal. ● vt taladrar, perforar; (train) entrenar. ● vi entrenarse

drily /'draɪlɪ/ adv secamente

drink /drɪŋk/ vt/i (pt **drank**, pp **drunk**) beber. ● n bebida f. ~**able** a bebible; ⟨water⟩ potable. ~**er** n bebedor m. ~**ing-water** n agua f potable

drip /drɪp/ vi (pt **dripped**) gotear. ● n gota f; (med) goteo m intravenoso; (person, sl) mentecato m. ~**-dry** a que no necesita plancharse

dripping /'drɪpɪŋ/ n (culin) pringue m

drive /draɪv/ vt (pt **drove**, pp **driven**) empujar; conducir, manejar (LAm) ⟨car etc⟩. ~ **in** clavar ⟨nail⟩. ~ **s.o. mad** volver loco a uno. ● vi conducir. ~ **in** (in car) entrar en coche. ● n paseo m; (road) calle f; (private road) camino m de entrada; (fig) energía f; (pol) campaña f. ~ **at** querer decir. ~**r** /'draɪvə(r)/ n conductor m, chófer m (LAm)

drivel /'drɪvl/ n tonterías fpl

driving /'draɪvɪŋ/ n conducción f. ~**licence** n carné m de conducir. ~**school** n autoescuela f

drizzl|e /'drɪzl/ n llovizna f. ● vi lloviznar. ~**y** a lloviznoso

dromedary /'drɒmədərɪ/ n dromedario m

drone /drəʊn/ n (noise) zumbido m; (bee) zángano m. ● vi zumbar; (fig) hablar en voz monótona; (idle, fam) holgazanear

drool /druːl/ vi babear

droop /druːp/ vt inclinar. ● vi inclinarse; ⟨flowers⟩ marchitarse

drop /drɒp/ n gota f; (fall) caída f; (decrease) baja f; (of cliff) precipicio m. ● vt (pt **dropped**) dejar caer; (lower) bajar. ● vi caer. ~ **in on** pasar por casa de. ~ **off** (sleep) dormirse. ~ **out** retirarse; ⟨student⟩ abandonar los estudios. ~**out** n marginado m

droppings /'drɒpɪŋz/ npl excremento m

dross /drɒs/ n escoria f

drought /draʊt/ n sequía f

drove[1] /drəʊv/ see **drive**

drove[2] /drəʊv/ n manada f

drown /draʊn/ vt ahogar. ● vi ahogarse

drowsy /'draʊzɪ/ a soñoliento

drudge /drʌdʒ/ n esclavo m del trabajo. ~**ry** /-ərɪ/ n trabajo m pesado

drug /drʌg/ n medicamento m. ● vt (pt **drugged**) drogar. ~ **addict** n toxicómano m

drugstore /'drʌgstɔː(r)/ n (Amer) farmacia f (que vende otros artículos también)

drum /drʌm/ n tambor m; (for oil) bidón m. ● vi (pt **drummed**) tocar el tambor. ● vt. ~ **into s.o.** inculcar en la mente de uno. ~**mer** n tambor m; (in group) batería f. ~**s** npl batería f. ~**stick** /'drʌmstɪk/ n baqueta f; (culin) pierna f (de pollo)

drunk /drʌŋk/ see **drink**. ● a borracho. **get** ~ emborracharse. ~**ard** n borracho m. ~**en** a borracho. ~**enness** n embriaguez f

dry /draɪ/ a (**drier**, **driest**) seco. ● vt secar. ● vi secarse. ~ **up** (dry) secar los platos. ~**-clean** vt limpiar en seco. ~**-cleaner** n tintorero m. ~**cleaner's** (shop) tintorería f. ~**ness** n sequedad f

dual /'djuːəl/ a doble. ~ **carriageway** n autovía f, carretera f de doble calzada. ~**-purpose** a de doble uso

dub /dʌb/ vt (pt **dubbed**) doblar ⟨film⟩; (nickname) apodar

dubious /'djuːbɪəs/ a dudoso; ⟨person⟩ sospechoso

duchess /'dʌtʃɪs/ n duquesa f

duck[1] /dʌk/ n pato m

duck[2] /dʌk/ vt sumergir; bajar ⟨head etc⟩. ● vi agacharse

duckling /'dʌklɪŋ/ n patito m

duct /dʌkt/ n conducto m

dud /dʌd/ a inútil; ⟨cheque⟩ sin fondos; ⟨coin⟩ falso

due /djuː/ a debido; (expected) esperado. ~ **to** debido a. ● adv. ~ **north** n derecho hacia el norte. ~**s** npl derechos mpl

duel /'djuːəl/ n duelo m

duet /djuː'et/ n dúo m

duffle /'dʌfl/ a. ~ **bag** n bolsa f de lona. ~**-coat** n trenca f

dug /dʌg/ see **dig**

duke /djuːk/ n duque m

dull /dʌl/ a (**-er, -est**) ⟨weather⟩ gris; ⟨colour⟩ apagado; ⟨person, play, etc⟩ pesado; ⟨sound⟩ sordo; (stupid) torpe. ● vt aliviar ⟨pain⟩; entorpecer ⟨mind⟩

duly /'dju:lɪ/ adv debidamente

dumb /dʌm/ a (**-er, -est**) mudo; (fam) estúpido

dumbfound /dʌm'faʊnd/ vt pasmar

dummy /'dʌmɪ/ n muñeco m; (of tailor) maniquí m; (of baby) chupete m. ● a falso. **~ run** n prueba f

dump /dʌmp/ vt descargar; (fam) deshacerse de. ● n vertedero m; (mil) depósito m; (fam) lugar m desagradable. **be down in the ~s** estar deprimido

dumpling /'dʌmplɪŋ/ n bola f de masa hervida

dumpy /'dʌmpɪ/ a (**-ier, -iest**) regordete

dunce /dʌns/ n burro m

dung /dʌŋ/ n excremento m; (manure) estiércol m

dungarees /dʌŋgə'ri:z/ npl mono m, peto m

dungeon /'dʌndʒən/ n calabozo m

dunk /dʌŋk/ vt remojar

duo /'dju:əʊ/ n dúo m

dupe /dju:p/ vt engañar. ● n inocentón m

duplicat|e /'dju:plɪkət/ a & n duplicado (m). /'dju:plɪkeɪt/ vt duplicar; (on machine) reproducir. **~or** n multicopista f

duplicity /dju:'plɪsətɪ/ n doblez f

durable /'djʊərəbl/ a resistente; (enduring) duradero

duration /djʊ'reɪʃn/ n duración f

duress /djʊ'res/ n coacción f

during /'djʊərɪŋ/ prep durante

dusk /dʌsk/ n crepúsculo m

dusky /'dʌskɪ/ a (**-ier, -iest**) oscuro

dust /dʌst/ n polvo m. ● vt quitar el polvo a; (sprinkle) espolvorear

dustbin /'dʌstbɪn/ n cubo m de la basura

dust-cover /'dʌstkʌvə(r)/ n sobrecubierta f

duster /'dʌstə(r)/ n trapo m

dust-jacket /'dʌstdʒækɪt/ n sobrecubierta f

dustman /'dʌstmən/ n (pl **-men**) basurero m

dustpan /'dʌstpæn/ n recogedor m

dusty /'dʌstɪ/ a (**-ier, -iest**) polvoriento

Dutch /dʌtʃ/ a & n holandés (m). **go ~** pagar a escote. **~man** m holandés m. **~woman** n holandesa f

dutiful /'dju:tɪfl/ a obediente

duty /'dju:tɪ/ n deber m; (tax) derechos mpl de aduana. **on ~** de servicio. **~-free** a libre de impuestos

duvet /'dju:veɪ/ n edredón m

dwarf /dwɔ:f/ n (pl **-s**) enano m. ● vt empequeñecer

dwell /dwel/ vi (pt **dwelt**) morar. **~ on** dilatarse. **~er** n habitante m & f. **~ing** n morada f

dwindle /'dwɪndl/ vi disminuir

dye /daɪ/ vt (pres p **dyeing**) teñir. ● n tinte m

dying /'daɪɪŋ/ see **die**

dynamic /daɪ'næmɪk/ a dinámico. **~s** npl dinámica f

dynamite /'daɪnəmaɪt/ n dinamita f. ● vt dinamitar

dynamo /'daɪnəməʊ/ n dinamo f, dínamo f

dynasty /'dɪnəstɪ/ n dinastía f

dysentery /'dɪsəntrɪ/ n disentería f

dyslexia /dɪs'leksɪə/ n dislexia f

E

each /i:tʃ/ a cada. ● pron cada uno. **~ one** cada uno. **~ other** uno a otro, el uno al otro. **they love ~ other** se aman

eager /'i:gə(r)/ a impaciente; (enthusiastic) ávido. **~ly** adv con impaciencia. **~ness** n impaciencia f, ansia f

eagle /'i:gl/ n águila f

ear¹ /ɪə(r)/ n oído m; (outer) oreja f

ear² /ɪə(r)/ n (of corn) espiga f

ear: **~ache** /'ɪəreɪk/ n dolor m de oído. **~-drum** n tímpano m

earl /ɜ:l/ n conde m

early /'ɜ:lɪ/ a (**-ier, -iest**) temprano; (before expected time) prematuro. **in the ~ spring** a principios de la primavera. ● adv temprano; (ahead of time) con anticipación

earmark /'ɪəma:k/ vt. **~ for** destinar a

earn /ɜ:n/ vt ganar; (deserve) merecer

earnest /'ɜ:nɪst/ a serio. **in ~** en serio

earnings /'ɜ:nɪŋz/ npl ingresos mpl; (com) ganacias fpl

ear: **~phones** /'ɪəfəʊnz/ npl auricular m. **~ring** n pendiente m

earshot /'ɪəʃɒt/ n. **within ~** al alcance del oído

earth /ɜ:θ/ n tierra f. ● vt (elec) conectar a tierra. **~ly** a terrenal

earthenware /'ɜ:θnweə(r)/ n loza f de barro

earthquake /'ɜ:θkweɪk/ n terremoto m

earthy /'ɜ:θɪ/ a terroso; (coarse) grosero

earwig /'ɪəwɪg/ n tijereta f

ease /i:z/ n facilidad f; (comfort) tranquilidad f. **at ~** a gusto; (mil) en posición de descanso. **ill at ~** molesto. **with ~** fácilmente. ● vt calmar; aliviar (pain); tranquilizar (mind); (loosen) aflojar. ● vi calmarse; (lessen) disminuir

easel /'i:zl/ n caballete m

east /i:st/ n este m, oriente m. ● a del este, oriental. ● adv hacia el este.

Easter /'i:stə(r)/ n Semana f Santa; (relig) Pascua f de Resurrección. **~ egg** n huevo m de Pascua

east: ~erly a este; (wind) del este. **~ern** a del este, oriental. **~ward** adv, **~wards** adv hacia el este

easy /'i:zɪ/ a (-ier, -iest) fácil; (relaxed) tranquilo. **go ~ on** (fam) tener cuidado con. **take it ~** no preocuparse. ● int ¡despacio! **~ chair** n sillón m. **~-going** a acomodadizo

eat /i:t/ vt/i (pt ate, pp eaten) comer. **~ into** corroer. **~able** a comestible. **~er** n comedor m

eau-de-Cologne /əʊdəkə'ləʊn/ n agua f de colonia

eaves /i:vz/ npl alero m

eavesdrop /'i:vzdrɒp/ vi (pt -dropped) escuchar a escondidas

ebb /eb/ n reflujo m. ● vi bajar; (fig) decaer

ebony /'ebənɪ/ n ébano m

ebullient /ɪ'bʌlɪənt/ a exuberante

EC /i:'si:/ abbr (European Community) CE (Comunidad f Europea)

eccentric /ɪk'sentrɪk/ a & n excéntrico (m). **~ity** /eksen'trɪsətɪ/ n excentricidad f

ecclesiastical /ɪkli:zɪ'æstɪkl/ a eclesiástico

echelon /'eʃəlɒn/ n escalón m

echo /'ekəʊ/ n (pl -oes) eco m. ● vt (pt echoed, pres p echoing) repetir; (imitate) imitar. ● vi hacer eco

eclectic /ɪk'lektɪk/ a & n ecléctico (m)

eclipse /ɪ'klɪps/ n eclipse m. ● vt eclipsar

ecology /ɪ'kɒlədʒɪ/ n ecología f

econom|ic /i:kə'nɒmɪk/ a económico. **~ical** a económico. **~ics** n economía f. **~ist** /ɪ'kɒnəmɪst/ n economista m & f. **~ize** /ɪ'kɒnəmaɪz/ vi economizar. **~y** /ɪ'kɒnəmɪ/ n economía f

ecsta|sy /'ekstəsɪ/ n éxtasis f. **~tic** /ɪk'stætɪk/ a extático. **~tically** adv con éxtasis

Ecuador /'ekwədɔ:(r)/ n el Ecuador m

ecumenical /i:kju:'menɪkl/ a ecuménico

eddy /'edɪ/ n remolino m

edge /edʒ/ n borde m, margen m; (of knife) filo m; (of town) afueras fpl. **have the ~ on** (fam) llevar la ventaja a. **on ~** nervioso. ● vt ribetear; (move) mover poco a poco. ● vi avanzar cautelosamente. **~ways** adv de lado

edging /'edʒɪŋ/ n borde m; (sewing) ribete m

edgy /'edʒɪ/ a nervioso

edible /'edɪbl/ a comestible

edict /'i:dɪkt/ n edicto m

edifice /'edɪfɪs/ n edificio m

edify /'edɪfaɪ/ vt edificar

edit /'edɪt/ vt dirigir (newspaper); preparar una edición de (text); (write) redactar; montar (film). **~ed by** a cargo de. **~ion** /ɪ'dɪʃn/ n edición f. **~or** /'edɪtə(r)/ n (of newspaper) director m; (of text) redactor m. **~orial** /edɪ'tɔ:rɪəl/ a editorial. ● n artículo m de fondo. **~or in chief** n jefe m de redacción

educat|e /'edʒʊkeɪt/ vt instruir, educar. **~ed** a culto. **~ion** /-'keɪʃn/ n enseñanza f; (culture) cultura f; (upbringing) educación f. **~ional** /-'keɪʃənl/ a instructivo

EEC /i:i:'si:/ abbr (European Economic Community) CEE (Comunidad f Económica Europea)

eel /i:l/ n anguila f

eerie /'ɪərɪ/ a (-ier, -iest) misterioso

efface /ɪ'feɪs/ vt borrar

effect /ɪ'fekt/ n efecto m. **in ~** efectivamente. **take ~** entrar en vigor. ● vt efectuar

effective /ɪ'fektɪv/ a eficaz; (striking) impresionante; (mil) efectivo. **~ly** adv eficazmente. **~ness** n eficacia f

effeminate /ɪ'femɪnət/ a afeminado

effervescent /efə'vesnt/ a efervescente

effete /ɪ'fi:t/ a agotado

efficien|cy /ɪ'fɪʃənsɪ/ n eficiencia f; (*mec*) rendimiento m. ~t /ɪ'fɪʃnt/ a eficiente. ~tly adv eficientemente

effigy /'efɪdʒɪ/ n efigie f

effort /'efət/ n esfuerzo m. ~less a fácil

effrontery /ɪ'frʌntərɪ/ n descaro m

effusive /ɪ'fju:sɪv/ a efusivo

e.g. /i:'dʒi:/ abbr (*exempli gratia*) p.ej., por ejemplo

egalitarian /ɪgælɪ'teərɪən/ a & n igualitario (m)

egg[1] /eg/ n huevo m

egg[2] /eg/ vt. ~ **on** (*fam*) incitar

egg-cup /'egkʌp/ n huevera f

egg-plant /'egplɑ:nt/ n berenjena f

eggshell /'egʃel/ n cáscara f de huevo

ego /'i:gəʊ/ n (*pl* -os) yo m. ~ism n egoísmo m. ~ist n egoísta m & f. ~centric /i:gəʊ'sentrɪk/ a egocéntrico. ~tism n egotismo m. ~tist n egotista m & f

Egypt /'i:dʒɪpt/ n Egipto m. ~ian /ɪ'dʒɪpʃn/ a & n egipcio (m)

eh /eɪ/ int (*fam*) ¡eh!

eiderdown /'aɪdədaʊn/ n edredón m

eight /eɪt/ a & n ocho (m)

eighteen /eɪ'ti:n/ a & n dieciocho (m). ~th a & n decimoctavo (m)

eighth /eɪtθ/ a & n octavo (m)

eight|ieth /'eɪtɪəθ/ a & n ochenta (m), octogésimo (m). ~y /'eɪtɪ/ a & n ochenta (m)

either /'aɪðə(r)/ a cualquiera de los dos; (*negative*) ninguno de los dos; (*each*) cada. ● *pron* uno u otro; (*with negative*) ni uno ni otro. ● *adv* (*negative*) tampoco. ● *conj* o. ~ **he or** o él o; (*with negative*) ni él ni

ejaculate /ɪ'dʒækjʊleɪt/ vt/i (*exclaim*) exclamar

eject /ɪ'dʒekt/ vt expulsar, echar

eke /i:k/ vt. ~ **out** hacer bastar; (*increase*) complementar

elaborate /ɪ'læbərət/ a complicado. /ɪ'læbəreɪt/ vt elaborar. ● vi explicarse

elapse /ɪ'læps/ vi (*of time*) transcurrir

elastic /ɪ'læstɪk/ a & n elástico (m). ~ **band** n goma f (elástica)

elasticity /ɪlæ'stɪsətɪ/ n elasticidad f

elat|ed /ɪ'leɪtɪd/ a regocijado. ~ion /-ʃn/ n regocijo m

elbow /'elbəʊ/ n codo m

elder[1] /'eldə(r)/ a & n mayor (m)

elder[2] /'eldə(r)/ n (*tree*) saúco m

elderly /'eldəlɪ/ a mayor, anciano

eldest /'eldɪst/ a & n el mayor (m)

elect /ɪ'lekt/ vt elegir. ~ **to do** decidir hacer. ● a electo. ~ion /-ʃn/ n elección f

elector /ɪ'lektə(r)/ n elector m. ~al a electoral. ~ate n electorado m

electric /ɪ'lektrɪk/ a eléctrico. ~al a eléctrico. ~ **blanket** n manta f eléctrica. ~ian /ɪlek'trɪʃn/ n electricista m & f. ~ity /ɪlek'trɪsətɪ/ n electricidad f

electrify /ɪ'lektrɪfaɪ/ vt electrificar; (*fig*) electrizar

electrocute /ɪ'lektrəkju:t/ vt electrocutar

electrolysis /ɪlek'trɒlɪsɪs/ n electrólisis f

electron /ɪ'lektrɒn/ n electrón m

electronic /ɪlek'trɒnɪk/ a electrónico. ~s n electrónica f

elegan|ce /'elɪgəns/ n elegancia f. ~t /'elɪgənt/ a elegante. ~tly adv elegantemente

element /'elɪmənt/ n elemento m. ~ary /-'mentrɪ/ a elemental

elephant /'elɪfənt/ n elefante m

elevat|e /'elɪveɪt/ vt elevar. ~ion /-'veɪʃn/ n elevación f. ~or /'elɪveɪtə(r)/ n (*Amer*) ascensor m

eleven /ɪ'levn/ a & n once (m). ~th a & n undécimo (m)

elf /elf/ n (*pl* elves) duende m

elicit /ɪ'lɪsɪt/ vt sacar

eligible /'elɪdʒəbl/ a elegible. **be** ~ **for** tener derecho a

eliminat|e /ɪ'lɪmɪneɪt/ vt eliminar. ~ion /-'neɪʃn/ n eliminación f

élite /eɪ'li:t/ n elite f, élite m

elixir /ɪ'lɪksɪə(r)/ n elixir m

ellip|se /ɪ'lɪps/ n elipse f. ~tical a elíptico

elm /elm/ n olmo m

elocution /elə'kju:ʃn/ n elocución f

elongate /'i:lɒŋgeɪt/ vt alargar

elope /ɪ'ləʊp/ vi fugarse con el amante. ~ment n fuga f

eloquen|ce /'eləkwəns/ n elocuencia f. ~t /'eləkwənt/ a elocuente. ~tly adv con elocuencia

El Salvador /el'sælvədɔ:(r)/ n El Salvador m

else /els/ *adv* más. **everybody ~** todos los demás. **nobody ~** ningún otro, nadie más. **nothing ~** nada más. **or ~** o bien. **somewhere ~** en otra parte

elsewhere /els'weə(r)/ *adv* en otra parte

elucidate /ɪ'luːsɪdeɪt/ *vt* aclarar

elude /ɪ'luːd/ *vt* eludir

elusive /ɪ'luːsɪv/ *a* esquivo

emaciated /ɪ'meɪsɪeɪtɪd/ *a* esquelético

emanate /'eməneɪt/ *vi* emanar

emancipat|e /ɪ'mænsɪpeɪt/ *vt* emancipar. **~ion** /-'peɪʃn/ *n* emancipación*f*

embalm /ɪm'bɑːm/ *vt* embalsamar

embankment /ɪm'bæŋkmənt/ *n* terraplén *m*; (*of river*) dique *m*

embargo /ɪm'bɑːgəʊ/ *n* (*pl* **-oes**) prohibición *f*

embark /ɪm'bɑːk/ *vi* embarcarse. ● *vi* embarcarse. **~ on** (*fig*) emprender. **~ation** /embɑː'keɪʃn/ *n* (*of people*) embarco *m*; (*of goods*) embarque *m*

embarrass /ɪm'bærəs/ *vt* desconcertar; (*shame*) dar vergüenza. **~ment** *n* desconcierto *m*; (*shame*) vergüenza*f*

embassy /'embəsɪ/ *n* embajada*f*

embed /ɪm'bed/ *vt* (*pt* **embedded**) embutir; (*fig*) fijar

embellish /ɪm'belɪʃ/ *vt* embellecer. **~ment** *n* embellecimiento *m*

embers /'embəz/ *npl* ascua*f*

embezzle /ɪm'bezl/ *vt* desfalcar. **~ment** *n* desfalco *m*

embitter /ɪm'bɪtə(r)/ *vt* amargar

emblem /'embləm/ *n* emblema *m*

embod|iment /ɪm'bɒdɪmənt/ *n* encarnación *f*. **~y** /ɪm'bɒdɪ/ *vt* encarnar; (*include*) incluir

emboss /ɪm'bɒs/ *vt* grabar en relieve, repujar. **~ed** *a* en relieve, repujado

embrace /ɪm'breɪs/ *vt* abrazar; (*fig*) abarcar. ● *vi* abrazarse. ● *n* abrazo *m*

embroider /ɪm'brɔɪdə(r)/ *vt* bordar. **~y** *n* bordado *m*

embroil /ɪm'brɔɪl/ *vt* enredar

embryo /'embrɪəʊ/ *n* (*pl* **-os**) embrión *m*. **~nic** /-'ɒnɪk/ *a* embrionario

emend /ɪ'mend/ *vt* enmendar

emerald /'emərəld/ *n* esmeralda*f*

emerge /ɪ'mɜːdʒ/ *vi* salir. **~nce** /-əns/ *n* aparición*f*

emergency /ɪ'mɜːdʒənsɪ/ *n* emergencia*f*. **in an ~** en caso de emergencia. **~ exit** *n* salida *f* de emergencia

emery /'emərɪ/ *n* esmeril *m*. **~board** *n* lima*f* de uñas

emigrant /'emɪɡrənt/ *n* emigrante *m & f*

emigrat|e /'emɪɡreɪt/ *vi* emigrar. **~ion** /-'ɡreɪʃn/ *n* emigración*f*

eminen|ce /'emɪnəns/ *n* eminencia *f*. **~t** /'emɪnənt/ *a* eminente. **~tly** *adv* eminentemente

emissary /'emɪsərɪ/ *n* emisario *m*

emission /ɪ'mɪʃn/ *n* emisión*f*

emit /ɪ'mɪt/ *vt* (*pt* **emitted**) emitir

emollient /ɪ'mɒlɪənt/ *a & n* emoliente (*m*)

emoti|on /ɪ'məʊʃn/ *n* emoción *f*. **~onal** *a* emocional; (*person*) emotivo; (*moving*) conmovedor. **~ve** /ɪ'məʊtɪv/ *a* emotivo

empathy /'empəθɪ/ *n* empatía*f*

emperor /'empərə(r)/ *n* emperador *m*

emphasi|s /'emfəsɪs/ *n* (*pl* **~ses** /-siːz/) énfasis *m*. **~ze** /'emfəsaɪz/ *vt* subrayar; (*single out*) destacar

emphatic /ɪm'fætɪk/ *a* categórico; (*resolute*) decidido

empire /'empaɪə(r)/ *n* imperio *m*

empirical /ɪm'pɪrɪkl/ *a* empírico

employ /ɪm'plɔɪ/ *vt* emplear. **~ee** /emplɔɪ'iː/ *n* empleado *m*. **~er** *n* patrón *m*. **~ment** *n* empleo *m*. **~ment agency** *n* agencia *f* de colocaciones

empower /ɪm'paʊə(r)/ *vt* autorizar (**to do** a hacer)

empress /'emprɪs/ *n* emperatriz*f*

empt|ies /'emptɪz/ *npl* envases *mpl*. **~iness** *n* vacío *m*. **~y** /'emptɪ/ *a* vacío; (*promise*) vano. **on an ~y stomach** con el estómago vacío. ● *vt* vaciar. ● *vi* vaciarse

emulate /'emjʊleɪt/ *vt* emular

emulsion /ɪ'mʌlʃn/ *n* emulsión*f*

enable /ɪ'neɪbl/ *vt*. **~ s.o. to** permitir a uno

enact /ɪ'nækt/ *vt* (*jurid*) decretar; (*in theatre*) representar

enamel /ɪ'næml/ *n* esmalte *m*. ● *vt* (*pt* **enamelled**) esmaltar

enamoured /ɪ'næməd/ *a*. **be ~ of** estar enamorado de

encampment /ɪn'kæmpmənt/ *n* campamento *m*

encase /ɪn'keɪs/ *vt* encerrar

enchant /ɪn'tʃɑːnt/ vt encantar. ~ing a encantador. ~ment n encanto m

encircle /ɪn'sɜːkl/ vt rodear

enclave /'enkleɪv/ n enclave m

enclos|e /ɪn'kləʊz/ vt cercar ⟨land⟩; (with letter) adjuntar; (in receptacle) encerrar. ~ed a ⟨space⟩ encerrado; (com) adjunto. ~ure /ɪn'kləʊʒə(r)/ n cercamiento m; (area) recinto m; (com) documento m adjunto

encompass /ɪn'kʌmpəs/ vt cercar; (include) incluir, abarcar

encore /'ɒŋkɔː(r)/ int ¡bis! ● n bis m, repetición f

encounter /ɪn'kaʊntə(r)/ vt encontrar. ● n encuentro m

encourage /ɪn'kʌrɪdʒ/ vt animar; (stimulate) estimular. ~ment n estímulo m

encroach /ɪn'krəʊtʃ/ vi. ~ on invadir ⟨land⟩; quitar ⟨time⟩. ~ment n usurpación f

encumb|er /ɪn'kʌmbə(r)/ vt (hamper) estorbar; (burden) cargar. be ~ered with estar cargado de. ~rance n estorbo m; (burden) carga f

encyclical /ɪn'sɪklɪkl/ n encíclica f

encyclopaedi|a /ɪnsaɪklə'piːdɪə/ n enciclopedia f. ~c a enciclopédico

end /end/ n fin m; (furthest point) extremo m. **in the** ~ por fin. **make** ~s meet poder llegar a fin de mes. **no** ~ (fam) muy. **no** ~ of muchísimos. **on** ~ de pie; (consecutive) seguido. ● vt/i terminar, acabar

endanger /ɪn'deɪndʒə(r)/ vt arriesgar

endear|ing /ɪn'dɪərɪŋ/ a simpático. ~ment n palabra f cariñosa

endeavour /ɪn'devə(r)/ n tentativa f. ● vi. ~ to esforzarse por

ending /'endɪŋ/ n fin m

endive /'endɪv/ n escarola f, endibia f

endless /'endlɪs/ a interminable; ⟨patience⟩ infinito

endorse /ɪn'dɔːs/ vt endosar; (fig) aprobar. ~ment n endoso m; aprobación f; (auto) nota f de inhabilitación

endow /ɪn'daʊ/ vt dotar

endur|able /ɪn'djʊərəbl/ a aguantable. ~ance n resistencia f. ~e /ɪn'djʊə(r)/ vt aguantar. ● vi durar. ~ing a perdurable

enemy /'enəmɪ/ n & a enemigo (m)

energ|etic /enə'dʒetɪk/ a enérgico. ~y /'enədʒɪ/ n energía f

enervat|e /'enəveɪt/ vt debilitar. ~ing a debilitante

enfold /ɪn'fəʊld/ vt envolver; (in arms) abrazar

enforce /ɪn'fɔːs/ vt aplicar; (impose) imponer; hacer cumplir ⟨law⟩. ~d a forzado

engage /ɪn'geɪdʒ/ vt emplear ⟨staff⟩; (reserve) reservar; ocupar ⟨attention⟩; (mec) hacer engranar. ● vi (mec) engranar. ~d a prometido; (busy) ocupado. **get** ~d prometerse. ~ment n compromiso m; (undertaking) obligación f

engaging /ɪn'geɪdʒɪŋ/ a atractivo

engender /ɪn'dʒendə(r)/ vt engendrar

engine /'endʒɪn/ n motor m; (of train) locomotora f. ~-driver n maquinista m

engineer /endʒɪ'nɪə(r)/ n ingeniero m; (mechanic) mecánico m. ● vt (contrive, fam) lograr. ~ing n ingeniería f

England /'ɪŋglənd/ n Inglaterra f

English /'ɪŋglɪʃ/ a inglés. ● n (lang) inglés m; (people) ingleses mpl. ~man n inglés m. ~woman n inglesa f. **the** ~ **Channel** n el canal m de la Mancha

engrav|e /ɪn'greɪv/ vt grabar. ~ing n grabado m

engrossed /ɪn'grəʊst/ a absorto

engulf /ɪn'gʌlf/ vt tragar(se)

enhance /ɪn'hɑːns/ vt aumentar

enigma /ɪ'nɪgmə/ n enigma m. ~tic /enɪg'mætɪk/ a enigmático

enjoy /ɪn'dʒɔɪ/ vt gozar de. ~ o.s. divertirse. **I** ~ **reading** me gusta la lectura. ~able a agradable. ~ment n placer m

enlarge /ɪn'lɑːdʒ/ vt agrandar; (foto) ampliar. ● vi agrandarse. ~ upon extenderse sobre. ~ment n (foto) ampliación f

enlighten /ɪn'laɪtn/ vt aclarar; (inform) informar. ~ment n aclaración f. **the E~ment** el siglo m de la luces

enlist /ɪn'lɪst/ vt alistar; (fig) conseguir. ● vi alistarse

enliven /ɪn'laɪvn/ vt animar

enmity /'enmətɪ/ n enemistad f

ennoble /ɪ'nəʊbl/ vt ennoblecer

enorm|ity /ɪ'nɔːmətɪ/ n enormidad f. ~ous /ɪ'nɔːməs/ a enorme

enough /ɪ'nʌf/ *a & adv* bastante. ● *n* bastante *m*, suficiente *m*. ● *int* ¡basta!

enquir|e /ɪn'kwaɪə(r)/ *vt/i* preguntar. ~**e about** informarse de. ~**y** *n* pregunta *f*; (*investigation*) investigación *f*

enrage /ɪn'reɪdʒ/ *vt* enfurecer

enrapture /ɪn'ræptʃə(r)/ *vt* extasiar

enrich /ɪn'rɪtʃ/ *vt* enriquecer

enrol /ɪn'rəʊl/ *vt* (*pt* **enrolled**) inscribir; matricular (*student*). ● *vi* inscribirse; (*student*) matricularse. ~**ment** *n* inscripción *f*; (*of student*) matrícula *f*

ensconce /ɪn'skɒns/ *vt*. ~ **o.s.** arrellanarse

ensemble /ɒn'sɒmbl/ *n* conjunto *m*

enshrine /ɪn'ʃraɪn/ *vt* encerrar

ensign /'ensaɪn/ *n* enseña *f*

enslave /ɪn'sleɪv/ *vt* esclavizar

ensue /ɪn'sju:/ *vi* resultar, seguirse

ensure /ɪn'ʃʊə(r)/ *vt* asegurar

entail /ɪn'teɪl/ *vt* suponer; acarrear (*trouble etc*)

entangle /ɪn'tæŋgl/ *vt* enredar. ~**ment** *n* enredo *m*; (*mil*) alambrada *f*

enter /'entə(r)/ *vt* entrar en; (*write*) escribir; matricular (*school etc*); hacerse socio de (*club*). ● *vi* entrar

enterprise /'entəpraɪz/ *n* empresa *f*; (*fig*) iniciativa *f*

enterprising /'entəpraɪzɪŋ/ *a* emprendedor

entertain /entə'teɪn/ *vt* divertir; recibir (*guests*); abrigar (*ideas, hopes*); (*consider*) considerar. ~**ment** *n* diversión *f*; (*performance*) espectáculo *m*; (*reception*) recepción *f*

enthral /ɪn'θrɔ:l/ *vt* (*pt* **enthralled**) cautivar

enthuse /ɪn'θju:z/ *vi*. ~ **over** entusiasmarse por

enthusias|m /ɪn'θju:zɪæzəm/ *n* entusiasmo *m*. ~**tic** /-'æstɪk/ *a* entusiasta; (*thing*) entusiástico. ~**tically** /-'æstɪklɪ/ *adv* con entusiasmo. ~**t** /ɪn'θju:zɪæst/ *n* entusiasta *m & f*

entice /ɪn'taɪs/ *vt* atraer. ~**ment** *n* atracción *f*

entire /ɪn'taɪə(r)/ *a* entero. ~**ly** *adv* completamente. ~**ty** /ɪn'taɪərətɪ/ *n*. **in its** ~**ty** en su totalidad

entitle /ɪn'taɪtl/ *vt* titular; (*give a right*) dar derecho a. **be** ~**d to** tener derecho a. ~**ment** *n* derecho *m*

entity /'entətɪ/ *n* entidad *f*

entomb /ɪn'tu:m/ *vt* sepultar

entrails /'entreɪlz/ *npl* entrañas *fpl*

entrance[1] /'entrəns/ *n* entrada *f*; (*right to enter*) admisión *f*

entrance[2] /ɪn'trɑ:ns/ *vt* encantar

entrant /'entrənt/ *n* participante *m & f*; (*in exam*) candidato *m*

entreat /ɪn'tri:t/ *vt* suplicar. ~**y** *n* súplica *f*

entrench /ɪn'trentʃ/ *vt* atrincherar

entrust /ɪn'trʌst/ *vt* confiar

entry /'entrɪ/ *n* entrada *f*; (*of street*) bocacalle *f*; (*note*) apunte *m*

entwine /ɪn'twaɪn/ *vt* entrelazar

enumerate /ɪ'nju:məreɪt/ *vt* enumerar

enunciate /ɪ'nʌnsɪeɪt/ *vt* pronunciar; (*state*) enunciar

envelop /ɪn'veləp/ *vt* (*pt* **enveloped**) envolver

envelope /'envələʊp/ *n* sobre *m*

enviable /'envɪəbl/ *a* envidiable

envious /'envɪəs/ *a* envidioso. ~**ly** *adv* con envidia

environment /ɪn'vaɪərənmənt/ *n* medio *m* ambiente. ~**al** /-'mentl/ *a* ambiental

envisage /ɪn'vɪzɪdʒ/ *vt* prever; (*imagine*) imaginar

envoy /'envɔɪ/ *n* enviado *m*

envy /'envɪ/ *n* envidia *f*. ● *vt* envidiar

enzyme /'enzaɪm/ *n* enzima *f*

epaulette /'epəlet/ *n* charretera *f*

ephemeral /ɪ'femərəl/ *a* efímero

epic /'epɪk/ *n* épica *f*. ● *a* épico

epicentre /'epɪsentə(r)/ *n* epicentro *m*

epicure /'epɪkjʊə(r)/ *n* sibarita *m & f*; (*gourmet*) gastrónomo *m*

epidemic /epɪ'demɪk/ *n* epidemia *f*. ● *a* epidémico

epilep|sy /'epɪlepsɪ/ *n* epilepsia *f*. ~**tic** /-'leptɪk/ *a & n* epiléptico (*m*)

epilogue /'epɪlɒg/ *n* epílogo *m*

episode /'epɪsəʊd/ *n* episodio *m*

epistle /ɪ'pɪsl/ *n* epístola *f*

epitaph /'epɪtɑ:f/ *n* epitafio *m*

epithet /'epɪθet/ *n* epíteto *m*

epitom|e /ɪ'pɪtəmɪ/ *n* epítome *m*, personificación *f*. ~**ize** *vt* epitomar, personificar, ser la personificación de

epoch /'i:pɒk/ *n* época *f*. ~**-making** *a* que hace época

equal /'i:kwəl/ *a & n* igual (*m & f*). ~ **to** (*a task*) a la altura de. ● *vt* (*pt* **equalled**) ser igual a; (*math*) ser. ~**ity** /ɪ'kwɒlətɪ/ *n* igualdad *f*. ~**ize**

/'i:kwəlaız/ *vt/i* igualar. **~izer** /-ə(r)/ *n* (*sport*) tanto *m* de empate. **~ly** *adv* igualmente

equanimity /ekwə'nımətı/ *n* ecuanimidad *f*

equate /ɪ'kweɪt/ *vt* igualar

equation /ɪ'kweɪʒn/ *n* ecuación *f*

equator /ɪ'kweɪtə(r)/ *n* ecuador *m*. **~ial** /ekwə'tɔ:rɪəl/ *a* ecuatorial

equestrian /ɪ'kwestrɪən/ *a* ecuestre

equilateral /i:kwɪ'lætərl/ *a* equilátero

equilibrium /i:kwɪ'lɪbrɪəm/ *n* equilibrio *m*

equinox /'i:kwɪnɒks/ *n* equinoccio *m*

equip /ɪ'kwɪp/ *vt* (*pt* **equipped**) equipar. **~ment** *n* equipo *m*

equitable /'ekwɪtəbl/ *a* equitativo

equity /'ekwɪtɪ/ *n* equidad *f*; (*pl*, *com*) acciones *fpl* ordinarias

equivalen|ce /ɪ'kwɪvələns/ *n* equivalencia *f*. **~t** /ɪ'kwɪvəkl/ *a* & *n* equivalente (*m*)

equivocal /ɪ'kwɪvəkl/ *a* equívoco

era /'ɪərə/ *n* era *f*

eradicate /ɪ'rædɪkeɪt/ *vt* extirpar

erase /ɪ'reɪz/ *vt* borrar. **~r** /-ə(r)/ *n* borrador *m*

erect /ɪ'rekt/ *a* erguido. ● *vt* levantar. **~ion** /-ʃn/ *n* erección *f*, montaje *m*

ermine /'ɜ:mɪn/ *n* armiño *m*

ero|de /ɪ'rəʊd/ *vt* desgastar. **~sion** /-ʒn/ *n* desgaste *m*

erotic /ɪ'rɒtɪk/ *a* erótico. **~ism** /-sɪzəm/ *n* erotismo *m*

err /ɜ:(r)/ *vi* errar; (*sin*) pecar

errand /'erənd/ *n* recado *m*

erratic /ɪ'rætɪk/ *a* irregular; ⟨*person*⟩ voluble

erroneous /ɪ'rəʊnɪəs/ *a* erróneo

error /'erə(r)/ *n* error *m*

erudit|e /'eru:daɪt/ *a* erudito. **~ion** /-'dɪʃn/ *n* erudición *f*

erupt /ɪ'rʌpt/ *vi* estar en erupción; (*fig*) estallar. **~ion** /-ʃn/ *n* erupción *f*

escalat|e /'eskəleɪt/ *vt* intensificar. ● *vi* intensificarse. **~ion** /-'leɪʃn/ *n* intensificación *f*

escalator /'eskəleɪtə(r)/ *n* escalera *f* mecánica

escapade /eskə'peɪd/ *n* aventura *f*

escap|e /ɪ'skeɪp/ *vi* escaparse. ● *vt* evitar. ● *n* fuga *f*, (*avoidance*) evasión *f*. **have a narrow ~e** escapar por un pelo. **~ism** /ɪ'skeɪpɪzəm/ *n* escapismo *m*

escarpment /ɪs'kɑ:pmənt/ *n* escarpa *f*

escort /'eskɔ:t/ *n* acompañante *m*; (*mil*) escolta *f*. /ɪ'skɔ:t/ *vt* acompañar; (*mil*) escoltar

Eskimo /'eskɪməʊ/ *n* (*pl* **-os, -o**) esquimal (*m & f*)

especial /ɪ'speʃl/ *a* especial. **~ly** *adv* especialmente

espionage /'espɪənɑ:ʒ/ *n* espionaje *m*

esplanade /esplə'neɪd/ *n* paseo *m* marítimo

Esq. /ɪ'skwaɪə(r)/ *abbr* (*Esquire*) (*in address*). **E. Ashton, ~** Sr. D. E. Ashton

essay /'eseɪ/ *n* ensayo *m*; (*at school*) composición *f*

essence /'esns/ *n* esencia *f*. **in ~** esencialmente

essential /ɪ'senʃl/ *a* esencial. ● *n* lo esencial. **~ly** *adv* esencialmente

establish /ɪ'stæblɪʃ/ *vt* establecer; (*prove*) probar. **~ment** *n* establecimiento *m*. **the E~ment** los que mandan, el sistema *m*

estate /ɪ'steɪt/ *n* finca *f*; (*possessions*) bienes *mpl*. **~ agent** *n* agente *m* inmobiliario. **~ car** *n* furgoneta *f*

esteem /ɪ'sti:m/ *vt* estimar. ● *n* estimación *f*, estima *f*

estimat|e /'estɪmət/ *n* cálculo *m*; (*com*) presupuesto *m*. /'estɪmeɪt/ *vt* calcular. **~ion** /-'meɪʃn/ *n* estima *f*, estimación *f*; (*opinion*) opinión *f*

estranged /ɪs'treɪndʒd/ *a* alejado

estuary /'estʃʊərɪ/ *n* estuario *m*

etc. /et'setrə/ *abbr* (*et cetera*) etc., etcétera

etching /'etʃɪŋ/ *n* aguafuerte *m*

eternal /ɪ'tɜ:nl/ *a* eterno

eternity /ɪ'tɜ:nətɪ/ *n* eternidad *f*

ether /'i:θə(r)/ *n* éter *m*

ethereal /ɪ'θɪərɪəl/ *a* etéreo

ethic /'eθɪk/ *n* ética *f*. **~s** *npl* ética *f*. **~al** *a* ético

ethnic /'eθnɪk/ *a* étnico

ethos /'i:θɒs/ *n* carácter *m* distintivo

etiquette /'etɪket/ *n* etiqueta *f*

etymology /etɪ'mɒlədʒɪ/ *n* etimología *f*

eucalyptus /ju:kə'lɪptəs/ *n* (*pl* **-tuses**) eucalipto *m*

eulogy /'ju:lədʒɪ/ *n* encomio *m*

euphemism /'ju:fəmɪzəm/ *n* eufemismo *m*

euphoria /ju:'fɔ:rɪə/ *n* euforia *f*

Europe /'jʊərəp/ n Europa f. **~an** /-'pɪən/ a & n europeo (m)

euthanasia /ju:θə'neɪzɪə/ n eutanasia f

evacuat|e /ɪ'vækjʊeɪt/ vt evacuar; desocupar ⟨building⟩. **~ion** /-'eɪʃn/ n evacuación f

evade /ɪ'veɪd/ vt evadir

evaluate /ɪ'væljʊeɪt/ vt evaluar

evangeli|cal /i:væn'dʒelɪkl/ a evangélico. **~st** /ɪ'vændʒəlɪst/ n evangelista m & f

evaporat|e /ɪ'væpəreɪt/ vi evaporarse. **~ion** /-'reɪʃn/ n evaporación f

evasion /ɪ'veɪʒn/ n evasión f

evasive /ɪ'veɪsɪv/ a evasivo

eve /i:v/ n víspera f

even /'i:vn/ a regular; ⟨flat⟩ llano; ⟨surface⟩ liso; ⟨amount⟩ igual; ⟨number⟩ par. **get ~ with** desquitarse con. • vt nivelar. **~ up** igualar. • adv aun, hasta, incluso. **~ if** aunque. **~ so** aun así. **not ~** ni siquiera

evening /'i:vnɪŋ/ n tarde f; ⟨after dark⟩ noche f. **~ class** n clase f nocturna. **~ dress** n ⟨man's⟩ traje m de etiqueta; ⟨woman's⟩ traje m de noche

evensong /'i:vənsɒŋ/ n vísperas fpl

event /ɪ'vent/ n acontecimiento m; ⟨sport⟩ prueba f. **in the ~ of** en caso de. **~ful** a lleno de acontecimientos

eventual /ɪ'ventʃʊəl/ a final, definitivo. **~ity** /-'ælətɪ/ n eventualidad f. **~ly** adv finalmente

ever /'evə(r)/ adv jamás, nunca; ⟨at all times⟩ siempre. **~ after** desde entonces. **~ since** desde entonces. • conj después de que. **~ so** ⟨fam⟩ muy. **for ~** para siempre. **hardly ~** casi nunca

evergreen /'evəgriːn/ a de hoja perenne. • n árbol m de hoja perenne

everlasting /'evəlɑːstɪŋ/ a eterno

every /'evrɪ/ a cada, todo. **~ child** todos los niños. **~ one** cada uno. **~ other day** cada dos días

everybody /'evrɪbɒdɪ/ pron todo el mundo

everyday /'evrɪdeɪ/ a todos los días

everyone /'evrɪwʌn/ pron todo el mundo. **~ else** todos los demás

everything /'evrɪθɪŋ/ pron todo

everywhere /'evrɪweə(r)/ adv en todas partes

evict /ɪ'vɪkt/ vt desahuciar. **~ion** /-ʃn/ n desahucio m

eviden|ce /'evɪdəns/ n evidencia f; ⟨proof⟩ pruebas fpl; ⟨jurid⟩ testimonio m. **~ce of** señales de. **in ~ce** visible. **~t** /'evɪdənt/ a evidente. **~tly** adv evidentemente

evil /'i:vl/ a malo. • n mal m, maldad f

evocative /ɪ'vɒkətɪv/ a evocador

evoke /ɪ'vəʊk/ vt evocar

evolution /i:və'lu:ʃn/ n evolución f

evolve /ɪ'vɒlv/ vt desarrollar. • vi desarrollarse, evolucionar

ewe /ju:/ n oveja f

ex... /eks/ pref ex...

exacerbate /ɪg'zæsəbeɪt/ vt exacerbar

exact /ɪg'zækt/ a exacto. • vt exigir ⟨from a⟩. **~ing** a exigente. **~itude** n exactitud f. **~ly** adv exactamente

exaggerat|e /ɪg'zædʒəreɪt/ vt exagerar. **~ion** /-'reɪʃn/ n exageración f

exalt /ɪg'zɔːlt/ vt exaltar

exam /ɪg'zæm/ n ⟨fam⟩ examen m. **~ination** /ɪgzæmɪ'neɪʃn/ n examen m. **~ine** /ɪg'zæmɪn/ vt examinar; interrogar ⟨witness⟩. **~iner** /-ə(r)/ n examinador m

example /ɪg'zɑːmpl/ n ejemplo m. **make an ~ of** infligir castigo ejemplar a

exasperat|e /ɪg'zæspəreɪt/ vt exasperar. **~ion** /-'reɪʃn/ n exasperación f

excavat|e /'ekskəveɪt/ vt excavar. **~ion** /-'veɪʃn/ n excavación f

exceed /ɪk'si:d/ vt exceder. **~ingly** adv extremadamente

excel /ɪk'sel/ vi ⟨pt **excelled**⟩ sobresalir. • vt superar

excellen|ce /'eksələns/ n excelencia f. **~t** /'eksələnt/ a excelente. **~tly** adv excelentemente

except /ɪk'sept/ prep excepto, con excepción de. **~ for** con excepción de. • vt exceptuar. **~ing** prep con excepción de

exception /ɪk'sepʃən/ n excepción f. **take ~ to** ofenderse por. **~al** /ɪk'sepʃənl/ a excepcional. **~ally** adv excepcionalmente

excerpt /'eksɜ:pt/ n extracto m

excess /ɪk'ses/ n exceso m. /'ekses/ a excedente. **~ fare** n suplemento m. **~ luggage** n exceso m de equipaje

excessive /ɪk'sesɪv/ a excesivo. **~ly** adv excesivamente

exchange /ɪk'stʃeɪndʒ/ vt cambiar.
● n cambio m. **(telephone)** ~ central f telefónica

exchequer /ɪks'tʃekə(r)/ n (pol) erario m, hacienda f

excise[1] /'eksaɪz/ n impuestos mpl
indirectos

excise[2] /ek'saɪz/ vt quitar

excit|able /ɪk'saɪtəbl/ a excitable.
~e /ɪk'saɪt/ vt emocionar; (stimulate) excitar. ~ed a entusiasmado.
~ement n emoción f; (enthusiasm)
entusiasmo m. ~ing a emocionante

excla|im /ɪk'skleɪm/ vi exclamar.
~mation /eksklə'meɪʃn/ n exclamación f. ~mation mark n signo m
de admiración f, punto m de
exclamación

exclu|de /ɪk'sklu:d/ vt excluir.
~sion /-ʒən/ n exclusión f

exclusive /ɪk'sklu:sɪv/ a exclusivo;
⟨club⟩ selecto. ~ of excluyendo. ~ly
adv exclusivamente

excommunicate /ekskə'mju:nɪkeɪt/
vt excomulgar

excrement /'ekskrɪmənt/ n excremento m

excruciating /ɪk'skru:ʃɪeɪtɪŋ/ a
atroz, insoportable

excursion /ɪk'skɜ:ʃn/ n excursión f

excus|able a /ɪk'skju:zəbl/ a per-
donable. ~e /ɪk'skju:z/ vt perdonar.
~e from dispensar de. ~e me!
¡perdón! /ɪk'skju:s/ n excusa f

ex-directory /eksdɪ'rektərɪ/ a que
no está en la guía telefónica

execrable /'eksɪkrəbl/ a execrable

execut|e /'eksɪkju:t/ vt ejecutar.
~ion /eksɪ'kju:ʃn/ n ejecución f. ~i-
oner n verdugo m

executive /ɪg'zekjʊtɪv/ a & n ejecutivo (m)

executor /ɪg'zekjʊtə(r)/ n (jurid)
testamentario m

exemplary /ɪg'zemplərɪ/ a ejemplar

exemplify /ɪg'zemplɪfaɪ/ vt ilustrar

exempt /ɪg'zempt/ a exento. ● vt dispensar. ~ion /-ʃn/ n exención f

exercise /'eksəsaɪz/ n ejercicio m.
● vt ejercer. ● vi hacer ejercicios. ~
book n cuaderno m

exert /ɪg'zɜ:t/ vt ejercer. ~ o.s. esforzarse. ~ion /-ʃn/ n esfuerzo m

exhal|ation /ekshə'leɪʃn/ n ex-
halación f. ~e /eks'heɪl/ vt/i
exhalar

exhaust /ɪg'zɔ:st/ vt agotar. ● n
(auto) tubo m de escape. ~ed a agotado. ~ion /-stʃən/ n agotamiento
m. ~ive /ɪg'zɔ:stɪv/ a exhaustivo

exhibit /ɪg'zɪbɪt/ vt exponer; (jurid)
exhibir; (fig) mostrar. ● n objeto m
expuesto; (jurid) documento m

exhibition /eksɪ'bɪʃn/ n exposición
f; (act of showing) demostración f;
(univ) beca f. ~ist n exhibicionista m
& f

exhibitor /ɪg'zɪbɪtə(r)/ n expositor m

exhilarat|e /ɪg'zɪləreɪt/ vt alegrar.
~ion /-'reɪʃn/ n regocijo m

exhort /ɪg'zɔ:t/ vt exhortar

exile /'eksaɪl/ n exilio m; (person)
exiliado m. ● vt desterrar

exist /ɪg'zɪst/ vi existir. ~ence n
existencia f. in ~ence existente

existentialism /egzɪs'tenʃəlɪzəm/ n
existencialismo m

exit /'eksɪt/ n salida f

exodus /'eksədəs/ n éxodo m

exonerate /ɪg'zɒnəreɪt/ vt disculpar

exorbitant /ɪg'zɔ:bɪtənt/ a exorbitante

exorcis|e /'eksɔ:saɪz/ vt exorcizar.
~m /-sɪzəm/ n exorcismo m

exotic /ɪg'zɒtɪk/ a exótico

expand /ɪk'spænd/ vt extender; dilatar ⟨metal⟩; (develop) desarrollar.
● vi extenderse; (develop) desarrollarse; ⟨metal⟩ dilatarse

expanse /ɪk'spæns/ n extensión f

expansion /ɪk'spænʃn/ n extensión
f; (of metal) dilatación f

expansive /ɪk'spænsɪv/ a expansivo

expatriate /eks'pætrɪət/ a & n
expatriado (m)

expect /ɪk'spekt/ vt esperar; (suppose) suponer; (demand) contar con. I
~ so supongo que sí

expectan|cy /ɪk'spektənsɪ/ n espe-
ranza f. **life** ~cy esperanza f de vida.
~t /ɪk'spektənt/ a expectante. ~t
mother n futura madre f

expectation /ekspek'teɪʃn/ n esperanza f

expedien|cy /ɪk'spi:dɪənsɪ/ n con-
veniencia f. ~t /ɪk'spi:dɪənt/ a con-
veniente

expedite /'ekspɪdaɪt/ vt acelerar

expedition /ekspɪ'dɪʃn/ n expedición f. ~ary a expedicionario

expel /ɪk'spel/ vt (pt expelled)
expulsar

expend /ɪk'spend/ vt gastar. ~able
a prescindible

expenditure /ɪk'spendɪtʃə(r)/ n gastos mpl

expens|e /ɪk'spens/ n gasto m; (fig) costa f. **at s.o.'s ~e** a costa de uno. **~ive** /ɪk'spensɪv/ a caro. **~ively** adv costosamente

experience /ɪk'spɪərɪəns/ n experiencia. ● vt experimentar. **~d** a experto

experiment /ɪk'sperɪmənt/ n experimento m. ● vi experimentar. **~al** /-'mentl/ a experimental

expert /'ekspɜːt/ a & n experto (m). **~ise** /eksp3ː'tiːz/ n pericia f. **~ly** adv hábilmente

expir|e /ɪk'spaɪə(r)/ vi expirar. **~y** n expiración f

expla|in /ɪk'spleɪn/ vt explicar. **~nation** /eksplə'neɪʃn/ n explicación f. **~natory** /ɪks'plænətərɪ/ a explicativo

expletive /ɪk'spliːtɪv/ n palabrota f

explicit /ɪk'splɪsɪt/ a explícito

explode /ɪk'spləʊd/ vt hacer explotar; (tec) explosionar. ● vi estallar

exploit /'eksplɔɪt/ n hazaña f. /ɪk'splɔɪt/ vt explotar. **~ation** /eksplɔɪ'teɪʃn/ n explotación f

explor|ation /eksplə'reɪʃn/ n exploración f. **~atory** /ɪk'splɒrətrɪ/ a exploratorio. **~e** /ɪk'splɔː(r)/ vt explorar. **~er** n explorador m

explosi|on /ɪk'spləʊʒn/ n explosión f. **~ve** a & n explosivo (m)

exponent /ɪk'spəʊnənt/ n exponente m

export /ɪk'spɔːt/ vt exportar. /'ekspɔːt/ n exportación f. **~er** /ɪks'pɔːtə(r)/ exportador m

expos|e /ɪk'spəʊz/ vt exponer; (reveal) descubrir. **~ure** /-ʒə(r)/ n exposición f. **die of ~ure** morir de frío

expound /ɪk'spaʊnd/ vt exponer

express[1] /ɪk'spres/ vt expresar

express[2] /ɪk'spres/ a expreso; (letter) urgente. ● adv (by express post) por correo urgente. ● n (train) rápido m, expreso m

expression /ɪk'spreʃn/ n expresión f

expressive /ɪk'spresɪv/ a expresivo

expressly /ɪk'spreslɪ/ adv expresamente

expulsion /ɪk'spʌlʃn/ n expulsión f

expurgate /'ekspɜːgeɪt/ vt expurgar

exquisite /'ekskwɪzɪt/ a exquisito. **~ly** adv primorosamente

ex-serviceman /eks'sɜːvɪsmən/ n (pl -men) excombatiente m

extant /ek'stænt/ a existente

extempore /ek'stempərɪ/ a improvisado. ● adv de improviso

exten|d /ɪk'stend/ vt extender; (prolong) prolongar; ensanchar (house). ● vi extenderse. **~sion** n extensión f; (of road, time) prolongación f; (building) anejo m; (com) prórroga f

extensive /ɪk'stensɪv/ a extenso. **~ly** adv extensamente

extent /ɪk'stent/ n extensión f; (fig) alcance. **to a certain ~** hasta cierto punto

extenuate /ɪk'stenjʊeɪt/ vt atenuar

exterior /ɪk'stɪərɪə(r)/ a & n exterior (m)

exterminat|e /ɪk'stɜːmɪneɪt/ vt exterminar. **~ion** /-'neɪʃn/ n exterminio m

external /ɪk'stɜːnl/ a externo. **~ly** adv externamente

extinct /ɪk'stɪŋkt/ a extinto. **~ion** /-ʃn/ n extinción f

extinguish /ɪk'stɪŋgwɪʃ/ vt extinguir. **~er** n extintor m

extol /ɪk'stəʊl/ vt (pt extolled) alabar

extort /ɪk'stɔːt/ vt sacar por la fuerza. **~ion** /-ʃn/ n exacción f. **~ionate** /ɪk'stɔːʃənət/ a exorbitante

extra /'ekstrə/ a suplementario. ● adv extraordinariamente. ● n suplemento m; (cinema) extra m & f

extract /'ekstrækt/ n extracto m. /ɪk'strækt/ vt extraer; (fig) arrancar. **~ion** /-ʃn/ n extracción f; (lineage) origen m

extradit|e /'ekstrədaɪt/ vt extraditar. **~ion** /-'dɪʃn/ n extradición f

extramarital /ekstrə'mærɪtl/ a fuera del matrimonio

extramural /ekstrə'mjʊərəl/ a fuera del recinto universitario; (for external students) para estudiantes externos

extraordinary /ɪk'strɔːdnrɪ/ a extraordinario

extra-sensory /ekstrə'sensərɪ/ a extrasensorial

extravagan|ce /ɪk'strævəgəns/ n prodigalidad f, extravagancia f. **~t** /ɪk'strævəgənt/ a pródigo, extravagante

extrem|e /ɪk'striːm/ a & n extremo (m). **~ely** adv extremadamente. **~ist** n extremista m & f. **~ity** /ɪk'stremətɪ/ n extremidad f

extricate /'ekstrɪkeɪt/ *vt* desenredar, librar

extrovert /'ekstrəvɜ:t/ *n* extrovertido *m*

exuberan|ce /ɪg'zju:bərəns/ *n* exuberancia *f*. ~**t** /ɪg'zju:bərənt/ *a* exuberante

exude /ɪg'zju:d/ *vt* rezumar

exult /ɪg'zʌlt/ *vi* exultar

eye /aɪ/ *n* ojo *m*. **keep an ~ on** no perder de vista. **see ~ to ~** estar de acuerdo con. ● *vt* (*pt* **eyed**, *pres p* **eyeing**) mirar. ~**ball** /'aɪbɔ:l/ *n* globo *m* del ojo. ~**brow** /'aɪbraʊ/ *n* ceja *f*. ~**ful** /'aɪfʊl/ *n* (*fam*) espectáculo *m* sorprendente. ~**lash** /'aɪlæʃ/ *n* pestaña *f*. ~**let** /'aɪlɪt/ *n* ojete *m*. ~**lid** /'aɪlɪd/ *n* párpado *m*. ~**opener** *n* (*fam*) revelación *f*. ~**shadow** *n* sombra *f* de ojos, sombreador *m*. ~**sight** /'aɪsaɪt/ *n* vista *f*. ~**sore** /'aɪsɔ:(r)/ *n* (*fig*, *fam*) monstruosidad *f*, horror *m*. ~**witness** /'aɪwɪtnɪs/ *n* testigo *m* ocular

F

fable /'feɪbl/ *n* fábula *f*

fabric /'fæbrɪk/ *n* tejido *m*, tela *f*

fabrication /fæbrɪ'keɪʃn/ *n* invención *f*

fabulous /'fæbjʊləs/ *a* fabuloso

facade /fə'sɑ:d/ *n* fachada *f*

face /feɪs/ *n* cara *f*, rostro *m*; (*of watch*) esfera *f*; (*aspect*) aspecto *m*. ~ **down(wards)** boca abajo. ~ **up-(wards)** boca arriba. **in the ~ of** frente a. **lose ~** quedar mal. **pull ~s** hacer muecas. ● *vt* mirar hacia; ⟨*house*⟩ dar a; (*confront*) enfrentarse con. ● *vi* volverse. ~ **up to** enfrentarse con. ~ **flannel** *n* paño *m* (para lavarse la cara). ~**less** *a* anónimo. ~**lift** *n* cirugía *f* estética en la cara

facet /'fæsɪt/ *n* faceta *f*

facetious /fə'si:ʃəs/ *a* chistoso, gracioso

facial /'feɪʃl/ *a* facial. ● *n* masaje *m* facial

facile /'fæsaɪl/ *a* fácil

facilitate /fə'sɪlɪteɪt/ *vt* facilitar

facility /fə'sɪlɪtɪ/ *n* facilidad *f*

facing /'feɪsɪŋ/ *n* revestimiento *m*. ~**s** *npl* (*on clothes*) vueltas *fpl*

facsimile /fæk'sɪmɪlɪ/ *n* facsímile *m*

fact /fækt/ *n* hecho *m*. **as a matter of ~**, **in ~** en realidad, a decir verdad

faction /'fækʃn/ *n* facción *f*

factor /'fæktə(r)/ *n* factor *m*

factory /'fæktərɪ/ *n* fábrica *f*

factual /'fæktʃʊəl/ *a* basado en hechos, factual

faculty /'fækltɪ/ *n* facultad *f*

fad /fæd/ *n* manía *f*, capricho *m*

fade /feɪd/ *vi* ⟨*colour*⟩ descolorarse; ⟨*flowers*⟩ marchitarse; ⟨*light*⟩ apagarse; ⟨*memory*, *sound*⟩ desvanecerse

faeces /'fi:si:z/ *npl* excrementos *mpl*

fag¹ /fæg/ *n* (*chore*, *fam*) faena *f*; (*cigarette*, *sl*) cigarillo *m*, pitillo *m*

fag² /fæg/ *n* (*homosexual*, *Amer*, *sl*) marica *m*

fagged /fægd/ *a*. ~ **(out)** rendido

fah /f/ *n* (*mus*, *fourth note of any musical scale*) fa *m*

fail /feɪl/ *vi* fallar; (*run short*) acabarse. **he ~ed to arrive** no llegó. ● *vt* no aprobar (*exam*); suspender ⟨*candidate*⟩; (*disappoint*) fallar. ~ **s.o.** ⟨*words etc*⟩ faltarle a uno. ● *n*. **without ~** sin falta

failing /'feɪlɪŋ/ *n* defecto *m*. ● *prep* a falta de

failure /'feɪljə(r)/ *n* fracaso *m*; (*person*) fracasado *m*; (*med*) ataque *m*; (*mec*) fallo *m*. ~ **to do** dejar *m* de hacer

faint /feɪnt/ *a* (**-er**, **-est**) (*weak*) débil; (*indistinct*) indistinto. **feel ~** estar mareado. **the ~est idea** la más remota idea. ● *vi* desmayarse. ● *n* desmayo *m*. ~**hearted** *a* pusilánime, cobarde. ~**ly** *adv* (*weakly*) débilmente; (*indistinctly*) indistintamente. ~**ness** *n* debilidad *f*

fair¹ /feə(r)/ *a* (**-er**, **-est**) (*just*) justo; ⟨*weather*⟩ bueno; ⟨*amount*⟩ razonable; ⟨*hair*⟩ rubio; ⟨*skin*⟩ blanco. ~ **play** *n* juego *m* limpio. ● *adv* limpio

fair² /feə(r)/ *n* feria *f*

fair: ~**ly** *adv* (*justly*) justamente; (*rather*) bastante. ~**ness** *n* justicia *f*

fairy /'feərɪ/ *n* hada *f*. ~**land** *n* país *m* de las hadas. ~ **story**, ~**tale** cuento *m* de hadas

fait accompli /feɪtə'kɒmpli:/ *n* hecho *m* consumado

faith /feɪθ/ *n* (*trust*) confianza *f*; (*relig*) fe *f*. ~**ful** *a* fiel. ~**fully** *adv* fielmente. ~**fulness** *n* fidelidad *f*. ~**healing** *n* curación *f* por la fe

fake /feɪk/ n falsificación f; (person) impostor m. ● a falso. ● vt falsificar; (pretend) fingir

fakir /'feɪkɪə(r)/ n faquir m

falcon /'fɔːlkən/ n halcón m

Falkland /'fɔːlklənd/ n. **the ~ Islands** npl las islas fpl Malvinas

fall /fɔːl/ vi (pt **fell**, pp **fallen**) caer. ● n caída f; (autumn, Amer) otoño m; (in price) baja f. **~ back on** recurrir a. **~ down** (fall) caer; (be unsuccessful) fracasar. **~ for** (fam) enamorarse de ⟨person⟩; (fam) dejarse engañar por ⟨trick⟩. **~ in** (mil) formar filas. **~ off** (diminish) disminuir. **~ out** (quarrel) reñir (**with** con); (drop out) caer. **~ over** caer(se). **~ over sth** tropezar con algo. **~ short** ser insuficiente. **~ through** fracasar

fallacy /'fæləsɪ/ n error m

fallible /'fælɪbl/ a falible

fallout /'fɔːlaʊt/ n lluvia f radiactiva

fallow /'fæləʊ/ a en barbecho

false /fɔːls/ a falso. **~hood** n mentira f. **~ly** adv falsamente. **~ness** n falsedad f

falsetto /fɔːl'setəʊ/ n (pl **-os**) falsete m

falsify /'fɔːlsɪfaɪ/ vt falsificar

falter /'fɔːltə(r)/ vi vacilar

fame /feɪm/ n fama f. **~d** a famoso

familiar /fə'mɪlɪə(r)/ a familiar. **be ~ with** conocer. **~ity** /-'ærətɪ/ n familiaridad f. **~ize** vt familiarizar

family /'fæməlɪ/ n familia f. ● a de (la) familia, familiar

famine /'fæmɪn/ n hambre f, hambruna f (LAm)

famished /'fæmɪʃt/ a hambriento

famous /'feɪməs/ a famoso. **~ly** adv (fam) a las mil maravillas

fan¹ /fæn/ n abanico m; (mec) ventilador m. ● vt (pt **fanned**) abanicar; soplar ⟨fire⟩. ● vi. **~ out** desparramarse en forma de abanico

fan² /fæn/ n (of person) admirador m; (enthusiast) aficionado m, entusiasta m & f

fanatic /fə'nætɪk/ n fanático m. **~al** a fanático. **~ism** /-sɪzəm/ n fanatismo m

fan belt /'fænbelt/ n correa f de ventilador

fancier /'fænsɪə(r)/ n aficionado m

fanciful /'fænsɪfl/ a (imaginative) imaginativo; (unreal) imaginario

fancy /'fænsɪ/ n fantasía f; (liking) gusto m. **take a ~ to** tomar cariño a ⟨person⟩; aficionarse a ⟨thing⟩. ● a de lujo; (extravagant) excesivo. ● vt (imagine) imaginar; (believe) creer; (want, fam) apetecer a. **~ dress** n disfraz m

fanfare /'fænfeə(r)/ n fanfarria f

fang /fæŋ/ n (of animal) colmillo m; (of snake) diente m

fanlight /'fænlaɪt/ n montante m

fantasize /'fæntəsaɪz/ vi fantasear

fantastic /fæn'tæstɪk/ a fantástico

fantasy /'fæntəsɪ/ n fantasía f

far /fɑː(r)/ adv lejos; (much) mucho. **as ~ as** hasta. **as ~ as I know** que yo sepa. **by ~** con mucho. ● a (**further, furthest** or **farther, farthest**) lejano

far-away /'fɑːrəweɪ/ a lejano

farc|e /fɑːs/ n farsa f. **~ical** a ridículo

fare /feə(r)/ n (for transport) tarifa f; (food) comida f. ● vi irle. **how did you ~?** ¿qué tal te fue?

Far East /fɑː(r)'iːst/ n Extremo/ Lejano Oriente m

farewell /feə'wel/ int & n adiós (m)

far-fetched /fɑː'fetʃt/ a improbable

farm /fɑːm/ n granja f. ● vt cultivar. **~ out** arrendar. ● vi ser agricultor. **~er** n agricultor m. **~house** n granja f. **~ing** n agricultura f. **~yard** n corral m

far: **~-off** a lejano. **~-reaching** a trascendental. **~-seeing** a clarividente. **~-sighted** a hipermétrope; (fig) clarividente

farther, farthest /'fɑːðə(r), 'fɑːðəst/ see **far**

fascinat|e /'fæsɪneɪt/ vt fascinar. **~ion** /-'neɪʃn/ n fascinación f

fascis|m /'fæʃɪzəm/ n fascismo m. **~t** /'fæʃɪst/ a & n fascista (m & f)

fashion /'fæʃn/ n (manner) manera f; (vogue) moda f. **~able** a de moda

fast¹ /fɑːst/ a (**-er, -est**) rápido; ⟨clock⟩ adelantado; (secure) fijo; ⟨colours⟩ sólido. ● adv rápidamente; (securely) firmemente. **~ asleep** profundamente dormido

fast² /fɑːst/ vi ayunar. ● n ayuno m

fasten /'fɑːsn/ vt/i sujetar; cerrar ⟨windows, doors⟩; abrochar ⟨belt etc⟩. **~er** n, **~ing** n (on box, window) cierre m; (on door) cerrojo m

fastidious /fə'stɪdɪəs/ a exigente, minucioso

fat /fæt/ n grasa f. ● a (**fatter, fat-test**) gordo; ‹*meat*› que tiene mucha grasa; (*thick*) grueso. **a ~ lot of** (*sl*) muy poco

fatal /'feɪtl/ a mortal; (*fateful*) fatídico

fatalis|m /'feɪtəlɪzəm/ n fatalismo m. **~t** n fatalista m & f

fatality /fə'tælətɪ/ n calamidad f; (*death*) muerte f

fatally /'feɪtəlɪ/ adv mortalmente; (*by fate*) fatalmente

fate /feɪt/ n destino m; (*one's lot*) suerte f. **~d** a predestinado. **~ful** a fatídico

fat-head /'fæthed/ n imbécil m

father /'fɑːðə(r)/ n padre m. **~hood** m paternidad f. **~-in-law** m (pl **fathers-in-law**) m suegro m. **~ly** a paternal

fathom /'fæðəm/ n braza f. ● vt. **~ (out)** comprender

fatigue /fə'tiːg/ n fatiga f. ● vt fatigar

fat: ~ness n gordura f. **~ten** vt/i engordar. **~tening** a que engorda. **~ty** a graso. ● n (*fam*) gordinflón m

fatuous /'fætjʊəs/ a fatuo

faucet /'fɔːsɪt/ n (*Amer*) grifo m

fault /fɔːlt/ n defecto m; (*blame*) culpa f; (*tennis*) falta f; (*geol*) falla f. **at ~** culpable. ● vt criticar. **~less** a impecable. **~y** a defectuoso

fauna /'fɔːnə/ n fauna f

faux pas /fəʊ'pɑː/ n (pl **faux pas** /fəʊ'pɑː/) n metedura f de pata, paso m en falso

favour /'feɪvə(r)/ n favor m. ● vt favorecer; (*support*) estar a favor de; (*prefer*) preferir. **~able** a favorable. **~ably** adv favorablemente

favourit|e /'feɪvərɪt/ a & n preferido (m). **~ism** n favoritismo m

fawn[1] /fɔːn/ n cervato m. ● a color de cervato, beige, beis

fawn[2] /fɔːn/ vi. **~ on** adular

fax /fæks/ n telefacsímil m, fax m

fear /fɪə(r)/ n miedo m. ● vt temer. **~ful** a (*frightening*) espantoso; (*frightened*) temeroso. **~less** a intrépido. **~lessness** n intrepidez f. **~some** a espantoso

feasib|ility /fiːzə'bɪlətɪ/ n viabilidad f. **~le** /'fiːzəbl/ a factible; (*likely*) posible

feast /fiːst/ n (*relig*) fiesta f; (*meal*) banquete m, comilona f. ● vt banquetear, festejar. **~ on** regalarse con

feat /fiːt/ n hazaña f

feather /'feðə(r)/ n pluma f. ● vt. **~ one's nest** hacer su agosto. **~brained** a tonto. **~weight** n peso m pluma

feature /'fiːtʃə(r)/ n (*on face*) facción f; (*characteristic*) característica f; (in *newspaper*) artículo m; **~ (film)** película f principal, largometraje m. ● vt presentar; (*give prominence to*) destacar. ● vi figurar

February /'februərɪ/ n febrero m

feckless /'feklɪs/ a inepto; (*irresponsible*) irreflexivo

fed /fed/ see **feed**. ● a. **~ up** (*sl*) harto (**with** de)

federal /'fedərəl/ a federal

federation /fedə'reɪʃn/ n federación f

fee /fiː/ n (*professional*) honorarios mpl; (*enrolment*) derechos mpl; (*club*) cuota f

feeble /'fiːbl/ a (**-er, -est**) débil. **~minded** a imbécil

feed /fiːd/ vt (pt **fed**) dar de comer a; (*supply*) alimentar. ● vi comer. ● n (*for animals*) pienso m; (*for babies*) comida f. **~back** n reacciones fpl, comentarios mpl

feel /fiːl/ vt (pt **felt**) sentir; (*touch*) tocar; (*think*) parecerle. **do you ~ it's a good idea?** te parece buena idea? **I ~ it is necessary** me parece necesario. **~ as if** tener la impresión de que. **~ hot/hungry** tener calor/ hambre. **~ like** (*want, fam*) tener ganas de. **~ up to** sentirse capaz de

feeler /'fiːlə(r)/ n (*of insects*) antena f. **put out a ~** (*fig*) hacer un sondeo

feeling /'fiːlɪŋ/ n sentimiento m; (*physical*) sensación f

feet /fiːt/ see **foot**

feign /feɪn/ vt fingir

feint /feɪnt/ n finta f

felicitous /fə'lɪsɪtəs/ a feliz, oportuno

feline /'fiːlaɪn/ a felino

fell[1] /fel/ see **fall**

fell[2] /fel/ vt derribar

fellow /'feləʊ/ n (*fam*) tipo m; (*comrade*) compañero m; (*society*) socio m. **~-countryman** n compatriota m & f. **~ passenger/traveller** n compañero de viaje. **~ship** n compañerismo m; (*group*) asociación f

felony /'felənɪ/ n crimen m

felt[1] /felt/ n fieltro m

felt[2] /felt/ see **feel**

female /'fi:meɪl/ a hembra; ⟨voice, sex etc⟩ femenino. ● n mujer f; ⟨animal⟩ hembra f

femini|ne /'femənɪn/ a & n femenino (m). ~**nity** /-'nɪnətɪ/ n feminidad f. ~**st** n feminista m & f

fenc|e /fens/ n cerca f; ⟨person, sl⟩ perista m & f ⟨fam⟩. ● vt. ~**e (in)** encerrar, cercar. ● vi ⟨sport⟩ practicar la esgrima. ~**er** n esgrimidor m. ~**ing** n ⟨sport⟩ esgrima f

fend /fend/ vi. ~ **for o.s.** valerse por sí mismo. ● vt. ~ **off** defenderse de

fender /'fendə(r)/ n guardafuego m; ⟨mudguard, Amer⟩ guardabarros m invar; ⟨naut⟩ defensa f

fennel /'fenl/ n hinojo m

ferment /'fɜ:ment/ n fermento m; ⟨fig⟩ agitación f. /fə'ment/ vt/i fermentar. ~**ation** /-'teɪʃn/ n fermentación f

fern /fɜ:n/ n helecho m

feroci|ous /fə'rəʊʃəs/ a feroz. ~**ty** /fə'rɒsətɪ/ n ferocidad f

ferret /'ferɪt/ n hurón m. ● vi ⟨pt **ferreted**⟩ huronear. ● vt. ~ **out** descubrir

ferry /'ferɪ/ n ferry m. ● vt transportar

fertil|e /'fɜ:taɪl/ a fértil; ⟨biol⟩ fecundo. ~**ity** /-'tɪlətɪ/ n fertilidad f; ⟨biol⟩ fecundidad f

fertilize /'fɜ:təlaɪz/ vt abonar; ⟨biol⟩ fecundar. ~**r** n abono m

fervent /'fɜ:vənt/ a ferviente

fervour /'fɜ:və(r)/ n fervor m

fester /'festə(r)/ vi enconarse

festival /'festəvl/ n fiesta f; ⟨of arts⟩ festival m

festive /'festɪv/ a festivo. ~ **season** n temporada f de fiestas

festivity /fe'stɪvətɪ/ n festividad f

festoon /fe'stu:n/ vi. ~ **with** adornar de

fetch /fetʃ/ vt ⟨go for⟩ ir a buscar; ⟨bring⟩ traer; ⟨be sold for⟩ venderse por

fetching /'fetʃɪŋ/ a atractivo

fête /feɪt/ n fiesta f. ● vt festejar

fetid /'fetɪd/ a fétido

fetish /'fetɪʃ/ n fetiche m; ⟨psych⟩ obsesión f

fetter /'fetə(r)/ vt encadenar. ~**s** npl grilletes mpl

fettle /'fetl/ n condición f

feud /fju:d/ n enemistad f ⟨inveterada⟩

feudal /fju:dl/ a feudal. ~**ism** n feudalismo m

fever /'fi:və(r)/ n fiebre f. ~**ish** a febril

few /fju:/ a pocos. ● n pocos mpl. **a** ~ unos (pocos). **a good** ~, **quite a** ~ ⟨fam⟩ muchos. ~**er** a & n menos. ~**est** a & n el menor número de

fiancé /fr'ɒnseɪ/ n novio m. ~**e** /fr'ɒnseɪ/ n novia f

fiasco /fr'æskəʊ/ n ⟨pl -**os**⟩ fiasco m

fib /fɪb/ n mentirijilla f. ~**ber** n mentiroso m

fibre /'faɪbə(r)/ n fibra f. ~**glass** n fibra f de vidrio

fickle /'fɪkl/ a inconstante

fiction /'fɪkʃn/ n ficción f. **(works of)** ~ novelas fpl. ~**al** a novelesco

fictitious /fɪk'tɪʃəs/ a ficticio

fiddle /'fɪdl/ n ⟨fam⟩ violín m; ⟨swindle, sl⟩ trampa f. ● vt ⟨sl⟩ falsificar. ~ **with** juguetear con, toquetear, manosear. ~**r** n ⟨fam⟩ violinista m & f; ⟨cheat, sl⟩ tramposo m

fidelity /fr'delətɪ/ n fidelidad f

fidget /'fɪdʒɪt/ vi ⟨pt **fidgeted**⟩ moverse, ponerse nervioso. ~ **with** juguetear con. ● n azogado m. ~**y** a azogado

field /fi:ld/ n campo m. ~ **day** n gran ocasión f. ~ **glasses** npl gemelos mpl. **F~ Marshal** n mariscal m de campo, capitán m general. ~**work** n investigaciones fpl en el terreno

fiend /fi:nd/ n demonio m. ~**ish** a diabólico

fierce /fɪəs/ a ⟨-**er**, -**est**⟩ feroz; ⟨attack⟩ violento. ~**ness** n ferocidad f, violencia f

fiery /'faɪərɪ/ a ⟨-**ier**, -**iest**⟩ ardiente

fifteen /fɪf'ti:n/ a & n quince (m). ~**th** a & n quince (m), decimoquinto (m). ● n ⟨fraction⟩ quinzavo m

fifth /fɪfθ/ a & n quinto (m). ~ **column** n quinta columna f

fift|ieth /'fɪftɪəθ/ a & n cincuenta (m). ~**y** a & n cincuenta (m). ~**y**-~**y** mitad y mitad, a medias. **a** ~**y**-~**y chance** una posibilidad f de cada dos

fig /fɪg/ n higo m

fight /faɪt/ vt/i ⟨pt **fought**⟩ luchar; ⟨quarrel⟩ disputar. ~ **shy of** evitar. ● n lucha f; ⟨quarrel⟩ disputa f; ⟨mil⟩ combate m. ~ **back** defenderse. ~ **off** rechazar ⟨attack⟩; luchar contra ⟨illness⟩. ~**er** n luchador m; ⟨mil⟩ combatiente m & f; ⟨aircraft⟩ avión m de caza. ~**ing** n luchas fpl

figment /'fɪgmənt/ n invención f
figurative /'fɪgjʊrətɪv/ a figurado
figure /'fɪgə(r)/ n (number) cifra f; (diagram) figura f; (shape) forma f; (of woman) tipo m. ● vt imaginar. ● vi figurar. **that ~s** (Amer, fam) es lógico. **~ out** explicarse. **~head** n testaferro m, mascarón m de proa. **~ of speech** n tropo m, figura f. **~s** npl (arithmetic) aritmética f
filament /'fɪləmənt/ n filamento m
filch /fɪltʃ/ vt hurtar
file¹ /faɪl/ n carpeta f; (set of papers) expediente m. ● vt archivar ⟨papers⟩
file² /faɪl/ n (row) fila f. ● vi. **~ in** entrar en fila. **~ past** desfilar ante
file³ /faɪl/ n (tool) lima f. ● vt limar
filings /'faɪlɪŋz/ npl limaduras fpl
fill /fɪl/ vt llenar. ● vi llenarse. **~ in** rellenar ⟨form⟩. **~ out** (get fatter) engordar. **~ up** (auto) llenar, repostar. ● n. **eat one's ~** hartarse de comer. **have had one's ~ of** estar harto de
fillet /'fɪlɪt/ n filete m. ● vt (pt **filleted**) cortar en filetes
filling /'fɪlɪŋ/ n (in tooth) empaste m. **~ station** n estación f de servicio
film /fɪlm/ n película f. ● vt filmar. **~ star** n estrella f de cine. **~-strip** n tira f de película
filter /'fɪltə(r)/ n filtro m. ● vt filtrar. ● vi filtrarse. **~-tipped** a con filtro
filth /fɪlθ/ n inmundicia f. **~iness** n inmundicia f. **~y** a inmundo
fin /fɪn/ n aleta f
final /'faɪnl/ a último; (conclusive) decisivo. ● n (sport) final f. **~s** npl (schol) exámenes mpl de fin de curso
finale /fɪ'nɑːlɪ/ n final m
final: **~ist** n finalista m & f. **~ize** vt concluir. **~ly** adv (lastly) finalmente, por fin; (once and for all) definitivamente
financ|e /'faɪnæns/ n finanzas fpl. ● vt financiar. **~ial** /faɪ'nænʃl/ a financiero. **~ially** adv económicamente. **~ier** /faɪ'nænsɪə(r)/ n financiero m
finch /fɪntʃ/ n pinzón m
find /faɪnd/ vt (pt **found**) encontrar. **~ out** enterarse de. **~er** n el m que encuentra, descubridor m. **~ings** npl resultados mpl
fine¹ /faɪn/ a (-er, -est) fino; (excellent) excelente. ● adv muy bien; (small) en trozos pequeños
fine² /faɪn/ n multa f. ● vt multar

fine: **~ arts** npl bellas artes fpl. **~ly** adv (admirably) espléndidamente; (cut) en trozos pequeños. **~ry** /'faɪnərɪ/ n galas fpl
finesse /fɪ'nes/ n tino m
finger /'fɪŋgə(r)/ n dedo m. ● vt tocar. **~-nail** n uña f. **~print** n huella f dactilar. **~-stall** n dedil m. **~-tip** n punta f del dedo
finicking /'fɪnɪkɪŋ/ a, **finicky** /'fɪnɪkɪ/ a melindroso
finish /'fɪnɪʃ/ vt/i terminar. **~ doing** terminar de hacer. **~ up doing** terminar por hacer. ● n fin m; (of race) llegada f, meta f; (appearance) acabado m
finite /'faɪnaɪt/ a finito
Fin|land /'fɪnlənd/ n Finlandia f. **~n** n finlandés m. **~nish** a & n finlandés (m)
fiord /fjɔːd/ n fiordo m
fir /fɜː(r)/ n abeto m
fire /faɪə(r)/ n fuego m; (conflagration) incendio m. ● vt disparar ⟨bullet etc⟩; (dismiss) despedir; (fig) excitar, enardecer, inflamar. ● vi tirar. **~arm** n arma f de fuego. **~ brigade** n cuerpo m de bomberos. **~cracker** n (Amer) petardo m. **~ department** n (Amer) cuerpo m de bomberos. **~-engine** n coche m de bomberos. **~-escape** n escalera f de incendios. **~light** n lumbre f. **~man** n bombero m. **~place** n chimenea f. **~side** n hogar m. **~ station** n parque m de bomberos. **~wood** n leña f. **~work** n fuego m artificial
firing-squad /'faɪərɪŋskwɒd/ n pelotón m de ejecución
firm¹ /fɜːm/ n empresa f
firm² /fɜːm/ a (-er, -est) firme. **~ly** adv firmemente. **~ness** n firmeza f
first /fɜːst/ a primero. **at ~** directamente. **at ~ sight** a primera vista. ● n primero m. ● adv primero; (first time) por primera vez. **~ of all** ante todo. **~ aid** n primeros auxilios mpl. **~-born** a primogénito. **~-class** a de primera clase. **~ floor** n primer piso m; (Amer) planta f baja. **F~ Lady** n (Amer) Primera Dama f. **~ly** adv en primer lugar. **~ name** n nombre m de pila. **~-rate** a excelente
fiscal /'fɪskl/ a fiscal
fish /fɪʃ/ n (usually invar) (alive in water) pez m; (food) pescado m. ● vi pescar. **~ for** pescar. **~ out** (take out, fam) sacar. **go ~ing** ir de pesca.

~**erman** /'fɪʃəmən/ n pescador m.
~**ing** n pesca f. ~**ing-rod** n caña f de
pesca. ~**monger** n pescadero m. ~
shop n pescadería f. ~**y** a ⟨smell⟩ a
pescado; ⟨questionable, fam⟩ sospechoso

fission /'fɪʃn/ n fisión f

fist /fɪst/ n puño m

fit[1] /fɪt/ a (**fitter, fittest**) con-
veniente; ⟨healthy⟩ sano; ⟨good
enough⟩ adecuado; ⟨able⟩ capaz. ● n
⟨of clothes⟩ corte m. ● vt ⟨pt **fitted**⟩
⟨adapt⟩ adaptar; ⟨be the right size for⟩
sentar bien a; ⟨install⟩ colocar. ● vi
encajar; ⟨in certain space⟩ caber;
⟨clothes⟩ sentar. ~ **out** equipar. ~
up equipar

fit[2] /fɪt/ n ataque m

fitful /'fɪtfl/ a irregular

fitment /'fɪtmənt/ n mueble m

fitness /'fɪtnɪs/ n ⟨buena⟩ salud f; ⟨of
remark⟩ conveniencia f

fitting /'fɪtɪŋ/ a apropiado. ● n ⟨of
clothes⟩ prueba f. ~**s** /'fɪtɪŋz/ npl ⟨in
house⟩ accesorios mpl

five /faɪv/ a & n cinco (m). ~**r**
/'faɪvə(r)/ n ⟨fam⟩ billete m de cinco
libras

fix /fɪks/ vt ⟨make firm, attach,
decide⟩ fijar; ⟨mend, deal with⟩ arreglar. ● n. **in a** ~ en un aprieto. ~**a-
tion** /-eɪʃn/ n fijación f. ~**ed** a
fijo

fixture /'fɪkstʃə(r)/ n ⟨sport⟩ partido
m. ~**s** ⟨in house⟩ accesorios mpl

fizz /fɪz/ vi burbujear. ● n efer-
vescencia f. ~**le** /fɪzl/ vi burbujear.
~**le out** fracasar. ~**y** a efervescente;
⟨water⟩ con gas

flab /flæb/ n ⟨fam⟩ flaccidez f

flabbergast /'flæbəgɑːst/ vt pasmar

flabby /'flæbɪ/ a flojo

flag /flæg/ n bandera f. ● vt ⟨pt
flagged⟩. ~ **down** hacer señales de
parada a. ● vi ⟨pt **flagged**⟩ ⟨weaken⟩
flaquear; ⟨interest⟩ decaer; ⟨con-
versation⟩ languidecer

flagon /'flægən/ n botella f grande,
jarro m

flag-pole /'flægpəʊl/ n asta f de
bandera

flagrant /'fleɪgrənt/ a ⟨glaring⟩
flagrante; ⟨scandalous⟩ escandaloso

flagstone /'flægstəʊn/ n losa f

flair /fleə(r)/ n don m ⟨for de⟩

flak|e /fleɪk/ n copo m; ⟨of paint,
metal⟩ escama f. ● vi desconcharse.
~**e out** ⟨fam⟩ caer rendido. ~**y** a
escamoso

flamboyant /flæm'bɔɪənt/ a ⟨clo-
thes⟩ vistoso; ⟨manner⟩ extravagante

flame /fleɪm/ n llama f. ● vi llamear

flamingo /flə'mɪŋgəʊ/ n (pl -**o(e)s**)
flamenco m

flammable /'flæməbl/ a inflamable

flan /flæn/ n tartaleta f, tarteleta f

flank /flæŋk/ n ⟨of animal⟩ ijada f,
flanco m; ⟨of person⟩ costado m; ⟨of
mountain⟩ falda f; ⟨mil⟩ flanco m

flannel /'flænl/ n franela f ⟨de lana⟩;
⟨for face⟩ paño m ⟨para lavarse la
cara⟩. ~**ette** n franela f ⟨de algodón⟩,
muletón m

flap /flæp/ vi ⟨pt **flapped**⟩ ondear;
⟨wings⟩ aletear; ⟨become agitated,
fam⟩ ponerse nervioso. ● vt sacudir;
batir ⟨wings⟩. ● n ⟨of pocket⟩ cartera
f; ⟨of table⟩ ala f. **get into a** ~ ponerse
nervioso

flare /fleə(r)/ ● n llamarada f; ⟨mil⟩
bengala f; ⟨in skirt⟩ vuelo m. ● vi. ~
up llamear; ⟨fighting⟩ estallar; ⟨per-
son⟩ encolerizarse. ~**d** a ⟨skirt⟩
acampanada

flash /flæʃ/ ● vi brillar; ⟨on and off⟩
destellar. ● vt despedir; ⟨aim torch⟩
dirigir; ⟨flaunt⟩ hacer ostentación
de. ~ **past** pasar como un rayo. ● n
relámpago m; ⟨of news, camera⟩ flash
m. ~**back** n escena f retrospectiva.
~**light** n ⟨torch⟩ linterna f

flashy /'flæʃɪ/ a ostentoso

flask /flɑːsk/ n frasco m; ⟨vacuum
flask⟩ termo m

flat[1] /flæt/ a (**flatter, flattest**) llano;
⟨tyre⟩ desinflado; ⟨refusal⟩ cate-
górico; ⟨fare, rate⟩ fijo; ⟨mus⟩
desafinado. ● adv. ~ **out** ⟨at top
speed⟩ a toda velocidad

flat[2] /flæt/ n ⟨rooms⟩ piso m, apartamento m; ⟨tyre⟩ ⟨fam⟩ pinchazo m;
⟨mus⟩ bemol m

flat: ~**ly** adv categóricamente.
~**ness** n llanura f. ~**ten** /'flætn/ vt
allanar, aplanar. ● vi allanarse,
aplanarse

flatter /flætə(r)/ vt adular. ~**er** n
adulador m. ~**ing** a ⟨person⟩ lison-
jero; ⟨clothes⟩ favorecedor. ~**y** n
adulación f

flatulence /'flætjʊləns/ n flatulencia f

flaunt /flɔːnt/ vt hacer ostentación
de

flautist /'flɔːtɪst/ n flautista m & f

flavour /'fleɪvə(r)/ n sabor m. ● vt condimentar. **~ing** n condimento m

flaw /flɔ:/ n defecto m. **~less** a perfecto

flax /flæks/ n lino m. **~en** a de lino; ⟨hair⟩ rubio

flea /fli:/ n pulga f

fleck /flek/ n mancha f, pinta f

fled /fled/ see **flee**

fledged /fledʒd/ a. **fully ~** ⟨doctor etc⟩ hecho y derecho; ⟨member⟩ de pleno derecho

fledg(e)ling /'fledʒlɪŋ/ n pájaro m volantón

flee /fli:/ vi (pt **fled**) huir. ● vt huir de

fleece /fli:s/ n vellón m. ● vt (rob) desplumar

fleet /fli:t/ n (naut, aviat) flota f; (of cars) parque m

fleeting /'fli:tɪŋ/ a fugaz

Flemish /'flemɪʃ/ a & n flamenco (m)

flesh /fleʃ/ n carne f. **in the ~** en persona. **one's own ~ and blood** los de su sangre. **~y** a ⟨fruit⟩ carnoso

flew /flu:/ see **fly**[1]

flex /fleks/ vt doblar; flexionar ⟨muscle⟩. ● n (elec) cable m, flexible m

flexib|ility /fleksə'bɪlətɪ/ n flexibilidad f. **~le** /'fleksəbl/ a flexible

flexitime /fleksɪ'taɪm/ n horario m flexible

flick /flɪk/ n golpecito m. ● vt dar un golpecito a. **~ through** hojear

flicker /'flɪkə(r)/ vi temblar; ⟨light⟩ parpadear. ● n temblor m; (of hope) resquicio m; (of light) parpadeo m

flick: **~-knife** n navaja f de muelle. **~s** npl cine m

flier /'flaɪə(r)/ n aviador m; (circular, Amer) prospecto m, folleto m

flies /flaɪz/ npl (on trousers, fam) bragueta f

flight /flaɪt/ n vuelo m; (fleeing) huida f, fuga f. **~ of stairs** tramo m de escalera f. **put to ~** poner en fuga. **take (to) ~** darse a la fuga. **~-deck** n cubierta f de vuelo

flighty /'flaɪtɪ/ a (-ier, -iest) frívolo

flimsy /'flɪmzɪ/ a (-ier, -iest) flojo, débil, poco substancioso

flinch /flɪntʃ/ vi (draw back) retroceder (**from** ante). **without ~ing** (without wincing) sin pestañear

fling /flɪŋ/ vt (pt **flung**) arrojar. ● n. **have a ~** echar una cana al aire

flint /flɪnt/ n pedernal m; (for lighter) piedra f

flip /flɪp/ vt (pt **flipped**) dar un golpecito a. **~ through** hojear. ● n golpecito m. **~ side** n otra cara f

flippant /'flɪpənt/ a poco serio; (disrespectful) irrespetuoso

flipper /'flɪpə(r)/ n aleta f

flirt /flɜ:t/ vi coquetear. ● n (woman) coqueta f; (man) mariposón m, coqueto m. **~ation** /-'teɪʃn/ n coqueteo m

flit /flɪt/ vi (pt **flitted**) revolotear

float /fləʊt/ vi flotar. ● vt hacer flotar. ● n flotador m; (on fishing line) corcho m; (cart) carroza f

flock /flɒk/ n (of birds) bandada f; (of sheep) rebaño m; (of people) muchedumbre f, multitud f. ● vi congregarse

flog /flɒg/ vt (pt **flogged**) (beat) azotar; (sell, sl) vender

flood /flʌd/ n inundación f; (fig) torrente m. ● vt inundar. ● vi ⟨building etc⟩ inundarse; ⟨river⟩ desbordar

floodlight /'flʌdlaɪt/ n foco m. ● vt (pt **floodlit**) iluminar (con focos)

floor /flɔ:(r)/ n suelo m; (storey) piso m; (for dancing) pista f. ● vt (knock down) derribar; (baffle) confundir

flop /flɒp/ vi (pt **flopped**) dejarse caer pesadamente; (fail, sl) fracasar. ● n (sl) fracaso m. **~py** a flojo

flora /'flɔ:rə/ n flora f

floral /'flɔ:rəl/ a floral

florid /'flɒrɪd/ a florido

florist /'flɒrɪst/ n florista m & f

flounce /flaʊns/ n volante m

flounder[1] /'flaʊndə(r)/ vi avanzar con dificultad, no saber qué hacer

flounder[2] /'flaʊndə(r)/ n (fish) platija f

flour /flaʊə(r)/ n harina f

flourish /'flʌrɪʃ/ vi prosperar. ● vt blandir. ● n ademán m elegante; (in handwriting) rasgo m. **~ing** a próspero

floury /'flaʊərɪ/ a harinoso

flout /flaʊt/ vt burlarse de

flow /fləʊ/ vi correr; (hang loosely) caer. **~ into** ⟨river⟩ desembocar en. ● n flujo m; (jet) chorro m; (stream) corriente f; (of words, tears) torrente m. **~ chart** n organigrama m

flower /'flaʊə(r)/ n flor f. **~-bed** n macizo m de flores. **~ed** a floreado, de flores. **~y** a florido

flown /fləʊn/ *see* **fly**[1]

flu /fluː/ *n* (*fam*) gripe *f*

fluctuat|e /'flʌktjʊeɪt/ *vi* fluctuar. ~ion /-eɪʃn/ *n* fluctuación *f*

flue /fluː/ *n* humero *m*

fluen|cy /'fluːənsɪ/ *n* facilidad *f*. ~t *a* (*style*) fluido; (*speaker*) elocuente. **be** ~t **(in a language)** hablar (un idioma) con soltura. ~tly *adv* con fluidez; (*lang*) con soltura

fluff /flʌf/ *n* pelusa *f*. ~y *a* (-ier, -iest) velloso

fluid /'fluːɪd/ *a & n* fluido (*m*)

fluke /fluːk/ *n* (*stroke of luck*) chiripa *f*

flung /flʌŋ/ *see* **fling**

flunk /flʌŋk/ *vt* (*Amer, fam*) ser suspendido en (*exam*); suspender (*person*). ● *vi* (*fam*) ser suspendido

fluorescent /flʊə'resnt/ *a* fluorescente

fluoride /'flʊəraɪd/ *n* fluoruro *m*

flurry /'flʌrɪ/ *n* (*squall*) ráfaga *f*; (*fig*) agitación *f*

flush[1] /flʌʃ/ *vi* ruborizarse. ● *vt* limpiar con agua. ~ **the toilet** tirar de la cadena. ● *n* (*blush*) rubor *m*; (*fig*) emoción *f*

flush[2] /flʌʃ/ *a.* ~ **(with)** a nivel (con)

flush[3] /flʌʃ/ *vt/i.* ~ **out** (*drive out*) echar fuera

fluster /'flʌstə(r)/ *vt* poner nervioso

flute /fluːt/ *n* flauta *f*

flutter /'flʌtə(r)/ *vi* ondear; (*bird*) revolotear. ● *n* (*of wings*) revoloteo *m*; (*fig*) agitación *f*

flux /flʌks/ *n* flujo *m*. **be in a state of** ~ estar siempre cambiando

fly[1] /flaɪ/ *vi* (*pt* **flew**, *pp* **flown**) volar; (*passenger*) ir en avión; (*flag*) flotar; (*rush*) correr. ● *vt* pilotar (*aircraft*); transportar en avión (*passengers, goods*); izar (*flag*). ● *n* (*of trousers*) bragueta *f*

fly[2] /flaɪ/ *n* mosca *f*

flyer /'flaɪə(r)/ *n* aviador *m*; (*circular, Amer*) prospecto *m*, folleto *m*

flying /'flaɪɪŋ/ *a* volante; (*hasty*) relámpago *invar*. ● *n* (*activity*) aviación *f*. ~ **visit** *n* visita *f* relámpago

fly: ~**leaf** *n* guarda *f*. ~**over** *n* paso *m* elevado. ~**weight** *n* peso *m* mosca

foal /fəʊl/ *n* potro *m*

foam /fəʊm/ *n* espuma *f*. ~**(rubber)** *n* goma *f* espuma. ● *vi* espumar

fob /fɒb/ *vt* (*pt* **fobbed**). ~ **off on s.o.** (*palm off*) encajar a uno

focal /'fəʊkl/ *a* focal

focus /'fəʊkəs/ *n* (*pl* **-cuses** *or* **-ci** /-saɪ/) foco *m*; (*fig*) centro *m*. **in** ~ enfocado. **out of** ~ desenfocado. ● *vt/i* (*pt* **focused**) enfocar(se); (*fig*) concentrar

fodder /'fɒdə(r)/ *n* forraje *m*

foe /fəʊ/ *n* enemigo *m*

foetus /'fiːtəs/ *n* (*pl* **-tuses**) feto *m*

fog /fɒg/ *n* niebla *f*. ● *vt* (*pt* **fogged**) envolver en niebla; (*photo*) velar. ● *vi.* ~ **(up)** empañarse; (*photo*) velarse

fog(e)y /'fəʊgɪ/ *n.* **be an old** ~ estar chapado a la antigua

foggy /'fɒgɪ/ *a* (-ier, -iest) nebuloso. **it is** ~ hay niebla

foghorn /'fɒghɔːn/ *n* sirena *f* de niebla

foible /'fɔɪbl/ *n* punto *m* débil

foil[1] /fɔɪl/ *vt* (*thwart*) frustrar

foil[2] /fɔɪl/ *n* papel *m* de plata; (*fig*) contraste *m*

foist /fɔɪst/ *vt* encajar (**on** a)

fold[1] /fəʊld/ *vt* doblar; cruzar (*arms*). ● *vi* doblarse; (*fail*) fracasar. ● *n* pliegue *m*

fold[2] /fəʊld/ *n* (*for sheep*) redil *m*

folder /'fəʊldə(r)/ *n* (*file*) carpeta *f*; (*leaflet*) folleto *m*

folding /'fəʊldɪŋ/ *a* plegable

foliage /'fəʊlɪɪdʒ/ *n* follaje *m*

folk /fəʊk/ *n* gente *f*. ● *a* popular. ~**lore** *n* folklore *m*. ~**s** *npl* (*one's relatives*) familia *f*

follow /'fɒləʊ/ *vt/i* seguir. ~ **up** seguir; (*investigate further*) investigar. ~**er** *n* seguidor *m*. ~**ing** *n* partidarios *mpl*. ● *a* siguiente. ● *prep* después de

folly /'fɒlɪ/ *n* locura *f*

foment /fə'ment/ *vt* fomentar

fond /fɒnd/ *a* (-er, -est) (*loving*) cariñoso; (*hope*) vivo. **be** ~ **of s.o.** tener(le) cariño a uno. **be** ~ **of sth** ser aficionado a algo

fondle /'fɒndl/ *vt* acariciar

fondness /'fɒndnɪs/ *n* cariño *m*; (*for things*) afición *f*

font /fɒnt/ *n* pila *f* bautismal

food /fuːd/ *n* alimento *m*, comida *f*. ~ **processor** *n* robot *m* de cocina, batidora *f*

fool /fuːl/ *n* tonto *m*. ● *vt* engañar. ● *vi* hacer el tonto

foolhardy /'fuːlhɑːdɪ/ *a* temerario

foolish /'fuːlɪʃ/ *a* tonto. ~**ly** *adv* tontamente. ~**ness** *n* tontería *f*

foolproof /'fuːlpruːf/ a infalible, a toda prueba, a prueba de tontos

foot /fut/ n (pl feet) pie m; (measure) pie m (= 30,48 cm); (of animal, furniture) pata f. **get under s.o.'s feet** estorbar a uno. **on ~** a pie. **on/to one's feet** de pie. **put one's ~ in it** meter la pata. ● vt pagar ⟨bill⟩. **~ it** ir andando

footage /'futɪdʒ/ n (of film) secuencia f

football /'futbɔːl/ n (ball) balón m; (game) fútbol m. **~er** n futbolista m & f

footbridge /'futbrɪdʒ/ n puente m para peatones

foothills /'futhɪlz/ npl estribaciones fpl

foothold /'futhəʊld/ n punto m de apoyo m

footing /'futɪŋ/ n pie m

footlights /'futlaɪts/ npl candilejas fpl

footloose /'futluːs/ a libre

footman /'futmən/ n lacayo m

footnote /'futnəʊt/ n nota f (al pie de la página)

foot: **~path** n (in country) senda f; (in town) acera f, vereda f (Arg), banqueta f (Mex). **~print** n huella f. **~sore** a. **be ~sore** tener los pies doloridos. **~step** n paso m. **~stool** n escabel m. **~wear** n calzado m

for /fɔː(r)/, unstressed /fə(r)/ prep (expressing purpose) para; (on behalf of) por; (in spite of) a pesar de; (during) durante; (in favour of) a favor de. **he has been in Madrid ~ two months** hace dos meses que está en Madrid. ● conj ya que

forage /'fɒrɪdʒ/ vi forrajear. ● n forraje m

foray /'fɒreɪ/ n incursión f

forbade /fə'bæd/ see **forbid**

forbear /fɔː'beər/ vt/i (pt **forbore**, pp **forborne**) contenerse. **~ance** n paciencia f

forbid /fə'bɪd/ vt (pt **forbade**, pp **forbidden**) prohibir (**s.o. to do** a uno hacer). **~s.o. sth** prohibir algo a uno

forbidding /fə'bɪdɪŋ/ a imponente

force /fɔːs/ n fuerza f. **come into ~** entrar en vigor. **the ~s** las fuerzas fpl armadas. ● vt forzar. **~ on** imponer a. **~d** a forzado. **~-feed** vt alimentar a la fuerza. **~ful** /'fɔːsfʊl/ a enérgico

forceps /'fɔːseps/ n invar tenazas fpl; (for obstetric use) fórceps m invar; (for dental use) gatillo m

forcibl|e /'fɔːsəbl/ a a la fuerza. **~y** adv a la fuerza

ford /fɔːd/ n vado m, botadero m (Mex). ● vt vadear

fore /fɔː(r)/ a anterior. ● n. **come to the ~** hacerse evidente

forearm /'fɔːrɑːm/ n antebrazo m

foreboding /fɔː'bəʊdɪŋ/ n presentimiento m

forecast /'fɔːkɑːst/ vt (pt **forecast**) pronosticar. ● n pronóstico m

forecourt /'fɔːkɔːt/ n patio m

forefathers /'fɔːfɑːðəz/ npl antepasados mpl

forefinger /'fɔːfɪŋgə(r)/ n (dedo m) índice m

forefront /'fɔːfrʌnt/ n vanguardia f. **in the ~** a/en vanguardia, en primer plano

foregone /'fɔːgɒn/ a. **~ conclusion** resultado m previsto

foreground /'fɔːgraʊnd/ n primer plano m

forehead /'fɒrɪd/ n frente f

foreign /'fɒrən/ a extranjero; ⟨trade⟩ exterior; ⟨travel⟩ al extranjero, en el extranjero. **~er** n extranjero m. **F~ Secretary** n ministro m de Asuntos Exteriores

foreman /'fɔːmən/ n capataz m, caporal m

foremost /'fɔːməʊst/ a primero. ● adv. **first and ~** ante todo

forensic /fə'rensɪk/ a forense

forerunner /'fɔːrʌnə(r)/ n precursor m

foresee /fɔː'siː/ vt (pt **-saw**, pp **-seen**) prever. **~able** a previsible

foreshadow /fɔː'ʃædəʊ/ vt presagiar

foresight /'fɔːsaɪt/ n previsión f

forest /'fɒrɪst/ n bosque m

forestall /fɔː'stɔːl/ vt anticiparse a

forestry /'fɒrɪstrɪ/ n silvicultura f

foretaste /'fɔːteɪst/ n anticipación f

foretell /fɔː'tel/ vt (pt **foretold**) predecir

forever /fə'revə(r)/ adv para siempre

forewarn /fɔː'wɔːn/ vt prevenir

foreword /'fɔːwɜːd/ n prefacio m

forfeit /'fɔːfɪt/ n (penalty) pena f; (in game) prenda f; (fine) multa f. ● vt perder

forgave /fə'geɪv/ see **forgive**

forge[1] /fɔːdʒ/ n fragua f. ● vt fraguar; (*copy*) falsificar

forge[2] /fɔːdʒ/ vi avanzar. **~ahead** adelantarse rápidamente

forge: **~r** /fɔːdʒə(r)/ n falsificador m. **~ry** n falsificación f

forget /fəˈget/ vt (pt **forgot**, pp **forgotten**) olvidar. **~ o.s.** propasarse, extralimitarse. ● vi olvidar(se). **I forgot** se me olvidó. **~ful** a olvidadizo. **~ful of** olvidando. **~menot** n nomeolvides f invar

forgive /fəˈgɪv/ vt (pt **forgave**, pp. **forgiven**) perdonar. **~ness** n perdón m

forgo /fɔːˈgəʊ/ vt (pt **forwent**, pp **forgone**) renunciar a

fork /fɔːk/ n tenedor m; (*for digging*) horca f; (*in road*) bifurcación f. ● vi (*road*) bifurcarse. **~ out** (*sl*) aflojar la bolsa (*fam*), pagar. **~ed** a ahorquillado; (*road*) bifurcado. **~-lift truck** n carretilla f elevadora

forlorn /fəˈlɔːn/ a (*hopeless*) desesperado; (*abandoned*) abandonado. **~ hope** n empresa f desesperada

form /fɔːm/ n forma f; (*document*) impreso m, formulario m; (*schol*) clase f. ● vt formar. ● vi formarse

formal /ˈfɔːml/ a formal; (*person*) formalista; (*dress*) de etiqueta. **~ity** /-ˈmælətɪ/ n formalidad f. **~ly** adv oficialmente

format /ˈfɔːmæt/ n formato m

formation /fɔːˈmeɪʃn/ n formación f

formative /ˈfɔːmətɪv/ a formativo

former /ˈfɔːmə(r)/ a anterior; (*first of two*) primero. **~ly** adv antes

formidable /ˈfɔːmɪdəbl/ a formidable

formless /ˈfɔːmlɪs/ a informe

formula /ˈfɔːmjʊlə/ n (pl **-ae** /-iː/ or **-as**) fórmula f

formulate /ˈfɔːmjʊleɪt/ vt formular

fornicat|e /ˈfɔːnɪkeɪt/ vi fornicar. **~ion** /-ˈkeɪʃn/ n fornicación f

forsake /fəˈseɪk/ vt (pt **forsook**, pp **forsaken**) abandonar

fort /fɔːt/ n (*mil*) fuerte m

forte /ˈfɔːteɪ/ n (*talent*) fuerte m

forth /fɔːθ/ adv en adelante. **and so ~** y así sucesivamente. **go back and ~** ir y venir

forthcoming /fɔːθˈkʌmɪŋ/ a próximo, venidero; (*sociable, fam*) comunicativo

forthright /ˈfɔːθraɪt/ a directo

forthwith /fɔːθˈwɪθ/ adv inmediatamente

fortieth /ˈfɔːtɪɪθ/ a cuarenta, cuadragésimo. ● n cuadragésima parte f

fortif|ication /fɔːtɪfɪˈkeɪʃn/ n fortificación f. **~y** /ˈfɔːtɪfaɪ/ vt fortificar

fortitude /ˈfɔːtɪtjuːd/ n valor m

fortnight /ˈfɔːtnaɪt/ n quince días mpl, quincena f. **~ly** a bimensual. ● adv cada quince días

fortress /ˈfɔːtrɪs/ n fortaleza f

fortuitous /fɔːˈtjuːɪtəs/ a fortuito

fortunate /ˈfɔːtʃənət/ a afortunado. **be ~** tener suerte. **~ly** adv afortunadamente

fortune /ˈfɔːtʃuːn/ n fortuna f. **have the good ~ to** tener la suerte de. **~teller** n adivino m

forty /ˈfɔːtɪ/ a & n cuarenta (m). **~ winks** un sueñecito m

forum /ˈfɔːrəm/ n foro m

forward /ˈfɔːwəd/ a delantero; (*advanced*) precoz; (*pert*) impertinente. ● n (*sport*) delantero m. ● adv adelante. **come ~** presentarse. **go ~** avanzar. ● vt hacer seguir (*letter*); enviar (*goods*); (*fig*) favorecer. **~ness** n precocidad f

forwards /ˈfɔːwədz/ adv adelante

fossil /ˈfɒsl/ a & n fósil (m)

foster /ˈfɒstə(r)/ vt (*promote*) fomentar; criar (*child*). **~-child** n hijo m adoptivo. **~-mother** n madre f adoptiva

fought /fɔːt/ see **fight**

foul /faʊl/ a (**-er**, **-est**) (*smell, weather*) asqueroso; (*dirty*) sucio; (*language*) obsceno; (*air*) viciado. **~ play** n jugada f sucia; (*crime*) delito m. ● n (*sport*) falta f. ● vt ensuciar; manchar (*reputation*). **~-mouthed** a obsceno

found[1] /faʊnd/ see **find**

found[2] /faʊnd/ vt fundar

found[3] /faʊnd/ vt (*tec*) fundir

foundation /faʊnˈdeɪʃn/ n fundación f; (*basis*) fundamento m. **~s** npl (*archit*) cimientos mpl

founder[1] /ˈfaʊndə(r)/ n fundador m

founder[2] /ˈfaʊndə(r)/ vi (*ship*) hundirse

foundry /ˈfaʊndrɪ/ n fundición f

fountain /ˈfaʊntɪn/ n fuente f. **~pen** n estilográfica f

four /fɔː(r)/ a & n cuatro (m). **~fold** a cuádruple. ● adv cuatro veces. **~poster** n cama f con cuatro columnas

foursome /'fɔːsəm/ *n* grupo *m* de cuatro personas

fourteen /'fɔːtiːn/ *a & n* catorce (*m*). ∼**th** *a & n* catorce (*m*), decimocuarto (*m*). ● *n* (*fraction*) catorceavo *m*

fourth /fɔːθ/ *a & n* cuarto (*m*)

fowl /faʊl/ *n* ave *f*

fox /fɒks/ *n* zorro *m*, zorra *f*. ● *vt* (*baffle*) dejar perplejo; (*deceive*) engañar

foyer /'fɔɪeɪ/ *n* (*hall*) vestíbulo *m*

fraction /'frækʃn/ *n* fracción *f*

fractious /'frækʃəs/ *a* díscolo

fracture /'fræktʃə(r)/ *n* fractura *f*. ● *vt* fracturar. ● *vi* fracturarse

fragile /'frædʒaɪl/ *a* frágil

fragment /'frægmənt/ *n* fragmento *m*. ∼**ary** *a* fragmentario

fragran|ce /'freɪgrəns/ *n* fragancia *f*. ∼**t** *a* fragante

frail /freɪl/ *a* (**-er, -est**) frágil

frame /freɪm/ *n* (*of picture, door, window*) marco *m*; (*of spectacles*) montura *f*; (*fig, structure*) estructura *f*; (*temporary state*) estado *m*. ∼ **of mind** estado *m* de ánimo. ● *vt* enmarcar; (*fig*) formular; (*jurid, sl*) incriminar falsamente. ∼**-up** *n* (*sl*) complot *m*

framework /'freɪmwɜːk/ *n* estructura *f*; (*context*) marco *m*

France /frɑːns/ *n* Francia *f*

franchise /'fræntʃaɪz/ *n* (*pol*) derecho *m* a votar; (*com*) concesión *f*

Franco... /'fræŋkəʊ/ *pref* franco...

frank /fræŋk/ *a* sincero. ● *vt* franquear. ∼**ly** *adv* sinceramente. ∼**ness** *n* sinceridad *f*

frantic /'fræntɪk/ *a* frenético. ∼ **with** loco de

fraternal /frə'tɜːnl/ *a* fraternal

fraternity /frə'tɜːnɪtɪ/ *n* fraternidad *f*; (*club*) asociación *f*

fraternize /'frætənaɪz/ *vi* fraternizar

fraud /frɔːd/ *n* (*deception*) fraude *m*; (*person*) impostor *m*. ∼**ulent** *a* fraudulento

fraught /frɔːt/ *a* (*tense*) tenso. ∼ **with** cargado de

fray[1] /freɪ/ *vt* desgastar. ● *vi* deshilacharse

fray[2] /freɪ/ *n* riña *f*

freak /friːk/ *n* (*caprice*) capricho *m*; (*monster*) monstruo *m*; (*person*) chalado *m*. ● *a* anormal. ∼**ish** *a* anormal

freckle /'frekl/ *n* peca *f*. ∼**d** *a* pecoso

free /friː/ *a* (**freer** /'friːə(r)/, **freest** /'friːɪst/) libre; (*gratis*) gratis; (*lavish*) generoso. ∼ **kick** *n* golpe *m* franco. ∼ **of charge** gratis. ∼ **speech** *n* libertad *f* de expresión. **give a** ∼ **hand** dar carta blanca. ● *vt* (*pt* **freed**) (*set at liberty*) poner en libertad; (*relieve from*) liberar (**from**); **of** de); (*untangle*) desenredar; (*loosen*) soltar

freedom /'friːdəm/ *n* libertad *f*

freehold /'friːhəʊld/ *n* propiedad *f* absoluta

freelance /'friːlɑːns/ *a* independiente

freely /'friːlɪ/ *adv* libremente

Freemason /'friːmeɪsn/ *n* masón *m*. ∼**ry** *n* masonería *f*

free-range /'friːreɪndʒ/ *a* (*eggs*) de granja

freesia /'friːzjə/ *n* fresia *f*

freeway /'friːweɪ/ *n* (*Amer*) autopista *f*

freez|e /'friːz/ *vt* (*pt* **froze**, *pp* **frozen**) helar; congelar (*food, wages*). ● *vi* helarse, congelarse; (*become motionless*) quedarse inmóvil. ● *n* helada *f*; (*of wages, prices*) congelación *f*. ∼**er** *n* congelador *m*. ∼**ing** *a* glacial. ● *n* congelación *f*. **below** ∼**ing** bajo cero

freight /freɪt/ *n* (*goods*) mercancías *fpl*; (*hire of ship etc*) flete *m*. ∼**er** *n* (*ship*) buque *m* de carga

French /frentʃ/ *a* francés. ● *n* (*lang*) francés *m*. ∼**man** *n* francés *m*. ∼**-speaking** *a* francófono. ∼ **window** *n* puertaventana *f*. ∼**woman** *f* francesa *f*

frenz|ied /'frenzɪd/ *a* frenético. ∼**y** *n* frenesí *m*

frequency /'friːkwənsɪ/ *n* frecuencia *f*

frequent /frɪ'kwent/ *vt* frecuentar. /'friːkwənt/ *a* frecuente. ∼**ly** *adv* frecuentemente

fresco /'freskəʊ/ *n* (*pl* **-o(e)s**) fresco *m*

fresh /freʃ/ *a* (**-er, -est**) fresco; (*different, additional*) nuevo; (*cheeky*) fresco, descarado; (*water*) dulce. ∼**en** *vi* refrescar. ∼**en up** (*person*) refrescarse. ∼**ly** *adv* recientemente. ∼**man** *n* estudiante *m* de primer año. ∼**ness** *n* frescura *f*

fret /fret/ *vi* (*pt* **fretted**) inquietarse. ∼**ful** *a* (*discontented*) quejoso; (*irritable*) irritable

Freudian /ˈfrɔɪdjən/ a freudiano

friar /ˈfraɪə(r)/ n fraile m

friction /ˈfrɪkʃn/ n fricción f

Friday /ˈfraɪdeɪ/ n viernes m. **Good** ~ Viernes Santo

fridge /frɪdʒ/ n (fam) nevera f, refrigerador m, refrigeradora f

fried /fraɪd/ see **fry**¹. ● a frito

friend /frend/ n amigo m. ~**liness** /ˈfrendlɪnɪs/ n simpatía f. ~**ly** a (-ier, -iest) simpático. **F~ly Society** n mutualidad f. ~**ship** /ˈfrendʃɪp/ n amistad f

frieze /friːz/ n friso m

frigate /ˈfrɪɡət/ n fragata f

fright /fraɪt/ n susto m; (person) espantajo m; (thing) horror m

frighten /ˈfraɪtn/ vt asustar. ~ **off** ahuyentar. ~**ed** a asustado. **be** ~**ed** tener miedo (**of** de)

frightful /ˈfraɪtfl/ a espantoso, horrible. ~**ly** adv terriblemente

frigid /ˈfrɪdʒɪd/ a frío; (psych) frígido. ~**ity** /-ˈdʒɪdətɪ/ n frigidez f

frill /frɪl/ n volante m. ~**s** npl (fig) adornos mpl. **with no** ~**s** sencillo

fringe /frɪndʒ/ n (sewing) fleco m; (ornamental border) franja f; (of hair) flequillo m; (of area) periferia f; (of society) margen m. ~ **benefits** npl beneficios mpl suplementarios. ~ **theatre** n teatro m de vanguardia

frisk /frɪsk/ vt (search) cachear

frisky /ˈfrɪskɪ/ a (-ier, -iest) retozón; ⟨horse⟩ fogoso

fritter¹ /ˈfrɪtə(r)/ vt. ~ **away** desperdiciar

fritter² /ˈfrɪtə(r)/ n buñuelo m

frivol|ity /frɪˈvɒlətɪ/ n frivolidad f. ~**ous** /ˈfrɪvələs/ a frívolo

frizzy /ˈfrɪzɪ/ a crespo

fro /frəʊ/ see **to and fro**

frock /frɒk/ n vestido m; (of monk) hábito m

frog /frɒɡ/ n rana f. **have a** ~ **in one's throat** tener carraspera

frogman /ˈfrɒɡmən/ n hombre m rana

frolic /ˈfrɒlɪk/ vi (pt **frolicked**) retozar. ● n broma f

from /frɒm/, unstressed /frəm/ prep de; (with time, prices, etc) a partir de; (habit, conviction) por; (according to) según. **take** ~ (away from) quitar a

front /frʌnt/ n parte f delantera; (of building) fachada f; (of clothes) delantera f; (mil, pol) frente f; (of book) principio m; (fig, appearance) apariencia f; (sea front) paseo m marítimo. **in** ~ **of** delante de. **put a bold** ~ **on** hacer de tripas corazón, mostrar firmeza. ● a delantero; (first) primero. ~**age** n fachada f. ~**al** a frontal; ⟨attack⟩ de frente. ~ **door** n puerta f principal. ~ **page** n (of newspaper) primera plana f

frontier /ˈfrʌntɪə(r)/ n frontera f

frost /frɒst/ n (freezing) helada f; (frozen dew) escarcha f. ~**bite** n congelación f. ~**bitten** a congelado. ~**ed** a ⟨glass⟩ esmerilado

frosting /ˈfrɒstɪŋ/ n (icing, Amer) azúcar m glaseado

frosty a ⟨weather⟩ de helada; ⟨window⟩ escarchado; (fig) glacial

froth /frɒθ/ n espuma f. ● vi espumar. ~**y** a espumoso

frown /fraʊn/ vi fruncir el entrecejo. ~ **on** desaprobar. ● n ceño m

froze /frəʊz/, **frozen** /ˈfrəʊzn/ see **freeze**

frugal /ˈfruːɡl/ a frugal. ~**ly** adv frugalmente

fruit /fruːt/ n (bot, on tree, fig) fruto m; (as food) fruta f. ~**erer** n frutero m. ~**ful** /ˈfruːtfl/ a fértil; (fig) fructífero. ~**less** a infructuoso. ~ **machine** n (máquina f) tragaperras m. ~ **salad** n macedonia f de frutas. ~**y** /ˈfruːtɪ/ a ⟨taste⟩ que sabe a fruta

fruition /fruːˈɪʃn/ n. **come to** ~ realizarse

frump /frʌmp/ n espantajo m

frustrat|e /frʌˈstreɪt/ vt frustrar. ~**ion** /-ʃn/ n frustración f; (disappointment) decepción f

fry¹ /fraɪ/ vt (pt **fried**) freír. ● vi freírse

fry² /fraɪ/ n (pl **fry**). **small** ~ gente f de poca monta

frying-pan /ˈfraɪŋpæn/ n sartén f

fuchsia /ˈfjuːʃə/ n fucsia f

fuddy-duddy /ˈfʌdɪdʌdɪ/ n. **be a** ~ (sl) estar chapado a la antigua

fudge /fʌdʒ/ n dulce m de azúcar

fuel /ˈfjuːəl/ n combustible m; (for car engine) carburante m; (fig) pábulo m. ● vt (pt **fuelled**) alimentar de combustible

fugitive /ˈfjuːdʒɪtɪv/ a & n fugitivo (m)

fugue /fjuːɡ/ n (mus) fuga f

fulfil /fʊlˈfɪl/ vt (pt **fulfilled**) cumplir (con) ⟨promise, obligation⟩; satisfacer ⟨condition⟩; realizar ⟨hopes, plans⟩; llevar a cabo ⟨task⟩. ~**ment**

n (*of promise, obligation*) cumplimiento *m*; (*of conditions*) satisfacción *f*; (*of hopes, plans*) realización *f*; (*of task*) ejecución *f*

full /fʊl/ *a* (**-er, -est**) lleno; (*bus, hotel*) completo; (*skirt*) amplio; (*account*) detallado. **at ~ speed** a máxima velocidad. **be ~ (up)** (*with food*) no poder más. **in ~ swing** en plena marcha. ● *n*. **in ~** sin quitar nada. **to the ~** completamente. **write in ~** escribir con todas las letras. **~ back** *n* (*sport*) defensa *m* & *f*. **~-blooded** *a* vigoroso. **~ moon** *n* plenilunio *m*. **~-scale** *a* (*drawing*) de tamaño natural; (*fig*) amplio. **~ stop** *n* punto *m*; (*at end of paragraph, fig*) punto *m* final. **~ time** *a* de jornada completa. **~y** *adv* completamente

fulsome /ˈfʊlsəm/ *a* excesivo

fumble /ˈfʌmbl/ *vi* buscar (torpemente)

fume /fjuːm/ *vi* humear; (*fig, be furious*) estar furioso. **~s** *npl* humo *m*

fumigate /ˈfjuːmɪɡeɪt/ *vt* fumigar

fun /fʌn/ *n* (*amusement*) diversión *f*; (*merriment*) alegría *f*. **for ~** en broma. **have ~** divertirse. **make ~ of** burlarse de

function /ˈfʌŋkʃn/ *n* (*purpose, duty*) función *f*; (*reception*) recepción *f*. ● *vi* funcionar. **~al** *a* funcional

fund /fʌnd/ *n* fondo *m*. ● *vt* proveer fondos para

fundamental /fʌndəˈmentl/ *a* fundamental

funeral /ˈfjuːnərəl/ *n* funeral *m*, funerales *mpl*. ● *a* fúnebre

fun-fair /ˈfʌnfeə(r)/ *n* parque *m* de atracciones

fungus /ˈfʌŋɡəs/ *n* (*pl* **-gi** /-ɡaɪ/) hongo *m*

funicular /fjuːˈnɪkjʊlə(r)/ *n* funicular *m*

funk /fʌŋk/ *m* (*fear, sl*) miedo *m*; (*state of depression, Amer, sl*) depresión *f*. **be in a (blue) ~** tener (mucho) miedo; (*Amer*) estar (muy) deprimido. ● *vi* rajarse

funnel /ˈfʌnl/ *n* (*for pouring*) embudo *m*; (*of ship*) chimenea *f*

funn|ily /ˈfʌnɪlɪ/ *adv* graciosamente; (*oddly*) curiosamente. **~y** *a* (**-ier, -iest**) divertido, gracioso; (*odd*) curioso, raro. **~y-bone** *n* cóndilo *m* del húmero. **~y business** *n* engaño *m*

fur /fɜː(r)/ *n* pelo *m*; (*pelt*) piel *f*; (*in kettle*) sarro *m*

furbish /ˈfɜːbɪʃ/ *vt* pulir; (*renovate*) renovar

furious /ˈfjʊərɪəs/ *a* furioso. **~ly** *adv* furiosamente

furnace /ˈfɜːnɪs/ *n* horno *m*

furnish /ˈfɜːnɪʃ/ *vt* (*with furniture*) amueblar; (*supply*) proveer. **~ings** *npl* muebles *mpl*, mobiliario *m*

furniture /ˈfɜːnɪtʃə(r)/ *n* muebles *mpl*, mobiliario *m*

furrier /ˈfʌrɪə(r)/ *n* peletero *m*

furrow /ˈfʌrəʊ/ *n* surco *m*

furry /ˈfɜːrɪ/ *a* peludo

furthe|r /ˈfɜːðə(r)/ *a* más lejano; (*additional*) nuevo. ● *adv* más lejos; (*more*) además. ● *vt* fomentar. **~rmore** *adv* además. **~rmost** *a* más lejano. **~st** *a* más lejano. ● *adv* más lejos

furtive /ˈfɜːtɪv/ *a* furtivo

fury /ˈfjʊərɪ/ *n* furia *f*

fuse[1] /fjuːz/ *vt* (*melt*) fundir; (*fig, unite*) fusionar. **~ the lights** fundir los plomos. ● *vi* fundirse; (*fig*) fusionarse. ● *n* fusible *m*, plomo *m*

fuse[2] /fjuːz/ *n* (*of bomb*) mecha *f*

fuse-box /ˈfjuːzbɒks/ *n* caja *f* de fusibles

fuselage /ˈfjuːzəlɑːʒ/ *n* fuselaje *m*

fusion /ˈfjuːʒn/ *n* fusión *f*

fuss /fʌs/ *n* (*commotion*) jaleo *m*. **kick up a ~** armar un lío, armar una bronca, protestar. **make a ~ of** tratar con mucha atención. **~y** *a* (**-ier, -iest**) (*finicky*) remilgado; (*demanding*) exigente; (*ornate*) recargado

fusty /ˈfʌstɪ/ *a* (**-ier, -iest**) que huele a cerrado

futile /ˈfjuːtaɪl/ *a* inútil, vano

future /ˈfjuːtʃə(r)/ *a* futuro. ● *n* futuro *m*, porvenir *m*; (*gram*) futuro *m*. **in ~** en lo sucesivo, de ahora en adelante

futuristic /fjuːtʃəˈrɪstɪk/ *a* futurista

fuzz /fʌz/ *n* (*fluff*) pelusa *f*; (*police, sl*) policía *f*, poli *f* (*fam*)

fuzzy /ˈfʌzɪ/ *a* (*hair*) crespo; (*photograph*) borroso

G

gab /ɡæb/ *n* charla *f*. **have the gift of the ~** tener un pico de oro

gabardine /ɡæbəˈdiːn/ *n* gabardina *f*

gabble /'gæbl/ vt decir atropelladamente. ● vi hablar atropelladamente. ● n torrente m de
palabras
gable /'geɪbl/ n aguilón m
gad /gæd/ vi (pt gadded). ~ about
callejear
gadget /'gædʒɪt/ n chisme m
Gaelic /'geɪlɪk/ a & n gaélico (m)
gaffe /gæf/ n plancha f, metedura f
de pata
gag /gæg/ n mordaza f; (joke) chiste
m. ● vt (pt gagged) amordazar
gaga /'gɑːgɑː/ a (sl) chocho
gaiety /'geɪətɪ/ n alegría f
gaily /'geɪlɪ/ adv alegremente
gain /geɪn/ vt ganar; (acquire)
adquirir; (obtain) conseguir. ● vi
‹clock› adelantar. ● n ganancia f; (increase) aumento m. ~ful a lucrativo
gainsay /geɪn'seɪ/ vt (pt gainsaid)
(formal) negar
gait /geɪt/ n modo m de andar
gala /'gɑːlə/ n fiesta f; (sport)
competición f
galaxy /'gæləksɪ/ n galaxia f
gale /geɪl/ n vendaval m; (storm)
tempestad f
gall /gɔːl/ n bilis f; (fig) hiel f; (impudence) descaro m
gallant /'gælənt/ a (brave) valiente;
(chivalrous) galante. ~ry n valor m
gall-bladder /'gɔːlblædə(r)/ n vesícula f biliar
galleon /'gælɪən/ n galeón m
gallery /'gælərɪ/ n galería f
galley /'gælɪ/ n (ship) galera f;
(ship's kitchen) cocina f. ~ (proof)
(typ) galerada f
Gallic /'gælɪk/ a gálico. ~ism n gali-
cismo m
gallivant /'gælɪvænt/ vi (fam) callejear
gallon /'gælən/ n galón m (imperial = 4,546l; Amer = 3,785l)
gallop /'gæləp/ n galope m. ● vi (pt
galloped) galopar
gallows /'gæləʊz/ n horca f
galore /gə'lɔː(r)/ adv en abundancia
galosh /gə'lɒʃ/ n chanclo m
galvanize /'gælvənaɪz/ vt galvanizar
gambit /'gæmbɪt/ n (in chess) gam-
bito m; (fig) táctica f
gamble /'gæmbl/ vt/i jugar. ~e on
contar con. ● n (venture) empresa f
arriesgada; (bet) jugada f; (risk)

riesgo m. ~er n jugador m. ~ing n
juego m
game[1] /geɪm/ n juego m; (match)
partido m; (animals, birds) caza f. ● a
valiente. ~ for listo para
game[2] /geɪm/ a (lame) cojo
gamekeeper /'geɪmkiːpə(r)/ n
guardabosque m
gammon /'gæmən/ n jamón m ahumado
gamut /'gæmət/ n gama f
gamy /'geɪmɪ/ a manido
gander /'gændə(r)/ n ganso m
gang /gæŋ/ n pandilla f; (of workmen) equipo m. ● vi. ~ up unirse (on
contra)
gangling /'gæŋglɪŋ/ a larguirucho
gangrene /'gæŋgriːn/ n gangrena f
gangster /'gæŋstə(r)/ n bandido m,
gangster m
gangway /'gæŋweɪ/ n pasillo m; (of
ship) pasarela f
gaol /dʒeɪl/ n cárcel f. ~bird n criminal m empedernido. ~er n carcelero
m
gap /gæp/ n vacío m; (breach) brecha
f; (in time) intervalo m; (deficiency)
laguna f; (difference) diferencia f
gap|e /geɪp/ vi quedarse boquia-
bierto; (be wide open) estar muy
abierto. ~ing a abierto; (person)
boquiabierto
garage /'gærɑːʒ/ n garaje m; (petrol
station) gasolinera f; (for repairs)
taller m. ● vt dejar en (el) garaje
garb /gɑːb/ n vestido m
garbage /'gɑːbɪdʒ/ n basura f
garble /'gɑːbl/ vt mutilar
garden /'gɑːdn/ n (of flowers) jardín
m; (of vegetables/fruit) huerto m. ● vi
trabajar en el jardín/huerto. ~er
n jardinero/hortelano m. ~ing n
jardinería/horticultura f
gargantuan /gɑː'gæntjʊən/ a gigantesco
gargle /'gɑːgl/ vi hacer gárgaras. ● n
gargarismo m
gargoyle /'gɑːgɔɪl/ n gárgola f
garish /'geərɪʃ/ a chillón
garland /'gɑːlənd/ n guirnalda f
garlic /'gɑːlɪk/ n ajo m
garment /'gɑːmənt/ n prenda f (de
vestir)
garnet /'gɑːnɪt/ n granate m
garnish /'gɑːnɪʃ/ vt aderezar. ● n
aderezo m
garret /'gærət/ n guardilla f,
buhardilla f

garrison /'gærɪsn/ n guarnición f

garrulous /'gærələs/ a hablador

garter /'gɑːtə(r)/ n liga f

gas /gæs/ n (pl **gases**) gas m; (med) anestésico m; (petrol, Amer, fam) gasolina f. ● vt (pt **gassed**) asfixiar con gas. ● vi (fam) charlar. ~ **fire** n estufa f de gas

gash /gæʃ/ n cuchillada f. ● vt acuchillar

gasket /'gæskɪt/ n junta f

gas: ~ **mask** n careta f antigás a invar. ~ **meter** n contador m de gas

gasoline /'gæsəliːn/ n (petrol, Amer) gasolina f

gasometer /gæ'sɒmɪtə(r)/ n gasómetro m

gasp /gɑːsp/ vi jadear; (with surprise) quedarse boquiabierto. ● n jadeo m

gas: ~ **ring** n hornillo m de gas. ~ **station** n (Amer) gasolinera f

gastric /'gæstrɪk/ a gástrico

gastronomy /gæ'strɒnəmɪ/ n gastronomía f

gate /geɪt/ n puerta f; (of metal) verja f; (barrier) barrera f

gateau /'gætəʊ/ n (pl **gateaux**) tarta f

gate: ~**crasher** n intruso m (que ha entrado sin ser invitado o sin pagar). ~**way** n puerta f

gather /'gæðə(r)/ vt reunir (people, things); (accumulate) acumular; (pick up) recoger; recoger (flowers); (fig, infer) deducir; (sewing) fruncir. ~ **speed** acelerar. ● vi (people) reunirse; (things) acumularse. ~**ing** n reunión f

gauche /gəʊʃ/ a torpe

gaudy /'gɔːdɪ/ a (-ier, -iest) chillón

gauge /geɪdʒ/ n (measurement) medida f; (rail) entrevía f; (instrument) indicador m. ● vt medir; (fig) estimar

gaunt /gɔːnt/ a macilento; (grim) lúgubre

gauntlet /'gɔːntlɪt/ n. **run the ~ of** estar sometido a

gauze /gɔːz/ n gasa f

gave /geɪv/ see **give**

gawk /gɔːk/ vi. ~ **at** mirar como un tonto

gawky /'gɔːkɪ/ a (-ier, -iest) torpe

gawp /gɔːp/ vi. ~ **at** mirar como un tonto

gay /geɪ/ a (-er, -est) (joyful) alegre; (homosexual, fam) homosexual, gay (fam)

gaze /geɪz/ vi. ~ **(at)** mirar (fijamente). ● n mirada f (fija)

gazelle /gə'zel/ n gacela f

gazette /gə'zet/ n boletín m oficial, gaceta f

gazump /gə'zʌmp/ vt aceptar un precio más elevado de otro comprador

GB abbr see **Great Britain**

gear /gɪə(r)/ n equipo m; (tec) engranaje m; (auto) marcha f. **in ~** engranado. **out of ~** desengranado. ● vt adaptar. ~**box** n (auto) caja f de cambios

geese /giːs/ see **goose**

geezer /'giːzə(r)/ n (sl) tipo m

gelatine /'dʒelətiːn/ n gelatina f

gelignite /'dʒelɪgnaɪt/ n gelignita f

gem /dʒem/ n piedra f preciosa

Gemini /'dʒemɪnaɪ/ n (astr) Gemelos mpl, Géminis mpl

gen /dʒen/ n (sl) información f

gender /'dʒendə(r)/ n género m

gene /dʒiːn/ n gene m

genealogy /dʒiːnɪ'ælədʒɪ/ n genealogía f

general /'dʒenərəl/ a general. ● n general m. **in ~** generalmente. ~ **election** n elecciones fpl generales

generaliz|ation /dʒenərəlaɪ'zeɪʃn/ n generalización f. ~**e** vt/i generalizar

generally /'dʒenərəlɪ/ adv generalmente

general practitioner /'dʒenərəl præk'tɪʃənə(r)/ n médico m de cabecera

generate /'dʒenəreɪt/ vt producir; (elec) generar

generation /dʒenə'reɪʃn/ n generación f

generator /'dʒenəreɪtə(r)/ n (elec) generador m

genero|sity /dʒenə'rɒsətɪ/ n generosidad f. ~**us** /'dʒenərəs/ a generoso; (plentiful) abundante

genetic /dʒɪ'netɪk/ a genético. ~**s** n genética f

Geneva /dʒɪ'niːvə/ n Ginebra f

genial /'dʒiːnɪəl/ a simpático, afable; (climate) suave, templado

genital /'dʒenɪtl/ a genital. ~**s** npl genitales mpl

genitive /'dʒenɪtɪv/ a & n genitivo (m)

genius /'dʒiːnɪəs/ n (pl -**uses**) genio m

genocide /'dʒenəsaɪd/ n genocidio m

genre /ʒɑːŋr/ n género m
gent /dʒent/ n (sl) señor m. ~s n aseo m de caballeros
genteel /dʒenˈtiːl/ a distinguido; (excessively refined) cursi
gentle /ˈdʒentl/ a (-er, -est) (mild, kind) amable, dulce; (slight) ligero; ⟨hint⟩ discreto
gentlefolk /ˈdʒentlfəʊk/ npl gente f de buena familia
gentleman /ˈdʒentlmən/ n señor m; (well-bred) caballero m
gentleness /ˈdʒentlnɪs/ n amabilidad f
gentlewoman /ˈdʒentlwʊmən/ n señora f (de buena familia)
gently /ˈdʒentlɪ/ adv amablemente; (slowly) despacio
gentry /ˈdʒentrɪ/ npl pequeña aristocracia f
genuflect /ˈdʒenjuːflekt/ vi doblar la rodilla
genuine /ˈdʒenjʊɪn/ a verdadero; ⟨person⟩ sincero
geograph|er /dʒɪˈɒɡrəfə(r)/ n geógrafo m. ~ical /dʒɪəˈɡræfɪkl/ a geográfico. ~y /dʒɪˈɒɡrəfɪ/ n geografía f
geolog|ical /dʒɪəˈlɒdʒɪkl/ a geológico. ~ist n geólogo m. ~y /dʒɪˈɒlədʒɪ/ n geología f
geometr|ic(al) /dʒɪəˈmetrɪk(l)/ a geométrico. ~y /dʒɪˈɒmetrɪ/ n geometría f
geranium /dʒəˈreɪnɪəm/ n geranio m
geriatrics /dʒerɪˈætrɪks/ n geriatría f
germ /dʒɜːm/ n (rudiment, seed) germen m; (med) microbio m
German /ˈdʒɜːmən/ a & n alemán (m). ~ic /dʒɜːˈmænɪk/ a germánico. ~ measles n rubéola f. ~ shepherd (dog) n (perro m) pastor m alemán. ~y n Alemania f
germicide /ˈdʒɜːmɪsaɪd/ n germicida m
germinate /ˈdʒɜːmɪneɪt/ vi germinar. ● vt hacer germinar
gerrymander /ˈdʒerɪmændə(r)/ n falsificación f electoral
gestation /dʒeˈsteɪʃn/ n gestación f
gesticulate /dʒeˈstɪkjʊleɪt/ vi hacer ademanes, gesticular
gesture /ˈdʒestʃə(r)/ n ademán m; (fig) gesto m
get /get/ vt (pt & pp got, pp Amer gotten, pres p getting) obtener,

tener; (catch) coger (not LAm), agarrar (esp LAm); (buy) comprar; (find) encontrar; (fetch) buscar, traer; (understand, sl) comprender, caer (fam). ~ s.o. to do sth conseguir que uno haga algo. ● vi (go) ir; (become) hacerse; (start to) empezar a; (manage) conseguir. ~ married casarse. ~ ready prepararse. ~ about ⟨person⟩ salir mucho; (after illness) levantarse. ~ along (manage) ir tirando; (progress) hacer progresos. ~ along with llevarse bien con. ~ at (reach) llegar a; (imply) querer decir. ~ away salir; (escape) escaparse. ~ back vi volver. ● vt (recover) recobrar. ~ by (manage) ir tirando; (pass) pasar. ~ down bajar; (depress) deprimir. ~ in entrar; subir ⟨vehicle⟩; (arrive) llegar. ~ off bajar de ⟨train, car etc⟩; (leave) irse; (jurid) salir absuelto. ~ on (progress) hacer progresos; (succeed) tener éxito. ~ on with (be on good terms with) llevarse bien con; (continue) seguir. ~ out ⟨person⟩ salir; (take out) sacar. ~ out of (fig) librarse de. ~ over reponerse de ⟨illness⟩. ~ round soslayar ⟨difficulty etc⟩; engatusar ⟨person⟩. ~ through (pass) pasar; (finish) terminar; (on phone) comunicar con. ~ up levantarse; (climb) subir; (organize) preparar. ~away n huida f. ~up n traje m
geyser /ˈɡiːzə(r)/ n calentador m de agua; (geog) géiser m
Ghana /ˈɡɑːnə/ n Ghana f
ghastly /ˈɡɑːstlɪ/ a (-ier, -iest) horrible; (pale) pálido
gherkin /ˈɡɜːkɪn/ n pepinillo m
ghetto /ˈɡetəʊ/ n (pl -os) (Jewish quarter) judería f; (ethnic settlement) barrio m pobre habitado por un grupo étnico
ghost /ɡəʊst/ n fantasma m. ~ly a espectral
ghoulish /ˈɡuːlɪʃ/ a macabro
giant /ˈdʒaɪənt/ n gigante m. ● a gigantesco
gibberish /ˈdʒɪbərɪʃ/ n jerigonza f
gibe /dʒaɪb/ n mofa f
giblets /ˈdʒɪblɪts/ npl menudillos mpl
Gibraltar /dʒɪˈbrɔːltə(r)/ n Gibraltar m
gidd|iness /ˈɡɪdɪnɪs/ n vértigo m. ~y a (-ier, -iest) mareado; (speed) vertiginoso. be/feel ~y estar/sentirse mareado

gift /gift/ *n* regalo *m*; (*ability*) don *m*. ∼**ed** *a* dotado de talento. ∼**wrap** *vt* envolver para regalo

gig /gig/ *n* (*fam*) concierto *m*

gigantic /dʒaɪˈgæntɪk/ *a* gigantesco

giggle /ˈgɪgl/ *vi* reírse tontamente. ● *n* risita *f*. **the** ∼**s** la risa *f* tonta

gild /gild/ *vt* dorar

gills /gɪlz/ *npl* agallas *fpl*

gilt /gilt/ *a* dorado. ∼**-edged** *a* (*com*) de máxima garantía

gimmick /ˈgɪmɪk/ *n* truco *m*

gin /dʒɪn/ *n* ginebra *f*

ginger /ˈdʒɪndʒə(r)/ *n* jengibre *m*. ● *a* rojizo. ● *vt*. ∼ **up** animar. ∼ **ale** *n*, ∼ **beer** *n* cerveza *f* de jengibre. ∼**bread** *n* pan *m* de jengibre

gingerly /ˈdʒɪndʒəlɪ/ *adv* cautelosamente

gingham /ˈgɪŋəm/ *n* guinga *f*

gipsy /ˈdʒɪpsɪ/ *n* gitano *m*

giraffe /dʒɪˈrɑːf/ *n* jirafa *f*

girder /ˈgɜːdə(r)/ *n* viga *f*

girdle /ˈgɜːdl/ *n* (*belt*) cinturón *m*; (*corset*) corsé *m*

girl /gɜːl/ *n* chica *f*, muchacha *f*; (*child*) niña *f*. ∼**friend** *n* amiga *f*; (*of boy*) novia *f*. ∼**hood** *n* (*up to adolescence*) niñez *f*; (*adolescence*) juventud *f*. ∼**ish** *a* de niña; ⟨*boy*⟩ afeminado

giro /ˈdʒaɪrəʊ/ *n* (*pl* **-os**) giro *m* (bancario)

girth /gɜːθ/ *n* circunferencia *f*

gist /dʒɪst/ *n* lo esencial *invar*

give /gɪv/ *vt* (*pt* **gave**, *pp* **given**) dar; (*deliver*) entregar; regalar ⟨*present*⟩; prestar ⟨*aid, attention*⟩; (*grant*) conceder; (*yield*) ceder; (*devote*) dedicar. ∼ **o.s. to** darse a. ● *vi* dar; (*yield*) ceder; (*stretch*) estirarse. ● *n* elasticidad *f*. ∼ **away** regalar; descubrir ⟨*secret*⟩. ∼ **back** devolver. ∼ **in** (*yield*) rendirse. ∼ **off** emitir. ∼ **o.s. up** entregarse (a). ∼ **out** distribuir; (*announce*) anunciar; (*become used up*) agotarse. ∼ **over** (*devote*) dedicar; (*stop, fam*) dejar (de). ∼ **up** (*renounce*) renunciar a; (*yield*) ceder

given /ˈgɪvn/ *see* **give**. ● *a* dado. ∼ **name** *n* nombre *m* de pila

glacier /ˈglæsɪə(r)/ *n* glaciar *m*

glad /glæd/ *a* contento. ∼**den** *vt* alegrar

glade /gleɪd/ *n* claro *m*

gladiator /ˈglædɪeɪtə(r)/ *n* gladiador *m*

gladiolus /ˌglædɪˈəʊləs/ *n* (*pl* **-li** /-laɪ/) estoque *m*, gladiolo *m*, gladíolo *m*

gladly /ˈglædlɪ/ *adv* alegremente; (*willingly*) con mucho gusto

glamo|rize /ˈglæməraɪz/ *vt* embellecer. ∼**rous** *a* atractivo. ∼**ur** *n* encanto *m*

glance /glɑːns/ *n* ojeada *f*. ● *vi*. ∼ **at** dar un vistazo a

gland /glænd/ *n* glándula *f*

glar|e /gleə(r)/ *vi* deslumbrar; (*stare angrily*) mirar airadamente. ● *n* deslumbramiento *m*; (*stare, fig*) mirada *f* airada. ∼**ing** *a* deslumbrador; (*obvious*) manifiesto

glass /glɑːs/ *n* (*material*) vidrio *m*; (*without stem or for wine*) vaso *m*; (*with stem*) copa *f*; (*for beer*) caña *f*; (*mirror*) espejo *m*. ∼**es** *npl* (*spectacles*) gafas *fpl*, anteojos (*LAm*) *mpl*. ∼**y** *a* vítreo

glaze /gleɪz/ *vt* poner cristales a ⟨*windows, doors*⟩; vidriar ⟨*pottery*⟩. ● *n* barniz *m*; (*for pottery*) esmalte *m*. ∼**d** ⟨*object*⟩ vidriado; ⟨*eye*⟩ vidrioso

gleam /gliːm/ *n* destello *m*. ● *vi* destellar

glean /gliːn/ *vt* espigar

glee /gliː/ *n* regocijo *m*. ∼ **club** *n* orfeón *m*. ∼**ful** *a* regocijado

glen /glen/ *n* cañada *f*

glib /glɪb/ *a* de mucha labia; ⟨*reply*⟩ fácil. ∼**ly** *adv* con poca sinceridad

glid|e /glaɪd/ *vi* deslizarse; ⟨*plane*⟩ planear. ∼**er** *n* planeador *m*. ∼**ing** *n* planeo *m*

glimmer /ˈglɪmə(r)/ *n* destello *m*. ● *vi* destellar

glimpse /glɪmps/ *n* vislumbre *f*. **catch a** ∼ **of** vislumbrar. ● *vt* vislumbrar

glint /glɪnt/ *n* destello *m*. ● *vi* destellar

glisten /ˈglɪsn/ *vi* brillar

glitter /ˈglɪtə(r)/ *vi* brillar. ● *n* brillo *m*

gloat /gləʊt/ *vi*. ∼ **on/over** regodearse

global /ˈgləʊbl/ *a* (*world-wide*) mundial; (*all-embracing*) global

globe /gləʊb/ *n* globo *m*

globule /ˈglɒbjuːl/ *n* glóbulo *m*

gloom /gluːm/ *n* oscuridad *f*; (*sadness, fig*) tristeza *f*. ∼**y** *a* (**-ier**, **-iest**) triste; (*pessimistic*) pesimista

glorify /ˈglɔːrɪfaɪ/ *vt* glorificar

glorious /'glɔːrɪəs/ a espléndido; ‹deed, hero etc› glorioso

glory /'glɔːrɪ/ n gloria f; ‹beauty› esplendor m. ● vi. ~ **in** enorgullecerse de. ~**-hole** n ‹untidy room› leonera f

gloss /glɒs/ n lustre m. ● a brillante. ● vi. ~ **over** ‹make light of› minimizar; ‹cover up› encubrir

glossary /'glɒsərɪ/ n glosario m

glossy /'glɒsɪ/ a brillante

glove /glʌv/ n guante m. ~ **compartment** n ‹auto› guantera f, gaveta f. ~**d** a enguantado

glow /gləʊ/ vi brillar; ‹with health› rebosar de; ‹with passion› enardecerse. ● n incandescencia f; ‹of cheeks› rubor m

glower /'glaʊə(r)/ vi. ~ **(at)** mirar airadamente

glowing /'gləʊɪŋ/ a incandescente; ‹account› entusiasta; ‹complexion› rojo; ‹with health› rebosante de

glucose /'gluːkəʊs/ n glucosa f

glue /gluː/ n cola f. ● vt ‹pres p gluing› pegar

glum /glʌm/ a ‹glummer, glummest› triste

glut /glʌt/ n superabundancia f

glutton /'glʌtn/ n glotón m. ~**ous** a glotón. ~**y** n glotonería f

glycerine /'glɪsəriːn/ n glicerina f

gnarled /nɑːld/ a nudoso

gnash /næʃ/ vt. ~ **one's teeth** rechinar los dientes

gnat /næt/ n mosquito m

gnaw /nɔː/ vt/i roer

gnome /nəʊm/ n gnomo m

go /gəʊ/ vi ‹pt went, pp gone› ir; ‹leave› irse; ‹work› funcionar; ‹become› hacerse; ‹be sold› venderse; ‹vanish› desaparecer. ~ **ahead!** ¡adelante! ~ **bad** pasarse. ~ **riding** montar a caballo. ~ **shopping** ir de compras. **be** ~**ing to do** ir a hacer. ● n ‹pl goes› ‹energy› energía f. **be on the** ~ trabajar sin cesar. **have a** ~ intentar. **it's your** ~ te toca a ti. **make a** ~ **of** tener éxito en. ~ **across** cruzar. ~ **away** irse. ~ **back** volver. ~ **back on** faltar a ‹promise etc›. ~ **by** pasar. ~ **down** bajar; ‹sun› ponerse. ~ **for** buscar, traer; ‹like› gustar; ‹attack, sl› atacar. ~ **in** entrar. ~ **in for** presentarse para ‹exam›. ~ **off** ‹leave› irse; ‹go bad› pasarse; ‹explode› estallar. ~ **on** seguir; ‹happen› pasar. ~ **out** salir; ‹light, fire› apagarse. ~ **over** ‹check›

examinar. ~ **round** ‹be enough› ser bastante. ~ **through** ‹suffer› sufrir; ‹check› examinar. ~ **under** hundirse. ~ **up** subir. ~ **without** pasarse sin

goad /gəʊd/ vt aguijonear

go-ahead /'gəʊəhed/ n luz f verde. ● a dinámico

goal /gəʊl/ n fin m, objeto m; ‹sport› gol m. ~**ie** n ‹fam› portero m. ~**keeper** n portero m. ~**post** n poste m (de la portería)

goat /gəʊt/ n cabra f

goatee /gəʊ'tiː/ n perilla f, barbas fpl de chivo

gobble /'gɒbl/ vt engullir

go-between /'gəʊbɪtwiːn/ n intermediario m

goblet /'gɒblɪt/ n copa f

goblin /'gɒblɪn/ n duende m

God /gɒd/ n Dios m. ~**-forsaken** a olvidado de Dios

god /gɒd/ n dios m. ~**child** n ahijado m. ~**daughter** n ahijada f. ~**dess** /'gɒdɪs/ n diosa f. ~**father** n padrino m. ~**ly** a devoto. ~**mother** n madrina f. ~**send** n beneficio m inesperado. ~**son** n ahijado m

go-getter /gəʊ'getə(r)/ n persona f ambiciosa

goggle /'gɒgl/ vi. ~ **(at)** mirar con los ojos desmesuradamente abiertos

goggles /'gɒglz/ npl gafas fpl protectoras

going /'gəʊɪŋ/ n camino m; ‹racing› ‹estado m del› terreno m. **it is slow/hard** ~ es lento/difícil. ● a ‹price› actual; ‹concern› en funcionamiento. ~**s-on** npl actividades fpl anormales, tejemaneje m

gold /gəʊld/ n oro m. ● a de oro. ~**en** /'gəʊldən/ a de oro; ‹in colour› dorado; ‹opportunity› único. ~**en wedding** n bodas fpl de oro. ~**fish** n invar pez m de colores, carpa f dorada. ~**mine** n mina f de oro; ‹fig› fuente f de gran riqueza. ~**-plated** a chapado en oro. ~**smith** n orfebre m

golf /gɒlf/ n golf m. ~**-course** n campo m de golf. ~**er** n jugador m de golf

golly /'gɒlɪ/ int ¡caramba!

golosh /gə'lɒʃ/ n chanclo m

gondola /'gɒndələ/ n góndola f. ~**ier** /gɒndə'lɪə(r)/ n gondolero m

gone /gɒn/ see **go**. ● a pasado. ~ **six o'clock** después de las seis

gong /gɒŋ/ n gong(o) m

good /gʊd/ a (**better**, **best**) bueno, (*before masculine singular noun*) buen. ~ **afternoon!** ¡buenas tardes! ~ **evening!** (*before dark*) ¡buenas tardes!; (*after dark*) ¡buenas noches! G~ **Friday** n Viernes m Santo. ~ **morning!** ¡buenos días! ~ **name** n (buena) reputación f. ~ **night!** ¡buenas noches! a ~ **deal** bastante. as ~ as (*almost*) casi. be ~ **with** entender. do ~ hacer bien. **feel** ~ sentirse bien. **have a** ~ **time** divertirse. **it is** ~ **for you** le sentará bien. ● n bien m. **for** ~ para siempre. **it is no** ~ **shouting/etc** es inútil gritar/etc.

goodbye /gʊd'baɪ/ int ¡adiós! ● n adiós m. **say** ~ to despedirse de

good: ~**-for-nothing** a & n inútil (m). ~**-looking** a guapo

goodness /'gʊdnɪs/ n bondad f. ~!, ~ **gracious!**, ~ **me!**, **my** ~! ¡Dios mío!

goods /gʊdz/ npl (*merchandise*) mercancías fpl

goodwill /gʊd'wɪl/ n buena voluntad f

goody /'gʊdɪ/ n (*culin, fam*) golosina f; (*in film*) bueno m. ~**-goody** n mojigato m

gooey /'guːɪ/ a (**gooier**, **gooiest**) (*sl*) pegajoso; (*fig*) sentimental

goof /guːf/ vi (*Amer, blunder*) cometer una pifia. ~**y** a (*sl*) necio

goose /guːs/ n (pl **geese**) oca f

gooseberry /'gʊzbərɪ/ n uva f espina, grosella f

goose-flesh /'guːsfleʃ/ n, **goose-pimples** /'guːspɪmplz/ n carne f de gallina

gore /gɔː(r)/ n sangre f. ● vt cornear

gorge /gɔːdʒ/ n (*geog*) garganta f. ● vt. ~ **o.s.** hartarse (**on** de)

gorgeous /'gɔːdʒəs/ a magnífico

gorilla /gə'rɪlə/ n gorila m

gormless /'gɔːmlɪs/ a (*sl*) idiota

gorse /gɔːs/ n aulaga f

gory /'gɔːrɪ/ a (**-ier**, **-iest**) (*covered in blood*) ensangrentado; (*horrific, fig*) horrible

gosh /gɒʃ/ int ¡caramba!

go-slow /gəʊ'sləʊ/ n huelga f de celo

gospel /'gɒspl/ n evangelio m

gossip /'gɒsɪp/ n (*idle chatter*) charla f; (*tittle-tattle*) comadreo m; (*person*) chismoso m. ● vi (pt **gossiped**) (*chatter*) charlar; (*repeat scandal*) comadrear. ~**y** a chismoso

got /gɒt/ *see* **get**. **have** ~ tener. **have** ~ **to** tener que hacer

Gothic /'gɒθɪk/ a (*archit*) gótico; (*people*) godo

gouge /gaʊdʒ/ vt. ~ **out** arrancar

gourmet /'gʊəmeɪ/ n gastrónomo m

gout /gaʊt/ n (*med*) gota f

govern /'gʌvn/ vt/i gobernar

governess /'gʌvənɪs/ n institutriz f

government /'gʌvənmənt/ n gobierno m. ~**al** /gʌvə'mentl/ a gubernamental

governor /'gʌvənə(r)/ n gobernador m

gown /gaʊn/ n vestido m; (*of judge, teacher*) toga f

GP *abbr see* **general practitioner**

grab /græb/ vt (pt **grabbed**) agarrar

grace /greɪs/ n gracia f. ~**ful** a elegante

gracious /'greɪʃəs/ a (*kind*) amable; (*elegant*) elegante

gradation /grə'deɪʃn/ n gradación f

grade /greɪd/ n clase f, categoría f; (*of goods*) clase f, calidad f; (*on scale*) grado m; (*school mark*) nota f; (*class, Amer*) curso m. ~ **school** n (*Amer*) escuela f primaria. ● vt clasificar; (*schol*) calificar

gradient /'greɪdɪənt/ n (*slope*) pendiente f

gradual /'grædʒʊəl/ a gradual. ~**ly** adv gradualmente

graduat|e /'grædʒʊət/ n (*univ*) licenciado. ● vi /'grædjʊeɪt/ licenciarse. ● vt graduar. ~**ion** /-'eɪʃn/ n entrega f de títulos

graffiti /grə'fiːtɪ/ npl pintada f

graft[1] /grɑːft/ n (*med, bot*) injerto m. ● vt injertar

graft[2] /grɑːft/ n (*bribery, fam*) corrupción f

grain /greɪn/ n grano m

gram /græm/ n gramo m

gramma|r /'græmə(r)/ n gramática f. ~**tical** /grə'mætɪkl/ a gramatical

gramophone /'græməfəʊn/ n toca-discos m invar

grand /grænd/ a (**-er**, **-est**) magnífico; (*excellent, fam*) estupendo. ~**child** n nieto m. ~**daughter** n nieta f

grandeur /'grændʒə(r)/ n grandiosidad f

grandfather /'grændfɑːðə(r)/ n abuelo m

grandiose /'grændɪəʊs/ a grandioso

grand: ~**mother** n abuela f. ~**parents** npl abuelos mpl. ~ **piano** n piano m de cola. ~**son** n nieto m

grandstand /'grænstænd/ n tribuna f

granite /'grænɪt/ n granito m

granny /'grænɪ/ n (fam) abuela f, nana f (fam)

grant /grɑːnt/ vt conceder; (give) donar; (admit) admitir (that que). **take for ~ed** dar por sentado. ● n concesión f; (univ) beca f

granulated /'grænjʊleɪtɪd/ a. ~ **sugar** n azúcar m granulado

granule /'grænuːl/ n gránulo m

grape /greɪp/ n uva f

grapefruit /'greɪpfruːt/ n invar toronja f, pomelo m

graph /grɑːf/ n gráfica f

graphic /'græfɪk/ a gráfico

grapple /'græpl/ vi. ~ **with** intentar vencer

grasp /grɑːsp/ vt agarrar. ● n (hold) agarro m; (strength of hand) apretón m; (reach) alcance m; (fig) comprensión f

grasping /'grɑːspɪŋ/ a avaro

grass /grɑːs/ n hierba f. ~**hopper** n saltamontes m invar. ~**land** n pradera f. ~ **roots** npl base f popular. ● a popular. ~**y** a cubierto de hierba

grate /greɪt/ n (fireplace) parrilla f. ● vt rallar. ~ **one's teeth** hacer rechinar los dientes. ● vi rechinar

grateful /'greɪtfl/ a agradecido. ~**ly** adv con gratitud

grater /'greɪtə(r)/ n rallador m

gratif|ied /'grætɪfaɪd/ a contento. ~**y** vt satisfacer; (please) agradar a. ~**ying** a agradable

grating /'greɪtɪŋ/ n reja f

gratis /'grɑːtɪs/ a & adv gratis (a invar)

gratitude /'grætɪtjuːd/ n gratitud f

gratuitous /grə'tjuːɪtəs/ a gratuito

gratuity /grə'tjuːətɪ/ n (tip) propina f; (gift of money) gratificación f

grave[1] /greɪv/ n sepultura f

grave[2] /greɪv/ a (-er, -est) (serious) serio. /grɑːv/ a. ~ **accent** n acento m grave

grave-digger /'greɪvdɪgə(r)/ n sepulturero m

gravel /'grævl/ n grava f

gravely /'greɪvlɪ/ a (seriously) seriamente

grave: ~**stone** n lápida f. ~**yard** n cementerio m

gravitat|e /'grævɪteɪt/ vi gravitar. ~**ion** /-'teɪʃn/ n gravitación f

gravity /'grævətɪ/ n gravedad f

gravy /'greɪvɪ/ n salsa f

graze[1] /greɪz/ vt/i (eat) pacer

graze[2] /greɪz/ vt (touch) rozar; (scrape) raspar. ● n rozadura f

greas|e /griːs/ n grasa f. ● vt engrasar. ~**e-paint** n maquillaje m. ~**e-proof paper** n papel m a prueba de grasa, apergaminado m. ~**y** a grasiento

great /greɪt/ a (-er, -est) grande, (before singular noun) gran; (very good, fam) estupendo. **G~ Britain** n Gran Bretaña f. ~**grandfather** n bisabuelo m. ~**grandmother** n bisabuela f. ~**ly** /'greɪtlɪ/ adv (very) muy; (much) mucho. ~**ness** n grandeza f

Greece /griːs/ n Grecia f

greed /griːd/ n avaricia f; (for food) glotonería f. ~**y** a avaro; (for food) glotón

Greek /griːk/ a & n griego (m)

green /griːn/ a (-er, -est) verde; (fig) crédulo. ● n verde m; (grass) césped m. ~ **belt** n zona f verde. ~**ery** n verdor m. ~ **fingers** npl habilidad f con las plantas

greengage /'griːngeɪdʒ/ n (plum) claudia f

greengrocer /'griːngrəʊsə(r)/ n verdulero m

greenhouse /'griːnhaʊs/ n invernadero m

green: ~ **light** n luz f verde. ~**s** npl verduras fpl

Greenwich Mean Time /grenɪtʃ 'miːntaɪm/ n hora f media de Greenwich

greet /griːt/ vt saludar; (receive) recibir. ~**ing** n saludo m. ~**ings** npl (in letter) recuerdos mpl

gregarious /grɪ'geərɪəs/ a gregario

grenade /grɪ'neɪd/ n granada f

grew /gruː/ see **grow**

grey /greɪ/ a & n (-er, -est) gris (m). ● vi ⟨hair⟩ encanecer

greyhound /'greɪhaʊnd/ n galgo m

grid /grɪd/ n reja f; (network, elec) red f; (culin) parrilla f; (on map) cuadrícula f

grief /griːf/ n dolor m. **come to ~** ⟨person⟩ sufrir un accidente; (fail) fracasar

grievance /'griːvns/ n queja f

grieve /griːv/ vt afligir. ● vi afligirse. ~ **for** llorar

grievous /'griːvəs/ a doloroso; (serious) grave

grill /grɪl/ n (cooking device) parrilla f; (food) parrillada f, asado m, asada f. ● vt asar a la parrilla; (interrogate) interrogar

grille /grɪl/ n rejilla f

grim /grɪm/ a (**grimmer, grimmest**) severo

grimace /'grɪməs/ n mueca f. ● vi hacer muecas

grim|e /graɪm/ n mugre f. ~**y** a mugriento

grin /grɪn/ vt (pt **grinned**) sonreír. ● n sonrisa f (abierta)

grind /graɪnd/ vt (pt **ground**) moler ⟨coffee, corn etc⟩; (pulverize) pulverizar; (sharpen) afilar. ~ **one's teeth** hacer rechinar los dientes. ● n faena f

grip /grɪp/ vt (pt **gripped**) agarrar; (interest) captar la atención de. ● n (hold) agarro m; (strength of hand) apretón m. **come to** ~**s** encararse (**with** a/con)

gripe /graɪp/ n. ~**s** npl (med) cólico m

grisly /'grɪzlɪ/ a (-ier, -iest) horrible

gristle /'grɪsl/ n cartílago m

grit /grɪt/ n arena f; (fig) valor m, aguante m. ● vt (pt **gritted**) echar arena en ⟨road⟩. ~ **one's teeth** (fig) acorazarse

grizzle /'grɪzl/ vi lloriquear

groan /grəʊn/ vi gemir. ● n gemido m

grocer /'grəʊsə(r)/ n tendero m. ~**ies** npl comestibles mpl. ~**y** n tienda f de comestibles

grog /grɒg/ n grog m

groggy /'grɒgɪ/ a (weak) débil; (unsteady) inseguro; (ill) malucho

groin /grɔɪn/ n ingle f

groom /gru:m/ n mozo m de caballos; (bridegroom) novio m. ● vt almohazar ⟨horses⟩; (fig) preparar. **well-**~**ed** a bien arreglado

groove /gru:v/ n ranura f; (in record) surco m

grope /grəʊp/ vi (find one's way) moverse a tientas. ~ **for** buscar a tientas

gross /grəʊs/ a (-er, -est) (coarse) grosero; (com) bruto; (fat) grueso; (flagrant) grave. ● n invar gruesa f. ~**ly** adv groseramente; (very) enormemente

grotesque /grəʊ'tesk/ a grotesco

grotto /'grɒtəʊ/ n (pl -**oes**) gruta f

grotty /'grɒtɪ/ a (sl) desagradable; (dirty) sucio

grouch /graʊtʃ/ vi (grumble, fam) rezongar

ground[1] /graʊnd/ n suelo m; (area) terreno m; (reason) razón f; (elec, Amer) toma f de tierra. ● vt varar ⟨ship⟩; prohibir despegar ⟨aircraft⟩. ~**s** npl jardines mpl; (sediment) poso m

ground[2] /graʊnd/ see **grind**

ground: ~ **floor** n planta f baja. ~ **rent** n alquiler m del terreno

grounding /'graʊndɪŋ/ n base f, conocimientos mpl (**in** de)

groundless /'graʊndlɪs/ a infundado

ground: ~**sheet** n tela f impermeable. ~**swell** n mar m de fondo. ~**work** n trabajo m preparatorio

group /gru:p/ n grupo m. ● vt agrupar. ● vi agruparse

grouse[1] /graʊs/ n invar (bird) urogallo m. **red** ~ lagópodo m escocés

grouse[2] /graʊs/ vi (grumble, fam) rezongar

grove /grəʊv/ n arboleda f. **lemon** ~ n limonar m. **olive** ~ n olivar m. **orange** ~ n naranjal m. **pine** ~ n pinar m

grovel /'grɒvl/ vi (pt **grovelled**) arrastrarse, humillarse. ~**ling** a servil

grow /grəʊ/ vi (pt **grew**, pp **grown**) crecer; ⟨cultivated plant⟩ cultivarse; (become) volverse, ponerse. ● vt cultivar. ~ **up** hacerse mayor. ~**er** n cultivador m

growl /graʊl/ vi gruñir. ● n gruñido m

grown /grəʊn/ see **grow**. ● a adulto. ~**-up** a & n adulto (m)

growth /grəʊθ/ n crecimiento m; (increase) aumento m; (development) desarrollo m; (med) tumor m

grub /grʌb/ n (larva) larva f; (food, sl) comida f

grubby /'grʌbɪ/ a (-ier, -iest) mugriento

grudg|e /grʌdʒ/ vt dar de mala gana; (envy) envidiar. ~**e doing** molestarle hacer. **he** ~**ed paying** le molestó pagar. ● n rencor m. **bear/have a** ~**e against s.o.** guardar rencor a alguien. ~**ingly** adv de mala gana

gruelling /'gru:əlɪŋ/ a agotador

gruesome /'gru:səm/ a horrible

gruff /grʌf/ a (-er, -est) ‹manners› brusco; ‹voice› ronco

grumble /'grʌmbl/ vi rezongar

grumpy /'grʌmpɪ/ a (-ier, -iest) mal-humorado

grunt /grʌnt/ vi gruñir. ● n gruñido m

guarant|ee /gærən'ti:/ n garantía f. ● vt garantizar. ~or n garante m & f

guard /gɑ:d/ vt proteger; ‹watch› vigilar. ● vi. ~ **against** guardar de. ● n (vigilance, mil group) guardia f; (person) guardia m; (on train) jefe m de tren

guarded /'gɑ:dɪd/ a cauteloso

guardian /'gɑ:dɪən/ n guardián m; (of orphan) tutor m

guer(r)illa /gə'rɪlə/ n guerrillero m. ~ **warfare** n guerra f de guerrillas

guess /ges/ vt/i adivinar; (suppose, Amer) creer. ● n conjetura f. ~**work** n conjetura(s) f(pl)

guest /gest/ n invitado m; (in hotel) huésped m. ~**house** n casa f de huéspedes

guffaw /gʌ'fɔː/ n carcajada f. ● vi reírse a carcajadas

guidance /'gaɪdəns/ n (advice) consejos mpl; (information) información f

guide /gaɪd/ n (person) guía m & f; (book) guía f. **Girl G~** exploradora f, guía f (fam). ● vt guiar. ~**book** n guía f. ~**d missile** n proyectil m teledirigido. ~**lines** npl pauta f

guild /gɪld/ n gremio m

guile /gaɪl/ n astucia f

guillotine /'gɪlətiːn/ n guillotina f

guilt /gɪlt/ n culpabilidad f. ~**y** a culpable

guinea-pig /'gɪnɪpɪg/ n (including fig) cobaya f

guise /gaɪz/ n (external appearance) apariencia f; (style) manera f

guitar /gɪ'tɑ:(r)/ n guitarra f. ~**ist** n guitarrista m & f

gulf /gʌlf/ n (part of sea) golfo m; (hollow) abismo m

gull /gʌl/ n gaviota f

gullet /'gʌlɪt/ n esófago m

gullible /'gʌləbl/ a crédulo

gully /'gʌlɪ/ n (ravine) barranco m

gulp /gʌlp/ vt. ~ **down** tragarse de prisa. ● vi tragar; (from fear etc) sentir dificultad para tragar. ● n trago m

gum[1] /gʌm/ n goma f; (for chewing) chicle m. ● vt (pt **gummed**) engomar

gum[2] /gʌm/ n (anat) encía f. ~**boil** /'gʌmbɔɪl/ n flemón m

gumboot /'gʌmbuːt/ n bota f de agua

gumption /'gʌmpʃn/ n (fam) iniciativa f; (common sense) sentido m común

gun /gʌn/ n (pistol) pistola f; (rifle) fusil m; (large) cañón m. ● vt (pt **gunned**). ~ **down** abatir a tiros. ~**fire** n tiros mpl

gunge /gʌndʒ/ n (sl) materia f sucia (y pegajosa)

gun: ~**man** /'gʌnmən/ n pistolero m. ~**ner** /'gʌnə(r)/ n artillero m. ~**powder** n pólvora f. ~**shot** n disparo m

gurgle /'gɜːgl/ n (of liquid) gorgoteo m; (of baby) gorjeo m. ● vi ‹liquid› gorgotear; ‹baby› gorjear

guru /'goruː/ n (pl **-us**) mentor m

gush /gʌʃ/ vi. ~ **(out)** salir a borbotones. ● n (of liquid) chorro m; (fig) torrente m. ~**ing** a efusivo

gusset /'gʌsɪt/ n escudete m

gust /gʌst/ n ráfaga f; (of smoke) bocanada f

gusto /'gʌstəʊ/ n entusiasmo m

gusty /'gʌstɪ/ a borrascoso

gut /gʌt/ n tripa f, intestino m. ● vt (pt **gutted**) destripar; ‹fire› destruir. ~**s** npl tripas fpl; (courage, fam) valor m

gutter /'gʌtə(r)/ n (on roof) canalón m; (in street) cuneta f; (slum, fig) arroyo m. ~**snipe** n golfillo m

guttural /'gʌtərəl/ a gutural

guy /gaɪ/ n (man, fam) hombre m, tío m (fam)

guzzle /'gʌzl/ vt/i soplarse, tragarse

gym /dʒɪm/ n (gymnasium, fam) gimnasio m; (gymnastics, fam) gimnasia f

gymkhana /dʒɪmkɑːnə/ n gincana f, gymkhana f

gymnasium /dʒɪm'neɪzɪəm/ n gimnasio m

gymnast /'dʒɪmnæst/ n gimnasta m & f. ~**ics** npl gimnasia f

gym-slip /'dʒɪmslɪp/ n túnica f (de gimnasia)

gynaecolog|ist /gaɪnɪ'kɒlədʒɪst/ n ginecólogo m. ~**y** n ginecología f

gypsy /'dʒɪpsɪ/ n gitano m

gyrate /dʒaɪə'reɪt/ vi girar

gyroscope /'dʒaɪərəskəʊp/ n giroscopio m

H

haberdashery /ˌhæbə'dæʃərɪ/ n mercería f

habit /'hæbɪt/ n costumbre f; (costume, relig) hábito m. **be in the ~ of** (+ gerund) tener la costumbre de (+ infintive), soler (+ infinitive). **get into the ~ of** (+ gerund) acostumbrarse a (+ infinitive)

habitable /'hæbɪtəbl/ a habitable

habitat /'hæbɪtæt/ n hábitat m

habitation /ˌhæbɪ'teɪʃn/ n habitación f

habitual /hə'bɪtjʊəl/ a habitual; ‹smoker, liar› inveterado. **~ly** adv de costumbre

hack /hæk/ n (old horse) jamelgo m; (writer) escritorzuelo m. ● vt cortar. **~ to pieces** cortar en pedazos

hackney /'hæknɪ/ a. **~ carriage** n coche m de alquiler, taxi m

hackneyed /'hæknɪd/ a manido

had /hæd/ see **have**

haddock /'hædək/ n invar eglefino m. **smoked ~** n eglefino m ahumado

haemorrhage /'hemərɪdʒ/ n hemorragia f

haemorrhoids /'hemərɔɪdz/ npl hemorroides fpl, almorranas fpl

hag /hæg/ n bruja f

haggard /'hægəd/ a ojeroso

haggle /'hægl/ vi regatear

Hague /heɪg/ n. **The ~** La Haya f

hail¹ /heɪl/ n granizo m. ● vi granizar

hail² /heɪl/ vt (greet) saludar; llamar ‹taxi›. ● vi. **~ from** venir de

hailstone /'heɪlstəʊn/ n grano m de granizo

hair /heə(r)/ n pelo m. **~brush** n cepillo m para el pelo. **~cut** n corte m de pelo. **have a ~cut** cortarse el pelo. **~do** n (fam) peinado m. **~dresser** n peluquero m. **~dresser's (shop)** n peluquería f. **~dryer** n secador m. **~pin** n horquilla f. **~pin bend** n curva f cerrada. **~raising** a espeluznante. **~style** n peinado m

hairy /'heərɪ/ a (-ier, -iest) peludo; (terrifying, sl) espeluznante

hake /heɪk/ n invar merluza f

halcyon /'hælsɪən/ a sereno. **~ days** npl época f feliz

hale /heɪl/ a robusto

half /hɑːf/ n (pl **halves**) mitad f. ● a medio. **~ a dozen** media docena f. **~ an hour** media hora f. ● adv medio, a medias. **~-back** n (sport) medio m. **~-caste** a & n mestizo (m). **~-hearted** a poco entusiasta. **~-term** n vacaciones fpl de medio trimestre. **~-time** n (sport) descanso m. **~way** a medio. ● adv a medio camino. **~-wit** n imbécil m & f. **at ~-mast** a media asta

halibut /'hælɪbət/ n invar hipogloso m, halibut m

hall /hɔːl/ n (room) sala f; (mansion) casa f solariega; (entrance) vestíbulo m. **~ of residence** n colegio m mayor

hallelujah /ˌhælɪ'luːjə/ int & n aleluya (f)

hallmark /'hɔːlmɑːk/ n (on gold etc) contraste m; (fig) sello m (distintivo)

hallo /hə'ləʊ/ int = **hello**

hallow /'hæləʊ/ vt santificar. **H~e'en** n víspera f de Todos los Santos

hallucination /həˌluːsɪ'neɪʃn/ n alucinación f

halo /'heɪləʊ/ n (pl **-oes**) aureola f

halt /hɔːlt/ n alto m. ● vt parar. ● vi pararse

halve /hɑːv/ vt dividir por mitad

ham /hæm/ n jamón m; (theatre, sl) racionista m & f

hamburger /'hæmbɜːgə(r)/ n hamburguesa f

hamlet /'hæmlɪt/ n aldea f, caserío m

hammer /'hæmə(r)/ n martillo m. ● vt martill(e)ar; (defeat, fam) machacar

hammock /'hæmək/ n hamaca f

hamper¹ /'hæmpə(r)/ n cesta f

hamper² /'hæmpə(r)/ vt estorbar, poner trabas

hamster /'hæmstə(r)/ n hámster m

hand /hænd/ n (including cards) mano f; (of clock) manecilla f; (writing) escritura f, letra f; (worker) obrero m. **at ~** a mano. **by ~** a mano. **lend a ~** echar una mano. **on ~** a mano. **on one's ~s** (fig) en (las) manos de uno. **on the one ~... on the other ~** por un lado... por otro. **out of ~** fuera de control. **to ~** a mano. ● vt dar. **~ down** pasar. **~ in** entregar. **~ over** entregar. **~ out** distribuir. **~bag** n bolso m, cartera f (LAm). **~book** n (manual) manual m; (guidebook) guía f. **~cuffs** npl esposas *fpl.* ∼**ful** /ˈhændfʊl/ *n* puñado *m*; (*person, fam*) persona *f* difícil. ∼**luggage** *n* equipaje *m* de mano. ∼**out** *n* folleto *m*; (*money*) limosna *f*

handicap /ˈhændɪkæp/ *n* desventaja *f*; (*sport*) handicap *m.* ● *vt* (*pt* **handicapped**) imponer impedimentos a

handicraft /ˈhændɪkrɑːft/ *n* artesanía *f*

handiwork /ˈhændɪwɜːk/ *n* obra *f*, trabajo *m* manual

handkerchief /ˈhæŋkətʃɪf/ *n* (*pl* **-fs**) pañuelo *m*

handle /ˈhændl/ *n* (*of door etc*) tirador *m*; (*of implement*) mango *m*; (*of cup, bag, basket etc*) asa *f.* ● *vt* manejar; (*touch*) tocar; (*control*) controlar

handlebar /ˈhændlbɑː(r)/ *n* (*on bicycle*) manillar *m*

handshake /ˈhændʃeɪk/ *n* apretón *m* de manos

handsome /ˈhænsəm/ *a* (*good-looking*) guapo; (*generous*) generoso; (*large*) considerable

handwriting /ˈhændraɪtɪŋ/ *n* escritura *f*, letra *f*

handy /ˈhændɪ/ *a* (**-ier, -iest**) (*useful*) cómodo; (*person*) diestro; (*near*) a mano. ∼**man** *n* hombre *m* habilidoso

hang /hæŋ/ *vt* (*pt* **hung**) colgar; (*pt* **hanged**) (*capital punishment*) ahorcar. ● *vi* colgar; (*hair*) caer. ● *n*. **get the** ∼ **of sth** coger el truco de algo. ∼ **about** holgazanear. ∼ **on** (*hold out*) resistir; (*wait, sl*) esperar. ∼ **out** *vi* tender; (*live, sl*) vivir. ∼ **up** (*telephone*) colgar

hangar /ˈhæŋə(r)/ *n* hangar *m*

hanger /ˈhæŋə(r)/ *n* (*for clothes*) percha *f.* ∼**on** *n* parásito *m*, pegote *m*

hang-gliding /ˈhæŋɡlaɪdɪŋ/ *n* vuelo *m* libre

hangman /ˈhæŋmən/ *n* verdugo *m*

hangover /ˈhæŋəʊvə(r)/ *n* (*after drinking*) resaca *f*

hang-up /ˈhæŋʌp/ *n* (*sl*) complejo *m*

hanker /ˈhæŋkə(r)/ *vi.* ∼ **after** anhelar. ∼**ing** *n* anhelo *m*

hanky-panky /ˈhæŋkɪpæŋkɪ/ *n* (*trickery, sl*) trucos *mpl*

haphazard /hæpˈhæzəd/ *a* fortuito. ∼**ly** *adv* al azar

hapless /ˈhæplɪs/ *a* desafortunado

happen /ˈhæpən/ *vi* pasar, suceder, ocurrir. **if he** ∼**s to come** si acaso viene. ∼**ing** *n* acontecimiento *m*

happ|ily /ˈhæpɪlɪ/ *adv* felizmente; (*fortunately*) afortunadamente. ∼**iness** *n* felicidad *f*. ∼**y** *a* (**-ier, -iest**) feliz. ∼**y-go-lucky** *a* despreocupado. ∼**y medium** *n* término *m* medio

harangue /həˈræŋ/ *n* arenga *f.* ● *vt* arengar

harass /ˈhærəs/ *vt* acosar. ∼**ment** *n* tormento *m*

harbour /ˈhɑːbə(r)/ *n* puerto *m.* ● *vt* encubrir (*criminal*); abrigar (*feelings*)

hard /hɑːd/ *a* (**-er, -est**) duro; (*difficult*) difícil. ∼ **of hearing** duro de oído. ● *adv* mucho; (*pull*) fuerte. ∼ **by** (muy) cerca. ∼ **done by** tratado injustamente. ∼ **up** (*fam*) sin un cuarto. ∼**board** *n* chapa *f* de madera, tabla *f*. ∼**-boiled egg** *n* huevo *m* duro. ∼**en** /ˈhɑːdn/ *vt* endurecer. ● *vi* endurecerse. ∼**-headed** *a* realista

hardly /ˈhɑːdlɪ/ *adv* apenas. ∼ **ever** casi nunca

hardness /ˈhɑːdnɪs/ *n* dureza *f*

hardship /ˈhɑːdʃɪp/ *n* apuro *m*

hard: ∼ **shoulder** *n* arcén *m*. ∼**ware** *n* ferretería *f*; (*computer*) hardware *m*. ∼**-working** *a* trabajador

hardy /ˈhɑːdɪ/ *a* (**-ier, -iest**) (*bold*) audaz; (*robust*) robusto; (*bot*) resistente

hare /heə(r)/ *n* liebre *f*. ∼**-brained** *a* aturdido

harem /ˈhɑːriːm/ *n* harén *m*

haricot /ˈhærɪkəʊ/ *n*. ∼ **bean** alubia *f*, judía *f*

hark /hɑːk/ *vi* escuchar. ∼ **back to** volver a

harlot /ˈhɑːlət/ *n* prostituta *f*

harm /hɑːm/ *n* daño *m*. **there is no** ∼ **in** (+ *gerund*) no hay ningún mal en (+ *infinitive*). ● *vt* hacer daño a (*person*); dañar (*thing*); perjudicar (*interests*). ∼**ful** *a* perjudicial. ∼**less** *a* inofensivo

harmonica /hɑːˈmɒnɪkə/ *n* armónica *f*

harmon|ious /hɑːˈməʊnɪəs/ *a* armonioso. ∼**ize** *vt/i* armonizar. ∼**y** *n* armonía *f*

harness /ˈhɑːnɪs/ *n* (*for horses*) guarniciones *fpl*; (*for children*) andadores *mpl.* ● *vt* poner guarniciones a (*horse*); (*fig*) aprovechar

harp /hɑːp/ *n* arpa *f.* ● *vi.* ∼ **on (about)** machacar. ∼**ist** /ˈhɑːpɪst/ *n* arpista *m & f*

harpoon /hɑːˈpuːn/ *n* arpón *m*

harpsichord /ˈhɑːpsɪkɔːd/ *n* clavicémbalo *m*, clave *m*

harrowing / ˈhærəʊɪŋ/ *a* desgarrador

harsh /hɑːʃ/ *a* (**-er, -est**) duro, severo; ⟨*taste, sound*⟩ áspero. **~ly** *adv* severamente. **~ness** *n* severidad *f*

harvest /ˈhɑːvɪst/ *n* cosecha *f*. ● *vt* cosechar. **~er** *n* ⟨*person*⟩ segador; ⟨*machine*⟩ cosechadora *f*

has /hæz/ *see* **have**

hash /hæʃ/ *n* picadillo *m*. **make a ~ of sth** hacer algo con los pies, estropear algo

hashish /ˈhæʃiːʃ/ *n* hachís *m*

hassle /ˈhæsl/ *n* ⟨*quarrel*⟩ pelea *f*; ⟨*difficulty*⟩ problema *m*, dificultad *f*; ⟨*bother, fam*⟩ pena *f*, follón *m*, lío *m*. ● *vt* ⟨*harass*⟩ acosar, dar la lata

haste /heɪst/ *n* prisa *f*. **in ~** de prisa. **make ~** darse prisa

hasten /ˈheɪsn/ *vt* apresurar. ● *vi* apresurarse; darse prisa

hast|ily /ˈheɪstɪlɪ/ *adv* de prisa. **~y** *a* (**-ier, -iest**) precipitado; ⟨*rash*⟩ irreflexivo

hat /hæt/ *n* sombrero *m*. **a ~ trick** *n* tres victorias *fpl* consecutivas

hatch[1] /hætʃ/ *n* ⟨*for food*⟩ ventanilla *f*; ⟨*naut*⟩ escotilla *f*

hatch[2] /hætʃ/ *vt* empollar ⟨*eggs*⟩; tramar ⟨*plot*⟩. ● *vi* salir del cascarón

hatchback /ˈhætʃbæk/ *n* ⟨coche *m*⟩ cincopuertas *m invar*, coche *m* con puerta trasera

hatchet /ˈhætʃɪt/ *n* hacha *f*

hate /heɪt/ *n* odio *m*. ● *vt* odiar. **~ful** *a* odioso

hatred /ˈheɪtrɪd/ *n* odio *m*

haughty /ˈhɔːtɪ/ *a* (**-ier, -iest**) altivo

haul /hɔːl/ *vt* arrastrar; transportar ⟨*goods*⟩. ● *n* ⟨*catch*⟩ redada *f*; ⟨*stolen goods*⟩ botín *m*; ⟨*journey*⟩ recorrido *m*. **~age** *n* transporte *m*. **~ier** *n* transportista *m & f*

haunch /hɔːntʃ/ *n* anca *f*

haunt /hɔːnt/ *vt* frecuentar. ● *n* sitio *m* preferido. **~ed house** *n* casa *f* frecuentada por fantasmas

Havana /həˈvænə/ *n* La Habana *f*

have /hæv/ *vt* (*3 sing pres tense* **has**, *pt* **had**) tener; ⟨*eat, drink*⟩ tomar. **~ it out with** resolver el asunto. **~ sth done** hacer algo. **~ to do** tener que hacer. ● *v aux* haber. **~ just done** acabar de hacer. ● *n*. **the ~s and ~-nots** los ricos *mpl* y los pobres *mpl*

haven /ˈheɪvn/ *n* puerto *m*; ⟨*refuge*⟩ refugio *m*

haversack /ˈhævəsæk/ *n* mochila *f*

havoc /ˈhævək/ *n* estragos *mpl*

haw /hɔː/ *see* **hum**

hawk[1] /hɔːk/ *n* halcón *m*

hawk[2] /hɔːk/ *vt* vender por las calles. **~er** *n* vendedor *m* ambulante

hawthorn /ˈhɔːθɔːn/ *n* espino *m* (blanco)

hay /heɪ/ *n* heno *m*. **~ fever** *n* fiebre *f* del heno. **~stack** *n* almiar *m*

haywire /ˈheɪwaɪə(r)/ *a*. **go ~** ⟨*plans*⟩ desorganizarse; ⟨*machine*⟩ estropearse

hazard /ˈhæzəd/ *n* riesgo *m*. ● *vt* arriesgar; aventurar ⟨*guess*⟩. **~ous** *a* arriesgado

haze /heɪz/ *n* neblina *f*

hazel /ˈheɪzl/ *n* avellano *m*. **~-nut** *n* avellana *f*

hazy /ˈheɪzɪ/ *a* (**-ier, -iest**) nebuloso

he /hiː/ *pron* él. ● *n* ⟨*animal*⟩ macho *m*; ⟨*man*⟩ varón *m*

head /hed/ *n* cabeza *f*; ⟨*leader*⟩ jefe *m*; ⟨*of beer*⟩ espuma *f*. **~s or tails** cara o cruz. ● *a* principal. **~ waiter** *n* jefe *m* de comedor. ● *vt* encabezar. **~ the ball** dar un cabezazo. **~ for** dirigirse a. **~ache** *n* dolor *m* de cabeza. **~dress** *n* tocado *m*. **~er** *n* ⟨*football*⟩ cabezazo *m*. **~ first** *adv* de cabeza. **~gear** *n* tocado *m*

heading /ˈhedɪŋ/ *n* título *m*, encabezamiento *m*

headlamp /ˈhedlæmp/ *n* faro *m*

headland /ˈhedland/ *n* promontorio *m*

headlight /ˈhedlaɪt/ *n* faro *m*

headline /ˈhedlaɪn/ *n* titular *m*

headlong /ˈhedlɒŋ/ *adv* de cabeza; ⟨*precipitately*⟩ precipitadamente

head: **~master** *n* director *m*. **~mistress** *n* directora *f*. **~-on** *a & adv* de frente. **~phone** *n* auricular *m*, audífono *m* (*LAm*)

headquarters /hedˈkwɔːtəz/ *n* ⟨*of organization*⟩ sede *f*; ⟨*of business*⟩ oficina *f* central; ⟨*mil*⟩ cuartel *m* general

headstrong /ˈhedstrɒŋ/ *a* testarudo

headway /ˈhedweɪ/ *n* progreso *m*. **make ~** hacer progresos

heady /ˈhedɪ/ *a* (**-ier, -iest**) ⟨*impetuous*⟩ impetuoso; ⟨*intoxicating*⟩ embriagador

heal /hiːl/ vt curar. ● vi cicatrizarse; (fig) curarse

health /helθ/ n salud f. ~y a sano

heap /hiːp/ n montón m. ● vt amontonar. ~s of (fam) montones de, muchísimos

hear /hɪə(r)/ vt/i (pt heard /hɜːd/) oír. ~, ~! ¡bravo! **not** ~ **of** (refuse to allow) no querer oír. ~ **about** oir hablar de. ~ **from** recibir noticias de. ~ **of** oir hablar de

hearing /'hɪərɪŋ/ n oído m; (of witness) audición f. ~-aid n audífono m

hearsay /'hɪəseɪ/ n rumores mpl. **from** ~ según los rumores

hearse /hɜːs/ n coche m fúnebre

heart /hɑːt/ n corazón m. **at** ~ en el fondo. **by** ~ de memoria. **lose** ~ descorazonarse. ~**ache** n pena f. ~ **attack** n ataque m al corazón. ~-**break** n pena f. ~-**breaking** a desgarrador. ~-**broken** a. **be** ~-**broken** partírsele el corazón

heartburn /'hɑːtbɜːn/ n acedía f

hearten /'hɑːtn/ vt animar

heartfelt /'hɑːtfelt/ a sincero

hearth /hɑːθ/ n hogar m

heartily /'hɑːtɪlɪ/ adv de buena gana; (sincerely) sinceramente

heart ~**less** a cruel. ~-**searching** n examen m de conciencia. ~-**to-**~ a abierto

hearty /'hɑːtɪ/ a (sincere) sincero; ⟨meal⟩ abundante

heat /hiːt/ n calor m; (contest) eliminatoria f. ● vt calentar. ● vi calentarse. ~**ed** a (fig) acalorado. ~**er** /'hiːtə(r)/ n calentador m

heath /hiːθ/ n brezal m, descampado m, terreno m baldío

heathen /'hiːðn/ n & a pagano (m)

heather /'heðə(r)/ n brezo m

heat: ~**ing** n calefacción f. ~-**stroke** n insolación f. ~-**wave** n ola f de calor

heave /hiːv/ vt (lift) levantar; exhalar ⟨sigh⟩; (throw, fam) lanzar. ● vi (retch) sentir náuseas

heaven /'hevn/ n cielo m. ~**ly** a celestial; (astronomy) celeste; (excellent, fam) divino

heav|ily /'hevɪlɪ/ adv pesadamente; (smoke, drink) mucho. ~**y** a (-ier, -iest) pesado; ⟨sea⟩ grueso; ⟨traffic⟩ denso; ⟨work⟩ duro. ~**yweight** n peso m pesado

Hebrew /'hiːbruː/ a & n hebreo (m)

heckle /'hekl/ vt interrumpir ⟨speaker⟩

hectic /'hektɪk/ a febril

hedge /hedʒ/ n seto m vivo. ● vt rodear con seto vivo. ● vi escaparse por la tangente

hedgehog /'hedʒhɒg/ n erizo m

heed /hiːd/ vt hacer caso de. ● n atención f. **pay** ~ **to** hacer caso de. ~**less** a desatento

heel /hiːl/ n talón m; (of shoe) tacón m. **down at** ~, **down at the** ~s (Amer) desharrapado

hefty /'heftɪ/ a (-ier, -iest) (sturdy) fuerte; (heavy) pesado

heifer /'hefə(r)/ n novilla f

height /haɪt/ n altura f; (of person) estatura f; (of fame, glory) cumbre f; (of joy, folly, pain) colmo m

heighten /'haɪtn/ vt (raise) elevar; (fig) aumentar

heinous /'heɪnəs/ a atroz

heir /eə(r)/ n heredero m. ~**ess** n heredera f. ~-**loom** /'eəluːm/ n reliquia f heredada

held /held/ see **hold**¹

helicopter /'helɪkɒptə(r)/ n helicóptero m

heliport /'helɪpɔːt/ n helipuerto m

hell /hel/ n infierno m. ~-**bent** a resuelto. ~**ish** a infernal

hello /hə'ləʊ/ int ¡hola!; (telephone, caller) ¡oiga!, ¡bueno! (Mex), ¡hola! (Arg); (telephone, person answering) ¡diga!, ¡bueno! (Mex), ¡hola! (Arg); (surprise) ¡vaya! **say** ~ **to** saludar

helm /helm/ n (of ship) timón m

helmet /'helmɪt/ n casco m

help /help/ vt/i ayudar. **he cannot** ~ **laughing** no puede menos de reír. ~ **o.s. to** servirse. **it cannot be** ~**ed** no hay más remedio. ● n ayuda f; (charwoman) asistenta f. ~**er** n ayudante m. ~**ful** a útil; ⟨person⟩ amable

helping /'helpɪŋ/ n porción f

helpless /'helplɪs/ a (unable to manage) incapaz; (powerless) impotente

helter-skelter /heltə'skeltə(r)/ n tobogán m. ● adv atropelladamente

hem /hem/ n dobladillo m. ● vt (pt **hemmed**) hacer un dobladillo. ~ **in** encerrar

hemisphere /'hemɪsfɪə(r)/ n hemisferio m

hemp /hemp/ n (plant) cáñamo m; (hashish) hachís m

hen /hen/ n gallina f

hence /hens/ adv de aquí. ~**forth** adv de ahora en adelante

henchman /'hentʃmən/ n secuaz m

henna /'henə/ n alheña f
hen-party /'henpɑ:tɪ/ n (fam) reunión f de mujeres
henpecked /'henpekt/ a dominado por su mujer
her /hɜ:(r)/ pron (accusative) la; (dative) le; (after prep) ella. **I know ~** la conozco. ● a su, sus pl
herald /'herəld/ vt anunciar
heraldry /'herəldrɪ/ n heráldica f
herb /hɜ:b/ n hierba f. **~s** npl hierbas fpl finas
herbaceous /hɜ:'beɪʃəs/ a herbáceo
herbalist /'hɜ:bəlɪst/ n herbolario m
herculean /hɜ:kjʊ'li:ən/ a hercúleo
herd /hɜ:d/ n rebaño m. ● vt. **~ together** reunir
here /hɪə(r)/ adv aquí. **~!** (take this) ¡tenga! **~abouts** adv por aquí. **~after** adv en el futuro. **~by** adv por este medio; (in letter) por la presente
heredit|ary /hɪ'redɪtərɪ/ a hereditario. **~y** /hɪ'redətɪ/ n herencia f
here|sy /'herəsɪ/ n herejía f. **~tic** n hereje m & f
herewith /hɪə'wɪð/ adv adjunto
heritage /'herɪtɪdʒ/ n herencia f; (fig) patrimonio m
hermetic /hɜ:'metɪk/ a hermético
hermit /'hɜ:mɪt/ n ermitaño m
hernia /'hɜ:nɪə/ n hernia f
hero /'hɪərəʊ/ n (pl **-oes**) héroe m. **~ic** a heroico
heroin /'herəʊɪn/ n heroína f
hero: ~ine /'herɔɪn/ n heroína f. **~ism** /'herəɪzm/ n heroísmo m
heron /'herən/ n garza f real
herring /'herɪŋ/ n arenque m
hers /hɜ:z/ poss pron suyo m, suya f, suyos mpl, suyas fpl, de ella
herself /hɜ:'self/ pron ella misma; (reflexive) se; (after prep) sí
hesitant /'hezɪtənt/ a vacilante
hesitat|e /'hezɪteɪt/ vi vacilar. **~ion** /-'teɪʃn/ n vacilación f
hessian /'hesɪən/ n arpillera f
het /het/ a. **~ up** (sl) nervioso
heterogeneous /hetərəʊ'dʒi:nɪəs/ a heterogéneo
heterosexual /hetərəʊ'seksjʊəl/ a heterosexual
hew /hju:/ vt (pp **hewn**) cortar; (cut into shape) tallar
hexagon /'heksəgən/ n hexágono m. **~al** /-'ægənl/ a hexagonal
hey /heɪ/ int ¡eh!
heyday /'heɪdeɪ/ n apogeo m

hi /haɪ/ int (fam) ¡hola!
hiatus /haɪ'eɪtəs/ n (pl **-tuses**) hiato m
hibernat|e /'haɪbəneɪt/ vi hibernar. **~ion** n hibernación f
hibiscus /hɪ'bɪskəs/ n hibisco m
hiccup /'hɪkʌp/ n hipo m. **have (the) ~s** tener hipo. ● vi tener hipo
hide¹ /haɪd/ vt (pt **hid**, pp **hidden**) esconder. ● vi esconderse
hide² /haɪd/ n piel f, cuero m
hideous /'hɪdɪəs/ a (dreadful) horrible; (ugly) feo
hide-out /'haɪdaʊt/ n escondrijo m
hiding¹ /'haɪdɪŋ/ n (thrashing) paliza f
hiding² /'haɪdɪŋ/ n. **go into ~** esconderse
hierarchy /'haɪərɑ:kɪ/ n jerarquía f
hieroglyph /'haɪərəglɪf/ n jeroglífico m
hi-fi /'haɪfaɪ/ a de alta fidelidad. ● n (equipo m de) alta fidelidad (f)
higgledy-piggledy /hɪgldɪ'pɪgldɪ/ adv en desorden
high /haɪ/ a (**-er**, **-est**) alto; (price) elevado; (number, speed) grande; (wind) fuerte; (intoxicated, fam) ebrio; (voice) agudo; (meat) manido. **in the ~ season** en plena temporada. ● n alto nivel m. **a (new) ~** un récord m. ● adv alto
highbrow /'haɪbrʊ/ a & n intelectual (m & f)
higher education /haɪər edʒʊ 'keɪʃn/ n enseñanza f superior
high-falutin /haɪfə'lu:tɪn/ a pomposo
high-handed /haɪ'hændɪd/ a despótico
high jump /'haɪdʒʌmp/ n salto m de altura
highlight /'haɪlaɪt/ n punto m culminante. ● vt destacar
highly /'haɪlɪ/ adv muy; (paid) muy bien. **~ strung** a nervioso
highness /'haɪnɪs/ n (title) alteza f
high: ~-rise building n rascacielos m. **~ school** n instituto m. **~-speed** a de gran velocidad. **~ spot** n (fam) punto m culminante. **~ street** n calle f mayor. **~-strung** a (Amer) nervioso. **~ tea** n merienda f substanciosa
highway /'haɪweɪ/ n carretera f. **~man** n salteador m de caminos
hijack /'haɪdʒæk/ vt secuestrar. ● n secuestro m. **~er** n secuestrador

hike /haɪk/ *n* caminata *f*. ● *vi* darse la caminata. **~r** *n* excursionista *m* & *f*

hilarious /hɪ'leərɪəs/ *a* (*funny*) muy divertido

hill /hɪl/ *n* colina *f*; (*slope*) cuesta *f*. **~billy** *n* rústico *m*. **~side** *n* ladera *f*. **~y** *a* montuoso

hilt /hɪlt/ *n* (*of sword*) puño *m*. **to the ~** totalmente

him /hɪm/ *pron* le, lo; (*after prep*) él. **I know ~** le/lo conozco

himself /hɪm'self/ *pron* él mismo; (*reflexive*) se

hind /haɪnd/ *a* trasero

hinder /'hɪndə(r)/ *vt* estorbar; (*prevent*) impedir

hindrance /'hɪndrəns/ *n* obstáculo *m*

hindsight /'haɪnsaɪt/ *n*. **with ~** retrospectivamente

Hindu /hɪn'duː/ *n* & *a* hindú (*m* & *f*). **~ism** *n* hinduismo *m*

hinge /hɪndʒ/ *n* bisagra *f*. ● *vi*. **~ on** (*depend on*) depender de

hint /hɪnt/ *n* indirecta *f*; (*advice*) consejo *m*. ● *vt* dar a entender. ● *vi* soltar una indirecta. **~ at** hacer alusión a

hinterland /'hɪntəlænd/ *n* interior *m*

hip /hɪp/ *n* cadera *f*

hippie /'hɪpɪ/ *n* hippie *m* & *f*

hippopotamus /hɪpə'pɒtəməs/ *n* (*pl* **-muses** *or* **-mi**) hipopótamo *m*

hire /haɪə(r)/ *vt* alquilar ⟨*thing*⟩; contratar ⟨*person*⟩. ● *n* alquiler *m*. **~purchase** *n* compra *f* a plazos

hirsute /'hɜːsjuːt/ *a* hirsuto

his /hɪz/ *a* su, sus *pl*. ● *poss pron* el suyo *m*, la suya *f*, los suyos *mpl*, las suyas *fpl*

Hispan|ic /hɪ'spænɪk/ *a* hispánico. **~ist** /'hɪspənɪst/ *n* hispanista *m* & *f*. **~o...** *pref* hispano...

hiss /hɪs/ *n* silbido. ● *vt/i* silbar

histor|ian /hɪ'stɔːrɪən/ *n* historiador *m*. **~ic(al)** /hɪ'stɒrɪkl/ *a* histórico. **~y** /'hɪstərɪ/ *n* historia *f*. **make ~y** pasar a la historia

histrionic /hɪstrɪ'ɒnɪk/ *a* histriónico

hit /hɪt/ *vt* (*pt* **hit**, *pres p* **hitting**) golpear; (*collide with*) chocar con; (*find*) dar con; (*affect*) afectar. **~ it off with** hacer buenas migas con. ● *n* (*blow*) golpe *m*; (*fig*) éxito *m*. **~ on** *vi* encontrar, dar con

hitch /hɪtʃ/ *vt* (*fasten*) atar. ● *n* (*snag*) problema *m*. **~ a lift**, **~-hike** *vi* hacer autostop, hacer dedo (*Arg*), pedir aventón (*Mex*). **~-hiker** *n* autostopista *m* & *f*

hither /'hɪðə(r)/ *adv* acá. **~ and thither** acá y allá

hitherto /'hɪðətuː/ *adv* hasta ahora

hit-or-miss /'hɪtɔː'mɪs/ *a* (*fam*) a la buena de Dios, a ojo

hive /haɪv/ *n* colmena *f*. ● *vt*. **~off** separar; (*industry*) desnacionalizar

hoard /hɔːd/ *vt* acumular. ● *n* provisión *f*; (*of money*) tesoro *m*

hoarding /'hɔːdɪŋ/ *n* cartelera *f*, valla *f* publicitaria

hoar-frost /'hɔːfrɒst/ *n* escarcha *f*

hoarse /hɔːs/ *a* (**-er**, **-est**) ronco. **~ness** *n* (*of voice*) ronquera *f*; (*of sound*) ronquedad *f*

hoax /həʊks/ *n* engaño *m*. ● *vt* engañar

hob /hɒb/ *n* repisa *f*; (*of cooker*) fogón *m*

hobble /'hɒbl/ *vi* cojear

hobby /'hɒbɪ/ *n* pasatiempo *m*

hobby-horse /'hɒbɪhɔːs/ *n* (*toy*) caballito *m* (de niño); (*fixation*) caballo *m* de batalla

hobnail /'hɒbneɪl/ *n* clavo *m*

hob-nob /'hɒbnɒb/ *vi* (*pt* **hob-nobbed**). **~ with** codearse con

hock¹ /hɒk/ *n* vino *m* del Rin

hock² /hɒk/ *vt* (*pawn*, *sl*) empeñar

hockey /'hɒkɪ/ *n* hockey *m*

hodgepodge /'hɒdʒpɒdʒ/ *n* mezcolanza *f*

hoe /həʊ/ *n* azada *f*. ● *vt* (*pres p* **hoeing**) azadonar

hog /hɒg/ *n* cerdo *m*. ● *vt* (*pt* **hogged**) (*fam*) acaparar

hoist /hɔɪst/ *vt* levantar; izar ⟨*flag*⟩. ● *n* montacargas *m invar*

hold¹ /həʊld/ *vt* (*pt* **held**) tener; (*grasp*) coger (*not LAm*), agarrar; (*contain*) contener; mantener ⟨*interest*⟩; (*believe*) creer; contener ⟨*breath*⟩. **~ one's tongue** callarse. ● *vi* mantenerse. ● *n* asidero *m*; (*influence*) influencia *f*. **get ~ of** agarrar; (*fig*, *acquire*) adquirir. **~ back** (*contain*) contener; (*conceal*) ocultar. **~ on** (*stand firm*) resistir; (*wait*) esperar. **~ on to** (*keep*) guardar; (*cling to*) agarrarse a. **~ out** *vt* (*offer*) ofrecer. ● *vi* (*resist*) resistir. **~ over** aplazar. **~ up** (*support*) sostener;

(*delay*) retrasar; (*rob*) atracar. ~ **with** aprobar

hold[2] /'həʊld/ n (*of ship*) bodega f

holdall /'həʊldɔːl/ n bolsa f (de viaje)

holder /'həʊldə(r)/ n tenedor m; (*of post*) titular m; (*for object*) soporte m

holding /'həʊldɪŋ/ n (*land*) propiedad f

hold-up /'həʊldʌp/ n atraco m

hole /həʊl/ n agujero m; (*in ground*) hoyo m; (*in road*) bache m. ● vt agujerear

holiday /'hɒlɪdeɪ/ n vacaciones fpl; (*public*) fiesta f. ● vi pasar las vacaciones. ~**maker** n veraneante m

holiness /'həʊlɪnɪs/ n santidad f

Holland /'hɒlənd/ n Holanda f

hollow /'hɒləʊ/ a & n hueco (m). ● vt ahuecar

holly /'hɒlɪ/ n acebo m. ~**hock** n malva f real

holocaust /'hɒləkɔːst/ n holocausto m

holster /'həʊlstə(r)/ n pistolera f

holy /'həʊlɪ/ a (-**ier, -iest**) santo, sagrado. **H~ Ghost** n, **H~ Spirit** n Espíritu m Santo. ~ **water** n agua f bendita

homage /'hɒmɪdʒ/ n homenaje m

home /həʊm/ n casa f; (*institution*) asilo m; (*for soldiers*) hogar m; (*native land*) patria f. **feel at ~ with** sentirse como en su casa. ● a casera, de casa; (*of family*) de familia; (*pol*) interior; ⟨*match*⟩ de casa. ● adv. (**at**) ~ en casa. **H~ Counties** npl región f alrededor de Londres. ~**land** n patria f. ~**less** a sin hogar. ~**ly** /'həʊmlɪ/ a (-**ier, -iest**) casero; (*ugly*) feo. **H~ Office** n Ministerio m del Interior. **H~ Secretary** n Ministro m del Interior. ~**sick** a. **be ~sick** tener morriña. ~**town** n ciudad f natal. ~ **truths** npl las verdades fpl del barquero, las cuatro verdades fpl. ~**ward** /'həʊmwəd/ a ⟨*journey*⟩ de vuelta. ● adv hacia casa. ~**work** n deberes mpl

homicide /'hɒmɪsaɪd/ n homicidio m

homoeopath|ic /həʊmɪəʊˈpæθɪk/ a homeopático. ~**y** /-'ɒpəθɪ/ n homeopatía f

homogeneous /həʊməʊˈdʒiːnɪəs/ a homogéneo

homosexual /həʊməʊˈseksjʊəl/ a & n homosexual (m)

hone /həʊn/ vt afilar

honest /'ɒnɪst/ a honrado; (*frank*) sincero. ~**ly** adv honradamente. ~**y** n honradez f

honey /'hʌnɪ/ n miel f; (*person, fam*) cielo m, cariño m. ~**comb** /'hʌnɪkəʊm/ n panal m

honeymoon /'hʌnɪmuːn/ n luna f de miel

honeysuckle /'hʌnɪsʌkl/ n madreselva f

honk /hɒŋk/ vi tocar la bocina

honorary /'ɒnərərɪ/ a honorario

honour /'ɒnə(r)/ n honor m. ● vt honrar. ~**able** a honorable

hood /hʊd/ n capucha f; (*car roof*) capota f; (*car bonnet*) capó m

hoodlum /'huːdləm/ n gamberro m, matón m

hoodwink /'hʊdwɪŋk/ vt engañar

hoof /huːf/ n (pl **hoofs** or **hooves**) casco m

hook /hʊk/ n gancho m; (*on garment*) corchete m; (*for fishing*) anzuelo m. **by ~ or by crook** por fas o por nefas, por las buenas o por las malas. **get s.o. off the ~** sacar a uno de un apuro. **off the ~** ⟨telephone⟩ descolgado. ● vt enganchar. ● vi engancharse

hooked /hʊkt/ a ganchudo. ~ **on** (*sl*) adicto a

hooker /'hʊkə(r)/ n (*rugby*) talonador m; (*Amer, sl*) prostituta f

hookey /'hʊkɪ/ n. **play ~** (*Amer, sl*) hacer novillos

hooligan /'huːlɪgən/ n gamberro m

hoop /huːp/ n aro m

hooray /hʊˈreɪ/ int & n ¡viva! (m)

hoot /huːt/ n (*of horn*) bocinazo m; (*of owl*) ululato m. ● vi tocar la bocina; ⟨owl⟩ ulular

hooter /'huːtə(r)/ n (*of car*) bocina f; (*of factory*) sirena f

Hoover /'huːvə(r)/ n (P) aspiradora f. ● vt pasar la aspiradora

hop[1] /hɒp/ vi (pt **hopped**) saltar a la pata coja. ~ **in** (*fam*) subir. ~ **it** (*sl*) largarse. ~ **out** (*fam*) bajar. ● n salto m; (*flight*) etapa f

hop[2] /hɒp/ n. ~**(s)** lúpulo m

hope /həʊp/ n esperanza f. ● vt/i esperar. ~ **for** esperar. ~**ful** a esperanzador. ~**fully** adv con optimismo; (*it is hoped*) se espera. ~**less** a desesperado. ~**lessly** adv sin esperanza

hopscotch /'hɒpskɒtʃ/ n tejo m

horde /hɔːd/ n horda f

horizon /hə'raɪzn/ n horizonte m
horizontal /hɒrɪ'zɒntl/ a horizontal. **~ly** adv horizontalmente
hormone /'hɔːməʊn/ n hormona f
horn /hɔːn/ n cuerno m; (of car) bocina f; (mus) trompa f. ● vt. **~ in** (sl) entrometerse. **~ed** a con cuernos
hornet /'hɔːnɪt/ n avispón m
horny /'hɔːnɪ/ a ⟨hands⟩ calloso
horoscope /'hɒrəskəʊp/ n horóscopo m
horri|ble /'hɒrəbl/ a horrible. **~d** /'hɒrɪd/ a horrible
horrif|ic /hə'rɪfɪk/ a horroroso. **~y** /'hɒrɪfaɪ/ vt horrorizar
horror /'hɒrə(r)/ n horror m. **~ film** n película f de miedo
hors-d'oevre /ɔː'dɜːvr/ n entremés m
horse /hɔːs/ n caballo m. **~back** n. **on ~back** a caballo
horse chestnut /hɔːs'tʃesnʌt/ n castaña f de Indias
horse: ~man n jinete m. **~play** n payasadas fpl. **~power** n (unit) caballo m (de fuerza). **~racing** n carreras fpl de caballos
horseradish /'hɔːsrædɪʃ/ n rábano m picante
horse: ~ sense n (fam) sentido m común. **~shoe** /'hɔːsʃuː/ n herradura f
horsy /'hɔːsɪ/ a ⟨face etc⟩ caballuno
horticultur|al /hɔːtɪ'kʌltʃərəl/ a hortícola. **~e** /'hɔːtɪkʌltʃə(r)/ n horticultura f
hose /həʊz/ n (tube) manga f. ● vt (water) regar con una manga; (clean) limpiar con una manga. **~pipe** n manga f
hosiery /'həʊzɪərɪ/ n calcetería f
hospice /'hɒspɪs/ n hospicio m
hospitabl|e /hɒ'spɪtəbl/ a hospitalario. **~y** adv con hospitalidad
hospital /'hɒspɪtl/ n hospital m
hospitality /hɒspɪ'tælətɪ/ n hospitalidad f
host[1] /həʊst/ n. **a ~ of** un montón de
host[2] /həʊst/ n (master of house) huésped m, anfitrión m
host[3] /həʊst/ n (relig) hostia f
hostage /'hɒstɪdʒ/ n rehén m
hostel /'hɒstl/ n (for students) residencia f. **youth ~** albergue m juvenil
hostess /'həʊstɪs/ n huéspeda f, anfitriona f

hostil|e /'hɒstaɪl/ a hostil. **~ity** n hostilidad f
hot /hɒt/ a (**hotter, hottest**) caliente; (culin) picante; ⟨news⟩ de última hora. **be/feel ~** tener calor. **in ~ water** (fam) en un apuro. **it is ~** hace calor. ● vt/i. **~ up** (fam) calentarse
hotbed /'hɒtbed/ n (fig) semillero m
hotchpotch /'hɒtʃpɒtʃ/ n mezcolanza f
hot dog /hɒt'dɒg/ n perrito m caliente
hotel /həʊ'tel/ n hotel m. **~ier** n hotelero m
hot: ~head n impetuoso m. **~headed** a impetuoso. **~house** n invernadero m. **~line** n teléfono m rojo. **~plate** n calentador m. **~water bottle** n bolsa f de agua caliente
hound /haʊnd/ n perro m de caza. ● vt perseguir
hour /aʊə(r)/ n hora f. **~ly** a & adv cada hora. **~ly pay** n sueldo m por hora. **paid ~ly** pagado por hora
house /haʊs/ n (pl **-s** /'haʊzɪz/) casa f; (theatre building) sala f; (theatre audience) público m; (pol) cámara f. /haʊz/ vt alojar; (keep) guardar. **~boat** n casa f flotante. **~breaking** n robo m de casa. **~hold** /'haʊshəʊld/ n casa f, familia f. **~holder** n dueño m de una casa; (head of household) cabeza f de familia. **~keeper** n ama f de llaves. **~keeping** n gobierno m de la casa. **~maid** n criada f, mucama f (LAm). **H~ of Commons** n Cámara f de los Comunes. **~proud** a meticuloso. **~warming** n inauguración f de una casa. **~wife** /'haʊswaɪf/ n ama f de casa. **~work** n quehaceres mpl domésticos
housing /'haʊzɪŋ/ n alojamiento m. **~ estate** n urbanización f
hovel /'hɒvl/ n casucha f
hover /'hɒvə(r)/ vi ⟨bird, threat etc⟩ cernerse; (loiter) rondar. **~craft** n aerodeslizador m
how /haʊ/ adv cómo. **~ about a walk?** ¿qué le parece si damos un paseo? **~ are you?** ¿cómo está Vd? **~ do you do?** (in introduction) mucho gusto. **~ long?** ¿cuánto tiempo? **~ many?** ¿cuántos? **~ much?** ¿cuánto? **~ often?** ¿cuántas veces? **and ~!** ¡y cómo!
however /haʊ'evə(r)/ adv (with verb) de cualquier manera que (+

subjunctive); (*with adjective or adverb*) por... que (+ *subjunctive*); (*nevertheless*) no obstante, sin embargo. ~ **much it rains** por mucho que llueva

howl /haʊl/ *n* aullido. ● *vi* aullar

howler /ˈhaʊlə(r)/ *n* (*fam*) plancha *f*

HP *abbr see* **hire-purchase**

hp *abbr see* **horsepower**

hub /hʌb/ *n* (*of wheel*) cubo *m*; (*fig*) centro *m*

hubbub /ˈhʌbʌb/ *n* barahúnda *f*

hub-cap /ˈhʌbkæp/ *n* tapacubos *m invar*

huddle /ˈhʌdl/ *vi* apiñarse

hue[1] /hju:/ *n* (*colour*) color *m*

hue[2] /hju:/ *n*. ~ **and cry** clamor *m*

huff /hʌf/ *n*. **in a** ~ enojado

hug /hʌg/ *vt* (*pt* **hugged**) abrazar; (*keep close to*) no apartarse de. ● *n* abrazo *m*

huge /hju:dʒ/ *a* enorme. ~**ly** *adv* enormemente

hulk /hʌlk/ *n* (*of ship*) barco *m* viejo; (*person*) armatoste *m*

hull /hʌl/ *n* (*of ship*) casco *m*

hullabaloo /hʌləbəˈlu:/ *n* tumulto *m*

hullo /həˈləʊ/ *int* = **hello**

hum /hʌm/ *vt/i* (*pt* **hummed**) (*person*) canturrear; (*insect, engine*) zumbar. ● *n* zumbido *m*. ~ **(or hem) and haw (or ha)** vacilar

human /ˈhju:mən/ *a* & *n* humano (*m*). ~ **being** *n* ser *m* humano

humane /hju:ˈmeɪn/ *a* humano

humanism /ˈhju:mənɪzəm/ *n* humanismo *m*

humanitarian /hju:mænɪˈteərɪən/ *a* humanitario

humanity /hju:ˈmænətɪ/ *n* humanidad *f*

humbl|e /ˈhʌmbl/ *a* (-**er**, -**est**) humilde. ● *vt* humillar. ~**y** *adv* humildemente

humbug /ˈhʌmbʌg/ *n* (*false talk*) charlatanería *f*; (*person*) charlatán *m*; (*sweet*) caramelo *m* de menta

humdrum /ˈhʌmdrʌm/ *a* monótono

humid /ˈhju:mɪd/ *a* húmedo. ~**ifier** *n* humedecedor *m*. ~**ity** /hju:-ˈmɪdətɪ/ *n* humedad *f*

humiliat|e /hju:ˈmɪlɪeɪt/ *vt* humillar. ~**ion** /-ˈeɪʃn/ *n* humillación *f*

humility /hju:ˈmɪlətɪ/ *n* humildad *f*

humorist /ˈhju:mərɪst/ *n* humorista *m* & *f*

humo|rous /ˈhju:mərəs/ *a* divertido. ~**rously** *adv* con gracia. ~**ur** *n*

humorismo *m*; (*mood*) humor *m*. **sense of** ~**ur** *n* sentido *m* del humor

hump /hʌmp/ *n* montecillo *m*; (*of the spine*) joroba *f*. **the** ~ (*sl*) malhumor *m*. ● *vt* encorvarse; (*hoist up*) llevar al hombro

hunch /hʌntʃ/ *vt* encorvar. ~**ed up** encorvado. ● *n* presentimiento *m*; (*lump*) joroba *f*. ~**back** /ˈhʌntʃbæk/ *n* jorobado *m*

hundred /ˈhʌndrəd/ *a* ciento, (*before noun*) cien. ● *n* ciento *m*. ~**fold** *a* céntuplo. ● *adv* cien veces. ~**s of** centenares de. ~**th** *a* centésimo. ● *n* centésimo *m*, centésima parte *f*

hundredweight /ˈhʌndrədweɪt/ *n* 50,8kg; (*Amer*) 45,36kg

hung /hʌŋ/ *see* **hang**

Hungar|ian /hʌŋˈgeərɪən/ *a* & *n* húngaro (*m*). ~**y** /ˈhʌŋgərɪ/ *n* Hungría *f*

hunger /ˈhʌŋgə(r)/ *n* hambre *f*. ● *vi*. ~ **for** tener hambre de. ~**-strike** *n* huelga *f* de hambre

hungr|ily /ˈhʌŋgrəlɪ/ *adv* ávidamente. ~**y** *a* (-**ier**, -**iest**) hambriento. **be** ~**y** tener hambre

hunk /hʌŋk/ *n* (buen) pedazo *m*

hunt /hʌnt/ *vt/i* cazar. ~ **for** buscar. ● *n* caza *f*. ~**er** *n* cazador *m*. ~**ing** *n* caza *f*

hurdle /ˈhɜ:dl/ *n* (*sport*) valla *f*; (*fig*) obstáculo *m*

hurdy-gurdy /ˈhɜ:dɪgɜ:dɪ/ *n* organillo *m*

hurl /hɜ:l/ *vt* lanzar

hurly-burly /ˈhɜ:lɪbɜ:lɪ/ *n* tumulto *m*

hurrah /hʊˈrɑ:/, **hurray** /hʊˈreɪ/ *int* & *n* ¡viva! (*m*)

hurricane /ˈhʌrɪkən/ *n* huracán *m*

hurried /ˈhʌrɪd/ *a* apresurado. ~**ly** *adv* apresuradamente

hurry /ˈhʌrɪ/ *vi* apresurarse, darse prisa. ● *vt* apresurar, dar prisa a. ● *n* prisa *f*. **be in a** ~ tener prisa

hurt /hɜ:t/ *vt/i* (*pt* **hurt**) herir. ● *n* (*injury*) herida *f*; (*harm*) daño *m*. ~**ful** *a* hiriente; (*harmful*) dañoso

hurtle /ˈhɜ:tl/ *vt* lanzar. ● *vi*. ~ **along** mover rápidamente

husband /ˈhʌzbənd/ *n* marido *m*

hush /hʌʃ/ *vt* acallar. ● *n* silencio *m*. ~ **up** ocultar (*affair*). ~~ *a* (*fam*) muy secreto

husk /hʌsk/ *n* cáscara *f*

husky /ˈhʌskɪ/ *a* (-**ier**, -**iest**) (*hoarse*) ronco; (*burly*) fornido

hussy /ˈhʌsɪ/ *n* desvergonzada *f*

hustle /'hʌsl/ vt (jostle) empujar. ● vi (hurry) darse prisa. ● n empuje m. ~ **and bustle** n bullicio m

hut /hʌt/ n cabaña f

hutch /hʌtʃ/ n conejera f

hyacinth /'haɪəsɪnθ/ n jacinto m

hybrid /'haɪbrɪd/ a & n híbrido (m)

hydrangea /haɪ'dreɪndʒə/ n hortensia f

hydrant /'haɪdrənt/ n. **(fire)** ~ n boca f de riego

hydraulic /haɪ'drɔːlɪk/ a hidráulico

hydroelectric /haɪdrəʊɪ'lektrɪk/ a hidroeléctrico

hydrofoil /'haɪdrəfɔɪl/ n aerodeslizador m

hydrogen /'haɪdrədʒən/ n hidrógeno m. ~ **bomb** n bomba f de hidrógeno. ~ **peroxide** n peróxido m de hidrógeno

hyena /haɪ'iːnə/ n hiena f

hygien|e /'haɪdʒiːn/ n higiene f. ~ic a higiénico

hymn /hɪm/ n himno m

hyper... /'haɪpə(r)/ pref hiper...

hypermarket /'haɪpəmɑːkɪt/ n hipermercado m

hyphen /'haɪfn/ n guión m. ~ate vt escribir con guión

hypno|sis /hɪp'nəʊsɪs/ n hipnosis f. ~tic /-'nɒtɪk/ a hipnótico. ~tism /hɪpnə'tɪzəm/ n hipnotismo m. ~tist n hipnotista m & f. ~tize vt hipnotizar

hypochondriac /haɪpə'kɒndrɪæk/ n hipocondríaco m

hypocrisy /hɪ'pɒkrəsɪ/ n hipocresía f

hypocrit|e /'hɪpəkrɪt/ n hipócrita m & f. ~ical a hipócrita

hypodermic /haɪpə'dɜːmɪk/ a hipodérmico. ● n jeringa f hipodérmica

hypothe|sis /haɪ'pɒθəsɪs/ n (pl -theses /-siːz/) hipótesis f. ~tical /-ə'θetɪkl/ a hipotético

hysteri|a /hɪ'stɪərɪə/ n histerismo m. ~cal /-'terɪkl/ a histérico. ~cs /hɪ'sterɪks/ npl histerismo m. **have** ~cs ponerse histérico; (laugh) morir de risa

I

I /aɪ/ pron yo

ice /aɪs/ n hielo m. ● vt helar; glasear (cake). ● vi. ~ **(up)** helarse. ~berg n iceberg m, témpano m. ~-cream n helado m. ~-cube n cubito m de hielo. ~ **hockey** n hockey m sobre hielo

Iceland /'aɪslənd/ n Islandia f. ~er n islandés m. ~ic /-'lændɪk/ a islandés

ice lolly /aɪs'lɒlɪ/ polo m, paleta f (LAm)

icicle /'aɪsɪkl/ n carámbano m

icing /'aɪsɪŋ/ n (sugar) azúcar m glaseado

icon /'aɪkɒn/ n icono m

icy /'aɪsɪ/ a (-ier, -iest) glacial

idea /aɪ'dɪə/ n idea f

ideal /aɪ'dɪəl/ a ideal. ● n ideal m. ~ism n idealismo m. ~ist n idealista m & f. ~istic /-'lɪstɪk/ a idealista. ~ize vt idealizar. ~ly adv idealmente

identical /aɪ'dentɪkl/ a idéntico

identif|ication /aɪdentɪfɪ'keɪʃn/ n identificación f. ~y /aɪ'dentɪfaɪ/ vt identificar. ● vi. ~y **with** identificarse con

identikit /aɪ'dentɪkɪt/ n retratorobot m

identity /aɪ'dentɪtɪ/ n identidad f

ideolog|ical /aɪdɪə'lɒdʒɪkl/ a ideológico. ~y /aɪdɪ'ɒlədʒɪ/ n ideología f

idiocy /'ɪdɪəsɪ/ n idiotez f

idiom /'ɪdɪəm/ n locución f. ~atic /-'mætɪk/ a idiomático

idiosyncrasy /ɪdɪəʊ'sɪŋkrəsɪ/ n idiosincrasia f

idiot /'ɪdɪət/ n idiota m & f. ~ic /-'ɒtɪk/ a idiota

idle /'aɪdl/ a (-er, -est) ocioso; (lazy) holgazán; (out of work) desocupado; (machine) parado. ● vi (engine) marchar en vacío. ● vt. ~ **away** perder. ~ness n ociosidad f. ~r /-ə(r)/ n ocioso m

idol /'aɪdl/ n ídolo m. ~ize vt idolatrar

idyllic /ɪ'dɪlɪk/ a idílico

i.e. /aɪ'iː/ abbr (id est) es decir

if /ɪf/ conj si

igloo /'ɪgluː/ n iglú m

ignite /ɪg'naɪt/ vt encender. ● vi encenderse

ignition /ɪg'nɪʃn/ n ignición f; (auto) encendido m. ~ **(switch)** n contacto m

ignoramus /ɪgnə'reɪməs/ n (pl -muses) ignorante

ignoran|ce /'ɪgnərəns/ n ignorancia f. ~t a ignorante. ~tly adv por ignorancia

ignore /ɪg'nɔː(r)/ vt no hacer caso de

ilk /ɪlk/ n ralea f

ill /ɪl/ a enfermo; (bad) malo. ~ **will** n mala voluntad f. ● adv mal. ~ **at ease** inquieto. ● n mal m. ~**advised** a imprudente. ~**-bred** a mal educado

illegal /ɪˈliːgl/ a ilegal

illegible /ɪˈledʒəbl/ a ilegible

illegitima|cy /ɪlɪˈdʒɪtɪməsɪ/ n ilegitimidad f. ~**te** a ilegítimo

ill: ~**-fated** a malogrado. ~**gotten** a mal adquirido

illitera|cy /ɪˈlɪtərəsɪ/ n analfabetismo m. ~**te** a & n analfabeto (m)

ill: ~**natured** a poco afable. ~**ness** n enfermedad f

illogical /ɪˈlɒdʒɪkl/ a ilógico

ill: ~**-starred** a malogrado. ~**treat** vt maltratar

illuminat|e /ɪˈluːmɪneɪt/ vt iluminar. ~**ion** /-ˈneɪʃn/ n iluminación f

illus|ion /ɪˈluːʒn/ n ilusión f. ~**sory** a ilusorio

illustrat|e /ˈɪləstreɪt/ vt ilustrar. ~**ion** n (example) ejemplo m; (picture in book) grabado m, lámina f. ~**ive** a ilustrativo

illustrious /ɪˈlʌstrɪəs/ a ilustre

image /ˈɪmɪdʒ/ n imagen f. ~**ry** n imágenes fpl

imagin|able /ɪˈmædʒɪnəbl/ a imaginable. ~**ary** a imaginario. ~**ation** /-ˈneɪʃn/ n imaginación f. ~**ative** a imaginativo. ~**e** vt imaginar(se)

imbalance /ɪmˈbæləns/ n desequilibrio m

imbecil|e /ˈɪmbəsiːl/ a & n imbécil (m & f). ~**ity** /-ˈsɪlətɪ/ n imbecilidad f

imbibe /ɪmˈbaɪb/ vt embeber; (drink) beber

imbue /ɪmˈbjuː/ vt empapar (with de)

imitat|e /ˈɪmɪteɪt/ vt imitar. ~**ion** /-ˈteɪʃn/ n imitación f. ~**or** n imitador m

immaculate /ɪˈmækjʊlət/ a inmaculado

immaterial /ɪməˈtɪərɪəl/ a inmaterial; (unimportant) insignificante

immature /ɪməˈtjʊə(r)/ a inmaduro

immediate /ɪˈmiːdɪət/ a inmediato. ~**ly** adv inmediatamente. ~**ly you hear me** en cuanto me oigas. ● conj en cuanto (+ subj)

immens|e /ɪˈmens/ a inmenso. ~**ely** adv inmensamente; (very much, fam) muchísimo. ~**ity** n inmensidad f

immers|e /ɪˈmɜːs/ vt sumergir. ~**ion** /ɪˈmɜːʃn/ n inmersión f. ~**ion heater** n calentador m de inmersión

immigra|nt /ˈɪmɪgrənt/ a & n inmigrante (m & f). ~**te** vi inmigrar. ~**tion** /-ˈgreɪʃn/ n inmigración f

imminen|ce /ˈɪmɪnəns/ n inminencia f. ~**t** a inminente

immobil|e /ɪˈməʊbaɪl/ a inmóvil. ~**ize** /-bɪlaɪz/ vt inmovilizar

immoderate /ɪˈmɒdərət/ a inmoderado

immodest /ɪˈmɒdɪst/ a inmodesto

immoral /ɪˈmɒrəl/ a inmoral. ~**ity** /ɪməˈrælətɪ/ n inmoralidad f

immortal /ɪˈmɔːtl/ a inmortal. ~**ity** /-ˈtælətɪ/ n inmortalidad f. ~**ize** vt inmortalizar

immun|e /ɪˈmjuːn/ a inmune (**from, to** a, contra). ~**ity** n inmunidad f. ~**ization** /ɪmjʊnaɪˈzeɪʃn/ n inmunización f. ~**ize** vt inmunizar

imp /ɪmp/ n diablillo m

impact /ˈɪmpækt/ n impacto m

impair /ɪmˈpeə(r)/ vt perjudicar

impale /ɪmˈpeɪl/ vt empalar

impart /ɪmˈpɑːt/ vt comunicar

impartial /ɪmˈpɑːʃl/ a imparcial. ~**ity** /-ɪˈælətɪ/ n imparcialidad f

impassable /ɪmˈpɑːsəbl/ a (barrier etc) infranqueable; (road) impracticable

impasse /æmˈpɑːs/ n callejón m sin salida

impassioned /ɪmˈpæʃnd/ a apasionado

impassive /ɪmˈpæsɪv/ a impasible

impatien|ce /ɪmˈpeɪʃəns/ n impaciencia f. ~**t** a impaciente. ~**tly** adv con impaciencia

impeach /ɪmˈpiːtʃ/ vt acusar

impeccable /ɪmˈpekəbl/ a impecable

impede /ɪmˈpiːd/ vt estorbar

impediment /ɪmˈpedɪmənt/ n obstáculo m. (**speech**) ~ n defecto m del habla

impel /ɪmˈpel/ vt (pt **impelled**) impeler

impending /ɪmˈpendɪŋ/ a inminente

impenetrable /ɪmˈpenɪtrəbl/ a impenetrable

imperative /ɪmˈperətɪv/ a imprescindible. ● n (gram) imperativo m

imperceptible /ɪmpə'septəbl/ a imperceptible

imperfect /ɪm'pɜːfɪkt/ a imperfecto. ∼**ion** /ə-'fekʃn/ n imperfección f

imperial /ɪm'pɪərɪəl/ a imperial. ∼**ism** n imperialismo m

imperil /ɪm'perəl/ vt (pt imperilled) poner en peligro

imperious /ɪm'pɪərɪəs/ a imperioso

impersonal /ɪm'pɜːsənl/ a impersonal

impersonat|e /ɪm'pɜːsəneɪt/ vt hacerse pasar por; (mimic) imitar. ∼**ion** /-'neɪʃn/ n imitación f. ∼**or** n imitador m

impertinen|ce /ɪm'pɜːtɪnəns/ n impertinencia f. ∼**t** a impertinente. ∼**tly** adv impertinentemente

impervious /ɪm'pɜːvɪəs/ a. ∼ **to** impermeable a; (fig) insensible a

impetuous /ɪm'petjʊəs/ a impetuoso

impetus /'ɪmpɪtəs/ n ímpetu m

impinge /ɪm'pɪndʒ/ vi. ∼ **on** afectar a

impish /'ɪmpɪʃ/ a travieso

implacable /ɪm'plækəbl/ a implacable

implant /ɪm'plɑːnt/ vt implantar

implement /'ɪmplɪmənt/ n herramienta f. /'ɪmplɪment/ vt realizar

implicat|e /'ɪmplɪkeɪt/ vt implicar. ∼**ion** /-'keɪʃn/ n implicación f

implicit /ɪm'plɪsɪt/ a (implied) implícito; (unquestioning) absoluto

implied /ɪm'plaɪd/ a implícito

implore /ɪm'plɔː(r)/ vt implorar

imply /ɪm'plaɪ/ vt implicar; (mean) querer decir; (insinuate) dar a entender

impolite /ɪmpə'laɪt/ a mal educado

imponderable /ɪm'pɒndərəbl/ a & n imponderable (m)

import /ɪm'pɔːt/ vt importar. /'ɪmpɔːt/ n (article) importación f; (meaning) significación f

importan|ce /ɪm'pɔːtəns/ n importancia f. ∼**t** a importante

importation /ɪmpɔː'teɪʃn/ n importación f

importer /ɪm'pɔːtə(r)/ n importador m

impose /ɪm'pəʊz/ vt imponer. ● vi. ∼ **on** abusar de la amabilidad de

imposing /ɪm'pəʊzɪŋ/ a imponente

imposition /ɪmpə'zɪʃn/ n imposición f; (fig) molestia f

impossib|ility /ɪmpɒsə'bɪlətɪ/ n imposibilidad f. ∼**le** a imposible

impostor /ɪm'pɒstə(r)/ n impostor m

impoten|ce /'ɪmpətəns/ n impotencia f. ∼**t** a impotente

impound /ɪm'paʊnd/ vt confiscar

impoverish /ɪm'pɒvərɪʃ/ vt empobrecer

impracticable /ɪm'præktɪkəbl/ a impracticable

impractical /ɪm'præktɪkl/ a poco práctico

imprecise /ɪmprɪ'saɪs/ a impreciso

impregnable /ɪm'pregnəbl/ a inexpugnable

impregnate /'ɪmpregneɪt/ vt impregnar (with de)

impresario /ɪmprɪ'sɑːrɪəʊ/ n (pl -os) empresario m

impress /ɪm'pres/ vt impresionar; (imprint) imprimir. ∼ **on s.o.** hacer entender a uno

impression /ɪm'preʃn/ n impresión f. ∼**able** a impresionable

impressive /ɪm'presɪv/ a impresionante

imprint /'ɪmprɪnt/ n impresión f. /ɪm'prɪnt/ vt imprimir

imprison /ɪm'prɪzn/ vt encarcelar. ∼**ment** n encarcelamiento m

improbab|ility /ɪmprɒbə'bɪlətɪ/ n improbabilidad f. ∼**le** a improbable

impromptu /ɪm'prɒmptjuː/ a improvisado. ● adv de improviso

improper /ɪm'prɒpə(r)/ a impropio; (incorrect) incorrecto

impropriety /ɪmprə'praɪətɪ/ n inconveniencia f

improve /ɪm'pruːv/ vt mejorar. ● vi mejorar(se). ∼**ment** n mejora f

improvis|ation /ɪmprəvaɪ'zeɪʃn/ n improvisación f. ∼**e** vt/i improvisar

imprudent /ɪm'pruːdənt/ a imprudente

impuden|ce /'ɪmpjʊdəns/ n insolencia f. ∼**t** a insolente

impulse /'ɪmpʌls/ n impulso m. **on** ∼ sin reflexionar

impulsive /ɪm'pʌlsɪv/ a irreflexivo. ∼**ly** adv sin reflexionar

impunity /ɪm'pjuːnətɪ/ n impunidad f. **with** ∼ impunemente

impur|e /ɪm'pjʊə(r)/ a impuro. ∼**ity** n impureza f

impute /ɪm'pjuːt/ vt imputar

in /ɪn/ prep en, dentro de. ∼ **a firm manner** de una manera terminante.

~ **an hour('s time)** dentro de una hora. ~ **doing** al hacer. ~ **so far as** en cuanto que. ~ **the evening** por la tarde. ~ **the main** por la mayor parte. ~ **the rain** bajo la lluvia. ~ **the sun** al sol. one ~ **ten** uno de cada diez. **the best** ~ el mejor de. ● *adv* (*inside*) dentro; (*at home*) en casa; (*in fashion*) de moda. ● *n.* **the** ~**s and outs of** los detalles *mpl* de

inability /ɪnə'bɪlətɪ/ *n* incapacidad *f*

inaccessible /ɪnæk'sesəbl/ *a* inaccesible

inaccura|cy /ɪn'ækjʊrəsɪ/ *n* inexactitud *f*. ~**te** *a* inexacto

inaction /ɪn'ækʃn/ *n* inacción *f*

inactiv|e /ɪn'æktɪv/ *a* inactivo. ~**ity** /-'tɪvətɪ/ *n* inactividad *f*

inadequa|cy /ɪn'ædɪkwəsɪ/ *a* insuficiencia *f*. ~**te** *a* insuficiente

inadmissible /ɪnəd'mɪsəbl/ *a* inadmisible

inadvertently /ɪnəd'vɜːtəntlɪ/ *adv* por descuido

inadvisable /ɪnəd'vaɪzəbl/ *a* no aconsejable

inane /ɪ'neɪn/ *a* estúpido

inanimate /ɪn'ænɪmət/ *a* inanimado

inappropriate /ɪnə'prəʊprɪət/ *a* inoportuno

inarticulate /ɪnɑː'tɪkjʊlət/ *a* incapaz de expresarse claramente

inasmuch as /ɪnəz'mʌtʃəz/ *adv* ya que

inattentive /ɪnə'tentɪv/ *a* desatento

inaudible /ɪn'ɔːdəbl/ *a* inaudible

inaugural /ɪ'nɔːgjʊrəl/ *a* inaugural

inaugurat|e /ɪ'nɔːgjʊreɪt/ *vt* inaugurar. ~**ion** /-'reɪʃn/ *n* inauguración *f*

inauspicious /ɪnɔː'spɪʃəs/ *a* poco propicio

inborn /'ɪnbɔːn/ *a* innato

inbred /ɪn'bred/ *a* (*inborn*) innato

incalculable /ɪn'kælkjʊləbl/ *a* incalculable

incapab|ility /ɪnkeɪpə'bɪlətɪ/ *n* incapacidad *f*. ~**le** *a* incapaz

incapacit|ate /ɪnkə'pæsɪteɪt/ *vt* incapacitar. ~**y** *n* incapacidad *f*

incarcerat|e /ɪn'kɑːsəreɪt/ *vt* encarcelar. ~**ion** /-'reɪʃn/ *n* encarcelamiento *m*

incarnat|e /ɪn'kɑːnət/ *a* encarnado. ~**ion** /-'neɪʃn/ *n* encarnación *f*

incautious /ɪn'kɔːʃəs/ *a* incauto. ~**ly** *adv* incautamente

incendiary /ɪn'sendɪərɪ/ *a* incendiario. ● *n* (*person*) incendiario *m*; (*bomb*) bomba *f* incendiaria

incense[1] /'ɪnsens/ *n* incienso *m*

incense[2] /ɪn'sens/ *vt* enfurecer

incentive /ɪn'sentɪv/ *n* incentivo *m*; (*payment*) prima *f* de incentivo

inception /ɪn'sepʃn/ *n* principio *m*

incertitude /ɪn'sɜːtɪtjuːd/ *n* incertidumbre *f*

incessant /ɪn'sesnt/ *a* incesante. ~**ly** *adv* sin cesar

incest /'ɪnsest/ *n* incesto *m*. ~**uous** /-'sestjʊəs/ *a* incestuoso

inch /ɪntʃ/ *n* pulgada *f* (= 2,54cm). ● *vi* avanzar palmo a palmo

incidence /'ɪnsɪdəns/ *n* frecuencia *f*

incident /'ɪnsɪdənt/ *n* incidente *m*

incidental /ɪnsɪ'dentl/ *a* fortuito. ~**ly** *adv* incidentemente; (*by the way*) a propósito

incinerat|e /ɪn'sɪnəreɪt/ *vt* incinerar. ~**or** *n* incinerador *m*

incipient /ɪn'sɪpɪənt/ *a* incipiente

incision /ɪn'sɪʒn/ *n* incisión *f*

incisive /ɪn'saɪsɪv/ *a* incisivo

incite /ɪn'saɪt/ *vt* incitar. ~**ment** *n* incitación *f*

inclement /ɪn'klemənt/ *a* inclemente

inclination /ɪnklɪ'neɪʃn/ *n* inclinación *f*

incline[1] /ɪn'klaɪn/ *vt* inclinar. ● *vi* inclinarse. **be** ~**d to** tener tendencia a

incline[2] /'ɪnklaɪn/ *n* cuesta *f*

inclu|de /ɪn'kluːd/ *vt* incluir. ~**ding** *prep* incluso. ~**sion** /-ʒn/ *n* inclusión *f*

inclusive /ɪn'kluːsɪv/ *a* inclusivo. **be** ~ **of** incluir. ● *adv* inclusive

incognito /ɪnkɒg'niːtəʊ/ *adv* de incógnito

incoherent /ɪnkəʊ'hɪərənt/ *a* incoherente

income /'ɪnkʌm/ *n* ingresos *mpl*. ~ **tax** *n* impuesto *m* sobre la renta

incoming /'ɪnkʌmɪŋ/ *a* ⟨*tide*⟩ ascendente; ⟨*tenant etc*⟩ nuevo

incomparable /ɪn'kɒmpərəbl/ *a* incomparable

incompatible /ɪnkəm'pætəbl/ *a* incompatible

incompeten|ce /ɪn'kɒmpɪtəns/ *n* incompetencia *f*. ~**t** *a* incompetente

incomplete /ɪnkəm'pliːt/ *a* incompleto

incomprehensible /ɪnkɒmprɪˈhen-səbl/ *a* incomprensible

inconceivable /ɪnkənˈsiːvəbl/ *a* inconcebible

inconclusive /ɪnkənˈkluːsɪv/ *a* poco concluyente

incongruous /ɪnˈkɒŋgruəs/ *a* incongruente

inconsequential /ɪnkɒnsɪˈkwenʃl/ *a* sin importancia

inconsiderate /ɪnkənˈsɪdərət/ *a* desconsiderado

inconsisten|cy /ɪnkənˈsɪstənsɪ/ *n* inconsecuencia *f.* ~t *a* inconsecuente. **be** ~t **with** no concordar con

inconspicuous /ɪnkənˈspɪkjuəs/ *a* que no llama la atención. ~ly *adv* sin llamar la atención

incontinen|ce /ɪnˈkɒntɪnəns/ *a* incontinencia *f.* ~t *a* incontinente

inconvenien|ce /ɪnkənˈviːnɪəns/ *a* incomodidad *f;* (*drawback*) inconveniente m. ~t *a* incómodo; (*time*) inoportuno

incorporat|e /ɪnˈkɔːpəreɪt/ *vt* incorporar; (*include*) incluir. ~ion /-ˈreɪʃn/ *n* incorporación *f*

incorrect /ɪnkəˈrekt/ *a* incorrecto

incorrigible /ɪnˈkɒrɪdʒəbl/ *a* incorregible

incorruptible /ɪnkəˈrʌptəbl/ *a* incorruptible

increase /ˈɪnkriːs/ *n* aumento m (**in**, **of** de). /ɪnˈkriːs/ *vt/i* aumentar

increasing /ɪnˈkriːsɪŋ/ *a* creciente. ~ly *adv* cada vez más

incredible /ɪnˈkredəbl/ *a* increíble

incredulous /ɪnˈkredjʊləs/ *a* incrédulo

increment /ˈɪnkrɪmənt/ *n* aumento m

incriminat|e /ɪnˈkrɪmɪneɪt/ *vt* acriminar. ~ing *a* acriminador

incubat|e /ˈɪnkjʊbeɪt/ *vt* incubar. ~ion /-ˈbeɪʃn/ *n* incubación *f.* ~or *n* incubadora *f*

inculcate /ˈɪnkʌlkeɪt/ *vt* inculcar

incumbent /ɪnˈkʌmbənt/ *n* titular. ● *a.* **be** ~ **on** incumbir a

incur /ɪnˈkɜː(r)/ *vt* (*pt* **incurred**) incurrir en; contraer (*debts*)

incurable /ɪnˈkjʊərəbl/ *a* incurable

incursion /ɪnˈkɜːʃn/ *n* incursión *f*

indebted /ɪnˈdetɪd/ *a.* ~ **to s.o.** estar en deuda con uno

indecen|cy /ɪnˈdiːsnsɪ/ *n* indecencia *f.* ~t *a* indecente

indecisi|on /ɪndɪˈsɪʒn/ *n* indecisión *f.* ~ve /ɪndɪˈsaɪsɪv/ *a* indeciso

indeed /ɪnˈdiːd/ *adv* en efecto; (*really?*) ¿de veras?

indefatigable /ɪndɪˈfætɪgəbl/ *a* incansable

indefinable /ɪndɪˈfaɪnəbl/ *a* indefinible

indefinite /ɪnˈdefɪnət/ *a* indefinido. ~ly *adv* indefinidamente

indelible /ɪnˈdelɪbl/ *a* indeleble

indemni|fy /ɪnˈdemnɪfaɪ/ *vt* indemnizar. ~ty /-ətɪ/ *n* indemnización *f*

indent /ɪnˈdent/ *vt* endentar (*text*). ~ation /-ˈteɪʃn/ *n* mella *f*

independen|ce /ɪndɪˈpendəns/ *n* independencia *f.* ~t *a* independiente. ~tly *adv* independientemente. ~tly **of** independientemente de

indescribable /ɪndɪˈskraɪbəbl/ *a* indescriptible

indestructible /ɪndɪˈstrʌktəbl/ *a* indestructible

indeterminate /ɪndɪˈtɜːmɪnət/ *a* indeterminate

index /ˈɪndeks/ *n* (*pl* **indexes**) índice m. ● *vt* poner índice a; (*enter in the/an index*) poner en el/un índice. ~ **finger** *n* (dedo m) índice m. ~**linked** *a* indexado

India /ˈɪndɪə/ *n* la India *f.* ~**n** *a* & *n* indio (m). ~**n summer** *n* veranillo m de San Martín

indicat|e /ˈɪndɪkeɪt/ *vt* indicar. ~ion /-ˈkeɪʃn/ *n* indicación *f.* ~ive /ɪnˈdɪkətɪv/ *a* & *n* indicativo (m). ~or /ˈɪndɪkeɪtə(r)/ *n* indicador m.

indict /ɪnˈdaɪt/ *vt* acusar. ~ment *n* acusación *f*

indifferen|ce /ɪnˈdɪfrəns/ *n* indiferencia *f.* ~t *a* indiferente; (*not good*) mediocre

indigenous /ɪnˈdɪdʒɪnəs/ *a* indígena

indigesti|ble /ɪndɪˈdʒestəbl/ *a* indigesto. ~on /-tʃən/ *n* indigestión *f*

indignant /ɪnˈdɪgnənt/ *a* indignado. ~tion /-ˈneɪʃn/ *n* indignación *f*

indignity /ɪnˈdɪgnətɪ/ *n* indignidad *f*

indigo /ˈɪndɪgəʊ/ *n* añil (m)

indirect /ɪndɪˈrekt/ *a* indirecto. ~ly *adv* indirectamente

indiscre|et /ɪndɪˈskriːt/ *a* indiscreto. ~tion /-ˈkreʃn/ *n* indiscreción *f*

indiscriminate /ɪndɪˈskrɪmɪnət/ *a* indistinto. ~ly *adv* indistintamente

indispensable /ɪndɪˈspensəbl/ *a* imprescindible

indispos|ed /ɪndɪˈspəʊzd/ a indispuesto. **~ition** /-əˈzɪʃn/ n indisposición f

indisputable /ɪndɪˈspjuːtəbl/ a indiscutible

indissoluble /ɪndɪˈsɒljʊbl/ a indisoluble

indistinct /ɪndɪˈstɪŋkt/ a indistinto

indistinguishable /ɪndɪˈstɪŋgwɪʃ-əbl/ a indistinguible

individual /ɪndɪˈvɪdjʊəl/ a individual. ● n individuo m. **~ist** n individualista m & f. **~ity** n individualidad f. **~ly** adv individualmente

indivisible /ɪndɪˈvɪzəbl/ a indivisible

Indo-China /ɪndəʊˈtʃaɪnə/ n Indochina f

indoctrinat|e /ɪnˈdɒktrɪneɪt/ vt adoctrinar. **~ion** /-ˈneɪʃn/ n adoctrinamiento m

indolen|ce /ˈɪndələns/ n indolencia f. **~t** a indolente

indomitable /ɪnˈdɒmɪtəbl/ a indomable

Indonesia /ɪndəʊˈniːzɪə/ n Indonesia f. **~n** a & n indonesio (m)

indoor /ˈɪndɔː(r)/ a interior; (clothes etc) de casa; (covered) cubierto. **~s** adv dentro; (at home) en casa

induce /ɪnˈdjuːs/ vt inducir; (cause) provocar. **~ment** n incentivo m

induct /ɪnˈdʌkt/ vt instalar; (mil, Amer) incorporar

indulge /ɪnˈdʌldʒ/ vt satisfacer (desires); complacer (person). ● vi. **~ in** entregarse a. **~nce** /ɪnˈdʌldʒəns/ n (of desires) satisfacción f; (relig) indulgencia f. **~nt** a indulgente

industrial /ɪnˈdʌstrɪəl/ a industrial; (unrest) laboral. **~ist** n industrial m & f. **~ized** a industrializado

industrious /ɪnˈdʌstrɪəs/ a trabajador

industry /ˈɪndəstrɪ/ n industria f; (zeal) aplicación f

inebriated /ɪˈniːbrɪeɪtɪd/ a borracho

inedible /ɪnˈedɪbl/ a incomible

ineffable /ɪnˈefəbl/ a inefable

ineffective /ɪnɪˈfektɪv/ a ineficaz; (person) incapaz

ineffectual /ɪnɪˈfektjʊəl/ a ineficaz

inefficien|cy /ɪnɪˈfɪʃnsɪ/ n ineficacia f; (of person) incompetencia f. **~t** a ineficaz; (person) incompetente

ineligible /ɪnˈelɪdʒəbl/ a inelegible. **be ~ for** no tener derecho a

inept /ɪˈnept/ a inepto

inequality /ɪnɪˈkwɒlətɪ/ n desigualdad f

inert /ɪˈnɜːt/ a inerte

inertia /ɪˈnɜːʃə/ n inercia f

inescapable /ɪnɪˈskeɪpəbl/ a ineludible

inestimable /ɪnˈestɪməbl/ a inestimable

inevitabl|e /ɪnˈevɪtəbl/ a inevitable. **~ly** adv inevitablemente

inexact /ɪnɪgˈzækt/ a inexacto

inexcusable /ɪnɪkˈskjuːsəbl/ a imperdonable

inexhaustible /ɪnɪgˈzɔːstəbl/ a inagotable

inexorable /ɪnˈeksərəbl/ a inexorable

inexpensive /ɪnɪkˈspensɪv/ a económico, barato

inexperience /ɪnɪkˈspɪərɪəns/ n falta f de experiencia. **~d** a inexperto

inexplicable /ɪnɪkˈsplɪkəbl/ a inexplicable

inextricable /ɪnɪkˈstrɪkəbl/ a inextricable

infallib|ility /ɪnfæləˈbɪlətɪ/ n infalibilidad f. **~le** a infalible

infam|ous /ˈɪnfəməs/ a infame. **~y** n infamia f

infan|cy /ˈɪnfənsɪ/ n infancia f. **~t** n niño m. **~tile** /ˈɪnfəntaɪl/ a infantil

infantry /ˈɪnfəntrɪ/ n infantería f

infatuat|ed /ɪnˈfætjʊeɪtɪd/ a. **be ~ed with** encapricharse por. **~ion** /-ˈeɪʃn/ n encaprichamiento m

infect /ɪnˈfekt/ vt infectar; (fig) contagiar. **~ s.o. with** contagiar a uno. **~ion** /-ˈfekʃn/ n infección f; (fig) contagio m. **~ious** /ɪnˈfekʃəs/ a contagioso

infer /ɪnˈfɜː(r)/ vt (pt **inferred**) deducir. **~ence** /ˈɪnfərəns/ n deducción f

inferior /ɪnˈfɪərɪə(r)/ a inferior. ● n inferior m & f. **~ity** /-ˈɒrətɪ/ n inferioridad f

infernal /ɪnˈfɜːnl/ a infernal. **~ly** adv (fam) atrozmente

inferno /ɪnˈfɜːnəʊ/ n (pl **-os**) infierno m

infertil|e /ɪnˈfɜːtaɪl/ a estéril. **~ity** /-ˈtɪlətɪ/ n esterilidad f

infest /ɪnˈfest/ vt infestar. **~ation** /-ˈsteɪʃn/ n infestación f

infidelity /ɪnfɪˈdelətɪ/ n infidelidad f

infighting /ˈɪnfaɪtɪŋ/ n lucha f cuerpo a cuerpo; (fig) riñas fpl (internas)

infiltrat|e /ɪnfɪlˈtreɪt/ vt infiltrar. ● vi infiltrarse. ~ion /-ˈtreɪʃn/ n infiltración f

infinite /ˈɪnfɪnət/ a infinito. ~ly adv infinitamente

infinitesimal /ɪnfɪnɪˈtesɪml/ a infinitesimal

infinitive /ɪnˈfɪnətɪv/ n infinitivo m

infinity /ɪnˈfɪnətɪ/ n (infinite distance) infinito m; (infinite quantity) infinidad f

infirm /ɪnˈfɜːm/ a enfermizo

infirmary /ɪnˈfɜːmərɪ/ n hospital m; (sick bay) enfermería f

infirmity /ɪnˈfɜːmətɪ/ n enfermedad f; (weakness) debilidad f

inflam|e /ɪnˈfleɪm/ vt inflamar. ~mable /ɪnˈflæməbl/ a inflamable. ~mation /-əˈmeɪʃn/ n inflamación f. ~matory /ɪnˈflæmətərɪ/ a inflamatorio

inflate /ɪnˈfleɪt/ vt inflar

inflation /ɪnˈfleɪʃn/ n inflación f. ~ary a inflacionario

inflection /ɪnˈflekʃn/ n inflexión f

inflexible /ɪnˈfleksəbl/ a inflexible

inflict /ɪnˈflɪkt/ vt infligir (on a)

inflow /ˈɪnfləʊ/ n afluencia f

influence /ˈɪnflʊəns/ n influencia f. **under the ~** (drunk, fam) borracho. ● vt influir, influenciar (esp LAm)

influential /ɪnflʊˈenʃl/ a influyente

influenza /ɪnflʊˈenzə/ n gripe f

influx /ˈɪnflʌks/ n afluencia f

inform /ɪnˈfɔːm/ vt informar. **keep ~ed** tener al corriente

informal /ɪnˈfɔːml/ a (simple) sencillo, sin ceremonia; (unofficial) oficioso. ~ity /ˈmælətɪ/ n falta f de ceremonia. ~ly adv sin ceremonia

inform|ant /ɪnˈfɔːmənt/ n informador m. ~ation /ɪnfəˈmeɪʃn/ n información f. ~ative /ɪnˈfɔːmətɪv/ a informativo. ~er /ɪnˈfɔːmə(r)/ n denunciante m

infra-red /ɪnfrəˈred/ a infrarrojo

infrequent /ɪnˈfriːkwənt/ a poco frecuente. ~ly adv raramente

infringe /ɪnˈfrɪndʒ/ vt infringir. ~ on usurpar. ~ment n infracción f

infuriate /ɪnˈfjʊərɪeɪt/ vt enfurecer

infus|e /ɪnˈfjuːz/ vt infundir. ~ion /-ʒn/ n infusión f

ingen|ious /ɪnˈdʒiːnɪəs/ a ingenioso. ~uity /ɪndʒɪˈnjuːətɪ/ n ingeniosidad f

ingenuous /ɪnˈdʒenjʊəs/ a ingenuo

ingest /ɪnˈdʒest/ vt ingerir

ingot /ˈɪŋgət/ n lingote m

ingrained /ɪnˈgreɪnd/ a arraigado

ingratiate /ɪnˈgreɪʃɪeɪt/ vt. ~ o.s. with congraciarse con

ingratitude /ɪnˈgrætɪtjuːd/ n ingratitud f

ingredient /ɪnˈgriːdɪənt/ n ingrediente m

ingrowing /ˈɪngrəʊɪŋ/ a. ~ nail n uñero m, uña f encarnada

inhabit /ɪnˈhæbɪt/ vt habitar. ~able a habitable. ~ant n habitante m

inhale /ɪnˈheɪl/ vt aspirar. ● vi (tobacco) aspirar el humo

inherent /ɪnˈhɪərənt/ a inherente. ~ly adv intrínsecamente

inherit /ɪnˈherɪt/ vt heredar. ~ance n herencia f

inhibit /ɪnˈhɪbɪt/ vt inhibir. **be ~ed** tener inhibiciones. ~ion /-ˈbɪʃn/ n inhibición f

inhospitable /ɪnhəˈspɪtəbl/ a (place) inhóspito; (person) inhospitalario

inhuman /ɪnˈhjuːmən/ a inhumano. ~e /ɪnhjuːˈmeɪn/ a inhumano. ~ity /ɪnhjuːˈmænətɪ/ n inhumanidad f

inimical /ɪˈnɪmɪkl/ a hostil

inimitable /ɪˈnɪmɪtəbl/ a inimitable

iniquit|ous /ɪˈnɪkwɪtəs/ a inicuo. ~y /-ətɪ/ n iniquidad f

initial /ɪˈnɪʃl/ n inicial f. ● vt (pt initialled) firmar con iniciales. **he ~led the document** firmó el documento con sus iniciales. ● a inicial. ~ly adv al principio

initiat|e /ɪˈnɪʃɪeɪt/ vt iniciar; promover (scheme etc). ~ion /-ˈeɪʃn/ n iniciación f

initiative /ɪˈnɪʃətɪv/ n iniciativa f

inject /ɪnˈdʒekt/ vt inyectar; (fig) injertar (new element). ~ion /-ʃn/ n inyección f

injunction /ɪnˈdʒʌŋkʃn/ n (court order) entredicho m

injur|e /ˈɪndʒə(r)/ vt (wound) herir; (fig, damage) perjudicar. ~y /ˈɪndʒərɪ/ n herida f; (damage) perjuicio m

injustice /ɪnˈdʒʌstɪs/ n injusticia f

ink /ɪŋk/ n tinta f

inkling /ˈɪŋklɪŋ/ n atisbo m

ink: **~-well** n tintero m. **~y** a manchado de tinta

inland /'ɪnlənd/ a interior. ● adv tierra adentro. **I~ Revenue** n Hacienda f

in-laws /'ɪnlɔːz/ npl parientes mpl políticos

inlay /ɪn'leɪ/ vt (pt inlaid) taracear, incrustar. /'ɪnleɪ/ n taracea f, incrustación f

inlet /'ɪnlet/ n ensenada f; (tec) entrada f

inmate /'ɪnmeɪt/ n (of asylum) internado m; (of prison) preso m

inn /ɪn/ n posada f

innards /'ɪnədz/ npl tripas fpl

innate /ɪ'neɪt/ a innato

inner /'ɪnə(r)/ a interior; (fig) íntimo. **~most** a más íntimo. **~ tube** n cámara f de aire, llanta f (LAm)

innings /'ɪnɪŋz/ n invar turno m

innkeeper /'ɪnkiːpə(r)/ n posadero m

innocen|ce /'ɪnəsns/ n inocencia f. **~t** a & n inocente (m & f)

innocuous /ɪ'nɒkjʊəs/ a inocuo

innovat|e /'ɪnəveɪt/ vi innovar. **~ion** /-'veɪʃn/ n innovación f. **~or** n innovador m

innuendo /ɪnjuː'endəʊ/ n (pl -oes) insinuación f

innumerable /ɪ'njuːmərəbl/ a innumerable

inoculat|e /ɪ'nɒkjʊleɪt/ vt inocular. **~ion** /-'leɪʃn/ n inoculación f

inoffensive /ɪnə'fensɪv/ a inofensivo

inoperative /ɪn'ɒpərətɪv/ a inoperante

inopportune /ɪn'ɒpətjuːn/ a inoportuno

inordinate /ɪ'nɔːdɪnət/ a excesivo. **~ly** adv excesivamente

in-patient /'ɪnpeɪʃnt/ n paciente m interno

input /'ɪnpʊt/ n (data) datos mpl; (comput process) entrada f, input m; (elec) energía f

inquest /'ɪnkwest/ n investigación f judicial

inquir|e /ɪn'kwaɪə(r)/ vi preguntar. **~y** n (question) pregunta f; (investigation) investigación f

inquisition /ɪnkwɪ'zɪʃn/ n inquisición f

inquisitive /ɪn'kwɪzətɪv/ a inquisitivo

inroad /'ɪnrəʊd/ n incursión f

inrush /'ɪnrʌʃ/ n irrupción f

insan|e /ɪn'seɪn/ a loco. **~ity** /-'sænətɪ/ n locura f

insanitary /ɪn'sænɪtərɪ/ a insalubre

insatiable /ɪn'seɪʃəbl/ a insaciable

inscri|be /ɪn'skraɪb/ vt inscribir; dedicar ‹book›. **~ption** /-ɪpʃn/ n inscripción f; (in book) dedicatoria f

inscrutable /ɪn'skruːtəbl/ a inescrutable

insect /'ɪnsekt/ n insecto m. **~icide** /ɪn'sektɪsaɪd/ n insecticida f

insecur|e /ɪnsɪ'kjʊə(r)/ a inseguro. **~ity** n inseguridad f

insemination /ɪnsemɪ'neɪʃn/ n inseminación f

insensible /ɪn'sensəbl/ a insensible; (unconscious) sin conocimiento

insensitive /ɪn'sensətɪv/ a insensible

inseparable /ɪn'sepərəbl/ a inseparable

insert /'ɪnsɜːt/ n materia f insertada. /ɪn'sɜːt/ vt insertar. **~ion** /-ʃn/ n inserción f

inshore /ɪn'ʃɔː(r)/ a costero

inside /ɪn'saɪd/ n interior m. **~ out** al revés; (thoroughly) a fondo. ● a interior. ● adv dentro. ● prep dentro de. **~s** npl tripas fpl

insidious /ɪn'sɪdɪəs/ a insidioso

insight /'ɪnsaɪt/ n (perception) penetración f, revelación f

insignia /ɪn'sɪgnɪə/ npl insignias fpl

insignificant /ɪnsɪg'nɪfɪkənt/ a insignificante

insincer|e /ɪnsɪn'sɪə(r)/ a poco sincero. **~ity** /-'serətɪ/ n falta f de sinceridad f

insinuat|e /ɪn'sɪnjʊeɪt/ vt insinuar. **~ion** /-'eɪʃn/ n insinuación f

insipid /ɪn'sɪpɪd/ a insípido

insist /ɪn'sɪst/ vt/i insistir. **~ on** insistir en; (demand) exigir

insisten|ce /ɪn'sɪstəns/ n insistencia f. **~t** a insistente. **~tly** adv con insistencia

insolen|ce /'ɪnsələns/ n insolencia f. **~t** a insolente

insoluble /ɪn'sɒljʊbl/ a insoluble

insolvent /ɪn'sɒlvənt/ a insolvente

insomnia /ɪn'sɒmnɪə/ n insomnio m. **~c** /-ɪæk/ n insomne m & f

inspect /ɪn'spekt/ vt inspeccionar; revisar ‹ticket›. **~ion** /-ʃn/ n inspección f. **~or** n inspector m; (on train, bus) revisor m

inspir|ation /ɪnspə'reɪʃn/ n inspiración f. **~e** /ɪn'spaɪə(r)/ vt inspirar

instability /ɪnstə'bɪlətɪ/ *n* inestabilidad *f*

install /ɪn'stɔːl/ *vt* instalar. **~ation** /-ə'leɪʃn/ *n* instalación *f*

instalment /ɪn'stɔːlmənt/ *n* (*payment*) plazo *m*; (*of serial*) entrega *f*

instance /'ɪnstəns/ *n* ejemplo *m*; (*case*) caso *m*. **for ~** por ejemplo. **in the first ~** en primer lugar

instant /'ɪnstənt/ *a* inmediato; (*food*) instantáneo. ● *n* instante *m*. **~aneous** /ɪnstən'teɪnɪəs/ *a* instantáneo. **~ly** /'ɪnstəntlɪ/ *adv* inmediatamente

instead /ɪn'sted/ *adv* en cambio. **~ of doing** en vez de hacer. **~ of s.o.** en lugar de uno

instep /'ɪnstep/ *n* empeine *m*

instigat|e /'ɪnstɪɡeɪt/ *vt* instigar. **~ion** /-'ɡeɪʃn/ *n* instigación *f*. **~or** *n* instigador *m*

instil /ɪn'stɪl/ *vt* (*pt* **instilled**) infundir

instinct /'ɪnstɪŋkt/ *n* instinto *m*. **~ive** /ɪn'stɪŋktɪv/ *a* instintivo

institut|e /'ɪnstɪtjuːt/ *n* instituto *m*. ● *vt* instituir; iniciar ⟨*enquiry etc*⟩. **~ion** /-'tjuːʃn/ *n* institución *f*

instruct /ɪn'strʌkt/ *vt* instruir; (*order*) mandar. **~ s.o. in sth** enseñar algo a uno. **~ion** /-ʃn/ *n* instrucción *f*. **~ions** /-ʃnz/ *npl* (*for use*) modo *m* de empleo. **~ive** *a* instructivo

instrument /'ɪnstrəmənt/ *n* instrumento *m*. **~al** /ɪnstrə'mentl/ *a* instrumental. **be ~al in** contribuir a. **~alist** *n* instrumentalista *m & f*

insubordinat|e /ɪnsə'bɔːdɪnət/ *a* insubordinado. **~ion** /-'neɪʃn/ *n* insubordinación *f*

insufferable /ɪn'sʌfərəbl/ *a* insufrible, insoportable

insufficient /ɪnsə'fɪʃnt/ *a* insuficiente. **~ly** *adv* insuficientemente

insular /'ɪnsjʊlə(r)/ *a* insular; (*narrow-minded*) de miras estrechas

insulat|e /'ɪnsjʊleɪt/ *vt* aislar. **~ing tape** *n* cinta *f* aisladora/aislante. **~ion** /-'leɪʃn/ *n* aislamiento *m*

insulin /'ɪnsjʊlɪn/ *n* insulina *f*

insult /ɪn'sʌlt/ *vt* insultar. /'ɪnsʌlt/ *n* insulto *m*

insuperable /ɪn'sjuːpərəbl/ *a* insuperable

insur|ance /ɪn'ʃʊərəns/ *n* seguro *m*. **~e** *vt* asegurar. **~e that** asegurarse de que

insurgent /ɪn'sɜːdʒənt/ *a & n* insurrecto (*m*)

insurmountable /ɪnsə'maʊntəbl/ *a* insuperable

insurrection /ɪnsə'rekʃn/ *n* insurrección *f*

intact /ɪn'tækt/ *a* intacto

intake /'ɪnteɪk/ *n* (*quantity*) número *m*; (*mec*) admisión *f*; (*of food*) consumo *m*

intangible /ɪn'tændʒəbl/ *a* intangible

integral /'ɪntɪɡrəl/ *a* íntegro. **be an ~ part of** ser parte integrante de

integrat|e /'ɪntɪɡreɪt/ *vt* integrar. ● *vi* integrarse. **~ion** /-'ɡreɪʃn/ *n* integración *f*

integrity /ɪn'teɡrətɪ/ *n* integridad *f*

intellect /'ɪntəlekt/ *n* intelecto *m*. **~ual** *a & n* intelectual (*m*)

intelligen|ce /ɪn'telɪdʒəns/ *n* inteligencia *f*; (*information*) información *f*. **~t** *a* inteligente. **~tly** *adv* inteligentemente. **~tsia** /ɪntelɪ'dʒentsɪə/ *n* intelectualidad *f*

intelligible /ɪn'telɪdʒəbl/ *a* inteligible

intemperance /ɪn'tempərəns/ *n* inmoderación *f*

intend /ɪn'tend/ *vt* destinar. **~ to do** tener la intención de hacer. **~ed** *a* intencionado. ● *n* (*future spouse*) novio *m*

intense /ɪn'tens/ *a* intenso; (*person*) apasionado. **~ly** *adv* intensamente; (*very*) sumamente

intensif|ication /ɪntensɪfɪ'keɪʃn/ *n* intensificación *f*. **~y** /-faɪ/ *vt* intensificar

intensity /ɪn'tensətɪ/ *n* intensidad *f*

intensive /ɪn'tensɪv/ *a* intensivo. **~ care** *n* asistencia *f* intensiva, cuidados *mpl* intensivos

intent /ɪn'tent/ *n* propósito *m*. ● *a* atento. **~ on** absorto en. **~ on doing** resuelto a hacer

intention /ɪn'tenʃn/ *n* intención *f*. **~al** *a* intencional

intently /ɪn'tentlɪ/ *adv* atentamente

inter /ɪn'tɜː(r)/ *vt* (*pt* **interred**) enterrar

inter... /'ɪntə(r)/ *pref* inter..., entre...

interact /ɪntər'ækt/ *vi* obrar recíprocamente. **~ion** /-ʃn/ *n* interacción *f*

intercede /ɪntə'siːd/ *vi* interceder

intercept /ɪntə'sept/ *vt* interceptar. **~ion** /-ʃn/ *n* interceptación *f*; (*in geometry*) intersección *f*

interchange /'ɪntətʃeɪndʒ/ n (road junction) cruce m. ~able /-'tʃeɪndʒəbl/ a intercambiable

intercom /'ɪntəkɒm/ n intercomunicador m

interconnected /ɪntəkə'nektɪd/ a relacionado

intercourse /'ɪntəkɔːs/ n trato m; (sexual) trato m sexual

interest /'ɪntrest/ n interés m; (advantage) ventaja f. ● vt interesar. ~ed a interesado. be ~ed in interesarse por. ~ing a interesante

interfere /ɪntə'fɪə(r)/ vi entrometerse. ~ in entrometerse en. ~ with entrometerse en, interferir en; interferir (radio). ~nce n interferencia f

interim a provisional. ● n. in the ~ entre tanto

interior /ɪn'tɪərɪə(r)/ a & n interior (m)

interjection /ɪntə'dʒekʃn/ n interjección f

interlock /ɪntə'lɒk/ vt/i (tec) engranar

interloper /'ɪntələʊpə(r)/ n intruso m

interlude /'ɪntəluːd/ n intervalo m; (theatre, music) interludio m

intermarr|iage /ɪntə'mærɪdʒ/ n matrimonio m entre personas de distintas razas. ~y vi casarse (con personas de distintas razas)

intermediary /ɪntə'miːdɪərɪ/ a & n intermediario (m)

intermediate /ɪntə'miːdɪət/ a intermedio

interminable /ɪn'tɜːmɪnəbl/ a interminable

intermission /ɪntə'mɪʃn/ n pausa f; (theatre) descanso m

intermittent /ɪntə'mɪtnt/ a intermitente. ~ly adv con discontinuidad

intern /ɪn'tɜːn/ vt internar. /'ɪntɜːn/ n (doctor, Amer) interno m

internal /ɪn'tɜːnl/ a interior. ~ly adv interiormente

international /ɪntə'næʃənl/ a & n internacional (m)

internee /ˌɪntɜː'niː/ n internado m

internment /ɪn'tɜːnmənt/ n internamiento m

interplay /'ɪntəpleɪ/ n interacción f

interpolate /ɪn'tɜːpəleɪt/ vt interpolar

interpret /ɪn'tɜːprɪt/ vt/i interpretar. ~ation /-'teɪʃn/ n interpretación f. ~er n intérprete m & f

interrelated /ɪntərɪ'leɪtɪd/ a interrelacionado

interrogat|e /ɪn'terəgeɪt/ vt interrogar. ~ion /-'geɪʃn/ n interrogación f; (session of questions) interrogatorio m

interrogative /ɪntə'rɒgətɪv/ a & n interrogativo (m)

interrupt /ɪntə'rʌpt/ vt interrumpir. ~ion /-ʃn/ n interrupción f

intersect /ɪntə'sekt/ vt cruzar. ● vi (roads) cruzarse; (geometry) intersecarse. ~ion /-ʃn/ n (roads) cruce m; (geometry) intersección f

interspersed /ɪntə'spɜːst/ a disperso. ~ with salpicado de

intertwine /ɪntə'twaɪn/ vt entrelazar. ● vi entrelazarse

interval /'ɪntəvl/ n intervalo m; (theatre) descanso m. at ~s a intervalos

interven|e /ɪntə'viːn/ vi intervenir. ~tion /-'venʃn/ n intervención f

interview /'ɪntəvjuː/ n entrevista f. ● vt entrevistarse con. ~er n entrevistador m

intestin|al /ɪnte'staɪnl/ a intestinal. ~e /ɪn'testɪn/ n intestino m

intimacy /'ɪntɪməsɪ/ n intimidad f

intimate[1] /'ɪntɪmət/ a íntimo

intimate[2] /'ɪntɪmeɪt/ vt (state) anunciar; (imply) dar a entender

intimately /'ɪntɪmətlɪ/ adv íntimamente

intimidat|e /ɪn'tɪmɪdeɪt/ vt intimidar. ~ion /-'deɪʃn/ n intimidación f

into /'ɪntuː/, unstressed /'ɪntə/ prep en; (translate) a

intolerable /ɪn'tɒlərəbl/ a intolerable

intoleran|ce /ɪn'tɒlərəns/ n intolerancia f. ~t a intolerante

intonation /ɪntə'neɪʃn/ n entonación f

intoxicat|e /ɪn'tɒksɪkeɪt/ vt embriagar; (med) intoxicar. ~ed a ebrio. ~ion /-'keɪʃn/ n embriaguez f; (med) intoxicación f

intra... /'ɪntrə/ pref intra...

intractable /ɪn'træktəbl/ a (person) intratable; (thing) muy difícil

intransigent /ɪn'trænsɪdʒənt/ a intransigente

intransitive /ɪnˈtrænsɪtɪv/ *a* intransitivo

intravenous /ɪntrəˈviːnəs/ *a* intravenoso

intrepid /ɪnˈtrepɪd/ *a* intrépido

intrica|cy /ˈɪntrɪkəsɪ/ *n* complejidad *f*. ~**te** *a* complejo

intrigu|e /ɪnˈtriːg/ *vt/i* intrigar. ● *n* intriga *f*. ~**ing** *a* intrigante

intrinsic /ɪnˈtrɪnsɪk/ *a* intrínseco. ~**ally** *adv* intrínsecamente

introduc|e /ɪntrəˈdjuːs/ *vt* introducir; presentar ‹*person*›. ~**tion** /ɪntrəˈdʌkʃn/ *n* introducción *f*; (*to person*) presentación *f*. ~**tory** /-tərɪ/ *a* preliminar

introspective /ɪntrəˈspektɪv/ *a* introspectivo

introvert /ˈɪntrəvɜːt/ *n* introvertido *m*

intru|de /ɪnˈtruːd/ *vi* entrometerse; (*disturb*) molestar. ~**der** *n* intruso *m*. ~**sion** *n* intrusión *f*

intuiti|on /ɪntjuːˈɪʃn/ *n* intuición *f*. ~**ve** /ɪnˈtjuːɪtɪv/ *a* intuitivo

inundat|e /ˈɪnʌndeɪt/ *vt* inundar. ~**ion** /-ˈdeɪʃn/ *n* inundación *f*

invade /ɪnˈveɪd/ *vt* invadir. ~**r** /-ə(r)/ *n* invasor *m*

invalid[1] /ˈɪnvəlɪd/ *n* enfermo *m*, inválido *m*

invalid[2] /ɪnˈvælɪd/ *a* nulo. ~**ate** *vt* invalidar

invaluable /ɪnˈvæljʊəbl/ *a* inestimable

invariabl|e /ɪnˈveərɪəbl/ *a* invariable. ~**y** *adv* invariablemente

invasion /ɪnˈveɪʒn/ *n* invasión *f*

invective /ɪnˈvektɪv/ *n* invectiva *f*

inveigh /ɪnˈveɪ/ *vi* dirigir invectivas (**against** contra)

inveigle /ɪnˈveɪgl/ *vt* engatusar, persuadir

invent /ɪnˈvent/ *vt* inventar. ~**ion** /-ˈvenʃn/ *n* invención *f*. ~**ive** *a* inventivo. ~**or** *n* inventor *m*

inventory /ˈɪnvəntərɪ/ *n* inventario *m*

invers|e /ɪnˈvɜːs/ *a & n* inverso (*m*). ~**ely** *adv* inversamente. ~**ion** /ɪnˈvɜːʃn/ *n* inversión *f*

invert /ɪnˈvɜːt/ *vt* invertir. ~**ed commas** *npl* comillas *fpl*

invest /ɪnˈvest/ *vt* invertir. ● *vi*. ~ **in** hacer una inversión *f*

investigat|e /ɪnˈvestɪgeɪt/ *vt* investigar. ~**ion** /-ˈgeɪʃn/ *n* investigación

f. **under** ~**ion** sometido a examen. ~**or** *n* investigador *m*

inveterate /ɪnˈvetərət/ *a* inveterado

invidious /ɪnˈvɪdɪəs/ *a* (*hateful*) odioso; (*unfair*) injusto

invigilat|e /ɪnˈvɪdʒɪleɪt/ *vi* vigilar. ~**or** *n* celador *m*

invigorate /ɪnˈvɪgəreɪt/ *vt* vigorizar; (*stimulate*) estimular

invincible /ɪnˈvɪnsɪbl/ *a* invencible

invisible /ɪnˈvɪzəbl/ *a* invisible

invit|ation /ɪnvɪˈteɪʃn/ *n* invitación *f*. ~**e** /ɪnˈvaɪt/ *vt* invitar; (*ask for*) pedir. ~**ing** *a* atrayente

invoice /ˈɪnvɔɪs/ *n* factura *f*. ● *vt* facturar

invoke /ɪnˈvəʊk/ *vt* invocar

involuntary /ɪnˈvɒləntərɪ/ *a* involuntario

involve /ɪnˈvɒlv/ *vt* enredar. ~**d** *a* (*complex*) complicado. ~**d in** embrollado en. ~**ment** *n* enredo *m*

invulnerable /ɪnˈvʌlnərəbl/ *a* invulnerable

inward /ˈɪnwəd/ *a* interior. ● *adv* interiormente. ~**s** *adv* hacia/para dentro

iodine /ˈaɪədiːn/ *n* yodo *m*

iota /aɪˈəʊtə/ *n* (*amount*) pizca *f*

IOU /aɪəʊˈjuː/ *abbr* (*I owe you*) pagaré *m*

IQ /aɪˈkjuː/ *abbr* (*intelligence quotient*) cociente *m* intelectual

Iran /ɪˈrɑːn/ *n* Irán *m*. ~**ian** /ɪˈreɪnɪən/ *a & n* iraní (*m*)

Iraq /ɪˈrɑːk/ *n* Irak *m*. ~**i** *a & n* iraquí (*m*)

irascible /ɪˈræsəbl/ *a* irascible

irate /aɪˈreɪt/ *a* colérico

ire /aɪə(r)/ *n* ira *f*

Ireland /ˈaɪələnd/ *n* Irlanda *f*

iris /ˈaɪərɪs/ *n* (*anat*) iris *m*; (*bot*) lirio *m*

Irish /ˈaɪərɪʃ/ *a* irlandés. ● *n* (*lang*) irlandés *m*. ~**man** *n* irlandés *m*. ~**woman** *n* irlandesa *f*

irk /ɜːk/ *vt* fastidiar. ~**some** *a* fastidioso

iron /ˈaɪən/ *n* hierro *m*; (*appliance*) plancha *f*. ● *a* de hierro. ● *vt* planchar. ~ **out** allanar. **I**~ **Curtain** *n* telón *m* de acero

ironic(al) /aɪˈrɒnɪk(l)/ *a* irónico

ironing-board /ˈaɪənɪŋbɔːd/ *n* tabla *f* de planchar

ironmonger /ˈaɪənmʌŋgə(r)/ *n* ferretero *m*. ~**y** *n* ferretería *f*

ironwork /ˈaɪənwɜːk/ *n* herraje *m*

irony /'aɪərənɪ/ n ironía f
irrational /ɪ'ræʃənl/ a irracional
irreconcilable /ɪrekən'saɪləbl/ a irreconciliable
irrefutable /ɪrɪ'fjuːtəbl/ a irrefutable
irregular /ɪ'regjʊlə(r)/ a irregular. **~ity** /-'lærɪtɪ/ n irregularidad f
irrelevan|ce /ɪ'reləvəns/ n inoportunidad f, impertinencia f. **~t** a no pertinente
irreparable /ɪ'repərəbl/ a irreparable
irreplaceable /ɪrɪ'pleɪsəbl/ a irreemplazable
irrepressible /ɪrɪ'presəbl/ a irreprimible
irresistible /ɪrɪ'zɪstəbl/ a irresistible
irresolute /ɪ'rezəluːt/ a irresoluto, indeciso
irrespective /ɪrɪ'spektɪv/ a. **~ of** sin tomar en cuenta
irresponsible /ɪrɪ'spɒnsəbl/ a irresponsable
irretrievable /ɪrɪ'triːvəbl/ a irrecuperable
irreverent /ɪ'revərənt/ a irreverente
irreversible /ɪrɪ'vɜːsəbl/ a irreversible; ⟨decision⟩ irrevocable
irrevocable /ɪ'revəkəbl/ a irrevocable
irrigat|e /'ɪrɪgeɪt/ vt regar; (med) irrigar. **~ion** /-'geɪʃn/ n riego m; (med) irrigación f
irritable /'ɪrɪtəbl/ a irritable
irritat|e /'ɪrɪteɪt/ vt irritar. **~ion** /-'teɪʃn/ n irritación f
is /ɪz/ see **be**
Islam /'ɪzlɑːm/ n Islam m. **~ic** /ɪz'læmɪk/ a islámico
island /'aɪlənd/ n isla f. **traffic ~** n refugio m (en la calle). **~er** n isleño m
isle /aɪl/ n isla f
isolat|e /'aɪsəleɪt/ vt aislar. **~ion** /-'leɪʃn/ n aislamiento m
isotope /'aɪsətəʊp/ n isótopo m
Israel /'ɪzreɪl/ n Israel m. **~i** /ɪz'reɪlɪ/ a & n israelí (m)
issue /'ɪʃuː/ n asunto m; (outcome) resultado m; (of magazine etc) número m; (of stamps) emisión f; (offspring) descendencia f. **at ~** en cuestión. **take ~ with** oponerse a. ● vt distribuir; emitir ⟨stamps etc⟩; publicar ⟨book⟩. ● vi. **~ from** salir de

isthmus /'ɪsməs/ n istmo m
it /ɪt/ pron (subject) el, ella, ello; (direct object) lo, la; (indirect object) le; (after preposition) él, ella, ello. **~ is hot** hace calor. **~ is me** soy yo. **far from ~** ni mucho menos. **that's ~** eso es. **who is ~?** ¿quién es?
italic /ɪ'tælɪk/ a bastardillo m. **~s** npl (letra f) bastardilla f
ital|ian /ɪ'tæljən/ a & n italiano (m). **I~y** /'ɪtəlɪ/ n Italia f
itch /ɪtʃ/ n picazón f. ● vi picar. **I'm ~ing to** rabio por. **my arm ~es** me pica el brazo. **~y** a que pica
item /'aɪtəm/ n artículo m; (on agenda) asunto m. **news ~** n noticia f. **~ize** vt detallar
itinerant /aɪ'tɪnərənt/ a ambulante
itinerary /aɪ'tɪnərərɪ/ n itinerario m
its /ɪts/ a su, sus (pl). ● pron (el) suyo m, (la) suya f, (los) suyos mpl, (las) suyas fpl
it's /ɪts/ = **it is, it has**
itself /ɪt'self/ pron él mismo, ella misma, ello mismo; (reflexive) se; (after prep) sí mismo, sí misma
ivory /'aɪvərɪ/ n marfil m. **~ tower** n torre f de marfil
ivy /'aɪvɪ/ n hiedra f

J

jab /dʒæb/ vt (pt jabbed) pinchar; (thrust) hurgonear. ● n pinchazo m
jabber /'dʒæbə(r)/ vi barbullar. ● n farfulla f
jack /dʒæk/ n (mec) gato m; (cards) sota f. ● vt. **~ up** alzar con gato
jackal /'dʒækl/ n chacal m
jackass /'dʒækæs/ n burro m
jackdaw /'dʒækdɔː/ n grajilla f
jacket /'dʒækɪt/ n chaqueta f, saco m (LAm); (of book) sobrecubierta f, camisa f
jack-knife /'dʒæknaɪf/ n navaja f
jackpot /'dʒækpɒt/ n premio m gordo. **hit the ~** sacar el premio gordo
jade /dʒeɪd/ n (stone) jade m
jaded /'dʒeɪdɪd/ a cansado
jagged /'dʒægɪd/ a dentado
jaguar /'dʒægjʊə(r)/ n jaguar m
jail /dʒeɪl/ n cárcel m. **~bird** n criminal m empedernido. **~er** n carcelero m
jalopy /dʒə'lɒpɪ/ n cacharro m

jam¹ /dʒæm/ *vt* (*pt* **jammed**) interferir con ⟨*radio*⟩; ⟨*traffic*⟩ embotellar; ⟨*people*⟩ agolparse en. ● *vi* obstruirse; ⟨*mechanism etc*⟩ atascarse. ● *n* (*of people*) agolpamiento *m*; (*of traffic*) embotellamiento *m*; (*situation, fam*) apuro *m*

jam² /dʒæm/ *n* mermelada *f*

Jamaica /dʒə'meɪkə/ *n* Jamaica *f*

jamboree /dʒæmbə'riː/ *n* reunión *f*

jam-packed /'dʒæm'pækt/ *a* atestado

jangle /'dʒæŋgl/ *n* sonido *m* metálico (y áspero). ● *vt/i* sonar discordemente

janitor /'dʒænɪtə(r)/ *n* portero *m*

January /'dʒænjʊərɪ/ *n* enero *m*

Japan /dʒə'pæn/ *n* el Japón *m*. ~**ese** /dʒæpə'niːz/ *a & n* japonés (*m*)

jar¹ /dʒɑː(r)/ *n* tarro *m*, frasco *m*

jar² /dʒɑː(r)/ *vi* (*pt* **jarred**) ⟨*sound*⟩ sonar mal; ⟨*colours*⟩ chillar. ● *vt* sacudir

jar³ /dʒɑː(r)/ *n*. **on the ~** (*ajar*) entreabierto

jargon /'dʒɑːgən/ *n* jerga *f*

jarring /'dʒɑːrɪŋ/ *a* discorde

jasmine /'dʒæsmɪn/ *n* jazmín *m*

jaundice /'dʒɔːndɪs/ *n* ictericia *f*. ~**d** *a* (*envious*) envidioso; (*bitter*) amargado

jaunt /dʒɔːnt/ *n* excursión *f*

jaunty /'dʒɔːntɪ/ *a* (**-ier, -iest**) garboso

javelin /'dʒævəlɪn/ *n* jabalina *f*

jaw /dʒɔː/ *n* mandíbula *f*. ● *vi* (*talk lengthily, sl*) hablar por los codos

jay /dʒeɪ/ *n* arrendajo *m*. ~**-walk** *vi* cruzar la calle descuidadamente

jazz /dʒæz/ *n* jazz *m*. ● *vt*. ~ **up** animar. ~**y** *a* chillón

jealous /dʒeləs/ *a* celoso. ~**y** *n* celos *mpl*

jeans /dʒiːnz/ *npl* (pantalones *mpl*) vaqueros *mpl*

jeep /dʒiːp/ *n* jeep *m*

jeer /dʒɪə(r)/ *vt/i*. ~ **at** mofarse de, befar; (*boo*) abuchear. ● *n* mofa *f*; (*boo*) abucheo *m*

jell /dʒel/ *vi* cuajar. ~**ied** *a* en gelatina

jelly /dʒelɪ/ *n* jalea *f*. ~**fish** *n* medusa *f*

jeopard|ize /'dʒepədaɪz/ *vt* arriesgar. ~**y** *n* peligro *m*

jerk /dʒɜːk/ *n* sacudida *f*; (*fool, sl*) idiota *m & f*. ● *vt* sacudir. ~**ily** *adv* a sacudidads. ~**y** *a* espasmódico

jersey /'dʒɜːzɪ/ *n* (*pl* **-eys**) jersey *m*

jest /dʒest/ *n* broma *f*. ● *vi* bromear. ~**er** *n* bufón *m*

Jesus /'dʒiːzəs/ *n* Jesús *m*

jet¹ /dʒet/ *n* (*stream*) chorro *m*; (*plane*) yet *m*, avión *m* de propulsión por reacción

jet² /dʒet/ *n* (*mineral*) azabache *m*. ~ **black** *a* de azabache, como el azabache

jet: ~ **lag** *n* cansancio *m* retardado después de un vuelo largo. **have ~ lag** estar desfasado. ~**-propelled** *a* (de propulsión) a reacción

jettison /'dʒetɪsn/ *vt* echar al mar; (*fig, discard*) deshacerse de

jetty /'dʒetɪ/ *n* muelle *m*

Jew /dʒuː/ *n* judío *m*

jewel /'dʒuːəl/ *n* joya *f*. ~**led** *a* enjoyado. ~**ler** *n* joyero *m*. ~**lery** *n* joyas *fpl*

Jew: ~**ess** *n* judía *f*. ~**ish** *a* judío. ~**ry** /'dʒʊərɪ/ *n* los judíos *mpl*

jib¹ /dʒɪb/ *n* (*sail*) foque *m*

jib² /dʒɪb/ *vi* (*pt* **jibbed**) rehusar. ~ **at** oponerse a.

jiffy /'dʒɪfɪ/ *n* momentito *m*. **do sth in a ~** hacer algo en un santiamén

jig /dʒɪg/ *n* (*dance*) giga *f*

jiggle /'dʒɪgl/ *vt* zangolotear

jigsaw /'dʒɪgsɔː/ *n* rompecabezas *m invar*

jilt /dʒɪlt/ *vt* plantar, dejar plantado

jingle /'dʒɪŋgl/ *vt* hacer sonar. ● *vi* tintinear. ● *n* tintineo *m*; (*advert*) anuncio *m* cantado

jinx /dʒɪŋks/ *n* (*person*) gafe *m*; (*spell*) maleficio *m*

jitter|s /'dʒɪtəz/ *npl*. **have the ~s** estar nervioso. ~**y** /-ərɪ/ *a* nervioso. **be ~y** estar nervioso

job /dʒɒb/ *n* trabajo *m*; (*post*) empleo *m*, puesto *m*. **have a ~ doing** costar trabajo hacer. **it is a good ~ that** menos mal que. ~**centre** *n* bolsa *f* de trabajo. ~**less** *a* sin trabajo.

jockey /'dʒɒkɪ/ *n* jockey *m*. ● *vi* (*manoeuvre*) maniobrar (**for** para)

jocular /'dʒɒkjʊlə(r)/ *a* jocoso

jog /dʒɒg/ *vt* (*pt* **jogged**) empujar; refrescar ⟨*memory*⟩. ● *vi* hacer footing. ~**ging** *n* jogging *m*

join /dʒɔɪn/ *vt* unir, juntar; hacerse socio de ⟨*club*⟩; hacerse miembro de ⟨*political group*⟩; alistarse en ⟨*army*⟩; reunirse con ⟨*another person*⟩. ● *vi* ⟨*roads etc*⟩ empalmar; ⟨*rivers*⟩ confluir. ~ **in** participar (en). **~ up** (*mil*) alistarse. ● *n* juntura

joiner /'dʒɔɪnə(r)/ *n* carpintero *m*

joint /dʒɔɪnt/ *a* común. **~ author** *n* coautor *m*. ● *n* (*join*) juntura *f*; (*anat*) articulación *f*; (*culin*) asado *m*; (*place*, *sl*) garito *m*; (*marijuana*, *sl*) cigarillo *m* de marijuana. **out of ~** descoyuntado. **~ly** *adv* conjuntamente

joist /dʒɔɪst/ *n* viga *f*

jok|e /dʒəʊk/ *n* broma *f*; (*funny story*) chiste *m*. ● *vi* bromear. **~er** *n* bromista *m & f*; (*cards*) comodín *m*. **~ingly** *adv* en broma

joll|ification /dʒɒlɪfɪ'keɪʃn/ *n* jolgorio *m*. **~ity** *n* jolgorio *m*. **~y** *a* (**-ier, -iest**) alegre. ● *adv* (*fam*) muy

jolt /dʒɒlt/ *vt* sacudir. ● *vt* (*vehicle*) traquetear. ● *n* sacudida *f*

Jordan /'dʒɔːdən/ *n* Jordania *f*. **~ian** *a & n* /-'deɪnɪən/ jordano (*m*)

jostle /'dʒɒsl/ *vt/i* empujar(se)

jot /dʒɒt/ *n* pizca *f*. ● *vt* (*pt* **jotted**) apuntar. **~ter** *n* bloc *m*

journal /'dʒɜːnl/ *n* (*diary*) diario *m*; (*newspaper*) periódico *m*; (*magazine*) revista *f*. **~ese** /dʒɜːnə'liːz/ *n* jerga *f* periodística. **~ism** *n* periodismo *m*. **~ist** *n* periodista *m & f*

journey /'dʒɜːnɪ/ *n* viaje *m*. ● *vi* viajar

jovial /'dʒəʊvɪəl/ *a* jovial

jowl /dʒaʊl/ *n* (*jaw*) quijada *f*; (*cheek*) mejilla *f*. **cheek by ~** muy cerca

joy /dʒɔɪ/ *n* alegría *f*. **~ful** *a* alegre. **~ride** *n* paseo *m* en coche sin permiso del dueño. **~ous** *a* alegre

jubila|nt /'dʒuːbɪlənt/ *a* jubiloso. **~tion** /-'leɪʃn/ *n* júbilo *m*

jubilee /'dʒuːbɪliː/ *n* aniversario *m* especial

Judaism /'dʒuːdeɪɪzəm/ *n* judaísmo *m*

judder /'dʒʌdə(r)/ *vi* vibrar. ● *n* vibración *f*

judge /dʒʌdʒ/ *n* juez *m*. ● *vt* juzgar. **~ment** *n* juicio *m*

judicia|l /dʒuː'dɪʃl/ *a* judicial. **~ry** *n* magistratura *f*

judicious /dʒuː'dɪʃəs/ *a* juicioso

judo /'dʒuːdəʊ/ *n* judo *m*

jug /dʒʌg/ *n* jarra *f*

juggernaut /'dʒʌgənɔːt/ *n* (*lorry*) camión *m* grande

juggle /'dʒʌgl/ *vt/i* hacer juegos malabares (con). **~r** *n* malabarista *m & f*

juic|e /dʒuːs/ *n* jugo *m*, zumo *m*. **~y** *a* jugoso, zumoso; (*story etc*) (*fam*) picante

juke-box /'dʒuːkbɒks/ *n* tocadiscos *m invar* tragaperras

July /dʒuː'laɪ/ *n* julio

jumble /'dʒʌmbl/ *vt* mezclar. ● *n* (*muddle*) revoltijo *m*. **~ sale** *n* venta *f* de objetos usados, mercadillo *m*

jumbo /'dʒʌmbəʊ/ *a*. **~ jet** *n* jumbo *m*

jump /dʒʌmp/ *vt/i* saltar. **~ the gun** obrar prematuramente. **~ the queue** colarse. ● *vi* saltar; (*start*) asustarse; (*prices*) alzarse. **~ at** apresurarse a aprovechar. ● *n* salto *m*; (*start*) susto *m*; (*increase*) aumento *m*

jumper /'dʒʌmpə(r)/ *n* jersey *m*; (*dress*, *Amer*) mandil *m*, falda *f* con peto

jumpy /'dʒʌmpɪ/ *a* nervioso

junction /'dʒʌŋkʃn/ *n* juntura *f*; (*of roads*) cruce *m*, entronque *m* (*LAm*); (*rail*) empalme *m*, entronque *m* (*LAm*)

juncture /'dʒʌŋktʃə(r)/ *n* momento *m*; (*state of affairs*) coyuntura *f*

June /dʒuːn/ *n* junio *m*

jungle /'dʒʌŋgl/ *n* selva *f*

junior /'dʒuːnɪə(r)/ *a* (*in age*) más joven (**to** que); (*in rank*) subalterno. ● *n* menor *m*. **~ school** *n* escuela *f*

junk /dʒʌŋk/ *n* trastos *mpl* viejos. ● *vt* (*fam*) tirar

junkie /'dʒʌŋkɪ/ *n* (*sl*) drogadicto *m*

junk shop /'dʒʌŋkʃɒp/ *n* tienda *f* de trastos viejos

junta /'dʒʌntə/ *n* junta *f*

jurisdiction /dʒʊərɪs'dɪkʃn/ *n* jurisdicción *f*

jurisprudence /dʒʊərɪs'pruːdəns/ *n* jurisprudencia *f*

juror /'dʒʊərə(r)/ *n* jurado *m*

jury /'dʒʊərɪ/ *n* jurado *m*

just /dʒʌst/ *a* (*fair*) justo. ● *adv* exactamente; (*slightly*) apenas; (*only*) sólo, solamente. **~ as tall** tan alto (**as** como). **~ listen!** ¡escucha! **he has ~ left** acaba de marcharse

justice /'dʒʌstɪs/ *n* justicia *f*. **J~ of the Peace** juez *m* de paz

justif|iable /dʒʌstɪ'faɪəbl/ *a* justificable. **~iably** *adv* con razón. **~ication** /dʒʌstɪfɪ'keɪʃn/ *n* justificación *f*. **~y** /'dʒʌstɪfaɪ/ *vt* justificar

justly /'dʒʌstlɪ/ *adv* con justicia

jut /dʒʌt/ vi (pt **jutted**). ∼ **out** sobresalir

juvenile /'dʒuːvənaɪl/ a juvenil; ⟨childish⟩ infantil. ● n joven m & f. ∼ **court** n tribunal m de menores

juxtapose /dʒʌkstə'pəʊz/ vt yuxtaponer

K

kaleidoscope /kə'laɪdəskəʊp/ n calidoscopio m

kangaroo /kæŋgə'ruː/ n canguro m

kapok /'keɪpɒk/ n miraguano m

karate /kə'rɑːtɪ/ n karate m

kebab /kɪ'bæb/ n broqueta f

keel /kiːl/ n ⟨of ship⟩ quilla f. ● vi. ∼ **over** volcarse

keen /kiːn/ a (**-er, -est**) ⟨interest, feeling⟩ vivo; ⟨wind, mind, analysis⟩ penetrante; ⟨edge⟩ afilado; ⟨appetite⟩ bueno; ⟨eyesight⟩ agudo; ⟨eager⟩ entusiasta. **be** ∼ **on** gustarle a uno. **he's** ∼ **on Shostakovich** le gusta Shostakovich. ∼**ly** adv vivamente; ⟨enthusiastically⟩ con entusiasmo. ∼**ness** n intensidad f; ⟨enthusiasm⟩ entusiasmo m.

keep /kiːp/ vt (pt **kept**) guardar; cumplir ⟨promise⟩; tener ⟨shop, animals⟩; mantener ⟨family⟩; observar ⟨rule⟩; ⟨celebrate⟩ celebrar; ⟨delay⟩ detener; ⟨prevent⟩ impedir. ● vi ⟨food⟩ conservarse; ⟨remain⟩ quedarse. ● n subsistencia f; ⟨of castle⟩ torreón m. **for** ∼**s** ⟨fam⟩ para siempre. ∼ **back** vt retener. ● vi no acercarse. ∼ **in** no dejar salir. ∼ **in with** mantenerse en buenas relaciones con. ∼ **out** no dejar entrar. ∼ **up** mantener. ∼ **up (with)** estar al día (en). ∼**er** n guarda m

keeping /'kiːpɪŋ/ n cuidado m. **in** ∼ **with** de acuerdo con

keepsake /'kiːpseɪk/ n recuerdo m

keg /keg/ n barrilete m

kennel /'kenl/ n perrera f

Kenya /'kenjə/ n Kenia f

kept /kept/ see **keep**

kerb /kɜːb/ n bordillo m

kerfuffle /kə'fʌfl/ n ⟨fuss, fam⟩ lío m

kernel /'kɜːnl/ n almendra f; ⟨fig⟩ meollo m

kerosene /'kerəsiːn/ n queroseno m

ketchup /'ketʃʌp/ n salsa f de tomate

kettle /'ketl/ n hervidor m

key /kiː/ n llave f; ⟨of typewriter, piano etc⟩ tecla f. ● a clave. ● vt. ∼ **up** excitar. ∼**board** n teclado m. ∼**hole** n ojo m de la cerradura. ∼**note** n ⟨mus⟩ tónica f; ⟨speech⟩ idea f fundamental. ∼**ring** n llavero m. ∼**stone** n piedra f clave

khaki /'kɑːkɪ/ a caqui

kibbutz /kɪ'bʊts/ n (pl **-im** /-iːm/ or **-es**) kibbutz m

kick /kɪk/ vt dar una patada a; ⟨animals⟩ tirar una coz a. ● vi dar patadas; ⟨firearm⟩ dar culatazo. ● n patada f; ⟨of animal⟩ coz f; ⟨of firearm⟩ culatazo m; ⟨thrill, fam⟩ placer m. ∼ **out** ⟨fam⟩ echar a patadas. ∼ **up** armar ⟨fuss etc⟩. ∼**back** n culatazo m; ⟨payment⟩ soborno m. ∼**-off** n ⟨sport⟩ saque m inicial

kid /kɪd/ n ⟨young goat⟩ cabrito m; ⟨leather⟩ cabritilla f; ⟨child, sl⟩ chaval m. ● vt (pt **kidded**) tomar el pelo a. ● vi bromear

kidnap /'kɪdnæp/ vt (pt **kidnapped**) secuestrar. ∼**ping** n secuestro m

kidney /'kɪdnɪ/ n riñón m. ● a renal

kill /kɪl/ vt matar; ⟨fig⟩ acabar con. ● n matanza f; ⟨in hunt⟩ pieza(s) f(pl). ∼**er** n matador m; ⟨murderer⟩ asesino m. ∼**ing** n matanza f; ⟨murder⟩ asesinato m. ● a ⟨funny, fam⟩ para morirse de risa; ⟨tiring, fam⟩ agotador. ∼**joy** n aguafiestas m & f invar

kiln /kɪln/ n horno m

kilo /'kiːləʊ/ n (pl **-os**) kilo m

kilogram(me) /'kɪləgræm/ n kilogramo m

kilohertz /'kɪləhɜːts/ n kilohercio m

kilometre /'kɪləmiːtə(r)/ n kilómetro m

kilowatt /'kɪləwɒt/ n kilovatio m

kilt /kɪlt/ n falda f escocesa

kin /kɪn/ n parientes mpl. **next of** ∼ pariente m más próximo, parientes mpl más próximos

kind¹ /kaɪnd/ n clase f. ∼ **of** ⟨somewhat, fam⟩ un poco. **in** ∼ en especie. **be two of a** ∼ ser tal para cual

kind² /kaɪnd/ a amable

kindergarten /'kɪndəgɑːtn/ n escuela f de párvulos

kind-hearted /kaɪnd'hɑːtɪd/ a bondadoso

kindle /'kɪndl/ vt/i encender(se)

kind: ∼**liness** n bondad f. ∼**ly** a (**-ier, -iest**) bondadoso. ● adv bondadosamente; ⟨please⟩ haga el favor de. ∼**ness** n bondad f

kindred /'kɪndrɪd/ a emparentado. ~ **spirits** npl almas fpl afines

kinetic /kɪ'netɪk/ a cinético

king /kɪŋ/ n rey m

kingdom /'kɪŋdəm/ n reino m

kingpin /'kɪŋpɪn/ n (person) persona f clave; (thing) piedra f angular

king-size(d) /'kɪŋsaɪz(d)/ a extraordinariamente grande

kink /kɪŋk/ n (in rope) retorcimiento m; (fig) manía f. ~**y** a (fam) pervertido

kiosk /'kiːɒsk/ n quiosco m. **telephone** ~ cabina f telefónica

kip /kɪp/ n (sl) sueño m. ● vi (pt **kipped**) dormir

kipper /'kɪpə(r)/ n arenque m ahumado

kiss /kɪs/ n beso m. ● vt/i besar(se)

kit /kɪt/ n avíos mpl; (tools) herramientas fpl. ● vt (pt **kitted**). ~ **out** equipar de. ~**bag** n mochila f

kitchen /'kɪtʃɪn/ n cocina f. ~**ette** /kɪtʃɪ'net/ n cocina f pequeña. ~ **garden** n huerto m

kite /kaɪt/ n (toy) cometa f

kith /kɪθ/ n. ~ **and kin** amigos mpl y parientes mpl

kitten /'kɪtn/ n gatito m

kitty /'kɪtɪ/ n (fund) fondo m común

kleptomaniac /kleptəʊ'meɪnɪæk/ n cleptómano m

knack /næk/ n truco m

knapsack /'næpsæk/ n mochila f

knave /neɪv/ n (cards) sota f

knead /niːd/ vt amasar

knee /niː/ n rodilla f. ~**cap** n rótula f

kneel /niːl/ vi (pt **knelt**). ~ **(down)** arrodillarse

knees-up /'niːzʌp/ n (fam) baile m

knell /nel/ n toque m de difuntos

knelt /nelt/ see **kneel**

knew /njuː/ see **know**

knickerbockers /'nɪkəbɒkəz/ npl pantalón m bombacho

knickers /'nɪkəz/ npl bragas fpl

knick-knack /'nɪknæk/ n chuchería f

knife /naɪf/ n (pl **knives**) cuchillo m. ● vt acuchillar

knight /naɪt/ n caballero m; (chess) caballo m. ● vt conceder el título de Sir a. ~**hood** n título m de Sir

knit /nɪt/ vt (pt **knitted** or **knit**) tejer. ● vi hacer punto. ~ **one's brow** fruncir el ceño. ~**ting** n labor f de punto. ~**wear** n artículos mpl de punto

knob /nɒb/ n botón m; (of door, drawer etc) tirador m. ~**bly** a nudoso

knock /nɒk/ vt golpear; (criticize) criticar. ● vi golpear; (at door) llamar. ● n golpe m. ~ **about** vt maltratar. ● vi rodar. ~ **down** derribar; atropellar (person); rebajar (prices). ~ **off** vt hacer caer; (complete quickly, fam) despachar; (steal, sl) birlar. ● vi (finish work, fam) terminar, salir del trabajo. ~ **out** (by blow) dejar sin conocimiento; (eliminate) eliminar; (tire) agotar. ~ **over** tirar; atropellar (person). ~ **up** preparar de prisa (meal etc). ~**down** a (price) de saldo. ~**er** n aldaba f. ~**kneed** a patizambo. ~**out** n (boxing) knock-out m

knot /nɒt/ n nudo m. ● vt (pt **knotted**) anudar. ~**ty** /'nɒtɪ/ a nudoso

know /nəʊ/ vt (pt **knew**) saber; (be acquainted with) conocer. ● vi saber. ● n. **be in the** ~ estar al tanto. ~ **about** entender de (cars etc). ~ **of** saber de. ~**all** n, ~**it-all** (Amer) n sabelotodo m & f. ~**how** n habilidad f. ~**ingly** adv deliberadamente

knowledge /'nɒlɪdʒ/ n conocimiento m; (learning) conocimientos mpl. ~**able** a informado

known /nəʊn/ see **know**. ● a conocido

knuckle /'nʌkl/ n nudillo m. ● vi. ~ **under** someterse

Koran /kə'rɑːn/ n Corán m, Alcorán m

Korea /kə'rɪə/ n Corea f

kosher /'kəʊʃə(r)/ a preparado según la ley judía

kowtow /kaʊ'taʊ/ vi humillarse (**to** ante)

kudos /'kjuːdɒs/ n prestigio m

L

lab /læb/ n (fam) laboratorio m

label /'leɪbl/ n etiqueta f. ● vt (pt **labelled**) poner etiqueta a; (fig, describe as) describir como

laboratory /lə'bɒrətərɪ/ n laboratorio m

laborious /lə'bɔːrɪəs/ a penoso

labour /'leɪbə(r)/ n trabajo m; (workers) mano f de obra. **in** ~ de parto. ● vi trabajar. ● vt insistir en

Labour /'leɪbə(r)/ n el partido m laborista. ● a laborista

laboured /'leɪbəd/ *a* penoso
labourer /'leɪbərə(r)/ *n* obrero *m*; (*on farm*) labriego *m*
labyrinth /'læbərɪnθ/ *n* laberinto *m*
lace /leɪs/ *n* encaje *m*; (*of shoe*) cordón *m*, agujeta *f* (*Mex*). ● *vt* (*fasten*) atar. ~ **with** echar a ⟨a drink⟩
lacerate /'læsəreɪt/ *vt* lacerar
lack /læk/ *n* falta *f*. **for ~ of** por falta de. ● *vt* faltarle a uno. **he ~s money** carece de dinero. **be ~ing** faltar
lackadaisical /lækə'deɪzɪkl/ *a* indolente, apático
lackey /'lækɪ/ *n* lacayo *m*
laconic /lə'kɒnɪk/ *a* lacónico
lacquer /'lækə(r)/ *n* laca *f*
lad /læd/ *n* muchacho *m*
ladder /'lædə(r)/ *n* escalera *f* (de mano); (*in stocking*) carrera *f*. ● *vt* hacer una carrera en. ● *vi* hacerse una carrera
laden /'leɪdn/ *a* cargado (**with** de)
ladle /'leɪdl/ *n* cucharón *m*
lady /'leɪdɪ/ *n* señora *f*. **young ~** señorita *f*. **~bird** *n*, **~bug** *n* (*Amer*) mariquita *f*. **~ friend** *n* amiga *f*. **~-in-waiting** *n* dama *f* de honor. **~like** *a* distinguido. **~ship** *n* Señora *f*
lag[1] /læg/ *vi* (*pt* **lagged**). ~ (**behind**) retrasarse. ● *n* (*interval*) intervalo *m*
lag[2] /læg/ *vt* (*pt* **lagged**) revestir ⟨pipes⟩
lager /'lɑːgə(r)/ *n* cerveza *f* dorada
laggard /'lægəd/ *n* holgazán *m*
lagging /'lægɪŋ/ *n* revestimiento *m* calorífugo
lagoon /lə'guːn/ *n* laguna *f*
lah /lɑː/ *n* (*mus, sixth note of any musical scale*) la *m*
laid /leɪd/ *see* **lay**[1]
lain /leɪn/ *see* **lie**[1]
lair /leə(r)/ *n* guarida *f*
laity /'leɪətɪ/ *n* laicado *m*
lake /leɪk/ *n* lago *m*
lamb /læm/ *n* cordero *m*. **~swool** *n* lana *f* de cordero
lame /leɪm/ *a* (**-er, -est**) cojo; ⟨excuse⟩ poco convincente. **~ly** *adv* (*argue*) con poca convicción *f*
lament /lə'ment/ *n* lamento *m*. ● *vt/i* lamentarse (de). **~able** /'læməntəbl/ *a* lamentable
laminated /'læmɪneɪtɪd/ *a* laminado
lamp /læmp/ *n* lámpara *f*. **~post** *n* farol *m*. **~shade** *n* pantalla *f*
lance /lɑːns/ *n* lanza *f*. ● *vt* (*med*) abrir con lanceta. **~corporal** *n* cabo *m* interino

lancet /'lɑːnsɪt/ *n* lanceta *f*
land /lænd/ *n* tierra *f*; (*country*) país *m*; (*plot*) terreno *m*. ● *a* terrestre; (*breeze*) de tierra; (*policy, reform*) agrario. ● *vt* desembarcar; (*obtain*) conseguir; dar ⟨blow⟩; (*put*) meter. ● *vi* (*from ship*) desembarcar; ⟨aircraft⟩ aterrizar; (*fall*) caer. ~ **up** ir a parar
landed /'lændɪd/ *a* hacendado
landing /'lændɪŋ/ *n* desembarque *m*; (*aviat*) aterrizaje *m*; (*top of stairs*) descanso *m*. **~-stage** *n* desembarcadero *m*
landlady /'lændleɪdɪ/ *n* propietaria *f*; (*of inn*) patrona *f*
land-locked /'lændlɒkt/ *a* rodeado de tierra
landlord /'lændlɔːd/ *n* propietario *m*; (*of inn*) patrón *m*
land: **~mark** *n* punto *m* destacado. **~scape** /'lændskeɪp/ *n* paisaje *m*. ● *vt* ajardinar. **~slide** *n* desprendimiento *m* de tierras; (*pol*) victoria *f* arrolladora
lane /leɪn/ *n* (*path, road*) camino *m*; (*strip of road*) carril *m*; (*aviat*) ruta *f*
language /'læŋgwɪdʒ/ *n* idioma *m*; (*speech, style*) lenguaje *m*
langu|id /'læŋgwɪd/ *a* lánguido. **~ish** /'læŋgwɪʃ/ *vi* languidecer. **~or** /'læŋgə(r)/ *n* languidez *f*
lank /læŋk/ *a* larguirucho; ⟨hair⟩ lacio. **~y** /'læŋkɪ/ *a* (**-ier, -iest**) larguirucho
lantern /'læntən/ *n* linterna *f*
lap[1] /læp/ *n* regazo *m*
lap[2] /læp/ *n* (*sport*) vuelta *f*. ● *vt/i* (*pt* **lapped**). ~ **over** traslapar(se)
lap[3] /læp/ *vt* (*pt* **lapped**). ~ **up** beber a lengüetazos; (*fig*) aceptar con entusiasmo. ● *vi* ⟨waves⟩ chapotear
lapel /lə'pel/ *n* solapa *f*
lapse /læps/ *vi* (*decline*) degradarse; (*expire*) caducar; ⟨time⟩ transcurrir. ~ **into** recaer en. ● *n* error *m*; (*of time*) intervalo *m*
larceny /'lɑːsənɪ/ *n* robo *m*
lard /lɑːd/ *n* manteca *f* de cerdo
larder /'lɑːdə(r)/ *n* despensa *f*
large /lɑːdʒ/ *a* (**-er, -est**) grande, (*before singular noun*) gran. ● *n*. **at ~** en libertad. **~ly** *adv* en gran parte. **~ness** *n* (gran) tamaño *m*
largesse /lɑː'ʒes/ *n* generosidad *f*
lark[1] /lɑːk/ *n* alondra *f*
lark[2] /lɑːk/ *n* broma *f*; (*bit of fun*) travesura *f*. ● *vi* andar de juerga

larva /ˈlɑːvə/ n (pl **-vae** /-viː/) larva f

laryn|gitis /ˌlærɪnˈdʒaɪtɪs/ n laringitis f. **~x** /ˈlærɪŋks/ n laringe f

lascivious /ləˈsɪvɪəs/ a lascivo

laser /ˈleɪzə(r)/ n láser m

lash /læʃ/ vt azotar. **~ out** (spend) gastar. **~ out against** atacar. ● n latigazo m; (eyelash) pestaña f

lashings /ˈlæʃɪŋz/ npl. **~ of** (cream etc, sl) montones de

lass /læs/ n muchacha f

lassitude /ˈlæsɪtjuːd/ n lasitud f

lasso /læˈsuː/ n (pl **-os**) lazo m

last¹ /lɑːst/ a último; ⟨week etc⟩ pasado. **~ Monday** n el lunes pasado. **have the ~ word** decir la última palabra. **the ~ straw** n el colmo m. ● adv por último; (most recently) la última vez. **he came ~** llegó el último. ● n último m; (remainder) lo que queda. **~ but one** penúltimo. **at (long) ~** en fin.

last² /lɑːst/ vi durar. **~ out** sobrevivir

last³ /lɑːst/ n horma f

lasting /ˈlɑːstɪŋ/ a duradero

last: **~ly** adv por último. **~ night** n anoche m

latch /lætʃ/ n picaporte m

late /leɪt/ a (**-er, -est**) (not on time) tarde; (recent) reciente; (former) antiguo, ex; ⟨fruit⟩ tardío; ⟨hour⟩ avanzado; (deceased) difunto. **in ~ July** a fines de julio. **the ~ Dr Phillips** el difunto Dr. Phillips. ● adv tarde. **of ~** últimamente. **~ly** adv últimamente. **~ness** n (delay) retraso m; (of hour) lo avanzado

latent /ˈleɪtnt/ a latente

lateral /ˈlætərəl/ a lateral

latest /ˈleɪtɪst/ a último. **at the ~** a más tardar

lathe /leɪð/ n torno m

lather /ˈlɑːðə(r)/ n espuma f. ● vt enjabonar. ● vi hacer espuma

Latin /ˈlætɪn/ n (lang) latín m. ● a latino

latitude /ˈlætɪtjuːd/ n latitud m

latrine /ləˈtriːn/ n letrina f

latter /ˈlætə(r)/ a último; (of two) segundo. ● n. **the ~** éste m, ésta f, éstos mpl, éstas fpl. **~-day** a moderno. **~ly** adv últimamente

lattice /ˈlætɪs/ n enrejado m

laudable /ˈlɔːdəbl/ a laudable

laugh /lɑːf/ vi reír(se) (**at** de). ● n risa f. **~able** a ridículo. **~ingstock** n hazmerreír m invar. **~ter** n

laugh /ˈlɑːftə(r)/ n (act) risa f; (sound of laughs) risas fpl

launch¹ /lɔːntʃ/ vt lanzar. ● n lanzamiento m. **~ (out) into** lanzarse a

launch² /lɔːntʃ/ n (boat) lancha f

launching pad /ˈlɔːntʃɪŋpæd/ n plataforma f de lanzamiento

laund|er /ˈlɔːndə(r)/ vt lavar (y planchar). **~erette** n lavandería f automática. **~ress** n lavandera f. **~ry** /ˈlɔːndrɪ/ n (place) lavandería f; (dirty clothes) ropa f sucia; (clean clothes) colada f

laurel /ˈlɒrəl/ n laurel m

lava /ˈlɑːvə/ n lava f

lavatory /ˈlævətərɪ/ n retrete m. **public ~** servicios mpl

lavender /ˈlævəndə(r)/ n lavanda f

lavish /ˈlævɪʃ/ a ⟨person⟩ pródigo; (plentiful) abundante; (lush) suntuoso. ● vt prodigar. **~ly** adv profusamente

law /lɔː/ n ley f; (profession, subject of study) derecho m. **~-abiding** a observante de la ley. **~ and order** n orden m público. **~ court** n tribunal m. **~ful** a (permitted by law) lícito; (recognized by law) legítimo. **~fully** adv legalmente. **~less** a sin leyes

lawn /lɔːn/ n césped m. **~-mower** n cortacésped f. **~ tennis** n tenis m (sobre hierba)

lawsuit /ˈlɔːsuːt/ n pleito m

lawyer /ˈlɔɪə(r)/ n abogado m

lax /læks/ a descuidado; ⟨morals etc⟩ laxo

laxative /ˈlæksətɪv/ n laxante m

laxity /ˈlæksətɪ/ n descuido m

lay¹ /leɪ/ vt (pt **laid**) poner ⟨incl table, eggs⟩; tender ⟨trap⟩; formar ⟨plan⟩. **~ hands on** echar mano a. **~ hold of** agarrar. **~ waste** asolar. **~ aside** dejar a un lado. **~ down** dejar a un lado; imponer ⟨condition⟩. **~ into** (sl) dar una paliza a. **~ off** vt despedir ⟨worker⟩. ● vi (fam) terminar. **~ on** (provide) proveer. **~ out** (design) disponer; (display) exponer; desembolsar ⟨money⟩. **~ up** (store) guardar; obligar a guardar cama ⟨person⟩

lay² /leɪ/ a (non-clerical) laico; ⟨opinion etc⟩ profano

lay³ /leɪ/ see **lie**

layabout /ˈleɪəbaʊt/ n holgazán m

lay-by /ˈleɪbaɪ/ n apartadero m

layer /ˈleɪə(r)/ n capa f

layette /leɪˈet/ n canastilla f

layman /'leɪmən/ n lego m
lay-off /'leɪɒf/ n paro m forzoso
layout /'leɪaʊt/ n disposición f
laze /leɪz/ vi holgazanear; (relax) descansar
laz|iness /'leɪzɪnɪs/ n pereza f. ~y a perezoso. ~y-bones n holgazán m
lb. abbr (pound) libra f
lead[1] /liːd/ vt (pt led) conducir; dirigir ⟨team⟩; llevar ⟨life⟩; (induce) inducir a. ● vi (go first) ir delante; ⟨road⟩ ir, conducir; (in cards) salir. ● n mando m; (clue) pista f; (leash) correa f; (in theatre) primer papel m; (wire) cable m; (example) ejemplo m. **in the** ~ en cabeza. ~ **away** llevar. ~ **up to** preparar el terreno para
lead[2] /led/ n plomo m; (of pencil) mina f. ~**en** /'ledn/ a de plomo
leader /'liːdə(r)/ n jefe m; (leading article) editorial m. ~**ship** n dirección f
leading /'liːdɪŋ/ a principal; (in front) delantero. ~ **article** n editorial m
leaf /liːf/ n (pl leaves) hoja f. ● vi. ~ **through** hojear
leaflet /'liːflɪt/ n folleto m
leafy /'liːfɪ/ a frondoso
league /liːg/ n liga f. **be in** ~ **with** conchabarse con
leak /liːk/ n (hole) agujero m; (of gas, liquid) escape m; (of information) filtración f; (in roof) gotera f; (in boat) vía f de agua. ● vi ⟨receptacle, gas, liquid⟩ salirse; (information) filtrarse; (drip) gotear; ⟨boat⟩ hacer agua. ● vt dejar escapar; filtrar (information). ~**age** n = leak. ~**y** a ⟨receptacle⟩ agujereado; ⟨roof⟩ que tiene goteras; ⟨boat⟩ que hace agua
lean[1] /liːn/ vt (pt leaned or leant /lent/) apoyar. ● vi inclinarse. ~ **against** apoyarse en. ~ **on** apoyarse en. ~**out** asomarse (of a). ~ **over** inclinarse
lean[2] /liːn/ a (-er, -est) magro. ● n carne f magra
leaning /'liːnɪŋ/ a inclinado. ● n inclinación f
leanness /'liːnnɪs/ n (of meat) magrez f; (of person) flaqueza f
lean-to /'liːntuː/ n colgadizo m
leap /liːp/ vi (pt leaped or leapt /lept/) saltar. ● n salto m. ~**-frog** n salto m, saltacabrilla f. ● vi (pt -frogged) jugar a saltacabrilla. ~ **year** n año m bisiesto

learn /lɜːn/ vt/i (pt **learned** or **learnt**) aprender (**to do** a hacer). ~**ed** /'lɜːnɪd/ a culto. ~**ing** /'lɜːnə(r)/ n principiante m; (apprentice) aprendiz m; (student) estudiante m & f. ~**ing** n saber m
lease /liːs/ n arriendo m. ● vt arrendar
leash /liːʃ/ n correa f
least /liːst/ a. **the** ~ (smallest amount of) mínimo; (slightest) menor; (smallest) más pequeño. ● n lo menos. **at** ~ por lo menos. **not in the** ~ en absoluto. ● adv menos
leather /'leðə(r)/ n piel f, cuero m
leave /liːv/ vt (pt **left**) dejar; (depart from) marcharse de. ~ **alone** dejar de tocar ⟨thing⟩; dejar en paz ⟨person⟩. **be left (over)** quedar. ● vi marcharse; ⟨train⟩ salir. ● n permiso m. **on** ~ (mil) de permiso. **take one's** ~ **of** despedirse de. ~ **out** omitir
leavings /'liːvɪŋz/ npl restos mpl
Leban|on /'lebənən/ n el Líbano m. ~**ese** /-'niːz/ a & n libanés (m)
lecher /'letʃə(r)/ n libertino m. ~**ous** a lascivo. ~**y** n lascivia f
lectern /'lektɜːn/ n atril m; (in church) facistol m
lecture /'lektʃə(r)/ n conferencia f; (univ) clase f; (rebuke) sermón m. ● vt/i dar una conferencia (a); (univ) dar clases (a); (rebuke) sermonear. ~**r** n conferenciante m; (univ) profesor m
led /led/ see **lead**[1]
ledge /ledʒ/ n repisa f, (of window) antepecho m
ledger /'ledʒə(r)/ n libro m mayor
lee /liː/ n sotavento m; (fig) abrigo m
leech /liːtʃ/ n sanguijuela f
leek /liːk/ n puerro m
leer /'lɪə(r)/ vi. ~ **(at)** mirar impúdicamente. ● n mirada f impúdica
leeway /'liːweɪ/ n deriva f; (fig, freedom of action) libertad f de acción. **make up** ~ recuperar los atrasos
left[1] /left/ a izquierdo. ● adv a la izquierda. ● n izquierda f
left[2] /left/ see **leave**
left: ~**-hand** a izquierdo. ~**-handed** a zurdo. ~**ist** n izquierdista m & f. ~**luggage** n consigna f. ~**-overs** npl restos mpl
left-wing /left'wɪŋ/ a izquierdista
leg /leg/ n pierna f; (of animal, furniture) pata f; (of pork) pernil m; (of

lamb) pierna *f*; (*of journey*) etapa *f*.
on its last ~s en las últimas
legacy /'legəsɪ/ *n* herencia *f*
legal /'li:gl/ *a* (*permitted by law*)
lícito; (*recognized by law*) legítimo;
⟨*affairs etc*⟩ jurídico. ~ **aid** *n* abogacía *f* de pobres. ~**ity** /-'gælətɪ/ *n*
legalidad *f*. ~**ize** *vt* legalizar. ~**ly**
adv legalmente
legation /lɪ'geɪʃn/ *n* legación *f*
legend /'ledʒənd/ *n* leyenda *f*. ~**ary**
a legendario
leggings /'legɪŋz/ *npl* polainas *fpl*
legib|ility /'ledʒəbɪlətɪ/ *n* legibilidad
f. ~**le** *a* legible. ~**ly** *a* legiblemente
legion /'li:dʒən/ *n* legión *f*
legislat|e /'ledʒɪsleɪt/ *vi* legislar.
~**ion** /-'leɪʃn/ *n* legislación *f*. ~**ive**
a legislativo. ~**ure** /-eɪtʃə(r)/ *n*
cuerpo *m* legislativo
legitima|cy /lɪ'dʒɪtɪməsɪ/ *f* legitimidad *f*. ~**te** *a* legítimo
leisure /'leʒə(r)/ *n* ocio *m*. **at one's**
~ cuando tenga tiempo. ~**ly** *adv* sin
prisa
lemon /'lemən/ *n* limón *m*. ~**ade**
/lemə'neɪd/ *n* (*fizzy*) gaseosa *f* (de
limón); (*still*) limonada *f*
lend /lend/ *vt* (*pt* lent) prestar. ~ **itself to** prestarse a. ~**er** *n* prestador
m; (*moneylender*) prestamista *m* & *f*.
~**ing** *n* préstamo *m*. ~**ing library** *n*
biblioteca *f* de préstamo
length /leŋθ/ *n* largo *m*; (*in time*)
duración *f*; (*of cloth*) largo *m*; (*of
road*) tramo *m*. **at** ~ (*at last*) por fin.
at (great) ~ detalladamente. ~**en**
/'leŋθən/ *vt* alargar. ● *vi* alargarse.
~**ways** *adv* a lo largo. ~**y** *a* largo
lenien|cy /'li:nɪənsɪ/ *n* indulgencia
f. ~**t** *a* indulgente. ~**tly** *adv* con
indulgencia
lens /lenz/ *n* lente *f*. **contact** ~**es** *npl*
lentillas *fpl*
lent /lent/ *see* **lend**
Lent /lent/ *n* cuaresma *f*
lentil /'lentl/ *n* (*bean*) lenteja *f*
Leo /'li:əʊ/ *n* (*astr*) Leo *m*
leopard /'lepəd/ *n* leopardo *m*
leotard /'li:ətɑ:d/ *n* leotardo *m*
lep|er /'lepə(r)/ *n* leproso *m*. ~**rosy**
/'leprəsɪ/ *n* lepra *f*
lesbian /'lezbɪən/ *n* lesbiana *f*. ● *a*
lesbiano
lesion /'li:ʒn/ *n* lesión *f*
less /les/ *a* (*in quantity*) menos; (*in
size*) menor. ● *adv & prep* menos. ~
than menos que; (*with numbers*)

menos de. ● *n* menor *m*. ~ **and** ~
cada vez menos. **none the** ~ sin embargo. ~**en** /'lesn/ *vt/i* disminuir.
~**er** /'lesə(r)/ *a* menor
lesson /'lesn/ *n* clase *f*
lest /lest/ *conj* por miedo de que
let /let/ *vt* (*pt* let, *pres p* letting) dejar; (*lease*) alquilar. ~ **me do it**
déjame hacerlo. ● *v aux*. ~**'s go!**
¡vamos!, ¡vámonos! ~**'s see** (vamos)
a ver. ~**'s talk/drink** hablemos/bebamos. ● *n* alquiler *m*. ~
down bajar; (*deflate*) desinflar; (*fig*)
defraudar. ~ **go** soltar. ~ **in** dejar
entrar. ~ **off** disparar ⟨*gun*⟩; (*cause
to explode*) hacer explotar; hacer estallar ⟨*firework*⟩; (*excuse*) perdonar.
~ **off steam** (*fig*) desfogarse. ~ **on**
(*sl*) revelar. ~ **o.s. in for** meterse en.
~ **out** dejar salir. ~ **through** dejar
pasar. ~ **up** disminuir. ~-**down** *n*
desilusión *f*
lethal /'li:θl/ *a* ⟨*dose, wound*⟩ mortal;
⟨*weapon*⟩ mortífero
letharg|ic /lɪ'tɑ:dʒɪk/ *a* letárgico.
~**y** /'leθədʒɪ/ *n* letargo *m*
letter /'letə(r)/ *n* (*of alphabet*) letra *f*;
(*written message*) carta *f*. ~-**bomb** *n*
carta *f* explosiva. ~-**box** *n* buzón *m*.
~-**head** *n* membrete *m*. ~**ing** *n* letras *fpl*
lettuce /'letɪs/ *n* lechuga *f*
let-up /'letʌp/ *n* (*fam*) descanso *m*
leukaemia /lu:'ki:mɪə/ *n* leucemia *f*
level /'levl/ *a* (*flat*) llano; (*on surface*)
horizontal; (*in height*) a nivel; (*in
score*) igual; ⟨*spoonful*⟩ raso. ~ *n*
nivel *m*. **be on the** ~ (*fam*) ser honrado. ● *vt* (*pt* levelled) nivelar; (*aim*)
apuntar. ~ **crossing** *n* paso *m* a
nivel. ~-**headed** *a* juicioso
lever /'li:və(r)/ *n* palanca *f*. ● *vt* apalancar. ~**age** /'li:vərɪdʒ/ *n* apalancamiento *m*
levity /'levətɪ/ *n* ligereza *f*
levy /'levɪ/ *vt* exigir ⟨*tax*⟩. ● *n* impuesto *m*
lewd /lu:d/ *a* (**-er, -est**) lascivo
lexicography /leksɪ'kɒgrəfɪ/ *n* lexicografía *f*
lexicon /'leksɪkən/ *n* léxico *m*
liable /'laɪəbl/ *a*. **be** ~ **to do** tener
tendencia a hacer. ~ **for** responsable
de. ~ **to** susceptible de; expuesto a
⟨*fine*⟩
liability /laɪə'bɪlətɪ/ *n* responsabilidad *f*; (*disadvantage, fam*) inconveniente *m*. **liabilities** *npl* (*debts*)
deudas *fpl*

liais|e /lɪˈeɪz/ vi hacer un enlace, enlazar. **~on** /lɪˈeɪzɒn/ n enlace m; (love affair) lío m

liar /ˈlaɪə(r)/ n mentiroso m

libel /ˈlaɪbl/ n libelo m. ● vt (pt libelled) difamar (por escrito)

Liberal /ˈlɪbərəl/ a & n liberal (m & f)

liberal /ˈlɪbərəl/ a liberal; (generous) generoso; (tolerant) tolerante. **~ly** adv liberalmente; (generously) generosamente; (tolerantly) tolerantemente

liberat|e /ˈlɪbəreɪt/ vt liberar. **~ion** /-ˈreɪʃn/ n liberación f

libertine /ˈlɪbətiːn/ n libertino m

liberty /ˈlɪbətɪ/ n libertad f. **be at ~ to** estar autorizado para. **take liberties** tomarse libertades. **take the ~ of** tomarse la libertad de

libido /lɪˈbiːdəʊ/ n (pl -os) libido m

Libra /ˈliːbrə/ n (astr) Libra f

librar|ian /laɪˈbreərɪən/ n bibliotecario m. **~y** /ˈlaɪbrərɪ/ n biblioteca f

libretto /lɪˈbretəʊ/ n (pl -os) libreto m

Libya /ˈlɪbɪə/ n Libia f. **~n** a & n libio (m)

lice /laɪs/ see **louse**

licence /ˈlaɪsns/ n licencia f, permiso m; (fig, liberty) libertad f. **~ plate** n (placa f de) matrícula f. **driving ~** carné m de conducir

license /ˈlaɪsns/ vt autorizar

licentious /laɪˈsenʃəs/ a licencioso

lichen /ˈlaɪkən/ n liquen m

lick /lɪk/ vt lamer; (defeat, sl) dar una paliza a. **~ one's chops** relamerse. ● n lametón m

licorice /ˈlɪkərɪs/ n (Amer) regaliz m

lid /lɪd/ n tapa f; (of pan) cobertera f

lido /ˈliːdəʊ/ n (pl -os) piscina f

lie[1] /laɪ/ vi (pt lay, pp lain, pres p lying) echarse; (state) estar echado; (remain) quedarse; (be) estar, encontrarse; (in grave) yacer. **be lying** estar echado. **~ down** acostarse. **~ low** quedarse escondido

lie[2] /laɪ/ n mentira f. ● vi (pt lied, pres p lying) mentir. **give the ~ to** desmentir

lie-in /laɪˈm/ n. **have a ~-in** quedarse en la cama

lieu /ljuː/ n. **in ~ of** en lugar de

lieutenant /lefˈtenənt/ n (mil) teniente m

life /laɪf/ n (pl lives) vida f. **~belt** n cinturón m salvavidas. **~boat** n lancha f de salvamento; (on ship) bote m

salvavidas. **~buoy** n boya f salvavidas. **~ cycle** n ciclo m vital. **~guard** n bañero m. **~jacket** n chaleco m salvavidas. **~less** a sin vida. **~like** a natural. **~line** n cuerda f salvavidas; (fig) cordón m umbilical. **~long** a de toda la vida. **~size(d)** a de tamaño natural. **~time** n vida f

lift /lɪft/ vt levantar; (steal, fam) robar. ● vi (fog) disiparse. ● n ascensor m, elevador m (LAm). **give a ~ to s.o.** llevar a uno en su coche, dar aventón a uno (LAm). **~off** n (aviat) despegue m

ligament /ˈlɪgəmənt/ n ligamento m

light[1] /laɪt/ n luz f; (lamp) lámpara f, luz f; (flame) fuego m; (headlight) faro m. **bring to ~** sacar a luz. **come to ~** salir a luz. **have you got a ~?** ¿tienes fuego? **the ~s** npl (auto, traffic signals) el semáforo m. ● a claro. ● vt (pt lit or lighted) encender; (illuminate) alumbrar. **~ up** vt/i iluminar(se)

light[2] /laɪt/ a (-er, -est) (not heavy) ligero

lighten[1] /ˈlaɪtn/ vt (make less heavy) aligerar

lighten[2] /ˈlaɪtn/ vt (give light to) iluminar; (make brighter) aclarar

lighter /ˈlaɪtə(r)/ n (for cigarettes) mechero m

light-fingered /laɪtˈfɪŋgəd/ a largo de uñas

light-headed /laɪtˈhedɪd/ a (dizzy) mareado; (frivolous) casquivano

light-hearted /laɪtˈhɑːtɪd/ a alegre

lighthouse /ˈlaɪthaʊs/ n faro m

lighting /ˈlaɪtɪŋ/ n (system) alumbrado m; (act) iluminación f

light: **~ly** adv ligeramente. **~ness** n ligereza f

lightning /ˈlaɪtnɪŋ/ n relámpago m. ● a relámpago

lightweight /ˈlaɪtweɪt/ a ligero. ● n (boxing) peso m ligero

light-year /ˈlaɪtjɪə(r)/ n año m luz

like[1] /laɪk/ a parecido. ● prep como. ● conj (fam) como. ● n igual. **the ~s of you** la gente como tú

like[2] /laɪk/ vt gustar le (a uno). **I ~ chocolate** me gusta el chocolate. **I should ~** quisiera. **they ~ swimming** (a ellos) les gusta nadar. **would you ~?** ¿quieres? **~able** a simpático. **~s** npl gustos mpl

likelihood /ˈlaɪklɪhʊd/ n probabilidad f

likely *a* (-ier, -iest) probable. **he is ~ to come** es probable que venga. ● *adv* probablemente. **not ~!** ¡ni hablar!

like-minded /laɪk'maɪndɪd/ *a*. **be ~** tener las mismas opiniones

liken /'laɪkən/ *vt* comparar

likeness /'laɪknɪs/ *n* parecido *m*. **be a good ~** parecerse mucho

likewise /'laɪkwaɪz/ *adv* (*also*) también; (*the same way*) lo mismo

liking /'laɪkɪŋ/ *n* (*for thing*) afición *f*; (*for person*) simpatía *f*

lilac /'laɪlək/ *n* lila *f*. ● *a* color de lila

lilt /lɪlt/ *n* ritmo *m*

lily /'lɪlɪ/ *n* lirio *m*. **~ of the valley** lirio *m* de los valles

limb /lɪm/ *n* miembro *m*. **out on a ~** aislado

limber /'lɪmbə(r)/ *vi*. **~ up** hacer ejercicios preliminares

limbo /'lɪmbəʊ/ *n* limbo *m*. **be in ~** (*forgotten*) estar olvidado

lime[1] /laɪm/ *n* (*white substance*) cal *f*

lime[2] /laɪm/ *n* (*fruit*) lima *f*

lime[3] /laɪm/ *n*. **~(-tree)** (*linden tree*) tilo *m*

limelight /'laɪmlaɪt/ *n*. **be in the ~** estar muy a la vista

limerick /'lɪmərɪk/ *n* quintilla *f* humorística

limestone /'laɪmstəʊn/ *n* caliza *f*

limit /'lɪmɪt/ *n* límite *m*. ● *vt* limitar. **~ation** /-'teɪʃn/ *n* limitación *f*. **~ed** *a* limitado. **~ed company** *n* sociedad *f* anónima

limousine /'lɪməziːn/ *n* limusina *f*

limp[1] /lɪmp/ *vi* cojear. ● *n* cojera *f*. **have a ~** cojear

limp[2] /lɪmp/ *a* (-er, -est) flojo

limpid /'lɪmpɪd/ *a* límpido

linctus /'lɪŋktəs/ *n* jarabe *m* (para la tos)

line[1] /laɪn/ *n* línea *f*; (*track*) vía *f*; (*wrinkle*) arruga *f*; (*row*) fila *f*; (*of poem*) verso *m*; (*rope*) cuerda *f*; (*of goods*) surtido *m*; (*queue*, *Amer*) cola *f*. **in ~ with** de acuerdo con. ● *vt* (*on paper etc*) rayar; bordear ‹*streets etc*›. **~ up** alinearse; (*in queue*) hacer cola

line[2] /laɪn/ *vt* forrar; (*fill*) llenar

lineage /'lɪnɪɪdʒ/ *n* linaje *m*

linear /'lɪnɪə(r)/ *a* lineal

linen /'lɪnɪn/ *n* (*sheets etc*) ropa *f* blanca; (*material*) lino *m*

liner /'laɪnə(r)/ *n* transatlántico *m*

linesman /'laɪnzmən/ *n* (*football*) juez *m* de línea

linger /'lɪŋgə(r)/ *vi* tardar en marcharse; ‹*smells etc*› persistir. **~ over** dilatarse en

lingerie /'læñərɪ/ *n* ropa *f* interior, lencería *f*

lingo /'lɪŋgəʊ/ *n* (*pl* -os) idioma *m*; (*specialized vocabulary*) jerga *f*

linguist /'lɪŋgwɪst/ *n* (*specialist in languages*) políglota *m* & *f*; (*specialist in linguistics*) lingüista *m* & *f*. **~ic** /lɪŋ'gwɪstɪk/ *a* lingüístico. **~ics** *n* lingüística *f*

lining /'laɪnɪŋ/ *n* forro *m*; (*auto, of brakes*) guarnición *f*

link /lɪŋk/ *n* (*of chain*) eslabón *m*; (*fig*) lazo *m*. ● *vt* eslabonar; (*fig*) enlazar. **~ up with** reunirse con. **~age** *n* enlace *m*

links /lɪŋks/ *n invar* campo *m* de golf

lino /'laɪnəʊ/ *n* (*pl* -os) linóleo *m*. **~leum** /lɪ'nəʊlɪəm/ *n* linóleo *m*

lint /lɪnt/ *n* (*med*) hilas *fpl*; (*fluff*) pelusa *f*

lion /'laɪən/ *n* león *m*. **the ~'s share** la parte *f* del león. **~ess** *n* leona *f*

lionize /'laɪənaɪz/ *vt* tratar como una celebridad

lip /lɪp/ *n* labio *m*; (*edge*) borde *m*. **pay ~ service to** aprobar de boquilla. **stiff upper ~** *n* imperturbabilidad *f*. **~-read** *vt/i* leer en los labios. **~salve** *n* crema *f* para los labios. **~stick** *n* lápiz *m* de labios.

liquefy /'lɪkwɪfaɪ/ *vt/i* licuar(se)

liqueur /lɪ'kjʊə(r)/ *n* licor *m*

liquid /'lɪkwɪd/ *a* & *n* líquido (*m*)

liquidat|e /'lɪkwɪdeɪt/ *vt* liquidar. **~ion** /-'deɪʃn/ *n* liquidación *f*

liquidize /'lɪkwɪdaɪz/ *vt* licuar. **~r** *n* licuadora *f*

liquor /'lɪkə(r)/ *n* bebida *f* alcohólica

liquorice /'lɪkərɪs/ *n* regaliz *m*

lira /'lɪərə/ *n* (*pl* lire /'lɪəreɪ/ or liras) lira *f*

lisle /laɪl/ *n* hilo *m* de Escocia

lisp /lɪsp/ *n* ceceo *m*. **speak with a ~** cecear. ● *vi* cecear

lissom /'lɪsəm/ *a* flexible, ágil

list[1] /lɪst/ *n* lista *f*. ● *vt* hacer una lista de; (*enter in a list*) inscribir

list[2] /lɪst/ *vi* ‹*ship*› escorar

listen /'lɪsn/ *vi* escuchar. **~ in (to)** escuchar. **~ to** escuchar. **~er** *n* oyente *m* & *f*

listless /'lɪstlɪs/ *a* apático

lit /lɪt/ *see* **light**[1]

litany /'lɪtənɪ/ *n* letanía *f*

literacy /'lɪtərəsɪ/ n capacidad f de leer y escribir

literal /'lɪtərəl/ a literal; (fig) prosaico. ~**ly** adv al pie de la letra, literalmente

literary /'lɪtərərɪ/ a literario

literate /'lɪtərət/ a que sabe leer y escribir

literature /'lɪtərətʃə(r)/ n literatura f; (fig) impresos mpl

lithe /laɪð/ a ágil

lithograph /'lɪθəgrɑːf/ n litografía f

litigation /lɪtɪ'geɪʃn/ n litigio m

litre /'liːtə(r)/ n litro m

litter /'lɪtə(r)/ n basura f; (of animals) camada f. ● vt ensuciar; (scatter) esparcir. ~**ed with** lleno de. ~**bin** n papelera f

little /'lɪtl/ a pequeño; (not much) poco de. ● n poco m. **a** ~ un poco. **a** ~ **water** un poco de agua. ● adv poco. ~ **by** ~ poco a poco. ~ **finger** n meñique m

liturgy /'lɪtədʒɪ/ n liturgia f

live[1] /lɪv/ vt/i vivir. ~ **down** lograr borrar. ~ **it up** echar una cana al aire. ~ **on** (feed o.s. on) vivir de; (continue) perdurar. ~ **up to** vivir de acuerdo con; cumplir ⟨a promise⟩

live[2] /laɪv/ a vivo; (wire) con corriente; ⟨broadcast⟩ en directo. **be a** ~ **wire** ser una persona enérgica

livelihood /'laɪvlɪhʊd/ n sustento m

livel|iness /'laɪvlɪnɪs/ n vivacidad f. ~**y** a (-ier, -iest) vivo

liven /'laɪvn/ vt/i. ~ **up** animar(se); (cheer up) alegrar(se)

liver /'lɪvə(r)/ n hígado m

livery /'lɪvərɪ/ n librea f

livestock /'laɪvstɒk/ n ganado m

livid /'lɪvɪd/ a lívido; (angry, fam) furioso

living /'lɪvɪŋ/ a vivo. ● n vida f. ~**room** n cuarto m de estar, cuarto m de estancia (LAm)

lizard /'lɪzəd/ n lagartija f; (big) lagarto m

llama /'lɑːmə/ n llama f

load /ləʊd/ n (incl elec) carga f; (quantity) cantidad f; (weight, strain) peso m. ● vt cargar. ~**ed** a ⟨incl dice⟩ cargado; (wealthy, sl) muy rico. ~**s of** (fam) montones de

loaf[1] /ləʊf/ n (pl loaves) pan m; (stick of bread) barra f

loaf[2] /ləʊf/ vi. ~ (**about**) holgazanear. ~**er** n holgazán m

loam /ləʊm/ n marga f

loan /ləʊn/ n préstamo m. **on** ~ prestado. ● vt prestar

loath /ləʊθ/ a poco dispuesto (**to** a)

loath|e /ləʊð/ vt odiar. ~**ing** n odio m (**of** a). ~**some** a odioso

lobby /'lɒbɪ/ n vestíbulo m; (pol) grupo m de presión. ● vt hacer presión sobre

lobe /ləʊb/ n lóbulo m

lobster /'lɒbstə(r)/ n langosta f

local /'ləʊkl/ a local. ● n (pub, fam) bar m. **the** ~**s** los vecinos mpl

locale /ləʊ'kɑːl/ n escenario m

local government /ləʊkl'gʌvənmənt/ n gobierno m municipal

locality /ləʊ'kælətɪ/ n localidad f

localized /'ləʊkəlaɪzd/ a localizado

locally /'ləʊkəlɪ/ adv localmente; (nearby) en la localidad

locate /ləʊ'keɪt/ vt (situate) situar; (find) encontrar

location /ləʊ'keɪʃn/ n colocación f; (place) situación f. **on** ~ fuera del estudio. **to film on** ~ **in Andalusia** rodar en Andalucía

lock[1] /lɒk/ n (of door etc) cerradura f; (on canal) esclusa f. ● vt/i cerrar(se) con llave. ~ **in** encerrar. ~ **out** cerrar la puerta a. ~ **up** encerrar

lock[2] /lɒk/ n (of hair) mechón m. ~**s** npl pelo m

locker /'lɒkə(r)/ n armario m

locket /'lɒkɪt/ n medallón m

lock-out /'lɒkaʊt/ n lock-out m

locksmith /'lɒksmɪθ/ n cerrajero m

locomotion /ləʊkə'məʊʃn/ n locomoción f

locomotive /ləʊkə'məʊtɪv/ n locomotora f

locum /'ləʊkəm/ n interino m

locust /'ləʊkəst/ n langosta f

lodge /lɒdʒ/ n (in park) casa f del guarda; (of porter) portería f. ● vt alojar; presentar ⟨complaint⟩; depositar ⟨money⟩. ● vi alojarse. ~**r** /-ə(r)/ n huésped m

lodgings /'lɒdʒɪŋz/ n alojamiento m; (room) habitación f

loft /lɒft/ n desván m

lofty /'lɒftɪ/ a (-ier, -iest) elevado; (haughty) altanero

log /lɒg/ n (of wood) leño m; (naut) cuaderno m de bitácora. **sleep like a** ~ dormir como un lirón. ● vt (pt **logged**) apuntar; (travel) recorrer

logarithm /'lɒgərɪðəm/ n logaritmo m

log-book /'lɒgbʊk/ n cuaderno m de bitácora; (aviat) diario m de vuelo

loggerheads /'lɒgəhedz/ npl. **be at ~ with** estar a matar con

logic /'lɒdʒɪk/ a lógica f. **~al** a lógico. **~ally** adv lógicamente

logistics /lə'dʒɪstɪks/ n logística f

logo /'ləʊgəʊ/ n (pl **-os**) logotipo m

loin /lɔɪn/ n (culin) solomillo m. **~s** npl ijadas fpl

loiter /'lɔɪtə(r)/ vi holgazanear

loll /lɒl/ vi repantigarse

loll‖ipop /'lɒlɪpɒp/ n (boiled sweet) piruli m. **~y** n (iced) polo m; (money, sl) dinero m

London /'lʌndən/ n Londres m. ● a londinense. **~er** n londinense m & f

lone /ləʊn/ a solitario. **~ly** /'ləʊnlɪ/ a (-ier, -iest) solitario. **feel ~ly** sentirse muy solo. **~r** /'ləʊnə(r)/ n solitario m. **~some** a solitario

long¹ /lɒŋ/ a (-er, -est) largo. **a ~ time** mucho tiempo. **how ~ is it?** ¿cuánto tiene de largo? **in the ~ run** a la larga. ● adv largo/mucho tiempo. **as ~ as** (while) mientras; (provided that) con tal que (+ subjunctive). **before ~** dentro de poco. **so ~!** ¡hasta luego! **so ~ as** (provided that) con tal que (+ subjunctive)

long² /lɒŋ/ vi. **~ for** anhelar

long-distance /lɒŋ'dɪstəns/ a de larga distancia. **~ (tele)phone call** n conferencia f

longer /'lɒŋgə(r)/ adv. **no ~er** ya no

longevity /lɒn'dʒevətɪ/ n longevidad f

long: **~ face** n cara f triste. **~hand** n escritura f a mano. **~ johns** npl (fam) calzoncillos mpl largos. **~ jump** n salto m de longitud

longing /'lɒŋɪŋ/ n anhelo m, ansia f

longitude /'lɒŋgɪtjuːd/ n longitud f

long: **~-playing record** n elepé m. **~-range** a de gran alcance. **~-sighted** a présbita. **~-standing** a de mucho tiempo. **~-suffering** a sufrido. **~-term** a a largo plazo. **~-wave** n onda f larga. **~-winded** a (speaker etc) prolijo

loo /luː/ n (fam) servicios mpl

look /lʊk/ vt mirar; (seem) parecer; representar (age). ● vi mirar; (seem) parecer; (search) buscar. ● n mirada f; (appearance) aspecto m. **~ after** ocuparse de; cuidar (person). **~ at** mirar. **~ down on** despreciar. **~ for** buscar. **~ forward to** esperar con ansia. **~ in on** pasar por casa de. **~ into** investigar. **~ like** (resemble) parecerse a. **~ on to** (room, window) dar a. **~ out** tener cuidado. **~ out for** buscar; (watch) tener cuidado con. **~ round** volver la cabeza. **~ through** hojear. **~ up** buscar (word); (visit) ir a ver. **~ up to** respetar. **~er-on** n espectador m. **~ing-glass** n espejo m. **~-out** n (mil) atalaya f; (person) vigía m. **~s** npl belleza f. **good ~s** mpl belleza f

loom¹ /luːm/ n telar m

loom² /luːm/ vi aparecerse

loony /'luːnɪ/ a & n (sl) chiflado (m) (fam), loco (m). **~ bin** n (sl) manicomio m

loop /luːp/ n lazo m. ● vt hacer presilla con

loophole /'luːphəʊl/ n (in rule) escapatoria f

loose /luːs/ a (-er, -est) (untied) suelto; (not tight) flojo; (inexact) vago; (immoral) inmoral; (not packed) suelto. **be at a ~ end, be at ~ ends** (Amer) no tener nada que hacer. **~ly** adv sueltamente; (roughly) aproximadamente. **~n** /'luːsn/ vt (slacken) aflojar; (untie) desatar

loot /luːt/ n botín m. ● vt saquear. **~er** n saqueador m. **~ing** n saqueo m

lop /lɒp/ vt (pt **lopped**). **~ off** cortar

lop-sided /lɒp'saɪdɪd/ a ladeado

loquacious /ləʊ'kweɪʃəs/ a locuaz

lord /lɔːd/ n señor m; (British title) lord m. **(good) L~!** ¡Dios mío! **the L~** el Señor m. **the (House of) L~s** la Cámara f de los Lores. **~ly** señorial; (haughty) altivo. **~ship** n señoría f

lore /lɔː(r)/ n tradiciones fpl

lorgnette /lɔː'njet/ n impertinentes mpl

lorry /'lɒrɪ/ n camión m

lose /luːz/ vt/i (pt **lost**) perder. **~r** n perdedor m

loss /lɒs/ n pérdida f. **be at a ~** estar perplejo. **be at a ~ for words** no encontrar palabras. **be at a ~ to** no saber cómo

lost /lɒst/ see **lose**. ● a perdido. **~ property** n, **~ and found** (Amer) n oficina f de objetos perdidos. **get ~** perderse

lot /lɒt/ n (fate) suerte f; (at auction) lote m; (land) solar m. **a ~ (of)** muchos. **quite a ~ of** (fam) bastante. **~s (of)** (fam) muchos. **the ~** todos mpl

lotion /'ləʊʃn/ n loción f

lottery /'lɒtərɪ/ n lotería f

lotto /'lɒtəʊ/ n lotería f

lotus /'ləʊtəs/ n (pl -uses) loto m

loud /laʊd/ a (-er, -est) fuerte; (noisy) ruidoso; (gaudy) chillón. **out ~** en voz alta. **~ hailer** n megáfono m. **~ly** adv (speak etc) en voz alta; (noisily) ruidosamente. **~speaker** n altavoz m

lounge /laʊndʒ/ vi repantigarse. ● n salón m. **~ suit** n traje m de calle

louse /laʊs/ n (pl lice) piojo m

lousy /'laʊzɪ/ a (-ier, -iest) piojoso; (bad, sl) malísimo

lout /laʊt/ n patán m

lovable /'lʌvəbl/ a adorable

love /lʌv/ n amor m; (tennis) cero m. **be in ~ with** estar enamorado de. **fall in ~ with** enamorarse de. ● vt querer (person); gustarle mucho a uno, encantarle a uno (things). **I ~ milk** me encanta la leche. **~ affair** n amores mpl

lovely /'lʌvlɪ/ a (-ier, -iest) hermoso; (delightful, fam) precioso. **have a ~ time** divertirse

lover /'lʌvə(r)/ n amante m & f

lovesick /'lʌvsɪk/ a atortolado

loving /'lʌvɪŋ/ a cariñoso

low¹ /ləʊ/ a & adv (-er, -est) bajo. ● n (low pressure) área f de baja presión

low² /ləʊ/ vi mugir

lowbrow /'ləʊbraʊ/ a poco culto

low-cut /'ləʊkʌt/ a escotado

low-down /'ləʊdaʊn/ a bajo. ● n (sl) informes mpl

lower /'ləʊə(r)/ a & adv see **low²**. ● vt bajar. **~ o.s.** envilecerse

low-key /'ləʊ'kiː/ a moderado

lowlands /'ləʊləndz/ npl tierra f baja

lowly /'ləʊlɪ/ a (-ier, -iest) humilde

loyal /'lɔɪəl/ a leal. **~ly** adv lealmente. **~ty** n lealtad f

lozenge /'lɒzɪndʒ/ n (shape) rombo m; (tablet) pastilla f

LP /el'piː/ abbr (long-playing record) elepé m

Ltd /'lɪmɪtɪd/ abbr (Limited) S.A., Sociedad Anónima

lubrica|nt /'luːbrɪkənt/ n lubricante m. **~te** /-'keɪt/ vt lubricar. **~tion** /-'keɪʃn/ n lubricación f

lucid /'luːsɪd/ a lúcido. **~ity** /-'sɪdətɪ/ n lucidez f

luck /lʌk/ n suerte f. **bad ~** n mala suerte f. **~ily** /'lʌkɪlɪ/ adv afortunadamente. **~y** a (-ier, -iest) afortunado

lucrative /'luːkrətɪv/ a lucrativo

lucre /'luːkə(r)/ n (pej) dinero m. **filthy ~** vil metal m

ludicrous /'luːdɪkrəs/ a ridículo

lug /lʌg/ vt (pt lugged) arrastrar

luggage /'lʌgɪdʒ/ n equipaje m. **~ rack** n rejilla f. **~-van** n furgón m

lugubrious /luː'guːbrɪəs/ a lúgubre

lukewarm /'luːkwɔːm/ a tibio

lull /lʌl/ vt (soothe, send to sleep) adormecer; (calm) calmar. ● n periodo m de calma

lullaby /'lʌləbaɪ/ n canción f de cuna

lumbago /lʌm'beɪgəʊ/ n lumbago m

lumber /'lʌmbə(r)/ n trastos mpl viejos; (wood) maderos mpl. ● vt. **s.o. with** hacer que uno cargue con. **~jack** n leñador m

luminous /'luːmɪnəs/ a luminoso

lump¹ /lʌmp/ n protuberancia f; (in liquid) grumo m; (of sugar) terrón m; (in throat) nudo m. ● vt. **~ together** agrupar

lump² /lʌmp/ vt. **~ it** (fam) aguantarlo

lump: ~ sum n suma f global. **~y** a (sauce) grumoso; (bumpy) cubierto de protuberancias

lunacy /'luːnəsɪ/ n locura f

lunar /'luːnə(r)/ a lunar

lunatic /'luːnətɪk/ n loco m

lunch /lʌntʃ/ n comida f, almuerzo m. ● vi comer

luncheon /'lʌntʃən/ n comida f, almuerzo m. **~ meat** n carne f en lata. **~ voucher** n vale m de comida

lung /lʌŋ/ n pulmón m

lunge /lʌndʒ/ n arremetida f

lurch¹ /lɜːtʃ/ vi tambalearse

lurch² /lɜːtʃ/ n. **leave in the ~** dejar en la estacada

lure /ljʊə(r)/ vt atraer. ● n (attraction) atractivo m

lurid /'ljʊərɪd/ a chillón; (shocking) espeluznante

lurk /lɜːk/ vi esconderse; (in ambush) estar al acecho; (prowl) rondar

luscious /'lʌʃəs/ a delicioso

lush /lʌʃ/ a exuberante. ● n (Amer, sl) borracho m

lust /lʌst/ n lujuria f; (fig) ansia f. ● vi. **~ after** codiciar. **~ful** a lujurioso

lustre /'lʌstə(r)/ n lustre m
lusty /'lʌstɪ/ a (**-ier, -iest**) fuerte
lute /luːt/ n laúd m
Luxemburg /'lʌksəmbɜːg/ n Luxemburgo m
luxuriant /lʌg'zjʊərɪənt/ a exuberante
luxur|ious /lʌg'zjʊərɪəs/ a lujoso. ~**y** /'lʌkʃərɪ/ n lujo m. ● a de lujo
lye /laɪ/ n lejía f
lying /'laɪɪŋ/ see **lie**[1], **lie**[2]. ● n mentiras fpl
lynch /lɪntʃ/ vt linchar
lynx /lɪŋks/ n lince m
lyre /'laɪə(r)/ n lira f
lyric /'lɪrɪk/ a lírico. ~**al** a lírico. ~**ism** /-sɪzəm/ n lirismo m. ~**s** npl letra f

M

MA abbr (Master of Arts) Master m, grado m universitario entre el de licenciado y doctor
mac /mæk/ n (fam) impermeable m
macabre /mə'kɑːbrə/ a macabro
macaroni /mækə'rəʊnɪ/ n macarrones mpl
macaroon /mækə'ruːn/ n mostachón m
mace[1] /meɪs/ n (staff) maza f
mace[2] /meɪs/ n (spice) macis f
Mach /mɑːk/ n. ~ (**number**) n (número m de) Mach (m)
machiavellian /mækɪə'velɪən/ a maquiavélico
machinations /mækɪ'neɪʃnz/ npl maquinaciones fpl
machine /mə'ʃiːn/ n máquina f. ● vt (sew) coser a máquina; (tec) trabajar a máquina. ~**gun** n ametralladora f. ~**ry** /mə'ʃiːnərɪ/ n maquinaria f; (working parts, fig) mecanismo m. ~**tool** n máquina f herramienta
machinist /mə'ʃiːnɪst/ n maquinista m & f
mach|ismo /mæ'tʃɪzməʊ/ n machismo m. ~**o** a macho
mackerel /'mækrəl/ n invar (fish) caballa f
mackintosh /'mækɪntɒʃ/ n impermeable m
macrobiotic /mækrəʊbaɪ'ɒtɪk/ a macrobiótico
mad /mæd/ a (**madder, maddest**) loco; (foolish) insensato; ⟨dog⟩ rabioso; (angry, fam) furioso. **be** ~

about estar loco por. **like** ~ como un loco; (a lot) muchísimo
Madagascar /mædə'gæskə(r)/ n Madagascar m
madam /'mædəm/ n señora f; (unmarried) señorita f
madcap /'mædkæp/ a atolondrado. ● n locuelo m
madden /'mædn/ vt (make mad) enloquecer; (make angry) enfurecer
made /meɪd/ see **make**. ~ **to measure** hecho a la medida
Madeira /mə'dɪərə/ n (wine) vino m de Madera
mad: ~**house** n manicomio m. ~**ly** adv (interested, in love etc) locamente; (frantically) como un loco. ~**man** n loco m. ~**ness** n locura f
madonna /mə'dɒnə/ n Virgen f María
madrigal /'mædrɪgl/ n madrigal m
maelstrom /'meɪlstrəm/ n remolino m
maestro /'maɪstrəʊ/ n (pl **maestri** /-striː/ or os) maestro m
Mafia /'mæfɪə/ n mafia f
magazine /mægə'ziːn/ n revista f; (of gun) recámara f
magenta /mə'dʒentə/ a rojo purpúreo
maggot /'mægət/ n gusano m. ~**y** a agusanado
Magi /'meɪdʒaɪ/ npl. the ~ los Reyes mpl Magos
magic /'mædʒɪk/ n magia f. ● a mágico. ~**al** a mágico. ~**ian** /mə'dʒɪʃn/ n mago m
magisterial /mædʒɪ'stɪərɪəl/ a magistral; (imperious) autoritario
magistrate /'mædʒɪstreɪt/ n magistrado m, juez m
magnanim|ity /mægnə'nɪmətɪ/ n magnanimidad f. ~**ous** /-'nænməs/ a magnánimo
magnate /'mægneɪt/ n magnate m
magnesia /mæg'niːʒə/ n magnesia f
magnet /'mægnɪt/ n imán m. ~**ic** /-'netɪk/ a magnético. ~**ism** n magnetismo m. ~**ize** vt magnetizar
magnificen|ce /mæg'nɪfɪsns/ a magnificencia f. ~**t** a magnífico
magnif|ication /mægnɪfɪ'keɪʃn/ n aumento m. ~**ier** /-'faɪə(r)/ n lupa f, lente f de aumento. ~**y** /-faɪ/ vt aumentar. ~**ying-glass** n lupa f, lente f de aumento
magnitude /'mægnɪtjuːd/ n magnitud f

magnolia /mæg'nəʊlɪə/ *n* magnolia *f*

magnum /'mægnəm/ *n* botella *f* de litro y medio

magpie /'mægpaɪ/ *n* urraca *f*

mahogany /mə'hɒgənɪ/ *n* caoba *f*

maid /meɪd/ *n* (*servant*) criada *f*; (*girl, old use*) doncella *f*. **old** ~ solterona *f*

maiden /'meɪdn/ *n* doncella *f*. ● *a* (*aunt*) soltera; (*voyage*) inaugural. ~**hood** *n* doncellez *f*, virginidad *f*, soltería *f*. ~**ly** *adv* virginal. ~ **name** *n* apellido *m* de soltera

mail[1] /meɪl/ *n* correo *m*; (*letters*) cartas *fpl*. ● *a* postal, de correos. ● *vt* (*post*) echar al correo; (*send*) enviar por correo

mail[2] /meɪl/ *n* (*armour*) (cota *f* de) malla *f*

mail: ~**ing list** *n* lista *f* de direcciones. ~**man** *n* (*Amer*) cartero *m*. ~ **order** *n* venta *f* por correo

maim /meɪm/ *vt* mutilar

main /meɪn/ *n*. (**water/gas**) ~ cañería *f* principal. **in the** ~ en su mayor parte. **the** ~**s** *npl* (*elec*) la red *f* eléctrica. ● *a* principal. **a** ~ **road** *n* una carretera *f*. ~**land** *n* continente *m*. ~**ly** *adv* principalmente. ~ **spring** *n* muelle *m* real; (*fig, motive*) móvil *m* principal. ~**stay** *n* sostén *m*. ~**stream** *n* corriente *f* principal. ~ **street** *n* calle *f* principal

maintain /meɪn'teɪn/ *vt* mantener

maintenance /'meɪntənəns/ *n* mantenimiento *m*; (*allowance*) pensión *f* alimenticia

maisonette /meɪzə'net/ *n* (*small house*) casita *f*; (*part of house*) dúplex *m*

maize /meɪz/ *n* maíz *m*

majestic /mə'dʒestɪk/ *a* majestuoso

majesty /'mædʒəstɪ/ *n* majestad *f*

major /'meɪdʒə(r)/ *a* mayor. **a** ~ **road** una calle *f* prioritaria. ● *n* comandante *m*. ● *vi*. ~ **in** (*univ, Amer*) especializarse en

Majorca /mə'jɔːkə/ *n* Mallorca *f*

majority /mə'dʒɒrətɪ/ *n* mayoría *f*. **the** ~ **of people** la mayoría *f* de la gente. ● *a* mayoritario

make /meɪk/ *vt/i* (*pt* **made**) hacer; (*manufacture*) fabricar; ganar (*money*); tomar (*decision*); llegar a (*destination*). ~ **s.o. do sth** obligar a uno a hacer algo. **be made of** estar hecho de. **I cannot** ~ **anything of it** no me lo explico. **I** ~ **it two o'clock** yo tengo las dos. ● *n* fabricación *f*; (*brand*) marca *f*. ~ **as if to** estar a punto de. ~ **believe** fingir. ~ **do** (*manage*) arreglarse. ~ **do with** (*content o.s.*) contentarse con. ~ **for** dirigirse a. ~ **good** *vi* tener éxito. ● *vt* compensar; (*repair*) reparar. ~ **it** llegar; (*succeed*) tener éxito. ~ **it up** (*become reconciled*) hacer las paces. ~ **much of** dar mucha importancia a. ~ **off** escaparse (**with** con). ~ **out** *vt* distinguir; (*understand*) entender; (*draw up*) extender; (*assert*) dar a entender. ● *vi* arreglárselas. ~ **over** ceder (**to** a). ~ **up** (*prepare*) preparar; inventar (*story*); (*compensate*) compensar. ● *vi* hacer las paces. ~ **up** (**one's face**) maquillarse. ~ **up for** compensar; recuperar (*time*). ~ **up to** congraciarse con. ~**believe** *a* fingido, simulado. ● *n* ficción *f*

maker /'meɪkə(r)/ *n* fabricante *m* & *f*. **the M**~ el Hacedor *m*, el Creador *m*

makeshift /'meɪkʃɪft/ *n* expediente *m*. ● *a* (*temporary*) provisional; (*improvised*) improvisado

make-up /'meɪkʌp/ *n* maquillaje *m*

makeweight /'meɪkweɪt/ *n* complemento *m*

making /'meɪkɪŋ/ *n*. **be the** ~ **of** ser la causa del éxito de. **he has the** ~**s of** tiene madera de. **in the** ~ en vías de formación

maladjust|ed /mælə'dʒʌstɪd/ *a* inadaptado. ~**ment** *n* inadaptación *f*

maladministration /mæləd mɪnɪ'streɪʃn/ *n* mala administración *f*

malady /'mælədɪ/ *n* enfermedad *f*

malaise /mæ'leɪz/ *n* malestar *m*

malaria /mə'leərɪə/ *n* paludismo *m*

Malay /mə'leɪ/ *a & n* malayo (*m*). ~**sia** *n* Malasia *f*

male /meɪl/ *a* masculino; (*bot, tec*) macho. ● *n* macho *m*; (*man*) varón *m*

malefactor /'mælɪfæktə(r)/ *n* malhechor *m*

malevolen|ce /mə'levəlns/ *n* malevolencia *f*. ~**t** *a* malévolo

malform|ation /mælfɔː'meɪʃn/ *n* malformación *f*. ~**ed** *a* deforme

malfunction /mæl'fʌŋkʃn/ *n* funcionamiento *m* defectuoso. ● *vi* funcionar mal

malic|e /'mælɪs/ *n* rencor *m*. **bear s.o.** ~**e** guardar rencor a uno. ~**ious**

/mə'lɪʃəs/ *a* malévolo. ∼**iously** *adv*
con malevolencia

malign /mə'laɪn/ *a* maligno. ● *vt*
calumniar

malignan|cy /mə'lɪgnənsɪ/ *n* mali-
gnidad *f*. ∼**t** *a* maligno

malinger /mə'lɪŋgə(r)/ *vi* fingirse
enfermo. ∼**er** *n* enfermo *m* fingido

malleable /'mælɪəbl/ *a* maleable

mallet /'mælɪt/ *n* mazo *m*

malnutrition /mælnju:'trɪʃn/ *n* des-
nutrición *f*

malpractice /mæl'præktɪs/ *n* falta *f*
profesional

malt /mɔ:lt/ *n* malta *f*

Malt|a /'mɔ:ltə/ *n* Malta *f*. ∼**ese**
/-'ti:z/ *a* & *n* maltés (*m*)

maltreat /mæl'tri:t/ *vt* maltratar.
∼**ment** *n* maltrato *m*

malt whisky /mɔ:lt'wɪskɪ/ *n* güisqui
m de malta

mammal /'mæml/ *n* mamífero *m*

mammoth /'mæməθ/ *n* mamut *m*.
● *a* gigantesco

man /mæn/ *n* (*pl* **men**) hombre *m*; (*in
sports team*) jugador *m*; (*chess*) pieza
f. ∼ **in the street** hombre *m* de la
calle. ∼ **to** ∼ de hombre a hombre.
● *vt* (*pt* **manned**) guarnecer (de hombres); tripular ⟨*ship*⟩; servir ⟨*guns*⟩

manacle /'mænəkl/ *n* manilla *f*. ● *vt*
poner esposas a

manage /'mænɪdʒ/ *vt* dirigir; llevar
⟨*shop, affairs*⟩; (*handle*) manejar.
● *vi* arreglárselas. ∼ **to do** lograr
hacer. ∼**able** *a* manejable. ∼**ment** *n*
dirección *f*

manager /'mænɪdʒə(r)/ *n* director
m; (*of actor*) empresario *m*. ∼**ess**
/-'res/ *n* directora *f*. ∼**ial** /-'dʒɪərɪəl/
a directivo. ∼**ial staff** *n* personal *m*
dirigente

managing director /mænɪdʒɪŋ daɪ-
'rektə(r)/ *n* director *m* gerente

mandarin /'mændərɪn/ *n* mandarín
m; (*orange*) mandarina *f*

mandate /'mændeɪt/ *n* mandato *m*

mandatory /'mændətərɪ/ *a* obligatorio

mane /meɪn/ *n* (*of horse*) crin *f*; (*of
lion*) melena *f*

manful /'mænfl/ *a* valiente

manganese /'mæŋgəni:z/ *n* man-
ganeso *m*

manger /'meɪndʒə(r)/ *n* pesebre *m*

mangle[1] /'mæŋgl/ *n* (*for wringing*)
exprimidor *m*; (*for smoothing*) máquina *f* de planchar

mangle[2] /'mæŋgl/ *vt* destrozar

mango /'mæŋgəʊ/ *n* (*pl* **-oes**) mango
m

mangy /'meɪndʒɪ/ *a* sarnoso

man: ∼**handle** *vt* maltratar. ∼**hole**
n registro *m*. ∼**hole cover** *n* tapa *f*
de registro. ∼**hood** *n* edad *f* viril;
(*quality*) virilidad *f*. ∼**-hour** *n* hora-
hombre *f*. ∼**-hunt** *n* persecución *f*

mania /'meɪnɪə/ *n* manía *f*. ∼**c**
/-ɪæk/ *n* maníaco *m*

manicur|e /'mænɪkjʊə(r)/ *n* mani-
cura *f*. ● *vt* hacer la manicura a ⟨*person*⟩. ∼**ist** *n* manicuro *m*

manifest /'mænɪfest/ *a* manifiesto.
● *vt* mostrar. ∼**ation** /-'steɪʃn/ *n*
manifestación *f*

manifesto /mænɪ'festəʊ/ *n* (*pl* **-os**)
manifiesto *m*

manifold /'mænɪfəʊld/ *a* múltiple

manipulat|e /mə'nɪpjʊleɪt/ *vt* mani-
pular. ∼**ion** /-'leɪʃn/ *n* manipulación *f*

mankind /mæn'kaɪnd/ *n* la humanidad *f*

man: ∼**ly** *adv* viril. ∼**-made** *a*
artificial

mannequin /'mænɪkɪn/ *n* maniquí
m

manner /'mænə(r)/ *n* manera *f*; (*behaviour*) comportamiento *m*; (*kind*)
clase *f*. ∼**ed** *a* amanerado. **bad-**∼**ed**
a mal educado. ∼**s** *npl* (*social behaviour*) educación *f*. **have no** ∼**s** no
tener educación

mannerism /'mænərɪzəm/ *n* peculiaridad *f*

mannish /'mænɪʃ/ *a* ⟨*woman*⟩ hom-
bruna

manoeuvre /mə'nu:və(r)/ *n* maniobra *f*. ● *vt/i* maniobrar

man-of-war /mænəv'wɔ:(r)/ *n*
buque *m* de guerra

manor /'mænə(r)/ *n* casa *f* solariega

manpower /'mænpaʊə(r)/ *n* mano *f*
de obra

manservant /'mænsɜ:vənt/ *n* criado *m*

mansion /'mænʃn/ *n* mansión *f*

man: ∼**-size(d)** *a* grande. ∼**slaughter** *n* homicidio *m* impremeditado

mantelpiece /'mæntlpi:s/ *n* repisa *f*
de chimenea

mantilla /mæn'tɪlə/ *n* mantilla *f*

mantle /'mæntl/ *n* manto *m*

manual /'mænjʊəl/ *a* manual. ● *n*
(*handbook*) manual *m*

manufacture /mænjʊ'fæktʃə(r)/ *vt*
fabricar. ● *n* fabricación *f*. ∼**r** /-ə(r)/
n fabricante *m*

manure /məˈnjʊə(r)/ n estiércol m

manuscript /ˈmænjʊskrɪpt/ n manuscrito m

many /ˈmenɪ/ a & n muchos (mpl). ∼ **people** mucha gente f. ∼ **a time** muchas veces. **a great/good** ∼ muchísimos

map /mæp/ n mapa m; (of streets etc) plano m. ● vt (pt **mapped**) levantar un mapa de. ∼ **out** organizar

maple /ˈmeɪpl/ n arce m

mar /mɑː/ vt (pt **marred**) estropear; aguar ⟨enjoyment⟩

marathon /ˈmærəθən/ n maratón m

maraud|er /məˈrɔːdə(r)/ n merodeador m. ∼**ing** a merodeador

marble /ˈmɑːbl/ n mármol m; (for game) canica f

March /mɑːtʃ/ n marzo m

march /mɑːtʃ/ vi (mil) marchar. ∼ **off** irse. ● vt. ∼ **off** (lead away) llevarse. ● n marcha f

marchioness /mɑːʃəˈnes/ n marquesa f

march-past /ˈmɑːtʃpɑːst/ n desfile m

mare /meə(r)/ n yegua f

margarine /mɑːdʒəˈriːn/ n margarina f

margin /ˈmɑːdʒɪn/ n margen f. ∼**al** a marginal. ∼**al seat** n (pol) escaño m inseguro. ∼**ally** adv muy poco

marguerite /mɑːgəˈriːt/ n margarita f

marigold /ˈmærɪgəʊld/ n caléndula f

marijuana /mærɪˈhwɑːnə/ n marihuana f

marina /məˈriːnə/ n puerto m deportivo

marina|de /mærɪˈneɪd/ n escabeche m. ∼**te** /ˈmærɪneɪt/ vt escabechar

marine /məˈriːn/ a marino. ● n (sailor) soldado m de infantería de marina; (shipping) marina f

marionette /mærɪəˈnet/ n marioneta f

marital /ˈmærɪtl/ a marital, matrimonial. ∼ **status** n estado m civil

maritime /ˈmærɪtaɪm/ a marítimo

marjoram /ˈmɑːdʒərəm/ n mejorana f

mark[1] /mɑːk/ n marca f; (trace) huella f; (schol) nota f; (target) blanco m. ● vt marcar; poner nota a ⟨exam⟩. ∼ **time** marcar el paso. ∼ **out** trazar; escoger ⟨person⟩

mark[2] /mɑːk/ n (currency) marco m

marked /mɑːkt/ a marcado. ∼**ly** /-kɪdlɪ/ adv marcadamente

marker /ˈmɑːkə(r)/ n marcador m; (for book) registro m

market /ˈmɑːkɪt/ n mercado m. **on the** ∼ en venta. ● vt (sell) vender; (launch) comercializar. ∼ **garden** n huerto m. ∼**ing** n marketing m

marking /ˈmɑːkɪŋ/ n (marks) marcas fpl

marksman /ˈmɑːksmən/ n tirador m. ∼**ship** n puntería f

marmalade /ˈmɑːməleɪd/ n mermelada f de naranja

marmot /ˈmɑːmət/ n marmota f

maroon /məˈruːn/ n granate m. ● a de color granate

marooned /məˈruːnd/ a abandonado; (snow-bound etc) aislado

marquee /mɑːˈkiː/ n tienda de campaña f grande; (awning, Amer) marquesina f

marquetry /ˈmɑːkɪtrɪ/ n marquetería f

marquis /ˈmɑːkwɪs/ n marqués m

marriage /ˈmærɪdʒ/ n matrimonio m; (wedding) boda f. ∼**able** a casadero

married /ˈmærɪd/ a casado; ⟨life⟩ conjugal

marrow /ˈmærəʊ/ n (of bone) tuétano m; (vegetable) calabacín m

marry /ˈmærɪ/ vt casarse con; (give or unite in marriage) casar. ● vi casarse. **get married** casarse

marsh /mɑːʃ/ n pantano m

marshal /ˈmɑːʃl/ n (mil) mariscal m; (master of ceremonies) maestro m de ceremonias; (at sports events) oficial m. ● vt (pt **marshalled**) ordenar; formar ⟨troops⟩

marsh mallow /mɑːʃˈmæləʊ/ n (plant) malvavisco m

marshmallow /mɑːʃˈmæləʊ/ n (sweet) caramelo m blando

marshy /ˈmɑːʃɪ/ a pantanoso

martial /ˈmɑːʃl/ a marcial. ∼ **law** n ley f marcial

Martian /ˈmɑːʃn/ a & n marciano (m)

martinet /mɑːtɪˈnet/ n ordenancista m & f

martyr /ˈmɑːtə(r)/ n mártir m & f. ● vt martirizar. ∼**dom** n martirio m

marvel /ˈmɑːvl/ n maravilla f. ● vi (pt **marvelled**) maravillarse (**at** con, de). ∼**lous** /ˈmɑːvələs/ a maravilloso

Marxis|m /'mɑ:ksɪzəm/ n marxismo m. ~t a & n marxista (m & f)

marzipan /'mɑ:zɪpæn/ n mazapán m

mascara /mæ'skɑ:rə/ n rimel m

mascot /'mæskɒt/ n mascota f

masculin|e /'mæskjʊlɪn/ a & n masculino (m). ~ity /-'lɪnɪtɪ/ n masculinidad f

mash /mæʃ/ n mezcla f; (potatoes, fam) puré m de patatas. ● vt (crush) machacar; (mix) mezclar. ~ed potatoes n puré m de patatas

mask /mɑ:sk/ n máscara f. ● vt enmascarar

masochis|m /'mæsəkɪzəm/ n masoquismo m. ~t n masoquista m & f

mason /'meɪsn/ n (builder) albañil m

Mason /'meɪsn/ n. ~ masón m. ~ic /mə'sɒnɪk/ a masónico

masonry /'meɪsnrɪ/ n albañilería f

masquerade /mɑ:skə'reɪd/ n mascarada f. ● vi. ~ as hacerse pasar por

mass[1] /mæs/ n masa f; (large quantity) montón m. **the ~es** npl las masas fpl. ● vt/i agrupar(se)

mass[2] /mæs/ n (relig) misa f. **high ~** misa f mayor

massacre /'mæsəkə(r)/ n masacre f, matanza f. ● vt masacrar

massage /'mæsɑ:ʒ/ n masaje m. ● vt dar masaje a

masseu|r /mæ'sɜ:(r)/ n masajista m. ~se /mæ'sɜ:z/ n masajista f

massive /'mæsɪv/ a masivo; (heavy) macizo; (huge) enorme

mass: ~ **media** n medios mpl de comunicación. ~**produce** vt fabricar en serie

mast /mɑ:st/ n mástil m; (for radio, TV) torre f

master /'mɑ:stə(r)/ n maestro m; (in secondary school) profesor m; (of ship) capitán m. ● vt dominar. ~**key** n llave f maestra. ~**ly** a magistral. ~**mind** n cerebro m. ● vt dirigir. **M~ of Arts** master m, grado m universitario entre el de licenciado y el de doctor

masterpiece /'mɑ:stəpi:s/ n obra f maestra

master-stroke /'mɑ:stəstrəʊk/ n golpe m maestro

mastery /'mɑ:stərɪ/ n dominio m; (skill) maestría f

masturbat|e /'mæstəbeɪt/ vi masturbarse. ~**ion** /-'beɪʃn/ n masturbación f

mat /mæt/ n estera f; (at door) felpudo m

match[1] /mætʃ/ n (sport) partido m; (equal) igual m; (marriage) matrimonio m; (s.o. to marry) partido m. ● vt emparejar; (equal) igualar; (clothes, colours) hacer juego con. ● vi hacer juego

match[2] /mætʃ/ n (of wood) fósforo m; (of wax) cerilla f. ~**box** /'mætʃbɒks/ n (for wooden matches) caja f de fósforos; (for wax matches) caja f de cerillas

matching /'mætʃɪŋ/ a que hace juego

mate[1] /meɪt/ n compañero m; (of animals) macho m, hembra f; (assistant) ayudante m. ● vt/i acoplar(se)

mate[2] /meɪt/ n (chess) mate m

material /mə'tɪərɪəl/ n material m; (cloth) tela f. ● a material; (fig) importante. ~**istic** /-'lɪstɪk/ a materialista. ~**s** npl materiales mpl. **raw ~s** npl materias fpl primas

materialize /mə'tɪərɪəlaɪz/ vi materializarse

maternal /mə'tɜ:nl/ a maternal; (relation) materno

maternity /mə'tɜ:nɪtɪ/ n maternidad f. ● a de maternidad. ~ **clothes** npl vestido m pre-mamá. ~ **hospital** n maternidad f

matey /'meɪtɪ/ a (fam) simpático

mathematic|ian /mæθəmə'tɪʃn/ n matemático m. ~**al** /-'mætɪkl/ a matemático. ~**s** /-'mætɪks/ n & npl matemáticas fpl

maths /mæθs/, **math** (Amer) n & npl matemáticas fpl

matinée /'mætɪneɪ/ n función f de tarde

matriculat|e /mə'trɪkjʊleɪt/ vt/i matricular(se). ~**ion** /-'leɪʃn/ n matriculación f

matrimon|ial /mætrɪ'məʊnɪəl/ a matrimonial. ~**y** /'mætrɪmənɪ/ n matrimonio m

matrix /'meɪtrɪks/ n (pl **matrices** /-si:z/) matriz f

matron /'meɪtrən/ n (married, elderly) matrona f; (in school) ama f de llaves; (former use, in hospital) enfermera f jefe. ~**ly** a matronil

matt /mæt/ a mate

matted /'mætɪd/ a enmarañado

matter /'mætə(r)/ n (substance) materia f; (affair) asunto m; (pus) pus *m.* **as a ~ of fact** en realidad. **no ~** no importa. **what is the ~?** ¿qué pasa? ● *vi* importar. **it does not ~** no importa. **~-of-fact** *a* realista

matting /'mætɪŋ/ *n* estera *f*

mattress /'mætrɪs/ *n* colchón *m*

matur|e /məˈtjʊə(r)/ *a* maduro. ● *vt/i* madurar. **~ity** *n* madurez *f*

maul /mɔːl/ *vt* maltratar

Mauritius /məˈrɪʃəs/ *n* Mauricio *m*

mausoleum /mɔːsəˈlɪəm/ *n* mausoleo *m*

mauve /məʊv/ *a & n* color (*m*) de malva

mawkish /'mɔːkɪʃ/ *a* empalagoso

maxim /'mæksɪm/ *n* máxima *f*

maxim|ize /'mæksɪmaɪz/ *vt* llevar al máximo. **~um** *a & n* (*pl* **-ima**) máximo (*m*)

may /meɪ/ *v aux* (*pt* **might**) poder. ~ **I smoke?** ¿se permite fumar? ~ **he be happy** ¡que sea feliz! **he ~/might come** puede que venga. **I ~/might as well stay** más vale quedarme. **it ~/ might be true** puede ser verdad

May /meɪ/ *n* mayo *m*. ~ **Day** *n* el primero *m* de mayo

maybe /'meɪbɪ/ *adv* quizá(s)

mayhem /'meɪhem/ *n* (*havoc*) alboroto *m*

mayonnaise /meɪəˈneɪz/ *n* mayonesa *f*

mayor /meə(r)/ *n* alcalde *m*, alcaldesa *f*. **~ess** *n* alcaldesa *f*

maze /meɪz/ *n* laberinto *m*

me[1] /miː/ *pron* me; (*after prep*) mí. **he knows ~** me conoce. **it's ~** soy yo

me[2] /miː/ *n* (*mus, third note of any musical scale*) mi *m*

meadow /'medəʊ/ *n* prado *m*

meagre /'miːgə(r)/ *a* escaso

meal[1] /miːl/ *n* comida *f*

meal[2] /miːl/ *n* (*grain*) harina *f*

mealy-mouthed /miːlɪˈmaʊðd/ *a* hipócrita

mean[1] /miːn/ *vt* (*pt* **meant**) (*intend*) tener la intención de, querer; (*signify*) querer decir, significar. ~ **to do** tener la intención de hacer. ~ **well** tener buenas intenciones. **be meant for** estar destinado a

mean[2] /miːn/ *a* (**-er**, **-est**) (*miserly*) tacaño; (*unkind*) malo; (*poor*) pobre

mean[3] /miːn/ *a* medio. ● *n* medio *m*; (*average*) promedio *m*

meander /mɪˈændə(r)/ *vi* ⟨*river*⟩ serpentear; ⟨*person*⟩ vagar

meaning /'miːnɪŋ/ *n* sentido *m*. **~ful** *a* significativo. **~less** *a* sin sentido

meanness /'miːnnɪs/ *n* (*miserliness*) tacañería *f*; (*unkindness*) maldad *f*

means /miːnz/ *n* medio *m*. **by all ~** por supuesto. **by no ~** de ninguna manera. ● *npl* (*wealth*) recursos *mpl*. ~ **test** *n* investigación *f* financial

meant /ment/ *see* **mean**[1]

meantime /'miːntaɪm/ *adv* entretanto. **in the ~** entretanto

meanwhile /'miːnwaɪl/ *adv* entretanto

measles /'miːzlz/ *n* sarampión *m*

measly /'miːzlɪ/ *a* (*sl*) miserable

measurable /'meʒərəbl/ *a* mensurable

measure /'meʒə(r)/ *n* medida *f*; (*ruler*) regla *f*. ● *vt/i* medir. ~ **up to** estar a la altura de. **~d** *a* (*rhythmical*) acompasado; (*carefully considered*) prudente. **~ment** *n* medida *f*

meat /miːt/ *n* carne *f*. **~y** *a* carnoso; (*fig*) sustancioso

mechanic /mɪˈkænɪk/ *n* mecánico *m*. **~al** /mɪˈkænɪkl/ *a* mecánico. **~s** *n* mecánica *f*

mechani|sm /'mekənɪzəm/ *n* mecanismo *m*. **~ze** *vt* mecanizar

medal /'medl/ *n* medalla *f*

medallion /mɪˈdælɪən/ *n* medallón *m*

medallist /'medəlɪst/ *n* ganador *m* de una medalla. **be a gold ~** ganar una medalla de oro

meddle /'medl/ *vi* entrometerse (**in** en); (*tinker*) tocar. ~ **with** (*tinker*) tocar. **~some** *a* entrometido

media /'miːdɪə/ *see* **medium**. ● *npl*. **the ~** *npl* los medios *mpl* de comunicación

mediat|e /'miːdɪeɪt/ *vi* mediar. **~ion** /-ˈeɪʃn/ *n* mediación *f*. **~or** *n* mediador *m*

medical /'medɪkl/ *a* médico; ⟨*student*⟩ de medicina. ● *n* (*fam*) reconocimiento *m* médico

medicat|ed /'medɪkeɪtɪd/ *a* medicinal. **~ion** /-ˈkeɪʃn/ *n* medicación *f*

medicin|e /'medsɪn/ *n* medicina *f*. **~al** /mɪˈdɪsɪnl/ *a* medicinal

medieval /medrˈiːvl/ *a* medieval

mediocr|e /miːdɪˈəʊkə(r)/ *a* mediocre. **~ity** /-ˈɒkrətɪ/ *n* mediocridad *f*

meditat|e /'medɪteɪt/ *vt/i* meditar. **~ion** /-ˈteɪʃn/ *n* meditación *f*

Mediterranean /medɪtə'reɪnɪən/ a mediterráneo. ● n. **the ~** el Mediterráneo m

medium /'miːdɪəm/ n (pl **media**) medio m; (pl **mediums**) (person) médium m. ● a mediano

medley /'medlɪ/ n popurrí m

meek /miːk/ a (-**er, -est**) manso

meet /miːt/ vt (pt **met**) encontrar; (bump into s.o.) encontrarse con; (see again) ver; (fetch) ir a buscar; (get to know, be introduced to) conocer. **~ the bill** pagar la cuenta. ● vi encontrarse; (get to know) conocerse; (in session) reunirse. **~ with** tropezar con ⟨obstacles⟩

meeting /'miːtɪŋ/ n reunión f; (accidental between two people) encuentro m; (arranged between two people) cita f

megalomania /megələʊ'meɪnɪə/ n megalomanía f

megaphone /'megəfəʊn/ n megáfono m

melanchol|ic /melən'kɒlɪk/ a melancólico. **~y** /'melənkɒlɪ/ n melancolía f. ● a melancólico

mêlée /me'leɪ/ n pelea f confusa

mellow /'meləʊ/ a (-**er, -est**) ⟨fruit, person⟩ maduro; ⟨sound, colour⟩ dulce. ● vt/i madurar(se)

melodi|c /mɪ'lɒdɪk/ a melódico. **~ous** /mɪ'ləʊdɪəs/ a melodioso

melodrama /'melədrɑːmə/ n melodrama m. **~tic** /-ə'mætɪk/ a melodramático

melody /'melədɪ/ n melodía f

melon /'melən/ n melón m

melt /melt/ vt (make liquid) derretir; fundir ⟨metals⟩. ● vi (become liquid) derretirse; ⟨metals⟩ fundirse. **~ing-pot** n crisol m

member /'membə(r)/ n miembro m. **M~ of Parliament** n diputado m. **~ship** n calidad f de miembro; (members) miembros mpl

membrane /'membreɪn/ n membrana f

memento /mɪ'mentəʊ/ n (pl **-oes**) recuerdo m

memo /'meməʊ/ n (pl **-os**) (fam) nota f

memoir /'memwɑː(r)/ n memoria f

memorable /'memərəbl/ a memorable

memorandum /memə'rændəm/ n (pl **-ums**) nota f

memorial /mɪ'mɔːrɪəl/ n monumento m. ● a conmemorativo

memorize /'meməraɪz/ vt aprender de memoria

memory /'memərɪ/ n (faculty) memoria f; (thing remembered) recuerdo m. **from ~** de memoria. **in ~ of** en memoria de

men /men/ see **man**

menac|e /'menəs/ n amenaza f; (nuisance) pesado m. ● vt amenazar. **~ingly** adv de manera amenazadora

menagerie /mɪ'nædʒərɪ/ n casa f de fieras

mend /mend/ vt reparar; (darn) zurcir. **~ one's ways** enmendarse. ● n remiendo m. **be on the ~** ir mejorando

menfolk /'menfəʊk/ n hombres mpl

menial /'miːnɪəl/ a servil

meningitis /menɪn'dʒaɪtɪs/ n meningitis f

menopause /'menəpɔːz/ n menopausia f

menstruat|e /'menstrʊeɪt/ vi menstruar. **~ion** /-eɪʃn/ n menstruación f

mental /'mentl/ a mental; ⟨hospital⟩ psiquiátrico

mentality /men'tælətɪ/ n mentalidad f

menthol /'menθɒl/ n mentol m. **~ated** a mentolado

mention /'menʃn/ vt mencionar. **don't ~ it!** ¡no hay de qué! ● n mención f

mentor /'mentɔː(r)/ n mentor m

menu /'menjuː/ n (set meal) menú m; (a la carte) lista f (de platos)

mercantile /'mɜːkəntaɪl/ a mercantil

mercenary /'mɜːsɪnərɪ/ a & n mercenario (m)

merchandise /'mɜːtʃəndaɪz/ n mercancías fpl

merchant /'mɜːtʃənt/ n comerciante m. ● a ⟨ship, navy⟩ mercante. **~ bank** n banco m mercantil

merci|ful /'mɜːsɪfl/ a misericordioso. **~fully** adv (fortunately, fam) gracias a Dios. **~less** /'mɜːsɪlɪs/ a despiadado

mercur|ial /mɜː'kjʊərɪəl/ a mercurial; (fig, active) vivo. **~y** /'mɜːkjʊrɪ/ n mercurio m

mercy /'mɜːsɪ/ n compasión f. **at the ~ of** a merced de

mere /mɪə(r)/ a simple. ~**ly** adv simplemente

merest /'mɪərɪst/ a mínimo

merge /mɜːdʒ/ vt unir; fusionar ‹companies›. ● vi unirse; ‹companies› fusionarse. ~**r** /-ə(r)/ n fusión f

meridian /mə'rɪdɪən/ n meridiano m

meringue /mə'ræŋ/ n merengue m

merit /'merɪt/ n mérito m. ● vt (pt **merited**) merecer. ~**orious** /-'tɔː-rɪəs/ a meritorio

mermaid /'mɜːmeɪd/ n sirena f

merr|ily /'merəlɪ/ adv alegremente. ~**iment** /'merɪmənt/ n alegría f. ~**y** /'merɪ/ a (-**ier**, -**iest**) alegre. **make** ~ divertirse. ~**y-go-round** n tiovivo m. ~**y-making** n holgorio m

mesh /meʃ/ n malla f; (network) red f

mesmerize /'mezməraɪz/ vt hipnotizar

mess /mes/ n desorden m; (dirt) suciedad f; (mil) rancho m. **make a** ~ **of** chapucear, estropear. ● vt. ~ **up** desordenar; (dirty) ensuciar. ● vi. ~ **about** entretenerse. ~ **with** (tinker with) manosear

message /'mesɪdʒ/ n recado m

messenger /'mesɪndʒə(r)/ n mensajero m

Messiah /mɪ'saɪə/ n Mesías m

Messrs /'mesəz/ npl. ~ **Smith** los señores mpl or Sres. Smith

messy /'mesɪ/ a (-**ier**, -**iest**) en desorden; (dirty) sucio

met /met/ see **meet**

metabolism /mɪ'tæbəlɪzəm/ n metabolismo m

metal /'metl/ n metal. ● a de metal. ~**lic** /mɪ'tælɪk/ a metálico

metallurgy /mɪ'tælədʒɪ/ n metalurgia f

metamorphosis /metə'mɔːfəsɪs/ n (pl -**phoses** /-siːz/) metamorfosis f

metaphor /'metəfə(r)/ n metáfora f. ~**ical** /-'fɔːrkl/ a metafórico

mete /miːt/ vt. ~ **out** repartir; dar ‹punishment›

meteor /'miːtɪə(r)/ n meteoro m

meteorite /'miːtɪəraɪt/ n meteorito m

meteorolog|ical /miːtɪərə'lɒdʒɪkl/ a meteorológico. ~**y** /-'rɒlədʒɪ/ n meteorología f

meter /'miːtə(r)/ n contador m

meter² /'miːtə(r)/ n (Amer) = **metre**

method /'meθəd/ n método m

methodical /mɪ'θɒdɪkl/ a metódico

Methodist /'meθədɪst/ a & n metodista (m & f)

methylated /'meθɪleɪtɪd/ a. ~ **spirit** n alcohol m desnaturalizado

meticulous /mɪ'tɪkjʊləs/ a meticuloso

metre /'miːtə(r)/ n metro m

metric /'metrɪk/ a métrico. ~**ation** /-'keɪʃn/ n cambio m al sistema métrico

metropolis /mɪ'trɒpəlɪs/ n metrópoli f

metropolitan /metrə'pɒlɪtən/ a metropolitano

mettle /'metl/ n valor m

mew /mjuː/ n maullido m. ● vi maullar

mews /mjuːz/ npl casas fpl pequeñas (que antes eran caballerizas)

Mexic|an /'meksɪkən/ a & n mejicano (m); (in Mexico) mexicano (m). ~**o** /-kəʊ/ n Méjico m; (in Mexico) México m

mezzanine /'metsəniːn/ n entresuelo m

mi /miː/ n (mus, third note of any musical scale) mi m

miaow /miː'aʊ/ n & vi = **mew**

mice /maɪs/ see **mouse**

mickey /'mɪkɪ/ n. **take the** ~ **out of** (sl) tomar el pelo a

micro... /'maɪkrəʊ/ pref micro...

microbe /'maɪkrəʊb/ n microbio m

microchip /'maɪkrəʊtʃɪp/ n pastilla f

microfilm /'maɪkrəʊfɪlm/ n microfilme m

microphone /'maɪkrəfəʊn/ n micrófono m

microprocessor /maɪkrəʊ'prəʊsesə(r)/ n microprocesador m

microscop|e /'maɪkrəskəʊp/ n microscopio m. ~**ic** /-'skɒpɪk/ a microscópico

microwave /'maɪkrəʊweɪv/ n microonda f. ~ **oven** n horno m de microondas

mid /mɪd/ a. **in** ~ **air** en pleno aire. **in** ~ **March** a mediados de marzo. **in** ~ **ocean** en medio del océano

midday /mɪd'deɪ/ n mediodía m

middle /'mɪdl/ a de en medio; ‹quality› mediano. ● n medio m. **in the** ~ **of** en medio de. ~**-aged** a de mediana edad. **M**~ **Ages** npl Edad f Media. ~ **class** n clase f media. **M**~ **class** a de la clase media. **M**~ **East** n

Oriente *m* Medio. **~man** *n* intermediario *m*

middling /'mɪdlɪŋ/ *a* regular

midge /mɪdʒ/ *n* mosquito *m*

midget /'mɪdʒɪt/ *n* enano *m*. ● *a* minúsculo

Midlands /'mɪdləndz/ *npl* región *f* central de Inglaterra

midnight /'mɪdnaɪt/ *n* medianoche *f*

midriff /'mɪdrɪf/ *n* diafragma *m*; (*fam*) vientre *m*

midst /mɪdst/ *n*. **in our ~** entre nosotros. **in the ~ of** en medio de

midsummer /mɪd'sʌmə(r)/ *n* pleno verano *m*; (*solstice*) solsticio *m* de verano

midway /mɪd'weɪ/ *adv* a medio camino

midwife /'mɪdwaɪf/ *n* comadrona *f*

midwinter /mɪd'wɪntə(r)/ *n* pleno invierno *m*

might[1] /maɪt/ *see* **may**

might[2] /maɪt/ *n* (*strength*) fuerza *f*; (*power*) poder *m*. **~y** *a* (*strong*) fuerte; (*powerful*) poderoso; (*very great, fam*) enorme. ● *adv* (*fam*) muy

migraine /'miːgreɪn/ *n* jaqueca *f*

migrant /'maɪgrənt/ *a* migratorio. ● *n* (*person*) emigrante *m* & *f*

migrat|e /maɪ'greɪt/ *vi* emigrar. **~ion** /-ʃn/ *n* migración *f*

mike /maɪk/ *n* (*fam*) micrófono *m*

mild /maɪld/ *a* (**-er, -est**) (*person*) apacible; (*climate*) templado; (*slight*) ligero; (*taste*) suave; (*illness*) benigno

mildew /'mɪldjuː/ *n* moho *m*

mild: **~ly** *adv* (*slightly*) ligeramente. **~ness** *n* (*of person*) apacibilidad *f*; (*of climate, illness*) benignidad *f*; (*of taste*) suavidad *f*

mile /maɪl/ *n* milla *f*. **~s better** (*fam*) mucho mejor. **~s too big** (*fam*) demasiado grande. **~age** *n* (*loosely*) kilometraje *m*. **~stone** *n* mojón *m*; (*event, stage, fig*) hito *m*

milieu /mɪ'ljɜː/ *n* ambiente *m*

militant /'mɪlɪtənt/ *a* & *n* militante (*m* & *f*)

military /'mɪlɪtərɪ/ *a* militar

militate /'mɪlɪteɪt/ *vi* militar (**against** contra)

militia /mɪ'lɪʃə/ *n* milicia *f*

milk /mɪlk/ *n* leche *f*. ● *a* (*product*) lácteo; (*chocolate*) con leche. ● *vt* ordeñar (*cow*); (*exploit*) chupar. **~man** *n* repartidor *m* de leche. **~**

shake *n* batido *m* de leche. **~y** *a* lechoso. **M~y Way** *n* Vía *f* Láctea

mill /mɪl/ *n* molino *m*; (*for coffee, pepper*) molinillo *m*; (*factory*) fábrica *f*. ● *vt* moler. ● *vi*. **~ about/around** apiñarse, circular

millennium /mɪ'lenɪəm/ *n* (*pl* **-ia** *or* **-iums**) milenio *m*

miller /'mɪlə(r)/ *n* molinero *m*

millet /'mɪlɪt/ *n* mijo *m*

milli... /'mɪlɪ/ *pref* mili...

milligram(me) /'mɪlɪgræm/ *n* miligramo *m*

millimetre /'mɪlɪmiːtə(r)/ *n* milímetro *m*

milliner /'mɪlɪnə(r)/ *n* sombrerero *m*

million /'mɪlɪən/ *n* millón *m*. **a ~ pounds** un millón *m* de libras. **~aire** *n* millonario *m*

millstone /'mɪlstəʊn/ *n* muela *f* (de molino); (*fig, burden*) losa *f*

mime /maɪm/ *n* pantomima *f*. ● *vt* hacer en pantomima. ● *vi* actuar de mimo

mimic /'mɪmɪk/ *vt* (*pt* **mimicked**) imitar. ● *n* imitador *m*. **~ry** *n* imitación *f*

mimosa /mɪ'məʊzə/ *n* mimosa *f*

minaret /mɪnə'ret/ *n* alminar *m*

mince /mɪns/ *vt* desmenuzar; picar (*meat*). **not to ~ matters/words** no tener pelos en la lengua. ● *n* carne *f* picada. **~meat** *n* conserva *f* de fruta picada. **make ~meat of s.o.** hacer trizas a uno. **~ pie** *n* pastel *m* con frutas picadas. **~r** *n* máquina *f* de picar carne

mind /maɪnd/ *n* mente *f*; (*sanity*) juicio *m*; (*opinion*) parecer *m*; (*intention*) intención *f*. **be on one's ~** preocuparle a uno. ● *vt* (*look after*) cuidar; (*heed*) hacer caso de. **I don't ~ me da igual. I don't ~ the noise** no me molesta el ruido. **never ~** no te preocupes, no se preocupe. **~er** *n* cuidador *m*. **~ful** *a* atento (**of** a). **~less** *a* estúpido

mine[1] /maɪn/ *poss pron* (el) mío *m*, (la) mía *f*, (los) míos *mpl*, (las) mías *fpl*. **it is ~** es mío

mine[2] /maɪn/ *n* mina *f*. ● *vt* extraer. **~field** *n* campo *m* de minas. **~r** *n* minero *m*

mineral /'mɪnərəl/ *a* & *n* mineral (*m*). **~ (water)** *n* (*fizzy soft drink*) gaseosa *f*. **~ water** *n* (*natural*) agua *f* mineral

minesweeper /'maɪnswi:pə(r)/ *n*
(*ship*) dragaminas *m invar*

mingle /'mɪŋgl/ *vt/i* mezclar(se)

mingy /'mɪndʒɪ/ *a* tacaño

mini... /'mɪnɪ/ *pref* mini...

miniature /'mɪnɪtʃə(r)/ *a & n* miniatura (*f*)

mini: ∼**bus** *n* microbús *m*. ∼**cab** *n*
taxi *m*

minim /'mɪnɪm/ *n* (*mus*) blanca *f*

minim|al /'mɪnɪml/ *a* mínimo. ∼**ize**
vt minimizar. ∼**um** *a & n* (*pl* **-ima**)
mínimo (*m*)

mining /'maɪnɪŋ/ *n* explotación *f*.
● *a* minero

miniskirt /'mɪnɪskɜːt/ *n* minifalda *f*

minist|er /'mɪnɪstə(r)/ *n* ministro *m*;
(*relig*) pastor *m*. ∼**erial** /-'stɪərɪəl/ *a*
ministerial. ∼**ry** *n* ministerio *m*

mink /mɪŋk/ *n* visón *m*

minor /'maɪnə(r)/ *a* (*incl mus*)
menor; (*of little importance*) sin importancia. ● *n* menor *m & f* de edad

minority /maɪ'nɒrətɪ/ *n* minoría *f*.
● *a* minoritario

minster /'mɪnstə(r)/ *n* catedral *f*

minstrel /'mɪnstrəl/ *n* juglar *m*

mint[1] /mɪnt/ *n* (*plant*) menta *f*;
(*sweet*) caramelo *m* de menta

mint[2] /mɪnt/ *n*. **the M**∼ *n* casa *f* de la
moneda. **a** ∼ un dineral *m*. ● *vt* acuñar. **in** ∼ **condition** como nuevo

minuet /mɪnjʊ'et/ *n* minué *m*

minus /'maɪnəs/ *prep* menos; (*without, fam*) sin. ● *n* (*sign*) menos *m*. ∼
sign *n* menos *m*

minuscule /'mɪnəskjuːl/ *a* minúsculo

minute[1] /'mɪnɪt/ *n* minuto *m*. ∼**s** *npl*
(*of meeting*) actas *fpl*

minute[2] /maɪ'njuːt/ *a* minúsculo;
(*detailed*) minucioso

minx /mɪŋks/ *n* chica *f* descarada

mirac|le /'mɪrəkl/ *n* milagro *m*. ∼**u-
lous** /mɪ'rækjʊləs/ *a* milagroso

mirage /'mɪrɑːʒ/ *n* espejismo *m*

mire /'maɪə(r)/ *n* fango *m*

mirror /'mɪrə(r)/ *n* espejo *m*. ● *vt* reflejar

mirth /mɜːθ/ *n* (*merriment*) alegría *f*;
(*laughter*) risas *fpl*

misadventure /mɪsəd'ventʃə(r)/ *n*
desgracia *f*

misanthropist /mɪ'zænθrəpɪst/ *n*
misántropo *m*

misapprehension /mɪsæprɪ'henʃn/
n malentendido *m*

misbehav|e /mɪsbɪ'heɪv/ *vi* portarse
mal. ∼**iour** *n* mala conducta *f*

miscalculat|e /mɪs'kælkjʊleɪt/ *vt/i*
calcular mal. ∼**ion** /-'leɪʃn/ *n*
desacierto *m*

miscarr|iage /'mɪskærɪdʒ/ *n* aborto
m. ∼**iage of justice** *n* error *m*
judicial. ∼**y** *vi* abortar

miscellaneous /mɪsə'leɪnɪəs/ *a*
vario

mischief /'mɪstʃɪf/ *n* (*foolish conduct*) travesura *f*; (*harm*) daño *m*. **get
into** ∼ cometer travesuras. **make** ∼
armar un lío

mischievous /'mɪstʃɪvəs/ *a* travieso; (*malicious*) perjudicial

misconception /mɪskən'sepʃn/ *n*
equivocación *f*

misconduct /mɪs'kɒndʌkt/ *n* mala
conducta *f*

misconstrue /mɪskən'struː/ *vt*
interpretar mal

misdeed /mɪs'diːd/ *n* fechoría *f*

misdemeanour /mɪsdɪ'miːnə(r)/ *n*
fechoría *f*

misdirect /mɪsdɪ'rekt/ *vt* dirigir mal
⟨*person*⟩

miser /'maɪzə(r)/ *n* avaro *m*

miserable /'mɪzərəbl/ *a* (*sad*) triste;
(*wretched*) miserable; (*weather*)
malo

miserly /'maɪzəlɪ/ *a* avariento

misery /'mɪzərɪ/ *n* (*unhappiness*)
tristeza *f*; (*pain*) sufrimiento *m*;
(*poverty*) pobreza *f*; (*person, fam*)
aguafiestas *m & f*

misfire /mɪs'faɪə(r)/ *vi* fallar

misfit /'mɪsfɪt/ *n* (*person*) inadaptado *m*; (*thing*) cosa *f* mal ajus-
tada

misfortune /mɪs'fɔːtʃuːn/ *n* desgracia *f*

misgiving /mɪs'gɪvɪŋ/ *n* (*doubt*)
duda *f*; (*apprehension*) presentimiento *m*

misguided /mɪs'gaɪdɪd/ *a* equivocado. **be** ∼ equivocarse

mishap /'mɪshæp/ *n* desgracia *f*

misinform /mɪsɪn'fɔːm/ *vt* informar
mal

misinterpret /mɪsɪn'tɜːprɪt/ *vt* interpretar mal

misjudge /mɪs'dʒʌdʒ/ *vt* juzgar mal

mislay /mɪs'leɪ/ *vt* (*pt* **mislaid**) extraviar

mislead /mɪs'liːd/ *vt* (*pt* **misled**)
engañar. ∼**ing** *a* engañoso

mismanage /mɪs'mænɪdʒ/ vt administrar mal. **~ment** n mala administración f

misnomer /mɪs'nəʊmə(r)/ n nombre m equivocado

misplace /mɪs'pleɪs/ vt colocar mal; ⟨lose⟩ extraviar

misprint /'mɪsprɪnt/ n errata f

misquote /mɪs'kwəʊt/ vt citar mal

misrepresent /ˌmɪsreprɪ'zent/ vt describir engañosamente

miss[1] /mɪs/ vt ⟨fail to hit⟩ errar; ⟨notice absence of⟩ echar de menos; perder ⟨train⟩. **~ the point** no comprender. ● n fallo m. **~ out** omitir

miss[2] /mɪs/ n (pl **misses**) señorita f

misshapen /mɪs'ʃeɪpən/ a deforme

missile /'mɪsaɪl/ n proyectil m

missing /'mɪsɪŋ/ a ⟨person⟩ ⟨absent⟩ ausente; ⟨person⟩ ⟨after disaster⟩ desaparecido; ⟨lost⟩ perdido. **be ~** faltar

mission /'mɪʃn/ n misión f. **~ary** /'mɪʃənərɪ/ n misionero m

missive /'mɪsɪv/ n misiva f

misspell /mɪs'spel/ vt (pt **misspelt** or **misspelled**) escribir mal

mist /mɪst/ n neblina f; ⟨at sea⟩ bruma f. ● vt/i empañar(se)

mistake /mɪ'steɪk/ n error m. ● vt (pt **mistook**, pp **mistaken**) equivocarse de; ⟨misunderstand⟩ entender mal. **~ for** tomar por. **~n** /-ən/ a equivocado. **be ~n** equivocarse. **~nly** adv equivocadamente

mistletoe /'mɪsltəʊ/ n muérdago m

mistreat /mɪs'triːt/ vt maltratar

mistress /'mɪstrɪs/ n ⟨of house⟩ señora f; ⟨primary school teacher⟩ maestra f; ⟨secondary school teacher⟩ profesora f; ⟨lover⟩ amante f

mistrust /mɪs'trʌst/ vt desconfiar de. ● n desconfianza f

misty /'mɪstɪ/ a (**-ier, -iest**) nebuloso; ⟨day⟩ de niebla; ⟨glass⟩ empañado. **it is ~** hay neblina

misunderstand /ˌmɪsʌndə'stænd/ vt (pt **-stood**) entender mal. **~ing** n malentendido m

misuse /mɪs'juːz/ vt emplear mal; abusar de ⟨power etc⟩. /mɪs'juːs/ n mal uso m; ⟨unfair use⟩ abuso m

mite /maɪt/ n ⟨insect⟩ ácaro m, garrapata f; ⟨child⟩ niño m pequeño

mitigate /'mɪtɪgeɪt/ vt mitigar

mitre /'maɪtə(r)/ n ⟨head-dress⟩ mitra f

mitten /'mɪtn/ n manopla f; ⟨leaving fingers exposed⟩ mitón m

mix /mɪks/ vt/i mezclar(se). **~ up** mezclar; ⟨confuse⟩ confundir. **~ with** frecuentar ⟨people⟩. ● n mezcla f

mixed /mɪkst/ a ⟨school etc⟩ mixto; ⟨assorted⟩ variado. **be ~ up** estar confuso

mixer /'mɪksə(r)/ n ⟨culin⟩ batidora f. **be a good ~** tener don de gentes

mixture /'mɪkstʃə(r)/ n mezcla f

mix-up /'mɪksʌp/ n lío m

moan /məʊn/ n gemido m. ● vi gemir; ⟨complain⟩ quejarse (**about** de). **~er** n refunfuñador m

moat /məʊt/ n foso m

mob /mɒb/ n ⟨crowd⟩ muchedumbre f; ⟨gang⟩ pandilla f; ⟨masses⟩ populacho m. ● vt (pt **mobbed**) acosar

mobil|e /'məʊbaɪl/ a móvil. **~e home** n caravana f. ● n móvil m. **~ity** /mə'bɪlətɪ/ n movilidad f

mobiliz|ation /ˌməʊbɪlaɪ'zeɪʃn/ n movilización f. **~e** /'məʊbɪlaɪz/ vt/i movilizar

moccasin /'mɒkəsɪn/ n mocasín m

mocha /'mɒkə/ n moca m

mock /mɒk/ vt burlarse de. ● vi burlarse. ● a fingido

mockery /'mɒkərɪ/ n burla f. **a ~ of** una parodia f de

mock-up /'mɒkʌp/ n maqueta f

mode /məʊd/ n ⟨way, method⟩ modo m; ⟨fashion⟩ moda f

model /'mɒdl/ n modelo m; ⟨mockup⟩ maqueta f; ⟨for fashion⟩ maniquí m. ● a ⟨exemplary⟩ ejemplar; ⟨car etc⟩ en miniatura. ● vt (pt **modelled**) modelar; presentar ⟨clothes⟩. ● vi ser maniquí; ⟨pose⟩ posar. **~ling** n profesión f de maniquí

moderate /'mɒdərət/ a & n moderado (m). /'mɒdəreɪt/ vt/i moderar(se). **~ly** /'mɒdərətlɪ/ adv ⟨in moderation⟩ moderadamente; ⟨fairly⟩ medianamente

moderation /mɒdə'reɪʃn/ n moderación f. **in ~** con moderación

modern /'mɒdn/ a moderno. **~ize** vt modernizar

modest /'mɒdɪst/ a modesto. **~y** n modestia f

modicum /'mɒdɪkəm/ n. **a ~ of** un poquito m de

modif|ication /ˌmɒdɪfɪ'keɪʃn/ n modificación f. **~y** /-faɪ/ vt/i modificar(se)

modulat|e /'mɒdjʊleɪt/ vt/i modular. **~ion** /-'leɪʃn/ n modulación f

module /'mɒdjuːl/ n módulo m

mogul /'məʊgəl/ n (fam) magnate m

mohair /'məʊheə(r)/ n mohair m

moist /mɔɪst/ a (-er, -est) húmedo. **~en** /'mɔɪsn/ vt humedecer

moistur|e /'mɔɪstʃə(r)/ n humedad f. **~ize** /'mɔɪstʃəraɪz/ vt humedecer. **~izer** n crema f hidratante

molar /'məʊlə(r)/ n muela f

molasses /mə'læsɪz/ n melaza f

mold /məʊld/ (Amer) = **mould**

mole[1] /məʊl/ n (animal) topo m

mole[2] /məʊl/ n (on skin) lunar m

mole[3] /məʊl/ n (breakwater) malecón m

molecule /'mɒlɪkjuːl/ n molécula f

molehill /'məʊlhɪl/ n topera f

molest /mə'lest/ vt importunar

mollify /'mɒlɪfaɪ/ vt apaciguar

mollusc /'mɒləsk/ n molusco m

mollycoddle /'mɒlɪkɒdl/ vt mimar

molten /'məʊltən/ a fundido

mom /mɒm/ n (Amer) mamá f

moment /'məʊmənt/ n momento m. **~arily** /'məʊməntərɪli/ adv momentáneamente. **~ary** a momentáneo

momentous /mə'mentəs/ a importante

momentum /mə'mentəm/ n momento m; (speed) velocidad f; (fig) ímpetu m

Monaco /'mɒnəkəʊ/ n Mónaco m

monarch /'mɒnək/ n monarca m. **~ist** n monárquico m. **~y** n monarquía f

monast|ery /'mɒnəstərɪ/ n monasterio m. **~ic** /mə'næstɪk/ a monástico

Monday /'mʌndeɪ/ n lunes m

monetar|ist /'mʌnɪtərɪst/ n monetarista m & f. **~y** a monetario

money /'mʌnɪ/ n dinero m. **~-box** n hucha f. **~ed** a adinerado. **~-lender** n prestamista m & f. **~ order** n giro m postal. **~s** npl cantidades fpl de dinero. **~-spinner** n mina f de dinero

mongol /'mɒŋgl/ n & a (med) mongólico (m)

mongrel /'mʌŋgrəl/ n perro m mestizo

monitor /'mɒnɪtə(r)/ n (pupil) monitor m & f; (tec) monitor m. ● vt controlar; escuchar ⟨a broadcast⟩

monk /mʌŋk/ n monje m

monkey /'mʌŋkɪ/ n mono m. **~-nut** n cacahuete m, maní m (LAm). **~-wrench** n llave f inglesa

mono /'mɒnəʊ/ a monofónico

monocle /'mɒnəkl/ n monóculo m

monogram /'mɒnəgræm/ n monograma m

monologue /'mɒnəlɒg/ n monólogo m

monopol|ize /mə'nɒpəlaɪz/ vt monopolizar. **~y** n monopolio m

monosyllab|ic /mɒnəsɪ'læbɪk/ a monosilábico. **~le** /-'sɪləbl/ n monosílabo m

monotone /'mɒnətəʊn/ n monotonía f. **speak in a ~** hablar con una voz monótona

monoton|ous /mə'nɒtənəs/ a monótono. **~y** n monotonía f

monsoon /mɒn'suːn/ n monzón m

monster /'mɒnstə(r)/ n monstruo m

monstrosity /mɒn'strɒsətɪ/ n monstruosidad f

monstrous /'mɒnstrəs/ a monstruoso

montage /mɒn'tɑːʒ/ n montaje m

month /mʌnθ/ n mes m. **~ly** /'mʌnθlɪ/ a mensual. ● adv mensualmente. ● n (periodical) revista f mensual

monument /'mɒnjʊmənt/ n monumento m. **~al** /-'mentl/ a monumental

moo /muː/ n mugido m. ● vi mugir

mooch /muːtʃ/ vi (sl) haraganear. ● vt (Amer, sl) birlar

mood /muːd/ n humor m. **be in the ~ for** tener ganas de. **in a good/bad ~** de buen/mal humor. **~y** a (-ier, -iest) de humor cambiadizo; (bad-tempered) malhumorado

moon /muːn/ n luna f. **~light** n luz f de la luna. **~lighting** n (fam) pluriempleo m. **~lit** a iluminado por la luna; ⟨night⟩ de luna

moor[1] /mʊə(r)/ n (open land) páramo m

moor[2] /mʊə(r)/ vt amarrar. **~ings** npl (ropes) amarras fpl; (place) amarradero m

Moor /mʊə(r)/ n moro m

moose /muːs/ n invar alce m

moot /muːt/ a discutible. ● vt proponer ⟨question⟩

mop /mɒp/ n fregona f. **~ of hair** pelambrera f. ● vt (pt **mopped**) fregar. **~ (up)** limpiar

mope /məʊp/ vi estar abatido

moped /'məʊped/ n ciclomotor m

moral /'mɒrəl/ a moral. ● n mora-leja f. ~s npl moralidad f

morale /mə'rɑːl/ n moral f

moral|ist /'mɒrəlɪst/ n moralista m & f. ~**ity** /mə'rælətɪ/ n moralidad f. ~**ize** vi moralizar. ~**ly** adv moral-mente

morass /mə'ræs/ n (marsh) pantano m; (fig, entanglement) embrollo m

morbid /'mɔːbɪd/ a morboso

more /mɔː(r)/ a & n & adv más. ~ **and** ~ cada vez más. ~ **or less** más o menos. **once** ~ una vez más. **some** ~ más

moreover /mɔː'rəʊvə(r)/ adv además

morgue /mɔːg/ n depósito m de cadá-veres

moribund /'mɒrɪbʌnd/ a mori-bundo

morning /'mɔːnɪŋ/ n mañana f; (early hours) madrugada f. **at 11 o'clock in the** ~ a las once de la mañana. **in the** ~ por la mañana

Morocc|an /mə'rɒkən/ a & n ma-rroquí (m & f). ~**o** /-kəʊ/ n Ma-rruecos mpl

moron /'mɔːrɒn/ n imbécil m & f

morose /mə'rəʊs/ a malhumorado

morphine /'mɔːfiːn/ n morfina f

Morse /mɔːs/ n Morse m. ~ **(code)** n alfabeto m Morse

morsel /'mɔːsl/ n pedazo m; (mouth-ful) bocado m

mortal /'mɔːtl/ a & n mortal (m). ~**ity** /-'tælətɪ/ n mortalidad f

mortar /'mɔːtə(r)/ n (all senses) mor-tero m

mortgage /'mɔːgɪdʒ/ n hipoteca f. ● vt hipotecar

mortify /'mɔːtɪfaɪ/ vt mortificar

mortuary /'mɔːtjʊərɪ/ n depósito m de cadáveres

mosaic /məʊ'zeɪk/ n mosaico m

Moscow /'mɒskəʊ/ n Moscú m

Moses /'məʊzɪz/ a. ~ **basket** n moisés m

mosque /mɒsk/ n mezquita f

mosquito /mɒs'kiːtəʊ/ n (pl -oes) mosquito m

moss /mɒs/ n musgo m. ~**y** n mus-goso

most /məʊst/ a más. **for the** ~ **part** en su mayor parte. ● n la mayoría f. ~ **of** la mayor parte de. **at** ~ a lo más. **make the** ~ **of** aprovechar al máximo. ● adv más; (very) muy. ~**ly** adv principalmente

MOT abbr (Ministry of Transport). ~ **(test)** ITV, inspección f técnica de vehículos

motel /məʊ'tel/ n motel m

moth /mɒθ/ n mariposa f (nocturna); (in clothes) polilla f. ~**-ball** n bola f de naftalina. ~**-eaten** a apolillado

mother /'mʌðə(r)/ n madre f. ● vt cuidar como a un hijo. ~**hood** n maternidad f. ~**-in-law** n (pl ~s-in-law) suegra f. ~**land** n patria f. ~**ly** adv maternalmente. ~**-of-pearl** n nácar m. **M~'s Day** n el día m de la Madre. ~**-to-be** n futura madre f. ~ **tongue** n lengua f materna

motif /məʊ'tiːf/ n motivo m

motion /'məʊʃn/ n movimiento m; (proposal) moción f. ● vt/i. ~ **(to) s.o. to** hacer señas a uno para que. ~**less** a inmóvil

motivat|e /'məʊtɪveɪt/ vt motivar. ~**ion** /-'veɪʃn/ n motivación f

motive /'məʊtɪv/ n motivo m

motley /'mɒtlɪ/ a abigarrado

motor /'məʊtə(r)/ n motor m; (car) coche m. ● a motor; (fem) motora, motriz. ● vi ir en coche. ~ **bike** n (fam) motocicleta f, moto f (fam). ~ **boat** n lancha f motora. ~**cade** /'məʊtəkeɪd/ n (Amer) desfile m de automóviles. ~ **car** n coche m, automóvil m. ~ **cycle** n motocicleta f. ~**cyclist** n motociclista m & f. ~**ing** n automovilismo m. ~**ist** n automovilista m & f. ~**ize** vt motor-izar. ~**way** n autopista f

mottled /'mɒtld/ a abigarrado

motto /'mɒtəʊ/ n (pl -oes) lema m

mould¹ /məʊld/ n molde m. ● vt mol-dear

mould² /məʊld/ n (fungus, rot) moho m

moulding /'məʊldɪŋ/ n (on wall etc) moldura f

mouldy /'məʊldɪ/ a mohoso

moult /məʊlt/ vi mudar

mound /maʊnd/ n montículo m; (pile, fig) montón m

mount¹ /maʊnt/ vt/i subir. ● n mon-tura f. ~ **up** aumentar

mount² /maʊnt/ n (hill) monte m

mountain /'maʊntɪn/ n montaña f. ~**eer** /maʊntɪ'nɪə(r)/ n alpinista m & f. ~**eering** n alpinismo m. ~**ous** /'maʊntɪnəs/ a montañoso

mourn /mɔːn/ vt llorar. • vi lamentarse. ~ **for** llorar la muerte de. ~**er** n persona f que acompaña el cortejo fúnebre. ~**ful** a triste. ~**ing** n luto m

mouse /maʊs/ n (pl **mice**) ratón m. ~**trap** n ratonera f

mousse /muːs/ n (dish) crema f batida

moustache /məˈstɑːʃ/ n bigote m

mousy /ˈmaʊsɪ/ a ⟨hair⟩ pardusco; (fig) tímido

mouth /maʊð/ vt formar con los labios. /maʊθ/ n boca f. ~**ful** n bocado m. ~**organ** n armónica f. ~**piece** n (mus) boquilla f; (fig, person) portavoz f, vocero m (LAm). ~**wash** n enjuague m

movable /ˈmuːvəbl/ a móvil, movible

move /muːv/ vt mover; mudarse de ⟨house⟩; (with emotion) conmover; (propose) proponer. • vi moverse; (be in motion) estar en movimiento; (progress) hacer progresos; (take action) tomar medidas; (depart) irse. ~ **(out)** irse. • n movimiento m; (in game) jugada f; (player's turn) turno m; (removal) mudanza f. **on the** ~ en movimiento. ~ **along** (hacer) circular. ~ **away** alejarse. ~ **back** (hacer) retroceder. ~ **forward** (hacer) avanzar. ~ **in** instalarse. ~ **on** (hacer) circular. ~ **over** apartarse. ~**ment** /ˈmuːvmənt/ n movimiento m

movie /ˈmuːvɪ/ n (Amer) película f. **the** ~s npl el cine m

moving /ˈmuːvɪŋ/ a en movimiento; (touching) conmovedor

mow /məʊ/ vt (pt **mowed** or **mown**) segar. ~ **down** derribar. ~**er** n (for lawn) cortacésped m invar

MP abbr see **Member of Parliament**

Mr /ˈmɪstə(r)/ abbr (pl **Messrs**) (Mister) señor m. ~ **Coldbeck** (el) Sr. Coldbeck

Mrs /ˈmɪsɪz/ abbr (pl **Mrs**) (Missis) señora f. ~ **Andrews** (la) Sra. Andrews. **the** ~ **Andrews** (las) Sras. Andrews

Ms /mɪz/ abbr (title of married or unmarried woman) señora f, señorita f. **Ms Lawton** (la) Sra. Lawton

much /mʌtʃ/ a & n mucho (m). • adv mucho; (before pp) muy. ~ **as** por mucho que. ~ **the same** más o

menos lo mismo. **so** ~ tanto. **too** ~ demasiado

muck /mʌk/ n estiércol m; (dirt, fam) suciedad f. • vi. ~ **about** (sl) perder el tiempo. ~ **about with** (sl) juguetear con. ~ **vt. ~ up** (sl) echar a perder. ~ **in** (sl) participar. ~**y** a sucio

mucus /ˈmjuːkəs/ n moco m

mud /mʌd/ n lodo m, barro m

muddle /ˈmʌdl/ vt embrollar. • vi. ~ **through** salir del paso. • n desorden m; (mix-up) lío m

muddy /ˈmʌdɪ/ a lodoso; ⟨hands etc⟩ cubierto de lodo

mudguard /ˈmʌdɡɑːd/ n guardabarros m invar

muff /mʌf/ n manguito m

muffin /ˈmʌfɪn/ n mollete m

muffle /ˈmʌfl/ vt tapar; amortiguar ⟨a sound⟩. ~**r** n (scarf) bufanda f

mug /mʌɡ/ n tazón m; (for beer) jarra f; (face, sl) cara f, jeta f (sl); (fool, sl) primo m. • vt (pt **mugged**) asaltar. ~**ger** n asaltador m. ~**ging** n asalto m

muggy /ˈmʌɡɪ/ a bochornoso

Muhammadan /məˈhæmɪdən/ a & n mahometano (m)

mule[1] /mjuːl/ n mula f, mulo m

mule[2] /mjuːl/ n (slipper) babucha f

mull[1] /mʌl/ vt. ~ **over** reflexionar sobre

mull[2] /mʌl/ vt calentar con especias ⟨wine⟩

multi... /ˈmʌltɪ/ pref multi...

multicoloured /mʌltɪˈkʌləd/ a multicolor

multifarious /mʌltɪˈfeərɪəs/ a múltiple

multinational /mʌltɪˈnæʃənl/ a & n multinacional (f)

multiple /ˈmʌltɪpl/ a & n múltiplo (m). ~**ication** /mʌltɪplɪˈkeɪʃn/ n multiplicación f. ~**y** /ˈmʌltɪplaɪ/ vt/i multiplicar(se)

multitude /ˈmʌltɪtjuːd/ n multitud f

mum[1] /mʌm/ n (fam) mamá f (fam)

mum[2] /mʌm/ a. **keep** ~ (fam) guardar silencio

mumble /ˈmʌmbl/ vt decir entre dientes. • vi hablar entre dientes

mummify /ˈmʌmɪfaɪ/ vt/i momificar(se)

mummy[1] /ˈmʌmɪ/ n (mother, fam) mamá f (fam)

mummy[2] /ˈmʌmɪ/ n momia f

mumps /mʌmps/ n paperas fpl

munch /mʌntʃ/ vt/i mascar

mundane /mʌn'deɪn/ a mundano

municipal /mju:'nɪsɪpl/ a municipal. **~ity** /-'pælɪtɪ/ n municipio m

munificent /mju:'nɪfɪsənt/ a munífico

munitions /mju:'nɪʃnz/ npl municiones fpl

mural /'mjʊərəl/ a & n mural (f)

murder /'mɜ:də(r)/ n asesinato m. ● vt asesinar. **~er** n asesino m. **~ess** n asesina f. **~ous** a homicida

murky /'mɜ:kɪ/ a (-ier, -iest) oscuro

murmur /'mɜ:mə(r)/ n murmullo m. ● vt/i murmurar

muscle /'mʌsl/ n músculo m. ● vi. **~ in** (Amer, sl) meterse por fuerza en

muscular /'mʌskjʊlə(r)/ a muscular; (having well-developed muscles) musculoso

muse /mju:z/ vi meditar

museum /mju:'zɪəm/ n museo m

mush /mʌʃ/ n pulpa f

mushroom /'mʌʃrʊm/ n champiñón m; (bot) seta f. ● vi (appear in large numbers) crecer como hongos

mushy /'mʌʃɪ/ a pulposo

music /'mju:zɪk/ n música f. **~al** a musical; (instrument) de música; (talented) que tiene don de música. ● n comedia f musical. **~ hall** n teatro m de variedades. **~ian** /mju:'zɪʃn/ n músico m

musk /mʌsk/ n almizcle m

Muslim /'mʊzlɪm/ a & n musulmán (m)

muslin /'mʌzlɪn/ n muselina f

musquash /'mʌskwɒʃ/ n ratón m almizclero

mussel /'mʌsl/ n mejillón m

must /mʌst/ v aux deber, tener que. he **~ be old** debe ser viejo. I **~ have done it** debo haberlo hecho. **you ~ go** debes marcharte. ● n. **be a ~** ser imprescindible

mustard /'mʌstəd/ n mostaza f

muster /'mʌstə(r)/ vt/i reunir(se)

musty /'mʌstɪ/ a (-ier, -iest) que huele a cerrado

mutation /mju:'teɪʃn/ n mutación f

mute /mju:t/ a & n mudo (m). **~d** a (sound) sordo; (criticism) callado

mutilat|e /'mju:tɪleɪt/ vt mutilar. **~ion** /-'leɪʃn/ n mutilación f

mutin|ous /'mju:tɪnəs/ a (sailor etc) amotinado; (fig) rebelde. **~y** n motín m. ● vi amotinarse

mutter /'mʌtə(r)/ vt/i murmurar

mutton /'mʌtn/ n cordero m

mutual /'mju:tʃʊəl/ a mutuo; (common, fam) común. **~ly** adv mutuamente

muzzle /mʌzl/ n (snout) hocico m; (device) bozal m; (of gun) boca f. ● vt poner el bozal a

my /maɪ/ a mi, mis pl

myopic /maɪ'ɒpɪk/ a miope

myriad /'mɪrɪəd/ n miríada f

myself /maɪ'self/ pron yo mismo m, yo misma f; (reflexive) me; (after prep) mí (mismo) m, mí (misma) f

myster|ious /mɪ'stɪərɪəs/ a misterioso. **~y** /'mɪstərɪ/ n misterio m

mystic /'mɪstɪk/ a & n místico (m). **~al** a místico. **~ism** /-sɪzəm/ n misticismo m

mystif|ication /mɪstɪfɪ'keɪʃn/ n confusión f. **~y** /-faɪ/ vt dejar perplejo

mystique /mɪ'sti:k/ n mística f

myth /mɪθ/ n mito m. **~ical** a mítico. **~ology** /mɪ'θɒlədʒɪ/ n mitología f

N

N abbr (north) norte m

nab /næb/ vt (pt nabbed) (arrest, sl) coger (not LAm), agarrar (esp LAm)

nag /næg/ vt (pt nagged) fastidiar; (scold) regañar. ● vi criticar

nagging /'nægɪŋ/ a persistente, regañón

nail /neɪl/ n clavo m; (of finger, toe) uña f. **pay on the ~** pagar a tocateja. ● vt clavar. **~ polish** n esmalte m para las uñas

naïve /naɪ'i:v/ a ingenuo

naked /'neɪkɪd/ a desnudo. **to the ~ eye** a simple vista. **~ly** adv desnudamente. **~ness** n desnudez f

namby-pamby /næmbɪ'pæmbɪ/ a & n ñoño (m)

name /neɪm/ n nombre m; (fig) fama f. ● vt nombrar; (fix) fijar. **be ~d after** llevar el nombre de. **~less** a anónimo. **~ly** /'neɪmlɪ/ adv a saber. **~sake** /'neɪmseɪk/ n (person) tocayo m

nanny /'nænɪ/ n niñera f. **~-goat** n cabra f

nap[1] /næp/ n (sleep) sueñecito m; (after lunch) siesta f. ● vi (pt napped) echarse un sueño. **catch s.o. ~ping** coger a uno desprevenido

nap[2] /næp/ n (fibres) lanilla f

nape /neɪp/ n nuca f

napkin /'næpkɪn/ n (at meals) servilleta f; (for baby) pañal m

nappy /'næpɪ/ n pañal m

narcotic /nɑː'kɒtɪk/ a & n narcótico (m)

narrat|e /nə'reɪt/ vt contar. ~ion /-ʃn/ n narración f. ~ive /'nærətɪv/ n relato m. ~or /nə'reɪtə(r)/ n narrador m

narrow /'nærəʊ/ a (-er, -est) estrecho. **have a ~ escape** escaparse por los pelos. ● vt estrechar; (limit) limitar. ● vi estrecharse. ~ly adv estrechamente; (just) por poco. ~ **minded** a de miras estrechas. ~**ness** n estrechez f

nasal /'neɪzl/ a nasal

nast|ily /'nɑːstɪlɪ/ adv desagradablemente; (maliciously) con malevolencia. ~**iness** n (malice) malevolencia f. ~y a /'nɑːstɪ/ (-ier, -iest) desagradable; (malicious) malévolo; (weather) malo; (taste, smell) asqueroso; (wound) grave; (person) antipático

natal /'neɪtl/ a natal

nation /'neɪʃn/ n nación f

national /'næʃənl/ a nacional. ● n súbdito m. ~ **anthem** n himno m nacional. ~**ism** n nacionalismo m. ~**ity** /næʃə'nælətɪ/ n nacionalidad f. ~**ize** vt nacionalizar. ~**ly** adv a nivel nacional

nationwide /'neɪʃnwaɪd/ a nacional

native /'neɪtɪv/ n natural m & f. **be a ~ of** ser natural de. ● a nativo; (country, town) natal; (inborn) innato. ~ **speaker of Spanish** hispanohablante m & f. ~ **language** n lengua f materna

Nativity /nə'tɪvətɪ/ n. **the ~** la Natividad f

NATO /'neɪtəʊ/ abbr (North Atlantic Treaty Organization) OTAN f, Organización f del Tratado del Atlántico Norte

natter /'nætə(r)/ vi (fam) charlar. ● n (fam) charla f

natural /'nætʃərəl/ a natural. ~ **history** n historia f natural. ~**ist** n naturalista m & f

naturaliz|ation /nætʃərəlaɪ'zeɪʃn/ n naturalización f. ~**e** vt naturalizar

naturally /'nætʃərəlɪ/ adv (of course) naturalmente; (by nature) por naturaleza

nature /'neɪtʃə(r)/ n naturaleza f; (kind) género m; (of person) carácter m

naught /nɔːt/ n (old use) nada f; (maths) cero m

naught|ily /'nɔːtɪlɪ/ adv mal. ~**y** a (-ier, -iest) malo; (child) travieso; (joke) verde

nause|a /'nɔːzɪə/ n náusea f. ~**ate** vt dar náuseas a. ~**ous** a nauseabundo

nautical /'nɔːtɪkl/ a náutico. ~ **mile** n milla f marina

naval /'neɪvl/ a naval; (officer) de marina

Navarre /nə'vɑː(r)/ n Navarra f. ~**se** a navarro

nave /neɪv/ n (of church) nave f

navel /'neɪvl/ n ombligo m

navigable /'nævɪgəbl/ a navegable

navigat|e /'nævɪgeɪt/ vt navegar por (sea etc); gobernar (ship). ● vi navegar. ~**ion** n navegación f. ~**or** n navegante m

navvy /'nævɪ/ n peón m caminero

navy /'neɪvɪ/ n marina f. ~ **(blue)** azul m marino

NE abbr (north-east) noreste m

near /'nɪə(r)/ adv cerca. ~ **at hand** muy cerca. ~ **by** adv cerca. **draw** ~ acercarse. ● prep. ~ **(to)** cerca de. ● a cercano. ● vt acercarse a. ~**by** a cercano. **N~ East** n Oriente m Próximo. ~**ly** /'nɪəlɪ/ adv casi. **not** ~**ly as pretty as** no es ni con mucho tan guapa como. ~**ness** n /'nɪənɪs/ n proximidad f

neat /niːt/ a (-er, -est) pulcro; (room etc) bien arreglado; (clever) diestro; (ingenious) hábil; (whisky, brandy etc) solo. ~**ly** adv pulcramente. ~**ness** n pulcritud f

nebulous /'nebjʊləs/ a nebuloso

necessar|ies /'nesəsərɪz/ npl lo indispensable. ~**ily** /nesə'serɪlɪ/ adv necesariamente. ~**y** a necesario, imprescindible

necessit|ate /nə'sesɪteɪt/ vt necesitar. ~**y** /nɪ'sesətɪ/ n necesidad f; (thing) cosa f indispensable

neck /nek/ n (of person, bottle, dress) cuello m; (of animal) pescuezo m. ~ **and** ~ parejos. ~**lace** /'nekləs/ n collar m. ~**line** n escote m. ~**tie** n corbata f

nectar /'nektə(r)/ n néctar m

nectarine /'nektəriːn/ n nectarina f

née /neɪ/ a de soltera

need /niːd/ *n* necesidad *f.* ● *vt* necesitar; (*demand*) exigir. **you ~ not speak** no tienes que hablar

needle /'niːdl/ *n* aguja *f.* ● *vt* (*annoy, fam*) pinchar

needless /'niːdlɪs/ *a* innecesario. **~ly** *adv* innecesariamente

needlework /'niːdlwɜːk/ *n* costura *f;* (*embroidery*) bordado *m*

needy /'niːdɪ/ *a* (**-ier, -iest**) necesitado

negation /nɪ'ɡeɪʃn/ *n* negación *f*

negative /'neɡətɪv/ *a* negativo. ● *n* (*of photograph*) negativo *m;* (*word, gram*) negativa *f.* **~ly** *adv* negativamente

neglect /nɪ'ɡlekt/ *vt* descuidar; no cumplir con (*duty*). **~ to do** dejar de hacer. ● *n* descuido *m,* negligencia *f.* **(state of) ~** abandono *m.* **~ful** *a* descuidado

négligé /'neɡlɪʒeɪ/ *n* bata *f,* salto *m* de cama

negligen|ce /'neɡlɪdʒəns/ *n* negligencia *f,* descuido *m.* **~t** *a* descuidado

negligible /'neɡlɪdʒəbl/ *a* insignificante

negotiable /nɪ'ɡəʊʃəbl/ *a* negociable

negotiat|e /nɪ'ɡəʊʃɪeɪt/ *vt/i* negociar. **~ion** /-'eɪʃn/ *n* negociación *f.* **~or** *n* negociador *m*

Negr|ess /'niːɡrɪs/ *n* negra *f.* **~o** *n* (*pl* **-oes**) negro *m.* ● *a* negro

neigh /neɪ/ *n* relincho *m.* ● *vi* relinchar

neighbour /'neɪbə(r)/ *n* vecino *m.* **~hood** *n* vecindad *f,* barrio *m.* **in the ~hood of** alrededor de. **~ing** *a* vecino. **~ly** /'neɪbəlɪ/ *a* amable

neither /'naɪðə(r)/ *a* & *pron* ninguno *m* de los dos, ni el uno *m* ni el otro *m.* ● *adv* ni. **~ big nor small** ni grande ni pequeño. **~ shall I come** no voy yo tampoco. ● *conj* tampoco

neon /'niːɒn/ *n* neón *m.* ● *a* (*lamp etc*) de neón

nephew /'nevjuː/ *n* sobrino *m*

nepotism /'nepətɪzəm/ *m* nepotismo *m*

nerve /nɜːv/ *n* nervio *m;* (*courage*) valor *m;* (*calm*) sangre *f* fría; (*impudence, fam*) descaro *m.* **~-racking** *a* exasperante. **~s** *npl* (*before exams etc*) nervios *mpl*

nervous /'nɜːvəs/ *a* nervioso. **be/feel ~** (*afraid*) tener miedo (**of** a).

~ly *adv* (*tensely*) nerviosamente; (*timidly*) tímidamente. **~ness** *n* nerviosidad *f;* (*fear*) miedo *m*

nervy /'nɜːvɪ/ *a see* **nervous**; (*Amer, fam*) descarado

nest /nest/ *n* nido *m.* ● *vi* anidar. **~ egg** *n* (*money*) ahorros *mpl*

nestle /'nesl/ *vi* acomodarse. **~ up to** arrimarse a

net /net/ *n* red *f.* ● *vt* (*pt* **netted**) coger (*not LAm*), agarrar (*esp LAm*). ● *a* (*weight etc*) neto

netball /'netbɔːl/ *n* baloncesto *m*

Netherlands /'neðələndz/ *npl.* **the ~** los Países *mpl* Bajos

netting /'netɪŋ/ *n* (*nets*) redes *fpl;* (*wire*) malla *f;* (*fabric*) tul *m*

nettle /'netl/ *n* ortiga *f*

network /'netwɜːk/ *n* red *f*

neuralgia /njʊə'rældʒɪə/ *n* neuralgia *f*

neuro|sis /njʊə'rəʊsɪs/ *n* (*pl* **-oses** /-siːz/) neurosis *f.* **~tic** *a* & *n* neurótico (*m*)

neuter /'njuːtə(r)/ *a* & *n* neutro (*m*). ● *vt* castrar (*animals*)

neutral /'njuːtrəl/ *a* neutral; (*colour*) neutro; (*elec*) neutro. **~ (gear)** (*auto*) punto *m* muerto. **~ity** /-'trælətɪ/ *n* neutralidad *f*

neutron /'njuːtrɒn/ *n* neutrón *m.* **~ bomb** *n* bomba *f* de neutrones

never /'nevə(r)/ *adv* nunca, jamás; (*not, fam*) no. **~ again** nunca más. **~ mind** (*don't worry*) no te preocupes, no se preocupe; (*it doesn't matter*) no importa. **he ~ smiles** no sonríe nunca. **I ~ saw him** (*fam*) no le vi. **~-ending** *a* interminable

nevertheless /nevəðə'les/ *adv* sin embargo, no obstante

new /njuː/ *a* (**-er, -est**) (*new to owner*) nuevo (*placed before noun*); (*brand new*) nuevo (*placed after noun*). **~-born** *a* recién nacido. **~comer** *n* recién llegado *m.* **~fangled** *a* (*pej*) moderno. **~-laid egg** *n* huevo *m* fresco. **~ly** *adv* nuevamente; (*recently*) recién. **~ly-weds** *npl* recién casados *mpl.* **~ moon** *n* luna *f* nueva. **~ness** *n* novedad *f*

news /njuːz/ *n* noticias *fpl;* (*broadcasting, press*) informaciones *fpl;* (*on TV*) telediario *m;* (*on radio*) diario *m* hablado. **~agent** *n* vendedor *m* de periódicos. **~caster** *n* locutor *m.* **~letter** *n* boletín *m.* **~paper** *n* periódico *m.* **~reader** *n* locutor *m.*

~reel n noticiario m, nodo m (in Spain)

newt /njuːt/ n tritón m

new year /njuːˈjɪə(r)/ n año m nuevo. **N~'s Day** n día m de Año Nuevo. **N~'s Eve** n noche f vieja

New Zealand /njuːˈziːlənd/ n Nueva Zelanda f. **~er** n neozelandés m

next /nekst/ a próximo; ⟨week, month etc⟩ que viene, próximo; (adjoining) vecino; (following) siguiente. ● adv la próxima vez; (afterwards) después. ● n siguiente m. **~ to** junto a. **~ to nothing** casi nada. **~ door** al lado (**to** de). **~-door** de al lado. **~-best** mejor alternativa f. **~ of kin** n pariente m más próximo, parientes mpl más próximos

nib /nɪb/ n (of pen) plumilla f

nibble /ˈnɪbl/ vt/i mordisquear. ● n mordisco m

nice /naɪs/ a (-er, -est) agradable; (likeable) simpático; (kind) amable; (pretty) bonito; ⟨weather⟩ bueno; (subtle) sutil. **~ly** adv agradablemente; (kindly) amablemente; (well) bien

nicety /ˈnaɪsətɪ/ n (precision) precisión f; (detail) detalle. **to a ~** exactamente

niche /nɪtʃ, niːʃ/ n (recess) nicho m; (fig) buena posición f

nick /nɪk/ n corte m pequeño; (prison, sl) cárcel f. **in the ~ of time** justo a tiempo. ● vt (steal, arrest, sl) birlar

nickel /ˈnɪkl/ n níquel m; (Amer) moneda f de cinco centavos

nickname /ˈnɪkneɪm/ n apodo m; (short form) diminutivo m. ● vt apodar

nicotine /ˈnɪkətiːn/ n nicotina f

niece /niːs/ n sobrina f

nifty /ˈnɪftɪ/ a (sl) (smart) elegante

Nigeria /naɪˈdʒɪərɪə/ n Nigeria f. **~n** a & n nigeriano (m)

niggardly /ˈnɪɡədlɪ/ a ⟨person⟩ tacaño; ⟨thing⟩ miserable

niggling /ˈnɪɡlɪŋ/ a molesto

night /naɪt/ n noche f; (evening) tarde f. ● a nocturno, de noche. **~cap** n (hat) gorro m de dormir; (drink) bebida f (tomada antes de acostarse). **~club** n sala f de fiestas, boite f. **~dress** n camisón m. **~fall** n anochecer m. **~gown** n camisón m

nightingale /ˈnaɪtɪŋɡeɪl/ n ruiseñor m

night: **~life** n vida f nocturna. **~ly** adv todas las noches. **~mare** n pesadilla f. **~-school** n escuela f nocturna. **~-time** n noche f. **~watchman** n sereno m

nil /nɪl/ n nada f; (sport) cero m

nimble /ˈnɪmbl/ a (-er, -est) ágil

nine /naɪn/ a & n nueve (m)

nineteen /naɪnˈtiːn/ a & n diecinueve (m). **~th** a & n diecinueve (m), decimonoveno (m)

ninet|ieth /ˈnaɪntɪəθ/ a noventa, nonagésimo. **~y** a & n noventa (m)

ninth /naɪnθ/ a & n noveno (m)

nip[1] /nɪp/ vt (pt nipped) (pinch) pellizcar; (bite) mordisquear. ● vi (rush, sl) correr. ● n (pinch) pellizco m; (cold) frío m

nip[2] /nɪp/ n (of drink) trago m

nipper /ˈnɪpə(r)/ n (sl) chaval m

nipple /ˈnɪpl/ n pezón m; (of baby's bottle) tetilla f

nippy /ˈnɪpɪ/ a (-ier, -iest) (nimble, fam) ágil; (quick, fam) rápido; (chilly, fam) fresquito

nitrogen /ˈnaɪtrədʒən/ n nitrógeno m

nitwit /ˈnɪtwɪt/ n (fam) imbécil m & f

no /nəʊ/ a ninguno. **~ entry** prohibido el paso. **~ man's land** n tierra f de nadie. **~ smoking** se prohibe fumar. **~ way!** (Amer, fam) ¡ni hablar! ● adv no. ● n (pl noes) no m

nobility /nəʊˈbɪlətɪ/ n nobleza f

noble /ˈnəʊbl/ a (-er, -est) noble. **~man** n noble m

nobody /ˈnəʊbədɪ/ pron nadie m. ● n nadie m. **~ is there** no hay nadie. **he knows ~** no conoce a nadie

nocturnal /nɒkˈtɜːnl/ a nocturno

nod /nɒd/ vt (pt nodded). **~ one's head** asentir con la cabeza. ● vi (in agreement) asentir con la cabeza; (in greeting) saludar; (be drowsy) dar cabezadas. ● n inclinación f de cabeza

nodule /ˈnɒdjuːl/ n nódulo m

nois|e /nɔɪz/ n ruido m. **~eless** a silencioso. **~ily** /ˈnɔɪzɪlɪ/ adv ruidosamente. **~y** a (-ier, -iest) ruidoso

nomad /ˈnəʊmæd/ n nómada m & f. **~ic** /-ˈmædɪk/ a nómada

nominal /ˈnɒmɪnl/ a nominal

nominat|e /ˈnɒmɪneɪt/ vt nombrar; (put forward) proponer. **~ion** /-ˈneɪʃn/ n nombramiento m

non-... /nɒn/ pref no ...
nonagenarian /nəʊnədʒɪ'neərɪən/ a & n nonagenario (m), noventón (m)
nonchalant /'nɒnʃələnt/ a imperturbable
non-commissioned /nɒnkə'mɪʃnd/ a. ~ **officer** n suboficial m
non-comittal /nɒnkə'mɪtl/ a evasivo
nondescript /'nɒndɪskrɪpt/ a inclasificable, anodino
none /nʌn/ pron (person) nadie, ninguno; (thing) ninguno, nada. ~ **of** nada de. ~ **of us** ninguno de nosotros. **I have** ~ no tengo nada. ● adv no, de ninguna manera. **he is** ~ **the happier** no está más contento
nonentity /nɒ'nentəti/ n nulidad f
non-existent /nɒnɪg'zɪstənt/ a inexistente
nonplussed /nɒn'plʌst/ a perplejo
nonsens|e /'nɒnsns/ n tonterías fpl, disparates mpl. ~**ical** /-'sensɪkl/ a absurdo
non-smoker /nɒn'sməʊkə(r)/ n persona f que no fuma; (rail) departamento m de no fumadores
non-starter /nɒn'stɑːtə(r)/ n (fam) proyecto m imposible
non-stop /nɒn'stɒp/ a ⟨train⟩ directo; ⟨flight⟩ sin escalas. ● adv sin parar; (by train) directamente; (by air) sin escalas
noodles /'nuːdlz/ npl fideos mpl
nook /nʊk/ n rincón m
noon /nuːn/ n mediodía m
no-one /'nəʊwʌn/ pron nadie. see **nobody**
noose /nuːs/ n nudo m corredizo
nor /nɔː(r)/ conj ni, tampoco. **neither blue** ~ **red** ni azul ni rojo. **he doesn't play the piano,** ~ **do I** no sabe tocar el piano, ni yo tampoco
Nordic /'nɔːdɪk/ a nórdico
norm /nɔːm/ n norma f; (normal) lo normal
normal /'nɔːml/ a normal. ~**cy** n (Amer) normalidad f. ~**ity** /-'mælətɪ/ n normalidad f. ~**ly** adv normalmente
Norman /'nɔːmən/ a & n normando (m)
Normandy /'nɔːməndɪ/ n Normandia f
north /nɔːθ/ n norte m. ● a del norte, norteño. ● adv hacia el norte. **N~ America** n América f del Norte, Norteamérica f. **N~ American** a & n

norteamericano (m). ~**east** n nordeste m. ~**erly** /'nɔːðəlɪ/ a del norte. ~**ern** /'nɔːðən/ a del norte. ~**erner** n norteño m. **N~ Sea** n mar m del Norte. ~**ward** a hacia el norte. ~**wards** adv hacia el norte. ~**west** n noroeste m
Norw|ay /'nɔːweɪ/ n Noruega f. ~**egian** a & n noruego (m)
nose /nəʊz/ n nariz f. ● vi. ~ **about** curiosear. ~**bleed** n hemorragia f nasal. ~**dive** n picado m
nostalgi|a /nɒ'stældʒə/ n nostalgia f. ~**c** a nostálgico
nostril /'nɒstrɪl/ n nariz f; (of horse) ollar m
nosy /'nəʊzɪ/ a (-ier, -iest) (fam) entrometido
not /nɒt/ adv no. ~ **at all** no... nada; (after thank you) de nada. ~ **yet** aún no. **I do** ~ **know** no sé. **I suppose** ~ supongo que no
notabl|e /'nəʊtəbl/ a notable. ● n (person) notabilidad f. ~**y** /'nəʊtəblɪ/ adv notablemente
notary /'nəʊtərɪ/ n notario m
notation /nəʊ'teɪʃn/ n notación f
notch /nɒtʃ/ n muesca f. ● vt. ~ **up** apuntar ⟨score etc⟩
note /nəʊt/ n nota f; (banknote) billete m. **take** ~**s** tomar apuntes. ● vt notar. ~**book** n libreta f. ~**d** a célebre. ~**paper** n papel m de escribir. ~**worthy** a notable
nothing /'nʌθɪŋ/ pron nada. **he eats** ~ no come nada. **for** ~ (free) gratis; (in vain) inútilmente. ● n nada f; (person) nulidad f; (thing of no importance) fruslería f; (zero) cero m. ● adv de ninguna manera. ~ **big** nada grande. ~ **else** nada más. ~ **much** poca cosa
notice /'nəʊtɪs/ n (attention) atención f; (advert) anuncio m; (sign) letrero m; (poster) cartel m; (termination of employment) despido m; (warning) aviso m. (advance) ~ previo aviso m. ~ (of dismissal) despido m. **take** ~ **of** prestar atención a, hacer caso a ⟨person⟩; hacer caso de ⟨thing⟩. ● vt notar. ~**able** a evidente. ~**ably** adv visiblemente. ~**board** n tablón m de anuncios
notif|ication /nəʊtɪfɪ'keɪʃn/ n aviso m, notificación f. ~**y** vt avisar
notion /'nəʊʃn/ n (concept) concepto m; (idea) idea f. ~**s** npl (sewing goods etc, Amer) artículos mpl de mercería

notori|ety /nəʊtə'raɪətɪ/ *n* notoriedad *f*; (*pej*) mala fama *f*. **~ous** /nəʊ'tɔ:rɪəs/ *a* notorio. **~ously** *adv* notoriamente

notwithstanding /nɒtwɪθ'stændɪŋ/ *prep* a pesar de. ● *adv* sin embargo

nougat /'nu:gɑ:/ *n* turrón *m*

nought /nɔ:t/ *n* cero *m*

noun /naʊn/ *n* sustantivo *m*, nombre *m*

nourish /'nʌrɪʃ/ *vt* alimentar; (*incl fig*) nutrir. **~ment** *n* alimento *m*

novel /'nɒvl/ *n* novela *f*. ● *a* nuevo. **~ist** *n* novelista *m* & *f*. **~ty** *n* novedad *f*

November /nəʊ'vembə(r)/ *n* noviembre *m*

novice /'nɒvɪs/ *n* principiante *m* & *f*

now /naʊ/ *adv* ahora. **~ and again**, **~ and then** de vez en cuando. **just ~** ahora mismo; (*a moment ago*) hace poco. ● *conj* ahora que

nowadays /'naʊədeɪz/ *adv* hoy (en) día

nowhere /'nəʊweə(r)/ *adv* en/por ninguna parte; (*after motion towards*) a ninguna parte

noxious /'nɒkʃəs/ *a* nocivo

nozzle /'nɒzl/ *n* boquilla *f*; (*tec*) tobera *f*

nuance /'njʊɑ:ns/ *n* matiz *m*

nuclear /'nju:klɪə(r)/ *a* nuclear

nucleus /'nju:klɪəs/ *n* (*pl* -lei /-lɪaɪ/) núcleo *m*

nude /nju:d/ *a* & *n* desnudo (*m*). **in the ~** desnudo

nudge /nʌdʒ/ *vt* dar un codazo a. ● *n* codazo *m*

nudi|sm /'nju:dɪzəm/ *n* desnudismo *m*. **~st** *n* nudista *m* & *f*. **~ty** /'nju:dətɪ/ *n* desnudez *f*

nuisance /'nju:sns/ *n* (*thing, event*) fastidio *m*; (*person*) pesado *m*. **be a ~** dar la lata

null /nʌl/ *a* nulo. **~ify** *vt* anular

numb /nʌm/ *a* entumecido. ● *vt* entumecer

number /'nʌmbə(r)/ *n* número *m*. ● *vt* numerar; (*count, include*) contar. **~plate** *n* matrícula *f*

numeracy /'nju:mərəsɪ/ *n* conocimientos *mpl* de matemáticas

numeral /'nju:mərəl/ *n* número *m*

numerate /'nju:mərət/ *a* que tiene buenos conocimientos de matemáticas

numerical /nju:'merɪkl/ *a* numérico

numerous /'nju:mərəs/ *a* numeroso

nun /nʌn/ *n* monja *f*

nurse /nɜ:s/ *n* enfermera *f*, enfermero *m*; (*nanny*) niñera *f*. **wet ~** *n* nodriza *f*. ● *vt* cuidar; abrigar (*hope etc*). **~maid** *n* niñera *f*

nursery /'nɜ:sərɪ/ *n* cuarto *m* de los niños; (*for plants*) vivero *m*. **(day) ~** *n* guardería *f* infantil. **~ rhyme** *n* canción *f* infantil. **~ school** *n* escuela *f* de párvulos

nursing home /'nɜ:sɪŋhəʊm/ *n* (*for old people*) asilo *m* de ancianos

nurture /'nɜ:tʃə(r)/ *vt* alimentar

nut /nʌt/ *n* (*walnut, Brazil nut etc*) nuez *f*; (*hazlenut*) avellana *f*; (*peanut*) cacahuete *m*; (*tec*) tuerca *f*; (*crazy person, sl*) chiflado *m*. **~crackers** *npl* cascanueces *m invar*

nutmeg /'nʌtmeg/ *n* nuez *f* moscada

nutrient /'nju:trɪənt/ *n* alimento *m*

nutrit|ion /nju:'trɪʃn/ *n* nutrición *f*. **~ious** *a* nutritivo

nuts /nʌts/ *a* (*crazy, sl*) chiflado

nutshell /'nʌtʃel/ *n* cáscara *f* de nuez. **in a ~** en pocas palabras

nuzzle /'nʌzl/ *vt* acariciar con el hocico

NW *abbr* (*north-west*) noroeste *m*

nylon /'naɪlɒn/ *n* nailon *m*. **~s** *npl* medias *fpl* de nailon

nymph /nɪmf/ *n* ninfa *f*

O

oaf /əʊf/ *n* (*pl* **oafs**) zoquete *m*

oak /əʊk/ *n* roble *m*

OAP /əʊeɪ'pi:/ *abbr* (*old-age pensioner*) *n* pensionista *m* & *f*

oar /ɔ:(r)/ *n* remo *m*. **~sman** /'ɔ:zmən/ *n* (*pl* -**men**) remero *m*

oasis /əʊ'eɪsɪs/ *n* (*pl* **oases** /-si:z/) oasis *m invar*

oath /əʊθ/ *n* juramento *m*; (*swearword*) palabrota *f*

oat|meal /'əʊtmi:l/ *n* harina *f* de avena. **~s** /əʊts/ *npl* avena *f*

obedien|ce /əʊ'bi:dɪəns/ *n* obediencia *f*. **~t** /əʊ'bi:dɪənt/ *a* obediente. **~tly** *adv* obedientemente

obelisk /'ɒbəlɪsk/ *n* obelisco *m*

obes|e /əʊ'bi:s/ *a* obeso. **~ity** *n* obesidad *f*

obey /əʊ'beɪ/ *vt* obedecer; cumplir (*instructions etc*)

obituary /ə'bɪtʃʊərɪ/ *n* necrología *f*

object /'ɒbdʒɪkt/ *n* objeto *m*. /əb'dʒekt/ *vi* oponerse

objection /əb'dʒekʃn/ n objeción f.
~able /əb'dʒekʃnəbl/ a censurable;
(*unpleasant*) desagradable
objective /əb'dʒektɪv/ a & n objetivo
(m). **~ively** adv objetivamente
objector /əb'dʒektə(r)/ n objetante
m & f
oblig|ation /ɒblɪ'geɪʃn/ n obliga-
ción f. **be under an ~ation to** tener
obligación de. **~atory** /ə'blɪgətrɪ/ a
obligatorio. **~e** /ə'blaɪdʒ/ vt obligar;
(*do a small service*) hacer un favor a.
~ed a agradecido. **much ~ed!** ¡muchas gracias! **~ing** a atento
oblique /ə'bliːk/ a oblicuo
obliterat|e /ə'blɪtəreɪt/ vt borrar.
~ion /-'reɪʃn/ n borradura f
oblivio|n /ə'blɪvɪən/ n olvido m.
~us /ə'blɪvɪəs/ a (*unaware*) inconsciente (**to, of** de)
oblong /'ɒblɒŋ/ a & n oblongo (m)
obnoxious /əb'nɒkʃəs/ a odioso
oboe /'əʊbəʊ/ n oboe m
obscen|e /əb'siːn/ a obsceno. **~ity**
/-enətɪ/ n obscenidad f
obscur|e /əb'skjʊə(r)/ a oscuro. ● vt
oscurecer; (*conceal*) esconder; (*confuse*) confundir. **~ity** n oscuridad f
obsequious /əb'siːkwɪəs/ a ob-
sequioso
observan|ce /əb'zɜːvəns/ n obser-
vancia f. **~t** /əb'zɜːvənt/ a
observador
observation /ɒbzə'veɪʃn/ n observación f
observatory /əb'zɜːvətrɪ/ n ob-
servatorio m
observe /əb'zɜːv/ vt observar. **~r** n
observador m
obsess /əb'ses/ vt obsesionar. **~ion**
/-ʃn/ n obsesión f. **~ive** a obsesivo
obsolete /'ɒbsəliːt/ a desusado
obstacle /'ɒbstəkl/ n obstáculo m
obstetrics /əb'stetrɪks/ n obstetricia
f
obstina|cy /'ɒbstɪnəsɪ/ n obstina-
ción f. **~te** /'ɒbstɪnət/ a obstinado.
~tely adv obstinadamente
obstreperous /ɒb'strepərəs/ a tur-
bulento, ruidoso, protestón
obstruct /əb'strʌkt/ vt obstruir.
~ion /-ʃn/ n obstrucción f
obtain /əb'teɪn/ vt obtener. ● vi prevalecer. **~able** a asequible
obtrusive /əb'truːsɪv/ a importuno
obtuse /əb'tjuːs/ a obtuso
obviate /'ɒbvɪeɪt/ vt evitar

obvious /'ɒbvɪəs/ a obvio. **~ly** adv
obviamente
occasion /ə'keɪʒn/ n ocasión f, oportunidad f. **on ~** de vez en cuando.
● vt ocasionar. **~al** /ə'keɪʒənl/ a
poco frecuente. **~ally** adv de vez en
cuando
occult /ɒ'kʌlt/ a oculto
occup|ant /'ɒkjʊpənt/ n ocupante m
& f. **~ation** /ɒkjʊ'peɪʃn/ n ocupación f; (*job*) trabajo m, profesión f.
~ational a profesional. **~ier** n
ocupante m & f. **~y** /'ɒkjʊpaɪ/ vt
ocupar
occur /ə'kɜː(r)/ vi (*pt* **occurred**)
ocurrir, suceder; (*exist*) encontrarse.
it ~red to me that se me ocurrió
que. **~rence** /ə'kʌrəns/ n suceso m,
acontecimiento m
ocean /'əʊʃn/ n océano m
o'clock /ə'klɒk/ adv. **it is 7 ~** son las
siete
octagon /'ɒktəgən/ n octágono m
octane /'ɒkteɪn/ n octano m
octave /'ɒktɪv/ n octava f
October /ɒk'təʊbə(r)/ n octubre m
octopus /'ɒktəpəs/ n (*pl* **-puses**)
pulpo m
oculist /'ɒkjʊlɪst/ n oculista m & f
odd /ɒd/ a (**-er**, **-est**) extraño, raro;
⟨*number*⟩ impar; (*one of pair*) sin
pareja; (*occasional*) poco frecuente;
(*left over*) sobrante. **fifty-~** unos cincuenta, cincuenta y pico. **the ~ one
out** la excepción f. **~ity** n (*thing*)
curiosidad f; (*person*) excéntrico m.
~ly adv extrañamente. **~ly enough**
por extraño que parezca. **~ment**
/'ɒdmənt/ n retazo m. **~s** /ɒdz/ npl
probabilidades fpl; (*in betting*)
apuesta f. **~s and ends** retazos mpl.
at ~s de punta, de malas
ode /əʊd/ n oda f
odious /'əʊdɪəs/ a odioso
odour /'əʊdə(r)/ n olor m. **~less** a
inodoro
of /əv, ɒv/ prep de. **a friend ~ mine**
un amigo mío. **how kind ~ you** es
Vd muy amable
off /ɒf/ adv lejos; ⟨*light etc*⟩ apagado;
⟨*tap*⟩ cerrado; ⟨*food*⟩ pasado. ● prep
de, desde; (*away from*) fuera de; (*dis-
tant from*) lejos de. **be better ~** estar
mejor. **be ~** marcharse. **day ~** n día
m de asueto, día m libre
offal /'ɒfl/ n menudos mpl, asaduras
fpl

off: ~**-beat** *a* insólito. ~ **chance** *n* posibilidad *f* remota. ~ **colour** *a* indispuesto

offen|ce /ə'fens/ *n* ofensa *f*; (*illegal act*) delito *m*. **take** ~**ce** ofenderse. ~**d** /ə'fend/ *vt* ofender. ~**der** *n* delincuente *m* & *f*. ~**sive** /ə'fensɪv/ *a* ofensivo; (*disgusting*) repugnante. ● *n* ofensiva *f*

offer /'ɒfə(r)/ *vt* ofrecer. ● *n* oferta *f*. **on** ~ en oferta

offhand /ɒf'hænd/ *a* (*casual*) desenvuelto; (*brusque*) descortés. ● *adv* de improviso

office /'ɒfɪs/ *n* oficina *f*; (*post*) cargo *m*

officer /'ɒfɪsə(r)/ *n* oficial *m*; (*policeman*) policía *f*, guardia *m*; (*of organization*) director *m*

official /ə'fɪʃl/ *a* & *n* oficial (*m*). ~**ly** *adv* oficialmente

officiate /ə'fɪʃɪeɪt/ *vi* oficiar. ~ **as** desempeñar las funciones de

officious /ə'fɪʃəs/ *a* oficioso

offing /'ɒfɪŋ/ *n*. **in the** ~ en perspectiva

off: ~**-licence** *n* tienda *f* de bebidas alcohólicas. ~**-load** *vt* descargar. ~**-putting** *a* (*disconcerting, fam*) desconcertante; (*repellent*) repugnante. ~**set** /'ɒfset/ *vt* (*pt* -**set**, *pres p* -**setting**) contrapesar. ~**shoot** /'ɒfʃuːt/ *n* retoño *m*; (*fig*) ramificación *f*. ~**side** /ɒf'saɪd/ *a* (*sport*) fuera de juego. ~**spring** /'ɒfsprɪŋ/ *n invar* progenie *f*. ~**stage** *a* entre bastidores. ~**white** *a* blancuzco, color hueso

often /'ɒfn/ *adv* muchas veces, con frecuencia, a menudo. **how** ~? ¿cuántas veces?

ogle /'əʊgl/ *vt* comerse con los ojos

ogre /'əʊgə(r)/ *n* ogro *m*

oh /əʊ/ *int* ¡oh!, ¡ay!

oil /ɔɪl/ *n* aceite *m*; (*petroleum*) petróleo *m*. ● *vt* lubricar. ~**field** /'ɔɪlfiːld/ *n* yacimiento *m* petrolífero. ~**painting** *n* pintura *f* al óleo. ~**-rig** /'ɔɪlrɪg/ *n* plataforma *f* de perforación. ~**skins** /'ɔɪlskɪnz/ *npl* chubasquero *m*. ~**y** *a* aceitoso; (*food*) grasiento

ointment /'ɔɪntmənt/ *n* ungüento *m*

OK /əʊ'keɪ/ *int* ¡vale!, ¡de acuerdo! ● *a* bien; (*satisfactory*) satisfactorio. ● *adv* muy bien

old /əʊld/ *a* (-**er**, -**est**) viejo; (*not modern*) anticuado; (*former*) antiguo. **how** ~ **is she?** ¿cuántos años tiene?

she is ten years ~ tiene diez años. ~ **of** ~ de antaño. ~ **age** *n* vejez *f*. ~**fashioned** *a* anticuado. ~ **maid** *n* solterona *f*. ~**world** *a* antiguo

oleander /əʊlɪ'ændə(r)/ *n* adelfa *f*

olive /'ɒlɪv/ *n* (*fruit*) aceituna *f*; (*tree*) olivo *m*. ● *a* de oliva; (*colour*) aceitunado

Olympic /ə'lɪmpɪk/ *a* olímpico. ~**s** *npl*, ~ **Games** *npl* Juegos *mpl* Olímpicos

omelette /'ɒmlɪt/ *n* tortilla *f*, tortilla *f* de huevos (*Mex*)

om|en /'əʊmen/ *n* agüero *m*. ~**inous** /'ɒmɪnəs/ *a* siniestro

omi|ssion /ə'mɪʃn/ *n* omisión *f*. ~**t** /ə'mɪt/ *vt* (*pt* **omitted**) omitir

omnipotent /ɒm'nɪpətənt/ *a* omnipotente

on /ɒn/ *prep* en, sobre. ~ **foot** a pie. ~ **Monday** el lunes. ~ **Mondays** los lunes. ~ **seeing** al ver. ~ **the way** de camino. ● *adv* (*light etc*) encendido; (*put on*) puesto, poco natural; (*machine*) en marcha; (*tap*) abierto. ~ **and off** de vez en cuando. ~ **and** ~ sin cesar. **and so** ~ y así sucesivamente. **be** ~ **at** (*fam*) criticar. **go** ~ continuar. **later** ~ más tarde

once /wʌns/ *adv* una vez; (*formerly*) antes. ● *conj* una vez que. **at** ~ en seguida. ~**-over** *n* (*fam*) ojeada *f*

oncoming /'ɒnkʌmɪŋ/ *a* que se acerca; (*traffic*) que viene en sentido contrario, de frente

one /wʌn/ *a* & *n* uno (*m*). ● *pron* uno. ~ **another** el uno al otro. ~ **by** ~ uno a uno. ~ **never knows** nunca se sabe. **the blue** ~ el azul. **this** ~ éste. ~**-off** *a* (*fam*) único

onerous /'ɒnərəs/ *a* oneroso

one: ~**self** /wʌn'self/ *pron* (*subject*) uno mismo; (*object*) se; (*after prep*) sí (mismo). **by** ~**self** solo. ~**-sided** *a* unilateral. ~**-way** *a* (*street*) de dirección única; (*ticket*) de ida

onion /'ʌnɪən/ *n* cebolla *f*

onlooker /'ɒnlʊkə(r)/ *n* espectador *m*

only /'əʊnlɪ/ *a* único. ~ **son** *n* hijo *m* único. ● *adv* sólo, solamente. ~ **just** apenas. ~ **too** de veras. ● *conj* pero, sólo que

onset /'ɒnset/ *n* principio *m*; (*attack*) ataque *m*

onslaught /'ɒnslɔːt/ *n* ataque *m* violento

onus /'əʊnəs/ *n* responsabilidad *f*

onward(s) /'ɒnwəd(z)/ *a* & *adv* hacia adelante

onyx /'ɒnɪks/ *n* ónice *f*

ooze /uːz/ *vt/i* rezumar

opal /'əʊpl/ *n* ópalo *m*

opaque /əʊ'peɪk/ *a* opaco

open /'əʊpən/ *a* abierto; (*free to all*) público; (*undisguised*) manifiesto; (*question*) discutible; (*view*) despejado. ~ **sea** *n* alta mar *f*. ~ **secret** *n* secreto *m* a voces. **O~ University** *n* Universidad *f* a Distancia. **half-~** *a* medio abierto. **in the** ~ *n* al aire libre. ● *vt/i* abrir. ~**ended** *a* abierto. ~**er** /'əʊpənə(r)/ *n* (*for tins*) abrelatas *m invar*; (*for bottles with caps*) abrebotellas *m invar*; (*corkscrew*) sacacorchos *m invar*. **eye-~er** *n* (*fam*) revelación *f*. ~**ing** /'əʊpənɪŋ/ *n* abertura *f*; (*beginning*) principio *m*; (*job*) vacante *m*. ~**ly** /'əʊpənlɪ/ *adv* abiertamente. ~**minded** *a* imparcial

opera /'ɒprə/ *n* ópera *f*. ~**glasses** *npl* gemelos *mpl* de teatro

operate /'ɒpəreɪt/ *vt* hacer funcionar. ● *vi* funcionar; (*medicine etc*) operar. ~ **on** (*med*) operar a

operatic /ɒpə'rætɪk/ *a* operístico

operation /ɒpə'reɪʃn/ *n* operación *f*; (*mec*) funcionamiento *m*. **in** ~ en vigor. ~**al** /ɒpə'reɪʃnl/ *a* operacional

operative /'ɒpərətɪv/ *a* operativo; (*law etc*) en vigor

operator *n* operario *m*; (*telephonist*) telefonista *m* & *f*

operetta /ɒpə'retə/ *n* opereta *f*

opinion /ə'pɪnɪən/ *n* opinión *f*. **in my** ~ a mi parecer. ~**ated** *a* dogmático

opium /'əʊpɪəm/ *n* opio *m*

opponent /ə'pəʊnənt/ *n* adversario *m*

opportun|e /'ɒpətjuːn/ *a* oportuno. ~**ist** /ɒpə'tjuːnɪst/ *n* oportunista *m* & *f*. ~**ity** /ɒpə'tjuːnətɪ/ *n* oportunidad *f*

oppos|e /ə'pəʊz/ *vt* oponerse a. ~**ed to** en contra de. **be** ~**ed to** oponerse a. ~**ing** *a* opuesto

opposite /'ɒpəzɪt/ *a* opuesto; (*facing*) de enfrente. ● *n* contrario *m*. ● *adv* enfrente. ● *prep* enfrente de. ~ **number** *n* homólogo *m*

opposition /ɒpə'zɪʃn/ *n* oposición *f*; (*resistence*) resistencia *f*

oppress /ə'pres/ *vt* oprimir. ~**ion** /-ʃn/ *n* opresión *f*. ~**ive** *a* (*cruel*) opresivo; (*heat*) sofocante. ~**or** *n* opresor *m*

opt /ɒpt/ *vi*. ~ **for** elegir. ~ **out** negarse a participar

optic|al /'ɒptɪkl/ *a* óptico. ~**ian** /ɒp'tɪʃn/ *n* óptico *m*

optimis|m /'ɒptɪmɪzəm/ *n* optimismo *m*. ~**t** /'ɒptɪmɪst/ *n* optimista *m* & *f*. ~**tic** /-'mɪstɪk/ *a* optimista

optimum /'ɒptɪməm/ *n* lo óptimo, lo mejor

option /'ɒpʃn/ *n* opción *f*. ~**al** /'ɒpʃənl/ *a* facultativo

opulen|ce /'ɒpjʊləns/ *n* opulencia *f*. ~**t** /'ɒpjʊlənt/ *a* opulento

or /ɔː(r)/ *conj* o; (*before Spanish o- and ho-*) u; (*after negative*) ni. ~ **else** si no, o bien

oracle /'ɒrəkl/ *n* oráculo *m*

oral /'ɔːrəl/ *a* oral. ● *n* (*fam*) examen *m* oral

orange /'ɒrɪndʒ/ *n* naranja *f*; (*tree*) naranjo *m*; (*colour*) color *m* naranja. ● *a* de color naranja. ~**ade** *n* naranjada *f*

orator /'ɒrətə(r)/ *n* orador *m*

oratorio /ɒrə'tɔːrɪəʊ/ *n* (*pl* -os) oratorio *m*

oratory /'ɒrətrɪ/ *n* oratoria *f*

orb /ɔːb/ *n* orbe *m*

orbit /'ɔːbɪt/ *n* órbita *f*. ● *vt* orbitar

orchard /'ɔːtʃəd/ *n* huerto *m*

orchestra /'ɔːkɪstrə/ *n* orquesta *f*. ~**l** /-'kestrəl/ *a* orquestal. ~**te** /'ɔːkɪstreɪt/ *vt* orquestar

orchid /'ɔːkɪd/ *n* orquídea *f*

ordain /ɔː'deɪn/ *vt* ordenar

ordeal /ɔː'diːl/ *n* prueba *f* dura

order /'ɔːdə(r)/ *n* orden *m*; (*com*) pedido *m*. **in** ~ **that** para que. **in** ~ **to** para. ● *vt* (*command*) mandar; (*com*) pedir

orderly /'ɔːdəlɪ/ *a* ordenado. ● *n* asistente *m* & *f*

ordinary /'ɔːdɪnrɪ/ *a* corriente; (*average*) medio; (*mediocre*) ordinario

ordination /ɔːdɪ'neɪʃn/ *n* ordenación *f*

ore /ɔː(r)/ *n* mineral *m*

organ /'ɔːgən/ *n* órgano *m*

organic /ɔː'gænɪk/ *a* orgánico

organism /'ɔːgənɪzəm/ *n* organismo *m*

organist /'ɔːgənɪst/ *n* organista *m* & *f*

organiz|ation /ˌɔːɡənaɪˈzeɪʃn/ n organización f. ~e /ˈɔːɡənaɪz/ vt organizar. ~er n organizador m

orgasm /ˈɔːɡæzəm/ n orgasmo m

orgy /ˈɔːdʒɪ/ n orgía f

Orient /ˈɔːrɪənt/ n Oriente m. ~al /-ˈentl/ a & n oriental (m & f)

orientat|e /ˈɔːrɪənteɪt/ vt orientar. ~ion /-ˈteɪʃn/ n orientación f

orifice /ˈɒrɪfɪs/ n orificio m

origin /ˈɒrɪdʒɪn/ n origen m. ~al /əˈrɪdʒənl/ a original. ~ality /-ˈnælətɪ/ n originalidad f. ~ally adv originalmente. ~ate /əˈrɪdʒɪneɪt/ vi. ~ate from provenir de. ~ator n autor m

ormolu /ˈɔːməluː/ n similor m

ornament /ˈɔːnəmənt/ n adorno m. ~al /-ˈmentl/ a de adorno. ~ation /-enˈteɪʃn/ n ornamentación f

ornate /ɔːˈneɪt/ a adornado; ⟨style⟩ florido

ornithology /ɔːnɪˈθɒlədʒɪ/ n ornitología f

orphan /ˈɔːfn/ n huérfano m. • vt dejar huérfano. ~age n orfanato m

orthodox /ˈɔːθədɒks/ a ortodoxo. ~y n ortodoxia f

orthopaedic /ɔːθəˈpiːdɪk/ a ortopédico. ~s n ortopedia f

oscillate /ˈɒsɪleɪt/ vi oscilar

ossify /ˈɒsɪfaɪ/ vt osificar. • vi osificarse

ostensibl|e /ɒsˈtensɪbl/ a aparente. ~y adv aparentemente

ostentat|ion /ɒstenˈteɪʃn/ n ostentación f. ~ious a ostentoso

osteopath /ˈɒstɪəpæθ/ n osteópata m & f. ~y /-ˈɒpəθɪ/ n osteopatía f

ostracize /ˈɒstrəsaɪz/ vt excluir

ostrich /ˈɒstrɪtʃ/ n avestruz m

other /ˈʌðə(r)/ a & n & pron otro (m). ~ than de otra manera que. **the ~ one** el otro. ~wise /ˈʌðəwaɪz/ adv de otra manera; (or) si no

otter /ˈɒtə(r)/ n nutria f

ouch /aʊtʃ/ int ¡ay!

ought /ɔːt/ v aux deber. **I ~ to see it** debería verlo. **he ~ to have done it** debería haberlo hecho

ounce /aʊns/ n onza f (= 28.35 gr.)

our /ˈaʊə(r)/ a nuestro. ~s /ˈaʊəz/ poss pron el nuestro, la nuestra, los nuestros, las nuestras. ~selves /aʊəˈselvz/ pron (subject) nosotros mismos, nosotras mismas; (reflexive) nos; (after prep) nosotros (mismos), nosotras (mismas)

oust /aʊst/ vt expulsar, desalojar

out /aʊt/ adv fuera; ⟨light⟩ apagado; (in blossom) en flor; (in error) equivocado. ~-and-~ a cien por cien. ~ of date anticuado; (not valid) caducado. ~ of doors fuera. ~ of order estropeado; (sign) no funciona. ~ of pity por compasión. ~ of place fuera de lugar; (fig) inoportuno. ~ of print agotado. ~ of sorts indispuesto. ~ of stock agotado. ~ of tune desafinado. ~ of work parado, desempleado. **be ~** equivocarse. **be ~ of** quedarse sin. **be ~ to** estar resuelto a. **five ~ of six** cinco de cada seis. **made ~** hecho de

outbid /aʊtˈbɪd/ vt (pt -bid, pres p -bidding) ofrecer más que

outboard /ˈaʊtbɔːd/ a fuera borda

outbreak /ˈaʊtbreɪk/ n (of anger) arranque m; (of war) comienzo m; (of disease) epidemia f

outbuilding /ˈaʊtbɪldɪŋ/ n dependencia f

outburst /ˈaʊtbɜːst/ n explosión f

outcast /ˈaʊtkɑːst/ n paria m & f

outcome /ˈaʊtkʌm/ n resultado m

outcry /ˈaʊtkraɪ/ n protesta f

outdated /aʊtˈdeɪtɪd/ a anticuado

outdo /aʊtˈduː/ vt (pt -did, pp -done) superar

outdoor /ˈaʊtdɔː(r)/ a al aire libre. ~s /-ˈdɔːz/ adv al aire libre

outer /ˈaʊtə(r)/ a exterior

outfit /ˈaʊtfɪt/ n equipo m; (clothes) traje m. ~ter n camisero m

outgoing /ˈaʊtɡəʊɪŋ/ a ⟨minister etc⟩ saliente; (sociable) abierto. ~s npl gastos mpl

outgrow /æʊtˈɡrəʊ/ vt (pt -grew, pp -grown) crecer más que ⟨person⟩; hacerse demasiado grande para ⟨clothes⟩. **he's ~n his trousers** le quedan pequeños los pantalones

outhouse /ˈaʊthaʊs/ n dependencia f

outing /ˈaʊtɪŋ/ n excursión f

outlandish /aʊtˈlændɪʃ/ a extravagante

outlaw /ˈaʊtlɔː/ n proscrito m. • vt proscribir

outlay /ˈaʊtleɪ/ n gastos mpl

outlet /ˈaʊtlet/ n salida f

outline /ˈaʊtlaɪn/ n contorno m; (summary) resumen m. • vt trazar; (describe) dar un resumen de

outlive /aʊtˈlɪv/ vt sobrevivir a

outlook /ˈaʊtlʊk/ n perspectiva f

outlying /'aʊtlaɪɪŋ/ a remoto

outmoded /aʊt'məʊdɪd/ a anticuado

outnumber /aʊt'nʌmbə(r)/ vt sobrepasar en número

outpatient /'aʊt'peɪʃnt/ n paciente m externo

outpost /'aʊtpəʊst/ n avanzada f

output /'aʊtpʊt/ n producción f

outrage /'aʊtreɪdʒ/ n ultraje m. ● vt ultrajar. ~ous /aʊt'reɪdʒəs/ a escandaloso, atroz

outright /'aʊtraɪt/ adv completamente; (at once) inmediatamente; (frankly) francamente. ● a completo; (refusal) rotundo

outset /'aʊtset/ n principio m

outside /'aʊtsaɪd/ a & n exterior (m). /aʊt'saɪd/ adv fuera. ● prep fuera de. ~r /aʊt'saɪdə(r)/ n forastero m; (in race) caballo m no favorito

outsize /'aʊtsaɪz/ a de tamaño extraordinario

outskirts /'aʊtskɜːts/ npl afueras fpl

outspoken /aʊt'spəʊkn/ a franco. be ~ no tener pelos en la lengua

outstanding /aʊt'stændɪŋ/ a excepcional; (not settled) pendiente; (conspicuous) sobresaliente

outstretched /aʊt'stretʃt/ a extendido

outstrip /aʊt'strɪp/ vt (pt -stripped) superar

outward /'aʊtwəd/ a externo; (journey) de ida. ~ly adv por fuera, exteriormente. ~(s) adv hacia fuera

outweigh /aʊt'weɪ/ vt pesar más que; (fig) valer más que

outwit /aʊt'wɪt/ vt (pt -witted) ser más listo que

oval /'əʊvl/ a oval(ado). ● n óvalo m

ovary /'əʊvərɪ/ n ovario m

ovation /əʊ'veɪʃn/ n ovación f

oven /'ʌvn/ n horno m

over /'əʊvə(r)/ prep por encima de; (across) al otro lado de; (during) durante; (more than) más de. ~ and above por encima de. ● adv por encima; (ended) terminado; (more) más; (in excess) de sobra. ~ again otra vez. ~ and ~ una y otra vez. ~ here por aquí. ~ there por allí. all ~ por todas partes

over... /'əʊvə(r)/ pref sobre..., super...

overall /əʊvər'ɔːl/ a global; (length, cost) total. ● adv en conjunto. /'əʊvərɔːl/ n, ~s npl mono m

overawe /əʊvər'ɔː/ vt intimidar

overbalance /əʊvə'bæləns/ vt hacer perder el equilibrio. ● vi perder el equilibrio

overbearing /əʊvə'beərɪŋ/ a dominante

overboard /'əʊvəbɔːd/ adv al agua

overbook /əʊvə'bʊk/ vt aceptar demasiadas reservaciones para

overcast /əʊvə'kɑːst/ a nublado

overcharge /əʊvə'tʃɑːdʒ/ vt (fill too much) sobrecargar; (charge too much) cobrar demasiado

overcoat /'əʊvəkəʊt/ n abrigo m

overcome /əʊvə'kʌm/ vt (pt -came, pp -come) superar, vencer. be ~ by estar abrumado de

overcrowded /əʊvə'kraʊdɪd/ a atestado (de gente)

overdo /əʊvə'duː/ vt (pt -did, pp -done) exagerar; (culin) cocer demasiado

overdose /'əʊvədəʊs/ n sobredosis f

overdraft /'əʊvədrɑːft/ n giro m en descubierto

overdraw /əʊvə'drɔː/ vt (pt -drew, pp -drawn) girar en descubierto. be ~n tener un saldo deudor

overdue /əʊvə'djuː/ a retrasado; (belated) tardío; (bill) vencido y no pagado

overestimate /əʊvər'estɪmeɪt/ vt sobrestimar

overflow /əʊvə'fləʊ/ vi desbordarse. /'əʊvəfləʊ/ n (excess) exceso m; (outlet) rebosadero m

overgrown /əʊvə'grəʊn/ a demasiado grande; (garden) cubierto de hierbas

overhang /əʊvə'hæŋ/ vt (pt -hung) sobresalir por encima de; (fig) amenazar. ● vi sobresalir. /'əʊvəhæŋ/ n saliente f

overhaul /əʊvə'hɔːl/ vt revisar. /'əʊvəhɔːl/ n revisión f

overhead /əʊvə'hed/ adv por encima. /'əʊvəhed/ a de arriba. ~s npl gastos mpl generales

overhear /əʊvə'hɪə(r)/ vt (pt -heard) oír por casualidad

overjoyed /əʊvə'dʒɔɪd/ a muy contento. he was ~ rebosaba de alegría

overland /'əʊvəlænd/ a terrestre. ● adv por tierra

overlap /əʊvə'læp/ vt (pt -lapped) traslapar. ● vi traslaparse

overleaf /əʊvə'liːf/ adv a la vuelta. see ~ véase al dorso

overload /əʊvə'ləʊd/ vt sobrecargar
overlook /əʊvə'lʊk/ vt dominar; ⟨building⟩ dar a; (forget) olvidar; (oversee) inspeccionar; (forgive) perdonar
overnight /əʊvə'naɪt/ adv por la noche, durante la noche; (fig, instantly) de la noche a la mañana. **stay ~** pasar la noche. ● a de noche
overpass /'əʊvəpɑːs/ n paso m a desnivel, paso m elevado
overpay /əʊvə'peɪ/ vt (pt **-paid**) pagar demasiado
overpower /əʊvə'paʊə(r)/ vt subyugar; dominar ⟨opponent⟩; (fig) abrumar. **~ing** a abrumador
overpriced /əʊvə'praɪst/ a demasiado caro
overrate /əʊvə'reɪt/ vt supervalorar
overreach /əʊvə'riːtʃ/ vr. **~ o.s.** extralimitarse
overreact /əʊvərɪ'ækt/ vi reaccionar excesivamente
overrid|e /əʊvə'raɪd/ vt (pt **-rode**, pp **-ridden**) pasar por encima de. **~ing** a dominante
overripe /'əʊvəraɪp/ a pasado, demasiado maduro
overrule /əʊvə'ruːl/ vt anular; denegar ⟨claim⟩
overrun /əʊvə'rʌn/ vt (pt **-ran**, pp **-run**, pres p **-running**) invadir; exceder ⟨limit⟩
overseas /əʊvə'siːz/ a de ultramar. ● adv al extranjero, en ultramar
oversee /əʊvə'siː/ vt (pt **-saw**, pp **-seen**) vigilar. **~r** /'əʊvəsɪə(r)/ n supervisor m
overshadow /əʊvə'ʃædəʊ/ vt (darken) sombrear; (fig) eclipsar
overshoot /əʊvə'ʃuːt/ vt (pt **-shot**) excederse. **~ the mark** pasarse de la raya
oversight /'əʊvəsaɪt/ n descuido m
oversleep /əʊvə'sliːp/ vi (pt **-slept**) despertarse tarde. **I overslept** se me pegaron las sábanas
overstep /əʊvə'step/ vt (pt **-stepped**) pasar de. **~ the mark** pasarse de la raya
overt /'əʊvɜːt/ a manifiesto
overtak|e /əʊvə'teɪk/ vt/i (pt **-took**, pp **-taken**) sobrepasar; (auto) adelantar. **~ing** n adelantamiento m
overtax /əʊvə'tæks/ vt exigir demasiado
overthrow /əʊvə'θrəʊ/ vt (pt **-threw**, pp **-thrown**) derrocar. /'əʊvəθrəʊ/ n derrocamiento m

overtime /'əʊvətaɪm/ n horas fpl extra
overtone /'əʊvətəʊn/ n (fig) matiz m
overture /'əʊvətjʊə(r)/ n obertura f. **~s** npl (fig) propuestas fpl
overturn /əʊvə'tɜːn/ vt/i volcar
overweight /əʊvə'weɪt/ a demasiado pesado. **be ~** pesar demasiado, ser gordo
overwhelm /əʊvə'welm/ vt aplastar; (with emotion) abrumar. **~ing** a aplastante; (fig) abrumador
overwork /əʊvə'wɜːk/ vt hacer trabajar demasiado. ● vi trabajar demasiado. ● n trabajo m excesivo
overwrought /əʊvə'rɔːt/ a agotado, muy nervioso
ovulation /ɒvjʊ'leɪʃn/ n ovulación f
ow|e /əʊ/ vt deber. **~ing** a debido. **~ing to** a causa de
owl /aʊl/ n lechuza f, búho m
own /əʊn/ a propio. **get one's back** (fam) vengarse. **hold one's ~** mantenerse firme, saber defenderse. **on one's ~** por su cuenta. ● vt poseer, tener. ● vi. **~ up (to)** (fam) confesar. **~er** n propietario m, dueño m. **~ership** n posesión f; (right) propiedad f
ox /ɒks/ n (pl **oxen**) buey m
oxide /'ɒksaɪd/ n óxido m
oxygen /'ɒksɪdʒən/ n oxígeno m
oyster /'ɔɪstə(r)/ n ostra f

P

p /piː/ abbr (pence, penny) penique(s) (m(pl))
pace /peɪs/ n paso m. ● vi. **~ up and down** pasearse de aquí para allá. **~maker** n (runner) el que marca el paso; (med) marcapasos m invar. **keep ~ with** andar al mismo paso que
Pacific /pə'sɪfɪk/ a pacífico. ● n. **~ (Ocean)** (Océano m) Pacífico m
pacif|ist /'pæsɪfɪst/ n pacifista m & f. **~y** /'pæsɪfaɪ/ vt apaciguar
pack /pæk/ n fardo m; (of cards) baraja f; (of hounds) jauría f; (of wolves) manada f; (large amount) montón m. ● vt empaquetar; hacer ⟨suitcase⟩; (press down) apretar. ● vi hacer la maleta. **~age** /'pækɪdʒ/ n paquete m. ● vt empaquetar. **~age deal** n acuerdo m global. **~age tour** n viaje

m organizado. **~ed lunch** *n* almuerzo *m* frío. **~ed out** (*fam*) de bote en bote. **~et** /'pækɪt/ *n* paquete *m*. **send ~ing** echar a paseo

pact /pækt/ *n* pacto *m*, acuerdo *m*

pad /pæd/ *n* almohadilla *f*; (*for writing*) bloc *m*; (*for ink*) tampón *m*; (*flat, fam*) piso *m*. ● *vt* (*pt* **padded**) rellenar. **~ding** *n* relleno *m*. ● *vi* andar a pasos quedos. **launching ~** plataforma *f* de lanzamiento

paddle[1] /'pædl/ *n* canalete *m*

paddle[2] /'pædl/ *vi* mojarse los pies

paddle-steamer /'pædlsti:mə(r)/ *n* vapor *m* de ruedas

paddock /'pædək/ *n* recinto *m*; (*field*) prado *m*

paddy /'pædɪ/ *n* arroz *m* con cáscara. **~-field** *n* arrozal *m*

padlock /'pædlɒk/ *n* candado *m*. ● *vt* cerrar con candado

paediatrician /pi:dɪə'trɪʃn/ *n* pediatra *m* & *f*

pagan /'peɪgən/ *a* & *n* pagano (*m*)

page[1] /peɪdʒ/ *n* página *f*. ● *vt* paginar

page[2] /peɪdʒ/ (*in hotel*) botones *m invar*. ● *vt* llamar

pageant /'pædʒənt/ *n* espectáculo *m* (histórico). **~ry** *n* boato *m*

pagoda /pə'gəʊdə/ *n* pagoda *f*

paid /peɪd/ *see* **pay**. ● *a*. **put ~ to** (*fam*) acabar con

pail /peɪl/ *n* cubo *m*

pain /peɪn/ *n* dolor *m*. **~ in the neck** (*fam*) (*persona*) pesado *m*; (*thing*) lata *f*. **be in ~** tener dolores. **~s** *npl* (*effort*) esfuerzos *mpl*. **be at ~s** esmerarse. ● *vt* doler. **~ful** /'peɪnfl/ *a* doloroso; (*laborious*) penoso. **~killer** *n* calmante *m*. **~less** *a* indoloro. **~staking** /'peɪnzteɪkɪŋ/ *a* esmerado

paint /peɪnt/ *n* pintura *f*. ● *vt/i* pintar. **~er** *n* pintor *m*. **~ing** *n* pintura *f*

pair /peə(r)/ *n* par *m*; (*of people*) pareja *f*. **~ of trousers** pantalón *m*, pantalones *mpl*. ● *vi* emparejarse. **~ off** emparejarse

pajamas /pə'dʒɑːməz/ *npl* pijama *m*

Pakistan /pɑːkɪ'stɑːn/ *n* el Pakistán *m*. **~i** *a* & *n* paquistaní (*m* & *f*)

pal /pæl/ *n* (*fam*) amigo *m*

palace /'pælɪs/ *n* palacio *m*

palat|able /'pælətəbl/ *a* sabroso; (*fig*) aceptable. **~e** /'pælət/ *n* paladar *m*

palatial /pə'leɪʃl/ *a* suntuoso

palaver /pə'lɑːvə(r)/ *n* (*fam*) lío *m*

pale[1] /peɪl/ *a* (**-er, -est**) pálido; (*colour*) claro. ● *vi* palidecer

pale[2] /peɪl/ *n* estaca *f*

paleness /'peɪlnɪs/ *n* palidez *f*

Palestin|e /'pælɪstaɪn/ *n* Palestina *f*. **~ian** /-'stɪnɪən/ *a* & *n* palestino (*m*)

palette /'pælɪt/ *n* paleta *f*. **~-knife** *n* espátula *f*

pall[1] /pɔːl/ *n* paño *m* mortuorio; (*fig*) capa *f*

pall[2] /pɔːl/ *vi*. **~ (on)** perder su sabor (para)

pallid /'pælɪd/ *a* pálido

palm /pɑːm/ *n* palma *f*. ● *vt*. **~ off** encajar (**on** a). **~ist** /'pɑːmɪst/ *n* quiromántico *m*. **P~ Sunday** *n* Domingo *m* de Ramos

palpable /'pælpəbl/ *a* palpable

palpitat|e /'pælpɪteɪt/ *vi* palpitar. **~ion** /-'teɪʃn/ *n* palpitación *f*

paltry /'pɔːltrɪ/ *a* (**-ier, -iest**) insignificante

pamper /'pæmpə(r)/ *vt* mimar

pamphlet /'pæmflɪt/ *n* folleto *m*

pan /pæn/ *n* cacerola *f*; (*for frying*) sartén *f*; (*of scales*) platillo *m*; (*of lavatory*) taza *f*

panacea /pænə'sɪə/ *n* panacea *f*

panache /pæ'næʃ/ *n* brío *m*

pancake /'pænkeɪk/ *n* hojuela *f*, crêpe *f*

panda /'pændə/ *n* panda *m*. **~ car** *n* coche *m* de la policía

pandemonium /pændɪ'məʊnɪəm/ *n* pandemonio *m*

pander /'pændə(r)/ *vi*. **~ to** complacer

pane /peɪn/ *n* (*of glass*) vidrio *m*

panel /'pænl/ *n* panel *m*; (*group of people*) jurado *m*. **~ling** *n* paneles *mpl*

pang /pæŋ/ *n* punzada *f*

panic /'pænɪk/ *n* pánico *m*. ● *vi* (*pt* **panicked**) ser preso de pánico. **~-stricken** *a* preso de pánico

panoram|a /pænə'rɑːmə/ *n* panorama *m*. **~ic** /-'ræmɪk/ *a* panorámico

pansy /'pænzɪ/ *n* pensamiento *m*; (*effeminate man, fam*) maricón *m*

pant /pænt/ *vi* jadear

pantechnicon /pæn'teknɪkən/ *n* camión *m* de mudanzas

panther /'pænθə(r)/ *n* pantera *f*

panties /'pæntɪz/ *npl* bragas *fpl*

pantomime /'pæntəmaɪm/ *n* pantomima *f*

pantry /'pæntri/ n despensa f
pants /pænts/ npl (man's underwear, fam) calzoncillos mpl; (woman's underwear, fam) bragas fpl; (trousers, fam) pantalones mpl
papa|cy /'peɪpəsɪ/ n papado m. **~l** a papal
paper /'peɪpə(r)/ n papel m; (newspaper) periódico m; (exam) examen m; (document) documento m. **on ~** en teoría. ● vt empapelar, tapizar (LAm). **~back** /'peɪpəbæk/ a en rústica. ● n libro m en rústica. **~clip** n sujetapapeles m invar, clip m. **~weight** /'peɪpəweɪt/ n pisapapeles m invar. **~work** n papeleo m, trabajo m de oficina
papier mâché /pæpɪer'mæʃeɪ/ n cartón m piedra
par /pɑ:(r)/ n par f; (golf) par m. **feel below ~** no estar en forma. **on a ~ with** a la par con
parable /'pærəbl/ n parábola f
parachut|e /'pærəʃu:t/ n paracaídas m invar. ● vi lanzarse en paracaídas. **~ist** n paracaidista m & f
parade /pə'reɪd/ n desfile m; (street) paseo m; (display) alarde m. ● vi desfilar. ● vt hacer alarde de
paradise /'pærədaɪs/ n paraíso m
paradox /'pærədɒks/ n paradoja f. **~ical** /-'dɒksɪkl/ a paradójico
paraffin /'pærəfɪn/ n queroseno m
paragon /'pærəgən/ n dechado m
paragraph /'pærəgrɑ:f/ n párrafo m
parallel /'pærəlel/ a paralelo. ● n paralelo m; (line) paralela f. ● vt ser paralelo a
paraly|se /'pærəlaɪz/ vt paralizar. **~sis** /pə'ræləsɪs/ n (pl -ses /-si:z/) parálisis f. **~tic** /pærə'lɪtɪk/ a & n paralítico (m)
parameter /pə'ræmɪtə(r)/ n parámetro m
paramount /'pærəmaʊnt/ a supremo
paranoia /pærə'nɔɪə/ n paranoia f
parapet /'pærəpɪt/ n parapeto m
paraphernalia /pærəfə'neɪlɪə/ n trastos mpl
paraphrase /'pærəfreɪz/ n paráfrasis f. ● vt parafrasear
paraplegic /pærə'pli:dʒɪk/ n parapléjico m
parasite /'pærəsaɪt/ n parásito m
parasol /'pærəsɒl/ n sombrilla f
paratrooper /'pærətru:pə(r)/ n paracaidista m

parcel /'pɑ:sl/ n paquete m
parch /pɑ:tʃ/ vt resecar. **be ~ed** tener mucha sed
parchment /'pɑ:tʃmənt/ n pergamino m
pardon /'pɑ:dn/ n perdón m; (jurid) indulto m. **I beg your ~!** ¡perdone Vd! **I beg your ~?** ¿cómo?, ¿mande? (Mex). ● vt perdonar
pare /peə(r)/ vt cortar ‹nails›; (peel) pelar, mondar
parent /'peərənt/ n (father) padre m; (mother) madre f; (source) origen m. **~s** npl padres mpl. **~al** /pə'rentl/ a de los padres
parenthesis /pə'renθəsɪs/ n (pl -theses /-si:z/) paréntesis m invar
parenthood /'peərənthʊd/ n paternidad f, maternidad f
Paris /'pærɪs/ n París m
parish /'pærɪʃ/ n parroquia f; (municipal) municipio m. **~ioner** /pə'rɪʃənə(r)/ n feligrés m
Parisian /pə'rɪzɪən/ a & n parisino (m)
parity /'pærətɪ/ n igualdad f
park /pɑ:k/ n parque m. ● vt/i aparcar. **~ oneself** vr (fam) instalarse
parka /'pɑ:kə/ n anorak m
parking-meter /'pɑ:kɪŋmi:tə(r)/ n parquímetro m
parliament /'pɑ:ləmənt/ n parlamento m. **~ary** /-'mentrɪ/ a parlamentario
parlour /'pɑ:lə(r)/ n salón m
parochial /pə'rəʊkɪəl/ a parroquial; (fig) pueblerino
parody /'pærədɪ/ n parodia f. ● vt parodiar
parole /pə'rəʊl/ n libertad f bajo palabra, libertad f provisional. **on ~** libre bajo palabra. ● vt liberar bajo palabra
paroxysm /'pærəksɪzəm/ n paroxismo m
parquet /'pɑ:keɪ/ n. **~ floor** n parqué m
parrot /'pærət/ n papagayo m
parry /'pærɪ/ vt parar; (avoid) esquivar. ● n parada f
parsimonious /pɑ:sɪ'məʊnɪəs/ a parsimonioso
parsley /'pɑ:slɪ/ n perejil m
parsnip /'pɑ:snɪp/ n pastinaca f
parson /'pɑ:sn/ n cura m, párroco m
part /pɑ:t/ n parte f; (of machine) pieza f; (of serial) entrega f; (in play) papel m; (side in dispute) partido m.

on the ~ of por parte de. ● *adv* en parte. ● *vt* separar. **~ with** *vt* separarse de. ● *vi* separarse

partake /pɑːˈteɪk/ *vt* (*pt* **-took**, *pp* **-taken**) participar. **~ of** compartir

partial /ˈpɑːʃl/ *a* parcial. **be ~ to** ser aficionado a. **~ity** /-ˈʃlætɪ/ *n* parcialidad *f*. **~ly** *adv* parcialmente

participa|nt /pɑːˈtɪsɪpənt/ *n* participante *m & f*. **~te** /pɑːˈtɪsɪpeɪt/ *vi* participar. **~tion** /-ˈpeɪʃn/ *n* participación *f*

participle /ˈpɑːtɪsɪpl/ *n* participio *m*

particle /ˈpɑːtɪkl/ *n* partícula *f*

particular /pəˈtɪkjʊlə(r)/ *a* particular; (*precise*) meticuloso; (*fastidious*) quisquilloso. ● *n*. **in ~** especialmente. **~ly** *adv* especialmente. **~s** *npl* detalles *mpl*

parting /ˈpɑːtɪŋ/ *n* separación *f*; (*in hair*) raya *f*. ● *a* de despedida

partisan /pɑːtɪˈzæn/ *n* partidario *m*

partition /pɑːˈtɪʃn/ *n* partición *f*; (*wall*) tabique *m*. ● *vt* dividir

partly /ˈpɑːtlɪ/ *adv* en parte

partner /ˈpɑːtnə(r)/ *n* socio *m*; (*sport*) pareja *f*. **~ship** *n* asociación *f*; (*com*) sociedad *f*

partridge /ˈpɑːtrɪdʒ/ *n* perdiz *f*

part-time /pɑːtˈtaɪm/ *a & adv* a tiempo parcial

party /ˈpɑːtɪ/ *n* reunión *f*, fiesta *f*; (*group*) grupo *m*; (*pol*) partido *m*; (*jurid*) parte *f*. **~ line** *n* (*telephone*) línea *f* colectiva

pass /pɑːs/ *vt* pasar; (*in front of*) pasar por delante de; (*overtake*) adelantar; (*approve*) aprobar ⟨*exam, bill, law*⟩; hacer ⟨*remark*⟩; pronunciar ⟨*judgement*⟩. **~ down** transmitir. **~ over** pasar por alto de. **~ round** distribuir. **~ through** pasar por; (*cross*) atravesar. **~ up** (*fam*) dejar pasar. ● *vi* pasar; (*in exam*) aprobar. **~ away** morir. **~ out** (*fam*) desmayarse. ● *n* (*permit*) permiso *m*; (*in mountains*) puerto *m*, desfiladero *m*; (*sport*) pase *m*; (*in exam*) aprobado *m*. **make a ~ at** (*fam*) hacer proposiciones amorosas a. **~able** /ˈpɑːsəbl/ *a* pasable; (*road*) transitable

passage /ˈpæsɪdʒ/ *n* paso *m*; (*voyage*) travesía *f*; (*corridor*) pasillo *m*; (*in book*) pasaje *m*

passenger /ˈpæsɪndʒə(r)/ *n* pasajero *m*

passer-by /pɑːsəˈbaɪ/ *n* (*pl* **passers-by**) transeúnte *m & f*

passion /ˈpæʃn/ *n* pasión *f*. **~ate** *a* apasionado. **~ately** *adv* apasionadamente

passive /ˈpæsɪv/ *a* pasivo. **~ness** *n* pasividad *f*

passmark /ˈpɑːsmɑːk/ *n* aprobado *m*

Passover /ˈpɑːsəʊvə(r)/ *n* Pascua *f* de los hebreos

passport /ˈpɑːspɔːt/ *n* pasaporte *m*

password /ˈpɑːswɜːd/ *n* contraseña *f*

past /pɑːst/ *a & n* pasado (*m*). **in times ~** en tiempos pasados. **the ~ week** *n* la semana *f* pasada. ● *prep* por delante de; (*beyond*) más allá de. ● *adv* por delante. **drive ~** pasar en coche. **go ~** pasar

paste /peɪst/ *n* pasta *f*; (*adhesive*) engrudo *m*. ● *vt* (*fasten*) pegar; (*cover*) engrudar. **~board** /peɪstbɔːd/ *n* cartón *m*. **~ jewellery** *n* joyas *fpl* de imitación

pastel /ˈpæstl/ *a & n* pastel (*m*)

pasteurize /ˈpæstʃəraɪz/ *vt* pasteurizar

pastiche /pæˈstiːʃ/ *n* pastiche *m*

pastille /ˈpæstɪl/ *n* pastilla *f*

pastime /ˈpɑːstaɪm/ *n* pasatiempo *m*

pastoral /ˈpɑːstərəl/ *a* pastoral

pastr|ies *npl* pasteles *mpl*, pastas *fpl*. **~y** /ˈpeɪstrɪ/ *n* pasta *f*

pasture /ˈpɑːstʃə(r)/ *n* pasto *m*

pasty¹ /ˈpæstɪ/ *n* empanada *f*

pasty² /ˈpeɪstɪ/ *a* pastoso; (*pale*) pálido

pat¹ /pæt/ *vt* (*pt* **patted**) dar palmaditas en; acariciar ⟨*dog etc*⟩. ● *n* palmadita *f*; (*of butter*) porción *f*

pat² /pæt/ *adv* en el momento oportuno

patch /pætʃ/ *n* pedazo *m*; (*period*) período *m*; (*repair*) remiendo *m*; (*piece of ground*) terreno *m*. **not a ~ on** (*fam*) muy inferior a. ● *vt* remendar. **~ up** arreglar. **~work** *n* labor *m* de retazos; (*fig*) mosaico *m*. **~y** *a* desigual

pâté /ˈpæteɪ/ *n* pasta *f*, paté *m*

patent /ˈpeɪtnt/ *a* patente. ● *n* patente *f*. ● *vt* patentar. **~ leather** *n* charol *m*. **~ly** *adv* evidentemente

patern|al /pəˈtɜːnl/ *a* paterno. **~ity** /pəˈtɜːnətɪ/ *n* paternidad *f*

path /pɑːθ/ *n* (*pl* **-s** /pɑːðz/) sendero *m*; (*sport*) pista *f*; (*of rocket*) trayectoria *f*; (*fig*) camino *m*

pathetic /pə'θetɪk/ *a* patético, lastimoso

pathology /pə'θɒlədʒɪ/ *n* patología *f*

pathos /'peɪθɒs/ *n* patetismo *m*

patien|ce /'peɪʃns/ *n* paciencia *f*. ~t /'peɪʃnt/ *a & n* paciente (*m & f*). ~tly *adv* con paciencia

patio /'pætɪəʊ/ *n* (*pl* -os) patio *m*

patriarch /'peɪtrɪɑːk/ *n* patriarca *m*

patrician /pə'trɪʃn/ *a & n* patricio (*m*)

patriot /'pætrɪət/ *n* patriota *m & f*. ~ic /-'ɒtɪk/ *a* patriótico. ~ism *n* patriotismo *m*

patrol /pə'trəʊl/ *n* patrulla *f*. ● *vt/i* patrullar

patron /'peɪtrən/ *n* (*of the arts etc*) mecenas *m & f*; (*customer*) cliente *m & f*; (*of charity*) patrocinador *m*. ~age /'pætrənɪdʒ/ *n* patrocinio *m*; (*of shop etc*) clientela *f*. ~ize *vt* ser cliente de; (*fig*) tratar con condescendencia

patter[1] /'pætə(r)/ *n* (*of steps*) golpeteo *m*; (*of rain*) tamborileo *m*. ● *vi* correr con pasos ligeros; (*rain*) tamborilear

patter[2] /'pætə(r)/ (*speech*) jerga *f*; (*chatter*) parloteo *m*

pattern /'pætn/ *n* diseño *m*; (*model*) modelo *m*; (*sample*) muestra *f*; (*manner*) modo *m*; (*in dressmaking*) patrón *m*

paunch /pɔːntʃ/ *n* panza *f*

pauper /'pɔːpə(r)/ *n* indigente *m & f*, pobre *m & f*

pause /pɔːz/ *n* pausa *f*. ● *vi* hacer una pausa

pave /peɪv/ *vt* pavimentar. ~ **the way for** preparar el terreno para

pavement /'peɪvmənt/ *n* pavimento *m*; (*at side of road*) acera *f*

pavilion /pə'vɪlɪən/ *n* pabellón *m*

paving-stone /'peɪvɪŋstəʊn/ *n* losa *f*

paw /pɔː/ *n* pata *f*; (*of cat*) garra *f*. ● *vi* tocar con la pata; (*person*) manosear

pawn[1] /pɔːn/ *n* (*chess*) peón *m*; (*fig*) instrumento *m*

pawn[2] /pɔːn/ *vt* empeñar. ● *n*. in ~ en prenda. ~broker /'pɔːnbrəʊkə(r)/ *n* prestamista *m & f*. ~shop *n* monte *m* de piedad

pawpaw /'pɔːpɔː/ *n* papaya *f*

pay /peɪ/ *vt* (*pt* **paid**) pagar; prestar (*attention*); hacer (*compliment, visit*). ~ **back** devolver. ~ **cash** pagar al contado. ~ **in** ingresar. ~ **off** pagar. ~ **out** pagar. ● *vi* pagar; (*be profitable*) rendir. ● *n* paga *f*. in the ~

of al servicio de. ~able /'peɪəbl/ *a* pagadero. ~ment /'peɪmənt/ *n* pago *m*. ~off *n* (*sl*) liquidación *f*; (*fig*) ajuste *m* de cuentas. ~roll /'peɪrəʊl/ *n* nómina *f*. ~ up pagar

pea /piː/ *n* guisante *m*

peace /piːs/ *n* paz *f*. ~ of mind tranquilidad *f*. ~able *a* pacífico. ~ful /'piːsfl/ *a* tranquilo. ~maker /'piːsmeɪkə(r)/ *n* pacificador *m*

peach /piːtʃ/ *n* melocotón *m*, durazno *m* (*LAm*); (*tree*) melocotonero *m*, duraznero *m* (*LAm*)

peacock /'piːkɒk/ *n* pavo *m* real

peak /piːk/ *n* cumbre *f*; (*maximum*) máximo *m*. ~ **hours** *npl* horas *fpl* punta. ~ed cap *n* gorra *f* de visera

peaky /'piːkɪ/ *a* pálido

peal /piːl/ *n* repique *m*. ~s of laughter risotadas *fpl*

peanut /'piːnʌt/ *n* cacahuete *m*, maní *m* (*Mex*). ~s (*sl*) una bagatela *f*

pear /peə(r)/ *n* pera *f*; (*tree*) peral *m*

pearl /pɜːl/ *n* perla *f*. ~y *a* nacarado

peasant /'peznt/ *n* campesino *m*

peat /piːt/ *n* turba *f*

pebble /'pebl/ *n* guijarro *m*

peck /pek/ *vt* picotear; (*kiss, fam*) dar un besito a. ● *n* picotazo *m*; (*kiss*) besito *m*. ~ish /'pekɪʃ/ *a*. be ~ish (*fam*) tener hambre, tener gazuza (*fam*)

peculiar /pɪ'kjuːlɪə(r)/ *a* raro; (*special*) especial. ~ity /-'ærətɪ/ *n* rareza *f*; (*feature*) particularidad *f*

pedal /'pedl/ *n* pedal *m*. ● *vi* pedalear

pedantic /pɪ'dæntɪk/ *a* pedante

peddle /'pedl/ *vt* vender por las calles

pedestal /'pedɪstl/ *n* pedestal *m*

pedestrian /pɪ'destrɪən/ *n* peatón *m*. ● *a* de peatones; (*dull*) prosaico. ~ crossing *n* paso *m* de peatones

pedigree /'pedɪgriː/ *n* linaje *m*; (*of animal*) pedigrí *m*. ● *a* (*animal*) de raza

pedlar /'pedlə(r)/ *n* buhonero *m*, vendedor *m* ambulante

peek /piːk/ *vi* mirar a hurtadillas

peel /piːl/ *n* cáscara *f*. ● *vt* pelar (*fruit, vegetables*). ● *vi* pelarse. ~ings *npl* peladuras *fpl*, monda *f*

peep[1] /piːp/ *vi* mirar a hurtadillas. ● *n* mirada *f* furtiva

peep[2] /piːp/ (*bird*) piar. ● *n* pío *m*

peep-hole /'piːphəʊl/ *n* mirilla *f*

peer[1] /pɪə(r)/ *vi* mirar. ~ at escudriñar

peer[2] /pɪə(r)/ n par m, compañero m. ~**age** n pares mpl

peev|ed /piːvd/ a (sl) irritado. ~**ish** /'piːvɪʃ/ a picajoso

peg /peg/ n clavija f; (for washing) pinza f; (hook) gancho m; (for tent) estaca f. **off the** ~ de percha. ● vt (pt **pegged**) fijar ⟨precios⟩. ~ **away at** afanarse por

pejorative /pɪ'dʒɒrətɪv/ a peyorativo, despectivo

pelican /'pelɪkən/ n pelícano m. ~ **crossing** n paso m de peatones (con semáforo)

pellet /'pelɪt/ n pelotilla f; (for gun) perdigón m

pelt[1] /pelt/ n pellejo m

pelt[2] /pelt/ vt tirar. ● vi llover a cántaros

pelvis /'pelvɪs/ n pelvis f

pen[1] /pen/ n (enclosure) recinto m

pen[2] /pen/ (for writing) pluma f, estilográfica f; (ball-point) bolígrafo m

penal /'piːnl/ a penal. ~**ize** vt castigar. ~**ty** /'penltɪ/ n castigo m; (fine) multa f. ~**ty kick** n (football) penalty m

penance /'penəns/ n penitencia f

pence /pens/ see **penny**

pencil /'pensl/ n lápiz m. ● vt (pt **pencilled**) escribir con lápiz. ~**sharpener** n sacapuntas m invar

pendant /'pendənt/ n dije m, medallón m

pending /'pendɪŋ/ a pendiente. ● prep hasta

pendulum /'pendjʊləm/ n péndulo m

penetrat|e /'penɪtreɪt/ vt/i penetrar. ~**ing** a penetrante. ~**ion** /-'treɪʃn/ n penetración f

penguin /'peŋgwɪn/ n pingüino m

penicillin /penɪ'sɪlɪn/ n penicilina f

peninsula /pə'nɪnsjʊlə/ n península f

penis /'piːnɪs/ n pene m

peniten|ce /'penɪtəns/ n penitencia f. ~**t** /'penɪtənt/ a & n penitente (m & f). ~**tiary** /penɪ'tenʃərɪ/ n (Amer) cárcel m

pen: ~**knife** /'pennaɪf/ n (pl **penknives**) navaja f; (small) cortaplumas m invar. ~**name** n seudónimo m

pennant /'penənt/ n banderín m

penn|iless /'penɪlɪs/ a sin un céntimo. ~**y** /'penɪ/ n (pl **pennies** or **pence**) penique m

pension /'penʃn/ n pensión f; (for retirement) jubilación f. ● vt pensionar. ~**able** a con derecho a pensión; ⟨age⟩ de la jubilación. ~**er** n jubilado m. ~ **off** jubilar

pensive /'pensɪv/ a pensativo

pent-up /pent'ʌp/ a reprimido; (confined) encerrado

pentagon /'pentəgən/ n pentágono m

Pentecost /'pentɪkɒst/ n Pentecostés m

penthouse /'penthaʊs/ n ático m

penultimate /pen'ʌltɪmət/ a penúltimo

penury /'penjʊərɪ/ n penuria f

peony /'piːənɪ/ n peonía f

people /'piːpl/ npl gente f; (citizens) pueblo m. ~ **say** se dice. **English** ~ los ingleses mpl. **my** ~ (fam) mi familia f. ● vt poblar

pep /pep/ n vigor m. ● vt. ~ **up** animar

pepper /'pepə(r)/ n pimienta f; (vegetable) pimiento m. ● vt sazonar con pimienta. ~**y** a picante. ~**corn** /'pepəkɔːn/ n grano m de pimienta. ~**corn rent** n alquiler m nominal

peppermint /'pepəmɪnt/ n menta f; (sweet) pastilla f de menta

pep talk /'peptɔːk/ n palabras fpl animadoras

per /pɜː(r)/ prep por. ~ **annum** al año. ~ **cent** por ciento. ~ **head** por cabeza, por persona. **ten miles** ~ **hour** diez millas por hora

perceive /pə'siːv/ vt percibir; (notice) darse cuenta de

percentage /pə'sentɪdʒ/ n porcentaje m

percepti|ble /pə'septəbl/ a perceptible. ~**on** /pə'sepʃn/ n percepción f. ~**ve** a perspicaz

perch[1] /pɜːtʃ/ n (of bird) percha f. ● vi posarse

perch[2] /pɜːtʃ/ (fish) perca f

percolat|e /'pɜːkəleɪt/ vt filtrar. ● vi filtrarse. ~**or** n cafetera f

percussion /pə'kʌʃn/ n percusión f

peremptory /pə'remptərɪ/ a perentorio

perennial /pə'renɪəl/ a & n perenne (m)

perfect /'pɜːfɪkt/ a perfecto. /pə'fekt/ vt perfeccionar. ~**ion** /pə'fekʃn/ n perfección f. **to** ~**ion** a la perfección. ~**ionist** n perfeccionista m & f. ~**ly** /'pɜːfɪktlɪ/ adv perfectamente

perforat|e /'pɜːfəreɪt/ vt perforar. **~ion** /-'reɪʃn/ n perforación f

perform /pə'fɔːm/ vt hacer, realizar; representar ‹play›; desempeñar ‹role›; (mus) interpretar. **~ an operation** (med) operar. **~ance** n ejecución f; (of play) representación f; (of car) rendimiento m; (fuss, fam) jaleo m. **~er** n artista m & f

perfume /'pɜːfjuːm/ n perfume m

perfunctory /pə'fʌŋktərɪ/ a superficial

perhaps /pə'hæps/ adv quizá(s), tal vez

peril /'perəl/ n peligro m. **~ous** a arriesgado, peligroso

perimeter /pə'rɪmɪtə(r)/ n perímetro m

period /'pɪərɪəd/ n período m; (lesson) clase f; (gram) punto m. ● a de (la) época. **~ic** /-'ɒdɪk/ a periódico. **~ical** /pɪərɪ'ɒdɪkl/ n revista f. **~ically** /-'ɒdɪklɪ/ adv periódico

peripher|al /pə'rɪfərəl/ a periférico. **~y** /pə'rɪfərɪ/ n periferia f

periscope /'perɪskəʊp/ n periscopio m

perish /'perɪʃ/ vi perecer; (rot) estropearse. **~able** a perecedero. **~ing** a (fam) glacial

perjur|e /'pɜːdʒə(r)/ vr. **~e o.s.** perjurarse. **~y** n perjurio m

perk[1] /pɜːk/ n gaje m

perk[2] /pɜːk/ vt/i. **~ up** vt reanimar. ● vi reanimarse. **~y** a alegre

perm /pɜːm/ n permanente f. ● vt hacer una permanente a

permanen|ce /'pɜːmənəns/ n permanencia f. **~t** /'pɜːmənənt/ a permanente. **~tly** adv permanentemente

permea|ble /'pɜːmɪəbl/ a permeable. **~te** /pɜːmɪeɪt/ vt penetrar; (soak) empapar

permissible /pə'mɪsəbl/ a permisible

permission /pə'mɪʃn/ n permiso m

permissive /pə'mɪsɪv/ a indulgente. **~ness** n tolerancia f. **~ society** n sociedad f permisiva

permit /pə'mɪt/ vt (pt **permitted**) permitir. /'pɜːmɪt/ n permiso m

permutation /pɜːmjuː'teɪʃn/ n permutación f

pernicious /pə'nɪʃəs/ a pernicioso

peroxide /pə'rɒksaɪd/ n peróxido m

perpendicular /pɜːpən'dɪkjʊlə(r)/ a & n perpendicular (f)

perpetrat|e /'pɜːpɪtreɪt/ vt cometer. **~or** n autor m

perpetua|l /pə'petʃʊəl/ a perpetuo. **~te** /pə'petʃʊeɪt/ vt perpetuar. **~tion** /-'eɪʃn/ n perpetuación f

perplex /pə'pleks/ vt dejar perplejo. **~ed** a perplejo. **~ing** a desconcertante. **~ity** n perplejidad f

persecut|e /'pɜːsɪkjuːt/ vt perseguir. **~ion** /-'kjuːʃn/ n persecución f

persever|ance /pɜːsɪ'vɪərəns/ n perseverancia f. **~e** /pɜːsɪ'vɪə(r)/ vi perseverar, persistir

Persian /'pɜːʃn/ a persa. **the ~ Gulf** n el golfo m Pérsico. ● n persa (m & f); (lang) persa m

persist /pə'sɪst/ vi persistir. **~ence** n persistencia f. **~ent** a persistente; (continual) continuo. **~ently** adv persistentemente

person /'pɜːsn/ n persona f

personal /'pɜːsənl/ a personal

personality /pɜːsə'nælətɪ/ n personalidad f; (on TV) personaje m

personally /'pɜːsənəlɪ/ adv personalmente; (in person) en persona

personify /pə'sɒnɪfaɪ/ vt personificar

personnel /pɜːsə'nel/ n personal m

perspective /pə'spektɪv/ n perspectiva f

perspicacious /pɜːspɪ'keɪʃəs/ a perspicaz

perspir|ation /pɜːspə'reɪʃn/ n sudor m. **~e** /pəs'paɪə(r)/ vi sudar

persua|de /pə'sweɪd/ vt persuadir. **~sion** n persuasión f. **~sive** /pə'sweɪsɪv/ a persuasivo. **~sively** adv de manera persuasiva

pert /pɜːt/ a (saucy) impertinente; (lively) animado

pertain /pə'teɪn/ vi. **~ to** relacionarse con

pertinent /'pɜːtɪnənt/ a pertinente. **~ly** adv pertinentemente

pertly /'pɜːtlɪ/ adv impertinentemente

perturb /pə'tɜːb/ vt perturbar

Peru /pə'ruː/ n el Perú m

perus|al /pə'ruːzl/ n lectura f cuidadosa. **~e** /pə'ruːz/ vt leer cuidadosamente

Peruvian /pə'ruːvɪən/ a & n peruano (m)

perva|de /pə'veɪd/ vt difundirse por. **~sive** a penetrante

perver|se /pə'vɜːs/ a (stubborn) terco; (wicked) perverso. **~sity** n terquedad f; (wickedness) perversidad f.

~sion *n* perversión *f*. **~t** /pə'vɜːt/ *vt* pervertir. /'pɜːvɜːt/ *n* pervertido *m*

pessimis|m /'pesɪmɪzəm/ *n* pesimismo *m*. **~t** /'pesɪmɪst/ *n* pesimista *m & f*. **~tic** /-'mɪstɪk/ *a* pesimista

pest /pest/ *n* insecto *m* nocivo, plaga *f*; (*person*) pelma *m*; (*thing*) lata *f*

pester /'pestə(r)/ *vt* importunar

pesticide /'pestɪsaɪd/ *n* pesticida *f*

pet /pet/ *n* animal *m* doméstico; (*favourite*) favorito *m*. ● *a* preferido. ● *vt* (*pt* petted) acariciar

petal /'petl/ *n* pétalo *m*

peter /'piːtə(r)/ *vi*. **~ out** ⟨*supplies*⟩ agotarse; (*disappear*) desparecer

petite /pə'tiːt/ *a* (*of woman*) chiquita

petition /pɪ'tɪʃn/ *n* petición *f*. ● *vt* dirigir una petición a

pet name /'petneɪm/ *n* apodo *m* cariñoso

petrify /'petrɪfaɪ/ *vt* petrificar. ● *vi* petrificarse

petrol /'petrəl/ *n* gasolina *f*. **~eum** /pɪ'trəʊlɪəm/ *n* petróleo *m*. **~ gauge** *n* indicador *m* de nivel de gasolina. **~ pump** *n* (*in car*) bomba *f* de gasolina; (*at garage*) surtidor *m* de gasolina. **~ station** *n* gasolinera *f*. **~ tank** *n* depósito *m* de gasolina

petticoat /'petɪkəʊt/ *n* enaguas *fpl*

pett|iness /'petnɪs/ *n* mezquindad *f*. **~y** /'petɪ/ *a* (**-ier, -iest**) insignificante; (*mean*) mezquino. **~y cash** *n* dinero *m* para gastos menores. **~y officer** *n* suboficial *m* de marina

petulan|ce /'petjʊləns/ *n* irritabilidad *f*. **~t** /'petjʊlənt/ *a* irritable

pew /pjuː/ *n* banco *m* (de iglesia)

pewter /'pjuːtə(r)/ *n* peltre *m*

phallic /'fælɪk/ *a* fálico

phantom /'fæntəm/ *n* fantasma *m*

pharmaceutical /fɑːmə'sjuːtɪkl/ *a* farmacéutico

pharmac|ist /'fɑːməsɪst/ *n* farmacéutico *m*. **~y** /'fɑːməsɪ/ *n* farmacia *f*

pharyngitis /færɪn'dʒaɪtɪs/ *n* faringitis *f*

phase /feɪz/ *n* etapa *f*. ● *vt*. **~ in** introducir progresivamente. **~ out** retirar progresivamente

PhD *abbr* (*Doctor of Philosophy*) *n* Doctor *m* en Filosofía

pheasant /'feznt/ *n* faisán *m*

phenomenal /fɪ'nɒmɪnl/ *a* fenomenal

phenomenon /fɪ'nɒmɪnən/ *n* (*pl* **-ena**) fenómeno *m*

phew /fjuː/ *int* ¡uy!

phial /'faɪəl/ *n* frasco *m*

philanderer /fɪ'lændərə(r)/ *n* mariposón *m*

philanthrop|ic /fɪlən'θrɒpɪk/ *a* filantrópico. **~ist** /fɪ'lænθrəpɪst/ *n* filántropo *m*

philatel|ist /fɪ'lætəlɪst/ *n* filatelista *m & f*. **~y** /fɪ'lætəlɪ/ *n* filatelia *f*

philharmonic /fɪlhɑː'mɒnɪk/ *a* filarmónico

Philippines /'fɪlɪpiːnz/ *npl* Filipinas *fpl*

philistine /'fɪlɪstaɪn/ *a & n* filisteo (*m*)

philosoph|er /fɪ'lɒsəfə(r)/ *n* filósofo *m*. **~ical** /-ə'sɒfɪkl/ *a* filosófico. **~y** /fɪ'lɒsəfɪ/ *n* filosofía *f*

phlegm /flem/ *n* flema *f*. **~atic** /fleg'mætɪk/ *a* flemático

phobia /'fəʊbɪə/ *n* fobia *f*

phone /fəʊn/ *n* (*fam*) teléfono *m*. ● *vt/i* llamar por teléfono. **~ back** ⟨*caller*⟩ volver a llamar; ⟨*person called*⟩ llamar. **~ box** *n* cabina *f* telefónica

phonetic /fə'netɪk/ *a* fonético. **~s** *n* fonética *f*

phoney /'fəʊnɪ/ *a* (**-ier, -iest**) (*sl*) falso. ● *n* (*sl*) farsante *m & f*

phosphate /'fɒsfeɪt/ *n* fosfato *m*

phosphorus /'fɒsfərəs/ *n* fósforo *m*

photo /'fəʊtəʊ/ *n* (*pl* **-os**) (*fam*) fotografía *f*, foto *f* (*fam*)

photocopy /'fəʊtəʊkɒpɪ/ *n* fotocopia *f*. ● *vt* fotocopiar

photogenic /fəʊtəʊ'dʒenɪk/ *a* fotogénico

photograph /'fəʊtəgrɑːf/ *n* fotografía *f*. ● *vt* hacer una fotografía de, sacar fotos de. **~er** /fə'tɒgrəfə(r)/ *n* fotógrafo *m*. **~ic** /-'græfɪk/ *a* fotográfico. **~y** /fə'tɒgrəfɪ/ *n* fotografía *f*

phrase /freɪz/ *n* frase *f*, locución *f*, expresión *f*. ● *vt* expresar. **~-book** *n* libro *m* de frases

physical /'fɪzɪkl/ *a* físico

physician /fɪ'zɪʃn/ *n* médico *m*

physic|ist /'fɪzɪsɪst/ *n* físico *m*. **~s** /'fɪzɪks/ *n* física *f*

physiology /fɪzɪ'ɒlədʒɪ/ *n* fisiología *f*

physiotherap|ist /fɪzɪəʊ'θerəpɪst/ *n* fisioterapeuta *m & f*. **~y** /fɪzɪəʊ-'θerəpɪ/ *n* fisioterapia *f*

physique /fɪˈziːk/ n constitución f; (appearance) físico m

pian|ist /ˈpiənɪst/ n pianista m & f. **∼o** /ˈpiænəʊ/ n (pl -os) piano m

piccolo /ˈpɪkələʊ/ n flautín m, píccolo m

pick[1] /pɪk/ (tool) pico m

pick[2] /pɪk/ vt escoger; recoger (flowers etc); forzar (a lock); (dig) picar. ∼ **a quarrel** buscar camorra. ∼ **holes in** criticar. ● n (choice) selección f; (the best) lo mejor. ∼ **on** vt (nag) meterse con. ∼ **out** vt escoger; (identify) identificar; destacar (colour). ∼ **up** vt recoger; (lift) levantar; (learn) aprender; adquirir (habit, etc); obtener (information); contagiarse de (illness). ● vi mejorar; (med) reponerse

pickaxe /ˈpɪkæks/ n pico m

picket /ˈpɪkɪt/ n (striker) huelguista m & f; (group of strikers) piquete m; (stake) estaca f. ∼ **line** n piquete m. ● vt vigilar por piquetes. ● vi estar de guardia

pickle /ˈpɪkl/ n (in vinegar) encurtido m; (in brine) salmuera f. **in a** ∼ (fam) en un apuro. ● vt encurtir. ∼**s** npl encurtido m

pick: ∼**pocket** /ˈpɪkpɒkɪt/ n ratero m. ∼**-up** n (sl) ligue m; (truck) camioneta f; (stylus-holder) fonocaptor m, brazo m

picnic /ˈpɪknɪk/ n comida f campestre. ● vi (pt picnicked) merendar en el campo

pictorial /pɪkˈtɔːrɪəl/ a ilustrado

picture /ˈpɪktʃə(r)/ n (painting) cuadro m; (photo) fotografía f; (drawing) dibujo m; (beautiful thing) preciosidad f; (film) película f; (fig) descripción f. **the** ∼**s** npl el cine m. ● vt imaginarse; (describe) describir

picturesque /pɪktʃəˈresk/ a pintoresco

piddling /ˈpɪdlɪŋ/ a (fam) insignificante

pidgin /ˈpɪdʒɪn/ a. ∼ **English** n inglés m corrompido

pie /paɪ/ n empanada f; (sweet) pastel m, tarta f

piebald /ˈpaɪbɔːld/ a pío

piece /piːs/ n pedazo m; (coin) moneda f; (in game) pieza f. **a** ∼ **of advice** un consejo m. **a** ∼ **of news** una noticia f. **take to** ∼**s** desmontar. ● vt. ∼ **together** juntar. ∼**meal** /ˈpiːsmiːl/ a gradual; (unsystematic)

poco sistemático. —adv poco a poco. ∼**-work** n trabajo m a destajo

pier /pɪə(r)/ n muelle m

pierc|e /pɪəs/ vt perforar. ∼**ing** a penetrante

piety /ˈpaɪətɪ/ n piedad f

piffl|e /ˈpɪfl/ n (sl) tonterías fpl. ∼**ing** a (sl) insignificante

pig /pɪg/ n cerdo m

pigeon /ˈpɪdʒɪn/ n paloma f; (culin) pichón m. ∼**-hole** n casilla f

pig: ∼**gy** /ˈpɪgɪ/ a (greedy, fam) glotón. ∼**gy-back** adv a cuestas. ∼**gy bank** n hucha f. ∼**-headed** a terco

pigment /ˈpɪgmənt/ n pigmento m. ∼**ation** /-ˈteɪʃn/ n pigmentación f

pig: ∼**skin** /ˈpɪgskɪn/ n piel m de cerdo. ∼**sty** /ˈpɪgstaɪ/ n pocilga f

pigtail /ˈpɪgteɪl/ n (plait) trenza f

pike /paɪk/ n invar (fish) lucio m

pilchard /ˈpɪltʃəd/ n sardina f

pile[1] /paɪl/ n (heap) montón m. ● vt amontonar. ∼ **it on** exagerar. ● vi amontonarse. ∼ **up** vt amontonar. ● vi amontonarse. ∼**s** /paɪlz/ npl (med) almorranas fpl

pile[2] /paɪl/ n (of fabric) pelo m

pile-up /ˈpaɪlʌp/ n accidente m múltiple

pilfer /ˈpɪlfə(r)/ vt/i hurtar. ∼**age** n, ∼**ing** n hurto m

pilgrim /ˈpɪlgrɪm/ n peregrino. ∼**age** n peregrinación f

pill /pɪl/ n píldora f

pillage /ˈpɪlɪdʒ/ n saqueo m. ● vt saquear

pillar /ˈpɪlə(r)/ n columna f. ∼**-box** n buzón m

pillion /ˈpɪlɪən/ n asiento m trasero. **ride** ∼ en el asiento trasero

pillory /ˈpɪlərɪ/ n picota f

pillow /ˈpɪləʊ/ n almohada f. ∼**case** /ˈpɪləʊkeɪs/ n funda f de almohada

pilot /ˈpaɪlət/ n piloto m. ● vt pilotar. ∼**-light** n fuego m piloto

pimp /pɪmp/ n alcahuete m

pimple /ˈpɪmpl/ n grano m

pin /pɪn/ n alfiler m; (mec) perno m. ∼**s and needles** hormigueo m. ● vt (pt pinned) prender con alfileres; (hold down) enclavijar; (fix) sujetar. ∼ **s.o. down** obligar a uno a que se decida. ∼ **up** fijar

pinafore /ˈpɪnəfɔː(r)/ n delantal m. ∼ **dress** n mandil m

pincers /ˈpɪnsəz/ npl tenazas fpl

pinch /pɪntʃ/ vt pellizcar; (*steal, sl*) hurtar. ● vi (*shoe*) apretar. ● n pellizco m; (*small amount*) pizca f. **at a** ∼ en caso de necesidad

pincushion /'pɪnkuʃn/ n acerico m

pine[1] /paɪn/ n pino m

pine[2] /paɪn/ vi. ∼ **away** consumirse. ∼ **for** suspirar por

pineapple /'paɪnæpl/ n piña f, ananás m

ping /pɪŋ/ n sonido m agudo. ∼-**pong** /'pɪŋpɒŋ/ n pimpón m, ping-pong m

pinion /'pɪnjən/ vt maniatar

pink /pɪŋk/ a & n color (m) de rosa

pinnacle /'pɪnəkl/ n pináculo m

pin: ∼**point** vt determinar con precisión f. ∼**stripe** /'pɪnstraɪp/ n raya f fina

pint /paɪnt/ n pinta f (= 0.57 litre)

pin-up /'pɪnʌp/ n (*fam*) fotografía f de mujer

pioneer /paɪə'nɪə(r)/ n pionero m. ● vt ser el primero, promotor de, promover

pious /'paɪəs/ a piadoso

pip[1] /pɪp/ n (*seed*) pepita f

pip[2] /pɪp/ n (*time signal*) señal f

pip[3] /pɪp/ n (*on uniform*) estrella f

pipe /paɪp/ n tubo m; (*mus*) caramillo m; (*for smoking*) pipa f. ● vt conducir por tuberías. ∼**down** (*fam*) bajar la voz, callarse. ∼-**cleaner** n limpiapipas m invar. ∼-**dream** n ilusión f. ∼**line** /'paɪplaɪn/ n tubería f; (*for oil*) oleoducto m. **in the** ∼**line** en preparación f. ∼**r** n flautista m & f

piping /'paɪpɪŋ/ n tubería f. ∼ **hot** muy caliente, hirviendo

piquant /'pi:kənt/ a picante

pique /pi:k/ n resentimiento m

pira|cy /'paɪərəsɪ/ n piratería f. ∼**te** /'paɪərət/ n pirata m

pirouette /pɪru'et/ n pirueta f. ● vi piruetear

Pisces /'paɪsi:z/ n (*astr*) Piscis m

pistol /'pɪstl/ n pistola f

piston /'pɪstən/ n pistón m

pit /pɪt/ n foso m; (*mine*) mina f; (*of stomach*) boca f. ● vt (*pt* **pitted**) marcar con hoyos; (*fig*) oponer. ∼ **o.s. against** medirse con

pitch[1] /pɪtʃ/ n brea f

pitch[2] /pɪtʃ/ n (*degree*) grado m; (*mus*) tono m; (*sport*) campo m. ● vt lanzar; armar ‹*tent*›. ∼ **into** (*fam*) atacar. ● vi caerse; ‹*ship*› cabecear. ∼ **in** (*fam*) contribuir. ∼**ed battle** n batalla f campal

pitch-black /pɪtʃ'blæk/ a oscuro como boca de lobo

pitcher /'pɪtʃə(r)/ n jarro m

pitchfork /'pɪtʃfɔːk/ n horca f

piteous /'pɪtɪəs/ a lastimoso

pitfall /'pɪtfɔːl/ n trampa f

pith /pɪθ/ n (*of orange, lemon*) médula f; (*fig*) meollo m

pithy /'pɪθɪ/ a (-**ier, -iest**) conciso

piti|ful /'pɪtɪfl/ a lastimoso. ∼**less** a despiadado

pittance /'pɪtns/ n sueldo m irrisorio

pity /'pɪtɪ/ n piedad f; (*regret*) lástima f. ● vt compadecerse de

pivot /'pɪvət/ n pivote m. ● vt montonar sobre un pivote. ● vi girar sobre un pivote; (*fig*) depender (**on** de)

pixie /'pɪksɪ/ n duende m

placard /'plækɑːd/ n pancarta f; (*poster*) cartel m

placate /plə'keɪt/ vt apaciguar

place /pleɪs/ n lugar m; (*seat*) asiento m; (*post*) puesto m; (*house, fam*) casa f. **take** ∼ tener lugar. ● vt poner, colocar; (*remember*) recordar; (*identify*) identificar. **be** ∼**d** (*in race*) colocarse. ∼-**mat** n salvamanteles m invar. ∼**ment** /'pleɪsmənt/ n colocación f

placid /'plæsɪd/ a plácido

plagiari|sm /'pleɪdʒərɪzm/ n plagio m. ∼**ze** /'pleɪdʒəraɪz/ vt plagiar

plague /pleɪg/ n peste f; (*fig*) plaga f. ● vt atormentar

plaice /pleɪs/ n invar platija f

plaid /plæd/ n tartán m

plain /pleɪn/ a (-**er, -est**) claro; (*simple*) sencillo; (*candid*) franco; (*ugly*) feo. **in** ∼ **clothes** en traje de paisano. ● adv claramente. ● n llanura f. ∼**ly** adv claramente; (*frankly*) francamente; (*simply*) sencillamente. ∼**ness** n claridad f; (*simplicity*) sencillez f

plaintiff /'pleɪntɪf/ n demandante m & f

plait /plæt/ vt trenzar. ● n trenza f

plan /plæn/ n proyecto m; (*map*) plano m. ● vt (*pt* **planned**) planear, proyectar; (*intend*) proponerse

plane[1] /pleɪn/ n (*tree*) plátano m

plane[2] /pleɪn/ n (*level*) nivel m; (*aviat*) avión m. ● a plano

plane³ /pleɪn/ (*tool*) cepillo *m*. ● *vt* cepillar

planet /'plænɪt/ *n* planeta *m*. **~ary** *a* planetario

plank /plæŋk/ *n* tabla *f*

planning /'plænɪŋ/ *n* planificación *f*. **~ family ~** *n* planificación familiar. **town ~** *n* urbanismo *m*

plant /plɑ:nt/ *n* planta *f*; (*mec*) maquinaria *f*; (*factory*) fábrica *f*. ● *vt* plantar; (*place in position*) colocar. **~ation** /plæn'teɪʃn/ *n* plantación *f*

plaque /plæk/ *n* placa *f*

plasma /'plæzmə/ *n* plasma *m*

plaster /'plɑ:stə(r)/ *n* yeso *m*; (*adhesive*) esparadrapo *m*; (*for setting bones*) escayola *f*. **~ of Paris** *n* yeso *m* mate. ● *vt* enyesar; (*med*) escayolar ‹*broken bone*›; (*cover*) cubrir (**with** de). **~ed** *a* (*fam*) borracho

plastic /'plæstɪk/ *a & n* plástico (*m*)

Plasticine /'plæstɪsi:n/ *n* (*P*) pasta *f* de modelar, plastilina *f*(*P*)

plastic surgery /plæstɪk'sɜ:dʒərɪ/ *n* cirugía *f* estética

plate /pleɪt/ *n* plato *m*; (*of metal*) chapa *f*, (*silverware*) vajilla *f* de plata; (*in book*) lámina *f*. ● *vt* (*cover with metal*) chapear ·

plateau /'plætəʊ/ *n* (*pl* **plateaux**) *n* meseta *f*

plateful /'pleɪtfl/ *n* (*pl* **-fuls**) plato *m*

platform /'plætfɔ:m/ *n* plataforma *f*; (*rail*) andén *m*

platinum /'plætɪnəm/ *n* platino *m*

platitude /'plætɪtju:d/ *n* tópico *m*, perogrullada *f*, lugar *m* común

platonic /plə'tɒnɪk/ *a* platónico

platoon /plə'tu:n/ *n* pelotón *m*

platter /'plætə(r)/ *n* fuente *f*, plato *m* grande

plausible /'plɔ:zəbl/ *a* plausible; ‹*person*› convincente

play /pleɪ/ *vt* jugar; (*act role*) desempeñar el papel de; tocar ‹*instrument*›. **~ safe** no arriesgarse. **~ up to** halagar. ● *vi* jugar. **~ed out** agotado. ● *n* juego *m*; (*drama*) obra *f* de teatro. **~ on words** *n* juego *m* de palabras. **~ down** *vt* minimizar. **~ on** *vi* aprovecharse de. **~ up** *vi* (*fam*) causar problemas. **~act** *vi* hacer la comedia. **~boy** /'pleɪbɔɪ/ *n* calavera *m*. **~er** *n* jugador *m*; (*mus*) músico *m*. **~ful** /'pleɪfl/ *a* juguetón. **~fully** *adv* jugando; (*jokingly*) en broma. **~ground** /'pleɪgraʊnd/ *n* parque *m* de juegos infantiles; (*in school*) campo

m de recreo. **~group** *n* jardín *m* de la infancia. **~ing** /'pleɪŋ/ *n* juego *m*. **~ing-card** *n* naipe *m*. **~ing-field** *n* campo *m* de deportes. **~mate** /'pleɪmeɪt/ *n* compañero *m* (de juego). **~pen** *n* corralito *m*. **~thing** *n* juguete *m*. **~wright** /'pleɪraɪt/ *n* dramaturgo *m*

plc /pi:el'si:/ *abbr* (*public limited company*) S.A., sociedad *f* anónima

plea /pli:/ *n* súplica *f*; (*excuse*) excusa *f*; (*jurid*) defensa *f*

plead /pli:d/ *vt* (*jurid*) alegar; (*as excuse*) pretextar. ● *vi* suplicar; (*jurid*) abogar. **~ with** suplicar

pleasant /'pleznt/ *a* agradable

pleas|e /pli:z/ *int* por favor. ● *vt* agradar, dar gusto a. ● *vi* agradar; (*wish*) querer. **~e o.s.** hacer lo que quiera. **do as you ~e** haz lo que quieras. **~ed with** *ed* contento, satisfecho de. **~ing** *a* agradable

pleasur|e /'pleʒə(r)/ *n* placer *m*. **~able** *a* agradable

pleat /pli:t/ *n* pliegue *m*. ● *vt* hacer pliegues en

plebiscite /'plebɪsɪt/ *n* plebiscito *m*

plectrum /'plektrəm/ *n* plectro *m*

pledge /pledʒ/ *n* prenda *f*; (*promise*) promesa *f*. ● *vt* empeñar; (*promise*) prometer

plent|iful /'plentɪfl/ *a* abundante. **~y** /'plentɪ/ *n* abundancia *f*. **~y (of)** muchos (de)

pleurisy /'plʊərəsɪ/ *n* pleuresía *f*

pliable /'plaɪəbl/ *a* flexible

pliers /'plaɪəz/ *npl* alicates *mpl*

plight /plaɪt/ *n* situación *f*(difícil)

plimsolls /'plɪmsəlz/ *npl* zapatillas *fpl* de lona

plinth /plɪnθ/ *n* plinto *m*

plod /plɒd/ *vi* (*pt* **plodded**) caminar con paso pesado; (*work hard*) trabajar laboriosamente. **~der** *n* empollón *m*

plonk /plɒŋk/ *n* (*sl*) vino *m* peleón

plop /plɒp/ *n* paf *m*. ● *vi* (*pt* **plopped**) caerse con un paf

plot /plɒt/ *n* complot *m*; (*of novel etc*) argumento *m*; (*piece of land*) parcela *f*. ● *vt* (*pt* **plotted**) tramar; (*mark out*) trazar. ● *vi* conspirar

plough /plaʊ/ *n* arado *m*. ● *vt/i* arar. **~ through** avanzar laboriosamente por

ploy /plɔɪ/ *n* (*fam*) estratagema *f*, truco *m*

pluck /plʌk/ *vt* arrancar; depilarse ⟨*eyebrows*⟩; desplumar ⟨*bird*⟩; recoger ⟨*flowers*⟩. **~ up courage** hacer de tripas corazón. ● *n* valor *m*. **~y** *a* (**-ier, -iest**) valiente

plug /plʌg/ *n* tapón *m*; (*elec*) enchufe *m*; (*auto*) bujía *f*. ● *vt* (*pt* **plugged**) tapar; (*advertise, fam*) dar publicidad a. **~ in** (*elec*) enchufar

plum /plʌm/ *n* ciruela *f*; (*tree*) ciruelo *m*

plumage /'plu:mɪdʒ/ *n* plumaje *m*

plumb /plʌm/ *a* vertical. ● *n* plomada *f*. ● *adv* verticalmente; (*exactly*) exactamente. ● *vt* sondar

plumb|er /'plʌmə(r)/ *n* fontanero *m*. **~ing** *n* instalación *f* sanitaria, instalación *f* de cañerías

plume /plu:m/ *n* pluma *f*

plum job /plʌm'dʒɒb/ *n* (*fam*) puesto *m* estupendo

plummet /'plʌmɪt/ *n* plomada *f*. ● *vi* caer a plomo, caer en picado

plump /plʌmp/ *a* (**-er, -est**) rechoncho. ● *vt*. **~ for** elegir. **~ness** *n* gordura *f*

plum pudding /plʌm'pʊdɪŋ/ *n* budín *m* de pasas

plunder /'plʌndə(r)/ *n* (*act*) saqueo *m*; (*goods*) botín *m*. ● *vt* saquear

plung|e /plʌndʒ/ *vt* hundir; (*in water*) sumergir. ● *vi* zambullirse; (*fall*) caer. ● *n* salto *m*. **~er** *n* (*for sink*) desatascador *m*; (*mec*) émbolo *m*. **~ing** *a* ⟨*neckline*⟩ bajo, escotado

plural /'plʊərəl/ *a* & *n* plural (*m*)

plus /plʌs/ *prep* más. ● *a* positivo. ● *n* signo *m* más; (*fig*) ventaja *f*. **five ~** más de cinco

plush /plʌʃ/ *n* felpa *f*. ● *a* de felpa, afelpado; (*fig*) lujoso. **~y** *a* lujoso

plutocrat /'plu:təkræt/ *n* plutócrata *m* & *f*

plutonium /plu:'təʊnjəm/ *n* plutonio *m*

ply /plaɪ/ *vt* manejar ⟨*tool*⟩; ejercer ⟨*trade*⟩. **~ s.o. with drink** dar continuamente de beber a uno. **~wood** *n* contrachapado *m*

p.m. /pi:'em/ *abbr* (*post meridiem*) de la tarde

pneumatic /nju:'mætɪk/ *a* neumático

pneumonia /nju:'məʊnjə/ *n* pulmonía *f*

PO /pi:'əʊ/ *abbr* (*Post Office*) oficina *f* de correos

poach /pəʊtʃ/ *vt* escalfar ⟨*egg*⟩; cocer ⟨*fish etc*⟩; (*steal*) cazar en vedado. **~er** *n* cazador *m* furtivo

pocket /'pɒkɪt/ *n* bolsillo *m*; (*of air, resistance*) bolsa *f*. **be in ~** salir ganando. **be out of ~** salir perdiendo. ● *vt* poner en el bolsillo. **~-book** *n* (*notebook*) libro *m* de bolsillo; (*purse, Amer*) cartera *f*; (*handbag, Amer*) bolso *m*. **~-money** *n* dinero *m* para los gastos personales

pock-marked /'pɒkmɑːkt/ *a* ⟨*face*⟩ picado de viruelas

pod /pɒd/ *n* vaina *f*

podgy /'pɒdʒɪ/ *a* (**-ier, -iest**) rechoncho

poem /'pəʊɪm/ *n* poesía *f*

poet /'pəʊɪt/ *n* poeta *m*. **~ess** *n* poetisa *f*. **~ic** /-'etɪk/ *a*, **~ical** /-'etɪkl/ *a* poético. **P~ Laureate** *n* poeta laureado. **~ry** /'pəʊɪtrɪ/ *n* poesía *f*

poignant /'pɔɪnjənt/ *a* conmovedor

point /pɔɪnt/ *n* punto *m*; (*sharp end*) punta *f*; (*significance*) lo importante; (*elec*) toma *f* de corriente. **good ~s** cualidades *fpl*. **to the ~** pertinente. **up to a ~** hasta cierto punto. **what is the ~?** ¿para qué?, ¿a qué fin? ● *vt* (*aim*) apuntar; (*show*) indicar. **~ out** señalar. ● *vi* señalar. **~-blank** *a* & *adv* a boca de jarro, a quemarropa. **~ed** /'pɔɪntɪd/ *a* puntiagudo; (*fig*) mordaz. **~er** /'pɔɪntə(r)/ *n* indicador *m*; (*dog*) perro *m* de muestra; (*clue, fam*) indicación *f*. **~less** /'pɔɪntlɪs/ *a* inútil

poise /pɔɪz/ *n* equilibrio *m*; (*elegance*) elegancia *f*; (*fig*) aplomo *m*. **~d** *a* en equilibrio. **~d for** listo para

poison /'pɔɪzn/ *n* veneno *m*. ● *vt* envenenar. **~ous** *a* venenoso; ⟨*chemical etc*⟩ tóxico

poke /pəʊk/ *vt* empujar; atizar ⟨*fire*⟩. **~ fun at** burlarse de. **~ out** asomar ⟨*head*⟩. ● *vi* hurgar; (*pry*) meterse. **~ about** fisgonear. ● *n* empuje *m*

poker[1] /'pəʊkə(r)/ *n* atizador *m*

poker[2] /'pəʊkə(r)/ (*cards*) póquer *m*. **~-face** *n* cara *f* inmutable

poky /'pəʊkɪ/ *a* (**-ier, -iest**) estrecho

Poland /'pəʊlənd/ *n* Polonia *f*

polar /'pəʊlə(r)/ *a* polar. **~ bear** *n* oso *m* blanco

polarize /'pəʊləraɪz/ *vt* polarizar

Pole /pəʊl/ *n* polaco *n*

pole[1] /pəʊl/ *n* palo *m*; (*for flag*) asta *f*

pole² /pəʊl/ (geog) polo m. ~**star** n estrella f polar

polemic /pə'lemɪk/ a polémico. ● n polémica f

police /pə'liːs/ n policía f. ● vt vigilar. ~**man** /pə'liːsmən/ n (pl -men) policía m, guardia m. ~ **record** n antecedentes mpl penales. ~ **state** n estado m policíaco. ~ **station** n comisaría f. ~**woman** /-wʊmən/ n (pl -women) mujer m policía

policy¹ /'pɒlɪsɪ/ n política f

policy² /'pɒlɪsɪ/ (insurance) póliza f (de seguros)

polio(myelitis) /'pəʊlɪəʊ(maɪə'laɪtɪs)/ n polio(mielitis) f

polish /'pɒlɪʃ/ n (for shoes) betún m; (for floor) cera f; (for nails) esmalte m de uñas; (shine) brillo m; (fig) finura f. **nail** ~ esmalte m de uñas. ● vt pulir; limpiar ⟨shoes⟩; encerar ⟨floor⟩. ~ **off** despachar. ~**ed** a pulido; (manner) refinado. ~**er** n pulidor m; (machine) pulidora f

Polish /'pəʊlɪʃ/ a & n polaco (m)

polite /pə'laɪt/ a cortés. ~**ly** adv cortésmente. ~**ness** n cortesía f

politic|al /pə'lɪtɪkl/ a político. ~**ian** /pɒlɪ'tɪʃn/ n político m. ~**s** /'pɒlətɪks/ n política f

polka /'pɒlkə/ n polca f. ~ **dots** npl diseño m de puntos

poll /pəʊl/ n elección f; (survey) encuesta f. ● vt obtener ⟨votes⟩

pollen /'pɒlən/ n polen m

polling-booth /'pəʊlɪŋbuːð/ n cabina f de votar

pollut|e /pə'luːt/ vt contaminar. ~**ion** /-ʃn/ n contaminación f

polo /'pəʊləʊ/ n polo m. ~**neck** n cuello m vuelto

poltergeist /'pɒltəgaɪst/ n duende m

polyester /pɒlɪ'estə(r)/ n poliéster m

polygam|ist /pə'lɪgəmɪst/ n polígamo m. ~**ous** a polígamo. ~**y** /pə'lɪgəmɪ/ n poligamia f

polyglot /'pɒlɪglɒt/ a & n políglota (m & f)

polygon /'pɒlɪgən/ n polígono m

polyp /'pɒlɪp/ n pólipo m

polystyrene /pɒlɪ'staɪriːn/ n poliestireno m

polytechnic /pɒlɪ'teknɪk/ n escuela f politécnica

polythene /'pɒlɪθiːn/ n polietileno m. ~ **bag** n bolsa f de plástico

pomegranate /'pɒmɪgrænɪt/ n (fruit) granada f

pommel /'pʌml/ n pomo m

pomp /pɒmp/ n pompa f

pompon /'pɒmpɒn/ n pompón m

pompo|sity /pɒm'pɒsɪtɪ/ n pomposidad f. ~**us** /'pɒmpəs/ a pomposo

poncho /'pɒntʃəʊ/ n (pl -os) poncho m

pond /pɒnd/ n charca f; (artificial) estanque m

ponder /'pɒndə(r)/ vt considerar. ● vi reflexionar. ~**ous** /'pɒndərəs/ a pesado

pong /pɒŋ/ n (sl) hedor m. ● vi (sl) apestar

pontif|f /'pɒntɪf/ n pontífice m. ~**ical** /-'tɪfɪkl/ a pontifical; (fig) dogmático. ~**icate** /pɒn'tɪfɪkeɪt/ vi pontificar

pontoon /pɒn'tuːn/ n pontón m. ~ **bridge** n puente m de pontones

pony /'pəʊnɪ/ n poni m. ~**tail** n cola f de caballo. ~**trekking** n excursionismo m en poni

poodle /'puːdl/ n perro m de lanas, caniche m

pool¹ /puːl/ n charca f; (artificial) estanque m. **(swimming-)**~ n piscina f

pool² /puːl/ (common fund) fondos mpl comunes; (snooker) billar m americano. ● vt aunar. ~**s** npl quinielas fpl

poor /pʊə(r)/ a (-er, -est) pobre; (not good) malo. **be in** ~ **health** estar mal de salud. ~**ly** a (fam) indispuesto. ● adv pobremente; (badly) mal

pop¹ /pɒp/ n ruido m seco; (of bottle) taponazo m. ● vt (pt popped) hacer reventar; (put) poner. ~ **in** vi entrar; (visit) pasar por. ~ **out** vi saltar; ⟨person⟩ salir un rato. ~ **up** vi surgir, aparecer

pop² /pɒp/ a (popular) pop invar. ● n (fam) música f pop. ~ **art** n arte m pop

popcorn /'pɒpkɔːn/ n palomitas fpl

pope /pəʊp/ n papa m

popgun /'pɒpgʌn/ n pistola f de aire comprimido

poplar /'pɒplə(r)/ n chopo m

poplin /'pɒplɪn/ n popelina f

poppy /'pɒpɪ/ n amapola f

popular /'pɒpjʊlə(r)/ a popular. ~**ity** /-'lærətɪ/ n popularidad f. ~**ize** vt popularizar

populat|e /'pɒpjʊleɪt/ vt poblar.
~ion /-'leɪʃn/ n población f; (number
of inhabitants) habitantes mpl

porcelain /'pɔ:səlɪn/ n porcelana f

porch /pɔ:tʃ/ n porche m

porcupine /'pɔ:kjʊpaɪn/ n puerco m
espín

pore[1] /pɔ:(r)/ n poro m

pore[2] /pɔ:(r)/ vi. **~ over** estudiar
detenidamente

pork /pɔ:k/ n cerdo m

porn /pɔ:n/ n (fam) pornografía f.
~ographic /-ə'ɡræfɪk/ a porno-
gráfico. **~ography** /pɔ:'nɒɡrəfɪ/ n
pornografía f

porous /'pɔ:rəs/ a poroso

porpoise /'pɔ:pəs/ n marsopa f

porridge /'pɒrɪdʒ/ n gachas fpl de
avena

port[1] /pɔ:t/ n puerto m; (porthole)
portilla f. **~ of call** puerto de escala

port[2] /pɔ:t/ (naut, left) babor m. ● a
de babor

port[3] /pɔ:t/ (wine) oporto m

portable /'pɔ:təbl/ a portátil

portal /'pɔ:tl/ n portal m

portent /'pɔ:tent/ n presagio m

porter /'pɔ:tə(r)/ n portero m; (for
luggage) mozo m. **~age** n porte m

portfolio /pɔ:t'fəʊljəʊ/ n (pl -os)
cartera f

porthole /'pɔ:thəʊl/ n portilla f

portico /'pɔ:tɪkəʊ/ n (pl -oes) pórtico
m

portion /'pɔ:ʃn/ n porción f. ● vt
repartir

portly /'pɔ:tlɪ/ a (-ier, -iest) corpulento

portrait /'pɔ:trɪt/ n retrato m

portray /pɔ:'treɪ/ vt retratar; (represent) representar. **~al** n retrato m

Portug|al /'pɔ:tjʊɡl/ n Portugal m.
~uese /-'ɡi:z/ a & n portugués (m)

pose /pəʊz/ n postura f. ● vt colocar;
hacer (question); plantear (problem).
● vi posar. **~ as** hacerse pasar por.
~r /'pəʊzə(r)/ n pregunta f difícil

posh /pɒʃ/ a (sl) elegante

position /pə'zɪʃn/ n posición f; (job)
puesto m; (status) rango m. ● vt
colocar

positive /'pɒzətɪv/ a positivo; (real)
verdadero; (certain) seguro. ● n
(foto) positiva f. **~ly** adv posi-
tivamente

possess /pə'zes/ vt poseer. **~ion**
/pə'zeʃn/ n posesión f. take **~ion of**

tomar posesión de. **~ions** npl pose-
siones fpl; (jurid) bienes mpl. **~ive**
/pə'zesɪv/ a posesivo. **~or** n
poseedor m

possib|ility /pɒsə'bɪlətɪ/ n posi-
bilidad f. **~le** /'pɒsəbl/ a posible.
~ly adv posiblemente

post[1] /pəʊst/ n (pole) poste m. ● vt
fijar (notice)

post[2] /pəʊst/ (place) puesto m

post[3] /pəʊst/ (mail) correo m. ● vt
echar (letter). keep s.o. **~ed** tener a
uno al corriente

post... /pəʊst/ pref post...

post: ~age /'pəʊstɪdʒ/ n franqueo m.
~al /'pəʊstl/ a postal. **~al order** n
giro m postal. **~box** n buzón m.
~card /'pəʊstkɑ:d/ n (tarjeta f)
postal f. **~code** n código m postal

post-date /pəʊst'deɪt/ vt poner
fecha posterior a

poster /'pəʊstə(r)/ n cartel m

poste restante /pəʊst'restɑ:nt/ n
lista f de correos

posteri|or /pɒ'stɪərɪə(r)/ a pos-
terior. ● n trasero m. **~ty**
/pɒs'terətɪ/ n posteridad f

posthumous /'pɒstjʊməs/ a póstumo. **~ly** adv después de la muerte

post: ~man /'pəʊstmən/ n (pl -men)
cartero m. **~mark** /'pəʊstmɑ:k/ n
matasellos m invar. **~master**
/'pəʊstmɑ:stə(r)/ n administrador m
de correos. **~mistress** /'pəʊst-
mɪstrɪs/ n administradora f de correos

post-mortem /'pəʊstmɔ:təm/ n
autopsia f

Post Office /'pəʊstɒfɪs/ n oficina f
de correos, correos mpl

postpone /pəʊst'pəʊn/ vt aplazar.
~ment n aplazamiento m

postscript /'pəʊstskrɪpt/ n posdata f

postulant /'pɒstjʊlənt/ n postulante
m & f

postulate /'pɒstjʊleɪt/ vt postular

posture /'pɒstʃə(r)/ n postura f. ● vi
adoptar una postura

posy /'pəʊzɪ/ n ramillete m

pot /pɒt/ n (for cooking) olla f; (for
flowers) tiesto m; (marijuana, sl)
mariguana f. go to **~** (sl) echarse a
perder. ● vt (pt potted) poner en
tiesto

potassium /pə'tæsjəm/ n potasio m

potato /pə'teɪtəʊ/ n (pl -oes) patata
f, papa f (LAm)

pot: **~-belly** *n* barriga *f*. **~-boiler** *n* obra *f* literaria escrita sólo para ganar dinero

poten|cy /'pəʊtənsɪ/ *n* potencia *f*. **~t** /'pəʊtnt/ *a* potente; ⟨*drink*⟩ fuerte

potentate /'pəʊtənteɪt/ *n* potentado *m*

potential /pəʊ'tenʃl/ *a & n* potencial (*m*). **~ity** /-ʃɪ'ræləti/ *n* potencialidad *f*. **~ly** *adv* potencialmente

pot-hole /'pɒthəʊl/ *n* caverna *f*; (in *road*) bache *m*. **~r** *n* espeleólogo *m*

potion /'pəʊʃn/ *n* poción *f*

pot: **~ luck** *n* lo que haya. **~-shot** *n* tiro *m* al azar. **~ted** /'pɒtɪd/ *see* pot. ● *a* ⟨*food*⟩ en conserva

potter[1] /'pɒtə(r)/ *n* alfarero *m*

potter[2] /'pɒtə(r)/ *vi* hacer pequeños trabajos agradables, no hacer nada de particular

pottery /'pɒtərɪ/ *n* cerámica *f*

potty /'pɒtɪ/ *a* (-ier, -iest) (*sl*) chiflado. ● *n* orinal *m*

pouch /paʊtʃ/ *n* bolsa *f* pequeña

pouffe /puːf/ *n* (*stool*) taburete *m*

poulterer /'pəʊltərə(r)/ *n* pollero *m*

poultice /'pəʊltɪs/ *n* cataplasma *f*

poultry /'pəʊltrɪ/ *n* aves *fpl* de corral

pounce /paʊns/ *vi* saltar, atacar de repente. ● *n* salto *m*, ataque *m* repentino

pound[1] /paʊnd/ *n* (*weight*) libra *f* (= 454g); (*money*) libra *f* (esterlina)

pound[2] /paʊnd/ *n* (*for cars*) depósito *m*

pound[3] /paʊnd/ *vt* (*crush*) machacar; (*bombard*) bombardear. ● *vi* golpear; ⟨*heart*⟩ palpitar; (*walk*) ir con pasos pesados

pour /pɔː(r)/ *vt* verter. **~ out** servir ⟨*drink*⟩. ● *vi* fluir; (*rain*) llover a cántaros. **~ in** (*people*) entrar en tropel. **~ing rain** *n* lluvia *f* torrencial. **~ out** (*people*) salir en tropel

pout /paʊt/ *vi* hacer pucheros. ● *n* puchero *m*, mala cara *f*

poverty /'pɒvətɪ/ *n* pobreza *f*

powder /'paʊdə(r)/ *n* polvo *m*; (*cosmetic*) polvos *mpl*. ● *vt* polvorear; (*pulverize*) pulverizar. **~ one's face** ponerse polvos en la cara. **~ed** *a* en polvo. **~y** *a* polvoriento

power /'paʊə(r)/ *n* poder *m*; (*elec*) corriente *f*; (*energy*) energía *f*; (*nation*) potencia *f*. **~ cut** *n* apagón *m*. **~ed** *a* con motor. **~ed by** impulsado por. **~ful** *a* poderoso. **~less** *a*

impotente. **~-station** *n* central *f* eléctrica

practicable /'præktɪkəbl/ *a* practicable

practical /'præktɪkl/ *a* práctico. **~ joke** *n* broma *f* pesada. **~ly** *adv* prácticamente

practi|ce /'præktɪs/ *n* práctica *f*; (*custom*) costumbre *f*; (*exercise*) ejercicio *m*; (*sport*) entrenamiento *m*; (*clients*) clientela *f*. **be in ~ce** ⟨*doctor, lawyer*⟩ ejercer. **be out of ~ce** no estar en forma. **in ~ce** (*in fact*) en la práctica; (*on form*) en forma. **~se** /'præktɪs/ *vt* hacer ejercicios en; (*put into practice*) poner en práctica; (*sport*) entrenarse en; ejercer ⟨*profession*⟩. ● *vi* ejercitarse; ⟨*professional*⟩ ejercer. **~sed** *a* experto

practitioner /præk'tɪʃənə(r)/ *n* profesional *m & f*. **general ~** médico *m* de cabecera. **medical ~** médico *m*

pragmatic /præg'mætɪk/ *a* pragmático

prairie /'preərɪ/ *n* pradera *f*

praise /preɪz/ *vt* alabar. ● *n* alabanza *f*. **~worthy** *a* loable

pram /præm/ *n* cochecito *m* de niño

prance /prɑːns/ *vi* ⟨*horse*⟩ hacer cabriolas; ⟨*person*⟩ pavonearse

prank /præŋk/ *n* travesura *f*

prattle /'prætl/ *vi* parlotear. ● *n* parloteo *m*

prawn /prɔːn/ *n* gamba *f*

pray /preɪ/ *vi* rezar. **~er** /preə(r)/ *n* oración *f*. **~ for** rogar

pre... /priː/ *pref* pre...

preach /priːtʃ/ *vt/i* predicar. **~er** *n* predicador *m*

preamble /priː'æmbl/ *n* preámbulo *m*

pre-arrange /priːə'reɪndʒ/ *vt* arreglar de antemano. **~ment** *n* arreglo *m* previo

precarious /prɪ'keərɪəs/ *a* precario. **~ly** *adv* precariamente

precaution /prɪ'kɔːʃn/ *n* precaución *f*. **~ary** *a* de precaución; (*preventive*) preventivo

precede /prɪ'siːd/ *vt* preceder

preceden|ce /'presɪdəns/ *n* precedencia *f*. **~t** /'presɪdənt/ *n* precedente *m*

preceding /prɪ'siːdɪŋ/ *a* precedente

precept /'priːsept/ *n* precepto *m*

precinct /'priːsɪŋkt/ *n* recinto *m*. **pedestrian ~** zona *f* peatonal. **~s** *npl* contornos *mpl*

precious /'preʃəs/ *a* precioso. ● *adv* (*fam*) muy

precipice /'presɪpɪs/ *n* precipicio *m*

precipitat|e /prɪ'sɪpɪteɪt/ *vt* precipitar. /prɪ'sɪpɪtət/ *n* precipitado *m*. ● *a* precipitado. ~**ion** /-'teɪʃn/ *n* precipitación *f*

precipitous /prɪ'sɪpɪtəs/ *a* escarpado

précis /'preɪsi:/ *n* (*pl* **précis** /-si:z/) resumen *m*

precis|e /prɪ'saɪs/ *a* preciso; (*careful*) meticuloso. ~**ely** *adv* precisamente. ~**ion** /-'sɪʒn/ *n* precisión *f*

preclude /prɪ'klu:d/ *vt* (*prevent*) impedir; (*exclude*) excluir

precocious /prɪ'kəʊʃəs/ *a* precoz. ~**ly** *adv* precozmente

preconce|ived /pri:kən'si:vd/ *a* preconcebido. ~**ption** /-'sepʃn/ *n* preconcepción *f*

precursor /pri:'kɜ:sə(r)/ *n* precursor *m*

predator /'predətə(r)/ *n* animal *m* de rapiña. ~**y** *a* de rapiña

predecessor /'pri:dɪsesə(r)/ *n* predecesor *m*, antecesor *m*

predestin|ation /prɪdestɪ'neɪʃn/ *n* predestinación *f*. ~**e** /pri:'destɪn/ *vt* predestinar

predicament /prɪ'dɪkəmənt/ *n* apuro *m*

predicat|e /'predɪkət/ *n* predicado *m*. ~**ive** /prɪ'dɪkətɪv/ *a* predicativo

predict /prɪ'dɪkt/ *vt* predecir. ~**ion** /-ʃn/ *n* predicción *f*

predilection /pri:dɪ'lekʃn/ *n* predilección *f*

predispose /pri:dɪ'spəʊz/ *vt* predisponer

predomina|nt /prɪ'dɒmɪnənt/ *a* predominante. ~**te** /prɪ'dɒmɪneɪt/ *vi* predominar

pre-eminent /pri:'emɪnənt/ *a* pre-eminente

pre-empt /pri:'empt/ *vt* adquirir por adelantado, adelantarse a

preen /pri:n/ *vt* limpiar, arreglar. ~ **o.s.** atildarse

prefab /'pri:fæb/ *n* (*fam*) casa *f* prefabricada. ~**ricated** /-'fæbrɪkeɪtɪd/ *a* prefabricado

preface /'prefəs/ *n* prólogo *m*

prefect /'pri:fekt/ *n* monitor *m*; (*official*) prefecto *m*

prefer /prɪ'fɜ:(r)/ *vt* (*pt* **preferred**) preferir. ~**able** /'prefrəbl/ *a* preferible. ~**ence** /'prefrəns/ *n* preferencia *f*. ~**ential** /-ə'renʃl/ *a* preferente

prefix /'pri:fɪks/ *n* (*pl* **-ixes**) prefijo *m*

pregnan|cy /'pregnənsɪ/ *n* embarazo *m*. ~**t** /'pregnənt/ *a* embarazada

prehistoric /pri:hɪ'stɒrɪk/ *a* prehistórico

prejudge /pri:'dʒʌdʒ/ *vt* prejuzgar

prejudice /'predʒʊdɪs/ *n* prejuicio *m*; (*harm*) perjuicio *m*. ● *vt* predisponer; (*harm*) perjudicar. ~**d** *a* parcial

prelate /'prelət/ *n* prelado *m*

preliminar|ies /prɪ'lɪmɪnərɪz/ *npl* preliminares *mpl*. ~**y** /prɪ'lɪmɪnərɪ/ *a* preliminar

prelude /'prelju:d/ *n* preludio *m*

pre-marital /pri:'mærɪtl/ *a* prematrimonial

premature /'premətjʊə(r)/ *a* prematuro

premeditated /pri:'medɪteɪtɪd/ *a* premeditado

premier /'premɪə(r)/ *a* primero. ● *n* (*pol*) primer ministro

première /'premɪə(r)/ *n* estreno *m*

premises /'premɪsɪz/ *npl* local *m*. **on the** ~ en el local

premiss /'premɪs/ *n* premisa *f*

premium /'pri:mɪəm/ *n* premio *m*. **at a** ~ muy solicitado

premonition /pri:mə'nɪʃn/ *n* presentimiento *m*

preoccup|ation /pri:ɒkjʊ'peɪʃn/ *n* preocupación *f*. ~**ied** /-'ɒkjʊpaɪd/ *a* preocupado

prep /prep/ *n* deberes *mpl*

preparation /prepə'reɪʃn/ *n* preparación *f*. ~**s** *npl* preparativos *mpl*

preparatory /prɪ'pærətrɪ/ *a* preparatorio. ~ **school** *n* escuela *f* primaria privada

prepare /prɪ'peə(r)/ *vt* preparar. ● *vi* prepararse. ~**d to** dispuesto a

prepay /pri:'peɪ/ *vt* (*pt* **-paid**) pagar por adelantado

preponderance /prɪ'pɒndərəns/ *n* preponderancia *f*

preposition /prepə'zɪʃn/ *n* preposición *f*

prepossessing /pri:pə'zesɪŋ/ *a* atractivo

preposterous /prɪ'pɒstərəs/ *a* absurdo

prep school /'prepsku:l/ *n* escuela *f* primaria privada

prerequisite /pri:'rekwɪzɪt/ *n* requisito *m* previo

prerogative /prɪˈrɒɡətɪv/ n prerrogativa f

Presbyterian /prezbɪˈtɪərɪən/ a & n presbiteriano (m)

prescri|be /prɪˈskraɪb/ vt prescribir; (med) recetar. ~ption /-ˈɪpʃn/ n prescripción f; (med) receta f

presence /ˈprezns/ n presencia f; (attendance) asistencia f. ~ of mind presencia f de ánimo

present¹ /ˈpreznt/ a & n presente (m & f). at ~ actualmente. for the ~ por ahora

present² /ˈpreznt/ n (gift) regalo m

present³ /prɪˈzent/ vt presentar; (give) obsequiar. ~ s.o. with obsequiar a uno con. ~able a presentable. ~ation /prezn'teɪʃn/ n presentación f; (ceremony) ceremonia f de entrega

presently /ˈprezntlɪ/ adv dentro de poco

preserv|ation /prezə'veɪʃn/ n conservación f. ~ative /prɪˈzɜːvətɪv/ n preservativo m. ~e /prɪˈzɜːv/ vt conservar; (maintain) mantener; (culin) poner en conserva. ● n coto m; (jam) confitura f

preside /prɪˈzaɪd/ vi presidir. ~ over presidir

presiden|cy /ˈprezɪdənsɪ/ n presidencia f. ~t /ˈprezɪdənt/ n presidente m. ~tial /-ˈdenʃl/ a presidencial

press /pres/ vt apretar; exprimir (fruit etc); (insist on) insistir en; (iron) planchar. be ~ed for tener poco. ● vi apretar; (time) apremiar; (fig) urgir. ~ on seguir adelante. ● n presión f; (mec, newspapers) prensa f; (printing) imprenta f. ~ conference n rueda f de prensa. ~ cutting n recorte m de periódico. ~ing /ˈpresɪŋ/ a urgente. ~stud n automático m. ~up n plancha f

pressure /ˈpreʃə(r)/ n presión f. ● vt hacer presión sobre. ~cooker n olla f a presión. ~ group n grupo m de presión

pressurize /ˈpreʃəraɪz/ vt hacer presión sobre

prestig|e /preˈstiːʒ/ n prestigio m. ~ious /preˈstɪdʒəs/ a prestigioso

presum|ably /prɪˈzjuːməblɪ/ adv presumiblemente, probablemente. ~e /prɪˈzjuːm/ vt presumir. ~e (up)on vi abusar de. ~ption

/-ˈzʌmpʃn/ n presunción f. ~ptuous /prɪˈzʌmptʃʊəs/ a presuntuoso

presuppose /priːsəˈpəʊz/ vt presuponer

preten|ce /prɪˈtens/ n fingimiento m; (claim) pretensión f; (pretext) pretexto m. ~d /prɪˈtend/ vt/i fingir. ~d to (lay claim) pretender

pretentious /prɪˈtenʃəs/ a pretencioso

pretext /ˈpriːtekst/ n pretexto m

pretty /ˈprɪtɪ/ a (-ier, -iest) adv bonito, lindo (esp LAm); ⟨person⟩ guapo

prevail /prɪˈveɪl/ vi predominar; (win) prevalecer. ~ on persuadir

prevalen|ce /ˈprevələns/ n costumbre f. ~t /ˈprevələnt/ a extendido

prevaricate /prɪˈværɪkeɪt/ vi despistar

prevent /prɪˈvent/ vt impedir. ~able a evitable. ~ion /-ʃn/ n prevención f. ~ive a preventivo

preview /ˈpriːvjuː/ n preestreno m, avance m

previous /ˈpriːvɪəs/ a anterior. ~ to antes de. ~ly adv anteriormente, antes

pre-war /priːˈwɔː(r)/ a de antes de la guerra

prey /preɪ/ n presa f; (fig) víctima f. bird of ~ n ave f de rapiña. ● vi. ~ on alimentarse de; (worry) atormentar

price /praɪs/ n precio m. ● vt fijar el precio de. ~less a inapreciable; (amusing, fam) muy divertido. ~y a (fam) caro

prick /prɪk/ vt/i pinchar. ~ up one's ears aguzar las orejas. ● n pinchazo m

prickl|e /ˈprɪkl/ n (bot) espina f; (of animal) púa f; (sensation) picor m. ~y a espinoso; ⟨animal⟩ lleno de púas; ⟨person⟩ quisquilloso

pride /praɪd/ n orgullo m. ~ of place n puesto m de honor. ● vr. ~ o.s. on enorgullecerse de

priest /priːst/ n sacerdote m. ~hood n sacerdocio m. ~ly a sacerdotal

prig /prɪg/ n mojigato m. ~gish a mojigato

prim /prɪm/ a (primmer, primmest) estirado; (prudish) gazmoño

primarily /ˈpraɪmərɪlɪ/ adv en primer lugar

primary /ˈpraɪmərɪ/ a primario; (chief) principal. ~ school n escuela f primaria

prime[1] /praɪm/ *vt* cebar ‹gun›; (*prepare*) preparar; aprestar ‹surface›

prime[2] /praɪm/ *a* principal; (*first rate*) excelente. ~ **minister** *n* primer ministro *m*. ● *n*. be in one's ~ estar en la flor de la vida

primer[1] /ˈpraɪmə(r)/ *n* (*of paint*) primera mano *f*

primer[2] /ˈpraɪmə(r)/ (*book*) silabario *m*

primeval /praɪˈmiːvl/ *a* primitivo

primitive /ˈprɪmɪtɪv/ *a* primitivo

primrose /ˈprɪmrəʊz/ *n* primavera *f*

prince /prɪns/ *n* príncipe *m*. ~**ly** *a* principesco. ~**ss** /prɪnˈses/ *n* princesa *f*

principal /ˈprɪnsəpl/ *a* principal. ● *n* (*of school etc*) director *m*

principality /prɪnsɪˈpælətɪ/ *n* principado *m*

principally /ˈprɪnsɪpəlɪ/ *adv* principalmente

principle /ˈprɪnsəpl/ *n* principio *m*. **in** ~ en principio. **on** ~ por principio

print /prɪnt/ *vt* imprimir; (*write in capitals*) escribir con letras de molde. ● *n* (*of finger, foot*) huella *f*; (*letters*) caracteres *mpl*; (*of design*) estampado *m*; (*picture*) grabado *m*; (*photo*) copia *f*. **in** ~ ‹book› disponible. **out of** ~ agotado. ~**ed matter** *n* impresos *mpl*. ~**er** /ˈprɪntə(r)/ *n* impresor *m*; (*machine*) impresora *f*. ~**ing** *n* tipografía *f*. ~**out** *n* listado *m*

prior /ˈpraɪə(r)/ *n* prior *m*. ● *a* anterior. ~ **to** antes de

priority /praɪˈɒrətɪ/ *n* prioridad *f*

priory /ˈpraɪərɪ/ *n* priorato *m*

prise /praɪz/ *vt* apalancar. ~ **open** abrir por fuerza

prism /ˈprɪzəm/ *n* prisma *m*

prison /ˈprɪzn/ *n* cárcel *m*. ~**er** *n* prisionero *m*; (*in prison*) preso *m*; (*under arrest*) detenido *m*. ~ **officer** *n* carcelero *m*

pristine /ˈprɪstiːn/ *a* prístino

privacy /ˈprɪvəsɪ/ *n* intimidad *f*; (*private life*) vida *f* privada. **in** ~ en la intimidad

private /ˈpraɪvət/ *a* privado; (*confidential*) personal; ‹lessons, house› particular; ‹ceremony› en la intimidad. ● *n* soldado *m* raso. **in** ~ en privado; (*secretly*) en secreto. ~ **eye** *n* (*fam*) detective *m* privado. ~**ly** *adv* en privado; (*inwardly*) interiormente

privation /praɪˈveɪʃn/ *n* privación *f*

privet /ˈprɪvɪt/ *n* alheña *f*

privilege /ˈprɪvɪlɪdʒ/ *n* privilegio *m*. ~**d** *a* privilegiado

privy /ˈprɪvɪ/ *a*. ~ **to** al corriente de

prize /praɪz/ *n* premio *m*. ● *a* ‹idiot etc› de remate. ● *vt* estimar. ~**-fighter** *n* boxeador *m* profesional. ~**-giving** *n* reparto *m* de premios. ~**winner** *n* premiado *m*

pro /prəʊ/ *n*. ~**s and cons** el pro *m* y el contra *m*

probab|ility /prɒbəˈbɪlətɪ/ *n* probabilidad *f*. ~**le** /ˈprɒbəbl/ *a* probable. ~**ly** *adv* probablemente

probation /prəˈbeɪʃn/ *n* prueba *f*; (*jurid*) libertad *f* condicional. ~**ary** *a* de prueba

probe /prəʊb/ *n* sonda *f*; (*fig*) encuesta *f*. ● *vt* sondar. ● *vi*. ~ **into** investigar

problem /ˈprɒbləm/ *n* problema *m*. ● *a* difícil. ~**atic** /-ˈmætɪk/ *a* problemático

procedure /prəˈsiːdʒə(r)/ *n* procedimiento *m*

proceed /prəˈsiːd/ *vi* proceder. ~**ing** *n* procedimiento *m*. ~**ings** /prəˈsiːdɪŋz/ *npl* (*report*) actas *fpl*; (*jurid*) proceso *m*

proceeds /ˈprəʊsiːdz/ *npl* ganancias *fpl*

process /ˈprəʊses/ *n* proceso *m*. **in** ~ **of** en vías de. **in the** ~ **of time** con el tiempo. ● *vt* tratar; revelar ‹photo›. ~**ion** /prəˈseʃn/ *n* desfile *m*

procla|im /prəˈkleɪm/ *vt* proclamar. ~**mation** /prɒkləˈmeɪʃn/ *n* proclamación *f*

procrastinate /prəʊˈkræstɪneɪt/ *vi* aplazar, demorar, diferir

procreation /prəʊkrɪˈeɪʃn/ *n* procreación *f*

procure /prəˈkjʊə(r)/ *vt* obtener

prod /prɒd/ *vt* (*pt* **prodded**) empujar; (*with elbow*) dar un codazo a. ● *vi* dar con el dedo. ● *n* empuje *m*; (*with elbow*) codazo *m*

prodigal /ˈprɒdɪgl/ *a* pródigo

prodigious /prəˈdɪdʒəs/ *a* prodigioso

prodigy /ˈprɒdɪdʒɪ/ *n* prodigio *m*

produce /prəˈdjuːs/ *vt* (*show*) presentar; (*bring out*) sacar; poner en escena ‹play›; (*cause*) causar; (*manufacture*) producir. /ˈprɒdjuːs/ *n* productos *mpl.* **~er** /prə'djuːsə(r)/ *n* productor *m*; (*in theatre*) director *m*

product /'prɒdʌkt/ *n* producto *m*. **~ion** /prə'dʌkʃn/ *n* producción *f*; (*of play*) representación *f*

productiv|e /prə'dʌktɪv/ *a* productivo. **~ity** /prɒdʌk'tɪvətɪ/ *n* productividad *f*

profan|e /prə'feɪn/ *a* profano; (*blasphemous*) blasfemo. **~ity** /-'fænətɪ/ *n* profanidad *f*

profess /prə'fes/ *vt* profesar; (*pretend*) pretender

profession /prə'feʃn/ *n* profesión *f*. **~al** *a & n* profesional (*m & f*)

professor /prə'fesə(r)/ *n* catedrático *m*; (*Amer*) profesor *m*

proffer /'prɒfə(r)/ *vt* ofrecer

proficien|cy /prə'fɪʃənsɪ/ *n* competencia *f*. **~t** /prə'fɪʃnt/ *a* competente

profile /'prəʊfaɪl/ *n* perfil *m*

profit /'prɒfɪt/ *n* ganancia *f*; (*fig*) provecho *m*. ● *vi.* **~ from** sacar provecho de. **~able** *a* provechoso

profound /prə'faʊnd/ *a* profundo. **~ly** *adv* profundamente

profus|e /prə'fjuːs/ *a* profuso. **~ely** *adv* profusamente. **~ion** /-ʒn/ *n* profusión *f*

progeny /'prɒdʒənɪ/ *n* progenie *f*

prognosis /prɒg'nəʊsɪs/ *n* (*pl* **-oses**) pronóstico *m*

program(|me) /'prəʊgræm/ *n* programa *m*. ● *vt* (*pt* **programmed**) programar. **~mer** *n* programador *m*

progress /'prəʊgres/ *n* progreso *m*, progresos *mpl*; (*development*) desarrollo *m.* **in ~** en curso. /prə'gres/ *vi* hacer progresos; (*develop*) desarrollarse. **~ion** /prə'greʃn/ *n* progresión *f*

progressive /prə'gresɪv/ *a* progresivo; (*reforming*) progresista. **~ly** *adv* progresivamente

prohibit /prə'hɪbɪt/ *vt* prohibir. **~ive** /-bətɪv/ *a* prohibitivo

project /prə'dʒekt/ *vt* proyectar. ● *vi* (*stick out*) sobresalir. /'prɒdʒekt/ *n* proyecto *m*

projectile /prə'dʒektaɪl/ *n* proyectil *m*

projector /prə'dʒektə(r)/ *n* proyector *m*

proletari|an /prəʊlɪ'teərɪən/ *a & n* proletario (*m*). **~at** /prəʊlɪ'teərɪət/ *n* proletariado *m*

prolif|erate /prə'lɪfəreɪt/ *vi* proliferar. **~eration** /-'reɪʃn/ *n* proliferación *f*. **~ic** /prə'lɪfɪk/ *a* prolífico

prologue /'prəʊlɒg/ *n* prólogo *m*

prolong /prə'lɒŋ/ *vt* prolongar

promenade /prɒmə'nɑːd/ *n* paseo *m*; (*along beach*) paseo *m* marítimo. ● *vt* pasear. ● *vi* pasearse. **~ concert** *n* concierto *m* (que forma parte de un festival de música clásica en Londres, en que no todo el público tiene asientos)

prominen|ce /'prɒmɪnəns/ *n* prominencia *f*; (*fig*) importancia *f*. **~t** /'prɒmɪnənt/ *a* prominente; (*important*) importante; (*conspicuous*) conspicuo

promiscu|ity /prɒmɪ'skjuːətɪ/ *n* libertinaje *m*. **~ous** /prə'mɪskjʊəs/ *a* libertino

promis|e /'prɒmɪs/ *n* promesa *f*. ● *vt/i* prometer. **~ing** *a* prometedor; ⟨*person*⟩ que promete

promontory /'prɒməntrɪ/ *n* promontorio *m*

promot|e /prə'məʊt/ *vt* promover. **~ion** /-'məʊʃn/ *n* promoción *f*

prompt /prɒmpt/ *a* pronto; (*punctual*) puntual. ● *adv* en punto. ● *vt* incitar; apuntar ⟨*actor*⟩. **~er** *n* apuntador *m*. **~ly** *adv* puntualmente. **~ness** *n* prontitud *f*

promulgate /'prɒməlgeɪt/ *vt* promulgar

prone /prəʊn/ *a* echado boca abajo. **~ to** propenso a

prong /prɒŋ/ *n* (*of fork*) diente *m*

pronoun /'prəʊnaʊn/ *n* pronombre *m*

pronounc|e /prə'naʊns/ *vt* pronunciar; (*declare*) declarar. **~ement** *n* declaración *f*. **~ed** /prə'naʊnst/ *a* pronunciado; (*noticeable*) marcado

pronunciation /prənʌnsɪ'eɪʃn/ *n* pronunciación *f*

proof /pruːf/ *n* prueba *f*; (*of alcohol*) graduación *f* normal. ● *a.* **~ against** a prueba de. **~-reading** *n* corrección *f* de pruebas

prop[1] /prɒp/ *n* puntal *m*; (*fig*) apoyo *m.* ● *vt* (*pt* **propped**) apoyar. **~ against** (*lean*) apoyar en

prop[2] /prɒp/ (*in theatre, fam*) accesorio *m*

propaganda /prɒpə'gændə/ *n* propaganda *f*

propagat|e /'prɒpəgeɪt/ *vt* propagar. ● *vi* propagarse. ∼**ion** /-'geɪʃn/ *n* propagación *f*

propel /prə'pel/ *vt* (*pt* **propelled**) propulsar. ∼**ler** /prə'pelə(r)/ *n* hélice *f*

propensity /prə'pensətɪ/ *n* propensión *f*

proper /'prɒpə(r)/ *a* correcto; (*suitable*) apropiado; (*gram*) propio; (*real, fam*) verdadero. ∼**ly** *adv* correctamente

property /'prɒpətɪ/ *n* propiedad *f*; (*things owned*) bienes *mpl*. ● *a* inmobiliario

prophe|cy /'prɒfəsɪ/ *n* profecía *f*. ∼**sy** /'prɒfɪsaɪ/ *vt/i* profetizar. ∼**t** /'prɒfɪt/ *n* profeta *m*. ∼**tic** /prə'fetɪk/ *a* profético

propitious /prə'pɪʃəs/ *a* propicio

proportion /prə'pɔːʃn/ *n* proporción *f*. ∼**al** *a*, ∼**ate** *a* proporcional

propos|al /prə'pəʊzl/ *n* propuesta *f*. ∼**al of marriage** oferta *f* de matrimonio. ∼**e** /prə'pəʊz/ *vt* proponer. ● *vi* hacer una oferta de matrimonio

proposition /prɒpə'zɪʃn/ *n* proposición *f*; (*project, fam*) asunto *m*

propound /prə'paʊnd/ *vt* proponer

proprietor /prə'praɪətə(r)/ *n* propietario *m*

propriety /prə'praɪətɪ/ *n* decoro *m*

propulsion /prə'pʌlʃn/ *n* propulsión *f*

prosaic /prə'zeɪk/ *a* prosaico

proscribe /prə'skraɪb/ *vt* proscribir

prose /prəʊz/ *n* prosa *f*

prosecut|e /'prɒsɪkjuːt/ *vt* procesar; (*carry on*) proseguir. ∼**ion** /-'kjuːʃn/ *n* proceso *m*. ∼**or** *n* acusador *m*. **Public P∼or** fiscal *m*

prospect /'prɒspekt/ *n* vista *f*; (*expectation*) perspectiva *f*. /prə'spekt/ *vi* prospectar

prospective /prə'spektɪv/ *a* probable; (*future*) futuro

prospector /prə'spektə(r)/ *n* prospector *m*, explorador *m*

prospectus /prə'spektəs/ *n* prospecto *m*

prosper /'prɒspə(r)/ *vi* prosperar. ∼**ity** /-'sperətɪ/ *n* prosperidad *f*. ∼**ous** /'prɒspərəs/ *a* próspero

prostitut|e /'prɒstɪtjuːt/ *n* prostituta *f*. ∼**ion** /-'tjuːʃn/ *n* prostitución *f*

prostrate /'prɒstreɪt/ *a* echado boca abajo; (*fig*) postrado

protagonist /prə'tægənɪst/ *n* protagonista *m & f*

protect /prə'tekt/ *vt* proteger. ∼**ion** /-ʃn/ *n* protección *f*. ∼**ive** /prə'tektɪv/ *a* protector. ∼**or** *n* protector *m*

protégé /'prɒtɪʒeɪ/ *n* protegido *m*. ∼**e** *n* protegida *f*

protein /'prəʊtiːn/ *n* proteína *f*

protest /'prəʊtest/ *n* protesta *f*. **under** ∼ bajo protesta. /prə'test/ *vt/i* protestar. ∼**er** *n* (*demonstrator*) manifestante *m & f*

Protestant /'prɒtɪstənt/ *a & n* protestante (*m & f*)

protocol /'prəʊtəkɒl/ *n* protocolo *m*

prototype /'prəʊtətaɪp/ *n* prototipo *m*

protract /prə'trækt/ *vt* prolongar

protractor /prə'træktə(r)/ *n* transportador *m*

protrude /prə'truːd/ *vi* sobresalir

protuberance /prə'tjuːbərəns/ *n* protuberancia *f*

proud /praʊd/ *a* orgulloso. ∼**ly** *adv* orgullosamente

prove /pruːv/ *vt* probar. ● *vi* resultar. ∼**n** *a* probado

provenance /'prɒvənəns/ *n* procedencia *f*

proverb /'prɒvɜːb/ *n* proverbio *m*. ∼**ial** /prə'vɜːbɪəl/ *a* proverbial

provide /prə'vaɪd/ *vt* proveer. ● *vi*. ∼ **against** precaverse de. ∼ **for** (*allow for*) prever; mantener (*person*). ∼**d** /prə'vaɪdɪd/ *conj*. ∼ **(that)** con tal que

providen|ce /'prɒvɪdəns/ *n* providencia *f*. ∼**t** *a* providente. ∼**tial** /prɒvɪ'denʃl/ *a* providencial

providing /prə'vaɪdɪŋ/ *conj*. ∼ **that** con tal que

provinc|e /'prɒvɪns/ *n* provincia *f*; (*fig*) competencia *f*. ∼**ial** /prə'vɪnʃl/ *a* provincial

provision /prə'vɪʒn/ *n* provisión *f*; (*supply*) suministro *m*; (*stipulation*) condición *f*. ∼**s** *npl* comestibles *mpl*

provisional /prə'vɪʒənl/ *a* provisional. ∼**ly** *adv* provisionalmente

proviso /prə'vaɪzəʊ/ *n* (*pl* **-os**) condición *f*

provo|cation /prɒvə'keɪʃn/ *n* provocación *f*. ∼**cative** /-'vɒkətɪv/ *a* provocador. ∼**ke** /prə'vəʊk/ *vt* provocar

prow /praʊ/ *n* proa *f*

prowess /'prauis/ n habilidad f; (valour) valor m

prowl /praul/ vi merodear. ● n ronda f. **be on the ~** merodear. **~er** n merodeador m

proximity /prɒk'sɪmətɪ/ n proximidad f

proxy /'prɒksɪ/ n poder m. **by ~** por poder

prude /pru:d/ n mojigato m

pruden|ce /'pru:dəns/ n prudencia f. **~t** /'pru:dənt/ a prudente. **~tly** adv prudentemente

prudish /'pru:dɪʃ/ a mojigato

prune[1] /pru:n/ n ciruela f pasa

prune[2] /pru:n/ vt podar

pry /praɪ/ vi entrometerse

psalm /sɑ:m/ n salmo m

pseudo... /'sju:dəʊ/ pref seudo...

pseudonym /'sju:dənɪm/ n seudónimo m

psychiatr|ic /saɪkɪ'ætrɪk/ a psiquiátrico. **~ist** /saɪ'kaɪətrɪst/ n psiquiatra m & f. **~y** /saɪ'kaɪətrɪ/ n psiquiatría f

psychic /'saɪkɪk/ a psíquico

psycho-analys|e /saɪkəʊ'ænəlaɪz/ vt psicoanalizar. **~is** /saɪkəʊə'næləsɪs/ n psicoanálisis m. **~t** /-ɪst/ n psicoanalista m & f

psycholog|ical /saɪkə'lɒdʒɪkl/ a psicológico. **~ist** /saɪ'kɒlədʒɪst/ n psicólogo m. **~y** /saɪ'kɒlədʒɪ/ n psicología f

psychopath /'saɪkəpæθ/ n psicópata m & f

pub /pʌb/ n bar m

puberty /'pju:bətɪ/ n pubertad f

pubic /'pju:bɪk/ a pubiano, púbico

public /'pʌblɪk/ a público

publican /'pʌblɪkən/ n tabernero m

publication /pʌblɪ'keɪʃn/ n publicación f

public house /pʌblɪk'haʊs/ n bar m

publicity /pʌb'lɪsətɪ/ n publicidad f

publicize /'pʌblɪsaɪz/ vt publicar, anunciar

publicly /'pʌblɪklɪ/ adv públicamente

public school /pʌblɪk'sku:l/ n colegio m privado; (Amer) instituto m

public-spirited /pʌblɪk'spɪrɪtɪd/ a cívico

publish /'pʌblɪʃ/ vt publicar. **~er** n editor m. **~ing** n publicación f

puck /pʌk/ n (ice hockey) disco m

pucker /'pʌkə(r)/ vt arrugar. ● vi arrugarse

pudding /'pʊdɪŋ/ n postre m; (steamed) budín m

puddle /'pʌdl/ n charco m

pudgy /'pʌdʒɪ/ a (-ier, -iest) rechoncho

puerile /'pjʊəraɪl/ a pueril

puff /pʌf/ n soplo m; (for powder) borla f. ● vt/i soplar. **~ at** chupar ⟨pipe⟩. **~ out** apagar ⟨candle⟩; (swell up) hinchar. **~ed** a (out of breath) sin aliento. **~ pastry** n hojaldre m. **~y** /'pʌfɪ/ a hinchado

pugnacious /pʌg'neɪʃəs/ a belicoso

pug-nosed /pʌg'nəʊzd/ a chato

pull /pʊl/ vt tirar de; sacar ⟨tooth⟩; torcer ⟨muscle⟩. **~ a face** hacer una mueca. **~ a fast one** hacer una mala jugada. **~ down** derribar ⟨building⟩. **~ off** quitarse; (fig) lograr. **~ one's weight** poner de su parte. **~ out** sacar. **~ s.o.'s leg** tomarle el pelo a uno. **~ up** (uproot) desarraigar; (reprimand) reprender. ● vi tirar (at de). **~ away** (auto) alejarse. **~ back** retirarse. **~ in** (enter) entrar; (auto) parar. **~ o.s. together** tranquilizarse. **~ out** (auto) salirse. **~ through** recobrar la salud. **~ up** (auto) parar. ● n tirón m; (fig) atracción f; (influence) influencia f. **give a ~** tirar

pulley /'pʊlɪ/ n polea f

pullover /'pʊləʊvə(r)/ n jersey m

pulp /pʌlp/ n pulpa f; (for paper) pasta f

pulpit /'pʊlpɪt/ n púlpito m

pulsate /'pʌlseɪt/ vi pulsar

pulse /pʌls/ n (med) pulso m

pulverize /'pʌlvəraɪz/ vt pulverizar

pumice /'pʌmɪs/ n piedra f pómez

pummel /'pʌml/ vt (pt pummelled) aporrear

pump[1] /pʌmp/ n bomba f. ● vt sacar con una bomba; (fig) sonsacar. **~ up** inflar

pump[2] /pʌmp/ (plimsoll) zapatilla f de lona; (dancing shoe) escarpín m

pumpkin /'pʌmpkɪn/ n calabaza f

pun /pʌn/ n juego m de palabras

punch[1] /pʌntʃ/ vt dar un puñetazo a; (perforate) perforar; hacer ⟨hole⟩. ● n puñetazo m; (vigour, sl) empuje m; (device) punzón m

punch[2] /pʌntʃ/ (drink) ponche m

punch: ~-drunk a aturdido a golpes. **~ line** n gracia f. **~-up** n riña f

punctilious /pʌŋk'tɪlɪəs/ a meticuloso

punctual /'pʌŋktʃʊəl/ a puntual. **~ity** /-'ælətɪ/ n puntualidad f. **~ly** adv puntualmente

punctuat|e /'pʌŋkʃʊeɪt/ vt puntuar. **~ion** /-'eɪʃn/ n puntuación f

puncture /'pʌŋktʃə(r)/ n (in tyre) pinchazo m. ● vt pinchar. ● vi pincharse

pundit /'pʌndɪt/ n experto m

pungen|cy /'pʌndʒənsɪ/ n acritud f; (fig) mordacidad f. **~t** /'pʌndʒənt/ a acre; ⟨remark⟩ mordaz

punish /'pʌnɪʃ/ vt castigar. **~able** a castigable. **~ment** n castigo m

punitive /'pjuːnɪtɪv/ a punitivo

punk /pʌŋk/ a ⟨music, person⟩ punk

punnet /'pʌnɪt/ n canastilla f

punt[1] /pʌnt/ n (boat) batea f

punt[2] /pʌnt/ vi apostar. **~er** n apostante m & f

puny /'pjuːnɪ/ a (-ier, -iest) diminuto; (weak) débil; (petty) insignificante

pup /pʌp/ n cachorro m

pupil[1] /'pjuːpl/ n alumno m

pupil[2] /'pjuːpl/ n (of eye) pupila f

puppet /'pʌpɪt/ n títere m

puppy /'pʌpɪ/ n cachorro m

purchase /'pɜːtʃəs/ vt comprar. ● n compra f. **~r** n comprador m

pur|e /pjʊə(r)/ a (-er, -est) puro. **~ely** adv puramente. **~ity** n pureza f

purée /'pjʊəreɪ/ n puré m

purgatory /'pɜːgətrɪ/ n purgatorio m

purge /pɜːdʒ/ vt purgar. ● n purga f

purif|ication /pjʊərɪfɪ'keɪʃn/ n purificación f. **~y** /'pjʊərɪfaɪ/ vt purificar

purist /'pjʊərɪst/ n purista m & f

puritan /'pjʊərɪtən/ n puritano m. **~ical** /-'tænɪkl/ a puritano

purl /pɜːl/ n (knitting) punto m del revés

purple /'pɜːpl/ a purpúreo, morado. ● n púrpura f

purport /pə'pɔːt/ vt. **~ to be** pretender ser

purpose /'pɜːpəs/ n propósito m; (determination) resolución f. **on ~** a propósito. **to no ~** en vano. **~-built** a construido especialmente. **~ful** a (resolute) resuelto. **~ly** adv a propósito

purr /pɜː(r)/ vi ronronear

purse /pɜːs/ n monedero m; (Amer) bolso m, cartera f (LAm). ● vt fruncir

pursu|e /pə'sjuː/ vt perseguir, seguir. **~er** n perseguidor m. **~it** /pə'sjuːt/ n persecución f; (fig) ocupación f

purveyor /pə'veɪə(r)/ n proveedor m

pus /pʌs/ n pus m

push /pʊʃ/ vt empujar; apretar ⟨button⟩. ● vi empujar. ● n empuje m; (effort) esfuerzo m; (drive) dinamismo m. **at a ~** en caso de necesidad. **get the ~** (sl) ser despedido. **~ aside** vt apartar. **~ back** vt hacer retroceder. **~ off** vi (sl) marcharse. **~ on** vi seguir adelante. **~ up** vt levantar. **~-button telephone** n teléfono m de teclas. **~-chair** n sillita f con ruedas. **~ing** /'pʊʃɪŋ/ a ambicioso. **~-over** n (fam) cosa f muy fácil, pan comido. **~y** a (pej) ambicioso

puss /pʊs/ n minino m

put /pʊt/ vt (pt put, pres p putting) poner; (express) expresar; (say) decir; (estimate) estimar; hacer ⟨question⟩. **~ across** comunicar; (deceive) engañar. **~ aside** poner aparte. **~ away** guardar. **~ back** devolver; retrasar ⟨clock⟩. **~ by** guardar; ahorrar ⟨money⟩. **~ down** depositar; (suppress) suprimir; (write) apuntar; (kill) sacrificar. **~ forward** avanzar. **~ in** introducir; (submit) presentar. **~ in for** pedir. **~ off** aplazar; (disconcert) desconcertar. **~ on** (wear) ponerse; cobrar ⟨speed⟩; encender ⟨light⟩. **~ one's foot down** mantenerse firme. **~ out** (extinguish) apagar; (inconvenience) incomodar; extender ⟨hand⟩; (disconcert) desconcertar. **~ to sea** hacerse a la mar. **~ through** (phone) poner. **~ up** levantar; subir ⟨price⟩; alojar ⟨guest⟩. **~ up with** soportar. **stay ~** (fam) no moverse

putrefy /'pjuːtrɪfaɪ/ vi pudrirse

putt /pʌt/ n (golf) golpe m suave

putty /'pʌtɪ/ n masilla f

put-up /'pʊtʌp/ a. **~ job** n confabulación f

puzzl|e /'pʌzl/ n enigma m; (game) rompecabezas m invar. ● vt dejar perplejo. ● vi calentarse los sesos. **~ing** a incomprensible; (odd) curioso

pygmy /'pɪgmɪ/ n pigmeo m

pyjamas /pə'dʒɑːməz/ npl pijama m

pylon /'paɪlɒn/ n pilón m

pyramid /'pɪrəmɪd/ n pirámide f

python /'paɪθn/ n pitón m

Q

quack[1] /kwæk/ n (of duck) graznido m

quack[2] /kwæk/ (person) charlatán m. ~ **doctor** n curandero m

quadrangle /'kwɒdræŋgl/ n cuadrilátero m; (court) patio m

quadruped /'kwɒdruped/ n cuadrúpedo m

quadruple /'kwɒdrupl/ a & n cuádruplo (m). ● vt cuadruplicar. ~t /-plət/ n cuatrillizo m

quagmire /'kwægmaɪə(r)/ n ciénaga f; (fig) atolladero m

quail /kweɪl/ n codorniz f

quaint /kweɪnt/ a (-er, -est) pintoresco; (odd) curioso

quake /kweɪk/ vi temblar. ● n (fam) terremoto m

Quaker /'kweɪkə(r)/ n cuáquero (m)

qualification /ˌkwɒlɪfɪ'keɪʃn/ n título m; (requirement) requisito m; (ability) capacidad f; (fig) reserva f

qualif|ied /'kwɒlɪfaɪd/ a cualificado; (limited) limitado; (with degree, diploma) titulado. ~y /'kwɒlɪfaɪ/ vt calificar; (limit) limitar. ● vi sacar el título; (sport) clasificarse; (fig) llenar los requisitos

qualitative /'kwɒlɪtətɪv/ a cualitativo

quality /'kwɒlɪtɪ/ n calidad f; (attribute) cualidad f

qualm /kwɑ:m/ n escrúpulo m

quandary /'kwɒndrɪ/ n. in a ~ en un dilema

quantitative /'kwɒntɪtətɪv/ a cuantitativo

quantity /'kwɒntɪtɪ/ n cantidad f

quarantine /'kwɒrəntiːn/ n cuarentena f

quarrel /'kwɒrəl/ n riña f. ● vi (pt quarrelled) reñir. ~some a pendenciero

quarry[1] /'kwɒrɪ/ n (excavation) cantera f

quarry[2] /'kwɒrɪ/ n (animal) presa f

quart /kwɔ:t/ n (poco más de un) litro m

quarter /'kwɔ:tə(r)/ n cuarto m; (of year) trimestre m; (district) barrio m. **from all ~s** de todas partes. ● vt dividir en cuartos; (mil) acuartelar. ~s npl alojamiento m

quartermaster /'kwɔ:təmɑ:stə(r)/ n intendente m

quarter: ~final n cuarto m de final. ~ly a trimestral. ● adv cada tres meses

quartet /kwɔ:'tet/ n cuarteto m

quartz /kwɔ:ts/ n cuarzo m. ● a (watch etc) de cuarzo

quash /kwɒʃ/ vt anular

quasi.. /'kweɪsaɪ/ pref cuasi...

quaver /'kweɪvə(r)/ vi temblar. ● n (mus) corchea f

quay /ki:/ n muelle m

queasy /'kwi:zɪ/ a (stomach) delicado

queen /kwi:n/ n reina f. ~ **mother** n reina f madre

queer /kwɪə(r)/ a (-er, -est) extraño; (dubious) sospechoso; (ill) indispuesto. ● n (sl) homosexual m

quell /kwel/ vt reprimir

quench /kwentʃ/ vt apagar; sofocar (desire)

querulous /'kwerʊləs/ a quejumbroso

query /'kwɪərɪ/ n pregunta f. ● vt preguntar; (doubt) poner en duda

quest /kwest/ n busca f

question /'kwestʃən/ n pregunta f; (for discussion) cuestión f. **in ~** en cuestión. **out of the ~** imposible. **without ~** sin duda. ● vt preguntar; (police etc) interrogar; (doubt) poner en duda. ~**able** /'kwestʃənəbl/ a discutible. ~ **mark** n signo m de interrogación. ~**naire** /kwestʃə'neə(r)/ n cuestionario m

queue /kju:/ n cola f. ● vi (pres p queuing) hacer cola

quibble /'kwɪbl/ vi discutir; (split hairs) sutilizar

quick /kwɪk/ a (-er, -est) rápido. **be ~!** ¡date prisa! ● adv rápidamente. ● n. **to the ~** en lo vivo. ~**en** /'kwɪkən/ vt acelerar. ● vi acelerarse. ~**ly** adv rápidamente. ~**sand** /'kwɪksænd/ n arena f movediza. ~**tempered** a irascible

quid /kwɪd/ n invar (sl) libra f (esterlina)

quiet /'kwaɪət/ a (-er, -est) tranquilo; (silent) callado; (discreet) discreto. ● n tranquilidad f. **on the ~** a escondidas. ~**en** /'kwaɪətn/ vt calmar. ● vi calmarse. ~**ly** adv tranquilamente; (silently) silenciosamente; (discreetly) discretamente. ~**ness** n tranquilidad f

quill /kwɪl/ n pluma f

quilt /kwɪlt/ n edredón m. ● vt acolchar

quince /kwɪns/ n membrillo m

quinine /kwɪˈniːn/ n quinina f

quintessence /kwɪnˈtesns/ n quintaesencia f

quintet /kwɪnˈtet/ n quinteto m

quintuplet /ˈkwɪntjuːplət/ n quintillizo m

quip /kwɪp/ n ocurrencia f

quirk /kwɜːk/ n peculiaridad f

quit /kwɪt/ vt (pt quitted) dejar. ● vi abandonar; (leave) marcharse; (resign) dimitir. ~ doing (cease, Amer) dejar de hacer

quite /kwaɪt/ adv bastante; (completely) totalmente; (really) verdaderamente. ~ (so)! ¡claro! ~ a few bastante

quits /kwɪts/ a a la par. call it ~ darlo por terminado

quiver /ˈkwɪvə(r)/ vi temblar

quixotic /kwɪkˈsɒtɪk/ a quijotesco

quiz /kwɪz/ n (pl quizzes) serie f de preguntas; (game) concurso m. ● vt (pt quizzed) interrogar. ~zical /ˈkwɪzɪkl/ a burlón

quorum /ˈkwɔːrəm/ n quórum m

quota /ˈkwəʊtə/ n cuota f

quot|ation /kwəʊˈteɪʃn/ n cita f; (price) presupuesto m. ~ation marks npl comillas fpl. ~e /kwəʊt/ vt citar; (com) cotizar. ● n (fam) cita f; (price) presupuesto m. in ~es npl entre comillas

quotient /ˈkwəʊʃnt/ n cociente m

R

rabbi /ˈræbaɪ/ n rabino m

rabbit /ˈræbɪt/ n conejo m

rabble /ˈræbl/ n gentío m. the ~ (pej) el populacho m

rabi|d /ˈræbɪd/ a feroz; (dog) rabioso. ~es /ˈreɪbiːz/ n rabia f

race[1] /reɪs/ n carrera f. ● vt hacer correr (horse); acelerar (engine). ● vi (run) correr, ir corriendo; (rush) ir de prisa

race[2] /reɪs/ (group) raza f

race: ~course /ˈreɪskɔːs/ n hipódromo m. ~horse /ˈreɪshɔːs/ n caballo m de carreras. ~riots /ˈreɪsraɪəts/ npl disturbios mpl raciales. ~track /ˈreɪstræk/ n hipódromo m

racial /ˈreɪʃl/ a racial. ~ism /-ɪzəm/ n racismo m

racing /ˈreɪsɪŋ/ n carreras fpl. ~ car n coche m de carreras

racis|m /ˈreɪsɪzəm/ n racismo m. ~t /ˈreɪsɪst/ a & n racista (m & f)

rack[1] /ræk/ n (shelf) estante m; (for luggage) rejilla f; (for plates) escurreplatos m invar. ● vt. ~ one's brains devanarse los sesos

rack[2] /ræk/ n. go to ~ and ruin quedarse en la ruina

racket[1] /ˈrækɪt/ n (for sports) raqueta f

racket[2] /ˈrækɪt/ (din) alboroto m; (swindle) estafa f. ~eer /-əˈtɪə(r)/ n estafador m

raconteur /rækɒnˈtɜː/ n anecdotista m & f

racy /ˈreɪsɪ/ a (-ier, -iest) vivo

radar /ˈreɪdɑː(r)/ n radar m

radian|ce /ˈreɪdɪəns/ n resplandor m. ~t /ˈreɪdɪənt/ a radiante. ~tly adv con resplandor

radiat|e /ˈreɪdɪeɪt/ vt irradiar. ● vi divergir. ~ion /-ˈeɪʃn/ n radiación f. ~or /ˈreɪdɪeɪtə(r)/ n radiador m

radical /ˈrædɪkl/ a & n radical (m)

radio /ˈreɪdɪəʊ/ n (pl -os) radio f. ● vt transmitir por radio

radioactiv|e /reɪdɪəʊˈæktɪv/ a radiactivo. ~ity /-ˈtɪvətɪ/ n radiactividad f

radiograph|er /reɪdɪˈɒɡrəfə(r)/ n radiógrafo m. ~y n radiografía f

radish /ˈrædɪʃ/ n rábano m

radius /ˈreɪdɪəs/ n (pl -dii /-dɪaɪ/) radio m

raffish /ˈræfɪʃ/ a disoluto

raffle /ˈræfl/ n rifa f

raft /rɑːft/ n balsa f

rafter /ˈrɑːftə(r)/ n cabrio m

rag[1] /ræg/ n andrajo m; (for wiping) trapo m; (newspaper) periodicucho m. in ~s (person) andrajoso; (clothes) hecho jirones

rag[2] /ræg/ n (univ) festival m estudiantil; (prank, fam) broma f pesada. ● vt (pt ragged) (sl) tomar el pelo a

ragamuffin /ˈræɡəmʌfɪn/ n granuja m, golfo m

rage /reɪdʒ/ n rabia f; (fashion) moda f. ● vi estar furioso; (storm) bramar

ragged /ˈræɡɪd/ a (person) andrajoso; (clothes) hecho jirones; (edge) mellado

raid /reɪd/ n (mil) incursión f; (by police, etc) redada f; (by thieves) asalto m. ● vt (mil) atacar; (police)

hacer una redada en; ⟨thieves⟩ asaltar. **~er** n invasor m; ⟨thief⟩ ladrón
m

rail[1] /reɪl/ n barandilla f; ⟨for train⟩
riel m; ⟨rod⟩ barra f. **by ~** por
ferrocarril

rail[2] /reɪl/ vi. **~ against, ~ at**
insultar

railing /ˈreɪlɪŋ/ n barandilla f; ⟨fence⟩
verja f

rail|road /ˈreɪlrəʊd/ n (Amer),
~way /ˈreɪlweɪ/ n ferrocarril m.
~wayman n (pl **-men**) ferroviario
m. **~way station** n estación f de
ferrocarril

rain /reɪn/ n lluvia f. ● vi llover.
~bow /ˈreɪnbəʊ/ n arco m iris.
~coat /ˈreɪnkəʊt/ n impermeable m.
~fall /ˈreɪnfɔːl/ n precipitación f. **~**
water n agua f de lluvia. **~y** /ˈreɪni/
a (**-ier, -iest**) lluvioso

raise /reɪz/ vt levantar; ⟨breed⟩ criar;
obtener ⟨money etc⟩; hacer ⟨question⟩;
plantear ⟨problem⟩; subir ⟨price⟩. **~**
one's glass to brindar por. **~ one's**
hat descubrirse. ● n (Amer) aumento m

raisin /ˈreɪzn/ n (uva f) pasa f

rake[1] /reɪk/ n rastrillo m. ● vt
rastrillar; ⟨search⟩ buscar en. **~ up**
remover

rake[2] /reɪk/ n (man) calavera m

rake-off /ˈreɪkɒf/ n (fam) comisión f

rally /ˈrælɪ/ vt reunir; ⟨revive⟩ reanimar. ● vi reunirse; ⟨in sickness⟩ re-
cuperarse. ● n reunión f; ⟨recovery⟩
recuperación f; ⟨auto⟩ rallye m

ram /ræm/ n carnero m. ● vt (pt
rammed) ⟨thrust⟩ meter por la
fuerza; ⟨crash into⟩ chocar con

rambl|e /ˈræmbl/ n excursión f a pie.
● vi ir de paseo; ⟨in speech⟩ divagar.
~e on divagar. **~er** n excursionista
m & f. **~ing** a ⟨speech⟩ divagador

ramification /ræmɪfɪˈkeɪʃn/ n
ramificación f

ramp /ræmp/ n rampa f

rampage /ræmˈpeɪdʒ/ vi alborotarse. /ˈræmpeɪdʒ/ n. **go on the ~**
alborotarse

rampant /ˈræmpənt/ a. **be ~** ⟨dis-
ease etc⟩ estar extendido

rampart /ˈræmpɑːt/ n muralla f

ramshackle /ˈræmʃækl/ a desvencijado

ran /ræn/ see **run**

ranch /rɑːntʃ/ n hacienda f

rancid /ˈrænsɪd/ a rancio

rancour /ˈræŋkə(r)/ n rencor m

random /ˈrændəm/ a hecho al azar;
⟨chance⟩ fortuito. ● n. **at ~** al azar

randy /ˈrændɪ/ a (**-ier, -iest**)
lujurioso, cachondo (fam)

rang /ræŋ/ see **ring**[2]

range /reɪndʒ/ n alcance m; ⟨dis-
tance⟩ distancia f; ⟨series⟩ serie f; ⟨of
mountains⟩ cordillera f; ⟨extent⟩
extensión f; ⟨com⟩ surtido m; ⟨open
area⟩ dehesa f; ⟨stove⟩ cocina f económica. ● vi extenderse; ⟨vary⟩ variar

ranger /ˈreɪndʒə(r)/ n guardabosque
m

rank[1] /ræŋk/ n posición f, categoría
f; ⟨row⟩ fila f; ⟨for taxis⟩ parada f. **the**
~ and file la masa f. ● vt clasificar.
● vi clasificarse. **~s** npl soldados
mpl rasos

rank[2] /ræŋk/ a (**-er, -est**) exuberante;
⟨smell⟩ fétido; ⟨fig⟩ completo

rankle /ˈræŋkl/ vi ⟨fig⟩ causar rencor

ransack /ˈrænsæk/ vt registrar; ⟨pil-
lage⟩ saquear

ransom /ˈrænsəm/ n rescate m. **hold**
s.o. to ~ exigir rescate por uno; ⟨fig⟩
hacer chantaje a uno. ● vt rescatar;
⟨redeem⟩ redimir

rant /rænt/ vi vociferar

rap /ræp/ n golpe m seco. ● vt/i (pt
rapped) golpear

rapacious /rəˈpeɪʃs/ a rapaz

rape /reɪp/ vt violar. ● n violación f

rapid /ˈræpɪd/ a rápido. **~ity**
/rəˈpɪdətɪ/ n rapidez f. **~s** /ˈræpɪdz/
npl rápido m

rapist /ˈreɪpɪst/ n violador m

rapport /ræˈpɔː(r)/ n armonía f,
relación f

rapt /ræpt/ a ⟨attention⟩ profundo. **~**
in absorto en

raptur|e /ˈræptʃə(r)/ n éxtasis m.
~ous a extático

rare[1] /reə(r)/ a (**-er, -est**) raro

rare[2] /reə(r)/ a ⟨culin⟩ poco hecho

rarefied /ˈreərɪfaɪd/ a enrarecido

rarely /ˈreəlɪ/ adv raramente

rarity /ˈreərətɪ/ n rareza f

raring /ˈreərɪŋ/ a (fam). **~ to**
impaciente por

rascal /ˈrɑːskl/ n tunante m & f

rash[1] /ræʃ/ a (**-er, -est**) imprudente,
precipitado

rash[2] /ræʃ/ n erupción f

rasher /ˈræʃə(r)/ n loncha f

rash|ly /ˈræʃlɪ/ adv impruden-
temente, a la ligera. **~ness** n imprudencia f

rasp /rɑːsp/ n (file) escofina f

raspberry /'rɑːzbrɪ/ n frambuesa f

rasping /'rɑːspɪŋ/ a áspero

rat /ræt/ n rata f. ● vi (pt ratted). ~ **on** (desert) desertar; (inform on) denunciar, chivarse

rate /reɪt/ n (ratio) proporción f; (speed) velocidad f; (price) precio m; (of interest) tipo m. **at any** ~ de todas formas. **at the** ~ **of** (on the basis of) a razón de. **at this** ~ así. ● vt valorar; (consider) considerar; (deserve, Amer) merecer. ● vi ser considerado. ~**able value** n valor m imponible. ~**payer** /'reɪtpeɪə(r)/ n contribuyente m & f. ~**s** npl (taxes) impuestos mpl municipales

rather /'rɑːðə(r)/ adv mejor dicho; (fairly) bastante; (a little) un poco. ● int claro. **I would** ~ **not** prefiero no

ratif|ication /rætɪfɪ'keɪʃn/ n ratificación f. ~**y** /'rætɪfaɪ/ vt ratificar

rating /'reɪtɪŋ/ n clasificación f; (sailor) marinero m; (number, TV) índice m

ratio /'reɪʃɪəʊ/ n (pl -os) proporción f

ration /'ræʃn/ n ración f. ● vt racionar

rational /'ræʃənəl/ a racional. ~**ize** /'ræʃənəlaɪz/ vt racionalizar

rat race /'rætreɪs/ n lucha f incesante para triunfar

rattle /'rætl/ vi traquetear. ● vt (shake) agitar; (sl) desconcertar. ● n traqueteo m; (toy) sonajero m. ~ **off** (fig) decir de corrida

rattlesnake /'rætlsneɪk/ n serpiente f de cascabel

ratty /'rætɪ/ a (-ier, -iest) (sl) irritable

raucous /'rɔːkəs/ a estridente

ravage /'rævɪdʒ/ vt estragar. ~**s** /'rævɪdʒɪz/ npl estragos mpl

rave /reɪv/ vi delirar; (in anger) enfurecerse. ~ **about** entusiasmarse por

raven /'reɪvn/ n cuervo m. ● a ⟨hair⟩ negro

ravenous /'rævənəs/ a voraz; ⟨person⟩ hambriento. **be** ~ morirse de hambre

ravine /rə'viːn/ n barranco m

raving /'reɪvɪŋ/ a. ~ **mad** loco de atar. ~**s** npl divagaciones fpl

ravish /'rævɪʃ/ vt (rape) violar. ~**ing** a (enchanting) encantador

raw /rɔː/ a (-er, -est) crudo; (not processed) bruto; ⟨wound⟩ en carne viva; (inexperienced) inexperto; ⟨weather⟩ crudo. ~ **deal** n tratamiento m injusto, injusticia f. ~ **materials** npl materias fpl primas

ray /reɪ/ n rayo m

raze /reɪz/ vt arrasar

razor /'reɪzə(r)/ n navaja f de afeitar; (electric) maquinilla f de afeitar

Rd abbr (Road) C/, Calle f

re[1] /riː/ prep con referencia a. ● pref re...

re[2] /reɪ/ n (mus, second note of any musical scale) re m

reach /riːtʃ/ vt alcanzar; (extend) extender; (arrive at) llegar a; (achieve) lograr; (hand over) pasar, dar. ● vi extenderse. ● n alcance m; (of river) tramo m recto. **within** ~ **of** al alcance de; (close to) a corta distancia de

react /rɪ'ækt/ vi reaccionar. ~**ion** /rɪ'ækʃn/ n reacción f. ~**ionary** a & n reaccionario (m)

reactor /rɪ'æktə(r)/ n reactor m

read /riːd/ vt (pt read /red/) leer; (study) estudiar; (interpret) interpretar. ● vi leer; ⟨instrument⟩ indicar. ● n (fam) lectura f. ~ **out** vt leer en voz alta. ~**able** a interesante, agradable; (clear) legible. ~**er** /'riːdə(r)/ n lector m. ~**ership** n lectores m

readi|ly /'redɪlɪ/ adv (willingly) de buena gana; (easily) fácilmente. ~**ness** /'redɪnɪs/ n prontitud f. **in** ~**ness** preparado, listo

reading /'riːdɪŋ/ n lectura f

readjust /riːə'dʒʌst/ vt reajustar. ● vi readaptarse (**to** a)

ready /'redɪ/ a (-ier, -iest) listo, preparado; (quick) pronto. ~**-made** a confeccionado. ~ **money** n dinero m contante. ~ **reckoner** n baremo m. **get** ~ prepararse

real /rɪəl/ a verdadero. ● adv (Amer, fam) verdaderamente. ~ **estate** n bienes mpl raíces

realis|m /'rɪəlɪzəm/ n realismo m. ~**t** /'rɪəlɪst/ n realista m & f. ~**tic** /-'lɪstɪk/ a realista. ~**tically** /-'lɪstɪklɪ/ adv de manera realista

reality /rɪ'ælətɪ/ n realidad f

realiz|ation /rɪəlaɪ'zeɪʃn/ n comprensión f; (com) realización f. ~**e** /'rɪəlaɪz/ vt darse cuenta de; (fulfil, com) realizar

really /'rɪəlɪ/ *adv* verdaderamente
realm /relm/ *n* reino *m*
ream /ri:m/ *n* resma *f*
reap /ri:p/ *vt* segar; *(fig)* cosechar
re: **~appear** /ri:ə'pɪə(r)/ *vi* reaparecer. **~appraisal** /ri:ə'preɪzl/ *n* revaluación *f*
rear[1] /rɪə(r)/ *n* parte *f* de atrás. ● *a* posterior, trasero
rear[2] /rɪə(r)/ *vt* *(bring up, breed)* criar. **~ one's head** levantar la cabeza. ● *vi* ⟨horse⟩ encabritarse. **~ up** ⟨horse⟩ encabritarse
rear: **~admiral** *n* contraalmirante *m*. **~guard** /'rɪəɡɑ:d/ *n* retaguardia *f*
re: **~arm** /ri:'ɑ:m/ *vt* rearmar. ● *vi* rearmarse. **~arrange** /ri:ə'reɪndʒ/ *vt* arreglar de otra manera
reason /'ri:zn/ *n* razón *f*, motivo *m*. **within ~** dentro de lo razonable. ● *vi* razonar
reasonable /'ri:zənəbl/ *a* razonable
reasoning /'ri:znɪŋ/ *n* razonamiento *m*
reassur|ance /ri:ə'ʃuərəns/ *n* promesa *f* tranquilizadora; *(guarantee)* garantía *f*. **~e** /ri:ə'ʃʊə(r)/ *vt* tranquilizar
rebate /'ri:beɪt/ *n* reembolso *m*; *(discount)* rebaja *f*
rebel /'rebl/ *n* rebelde *m & f*. /rɪ'bel/ *vi* *(pt* **rebelled**) rebelarse. **~lion** *n* rebelión *f*. **~lious** *a* rebelde
rebound /rɪ'baʊnd/ *vi* rebotar; *(fig)* recaer. /'ri:baʊnd/ *n* rebote *m*. **on the ~** *(fig)* por reacción
rebuff /rɪ'bʌf/ *vt* rechazar. ● *n* desaire *m*
rebuild /ri:'bɪld/ *vt* *(pt* **rebuilt**) reconstruir
rebuke /rɪ'bju:k/ *vt* reprender. ● *n* reprensión *f*
rebuttal /rɪ'bʌtl/ *n* refutación *f*
recall /rɪ'kɔ:l/ *vt* *(call s.o. back)* llamar; *(remember)* recordar. ● *n* llamada *f*
recant /rɪ'kænt/ *vi* retractarse
recap /'ri:kæp/ *vt/i* *(pt* **recapped**) *(fam)* resumir. ● *n* *(fam)* resumen *m*
recapitulat|e /ri:kə'pɪtʃʊleɪt/ *vt/i* resumir. **~ion** /-'leɪʃn/ *n* resumen *m*
recapture /ri:'kæptʃə(r)/ *vt* recobrar; *(recall)* hacer revivir
reced|e /rɪ'si:d/ *vi* retroceder. **~ing** *a* ⟨forehead⟩ huidizo
receipt /rɪ'si:t/ *n* recibo *m*. **~s** *npl* *(com)* ingresos *mpl*

receive /rɪ'si:v/ *vt* recibir. **~r** /-ə(r)/ *n* *(of stolen goods)* perista *m & f*; *(of phone)* auricular *m*
recent /'ri:snt/ *a* reciente. **~ly** *adv* recientemente
receptacle /rɪ'septəkl/ *n* recipiente *m*
reception /rɪ'sepʃn/ *n* recepción *f*; *(welcome)* acogida *f*. **~ist** *n* recepcionista *m & f*
receptive /rɪ'septɪv/ *a* receptivo
recess /rɪ'ses/ *n* hueco *m*; *(holiday)* vacaciones *fpl*; *(fig)* parte *f* recóndita
recession /rɪ'seʃn/ *n* recesión *f*
recharge /ri:'tʃɑ:dʒ/ *vt* cargar de nuevo, recargar
recipe /'resəpɪ/ *n* receta *f*
recipient /rɪ'sɪpɪənt/ *n* recipiente *m & f*; *(of letter)* destinatario *m*
reciprocal /rɪ'sɪprəkl/ *a* recíproco
reciprocate /rɪ'sɪprəkeɪt/ *vt* corresponder a
recital /rɪ'saɪtl/ *n* *(mus)* recital *m*
recite /rɪ'saɪt/ *vt* recitar; *(list)* enumerar
reckless /'reklɪs/ *a* imprudente. **~ly** *adv* imprudentemente. **~ness** *n* imprudencia *f*
reckon /'rekən/ *vt/i* calcular; *(consider)* considerar; *(think)* pensar. **~ on** *(rely)* contar con. **~ing** *n* cálculo *m*
reclaim /rɪ'kleɪm/ *vt* reclamar; recuperar ⟨land⟩
reclin|e /rɪ'klaɪm/ *vi* recostarse. **~ing** *a* acostado; ⟨seat⟩ reclinable
recluse /rɪ'klu:s/ *n* solitario *m*
recogni|tion /rekəg'nɪʃn/ *n* reconocimiento *m*. **beyond ~tion** irreconocible. **~ze** /'rekəgnaɪz/ *vt* reconocer
recoil /rɪ'kɔɪl/ *vi* retroceder. ● *n* *(of gun)* culatazo *m*
recollect /rekə'lekt/ *vt* recordar. **~ion** /-ʃn/ *n* recuerdo *m*
recommend /rekə'mend/ *vt* recomendar. **~ation** /-'deɪʃn/ *n* recomendación *f*
recompense /'rekəmpens/ *vt* recompensar. ● *n* recompensa *f*
reconcil|e /'rekənsaɪl/ *vt* reconciliar ⟨people⟩; conciliar ⟨facts⟩. **~e o.s.** resignarse **(to** a). **~iation** /-sɪlɪ'eɪʃn/ *n* reconciliación *f*
recondition /ri:kən'dɪʃn/ *vt* reacondicionar, arreglar
reconnaissance /rɪ'kɒnɪsns/ *n* reconocimiento *m*

reconnoitre /rekəˈnɔɪtə(r)/ vt (pres p **-tring**) (mil) reconocer. ● vi hacer un reconocimiento

re: ~**consider** /riːkənˈsɪdə(r)/ vt volver a considerar. ~**construct** /riːkənˈstrʌkt/ vt reconstruir. ~**construction** /-ʃn/ n reconstrucción f

record /rɪˈkɔːd/ vt (in register) registrar; (in diary) apuntar; (mus) grabar. /ˈrekɔːd/ n (file) documentación f, expediente m; (mus) disco m; (sport) récord m. **off the** ~ en confianza. ~**er** /rɪˈkɔːdə(r)/ n registrador m; (mus) flauta f dulce. ~**ing** n grabación f. ~**player** n tocadiscos m invar

recount /rɪˈkaʊnt/ vt contar, relatar, referir

re-count /riːˈkaʊnt/ vt recontar. /ˈriːkaʊnt/ n (pol) recuento m

recoup /rɪˈkuːp/ vt recuperar

recourse /rɪˈkɔːs/ n recurso m. **have** ~ **to** recurrir a

recover /rɪˈkʌvə(r)/ vt recuperar. ● vi reponerse. ~**y** n recuperación f

recreation /rekrɪˈeɪʃn/ n recreo m. ~**al** a de recreo

recrimination /rɪkrɪmɪˈneɪʃn/ n recriminación f

recruit /rɪˈkruːt/ n recluta m. ● vt reclutar. ~**ment** n reclutamiento m

rectangle /ˈrektæŋgl/ n rectángulo m. ~**ular** /-ˈtæŋgjʊlə(r)/ a rectangular

rectification /rektɪfɪˈkeɪʃn/ n rectificación f. ~**y** /ˈrektɪfaɪ/ vt rectificar

rector /ˈrektə(r)/ n párroco m; (of college) rector m. ~**y** n rectoría f

recumbent /rɪˈkʌmbənt/ a recostado

recuperate /rɪˈkuːpəreɪt/ vt recuperar. ● vi reponerse. ~**ion** /-ˈreɪʃn/ n recuperación f

recur /rɪˈkɜː(r)/ vi (pt **recurred**) repetirse. ~**rence** /rɪˈkʌrns/ n repetición f. ~**rent** /rɪˈkʌrənt/ a repetido

recycle /riːˈsaɪkl/ vt reciclar

red /red/ a (**redder, reddest**) rojo. ● n rojo. **in the** ~ ⟨account⟩ en descubierto. ~**breast** /ˈredbrest/ n petirrojo m. ~**brick** /ˈredbrɪk/ a ⟨univ⟩ de reciente fundación. ~**den** /ˈredn/ vt enrojecer. ● vi enrojecerse. ~**dish** a rojizo

redecorate /riːˈdekəreɪt/ vt pintar de nuevo

redeem /rɪˈdiːm/ vt redimir. ~**eming quality** n cualidad f compensadora. ~**mption** /-ˈdempʃn/ n redención f

redeploy /riːdɪˈplɔɪ/ vt disponer de otra manera; (mil) cambiar de frente

red: ~**handed** a en flagrante. ~**herring** n (fig) pista f falsa. ~**hot** a al rojo; ⟨news⟩ de última hora

Red Indian /red ˈɪndjən/ n piel m & f roja

redirect /riːdaɪˈrekt/ vt reexpedir

red: ~**letter day** n día m señalado, día m memorable. ~ **light** n luz f roja. ~**ness** n rojez f

redo /riːˈduː/ vt (pt **redid**, pp **redone**) rehacer

redouble /rɪˈdʌbl/ vt redoblar

redress /rɪˈdres/ vt reparar. ● n reparación f

red tape /red ˈteɪp/ n (fig) papeleo m

reduce /rɪˈdjuːs/ vt reducir. ● vi reducirse; (slim) adelgazar. ~**tion** /-ˈdʌkʃn/ n reducción f

redundancy /rɪˈdʌndənsɪ/ n superfluidad f; (unemployment) desempleo m. ~**t** /rɪˈdʌndənt/ superfluo. **be made** ~**t** perder su empleo

reed /riːd/ n caña f; (mus) lengüeta f

reef /riːf/ n arrecife m

reek /riːk/ n mal olor m. ● vi. ~ **(of)** apestar a

reel /riːl/ n carrete m. ● vi dar vueltas; (stagger) tambalearse. ● vt. ~ **off** (fig) enumerar

refectory /rɪˈfektərɪ/ n refectorio m

refer /rɪˈfɜː(r)/ vt (pt **referred**) remitir. ● vi referirse. ~ **to** referirse a; (consult) consultar

referee /refəˈriː/ n árbitro m; (for job) referencia f. ● vi (pt **refereed**) arbitrar

reference /ˈrefrəns/ n referencia f. ~ **book** n libro m de consulta. **in** ~ **to, with** ~ **to** en cuanto a; (com) respecto a

referendum /refəˈrendəm/ n (pl **-ums**) referéndum m

refill /riːˈfɪl/ vt rellenar. /ˈriːfɪl/ n recambio m

refine /rɪˈfaɪn/ vt refinar. ~**d** a refinado. ~**ment** n refinamiento m; (tec) refinación f. ~**ry** /-ərɪ/ n refinería f

reflect /rɪˈflekt/ vt reflejar. ● vi reflejar; (think) reflexionar. ~ **upon** perjudicar. ~**ion** /-ʃn/ n reflexión f;

(*image*) reflejo *m*. **~ive** /rɪ'flektɪv/ *a* reflector; (*thoughtful*) pensativo. **~or** *n* reflector *m*

reflex /'riːfleks/ *a & n* reflejo (*m*)

reflexive /rɪ'fleksɪv/ *a* (*gram*) reflexivo

reform /rɪ'fɔːm/ *vt* reformar. ● *vi* reformarse. ● *n* reforma *f*. **~er** *n* reformador *m*

refract /rɪ'frækt/ *vt* refractar

refrain[1] /rɪ'freɪn/ *n* estribillo *m*

refrain[2] /rɪ'freɪn/ *vi* abstenerse (**from** de)

refresh /rɪ'freʃ/ *vt* refrescar. **~er** /rɪ'freʃə(r)/ *a* ⟨*course*⟩ de repaso. **~ing** *a* refrescante. **~ments** *npl* (*food and drink*) refrigerio *m*

refrigerat|e /rɪ'frɪdʒəreɪt/ *vt* refrigerar. **~or** *n* nevera *f*, refrigeradora *f* (*LAm*)

refuel /riː'fjuːəl/ *vt/i* (*pt* **refuelled**) repostar

refuge /'refjuːdʒ/ *n* refugio *m*. **take ~** refugiarse. **~e** /refjʊ'dʒiː/ *n* refugiado *m*

refund /rɪ'fʌnd/ *vt* reembolsar. /'riː fʌnd/ *n* reembolso *m*

refurbish /riː'fɜːbɪʃ/ *vt* renovar

refusal /rɪ'fjuːzl/ *n* negativa *f*

refuse[1] /rɪ'fjuːz/ *vt* rehusar. ● *vi* negarse

refuse[2] /'refjuːs/ *n* basura *f*

refute /rɪ'fjuːt/ *vt* refutar

regain /rɪ'geɪn/ *vt* recobrar

regal /'riːgl/ *a* real

regale /rɪ'geɪl/ *vt* festejar

regalia /rɪ'geɪlɪə/ *npl* insignias *fpl*

regard /rɪ'gɑːd/ *vt* mirar; (*consider*) considerar. **as ~s** en cuanto a. ● *n* mirada *f*; (*care*) atención *f*; (*esteem*) respeto *m*. **~ing** *prep* en cuanto a. **~less** /rɪ'gɑːdlɪs/ *adv* a pesar de todo. **~less of** sin tener en cuenta. **~s** *npl* saludos *mpl*. **kind ~s** *npl* recuerdos *mpl*

regatta /rɪ'gætə/ *n* regata *f*

regency /'riːdʒənsɪ/ *n* regencia *f*

regenerate /rɪ'dʒenəreɪt/ *vt* regenerar

regent /'riːdʒənt/ *n* regente *m & f*

regime /reɪ'ʒiːm/ *n* régimen *m*

regiment /'redʒɪmənt/ *n* regimiento *m*. **~al** /-'mentl/ *a* del regimiento. **~ation** /-en'teɪʃn/ *n* reglamentación rígida

region /'riːdʒən/ *n* región *f*. **in the ~ of** alrededor de. **~al** *a* regional

register /'redʒɪstə(r)/ *n* registro *m*. ● *vt* registrar; matricular ⟨*vehicle*⟩; declarar ⟨*birth*⟩; certificar ⟨*letter*⟩; facturar ⟨*luggage*⟩; (*indicate*) indicar; (*express*) expresar. ● *vi* (*enrol*) inscribirse; (*fig*) producir impresión. **~ office** *n* registro *m* civil

registrar /redʒɪ'strɑː(r)/ *n* secretario *m* del registro civil; (*univ*) secretario *m* general

registration /redʒɪ'streɪʃn/ *n* registración *f*; (*in register*) inscripción *f*; (*of vehicle*) matricula *f*

registry /'redʒɪstrɪ/ *n*. **~ office** *n* registro *m* civil

regression /rɪ'greʃn/ *n* regresión *f*

regret /rɪ'gret/ *n* pesar *m*. ● *vt* (*pt* **regretted**) lamentar. **I ~ that** siento (que). **~fully** *adv* con pesar. **~table** *a* lamentable. **~tably** *adv* lamentablemente

regular /'regjʊlə(r)/ *a* regular; (*usual*) habitual. ● *n* (*fam*) cliente *m* habitual. **~ity** /-'lærətɪ/ *n* regularidad *f*. **~ly** *adv* regularmente

regulat|e /'regjʊleɪt/ *vt* regular. **~ion** /-'leɪʃn/ *n* arreglo *m*; (*rule*) regla *f*

rehabilitat|e /riːhə'bɪlɪteɪt/ *vt* rehabilitar. **~ion** /-'teɪʃn/ *n* rehabilitación *f*

rehash /riː'hæʃ/ *vt* volver a presentar. /'riːhæʃ/ *n* refrito *m*

rehears|al /rɪ'hɜːsl/ *n* ensayo *m*. **~e** /rɪ'hɜːs/ *vt* ensayar

reign /reɪn/ *n* reinado *m*. ● *vi* reinar

reimburse /riːɪm'bɜːs/ *vt* reembolsar

reins /reɪnz/ *npl* riendas *fpl*

reindeer /'reɪndɪə(r)/ *n invar* reno *m*

reinforce /riːɪn'fɔːs/ *vt* reforzar. **~ment** *n* refuerzo *m*

reinstate /riːɪn'steɪt/ *vt* reintegrar

reiterate /riː'ɪtəreɪt/ *vt* reiterar

reject /rɪ'dʒekt/ *vt* rechazar. /'riː dʒekt/ *n* producto *m* defectuoso. **~ion** /'dʒekʃn/ *n* rechazamiento *m*, rechazo *m*

rejoic|e /rɪ'dʒɔɪs/ *vi* regocijarse. **~ing** *n* regocijo *m*

rejoin /rɪ'dʒɔɪn/ *vt* reunirse con; (*answer*) replicar. **~der** /rɪ'dʒɔɪndə(r)/ *n* réplica *f*

rejuvenate /rɪ'dʒuːvəneɪt/ *vt* rejuvenecer

rekindle /riː'kɪndl/ *vt* reavivar

relapse /rɪˈlæps/ n recaída f. ● vi recaer; (into crime) reincidir

relate /rɪˈleɪt/ vt contar; (connect) relacionar. ● vi relacionarse (to con). ~d a emparentado; ⟨ideas etc⟩ relacionado

relation /rɪˈleɪʃn/ n relación f; (person) pariente m & f. ~ship n relación f; (blood tie) parentesco m; (affair) relaciones fpl

relative /ˈrelətɪv/ n pariente m & f. ● a relativo. ~ly adv relativamente

relax /rɪˈlæks/ vt relajar. ● vi relajarse. ~ation /riːlækˈseɪʃn/ n relajación f; (rest) descanso m; (recreation) recreo m. ~ing a relajante

relay /ˈriːleɪ/ n relevo m. ~ (race) n carrera f de relevos. /rɪˈleɪ/ vt retransmitir

release /rɪˈliːs/ vt soltar; poner en libertad ⟨prisoner⟩; estrenar ⟨film⟩; (mec) desenganchar; publicar ⟨news⟩; emitir ⟨smoke⟩. ● n liberación f; (of film) estreno m; (record) disco m nuevo

relegate /ˈrelɪɡeɪt/ vt relegar

relent /rɪˈlent/ vi ceder. ~less a implacable; (continuous) incesante

relevan|ce /ˈreləvəns/ n pertinencia f. ~t /ˈreləvənt/ a pertinente

reliab|ility /rɪlaɪəˈbɪlətɪ/ n fiabilidad f. ~le /rɪˈlaɪəbl/ a seguro; ⟨person⟩ de fiar; (com) serio

relian|ce /rɪˈlaɪəns/ n dependencia f; (trust) confianza f. ~t a confiado

relic /ˈrelɪk/ n reliquia f. ~s npl restos mpl

relie|f /rɪˈliːf/ n alivio m; (assistance) socorro m; (outline) relieve m. ~ve /rɪˈliːv/ vt aliviar; (take over from) relevar

religio|n /rɪˈlɪdʒən/ n religión f. ~us /rɪˈlɪdʒəs/ a religioso

relinquish /rɪˈlɪŋkwɪʃ/ vt abandonar, renunciar

relish /ˈrelɪʃ/ n gusto m; (culin) salsa f. ● vt saborear. **I don't ~ the idea** no me gusta la idea

relocate /riːləʊˈkeɪt/ vt colocar de nuevo

reluctan|ce /rɪˈlʌktəns/ n desgana f. ~t /rɪˈlʌktənt/ a mal dispuesto. **be ~t to** no tener ganas de. ~tly adv de mala gana

rely /rɪˈlaɪ/ vi. ~ **on** contar con; (trust) fiarse de; (depend) depender

remain /rɪˈmeɪn/ vi quedar. ~der /rɪˈmeɪndə(r)/ n resto m. ~s npl restos mpl; (left-overs) sobras fpl

remand /rɪˈmɑːnd/ vt. ~ **in custody** mantener bajo custodia. ● n. **on ~** bajo custodia

remark /rɪˈmɑːk/ n observación f. ● vt observar. ~able a notable

remarry /riːˈmærɪ/ vi volver a casarse

remedial /rɪˈmiːdɪəl/ a remediador

remedy /ˈremədɪ/ n remedio m. ● vt remediar

rememb|er /rɪˈmembə(r)/ vt acordarse de. ● vi acordarse. ~rance n recuerdo m

remind /rɪˈmaɪnd/ vt recordar. ~er n recordatorio m; (letter) notificación f

reminisce /remɪˈnɪs/ vi recordar el pasado. ~nces npl recuerdos mpl. ~nt /remɪˈnɪsnt/ a. **be ~nt of** recordar

remiss /rɪˈmɪs/ a negligente

remission /rɪˈmɪʃn/ n remisión f; (of sentence) reducción f de condena

remit /rɪˈmɪt/ vt (pt **remitted**) perdonar; enviar ⟨money⟩. ● vi moderarse. ~tance n remesa f

remnant /ˈremnənt/ n resto m; (of cloth) retazo m; (trace) vestigio m

remonstrate /ˈremənstreɪt/ vi protestar

remorse /rɪˈmɔːs/ n remordimiento m. ~ful a lleno de remordimiento. ~less a implacable

remote /rɪˈməʊt/ a remoto; (slight) leve; ⟨person⟩ distante. ~ **control** n mando m a distancia. ~ly adv remotamente. ~ness n lejanía f; (isolation) aislamiento m, alejamiento m; (fig) improbabilidad f

remov|able /rɪˈmuːvəbl/ a movible; (detachable) de quita y pon, separable. ~al n eliminación f; (from house) mudanza f. ~e /rɪˈmuːv/ vt quitar; (dismiss) despedir; (get rid of) eliminar; (do away with) suprimir

remunerat|e /rɪˈmjuːnəreɪt/ vt remunerar. ~ion /-ˈreɪʃn/ n remuneración f. ~ive a remunerador

Renaissance /rəˈneɪsəns/ n Renacimiento m

rend /rend/ vt (pt **rent**) rasgar

render /ˈrendə(r)/ vt rendir; (com) presentar; (mus) interpretar; prestar ⟨help etc⟩. ~ing n (mus) interpretación f

rendezvous /ˈrɒndɪvuː/ n (pl **-vous** /-vuːz/) cita f

renegade /'renɪgeɪd/ n renegado
renew /rɪ'nju:/ vt renovar; (resume) reanudar. ∼**able** a renovable. ∼**al** n renovación f
renounce /rɪ'naʊns/ vt renunciar a; (disown) repudiar
renovat|e /'renəveɪt/ vt renovar. ∼**ion** /-'veɪʃn/ n renovación f
renown /rɪ'naʊn/ n fama f. ∼**ed** a célebre
rent[1] /rent/ n alquiler m. ● vt alquilar
rent[2] /rent/ see **rend**
rental /rentl/ n alquiler m
renunciation /rɪnʌnsɪ'eɪʃn/ n renuncia f
reopen /ri:'əʊpən/ vt reabrir. ● vi reabrirse. ∼**ing** n reapertura f
reorganize /ri:'ɔ:gənaɪz/ vt reorganizar
rep[1] /rep/ n (com, fam) representante m & f
rep[2] /rep/ (theatre, fam) teatro m de repertorio
repair /rɪ'peə(r)/ vt reparar; remendar ⟨clothes, shoes⟩. ● n reparación f; (patch) remiendo m. **in good** ∼ en buen estado
repartee /repɑː'tiː/ n ocurrencias fpl
repatriat|e /ri:'pætrɪeɪt/ vt repatriar. ∼**ion** /-'eɪʃn/ n repatriación f
repay /ri:'peɪ/ vt (pt **repaid**) reembolsar; pagar ⟨debt⟩; (reward) recompensar. ∼**ment** n reembolso m, pago m
repeal /rɪ'piːl/ vt abrogar. ● n abrogación f
repeat /rɪ'piːt/ vt repetir. ● vi repetir(se). ● n repetición f. ∼**edly** /rɪ'piːtɪdlɪ/ adv repetidas veces
repel /rɪ'pel/ vt (pt **repelled**) repeler. ∼**lent** a repelente
repent /rɪ'pent/ vi arrepentirse. ∼**ance** n arrepentimiento m. ∼**ant** a arrepentido
repercussion /ri:pə'kʌʃn/ n repercusión f
reperto|ire /'repətwɑː(r)/ n repertorio m. ∼**ry** /'repətrɪ/ n repertorio m. ∼**ry (theatre)** n teatro m de repertorio
repetit|ion /repɪ'tɪʃn/ n repetición f. ∼**ious** /-'tɪʃəs/ a, ∼**ive** /rɪ'petətɪv/ a que se repite; (dull) monótono
replace /rɪ'pleɪs/ vt reponer; (take the place of) sustituir. ∼**ment** n

sustitución f; (person) sustituto m. ∼**ment part** n recambio m
replay /'riːpleɪ/ n (sport) repetición f del partido; (recording) repetición f inmediata
replenish /rɪ'plenɪʃ/ vt reponer; (refill) rellenar
replete /rɪ'pliːt/ a repleto
replica /'replɪkə/ n copia f
reply /rɪ'plaɪ/ vt/i contestar. ● n respuesta f
report /rɪ'pɔːt/ vt anunciar; (denounce) denunciar. ● vi presentar un informe; (present o.s.) presentarse. ● n informe m; (schol) boletín m; (rumour) rumor m; (newspaper) reportaje m; (sound) estallido m. ∼**age** /repɔː'tɑːʒ/ n reportaje m. ∼**edly** adv según se dice. ∼**er** /rɪ'pɔːtə(r)/ n reportero m, informador m
repose /rɪ'pəʊz/ n reposo m
repository /rɪ'pɒzɪtrɪ/ n depósito m
repossess /ri:pə'zes/ vt recuperar
reprehen|d /reprɪ'hend/ vt reprender. ∼**sible** /-səbl/ a reprensible
represent /reprɪ'zent/ vt representar. ∼**ation** /-'teɪʃn/ n representación f. ∼**ative** /reprɪ'zentətɪv/ a representativo. ● n representante m & f
repress /rɪ'pres/ vt reprimir. ∼**ion** /-ʃn/ n represión f. ∼**ive** a represivo
reprieve /rɪ'priːv/ n indulto m; (fig) respiro m. ● vt indultar; (fig) aliviar
reprimand /'reprɪmɑːnd/ vt reprender. ● n reprensión f
reprint /'riːprɪnt/ n reimpresión f; (offprint) tirada f aparte. /riː'prɪnt/ vt reimprimir
reprisal /rɪ'praɪzl/ n represalia f
reproach /rɪ'prəʊtʃ/ vt reprochar. ● n reproche m. ∼**ful** a de reproche, reprobador. ∼**fully** adv con reproche
reprobate /'reprəbeɪt/ n malvado m; (relig) réprobo m
reproduc|e /ri:prə'djuːs/ vt reproducir. ● vi reproducirse. ∼**tion** /-'dʌkʃn/ n reproducción f. ∼**tive** /-'dʌktɪv/ a reproductor
reprove /rɪ'pruːv/ vt reprender
reptile /'reptaɪl/ n reptil m
republic /rɪ'pʌblɪk/ n república f. ∼**an** a & n republicano (m)
repudiate /rɪ'pjuːdɪeɪt/ vt repudiar; (refuse to recognize) negarse a reconocer

repugnan|ce /rɪ'pʌgnəns/ *n* repugnancia *f*. ~**t** /rɪ'pʌgnənt/ *a* repugnante

repuls|e /rɪ'pʌls/ *vt* rechazar, repulsar. ~**ion** /-ʃn/ *n* repulsión *f*. ~**ive** *a* repulsivo

reputable /'repjʊtəbl/ *a* acreditado, de confianza, honroso

reputation /repjʊ'teɪʃn/ *n* reputación *f*

repute /rɪ'pju:t/ *n* reputación *f*. ~**d** /-ɪd/ *a* supuesto. ~**dly** *adv* según se dice

request /rɪ'kwest/ *n* petición *f*. ● *vt* pedir. ~ **stop** *n* parada *f* discrecional

require /rɪ'kwaɪə(r)/ *vt* requerir; (*need*) necesitar; (*demand*) exigir. ~**d** *a* necesario. ~**ment** *n* requisito *m*

requisite /'rekwɪzɪt/ *a* necesario. ● *n* requisito *m*

requisition /rekwɪ'zɪʃn/ *n* requisición *f*. ● *vt* requisar

resale /'ri:seɪl/ *n* reventa *f*

rescind /rɪ'sɪnd/ *vt* rescindir

rescue /'reskju:/ *vt* salvar. ● *n* salvamento *m*. ~**r** /-ə(r)/ *n* salvador *m*

research /rɪ'sɜ:tʃ/ *n* investigación *f*. ● *vt* investigar. ~**er** *n* investigador *m*

resembl|ance /rɪ'zembləns/ *n* parecido *m*. ~**e** /rɪ'zembl/ *vt* parecerse a

resent /rɪ'zent/ *vt* resentirse por. ~**ful** *a* resentido. ~**ment** *n* resentimiento *m*

reservation /rezə'veɪʃn/ *n* reserva *f*; (*booking*) reservación *f*

reserve /rɪ'zɜ:v/ *vt* reservar. ● *n* reserva *f*; (*in sports*) suplente *m* & *f*. ~**d** *a* reservado

reservist /rɪ'zɜ:vɪst/ *n* reservista *m* & *f*

reservoir /'rezəvwɑ:(r)/ *n* embalse *m*; (*tank*) depósito *m*

reshape /ri:'ʃeɪp/ *vt* formar de nuevo, reorganizar

reshuffle /ri:'ʃʌfl/ *vt* (*pol*) reorganizar. ● *n* (*pol*) reorganización *f*

reside /rɪ'zaɪd/ *vi* residir

residen|ce /'rezɪdəns/ *n* residencia *f*. ~**ce permit** *n* permiso *m* de residencia. **be in** ~**ce** ‹*doctor etc*› interno. ~**t** /'rezɪdənt/ *a* & *n* residente (*m* & *f*). ~**tial** /rezɪ'denʃl/ *a* residencial

residue /'rezɪdju:/ *n* residuo *m*

resign /rɪ'zaɪn/ *vt/i* dimitir. ~ **o.s. to** resignarse a. ~**ation** /rezɪg'neɪʃn/ *n* resignación *f*; (*from job*) dimisión *f*. ~**ed** *a* resignado

resilien|ce /rɪ'zɪlɪəns/ *n* elasticidad *f*; (*of person*) resistencia *f*. ~**t** /rɪ'zɪlɪənt/ *a* elástico; ‹*person*› resistente

resin /'rezɪn/ *n* resina *f*

resist /rɪ'zɪst/ *vt* resistir. ● *vi* resistirse. ~**ance** *n* resistencia *f*. ~**ant** *a* resistente

resolut|e /'rezəlu:t/ *a* resuelto. ~**ion** /-'lu:ʃn/ *n* resolución *f*

resolve /rɪ'zɒlv/ *vt* resolver. ~ **to do** resolverse a hacer. ● *n* resolución *f*. ~**d** *a* resuelto

resonan|ce /'rezənəns/ *n* resonancia *f*. ~**t** /'rezənənt/ *a* resonante

resort /rɪ'zɔ:t/ *vi*. ~ **to** recurrir a. ● *n* recurso *m*; (*place*) lugar *m* turístico. **in the last** ~ como último recurso

resound /rɪ'zaʊnd/ *vi* resonar. ~**ing** *a* resonante

resource /rɪ'sɔ:s/ *n* recurso *m*. ~**ful** *a* ingenioso. ~**fulness** *n* ingeniosidad *f*

respect /rɪ'spekt/ *n* (*esteem*) respeto *m*; (*aspect*) respecto *m*. **with** ~ **to** con respecto a. ● *vt* respetar

respectab|ility /rɪspektə'bɪlətɪ/ *n* respetabilidad *f*. ~**le** /rɪ'spektəbl/ *a* respetable. ~**ly** *adv* respetablemente

respectful /rɪ'spektfl/ *a* respetuoso

respective /rɪ'spektɪv/ *a* respectivo. ~**ly** *adv* respectivamente

respiration /respə'reɪʃn/ *n* respiración *f*

respite /'respaɪt/ *n* respiro *m*, tregua *f*

resplendent /rɪ'splendənt/ *a* resplandeciente

respon|d /rɪ'spɒnd/ *vi* responder. ~**se** /rɪ'spɒns/ *n* respuesta *f*; (*reaction*) reacción *f*

responsib|ility /rɪspɒnsə'bɪlətɪ/ *n* responsabilidad *f*. ~**le** /rɪ'spɒnsəbl/ *a* responsable; ‹*job*› de responsabilidad. ~**ly** *adv* con formalidad

responsive /rɪ'spɒnsɪv/ *a* que reacciona bien. ~ **to** sensible a

rest[1] /rest/ *vt* descansar; (*lean*) apoyar; (*place*) poner, colocar. ● *vi* descansar; (*lean*) apoyarse. ● *n* descanso *m*; (*mus*) pausa *f*

rest[2] /rest/ *n* (*remainder*) resto *m*, lo demás; (*people*) los demás, los otros *mpl*. ● *vi* (*remain*) quedar

restaurant /'restərɒnt/ *n* restaurante *m*

restful /'restfl/ *a* sosegado

restitution /restɪ'tjuːʃn/ *n* restitución *f*

restive /'restɪv/ *a* inquieto

restless /'restlɪs/ *a* inquieto. **~ly** *adv* inquietamente. **~ness** *n* inquietud *f*

restor|ation /restə'reɪʃn/ *n* restauración *f*. **~e** /rɪ'stɔː(r)/ *vt* restablecer; restaurar ⟨building⟩; (put back in position) reponer; (return) devolver

restrain /rɪ'streɪn/ *vt* contener. **~ o.s.** contenerse. **~ed** *a* (moderate) moderado; (in control of self) comedido. **~t** *n* restricción *f*; (moderation) moderación *f*

restrict /rɪ'strɪkt/ *vt* restringir. **~ion** /-ʃn/ *n* restricción *f*. **~ive** /rɪ'strɪktɪv/ *a* restrictivo

result /rɪ'zʌlt/ *n* resultado *m*. ● *vi*. **~ from** resultar de. **~ in** dar como resultado

resume /rɪ'zjuːm/ *vt* reanudar. ● *vi* continuar

résumé /'rezjʊmeɪ/ *n* resumen *m*

resumption /rɪ'zʌmpʃn/ *n* continuación *f*

resurgence /rɪ'sɜːdʒəns/ *n* resurgimiento *m*

resurrect /rezə'rekt/ *vt* resucitar. **~ion** /-ʃn/ *n* resurrección *f*

resuscitat|e /rɪ'sʌsɪteɪt/ *vt* resucitar. **~ion** /-'teɪʃn/ *n* resucitación *f*

retail /'riːteɪl/ *n* venta *f* al por menor. ● *a & adv* al por menor. ● *vt* vender al por menor. ● *vi* venderse al por menor. **~er** *n* minorista *m & f*

retain /rɪ'teɪn/ *vt* retener; (keep) conservar

retainer /rɪ'teɪnə(r)/ *n* (fee) anticipo *m*

retaliat|e /rɪ'tælɪeɪt/ *vi* desquitarse. **~ion** /-'eɪʃn/ *n* represalias *fpl*

retarded /rɪ'tɑːdɪd/ *a* retrasado

retentive /rɪ'tentɪv/ *a* ⟨memory⟩ bueno

rethink /riː'θɪŋk/ *vt* (pt rethought) considerar de nuevo

reticen|ce /'retɪsns/ *n* reserva *f*. **~t** /'retɪsnt/ *a* reservado, callado

retina /'retɪnə/ *n* retina *f*

retinue /'retɪnjuː/ *n* séquito *m*

retir|e /rɪ'taɪə(r)/ *vi* (from work) jubilarse; (withdraw) retirarse; (go to bed) acostarse. ● *vt* jubilar. **~ed** *a* jubilado. **~ement** *n* jubilación *f*. **~ing** /rɪ'taɪərɪŋ/ *a* reservado

retort /rɪ'tɔːt/ *vt/i* replicar. ● *n* réplica *f*

retrace /riː'treɪs/ *vt* repasar. **~ one's steps** volver sobre sus pasos

retract /rɪ'trækt/ *vt* retirar. ● *vi* retractarse

retrain /riː'treɪn/ *vt* reciclar, reeducar

retreat /rɪ'triːt/ *vi* retirarse. ● *n* retirada *f*; (place) refugio *m*

retrial /riː'traɪəl/ *n* nuevo proceso *m*

retribution /retrɪ'bjuːʃn/ *n* justo *m* castigo

retriev|al /rɪ'triːvl/ *n* recuperación *f*. **~e** /rɪ'triːv/ *vt* (recover) recuperar; (save) salvar; (put right) reparar. **~er** *n* (dog) perro *m* cobrador

retrograde /'retrəgreɪd/ *a* retrógrado

retrospect /'retrəspekt/ *n* retrospección *f*. **in ~** retrospectivamente. **~ive** /-'spektɪv/ *a* retrospectivo

return /rɪ'tɜːn/ *vi* volver; (reappear) reaparecer. ● *vt* devolver; (com) declarar; (pol) elegir. ● *n* vuelta *f*; (com) ganancia *f*; (restitution) devolución *f*. **~ of income** *n* declaración *f* de ingresos. **in ~ for** a cambio de. **many happy ~s!** ¡feliz cumpleaños! **~ing** /rɪ'tɜːnɪŋ/ *a*. **~ing officer** *n* escrutador *m*. **~ match** *n* partido *m* de desquite. **~ ticket** *n* billete *m* de ida y vuelta. **~s** *npl* (com) ingresos *mpl*

reunion /riː'juːnɪən/ *n* reunión *f*

reunite /riːjuː'naɪt/ *vt* reunir

rev /rev/ *n* (auto, fam) revolución *f*. ● *vt/i*. **~ (up)** (pt revved) (auto, fam) acelerar(se)

revamp /riː'væmp/ *vt* renovar

reveal /rɪ'viːl/ *vt* revelar. **~ing** *a* revelador

revel /'revl/ *vi* (pt revelled) jaranear. **~ in** deleitarse en. **~ry** *n* juerga *f*

revelation /revə'leɪʃn/ *n* revelación *f*

revenge /rɪ'vendʒ/ *n* venganza *f*; (sport) desquite *m*. **take ~** vengarse. ● *vt* vengar. **~ful** *a* vindicativo, vengativo

revenue /'revənjuː/ *n* ingresos *mpl*

reverberate /rɪ'vɜːbəreɪt/ *vi* ⟨light⟩ reverberar; ⟨sound⟩ resonar

revere /rɪ'vɪə(r)/ *vt* venerar

reverence /'revərəns/ *n* reverencia *f*

reverend /'revərənd/ *a* reverendo
reverent /'revərənt/ *a* reverente
reverie /'revəri/ *n* ensueño *m*
revers /rɪ'vɪə/ *n* (*pl* **revers** /rɪ'vɪəz/) *n* solapa *f*
revers|al /rɪ'vɜ:sl/ *n* inversión *f*. **~e** /rɪ'vɜ:s/ *a* inverso. ● *n* contrario *m*; (*back*) revés *m*; (*auto*) marcha *f* atrás. ● *vt* invertir; anular ⟨*decision*⟩; (*auto*) dar marcha atrás a. ● *vi* (*auto*) dar marcha atrás
revert /rɪ'vɜ:t/ *vi*. **~ to** volver a
review /rɪ'vju:/ *n* repaso *m*; (*mil*) revista *f*; (*of book, play, etc*) crítica *f*. ● *vt* analizar ⟨*situation*⟩; reseñar ⟨*book, play, etc*⟩. **~er** *n* crítico *m*
revile /rɪ'vaɪl/ *vt* injuriar
revis|e /rɪ'vaɪz/ *vt* revisar; (*schol*) repasar. **~ion** /-ɪʒn/ *n* revisión *f*; (*schol*) repaso *m*
reviv|al /rɪ'vaɪvl/ *n* restablecimiento *m*; (*of faith*) despertar *m*; (*of play*) reestreno *m*. **~e** /rɪ'vaɪv/ *vt* restablecer; resucitar ⟨*person*⟩. ● *vi* restablecerse; ⟨*person*⟩ volver en sí
revoke /rɪ'vəʊk/ *vt* revocar
revolt /rɪ'vəʊlt/ *vi* sublevarse. ● *vt* dar asco a. **~ing** *a* repugnante *f*
revolting /rɪ'vəʊltɪŋ/ *a* asqueroso
revolution /revə'lu:ʃn/ *n* revolución *f*. **~ary** *a & n* revolucionario (*m*). **~ize** *vt* revolucionar
revolve /rɪ'vɒlv/ *vi* girar
revolver /rɪ'vɒlvə(r)/ *n* revólver *m*
revolving /rɪ'vɒlvɪŋ/ *a* giratorio
revue /rɪ'vju:/ *n* revista *f*
revulsion /rɪ'vʌlʃn/ *n* asco *m*
reward /rɪ'wɔ:d/ *n* recompensa *f*. ● *vt* recompensar. **~ing** *a* remunerador; (*worthwhile*) que vale la pena
rewrite /ri:'raɪt/ *vt* (*pt* **rewrote**, *pp* **rewritten**) escribir de nuevo; (*change*) redactar de nuevo
rhapsody /'ræpsədɪ/ *n* rapsodia *f*
rhetoric /'retərɪk/ *n* retórica *f*. **~al** /rɪ'tɒrɪkl/ *a* retórico
rheumati|c /ru:'mætɪk/ *a* reumático. **~sm** /'ru:mətɪzəm/ *n* reumatismo *m*
rhinoceros /raɪ'nɒsərəs/ *n* (*pl* **-oses**) rinoceronte *m*
rhubarb /'ru:bɑ:b/ *n* ruibarbo *m*
rhyme /raɪm/ *n* rima *f*; (*poem*) poesía *f*. ● *vt/i* rimar
rhythm /'rɪðəm/ *n* ritmo *m*. **~ic(al)** /'rɪðmɪk(l)/ *a* rítmico

rib /rɪb/ *n* costilla *f*. —*vt* (*pt* **ribbed**) (*fam*) tomar el pelo a
ribald /'rɪbld/ *a* obsceno, verde
ribbon /'rɪbən/ *n* cinta *f*
rice /raɪs/ *n* arroz *m*. **~ pudding** *n* arroz con leche
rich /rɪtʃ/ *a* (**-er, -est**) rico. ● *n* ricos *mpl*. **~es** *npl* riquezas *fpl*. **~ly** *adv* ricamente. **~ness** *n* riqueza *f*
rickety /'rɪkətɪ/ *a* (*shaky*) cojo, desvencijado
ricochet /'rɪkəʃeɪ/ *n* rebote *m*. ● *vi* rebotar
rid /rɪd/ *vt* (*pt* **rid**, *pres p* **ridding**) librar (**of** de). **get ~ of** deshacerse de. **~dance** /'rɪdns/ *n*. **good ~ dance!** ¡qué alivio!
ridden /'rɪdn/ *see* **ride**. ● *a* (*infested*) infestado. **~ by** (*oppressed*) agobiado de
riddle¹ /'rɪdl/ *n* acertijo *m*
riddle² /'rɪdl/ *vt* acribillar. **be ~d with** estar lleno de
ride /raɪd/ *vi* (*pt* **rode**, *pp* **ridden**) (*on horseback*) montar; (*go*) ir (en bicicleta, a caballo etc). **take s.o. for a ~** (*fam*) engañarle a uno. ● *vt* montar a ⟨*horse*⟩; ir en ⟨*bicycle*⟩; recorrer ⟨*distance*⟩. ● *n* (*on horse*) cabalgata *f*; (*in car*) paseo *m* en coche. **~r** /-ə(r)/ *n* (*on horse*) jinete *m*; (*cyclist*) ciclista *m & f*; (*in document*) cláusula *f* adicional
ridge /rɪdʒ/ *n* línea *f*, arruga *f*; (*of mountain*) cresta *f*; (*of roof*) caballete *m*
ridicul|e /'rɪdɪkju:l/ *n* irrisión *f*. ● *vt* ridiculizar. **~ous** /rɪ'dɪkjʊləs/ *a* ridículo
riding /'raɪdɪŋ/ *n* equitación *f*
rife /raɪf/ *a* difundido. **~ with** lleno de
riff-raff /'rɪfræf/ *n* gentuza *f*
rifle¹ /'raɪfl/ *n* fusil *m*
rifle² /'raɪfl/ *vt* saquear
rifle-range /'raɪflreɪndʒ/ *n* campo *m* de tiro
rift /rɪft/ *n* grieta *f*; (*fig*) ruptura *f*
rig¹ /rɪg/ *vt* (*pt* **rigged**) aparejar. ● *n* (*at sea*) plataforma *f* de perforación. **~ up** *vt* improvisar
rig² /rɪg/ *vt* (*pej*) amañar
right /raɪt/ *a* (*correct, fair*) exacto, justo; (*morally*) bueno; (*not left*) derecho; (*suitable*) adecuado. ● *n* (*entitlement*) derecho *m*; (*not left*) derecha *f*; (*not evil*) bien *m*. **~ of way** *n* (*auto*) prioridad *f*. **be in the ~**

tener razón. **on the** ~ a la derecha.
put ~ rectificar. ● *vt* enderezar; *(fig)*
corregir. ● *adv* a la derecha; *(directly)* derecho; *(completely)* completamente; *(well)* bien. ~ **away** *adv*
inmediatamente. ~ **angle** *n* ángulo
m recto

righteous /'raɪtʃəs/ *a* recto; *(cause)*
justo

right /~**ful** /'raɪtfl/ *a* legítimo.
~**fully** *adv* legítimamente. ~**-hand
man** *n* brazo *m* derecho. ~**ly** *adv*
justamente. ~ **wing** *a* *(pol)* *n* de-
rechista

rigid /'rɪdʒɪd/ *a* rígido. ~**ity**
/·'dʒɪdəti/ *n* rigidez *f*

rigmarole /'rɪgmərəʊl/ *n* galimatías
m invar

rig|orous /'rɪgərəs/ *a* riguroso.
~**our** /'rɪgə(r)/ *n* rigor *m*

rig-out /'rɪgaʊt/ *n* *(fam)* atavío *m*

rile /raɪl/ *vt* *(fam)* irritar

rim /rɪm/ *n* borde *m*; *(of wheel)* llanta
f; *(of glasses)* montura *f*. ~**med** *a* bor-
deado

rind /raɪnd/ *n* corteza *f*; *(of fruit)*
cáscara *f*

ring[1] /rɪŋ/ *n* *(circle)* círculo *m*; *(circle
of metal etc)* aro *m*; *(on finger)* anillo
m; *(on finger with stone)* sortija *f*;
(boxing) cuadrilátero *m*; *(bullring)*
ruedo *m*, redondel *m*, plaza *f*; *(for circus)* pista *f*. ● *vt* rodear

ring[2] /rɪŋ/ *n* *(of bell)* toque *m*; *(tinkle)*
tintíneo *m*; *(telephone call)* llamada *f*.
● *vt* *(pt* **rang**, *pp* **rung**) hacer sonar;
(telephone) llamar por teléfono. ~
the bell tocar el timbre. ● *vi* sonar.
~ **back** *vt/i* volver a llamar. ~ **off** *vi*
colgar. ~ **up** *vt* llamar por teléfono

ring /~**leader** /'rɪŋliːdə(r)/ *n* cabecilla *f*. ~ **road** *n* carretera *f* de
circunvalación

rink /rɪŋk/ *n* pista *f*

rinse /rɪns/ *vt* enjuagar. ● *n* aclarado
m; *(of dishes)* enjuague *m*; *(for hair)*
reflejo *m*

riot /'raɪət/ *n* disturbio *m*; *(of colours)*
profusión *f*. **run** ~ desenfrenarse.
● *vi* amotinarse. ~**er** *n* amotinador
m. ~**ous** *a* tumultuoso

rip /rɪp/ *vt* *(pt* **ripped**) rasgar. ● *vi*
rasgarse. **let** ~ *(fig)* soltar. ● *n* ras-
gadura *f*. ~ **off** *vt* *(sl)* robar. ~**-cord**
n *(of parachute)* cuerda *f* de abertura

ripe /raɪp/ *a* (**-er**, **-est**) maduro. ~**n**
/'raɪpən/ *vt/i* madurar. ~**ness** *n*
madurez *f*

rip-off /'rɪpɒf/ *n* *(sl)* timo *m*

ripple /'rɪpl/ *n* rizo *m*; *(sound)* murmullo *m*. ● *vt* rizar. ● *vi* rizarse

rise /raɪz/ *vi* *(pt* **rose**, *pp* **risen**)
levantarse; *(rebel)* sublevarse; *(river)*
crecer; *(prices)* subir. ● *n* subida *f*;
(land) altura *f*; *(increase)* aumento *m*;
(to power) ascenso *m*. **give** ~ **to**
ocasionar. ~**r** /·-ə(r)/ *n*. **early** ~**r** *n*
madrugador *m*

rising /'raɪzɪŋ/ *n* *(revolt)* sublevación
f. ● *a* *(sun)* naciente. ~ **generation**
n nueva generación *f*

risk /rɪsk/ *n* riesgo *m*. ● *vt* arriesgar.
~**y** *a* (**-ier**, **-iest**) arriesgado

risqué /'riːskeɪ/ *a* subido de color

rissole /'rɪsəʊl/ *n* croqueta *f*

rite /raɪt/ *n* rito *m*

ritual /'rɪtʃʊəl/ *a & n* ritual (*m*)

rival /'raɪvl/ *a & n* rival (*m*). ● *vt* *(pt*
rivalled) rivalizar con. ~**ry** *n* rivalidad *f*

river /'rɪvə(r)/ *n* río *m*

rivet /'rɪvɪt/ *n* remache *m*. ● *vt* re-
machar. ~**ing** *a* fascinante

Riviera /rɪvɪ'erə/ *n*. **the (French)** ~
la Costa *f* Azul. **the (Italian)** ~ la
Riviera *f* (Italiana)

rivulet /'rɪvjʊlɪt/ *n* riachuelo *m*

road /rəʊd/ *n* *(in town)* calle *f*; *(between towns)* carretera *f*; *(way)* camino *m*. **on the** ~ en camino. ~**-hog**
n conductor *m* descortés. ~**house** *n*
albergue *m*. ~**-map** *n* mapa *m* de carreteras. ~**side** /'rəʊdsaɪd/ *n* borde
m de la carretera. ~ **sign** *n* señal *f* de
tráfico. ~**way** /'rəʊdweɪ/ *n* calzada
f. ~**works** *npl* obras *fpl*. ~**worthy**
/'rəʊdwɜːðɪ/ *a* *(vehicle)* seguro

roam /rəʊm/ *vi* vagar

roar /rɔː(r)/ *n* rugido *m*; *(laughter)*
carcajada *f*. ● *vt/i* rugir. ~ **past**
(vehicles) pasar con estruendo. ~
with laughter reírse a carcajadas.
~**ing** /'rɔːrɪŋ/ *a* *(trade etc)* activo

roast /rəʊst/ *vt* asar; tostar *(coffee)*.
● *vi* asarse; *(person, coffee)* tostarse.
● *a & n* asado (*m*). ~ **beef** *n* rosbif *m*

rob /rɒb/ *vt* *(pt* **robbed**) robar;
asaltar *(bank)*. ~ **of** privar de,
~**ber** *n* ladrón *m*; *(of bank)* atracador
m. ~**bery** *n* robo *m*

robe /rəʊb/ *n* manto *m*; *(univ etc)*
toga *f*. **bath-**~ *n* albornoz *m*

robin /'rɒbɪn/ *n* petirrojo *m*

robot /'rəʊbɒt/ *n* robot *m*, autómata
m

robust /rəʊ'bʌst/ *a* robusto

rock[1] /rɒk/ n roca f; (*boulder*) peñasco m; (*sweet*) caramelo m en forma de barra; (*of Gibraltar*) peñón m. **on the ~s** (*drink*) con hielo; (*fig*) arruinado. **be on the ~s** (*marriage etc*) andar mal

rock[2] /rɒk/ vt mecer; (*shake*) sacudir. ● vi mecerse; (*shake*) sacudirse. ● n (*mus*) música f rock

rock: **~-bottom** a (*fam*) bajísimo. **~ery** /'rɒkərɪ/ n cuadro m alpino, rocalla f

rocket /'rɒkɪt/ n cohete m

rock: **~ing-chair** n mecedora f. **~ing-horse** n caballo m de balancín. **~y** /'rɒkɪ/ a (-ier, -iest) rocoso; (*fig, shaky*) bamboleante

rod /rɒd/ n vara f; (*for fishing*) caña f; (*metal*) barra f

rode /rəʊd/ see **ride**

rodent /'rəʊdnt/ n roedor m

rodeo /rə'deɪəʊ/ n (*pl -os*) rodeo m

roe[1] /rəʊ/ n (*fish eggs*) hueva f

roe[2] /rəʊ/ (*pl* **roe**, *or* **roes**) (*deer*) corzo m

rogu|e /rəʊg/ n pícaro m. **~ish** a picaresco

role /rəʊl/ n papel m

roll /rəʊl/ vt hacer rodar; (*roll up*) enrollar; (*flatten lawn*) allanar; aplanar (*pastry*). ● vi rodar; (*ship*) balancearse; (*on floor*) revolcarse. **be ~ing (in money)** (*fam*) nadar (en dinero). ● n rollo m; (*of ship*) balanceo m; (*of drum*) redoble m; (*of thunder*) retumbo m; (*bread*) panecillo m; (*list*) lista f. **~ over** vi (*turn over*) dar una vuelta. **~ up** vt enrollar; arremangar (*sleeve*). ● vi (*fam*) llegar. **~-call** n lista f

roller /'rəʊlə(r)/ n rodillo m; (*wheel*) rueda f; (*for hair*) rulo m, bigudí m. **~-coaster** n montaña f rusa. **~-skate** n patín m de ruedas

rollicking /'rɒlɪkɪŋ/ a alegre

rolling /'rəʊlɪŋ/ a ondulado. **~-pin** n rodillo m

Roman /'rəʊmən/ a & n romano (m). **~ Catholic** a & n católico (m) (romano)

romance /rə'mæns/ n novela f romántica; (*love*) amor m; (*affair*) aventura f

Romania /rə'meɪnɪə/ n Rumania f. **~n** a & n rumano (m)

romantic /rə'mæntɪk/ a romántico. **~ism** n romanticismo m

Rome /rəʊm/ n Roma f

romp /rɒmp/ vi retozar. ● n retozo m

rompers /'rɒmpəz/ npl pelele m

roof /ru:f/ n techo m, tejado m; (*of mouth*) paladar m. ● vt techar. **~-garden** n jardín m en la azotea. **~-rack** n baca f. **~-top** n tejado m

rook[1] /rʊk/ n grajo m

rook[2] /rʊk/ (*in chess*) torre f

room /ru:m/ n cuarto m, habitación f; (*bedroom*) dormitorio m; (*space*) sitio m; (*large hall*) sala f. **~y** a espacioso; (*clothes*) holgado

roost /ru:st/ n percha f. ● vi descansar. **~er** n gallo m

root[1] /ru:t/ n raíz f. **take ~** echar raíces. ● vt hacer arraigar. ● vi echar raíces, arraigarse

root[2] /ru:t/ vt/i. **~ about** vi hurgar. **~ for** vi (*Amer, sl*) alentar. **~ out** vt extirpar

rootless /'ru:tlɪs/ a desarraigado

rope /rəʊp/ n cuerda f. **know the ~s** estar al corriente. ● vt atar. **~ in** vt agarrar

rosary /'rəʊzərɪ/ n (*relig*) rosario m

rose[1] /rəʊz/ n rosa f; (*nozzle*) roseta f

rose[2] /rəʊz/ see **rise**

rosé /'rəʊzeɪ/ n (*vino m*) rosado m

rosette /rəʊ'zet/ n escarapela f

roster /'rɒstə(r)/ n lista f

rostrum /'rɒstrəm/ n tribuna f

rosy /'rəʊzɪ/ a (-ier, -iest) rosado; (*skin*) sonrosado

rot /rɒt/ vt (*pt* **rotted**) pudrir. ● vi pudrirse. ● n putrefacción f; (*sl*) tonterías fpl

rota /'rəʊtə/ n lista f

rotary /'rəʊtərɪ/ a giratorio, rotativo

rotat|e /rəʊ'teɪt/ vt girar; (*change round*) alternar. ● vi girar; (*change round*) alternarse. **~ion** /-ʃn/ n rotación f

rote /rəʊt/ n. **by ~** maquinalmente, de memoria

rotten /'rɒtn/ a podrido; (*fam*) desagradable

rotund /rəʊ'tʌnd/ a redondo; (*person*) regordete

rouge /ru:ʒ/ n colorete m

rough /rʌf/ a (-er, -est) áspero; (*person*) tosco; (*bad*) malo; (*ground*) accidentado; (*violent*) brutal; (*approximate*) aproximado; (*diamond*) bruto. ● adv duro. **~ copy** n, **~ draft** n borrador m. **~** (*ruffian*) matón m. ● vt. **~ it** vivir sin comodidades. **~ out** vt esbozar

roughage /'rʌfɪdʒ/ n alimento m indigesto, afrecho m; (for animals) forraje m

rough: ~-and-ready a improvisado. ~-and-tumble n riña f. ~ly adv toscamente; (more or less) más o menos. ~ness n aspereza f; (lack of manners) incultura f; (crudeness) tosquedad f

roulette /ru:'let/ n ruleta f

round /raʊnd/ a (-er, -est) redondo. ● n círculo m; (slice) tajada f; (of visits, drinks) ronda f; (of competition) vuelta f; (boxing) asalto m.● prep alrededor de. ● adv alrededor. ~ about (approximately) aproximadamente. come ~ to, go ~ to (a friend etc) pasar por casa de. ● vt redondear; doblar ⟨corner⟩. ~ off vt terminar. ~ up vt reunir; redondear ⟨price⟩

roundabout /'raʊndəbaʊt/ n tiovivo m; (for traffic) glorieta f. ● a indirecto

rounders /'raʊndəz/ n juego m parecido al béisbol

round: ~ly adv (bluntly) francamente. ~ trip n viaje m de ida y vuelta. ~-up n reunión f; (of suspects) redada f

rous|e /raʊz/ vt despertar. ~ing a excitante

rout /raʊt/ n derrota f. ● vt derrotar

route /ru:t/ n ruta f; (naut, aviat) rumbo m; (of bus) línea f

routine /ru:'ti:n/ n rutina f. ● a rutinario

rov|e /rəʊv/ vt/i vagar (por). ~ing a errante

row[1] /rəʊ/ n fila f

row[2] /rəʊ/ n (in boat) paseo m en bote (de remos). ● vi remar

row[3] /raʊ/ n (noise, fam) ruido m; (quarrel) pelea f. ● vi (fam) pelearse

rowdy /'raʊdɪ/ a (-ier, -iest) n ruidoso

rowing /'rəʊɪŋ/ n remo m. ~-boat n bote m de remos

royal /'rɔɪəl/ a real. ~ist a & n monárquico (m). ~ly adv magníficamente. ~ty /'rɔɪəltɪ/ n familia f real; (payment) derechos mpl de autor

rub /rʌb/ vt (pt rubbed) frotar. ~ it in insistir en algo. ● n frotamiento m. ~ off on s.o. vi pegársele a uno. ~ out vt borrar

rubber /'rʌbə(r)/ n goma f. ~ band n goma f (elástica). ~ stamp n sello m de goma. ~-stamp vt (fig) aprobar maquinalmente. ~y a parecido al caucho

rubbish /'rʌbɪʃ/ n basura f; (junk) trastos mpl; (fig) tonterías fpl. ~y a sin valor

rubble /'rʌbl/ n escombros; (small) cascajo m

ruby /'ru:bɪ/ n rubí m

rucksack /'rʌksæk/ n mochila f

rudder /'rʌdə(r)/ n timón m

ruddy /'rʌdɪ/ a (-ier, -iest) rubicundo; (sl) maldito

rude /ru:d/ a (-er, -est) descortés, mal educado; (improper) indecente; (brusque) brusco. ~ly adv con descortesía. ~ness n descortesía f

rudiment /'ru:dɪmənt/ n rudimento m. ~ary /-'mentrɪ/ a rudimentario

rueful /'ru:fl/ a triste

ruffian /'rʌfɪən/ n rufián m

ruffle /'rʌfl/ vt despeinar ⟨hair⟩; arrugar ⟨clothes⟩. ● n (frill) volante m, fruncido m

rug /rʌg/ n tapete m; (blanket) manta f

Rugby /'rʌgbɪ/ n. ~ (football) n rugby m

rugged /'rʌgɪd/ a desigual; (landscape) accidentado; (fig) duro

ruin /'ru:ɪn/ n ruina f. ● vt arruinar. ~ous a ruinoso

rule /ru:l/ n regla f; (custom) costumbre f; (pol) dominio m. as a ~ por regla general. ● vt gobernar; (master) dominar; (jurid) decretar; (decide) decidir. ~ out vt descartar. ~d paper n papel m rayado

ruler /'ru:lə(r)/ n (sovereign) soberano m; (leader) gobernante m & f; (measure) regla f

ruling /'ru:lɪŋ/ a ⟨class⟩ dirigente. ● n decisión f

rum /rʌm/ n ron m

rumble /'rʌmbl/ vi retumbar; ⟨stomach⟩ hacer ruidos. ● n retumbo m; (of stomach) ruido m

ruminant /'ru:mɪnənt/ a & n rumiante (m)

rummage /'rʌmɪdʒ/ vi hurgar

rumour /'ru:mə(r)/ n rumor m. ● vt. it is ~ed that se dice que

rump /rʌmp/ n (of horse) grupa f; (of fowl) rabadilla f. ~ steak n filete m

rumpus /'rʌmpəs/ n (fam) jaleo m

run /rʌn/ *vi* (*pt* **ran**, *pp* **run**, *pres p*
running) correr; (*flow*) fluir; (*pass*)
pasar; (*function*) funcionar; (*melt*)
derretirse; ⟨*bus etc*⟩ circular; ⟨*play*⟩
representarse (continuamente); ⟨*colours*⟩ correrse; (*in election*) presentarse. ● *vt* tener ⟨*house*⟩; (*control*)
dirigir; correr ⟨*risk*⟩; (*drive*) conducir; (*pass*) pasar; (*present*) presentar; forzar ⟨*blockade*⟩. **~ a
temperature** tener fiebre. ● *n* corrida *f*, carrera *f*; (*journey*) viaje *m*;
(*outing*) paseo *m*, excursión *f*; (*distance travelled*) recorrido *m*; (*ladder*)
carrera *f*; (*ski*) pista *f*; (*series*) serie *f*.
at a ~ corriendo. **have the ~ of**
tener a su disposición. **in the long ~**
a la larga. **on the ~** de fuga. **~
across** *vt* toparse con ⟨*friend*⟩. **~
away** *vi* escaparse. **~ down** *vi* bajar
corriendo; ⟨*clock*⟩ quedarse sin
cuerda. ● *vt* (*auto*) atropellar; (*belittle*) denigrar. **~ in** *vt* rodar
⟨*vehicle*⟩. ● *vi* entrar corriendo. **~
into** *vt* toparse con ⟨*friend*⟩; (*hit*)
chocar con. **~ off** *vt* tirar ⟨*copies etc*⟩.
~ out *vi* salir corriendo; ⟨*liquid*⟩
salirse; (*fig*) agotarse. **~ out of** quedar sin. **~ over** *vt* (*auto*) atropellar.
~ through *vt* traspasar; (*revise*) repasar. **~ up** *vt* hacerse ⟨*bill*⟩. ● *vi*
subir corriendo. **~ up against**
tropezar con ⟨*difficulties*⟩. **~away**
/'rʌnəweɪ/ *a* fugitivo; (*success*)
decisivo; ⟨*inflation*⟩ galopante. ● *n*
fugitivo *m*. **~ down** *a* ⟨*person*⟩ agotado. **~down** *n* informe *m* detallado
rung[1] /rʌŋ/ *n* (*of ladder*) peldaño *m*
rung[2] /rʌŋ/ *see* **ring**
run: **~ner** /'rʌnə(r)/ *n* corredor *m*;
(*on sledge*) patín *m*. **~ner bean** *n*
judía *f* escarlata. **~ner-up** *n* subcampeón *m*, segundo *m*. **~ning**
/'rʌnɪŋ/ *n* (*race*) carrera *f*. **be in the
~ning** tener posibilidades de ganar.
● *a* en marcha; ⟨*water*⟩ corriente;
⟨*commentary*⟩ en directo. **four times
~ning** cuatro veces seguidas. **~ny**
/'rʌnɪ/ *a* líquido; ⟨*nose*⟩ que moquea.
~of-the-mill *a* ordinario. **~up** *n*
período *m* que precede. **~way**
/'rʌnweɪ/ *n* pista *f*
rupture /'rʌptʃə(r)/ *n* ruptura *f*;
(*med*) hernia *f*. ● *vt/i* quebrarse
rural /'rʊərəl/ *a* rural
ruse /ruːz/ *n* ardid *m*

rush[1] /rʌʃ/ *n* (*haste*) prisa *f*; (*crush*)
bullicio *m*. ● *vi* precipitarse. ● *vt*
apresurar; (*mil*) asaltar
rush[2] /rʌʃ/ *n* (*plant*) junco *m*
rush-hour /'rʌʃaʊə(r)/ *n* hora *f*
punta
rusk /rʌsk/ *n* galleta *f*, tostada *f*
russet /'rʌsɪt/ *a* rojizo. ● *n* (*apple*)
manzana *f* rojiza
Russia /'rʌʃə/ *n* Rusia *f*. **~n** *a & n*
ruso (*m*)
rust /rʌst/ *n* orín *m*. ● *vt* oxidar. ● *vi*
oxidarse
rustic /'rʌstɪk/ *a* rústico
rustle /'rʌsl/ *vt* hacer susurrar;
(*Amer*) robar. **~ up** (*fam*) preparar.
● *vi* susurrar
rust: **~proof** *a* inoxidable. **~y**
(**-ier, -iest**) oxidado
rut /rʌt/ *n* surco *m*. **in a ~** en la rutina de siempre
ruthless /'ruːθlɪs/ *a* despiadado.
~ness *n* crueldad *f*
rye /raɪ/ *n* centeno *m*

S

S *abbr* (*south*) sur *m*
sabbath /'sæbəθ/ *n* día *m* de descanso; (*Christian*) domingo *m*; (*Jewish*) sábado *m*
sabbatical /sə'bætɪkl/ *a* sabático
sabot|**age** /'sæbətɑːʒ/ *n* sabotaje *m*.
● *vt* sabotear. **~eur** /-'tɜː(r)/ *n*
saboteador *m*
saccharin /'sækərɪn/ *n* sacarina *f*
sachet /'sæʃeɪ/ *n* bolsita *f*
sack[1] /sæk/ *n* saco *m*. **get the ~** (*fam*)
ser despedido. ● *vt* (*fam*) despedir.
~ing *n* arpillera *f*; (*fam*) despido *m*
sack[2] /sæk/ *vt* (*plunder*) saquear
sacrament /'sækrəmənt/ *n* sacramento *m*
sacred /'seɪkrɪd/ *a* sagrado
sacrifice /'sækrɪfaɪs/ *n* sacrificio *m*.
● *vt* sacrificar
sacrileg|**e** /'sækrɪlɪdʒ/ *n* sacrilegio
m. **~ious** /-'lɪdʒəs/ *a* sacrílego
sacrosanct /'sækrəʊsæŋkt/ *a* sacrosanto
sad /sæd/ *a* (**sadder, saddest**) triste.
~den /'sædn/ *vt* entristecer
saddle /'sædl/ *n* silla *f*. **be in the ~**
(*fig*) tener las riendas. ● *vt* ensillar
⟨*horse*⟩. **~ s.o. with** (*fig*) cargar a
uno con. **~bag** *n* alforja *f*

sad: ~**ly** *adv* tristemente; (*fig*) desgraciadamente. ~**ness** *n* tristeza *f*

sadis|m /'seɪdɪzəm/ *n* sadismo *m*. ~**t** /'seɪdɪst/ *n* sádico *m*. ~**tic** /sə'dɪstɪk/ *a* sádico

safari /sə'fɑːrɪ/ *n* safari *m*

safe /seɪf/ *a* (**-er**, **-est**) seguro; (*out of danger*) salvo; (*cautious*) prudente. ~ **and sound** sano y salvo. ● *n* caja *f* fuerte. ~ **deposit** *n* caja *f* de seguridad. ~**guard** /'seɪfgɑːd/ *n* salvaguardia *f*. ● *vt* salvaguardar. ~**ly** *adv* sin peligro; (*in safe place*) en lugar seguro. ~**ty** /'seɪftɪ/ *n* seguridad *f*. ~**ty belt** *n* cinturón *m* de seguridad. ~**ty-pin** *n* imperdible *m*. ~**ty-valve** *n* válvula *f* de seguridad

saffron /'sæfrən/ *n* azafrán *m*

sag /sæg/ *vi* (*pt* **sagged**) hundirse; (*give*) aflojarse

saga /'sɑːgə/ *n* saga *f*

sage[1] /seɪdʒ/ *n* (*wise person*) sabio *m*. ● *a* sabio

sage[2] /seɪdʒ/ *n* (*herb*) salvia *f*

sagging /'sægɪŋ/ *a* hundido; (*fig*) decaído

Sagittarius /sædʒɪ'teərɪəs/ *n* (*astr*) Sagitario *m*

sago /'seɪgəʊ/ *n* sagú *m*

said /sed/ *see* **say**

sail /seɪl/ *n* vela *f*; (*trip*) paseo *m* (en barco). ● *vi* navegar; (*leave*) partir; (*sport*) practicar la vela; (*fig*) deslizarse. ● *vt* manejar ‹*boat*›. ~**ing** *n* (*sport*) vela *f*. ~**ing-boat** *n*, ~**ing-ship** *n* barco *m* de vela. ~**or** /'seɪlə(r)/ *n* marinero *m*

saint /seɪnt, *before name* sənt/ *n* santo *m*. ~**ly** *a* santo

sake /seɪk/ *n*. **for the** ~ **of** por, por el amor de

salacious /sə'leɪʃəs/ *a* salaz

salad /'sæləd/ *n* ensalada *f*. ~ **bowl** *n* ensaladera *f*. ~ **cream** *n* mayonesa *f*. ~**dressing** *n* aliño *m*

salar|ied /'sælərɪd/ *a* asalariado. ~**y** /'sælərɪ/ *n* sueldo *m*

sale /seɪl/ *n* venta *f*; (*at reduced prices*) liquidación *f*. **for** ~ (*sign*) se vende. **on** ~ en venta. ~**able** /'seɪləbl/ *a* vendible. ~**sman** /'seɪlzmən/ *n* (*pl* **-men**) vendedor *m*; (*in shop*) dependiente *m*; (*traveller*) viajante *m*. ~**swoman** *n* (*pl* **-women**) vendedora *f*; (*in shop*) dependienta *f*

salient /'seɪlɪənt/ *a* saliente, destacado

saliva /sə'laɪvə/ *n* saliva *f*

sallow /'sæləʊ/ *a* (**-er**, **-est**) amarillento

salmon /'sæmən/ *n invar* salmón *m*. ~ **trout** *n* trucha *f* salmonada

salon /'sælɒn/ *n* salón *m*

saloon /sə'luːn/ *n* (*on ship*) salón *m*; (*Amer, bar*) bar *m*; (*auto*) turismo *m*

salt /sɔːlt/ *n* sal *f*. ● *a* salado. ● *vt* salar. ~**cellar** *n* salero *m*. ~**y** *a* salado

salutary /'sæljʊtrɪ/ *a* saludable

salute /sə'luːt/ *n* saludo *m*. ● *vt* saludar. ● *vi* hacer un saludo

salvage /'sælvɪdʒ/ *n* salvamento *m*; (*goods*) objetos *mpl* salvados. ● *vt* salvar

salvation /sæl'veɪʃn/ *n* salvación *f*

salve /sælv/ *n* ungüento *m*

salver /'sælvə(r)/ *n* bandeja *f*

salvo /'sælvəʊ/ *n* (*pl* **-os**) salva *f*

same /seɪm/ *a* igual (**as** que); (*before noun*) mismo (**as** que). **at the** ~ **time** al mismo tiempo. ● *pron*. **the** ~ el mismo, la misma, los mismos, las mismas. **do the** ~ **as** hacer como. ● *adv*. **the** ~ de la misma manera. **all the** ~ de todas formas

sample /'sɑːmpl/ *n* muestra *f*. ● *vt* probar ‹*food*›

sanatorium /sænə'tɔːrɪəm/ *n* (*pl* **-ums**) sanatorio *m*

sanctify /'sæŋktɪfaɪ/ *vt* santificar

sanctimonious /sæŋktɪ'məʊnɪəs/ *a* beato

sanction /'sæŋkʃn/ *n* sanción *f*. ● *vt* sancionar

sanctity /'sæŋktɪtɪ/ *n* santidad *f*

sanctuary /'sæŋktʃʊərɪ/ *n* (*relig*) santuario *m*; (*for wildlife*) reserva *f*; (*refuge*) asilo *m*

sand /sænd/ *n* arena *f*. ● *vt* enarenar. ~**s** *npl* (*beach*) playa *f*

sandal /'sændl/ *n* sandalia *f*

sand: ~**castle** *n* castillo *m* de arena. ~**paper** /'sændpeɪpə(r)/ *n* papel *m* de lija. ● *vt* lijar. ~**storm** /'sændstɔːm/ *n* tempestad *f* de arena

sandwich /'sænwɪdʒ/ *n* bocadillo *m*, sandwich *m*. ● *vt*. ~**ed between** intercalado

sandy /'sændɪ/ *a* arenoso

sane /seɪn/ *a* (**-er**, **-est**) ‹*person*› cuerdo; ‹*judgement, policy*› razonable. ~**ly** *adv* sensatamente

sang /sæŋ/ *see* **sing**

sanitary /'sænɪtrɪ/ *a* higiénico; ‹*system etc*› sanitario. ~ **towel** *n*, ~ **napkin** *n* (*Amer*) compresa *f* (higiénica)

sanitation /sænɪˈteɪʃn/ n higiene f; (drainage) sistema m sanitario

sanity /ˈsænɪtɪ/ n cordura f; (fig) sensatez f

sank /sæŋk/ see **sink**

Santa Claus /ˈsæntəklɔːz/ n Papá m Noel

sap /sæp/ n (in plants) savia f. ● vt (pt sapped) agotar

sapling /ˈsæplɪŋ/ n árbol m joven

sapphire /ˈsæfaɪə(r)/ n zafiro m

sarcas|m /ˈsɑːkæzəm/ n sarcasmo m. ~tic /-ˈkæstɪk/ a sarcástico

sardine /sɑːˈdiːn/ n sardina f

Sardinia /sɑːˈdɪnɪə/ n Cerdeña f. ~n a & n sardo (m)

sardonic /sɑːˈdɒnɪk/ a sardónico

sash /sæʃ/ n (over shoulder) banda f; (round waist) fajín m. ~-window n ventana f de guillotina

sat /sæt/ see **sit**

satanic /səˈtænɪk/ a satánico

satchel /ˈsætʃl/ n cartera f

satellite /ˈsætəlaɪt/ n & a satélite (m)

satiate /ˈseɪʃɪeɪt/ vt saciar

satin /ˈsætɪn/ n raso m. ● a de raso; (like satin) satinado

satir|e /ˈsætaɪə(r)/ n sátira f. ~ical /səˈtɪrɪkl/ a satírico. ~ist /ˈsætərɪst/ n satírico m. ~ize /ˈsætəraɪz/ vt satirizar

satisfaction /sætɪsˈfækʃn/ n satisfacción f

satisfactor|ily /sætɪsˈfæktərɪlɪ/ adv satisfactoriamente. ~y /sætɪsˈfæktərɪ/ a satisfactorio

satisfy /ˈsætɪsfaɪ/ vt satisfacer; (convince) convencer. ~ing a satisfactorio

satsuma /sætˈsuːmə/ n mandarina f

saturat|e /ˈsætʃəreɪt/ vt saturar, empapar. ~ed a saturado, empapado. ~ion /-ˈreɪʃn/ n saturación f

Saturday /ˈsætədeɪ/ n sábado m

sauce /sɔːs/ n salsa f; (cheek) descaro m. ~pan /ˈsɔːspən/ n cazo m

saucer /ˈsɔːsə(r)/ n platillo m

saucy /ˈsɔːsɪ/ a (-ier, -iest) descarado

Saudi Arabia /saʊdɪəˈreɪbɪə/ n Arabia f Saudí

sauna /ˈsɔːnə/ n sauna f

saunter /ˈsɔːntə(r)/ vi deambular, pasearse

sausage /ˈsɒsɪdʒ/ n salchicha f

savage /ˈsævɪdʒ/ a salvaje; (fierce) feroz; (furious, fam) rabioso. ● n salvaje m & f. ● vt atacar. ~ry n ferocidad f

sav|e /seɪv/ vt salvar; ahorrar ⟨money, time⟩; (prevent) evitar. ● n (football) parada f. ● prep salvo, con excepción de. ~er n ahorrador m. ~ing n ahorro m. ~ings npl ahorros mpl

saviour /ˈseɪvɪə(r)/ n salvador m

savour /ˈseɪvə(r)/ n sabor m. ● vt saborear. ~y a (appetizing) sabroso; (not sweet) no dulce. ● n aperitivo m (no dulce)

saw[1] /sɔː/ see **see**[1]

saw[2] /sɔː/ n sierra f. ● vt (pt sawed, pp sawn) serrar. ~dust /ˈsɔːdʌst/ n serrín m. ~n /sɔːn/ see **saw**[1]

saxophone /ˈsæksəfəʊn/ n saxófono m

say /seɪ/ vt/i (pt said /sed/) decir; rezar ⟨prayer⟩. **I ~!** ¡no me digas! ● n. **have a ~** expresar una opinión; (in decision) tener voz en capítulo. **have no ~** no tener ni voz ni voto. ~ing /ˈseɪɪŋ/ n refrán m

scab /skæb/ n costra f; (blackleg, fam) esquirol m

scaffold /ˈskæfəʊld/ n (gallows) cadalso m, patíbulo m. ~ing /ˈskæfəldɪŋ/ n (for workmen) andamio m

scald /skɔːld/ vt escaldar; calentar ⟨milk etc⟩. ● n escaldadura f

scale[1] /skeɪl/ n escala f

scale[2] /skeɪl/ n (of fish) escama f

scale[3] /skeɪl/ vt (climb) escalar. ~ down vt reducir (proporcionalmente)

scales /skeɪlz/ npl (for weighing) balanza f, peso m

scallop /ˈskɒləp/ n venera f; (on dress) festón m

scalp /skælp/ n cuero m cabelludo. ● vt quitar el cuero cabelludo a

scalpel /ˈskælpəl/ n escalpelo m

scamp /skæmp/ n bribón m

scamper /ˈskæmpə(r)/ vi. ~ away marcharse corriendo

scampi /ˈskæmpɪ/ npl gambas fpl grandes

scan /skæn/ vt (pt scanned) escudriñar; (quickly) echar un vistazo a; ⟨radar⟩ explorar. ● vi ⟨poetry⟩ estar bien medido

scandal /ˈskændl/ n escándalo m; (gossip) chismorreo m. ~ize /ˈskændəlaɪz/ vt escandalizar. ~ous a escandaloso

Scandinavia /skændɪˈneɪvɪə/ n Escandinavia f. ~n a & n escandinavo (m)

scant /skænt/ a escaso. **~ily** adv insuficientemente. **~y** /'skæntɪ/ a (-ier, -iest) escaso

scapegoat /'skeɪpgəʊt/ n cabeza f de turco

scar /skɑ:(r)/ n cicatriz f. ● vt (pt scarred) dejar una cicatriz en. ● vi cicatrizarse

scarc|e /skeəs/ a (-er, -est) escaso. **make o.s. ~e** (fam) mantenerse lejos. **~ely** /'skeəslɪ/ adv apenas. **~ity** n escasez f

scare /'skeə(r)/ vt asustar. **be ~d** tener miedo. ● n susto m. **~crow** /'skeəkrəʊ/ n espantapájaros m invar. **~monger** /'skeəmʌŋgə(r)/ n alarmista m & f

scarf /skɑ:f/ n (pl scarves) bufanda f; (over head) pañuelo m

scarlet /'skɑ:lət/ a escarlata f. **~ fever** n escarlatina f

scary /'skeərɪ/ a (-ier, -iest) que da miedo

scathing /'skeɪðɪŋ/ a mordaz

scatter /'skætə(r)/ vt (throw) esparcir; (disperse) dispersar. ● vi dispersarse. **~-brained** a atolondrado. **~ed** a disperso; (occasional) esporádico

scatty /'skætɪ/ a (-ier, -iest) (sl) atolondrado

scavenge /'skævɪndʒ/ vi buscar (en la basura). **~r** /-ə(r)/ n (vagrant) persona f que busca objetos en la basura

scenario /sɪ'nɑ:rɪəʊ/ n (pl -os) argumento m; (of film) guión m

scen|e /si:n/ n escena f; (sight) vista f; (fuss) lío m. **behind the ~es** entre bastidores. **~ery** /'si:nərɪ/ n paisaje m; (in theatre) decorado m. **~ic** /'si:nɪk/ a pintoresco

scent /sent/ n olor m; (perfume) perfume m; (trail) pista f. ● vt presentir; (make fragrant) perfumar

sceptic /'skeptɪk/ n escéptico m. **~al** a escéptico. **~ism** /-sɪzəm/ n escepticismo m

sceptre /'septə(r)/ n cetro m

schedule /'ʃedju:l, 'skedju:l/ n programa f; (timetable) horario m. **behind ~** con retraso. **on ~** sin retraso. ● vt proyectar. **~d flight** n vuelo m regular

scheme /ski:m/ n proyecto m; (plot) intriga f. ● vi hacer proyectos (pej) intrigar. **~r** n intrigante m & f

schism /'sɪzəm/ n cisma m

schizophrenic /skɪtsə'frenɪk/ a & n esquizofrénico (m)

scholar /'skɒlə(r)/ n erudito m. **~ly** a erudito. **~ship** n erudición f; (grant) beca f

scholastic /skə'læstɪk/ a escolar

school /sku:l/ n escuela f; (of univ) facultad f. ● a ⟨age, holidays, year⟩ escolar. ● vt enseñar; (discipline) disciplinar. **~boy** /'sku:lbɔɪ/ n colegial m. **~girl** /-gə:l/ n colegiala f. **~ing** n instrucción f. **~master** /'sku:lmɑ:stə(r)/ n (primary) maestro m; (secondary) profesor m. **~mistress** n (primary) maestra f; (secondary) profesora f. **~teacher** n (primary) maestro m; (secondary) profesor m

schooner /'sku:nə(r)/ n goleta f; (glass) vaso m grande

sciatica /saɪ'ætɪkə/ n ciática f

scien|ce /'saɪəns/ n ciencia f. **~ce fiction** n ciencia f ficción. **~tific** /-'tɪfɪk/ a científico. **~tist** /'saɪəntɪst/ n científico m

scintillate /'sɪntɪleɪt/ vi centellear

scissors /'sɪsəz/ npl tijeras fpl

sclerosis /sklə'rəʊsɪs/ n esclerosis f

scoff /skɒf/ vt (sl) zamparse. ● vi. **~ at** mofarse de

scold /skəʊld/ vt regañar. **~ing** n regaño m

scone /skɒn/ n (tipo m de) bollo m

scoop /sku:p/ n paleta f; (news) noticia f exclusiva. ● vt. **~ out** excavar. **~ up** recoger

scoot /sku:t/ vi (fam) largarse corriendo. **~er** /'sku:tə(r)/ n escúter m; (for child) patinete m

scope /skəʊp/ n alcance m; (opportunity) oportunidad f

scorch /skɔ:tʃ/ vt chamuscar. **~er** n (fam) día m de mucho calor. **~ing** a (fam) de mucho calor

score /skɔ:(r)/ n tanteo m; (mus) partitura f; (twenty) veintena f; (reason) motivo m. **on that ~** en cuanto a eso. ● vt marcar; (slash) rayar; (mus) instrumentar; conseguir ⟨success⟩. ● vi marcar un tanto; (keep score) tantear. **~ over s.o.** aventajar a. **~r** /-ə(r)/ n tanteador m

scorn /skɔ:n/ n desdén m. ● vt desdeñar. **~ful** a desdeñoso. **~fully** adv desdeñosamente

Scorpio /'skɔ:pɪəʊ/ n (astr) Escorpión m

scorpion /'skɔ:pɪən/ n escorpión m

Scot /skɒt/ *n* escocés *m*. ∼**ch** /skɒtʃ/ *a* escocés. ● *n* güisqui *m*

scotch /skɒtʃ/ *vt* frustrar; *(suppress)* suprimir

scot-free /skɒt'friː/ *a* impune; *(gratis)* sin pagar

Scot ∼**land** /'skɒtlənd/ *n* Escocia *f*. ∼**s** *a* escocés. ∼**sman** *n* escocés *m*. ∼**swoman** *n* escocesa *f*. ∼**tish** *a* escocés

scoundrel /'skaʊndrəl/ *n* canalla *f*

scour /'skaʊə(r)/ *vt* estregar; *(search)* registrar. ∼**er** *n* estropajo *m*

scourge /skɜːdʒ/ *n* azote *m*

scout /skaʊt/ *n* explorador *m*. **Boy S**∼ explorador *m*. ● *vi*. ∼ **(for)** buscar

scowl /skaʊl/ *n* ceño *m*. ● *vi* fruncir el entrecejo

scraggy /'skrægɪ/ *a* **(-ier, -iest)** descarnado

scram /skræm/ *vi (sl)* largarse

scramble /'skræmbl/ *vi (clamber)* gatear. ∼ **for** pelearse para obtener. ● *vt* revolver *(eggs)*. ● *n (difficult climb)* subida *f* difícil; *(struggle)* lucha *f*

scrap /skræp/ *n* pedacito *m*; *(fight, fam)* pelea *f*. ● *vt (pt* **scrapped)** desechar. ∼**s** *npl* sobras *fpl*

scrape /skreɪp/ *n* raspadura *f*; *(fig)* apuro *m*. ● *vt* raspar; *(graze)* arañar; *(rub)* frotar. ● *vi*. ∼ **through** lograr pasar; aprobar por los pelos *(exam)*. ∼ **together** reunir. ∼**r** /-ə(r)/ *n* raspador *m*

scrap: ∼ **heap** *n* montón *m* de deshechos. ∼**iron** *n* chatarra *f*

scrappy /'skræpɪ/ *a* fragmentario, pobre, de mala calidad

scratch /skrætʃ/ *vt* rayar; *(with nail etc)* arañar; rascar *(itch)*. ● *vi* arañar. ● *n* raya *f*; *(from nail etc)* arañazo *m*. **start from** ∼ empezar sin nada, empezar desde el principio. **up to** ∼ al nivel requerido

scrawl /skrɔːl/ *n* garrapato *m*. ● *vt/i* garrapatear

scrawny /'skrɔːnɪ/ *a* **(-ier, -iest)** descarnado

scream /skriːm/ *vt/i* gritar. ● *n* grito *m*

screech /skriːtʃ/ *vi* gritar; *(brakes etc)* chirriar. ● *n* grito *m*; *(of brakes etc)* chirrido *m*

screen /skriːn/ *n* pantalla *f*; *(folding)* biombo *m*. ● *vt (hide)* ocultar; *(protect)* proteger; proyectar *(film)*; seleccionar *(candidates)*

screw /skruː/ *n* tornillo *m*. ● *vt* atornillar. ∼**driver** /'skruːdraɪvə(r)/ *n* destornillador *m*. ∼ **up** atornillar; entornar *(eyes)*; torcer *(face)*; *(ruin, sl)* arruinar. ∼**y** /'skruːɪ/ *a* **(-ier, -iest)** *(sl)* chiflado

scribble /'skrɪbl/ *vt/i* garrapatear. ● *n* garrapato *m*

scribe /skraɪb/ *n* copista *m* & *f*

script /skrɪpt/ *n* escritura *f*; *(of film etc)* guión *m*

Scriptures /'skrɪptʃəz/ *npl* Sagradas Escrituras *fpl*

script-writer /'skrɪptraɪtə(r)/ *n* guionista *m* & *f*

scroll /skrəʊl/ *n* rollo *m* (de pergamino)

scrounge /skraʊndʒ/ *vt/i* obtener de gorra; *(steal)* birlar. ∼**r** /-ə(r)/ *n* gorrón *m*

scrub /skrʌb/ *n (land)* maleza *f*; *(clean)* fregado *m*. ● *vt/i (pt* **scrubbed)** fregar

scruff /skrʌf/ *n*. **the** ∼ **of the neck** el cogote *m*

scruffy /'skrʌfɪ/ *a* **(-ier, -iest)** desaliñado

scrum /skrʌm/ *n*, **scrummage** /'skrʌmɪdʒ/ *n (Rugby)* melée *f*

scrup||**le** /'skruːpl/ *n* escrúpulo *m*. ∼**ulous** /'skruːpjʊləs/ *a* escrupuloso. ∼**ulously** *adv* escrupulosamente

scrutin|**ize** /'skruːtɪnaɪz/ *vt* escudriñar. ∼**y** /'skruːtɪnɪ/ *n* examen *m* minucioso

scuff /skʌf/ *vt* arañar *(shoes)*

scuffle /'skʌfl/ *n* pelea *f*

scullery /'skʌlərɪ/ *n* trascocina *f*

sculpt /skʌlpt/ *vt/i* esculpir. ∼**or** *n* escultor *m*. ∼**ure** /-tʃə(r)/ *n* escultura *f*. ● *vt/i* esculpir

scum /skʌm/ *n* espuma *f*; *(people, pej)* escoria *f*

scurf /skɜːf/ *n* caspa *f*

scurrilous /'skʌrɪləs/ *a* grosero

scurry /'skʌrɪ/ *vi* correr

scurvy /'skɜːvɪ/ *n* escorbuto *m*

scuttle[1] /'skʌtl/ *n* cubo *m* del carbón

scuttle[2] /'skʌtl/ *vt* barrenar *(ship)*

scuttle[3] /'skʌtl/ *vi*. ∼ **away** correr, irse de prisa

scythe /saɪð/ *n* guadaña *f*

SE *abbr (south-east)* sudeste *m*

sea /si:/ *n* mar *m*. **at ~** en el mar; (*fig*) confuso. **by ~** por mar. **~board** /'si:bɔ:d/ *n* litoral *m*. **~farer** /'si:feərə(r)/ *n* marinero *m*. **~food** /'si:fu:d/ *n* mariscos *mpl*. **~gull** /'si:gʌl/ *n* gaviota *f*. **~horse** *n* caballito *m* de mar, hipocampo *m*

seal[1] /si:l/ *n* sello *m*. ● *vt* sellar. **~ off** acordonar ⟨*area*⟩

seal[2] /si:l/ (*animal*) foca *f*

sea level /'si:levl/ *n* nivel *m* del mar

sealing-wax /'si:lɪŋwæks/ *n* lacre *m*

sea lion /'si:laɪən/ *n* león *m* marino

seam /si:m/ *n* costura *f*; (*of coal*) veta *f*

seaman /'si:mən/ *n* (*pl* **-men**) marinero *m*

seamy /'si:mɪ/ *a*. **the ~ side** *n* el lado *m* sórdido, el revés *m*

seance /'seɪɑ:ns/ *n* sesión *f* de espiritismo

sea: **~plane** /'si:pleɪn/ *n* hidroavión *f*. **~port** /'si:pɔ:t/ *n* puerto *m* de mar

search /sɜ:tʃ/ *vt* registrar; (*examine*) examinar. ● *vi* buscar. ● *n* (*for sth*) búsqueda *f*; (*of sth*) registro *m*. **in ~ of** en busca de. **~ for** buscar. **~ing** *a* penetrante. **~party** *n* equipo *m* de salvamento. **~light** /'sɜ:tʃlaɪt/ *n* reflector *m*

sea: **~scape** /'si:skeɪp/ *n* marina *f*. **~shore** *n* orilla *f* del mar. **~sick** /'si:-sɪk/ *a* mareado. **be ~sick** marearse. **~side** /'si:saɪd/ *n* playa *f*

season /'si:zn/ *n* estación *f*; (*period*) temporada *f*. ● *vt* (*culin*) sazonar; secar ⟨*wood*⟩. **~able** *a* propio de la estación. **~al** *a* estacional. **~ed** /'si:znd/ *a* (*fig*) experto. **~ing** *n* condimento *m*. **~ticket** *n* billete *m* de abono

seat /si:t/ *n* asiento *m*; (*place*) lugar *m*; (*of trousers*) fondillos *mpl*; (*bottom*) trasero *m*. **take a ~** sentarse. ● *vt* sentar; (*have seats for*) tener asientos para. **~belt** *n* cinturón *m* de seguridad

sea: **~urchin** *n* erizo *m* de mar. **~weed** /'si:wi:d/ *n* alga *f*. **~worthy** /'si:wɜ:ðɪ/ *a* en estado de navegar

secateurs /'sekətɜ:z/ *npl* tijeras *fpl* de podar

sece|de /sɪ'si:d/ *vi* separarse. **~sion** /-eʃn/ *n* secesión *f*

seclu|de /sɪ'klu:d/ *vt* aislar. **~ded** *a* aislado. **~sion** /-ʒn/ *n* aislamiento *m*

second[1] /'sekənd/ *a & n* segundo (*m*). **on ~ thoughts** pensándolo bien.

● *adv* (*in race etc*) en segundo lugar. ● *vt* apoyar. **~s** *npl* (*goods*) artículos *mpl* de segunda calidad; (*more food, fam*) otra porción *f*

second[2] /sɪ'kɒnd/ *vt* (*transfer*) trasladar temporalmente

secondary /'sekəndrɪ/ *a* secundario. **~ school** *n* instituto *m*

second: **~best** *a* segundo. **~class** *a* de segunda clase. **~hand** *a* de segunda mano. **~ly** *adv* en segundo lugar. **~rate** *a* mediocre

secre|cy /'si:krəsɪ/ *n* secreto *m*. **~t** /'si:krɪt/ *a & n* secreto (*m*). **in ~t** en secreto

secretar|ial /sekrə'teərɪəl/ *a* de secretario. **~iat** /sekrə'teərɪət/ *n* secretaría *f*. **~y** /sekrətrɪ/ *n* secretario *m*. **S~y of State** ministro *m*: (*Amer*) Ministro *m* de Asuntos Exteriores

secret|e /sɪ'kri:t/ *vt* (*med*) secretar. **~ion** /-ʃn/ *n* secreción *f*

secretive /'si:krɪtɪv/ *a* reservado

secretly /'si:krɪtlɪ/ *adv* en secreto

sect /sekt/ *n* secta *f*. **~arian** /-'teərɪən/ *a* sectario

section /'sekʃn/ *n* sección *f*; (*part*) parte *f*

sector /'sektə(r)/ *n* sector *m*

secular /'sekjʊlə(r)/ *a* seglar

secur|e /sɪ'kjʊə(r)/ *a* seguro; (*fixed*) fijo. ● *vt* asegurar; (*obtain*) obtener. **~ely** *adv* seguramente. **~ity** /sɪ'kjʊərətɪ/ *n* seguridad *f*; (*for loan*) garantía *f*, fianza *f*

sedate /sɪ'deɪt/ *a* sosegado

sedat|ion /sɪ'deɪʃn/ *n* sedación *f*. **~ive** /'sedətɪv/ *a & n* sedante (*m*)

sedentary /'sedəntrɪ/ *a* sedentario

sediment /'sedɪmənt/ *n* sedimento *m*

seduc|e /sɪ'dju:s/ *vt* seducir. **~er** /-ə(r)/ *n* seductor *m*. **~tion** /sɪ'dʌkʃn/ *n* seducción *f*. **~tive** /-tɪv/ *a* seductor

see[1] /si:/ ● *vt* (*pt* **saw**, *pp* **seen**) ver; (*understand*) comprender; (*notice*) notar; (*escort*) acompañar. **~ing that** visto que. **~ you later!** ¡hasta luego! ● *vi* ver; (*understand*) comprender. **~ about** ocuparse de. **~ off** despedirse de. **~ through** llevar a cabo; descubrir el juego de ⟨*person*⟩. **~ to** ocuparse de

see[2] /si:/ *n* diócesis *f*

seed /si:d/ *n* semilla *f*; (*fig*) germen *m*; (*tennis*) preseleccionado *m*. **~ling**

n plantón *m*. **go to** ~ granar; (*fig*) echarse a perder. ~**y** /'si:dɪ/ *a* (**-ier, -iest**) sórdido

seek /si:k/ *vt* (*pt* **sought**) buscar. ~ **out** buscar

seem /si:m/ *vi* parecer. ~**ingly** *adv* aparentemente

seemly /'si:mlɪ/ *a* (**-ier, -iest**) correcto

seen /si:n/ *see* **see**[1]

seep /si:p/ *vi* filtrarse. ~**age** *n* filtración *f*

see-saw /'si:sɔ:/ *n* balancín *m*

seethe /si:ð/ *vi* (*fig*) hervir. **be seething with anger** estar furioso

see-through /'si:θru:/ *a* transparente

segment /'segmənt/ *n* segmento *m*; (*of orange*) gajo *m*

segregat|e /'segrɪgeɪt/ *vt* segregar. ~**ion** /-'geɪʃn/ *n* segregación *f*

seiz|e /si:z/ *vt* agarrar; (*jurid*) incautarse de. ~**e on** *vi* valerse de. ~**e up** *vi* (*tec*) agarrotarse. ~**ure** /'si:ʒə(r)/ *n* incautación *f*; (*med*) ataque *m*

seldom /'seldəm/ *adv* raramente

select /sɪ'lekt/ *vt* escoger; (*sport*) seleccionar. ● *a* selecto; (*exclusive*) exclusivo. ~**ion** /-ʃn/ *n* selección *f*. ~**ive** *a* selectivo

self /self/ *n* (*pl* **selves**) sí mismo. ~**addressed** *a* con su propia dirección. ~**assurance** *n* confianza *f* en sí mismo. ~**assured** *a* seguro de sí mismo. ~**catering** *a* con facilidades para cocinar. ~**centred** *a* egocéntrico. ~**confidence** *n* confianza *f* en sí mismo. ~**confident** *a* seguro de sí mismo. ~**conscious** *a* cohibido. ~**contained** *a* independiente. ~**control** *n* dominio *m* de sí mismo. ~**defence** *n* defensa *f* propia. ~**denial** *n* abnegación *f*. ~**employed** *a* que trabaja por cuenta propia. ~**esteem** *n* amor *m* propio. ~**evident** *a* evidente. ~**government** *n* autonomía *f*. ~**important** *a* presumido. ~**indulgent** *a* inmoderado. ~**interest** *n* interés *m* propio. ~**ish** /'selfɪʃ/ *a* egoísta. ~**ishness** *n* egoísmo *m*. ~**less** /'selflɪs/ *a* desinteresado. ~**made** *a* rico por su propio esfuerzo. ~**opinionated** *a* intransigente; (*arrogant*) engreído. ~**pity** *n* compasión *f* de sí mismo. ~**portrait** *n* autorretrato *m*. ~**possessed** *a* dueño de sí mismo. ~**reliant** *a* independiente. ~**respect** *n*

amor *m* propio. ~**righteous** *a* santurrón. ~**sacrifice** *n* abnegación *f*. ~**satisfied** *a* satisfecho de sí mismo. ~**seeking** *a* egoísta. ~**service** *a* & *n* autoservicio (*m*). ~**styled** *a* sedicente, llamado. ~**sufficient** *a* independiente. ~**willed** *a* terco

sell /sel/ *vt* (*pt* **sold**) vender. **be sold on** (*fam*) entusiasmarse por. **be sold out** estar agotado. ● *vi* venderse. ~ **by date** *n* fecha *f* de caducidad. ~ **off** *vt* liquidar. ~ **up** *vt* vender todo. ~**er** *n* vendedor *m*

Sellotape /'seləteɪp/ *n* (*P*) (papel *m*) celo *m*, cinta *f* adhesiva

sell-out /'selaʊt/ *n* (*betrayal, fam*) traición *f*

semantic /sɪ'mæntɪk/ *a* semántico. ~**s** *n* semántica *f*

semaphore /'seməfɔ:(r)/ *n* semáforo *m*

semblance /'sembləns/ *n* apariencia *f*

semen /'si:mən/ *n* semen *m*

semester /sɪ'mestə(r)/ *n* (*Amer*) semestre *m*

semi... /'semɪ/ *pref* semi...

semi|breve /'semɪbri:v/ *n* semibreve *f*, redonda *f*. ~**circle** /'semɪsɜ:kl/ *n* semicírculo *m*. ~**circular** /-'sɜ:kjʊlə(r)/ *a* semicircular. ~**colon** /semɪ'kəʊlən/ *n* punto *m* y coma. ~**detached** /semɪdɪ'tætʃt/ *a* ⟨*house*⟩ adosado. ~**final** /semɪ'faɪnl/ *n* semifinal *f*

seminar /'semɪnɑ:(r)/ *n* seminario *m*

seminary /'semɪnərɪ/ *n* (*college*) seminario *m*

semiquaver /'semɪkweɪvə(r)/ *n* (*mus*) semicorchea *f*

Semit|e /'si:maɪt/ *n* semita *m* & *f*. ~**ic** /sɪ'mɪtɪk/ *a* semítico

semolina /semə'li:nə/ *n* sémola *f*

senat|e /'senɪt/ *n* senado *m*. ~**or** /-ətə(r)/ *n* senador *m*

send /send/ *vt/i* (*pt* **sent**) enviar. ~ **away** despedir. ~ **away for** pedir (por correo). ~ **for** enviar a buscar. ~ **off for** pedir (por correo). ~ **up** (*fam*) parodiar. ~**er** *n* remitente *m*. ~**off** *n* despedida *f*

senil|e /'si:naɪl/ *a* senil. ~**ity** /sɪ'nɪlətɪ/ *n* senilidad *f*

senior /'si:nɪə(r)/ *a* mayor; (*in rank*) superior; ⟨*partner etc*⟩ principal. ● *n* mayor *m* & *f*. ~ **citizen** *n* jubilado *m*. ~**ity** /-'ɒrətɪ/ *n* antigüedad *f*

sensation /sen'seɪʃn/ n sensación f.
  ∼**al** a sensacional
sense /sens/ n sentido m; (common
  sense) juicio m; (feeling) sensación f.
  make ∼ vt tener sentido. **make** ∼ **of**
  comprender. ∼**less** a insensato;
  (med) sin sentido
sensibilities /sensɪ'bɪlətɪz/ npl sus-
  ceptibilidad f. ∼**ibility** /sensɪ'bɪlətɪ/
  n sensibilidad f
sensible /'sensəbl/ a sensato; (clothing) práctico
sensitiv|e /'sensɪtɪv/ a sensible;
  (touchy) susceptible. ∼**ity** /-'tɪvətɪ/ n
  sensibilidad f
sensory /'sensərɪ/ a sensorio
sensual /'senʃʊəl/ a sensual. ∼**ity**
  /-'ælətɪ/ n sensualidad f
sensuous /'sensʊəs/ a sensual
sent /sent/ see **send**
sentence /'sentəns/ n frase f; (jurid)
  sentencia f; (punishment) condena f.
  ● vt. ∼ **to** condenar a
sentiment /'sentɪmənt/ n sentimiento m; (opinion) opinión f. ∼**al**
  /sentɪ'mentl/ a sentimental. ∼**ality**
  /-'tælətɪ/ n sentimentalismo m
sentry /'sentrɪ/ n centinela f
separable /'sepərəbl/ a separable
separate[1] /'sepərət/ a separado;
  (independent) independiente. ∼**ly**
  adv por separado. ∼**s** npl coordina-
  dos mpl
separat|e[2] /'sepəreɪt/ vt separar. ● vi
  separarse. ∼**ion** /-'reɪʃn/ n
  separación f. ∼**ist** /'sepərətɪst/ n
  separatista m & f
September /sep'tembə(r)/ n se(p)-
  tiembre m
septic /'septɪk/ a séptico. ∼ **tank** n
  fosa f séptica
sequel /'siːkwəl/ n continuación f;
  (consequence) consecuencia f
sequence /'siːkwəns/ n sucesión f;
  (of film) secuencia f
sequin /'siːkwɪn/ n lentejuela f
serenade /serə'neɪd/ n serenata f.
  ● vt dar serenata a
seren|e /sɪ'riːn/ a sereno. ∼**ity**
  /-enətɪ/ n serenidad f
sergeant /'sɑːdʒənt/ n sargento m
serial /'sɪərɪəl/ n serial m. ● a de
  serie. ∼**ize** vt publicar por entregas
series /'sɪərɪːz/ n serie f
serious /'sɪərɪəs/ a serio. ∼**ly** adv
  seriamente; (ill) gravemente. **take**
  ∼**ly** tomar en serio. ∼**ness** n
  seriedad f

sermon /'sɜːmən/ n sermón m
serpent /'sɜːpənt/ n serpiente f
serrated /sɪ'reɪtɪd/ a serrado
serum /'sɪərəm/ n (pl -a) suero m
servant /'sɜːvənt/ n criado m; (fig)
  servidor m
serve /sɜːv/ vt servir; (in the army
  etc) prestar servicio; cumplir ⟨sen-
  tence⟩. ∼ **as** servir de. ∼ **its purpose**
  servir para el caso. **it** ∼**s you right**
  ¡bien te lo mereces! ¡te está bien
  merecido! ● vi servir. ● n (in tennis)
  saque m
service /'sɜːvɪs/ n servicio m; (maintenance) revisión f. **of** ∼ **to** útil a.
  ● vt revisar ⟨car etc⟩. ∼**able** /'sɜː-
  vɪsəbl/ a práctico; (durable) duradero. ∼ **charge** n servicio m. ∼**man**
  /'sɜːvɪsmən/ n (pl -**men**) militar m.
  ∼**s** npl (mil) fuerzas fpl armadas. ∼
  station n estación f de servicio
serviette /sɜːvɪ'et/ n servilleta f
servile /'sɜːvaɪl/ a servil
session /'seʃn/ n sesión f; (univ)
  curso m
set /set/ vt (pt **set**, pres p **setting**)
  poner; poner en hora ⟨clock etc⟩; fijar
  ⟨limit etc⟩; (typ) componer. ∼ **fire to**
  pegar fuego a. ∼ **free** vt poner en
  libertad. ● vi ⟨sun⟩ ponerse; ⟨jelly⟩
  cuajarse. ● n serie f; (of cutlery etc)
  juego m; (tennis) set m; (TV, radio)
  aparato m; (of hair) marcado m; (in
  theatre) decorado m; (of people)
  círculo m. ● a fijo. **be** ∼ **on** estar
  resuelto a. ∼ **about** vi empezar a. ∼
  back vt (delay) retardar; (cost, sl)
  costar. ∼ **off** vi salir. ● vt (make
  start) poner en marcha; hacer estallar ⟨bomb⟩. ∼ **out** vi (declare) declarar; (leave) salir. ∼ **sail** salir. ∼
  the table poner la mesa. ∼ **up** vt establecer. ∼**back** n revés m. ∼
  square n escuadra f de dibujar
settee /se'tiː/ n sofá m
setting /'setɪŋ/ n (of sun) puesta f;
  (of jewel) engaste m; (in theatre)
  escenario m; (typ) composición f. ∼
  -**lotion** n fijador m
settle /'setl/ vt (arrange) arreglar;
  (pay) pagar; fijar ⟨date⟩; calmar
  ⟨nerves⟩. ● vi (come to rest) posarse;
  (live) instalarse. ∼ **down** calmarse;
  (become orderly) sentar la cabeza. ∼
  for aceptar. ∼ **up** ajustar cuentas.
  ∼**ment** /'setlmənt/ n establecimiento m; (agreement) acuerdo m;

(*com*) liquidación *f*; (*place*) colonia *f*. ~**r** /-ə(r)/ *n* colonizador *m*

set: ~**-to** *n* pelea *f*. ~**-up** *n* (*fam*) sistema *m*

seven /'sevn/ *a & n* siete (*m*). ~**teen** /sevn'tiːn/ *a & n* diecisiete (*m*). ~**teenth** *a & n* decimoséptimo (*m*). ~**th** *a & n* séptimo (*m*). ~**tieth** *a & n* setenta (*m*), septuagésimo (*m*). ~**ty** /'sevntɪ/ *a & n* setenta (*m*)

sever /'sevə(r)/ *vt* cortar; (*fig*) romper

several /'sevrəl/ *a & pron* varios

severance /'sevərəns/ *n* (*breaking off*) ruptura *f*

sever|e /sɪ'vɪə(r)/ *a* (**-er, -est**) severo; (*violent*) violento; (*serious*) grave; (*weather*) riguroso. ~**ely** *adv* severamente; (*seriously*) gravemente. ~**ity** /-'verətɪ/ *n* severidad *f*; (*violence*) violencia *f*; (*seriousness*) gravedad *f*

sew /səʊ/ *vt/i* (*pt* sewed, *pp* sewn, *or* sewed) coser

sew|age /'suːɪdʒ/ *n* aguas *fpl* residuales. ~**er** /'suːə(r)/ *n* cloaca *f*

sewing /'səʊɪŋ/ *n* costura *f*. ~**machine** *n* máquina *f* de coser

sewn /səʊn/ *see* **sew**

sex /seks/ *n* sexo *m*. have ~ tener relaciones sexuales. ● *a* sexual. ~**ist** /'seksɪst/ *a & n* sexista (*m & f*)

sextet /seks'tet/ *n* sexteto *m*

sexual /'seksjʊəl/ *a* sexual. ~ **intercourse** *n* relaciones *fpl* sexuales. ~**ity** /-'ælətɪ/ *n* sexualidad *f*

sexy /'seksɪ/ *a* (**-ier, -iest**) excitante, sexy, provocativo

shabb|ily /'ʃæbɪlɪ/ *adv* pobremente; (*act*) mezquinamente. ~**iness** *n* pobreza *f*; (*meanness*) mezquindad *f*. ~**y** /'ʃæbɪ/ *a* (**-ier, -iest**) (*clothes*) gastado; (*person*) pobremente vestido; (*mean*) mezquino

shack /ʃæk/ *n* choza *f*

shackles /'ʃæklz/ *npl* grillos *mpl*, grilletes *mpl*

shade /ʃeɪd/ *n* sombra *f*; (*of colour*) matiz *m*; (*for lamp*) pantalla *f*. **a ~ better** un poquito mejor. ● *vt* dar sombra a

shadow /'ʃædəʊ/ *n* sombra *f*. **S~ Cabinet** *n* gobierno *m* en la sombra. ● *vt* (*follow*) seguir. ~**y** *a* (*fig*) vago

shady /'ʃeɪdɪ/ *a* (**-ier, -iest**) sombreado; (*fig*) dudoso

shaft /ʃɑːft/ *n* (*of arrow*) astil *m*; (*mec*) eje *m*; (*of light*) rayo *m*; (*of lift, mine*) pozo *m*

shaggy /'ʃægɪ/ *a* (**-ier, -iest**) peludo

shak|e /ʃeɪk/ *vt* (*pt* shook, *pp* shaken) sacudir; agitar (*bottle*); (*shock*) desconcertar. ~**e hands with** estrechar la mano a. ● *vi* temblar. ~**e off** *vi* deshacerse de. ● *n* sacudida *f*. ~**e-up** *n* reorganización *f*. ~**y** /'ʃeɪkɪ/ *a* (**-ier, -iest**) tembloroso; (*table etc*) inestable; (*unreliable*) incierto

shall /ʃæl/ *v aux* (*first person in future tense*). **I ~ go** iré. **we ~ see** veremos

shallot /ʃə'lɒt/ *n* chalote *m*

shallow /'ʃæləʊ/ *a* (**-er, -est**) poco profundo; (*fig*) superficial

sham /ʃæm/ *n* farsa *f*; (*person*) impostor *m*. ● *a* falso; (*affected*) fingido. ● *vt* (*pt* shammed) fingir

shambles /'ʃæmblz/ *npl* (*mess, fam*) desorden *m* total

shame /ʃeɪm/ *n* vergüenza *f*. **what a ~!** ¡qué lástima! ● *vt* avergonzar. ~**faced** /'ʃeɪmfeɪst/ *a* avergonzado. ~**ful** *a* vergonzoso. ~**fully** *adv* vergonzosamente. ~**less** *a* desvergonzado

shampoo /ʃæm'puː/ *n* champú *m*. ● *vt* lavar

shamrock /'ʃæmrɒk/ *n* trébol *m*

shandy /'ʃændɪ/ *n* cerveza *f* con gaseosa, clara *f*

shan't /ʃɑːnt/ = **shall not**

shanty /'ʃæntɪ/ *n* chabola *f*. ~ **town** *n* chabolas *fpl*

shape /ʃeɪp/ *n* forma *f*. ● *vt* formar; determinar (*future*). ● *vi* formarse. ~ **up** prometer. ~**less** *a* informe. ~**ly** /'ʃeɪplɪ/ *a* (**-ier, -iest**) bien proporcionado

share /ʃeə(r)/ *n* porción *f*; (*com*) acción *f*. **go ~s** compartir. ● *vt* compartir; (*divide*) dividir. ● *vi* participar. ~ **in** participar en. ~**holder** /'ʃeəhəʊldə(r)/ *n* accionista *m & f*. ~**out** *n* reparto *m*

shark /ʃɑːk/ *n* tiburón *m*; (*fig*) estafador *m*

sharp /ʃɑːp/ *a* (**-er, -est**) (*knife etc*) afilado; (*pin etc*) puntiagudo; (*pain, sound*) agudo; (*taste*) acre; (*sudden, harsh*) brusco; (*well defined*) marcado; (*dishonest*) poco escrupuloso; (*clever*) listo. ● *adv* en punto. **at seven o'clock** ~ a las siete en punto. ● *n* (*mus*) sostenido *m*. ~**en** /'ʃɑːpn/ *vt* afilar; sacar punta a (*pencil*).

~ener *n* (*mec*) afilador *m*; (*for pencils*) sacapuntas *m invar.* **~ly** *adv* bruscamente

shatter /'ʃætə(r)/ *vt* hacer añicos; (*upset*) perturbar. ● *vi* hacerse añicos. **~ed** *a* (*exhausted*) agotado

shav|e /ʃeɪv/ *vt* afeitar. ● *vi* afeitarse. ● *n* afeitado *m*. **have a ~e** afeitarse. **~en** *a* (*face*) afeitado; (*head*) rapado. **~er** *n* maquinilla *f* (de afeitar). **~ing-brush** *n* brocha *f* de afeitar. **~ing-cream** *n* crema *f* de afeitar

shawl /ʃɔ:l/ *n* chal *m*

she /ʃi:/ *pron* ella. ● *n* hembra *f*

sheaf /ʃi:f/ *n* (*pl* **sheaves**) gavilla *f*

shear /ʃɪə(r)/ *vt* (*pp* **shorn**, *or* **sheared**) esquilar. **~s** /ʃɪəz/ *npl* tijeras *fpl* grandes

sheath /ʃi:θ/ *n* (*pl* **-s** /ʃi:ðz/) vaina *f*; (*contraceptive*) condón *m*. **~e** /ʃi:ð/ *vt* envainar

shed[1] /ʃed/ *n* cobertizo *m*

shed[2] /ʃed/ *vt* (*pt* **shed**, *pres p* **shedding**) perder; derramar (*tears*); despojarse de (*clothes*). **~ light on** aclarar

sheen /ʃi:n/ *n* lustre *m*

sheep /ʃi:p/ *n invar* oveja *f*. **~-dog** *n* perro *m* pastor. **~ish** /ʃi:pɪʃ/ *a* vergonzoso. **~ishly** *adv* tímidamente. **~skin** /ʃi:pskɪn/ *n* piel *f* de carnero, zamarra *f*

sheer /ʃɪə(r)/ *a* puro; (*steep*) perpendicular; (*fabric*) muy fino. ● *adv* a pico

sheet /ʃi:t/ *n* sábana *f*; (*of paper*) hoja *f*; (*of glass*) lámina *f*; (*of ice*) capa *f*

sheikh /ʃeɪk/ *n* jeque *m*

shelf /ʃelf/ *n* (*pl* **shelves**) estante *m*. **be on the ~** quedarse para vestir santos

shell /ʃel/ *n* concha *f*; (*of egg*) cáscara *f*; (*of building*) casco *m*; (*explosive*) proyectil *m*. ● *vt* desgranar (*peas etc*); (*mil*) bombardear. **~fish** /'ʃelfɪʃ/ *n invar* (*crustacean*) crustáceo *m*; (*mollusc*) marisco *m*

shelter /'ʃeltə(r)/ *n* refugio *m*, abrigo *m*. ● *vt* abrigar; (*protect*) proteger; (*give lodging to*) dar asilo a. ● *vi* abrigarse. **~ed** *a* (*spot*) abrigado; (*life etc*) protegido

shelv|e /ʃelv/ *vt* (*fig*) dar carpetazo a. **~ing** /ʃelvɪŋ/ *n* estantería *f*

shepherd /'ʃepəd/ *n* pastor *m*. ● *vt* guiar. **~ess** /-'des/ *n* pastora *f*. **~'s pie** *n* carne *f* picada con puré de patatas

sherbet /'ʃɜ:bət/ *n* (*Amer, water-ice*) sorbete *m*

sheriff /'ʃerɪf/ *n* alguacil *m*, sheriff *m*

sherry /'ʃerɪ/ *n* (vino *m* de) jerez *m*

shield /ʃi:ld/ *n* escudo *m*. ● *vt* proteger

shift /ʃɪft/ *vt* cambiar; cambiar de sitio (*furniture etc*); echar (*blame etc*). ● *n* cambio *m*; (*work*) turno *m*; (*workers*) tanda *f*. **make ~** arreglárselas. **~less** /'ʃɪftlɪs/ *a* holgazán

shifty /'ʃɪftɪ/ *a* (**-ier, -iest**) taimado

shilling /'ʃɪlɪŋ/ *n* chelín *m*

shilly-shally /'ʃɪlɪʃælɪ/ *vi* titubear

shimmer /'ʃɪmə(r)/ *vi* rielar, relucir. ● *n* luz *f* trémula

shin /ʃɪn/ *n* espinilla *f*

shine /ʃaɪn/ *vi* (*pt* **shone**) brillar. ● *vt* sacar brillo a. **~ on** dirigir (*torch*). ● *n* brillo *m*

shingle /'ʃɪŋgl/ *n* (*pebbles*) guijarros *mpl*

shingles /'ʃɪŋglz/ *npl* (*med*) herpes *mpl* & *fpl*

shiny /'ʃaɪnɪ/ *a* (**-ier, -iest**) brillante

ship /ʃɪp/ *n* buque *m*, barco *m*. ● *vt* (*pt* **shipped**) transportar; (*send*) enviar; (*load*) embarcar. **~building** /'ʃɪpbɪldɪŋ/ *n* construcción *f* naval. **~ment** *n* envío *m*. **~per** *n* expedidor *m*. **~ping** *n* envío *m*; (*ships*) barcos *mpl*. **~shape** /'ʃɪpʃeɪp/ *adv* & *a* en buen orden, en regla. **~wreck** /'ʃɪprek/ *n* naufragio *m*. **~wrecked** *a* naufragado. **be ~wrecked** naufragar. **~yard** /'ʃɪpja:d/ *n* astillero *m*

shirk /ʃɜ:k/ *vt* esquivar. **~er** *n* gandul *m*

shirt /ʃɜ:t/ *n* camisa *f*. **in ~-sleeves** en mangas de camisa. **~y** /'ʃɜ:tɪ/ *a* (*sl*) enfadado

shiver /'ʃɪvə(r)/ *vi* temblar. ● *n* escalofrío *m*

shoal /ʃəʊl/ *n* banco *m*

shock /ʃɒk/ *n* sacudida *f*; (*fig*) susto *m*; (*elec*) descarga *f*; (*med*) choque *m*. ● *vt* escandalizar. **~ing** *a* escandaloso; (*fam*) espantoso. **~ingly** *adv* terriblemente

shod /ʃɒd/ *see* **shoe**

shodd|ily /'ʃɒdɪlɪ/ *adv* mal. **~y** /'ʃɒdɪ/ *a* (**-ier, -iest**) mal hecho, de pacotilla

shoe /ʃu:/ *n* zapato *m*; (*of horse*) herradura *f*. ● *vt* (*pt* **shod**, *pres p* **shoeing**) herrar (*horse*). **be well shod** estar bien calzado. **~horn** /'ʃu:hɔ:n/

n calzador *m*. **~‑lace** *n* cordón *m* de zapato. **~maker** /'ʃuːmeɪkə(r)/ *n* zapatero *m*. **~polish** *n* betún *m*. **~string** *n*. **on a ~string** con poco dinero. **~tree** *n* horma *f*

shone /ʃɒn/ *see* **shine**

shoo /ʃuː/ *vt* ahuyentar

shook /ʃʊk/ *see* **shake**

shoot /ʃuːt/ *vt* (*pt* **shot**) disparar; rodar ⟨*film*⟩. ● *vi* ⟨*hunt*⟩ cazar. ● *n* ⟨*bot*⟩ retoño *m*; ⟨*hunt*⟩ cacería *f*. **~ down** *vt* derribar. **~ out** *vi* ⟨*rush*⟩ salir disparado. **~ up** ⟨*prices*⟩ subir de repente; ⟨*grow*⟩ crecer. **~ing‑range** *n* campo *m* de tiro

shop /ʃɒp/ *n* tienda *f*; ⟨*work‑shop*⟩ taller *m*. **talk ~** hablar de su trabajo. ● *vi* (*pt* **shopping**) hacer compras. **~ around** buscar el mejor precio. **go ~ping** ir de compras. **~ assistant** *n* dependiente *m*. **~keeper** /'ʃɒpkiːpə(r)/ *n* tendero *m*. **~lifter** *n* ratero *m* (de tiendas). **~lifting** *n* ratería *f* (de tiendas). **~per** *n* comprador *m*. **~ping** /'ʃɒpɪŋ/ *n* compras *fpl*. **~ping bag** *n* bolsa *f* de la compra. **~ping centre** *n* centro *m* comercial. **~ steward** *n* enlace *m* sindical. **~window** *n* escaparate *m*

shore /ʃɔː(r)/ *n* orilla *f*

shorn /ʃɔːn/ *see* **shear**

short /ʃɔːt/ *a* (**‑er, ‑est**) corto; (*not lasting*) breve; ⟨*person*⟩ bajo; (*curt*) brusco. **a ~ time ago** hace poco. **be ~ of** necesitar. **Mick is ~ for Michael** Mick es el diminutivo de Michael. ● *adv* (*stop*) en seco. **~ of doing** a menos que no hagamos. ● *n*. **in ~** en resumen. **~age** /'ʃɔːtɪdʒ/ *n* escasez *f*. **~bread** /'ʃɔːtbred/ *n* galleta *f* de mantequilla. **~change** *vt* estafar, engañar. **~ circuit** *n* cortocircuito *m*. **~coming** /'ʃɔːtkʌmɪŋ/ *n* deficiencia *f*. **~ cut** *n* atajo *m*. **~en** /'ʃɔːtn/ *vt* acortar. **~hand** /'ʃɔːthænd/ *n* taquigrafía *f*. **~hand typist** *n* taquimecanógrafo *m*, taquimeca *f* (*fam*). **~lived** *a* efímero. **~ly** /'ʃɔːtlɪ/ *adv* dentro de poco. **~s** *npl* pantalón *m* corto. **~sighted** *a* miope. **~tempered** *a* de mal genio

shot /ʃɒt/ *see* **shoot**. ● *n* tiro *m*; (*person*) tirador *m*; (*photo*) foto *f*; (*injection*) inyección *f*. **like a ~** como una bala; (*willingly*) de buena gana. **~gun** *n* escopeta *f*

should /ʃʊd, ʃəd/ *v aux*. **I ~ go** debería ir. **I ~ have seen him** debiera haberlo visto. **I ~ like** me gustaría. **if he ~ come** si viniese

shoulder /'ʃəʊldə(r)/ *n* hombro *m*. ● *vt* cargar con ⟨*responsibility*⟩; llevar a hombros ⟨*burden*⟩. **~‑blade** *n* omóplato *m*. **~‑strap** *n* correa *f* del hombro; (*of bra etc*) tirante *m*

shout /ʃaʊt/ *n* grito *m*. ● *vt/i* gritar. **~ at s.o.** gritarle a uno. **~ down** hacer callar a gritos

shove /ʃʌv/ *n* empujón *m*. ● *vt* empujar; (*put, fam*) poner. ● *vi* empujar. **~ off** *vi* (*fam*) largarse

shovel /'ʃʌvl/ *n* pala *f*. ● *vt* (*pt* **shovelled**) mover con la pala

show /ʃəʊ/ *vt* (*pt* **showed**, *pp* **shown**) mostrar; (*put on display*) exponer; poner ⟨*film*⟩. ● *vi* (*be visible*) verse. ● *n* demostración *f*; (*exhibition*) exposición *f*; (*ostentation*) pompa *f*; (*in theatre*) espectáculo *m*; (*in cinema*) sesión *f*. **on ~** expuesto. **~ off** *vt* lucir; (*pej*) ostentar. ● *vi* presumir. **~ up** *vi* destacar; (*be present*) presentarse. ● *vt* (*unmask*) desenmascarar. **~case** *n* vitrina *f*. **~down** *n* confrontación *f*

shower /'ʃaʊə(r)/ *n* chaparrón *m*; (*of blows etc*) lluvia *f*; (*for washing*) ducha *f*. **have a ~** ducharse. ● *vi* ducharse. ● *vt*. **~ with** colmar de. **~proof** /'ʃaʊəpruːf/ *a* impermeable. **~y** *a* lluvioso

show: **~jumping** *n* concurso *m* hípico. **~manship** /'ʃəʊmənʃɪp/ *n* teatralidad *f*, arte *f* de presentar espectáculos

shown /ʃəʊn/ *see* **show**

show: **~‑off** *n* fanfarrón *m*. **~place** *n* lugar *m* de interés turístico. **~room** /'ʃəʊruːm/ *n* sala *f* de exposición *f*

showy /'ʃəʊɪ/ *a* (**‑ier, ‑iest**) llamativo; ⟨*person*⟩ ostentoso

shrank /ʃræŋk/ *see* **shrink**

shrapnel /'ʃræpnəl/ *n* metralla *f*

shred /ʃred/ *n* pedazo *m*; (*fig*) pizca *f*. ● *vt* (*pt* **shredded**) hacer tiras; (*culin*) cortar en tiras. **~der** *n* desfibradora *f*, trituradora *f*

shrew /ʃruː/ *n* musaraña *f*; (*woman*) arpía *f*

shrewd /ʃruːd/ *a* (**‑er, ‑est**) astuto. **~ness** *n* astucia *f*

shriek /ʃriːk/ *n* chillido *m*. ● *vt/i* chillar

shrift /ʃrɪft/ *n.* give s.o. short ∼ despachar a uno con brusquedad

shrill /ʃrɪl/ *a* agudo

shrimp /ʃrɪmp/ *n* camarón *m*

shrine /ʃraɪn/ *n* (*place*) lugar *m* santo; (*tomb*) sepulcro *m*

shrink /ʃrɪŋk/ *vt* (*pt* **shrank**, *pp* **shrunk**) encoger. ● *vi* encogerse; (*draw back*) retirarse; (*lessen*) disminuir. ∼**age** *n* encogimiento *m*

shrivel /ʃrɪvl/ *vi* (*pt* **shrivelled**) (*dry up*) secarse; (*become wrinkled*) arrugarse

shroud /ʃraʊd/ *n* sudario *m*; (*fig*) velo *m*. ● *vt* (*veil*) velar

Shrove /ʃrəʊv/ *n.* ∼ **Tuesday** *n* martes *m* de carnaval

shrub /ʃrʌb/ *n* arbusto *m*

shrug /ʃrʌg/ *vt* (*pt* **shrugged**) encogerse de hombros. ● *n* encogimiento *m* de hombros

shrunk /ʃrʌŋk/ *see* **shrink**

shrunken /ʃrʌŋkən/ *a* encogido

shudder /ʃʌdə(r)/ *vi* estremecerse. ● *n* estremecimiento *m*

shuffle /ʃʌfl/ *vi* arrastrar los pies. ● *vt* barajar (*cards*). ● *n* arrastramiento *m* de los pies; (*of cards*) barajadura *f*

shun /ʃʌn/ *vt* (*pt* **shunned**) evitar

shunt /ʃʌnt/ *vt* apartar, desviar

shush /ʃʊʃ/ *int* ¡chitón!

shut /ʃʌt/ *vt* (*pt* **shut**, *pres p* **shutting**) cerrar. ● *vi* cerrarse. ∼ **down** cerrar. ∼ **up** *vt* cerrar; (*fam*) hacer callar. ● *vi* callarse. ∼**down** *n* cierre *m*. ∼**ter** /ʃʌtə(r)/ *n* contraventana *f*; (*photo*) obturador *m*

shuttle /ʃʌtl/ *n* lanzadera *f*; (*train*) tren *m* de enlace. ● *vt* transportar. ● *vi* ir y venir. ∼**cock** /ʃʌtlkɒk/ *n* volante *m*. ∼ **service** *n* servicio *m* de enlace

shy /ʃaɪ/ *a* (**-er**, **-est**) tímido. ● *vi* (*pt* **shied**) asustarse. ∼ **away from** huir. ∼**ness** *n* timidez *f*

Siamese /saɪə'miːz/ *a* siamés

sibling /sɪblɪŋ/ *n* hermano *m*, hermana *f*

Sicil|ian /sɪ'sɪljən/ *a* & *n* siciliano (*m*). ∼**y** /sɪsɪlɪ/ *n* Sicilia *f*

sick /sɪk/ *a* enfermo; (*humour*) negro; (*fed up, fam*) harto. **be** ∼ (*vomit*) vomitar. **be** ∼ **of** (*fig*) estar harto de. **feel** ∼ sentir náuseas. ∼**en** /sɪkən/ *vt* dar asco. ● *vi* caer enfermo. **be** ∼**ening for** incubar

sickle /sɪkl/ *n* hoz *f*

sick /sɪk/: ∼**ly** /sɪklɪ/ *a* (**-ier**, **-iest**) enfermizo; (*taste, smell etc*) nauseabundo. ∼**ness** /sɪknɪs/ *n* enfermedad *f*. ∼ **room** *n* cuarto *m* del enfermo

side /saɪd/ *n* lado *m*; (*of river*) orilla *f*; (*of hill*) ladera *f*; (*team*) equipo *m*; (*fig*) parte *f*. ∼ **by** ∼ uno al lado del otro. **on the** ∼ (*sideline*) como actividad secundaria; (*secretly*) a escondidas. ● *a* lateral. ● *vi.* ∼ **with** tomar el partido de. ∼**board** /saɪdbɔːd/ *n* aparador *m*. ∼**boards** *npl*, ∼**burns** *npl* (*sl*) patillas *fpl*. ∼**car** *n* sidecar *m*. ∼**effect** *n* efecto *m* secundario. ∼**light** /saɪdlaɪt/ *n* luz *f* de posición. ∼**line** /saɪdlaɪn/ *n* actividad *f* secundaria. ∼**long** /-lɒŋ/ *a* & *adv* de soslayo. ∼**road** *n* calle *f* secundaria. ∼**saddle** *n* silla *f* de mujer. **ride** ∼**saddle** *adv* a mujeriegas. ∼**show** *n* atracción *f* secundaria. ∼**step** *vt* evitar. ∼**track** *vt* desviar del asunto. ∼**walk** /saɪdwɔːk/ *n* (*Amer*) acera *f*, vereda *f* (*LAm*). ∼**ways** /saɪdweɪz/ *a* & *adv* de lado. ∼**whiskers** *npl* patillas *fpl*

siding /saɪdɪŋ/ *n* apartadero *m*

sidle /saɪdl/ *vi* avanzar furtivamente. ∼ **up to** acercarse furtivamente

siege /siːdʒ/ *n* sitio *m*, cerco *m*

siesta /sɪ'estə/ *n* siesta *f*

sieve /sɪv/ *n* cernedor *m*. ● *vt* cerner

sift /sɪft/ *vt* cerner. ● *vi.* ∼ **through** examinar

sigh /saɪ/ *n* suspiro *m*. ● *vi* suspirar

sight /saɪt/ *n* vista *f*; (*spectacle*) espectáculo *m*; (*on gun*) mira *f*. **at** (**first**) ∼ a primera vista. **catch** ∼ **of** vislumbrar. **lose** ∼ **of** perder de vista. **on** ∼ a primera vista. **within** ∼ **of** (*near*) cerca de. ● *vt* ver, divisar. ∼**seeing** /saɪtsiːɪŋ/ *n* visita *f* turística. ∼**seer** /-ə(r)/ *n* turista *m* & *f*

sign /saɪn/ *n* señal *f*. ● *vt* firmar. ∼ **on**, ∼ **up** *vt* inscribir. ● *vi* inscribirse

signal /sɪgnəl/ *n* señal *f*. ● *vt* (*pt* **signalled**) comunicar; hacer señas a (*person*). ∼**box** *n* casilla *f* del guardavía. ∼**man** /sɪgnəlmən/ *n* (*pl* **-men**) guardavía *f*

signatory /sɪgnətrɪ/ *n* firmante *m* & *f*

signature /sɪgnətʃə(r)/ *n* firma *f*. ∼ **tune** *n* sintonía *f*

signet-ring /sɪgnɪtrɪŋ/ *n* anillo *m* de sello

significan|ce /sɪg'nɪfɪkəns/ n significado m. **~t** /sɪg'nɪfɪkənt/ a significativo; (important) importante. **~tly** adv significativamente

signify /'sɪgnɪfaɪ/ vt significar. ● vi (matter) importar, tener importancia

signpost /'saɪnpəʊst/ n poste m indicador

silen|ce /'saɪləns/ n silencio m. ● vt hacer callar. **~cer** /-ə(r)/ n silenciador m. **~t** /'saɪlənt/ a silencioso; (film) mudo. **~tly** adv silenciosamente

silhouette /sɪlu:'et/ n silueta f. ● vt. **be ~d** perfilarse, destacarse (against contra)

silicon /'sɪlɪkən/ n silicio m. **~ chip** n pastilla f de silicio

silk /sɪlk/ n seda f. **~en** a, **~y** a (of silk) de seda; (like silk) sedoso. **~worm** n gusano m de seda

sill /sɪl/ n antepecho m; (of window) alféizar m; (of door) umbral m

silly /'sɪlɪ/ a (-ier, -iest) tonto. ● n. **~billy** (fam) tonto m

silo /'saɪləʊ/ n (pl -os) silo m

silt /sɪlt/ n sedimento m

silver /'sɪlvə(r)/ n plata f. ● a de plata. **~ plated** a bañado en plata, plateado. **~side** /'sɪlvəsaɪd/ n (culin) contra f. **~smith** /'sɪlvəsmɪθ/ n platero m. **~ware** /'sɪlvəweə(r)/ n plata f. **~ wedding** n bodas fpl de plata. **~y** a plateado; (sound) argentino

simil|ar /'sɪmɪlə(r)/ a parecido. **~arity** /-ɪ'lærətɪ/ n parecido m. **~arly** adv de igual manera

simile /'sɪmɪlɪ/ n símil m

simmer /'sɪmə(r)/ vt/i hervir a fuego lento; (fig) hervir. **~ down** calmarse

simpl|e /'sɪmpl/ a (-er, -est) sencillo; (person) ingenuo. **~e-minded** a ingenuo. **~eton** /'sɪmpltən/ n simplón m. **~icity** /-'plɪsetɪ/ n sencillez f. **~ification** /-ɪ'keɪʃn/ n simplificación f. **~ify** /'sɪmplɪfaɪ/ vt simplificar. **~y** adv sencillamente; (absolutely) absolutamente

simulat|e /'sɪmjʊleɪt/ vt simular. **~ion** /-'leɪʃn/ n simulación f

simultaneous /sɪml'teɪnɪəs/ a simultáneo. **~ly** adv simultáneamente

sin /sɪn/ n pecado m. ● vi (pt sinned) pecar

since /sɪns/ prep desde. ● adv desde entonces. ● conj desde que; (because) ya que

sincer|e /sɪn'sɪə(r)/ a sincero. **~ely** adv sinceramente. **~ity** /-'serətɪ/ n sinceridad f

sinew /'sɪnju:/ n tendón m. **~s** npl músculos mpl

sinful /'sɪnfl/ a pecaminoso; (shocking) escandaloso

sing /sɪŋ/ vt/i (pt sang, pp sung) cantar

singe /sɪndʒ/ vt (pres p singeing) chamuscar

singer /'sɪŋə(r)/ n cantante m & f

singl|e /'sɪŋgl/ a único; (not double) sencillo; (unmarried) soltero; (bed, room) individual. ● n (tennis) juego m individual; (ticket) billete m sencillo. ● vt. **~e out** escoger; (distinguish) distinguir. **~e-handed** a & adv sin ayuda. **~e-minded** a resuelto

singlet /'sɪŋglɪt/ n camiseta f

singly /'sɪŋglɪ/ adv uno a uno

singsong /'sɪŋsɒŋ/ a monótono. ● n. **have a ~** cantar juntos

singular /'sɪŋgjʊlə(r)/ n singular f. ● a singular; (uncommon) raro; (noun) en singular. **~ly** adv singularmente

sinister /'sɪnɪstə(r)/ a siniestro

sink /sɪŋk/ vt (pt sank, pp sunk) hundir; perforar (well); invertir (money). ● vi hundirse; (patient) debilitarse. ● n fregadero m. **~ in** vi penetrar

sinner /'sɪnə(r)/ n pecador m

sinuous /'sɪnjuəs/ a sinuoso

sinus /'saɪnəs/ n (pl -uses) seno m

sip /sɪp/ n sorbo m. ● vt (pt sipped) sorber

siphon /'saɪfən/ n sifón m. vt. **~ out** sacar con sifón

sir /sɜ:(r)/ n señor m. **S~** n (title) sir m

siren /'saɪərən/ n sirena f

sirloin /'sɜ:lɔɪn/ n solomillo m, lomo m bajo

sirocco /sɪ'rɒkəʊ/ n siroco m

sissy /'sɪsɪ/ n hombre m afeminado, marica m, mariquita m; (coward) gallina m & f

sister /'sɪstə(r)/ n hermana f; (nurse) enfermera f jefe. **S~ Mary** Sor María. **~-in-law** n (pl **~s-in-law**) cuñada f. **~ly** a de hermana; (like sister) como hermana

sit /sɪt/ vt (pt **sat**, pres p **sitting**) sentar. ● vi sentarse; ⟨committee etc⟩ reunirse. **be ~ting** estar sentado. **~ back** vi (fig) relajarse. **~ down** vi sentarse. **~ for** vi presentarse a ⟨exam⟩; posar para ⟨portrait⟩. **~ up** vi enderezarse; (stay awake) velar. **~-in** n ocupación f

site /saɪt/ n sitio m. **building ~** n solar m. ● vt situar

sit: **~ting** n sesión f; (in restaurant) turno m. **~ting-room** n cuarto m de estar

situat|e /'sɪtjʊeɪt/ vt situar. **~ed** a situado. **~ion** /-'eɪʃn/ n situación f; (job) puesto m

six /sɪks/ a & n seis (m). **~teen** /sɪk'stiːn/ a & n dieciséis (m). **~teenth** a & n decimosexto (m). **~th** a & n sexto (m). **~tieth** a & n sesenta (m), sexagésimo (m). **~ty** /'sɪkstɪ/ a & n sesenta (m)

size /saɪz/ n tamaño m; (of clothes) talla f; (of shoes) número m; (extent) magnitud f. ● vt. **~ up** (fam) juzgar. **~able** a bastante grande

sizzle /'sɪzl/ vi crepitar

skate¹ /skeɪt/ n patín m. ● vi patinar. **~board** /'skeɪtbɔːd/ n monopatín m. **~r** n patinador m

skate² /skeɪt/ n invar (fish) raya f

skating /'skeɪtɪŋ/ n patinaje m. **~rink** n pista f de patinaje

skein /skeɪn/ n madeja f

skelet|al /'skelɪtl/ a esquelético. **~on** /'skelɪtn/ n esqueleto m. **~on staff** n personal m reducido

sketch /sketʃ/ n esbozo m; (drawing) dibujo m; (in theatre) pieza f corta y divertida. ● vt esbozar. ● vi dibujar. **~y** /'sketʃɪ/ a (-ier, -iest) incompleto

skew /skju:/ n. **on the ~** sesgado

skewer /'skju:ə(r)/ n broqueta f

ski /ski:/ n (pl **skis**) esquí m. ● vi (pt **skied**, pres p **skiing**) esquiar. **go ~ing** ir a esquiar

skid /skɪd/ vi (pt **skidded**) patinar. ● n patinazo m

ski: **~er** n esquiador m. **~ing** n esquí m

skilful /'skɪlfl/ a diestro

ski-lift /'ski:lɪft/ n telesquí m

skill /skɪl/ n destreza f, habilidad f. **~ed** a hábil; ⟨worker⟩ cualificado

skim /skɪm/ vt (pt **skimmed**) espumar; desnatar ⟨milk⟩; (glide over) rozar. **~ over** vt rasar. **~ through** vi hojear

skimp /skɪmp/ vt escatimar. **~y** /'skɪmpɪ/ a (-ier, -iest) insuficiente; ⟨skirt, dress⟩ corto

skin /skɪn/ n piel f. ● vt (pt **skinned**) despellejar; pelar ⟨fruit⟩. **~-deep** a superficial. **~-diving** n natación f submarina. **~flint** /'skɪnflɪnt/ n tacaño m. **~ny** /'skɪnɪ/ a (-ier, -iest) flaco

skint /skɪnt/ a (sl) sin una perra

skip¹ /skɪp/ vi (pt **skipped**) saltar; (with rope) saltar a la comba. ● vt saltarse. ● n salto m

skip² /skɪp/ n (container) cuba f

skipper /'skɪpə(r)/ n capitán m

skipping-rope /'skɪpɪŋrəʊp/ n comba f

skirmish /'skɜːmɪʃ/ n escaramuza f

skirt /skɜːt/ n falda f. ● vt rodear; (go round) ladear

skirting-board /'skɜːtɪŋbɔːd/ n rodapié m, zócalo m

skit /skɪt/ n pieza f satírica

skittish /'skɪtɪʃ/ a juguetón; ⟨horse⟩ nervioso

skittle /'skɪtl/ n bolo m

skive /skaɪv/ vi (sl) gandulear

skivvy /'skɪvɪ/ n (fam) criada f

skulk /skʌlk/ vi avanzar furtivamente; (hide) esconderse

skull /skʌl/ n cráneo m; (remains) calavera f. **~-cap** n casquete m

skunk /skʌŋk/ n mofeta f; (person) canalla f

sky /skaɪ/ n cielo m. **~-blue** a & n azul (m) celeste. **~jack** /'skaɪdʒæk/ vt secuestrar. **~jacker** n secuestrador m. **~light** /'skaɪlaɪt/ n tragaluz m. **~scraper** /'skaɪskreɪpə(r)/ n rascacielos m invar

slab /slæb/ n bloque m; (of stone) losa f; (of chocolate) tableta f

slack /slæk/ a (-er, -est) flojo; ⟨person⟩ negligente; ⟨period⟩ de poca actividad. ● n (of rope) parte f floja. ● vt aflojar. ● vi aflojarse; ⟨person⟩ descansar. **~en** /'slækən/ vt aflojar. ● vi aflojarse; ⟨person⟩ descansar. **~en (off)** vt aflojar. **~ off** (fam) aflojar

slacks /slæks/ npl pantalones mpl

slag /slæg/ n escoria f

slain /sleɪn/ see **slay**

slake /sleɪk/ vt apagar

slam /slæm/ vt (pt **slammed**) golpear; (throw) arrojar; (criticize, sl) criticar. **~ the door** dar un portazo.

● *vi* cerrarse de golpe. ● *n* golpe *m*; (*of door*) portazo *m*

slander /'slɑ:ndə(r)/ *n* calumnia *f*. ● *vt* difamar. ~**ous** *a* calumnioso

slang /slæŋ/ *n* jerga *f*, argot *m*. ~**y** *a* vulgar

slant /slɑ:nt/ *vt* inclinar; presentar con parcialidad (*news*). ● *n* inclinación *f*; (*point of view*) punto *m* de vista

slap /slæp/ *vt* (*pt* **slapped**) abofetear; (*on the back*) dar una palmada; (*put*) arrojar. ● *n* bofetada *f*; (*on back*) palmada *f*. ● *adv* de lleno. ~**dash** /'slæpdæʃ/ *a* descuidado. ~**happy** *a* (*fam*) despreocupado; (*dazed, fam*) aturdido. ~**stick** /'slæpstɪk/ *n* payasada *f*. ~**up** *a* (*sl*) de primera categoría

slash /slæʃ/ *vt* acuchillar; (*fig*) reducir radicalmente. ● *n* cuchillada *f*

slat /slæt/ *n* tablilla *f*

slate /sleɪt/ *n* pizarra *f*. ● *vt* (*fam*) criticar

slaughter /'slɔ:tə(r)/ *vt* masacrar; matar (*animal*). ● *n* carnicería *f*; (*of animals*) matanza *f*. ~**house** /'slɔ:təhaʊs/ *n* matadero *m*

Slav /slɑ:v/ *a & n* eslavo (*m*)

slav|e /sleɪv/ *n* esclavo *m*. ● *vi* trabajar como un negro. ~**e-driver** *n* negrero *m*. ~**ery** /-ərɪ/ *n* esclavitud *f*. ~**ish** /'sleɪvɪʃ/ *a* servil

Slavonic /slə'vɒnɪk/ *a* eslavo

slay /sleɪ/ *vt* (*pt* **slew**, *pp* **slain**) matar

sleazy /'sli:zɪ/ *a* (**-ier, -iest**) (*fam*) sórdido

sledge /sledʒ/ *n* trineo *m*. ~**hammer** *n* almádena *f*

sleek /sli:k/ *a* (**-er, -est**) liso, brillante; (*elegant*) elegante

sleep /sli:p/ *n* sueño *m*. **go to** ~ dormirse. ● *vi* (*pt* **slept**) dormir. ● *vt* poder alojar. ~**er** *n* durmiente *m & f*; (*on track*) traviesa *f*; (*berth*) cochecama *m*. ~**ily** *adv* soñolientamente. ~**ing-bag** *n* saco *m* de dormir. ~**ing-pill** *n* somnífero *m*. ~**less** *a* insomne. ~**lessness** *n* insomnio *m*. ~**walker** *n* sonámbulo *m*. ~**y** /'sli:pɪ/ *a* (**-ier, -iest**) soñoliento. **be** ~**y** tener sueño

sleet /sli:t/ *n* aguanieve *f*. ● *vi* caer aguanieve

sleeve /sli:v/ *n* manga *f*; (*for record*) funda *f*. **up one's** ~ en reserva. ~**less** *a* sin mangas

sleigh /sleɪ/ *n* trineo *m*

sleight /slaɪt/ *n*. ~ **of hand** prestidigitación *f*

slender /'slendə(r)/ *a* delgado; (*fig*) escaso

slept /slept/ *see* **sleep**

sleuth /slu:θ/ *n* investigador *m*

slew[1] /slu:/ *see* **slay**

slew[2] /slu:/ *vi* (*turn*) girar

slice /slaɪs/ *n* lonja *f*; (*of bread*) rebanada *f*; (*of sth round*) rodaja *f*; (*implement*) paleta *f*. ● *vt* cortar; rebanar (*bread*)

slick /slɪk/ *a* liso; (*cunning*) astuto. ● *n*. (**oil**)~ capa *f* de aceite

slid|e /slaɪd/ *vt* (*pt* **slid**) deslizar. ● *vi* resbalar. ~**e over** pasar por alto de. ● *n* resbalón *m*; (*in playground*) tobogán *m*; (*for hair*) pasador *m*; (*photo*) diapositiva *f*; (*fig, fall*) baja *f*. ~**e-rule** *n* regla *f* de cálculo. ~**ing** *a* corredizo. ~**ing scale** *n* escala *f* móvil

slight /slaɪt/ *a* (**-er, -est**) ligero; (*slender*) delgado. ● *vt* ofender. ● *n* desaire *m*. ~**est** *a* mínimo. **not in the** ~**est** en absoluto. ~**ly** *adv* un poco

slim /slɪm/ *a* (**slimmer, slimmest**) delgado. ● *vi* (*pt* **slimmed**) adelgazar

slime /slaɪm/ *n* légamo *m*, lodo *m*, fango *m*

sliminess /'slɪmɪnɪs/ *n* delgadez *f*

slimy /'slaɪmɪ/ *a* legamoso, fangoso, viscoso; (*fig*) rastrero

sling /slɪŋ/ *n* honda *f*; (*toy*) tirador; (*med*) cabestrillo *m*. ● *vt* (*pt* **slung**) lanzar

slip /slɪp/ *vt* (*pt* **slipped**) deslizar. ~ **s.o.'s mind** olvidársele a uno. ● *vi* deslizarse. ● *n* resbalón *m*; (*mistake*) error *m*; (*petticoat*) combinación *f*; (*paper*) trozo *m*. ~ **of the tongue** *n* lapsus *m* linguae. **give the** ~ **to** zafarse de, dar esquinazo a. ~ **away** *vi* escabullirse. ~ **into** *vi* ponerse (*clothes*). ~ **up** *vi* (*fam*) equivocarse

slipper /'slɪpə(r)/ *n* zapatilla *f*

slippery /'slɪpərɪ/ *a* resbaladizo

slip: ~**road** *n* rampa *f* de acceso. ~**shod** /'slɪpʃɒd/ *a* descuidado. ~**up** *n* (*fam*) error *m*

slit /slɪt/ *n* raja *f*; (*cut*) corte *m*. ● *vt* (*pt* **slit**, *pres p* **slitting**) rajar; (*cut*) cortar

slither /'slɪðə(r)/ *vi* deslizarse

sliver /'slɪvə(r)/ *n* trocito *m*; (*splinter*) astilla *f*

slobber /'slɒbə(r)/ *vi* babear

slog /slɒg/ vt (pt **slogged**) golpear. ● vi trabajar como un negro. ● n golpetazo m; (hard work) trabajo m penoso

slogan /'sləʊgən/ n eslogan m

slop /slɒp/ vt (pt **slopped**) derramar. ● vi derramarse. **~s** npl (fam) agua f sucia

slop|e /sləʊp/ vi inclinarse. ● vt inclinar. ● n declive m, pendiente m. **~ing** a inclinado

sloppy /'slɒpɪ/ a (-ier, -iest) (wet) mojado; (food) líquido; (work) descuidado; (person) desaliñado; (fig) sentimental

slosh /slɒʃ/ vi (fam) chapotear. ● vt (hit, sl) pegar

slot /slɒt/ n ranura f. ● vt (pt **slotted**) encajar

sloth /sləʊθ/ n pereza f

slot-machine /'slɒtməʃiːn/ n distribuidor m automático; (for gambling) máquina f tragaperras

slouch /slaʊtʃ/ vi andar cargado de espaldas; (in chair) repanchigarse

Slovak /'sləʊvæk/ a & n eslovaco (m). **~ia** /sləʊ'vækɪə/ n Eslovaquia f

sloven|liness /'slʌvnlɪnɪs/ n despreocupación f. **~y** /'slʌvnlɪ/ a descuidado

slow /sləʊ/ a (-er, -est) lento. be **~** (clock) estar atrasado. in **~** motion a cámara lenta. ● adv despacio. ● vt retardar. ● vi ir más despacio. **~ down**, **~ up** vt retardar. ● vi ir más despacio. **~coach** /'sləʊkəʊtʃ/ n tardón m. **~ly** adv despacio. **~ness** n lentitud f

sludge /slʌdʒ/ n fango m; (sediment) sedimento m

slug /slʌg/ n babosa f; (bullet) posta f. **~gish** /'slʌgɪʃ/ a lento

sluice /sluːs/ n (gate) compuerta f; (channel) canal m

slum /slʌm/ n tugurio m

slumber /'slʌmbə(r)/ n sueño m. ● vi dormir

slump /slʌmp/ n baja f repentina; (in business) depresión f. ● vi bajar repentinamente; (flop down) dejarse caer pesadamente; (collapse) desplomarse

slung /slʌŋ/ see **sling**

slur /slɜː(r)/ vt/i (pt **slurred**) articular mal. ● n dicción f defectuosa; (discredit) calumnia f

slush /slʌʃ/ n nieve f medio derretida; (fig) sentimentalismo m. **~**

fund n fondos mpl secretos para fines deshonestos. **~y** a (road) cubierto de nieve medio derretida

slut /slʌt/ n mujer f desaseada

sly /slaɪ/ a (slyer, slyest) (crafty) astuto; (secretive) furtivo. ● n. on the **~** a escondidas. **~ly** adv astutamente

smack[1] /smæk/ n golpe m; (on face) bofetada f. ● adv (fam) de lleno. ● vt pegar

smack[2] /smæk/ vi. **~** of saber a; (fig) oler a

small /smɔːl/ a (-er, -est) pequeño. ● n. the **~** of the back la región f lumbar. **~ ads** npl anuncios mpl por palabras. **~ change** n cambio m. **~holding** /'smɔːlhəʊldɪŋ/ n parcela f. **~pox** /'smɔːlpɒks/ n viruela f. **~ talk** n charla f. **~-time** a (fam) de poca monta

smarmy /'smɑːmɪ/ a (-ier, -iest) (fam) zalamero

smart /smɑːt/ a (-er, -est) elegante; (clever) inteligente; (brisk) rápido. ● vi escocer. **~en** /'smɑːtn/ vt arreglar. ● vi arreglarse. **~en up** vi arreglarse. **~ly** adv elegantemente; (quickly) rápidamente. **~ness** n elegancia f

smash /smæʃ/ vt romper; (into little pieces) hacer pedazos; batir (record). ● vi romperse; (collide) chocar (into con). ● n (noise) estruendo m; (collision) choque m; (com) quiebra f. **~ing** /'smæʃɪŋ/ a (fam) estupendo

smattering /'smætərɪŋ/ n conocimientos mpl superficiales

smear /smɪə(r)/ vt untar (with de); (stain) manchar (with de); (fig) difamar. ● n mancha f; (med) frotis m

smell /smel/ n olor m; (sense) olfato m. ● vt/i (pt **smelt**) oler. **~y** a maloliente

smelt[1] /smelt/ see **smell**

smelt[2] /smelt/ vt fundir

smile /smaɪl/ n sonrisa f. ● vi sonreír(se)

smirk /smɜːk/ n sonrisa f afectada

smite /smaɪt/ vt (pt **smote**, pp **smitten**) golpear

smith /smɪθ/ n herrero m

smithereens /smɪðə'riːnz/ npl añicos mpl. **smash to ~** hacer añicos

smitten /'smɪtn/ see **smite**. ● a encaprichado (with por)

smock /smɒk/ n blusa f, bata f

smog /smɒg/ *n* niebla *f* con humo

smok|e /sməʊk/ *n* humo *m*. ● *vt/i* fumar. ~**eless** *a* sin humo. ~**er** /-ə(r)/ *n* fumador *m*. ~**e-screen** *n* cortina *f* de humo. ~**y** *a* ⟨*room*⟩ lleno de humo

smooth /smuːð/ *a* (**-er, -est**) liso; ⟨*sound, movement*⟩ suave; ⟨*sea*⟩ tranquilo; ⟨*manners*⟩ zalamero. ● *vt* alisar; ⟨*fig*⟩ allanar. ~**ly** *adv* suavemente

smote /sməʊt/ *see* **smite**

smother /ˈsmʌðə(r)/ *vt* sofocar; ⟨*cover*⟩ cubrir

smoulder /ˈsməʊldə(r)/ *vi* arder sin llama; ⟨*fig*⟩ arder

smudge /smʌdʒ/ *n* borrón *m*, mancha *f*. ● *vt* tiznar. ● *vi* tiznarse

smug /smʌg/ *a* (**smugger, smuggest**) satisfecho de sí mismo

smuggl|e /ˈsmʌgl/ *vt* pasar de contrabando. ~**er** *n* contrabandista *m* & *f*. ~**ing** *n* contrabando *m*

smug| ~**ly** *adv* con suficiencia. ~**ness** *n* suficiencia *f*

smut /smʌt/ *n* tizne *m*; ⟨*mark*⟩ tiznajo *m*. ~**ty** *a* (**-ier, -iest**) tiznado; ⟨*fig*⟩ obsceno

snack /snæk/ *n* tentempié *m*. ~**bar** *n* cafetería *f*

snag /snæg/ *n* problema *m*; ⟨*in cloth*⟩ rasgón *m*

snail /sneɪl/ *n* caracol *m*. ~**'s pace** *n* paso *m* de tortuga

snake /sneɪk/ *n* serpiente *f*

snap /snæp/ *vt* (*pt* **snapped**) ⟨*break*⟩ romper; castañetear ⟨*fingers*⟩. ● *vi* romperse; ⟨*dog*⟩ intentar morder; ⟨*say*⟩ contestar bruscamente; ⟨*whip*⟩ chasquear. ~ **at** ⟨*dog*⟩ intentar morder; ⟨*say*⟩ contestar bruscamente. ● *n* chasquido *m*; ⟨*photo*⟩ foto *f*. ● *a* instantáneo. ~ **up** *vt* agarrar. ~**py** /ˈsnæpɪ/ *a* (**-ier, -iest**) ⟨*fam*⟩ rápido. **make it** ~**py!** ⟨*fam*⟩ ¡date prisa! ~**shot** /ˈsnæpʃɒt/ *n* foto *f*

snare /sneə(r)/ *n* trampa *f*

snarl /snɑːl/ *vi* gruñir. ● *n* gruñido *m*

snatch /snætʃ/ *vt* agarrar; ⟨*steal*⟩ robar. ● *n* arrebatamiento *m*; ⟨*short part*⟩ trocito *m*; ⟨*theft*⟩ robo *m*

sneak /sniːk/ ● *n* soplón *m*. ● *vi*. ~ **in** entrar furtivamente. ~ **out** salir furtivamente

sneakers /ˈsniːkəz/ *npl* zapatillas *fpl* de lona

sneak|ing /ˈsniːkɪŋ/ *a* furtivo. ~**y** *a* furtivo

sneer /snɪə(r)/ *n* sonrisa *f* de desprecio. ● *vi* sonreír con desprecio. ~ **at** hablar con desprecio a

sneeze /sniːz/ *n* estornudo *m*. ● *vi* estornudar

snide /snaɪd/ *a* ⟨*fam*⟩ despreciativo

sniff /snɪf/ *vt* oler. ● *vi* aspirar por la nariz. ● *n* aspiración *f*

snigger /ˈsnɪgə(r)/ *n* risa *f* disimulada. ● *vi* reír disimuladamente

snip /snɪp/ *vt* (*pt* **snipped**) tijeretear. ● *n* tijeretada *f*; ⟨*bargain, sl*⟩ ganga *f*

snipe /snaɪp/ *vi* disparar desde un escondite. ~**r** /ə(r)/ *n* tirador *m* emboscado, francotirador *m*

snippet /ˈsnɪpɪt/ *n* retazo *m*

snivel /ˈsnɪvl/ *vi* (*pt* **snivelled**) lloriquear. ~**ling** *a* llorón

snob /snɒb/ *n* esnob *m*. ~**bery** *n* esnobismo *m*. ~**bish** *a* esnob

snooker /ˈsnuːkə(r)/ *n* billar *m*

snoop /snuːp/ *vi* ⟨*fam*⟩ curiosear

snooty /ˈsnuːtɪ/ *a* ⟨*fam*⟩ desdeñoso

snooze /snuːz/ *n* sueñecito *m*. ● *vi* echarse un sueñecito

snore /snɔː(r)/ *n* ronquido *m*. ● *vi* roncar

snorkel /ˈsnɔːkl/ *n* tubo *m* respiratorio

snort /snɔːt/ *n* bufido *m*. ● *vi* bufar

snout /snaʊt/ *n* hocico *m*

snow /snəʊ/ *n* nieve *f*. ● *vi* nevar. **be** ~**ed under with** estar inundado por. ~**ball** /ˈsnəʊbɔːl/ *n* bola *f* de nieve. ~**drift** *n* nieve amontonada. ~**drop** /ˈsnəʊdrɒp/ *n* campanilla *f* de invierno. ~**fall** /ˈsnəʊfɔːl/ *n* nevada *f*. ~**flake** /ˈsnəʊfleɪk/ *n* copo *m* de nieve. ~**man** /ˈsnəʊmæn/ *n* (*pl* **-men**) muñeco *m* de nieve. ~**plough** *n* quitanieves *m invar*. ~**storm** /ˈsnəʊstɔːm/ *n* nevasca *f*. ~**y** *a* ⟨*place*⟩ de nieves abundantes; ⟨*weather*⟩ con nevadas seguidas

snub /snʌb/ *vt* (*pt* **snubbed**) desairar. ● *n* desaire *m*. ~**-nosed** /ˈsnʌbnəʊzd/ *a* chato

snuff /snʌf/ *n* rapé *m*. ● *vt* despabilar ⟨*candle*⟩. ~ **out** apagar ⟨*candle*⟩

snuffle /ˈsnʌfl/ *vi* respirar ruidosamente

snug /snʌg/ *a* (**snugger, snuggest**) cómodo; ⟨*tight*⟩ ajustado

snuggle /ˈsnʌgl/ *vi* acomodarse

so /səʊ/ *adv* (*before a or adv*) tan; ⟨*thus*⟩ así. ● *conj* así que. ~ **am I** yo también. ~ **as to** para. ~ **far** *adv* (*time*) hasta ahora; (*place*) hasta aquí. ~ **far as I know** que yo sepa. ~ **long!** (*fam*) ¡hasta luego! ~ **much** tanto. ~ **that** *conj* para que. **and** ~ **forth, and** ~ **on** y así sucesivamente. **if** ~ si es así. **I think** ~ creo que sí. **or** ~ más o menos

soak /səʊk/ *vt* remojar. ● *vi* remojarse. ~ **in** penetrar. ~ **up** absorber. ~**ing** *a* empapado. ● *n* remojón *m*

so-and-so /ˈsəʊənsəʊ/ *n* fulano *m*

soap /səʊp/ *n* jabón *m*. ● *vt* enjabonar. ~ **powder** *n* jabón en polvo. ~**y** *a* jabonoso

soar /sɔː(r)/ *vi* elevarse; ⟨*price etc*⟩ ponerse por las nubes

sob /sɒb/ *n* sollozo *m*. ● *vi* (*pt* **sobbed**) sollozar

sober /ˈsəʊbə(r)/ *a* sobrio; ⟨*colour*⟩ discreto

so-called /ˈsəʊkɔːld/ *a* llamado, supuesto

soccer /ˈsɒkə(r)/ *n* (*fam*) fútbol *m*

sociable /ˈsəʊʃəbl/ *a* sociable

social /ˈsəʊʃl/ *a* social; (*sociable*) sociable. ● *n* reunión *f*. ~**ism** /-zəm/ *n* socialismo *m*. ~**ist** /ˈsəʊʃəlɪst/ *a* & *n* socialista *m* & *f*. ~**ize** /ˈsəʊʃəlaɪz/ *vt* socializar. ~**ly** *adv* socialmente. ~ **security** *n* seguridad *f* social. ~ **worker** *n* asistente *m* social

society /səˈsaɪətɪ/ *n* sociedad *f*

sociolog|ical /səʊsɪəˈlɒdʒɪkl/ *a* sociológico. ~**ist** *n* sociólogo *m*. ~**y** /səʊsɪˈɒlədʒɪ/ *n* sociología *f*

sock[1] /sɒk/ *n* calcetín *m*

sock[2] /sɒk/ *vt* (*sl*) pegar

socket /ˈsɒkɪt/ *n* hueco *m*; (*of eye*) cuenca *f*; (*wall plug*) enchufe *m*; (*for bulb*) portalámparas *m invar*, casquillo *m*

soda /ˈsəʊdə/ *n* sosa *f*; (*water*) soda *f*. ~**-water** *n* soda *f*

sodden /ˈsɒdn/ *a* empapado

sodium /ˈsəʊdɪəm/ *n* sodio *m*

sofa /ˈsəʊfə/ *n* sofá *m*

soft /sɒft/ *a* (**-er, -est**) blando; ⟨*sound, colour*⟩ suave; (*gentle*) dulce, tierno; (*silly*) estúpido. ~ **drink** *n* bebida *f* no alcohólica. ~ **spot** *n* debilidad *f*. ~**en** /ˈsɒfn/ *vt* ablandar; (*fig*) suavizar. ● *vi* ablandarse; (*fig*) suavizarse. ~**ly** *adv* dulcemente. ~**ness** *n* blandura *f*; (*fig*) dulzura *f*. ~**ware** /ˈsɒftweə(r)/ *n* programación *f*, software *m*

soggy /ˈsɒgɪ/ *a* (**-ier, -iest**) empapado

soh /səʊ/ *n* (*mus, fifth note of any musical scale*) sol *m*

soil[1] /sɔɪl/ *n* suelo *m*

soil[2] /sɔɪl/ *vt* ensuciar. ● *vi* ensuciarse

solace /ˈsɒləs/ *n* consuelo *m*

solar /ˈsəʊlə(r)/ *a* solar. ~**ium** /səˈleərɪəm/ *n* (*pl* **-a**) solario *m*

sold /səʊld/ *see* **sell**

solder /ˈsɒldə(r)/ *n* soldadura *f*. ● *vt* soldar

soldier /ˈsəʊldʒə(r)/ *n* soldado *m*. ● *vi.* ~ **on** (*fam*) perseverar

sole[1] /səʊl/ *n* (*of foot*) planta *f*; (*of shoe*) suela *f*

sole[2] /səʊl/ (*fish*) lenguado *m*

sole[3] /səʊl/ *a* único, solo. ~**ly** *adv* únicamente

solemn /ˈsɒləm/ *a* solemne. ~**ity** /səˈlemnətɪ/ *n* solemnidad *f*. ~**ly** *adv* solemnemente

solicit /səˈlɪsɪt/ *vt* solicitar. ● *vi* importunar

solicitor /səˈlɪsɪtə(r)/ *n* abogado *m*; (*notary*) notario *m*

solicitous /səˈlɪsɪtəs/ *a* solícito

solid /ˈsɒlɪd/ *a* sólido; ⟨*gold etc*⟩ macizo; (*unanimous*) unánime; ⟨*meal*⟩ sustancioso. ● *n* sólido *m*. ~**arity** /sɒlɪˈdærətɪ/ *n* solidaridad *f*. ~**ify** /səˈlɪdɪfaɪ/ *vi* solidificar. ● *vi* solidificarse. ~**ity** /səˈlɪdətɪ/ *n* solidez *f*. ~**ly** *adv* sólidamente. ~**s** *npl* alimentos *mpl* sólidos

soliloquy /səˈlɪləkwɪ/ *n* soliloquio *m*

solitaire /sɒlɪˈteə(r)/ *n* solitario *m*

solitary /ˈsɒlɪtrɪ/ *a* solitario

solitude /ˈsɒlɪtjuːd/ *n* soledad *f*

solo /ˈsəʊləʊ/ *n* (*pl* **-os**) (*mus*) solo *m*. ~**ist** *n* solista *m* & *f*

solstice /ˈsɒlstɪs/ *n* solsticio *m*

soluble /ˈsɒljʊbl/ *a* soluble

solution /səˈluːʃn/ *n* solución *f*

solvable *a* soluble

solve /sɒlv/ *vt* resolver

solvent /ˈsɒlvənt/ *a* & *n* solvente (*m*)

sombre /ˈsɒmbə(r)/ *a* sombrío

some /sʌm/ *a* alguno; (*a little*) un poco de. ~ **day** algún día. ~ **two hours** unas dos horas. **will you have** ~ **wine?** ¿quieres vino? ● *pron* algunos; (*a little*) un poco. ~ **of us** algunos de nosotros. **I want** ~ quiero un poco. ● *adv* (*approximately*) unos. ~**body** /ˈsʌmbədɪ/ *pron* alguien. ● *n* personaje *m*. ~**how** /ˈsʌmhaʊ/ *adv* de algún modo. ~**how or other** de una manera u otra. ~**one**

/'sʌmwʌn/ *pron* alguien. ● *n* personaje *m*

somersault /'sʌməsɔːlt/ *n* salto *m* mortal. ● *vi* dar un salto mortal

some: ~**thing** /'sʌmθɪŋ/ *pron* algo *m*. ~**thing like** algo como; (*approximately*) cerca de. ~**time** /'sʌmtaɪm/ *a* ex. ● *adv* algún día; (*in past*) durante. ~**time last summer** *a* (durante) el verano pasado. ~ **times** /'sʌmtaɪmz/ *adv* de vez en cuando, a veces. ~**what** /'sʌmwɒt/ *adv* algo, un poco. ~**where** /'sʌmweə(r)/ *adv* en alguna parte

son /sʌn/ *n* hijo *m*

sonata /sə'nɑːtə/ *n* sonata *f*

song /sɒŋ/ *n* canción *f*. **sell for a** ~ vender muy barato. ~**-book** *n* cancionero *m*

sonic /'sɒnɪk/ *a* sónico

son-in-law /'sʌnɪnlɔː/ *n* (*pl* **sons-in-law**) yerno *m*

sonnet /'sɒnɪt/ *n* soneto *m*

sonny /'sʌnɪ/ *n* (*fam*) hijo *m*

soon /suːn/ *adv* (**-er, -est**) pronto; (*in a short time*) dentro de poco; (*early*) temprano. ~ **after** poco después. ~**er or later** tarde o temprano. **as** ~ **as** en cuanto; **as** ~ **as possible** lo antes posible. **I would** ~**er not go** prefiero no ir

soot /sʊt/ *n* hollín *m*

sooth|e /suːð/ *vt* calmar. ~**ing** *a* calmante

sooty /'sʊtɪ/ *a* cubierto de hollín

sophisticated /sə'fɪstɪkeɪtɪd/ *a* sofisticado; (*complex*) complejo

soporific /sɒpə'rɪfɪk/ *a* soporífero

sopping /'sɒpɪŋ/ *a*. ~ (**wet**) empapado

soppy /'sɒpɪ/ *a* (**-ier, -iest**) (*fam*) sentimental; (*silly, fam*) tonto

soprano /sə'prɑːnəʊ/ *n* (*pl* **-os**) (*voice*) soprano *m*; (*singer*) soprano *f*

sorcerer /'sɔːsərə(r)/ *n* hechicero *m*

sordid /'sɔːdɪd/ *a* sórdido

sore /sɔː(r)/ *a* (**-er, -est**) que duele, dolorido; (*distressed*) penoso; (*vexed*) enojado. ● *n* llaga *f*. ~**ly** /'sɔːlɪ/ *adv* gravemente. ~ **throat** *n* dolor *m* de garganta. **I've got a** ~ **throat** me duele la garganta

sorrow /'sɒrəʊ/ *n* pena *f*, tristeza *f*. ~**ful** *a* triste

sorry /'sɒrɪ/ *a* (**-ier, -ier**) arrepentido; (*wretched*) lamentable; (*sad*) triste. **be** ~ sentirlo; (*repent*) arrepentirse.

be ~ **for s.o.** (*pity*) compadecerse de uno. ~**!** ¡perdón!, ¡perdone!

sort /sɔːt/ *n* clase *f*; (*person, fam*) tipo *m*. **be out of** ~**s** estar indispuesto; (*irritable*) estar de mal humor. ● *vt* clasificar. ~ **out** (*choose*) escoger; (*separate*) separar; resolver (*problem*)

so-so /'səʊsəʊ/ *a* & *adv* regular

soufflé /'suːfleɪ/ *n* suflé *m*

sought /sɔːt/ *see* **seek**

soul /səʊl/ *n* alma *f*. ~**ful** *a* sentimental

sound[1] /saʊnd/ *n* sonido *m*; ruido *m*. ● *vt* sonar; (*test*) sondar. ● *vi* sonar; (*seem*) parecer ⟨**as if** que⟩

sound[2] /saʊnd/ *a* (**-er, -est**) sano; ⟨*argument etc*⟩ lógico; (*secure*) seguro. ~ **asleep** profundamente dormido

sound[3] /saʊnd/ *n* (*strait*) estrecho *m*

sound barrier /'saʊndbæriə(r)/ *n* barrera *f* del sonido

soundly /'saʊndlɪ/ *adv* sólidamente; (*asleep*) profundamente

sound: ~**-proof** *a* insonorizado. ~ **track** *n* banda *f* sonora

soup /suːp/ *n* sopa *f*. **in the** ~ (*sl*) en apuros

sour /'saʊə(r)/ *a* (**-er, -est**) agrio; ⟨*cream, milk*⟩ cortado. ● *vt* agriar. ● *vi* agriarse

source /sɔːs/ *n* fuente *f*

south /saʊθ/ *n* sur *m*. ● *a* del sur. ● *adv* hacia el sur. **S**~ **Africa** *n* Africa *f* del Sur. **S**~ **America** *n* América *f* (del Sur), Sudamérica *f*. **S**~ **American** *a* & *n* sudamericano (*m*). ~**-east** *n* sudeste *m*. ~**erly** /'sʌðəlɪ/ *a* sur; ⟨*wind*⟩ del sur. ~**ern** /'sʌðən/ *a* del sur, meridional. ~**e-rner** *n* meridional *m*. ~**ward** *a* sur; ● *adv* hacia el sur. ~**wards** *adv* hacia el sur. ~**-west** *n* sudoeste *m*

souvenir /suːvə'nɪə(r)/ *n* recuerdo *m*

sovereign /'sɒvrɪn/ *n* & *a* soberano (*m*). ~**ty** *n* soberanía *f*

Soviet /'səʊvɪət/ *a* (*history*) soviético. **the** ~ **Union** *n* la Unión *f* Soviética

sow[1] /səʊ/ *vt* (*pt* **sowed**, *pp* **sowed** *or* **sown**) sembrar

sow[2] /saʊ/ *n* cerda *f*

soya /'sɔɪə/ *n*. ~ **bean** *n* soja *f*

spa /spɑː/ *n* balneario *m*

space /speɪs/ *n* espacio *m*; (*room*) sitio *m*; (*period*) período *m*. ● *a* ⟨*research etc*⟩ espacial. ● *vt* espaciar. ~ **out** espaciar. ~**craft** /'speɪs-

krɑːft/ n, ~ship n nave f espacial.
~suit n traje m espacial

spacious /'speıʃəs/ a espacioso

spade /speıd/ n pala f. ~s npl (cards)
picos mpl, picas fpl; (in Spanish
pack) espadas fpl. ~work /'speıdwɜː
k/ n trabajo m preparatorio

spaghetti /spə'getı/ n espaguetis
mpl

Spain /speın/ n España f

span¹ /spæn/ n (of arch) luz f; (of time)
espacio m; (of wings) envergadura f.
● vt (pt spanned) extenderse sobre

span² /spæn/ see **spick**

Spaniard /'spænjəd/ n español m

spaniel /'spænjəl/ n perro m de a-
guas

Spanish /'spænıʃ/ a & n español (m)

spank /spæŋk/ vt dar un azote a.
~ing n azote m

spanner /'spænə(r)/ n llave f

spar /spɑː(r)/ vi (pt sparred) entrenarse en el boxeo; (argue) disputar

spare /speə(r)/ vt salvar; (do without) prescindir de; (afford to give)
dar; (use with restraint) escatimar.
● a de reserva; (surplus) sobrante;
(person) enjuto; (meal etc) frugal. ~
(part) n repuesto m. ~ time n
tiempo m libre. ~ tyre n neumático
m de repuesto

sparing /'speərıŋ/ a frugal. ~ly adv
frugalmente

spark /spɑːk/ n chispa f. ● vt. ~ off
(initiate) provocar. ~ing-plug n
(auto) bujía f

sparkl|e /'spɑːkl/ vi centellear. ● n
centelleo m. ~ing a centelleante;
(wine) espumoso

sparrow /'spærəʊ/ n gorrión m

sparse /spɑːs/ a escaso; (population)
poco denso. ~ly adv escasamente

spartan /'spɑːtn/ a espartano

spasm /'spæzəm/ n espasmo m; (of
cough) acceso m. ~odic /spæz'-
mɒdık/ a espasmódico

spastic /'spæstık/ n víctima f de pará-
lisis cerebral

spat /spæt/ see **spit**¹

spate /speıt/ n avalancha f

spatial /'speıʃl/ a espacial

spatter /'spætə(r)/ vt salpicar (**with**
de)

spatula /'spætjʊlə/ n espátula f

spawn /spɔːn/ n hueva f. ● vt
engendrar. ● vi desovar

speak /spiːk/ vt/i (pt spoke, pp
spoken) hablar. ~ for vi hablar en

nombre de. ~ up vi hablar más
fuerte. ~er /'spiːkə(r)/ n (in public)
orador m; (loudspeaker) altavoz m.
be a Spanish ~er hablar español

spear /spıə(r)/ n lanza f. ~head
/'spıəhed/ n punta f de lanza. ● vt
(lead) encabezar. ~mint /'spıəmınt/
n menta f verde

spec /spek/ n. **on ~** (fam) por si
acaso

special /'speʃl/ a especial. ~ist
/'speʃəlıst/ n especialista m & f.
~ity /-ı'ælətı/ n especialidad f. ~
ization /-'zeıʃn/ n especialización f.
~ize /'speʃəlaız/ vi especializarse.
~ized a especializado. ~ty n especialidad f. ~ly adv especialmente

species /'spiːʃiːz/ n especie f

specif|ic /spə'sıfık/ a específico. ~
ically adv específicamente. ~i-
cation /-ı'keıʃn/ n especificación f;
(details) descripción f. ~y /'spesıfaı/
vt especificar

specimen /'spesımın/ n muestra f

speck /spek/ n manchita f; (particle)
partícula f

speckled /'spekld/ a moteado

specs /speks/ npl (fam) gafas fpl,
anteojos mpl (LAm)

spectac|le /'spektəkl/ n espectáculo
m. ~les npl gafas fpl, anteojos mpl
(LAm). ~ular /spek'tækjʊlə(r)/ a es-
pectacular

spectator /spek'teıtə(r)/ n espectador m

spectre /'spektə(r)/ n espectro m

spectrum /'spektrəm/ n (pl -tra)
espectro m; (of ideas) gama f

speculat|e /'spekjʊleıt/ vi especular.
~ion /-'leıʃn/ n especulación f. ~ive
/-lətıv/ a especulativo. ~or n es-
peculador m

sped /sped/ see **speed**

speech /spiːtʃ/ n (faculty) habla f;
(address) discurso m. ~less a mudo

speed /spiːd/ n velocidad f;
(rapidity) rapidez f; (haste) prisa f.
● vi (pt sped) apresurarse. (pt
speeded) (drive too fast) ir a una velocidad excesiva. ~ up vt acelerar.
● vi acelerarse. ~boat /'spiːdbəʊt/
n lancha f motora. ~ily adv rápidamente. ~ing n exceso m de velocidad. ~ometer /spiː'dɒmıtə(r)/ n
velocímetro m. ~way /'spiːdweı/ n
pista f; (Amer) autopista f. ~y
/'spiːdı/ a (-ier, -iest) rápido

spell¹ /spel/ n (magic) hechizo m

spell[2] /spel/ *vt/i* (*pt* **spelled** *or* **spelt**) escribir; (*mean*) significar. ~ **out** *vt* deletrear; (*fig*) explicar. ~**ing** *n* ortografía *f*

spell[3] /spel/ (*period*) período *m*

spellbound /'spelbaʊnd/ *a* hechizado

spelt /spelt/ *see* **spell**[2]

spend /spend/ *vt* (*pt* **spent**) gastar; pasar ⟨*time etc*⟩; dedicar ⟨*care etc*⟩. ● *vi* gastar dinero. ~**thrift** /'spend-θrɪft/ *n* derrochador *m*

spent /spent/ *see* **spend**

sperm /spɜ:m/ *n* (*pl* **sperms** *or* **sperm**) esperma *f*

spew /spju:/ *vt/i* vomitar

spher|e /sfɪə(r)/ *n* esfera *f*. ~**ical** /'sferɪkl/ *a* esférico

sphinx /sfɪŋks/ *n* esfinge *f*

spice /spaɪs/ *n* especia *f*; (*fig*) sabor *m*

spick /spɪk/ *a.* ~ **and span** impecable

spicy /'spaɪsɪ/ *a* picante

spider /'spaɪdə(r)/ *n* araña *f*

spik|e /spaɪk/ *n* (*of metal etc*) punta *f*. ~**y** *a* puntiagudo; ⟨*person*⟩ quisquilloso

spill /spɪl/ *vt* (*pt* **spilled** *or* **spilt**) derramar. ● *vi* derramarse. ~ **over** *vi* desbordarse

spin /spɪn/ *vt* (*pt* **spun**, *pres p* **spinning**) hacer girar; hilar ⟨*wool etc*⟩. ● *vi* girar. ● *n* vuelta *f*; (*short drive*) paseo *m*

spinach /'spɪnɪdʒ/ *n* espinacas *fpl*

spinal /'spaɪnl/ *a* espinal. ~ **cord** *n* médula *f* espinal

spindl|e /'spɪndl/ *n* (*for spinning*) huso *m*. ~**y** *a* larguirucho

spin-drier /spɪn'draɪə(r)/ *n* secador *m* centrífugo

spine /spaɪn/ *n* columna *f* vertebral; (*of book*) lomo *m*. ~**less** *a* (*fig*) sin carácter

spinning /'spɪnɪŋ/ *n* hilado *m*. ~ **top** *n* trompa *f*, peonza *f*. ~**-wheel** *n* rueca *f*

spin-off /'spɪnɒf/ *n* beneficio *m* incidental; (*by-product*) subproducto *m*

spinster /'spɪnstə(r)/ *n* soltera *f*; (*old maid, fam*) solterona *f*

spiral /'spaɪərəl/ *a* espiral, helicoidal. ● *n* hélice *f*. ● *vi* (*pt* **spiralled**) moverse en espiral. ~ **staircase** *n* escalera *f* de caracol

spire /spaɪə(r)/ *n* (*archit*) aguja *f*

spirit /'spɪrɪt/ *n* espíritu *m*; (*boldness*) valor *m*. **in low** ~**s** abatido. ● *vt*. ~ **away** hacer desaparecer. ~**ed** /'spɪrɪtɪd/ *a* animado, fogoso. ~**-lamp** *n* lamparilla *f* de alcohol. ~**level** *n* nivel *m* de aire. ~**s** *npl* (*drinks*) bebidas *fpl* alcohólicas

spiritual /'spɪrɪtjʊəl/ *a* espiritual. ● *n* canción *f* religiosa de los negros. ~**ualism** /-zəm/ *n* espiritismo *m*. ~**ualist** /'spɪrɪtjʊəlɪst/ *n* espiritista *m & f*

spit[1] /spɪt/ *vt* (*pt* **spat** *or* **spit**, *pres p* **spitting**) escupir. ● *vi* escupir; (*rain*) lloviznar. ● *n* esputo *m*; (*spittle*) saliva *f*

spit[2] /spɪt/ (*for roasting*) asador *m*

spite /spaɪt/ *n* rencor *m*. **in** ~ **of** a pesar de. ● *vt* fastidiar. ~**ful** *a* rencoroso. ~**fully** *adv* con rencor

spitting image /spɪtɪŋ'ɪmɪdʒ/ *n* vivo retrato *m*

spittle /'spɪtl/ *n* saliva *f*

splash /splæʃ/ *vt* salpicar. ● *vi* esparcirse; ⟨*person*⟩ chapotear. ● *n* salpicadura *f*; (*sound*) chapoteo *m*; (*of colour*) mancha *f*; (*drop, fam*) gota *f*. ~ **about** *vi* chapotear. ~ **down** *vi* ⟨*spacecraft*⟩ amerizar

spleen /spli:n/ *n* bazo *m*; (*fig*) esplín *m*

splendid /'splendɪd/ *a* espléndido

splendour /'splendə(r)/ *n* esplendor *m*

splint /splɪnt/ *n* tablilla *f*

splinter /'splɪntə(r)/ *n* astilla *f*. ● *vi* astillarse. ~ **group** *n* grupo *m* disidente

split /splɪt/ *vt* (*pt* **split**, *pres p* **splitting**) hender, rajar; (*tear*) rajar; (*divide*) dividir; (*share*) repartir. ~ **one's sides** caerse de risa. ● *vi* partirse; (*divide*) dividirse. ~ **on s.o.** (*sl*) traicionar. ● *n* hendidura *f*; (*tear*) desgarrón *m*; (*quarrel*) ruptura *f*; (*pol*) escisión *f*. ~ **up** *vi* separarse. ~ **second** *n* fracción *f* de segundo

splurge /splɜ:dʒ/ *vi* (*fam*) derrochar

splutter /'splʌtə(r)/ *vi* chisporrotear; ⟨*person*⟩ farfullar. ● *n* chisporroteo *m*; (*speech*) farfulla *f*

spoil /spɔɪl/ *vt* (*pt* **spoilt** *or* **spoiled**) estropear, echar a perder; (*ruin*) arruinar; (*indulge*) mimar. ● *n* botín *m*. ~**s** *npl* botín *m*. ~**-sport** *n* aguafiestas *m invar*

spoke[1] /spəʊk/ *see* **speak**

spoke[2] /spəʊk/ *n* (*of wheel*) radio *m*

spoken /ˈspəʊkən/ *see* **speak**

spokesman /ˈspəʊksmən/ *n* (*pl* **-men**) portavoz *m*

spong|e /spʌndʒ/ *n* esponja *f*. ● *vt* limpiar con una esponja. ● *vi.* **~e on** vivir a costa de. **~e-cake** *n* bizcocho *m*. **~er** /-ə(r)/ *n* gorrón *m*. **~y** *a* esponjoso

sponsor /ˈspɒnsə(r)/ *n* patrocinador *m*; (*surety*) garante *m*. ● *vt* patrocinar. **~ship** *n* patrocinio *m*

spontane|ity /spɒntəˈneɪɪtɪ/ *n* espontaneidad *f*. **~ous** /spɒnˈteɪnjəs/ *a* espontáneo. **~ously** *adv* espontáneamente

spoof /spuːf/ *n* (*sl*) parodia *f*

spooky /ˈspuːkɪ/ *a* (**-ier, -iest**) (*fam*) escalofriante

spool /spuːl/ *n* carrete *m*; (*of sewing-machine*) canilla *f*

spoon /spuːn/ *n* cuchara *f*. **~fed** *a* (*fig*) mimado. **~feed** *vt* (*pt* **-fed**) dar de comer con cuchara. **~ful** *n* (*pl* **-fuls**) cucharada *f*

sporadic /spəˈrædɪk/ *a* esporádico

sport /spɔːt/ *n* deporte *m*; (*amusement*) pasatiempo *m*; (*person, fam*) persona *f* alegre, buen chico *m*, buena chica *f*. **be a good ~** ser buen perdedor. ● *vt* lucir. **~ing** *a* deportivo. **~ing chance** *n* probabilidad *f* de éxito. **~s car** *n* coche *m* deportivo. **~s coat** *n* chaqueta *f* de sport. **~sman** /ˈspɔːtsmən/ *n*, (*pl* **-men**), **~swoman** /ˈspɔːtswʊmən/ *n* (*pl* **-women**) deportista *m & f*

spot /spɒt/ *n* mancha *f*; (*pimple*) grano *m*; (*place*) lugar *m*; (*drop*) gota *f*; (*a little, fam*) poquito *m*. **in a ~** (*fam*) en un apuro. **on the ~** en el lugar; (*without delay*) en el acto. ● *vt* (*pt* **spotted**) manchar; (*notice, fam*) observar, ver. **~ check** *n* control *m* hecho al azar. **~less** *a* inmaculado. **~light** /ˈspɒtlaɪt/ *n* reflector *m*. **~ted** *a* moteado; (*cloth*) a puntos. **~ty** *a* (**-ier, -iest**) manchado; (*skin*) con granos

spouse /spaʊz/ *n* cónyuge *m & f*

spout /spaʊt/ *n* pico *m*; (*jet*) chorro *m*. **up the ~** (*ruined, sl*) perdido. ● *vi* chorrear

sprain /spreɪn/ *vt* torcer. ● *n* torcedura *f*

sprang /spræŋ/ *see* **spring**

sprat /spræt/ *n* espadín *m*

sprawl /sprɔːl/ *vi* (*person*) repanchigarse; (*city etc*) extenderse

spray /spreɪ/ *n* (*of flowers*) ramo *m*; (*water*) rociada *f*; (*from sea*) espuma *f*; (*device*) pulverizador *m*. ● *vt* rociar. **~gun** *n* pistola *f* pulverizadora

spread /spred/ *vt* (*pt* **spread**) (*stretch, extend*) extender; untar (*jam etc*); difundir (*idea, news*). ● *vi* extenderse; (*disease*) propagarse; (*idea, news*) difundirse. ● *n* extensión *f*; (*paste*) pasta *f*; (*of disease*) propagación *f*; (*feast, fam*) comilona *f*. **~eagled** *a* con los brazos y piernas extendidos

spree /spriː/ *n*. **go on a ~** (*have fun, fam*) ir de juerga

sprig /sprɪg/ *n* ramito *m*

sprightly /ˈspraɪtlɪ/ *a* (**-ier, -iest**) vivo

spring /sprɪŋ/ *n* (*season*) primavera *f*; (*device*) muelle *m*; (*elasticity*) elasticidad *f*; (*water*) manantial *m*. ● *a* de primavera. ● *vt* (*pt* **sprang**, *pp* **sprung**) hacer inesperadamente. ● *vi* saltar; (*issue*) brotar. **~ from** *vi* provenir de. **~ up** *vi* surgir. **~board** *n* trampolín *m*. **~time** *n* primavera *f*. **~y** *a* (**-ier, -iest**) elástico

sprinkl|e /ˈsprɪŋkl/ *vt* salpicar; (*with liquid*) rociar. ● *n* salpicadura *f*; (*of liquid*) rociada *f*. **~ed with** salpicado de. **~er** /-ə(r)/ *n* regadera *f*. **~ing** /ˈsprɪŋklɪŋ/ *n* (*fig, amount*) poco *m*

sprint /sprɪnt/ *n* carrera *f*. ● *vi* correr. **~er** *n* corredor *m*

sprite /spraɪt/ *n* duende *m*, hada *f*

sprout /spraʊt/ *vi* brotar. ● *n* brote *m*. **(Brussels) ~s** *npl* coles *fpl* de Bruselas

spruce /spruːs/ *a* elegante

sprung /sprʌŋ/ *see* **spring**. ● *a* de muelles

spry /spraɪ/ *a* (**spryer, spryest**) vivo

spud /spʌd/ *n* (*sl*) patata *f*, papa *f* (*LAm*)

spun /spʌn/ *see* **spin**

spur /spɜː(r)/ *n* espuela *f*; (*stimulus*) estímulo *m*. **on the ~ of the moment** impulsivamente. ● *vt* (*pt* **spurred**). **~ (on)** espolear; (*fig*) estimular

spurious /ˈspjʊərɪəs/ *a* falso. **~ly** *adv* falsamente

spurn /spɜːn/ *vt* despreciar; (*reject*) rechazar

spurt /spɜːt/ *vi* chorrear; *(make sudden effort)* hacer un esfuerzo repentino. ● *n* chorro *m*; *(effort)* esfuerzo *m* repentino

spy /spaɪ/ *n* espía *m & f.* ● *vt* divisar. ● *vi* espiar. ~ **out** *vt* reconocer. ~**ing** *n* espionaje *m*

squabble /'skwɒbl/ *n* riña *f.* ● *vi* reñir

squad /skwɒd/ *n* *(mil)* pelotón *m*; *(of police)* brigada *f*; *(sport)* equipo *m*

squadron /'skwɒdrən/ *n* *(mil)* escuadrón *m*; *(naut, aviat)* escuadrilla *f*

squalid /'skwɒlɪd/ *a* asqueroso; *(wretched)* miserable

squall /skwɔːl/ *n* turbión *m.* ● *vi* chillar. ~**y** *a* borrascoso

squalor /'skwɒlə(r)/ *n* miseria *f*

squander /'skwɒndə(r)/ *vt* derrochar

square /skweə(r)/ *n* cuadrado *m*; *(open space in town)* plaza *f*; *(for drawing)* escuadra *f.* ● *a* cuadrado; *(not owing)* sin deudas, iguales; *(honest)* honrado; *(meal)* satisfactorio; *(old-fashioned, sl)* chapado a la antigua. **all** ~ iguales. ● *vt* *(settle)* arreglar; *(math)* cuadrar. ● *vi* *(agree)* cuadrar. ~ **up to** enfrentarse con. ~**ly** *adv* directamente

squash /skwɒʃ/ *vt* aplastar; *(suppress)* suprimir. ● *n* apiñamiento *m*; *(drink)* zumo *m*; *(sport)* squash *m.* ~**y** *a* blando

squat /skwɒt/ *vi* *(pt* **squatted***)* ponerse en cuclillas; *(occupy illegally)* ocupar sin derecho. ● *n* casa *f* ocupada sin derecho. ● *a* *(dumpy)* achaparrado. ~**ter** /-ə(r)/ *n* ocupante *m & f* ilegal

squawk /skwɔːk/ *n* graznido *m.* ● *vi* graznar

squeak /skwiːk/ *n* chillido *m*; *(of door etc)* chirrido *m.* ● *vi* chillar; *(door etc)* chirriar. ~**y** *a* chirriador

squeal /skwiːl/ *n* chillido *m.* ● *vi* chillar. ~ **on** *(inform on, sl)* denunciar

squeamish /'skwiːmɪʃ/ *a* delicado; *(scrupulous)* escrupuloso. **be ~ about snakes** tener horror a las serpientes

squeeze /skwiːz/ *vt* apretar; exprimir *(lemon etc)*; *(extort)* extorsionar *(from* de). ● *vi* *(force one's way)* abrirse paso. ● *n* estrujón *m*; *(of hand)* apretón *m.* **credit ~** *n* restricción *f* de crédito

squelch /skweltʃ/ *vi* chapotear. ● *n* chapoteo *m*

squib /skwɪb/ *n* *(firework)* buscapiés *m* invar

squid /skwɪd/ *n* calamar *m*

squiggle /'skwɪgl/ *n* garabato *m*

squint /skwɪnt/ *vi* ser bizco; *(look sideways)* mirar de soslayo. ● *n* estrabismo *m*

squire /'skwaɪə(r)/ *n* terrateniente *m*

squirm /skwɜːm/ *vi* retorcerse

squirrel /'skwɪrəl/ *n* ardilla *f*

squirt /skwɜːt/ *vt* arrojar a chorros. ● *vi* salir a chorros. ● *n* chorro *m*

St *abbr* *(saint)* /sənt/ S, San(to); *(street)* C/, Calle *f*

stab /stæb/ *vt* *(pt* **stabbed***)* apuñalar. ● *n* puñalada *f*; *(pain)* punzada *f*; *(attempt, fam)* tentativa *f*

stabili|ty /stə'bɪlətɪ/ *n* estabilidad *f.* ~**ze** /'steɪbɪlaɪz/ *vt* estabilizar. ~**zer** /-ə(r)/ *n* estabilizador *m*

stable[1] /'steɪbl/ *a* *(-er, -est)* estable

stable[2] /'steɪbl/ *n* cuadra *f.* ● *vt* poner en una cuadra. ~**boy** *n* mozo *m* de cuadra

stack /stæk/ *n* montón *m.* ● *vt* amontonar

stadium /'steɪdjəm/ *n* estadio *m*

staff /stɑːf/ *n* *(stick)* palo *m*; *(employees)* personal *m*; *(mil)* estado *m* mayor; *(in school)* profesorado *m.* ● *vt* proveer de personal

stag /stæg/ *n* ciervo *m.* ~**party** *n* reunión *f* de hombres, fiesta *f* de despedida de soltero

stage /steɪdʒ/ *n* *(in theatre)* escena *f*; *(phase)* etapa *f*; *(platform)* plataforma *f.* **go on the** ~ hacerse actor. ● *vt* representar; *(arrange)* organizar. ~**coach** *n* *(hist)* diligencia *f.* ~ **fright** *n* miedo *m* al público. ~**manager** *n* director *m* de escena. ~ **whisper** *n* aparte *m*

stagger /'stægə(r)/ *vi* tambalearse. ● *vt* asombrar; escalonar *(holidays etc)*. ● *n* tambaleo *m.* ~**ing** *a* asombroso

stagna|nt /'stægnənt/ *a* estancado. ~**te** /stæg'neɪt/ *vi* estancarse. ~**tion** /-ʃn/ *n* estancamiento *m*

staid /steɪd/ *a* serio, formal

stain /steɪn/ *vt* manchar; *(colour)* teñir. ● *n* mancha *f*; *(liquid)* tinte *m.* ~**ed glass window** *n* vidriera *f* de colores. ~**less** /'steɪnlɪs/ *a* inmaculado. ~**less steel** *n* acero *m* inoxidable. **~ remover** *n* quitamanchas *m invar*

stair /steə(r)/ *n* escalón *m.* **~s** *npl* escalera *f.* **flight of ~s** tramo *m* de escalera. **~case** /'steəkeɪs/ *n,* **~ way** *n* escalera *f*

stake /steɪk/ *n* estaca *f*; *(for execution)* hoguera *f*; *(wager)* apuesta *f*; *(com)* intereses *mpl.* **at ~** en juego. ● *vt* estacar; *(wager)* apostar. **~ a claim** reclamar

stalactite /'stæləktaɪt/ *n* estalactita *f*

stalagmite /'stæləgmaɪt/ *n* estalagmita *f*

stale /steɪl/ *a* (**-er, -est**) no fresco; *‹bread›* duro; *‹smell›* viciado; *‹news›* viejo; *(uninteresting)* gastado. **~mate** /'steɪlmeɪt/ *n* *(chess)* ahogado *m*; *(deadlock)* punto *m* muerto

stalk[1] /stɔːk/ *n* tallo *m*

stalk[2] /stɔːk/ *vi* andar majestuosamente. ● *vt* seguir; *‹animal›* acechar

stall[1] /stɔːl/ *n* *(stable)* cuadra *f*; *(in stable)* casilla *f*; *(in theatre)* butaca *f*; *(in market)* puesto *m*; *(kiosk)* quiosco *m*

stall[2] /stɔːl/ *vt* parar *‹engine›.* ● *vi* *‹engine›* pararse; *(fig)* andar con rodeos

stallion /'stæljən/ *n* semental *m*

stalwart /'stɔːlwət/ *n* partidario *m* leal

stamina /'stæmɪnə/ *n* resistencia *f*

stammer /'stæmə(r)/ *vi* tartamudear. ● *n* tartamudeo *m*

stamp /stæmp/ *vt* *(with feet)* patear; *(press)* estampar; poner un sello en *‹envelope›*; *(with rubber stamp)* sellar; *(fig)* señalar. ● *vi* patear. ● *n* sello *m*; *(with foot)* patada *f*; *(mark)* marca *f*, señal *f.* **~ out** *(fig)* acabar con

stampede /stæm'piːd/ *n* desbandada *f*; *(fam)* pánico *m.* ● *vi* huir en desorden

stance /stɑːns/ *n* postura *f*

stand /stænd/ *vi* *(pt* **stood***)* estar de pie; *(rise)* ponerse de pie; *(be)* encontrarse; *(stay firm)* permanecer; *(pol)* presentarse como candidato *(for* en). **~ to reason** ser lógico. ● *vt* *(endure)* soportar; *(place)* poner; *(offer)* ofrecer. **~ a chance** tener una posibilidad. **~ one's ground** mantenerse firme. **I'll ~ you a drink** te invito a una copa. ● *n* posición *f*, postura *f*; *(mil)* resistencia *f*; *(for lamp etc)* pie *m*, sostén *m*; *(at market)* puesto *m*; *(booth)* quiosco *m*; *(sport)* tribuna *f.* **~ around** no hacer nada. **~ back** retroceder. **~ by** *vi* estar preparado. ● *vt* *(support)* apoyar. **~ down** *vi* retirarse. **~ for** *vt* representar. **~ in for** suplir a. **~ out** destacarse. **~ up** *vi* ponerse de pie. **~ up for** defender. **~ up to** *vt* resistir a

standard /'stændəd/ *n* norma *f*; *(level)* nivel *m*; *(flag)* estandarte *m.* ● *a* normal, corriente. **~ize** *vt* uniformar. **~ lamp** *n* lámpara *f* de pie. **~s** *npl* valores *mpl*

stand: **~-by** *n* *(person)* reserva *f*; *(at airport)* lista *f* de espera. **~-in** *n* suplente *m & f.* **~ing** /'stændɪŋ/ *a* de pie; *(upright)* derecho. ● *n* posición *f*; *(duration)* duración *f.* **~-offish** *a* *(fam)* frío. **~point** /'stændpɔɪnt/ *n* punto *m* de vista. **~still** /'stændstɪl/ *n.* **at a ~still** parado. **come to a ~still** pararse

stank /stæŋk/ *see* **stink**

staple[1] /'steɪpl/ *a* principal

staple[2] /'steɪpl/ *n* grapa *f.* ● *vt* sujetar con una grapa. **~r** /-ə(r)/ *n* grapadora *f*

star /stɑː/ *n* *(incl cinema, theatre)* estrella *f*; *(asterisk)* asterisco *m.* ● *vi* *(pt* **starred***)* ser el protagonista

starboard /'stɑːbəd/ *n* estribor *m*

starch /stɑːtʃ/ *n* almidón *m*; *(in food)* fécula *f.* ● *vt* almidonar. **~y** *a* almidonado; *‹food›* feculento; *(fig)* formal

stardom /'stɑːdəm/ *n* estrellato *m*

stare /steə(r)/ *n* mirada *f* fija. ● *vi.* **~ at** mirar fijamente

starfish /'stɑːfɪʃ/ *n* estrella *f* de mar

stark /stɑːk/ *a* (**-er, -est**) rígido; *(utter)* completo. ● *adv* completamente

starlight /'stɑːlaɪt/ *n* luz *f* de las estrellas

starling /'stɑːlɪŋ/ *n* estornino *m*

starry /'stɑːrɪ/ *a* estrellado. **~-eyed** *a* *(fam)* ingenuo, idealista

start /stɑːt/ *vt* empezar; poner en marcha *‹machine›*; *(cause)* provocar. ● *vi* empezar; *(jump)* sobresaltarse; *(leave)* partir; *‹car etc›* arrancar. ● *n* principio *m*; *(leaving)* salida *f*; *(sport)* ventaja *f*; *(jump)* susto *m.* **~er** *n* *(sport)* participante *m & f*; *(auto)* motor *m* de arranque; *(culin)* primer plato *m.* **~ing-point** *n* punto *m* de partida

startle /'stɑːtl/ vt asustar

starv|ation /stɑː'veɪʃn/ n hambre f. **~e** /stɑːv/ vt hacer morir de hambre; (deprive) privar. ● vi morir de hambre

stash /stæʃ/ vt (sl) esconder

state /steɪt/ n estado m; (grand style) pompa f. **S~** n Estado m. **be in a ~** estar agitado. ● vt declarar; expresar (views); (fix) fijar. ● a del Estado; (schol) público; (with ceremony) de gala. **~less** a sin patria

stately /'steɪtlɪ/ a (-ier, -iest) majestuoso

statement /'steɪtmənt/ n declaración f; (account) informe m. **bank ~** n estado m de cuenta

stateroom /'steɪtrʊm/ n (on ship) camarote m

statesman /'steɪtsmən/ n (pl -men) estadista m

static /'stætɪk/ a inmóvil. **~s** n estática f; (radio, TV) parásitos mpl atmosféricos, interferencias fpl

station /'steɪʃn/ n estación f; (status) posición f social. ● vt colocar; (mil) estacionar

stationary /'steɪʃənərɪ/ a estacionario

stationer /'steɪʃənə(r)/ n papelero m. **~'s (shop)** n papelería f. **~y** n artículos mpl de escritorio

station-wagon /'steɪʃnwægən/ n furgoneta f

statistic /stə'tɪstɪk/ n estadística f. **~al** /stə'tɪstɪkl/ a estadístico. **~s** /stə'tɪstɪks/ n (science) estadística f

statue /'stætʃuː/ n estatua f. **~sque** /-ʊ'esk/ a escultural. **~tte** /-ʊ'et/ n figurilla f

stature /'stætʃə(r)/ n talla f, estatura f

status /'steɪtəs/ n posición f social; (prestige) categoría f; (jurid) estado m

statut|e /'stætʃuːt/ n estatuto m. **~ory** /-ʊtrɪ/ a estatutario

staunch /stɔːnʃ/ a (-er, -est) leal. **~ly** adv lealmente

stave /steɪv/ n (mus) pentagrama m. ● vt. **~ off** evitar

stay /steɪ/ n soporte m, sostén m; (of time) estancia f; (jurid) suspensión f. ● vi quedar; (spend time) detenerse; (reside) alojarse. ● vt matar (hunger). **~ the course** terminar. **~ in** quedar en casa. **~ put** mantenerse firme. **~**

up no acostarse. **~ing-power** n resistencia f

stays /steɪz/ npl (old use) corsé m

stead /sted/ n. **in s.o.'s ~** en lugar de uno. **stand s.o. in good ~** ser útil a uno

steadfast /'stedfɑːst/ a firme

stead|ily /'stedɪlɪ/ adv firmemente; (regularly) regularmente. **~y** /'stedɪ/ a (-ier, -iest) firme; (regular) regular; (dependable) serio

steak /steɪk/ n filete m

steal /stiːl/ vt (pt **stole**, pp **stolen**) robar. **~ the show** llevarse los aplausos. **~ in** vi entrar a hurtadillas. **~ out** vi salir a hurtadillas

stealth /stelθ/ n. **by ~** sigilosamente. **~y** a sigiloso

steam /stiːm/ n vapor m; (energy) energía f. ● vt (cook) cocer al vapor; empañar (window). ● vi echar vapor. **~ ahead** (fam) hacer progresos. **~ up** vi (glass) empañar. **~-engine** n máquina f de vapor. **~er** /'stiːmə(r)/ n (ship) barco m de vapor. **~-roller** /'stiːmrəʊlə(r)/ n apisonadora f. **~y** a húmedo

steel /stiːl/ n acero m. ● vt. **~ o.s.** fortalecerse. **~ industry** n industria f siderúrgica. **~ wool** n estropajo m de acero. **~y** a acerado; (fig) duro, inflexible

steep /stiːp/ a (-er, -est) escarpado; (price) (fam) exorbitante. ● vt (soak) remojar. **~ed in** (fig) empapado de

steeple /'stiːpl/ n aguja f, campanario m. **~chase** /'stiːpltʃeɪs/ n carrera f de obstáculos

steep: **~ly** adv de modo empinado. **~ness** n lo escarpado

steer /stɪə(r)/ vt guiar; gobernar (ship). ● vi (in ship) gobernar. **~ clear of** evitar. **~ing** n (auto) dirección f. **~ing-wheel** n volante m

stem /stem/ n tallo m; (of glass) pie m; (of word) raíz f; (of ship) roda f. ● vt (pt **stemmed**) detener. ● vi. **~ from** provenir de

stench /stentʃ/ n hedor m

stencil /'stensl/ n plantilla f; (for typing) cliché m. ● vt (pt **stencilled**) estarcir

stenographer /ste'nɒɡrəfə(r)/ n (Amer) estenógrafo m

step /step/ vi (pt **stepped**) ir. **~ down** retirarse. **~ in** entrar; (fig) intervenir. **~ up** vt aumentar. ● n paso *m*; (*surface*) escalón *m*; (*fig*) medida *f*. **in ~** (*fig*) de acuerdo con. **out of ~** (*fig*) en desacuerdo con. **~brother** /'stepbrʌðə(r)/ *n* hermanastro *m*. **~daughter** *n* hijastra *f*. **~father** *n* padrastro *m*. **~ladder** *n* escalera *f* de tijeras. **~mother** *n* madrastra *f*. **~ping-stone** /'stepɪŋstəʊn/ *n* pasadera *f*; (*fig*) escalón *m*. **~sister** *n* hermanastra *f*. **~son** *n* hijastro *m*

stereo /'steriəʊ/ *n* (*pl* **-os**) cadena *f* estereofónica. ● *a* estereofónico. **~phonic** /steriəʊ'fɒnɪk/ *a* estereofónico. **~type** /'steriəʊtaɪp/ *n* estereotipo *m*. **~typed** *a* estereotipado

steril|e /'steraɪl/ *a* estéril. **~ity** /stə'rɪlətɪ/ *n* esterilidad *f*. **~ization** /-'zeɪʃn/ *n* esterilización *f*. **~ize** /'sterɪlaɪz/ *vt* esterilizar

sterling /'stɜːlɪŋ/ *n* libras *fpl* esterlinas. ● *a* (*pound*) esterlina; (*fig*) excelente. **~ silver** *n* plata *f* de ley

stern[1] /stɜːn/ *n* (*of boat*) popa *f*

stern[2] /stɜːn/ *a* (**-er**, **-est**) severo. **~ly** *adv* severamente

stethoscope /'steθəskəʊp/ *n* estetoscopio *m*

stew /stjuː/ *vt/i* guisar. ● *n* guisado *m*. **in a ~** (*fam*) en un apuro

steward /stjʊəd/ *n* administrador *m*; (*on ship, aircraft*) camarero *m*. **~ess** /-'des/ *n* camarera *f*; (*on aircraft*) azafata *f*

stick /stɪk/ *n* palo *m*; (*for walking*) bastón *m*; (*of celery etc*) tallo *m*. ● *vt* (*pt* **stuck**) (*glue*) pegar; (*put, fam*) poner; (*thrust*) clavar; (*endure, sl*) soportar. ● *vi* pegarse; (*remain, fam*) quedarse; (*jam*) bloquearse. **~ at** (*fam*) perseverar en. **~ out** sobresalir; (*catch the eye, fam*) resaltar. **~ to** aferrarse a; cumplir (*promise*). **~ up for** (*fam*) defender. **~er** /'stɪkə(r)/ *n* pegatina *f*. **~ing-plaster** *n* esparadrapo *m*. **~-in-the-mud** *n* persona *f* chapada a la antigua

stickler /'stɪklə(r)/ *n*. **be a ~ for** insistir en

sticky /'stɪkɪ/ *a* (**-ier**, **-iest**) pegajoso; (*label*) engomado; (*sl*) difícil

stiff /stɪf/ *a* (**-er**, **-est**) rígido; (*difficult*) difícil; (*manner*) estirado; (*drink*) fuerte; (*price*) subido; (*joint*) tieso; (*muscle*) con agujetas. **~en** /'stɪfn/ *vt* poner tieso. **~ly** *adv* rígidamente. **~ neck** *n* torticolis *f*. **~ness** *n* rigidez *f*

stifl|e /'staɪfl/ *vt* sofocar. **~ing** *a* sofocante

stigma /'stɪgmə/ *n* (*pl* **-as**) estigma *m*. (*pl* **stigmata** /'stɪgmətə/) (*relig*) estigma *m*. **~tize** *vt* estigmatizar

stile /staɪl/ *n* portillo *m* con escalones

stiletto /stɪ'letəʊ/ *n* (*pl* **-os**) estilete *m*. **~ heels** *npl* tacones *mpl* aguja

still[1] /stɪl/ *a* inmóvil; (*peaceful*) tranquilo; (*drink*) sin gas. ● *n* silencio *m*. ● *adv* todavía; (*nevertheless*) sin embargo

still[2] /stɪl/ *n* (*apparatus*) alambique *m*

still: **~born** *a* nacido muerto. **~ life** *n* (*pl* **-s**) bodegón *m*. **~ness** *n* tranquilidad *f*

stilted /'stɪltɪd/ *a* artificial

stilts /stɪlts/ *npl* zancos *mpl*

stimul|ant /'stɪmjʊlənt/ *n* estimulante *m*. **~ate** /'stɪmjʊleɪt/ *vt* estimular. **~ation** /-'leɪʃn/ *n* estímulo *m*. **~us** /'stɪmjʊləs/ *n* (*pl* **-li** /-laɪ/) estímulo *m*

sting /stɪŋ/ *n* picadura *f*; (*organ*) aguijón *m*. ● *vt/i* (*pt* **stung**) picar

sting|iness /'stɪndʒɪnɪs/ *n* tacañería *f*. **~y** /'stɪndʒɪ/ *a* (**-ier**, **-iest**) tacaño

stink /stɪŋk/ *n* hedor *m*. ● *vi* (*pt* **stank** *or* **stunk**, *pp* **stunk**) oler mal. ● *vt*. **~ out** apestar (*room*); ahuyentar (*person*). **~er** /-ə(r)/ *n* (*sl*) problema *m* difícil; (*person*) mal bicho *m*

stint /stɪnt/ *n* (*work*) trabajo *m*. ● *vi*. **~ on** escatimar

stipple /'stɪpl/ *vt* puntear

stipulat|e /'stɪpjʊleɪt/ *vt/i* estipular. **~ion** /-'leɪʃn/ *n* estipulación *f*

stir /stɜː(r)/ *vt* (*pt* **stirred**) remover, agitar; (*mix*) mezclar; (*stimulate*) estimular. ● *vi* moverse. ● *n* agitación *f*; (*commotion*) conmoción *f*

stirrup /'stɪrəp/ *n* estribo *m*

stitch /stɪtʃ/ *n* (*in sewing*) puntada *f*; (*in knitting*) punto *m*; (*pain*) dolor *m* de costado; (*med*) punto *m* de sutura. **be in ~es** (*fam*) desternillarse de risa. ● *vt* coser

stoat /stəʊt/ *n* armiño *m*

stock /stɒk/ *n* (*com*, *supplies*) existencias *fpl*; (*com*, *variety*) surtido *m*; (*livestock*) ganado *m*; (*lineage*) linaje *m*; (*finance*) acciones *fpl*; (*culin*) caldo *m*; (*plant*) alhelí *m*. **out of ~** agotado. **take ~** (*fig*) evaluar. ● *a* corriente; (*fig*) trillado. ● *vt* abastecer

(with de). ● *vi.* ~ **up** abastecerse
(with de). ~**broker** /'stɒkbrəʊkə(r)/ *n*
corredor *m* de bolsa. **S**~ **Exchange** *n*
bolsa *f*. **well-**~**ed** *a* bien provisto
stocking /'stɒkɪŋ/ *n* media *f*
stock: ~**in-trade** /'stɒkɪntreɪd/ *n*
existencias *fpl*. ~**ist** /'stɒkɪst/ *n* distribuidor *m*. ~**pile** /'stɒkpaɪl/ *n* reservas *fpl*. ● *vt* acumular. ~**still** *a*
inmóvil. ~**taking** *n* (*com*) inventario *m*
stocky /'stɒkɪ/ *a* (**-ier, -iest**) achaparrado
stodg|e /stɒdʒ/ *n* (*fam*) comida *f*
pesada. ~**y** *a* pesado
stoic /'stəʊɪk/ *n* estoico. ~**al** *a*
estoico. ~**ally** *adv* estoicamente.
~**ism** /-sɪzəm/ *n* estoicismo *m*
stoke /stəʊk/ *vt* alimentar. ~**r**
/'stəʊkə(r)/ *n* fogonero *m*
stole[1] /stəʊl/ *see* **steal**
stole[2] /stəʊl/ *n* estola *f*
stolen /'stəʊlən/ *see* **steal**
stolid /'stɒlɪd/ *a* impasible. ~**ly** *adv*
impasiblemente
stomach /'stʌmək/ *n* estómago *m*.
● *vt* soportar. ~**-ache** *n* dolor *m* de
estómago
ston|e /stəʊn/ *n* piedra *f*; (*med*)
cálculo *m*; (*in fruit*) hueso *m*; (*weight,
pl* **stone**) peso *m* de 14 libras (= *6,
348 kg*). ● *a* de piedra. ● *vt* apedrear;
deshuesar ⟨*fruit*⟩. ~**e-deaf** *a* sordo
como una tapia. ~**emason** /'stəʊn-
meɪsn/ *n* albañil *m*. ~**ework**
/'stəʊnwɜːk/ *n* cantería *f*. ~**y** *a*
pedregoso; (*like stone*) pétreo
stood /stʊd/ *see* **stand**
stooge /stuːdʒ/ *n* (*in theatre*)
compañero *m*; (*underling*) lacayo *m*
stool /stuːl/ *n* taburete *m*
stoop /stuːp/ *vi* inclinarse; (*fig*)
rebajarse. ● *n.* **have a** ~ ser cargado
de espaldas
stop /stɒp/ *vt* (*pt* **stopped**) parar;
(*cease*) terminar; tapar ⟨*a leak etc*⟩;
(*prevent*) impedir; (*interrupt*) interrumpir. ● *vi* pararse; (*stay, fam*)
quedarse. ● *n* (*bus etc*) parada *f*;
(*gram*) punto *m*; (*mec*) tope *m*. ~
dead *vi* pararse en seco. ~**cock**
/'stɒpkɒk/ *n* llave *f* de paso. ~**gap**
/'stɒpgæp/ *n* remedio *m* provisional.
~(**-over**) *n* escala *f*. ~**page**
/'stɒpɪdʒ/ *n* parada *f*; (*of work*) paro
m; (*interruption*) interrupción *f*.
~**per** /'stɒpə(r)/ *n* tapón *m*. ~**press**
n noticias *fpl* de última hora. ~ **light**

n luz *f* de freno. ~**watch** *n* cronómetro *m*
storage /'stɔːrɪdʒ/ *n* almacena-
miento *m*. ~ **heater** *n* acumulador
m. **in cold** ~ almacenaje *m* frigorífico
store /stɔː(r)/ *n* provisión *f*; (*shop,
depot*) almacén *m*; (*fig*) reserva *f*. **in**
~ en reserva. **set** ~ **by** dar importancia a. ● *vt* (*for future*) poner en
reserva; (*in warehouse*) almacenar.
~ **up** *vt* acumular
storeroom /'stɔːruːm/ *n* despensa *f*
storey /'stɔːrɪ/ *n* (*pl* **-eys**) piso *m*
stork /stɔːk/ *n* cigüeña *f*
storm /stɔːm/ *n* tempestad *f*; (*mil*)
asalto *m*. ● *vi* rabiar. ● *vt* (*mil*) a-
saltar. ~**y** *a* tempestuoso
story /'stɔːrɪ/ *n* historia *f*; (*in newspaper*) artículo *m*; (*fam*) mentira *f*,
cuento *m*. ~**teller** *n* cuentista *m & f*
stout /staʊt/ *a* (**-er, -est**) (*fat*) gordo;
(*brave*) valiente. ● *n* cerveza *f* negra.
~**ness** *n* corpulencia *f*
stove /stəʊv/ *n* estufa *f*
stow /stəʊ/ *vt* guardar; (*hide*)
esconder. ● *vi.* ~ **away** viajar
de polizón. ~**away** /'stəʊəweɪ/ *n*
polizón *m*
straddle /'strædl/ *vt* estar a horcajadas
straggl|e /'strægl/ *vi* rezagarse. ~**y**
a desordenado
straight /streɪt/ *a* (**-er, -est**) derecho,
recto; (*tidy*) en orden; (*frank*) franco;
⟨*drink*⟩ solo, puro; ⟨*hair*⟩ lacio. ● *adv*
derecho; (*direct*) directamente;
(*without delay*) inmediatamente. ~
on todo recto. ~ **out** sin vacilar. **go**
~ enmendarse. ● *n* recta *f*. ~ **away**
inmediatamente. ~**en** /'streɪtn/ *vt*
enderezar. ● *vi* enderezarse. ~
forward /streɪt'fɔːwəd/ *a* franco;
(*easy*) sencillo. ~**forwardly** *adv*
francamente. ~**ness** *n* rectitud *f*
strain[1] /streɪn/ *n* (*tension*) tensión *f*;
(*injury*) torcedura *f*. ● *vt* estirar;
(*tire*) cansar; (*injure*) torcer; (*sieve*)
colar
strain[2] /streɪn/ *n* (*lineage*) linaje *m*;
(*streak*) tendencia *f*
strained /streɪnd/ *a* forzado; ⟨*rela-
tions*⟩ tirante
strainer /-ə(r)/ *n* colador *m*
strains /streɪnz/ *npl* (*mus*) acordes
mpl
strait /streɪt/ *n* estrecho *m*. ~**-jacket**
n camisa *f* de fuerza. ~**-laced** *a* remilgado, gazmoño. ~**s** *npl* apuro *m*

strand /strænd/ n (thread) hebra f; (sand) playa f. ● vi ⟨ship⟩ varar. **be ~ed** quedarse sin recursos

strange /streɪndʒ/ a (-er, -est) extraño, raro; (not known) desconocido; (unaccustomed) nuevo. **~ly** adv extrañamente. **~ness** n extrañeza f. **~r** /'streɪndʒə(r)/ n desconocido m

strang|le /'stræŋgl/ vt estrangular; (fig) ahogar. **~lehold** /'stræŋglhəʊld/ n (fig) dominio m completo. **~ler** /-ə(r)/ n estrangulador m. **~ulation** /stræŋgjʊ'leɪʃn/ n estrangulación f

strap /stræp/ n correa f; (of garment) tirante m. ● vt (pt strapped) atar con correa; (flog) azotar

strapping /'stræpɪŋ/ a robusto

strata /'strɑːtə/ see **stratum**

strat|agem /'strætədʒəm/ n estratagema f. **~egic** /strə'tiːdʒɪk/ a estratégico. **~egically** adv estratégicamente. **~egist** n estratega m & f. **~egy** /'strætədʒɪ/ n estrategia f

stratum /'strɑːtəm/ n (pl strata) estrato m

straw /strɔː/ n paja f. **the last ~** el colmo

strawberry /'strɔːbərɪ/ n fresa f

stray /streɪ/ vi vagar; (deviate) desviarse (**from** de). ● a ⟨animal⟩ extraviado, callejero; (isolated) aislado. ● n animal m extraviado, animal m callejero

streak /striːk/ n raya f; (of madness) vena f. ● vt rayar. ● vi moverse como un rayo. **~y** a (-ier, -iest) rayado; ⟨bacon⟩ entreverado

stream /striːm/ n arroyo m; (current) corriente f; (of people) desfile m; (schol) grupo m. ● vi correr. **~ out** vi ⟨people⟩ salir en tropel

streamer /'striːmə(r)/ n (paper) serpentina f; (flag) gallardete m

streamline /'striːmlaɪn/ vt dar línea aerodinámica a; (simplify) simplificar. **~d** a aerodinámico

street /striːt/ n calle f. **~car** /'striːtkɑː/ n (Amer) tranvía m. **~ lamp** n farol m. **~ map** n, **~ plan** n plano m

strength /streŋθ/ n fuerza f; (of wall etc) solidez f. **on the ~ of** a base de. **~en** /'streŋθn/ vt reforzar

strenuous /'strenjʊəs/ a enérgico; (arduous) arduo; (tiring) fatigoso. **~ly** adv enérgicamente

stress /stres/ n énfasis f; (gram) acento m; (mec, med, tension) tensión f. ● vt insistir en

stretch /stretʃ/ vt estirar; (extend) extender; (exaggerate) forzar. **~ a point** hacer una excepción. ● vi estirarse; (extend) extenderse. ● n estirón m; (period) período m; (of road) tramo m. **at a ~** seguido; (in one go) de un tirón. **~er** /'stretʃə(r)/ n camilla f

strew /struː/ vt (pt strewed, pp strewn or strewed) esparcir; (cover) cubrir

stricken /'strɪkən/ a. **~ with** afectado de

strict /strɪkt/ a (-er, -est) severo; (precise) estricto, preciso. **~ly** adv estrictamente. **~ly speaking** en rigor

stricture /'strɪktʃə(r)/ n crítica f; (constriction) constricción f

stride /straɪd/ vi (pt strode, pp stridden) andar a zancadas. ● n zancada f. **take sth in one's ~** hacer algo con facilidad, tomarse las cosas con calma

strident /'straɪdnt/ a estridente

strife /straɪf/ n conflicto m

strike /straɪk/ vt (pt struck) golpear; encender ⟨match⟩; encontrar ⟨gold etc⟩; ⟨clock⟩ dar. ● vi golpear; (go on strike) declararse en huelga; (be on strike) estar en huelga; (attack) atacar; ⟨clock⟩ dar la hora. ● n (of workers) huelga f; (attack) ataque m; (find) descubrimiento m. **on ~** en huelga. **~ off, ~ out** tachar. **~ up a friendship** trabar amistad. **~r** /'straɪkə(r)/ n huelguista m & f

striking /'straɪkɪŋ/ a impresionante

string /strɪŋ/ n cuerda f; (of lies, pearls) sarta f. **pull ~s** tocar todos los resortes. ● vt (pt strung) (thread) ensartar. **~ along** (fam) engañar. **~ out** extender(se). **~ed** a (mus) de cuerda

stringen|cy /'strɪndʒənsɪ/ n rigor m. **~t** /'strɪndʒənt/ a riguroso

stringy /'strɪŋɪ/ a fibroso

strip /strɪp/ vt (pt stripped) desnudar; (tear away, deprive) quitar; desmontar ⟨machine⟩. ● vi desnudarse. ● n tira f. **~ cartoon** n historieta f

stripe /straɪp/ n raya f; (mil) galón m. **~d** a a rayas, rayado

strip: ~ **light** n tubo m fluorescente. ~**per** /-ə(r)/ n artista m & f de strip-tease. ~**tease** n número m del desnudo, striptease m

strive /straɪv/ vi (pt **strove**, pp **striven**). ~ **to** esforzarse por

strode /strəʊd/ see **stride**

stroke /strəʊk/ n golpe m; (in swimming) brazada f; (med) apoplejía f; (of pen etc) rasgo m; (of clock) campanada f; (caress) caricia f. ● vt acariciar

stroll /strəʊl/ vi pasearse. ● n paseo m

strong /strɒŋ/ a (-er, -est) fuerte. ~**box** n caja f fuerte. ~**hold** /strɒŋhəʊld/ n fortaleza f; (fig) baluarte m. ~ **language** n palabras fpl fuertes, palabras fpl subidas de tono. ~**ly** adv (greatly) fuertemente; (with energy) enérgicamente; (deeply) profundamente. ~ **measures** npl medidas fpl enérgicas. ~**minded** a resuelto. ~**room** n cámara f acorazada

stroppy /strɒpɪ/ a (sl) irascible

strove /strəʊv/ see **strive**

struck /strʌk/ see **strike**. ~ **on** (sl) entusiasta de

structur|al /strʌktʃərəl/ a estructural. ~**e** /strʌktʃə(r)/ n estructura f

struggle /strʌgl/ vi luchar. ~ **to one's feet** levantarse con dificultad. ● n lucha f

strum /strʌm/ vt/i (pt **strummed**) rasguear

strung /strʌŋ/ see **string**. ● a. ~ **up** (tense) nervioso

strut /strʌt/ n puntal m; (walk) pavoneo m. ● vi (pt **strutted**) pavonearse

stub /stʌb/ n cabo m; (counterfoil) talón m; (of cigarette) colilla f; (of tree) tocón m. ● vt (pt **stubbed**). ~ **out** apagar

stubble /stʌbl/ n rastrojo m; (beard) barba f de varios días

stubborn /stʌbən/ a terco. ~**ly** adv tercamente. ~**ness** n terquedad f

stubby /stʌbɪ/ a (-ier, -iest) achaparrado

stucco /stʌkəʊ/ n (pl -oes) estuco m

stuck /stʌk/ see **stick**. ● a (jammed) bloqueado; (in difficulties) en un apuro. ~ **on** (sl) encantado con. ~ **up** a (sl) presumido

stud[1] /stʌd/ n tachón m; (for collar) botón m. ● vt (pt **studded**) tachonar. ~**ded with** sembrado de

stud[2] /stʌd/ n (of horses) caballeriza f

student /stjuːdənt/ n estudiante m & f

studied /stʌdɪd/ a deliberado

studio /stjuːdɪəʊ/ n (pl -os) estudio m. ~ **couch** n sofá m cama. ~ **flat** n estudio m de artista

studious /stjuːdɪəs/ a estudioso; (studied) deliberado. ~**ly** adv estudiosamente; (carefully) cuidadosamente

study /stʌdɪ/ n estudio m; (office) despacho m. ● vt/i estudiar

stuff /stʌf/ n materia f, sustancia f; (sl) cosas fpl. ● vt rellenar; disecar ⟨animal⟩; (cram) atiborrar; (block up) tapar; (put) meter de prisa. ~**ing** n relleno m

stuffy /stʌfɪ/ a (-ier, -iest) mal ventilado; (old-fashioned) chapado a la antigua

stumbl|e /stʌmbl/ vi tropezar. ~**e across**, ~**e on** tropezar con. ● n tropezón m. ~**ing-block** n tropiezo m, impedimento m

stump /stʌmp/ n cabo m; (of limb) muñón m; (of tree) tocón m. ~**ed** /stʌmpt/ a (fam) perplejo. ~**y** /stʌmpɪ/ a (-ier, -iest) achaparrado

stun /stʌn/ vt (pt **stunned**) aturdir; (bewilder) pasmar. ~**ning** a (fabulous, fam) estupendo

stung /stʌŋ/ see **sting**

stunk /stʌŋk/ see **stink**

stunt[1] /stʌnt/ n (fam) truco m publicitario

stunt[2] /stʌnt/ vt impedir el desarrollo de. ~**ed** a enano

stupefy /stjuːpɪfaɪ/ vt dejar estupefacto

stupendous /stjuːpendəs/ a estupendo. ~**ly** adv estupendamente

stupid /stjuːpɪd/ a estúpido. ~**ity** /-pɪdətɪ/ n estupidez f. ~**ly** adv estúpidamente

stupor /stjuːpə(r)/ n estupor m

sturd|iness /stɜːdɪnɪs/ n robustez f. ~**y** /stɜːdɪ/ a (-ier, -iest) robusto

sturgeon /stɜːdʒən/ n (pl **sturgeon**) esturión m

stutter /stʌtə(r)/ vi tartamudear. ● n tartamudeo m

sty[1] /staɪ/ n (pl **sties**) pocilga f

sty[2] /staɪ/ n (pl **sties**) (med) orzuelo m

styl|e /staɪl/ n estilo m; (fashion) moda f. **in** ~ con todo lujo. ● vt diseñar. ~**ish** /'staɪlɪʃ/ a elegante. ~**ishly** adv elegantemente. ~**ist** /'staɪlɪst/ n estilista m & f. **hair** ~**ist** n peluquero m. ~**ized** /'staɪlaɪzd/ a estilizado

stylus /'staɪləs/ n (pl **-uses**) aguja f (de tocadiscos)

suave /swɑ:v/ a (pej) zalamero

sub... /sʌb/ pref sub...

subaquatic /sʌbə'kwætɪk/ a sub-acuático

subconscious /sʌb'kɒnʃəs/ a & n subconsciente (m). ~**ly** adv de modo subconsciente

subcontinent /sʌb'kɒntɪnənt/ n subcontinente m

subcontract /sʌbkən'trækt/ vt sub-contratar. ~**or** /-ə(r)/ n subcon-tratista m & f

subdivide /sʌbdɪ'vaɪd/ vt subdividir

subdue /səb'dju:/ vt dominar (feel-ings); sojuzgar (country). ~**d** a (de-pressed) abatido; (light) suave

subhuman /sʌb'hju:mən/ a infra-humano

subject /'sʌbdʒɪkt/ a sometido. ~ **to** sujeto a. ● n súbdito m; (theme) asunto m; (schol) asignatura f; (gram) sujeto m; (of painting, play, book etc) tema m. /səb'dʒekt/ vt so-juzgar; (submit) someter. ~**ion** /-ʃn/ n sometimiento m

subjective /səb'dʒektɪv/ a sub-jetivo. ~**ly** adv subjetivamente

subjugate /'sʌbdʒʊgeɪt/ vt sub-yugar

subjunctive /səb'dʒʌŋktɪv/ a & n subjuntivo (m)

sublet /sʌb'let/ vt (pt **sublet**, pres p **subletting**) subarrendar

sublimat|e /'sʌblɪmeɪt/ vt sublimar. ~**ion** /-'meɪʃn/ n sublimación f

sublime /sə'blaɪm/ a sublime. ~**ly** adv sublimemente

submarine /sʌbmə'ri:n/ n sub-marino m

submerge /səb'mɜ:dʒ/ vt sumergir. ● vi sumergirse

submi|ssion /səb'mɪʃn/ n sumisión f. ~**ssive** /-sɪv/ a sumiso. ~**t** /səb'mɪt/ vt (pt **submitted**) someter. ● vi someterse

subordinat|e /sə'bɔ:dɪnət/ a & n subordinado (m). /sə'bɔ:dɪneɪt/ vt subordinar. ~**ion** /-'neɪʃn/ n subordinación f

subscri|be /səb'skraɪb/ vi suscribir. ~**be to** suscribir (fund); (agree) es-tar de acuerdo con; abonarse a (news-paper). ~**ber** /-ə(r)/ n abonado m. ~**ption** /-rɪpʃn/ n suscripción f

subsequent /'sʌbsɪkwənt/ a sub-siguiente. ~**ly** adv posteriormente

subservient /səb'sɜ:vjənt/ a servil

subside /səb'saɪd/ vi (land) hun-dirse; (flood) bajar; (storm, wind) amainar. ~**nce** n hundimiento m

subsidiary /səb'sɪdɪərɪ/ a sub-sidiario. ● n (com) sucursal m

subsid|ize /'sʌbsɪdaɪz/ vt sub-vencionar. ~**y** /'sʌbsɪdɪ/ n sub-vención f

subsist /səb'sɪst/ vi subsistir. ~**ence** n subsistencia f

subsoil /'sʌbsɔɪl/ n subsuelo m

subsonic /sʌb'sɒnɪk/ a subsónico

substance /'sʌbstəns/ n substancia f

substandard /sʌb'stændəd/ a infe-rior

substantial /səb'stænʃl/ a sólido; (meal) substancial; (considerable) considerable. ~**ly** adv conside-rablemente

substantiate /səb'stænʃɪeɪt/ vt justificar

substitut|e /'sʌbstɪtju:t/ n subs-tituto m. ● vt/i substituir. ~**ion** /-'tju:ʃn/ n substitución f

subterfuge /'sʌbtəfju:dʒ/ n sub-terfugio m

subterranean /sʌbtə'reɪnjən/ a subterráneo

subtitle /'sʌbtaɪtl/ n subtítulo m

subtle /'sʌtl/ a (**-er, -est**) sutil. ~**ty** n sutileza f

subtract /səb'trækt/ vt restar. ~**ion** /-ʃn/ n resta f

suburb /'sʌbɜ:b/ n barrio m. **the** ~**s** las afueras fpl. ~**an** /sə'bɜ:bən/ a suburbano. ~**ia** /sə'bɜ:bɪə/ n las afue-ras fpl

subvention /səb'venʃn/ n sub-vención f

subver|sion /səb'vɜ:ʃn/ n sub-versión f. ~**sive** /səb'vɜ:sɪv/ a sub-versivo. ~**t** /səb'vɜ:t/ vt subvertir

subway /'sʌbweɪ/ n paso m subterráneo; (Amer) metro m

succeed /sək'si:d/ vi tener éxito. ● vt suceder a. ~ **in doing** lograr hacer. ~**ing** a sucesivo

success /sək'ses/ n éxito m. ~**ful** a que tiene éxito; (chosen) elegido

succession /sək'seʃn/ *n* sucesión *f*. **in** ~ sucesivamente, seguidos

successive /sək'sesɪv/ *a* sucesivo. ~**ly** *adv* sucesivamente

successor /sək'sesə(r)/ *n* sucesor *m*

succinct /sək'sɪŋkt/ *a* sucinto

succour /'sʌkə(r)/ *vt* socorrer. ● *n* socorro *m*

succulent /'sʌkjʊlənt/ *a* suculento

succumb /sə'kʌm/ *vi* sucumbir

such /sʌtʃ/ *a* tal. ● *pron* los que, las que; (*so much*) tanto. **and** ~ y tal. ● *adv* tan. ~ **a big house** una casa tan grande. ~ **and** ~ tal o cual. ~ **as it is** tal como es. ~**like** *a* (*fam*) semejante, de ese tipo

suck /sʌk/ *vt* chupar; sorber (*liquid*). ~ **up** absorber. ~ **up to** (*sl*) dar coba a. ~**er** /'sʌkə(r)/ *n* (*plant*) chupón *m*; (*person, fam*) primo *m*

suckle /sʌkl/ *vt* amamantar

suction /'sʌkʃn/ *n* succión *f*

sudden /'sʌdn/ *a* repentino. **all of a** ~ de repente. ~**ly** *adv* de repente. ~**ness** *n* lo repentino

suds /sʌds/ *npl* espuma *f* (de jabón)

sue /su:/ *vt* (*pres p* **suing**) demandar (**for** por)

suede /sweɪd/ *n* ante *m*

suet /'su:ɪt/ *n* sebo *m*

suffer /'sʌfə(r)/ *vt* sufrir; (*tolerate*) tolerar. ● *vi* sufrir. ~**ance** /'sʌfərəns/ *n*. **on** ~**ance** por tolerancia. ~**ing** *n* sufrimiento *m*

suffic|e /sə'faɪs/ *vi* bastar. ~**iency** /sə'fɪʃənsɪ/ *n* suficiencia *f*. ~**ient** /sə'fɪʃnt/ *a* suficiente; (*enough*) bastante. ~**iently** *adv* suficientemente, bastante

suffix /'sʌfɪks/ *n* (*pl* **-ixes**) sufijo *m*

suffocat|e /'sʌfəkeɪt/ *vt* ahogar. ● *vi* ahogarse. ~**ion** /-'keɪʃn/ *n* asfixia *f*

sugar /'ʃʊgə(r)/ *n* azúcar *m* & *f*. ● *vt* azucarar. ~**bowl** *n* azucarero *m*. ~ **lump** *n* terrón *m* de azúcar. ~**y** *a* azucarado

suggest /sə'dʒest/ *vt* sugerir. ~**ible** /sə'dʒestɪbl/ *a* sugestionable. ~**ion** /-tʃən/ *n* sugerencia *f*; (*trace*) traza *f*. ~**ive** /sə'dʒestɪv/ *a* sugestivo. **be** ~**ive** of evocar, recordar. ~**ively** *adv* sugestivamente

suicid|al /su:ɪ'saɪdl/ *a* suicida. ~**e** /'su:ɪsaɪd/ *n* suicidio *m*; (*person*) suicida *m* & *f*. **commit** ~**e** suicidarse

suit /su:t/ *n* traje *m*; (*woman's*) traje *m* de chaqueta; (*cards*) palo *m*; (*jurid*) pleito *m*. ● *vt* convenir; (*clothes*) sentar bien a; (*adapt*) adaptar. **be** ~**ed for** ser apto para. ~**ability** *n* conveniencia *f*. ~**able** *a* adecuado. ~**ably** *adv* convenientemente. ~**case** /'su:tkeɪs/ *n* maleta *f*, valija *f* (*LAm*)

suite /swi:t/ *n* (*of furniture*) juego *m*; (*of rooms*) apartamento *m*; (*retinue*) séquito *m*

suitor /'su:tə(r)/ *n* pretendiente *m*

sulk /sʌlk/ *vi* enfurruñarse. ~**s** *npl* enfurruñamiento *m*. ~**y** *a* enfurruñado

sullen /'sʌlən/ *a* resentido. ~**ly** *adv* con resentimiento

sully /'sʌlɪ/ *vt* manchar

sulphur /'sʌlfə(r)/ *n* azufre *m*. ~**ic** /-'fjʊərɪk/ *a* sulfúrico. ~**ic acid** *n* ácido *m* sulfúrico

sultan /'sʌltən/ *n* sultán *m*

sultana /sʌl'tɑ:nə/ *n* pasa *f* gorrona

sultry /'sʌltrɪ/ *a* (**-ier**, **-iest**) (*weather*) bochornoso; (*fig*) sensual

sum /sʌm/ *n* suma *f*. ● *vt* (*pt* **summed**). ~ **up** resumir (*situation*); (*assess*) evaluar

summar|ily /'sʌmərɪlɪ/ *adv* sumariamente. ~**ize** *vt* resumir. ~**y** /'sʌmərɪ/ *a* sumario. ● *n* resumen *m*

summer /'sʌmə(r)/ *n* verano *m*. ~**house** *n* glorieta *f*, cenador *m*. ~**time** *n* verano *m*. ~ **time** *n* hora *f* de verano. ~**y** *a* veraniego

summit /'sʌmɪt/ *n* cumbre *f*. ~ **conference** *n* conferencia *f* cumbre

summon /'sʌmən/ *vt* llamar; convocar (*meeting, s.o. to meeting*); (*jurid*) citar. ~ **up** armarse de. ~**s** /'sʌmənz/ *n* llamada *f*; (*jurid*) citación *f*. ● *vt* citar

sump /sʌmp/ *n* (*mec*) cárter *m*

sumptuous /'sʌmptjʊəs/ *a* suntuoso. ~**ly** *adv* suntuosamente

sun /sʌn/ *n* sol *m*. ● *vt* (*pt* **sunned**). ~ **o.s.** tomar el sol. ~**bathe** /'sʌnbeɪð/ *vi* tomar el sol. ~**beam** /'sʌnbi:m/ *n* rayo *m* de sol. ~**burn** /'sʌnbɜ:n/ *n* quemadura *f* de sol. ~**burnt** *a* quemado por el sol

sundae /'sʌndeɪ/ *n* helado *m* con frutas y nueces

Sunday /'sʌndeɪ/ *n* domingo *m*. ~ **school** *n* catequesis *f*

sun: ~**dial** /'sʌndaɪl/ *n* reloj *m* de sol. ~**down** /'sʌndaʊn/ *n* puesta *f* del sol

sundry /'sʌndrɪ/ *a* diversos. **all and** ~ todo el mundo. **sundries** *npl* artículos *mpl* diversos

sunflower /'sʌnflaʊə(r)/ n girasol m
sung /sʌŋ/ see **sing**
sun-glasses /'sʌnglɑːsɪz/ npl gafas fpl de sol
sunk /sʌŋk/ see **sink**. ~**en** /'sʌŋkən/ ● a hundido
sunlight /'sʌnlaɪt/ n luz f del sol
sunny /'sʌnɪ/ a (-ier, -iest) ⟨day⟩ de sol; ⟨place⟩ soleado. **it is** ~ hace sol
sun: ~**rise** /'sʌnraɪz/ n amanecer m, salida f del sol. ~**roof** n techo m corredizo. ~**set** /'sʌnset/ n puesta f del sol. ~**shade** /'sʌnʃeɪd/ n quitasol m, sombrilla f; ⟨awning⟩ toldo m. ~**shine** /'sʌnʃaɪn/ n sol m. ~**spot** /'sʌnspɒt/ n mancha f solar. ~**stroke** /'sʌnstrəʊk/ n insolación f. ~**tan** /'sʌntæn/ n bronceado m. ~**tanned** a bronceado. ~**tan lotion** n bronceador m
sup /sʌp/ vt (pt **supped**) sorber
super /'suːpə(r)/ a (fam) estupendo
superannuation /suːpərænjʊ'eɪʃn/ n jubilación f
superb /suː'pɜːb/ a espléndido. ~**ly** adv espléndidamente
supercilious /suːpə'sɪlɪəs/ a desdeñoso
superficial /suːpə'fɪʃl/ a superficial. ~**ity** /-ɪ'rælətɪ/ n superficialidad f. ~**ly** adv superficialmente
superfluous /suː'pɜːflʊəs/ a superfluo
superhuman /suːpə'hjuːmən/ a sobrehumano
superimpose /suːpərɪm'pəʊz/ vt sobreponer
superintend /suːpərɪn'tend/ vt vigilar. ~**ence** n dirección f. ~**ent** n director m; ⟨of police⟩ comisario m
superior /suː'pɪərɪə(r)/ a & n superior (m). ~**ity** /-ɪ'ɒrətɪ/ n superioridad f
superlative /suː'pɜːlətɪv/ a & n superlativo (m)
superman /'suːpəmæn/ n (pl **-men**) superhombre m
supermarket /'suːpəmɑːkɪt/ n supermercado m
supernatural /suːpə'nætʃrəl/ a sobrenatural
superpower /'suːpəpaʊə(r)/ n superpotencia f
supersede /suːpə'siːd/ vt reemplazar, suplantar
supersonic /suːpə'sɒnɪk/ a supersónico
superstitio|n /suːpə'stɪʃn/ n superstición f. ~**us** a supersticioso

superstructure /'suːpəstrʌktʃə(r)/ n superestructura f
supertanker /'suːpətæŋkə(r)/ n petrolero m gigante
supervene /suːpə'viːn/ vi sobrevenir
supervis|e /'suːpəvaɪz/ vt supervisar. ~**ion** /-'vɪʒn/ n supervisión f. ~**or** /-zə(r)/ n supervisor m. ~**ory** a de supervisión
supper /'sʌpə(r)/ n cena f
supplant /sə'plɑːnt/ vt suplantar
supple /sʌpl/ a flexible. ~**ness** n flexibilidad f
supplement /'sʌplɪmənt/ n suplemento m. ● vt completar; ⟨increase⟩ aumentar. ~**ary** /-'mentərɪ/ a suplementario
suppl|ier /sə'plaɪə(r)/ n suministrador m; ⟨com⟩ proveedor m. ~**y** /sə'plaɪ/ vt proveer; ⟨feed⟩ alimentar; satisfacer ⟨a need⟩. ~**y with** abastecer de. ● n provisión f, suministro m. ~**y and demand** oferta f y demanda
support /sə'pɔːt/ vt sostener; ⟨endure⟩ soportar, aguantar; ⟨fig⟩ apoyar. ● n apoyo m; ⟨tec⟩ soporte m. ~**er** /-ə(r)/ n soporte m; ⟨sport⟩ seguidor m, hincha m & f. ~**ive** a alentador
suppos|e /sə'pəʊz/ vt suponer; ⟨think⟩ creer. **be** ~**ed to** deber. **not be** ~**ed to** (fam) no tener permiso para, no tener derecho a. ~**edly** adv según cabe suponer; ⟨before adjective⟩ presuntamente. ~**ition** /sʌpə'zɪʃn/ n suposición f
suppository /sə'pɒzɪtərɪ/ n supositorio m
suppress /sə'pres/ vt suprimir. ~**ion** n supresión f. ~**or** /-ə(r)/ n supresor m
suprem|acy /suː'preməsɪ/ n supremacía f. ~**e** /suː'priːm/ a supremo
surcharge /'sɜːtʃɑːdʒ/ n sobreprecio m; ⟨tax⟩ recargo m
sure /ʃʊə(r)/ a (-er, -est) seguro, cierto. **make** ~ asegurarse. ● adv (Amer, fam) ¡claro! **enough** efectivamente. ~**-footed** a de pie firme. ~**ly** adv seguramente
surety /'ʃʊərətɪ/ n garantía f
surf /sɜːf/ n oleaje m; ⟨foam⟩ espuma f
surface /'sɜːfɪs/ n superficie f. ● a superficial, de la superficie. ● vt ⟨smoothe⟩ alisar; ⟨cover⟩ recubrir (**with** de). ● vi salir a la superficie;

(*emerge*) emerger. ~ **mail** *n* por vía marítima

surfboard /'sɜːfbɔːd/ *n* tabla *f* de surf

surfeit /'sɜːfɪt/ *n* exceso *m*

surfing /'sɜːfɪŋ/ *n*, **surf-riding** /'sɜːfraɪdɪŋ/ *n* surf *m*

surge /sɜːdʒ/ *vi* ⟨crowd⟩ moverse en tropel; ⟨waves⟩ encresparse. ● *n* oleada *f*; (*elec*) sobretensión *f*

surgeon /'sɜːdʒən/ *n* cirujano *m*

surgery /'sɜːdʒərɪ/ *n* cirugía *f*; (*consulting room*) consultorio *m*; (*consulting hours*) horas *fpl* de consulta

surgical /'sɜːrdʒɪkl/ *a* quirúrgico

surl|iness /'sɜːlɪnɪs/ *n* aspereza *f*. ~**y** /'sɜːlɪ/ *a* (**-ier, -iest**) áspero

surmise /sə'maɪz/ *vt* conjeturar

surmount /sə'maʊnt/ *vt* superar

surname /'sɜːneɪm/ *n* apellido *m*

surpass /sə'pɑːs/ *vt* sobrepasar, exceder

surplus /'sɜːpləs/ *a & n* excedente (*m*)

surpris|e /sə'praɪz/ *n* sorpresa *f*. ● *vt* sorprender. ~**ing** *a* sorprendente. ~**ingly** *adv* asombrosamente

surrealis|m /sə'rɪəlɪzəm/ *n* surrealismo *m*. ~**t** *n* surrealista *m & f*

surrender /sə'rendə(r)/ *vt* entregar. ● *vi* entregarse. ● *n* entrega *f*; (*mil*) rendición *f*

surreptitious /sʌrəp'tɪʃəs/ *a* clandestino

surrogate /'sʌrəgət/ *n* substituto *m*

surround /sə'raʊnd/ *vt* rodear; (*mil*) cercar. ● *n* borde *m*. ~**ing** *a* circundante. ~**ings** *npl* alrededores *mpl*

surveillance /sɜː'veɪləns/ *n* vigilancia *f*

survey /'sɜːveɪ/ *n* inspección *f*; (*report*) informe *m*; (*general view*) vista *f* de conjunto. /sə'veɪ/ *vt* examinar, inspeccionar; (*inquire into*) hacer una encuesta de. ~**or** *n* topógrafo *m*, agrimensor *m*

surviv|al /sə'vaɪvl/ *n* supervivencia *f*. ~**e** /sə'vaɪv/ *vt/i* sobrevivir. ~**or** /-ə(r)/ *n* superviviente *m & f*

susceptib|ility /səseptə'bɪlətɪ/ *n* susceptibilidad *f*. ~**le** /sə'septəbl/ *a* susceptible. ~**le to** propenso a

suspect /sə'spekt/ *vt* sospechar. /'sʌspekt/ *a & n* sospechoso (*m*)

suspend /sə'spend/ *vt* suspender. ~**er** /sə'spendə(r)/ *n* liga *f*. ~**er belt** *n* liguero *m*. ~**ers** *npl* (*Amer*) tirantes *mpl*

suspense /sə'spens/ *n* incertidumbre *f*; (*in film etc*) suspense *m*

suspension /sə'spenʃn/ *n* suspensión *f*. ~ **bridge** *n* puente *m* colgante

suspicion /sə'spɪʃn/ *n* sospecha *f*; (*trace*) pizca *f*

suspicious /sə'spɪʃəs/ *a* desconfiado; (*causing suspicion*) sospechoso

sustain /sə'steɪn/ *vt* sostener; (*suffer*) sufrir

sustenance /'sʌstɪnəns/ *n* sustento *m*

svelte /svelt/ *a* esbelto

SW *abbr* (*south-west*) sudoeste *m*

swab /swɒb/ *n* (*med*) tapón *m*

swagger /'swægə(r)/ *vi* pavonearse

swallow[1] /'swɒləʊ/ *vt/i* tragar. ● *n* trago *m*. ~ **up** tragar; consumir ⟨savings etc⟩

swallow[2] /'swɒləʊ/ *n* (*bird*) golondrina *f*

swam /swæm/ *see* **swim**

swamp /swɒmp/ *n* pantano *m*. ● *vt* inundar; (*with work*) agobiar. ~**y** *a* pantanoso

swan /swɒn/ *n* cisne *m*

swank /swæŋk/ *n* (*fam*) ostentación *f*. ● *vi* (*fam*) fanfarronear

swap /swɒp/ *vt/i* (*pt* **swapped**) (*fam*) (inter)cambiar. ● *n* (*fam*) (inter) cambio *m*

swarm /swɔːm/ *n* enjambre *m*. ● *vi* ⟨bees⟩ enjambrar; (*fig*) hormiguear

swarthy /'swɔːðɪ/ *a* (**-ier, -iest**) moreno

swastika /'swɒstɪkə/ *n* cruz *f* gamada

swat /swɒt/ *vt* (*pt* **swatted**) aplastar

sway /sweɪ/ *vi* balancearse. ● *vt* (*influence*) influir en. ● *n* balanceo *m*; (*rule*) imperio *m*

swear /sweə(r)/ *vt/i* (*pt* **swore**, *pp* **sworn**) jurar. ~ **by** (*fam*) creer ciegamente en. ~-**word** *n* palabrota *f*

sweat /swet/ *n* sudor *m*. ● *vi* sudar

sweat|er /'swetə(r)/ *n* jersey *m*. ~-**shirt** *n* sudadera *f*

swede /swiːd/ *n* naba *f*

Swede /swiːd/ *n* sueco *m*

Sweden /'swiːdn/ *n* Suecia *f*

Swedish /'swiːdɪʃ/ *a & n* sueco (*m*)

sweep /swiːp/ *vt* (*pt* **swept**) barrer; deshollinar ⟨chimney⟩. ~ **the board** ganar todo. ● *vi* barrer; ⟨road⟩ extenderse; (*go majestically*) moverse majestuosamente. ● *n* barrido *m*;

(*curve*) curva *f*; (*movement*) movimiento *m*; (*person*) deshollinador *m*. **~ away** *vt* barrer. **~ing** *a* (*gesture*) amplio; (*changes etc*) radical; (*statement*) demasiado general. **~stake** /'swi:psteɪk/ *n* lotería *f*

sweet /swi:t/ *a* (**-er**, **-est**) dulce; (*fragrant*) fragante; (*pleasant*) agradable. **have a ~ tooth** ser dulcero. ● *n* caramelo *m*; (*dish*) postre *m*. **~bread** /'swi:tbred/ *n* lechecillas *fpl*. **~en** /'swi:tn/ *vt* endulzar. **~ener** /-ə(r)/ *n* dulcificante *m*. **~heart** /'swi:thɑ:t/ *n* amor *m*. **~ly** *adv* dulcemente. **~ness** *n* dulzura *f*. **~ pea** *n* guisante *m* de olor

swell /swel/ *vt* (*pt* **swelled**, *pp* **swollen** *or* **swelled**) hinchar; (*increase*) aumentar. ● *vi* hincharse; (*increase*) aumentarse; (*river*) crecer. ● *a* (*fam*) estupendo. ● *n* (*of sea*) oleaje *m*. **~ing** *n* hinchazón *m*

swelter /'sweltə(r)/ *vi* sofocarse de calor

swept /swept/ *see* **sweep**

swerve /swɜ:v/ *vi* desviarse

swift /swɪft/ *a* (**-er**, **-est**) rápido. ● *n* (*bird*) vencejo *m*. **~ly** *adv* rápidamente. **~ness** *n* rapidez *f*

swig /swɪg/ *vt* (*pt* **swigged**) (*fam*) beber a grandes tragos. ● *n* (*fam*) trago *m*

swill /swɪl/ *vt* enjuagar; (*drink*) beber a grandes tragos. ● *n* (*food for pigs*) bazofia *f*

swim /swɪm/ *vi* (*pt* **swam**, *pp* **swum**) nadar; (*room, head*) dar vueltas. ● *n* baño *m*. **~mer** *n* nadador *m*. **~ming-bath** *n* piscina *f*. **~mingly** /'swɪmɪŋlɪ/ *adv* a las mil maravillas. **~ming-pool** *n* piscina *f*. **~ming-trunks** *npl* bañador *m*. **~suit** *n* traje *m* de baño

swindle /'swɪndl/ *vt* estafar. ● *n* estafa *f*. **~r** /-ə(r)/ *n* estafador *m*

swine /swaɪn/ *npl* cerdos *mpl*. ● *n* (*pl* **swine**) (*person, fam*) canalla *m*

swing /swɪŋ/ *vt* (*pt* **swung**) balancear. ● *vi* oscilar; (*person*) balancearse; (*turn round*) girar. ● *n* balanceo *m*, vaivén *m*; (*seat*) columpio *m*; (*mus*) ritmo *m*. **in full ~** en plena actividad. **~ bridge** *n* puente *m* giratorio

swingeing /'swɪndʒɪŋ/ *a* enorme

swipe /swaɪp/ *vt* golpear; (*snatch, sl*) birlar. ● *n* (*fam*) golpe *m*

swirl /swɜ:l/ *vi* arremolinarse. ● *n* remolino *m*

swish /swɪʃ/ *vt* silbar. ● *a* (*fam*) elegante

Swiss /swɪs/ *a & n* suizo (*m*). **~ roll** *n* bizcocho *m* enrollado

switch /swɪtʃ/ *n* (*elec*) interruptor *m*; (*change*) cambio *m*. ● *vt* cambiar; (*deviate*) desviar. **~ off** (*elec*) desconectar; apagar (*light*). **~ on** (*elec*) encender; arrancar (*engine*). **~back** /'swɪtʃbæk/ *n* montaña *f* rusa. **~board** /'swɪtʃbɔ:d/ *n* centralita *f*

Switzerland /'swɪtsələnd/ *n* Suiza *f*

swivel /'swɪvl/ ● *vi* (*pt* **swivelled**) girar

swollen /'swəʊlən/ *see* **swell**. ● *a* hinchado

swoon /swu:n/ *vi* desmayarse

swoop /swu:p/ *vi* (*bird*) calarse; (*plane*) bajar en picado. ● *n* calada *f*; (*by police*) redada *f*

sword /sɔ:d/ *n* espada *f*. **~fish** /'sɔ:dfɪʃ/ *n* pez *m* espada

swore /swɔ:(r)/ *see* **swear**

sworn /swɔ:n/ *see* **swear**. ● *a* (*enemy*) jurado; (*friend*) leal

swot /swɒt/ *vt/i* (*pt* **swotted**) (*schol, sl*) empollar. ● *n* (*schol, sl*) empollón *m*

swum /swʌm/ *see* **swim**

swung /swʌŋ/ *see* **swing**

sycamore /'sɪkəmɔ:(r)/ *n* plátano *m* falso

syllable /'sɪləbl/ *n* sílaba *f*

syllabus /'sɪləbəs/ *n* (*pl* **-buses**) programa *m* (de estudios)

symbol /'sɪmbl/ *n* símbolo *m*. **~ic(al)** /-'bɒlɪk(l)/ *a* simbólico. **~ism** *n* simbolismo *m*. **~ize** *vt* simbolizar

symmetr|ical /sɪ'metrɪkl/ *a* simétrico. **~y** /'sɪmətrɪ/ *n* simetría *f*

sympath|etic /sɪmpə'θetɪk/ *a* comprensivo; (*showing pity*) compasivo. **~ize** /-aɪz/ *vi* comprender; (*pity*) compadecerse (**with** de). **~izer** *n* (*pol*) simpatizante *m & f*. **~y** /'sɪmpəθɪ/ *n* comprensión *f*; (*pity*) compasión *f*; (*condolences*) pésame *m*. **be in ~y with** estar de acuerdo con

symphon|ic /sɪm'fɒnɪk/ *a* sinfónico. **~y** /'sɪmfənɪ/ *n* sinfonía *f*

symposium /sɪm'pəʊzɪəm/ *n* (*pl* **-ia**) simposio *m*

symptom /'sɪmptəm/ *n* síntoma *m*. **~atic** /-'mætɪk/ *a* sintomático

synagogue /'sɪnəgɒg/ *n* sinagoga *f*

synchroniz|ation /sɪnkrənaɪ'zeɪʃn/ *n* sincronización *f*. **~e** /'sɪŋkrənaɪz/ *vt* sincronizar

syncopat|e /'sɪnkəpeɪt/ *vt* sincopar. **~ion** /-'peɪʃn/ *n* síncopa *f*

syndicate /'sɪndɪkət/ *n* sindicato *m*

syndrome /'sɪndrəʊm/ *n* síndrome *m*

synod /'sɪnəd/ *n* sínodo *m*

synonym /'sɪnənɪm/ *n* sinónimo *m*. **~ous** /-'nɒnɪməs/ *a* sinónimo

synopsis /sɪ'nɒpsɪs/ *n* (*pl* **-opses** /-siːz/) sinopsis *f*, resumen *m*

syntax /'sɪntæks/ *n* sintaxis *f invar*

synthesi|s /'sɪnθəsɪs/ *n* (*pl* **-theses** /-siːz/) síntesis *f*. **~ze** *vt* sintetizar

synthetic /sɪn'θetɪk/ *a* sintético

syphilis /'sɪfɪlɪs/ *n* sífilis *f*

Syria /'sɪrɪə/ *n* Siria *f*. **~n** *a* & *n* sirio (*m*)

syringe /'sɪrɪndʒ/ *n* jeringa *f*. ● *vt* jeringar

syrup /'sɪrəp/ *n* jarabe *m*, almíbar *m*; (*treacle*) melaza *f*. **~y** *a* almibarado

system /'sɪstəm/ *n* sistema *m*; (*body*) organismo *m*; (*order*) método *m*. **~atic** /-ə'mætɪk/ *a* sistemático. **~atically** /-ə'mætɪkli/ *adv* sistemáticamente. **~s analyst** *n* analista *m* & *f* de sistemas

T

tab /tæb/ *n* (*flap*) lengüeta *f*; (*label*) etiqueta *f*. **keep ~s on** (*fam*) vigilar

tabby /'tæbɪ/ *n* gato *m* atigrado

tabernacle /'tæbənækl/ *n* tabernáculo *m*

table /'teɪbl/ *n* mesa *f*; (*list*) tabla *f*. **~ of contents** índice *m*. ● *vt* presentar; (*postpone*) aplazar. **~cloth** *n* mantel *m*. **~mat** *n* salvamanteles *m invar*. **~spoon** /'teɪblspuːn/ *n* cucharón *m*, cuchara *f* sopera. **~spoonful** *n* (*pl* **-fuls**) cucharada *f*

table tennis /'teɪbltenɪs/ *n* tenis *m* de mesa, ping-pong *m*

tabloid /'tæblɔɪd/ *n* tabloide *m*

taboo /tə'buː/ *a* & *n* tabú (*m*)

tabulator /'tæbjʊleɪtə(r)/ *n* tabulador *m*

tacit /'tæsɪt/ *a* tácito

taciturn /'tæsɪtɜːn/ *a* taciturno

tack /tæk/ *n* tachuela *f*; (*stitch*) hilván *m*; (*naut*) virada *f*; (*fig*) línea *f*

de conducta. ● *vt* sujetar con tachuelas; (*sew*) hilvanar. **~ on** añadir. ● *vi* virar

tackle /'tækl/ *n* (*equipment*) equipo *m*; (*football*) placaje *m*. ● *vt* abordar ⟨*problem etc*⟩; (*in rugby*) hacer un placaje a

tacky /'tækɪ/ *a* pegajoso; (*in poor taste*) vulgar, de pacotilla

tact /tækt/ *n* tacto *m*. **~ful** *a* discreto. **~fully** *adv* discretamente

tactic|al /'tæktɪkl/ *a* táctico. **~s** /'tæktɪks/ *npl* táctica *f*

tactile /'tæktaɪl/ *a* táctil

tact~less *a* indiscreto. **~lessly** *adv* indiscretamente

tadpole /'tædpəʊl/ *n* renacuajo *m*

tag /tæg/ *n* (*on shoe-lace*) herrete *m*; (*label*) etiqueta *f*. ● *vt* (*pt* **tagged**) poner etiqueta a; (*trail*) seguir. ● *vi*. **~ along** (*fam*) seguir

tail /teɪl/ *n* cola *f*. **~s** *npl* (*tailcoat*) frac *m*; (*of coin*) cruz *f*. ● *vt* (*sl*) seguir. ● *vi*. **~ off** disminuir. **~-end** *n* extremo *m* final, cola *f*

tailor /'teɪlə(r)/ *n* sastre *m*. ● *vt* confeccionar. **~-made** *n* hecho a la medida. **~-made for** (*fig*) hecho para

tailplane /'teɪlpleɪn/ *n* plano *m* de cola

taint /teɪnt/ *n* mancha *f*. ● *vt* contaminar

take /teɪk/ *vt* (*pt* **took**, *pp* **taken**) tomar, coger (*not LAm*), agarrar (*esp LAm*); (*contain*) contener; (*capture*) capturar; (*endure*) aguantar; (*require*) requerir; tomar ⟨*bath*⟩; dar ⟨*walk*⟩; (*carry*) llevar; (*accompany*) acompañar; presentarse para ⟨*exam*⟩; sacar ⟨*photo*⟩; ganar ⟨*prize*⟩. **~ advantage of** aprovechar. **~ after** parecerse a. **~ away** quitar. **~ back** retirar ⟨*statement etc*⟩. **~ in** achicar ⟨*garment*⟩; (*understand*) comprender; (*deceive*) engañar. **~ off** quitarse ⟨*clothes*⟩; (*mimic*) imitar; (*aviat*) despegar. **~ o.s. off** marcharse. **~ on** (*undertake*) emprender; contratar ⟨*employee*⟩. **~ out** (*remove*) sacar. **~ over** tomar posesión de; (*assume control*) tomar el poder. **~ part** participar. **~ place** tener lugar. **~ sides** tomar partido. **~ to** dedicarse a; (*like*) tomar simpatía a ⟨*person*⟩; (*like*) aficionarse a ⟨*thing*⟩. **~ up** dedicarse a ⟨*hobby*⟩; (*occupy*) ocupar; (*resume*) reanudar. **~ up with** trabar amistad con. **be ~n ill** ponerse enfermo. ● *n* presa *f*; (*photo, cinema, TV*) toma *f*

takings /'teɪkɪŋz/ *npl* ingresos *mpl*

take: **~off** *n* despegue *m*. **~over** *n* toma *f* de posesión.

talcum /'tælkəm/ *n*. **~ powder** *n* (polvos *mpl* de) talco (*m*)

tale /teɪl/ *n* cuento *m*

talent /'tælənt/ *n* talento *m*. **~ed** *a* talentoso

talisman /'tælɪzmən/ *n* talismán *m*

talk /tɔːk/ *vt/i* hablar. **~ about** hablar de. **~ over** discutir. ● *n* conversación *f*; (*lecture*) conferencia *f*. **small ~** charla *f*. **~ative** *a* hablador. **~er** *n* hablador *m*; (*chatterbox*) parlanchín *m*. **~ing-to** *n* represión *f*

tall /tɔːl/ *a* (**-er, -est**) alto. **~ story** *n* (*fam*) historia *f* inverosímil. **that's a ~ order** *n* (*fam*) eso es pedir mucho

tallboy /'tɔːlbɔɪ/ *n* cómoda *f* alta

tally /'tælɪ/ *n* tarja *f*; (*total*) total *m*. ● *vi* corresponder (**with** a)

talon /'tælən/ *n* garra *f*

tambourine /tæmbə'riːn/ *n* pandereta *f*

tame /teɪm/ *a* (**-er, -est**) ⟨*animal*⟩ doméstico; ⟨*person*⟩ dócil; (*dull*) insípido. ● *vt* domesticar; domar ⟨*wild animal*⟩. **~ly** *adv* dócilmente. **~r** /-ə(r)/ *n* domador *m*

tamper /'tæmpə(r)/ *vi*. **~ with** manosear; (*alter*) alterar, falsificar

tampon /'tæmpən/ *n* tampón *m*

tan /tæn/ *vt* (*pt* **tanned**) curtir ⟨*hide*⟩; ⟨*sun*⟩ broncear. ● *vi* ponerse moreno. ● *n* bronceado *m*. ● *a* (*colour*) de color canela

tandem /'tændəm/ *n* tándem *m*

tang /tæŋ/ *n* sabor *m* fuerte; (*smell*) olor *m* fuerte

tangent /'tændʒənt/ *n* tangente *f*

tangerine /tændʒə'riːn/ *n* mandarina *f*

tangibl|e /'tændʒəbl/ *a* tangible. **~y** *adv* perceptiblemente

tangle /'tæŋgl/ *vt* enredar. ● *vi* enredarse. ● *n* enredo *m*

tango /'tæŋgəʊ/ *n* (*pl* **-os**) tango *m*

tank /tæŋk/ *n* depósito *m*; (*mil*) tanque *m*

tankard /'tæŋkəd/ *n* jarra *f*, bock *m*

tanker /'tæŋkə(r)/ *n* petrolero *m*; (*truck*) camión *m* cisterna

tantaliz|e /'tæntəlaɪz/ *vt* atormentar. **~ing** *a* atormentador; (*tempting*) tentador

tantamount /'tæntəmaʊnt/ *a*. **~ to** equivalente a

tantrum /'tæntrəm/ *n* rabieta *f*

tap¹ /tæp/ *n* grifo *m*. **on ~** disponible. ● *vt* explotar ⟨*resources*⟩; interceptar ⟨*phone*⟩

tap² /tæp/ *n* (*knock*) golpe *m* ligero. ● *vt* (*pt* **tapped**) golpear ligeramente. **~-dance** *n* zapateado *m*

tape /teɪp/ *n* cinta *f*. ● *vt* atar con cinta; (*record*) grabar. **have sth ~d** (*sl*) comprender perfectamente. **~ measure** *n* cinta *f* métrica

taper /'teɪpə(r)/ *n* bujía *f*. ● *vt* ahusar. ● *vi* ahusarse. **~ off** disminuir

tape: **~ recorder** *n* magnetófon *m*, magnetófono *m*. **~ recording** *n* grabación *f*

tapestry /'tæpɪstrɪ/ *n* tapicería *f*; (*product*) tapiz *m*

tapioca /tæpɪ'əʊkə/ *n* tapioca *f*

tar /tɑː(r)/ *n* alquitrán *m*. ● *vt* (*pt* **tarred**) alquitranar

tard|ily /'tɑːdɪlɪ/ *adv* lentamente; (*late*) tardíamente. **~y** /'tɑːdɪ/ *a* (**-ier, -iest**) (*slow*) lento; (*late*) tardío

target /'tɑːgɪt/ *n* blanco *m*; (*fig*) objetivo *m*

tariff /'tærɪf/ *n* tarifa *f*

tarmac /'tɑːmæk/ *n* pista *f* de aterrizaje. **T~** *n* (*P*) macadán *m*

tarnish /'tɑːnɪʃ/ *vt* deslustrar. ● *vi* deslustrarse

tarpaulin /tɑː'pɔːlɪn/ *n* alquitranado *m*

tarragon /'tærəgən/ *n* estragón *m*

tart¹ /tɑːt/ *n* pastel *m*; (*individual*) pastelillo *m*

tart² /tɑːt/ *n* (*sl, woman*) prostituta *f*, fulana *f* (*fam*). ● *vt*. **~ o.s. up** (*fam*) engalanarse

tart³ /tɑːt/ *a* (**-er, -est**) ácido; (*fig*) áspero

tartan /'tɑːtn/ *n* tartán *m*, tela *f* escocesa

tartar /'tɑːtə(r)/ *n* tártaro *m*. **~ sauce** *n* salsa *f* tártara

task /tɑːsk/ *n* tarea *f*. **take to ~** reprender. **~ force** *n* destacamento *m* especial

tassel /'tæsl/ *n* borla *f*

tast|e /teɪst/ *n* sabor *m*, gusto *m*; (*small quantity*) poquito *m*. ● *vt* probar. ● *vi*. **~e of** saber a. **~eful** *a* de buen gusto. **~eless** *a* soso; (*fig*) de mal gusto. **~y** *a* (**-ier, -iest**) sabroso

tat /tæt/ *see* **tit²**

tatter|ed /'tætəd/ a hecho jirones. ~**s** /'tætəz/ npl andrajos mpl

tattle /'tætl/ vi charlar. ● n charla f

tattoo[1] /tə'tu:/ (mil) espectáculo m militar

tattoo[2] /tə'tu:/ vt tatuar. ● n tatuaje m

tatty /'tætɪ/ a (-ier, -iest) gastado, en mal estado

taught /tɔ:t/ see **teach**

taunt /tɔ:nt/ vt mofarse de. ~ **s.o. with sth** echar algo en cara a uno. ● n mofa f

Taurus /'tɔ:rəs/ n (astr) Tauro m

taut /tɔ:t/ a tenso

tavern /'tævən/ n taberna f

tawdry /'tɔ:drɪ/ a (-ier, -iest) charro

tawny /'tɔ:nɪ/ a bronceado

tax /tæks/ n impuesto m. ● vt imponer contribuciones a ⟨person⟩; gravar con un impuesto ⟨thing⟩; (fig) poner a prueba. ~**able** a imponible. ~**ation** /-'seɪʃn/ n impuestos mpl. ~**-collector** n recaudador m de contribuciones. ~**-free** a libre de impuestos

taxi /'tæksɪ/ n (pl -is) taxi m. ● vi (pt taxied, pres p taxiing) ⟨aircraft⟩ rodar por la pista. ~ **rank** n parada f de taxis

taxpayer /'tækspeɪə(r)/ n contribuyente m & f

te /ti:/ n (mus, seventh note of any musical scale) si m

tea /ti:/ n té m. ~**-bag** n bolsita f de té. ~**-break** n descanso m para el té

teach /ti:tʃ/ vt/i (pt taught) enseñar. ~**er** n profesor m; (primary) maestro m. ~**-in** n seminario m. ~**ing** n enseñanza f. ● a docente. ~**ing staff** n profesorado m

teacup /'ti:kʌp/ n taza f de té

teak /ti:k/ n teca f

tea-leaf /'ti:li:f/ n hoja f de té

team /ti:m/ n equipo m; (of horses) tiro m. ● vi. ~ **up** unirse. ~**-work** n trabajo m en equipo

teapot /'ti:pɒt/ n tetera f

tear[1] /teə(r)/ vt (pt tore, pp torn) rasgar. ● vi rasgarse; (run) precipitarse. ● n rasgón m; (fig) apart desgarrar. ~ **o.s. away** separarse

tear[2] /tɪə(r)/ n lágrima f. **in** ~**s** llorando

tearaway /'teərəweɪ/ n gamberro f

tear /tɪə(r)/: ~**ful** a lloroso. ~**-gas** n gas m lacrimógeno

tease /ti:z/ vt tomar el pelo a; cardar ⟨cloth etc⟩. ● n guasón m. ~**r** /-ə(r)/ n (fam) problema m difícil

tea: ~**-set** n juego m de té. ~**spoon** /'ti:spu:n/ n cucharilla f. ~**spoonful** n (pl -fuls) (amount) cucharadita f

teat /ti:t/ n (of animal) teta f; (for bottle) tetilla f

tea-towel /'ti:taʊəl/ n paño m de cocina

technical /'teknɪkl/ a técnico. ~**ity** n /-'kælətɪ/ n detalle m técnico. ~**ly** adv técnicamente

technician /tek'nɪʃn/ n técnico m

technique /tek'ni:k/ n técnica f

technolog|ist /tek'nɒlədʒɪst/ n tecnólogo m. ~**y** /tek'nɒlədʒɪ/ n tecnología f

teddy bear /'tedɪbeə/ n osito m de felpa, osito m de peluche

tedious /'ti:dɪəs/ a pesado. ~**ly** adv pesadamente

tedium /'ti:dɪəm/ n aburrimiento m

tee /ti:/ n (golf) tee m

teem /ti:m/ vi abundar; (rain) llover a cántaros

teen|age /'ti:neɪdʒ/ a adolescente; (for teenagers) para jóvenes. ~**ager** /-ə(r)/ n adolescente m & f, joven m & f. ~**s** /ti:nz/ npl. **the** ~**s** la adolescencia f

teeny /'ti:nɪ/ a (-ier, -iest) (fam) chiquito

teeter /'ti:tə(r)/ vi balancearse

teeth /ti:θ/ see **tooth**. ~**e** /ti:ð/ vi echar los dientes. ~**ing troubles** npl (fig) dificultades fpl iniciales

teetotaller /ti:'təʊtələ(r)/ n abstemio m

telecommunications /telɪkəmju:nɪ'keɪʃnz/ npl telecomunicaciones fpl

telegram /'telɪgræm/ n telegrama m

telegraph /'telɪgrɑ:f/ n telégrafo m. ● vt telegrafiar. ~**ic** /-'græfɪk/ a telegráfico

telepath|ic /telɪ'pæθɪk/ a telepático. ~**y** /tɪ'lepəθɪ/ n telepatía f

telephon|e /'telɪfəʊn/ n teléfono m. ● vt llamar por teléfono. ~**e booth** n cabina f telefónica. ~**e directory** n guía f telefónica. ~**e exchange** n central f telefónica. ~**ic** /-'fɒnɪk/ a telefónico. ~**ist** /tɪ'lefənɪst/ n telefonista m & f

telephoto /telɪ'fəʊtəʊ/ a. ~ **lens** n teleobjetivo m

teleprinter /'telɪprɪntə(r)/ n tele-impresor m

telescop|e /'telɪskəʊp/ n telescopio m. ~**ic** /-'kɒpɪk/ a telescópico

televis|e /'telɪvaɪz/ vt televisar. ~**ion** /-vɪʒn/ n televisión f. ~**ion set** n televisor m

telex /'teleks/ n télex m. ● vt enviar por télex

tell /tel/ vt (pt **told**) decir; contar ‹story›; (distinguish) distinguir. ● vi (produce an effect) tener efecto; (know) saber. ~ **off** vt reprender. ~**er** /'telə(r)/ n (in bank) cajero m

telling /'telɪŋ/ a eficaz

tell-tale /'telteɪl/ n soplón m. ● a revelador

telly /'telɪ/ n (fam) televisión f, tele f (fam)

temerity /tɪ'merətɪ/ n temeridad f

temp /temp/ n (fam) empleado m temporal

temper /'tempə(r)/ n (disposition) disposición f; (mood) humor m; (fit of anger) cólera f; (of metal) temple m. **be in a** ~ estar de mal humor. **keep one's** ~ contenerse. **lose one's** ~ enfadarse, perder la paciencia. ● vt templar ‹metal›

temperament /'temprəmənt/ n temperamento m. ~**al** /-'mentl/ a caprichoso

temperance /'tempərəns/ n moderación f

temperate /'tempərət/ a moderado; ‹climate› templado

temperature /'temprɪtʃə(r)/ n temperatura f. **have a** ~ tener fiebre

tempest /'tempɪst/ n tempestad f. ~**uous** /-'pestjʊəs/ a tempestuoso

temple[1] /'templ/ n templo m

temple[2] /'templ/ (anat) sien f

tempo /'tempəʊ/ n (pl **-os** or **tempi**) ritmo m

temporar|ily /'tempərərəlɪ/ adv temporalmente. ~**y** /'tempərərɪ/ a temporal, provisional

tempt /tempt/ vt tentar. ~ **s.o. to** inducir a uno a. ~**ation** /-'teɪʃn/ n tentación f. ~**ing** a tentador

ten /ten/ a & n diez (m)

tenable /'tenəbl/ a sostenible

tenaci|ous /tɪ'neɪʃəs/ a tenaz. ~**ty** /-'æsətɪ/ n tenacidad f

tenan|cy /'tenənsɪ/ n alquiler m. ~**t** /'tenənt/ n inquilino m

tend[1] /tend/ vi. ~ **to** tener tendencia a

tend[2] /tend/ vt cuidar

tendency /'tendənsɪ/ n tendencia f

tender[1] /'tendə(r)/ a tierno; (painful) dolorido

tender[2] /'tendə(r)/ n (com) oferta f. **legal** ~ n curso m legal. ● vt ofrecer, presentar

tender: ~**ly** adv tiernamente. ~**ness** n ternura f

tendon /'tendən/ n tendón m

tenement /'tenəmənt/ n vivienda f

tenet /'tenɪt/ n principio m

tenfold /'tenfəʊld/ a diez veces mayor, décuplo. ● adv diez veces

tenner /'tenə(r)/ n (fam) billete m de diez libras

tennis /'tenɪs/ n tenis m

tenor /'tenə(r)/ n tenor m

tens|e /tens/ a (**-er**, **-est**) tieso; (fig) tenso. ● n (gram) tiempo m. ● vi. ~ **up** tensarse. ~**eness** n, ~**ion** /'tenʃn/ n tensión f

tent /tent/ n tienda f, carpa f(LAm)

tentacle /'tentəkl/ n tentáculo m

tentative /'tentətɪv/ a provisional; (hesitant) indeciso. ~**ly** adv provisionalmente; (timidly) tímidamente

tenterhooks /'tentəhʊks/ npl. **on** ~ en ascuas

tenth /tenθ/ a & n décimo (m)

tenuous /'tenjʊəs/ a tenue

tenure /'tenjʊə(r)/ n posesión f

tepid /'tepɪd/ a tibio

term /tɜːm/ n (of time) período m; (schol) trimestre m; (word etc) término m. ● vt llamar. ~**s** npl condiciones fpl; (com) precio m. **on bad** ~**s** en malas relaciones. **on good** ~**s** en buenas relaciones

terminal /'tɜːmɪnl/ a terminal, final. ● n (rail) estación f terminal; (elec) borne m. (**air**) ~ n término m, terminal m

terminat|e /'tɜːmɪneɪt/ vt terminar. ● vi terminarse. ~**tion** /-'neɪʃn/ n terminación f

terminology /tɜːmɪ'nɒlədʒɪ/ n terminología f

terrace /'terəs/ n terraza f; (houses) hilera f de casas. **the** ~**s** npl (sport) las gradas fpl

terrain /tə'reɪn/ n terreno m

terrestrial /tɪ'restrɪəl/ a terrestre

terribl|e /'terəbl/ a terrible. ~**y** adv terriblemente

terrier /'terɪə(r)/ n terrier m

terrific /tə'rıfık/ a (*excellent*, *fam*) estupendo; (*huge*, *fam*) enorme. **~ally** adv (*fam*) terriblemente; (*very well*) muy bien

terrify /'terıfaı/ vt aterrorizar. **~ing** a espantoso

territor|ial /terı'tɔ:rıəl/ a territorial. **~y** /'terıtrı/ n territorio m

terror /'terə(r)/ n terror m. **~ism** /-zəm/ n terrorismo m. **~ist** /'terərıst/ n terrorista m & f. **~ize** /'terəraız/ vt aterrorizar

terse /tɜ:s/ a conciso; (*abrupt*) brusco

test /test/ n prueba f; (*exam*) examen m. ● vt probar; (*examine*) examinar

testament /'testəmənt/ n testamento m. **New T~** Nuevo Testamento. **Old T~** Antiguo Testamento

testicle /'testıkl/ n testículo m

testify /'testıfaı/ vt atestiguar. ● vi declarar

testimon|ial /testı'məʊnıəl/ n certificado m; (*of character*) recomendación f. **~y** /'testımənı/ n testimonio m

test: ~ match n partido m internacional. **~tube** n tubo m de ensayo, probeta f

testy /'testı/ a irritable

tetanus /'tetənəs/ n tétanos m invar

tetchy /'tetʃı/ a irritable

tether /'teðə(r)/ vt atar. ● n. **be at the end of one's ~** no poder más

text /tekst/ n texto m. **~book** n libro m de texto

textile /'tekstaıl/ a & n textil (m)

texture /'tekstʃə(r)/ n textura f

Thai /taı/ a & n tailandés (m). **~land** n Tailandia f

Thames /temz/ n Támesis m

than /ðæn, ðən/ conj que; (*with numbers*) de

thank /θæŋk/ vt dar las gracias a, agradecer. **~ you** gracias. **~ful** /'θæŋkfl/ a agradecido. **~fully** adv con gratitud; (*happily*) afortunadamente. **~less** /'θæŋklıs/ a ingrato. **~s** npl gracias fpl. **~s!** (*fam*) ¡gracias! **~s to** gracias a

that /ðæt, ðət/ a (pl **those**) ese, aquel, esa, aquella. ● pron (pl **those**) ése, aquél, ésa, aquélla. **~ is** es decir. **~'s it!** ¡eso es! **~ is why** por eso. **is ~ you?** ¿eres tú? **like ~** así. ● adv tan. ● rel pron que; (*with prep*) el que, la que, el cual, la cual. ● conj que

thatch /θætʃ/ n techo m de paja. **~ed** a con techo de paja

thaw /θɔ:/ vt deshelar. ● vi deshelarse; (*snow*) derretirse. ● n deshielo m

the /ðə, ðı: *def art* el, la, los, las. **at ~** al, a la, a los, a las. **from ~** del, de la, de los, de las. **to ~** al, a la, a los, a las. ● adv. **all ~ better** tanto mejor

theatr|e /'θıətə(r)/ n teatro m. **~ical** /-'ætrıkl/ a teatral

theft /θeft/ n hurto m

their /ðeə(r)/ a su, sus

theirs /ðeəz/ poss pron (el) suyo, (la) suya, (los) suyos, (las) suyas

them /ðem, ðəm/ pron (*accusative*) los, las; (*dative*) les; (*after prep*) ellos, ellas

theme /θi:m/ n tema m. **~ song** n motivo m principal

themselves /ðəm'selvz/ pron ellos mismos, ellas mismas; (*reflexive*) se; (*after prep*) sí mismos, sí mismas

then /ðen/ adv entonces; (*next*) luego, después. **by ~** para entonces. **now and ~** de vez en cuando. **since ~** desde entonces. ● a de entonces

theolog|ian /θıə'ləʊdʒən/ n teólogo m. **~y** /θı'ɒlədʒı/ n teología f

theorem /'θıərəm/ n teorema m

theor|etical /θıə'retıkl/ a teórico. **~y** /'θıərı/ n teoría f

therap|eutic /θerə'pju:tık/ a terapéutico. **~ist** n terapeuta m & f. **~y** /'θerəpı/ n terapia f

there /ðeə(r)/ adv ahí, allí. **~ are** hay. **~ he is** ahí está. **~ is** hay. **~ it is** ahí está. **down ~** ahí abajo. **up ~** ahí arriba. ● int ¡vaya! **~, ~!** ¡ya, ya! **~abouts** adv por ahí. **~after** adv después. **~by** adv por eso. **~fore** /'ðeəfɔ:(r)/ adv por lo tanto.

thermal /'θɜ:ml/ a termal

thermometer /θə'mɒmıtə(r)/ n termómetro m

thermonuclear /θɜ:məʊ'nju:klıə(r)/ a termonuclear

Thermos /'θɜ:məs/ n (P) termo m

thermostat /'θɜ:məstæt/ n termostato m

thesaurus /θı'sɔ:rəs/ n (pl -ri /-raı/) diccionario m de sinónimos

these /ði:z/ a estos, estas. ● pron éstos, éstas

thesis /'θi:sıs/ n (pl **theses** /-si:z/) tesis f

they /ðeı/ pron ellos, ellas. **~ say that** se dice que

thick /θɪk/ a (**-er, -est**) espeso; (*dense*) denso; (*stupid, fam*) torpe; (*close, fam*) íntimo. ● *adv* espesamente, densamente. ● *n*. **in the ~ of** en medio de. **~en** /'θɪkən/ *vt* espesar. ● *vi* espesarse

thicket /'θɪkɪt/ *n* matorral *m*

thick: **~ly** *adv* espesamente, densamente. **~ness** *n* espesor *m*

thickset /θɪk'set/ *a* fornido

thick-skinned /θɪk'skɪnd/ *a* insensible

thief /θiːf/ *n* (*pl* **thieves**) ladrón *m*

thiev|e /θiːv/ *vt/i* robar. **~ing** *n* ladrón

thigh /θaɪ/ *n* muslo *m*

thimble /'θɪmbl/ *n* dedal *m*

thin /θɪn/ *a* (**thinner, thinnest**) delgado; (*person*) flaco; (*weak*) débil; (*fine*) fino; (*sparse*) escaso. ● *adv* ligeramente. ● *vt* (*pt* **thinned**) adelgazar; (*dilute*) diluir. **~ out** hacer menos denso. ● *vi* adelgazarse; (*diminish*) disminuir

thing /θɪŋ/ *n* cosa *f*. **for one ~** en primer lugar. **just the ~** exactamente lo que se necesita. **poor ~!** ¡pobrecito! **~s** *npl* (*belongings*) efectos *mpl*; (*clothing*) ropa *f*

think /θɪŋk/ *vt* (*pt* **thought**) pensar, creer. ● *vi* pensar (**about, of** en); (*carefully*) reflexionar; (*imagine*) imaginarse. **~ better of it** cambiar de idea. **I ~ so** creo que sí. **~ over** *vt* pensar bien. **~ up** *vt* idear, inventar. **~er** *n* pensador *m*. **~-tank** *n* grupo *m* de expertos

thin: **~ly** *adv* ligeramente. **~ness** *n* delgadez *f*; (*of person*) flaqueza *f*

third /θɜːd/ *a* tercero. ● *n* tercio *m*, tercera parte *f*. **~-rate** *a* muy inferior. **T~ World** *n* Tercer Mundo *m*

thirst /θɜːst/ *n* sed *f*. **~y** *a* sediento. **be ~y** tener sed

thirteen /θɜː'tiːn/ *a & n* trece (*m*). **~th** *a & n* decimotercero (*m*)

thirt|ieth /'θɜːtɪəθ/ *a & n* trigésimo (*m*). **~y** /'θɜːtɪ/ *a & n* treinta (*m*)

this /ðɪs/ *a* (*pl* **these**) este, esta. **~ one** éste, ésta. ● *pron* (*pl* **these**) éste, ésta, esto. **like ~** así

thistle /'θɪsl/ *n* cardo *m*

thong /θɒŋ/ *n* correa *f*

thorn /θɔːn/ *n* espina *f*. **~y** *a* espinoso

thorough /'θʌrə/ *a* completo; (*deep*) profundo; (*cleaning etc*) a fondo; (*person*) concienzudo

thoroughbred /'θʌrəbred/ *a* de pura sangre

thoroughfare /'θʌrəfeə(r)/ *n* calle *f*. **no ~** prohibido el paso

thoroughly /'θʌrəlɪ/ *adv* completamente

those /ðəʊz/ *a* esos, aquellos, esas, aquellas. ● *pron* ésos, aquéllos, ésas, aquéllas

though /ðəʊ/ *conj* aunque. ● *adv* sin embargo. **as ~** como si

thought /θɔːt/ *see* **think**. ● *n* pensamiento *m*; (*idea*) idea *f*. **~ful** /'θɔːtfl/ *a* pensativo; (*considerate*) atento. **~fully** *adv* pensativamente; (*considerately*) atentamente. **~less** /'θɔːtlɪs/ *a* irreflexivo; (*inconsiderate*) desconsiderado

thousand /'θaʊznd/ *a & n* mil (*m*). **~th** *a & n* milésimo (*m*)

thrash /θræʃ/ *vt* azotar; (*defeat*) derrotar. **~ out** discutir a fondo

thread /θred/ *n* hilo *m*; (*of screw*) rosca *f*. ● *vt* ensartar. **~ one's way** abrirse paso. **~bare** /'θredbeə(r)/ *a* raído

threat /θret/ *n* amenaza *f*. **~en** /'θretn/ *vt/i* amenazar. **~ening** *a* amenazador. **~eningly** *adv* de modo amenazador

three /θriː/ *a & n* tres (*m*). **~fold** *a* triple. ● *adv* tres veces. **~some** /'θriːsəm/ *n* conjunto *m* de tres personas

thresh /θreʃ/ *vt* trillar

threshold /'θreʃhəʊld/ *n* umbral *m*

threw /θruː/ *see* **throw**

thrift /θrɪft/ *n* economía *f*, ahorro *m*. **~y** *a* frugal

thrill /θrɪl/ *n* emoción *f*. ● *vt* emocionar. ● *vi* emocionarse; (*quiver*) estremecerse. **be ~ed with** estar encantado de. **~er** /'θrɪlə(r)/ *n* (*book*) libro *m* de suspense; (*film*) película *f* de suspense. **~ing** *a* emocionante

thriv|e /θraɪv/ *vi* prosperar. **~ing** *a* próspero

throat /θrəʊt/ *n* garganta *f*. **have a sore ~** dolerle la garganta

throb /θrɒb/ *vi* (*pt* **throbbed**) palpitar; (*with pain*) dar punzadas; (*fig*) vibrar. ● *n* palpitación *f*; (*pain*) punzada *f*; (*fig*) vibración *f*. **~bing** *a* (*pain*) punzante

throes /θrəʊz/ *npl*. **in the ~ of** en medio de

thrombosis /θrɒm'bəʊsɪs/ *n* trombosis *f*

throne /θrəʊn/ *n* trono *m*

throng /θrɒŋ/ *n* multitud *f*

throttle /'θrɒtl/ *n* (*auto*) acelerador *m*. ● *vt* ahogar

through /θruː/ *prep* por, a través de; (*during*) durante; (*by means of*) por medio de; (*thanks to*) gracias a. ● *adv* de parte a parte, de un lado a otro; (*entirely*) completamente; (*to the end*) hasta el final. **be ~** (*finished*) haber terminado. ● *a* ⟨*train etc*⟩ directo

throughout /θruː'aʊt/ *prep* por todo; (*time*) en todo. ● *adv* en todas partes; (*all the time*) todo el tiempo

throve /θrəʊv/ *see* **thrive**

throw /θrəʊ/ *vt* (*pt* **threw**, *pp* **thrown**) arrojar; (*baffle etc*) desconcertar. **~ a party** (*fam*) dar una fiesta. ● *n* tiro *m*; (*of dice*) lance *m*. **~ away** *vt* tirar. **~ over** *vt* abandonar. **~ up** *vi* (*vomit*) vomitar. **~-away** *a* desechable

thrush /θrʌʃ/ *n* tordo *m*

thrust /θrʌst/ *vt* (*pt* **thrust**) empujar; (*push in*) meter. ● *n* empuje *m*. **~ (up)on** imponer a

thud /θʌd/ *n* ruido *m* sordo

thug /θʌg/ *n* bruto *m*

thumb /θʌm/ *n* pulgar *m*. **under the ~ of** dominado por. ● *vt* hojear ⟨*book*⟩. **~ a lift** hacer autostop. **~-index** *n* uñeros *mpl*

thump /θʌmp/ *vt* golpear. ● *vi* ⟨*heart*⟩ latir fuertemente. ● *n* porrazo *m*; (*noise*) ruido *m* sordo

thunder /'θʌndə(r)/ *n* trueno *m*. ● *vi* tronar. **~ past** pasar con estruendo. **~bolt** /'θʌndəbəʊlt/ *n* rayo *m*. **~clap** /'θʌndəklæp/ *n* trueno *m*. **~storm** /'θʌndəstɔːm/ *n* tronada *f*. **~y** *a* con truenos

Thursday /'θɜːzdeɪ/ *n* jueves *m*

thus /ðʌs/ *adv* así

thwart /θwɔːt/ *vt* frustrar

thyme /taɪm/ *n* tomillo *m*

thyroid /'θaɪrɔɪd/ *n* tiroides *m invar*

tiara /tɪ'ɑːrə/ *n* diadema *f*

tic /tɪk/ *n* tic *m*

tick[1] /tɪk/ *n* tictac *m*; (*mark*) señal *f*, marca *f*; (*instant, fam*) momentito *m*. ● *vi* hacer tictac. ● *vt*. **~ (off)** marcar. **~ off** *vt* (*sl*) reprender. **~ over** *vi* ⟨*of engine*⟩ marchar en vacío

tick[2] /tɪk/ *n* (*insect*) garrapata *f*

tick[3] /tɪk/ *n*. **on ~** (*fam*) a crédito

ticket /'tɪkɪt/ *n* billete *m*, boleto *m* (*LAm*); (*label*) etiqueta *f*; (*fine*) multa *f*. **~-collector** *n* revisor *m*. **~-office** *n* taquilla *f*

tickl|e /'tɪkl/ *vt* hacer cosquillas a; (*amuse*) divertir. ● *n* cosquilleo *m*. **~ish** /'tɪklɪʃ/ *a* cosquilloso; (*problem*) delicado. **be ~ish** tener cosquillas

tidal /'taɪdl/ *a* de marea. **~ wave** *n* maremoto *m*

tiddly-winks /'tɪdlɪwɪŋks/ *n* juego *m* de pulgas

tide /taɪd/ *n* marea *f*; (*of events*) curso *m*. ● *vt*. **~ over** ayudar a salir de un apuro

tidings /'taɪdɪŋz/ *npl* noticias *fpl*

tid|ily /'taɪdɪlɪ/ *adv* en orden; (*well*) bien. **~iness** *n* orden *m*. **~y** /'taɪdɪ/ *a* (**-ier**, **-iest**) ordenado; ⟨*amount, fam*⟩ considerable. ● *vt/i*. **~y (up)** ordenar. **~y o.s. up** arreglarse

tie /taɪ/ *vt* (*pres p* **tying**) atar; hacer ⟨*a knot*⟩; (*link*) vincular. ● *vi* (*sport*) empatar. ● *n* atadura *f*; (*necktie*) corbata *f*; (*link*) lazo *m*; (*sport*) empate *m*. **~ in with** relacionar con. **~ up** atar; (*com*) inmovilizar. **be ~d up** (*busy*) estar ocupado

tier /tɪə(r)/ *n* fila *f*; (*in stadium etc*) grada *f*; (*of cake*) piso *m*

tie-up /'taɪʌp/ *n* enlace *m*

tiff /tɪf/ *n* riña *f*

tiger /'taɪgə(r)/ *n* tigre *m*

tight /taɪt/ *a* (**-er**, **-est**) ⟨*clothes*⟩ ceñido; (*taut*) tieso; ⟨*control etc*⟩ riguroso; ⟨*knot, nut*⟩ apretado; (*drunk, fam*) borracho. ● *adv* bien; (*shut*) herméticamente. **~ corner** *n* (*fig*) apuro *m*. **~en** /'taɪtn/ *vt* apretar. ● *vi* apretarse. **~-fisted** *a* tacaño. **~ly** *adv* bien; (*shut*) herméticamente. **~ness** *n* estrechez *f*. **~rope** /'taɪtrəʊp/ *n* cuerda *f* floja. **~s** /taɪts/ *npl* leotardos *mpl*

tile /taɪl/ *n* (*decorative*) azulejo *m*; (*on roof*) teja *f*; (*on floor*) baldosa *f*. ● *vt* azulejar; tejar ⟨*roof*⟩; embaldosar ⟨*floor*⟩

till[1] /tɪl/ *prep* hasta. ● *conj* hasta que

till[2] /tɪl/ *n* caja *f*

till[3] /tɪl/ *vt* cultivar

tilt /tɪlt/ *vt* inclinar. ● *vi* inclinarse. ● *n* inclinación *f*. **at full ~** a toda velocidad

timber /'tɪmbə(r)/ *n* madera *f* (de construcción); (*trees*) árboles *mpl*

time /taɪm/ *n* tiempo *m*; (*moment*) momento *m*; (*occasion*) ocasión *f*; (*by clock*) hora *f*; (*epoch*) época *f*; (*rhythm*) compás *m*. **~ off** tiempo libre. **at ~s** a veces. **behind the ~s** anticuado. **behind ~** atrasado. **for the ~ being** por ahora. **from ~ to ~** de vez en cuando. **have a good ~** divertirse, pasarlo bien. **in a year's ~** dentro de un año. **in no ~** en un abrir y cerrar de ojos. **in ~** a tiempo; (*eventually*) con el tiempo. **on ~** a la hora, puntual. ● *vt* elegir el momento; cronometrar ⟨*race*⟩. **~ bomb** *n* bomba *f* de tiempo. **~-honoured** *a* consagrado. **~-lag** *n* intervalo *m*
timeless /'taɪmlɪs/ *a* eterno
timely /'taɪmlɪ/ *a* oportuno
timer /'taɪmə(r)/ *n* cronómetro *m*; (*culin*) avisador *m*; (*with sand*) reloj *m* de arena; (*elec*) interruptor *m* de reloj
timetable /'taɪmteɪbl/ *n* horario *m*
time zone /'taɪmzəʊn/ *n* huso *m* horario
timid /'tɪmɪd/ *a* tímido; (*fearful*) miedoso. **~ly** *adv* tímidamente
timing /'taɪmɪŋ/ *n* medida *f* del tiempo; (*moment*) momento *m*; (*sport*) cronometraje *m*
timorous /'tɪmərəs/ *a* tímido; (*fearful*) miedoso. **~ly** *adv* tímidamente
tin /tɪn/ *n* estaño *m*; (*container*) lata *f*. **~ foil** *n* papel *m* de estaño. ● *vt* (*pt* **tinned**) conservar en lata, enlatar
tinge /tɪndʒ/ *vt* teñir (**with** de); (*fig*) matizar (**with** de). ● *n* matiz *m*
tingle /'tɪŋgl/ *vi* sentir hormigueo; (*with excitement*) estremecerse
tinker /'tɪŋkə(r)/ *n* hojalatero *m*. ● *vi*. **~ (with)** jugar con; (*repair*) arreglar
tinkle /'tɪŋkl/ *n* retintín *m*; (*phone call, fam*) llamada *f*
tin: **~ned** *a* en lata. **~ny** *a* metálico. **~-opener** *n* abrelatas *m invar*. **~ plate** *n* hojalata *f*
tinpot /'tɪnpɒt/ *a* (*pej*) inferior
tinsel /'tɪnsl/ *n* oropel *m*
tint /tɪnt/ *n* matiz *m*
tiny /'taɪnɪ/ *a* (**-ier, -iest**) diminuto
tip[1] /tɪp/ *n* punta *f*
tip[2] /tɪp/ *vt* (*pt* **tipped**) (*tilt*) inclinar; (*overturn*) volcar; (*pour*) verter● *vi* inclinarse; (*overturn*) volcarse. ● *n* (*for rubbish*) vertedero *m*. **~ out** verter

tip[3] /tɪp/ *vt* (*reward*) dar una propina a. **~ off** advertir. ● *n* (*reward*) propina *f*; (*advice*) consejo *m*
tip-off /'tɪpɒf/ *n* advertencia *f*
tipped /'tɪpt/ *a* ⟨*cigarette*⟩ con filtro
tipple /'tɪpl/ *vi* beborrotear. ● *n* bebida *f* alcohólica. **have a ~** tomar una copa
tipsy /'tɪpsɪ/ *a* achispado
tiptoe /'tɪptəʊ/ *n*. **on ~** de puntillas
tiptop /'tɪptɒp/ *a* (*fam*) de primera
tirade /taɪ'reɪd/ *n* diatriba *f*
tire /'taɪə(r)/ *vt* cansar. ● *vi* cansarse. **~d** /'taɪəd/ *a* cansado. **~d of** harto de. **~d out** agotado. **~less** *a* incansable
tiresome /'taɪəsəm/ *a* (*annoying*) fastidioso; (*boring*) pesado
tiring /'taɪərɪŋ/ *a* cansado
tissue /'tɪʃu:/ *n* tisú *m*; (*handkerchief*) pañuelo *m* de papel. **~-paper** *n* papel *m* de seda
tit[1] /tɪt/ *n* (*bird*) paro *m*
tit[2] /tɪt/ *n*. **~ for tat** golpe por golpe
titbit /'tɪtbɪt/ *n* golosina *f*
titillate /'tɪtɪleɪt/ *vt* excitar
title /'taɪtl/ *n* título *m*. **~d** *a* con título nobiliario. **~-deed** *n* título *m* de propiedad. **~-role** *n* papel *m* principal
tittle-tattle /'tɪtltætl/ *n* cháchara *f*
titular /'tɪtjʊlə(r)/ *a* nominal
tizzy /'tɪzɪ/ *n* (*sl*). **get in a ~** ponerse nervioso
to /tu:, tə/ *prep* a; (*towards*) hacia; (*in order to*) para; (*according to*) según; (*as far as*) hasta; (*with times*) menos; (*of*) de. **give it ~ me** dámelo. **I don't want ~** no quiero. **twenty ~ seven** (*by clock*) las siete menos veinte. ● *adv*. **push ~**, **pull ~** cerrar. **~ and fro** *adv* de aquí para allá
toad /təʊd/ *n* sapo *m*
toadstool /'təʊdstu:l/ *n* seta *f* venenosa
toast /təʊst/ *n* pan *m* tostado, tostada *f*; (*drink*) brindis *m*. **drink a ~ to** brindar por. ● *vt* brindar por. **~er** *n* tostador *m* de pan
tobacco /tə'bækəʊ/ *n* tabaco *m*. **~nist** *n* estanquero *m*. **~nist's shop** *n* estanco *m*
to-be /tə'bi:/ *a* futuro
toboggan /tə'bɒgən/ *n* tobogán *m*
today /tə'deɪ/ *n* & *adv* hoy (*m*). **~ week** dentro de una semana
toddler /'tɒdlə(r)/ *n* niño *m* que empieza a andar

toddy /'tɒdɪ/ n ponche m
to-do /təˈduː/ n lío m
toe /təʊ/ n dedo m del pie; (of shoe) punta f. **big ~** dedo m gordo (del pie). **on one's ~s** (fig) alerta. ● vt. **~ the line** conformarse. **~-hold** n punto m de apoyo
toff /tɒf/ n (sl) petimetre m
toffee /'tɒfɪ/ n caramelo m
together /təˈgeðə(r)/ adv junto, juntos; (at same time) a la vez. **~ with** junto con. **~ness** n compañerismo m
toil /tɔɪl/ vi afanarse. ● n trabajo m
toilet /'tɔɪlɪt/ n servicio m, retrete m; (grooming) arreglo m, tocado m. **~paper** n papel m higiénico. **~ries** /'tɔɪlɪtrɪz/ npl artículos mpl de tocador. **~ water** n agua f de Colonia
token /'təʊkən/ n señal f; (voucher) vale m; (coin) ficha f. ● a simbólico
told /təʊld/ see **tell**. ● a. **all ~** con todo
tolerabl|e /'tɒlərəbl/ a tolerable; (not bad) regular. **~y** adv pasablemente
toleran|ce /'tɒlərəns/ n tolerancia f. **~t** /'tɒlərənt/ a tolerante. **~tly** adv con tolerancia
tolerate /'tɒləreɪt/ vt tolerar
toll[1] /təʊl/ n peaje m. **death ~** número m de muertos. **take a heavy ~** dejar muchas víctimas
toll[2] /təʊl/ vi doblar, tocar a muerto
tom /tɒm/ n gato m (macho)
tomato /təˈmɑːtəʊ/ n (pl **~oes**) tomate m
tomb /tuːm/ n tumba f, sepulcro m
tomboy /'tɒmbɔɪ/ n marimacho m
tombstone /'tuːmstəʊn/ n lápida f sepulcral
tom-cat /'tɒmkæt/ n gato m (macho)
tome /təʊm/ n librote m
tomfoolery /tɒmˈfuːlərɪ/ n payasadas fpl, tonterías fpl
tomorrow /təˈmɒrəʊ/ n & adv mañana (f). **see you ~!** ¡hasta mañana!
ton /tʌn/ n tonelada f (= 1,016 kg). **~s of** (fam) montones de. **metric ~** tonelada f (métrica) (= 1,000 kg)
tone /təʊn/ n tono m. ● vt. **~ down** atenuar. **~ up** tonificar (muscles). ● vi. **~ in** armonizar. **~-deaf** a que no tiene buen oído
tongs /tɒŋz/ npl tenazas fpl; (for hair, sugar) tenacillas fpl
tongue /tʌŋ/ n lengua f. **~ in cheek** adv irónicamente. **~-tied** a mudo.

tonic /'tɒnɪk/ a tónico. ● n (tonic water) tónica f; (med, fig) tónico m. **~ water** n tónica f
tonight /təˈnaɪt/ adv & n esta noche (f); (evening) esta tarde (f)
tonne /tʌn/ n tonelada f (métrica)
tonsil /'tɒnsl/ n amígdala f. **~litis** /-'laɪtɪs/ n amigdalitis f
too /tuː/ adv demasiado; (also) también. **~ many** a demasiados. **~ much** a & adv demasiado
took /tʊk/ see **take**
tool /tuːl/ n herramienta f. **~-bag** n bolsa f de herramientas
toot /tuːt/ n bocinazo m. ● vi tocar la bocina
tooth /tuːθ/ n (pl **teeth**) diente m; (molar) muela f. **~ache** /'tuːθeɪk/ n dolor m de muelas. **~brush** /'tuːθbrʌʃ/ n cepillo m de dientes. **~comb** /'tuːθkəʊm/ n peine m de púa fina. **~less** a desdentado, sin dientes. **~paste** /'tuːθpeɪst/ n pasta f dentífrica. **~pick** /'tuːθpɪk/ n palillo m de dientes
top[1] /tɒp/ n cima f; (upper part) parte f de arriba; (upper surface) superficie f; (lid, of bottle) tapa f; (of list) cabeza f. **~ from ~ to bottom** de arriba abajo. **on ~ (of)** encima de; (besides) además. ● a más alto; (in rank) superior, principal; (maximum) máximo. **~ floor** n último piso m. ● vt (pt **topped**) cubrir; (exceed) exceder. **~ up** vt llenar
top[2] /tɒp/ n (toy) trompa f, peonza f
top: **~ hat** n chistera f. **~-heavy** a más pesado arriba que abajo
topic /'tɒpɪk/ n tema m. **~al** /'tɒpɪkl/ a de actualidad
top: **~less** /'tɒplɪs/ a (bather) con los senos desnudos. **~most** /'tɒpməʊst/ a (el) más alto. **~-notch** a (fam) excelente
topography /təˈpɒgrəfɪ/ n topografía f
topple /'tɒpl/ vi derribar; (overturn) volcar
top secret /tɒp'siːkrɪt/ a sumamente secreto
topsy-turvy /tɒpsɪ'tɜːvɪ/ adv & a patas arriba
torch /tɔːtʃ/ n lámpara f de bolsillo; (flaming) antorcha f
tore /tɔː(r)/ see **tear**[1]
toreador /'tɒrɪədɔː(r)/ n torero m

torment /'tɔːment/ *n* tormento *m*. /tɔː'ment/ *vt* atormentar

torn /tɔːn/ *see* tear¹

tornado /tɔː'neɪdəʊ/ *n* (*pl* -**oes**) tornado *m*

torpedo /tɔː'piːdəʊ/ *n* (*pl* -**oes**) torpedo *m*. ● *vt* torpedear

torpor /'tɔːpə(r)/ *n* apatía *f*

torrent /'tɒrənt/ *n* torrente *m*. ~**ial** /tə'renʃl/ *a* torrencial

torrid /'tɒrɪd/ *a* tórrido

torso /'tɔːsəʊ/ *n* (*pl* -**os**) torso *m*

tortoise /'tɔːtəs/ *n* tortuga *f*. ~**shell** *n* carey *m*

tortuous /'tɔːtjʊəs/ *a* tortuoso

torture /'tɔːtʃə(r)/ *n* tortura *f*, tormento *m*. ● *vt* atormentar. ~**r** /-ə(r)/ *n* atormentador *m*, verdugo *m*

Tory /'tɔːrɪ/ *a* & *n* (*fam*) conservador (*m*)

toss /tɒs/ *vt* echar; (*shake*) sacudir. ● *vi* agitarse. ~ **and turn** (*in bed*) revolverse. ~ **up** echar a cara o cruz

tot¹ /tɒt/ *n* nene *m*; (*of liquor, fam*) trago *m*

tot² /tɒt/ *vt* (*pt* **totted**). ~ **up** (*fam*) sumar

total /'təʊtl/ *a* & *n* total (*m*). ● *vt* (*pt* **totalled**) sumar

totalitarian /təʊtælɪ'teərɪən/ *a* totalitario

total: ~**ity** /təʊ'tælətɪ/ *n* totalidad *f*. ~**ly** *adv* totalmente

totter /'tɒtə(r)/ *vi* tambalearse. ~**y** *a* inseguro

touch /tʌtʃ/ *vt* tocar; (*reach*) alcanzar; (*move*) conmover. ● *vi* tocarse. ● *n* toque *m*; (*sense*) tacto *m*; (*contact*) contacto *m*; (*trace*) pizca *f*. **get in** ~ **with** ponerse en contacto con. ~ **down** (*aircraft*) aterrizar. ~ **off** disparar (*gun*); (*fig*) desencadenar. ~ **on** tratar levemente. ~ **up** retocar. ~**-and-go** *a* incierto, dudoso

touching /'tʌtʃɪŋ/ *a* conmovedor

touchstone /'tʌtʃstəʊn/ *n* (*fig*) piedra *f* de toque

touchy /'tʌtʃɪ/ *a* quisquilloso

tough /tʌf/ *a* (-**er**, -**est**) duro; (*strong*) fuerte, resistente. ~**en** /'tʌfn/ *vt* endurecer. ~**ness** *n* dureza *f*; (*strength*) resistencia *f*

toupee /'tuːpeɪ/ *n* postizo *m*, tupé *m*

tour /tʊə(r)/ *n* viaje *m*; (*visit*) visita *f*; (*excursion*) excursión *f*; (*by team etc*) gira *f*. ● *vt* recorrer; (*visit*) visitar

touris|m /'tʊərɪzəm/ *n* turismo *m*. ~**t** /'tʊərɪst/ *n* turista *m* & *f*. ● *a*

turístico. ~**t office** *n* oficina *f* de turismo

tournament /'tɔːnəmənt/ *n* torneo *m*

tousle /'taʊzl/ *vt* despeinar

tout /taʊt/ *vi*. ~ (**for**) solicitar. ● *n* solicitador *m*

tow /təʊ/ *vt* remolcar. ● *n* remolque *m*. **on** ~ a remolque. **with his family in** ~ (*fam*) acompañado por su familia

toward(s) /tə'wɔːd(z)/ *prep* hacia

towel /'taʊəl/ *n* toalla *f*. ~**ling** *n* (*fabric*) toalla *f*

tower /'taʊə(r)/ *n* torre *f*. ● *vi*. ~ **above** dominar. ~ **block** *n* edificio *m* alto. ~**ing** *a* altísimo; (*rage*) violento

town /taʊn/ *n* ciudad *f*, pueblo *m*. **go to** ~ (*fam*) no escatimar dinero. ~ **hall** *n* ayuntamiento *m*. ~ **planning** *n* urbanismo *m*

tow-path /'təʊpɑːθ/ *n* camino *m* de sirga

toxi|c /'tɒksɪk/ *a* tóxico. ~**n** /'tɒksɪn/ *n* toxina *f*

toy /tɔɪ/ *n* juguete *m*. ● *vi*. ~ **with** jugar con (*object*); acariciar (*idea*). ~**shop** *n* juguetería *f*

trac|e /treɪs/ *n* huella *f*; (*small amount*) pizca *f*. ● *vt* seguir la pista de; (*draw*) dibujar; (*with tracing-paper*) calcar; (*track down*) encontrar. ~**ing** /'treɪsɪŋ/ *n* calco *m*. ~**ing-paper** *n* papel *m* de calcar

track /træk/ *n* huella *f*; (*path*) sendero *m*; (*sport*) pista *f*; (*of rocket etc*) trayectoria *f*; (*rail*) vía *f*. **keep** ~ **of** vigilar. **make** ~**s** (*sl*) marcharse. ● *vt* seguir la pista de. ~ **down** *vt* localizar. ~ **suit** *n* traje *m* de deporte, chandal *m*

tract¹ /trækt/ *n* (*land*) extensión *f*; (*anat*) aparato *m*

tract² /trækt/ *n* (*pamphlet*) opúsculo *m*

traction /'trækʃn/ *n* tracción *f*

tractor /'træktə(r)/ *n* tractor *m*

trade /treɪd/ *n* comercio *m*; (*occupation*) oficio *m*; (*exchange*) cambio *m*; (*industry*) industria *f*. ● *vt* cambiar. ● *vi* comerciar. ~ **in** (*give in part-exchange*) dar como parte del pago. ~ **on** aprovecharse de. ~ **mark** *n* marca *f* registrada. ~**r** /-ə(r)/ *n* comerciante *m* & *f*. ~**sman** /'treɪdzmən/ *n* (*pl* -**men**) (*shopkeeper*) tendero *m*. ~ **union** *n* sindicato *m*. ~ **unionist** *n* sindicalista *m* & *f*. ~ **wind** *n* viento *m* alisio

trading /'treɪdɪŋ/ n comercio m. ~ **estate** n zona f industrial

tradition /trə'dɪʃn/ n tradición f. ~**al** a tradicional. ~**alist** n tradicionalista m & f. ~**ally** adv tradicionalmente

traffic /'træfɪk/ n tráfico m. ● vi (pt **trafficked**) comerciar (**in** en). ~ **lights** npl semáforo m. ~ **warden** n guardia m, controlador m de tráfico

trag|edy /'trædʒɪdɪ/ n tragedia f. ~**ic** /'trædʒɪk/ a trágico. ~**ically** adv trágicamente

trail /treɪl/ vi arrastrarse; (lag) rezagarse. ● vt (track) seguir la pista de. ● n estela f; (track) pista f. (path) sendero m. ~**er** /'treɪlə(r)/ n remolque m; (film) avance m

train /treɪn/ n tren m; (of dress) cola f; (series) sucesión f; (retinue) séquito m. ● vt adiestrar; (sport) entrenar; educar ⟨child⟩; guiar ⟨plant⟩; domar ⟨animal⟩. ● vi adiestrarse; (sport) entrenarse. ~**ed** a (skilled) cualificado; ⟨doctor⟩ diplomado. ~**ee** n aprendiz m. ~**er** n (sport) entrenador m; (of animals) domador m. ~**ers** mpl zapatillas fpl de deporte. ~**ing** n instrucción f; (sport) entrenamiento m

traipse /treɪps/ vi (fam) vagar

trait /treɪ(t)/ n característica f, rasgo m

traitor /'treɪtə(r)/ n traidor m

tram /træm/ n tranvía m

tramp /træmp/ vt recorrer a pie. ● vi andar con pasos pesados. ● n (vagrant) vagabundo m; (sound) ruido m de pasos; (hike) paseo m largo

trample /'træmpl/ vt/i pisotear. ~ **(on)** pisotear

trampoline /'træmpəli:n/ n trampolín m

trance /trɑːns/ n trance m

tranquil /'træŋkwɪl/ a tranquilo. ~**lity** /-'kwɪlətɪ/ n tranquilidad f

tranquillize /'træŋkwɪlaɪz/ vt tranquilizar. ~**r** /-ə(r)/ n tranquilizante m

transact /træn'zækt/ vt negociar. ~**ion** /-ʃn/ n transacción f

transatlantic /trænzət'læntɪk/ a transatlántico

transcend /træn'send/ vt exceder. ~**ent** a sobresaliente

transcendental /trænsen'dentl/ a trascendental

transcribe /træns'kraɪb/ vt transcribir; grabar ⟨recorded sound⟩

transcript /'trænskrɪpt/ n copia f. ~**ion** /-ɪpʃn/ n transcripción f

transfer /træns'fɜː(r)/ vt (pt **transferred**) trasladar; calcar ⟨drawing⟩. ● vi trasladarse. ~ **the charges** (on telephone) llamar a cobro revertido. /'trænsfɜː(r)/ n traslado m; (paper) calcomanía f. ~**able** a transferible

transfigur|ation /trænsfɪgjʊ'reɪʃn/ n transfiguración f. ~**e** /træns'fɪgə(r)/ vt transfigurar

transfix /træns'fɪks/ vt traspasar; (fig) paralizar

transform /træns'fɔːm/ vt transformar. ~**ation** /-ə'meɪʃn/ n transformación f. ~**er** /-ə(r)/ n transformador m

transfusion /træns'fjuːʒn/ n transfusión f

transgress /træns'gres/ vt traspasar, infringir. ~**ion** /-ʃn/ n transgresión f; (sin) pecado m

transient /'trænzɪənt/ a pasajero

transistor /træn'zɪstə(r)/ n transistor m

transit /'trænsɪt/ n tránsito m

transition /træn'zɪʒn/ n transición f

transitive /'trænsɪtɪv/ a transitivo

transitory /'trænsɪtrɪ/ a transitorio

translat|e /trænz'leɪt/ vt traducir. ~**ion** /-ʃn/ n traducción f. ~**or** /-ə(r)/ n traductor m

translucen|ce /trænz'luːsns/ n traslucidez f. ~**t** /trænz'luːsnt/ a traslúcido

transmission /træns'mɪʃn/ n transmisión f

transmit /trænz'mɪt/ vt (pt **transmitted**) transmitir. ~**ter** /-ə(r)/ n transmisor m; (TV, radio) emisora f

transparen|cy /træns'pærənsɪ/ n transparencia f. (photo) diapositiva f. ~**t** /træns'pærənt/ a transparente

transpire /træn'spaɪə(r)/ vi transpirar; (happen, fam) suceder, revelarse

transplant /træns'plɑːnt/ vt trasplantar. /'trænsplɑːnt/ n trasplante m

transport /træn'spɔːt/ vt transportar. /'trænspɔːt/ n transporte m. ~**ation** /-'teɪʃn/ n transporte m

transpos|e /træn'spəʊz/ vt transponer; (mus) transportar. ~**ition** /-pə'zɪʃn/ n transposición f; (mus) transporte m

transverse /'trænzvɜ:s/ a transverso

transvestite /trænz'vestaɪt/ n travestido m

trap /træp/ n trampa f. ● vt (pt trapped) atrapar; (jam) atascar; (cut off) bloquear. ~door /'træpdɔ:(r)/ n trampa f; (in theatre) escotillón m

trapeze /trə'pi:z/ n trapecio m

trappings /'træpɪŋz/ npl (fig) atavíos mpl

trash /træʃ/ n pacotilla f; (refuse) basura f; (nonsense) tonterías fpl. ~ can n (Amer) cubo m de la basura. ~y a de baja calidad

trauma /'trɔ:mə/ n trauma m. ~tic /-'mætɪk/ a traumático

travel /'trævl/ vi (pt travelled) viajar. ● vt recorrer. ● n viajar m. ~ler /-ə(r)/ n viajero m. ~ler's cheque n cheque m de viaje. ~ling n viajar m

traverse /'trævɜ:s/ vt atravesar, recorrer

travesty /'trævɪstɪ/ n parodia f

trawler /'trɔ:lə(r)/ n pesquero m de arrastre

tray /treɪ/ n bandeja f

treacher|ous /'tretʃərəs/ a traidor; (deceptive) engañoso. ~ously adv traidoramente. ~y /'tretʃərɪ/ n traición f

treacle /'tri:kl/ n melaza f

tread /tred/ vi (pt trod, pp trodden) andar. ~ on pisar. ● vt pisar. ● n (step) paso m; (of tyre) banda f de rodadura. ~le /'tredl/ n pedal m. ~mill /'tredmɪl/ n rueda f de molino; (fig) rutina f

treason /'tri:zn/ n traición f

treasure /'treʒə(r)/ n tesoro m. ● vt apreciar mucho; (store) guardar

treasur|er /'treʒərə(r)/ n tesorero m. ~y /'treʒərɪ/ n tesorería f. the T~y n el Ministerio m de Hacienda

treat /tri:t/ vt tratar; (consider) considerar. ~ s.o. invitar a uno. ● n placer m; (present) regalo m

treatise /'tri:tɪz/ n tratado m

treatment /'tri:tmənt/ n tratamiento m

treaty /'tri:tɪ/ n tratado m

treble /'trebl/ a triple; (clef) de sol; (voice) de tiple. ● vt triplicar. ● vi triplicarse. ● n tiple m & f

tree /tri:/ n árbol m

trek /trek/ n viaje m arduo, caminata f. ● vi (pt trekked) hacer un viaje arduo

trellis /'trelɪs/ n enrejado m

tremble /'trembl/ vi temblar

tremendous /trɪ'mendəs/ a tremendo; (huge, fam) enorme. ~ly adv tremendamente

tremor /'tremə(r)/ n temblor m

tremulous /'tremjʊləs/ a tembloroso

trench /trentʃ/ n foso m, zanja f; (mil) trinchera f. ~ coat n trinchera f

trend /trend/ n tendencia f; (fashion) moda f. ~-setter n persona f que lanza la moda. ~y a (-ier, -iest) (fam) a la última

trepidation /trepɪ'deɪʃn/ n inquietud f

trespass /'trespəs/ vi. ~ on entrar sin derecho; (fig) abusar de. ~er /-ə(r)/ n intruso m

tress /tres/ n trenza f

trestle /'tresl/ n caballete m. ~table n mesa f de caballete

trews /tru:z/ npl pantalón m

trial /'traɪəl/ n prueba f; (jurid) proceso m; (ordeal) prueba f dura. ~ and error n tanteo m. be on ~ estar a prueba; (jurid) ser procesado

triang|le /'traɪæŋgl/ n triángulo m. ~ular /-'æŋgjʊlə(r)/ a triangular

trib|al /'traɪbl/ a tribal. ~e /traɪb/ n tribu f

tribulation /trɪbjʊ'leɪʃn/ n tribulación f

tribunal /traɪ'bju:nl/ n tribunal m

tributary /'trɪbjʊtrɪ/ n (stream) afluente m

tribute /'trɪbju:t/ n tributo m. pay ~ to rendir homenaje a

trice /traɪs/ n. in a ~ en un abrir y cerrar de ojos

trick /trɪk/ n trampa f; engaño m; (joke) broma f; (at cards) baza f; (habit) manía f. do the ~ servir. play a ~ on gastar una broma a. ● vt engañar. ~ery /'trɪkərɪ/ n engaño m

trickle /'trɪkl/ vi gotear. ~ in (fig) entrar poco a poco. ~ out (fig) salir poco a poco

trickster /'trɪkstə(r)/ n estafador m

tricky /'trɪkɪ/ a delicado, difícil

tricolour /'trɪkələ(r)/ n bandera f tricolor

tricycle /'traɪsɪkl/ n triciclo m

trident /'traɪdənt/ n tridente m

tried /traɪd/ see **try**

trifl|e /'traɪfl/ n bagatela f; (culin) bizcocho m con natillas, jalea, frutas y nata. ● *vi.* ~**e with** jugar con. ~**ing** *a* insignificante

trigger /'trɪgə(r)/ *n* (*of gun*) gatillo *m.* ● *vt.* ~ (**off**) desencadenar

trigonometry /ˌtrɪgə'nɒmɪtrɪ/ *n* trigonometría *f*

trilby /'trɪlbɪ/ *n* sombrero *m* de fieltro

trilogy /'trɪlədʒɪ/ *n* trilogía *f*

trim /trɪm/ *a* (**trimmer**, **trimmest**) arreglado. ● *vt* (*pt* **trimmed**) cortar; recortar ⟨*hair etc*⟩; (*adorn*) adornar. ● *n* (*cut*) recorte *m*; (*decoration*) adorno *m*; (*state*) estado *m*. **in** ~ en buen estado; (*fit*) en forma. ~**ming** *n* adorno *m*. ~**mings** *npl* recortes *mpl*; (*decorations*) adornos *mpl*; (*culin*) guarnición *f*

trinity /'trɪnɪtɪ/ *n* trinidad *f*. **the T**~ la Trinidad

trinket /'trɪŋkɪt/ *n* chuchería *f*

trio /'triːəʊ/ *n* (*pl* -**os**) trío *m*

trip /trɪp/ *vt* (*pt* **tripped**) hacer tropezar. ● *vi* tropezar; (*go lightly*) andar con paso ligero. ● *n* (*journey*) viaje *m*; (*outing*) excursión *f*; (*stumble*) traspié *m*. ~ **up** *vi* tropezar. ● *vt* hacer tropezar

tripe /traɪp/ *n* callos *mpl*; (*nonsense*, *sl*) tonterías *fpl*

triple /'trɪpl/ *a* triple. ● *vt* triplicar. ● *vi* triplicarse. ~**ts** /'trɪplɪts/ *npl* trillizos *mpl*

triplicate /'trɪplɪkət/ *a* triplicado. **in** ~ por triplicado

tripod /'traɪpɒd/ *n* trípode *m*

tripper /'trɪpə(r)/ *n* (*on day trip etc*) excursionista *m & f*

triptych /'trɪptɪk/ *n* tríptico *m*

trite /traɪt/ *a* trillado

triumph /'traɪʌmf/ *n* triunfo *m*. ● *vi* triunfar (**over** sobre). ~**al** /-'ʌmfl/ *a* triunfal. ~**ant** /-'ʌmfnt/ *a* triunfante

trivial /'trɪvɪəl/ *a* insignificante. ~**ity** /-'ælətɪ/ *n* insignificancia *f*

trod, trodden /trɒd, trɒdn/ *see* **tread**

trolley /'trɒlɪ/ *n* (*pl* -**eys**) carretón *m*. **tea** ~ *n* mesita *f* de ruedas. ~**bus** *n* trolebús *m*

trombone /trɒm'bəʊn/ *n* trombón *m*

troop /truːp/ *n* grupo *m*. ● *vi.* ~ **in** entrar en tropel. ~ **out** salir en tropel. ● *vt.* ~**ing the colour** saludo *m* a la bandera. ~**s** *npl* (*mil*) tropas *fpl*

trophy /'trəʊfɪ/ *n* trofeo *m*

tropic /'trɒpɪk/ *n* trópico *m*. ~**al** *a* tropical. ~**s** *npl* trópicos *mpl*

trot /trɒt/ *n* trote *m*. **on the** ~ (*fam*) seguidos. ● *vi* (*pt* **trotted**) trotar. ~ **out** (*produce*, *fam*) producir

trotter /'trɒtə(r)/ *n* (*culin*) pie *m* de cerdo

trouble /'trʌbl/ *n* problema *m*; (*awkward situation*) apuro *m*; (*inconvenience*) molestia *f*; (*conflict*) conflicto *m*; (*med*) enfermedad *f*; (*mec*) avería *f*. **be in** ~ estar en un apuro. **make** ~ armar un lío. **take** ~ tomarse la molestia. ● *vt* (*bother*) molestar; (*worry*) preocupar. ● *vi* molestarse; (*worry*) preocuparse. **be** ~**d about** preocuparse por. ~**maker** *n* alborotador *m*. ~**some** *a* molesto

trough /trɒf/ *n* (*for drinking*) abrevadero *m*; (*for feeding*) pesebre *m*; (*of wave*) seno *m*; (*atmospheric*) mínimo *m* de presión

trounce /traʊns/ *vt* (*defeat*) derrotar; (*thrash*) pegar

troupe /truːp/ *n* compañía *f*

trousers /'traʊzəz/ *npl* pantalón *m*; pantalones *mpl*

trousseau /'truːsəʊ/ *n* (*pl* -**s** /-əʊz/) ajuar *m*

trout /traʊt/ *n* (*pl* **trout**) trucha *f*

trowel /'traʊəl/ *n* (*garden*) desplantador *m*; (*for mortar*) paleta *f*

truant /'truːənt/ *n*. **play** ~ hacer novillos

truce /truːs/ *n* tregua *f*

truck[1] /trʌk/ *n* carro *m*; (*rail*) vagón *m*; (*lorry*) camión *m*

truck[2] /trʌk/ *n* (*dealings*) trato *m*

truculent /'trʌkjʊlənt/ *a* agresivo

trudge /trʌdʒ/ *vi* andar penosamente. ● *n* caminata *f* penosa

true /truː/ *a* (-**er**, -**est**) verdadero; (*loyal*) leal; (*genuine*) auténtico; (*accurate*) exacto. **come** ~ realizarse

truffle /'trʌfl/ *n* trufa *f*; (*chocolate*) trufa *f* de chocolate

truism /'truːɪzəm/ *n* perogrullada *f*

truly /'truːlɪ/ *adv* verdaderamente; (*sincerely*) sinceramente; (*faithfully*) fielmente. **yours** ~ (*in letters*) le saluda atentamente

trump /trʌmp/ *n* (*cards*) triunfo *m*. ● *vt* fallar. ~ **up** inventar

trumpet /'trʌmpɪt/ *n* trompeta *f*. ~**er** /-ə(r)/ *n* trompetero *m*, trompeta *m & f*

truncated /trʌŋ'keɪtɪd/ *a* truncado

truncheon /'trʌntʃən/ n porra f
trundle /'trʌndl/ vt hacer rodar. ● vi rodar
trunk /trʌŋk/ n tronco m; (box) baúl m; (of elephant) trompa f. ~**-call** n conferencia f. ~**-road** n carretera f (nacional). ~**s** npl bañador m
truss /trʌs/ n (med) braguero m. ~ **up** vt (culin) espetar
trust /trʌst/ n confianza f; (association) trust m. **on** ~ a ojos cerrados; (com) al fiado. ● vi confiar. ~ **to** confiar en. ● vt confiar en; (hope) esperar. ~**ed** a leal
trustee /trʌ'sti:/ n administrador m
trust /~**ful** a confiado. ~**fully** adv confiadamente. ~**worthy** a, ~**y** a digno de confianza
truth /tru:θ/ n (pl -s /tru:ðz/) verdad f. ~**ful** a veraz; (true) verídico. ~**fully** adv sinceramente
try /traɪ/ vt (pt **tried**) probar; (be a strain on) poner a prueba; (jurid) procesar. ~ **on** vt probarse (garment). ~ **out** vt probar. ● vi probar. ~ **for** vi intentar conseguir. ● n tentativa f, prueba f; (rugby) ensayo m. ~**ing** a difícil; (annoying) molesto. ~**-out** n prueba f
tryst /trɪst/ n cita f
T-shirt /'ti:ʃɜ:t/ n camiseta f
tub /tʌb/ n tina f; (bath, fam) baño m
tuba /'tju:bə/ n tuba f
tubby /'tʌbɪ/ a (-ier, -iest) rechoncho
tube /tju:b/ n tubo m; (rail, fam) metro m. **inner** ~ n cámara f de aire
tuber /'tju:bə(r)/ n tubérculo m
tuberculosis /tju:bɜ:kju'ləʊsɪs/ n tuberculosis f
tub|ing /'tju:bɪŋ/ n tubería f, tubos mpl. ~**ular** a tubular
tuck /tʌk/ n pliegue m. ● vt plegar; (put) meter; (put away) remeter; (hide) esconder. ~ **up** vt arropar (child). ● vi. ~ **in(to)** (eat, sl) comer con buen apetito. ~**-shop** n confitería f
Tuesday /'tju:zdeɪ/ n martes m
tuft /tʌft/ n (of hair) mechón m; (of feathers) penacho m; (of grass) manojo m
tug /tʌg/ vt (pt **tugged**) tirar de; (tow) remolcar. ● vi tirar fuerte. ● n tirón m; (naut) remolcador m. ~**-of-war** n lucha f de la cuerda; (fig) tira m y afloja
tuition /tju:'ɪʃn/ n enseñanza f
tulip /'tju:lɪp/ n tulipán m

tumble /'tʌmbl/ vi caerse. ~ **to** (fam) comprender. ● n caída f
tumbledown /'tʌmbldaʊn/ a ruinoso
tumble-drier /tʌmbl'draɪə(r)/ n secadora f (eléctrica con aire de salida)
tumbler /'tʌmblə(r)/ n (glass) vaso m
tummy /'tʌmɪ/ n (fam) estómago m
tumour /'tju:mə(r)/ n tumor m
tumult /'tju:mʌlt/ n tumulto m. ~**uous** a tumultuoso
tuna /'tju:nə/ n (pl **tuna**) atún m
tune /tju:n/ n aire m. **be in** ~ estar afinado. **be out of** ~ estar desafinado. ● vt afinar; sintonizar (radio, TV); (mec) poner a punto. ● vi. ~ **in (to)** (radio, TV) sintonizarse. ~ **up** afinar. ~**ful** a melodioso. ~**r** /-ə(r)/ n afinador m; (radio, TV) sintonizador m
tunic /'tju:nɪk/ n túnica f
tuning-fork /'tju:nɪŋfɔ:k/ n diapasón m
Tunisia /tju:'nɪzɪə/ n Túnez m. ~**n** a & n tunecino (m)
tunnel /'tʌnl/ n túnel m. ● vi (pt **tunnelled**) construir un túnel en
turban /'tɜ:bən/ n turbante m
turbid /'tɜ:bɪd/ a túrbido
turbine /'tɜ:baɪn/ n turbina f
turbo-jet /'tɜ:bəʊdʒet/ n turborreactor m
turbot /'tɜ:bət/ n rodaballo m
turbulen|ce /'tɜ:bjʊləns/ n turbulencia f. ~**t** /'tɜ:bjʊlənt/ a turbulento
tureen /tjʊ'ri:n/ n sopera f
turf /tɜ:f/ n (pl **turfs** or **turves**) césped m; (segment) tepe m. **the** ~ n las carreras fpl de caballos. ● vt. ~ **out** (sl) echar
turgid /'tɜ:dʒɪd/ a (language) pomposo
Turk /tɜ:k/ n turco m
turkey /'tɜ:kɪ/ n (pl -**eys**) pavo m
Turk|ey /'tɜ:kɪ/ f Turquía f. **T~ish** a & n turco (m)
turmoil /'tɜ:mɔɪl/ n confusión f
turn /tɜ:n/ vt hacer girar, dar vueltas a; volver (direction, page, etc); cumplir (age); dar (hour); doblar (corner); (change) cambiar; (deflect) desviar. ~ **the tables** volver las tornas. ● vi girar, dar vueltas; (become) hacerse; (change) cambiar. ● n vuelta f; (in road) curva f; (change)

cambio *m*; (*sequence*) turno *m*; (*of mind*) disposición *f*; (*in theatre*) número *m*; (*fright*) susto *m*; (*of illness, fam*) ataque *m*. **bad** ~ mala jugada *f*. **good** ~ favor *m*. **in** ~ a su vez. **out of** ~ fuera de lugar. **to a** ~ (*culin*) en su punto. ~ **against** *vt* volverse en contra de. ~ **down** *vt* (*fold*) doblar; (*reduce*) bajar; (*reject*) rechazar. ~ **in** *vt* entregar. ● *vi* (*go to bed, fam*) acostarse. ~ **off** *vt* cerrar ⟨*tap*⟩; apagar ⟨*light, TV, etc*⟩. ● *vi* desviarse. ~ **on** *vt* abrir ⟨*tap*⟩; encender ⟨*light etc*⟩; (*attack*) atacar; (*attract, fam*) excitar. ~ **out** *vt* expulsar; apagar ⟨*light etc*⟩; (*produce*) producir; (*empty*) vaciar. ● *vi* (*result*) resultar. ~ **round** *vi* dar la vuelta. ~ **up** *vi* aparecer. ● *vt* (*find*) encontrar; levantar ⟨*collar*⟩; poner más fuerte ⟨*gas*⟩. ~**ed-up** *a* ⟨*nose*⟩ respingona. ~**ing** /'tɜːnɪŋ/ *n* vuelta *f*; ⟨*road*⟩ bocacalle *f*. ~**ing-point** *n* punto *m* decisivo.

turnip /'tɜːnɪp/ *n* nabo *m*

turn: ~**out** *n* (*of people*) concurrencia *f*; (*of goods*) producción *f*. ~**over** /'tɜːnəʊvə(r)/ *n* (*culin*) empanada *f*; (*com*) volumen *m* de negocios; (*of staff*) rotación *f*. ~**pike** /'tɜːnpaɪk/ *n* (*Amer*) autopista *f* de peaje. ~**stile** /'tɜːnstaɪl/ *n* torniquete *m*. ~**table** /'tɜːnteɪbl/ *n* plataforma *f* giratoria; (*on record-player*) plato *m* giratorio. ~**-up** *n* (*of trousers*) vuelta *f*

turpentine /'tɜːpəntaɪn/ *n* trementina *f*

turquoise /'tɜːkwɔɪz/ *a & n* turquesa (*f*)

turret /'tʌrɪt/ *n* torrecilla *f*; (*mil*) torreta *f*

turtle /'tɜːtl/ *n* tortuga *f* de mar. ~**neck** *n* cuello *m* alto

tusk /tʌsk/ *n* colmillo *m*

tussle /'tʌsl/ *vi* pelearse. ● *n* pelea *f*

tussock /'tʌsək/ *n* montecillo *m* de hierbas

tutor /'tjuːtə(r)/ *n* preceptor *m*; (*univ*) director *m* de estudios, profesor *m*. ~**ial** /tjuː'tɔːrɪəl/ *n* clase *f* particular

tuxedo /tʌk'siːdəʊ/ *n* (*pl* **-os**) (*Amer*) esmoquin *m*

TV /tiː'viː/ *n* televisión *f*

twaddle /'twɒdl/ *n* tonterías *fpl*

twang /twæŋ/ *n* tañido *m*; (*in voice*) gangueo *m*. ● *vt* hacer vibrar. ● *vi* vibrar

tweed /twiːd/ *n* tela *f* gruesa de lana

tweet /twiːt/ *n* piada *f*. ● *vi* piar

tweezers /'twiːzəz/ *npl* pinzas *fpl*

twelfth /twelfθ/ *a & n* duodécimo (*m*). ~**ve** /twelv/ *a & n* doce (*m*)

twent|ieth /'twentɪəθ/ *a & n* vigésimo (*m*). ~**y** /'twentɪ/ *a & n* veinte (*m*)

twerp /twɜːp/ *n* (*sl*) imbécil *m*

twice /twaɪs/ *adv* dos veces

twiddle /'twɪdl/ *vt* hacer girar. ~ **one's thumbs** (*fig*) no tener nada que hacer. ● *vi* jugar con

twig[1] /twɪg/ *n* ramita *f*

twig[2] /twɪg/ *vt/i* (*pt* **twigged**) (*fam*) comprender

twilight /'twaɪlaɪt/ *n* crepúsculo *m*

twin /twɪn/ *a & n* gemelo (*m*)

twine /twaɪn/ *n* bramante *m*. ● *vt* torcer. ● *vi* enroscarse

twinge /twɪndʒ/ *n* punzada *f*; (*fig*) remordimiento *m* (de conciencia)

twinkle /'twɪŋkl/ *vi* centellear. ● *n* centelleo *m*

twirl /twɜːl/ *vt* dar vueltas a. ● *vi* dar vueltas. ● *n* vuelta *f*

twist /twɪst/ *vt* torcer; (*roll*) enrollar; (*distort*) deformar. ● *vi* torcerse; (*coil*) enroscarse; ⟨*road*⟩ serpentear. ● *n* torsión *f*; (*curve*) vuelta *f*; (*of character*) peculiaridad *f*

twit[1] /twɪt/ *n* (*sl*) imbécil *m*

twit[2] /twɪt/ *vt* (*pt* **twitted**) tomar el pelo a

twitch /twɪtʃ/ *vt* crispar. ● *vi* crisparse. ● *n* tic *m*; (*jerk*) tirón *m*

twitter /'twɪtə(r)/ *vi* gorjear. ● *n* gorjeo *m*

two /tuː/ *a & n* dos (*m*). **in** ~ **minds** indeciso. ~**-faced** *a* falso, insincero. ~**-piece** (*suit*) *n* traje *m* (de dos piezas). ~**some** /'tuːsəm/ *n* pareja *f*. ~**-way** *a* ⟨*traffic*⟩ de doble sentido

tycoon /taɪ'kuːn/ *n* magnate *m*

tying /'taɪɪŋ/ *see* **tie**

type /taɪp/ *n* tipo *m*. ● *vt/i* escribir a máquina. ~**cast** *a* ⟨*actor*⟩ encasillado. ~**script** /'taɪpskrɪpt/ *n* texto *m* escrito a máquina. ~**writer** /'taɪpraɪtə(r)/ *n* máquina *f* de escribir. ~**written** /-ɪtn/ *a* escrito a máquina, mecanografiado

typhoid /'taɪfɔɪd/ *n*. ~ (**fever**) fiebre *f* tifoidea

typhoon /taɪ'fuːn/ *n* tifón *m*

typical /'tɪpɪkl/ *a* típico. ~**ly** *adv* típicamente

typify /'tɪpɪfaɪ/ *vt* tipificar

typi|ng /ˈtaɪpɪŋ/ n mecanografía f.
~st n mecanógrafo m

typography /taɪˈpɒgrəfɪ/ n tipografía f

tyran|nical /tɪˈrænɪkl/ a tiránico.
~nize vi tiranizar. **~ny** /ˈtɪrənɪ/ n tiranía f. **~t** /ˈtaɪərənt/ n tirano m

tyre /ˈtaɪə(r)/ n neumático m, llanta f (Amer)

U

ubiquitous /juːˈbɪkwɪtəs/ a omnipresente, ubicuo

udder /ˈʌdə(r)/ n ubre f

UFO /ˈjuːfəʊ/ abbr (unidentified flying object) OVNI m, objeto m volante no identificado

ugl|iness /ˈʌglɪnɪs/ n fealdad f. **~y** /ˈʌglɪ/ a (-ier, -iest) feo

UK /juːˈkeɪ/ abbr (United Kingdom) Reino m Unido

ulcer /ˈʌlsə(r)/ n úlcera f. **~ous** a ulceroso

ulterior /ʌlˈtɪərɪə(r)/ a ulterior. **~ motive** n segunda intención f

ultimate /ˈʌltɪmət/ a último; (definitive) definitivo; (fundamental) fundamental. **~ly** adv al final; (basically) en el fondo

ultimatum /ʌltɪˈmeɪtəm/ n (pl -ums) ultimátum m invar

ultra... /ˈʌltrə/ pref ultra...

ultramarine /ʌltrəməˈriːn/ n azul m marino

ultrasonic /ʌltrəˈsɒnɪk/ a ultrasónico

ultraviolet /ʌltrəˈvaɪələt/ a ultravioleta a invar

umbilical /ʌmˈbɪlɪkl/ a umbilical. **~ cord** n cordón m umbilical

umbrage /ˈʌmbrɪdʒ/ n resentimiento m. **take ~** ofenderse (**at** por)

umbrella /ʌmˈbrelə/ n paraguas m invar

umpire /ˈʌmpaɪə(r)/ n árbitro m.
● vt arbitrar

umpteen /ˈʌmptiːn/ a (sl) muchísimos. **~th** a (sl) enésimo

UN /juːˈen/ abbr (United Nations) ONU f, Organización f de las Naciones Unidas

un... /ʌn/ pref in..., des..., no, poco, sin

unabated /ʌnəˈbeɪtɪd/ a no disminuido

unable /ʌnˈeɪbl/ a incapaz (**to** de). **be ~ to** no poder

unabridged /ʌnəˈbrɪdʒd/ a íntegro

unacceptable /ʌnəkˈseptəbl/ a inaceptable

unaccountabl|e /ʌnəˈkaʊntəbl/ a inexplicable. **~y** adv inexplicablemente

unaccustomed /ʌnəˈkʌstəmd/ a insólito. **be ~ to** a no estar acostumbrado a

unadopted /ʌnəˈdɒptɪd/ a ‹of road› privado

unadulterated /ʌnəˈdʌltəreɪtɪd/ a puro

unaffected /ʌnəˈfektɪd/ a sin afectación, natural

unaided /ʌnˈeɪdɪd/ a sin ayuda

unalloyed /ʌnəˈlɔɪd/ a puro

unanimous /juːˈnænɪməs/ a unánime. **~ly** adv unánimemente

unannounced /ʌnəˈnaʊnst/ a sin previo aviso; (unexpected) inesperado

unarmed /ʌnˈɑːmd/ a desarmado

unassuming /ʌnəˈsjuːmɪŋ/ a modesto, sin pretensiones

unattached /ʌnəˈtætʃt/ a suelto; (unmarried) soltero

unattended /ʌnəˈtendɪd/ a sin vigilar

unattractive /ʌnəˈtræktɪv/ a poco atractivo

unavoidabl|e /ʌnəˈvɔɪdəbl/ a inevitable. **~y** adv inevitablemente

unaware /ʌnəˈweə(r)/ a ignorante (**of** de). **be ~ of** ignorar. **~s** /-eəz/ adv desprevenido

unbalanced /ʌnˈbælənst/ a desequilibrado

unbearabl|e /ʌnˈbeərəbl/ a inaguantable. **~y** adv inaguantablemente

unbeat|able /ʌnˈbiːtəbl/ a insuperable. **~en** a no vencido

unbeknown /ʌnbɪˈnəʊn/ a desconocido. **~ to me** (fam) sin saberlo yo

unbelievable /ʌnbɪˈliːvəbl/ a increíble

unbend /ʌnˈbend/ vt (pt unbent) enderezar. ● vi (relax) relajarse. **~ing** a inflexible

unbiased /ʌnˈbaɪəst/ a imparcial

unbidden /ʌnˈbɪdn/ a espontáneo; (without invitation) sin ser invitado

unblock /ʌnˈblɒk/ vt desatascar

unbolt /ʌnˈbəʊlt/ vt desatrancar

unborn /ʌnˈbɔːn/ a no nacido todavía

unbounded /ʌnˈbaʊndɪd/ a ilimitado

unbreakable /ʌnˈbreɪkəbl/ a irrompible

unbridled /ʌnˈbraɪdld/ a desenfrenado

unbroken /ʌnˈbrəʊkən/ a (intact) intacto; (continuous) continuo

unburden /ʌnˈbɜːdn/ vt. ~ o.s. desahogarse

unbutton /ʌnˈbʌtn/ vt desabotonar, desabrochar

uncalled-for /ʌnˈkɔːldfɔː(r)/ a fuera de lugar; (unjustified) injustificado

uncanny /ʌnˈkænɪ/ a (-ier, -iest) misterioso

unceasing /ʌnˈsiːsɪŋ/ a incesante

unceremonious /ʌnserɪˈməʊnɪəs/ a informal; (abrupt) brusco

uncertain /ʌnˈsɜːtn/ a incierto; (changeable) variable. **be ~ whether** no saber exactamente si. **~ty** n incertidumbre f

unchang|ed /ʌnˈtʃeɪndʒd/ a igual. **~ing** a inmutable

uncharitable /ʌnˈtʃærɪtəbl/ a severo

uncivilized /ʌnˈsɪvɪlaɪzd/ a incivilizado

uncle /ˈʌŋkl/ n tío m

unclean /ʌnˈkliːn/ a sucio

unclear /ʌnˈklɪə(r)/ a poco claro

uncomfortable /ʌnˈkʌmfətəbl/ a incómodo; (unpleasant) desagradable. **feel ~** no estar a gusto

uncommon /ʌnˈkɒmən/ a raro. **~ly** adv extraordinariamente

uncompromising /ʌnˈkɒmprəmaɪzɪŋ/ a intransigente

unconcerned /ʌnkənˈsɜːnd/ a indiferente

unconditional /ʌnkənˈdɪʃənl/ a incondicional. **~ly** adv incondicionalmente

unconscious /ʌnˈkɒnʃəs/ a inconsciente; (med) sin sentido. **~ly** adv inconscientemente

unconventional /ʌnkənˈvenʃənl/ a poco convencional

uncooperative /ʌnkəʊˈɒpərətɪv/ a poco servicial

uncork /ʌnˈkɔːk/ vt descorchar, destapar

uncouth /ʌnˈkuːθ/ a grosero

uncover /ʌnˈkʌvə(r)/ vt descubrir

unctuous /ˈʌŋktjʊəs/ a untuoso; (fig) empalagoso

undecided /ʌndɪˈsaɪdɪd/ a indeciso

undeniabl|e /ʌndɪˈnaɪəbl/ a innegable. **~y** adv indiscutiblemente

under /ˈʌndə(r)/ prep debajo de; (less than) menos de; (in the course of) bajo, en. ● adv debajo, abajo. **~ age** a menor de edad. **~ way** adv en curso; (on the way) en marcha

under... pref sub...

undercarriage /ˈʌndəkærɪdʒ/ n (aviat) tren m de aterrizaje

underclothes /ˈʌndəkləʊðz/ npl ropa f interior

undercoat /ˈʌndəkəʊt/ n (of paint) primera mano f

undercover /ʌndəˈkʌvə(r)/ a secreto

undercurrent /ˈʌndəkʌrənt/ n corriente f submarina; (fig) tendencia f oculta

undercut /ˈʌndəkʌt/ vt (pt undercut) (com) vender más barato que

underdeveloped /ʌndədɪˈveləpt/ a subdesarrollado

underdog /ˈʌndədɒg/ n perdedor m. **the ~s** npl los de abajo

underdone /ʌndəˈdʌn/ a ⟨meat⟩ poco hecho

underestimate /ʌndərˈestɪmeɪt/ vt subestimar

underfed /ʌndəˈfed/ a desnutrido

underfoot /ʌndəˈfʊt/ adv bajo los pies

undergo /ˈʌndəgəʊ/ vt (pt -went, pp -gone) sufrir

undergraduate /ʌndəˈgrædjʊət/ n estudiante m & f universitario (no licenciado)

underground /ʌndəˈgraʊnd/ adv bajo tierra; (in secret) clandestinamente. /ˈʌndəgraʊnd/ a subterráneo; (secret) clandestino. ● n metro m

undergrowth /ˈʌndəgrəʊθ/ n maleza f

underhand /ˈʌndəhænd/ a (secret) clandestino; (deceptive) fraudulento

underlie /ʌndəˈlaɪ/ vt (pt -lay, pp -lain, pres p -lying) estar debajo de; (fig) estar a la base de

underline /ʌndəˈlaɪn/ vt subrayar

underling /ˈʌndəlɪŋ/ n subalterno m

underlying /ʌndəˈlaɪɪŋ/ a fundamental

undermine /ʌndəˈmaɪn/ vt socavar

underneath /ʌndə'ni:θ/ *prep* debajo de. ● *adv* por debajo

underpaid /ʌndə'peɪd/ *a* mal pagado

underpants /'ʌndəpænts/ *npl* calzoncillos *mpl*

underpass /'ʌndəpa:s/ *n* paso *m* subterráneo

underprivileged /ʌndə'prɪvɪlɪdʒd/ *a* desvalido

underrate /ʌndə'reɪt/ *vt* subestimar

undersell /ʌndə'sel/ *vt* (*pt* **-sold**) vender más barato que

undersigned /'ʌndəsaɪnd/ *a* abajo firmante

undersized /ʌndə'saɪzd/ *a* pequeño

understand /ʌndə'stænd/ *vt/i* (*pt* **-stood**) entender, comprender. **~able** *a* comprensible. **~ing** /ʌndə'stændɪŋ/ *a* comprensivo. ● *n* comprensión *f*; (*agreement*) acuerdo *m*

understatement /ʌndə'steɪtmənt/ *n* subestimación *f*

understudy /'ʌndəstʌdɪ/ *n* sobresaliente *m & f* (en el teatro)

undertake /ʌndə'teɪk/ *vt* (*pt* **-took**, *pp* **-taken**) emprender; (*assume responsibility*) encargarse de

undertaker /'ʌndəteɪkə(r)/ *n* empresario *m* de pompas fúnebres

undertaking /ʌndə'teɪkɪŋ/ *n* empresa *f*; (*promise*) promesa *f*

undertone /'ʌndətəʊn/ *n*. **in an ~** en voz baja

undertow /'ʌndətəʊ/ *n* resaca *f*

undervalue /ʌndə'vælju:/ *vt* subvalorar

underwater /ʌndə'wɔ:tə(r)/ *a* submarino. ● *adv* bajo el agua

underwear /'ʌndəweə(r)/ *n* ropa *f* interior

underweight /'ʌndəweɪt/ *a* de peso insuficiente. **be ~** estar flaco

underwent /ʌndə'went/ *see* **undergo**

underworld /'ʌndəwɜ:ld/ *n* (*criminals*) hampa *f*

underwrite /ʌndə'raɪt/ *vt* (*pt* **-wrote**, *pp* **-written**) (*com*) asegurar. **~r** /-ə(r)/ *n* asegurador *m*

undeserved /ʌndɪ'zɜ:vd/ *a* inmerecido

undesirable /ʌndɪ'zaɪərəbl/ *a* indeseable

undeveloped /ʌndɪ'veləpt/ *a* sin desarrollar

undies /'ʌndɪz/ *npl* (*fam*) ropa *f* interior

undignified /ʌn'dɪgnɪfaɪd/ *a* indecoroso

undisputed /ʌndɪs'pju:tɪd/ *a* incontestable

undistinguished /ʌndɪs'tɪŋgwɪʃt/ *a* mediocre

undo /ʌn'du:/ *vt* (*pt* **-did**, *pp* **-done**) deshacer; (*ruin*) arruinar; reparar (*wrong*). **leave ~ne** dejar sin hacer

undoubted /ʌn'daʊtɪd/ *a* indudable. **~ly** *adv* indudablemente

undress /ʌn'dres/ *vt* desnudar. ● *vi* desnudarse

undue /ʌn'dju:/ *a* excesivo

undulat|e /'ʌndjʊleɪt/ *vi* ondular. **~ion** /-'leɪʃn/ *n* ondulación *f*

unduly /ʌn'dju:lɪ/ *adv* excesivamente

undying /ʌn'daɪɪŋ/ *a* eterno

unearth /ʌn'ɜ:θ/ *vt* desenterrar

unearthly /ʌn'ɜ:θlɪ/ *a* sobrenatural; (*impossible, fam*) absurdo. **~ hour** *n* hora intempestiva

uneas|ily /ʌn'i:zɪlɪ/ *adv* inquietamente. **~y** /ʌn'i:zɪ/ *a* incómodo; (*worrying*) inquieto

uneconomic /ʌni:kə'nɒmɪk/ *a* poco rentable

uneducated /ʌn'edjʊkeɪtɪd/ *a* inculto

unemploy|ed /ʌnɪm'plɔɪd/ *a* parado, desempleado; (*not in use*) inutilizado. **~ment** *n* paro *m*, desempleo *m*

unending /ʌn'endɪŋ/ *a* interminable, sin fin

unequal /ʌn'i:kwəl/ *a* desigual

unequivocal /ʌnɪ'kwɪvəkl/ *a* inequívoco

unerring /ʌn'ɜ:rɪŋ/ *a* infalible

unethical /ʌn'eθɪkl/ *a* sin ética, inmoral

uneven /ʌn'i:vn/ *a* desigual

unexceptional /ʌnɪk'sepʃənl/ *a* corriente

unexpected /ʌnɪk'spektɪd/ *a* inesperado

unfailing /ʌn'feɪlɪŋ/ *a* inagotable; (*constant*) constante; (*loyal*) leal

unfair /ʌn'feə(r)/ *a* injusto. **~ly** *adv* injustamente. **~ness** *n* injusticia *f*

unfaithful /ʌn'feɪθfl/ *a* infiel. **~ness** *n* infidelidad *f*

unfamiliar /ʌnfə'mɪlɪə(r)/ *a* desconocido. **be ~ with** desconocer

unfasten /ʌnˈfɑːsn/ vt desabrochar ‹clothes›; (untie) desatar

unfavourable /ʌnˈfeɪvərəbl/ a desfavorable

unfeeling /ʌnˈfiːlɪŋ/ a insensible

unfit /ʌnˈfɪt/ a inadecuado, no apto; (unwell) en mal estado físico; (incapable) incapaz

unflinching /ʌnˈflɪntʃɪŋ/ a resuelto

unfold /ʌnˈfəʊld/ vt desdoblar; (fig) revelar. ● vi ‹view etc› extenderse

unforeseen /ʌnfɔːˈsiːn/ a imprevisto

unforgettable /ʌnfəˈgetəbl/ a inolvidable

unforgivable /ʌnfəˈgɪvəbl/ a imperdonable

unfortunate /ʌnˈfɔːtʃənət/ a desgraciado; (regrettable) lamentable. ~ly adv desgraciadamente

unfounded /ʌnˈfaʊndɪd/ a infundado

unfriendly /ʌnˈfrendlɪ/ a poco amistoso, frío

unfurl /ʌnˈfɜːl/ vt desplegar

ungainly /ʌnˈgeɪnlɪ/ a desgarbado

ungodly /ʌnˈgɒdlɪ/ a impío. ~ hour n (fam) hora f intempestiva

ungrateful /ʌnˈgreɪtfl/ a desagradecido

unguarded /ʌnˈgɑːdɪd/ a indefenso; (incautious) imprudente, incauto

unhapp|ily /ʌnˈhæpɪlɪ/ adv infelizmente; (unfortunately) desgraciadamente. ~iness n tristeza f. ~y /ʌnˈhæpɪ/ a (-ier, -iest) infeliz, triste; (unsuitable) inoportuno. ~y with insatisfecho de ‹plans etc›

unharmed /ʌnˈhɑːmd/ a ileso, sano y salvo

unhealthy /ʌnˈhelθɪ/ a (-ier, -iest) enfermizo; (insanitary) malsano

unhinge /ʌnˈhɪndʒ/ vt desquiciar

unholy /ʌnˈhəʊlɪ/ a (-ier, -iest) impío; (terrible, fam) terrible

unhook /ʌnˈhʊk/ vt desenganchar

unhoped /ʌnˈhəʊpt/ a. ~ for inesperado

unhurt /ʌnˈhɜːt/ a ileso

unicorn /ˈjuːnɪkɔːn/ n unicornio m

unification /juːnɪfɪˈkeɪʃn/ n unificación f

uniform /ˈjuːnɪfɔːm/ a & n uniforme (m). ~ity /-ˈfɔːmətɪ/ n uniformidad f. ~ly adv uniformemente

unify /ˈjuːnɪfaɪ/ vt unificar

unilateral /juːnɪˈlætərəl/ a unilateral

unimaginable /ʌnɪˈmædʒɪnəbl/ a inconcebible

unimpeachable /ʌnɪmˈpiːtʃəbl/ a irreprensible

unimportant /ʌnɪmˈpɔːtnt/ a insignificante

uninhabited /ʌnɪnˈhæbɪtɪd/ a inhabitado; (abandoned) despoblado

unintentional /ʌnɪnˈtenʃnl/ a involuntario

union /ˈjuːnjən/ n unión f; (trade union) sindicato m. ~ist n sindicalista m & f. U~ Jack n bandera f del Reino Unido

unique /juːˈniːk/ a único. ~ly adv extraordinariamente

unisex /ˈjuːnɪseks/ a unisex(o)

unison /ˈjuːnɪsn/ n. in ~ al unísono

unit /ˈjuːnɪt/ n unidad f; (of furniture etc) elemento m

unite /juːˈnaɪt/ vt unir. ● vi unirse. U~d Kingdom (UK) n Reino m Unido. U~d Nations (UN) n Organización f de las Naciones Unidas (ONU). U~d States (of America) (USA) n Estados mpl Unidos (de América) (EE.UU.)

unity /ˈjuːnɪtɪ/ n unidad f; (fig) acuerdo m

univers|al /juːnɪˈvɜːsl/ a universal. ~e /ˈjuːnɪvɜːs/ n universo m

university /juːnɪˈvɜːsətɪ/ n universidad f. ● a universitario

unjust /ʌnˈdʒʌst/ a injusto

unkempt /ʌnˈkempt/ a desaseado

unkind /ʌnˈkaɪnd/ a poco amable; (cruel) cruel. ~ly adv poco amablemente. ~ness n falta f de amabilidad; (cruelty) crueldad f

unknown /ʌnˈnəʊn/ a desconocido

unlawful /ʌnˈlɔːfl/ a ilegal

unleash /ʌnˈliːʃ/ vt soltar; (fig) desencadenar

unless /ʌnˈles, ənˈles/ conj a menos que, a no ser que

unlike /ʌnˈlaɪk/ a diferente; (not typical) impropio de. ● prep a diferencia de. ~lihood n improbabilidad f. ~ly /ʌnˈlaɪklɪ/ a improbable

unlimited /ʌnˈlɪmɪtɪd/ a ilimitado

unload /ʌnˈləʊd/ vt descargar

unlock /ʌnˈlɒk/ vt abrir (con llave)

unluck|ily /ʌnˈlʌkɪlɪ/ adv desgraciadamente. ~y /ʌnˈlʌkɪ/ a (-ier, -iest) desgraciado; ‹number› de mala suerte

unmanly /ʌnˈmænlɪ/ a poco viril

unmanned /ʌn'mænd/ a no tripulado

unmarried /ʌn'mærɪd/ a soltero. ~ **mother** n madre f soltera

unmask /ʌn'mɑːsk/ vt desenmascarar. ● vi quitarse la máscara

unmentionable /ʌn'menʃənəbl/ a a que no se debe aludir

unmistakabl|e /ʌnmɪ'steɪkəbl/ a inconfundible. ~**y** adv claramente

unmitigated /ʌn'mɪtɪgeɪtɪd/ a (absolute) absoluto

unmoved /ʌn'muːvd/ a (fig) indiferente (**by** a), insensible (**by** a)

unnatural /ʌn'nætʃərəl/ a no natural; (not normal) anormal

unnecessar|ily /ʌn'nesəsərɪlɪ/ adv innecesariamente. ~**y** /ʌn'nesəsərɪ/ a innecesario

unnerve /ʌn'nɜːv/ vt desconcertar

unnoticed /ʌn'nəʊtɪst/ a inadvertido

unobtainable /ʌnəb'teɪnəbl/ a inaseguible; (fig) inalcanzable

unobtrusive /ʌnəb'truːsɪv/ a discreto

unofficial /ʌnə'fɪʃl/ a no oficial. ~**ly** adv extraoficialmente

unpack /ʌn'pæk/ vt desempaquetar ⟨parcel⟩; deshacer ⟨suitcase⟩. ● vi deshacer la maleta

unpalatable /ʌn'pælətəbl/ a desagradable

unparalleled /ʌn'pærəleld/ a sin par

unpick /ʌn'pɪk/ vt descoser

unpleasant /ʌn'pleznt/ a desagradable. ~**ness** n lo desagradable

unplug /ʌn'plʌg/ vt (elec) desenchufar

unpopular /ʌn'pɒpjʊlə(r)/ a impopular

unprecedented /ʌn'presɪdentɪd/ a sin precedente

unpredictable /ʌnprɪ'dɪktəbl/ a imprevisible

unpremeditated /ʌnprɪ'medɪteɪtɪd/ a impremeditado

unprepared /ʌnprɪ'peəd/ a no preparado; (unready) desprevenido

unprepossessing /ʌnpriː'pəzesɪŋ/ a poco atractivo

unpretentious /ʌnprɪ'tenʃəs/ a sin pretensiones, modesto

unprincipled /ʌn'prɪnsɪpld/ a sin principios

unprofessional /ʌnprə'feʃənəl/ a contrario a la ética profesional

unpublished /ʌn'pʌblɪʃt/ a inédito

unqualified /ʌn'kwɒlɪfaɪd/ a sin título; (fig) absoluto

unquestionabl|e /ʌn'kwestʃənəbl/ a indiscutible. ~**y** adv indiscutiblemente

unquote /ʌn'kwəʊt/ vi cerrar comillas

unravel /ʌn'rævl/ vt (pt **unravelled**) desenredar; deshacer ⟨knitting etc⟩. ● vi desenredarse

unreal /ʌn'rɪəl/ a irreal. ~**istic** a poco realista

unreasonable /ʌn'riːzənəbl/ a irrazonable

unrecognizable /ʌnrekəg'naɪzəbl/ a irreconocible

unrelated /ʌnrɪ'leɪtɪd/ a ⟨facts⟩ inconexo, sin relación; ⟨people⟩ no emparentado

unreliable /ʌnrɪ'laɪəbl/ a ⟨person⟩ poco formal; ⟨machine⟩ poco fiable

unrelieved /ʌnrɪ'liːvd/ a no aliviado

unremitting /ʌnrɪ'mɪtɪŋ/ a incesante

unrepentant /ʌnrɪ'pentənt/ a impenitente

unrequited /ʌnrɪ'kwaɪtɪd/ a no correspondido

unreservedly /ʌnrɪ'zɜːvɪdlɪ/ adv sin reserva

unrest /ʌn'rest/ n inquietud f; (pol) agitación f

unrivalled /ʌn'raɪvld/ a sin par

unroll /ʌn'rəʊl/ vt desenrollar. ● vi desenrollarse

unruffled /ʌn'rʌfld/ a ⟨person⟩ imperturbable

unruly /ʌn'ruːlɪ/ a indisciplinado

unsafe /ʌn'seɪf/ a peligroso; ⟨person⟩ en peligro

unsaid /ʌn'sed/ a sin decir

unsatisfactory /ʌnsætɪs'fæktərɪ/ a insatisfactorio

unsavoury /ʌn'seɪvərɪ/ a desagradable

unscathed /ʌn'skeɪðd/ a ileso

unscramble /ʌn'skræmbl/ vt descifrar

unscrew /ʌn'skruː/ vt destornillar

unscrupulous /ʌn'skruːpjʊləs/ a sin escrúpulos

unseat /ʌn'siːt/ vt (pol) quitar el escaño a

unseemly /ʌn'siːmlɪ/ a indecoroso

unseen /ʌn'siːn/ a inadvertido. ● n (translation) traducción f a primera vista

unselfish /ʌnˈselfɪʃ/ a desinteresado

unsettle /ʌnˈsetl/ vt perturbar. ~**d** a perturbado; ⟨weather⟩ variable; ⟨bill⟩ por pagar

unshakeable /ʌnˈʃeɪkəbl/ a firme

unshaven /ʌnˈʃeɪvn/ a sin afeitar

unsightly /ʌnˈsaɪtlɪ/ a feo

unskilled /ʌnˈskɪld/ a inexperto. ~ **worker** n obrero m no cualificado

unsociable /ʌnˈsəʊʃəbl/ a insociable

unsolicited /ʌnsəˈlɪsɪtɪd/ a no solicitado

unsophisticated /ʌnsəˈfɪstɪkeɪtɪd/ a sencillo

unsound /ʌnˈsaʊnd/ a defectuoso, erróneo. **of** ~ **mind** demente

unsparing /ʌnˈspeərɪŋ/ a pródigo; ⟨cruel⟩ cruel

unspeakable /ʌnˈspiːkəbl/ a indecible

unspecified /ʌnˈspesɪfaɪd/ a no especificado

unstable /ʌnˈsteɪbl/ a inestable

unsteady /ʌnˈstedɪ/ a inestable; ⟨hand⟩ poco firme; ⟨step⟩ inseguro

unstinted /ʌnˈstɪntɪd/ a abundante

unstuck /ʌnˈstʌk/ a suelto. **come** ~ despegarse; ⟨fail, fam⟩ fracasar

unstudied /ʌnˈstʌdɪd/ a natural

unsuccessful /ʌnsəkˈsesfʊl/ a fracasado. **be** ~ no tener éxito, fracasar

unsuitable /ʌnˈsuːtəbl/ a inadecuado; ⟨inconvenient⟩ inconveniente

unsure /ʌnˈʃʊə(r)/ a inseguro

unsuspecting /ʌnsəˈspektɪŋ/ a confiado

unthinkable /ʌnˈθɪŋkəbl/ a inconcebible

untid|ily /ʌnˈtaɪdɪlɪ/ adv desordenadamente. ~**iness** n desorden m. ~**y** /ʌnˈtaɪdɪ/ a (-ier, -iest) desordenado; ⟨person⟩ desaseado

untie /ʌnˈtaɪ/ vt desatar

until /ənˈtɪl, ʌnˈtɪl/ prep hasta. ● conj hasta que

untimely /ʌnˈtaɪmlɪ/ a inoportuno; ⟨premature⟩ prematuro

untiring /ʌnˈtaɪərɪŋ/ a incansable

untold /ʌnˈtəʊld/ a incalculable

untoward /ʌntəˈwɔːd/ a ⟨inconvenient⟩ inconveniente

untried /ʌnˈtraɪd/ a no probado

untrue /ʌnˈtruː/ a falso

unused /ʌnˈjuːzd/ a nuevo. /ʌnˈjuːst/ a. ~ **to** no acostumbrado a

unusual /ʌnˈjuːʒʊəl/ a insólito; ⟨exceptional⟩ excepcional. ~**ly** adv excepcionalmente

unutterable /ʌnˈʌtərəbl/ a indecible

unveil /ʌnˈveɪl/ vt descubrir; ⟨disclose⟩ revelar

unwanted /ʌnˈwɒntɪd/ a superfluo; ⟨child⟩ no deseado

unwarranted /ʌnˈwɒrəntɪd/ a injustificado

unwelcome /ʌnˈwelkəm/ a desagradable; ⟨guest⟩ inoportuno

unwell /ʌnˈwel/ a indispuesto

unwieldy /ʌnˈwiːldɪ/ a difícil de manejar

unwilling /ʌnˈwɪlɪŋ/ a no dispuesto. **be** ~ no querer. ~**ly** adv de mala gana

unwind /ʌnˈwaɪnd/ vt (pt un- **wound**) desenvolver. ● vi desenvolverse; ⟨relax, fam⟩ relajarse

unwise /ʌnˈwaɪz/ a imprudente

unwitting /ʌnˈwɪtɪŋ/ a inconsciente; ⟨involuntary⟩ involuntario. ~**ly** adv involuntariamente

unworthy /ʌnˈwɜːðɪ/ a indigno

unwrap /ʌnˈræp/ vt (pt un- **wrapped**) desenvolver, deshacer

unwritten /ʌnˈrɪtn/ a no escrito; ⟨agreement⟩ tácito

up /ʌp/ adv arriba; ⟨upwards⟩ hacia arriba; ⟨higher⟩ más arriba; ⟨out of bed⟩ levantado; ⟨finished⟩ terminado. ~ **here** aquí arriba. ~ **in** ⟨fam⟩ versado en, fuerte en. ~ **there** allí arriba. ~ **to** hasta. **be one** ~ **on** llevar la ventaja a. **be** ~ **against** enfrentarse con. **be** ~ **to** tramar ⟨plot⟩; ⟨one's turn⟩ tocar a; a la altura de ⟨task⟩; ⟨reach⟩ llegar a. **come** ~ subir. **feel** ~ **to it** sentirse capaz. **go** ~ subir. **it's** ~ **to you** depende de tí. **what is** ~? ¿qué pasa? ● prep arriba; ⟨on top of⟩ en lo alto de. ● vt (pt **upped**) aumentar. ● n. ~**s and downs** npl altibajos mpl

upbraid /ʌpˈbreɪd/ vt reprender

upbringing /ˈʌpbrɪŋɪŋ/ n educación f

update /ʌpˈdeɪt/ vt poner al día

upgrade /ʌpˈgreɪd/ vt ascender ⟨person⟩; mejorar ⟨equipment⟩

upheaval /ʌpˈhiːvl/ n trastorno m

uphill /ˈʌphɪl/ a ascendente; ⟨fig⟩ arduo. ● adv /ʌpˈhɪl/ cuesta arriba. **go** ~ subir

uphold /ʌp'həʊld/ vt (pt **upheld**) sostener

upholster /ʌp'həʊlstə(r)/ vt tapizar. **~er** /-rə(r)/ n tapicero m. **~y** n tapicería f

upkeep /'ʌpkiːp/ n mantenimiento m

up-market /ʌp'mɑːkɪt/ a superior

upon /ə'pɒn/ prep en; (on top of) encima de. **once ~ a time** érase una vez

upper /'ʌpə(r)/ a superior. **~ class** n clases fpl altas. **~ hand** n dominio m, ventaja f. **~most** a (el) más alto. ● n (of shoe) pala f

uppish /'ʌpɪʃ/ a engreído

upright /'ʌpraɪt/ a derecho; ⟨piano⟩ vertical. ● n montante m

uprising /'ʌpraɪzɪŋ/ n sublevación f

uproar /'ʌprɔː(r)/ n tumulto m. **~ious** /-'rɔːrɪəs/ a tumultuoso

uproot /ʌp'ruːt/ vt desarraigar

upset /ʌp'set/ vt (pt upset, presp **upsetting**) trastornar; desbaratar ⟨plan etc⟩; ⟨distress⟩ alterar. /'ʌpset/ n trastorno m

upshot /'ʌpʃɒt/ n resultado m

upside-down /ʌpsaɪd'daʊn/ adv al revés; (in disorder) patas arriba. **turn ~** volver

upstairs /ʌp'steəz/ adv arriba. /'ʌpsteəz/ a de arriba

upstart /'ʌpstɑːt/ n arribista m & f

upstream /'ʌpstriːm/ adv río arriba; (against the current) contra la corriente

upsurge /'ʌpsɜːdʒ/ n aumento m; (of anger etc) arrebato m

uptake /'ʌpteɪk/ n. **quick on the ~** muy listo

uptight /'ʌptaɪt/ a (fam) nervioso

up-to-date /ʌptə'deɪt/ a al día; ⟨news⟩ de última hora; (modern) moderno

upturn /'ʌptɜːn/ n aumento m; (improvement) mejora f

upward /'ʌpwəd/ a ascendente. ● adv hacia arriba. **~s** adv hacia arriba

uranium /jʊ'reɪnɪəm/ n uranio m

urban /'ɜːbən/ a urbano

urbane /ɜː'beɪn/ a cortés

urbanize /'ɜːbənaɪz/ vt urbanizar

urchin /'ɜːtʃɪn/ n pilluelo m

urge /ɜːdʒ/ vt incitar, animar. ● n impulso m. **~ on** animar

urgen|cy /'ɜːdʒənsɪ/ n urgencia f. **~t** /'ɜːdʒənt/ a urgente. **~tly** adv urgentemente

urin|ate /'jʊərɪneɪt/ vi orinar. **~e** /'jʊərɪn/ n orina f

urn /ɜːn/ n urna f

Uruguay /jʊərəgwaɪ/ n el Uruguay m. **~an** a & n uruguayo (m)

us /ʌs, əs/ pron nos; (after prep) nosotros, nosotras

US(A) /juːes'eɪ/ abbr (United States (of America)) EE.UU., Estados mpl Unidos

usage /'juːzɪdʒ/ n uso m

use /juːz/ vt emplear. /juːs/ n uso m, empleo m. **be of ~** servir. **it is no ~** es inútil, no sirve para nada. **make ~ of** servirse de. **~ up** agotar, consumir. **~d** /juːzd/ a ⟨clothes⟩ gastado. /juːst/ pt. **he ~d to say** decía, solía decir. ● a. **~d to** acostumbrado a. **~ful** /'juːsfl/ a útil. **~fully** adv útilmente. **~less** a inútil; ⟨person⟩ incompetente. **~r** /-zə(r)/ n usuario m

usher /'ʌʃə(r)/ n ujier m; (in theatre etc) acomodador m. ● vt. **~ in** hacer entrar. **~ette** n acomodadora f

USSR abbr (history) (Union of Soviet Socialist Republics) URSS

usual /'juːʒʊəl/ a usual, corriente; (habitual) acostumbrado, habitual. **as ~** como de costumbre, como siempre. **~ly** adv normalmente. **he ~ly wakes up early** suele despertarse temprano

usurer /'juːʒərə(r)/ n usurero m

usurp /juː'zɜːp/ vt usurpar. **~er** /-ə(r)/ n usurpador m

usury /'juːʒərɪ/ n usura f

utensil /juː'tensl/ n utensilio m

uterus /'juːtərəs/ n útero m

utilitarian /juːtɪlɪ'teərɪən/ a utilitario

utility /juː'tɪlətɪ/ n utilidad f. **public ~** n servicio m público. ● a utilitario

utilize /'juːtɪlaɪz/ vt utilizar

utmost /'ʌtməʊst/ a extremo. ● n. **one's ~** todo lo posible

utter[1] /'ʌtə(r)/ a completo

utter[2] /'ʌtə(r)/ vt (speak) pronunciar; dar ⟨sigh⟩; emitir ⟨sound⟩. **~ance** n expresión f

utterly /'ʌtəlɪ/ adv totalmente

U-turn /'juːtɜːn/ n vuelta f

V

vacan|cy /'veɪkənsɪ/ n (job) vacante f; (room) habitación f libre. **~t** a libre; (empty) vacío; ⟨look⟩ vago

vacate /vəˈkeɪt/ *vt* dejar

vacation /vəˈkeɪʃn/ *n* (*Amer*) vacaciones *fpl*

vaccin|ate /ˈvæksɪmeɪt/ *vt* vacunar. **~ation** /-ˈneɪʃn/ *n* vacunación *f*. **~e** /ˈvæksiːn/ *n* vacuna *f*

vacuum /ˈvækjʊəm/ *n* (*pl* **-cuums** *or* **-cua**) vacío *m*. **~ cleaner** *n* aspiradora *f*. **~ flask** *n* termo *m*

vagabond /ˈvægəbɒnd/ *n* vagabundo *m*

vagary /ˈveɪgəri/ *n* capricho *m*

vagina /vəˈdʒaɪnə/ *n* vagina *f*

vagrant /ˈveɪgrənt/ *n* vagabundo *m*

vague /veɪg/ *a* (**-er, -est**) vago; ⟨*outline*⟩ indistinto. **be ~ about** no precisar. **~ly** *adv* vagamente

vain /veɪn/ *a* (**-er, -est**) vanidoso; (*useless*) vano, inútil. **in ~** en vano. **~ly** *adv* vanamente

valance /ˈvæləns/ *n* cenefa *f*

vale /veɪl/ *n* valle *m*

valentine /ˈvæləntaɪn/ *n* (*card*) tarjeta *f* del día de San Valentín

valet /ˈvælɪt, ˈvæleɪ/ *n* ayuda *m* de cámara

valiant /ˈvæliənt/ *a* valeroso

valid /ˈvælɪd/ *a* válido; ⟨*ticket*⟩ valedero. **~ate** *vt* dar validez a; (*confirm*) convalidar. **~ity** /-ˈɪdətɪ/ *n* validez *f*

valley /ˈvælɪ/ *n* (*pl* **-eys**) valle *m*

valour /ˈvælə(r)/ *n* valor *m*

valuable /ˈvæljʊəbl/ *a* valioso. **~s** *npl* objetos *mpl* de valor

valuation /væljʊˈeɪʃn/ *n* valoración *f*

value /ˈvæljuː/ *n* valor *m*; (*usefulness*) utilidad *f*. **face ~** *n* valor *m* nominal; (*fig*) significado *m* literal. ● *vt* valorar; (*cherish*) apreciar. **~ added tax (VAT)** *n* impuesto *m* sobre el valor añadido (IVA). **~d** *a* (*appreciated*) apreciado, estimado. **~r** /-ə(r)/ *n* tasador *m*

valve /vælv/ *n* válvula *f*

vampire /ˈvæmpaɪə(r)/ *n* vampiro *m*

van /væn/ *n* furgoneta *f*; (*rail*) furgón *m*

vandal /ˈvændl/ *n* vándalo *m*. **~ism** /-əlɪzəm/ *n* vandalismo *m*. **~ize** *vt* destruir

vane /veɪn/ *n* (*weathercock*) veleta *f*; (*naut, aviat*) paleta *f*

vanguard /ˈvængɑːd/ *n* vanguardia *f*

vanilla /vəˈnɪlə/ *n* vainilla *f*

vanish /ˈvænɪʃ/ *vi* desaparecer

vanity /ˈvænɪtɪ/ *n* vanidad *f*. **~ case** *n* neceser *m*

vantage /ˈvɑːntɪdʒ/ *n* ventaja *f*. **~point** *n* posición *f* ventajosa

vapour /ˈveɪpə(r)/ *n* vapor *m*

variable /ˈveərɪəbl/ *a* variable

varian|ce /ˈveərɪəns/ *n*. **at ~ce** en desacuerdo. **~t** /ˈveərɪənt/ *a* diferente. ● *n* variante *m*

variation /veərɪˈeɪʃn/ *n* variación *f*

varicoloured /ˈveərɪkʌləd/ *a* multicolor

varied /ˈveərɪd/ *a* variado

varicose /ˈværɪkəʊs/ *a* varicoso. **~ veins** *npl* varices *fpl*

variety /vəˈraɪətɪ/ *n* variedad *f*. **~ show** *n* espectáculo *m* de variedades

various /ˈveərɪəs/ *a* diverso. **~ly** *adv* diversamente

varnish /ˈvɑːnɪʃ/ *n* barniz *m*; (*for nails*) esmalte *m*. ● *vt* barnizar

vary /ˈveərɪ/ *vt/i* variar. **~ing** *a* diverso

vase /vɑːz, *Amer* veɪs/ *n* jarrón *m*

vasectomy /vəˈsektəmɪ/ *n* vasectomía *f*

vast /vɑːst/ *a* vasto, enorme. **~ly** *adv* enormemente. **~ness** *n* inmensidad *f*

vat /væt/ *n* tina *f*

VAT /viːeɪˈtiː/ *abbr* (*value added tax*) IVA *m*, impuesto *m* sobre el valor añadido

vault /vɔːlt/ *n* (*roof*) bóveda *f*; (*in bank*) cámara *f* acorazada; (*tomb*) cripta *f*; (*cellar*) sótano *m*; (*jump*) salto *m*. ● *vt/i* saltar

vaunt /vɔːnt/ *vt* jactarse de

veal /viːl/ *n* ternera *f*

veer /vɪə(r)/ *vi* cambiar de dirección; (*naut*) virar

vegetable /ˈvedʒɪtəbl/ *a* vegetal. ● *n* legumbre *m*; (*greens*) verduras *fpl*

vegetarian /vedʒɪˈteərɪən/ *a & n* vegetariano (*m*)

vegetate /ˈvedʒɪteɪt/ *vi* vegetar

vegetation /vedʒɪˈteɪʃn/ *n* vegetación *f*

vehemen|ce /ˈviːəməns/ *n* vehemencia *f*. **~t** /ˈviːəmənt/ *a* vehemente. **~tly** *adv* con vehemencia

vehicle /ˈviːɪkl/ *n* vehículo *m*

veil /veɪl/ *n* velo *m*. **take the ~** hacerse monja. ● *vt* velar

vein /veɪn/ *n* vena *f*; (*mood*) humor *m*. **~ed** *a* veteado

velocity /vɪˈlɒsɪtɪ/ *n* velocidad *f*

velvet /ˈvelvɪt/ *n* terciopelo *m*. **~y** *a* aterciopelado

venal /'vi:nl/ *a* venal. **~ity** /-'næləti/ *n* venalidad *f*

vendetta /ven'detə/ *n* enemistad *f* prolongada

vending-machine /'vendɪŋ məʃi:n/ *n* distribuidor *m* automático

vendor /'vendə(r)/ *n* vendedor *m*

veneer /və'nɪə(r)/ *n* chapa *f*; *(fig)* barniz *m*, apariencia *f*

venerable /'venərəbl/ *a* venerable

venereal /və'nɪərɪəl/ *a* venéreo

Venetian /və'ni:ʃn/ *a & n* veneciano *(m)*. **v~ blind** *n* persiana *f* veneciana

vengeance /'vendʒəns/ *n* venganza *f*. **with a ~** *(fig)* con creces

venison /'venɪzn/ *n* carne *f* de venado

venom /'venəm/ *n* veneno *m*. **~ous** *a* venenoso

vent /vent/ *n* abertura *f*; *(for air)* respiradero *m*. **give ~ to** dar salida a. ● *vt* hacer un agujero en; *(fig)* desahogar

ventilat|e /'ventɪleɪt/ *vt* ventilar. **~ion** /-'leɪʃn/ *n* ventilación *f*. **~or** /-ə(r)/ *n* ventilador *m*

ventriloquist /ven'trɪləkwɪst/ *n* ventrílocuo *m*

venture /'ventʃə(r)/ *n* empresa *f* (arriesgada). **at a ~** a la ventura. ● *vt* arriesgar. ● *vi* atreverse

venue /'venju:/ *n* lugar *m* (de reunión)

veranda /və'rændə/ *n* terraza *f*

verb /vɜ:b/ *n* verbo *m*

verbal /'vɜ:bl/ *a* verbal. **~ly** *adv* verbalmente

verbatim /vɜ:'beɪtɪm/ *adv* palabra por palabra, al pie de la letra

verbose /vɜ:'bəʊs/ *a* prolijo

verdant /'vɜ:dənt/ *a* verde

verdict /'vɜ:dɪkt/ *n* veredicto *m*; *(opinion)* opinión *f*

verge /vɜ:dʒ/ *n* borde *m*. ● *vt*. **~ on** acercarse a

verger /'vɜ:dʒə(r)/ *n* sacristán *m*

verif|ication /verɪfɪ'keɪʃn/ *n* verificación *f*. **~y** /'verɪfaɪ/ *vt* verificar

veritable /'verɪtəbl/ *a* verdadero

vermicelli /vɜ:mɪ'tʃelɪ/ *n* fideos *mpl*

vermin /'vɜ:mɪn/ *n* sabandijas *fpl*

vermouth /'vɜ:məθ/ *n* vermut *m*

vernacular /və'nækjʊlə(r)/ *n* lengua *f*; *(regional)* dialecto *m*

versatil|e /'vɜ:sətaɪl/ *a* versátil. **~ity** /-'tɪlətɪ/ *n* versatilidad *f*

verse /vɜ:s/ *n* estrofa *f*; *(poetry)* poesías *fpl*; *(of Bible)* versículo *m*

versed /vɜ:st/ *a*. **~ in** versado en

version /'vɜ:ʃn/ *n* versión *f*

versus /'vɜ:səs/ *prep* contra

vertebra /'vɜ:tɪbrə/ *n* (*pl* **-brae** /-briː/) vértebra *f*

vertical /'vɜ:tɪkl/ *a & n* vertical *(f)*. **~ly** *adv* verticalmente

vertigo /'vɜ:tɪgəʊ/ *n* vértigo *m*

verve /vɜ:v/ *n* entusiasmo *m*, vigor *m*

very /'verɪ/ *adv* muy. **~ much** muchísimo. **~ well** muy bien. **the ~ first** el primero de todos. ● *a* mismo. **the ~ thing** exactamente lo que hace falta

vespers /'vespəz/ *npl* vísperas *fpl*

vessel /'vesl/ *n* (*receptacle*) recipiente *m*; *(ship)* buque *m*; *(anat)* vaso *m*

vest /vest/ *n* camiseta *f*; *(Amer)* chaleco *m*. ● *vt* conferir. **~ed interest** *n* interés *m* personal; *(jurid)* derecho *m* adquirido

vestige /'vestɪdʒ/ *n* vestigio *m*

vestment /'vestmənt/ *n* vestidura *f*

vestry /'vestrɪ/ *n* sacristía *f*

vet /vet/ *n* *(fam)* veterinario *m*. ● *vt* (*pt* **vetted**) examinar

veteran /'vetərən/ *n* veterano *m*

veterinary /'vetərɪnərɪ/ *a* veterinario. **~ surgeon** *n* veterinario *m*

veto /'vi:təʊ/ *n* (*pl* **-oes**) veto *m*. ● *vt* poner el veto a

vex /veks/ *vt* fastidiar. **~ation** /-'seɪʃn/ *n* fastidio *m*. **~ed question** *n* cuestión *f* controvertida. **~ing** *a* fastidioso

via /'vaɪə/ *prep* por, por vía de

viab|ility /vaɪə'bɪlətɪ/ *n* viabilidad *f*. **~le** /'vaɪəbl/ *a* viable

viaduct /'vaɪədʌkt/ *n* viaducto *m*

vibrant /'vaɪbrənt/ *a* vibrante

vibrat|e /vaɪ'breɪt/ *vt/i* vibrar. **~ion** /-ʃn/ *n* vibración *f*

vicar /'vɪkə(r)/ *n* párroco *m*. **~age** /-rɪdʒ/ *n* casa *f* del párroco

vicarious /vɪ'keərɪəs/ *a* indirecto

vice[1] /vaɪs/ *n* vicio *m*

vice[2] /vaɪs/ *n* *(tec)* torno *m* de banco

vice... /'vaɪs/ *pref* vice...

vice versa /vaɪsɪ'vɜ:sə/ *adv* viceversa

vicinity /vɪ'sɪnɪtɪ/ *n* vecindad *f*. **in the ~ of** cerca de

vicious /'vɪʃəs/ *a* (*spiteful*) malicioso; *(violent)* atroz. **~ circle** *n* círculo *m* vicioso. **~ly** *adv* cruelmente

vicissitudes /vɪˈsɪsɪtjuːdz/ *npl* vicisitudes *fpl*

victim /ˈvɪktɪm/ *n* víctima *f*. **~ization** /-aɪˈzeɪʃn/ *n* persecución *f*. **~ize** *vt* victimizar

victor /ˈvɪktə(r)/ *n* vencedor *m*

Victorian /vɪkˈtɔːrɪən/ *a* victoriano

victor|ious /vɪkˈtɔːrɪəs/ *a* victorioso. **~y** /ˈvɪktərɪ/ *n* victoria *f*

video /ˈvɪdɪəʊ/ *a* video. ● *n* (*fam*) magnetoscopio *m*. **~ recorder** *n* magnetoscopio *m*. **~tape** *n* videocassette *f*

vie /vaɪ/ *vi* (*pres p* **vying**) rivalizar

view /vjuː/ *n* vista *f*; (*mental survey*) visión *f* de conjunto; (*opinion*) opinión *f*. **in my ~** a mi juicio. **in ~ of** en vista de. **on ~** expuesto. **with a ~ to** con miras a. ● *vt* ver; (*visit*) visitar; (*consider*) considerar. **~er** /-ə(r)/ *n* espectador *m*; (*TV*) televidente *m & f*. **~finder** /ˈvjuːfaɪndə(r)/ *n* visor *m*. **~point** /ˈvjuːpɔɪnt/ *n* punto *m* de vista

vigil /ˈvɪdʒɪl/ *n* vigilia *f*. **~ance** *n* vigilancia *f*. **~ant** *a* vigilante. **keep ~** velar

vigo|rous /ˈvɪgərəs/ *a* vigoroso. **~ur** /ˈvɪgə(r)/ *n* vigor *m*

vile /vaɪl/ *a* (*base*) vil; (*bad*) horrible; ⟨*weather, temper*⟩ de perros

vilif|ication /vɪlɪfɪˈkeɪʃn/ *n* difamación *f*. **~y** /ˈvɪlɪfaɪ/ *vt* difamar

village /ˈvɪlɪdʒ/ *n* aldea *f*. **~r** /-ə(r)/ *n* aldeano *m*

villain /ˈvɪlən/ *n* malvado *m*; (*in story etc*) malo *m*. **~ous** *a* infame. **~y** *n* infamia *f*

vim /vɪm/ *n* (*fam*) energía *f*

vinaigrette /vɪnɪˈgret/ *n*. **~ sauce** *n* vinagreta *f*

vindicat|e /ˈvɪndɪkeɪt/ *vt* vindicar. **~ion** /-ˈkeɪʃn/ *n* vindicación *f*

vindictive /vɪnˈdɪktɪv/ *a* vengativo. **~ness** *n* carácter *m* vengativo

vine /vaɪn/ *n* vid *f*

vinegar /ˈvɪnɪgə(r)/ *n* vinagre *m*. **~y** *a* ⟨*person*⟩ avinagrado

vineyard /ˈvɪnjəd/ *n* viña *f*

vintage /ˈvɪntɪdʒ/ *n* (*year*) cosecha *f*. ● *a* ⟨*wine*⟩ añejo; ⟨*car*⟩ de época

vinyl /ˈvaɪnɪl/ *n* vinilo *m*

viola /vɪˈəʊlə/ *n* viola *f*

violat|e /ˈvaɪəleɪt/ *vt* violar. **~ion** /-ˈleɪʃn/ *n* violación *f*

violen|ce /ˈvaɪələns/ *n* violencia *f*. **~t** /ˈvaɪələnt/ *a* violento. **~tly** *adv* violentamente

violet /ˈvaɪələt/ *a & n* violeta (*f*)

violin /ˈvaɪəlɪn/ *n* violín *m*. **~ist** *n* violinista *m & f*

VIP /viːaɪˈpiː/ *abbr* (*very important person*) personaje *m*

viper /ˈvaɪpə(r)/ *n* víbora *f*

virgin /ˈvɜːdʒɪn/ *a & n* virgen (*f*). **~al** *a* virginal. **~ity** /vəˈdʒɪnətɪ/ *n* virginidad *f*

Virgo /ˈvɜːgəʊ/ *n* (*astr*) Virgo *f*

viril|e /ˈvɪraɪl/ *a* viril. **~ity** /-ˈrɪlətɪ/ *n* virilidad *f*

virtual /ˈvɜːtʃʊəl/ *a* verdadero. **a ~ failure** prácticamente un fracaso. **~ly** *adv* prácticamente

virtue /ˈvɜːtʃuː/ *n* virtud *f*. **by ~ of**, **in ~ of** en virtud de

virtuoso /vɜːtʃʊˈəʊzəʊ/ *n* (*pl* **-si** /-ziː/) virtuoso *m*

virtuous /ˈvɜːtʃʊəs/ *a* virtuoso

virulent /ˈvɪrʊlənt/ *a* virulento

virus /ˈvaɪərəs/ *n* (*pl* **-uses**) virus *m*

visa /ˈviːzə/ *n* visado *m*, visa *f* (*LAm*)

vis-a-vis /viːzɑːˈviː/ *adv* frente a frente. ● *prep* respecto a; (*opposite*) en frente de

viscount /ˈvaɪkaʊnt/ *n* vizconde *m*. **~ess** *n* vizcondesa *f*

viscous /ˈvɪskəs/ *a* viscoso

visib|ility /vɪzɪˈbɪlətɪ/ *n* visibilidad *f*. **~le** /ˈvɪzɪbl/ *a* visible. **~ly** *adv* visiblemente

vision /ˈvɪʒn/ *n* visión *f*; (*sight*) vista *f*. **~ary** /ˈvɪʒənərɪ/ *a & n* visionario (*m*)

visit /ˈvɪzɪt/ *vt* visitar; hacer una visita a ⟨*person*⟩. ● *vi* hacer visitas. ● *n* visita *f*. **~or** *n* visitante *m & f*; (*guest*) visita *f*; (*in hotel*) cliente *m & f*

visor /ˈvaɪzə(r)/ *n* visera *f*

vista /ˈvɪstə/ *n* perspectiva *f*

visual /ˈvɪʒʊəl/ *a* visual. **~ize** /ˈvɪʒʊəlaɪz/ *vt* imaginar(se); (*foresee*) prever. **~ly** *adv* visualmente

vital /ˈvaɪtl/ *a* vital; (*essential*) esencial

vitality /vaɪˈtælətɪ/ *n* vitalidad *f*

vital: **~ly** /ˈvaɪtəlɪ/ *adv* extremadamente. **~s** *npl* órganos *mpl* vitales. **~ statistics** *npl* (*fam*) medidas *fpl*

vitamin /ˈvɪtəmɪn/ *n* vitamina *f*

vitiate /ˈvɪʃɪeɪt/ *vt* viciar

vitreous /ˈvɪtrɪəs/ *a* vítreo

vituperat|e /vɪˈtjuːpəreɪt/ *vt* vituperar. **~ion** /-ˈreɪʃn/ *n* vituperación *f*

vivaci|ous /vɪ'veɪʃəs/ a animado, vivo. **~ously** adv animadamente. **~ty** /-'væsətɪ/ n viveza f

vivid /'vɪvɪd/ a vivo. **~ly** adv intensamente; (describe) gráficamente. **~ness** n viveza f

vivisection /vɪvɪ'sekʃn/ n vivisección f

vixen /'vɪksn/ n zorra f

vocabulary /və'kæbjʊlərɪ/ n vocabulario m

vocal /'vəʊkl/ a vocal; (fig) franco. **~ist** n cantante m & f

vocation /vəʊ'keɪʃn/ n vocación f. **~al** a profesional

vocifer|ate /və'sɪfəreɪt/ vt/i vociferar. **~ous** a vociferador

vogue /vəʊg/ n boga f. **in ~** de moda

voice /vɔɪs/ n voz f. ● vt expresar

void /vɔɪd/ a vacío; (not valid) nulo. **~ of** desprovisto de. ● n vacío m. ● vt anular

volatile /'vɒlətaɪl/ a volátil; ⟨person⟩ voluble

volcan|ic /vɒl'kænɪk/ a volcánico. **~o** /vɒl'keɪnəʊ/ n (pl **-oes**) volcán m

volition /və'lɪʃn/ n. **of one's own ~** de su propia voluntad

volley /'vɒlɪ/ n (pl **-eys**) (of blows) lluvia f; (of gunfire) descarga f cerrada

volt /vəʊlt/ n voltio m. **~age** n voltaje m

voluble /'vɒljʊbl/ a locuaz

volume /'vɒljuːm/ n volumen m; (book) tomo m

voluminous /və'ljuːmɪnəs/ a voluminoso

voluntar|ily /'vɒləntərəlɪ/ adv voluntariamente. **~y** /'vɒləntərɪ/ a voluntario

volunteer /vɒlən'tɪə(r)/ n voluntario m. ● vt ofrecer. ● vi ofrecerse voluntariamente; (mil) alistarse como voluntario

voluptuous /və'lʌptjʊəs/ a voluptuoso

vomit /'vɒmɪt/ vt/i vomitar. ● n vómito m

voracious /və'reɪʃəs/ a voraz

vot|e /vəʊt/ n voto m; (right) derecho m de votar. ● vi votar. **~er** /-ə(r)/ n votante m & f. **~ing** n votación f

vouch /vaʊtʃ/ vi. **~ for** garantizar

voucher /'vaʊtʃə(r)/ n vale m

vow /vaʊ/ n voto m. ● vi jurar

vowel /'vaʊəl/ n vocal f

voyage /'vɔɪɪdʒ/ n viaje m (en barco)

vulgar /'vʌlgə(r)/ a vulgar. **~ity** /-'gærətɪ/ n vulgaridad f. **~ize** vt vulgarizar

vulnerab|ility /vʌlnərə'bɪlətɪ/ n vulnerabilidad f. **~le** /'vʌlnərəbl/ a vulnerable

vulture /'vʌltʃə(r)/ n buitre m

vying /'vaɪɪŋ/ see **vie**

W

wad /wɒd/ n (pad) tapón m; (bundle) lío m; (of notes) fajo m; (of cotton wool etc) bolita f

wadding /'wɒdɪŋ/ n relleno m

waddle /'wɒdl/ vi contonearse

wade /weɪd/ vt vadear. ● vi. **~ through** abrirse paso entre; leer con dificultad ⟨book⟩

wafer /'weɪfə(r)/ n barquillo m; (relig) hostia f

waffle¹ /'wɒfl/ n (fam) palabrería f. ● vi (fam) divagar

waffle² /'wɒfl/ n (culin) gofre m

waft /wɒft/ vt llevar por el aire. ● vi flotar

wag /wæg/ vt (pt **wagged**) menear. ● vi menearse

wage /weɪdʒ/ n. **~s** npl salario m. ● vt. **~ war** hacer la guerra. **~r** /'weɪdʒə(r)/ n apuesta f. ● vt apostar

waggle /'wægl/ vt menear. ● vi menearse

wagon /'wægən/ n carro m; (rail) vagón m. **be on the ~** (sl) no beber

waif /weɪf/ n niño m abandonado

wail /weɪl/ vi lamentarse. ● n lamento m

wainscot /'weɪnskət/ n revestimiento m, zócalo m

waist /weɪst/ n cintura f. **~band** n cinturón m

waistcoat /'weɪstkəʊt/ n chaleco m

waistline /'weɪstlaɪn/ n cintura f

wait /weɪt/ vt/i esperar; (at table) servir. **~ for** esperar. **~ on** servir. ● n espera f. **lie in ~** acechar

waiter /'weɪtə(r)/ n camarero m

wait: **~ing-list** n lista f de espera. **~ing-room** n sala f de espera

waitress /'weɪtrɪs/ n camarera f

waive /weɪv/ vt renunciar a

wake¹ /weɪk/ vt (pt **woke**, pp **woken**) despertar. ● vi despertarse. ● n velatorio m. **~ up** vt despertar. ● vi despertarse

wake² /weɪk/ *n* (*naut*) estela *f*. **in the ~ of** como resultado de, tras

waken /'weɪkən/ *vt* despertar. ● *vi* despertarse

wakeful /'weɪkfl/ *a* insomne

Wales /weɪlz/ *n* País *m* de Gales

walk /wɔːk/ *vi* andar; (*not ride*) ir a pie; (*stroll*) pasearse. **~ out** salir; ‹*workers*› declararse en huelga. **~ out on** abandonar. ● *vt* andar por ‹*streets*›; llevar de paseo ‹*dog*›. ● *n* paseo *m*; (*gait*) modo *m* de andar; (*path*) sendero *m*. **~ of life** clase *f* social. **~about** /'wɔːkəbaʊt/ *n* (*of royalty*) encuentro *m* con el público. **~er** /-ə(r)/ *n* paseante *m* & *f*

walkie-talkie /wɔːkɪ'tɔːkɪ/ *n* transmisor-receptor *m* portátil

walking /'wɔːkɪŋ/ *n* paseo *m*. **~ stick** *n* bastón *m*

Walkman /'wɔːkmən/ *n* (P) estereo *m* personal, Walkman *m* (P), magnetófono *m* de bolsillo

walk: **~-out** *n* huelga *f*. **~-over** *n* victoria *f* fácil

wall /wɔːl/ *n* (*interior*) pared *f*; (*exterior*) muro *m*; (*in garden*) tapia *f*; (*of city*) muralla *f*. **go to the ~** fracasar. **up the ~** (*fam*) loco. ● *vt* amurallar ‹*city*›

wallet /'wɒlɪt/ *n* cartera *f*, billetera *f* (*LAm*)

wallflower /'wɔːlflaʊə(r)/ *n* alhelí *m*

wallop /'wɒləp/ *vt* (*pt* **walloped**) (*sl*) golpear con fuerza. ● *n* (*sl*) golpe *m* fuerte

wallow /'wɒləʊ/ *vi* revolcarse

wallpaper /'wɔːlpeɪpə(r)/ *n* papel *m* pintado

walnut /'wɔːlnʌt/ *n* nuez *f*; (*tree*) nogal *m*

walrus /'wɔːlrəs/ *n* morsa *f*

waltz /wɔːls/ *n* vals *m*. ● *vi* valsar

wan /wɒn/ *a* pálido

wand /wɒnd/ *n* varita *f*

wander /'wɒndə(r)/ *vi* vagar; (*stroll*) pasearse; (*digress*) divagar; ‹*road, river*› serpentear. ● *n* paseo *m*. **~er** /-ə(r)/ *n* vagabundo *m*. **~lust** /'wɒndəlʌst/ *n* pasión *f* por los viajes

wane /weɪn/ *vi* menguar. ● *n*. **on the ~** disminuyendo

wangle /'wæŋgl/ *vt* (*sl*) agenciarse

want /wɒnt/ *vt* querer; (*need*) necesitar; (*require*) exigir. ● *vi*. **~ for** carecer de. ● *n* necesidad *f*; (*lack*) falta *f*; (*desire*) deseo *m*. **~ed** *a* (*criminal*) buscado. **~ing** *a* (*lacking*) falto de. **be ~ing** carecer de

wanton /'wɒntən/ *a* (*licentious*) lascivo; (*motiveless*) sin motivo

war /wɔː(r)/ *n* guerra *f*. **at ~** en guerra

warble /'wɔːbl/ *vt* cantar trinando. ● *vi* gorjear. ● *n* gorjeo *m*. **~r** /-ə(r)/ *n* curruca *f*

ward /wɔːd/ *n* (*in hospital*) sala *f*; (*of town*) barrio *m*; (*child*) pupilo *m*. ● *vt*. **~ off** parar

warden /'wɔːdn/ *n* guarda *m*

warder /'wɔːdə(r)/ *n* carcelero *m*

wardrobe /'wɔːdrəʊb/ *n* armario *m*; (*clothes*) vestuario *m*

warehouse /'weəhaʊs/ *n* almacén *m*

wares /weəz/ *npl* mercancías *fpl*

war: **~fare** /'wɔːfeə(r)/ *n* guerra *f*. **~head** /'wɔːhed/ *n* cabeza *f* explosiva

warily /'weərɪlɪ/ *adv* cautelosamente

warlike /'wɔːlaɪk/ *a* belicoso

warm /wɔːm/ *a* (**-er, -est**) caliente; (*hearty*) caluroso. **be ~** ‹*person*› tener calor. **it is ~** hace calor. ● *vt*. **~ (up)** calentar; recalentar ‹*food*›; (*fig*) animar. ● *vi*. **~ (up)** calentarse; (*fig*) animarse. **~ to** tomar simpatía a ‹*person*›; ir entusiasmándose por ‹*idea etc*›. **~-blooded** *a* de sangre caliente. **~-hearted** *a* simpático. **~ly** *adv* (*heartily*) calurosamente

warmonger /'wɔːmʌŋgə(r)/ *n* belicista *m* & *f*

warmth /wɔːmθ/ *n* calor *m*

warn /wɔːn/ *vt* avisar, advertir. **~ing** *n* advertencia *f*; (*notice*) aviso *m*. **~ off** (*advise against*) aconsejar en contra de; (*forbid*) impedir

warp /wɔːp/ *vt* deformar; (*fig*) pervertir. ● *vi* deformarse

warpath /'wɔːpɑːθ/ *n*. **be on the ~** buscar camorra

warrant /'wɒrənt/ *n* autorización *f*; (*for arrest*) orden *f*. ● *vt* justificar. **~ officer** *n* suboficial *m*

warranty /'wɒrəntɪ/ *n* garantía *f*

warring /'wɔːrɪŋ/ *a* en guerra

warrior /'wɒrɪə(r)/ *n* guerrero *m*

warship /'wɔːʃɪp/ *n* buque *m* de guerra

wart /wɔːt/ *n* verruga *f*

wartime /'wɔːtaɪm/ *n* tiempo *m* de guerra

wary /'weərɪ/ *a* (**-ier, -iest**) cauteloso

was /wəz, wɒz/ *see* **be**

wash /wɒʃ/ *vt* lavar; (*flow over*) bañar. ● *vi* lavarse. ● *n* lavado *m*;

weak

(*dirty clothes*) ropa *f* sucia; (*wet clothes*) colada *f*; (*of ship*) estela *f*. **have a ~** lavarse. **~ out** *vt* enjuagar; (*fig*) cancelar. **~ up** *vi* fregar los platos. **~able** *a* lavable. **~basin** *n* lavabo *m*. **~ed-out** *a* (*pale*) pálido; (*tired*) rendido. **~er** /'wɒʃə(r)/ *n* arandela *f*; (*washing-machine*) lavadora *f*. **~ing** /'wɒʃɪŋ/ *n* lavado *m*; (*dirty clothes*) ropa *f* sucia; (*wet clothes*) colada *f*. **~ing-machine** *n* lavadora *f*. **~ing-powder** *n* jabón *m* en polvo. **~ing-up** *n* fregado *m*; (*dirty plates etc*) platos *mpl* para fregar. **~out** *n* (*sl*) desastre *m*. **~room** *n* (*Amer*) servicios *mpl*. **~stand** *n* lavabo *m*. **~tub** *n* tina *f* de lavar

wasp /wɒsp/ *n* avispa *f*

wastage /'weɪstɪdʒ/ *n* desperdicios *mpl*

waste /weɪst/ ● *a* de desecho; ‹*land*› yermo. ● *n* derroche *m*; (*rubbish*) desperdicio *m*; (*of time*) pérdida *f*. ● *vt* derrochar; (*not use*) desperdiciar; perder ‹*time*›. ● *vi*. **~ away** consumirse. **~disposal unit** *n* trituradora *f* de basuras. **~ful** *a* dispendioso; ‹*person*› derrochador. **~-paper basket** *n* papelera *f*. **~s** *npl* tierras *fpl* baldías

watch /wɒtʃ/ *vt* mirar; (*keep an eye on*) vigilar; (*take heed*) tener cuidado con; ver ‹*TV*›. ● *vi* mirar; (*keep an eye on*) vigilar. ● *n* vigilancia *f*; (*period of duty*) guardia *f*; (*timepiece*) reloj *m*. **on the ~** alerta. **~ out** *vi* tener cuidado. **~dog** *n* perro *m* guardián; (*fig*) guardián *m*. **~ful** *a* vigilante. **~maker** /'wɒtʃmeɪkə(r)/ *n* relojero *m*. **~man** /'wɒtʃmən/ *n* (*pl* -men) vigilante *m*. **~tower** *n* atalaya *f*. **~word** /'wɒtʃwɜːd/ *n* santo *m* y seña

water /'wɔːtə(r)/ *n* agua *f*. **by ~** (*of travel*) por mar. **in hot ~** (*fam*) en un apuro. ● *vt* regar ‹*plants etc*›; (*dilute*) aguar, diluir. ● *vi* ‹*eyes*› llorar. **make s.o.'s mouth ~** hacérsele la boca agua. **~ down** *vt* diluir; (*fig*) suavizar. **~closet** *n* wáter *m*. **~colour** *n* acuarela *f*. **~course** /'wɔːtəkɔː s/ *n* arroyo *m*; (*artificial*) canal *m*. **~cress** /'wɔːtəkres/ *n* berro *m*. **~fall** /'wɔːtəfɔːl/ *n* cascada *f*. **~ice** *n* sorbete *m*. **~ing-can** /'wɔːtərɪŋkæn/ *n* regadera *f*. **~lily** *n* nenúfar *m*. **~line** *n* línea *f* de flotación. **~logged** /'wɔːtəlɒgd/ *a* saturado de agua, empapado. **~ main** *n* cañería *f* principal. **~ melon** *n* sandía *f*. **~mill** *n*

molino *m* de agua. **~ polo** *n* polo *m* acuático. **~-power** *n* energía *f* hidráulica. **~proof** /'wɔːtəpruːf/ *a* & *n* impermeable (*m*); ‹*watch*› sumergible. **~shed** /'wɔːtəʃed/ *n* punto *m* decisivo. **~-skiing** *n* esquí *m* acuático. **~-softener** *n* ablandador *m* de agua. **~tight** /'wɔːtətaɪt/ *a* hermético, estanco; (*fig*) irrecusable. **~way** *n* canal *m* navegable. **~wheel** *n* rueda *f* hidráulica. **~wings** *npl* flotadores *mpl*. **~works** /'wɔːtəwɜːks/ *n* sistema *m* de abastecimiento de agua. **~y** /'wɔːtərɪ/ *a* acuoso; ‹*colour*› pálido; ‹*eyes*› lloroso

watt /wɒt/ *n* vatio *m*

wave /weɪv/ *n* onda *f*; (*of hand*) señal *f*; (*fig*) oleada *f*. ● *vt* agitar; ondular ‹*hair*›. ● *vi* (*signal*) hacer señales con la mano; ‹*flag*› flotar. **~band** /'weɪvbænd/ *n* banda *f* de ondas. **~length** /'weɪvleŋθ/ *n* longitud *f* de onda

waver /'weɪvə(r)/ *vi* vacilar

wavy /'weɪvɪ/ *a* (-ier, -iest) ondulado

wax[1] /wæks/ *n* cera *f*. ● *vt* encerar

wax[2] /wæks/ *vi* ‹*moon*› crecer

wax: **~en** *a* céreo. **~work** /'wækswɜːk/ *n* figura *f* de cera. **~y** *a* céreo

way /weɪ/ *n* camino *m*; (*distance*) distancia *f*; (*manner*) manera *f*, modo *m*; (*direction*) dirección *f*; (*means*) medio *m*; (*habit*) costumbre *f*. **be in the ~** estorbar. **by the ~** a propósito. **by ~ of** a título de, por. **either ~** de cualquier modo. **in a ~** en cierta manera. **in some ~s** en ciertos modos. **lead the ~** mostrar el camino. **make ~** dejar paso a. **on the ~** en camino. **out of the ~** remoto; (*extraordinary*) fuera de lo común. **that ~** por allí. **this ~** por aquí. **under ~** en curso. **~-bill** *n* hoja *f* de ruta. **~farer** /'weɪfeərə(r)/ *n* viajero *m*. **~ in** *n* entrada *f*

waylay /weɪ'leɪ/ *vt* (*pt* -laid) acechar; (*detain*) detener

way: **~ out** *n* salida *f*. **~-out** *a* ultramoderno, original. **~s** *npl* costumbres *fpl*. **~side** /'weɪsaɪd/ *n* borde *m* del camino

wayward /'weɪwəd/ *a* caprichoso

we /wiː/ *pron* nosotros, nosotras

weak /wiːk/ *a* (-er, -est) débil; ‹*liquid*› aguado, acuoso; (*fig*) flojo.

~en *vt* debilitar. ~**-kneed** *a* irresoluto. ~**ling** /'wiːklɪŋ/ *n* persona *f* débil. ~**ly** *adv* débilmente. ● *a* enfermizo. ~**ness** *n* debilidad *f*

weal /wiːl/ *n* verdugón *m*

wealth /welθ/ *n* riqueza *f*. ~**y** *a* (**-ier, -iest**) rico

wean /wiːn/ *vt* destetar

weapon /'wepən/ *n* arma *f*

wear /weə(r)/ *vt* (*pt* **wore**, *pp* **worn**) llevar; (*put on*) ponerse; tener ‹*expression etc*›; (*damage*) desgastar. ● *vi* desgastarse; (*last*) durar. ● *n* uso *m*; (*damage*) desgaste *m*; (*clothing*) ropa *f*. ~ **down** *vt* desgastar; agotar ‹*opposition etc*›. ~ **off** *vi* desaparecer. ~ **on** *vi* ‹*time*› pasar. ~ **out** *vt* desgastar; (*tire*) agotar. ~**able** *a* que se puede llevar. ~ **and tear** desgaste *m*

wear|ily /'wɪərɪlɪ/ *adv* cansadamente. ~**iness** *n* cansancio *m*. ~**isome** /'wɪərɪsəm/ *a* cansado. ~**y** /'wɪərɪ/ *a* (**-ier, -iest**) cansado. ● *vt* cansar. ● *vi* cansarse. ~**y of** cansarse de

weasel /'wiːzl/ *n* comadreja *f*

weather /'weðə(r)/ *n* tiempo *m*. **under the** ~ (*fam*) indispuesto. ● *a* meteorológico. ● *vt* curar ‹*wood*›; (*survive*) superar. ~**-beaten** *a* curtido. ~**cock** /'weðəkɒk/ *n*, ~**-vane** *n* veleta *f*

weave /wiːv/ *vt* (*pt* **wove**, *pp* **woven**) tejer; entretejer ‹*story etc*›; entrelazar ‹*flowers etc*›. ~ **one's way** abrirse paso. ● *n* tejido *m*. ~**r** /-ə(r)/ *n* tejedor *m*

web /web/ *n* tela *f*; (*of spider*) telaraña *f*; (*on foot*) membrana *f*. ~**bing** *n* cincha *f*

wed /wed/ *vt* (*pt* **wedded**) casarse con; ‹*priest etc*› casar. ● *vi* casarse. ~**ded to** (*fig*) unido a

wedding /'wedɪŋ/ *n* boda *f*. ~**-cake** *n* pastel *m* de boda. ~**-ring** *n* anillo *m* de boda

wedge /wedʒ/ *n* cuña *f*; (*space filler*) calce *m*. ● *vt* acuñar; (*push*) apretar

wedlock /'wedlɒk/ *n* matrimonio *m*

Wednesday /'wenzdeɪ/ *n* miércoles *m*

wee /wiː/ *a* (*fam*) pequeñito

weed /wiːd/ *n* mala hierba *f*. ● *vt* desherbar. ~**-killer** *n* herbicida *m*. ~ **out** eliminar. ~**y** *a* ‹*person*› débil

week /wiːk/ *n* semana *f*. ~**day** /'wiːkdeɪ/ *n* día *m* laborable. ~**end** *n* fin *m* de semana. ~**ly** /'wiːklɪ/ *a*

semanal. ● *n* semanario *m*. ● *adv* semanalmente

weep /wiːp/ *vi* (*pt* **wept**) llorar. ~**ing willow** *n* sauce *m* llorón

weevil /'wiːvɪl/ *n* gorgojo *m*

weigh /weɪ/ *vt/i* pesar. ~ **anchor** levar anclas. ~ **down** *vt* (*fig*) oprimir. ~ **up** *vt* pesar; (*fig*) considerar

weight /weɪt/ *n* peso *m*. ~**less** *a* ingrávido. ~**lessness** *n* ingravidez *f*. ~**-lifting** *n* halterofilia *f*, levantamiento *m* de pesos. ~**y** *a* (**-ier, -iest**) pesado; (*influential*) influyente

weir /wɪə(r)/ *n* presa *f*

weird /wɪəd/ *a* (**-er, -est**) misterioso; (*bizarre*) extraño

welcome /'welkəm/ *a* bienvenido. ~ **to do** libre de hacer. **you're** ~**e!** (*after thank you*) ¡de nada! ● *n* bienvenida *f*; (*reception*) acogida *f*. ● *vt* dar la bienvenida a; (*appreciate*) alegrarse de

welcoming /'welkəmɪŋ/ *a* acogedor

weld /weld/ *vt* soldar. ● *n* soldadura *f*. ~**er** *n* soldador *m*

welfare /'welfeə(r)/ *n* bienestar *m*; (*aid*) asistencia *f* social. **W~ State** *n* estado *m* benefactor. ~ **work** *n* asistencia *f* social

well[1] /wel/ *adv* (**better**, **best**) bien. ~ **done!** ¡bravo! **as** ~ también. **as as** tanto... como. **be** ~ estar bien. **do** ~ (*succeed*) tener éxito. **very** ~ muy bien. ● *a* bien. ● *int* bueno; (*surprise*) ¡vaya! ~ **I never!** ¡no me digas!

well[2] /wel/ *n* pozo *m*; (*of staircase*) caja *f*

well: ~**-appointed** *a* bien equipado. ~**-behaved** *a* bien educado. ~**being** *n* bienestar *m*. ~**-bred** *a* bien educado. ~**-disposed** *a* benévolo. ~**groomed** *a* bien aseado. ~**-heeled** *a* (*fam*) rico

wellington /'welɪŋtən/ *n* bota *f* de agua

well: ~**-knit** *a* robusto. ~**-known** *a* conocido. ~**-meaning** *a*, ~ **meant** *a* bienintencionado. ~ **off** *a* acomodado. ~**-read** *a* culto. ~**-spoken** *a* bienhablado. ~**-to-do** *a* rico. ~**-wisher** *n* bienqueriente *m & f*

Welsh /welʃ/ *a & n* galés (*m*). ~ **rabbit** *n* pan *m* tostado con queso

welsh /welʃ/ *vi*. ~ **on** no cumplir con

wench /wentʃ/ *n* (*old use*) muchacha *f*

wend /wend/ vt. ~ **one's way** encaminarse

went /went/ see **go**

wept /wept/ see **weep**

were /wɜː(r), wə(r)/ see **be**

west /west/ n oeste m. **the** ~ el Occidente m. ● a del oeste. ● adv hacia el oeste, al oeste. **go** ~ (sl) morir. **W~ Germany** n Alemania f Occidental. **~erly** a del oeste. **~ern** a occidental. ● n (film) película f del Oeste. **~erner** /-ənə(r)/ n occidental m & f. **W~ Indian** a & n antillano (m). **W~ Indies** npl Antillas fpl. **~ward** a, **~ward(s)** adv hacia el oeste

wet /wet/ a (wetter, wettest) mojado; (rainy) lluvioso, de lluvia; (person, sl) soso. ~ **paint** recién pintado. **get** ~ mojarse. ● vt (pt wetted) mojar, humedecer. ~ **blanket** n aguafiestas m & f invar. ~ **suit** n traje m de buzo

whack /wæk/ vt (fam) golpear. ● n (fam) golpe m. **~ed** /wækt/ a (fam) agotado. **~ing** a (huge, sl) enorme. ● n paliza f

whale /weɪl/ n ballena f. **a** ~ **of a** (fam) maravilloso, enorme

wham /wæm/ int ¡zas!

wharf /wɔːf/ n (pl wharves or wharfs) muelle m

what /wɒt/ a el que, la que, lo que, los que, las que; (in questions & exclamations) qué. ● pron lo que; (interrogative) qué. ~ **about going?** ¿si fuésemos? ~ **about me?** ¿y yo? ~ **for?** ¿para qué? ~ **if?** ¿y si? ~ **is it?** ¿qué es? ~ **you need** lo que te haga falta. ● int ¡cómo! ~ **a fool!** ¡qué tonto!

whatever /wɒt'evə(r)/ a cualquiera. ● pron (todo) lo que, cualquier cosa que

whatnot /'wɒtnɒt/ n chisme m

whatsoever /wɒtsəu'evə(r)/ a & pron = **whatever**

wheat /wiːt/ n trigo m. **~en** a de trigo

wheedle /'wiːdl/ vt engatusar

wheel /wiːl/ n rueda f. **at the** ~ al volante. **steering-**~ n volante m. ● vt empujar (bicycle etc). ● vi girar. ~ **round** girar. **~barrow** /'wiːlbærəu/ n carretilla f. **~chair** /'wiːltʃeə(r)/ n silla f de ruedas

wheeze /wiːz/ vi resollar. ● n resuello m

when /wen/ adv cuándo. ● conj cuando

whence /wens/ adv de dónde

whenever /wen'evə(r)/ adv en cualquier momento; (every time that) cada vez que

where /weə(r)/ adv & conj donde; (interrogative) dónde. ~ **are you going?** ¿adónde vas? ~ **are you from?** ¿de dónde eres?

whereabouts /'weərəbauts/ adv dónde. ● n paradero m

whereas /weər'æz/ conj por cuanto; (in contrast) mientras (que)

whereby /weə'baɪ/ adv por lo cual

whereupon /weərə'pɒn/ adv después de lo cual

wherever /weər'evə(r)/ adv (in whatever place) dónde (diablos). ● conj dondequiera que

whet /wet/ vt (pt whetted) afilar; (fig) aguzar

whether /'weðə(r)/ conj si. ~ **you like it or not** que te guste o no te guste. **I don't know** ~ **she will like it** no sé si le gustará

which /wɪtʃ/ a (in questions) qué. ~ **one** cuál. ~ **one of you** cuál de vosotros. ● pron (in questions) qué; (relative) que; (object) el cual, la cual, lo cual, los cuales, las cuales

whichever /wɪtʃ'evə(r)/ a cualquier. ● pron cualquiera que, el que, la que

whiff /wɪf/ n soplo m; (of smoke) bocanada f; (smell) olorcillo m

while /waɪl/ n rato m. ● conj mientras; (although) aunque. ● vt. ~ **away** pasar (time)

whilst /waɪlst/ conj = **while**

whim /wɪm/ n capricho m

whimper /'wɪmpə(r)/ vi lloriquear. ● n lloriqueo m

whimsical /'wɪmzɪkl/ a caprichoso; (odd) extraño

whine /waɪn/ vi gimotear. ● n gimoteo m

whip /wɪp/ n látigo m; (pol) oficial m disciplinario. ● vt (pt whipped) azotar; (culin) batir; (seize) agarrar. ~ **cord** n tralla f. **~ped cream** n nata f batida. **~ping-boy** /'wɪpɪŋbɔɪ/ n cabeza f de turco. **~round** n colecta f. ~ **up** (incite) estimular

whirl /wɜːl/ vt hacer girar rápidamente. ● vi girar rápidamente; (swirl) arremolinarse. ● n giro m;

(*swirl*) remolino *m.* **~pool** /'wɜːl-puːl/ *n* remolino *m.* **~wind** /'wɜːl-wɪnd/ *n* torbellino *m*

whirr /wɜː(r)/ *n* zumbido *m.* ● *vi* zumbar

whisk /wɪsk/ *vt* (*culin*) batir. ● *n* (*culin*) batidor *m.* **~ away** llevarse

whisker /'wɪskə(r)/ *n* pelo *m.* **~s** *npl* (*of man*) patillas *fpl*; (*of cat etc*) bigotes *mpl*

whisky /'wɪskɪ/ *n* güisqui *m*

whisper /'wɪspə(r)/ *vt* decir en voz baja. ● *vi* cuchichear; ⟨*leaves etc*⟩ susurrar. ● *n* cuchicheo *m*; (*of leaves*) susurro *m*; (*rumour*) rumor *m*

whistle /'wɪsl/ *n* silbido *m*; (*instrument*) silbato *m.* ● *vi* silbar. **~stop** *n* (*pol*) breve parada *f* (en gira electoral)

white /waɪt/ *a* (**-er, -est**) blanco. **go ~** ponerse pálido. ● *n* blanco; (*of egg*) clara *f.* **~bait** /'waɪtbeɪt/ *n* (*pl* **~bait**) chanquetes *mpl.* **~ coffee** *n* café *m* con leche. **~collar worker** *n* empleado *m* de oficina. **~ elephant** *n* objeto *m* inútil y costoso

Whitehall /'waɪthɔːl/ *n* el gobierno *m* británico

white: **~ horses** *n* cabrillas *fpl.* **~hot** *a* ⟨*metal*⟩ candente. **~ lie** *n* mentirijilla *f.* **~n** *vt/i* blanquear. **~ness** *n* blancura *f.* **W~ Paper** *n* libro *m* blanco. **~wash** /'waɪtwɒʃ/ *n* jalbegue *m*; (*fig*) encubrimiento *m.* ● *vt* enjalbegar; (*fig*) encubrir

whiting /'waɪtɪŋ/ *n* (*pl* **whiting**) (*fish*) pescadilla *f*

whitlow /'wɪtləʊ/ *n* panadizo *m*

Whitsun /'wɪtsn/ *n* Pentecostés *m*

whittle /'wɪtl/ *vt.* **~ (down)** tallar; (*fig*) reducir

whiz /wɪz/ *vi* (*pt* **whizzed**) silbar; (*rush*) ir a gran velocidad. **~ past** pasar como un rayo. **~kid** *n* (*fam*) joven *m* prometedor, promesa *f*

who /huː/ *pron* que, quien; (*interrogative*) quién; (*particular person*) el que, la que, los que, las que

whodunit /huː'dʌnɪt/ *n* (*fam*) novela *f* policíaca

whoever /huː'evə(r)/ *pron* quienquiera que; (*interrogative*) quién (diablos)

whole /həʊl/ *a* entero; (*not broken*) intacto. ● *n* todo *m*, conjunto *m*; (*total*) total *m.* **as a ~** en conjunto. **on the ~** por regla general. **~hearted** *a* sincero. **~meal** *a* integral

wholesale /'həʊlseɪl/ *n* venta *f* al por mayor. ● *a & adv* al por mayor. **~r** /-ə(r)/ *n* comerciante *m & f* al por mayor

wholesome /'həʊlsəm/ *a* saludable

wholly /'həʊlɪ/ *adv* completamente

whom /huːm/ *pron* que, a quien; (*interrogative*) a quién

whooping cough /'huːpɪŋkɒf/ *n* tos *f* ferina

whore /hɔː(r)/ *n* puta *f*

whose /huːz/ *pron* de quién. ● *a* de quién; (*relative*) cuyo

why /waɪ/ *adv* por qué. ● *int* ¡toma!

wick /wɪk/ *n* mecha *f*

wicked /'wɪkɪd/ *a* malo; (*mischievous*) travieso; (*very bad, fam*) malísimo. **~ness** *n* maldad *f*

wicker /'wɪkə(r)/ *n* mimbre *m & f.* ● *a* de mimbre. **~work** *n* artículos *mpl* de mimbre

wicket /'wɪkɪt/ *n* (*cricket*) rastrillo *m*

wide /waɪd/ *a* (**-er, -est**) ancho; (*fully opened*) de par en par; (*far from target*) lejano; ⟨*knowledge etc*⟩ amplio. ● *adv* lejos. **far and ~** por todas partes. **~ awake** *a* completamente despierto; (*fig*) despabilado. **~ly** *adv* extensamente; (*believed*) generalmente; (*different*) muy. **~n** *vt* ensanchar

widespread /'waɪdspred/ *a* extendido; (*fig*) difundido

widow /'wɪdəʊ/ *n* viuda *f.* **~ed** *a* viudo. **~er** *n* viudo *m.* **~hood** *n* viudez *f*

width /wɪdθ/ *n* anchura *f.* **in ~** de ancho

wield /wiːld/ *vt* manejar; ejercer ⟨*power*⟩

wife /waɪf/ *n* (*pl* **wives**) mujer *f*, esposa *f*

wig /wɪg/ *n* peluca *f*

wiggle /'wɪgl/ *vt* menear. ● *vi* menearse

wild /waɪld/ *a* (**-er, -est**) salvaje; (*enraged*) furioso; ⟨*idea*⟩ extravagante; (*with joy*) loco; (*random*) al azar. ● *adv* en estado salvaje. **run ~** crecer en estado salvaje. **~s** *npl* regiones *fpl* salvajes

wildcat /'waɪldkæt/ *a.* **~ strike** *n* huelga *f* salvaje

wilderness /'wɪldənɪs/ *n* desierto *m*

wild: **~fire** /'waɪldfaɪə(r)/ *n.* **spread like ~fire** correr como un reguero de pólvora. **~goose chase** *n* empresa *f* inútil. **~life** /'waɪldlaɪf/ *n* fauna f. **∼ly** adv violentamente; (fig) locamente

wilful /'wɪlfʊl/ a intencionado; (self-willed) terco. **∼ly** adv intencionadamente; (obstinately) obstinadamente

will[1] /wɪl/ v aux. **∼ you have some wine?** ¿quieres vino? **he ∼ be** será. **you ∼ be back soon, won't you?** volverás pronto, ¿no?

will[2] /wɪl/ n voluntad f; (document) testamento m

willing /'wɪlɪŋ/ a complaciente. **∼to** dispuesto a. **∼ly** adv de buena gana. **∼ness** n buena voluntad f

willow /'wɪləʊ/ n sauce m

will-power /'wɪlpaʊə(r)/ n fuerza f de voluntad

willy-nilly /wɪlɪ'nɪlɪ/ adv quieras que no

wilt /wɪlt/ vi marchitarse

wily /'waɪlɪ/ a (-ier, -iest) astuto

win /wɪn/ vt (vb won, pres p winning) ganar; (achieve, obtain) conseguir. ● vi ganar. ● n victoria f. **∼ back** vi reconquistar. **∼ over** vt convencer

wince /wɪns/ vi hacer una mueca de dolor. **without wincing** sin pestañear. ● n mueca f de dolor

winch /wɪntʃ/ n cabrestante m. ● vt levantar con el cabrestante

wind[1] /wɪnd/ n viento m; (in stomach) flatulencia f. **get the ∼ up** (sl) asustarse. **get ∼ of** enterarse de. **in the ∼** en el aire. ● vt dejar sin aliento.

wind[2] /waɪnd/ vt (pt wound) (wrap around) enrollar; dar cuerda a (clock etc). ● vi (road etc) serpentear. **∼ up** vt dar cuerda a (watch, clock); (provoke) agitar, poner nervioso; (fig) terminar, concluir

wind /wɪnd/: **∼bag** n charlatán m. **∼cheater** n cazadora f

winder /'waɪndə(r)/ n devanador m; (of clock, watch) llave f

windfall /'wɪndfɔːl/ n fruta f caída; (fig) suerte f inesperada

winding /'waɪndɪŋ/ a tortuoso

wind instrument /'wɪndɪnstrəmənt/ n instrumento m de viento

windmill /'wɪndmɪl/ n molino m (de viento)

window /'wɪndəʊ/ n ventana f; (in shop) escaparate m; (of vehicle, booking-office) ventanilla f. **∼-box** n

jardinera f. **∼-dresser** n escaparatista m & f. **∼-shop** vi mirar los escaparates

windpipe /'wɪndpaɪp/ n tráquea f

windscreen /'wɪndskriːn/ n, **windshield** n (Amer) parabrisas m invar. **∼ wiper** n limpiaparabrisas m invar

wind /wɪnd/: **∼y** a (-ier, -iest) ventoso, de mucho viento. **it is ∼y** hace viento

wine /waɪn/ n vino m. **∼-cellar** n bodega f. **∼glass** n copa f. **∼-grower** n vinicultor m. **∼-growing** n vinicultura f. ● a vinícola. **∼ list** n lista f de vinos. **∼-tasting** n cata f de vinos

wing /wɪŋ/ n ala f; (auto) aleta f. **under one's ∼** bajo la protección de uno. **∼ed** a alado. **∼er** /-ə(r)/ n (sport) ala m & f. **∼s** npl (in theatre) bastidores mpl

wink /wɪŋk/ vi guiñar el ojo; (light etc) centellear. ● n guiño m. **not to sleep a ∼** no pegar ojo

winkle /'wɪŋkl/ n bígaro m

win: **∼ner** /-ə(r)/ n ganador m. **∼ning-post** n poste m de llegada. **∼ning smile** n sonrisa f encantadora. **∼nings** npl ganancias fpl

winsome /'wɪnsəm/ a atractivo

wint|er /'wɪntə(r)/ n invierno m. ● vi invernar. **∼ry** a invernal

wipe /waɪp/ vt limpiar; (dry) secar. ● n limpión m. **give sth a ∼** limpiar algo. **∼ out** (cancel) cancelar; (destroy) destruir; (obliterate) borrar. **∼ up** limpiar; (dry) secar

wire /'waɪə(r)/ n alambre m; (elec) cable m; (telegram, fam) telegrama m

wireless /'waɪəlɪs/ n radio f

wire netting /waɪə'netɪŋ/ n alambrera f, tela f metálica

wiring n instalación f eléctrica

wiry /'waɪərɪ/ a (-ier, -iest) (person) delgado

wisdom /'wɪzdəm/ n sabiduría f. **∼ tooth** n muela f del juicio

wise /waɪz/ a (-er, -est) sabio; (sensible) prudente. **∼crack** /'waɪzkræk/ n (fam) salida f. **∼ly** adv sabiamente; (sensibly) prudentemente

wish /wɪʃ/ n deseo m; (greeting) saludo m. **with best ∼es** (in letters) un fuerte abrazo. ● vt desear. **∼ on** (fam) encajar a. **∼ s.o. well** desear buena suerte a uno. **∼bone** n espoleta f (de las aves). **∼ful** a deseoso. **∼ful thinking** n ilusiones fpl

wishy-washy /'wɪʃɪwɒʃɪ/ *a* soso; ⟨*person*⟩ sin convicciones, falto de entereza

wisp /wɪsp/ *n* manojito *m*; (*of smoke*) voluta *f*; (*of hair*) mechón *m*

wisteria /wɪs'tɪərɪə/ *n* glicina *f*

wistful /'wɪstfl/ *a* melancólico

wit /wɪt/ *n* gracia *f*; (*person*) persona *f* chistosa; (*intelligence*) ingenio *m*. **be at one's ∼s' end** no saber qué hacer. **live by one's ∼s** vivir de expedientes, vivir del cuento

witch /wɪtʃ/ *n* bruja *f*. **∼craft** *n* brujería *f*. **∼doctor** *n* hechicero *m*

with /wɪð/ *prep* con; (*cause, having*) de. **be ∼ it** (*fam*) estar al día, estar al tanto. **the man ∼ the beard**, el hombre de la barba

withdraw /wɪð'drɔ:/ *vt* (*pt* **withdrew**, *pp* **withdrawn**) retirar. ● *vi* apartarse. **∼al** *n* retirada *f*. **∼n** *a* ⟨*person*⟩ introvertido

wither /'wɪðə(r)/ *vi* marchitarse. ● *vt* (*fig*) fulminar

withhold /wɪð'həʊld/ *vt* (*pt* **withheld**) retener; (*conceal*) ocultar (**from** a)

within /wɪð'ɪn/ *prep* dentro de. ● *adv* dentro. **∼ sight** a la vista

without /wɪð'aʊt/ *prep* sin

withstand /wɪð'stænd/ *vt* (*pt* **∼stood**) resistir a

witness /'wɪtnɪs/ *n* testigo *m*; (*proof*) testimonio *m*. ● *vt* presenciar; firmar como testigo ⟨*document*⟩. **∼box** *n* tribuna *f* de los testigos

witticism /'wɪtɪsɪzəm/ *n* ocurrencia *f*

wittingly /'wɪtɪŋlɪ/ *adv* a sabiendas

witty /'wɪtɪ/ *a* (**-ier, -iest**) gracioso

wives /waɪvz/ *see* **wife**

wizard /'wɪzəd/ *n* hechicero *m*. **∼ry** *n* hechicería *f*

wizened /'wɪznd/ *a* arrugado

wobbl|e /'wɒbl/ *vi* tambalearse; ⟨*voice, jelly, hand*⟩ temblar; ⟨*chair etc*⟩ balancearse. **∼y** *a* ⟨*chair etc*⟩ cojo

woe /wəʊ/ *n* aflicción *f*. **∼ful** *a* triste. **∼begone** /'wəʊbɪgɒn/ *a* desconsolado

woke, woken /wəʊk, 'wəʊkən/ *see* **wake**[1]

wolf /wʊlf/ *n* (*pl* **wolves**) lobo *m*. **cry ∼** gritar al lobo. ● *vt* zamparse. **∼whistle** *n* silbido *m* de admiración

woman /'wʊmən/ *n* (*pl* **women**) mujer *f*. **single ∼** soltera *f*. **∼ize**

/'wʊmənaɪz/ *vi* ser mujeriego. **∼ly** *a* femenino

womb /wu:m/ *n* matriz *f*

women /'wɪmɪn/ *npl see* **woman**. **∼folk** /'wɪmɪnfəʊk/ *npl* mujeres *fpl*. **∼'s lib** *n* movimiento *m* de liberación de la mujer

won /wʌn/ *see* **win**

wonder /'wʌndə(r)/ *n* maravilla *f*; (*bewilderment*) asombro *m*. **no ∼** no es de extrañarse (**that** que). ● *vi* admirarse; (*reflect*) preguntarse

wonderful /'wʌndəfl/ *a* maravilloso. **∼ly** *adv* maravillosamente

won't /wəʊnt/ = **will not**

woo /wu:/ *vt* cortejar

wood /wʊd/ *n* madera *f*; (*for burning*) leña *f*; (*area*) bosque *m*; (*in bowls*) bola *f*. **out of the ∼** (*fig*) fuera de peligro. **∼cutter** /'wʊdkʌtə(r)/ *n* leñador *m*. **∼ed** *a* poblado de árboles, boscoso. **∼en** *a* de madera. **∼land** *n* bosque *m*

woodlouse /'wʊdlaʊs/ *n* (*pl* **-lice**) cochinilla *f*

woodpecker /'wʊdpekə(r)/ *n* pájaro *m* carpintero

woodwind /'wʊdwɪnd/ *n* instrumentos *mpl* de viento de madera

woodwork /'wʊdwɜ:k/ *n* carpintería *f*; (*in room etc*) maderaje *m*

woodworm /'wʊdwɜ:m/ *n* carcoma *f*

woody /'wʊdɪ/ *a* leñoso

wool /wʊl/ *n* lana *f*. **pull the ∼ over s.o.'s eyes** engañar a uno. **∼len** *a* de lana. **∼lens** *npl* ropa *f* de lana. **∼ly** *a* (**-ier, -iest**) de lana; (*fig*) confuso. ● *n* jersey *m*

word /wɜ:d/ *n* palabra *f*; (*news*) noticia *f*. **by ∼ of mouth** de palabra. **have ∼s with** reñir con. **in one** ∼ en una palabra. **in other ∼s** es decir. ● *vt* expresar. **∼ing** *n* expresión *f*, términos *mpl*. **∼perfect** *a*. **be ∼perfect** saber de memoria. **∼ processor** *n* procesador *m* de textos. **∼y** *a* prolijo

wore /wɔ:(r)/ *see* **wear**

work /wɜ:k/ *n* trabajo *m*; (*arts*) obra *f*. ● *vt* hacer trabajar; manejar ⟨*machine*⟩. ● *vi* trabajar; ⟨*machine*⟩ funcionar; ⟨*student*⟩ estudiar; ⟨*drug etc*⟩ tener efecto; (*be successful*) tener éxito. **∼ in** introducir(se). **∼ off** desahogar. **∼ out** *vt* resolver; (*calculate*) calcular; elaborar ⟨*plan*⟩. ● *vi* (*succeed*) salir bien; (*sport*) entrenarse. ~ **up** *vt* desarrollar. ● *vi* excitarse. ~**able** /'wɜː kəbl/ *a* ⟨*project*⟩ factible. ~**aholic** /wɜːkəˈhɒlɪk/ *n* trabajador *m* obsesivo. ~**ed up** *a* agitado. ~**er** /'wɜːkə(r)/ *n* trabajador *m*; (*manual*) obrero *m*

workhouse /'wɜːkhaʊs/ *n* asilo *m* de pobres

work /wɜːk/ ~**ing** /'wɜːkɪŋ/ *a* ⟨*day*⟩ laborable; ⟨*clothes etc*⟩ de trabajo. ● *n* (*mec*) funcionamiento *m*. **in** ~**ing order** en estado de funcionamiento. ~**ing class** *n* clase *f* obrera. ~**ing-class** *a* de la clase obrera. ~**man** /'wɜːkmən/ *n* (*pl* **-men**) obrero *m*. ~**manlike** /'wɜːkmənlaɪk/ *a* concienzudo. ~**manship** *n* destreza *f*. ~**s** *npl* (*building*) fábrica *f*; (*mec*) mecanismo *m*. ~**shop** /'wɜːkʃɒp/ *n* taller *m*. ~**-to-rule** *n* huelga *f* de celo

world /wɜːld/ *n* mundo *m*. **a** ~ **of** enorme. **out of this** ~ maravilloso. ● *a* mundial. ~**ly** *a* mundano. ~**wide** *a* universal

worm /wɜːm/ *n* lombriz *f*; (*grub*) gusano *m*. ● *vi*. ~ **one's way** insinuarse. ~**eaten** *a* carcomido

worn /wɔːn/ *see* **wear**. ● *a* gastado. ~**out** *a* gastado; ⟨*person*⟩ rendido

worr|ied /'wʌrɪd/ *a* preocupado. ~**ier** /-ə(r)/ *n* aprensivo *m*. ~**y** /'wʌrɪ/ *vt* preocupar; (*annoy*) molestar. ● *vi* preocuparse. ● *n* preocupación *f*. ~**ying** *a* inquietante

worse /wɜːs/ *a* peor. ● *adv* peor; (*more*) más. ● *n* lo peor. ~**n** *vt/i* empeorar

worship /'wɜːʃɪp/ *n* culto *m*; (*title*) señor, su señoría. ● *vt* (*pt* **worshipped**) adorar

worst /wɜːst/ *a* (el) peor. ● *adv* peor. ● *n* lo peor. **get the** ~ **of it** llevar la peor parte

worsted /'wʊstɪd/ *n* estambre *m*

worth /wɜːθ/ *n* valor *m*. ● *a*. **be** ~ valer. **it is** ~ **trying** vale la pena probarlo. **it was** ~ **my while** (me) valió la pena. ~**less** *a* sin valor. ~**while** /'wɜːθwaɪl/ *a* que vale la pena

worthy /'wɜːðɪ/ *a* meritorio; (*respectable*) respetable; (*laudable*) loable

would /wʊd/ *v aux*. ~ **you come here please?** ¿quieres venir aquí? ~ **you go?** ¿irías tú? **he** ~ **come if he could** vendría si pudiese. **I** ~ **come every day** (*used to*) venía todos los

días. **I** ~ **do it** lo haría yo. ~**-be** *a* supuesto

wound[1] /wuːnd/ *n* herida *f*. ● *vt* herir

wound[2] /waʊnd/ *see* **wind**[2]

wove, woven /wəʊv, 'wəʊvn/ *see* **weave**

wow /waʊ/ *int* ¡caramba!

wrangle /'ræŋɡl/ *vi* reñir. ● *n* riña *f*

wrap /ræp/ *vt* (*pt* **wrapped**) envolver. **be** ~**ped up in** (*fig*) estar absorto en. ● *n* bata *f*; (*shawl*) chal *m*. ~**per** /-ə(r)/ *n*, ~**ping** *n* envoltura *f*

wrath /rɒθ/ *n* ira *f*. ~**ful** *a* iracundo

wreath /riːθ/ *n* (*pl* **-ths** /-ðz/) guirnalda *f*; (*for funeral*) corona *f*

wreck /rek/ *n* ruina *f*; (*sinking*) naufragio *m*; (*remains of ship*) buque *m* naufragado. **be a nervous** ~ tener los nervios destrozados. ● *vt* hacer naufragar; (*fig*) arruinar. ~**age** *n* restos *mpl*; (*of building*) escombros *mpl*

wren /ren/ *n* troglodito *m*

wrench /rentʃ/ *vt* arrancar; (*twist*) torcer. ● *n* arranque *m*; (*tool*) llave *f* inglesa

wrest /rest/ *vt* arrancar (**from** a)

wrestl|e /'resl/ *vi* luchar. ~**er** /-ə(r)/ *n* luchador *m*. ~**ing** *n* lucha *f*

wretch /retʃ/ *n* desgraciado *m*; (*rascal*) tunante *m & f*. ~**ed** *a* miserable; ⟨*weather*⟩ horrible, de perros; ⟨*dog etc*⟩ maldito

wriggle /'rɪɡl/ *vi* culebrear. ~ **out of** escaparse de. ~ **through** deslizarse por. ● *n* serpenteo *m*

wring /rɪŋ/ *vt* (*pt* **wrung**) retorcer. ~ **out of** (*obtain from*) arrancar. ~**ing wet** empapado

wrinkle /'rɪŋkl/ *n* arruga *f*. ● *vt* arrugar. ● *vi* arrugarse

wrist /rɪst/ *n* muñeca *f*. ~**-watch** *n* reloj *m* de pulsera

writ /rɪt/ *n* decreto *m* judicial

write /raɪt/ *vt/i* (*pt* **wrote**, *pp* **written**, *pres p* **writing**) escribir. ~ **down** *vt* anotar. ~ **off** *vt* cancelar; (*fig*) dar por perdido. ~ **up** *vt* hacer un reportaje de; (*keep up to date*) poner al día. ~**-off** *n* pérdida *f* total. ~**r** /-ə(r)/ *n* escritor *m*; (*author*) autor *m*. ~**-up** *n* reportaje *m*; (*review*) crítica *f*

writhe /raɪð/ *vi* retorcerse

writing /'raɪtɪŋ/ *n* escribir *m*; (*handwriting*) letra *f*. **in** ~ por escrito. ~**s**

npl obras *fpl.* ∼**-paper** *n* papel *m* de escribir

written /'rɪtn/ *see* **write**

wrong /rɒŋ/ *a* incorrecto; (*not just*) injusto; (*mistaken*) equivocado. **be** ∼ no tener razón; (*be mistaken*) equivocarse. ● *adv* mal. **go** ∼ equivocarse; ⟨*plan*⟩ salir mal; ⟨*car etc*⟩ estropearse. ● *n* injusticia *f*; (*evil*) mal *m*. **in the** ∼ equivocado. ● *vt* ser injusto con. ∼**ful** *a* injusto. ∼**ly** *adv* mal; (*unfairly*) injustamente

wrote /rəʊt/ *see* **write**

wrought /rɔːt/ *a.* ∼ **iron** *n* hierro *m* forjado

wrung /rʌŋ/ *see* **wring**

wry /raɪ/ *a* (**wryer, wryest**) torcido; ⟨*smile*⟩ forzado. ∼ **face** *n* mueca *f*

X

xenophobia /zenə'fəʊbɪə/ *n* xenofobia *f*

Xerox /'zɪərɒks/ *n* (*P*) fotocopiadora *f*. **xerox** *n* fotocopia *f*

Xmas /'krɪsməs/ *n abbr* (*Christmas*) Navidad *f*, Navidades *fpl*

X-ray /'eksreɪ/ *n* radiografía *f*. ∼**s** *npl* rayos *mpl* X. ● *vt* radiografiar

xylophone /'zaɪləfəʊn/ *n* xilófono *m*

Y

yacht /jɒt/ *n* yate *m*. ∼**ing** *n* navegación *f* a vela

yam /jæm/ *n* ñame *m*, batata *f*

yank /jæŋk/ *vt* (*fam*) arrancar violentamente

Yankee /'jæŋkɪ/ *n* (*fam*) yanqui *m* & *f*

yap /jæp/ *vi* (*pt* **yapped**) ⟨*dog*⟩ ladrar

yard[1] /jɑːd/ *n* (*measurement*) yarda *f* (= *0.9144 metre*)

yard[2] /jɑːd/ *n* patio *m*; (*Amer, garden*) jardín *m*

yardage /'jɑːdɪdʒ/ *n* metraje *m*

yardstick /'jɑːdstɪk/ *n* (*fig*) criterio *m*

yarn /jɑːn/ *n* hilo *m*; (*tale, fam*) cuento *m*

yashmak /'jæʃmæk/ *n* velo *m*

yawn /jɔːn/ *vi* bostezar. ● *n* bostezo *m*

year /jɪə(r)/ *n* año *m*. **be three** ∼**s old** tener tres años. ∼**-book** *n*

anuario *m*. ∼**ling** /'jɜːlɪŋ/ *n* primal *m*. ∼**ly** *a* anual. ● *adv* anualmente

yearn /jɜːn/ *vi*. ∼ **for** anhelar. ∼**ing** *n* ansia *f*

yeast /jiːst/ *n* levadura *f*

yell /jel/ *vi* gritar. ● *n* grito *m*

yellow /'jeləʊ/ *a* & *n* amarillo (*m*). ∼**ish** *a* amarillento

yelp /jelp/ *n* gañido *m*. ● *vi* gañir

yen /jen/ *n* muchas ganas *fpl*

yeoman /'jəʊmən/ *n* (*pl* **-men**). **Y**∼ **of the Guard** alabardero *m* de la Casa Real

yes /jes/ *adv* & *n* sí (*m*)

yesterday /'jestədeɪ/ *adv* & *n* ayer (*m*). **the day before** ∼ anteayer *m*

yet /jet/ *adv* todavía, aún; (*already*) ya. **as** ∼ hasta ahora. ● *conj* sin embargo

yew /juː/ *n* tejo *m*

Yiddish /'jɪdɪʃ/ *n* judeoalemán *m*

yield /jiːld/ *vt* producir. ● *vi* ceder. ● *n* producción *f*; (*com*) rendimiento *m*

yoga /'jəʊgə/ *n* yoga *m*

yoghurt /'jɒgət/ *n* yogur *m*

yoke /jəʊk/ *n* yugo *m*; (*of garment*) canesú *m*

yokel /'jəʊkl/ *n* patán *m*, palurdo *m*

yolk /jəʊk/ *n* yema *f* (de huevo)

yonder /'jɒndə(r)/ *adv* a lo lejos

you /juː/ *pron* (*familiar form*) tú, vos (*Arg*), (*pl*) vosotros, vosotras, (*LAm*); (*polite form*) usted, (*pl*) ustedes; (*familiar, object*) te, (*pl*) os, les (*LAm*); (*polite, object*) le, la, (*pl*) les; (*familiar, after prep*) ti, (*pl*) vosotros, vosotras, ustedes (*LAm*); (*polite, after prep*) usted, (*pl*) ustedes. **with** ∼ (*familiar*) contigo, (*pl*) con vosotros, con vosotras, con ustedes (*LAm*); (*polite*) con usted, (*pl*) con ustedes; (*polite reflexive*) consigo. **I know** ∼ te conozco, le conozco a usted. **you can't smoke here** aquí no se puede fumar

young /jʌŋ/ *a* (**-er, -est**) joven. ∼ **lady** *n* señorita *f*. ∼ **man** *n* joven *m*. **her** ∼ **man** (*boyfriend*) su novio *m*. **the** ∼ *npl* los jóvenes *mpl*; (*of animals*) la cría *f*. ∼**ster** /'jʌŋstə(r)/ *n* joven *m*

your /jɔː(r)/ *a* (*familiar*) tu, (*pl*) vuestro; (*polite*) su

yours /jɔːz/ *poss pron* (el) tuyo, (*pl*) (el) vuestro, el de ustedes (*LAm*);

(*polite*) el suyo. **a book of** ~**s** un libro tuyo, un libro suyo. **Y~s faithfully, Y~s sincerely** le saluda atentamente

yourself /jɔː'self/ *pron* (*pl* **yourselves**) (*familiar, subject*) tú mismo, tú misma, (*pl*) vosotros mismos, vosotras mismas, ustedes mismos (*LAm*), ustedes mismas (*LAm*); (*polite, subject*) usted mismo, usted misma, (*pl*) ustedes mismos, ustedes mismas; (*familiar, object*) te, (*pl*) os, se (*LAm*); (*polite, object*) se; (*familiar, after prep*) ti, (*pl*) vosotros, vosotras, ustedes (*LAm*); (*polite, after prep*) sí

youth /juːθ/ *n* (*pl* **youths** /juːðz/) juventud *f*; (*boy*) joven *m*; (*young people*) jóvenes *mpl*. ~**ful** *a* joven, juvenil. ~**hostel** *n* albergue *m* para jóvenes

yowl /jaʊl/ *vi* aullar. ● *n* aullido *m*

Yugoslav /'juːgəslɑːv/ *a* & *n* yugoslavo (*m*). ~**ia** /-'slɑːvɪə/ *n* Yugoslavia *f*

yule /juːl/ *n*, **yule-tide** /'juːltaɪd/ *n* (*old use*) Navidades *fpl*

Z

zany /'zeɪnɪ/ *a*(**-ier,-iest**)estrafalario

zeal /ziːl/ *n* celo *m*

zealot /'zelət/ *n* fanático *m*

zealous /'zeləs/ *a* entusiasta. ~**ly** /'zeləslɪ/ *adv* con entusiasmo

zebra /'zebrə/ *n* cebra *f*. ~ **crossing** *n* paso *m* de cebra

zenith /'zenɪθ/ *n* cenit *m*

zero /'zɪərəʊ/ *n* (*pl* **-os**) cero *m*

zest /zest/ *n* gusto *m*; (*peel*) cáscara *f*

zigzag /'zɪgzæg/ *n* zigzag *m*. ● *vi* (*pt* **zigzagged**) zigzaguear

zinc /zɪŋk/ *n* cinc *m*

Zionis|m /'zaɪənɪzəm/ *n* sionismo *m*. ~**t** *n* sionista *m* & *f*

zip /zɪp/ *n* cremallera *f*. ● *vt*. ~ (**up**) cerrar (la cremallera)

Zip code /'zɪpkəʊd/ *n* (*Amer*) código *m* postal

zip fastener /zɪp'fɑːsnə(r)/ *n* cremallera *f*

zircon /'zɜːkən/ *n* circón *m*

zither /'zɪðə(r)/ *n* cítara *f*

zodiac /'zəʊdɪæk/ *n* zodiaco *m*

zombie /'zɒmbɪ/ *n* (*fam*) autómata *m* & *f*

zone /zəʊn/ *n* zona *f*

zoo /zuː/ *n* (*fam*) zoo *m*, jardín *m* zoológico. ~**logical** /zəʊə'lɒdʒɪkl/ *a* zoológico

zoolog|ist /zəʊ'ɒlədʒɪst/ *n* zoólogo *m*. ~**y** /zəʊ'ɒlədʒɪ/ *n* zoología *f*

zoom /zuːm/ *vi* ir a gran velocidad. ~ **in** (*photo*) acercarse rápidamente. ~ **past** pasar zumbando. ~ **lens** *n* zoom *m*

Zulu /'zuːluː/ *n* zulú *m* & *f*

Numbers · Números

zero	0	cero
one (first)	1	uno (primero)
two (second)	2	dos (segundo)
three (third)	3	tres (tercero)
four (fourth)	4	cuatro (cuarto)
five (fifth)	5	cinco (quinto)
six (sixth)	6	seis (sexto)
seven (seventh)	7	siete (séptimo)
eight (eighth)	8	ocho (octavo)
nine (ninth)	9	nueve (noveno)
ten (tenth)	10	diez (décimo)
eleven (eleventh)	11	once (undécimo)
twelve (twelfth)	12	doce (duodécimo)
thirteen (thirteenth)	13	trece (decimotercero)
fourteen (fourteenth)	14	catorce (decimocuarto)
fifteen (fifteenth)	15	quince (decimoquinto)
sixteen (sixteenth)	16	dieciséis (decimosexto)
seventeen (seventeenth)	17	diecisiete (decimoséptimo)
eighteen (eighteenth)	18	dieciocho (decimoctavo)
nineteen (nineteenth)	19	diecinueve (decimonoveno)
twenty (twentieth)	20	veinte (vigésimo)
twenty-one (twenty-first)	21	veintiuno (vigésimo primero)
twenty-two (twenty-second)	22	veintidós (vigésimo segundo)
twenty-three (twenty-third)	23	veintitrés (vigésimo tercero)
twenty-four (twenty-fourth)	24	veinticuatro (vigésimo cuarto)
twenty-five (twenty-fifth)	25	veinticinco (vigésimo quinto)
twenty-six (twenty-sixth)	26	veintiséis (vigésimo sexto)
thirty (thirtieth)	30	treinta (trigésimo)
thirty-one (thirty-first)	31	treinta y uno (trigésimo primero)
forty (fortieth)	40	cuarenta (cuadragésimo)
fifty (fiftieth)	50	cincuenta (quincuagésimo)
sixty (sixtieth)	60	sesenta (sexagésimo)
seventy (seventieth)	70	setenta (septuagésimo)
eighty (eightieth)	80	ochenta (octogésimo)

ninety (ninetieth)	90	noventa (nonagésimo)
a/one hundred (hundredth)	100	cien (centésimo)
a/one hundred and one (hundred and first)	101	ciento uno (centésimo primero)
two hundred (two hundredth)	200	doscientos (ducentésimo)
three hundred (three hundredth)	300	trescientos (tricentésimo)
four hundred (four hundredth)	400	cuatrocientos (cuadringentésimo)
five hundred (five hundredth)	500	quinientos (quingentésimo)
six hundred (six hundredth)	600	seiscientos (sexcentésimo)
seven hundred (seven hundredth)	700	setecientos (septingentésimo)
eight hundred (eight hundredth)	800	ochocientos (octingentésimo)
nine hundred (nine hundredth)	900	novecientos (noningentésimo)
a/one thousand (thousandth)	1000	mil (milésimo)
two thousand (two thousandth)	2000	dos mil (dos milésimo)
a/one million (millionth)	1,000,000	un millón (millonésimo)

Spanish Verbs · Verbos españoles

Regular verbs:

in **-ar** (*e.g.* **comprar**)
Present; compr|o, ~as, ~a, ~amos,
~áis, ~an
Future: comprar|é, ~ás, ~á,
~emos, ~éis, ~án
Imperfect: compr|aba, ~abas, ~aba,
~ábamos, ~abais, ~aban
Preterite: compr|é, ~aste, ~ó,
~amos, ~asteis, ~aron
Present subjunctive: compr|e, ~es,
~e, ~emos, ~éis, ~en
Imperfect subjunctive: compr|ara,
~aras ~ara, ~áramos, ~arais,
~aran
compr|ase, ~ases, ~ase,
~ásemos, ~aseis, ~asen
Conditional: comprar|ía, ~ías, ~ía,
~íamos, ~íais, ~ían
Present participle: comprando
Past participle: comprado
Imperative: compra, comprad

in **-er** (*e.g.* **beber**)
Present: beb|o, ~es, ~e, ~emos,
~éis, ~en
Future: beber|é, ~ás, ~á, ~emos,
~éis, ~án
Imperfect: beb|ía, ~ías, ~ía,
~íamos, ~íais, ~ían
Preterite: beb|í, ~iste, ~ió, ~imos,
~isteis, ~ieron
Present subjunctive: beb|a, ~as, ~a,
~amos, ~áis, ~an
Imperfect subjunctive: beb|iera,
~ieras, ~iera, ~iéramos,
~ierais, ~ieran
beb|iese, ~ieses, ~iese,
~iésemos, ~ieseis, ~iesen
Conditional: beber|ía, ~ías, ~ía,
~íamos, ~íais, ~ían
Present participle: bebiendo
Past participle: bebido
Imperative: bebe, bebed

in **-ir** (*e.g.* **vivir**)
Present: viv|o, ~es, ~e, ~imos, ~ís,
~en
Future: vivir|é, ~ás, ~á, ~emos,
~éis, ~án
Imperfect: viv|ía, ~ías, ~ía,
~íamos, ~íais, ~ían
Preterite: viv|í, ~iste, ~ió, ~imos,
~isteis, ~ieron

Present subjunctive: viv|a, ~as, ~a,
~amos, ~áis, ~an
Imperfect subjunctive: viv|iera,
~ieras, ~iera, ~iéramos,
~ierais, ~ieran
viv|iese, ~ieses, ~iese,
~iésemos, ~ieseis, ~iesen
Conditional: vivir|ía, ~ías, ~ía,
~íamos, ~íais, ~ían
Present participle: viviendo
Past participle: vivido
Imperative: vive, vivid

Irregular verbs:

[1] **cerrar**
Present: cierro, cierras, cierra,
cerramos, cerráis, cierran
Present subjunctive: cierre, cierres,
cierre, cerremos, cerréis, cierren
Imperative: cierra, cerrad

[2] **contar, mover**
Present: cuento, cuentas, cuenta,
contamos, contáis, cuentan
muevo, mueves, mueve, movemos,
movéis, mueven
Present subjunctive: cuente, cuentes,
cuente, contemos, contéis, cuenten
mueva, muevas, mueva, movamos,
mováis, muevan
Imperative: cuenta, contad
mueve, moved

[3] **jugar**
Present: juego, juegas, juega, jugamos,
jugáis, juegan
Preterite: jug|ué, jugaste, jugó, jugamos,
jugasteis, jugaron
Present subjunctive: juegue, juegues,
juegue, juguemos, juguéis, jueguen

[4] **sentir**
Present: siento, sientes, siente, sentimos,
sentís, sienten
Preterite: sentí, sentiste, sintió,
sentimos, sentisteis, sintieron
Present subjunctive: sienta, sientas,
sienta, sintamos, sintáis, sientan
Imperfect subjunctive: sint|iera, ~ieras,
~iera, ~iéramos, ~ierais,
~ieran

sint|iese, ~ieses, ~iese,
~iésemos, ~ieseis, ~iesen
Present participle: sintiendo
Imperative: siente, sentid

[5] pedir
Present: pido, pides, pide, pedimos,
pedís, piden
Preterite: pedí, pediste, pidió,
pedimos, pedisteis, pidieron
Present subjunctive: pid|a, ~as, ~a,
~amos, ~áis, ~an
Imperfect subjunctive: pid|iera,
~ieras, ~iera, ~iéramos,
~ierais, ~ieran
pid|iese, ~ieses, ~iese,
~iésemos, ~ieseis, ~iesen
Present participle: pidiendo
Imperative: pide, pedid

[6] dormir
Present: duermo, duermes, duerme,
dormimos, dormís, duermen
Preterite: dormí, dormiste, durmió,
dormimos, dormisteis, durmieron
Present subjunctive: duerma,
duermas, duerma, durmamos,
durmáis, duerman
Imperfect subjunctive: durm|iera,
~ieras, ~iera, ~iéramos,
~ierais, ~ieran
durm|iese, ~ieses, ~iese,
~iésemos, ~ieseis, ~iesen
Present participle: durmiendo
Imperative: duerme, dormid

[7] dedicar
Preterite: dediqué, dedicaste, dedicó,
dedicamos, dedicasteis, dedicaron
Present subjunctive: dediqu|e, ~es,
~e, ~emos, ~éis, ~en

[8] delinquir
Present: delinco, delinques, delinque,
delinquimos, delinquís, delinquen
Present subjunctive: delinc|a, ~as,
~a, ~amos, ~áis, ~an

[9] vencer, esparcir
Present: venzo, vences, vence,
vencemos, vencéis, vencen
esparzo, esparces, esparce,
esparcimos, esparcís, esparcen
Present subjunctive: venz|a, ~as, ~a,
~amos, ~áis, ~an
esparz|a, ~as, ~a, ~amos, ~áis,
~an

[10] rechazar
Preterite: rechacé, rechazaste,
rechazó, rechazamos, rechazasteis,
rechazaron
Present subjunctive: rechac|e, ~es,
~e, ~emos, ~éis, ~en

[11] conocer, lucir
Present: conozco, conoces, conoce,
conocemos, conocéis, conocen
luzco, luces, luce, lucimos, lucís,
lucen
Present subjunctive: conozc|a, ~as,
~a, ~amos, ~áis, ~an
luzc|a, ~as, ~a, ~amos, ~áis,
~an

[12] pagar
Preterite: pagué, pagaste, pagó,
pagamos, pagasteis, pagaron
Present subjunctive: pagu|e, ~es, ~e,
~emos, ~éis, ~en

[13] distinguir
Present: distingo, distingues,
distingue, distinguimos,
distinguís, distinguen
Present subjunctive: disting|a, ~as,
~a, ~amos, ~áis, ~an

[14] acoger, afligir
Present: acojo, acoges, acoge,
acogemos, acogéis, acogen
aflijo, afliges, aflige, afligimos,
afligís, afligen
Present subjunctive: acoj|a, ~as, ~a,
~amos, ~áis, ~an
aflij|a, ~as, ~a, ~amos, ~áis,
~an

[15] averiguar
Preterite: averigüé, averiguaste,
averiguó, averiguamos,
averiguasteis, averiguaron
Present subjunctive: averigü|e, ~es,
~e, ~emos, ~éis, ~en

[16] agorar
Present: agüero, agüeras, agüera,
agoramos, agoráis, agüeran
Present subjunctive: agüere, agüeres,
agüere, agoremos, agoréis, agüeren
Imperative: agüera, agorad

[17] huir
Present: huyo, huyes, huye, huimos,
huís, huyen

Preterite: huí, huiste, huyó, huimos, huisteis, huyeron
Present subjunctive: huy|a, ~as, ~a, ~amos, ~áis, ~an
Imperfect subjunctive: huy|era, ~eras, ~era, ~éramos, ~erais, ~eran
huy|ese, ~eses, ~ese, ~ésemos, ~eseis, ~esen
Present participle: huyendo
Imperative: huye, huid

[18] creer
Preterite: creí, creíste, creyó, creímos, creísteis, creyeron
Imperfect subjunctive: crey|era, ~eras, ~era, ~éramos, ~erais, ~eran
crey|ese, ~eses, ~ese, ~ésemos, ~eseis, ~esen
Present participle: creyendo
Past participle: creído

[19] argüir
Present: arguyo, arguyes, arguye, argüimos, argüís, arguyen
Preterite: argüí, argüiste, arguyó, argüimos, argüisteis, arguyeron
Present subjunctive: arguy|a, ~as, ~a, ~amos, ~áis, ~an
Imperfect subjunctive: arguy|era, ~eras, ~era, ~éramos, ~erais, ~eran
arguy|ese, ~eses, ~ese, ~ésemos, ~eseis, ~esen
Present participle: arguyendo
Imperative: arguye, argüid

[20] vaciar
Present: vacío, vacías, vacía, vaciamos, vaciáis, vacían
Present subjunctive: vacíe, vacíes, vacíe, vaciemos, vaciéis, vacíen
Imperative: vacía, vaciad

[21] acentuar
Present: acentúo, acentúas, acentúa, acentuamos, acentuáis, acentúan
Present subjunctive: acentúe, acentúes, acentúe, acentuemos, acentuéis, acentúen
Imperative: acentúa, acentuad

[22] atañer, engullir
Preterite: atañ|í, ~iste, ~ó, ~imos, ~isteis, ~eron
engull|í ~iste, ~ó, ~imos, ~isteis, ~eron

Imperfect subjunctive: atañ|era, ~eras, ~era, ~éramos, ~erais, ~eran
atañ|ese, ~eses, ~ese, ~ésemos, ~eseis, ~esen
engull|era, ~eras, ~era, ~éramos, ~erais, ~eran
engull|ese, ~eses, ~ese, ~ésemos, ~eseis, ~esen
Present participle: atañendo
engullendo

[23] aislar, aullar
Present: aíslo, aíslas, aísla, aislamos, aisláis, aíslan
aúllo, aúllas, aúlla, aullamos, aulláis, aúllan
Present subjunctive: aísle, aísles, aísle, aislemos, aisléis, aíslen
aúlle, aúlles, aúlle, aullemos, aulléis, aúllen
Imperative: aísla, aislad
aúlla, aullad

[24] abolir, garantir
Present: abolimos, abolís
garantimos, garantís
Present subjunctive: not used
Imperative: abolid
garantid

[25] andar
Preterite: anduv|e, ~iste, ~o, ~imos, ~isteis, ~ieron
Imperfect subjunctive: anduv|iera, ~ieras, ~iera, ~iéramos, ~ierais, ~ieran
anduv|iese, ~ieses, ~iese, ~iésemos, ~ieseis, ~iesen

[26] dar
Present: doy, das, da, damos, dais, dan
Preterite: di, diste, dio, dimos, disteis, dieron
Present subjunctive: dé, des, dé, demos, deis, den
Imperfect subjunctive: diera, dieras, diera, diéramos, dierais, dieran
diese, dieses, diese, diésemos, dieseis, diesen

[27] estar
Present: estoy, estás, está, estamos, estáis, están
Preterite: estuv|e, ~iste, ~o, ~imos, ~isteis, ~ieron
Present subjunctive: esté, estés, esté, estemos, estéis, estén

Imperfect subjunctive: estuv|iera,
~ieras, ~iera, ~iéramos,
~ierais, ~ieran
estuv|iese, ~ieses, ~iese,
~iésemos, ~ieseis, ~iesen
Imperative: está, estad

[28] caber
Present: quepo, cabes, cabe, cabemos,
cabéis, caben
Future: cabr|é, ~ás, ~á, ~emos,
~éis, ~án
Preterite: cup|e, ~iste, ~o, ~imos,
~isteis, ~ieron
Present subjunctive: quep|a, ~as, ~a,
~amos, ~áis, ~an
Imperfect subjunctive: cup|iera,
~ieras, ~iera, ~iéramos,
~ierais, ~ieran
cup|iese, ~ieses, ~iese,
~iésemos, ~ieseis, ~iesen
Conditional: cabr|ía, ~ías, ~ía,
~íamos, ~íais, ~ían

[29] caer
Present: caigo, caes, cae, caemos,
caéis, caen
Preterite: caí, caiste, cayó, caímos,
caísteis, cayeron
Present subjunctive: caig|a, ~as, ~a,
~amos, ~áis, ~an
Imperfect subjunctive: cay|era,
~eras, ~era, ~éramos, ~erais,
~eran
cay|ese, ~eses, ~ese, ~ésemos,
~eseis, ~esen
Present participle: cayendo
Past participle: caído

[30] haber
Present: he, has, ha, hemos, habéis,
han
Future: habr|é ~ás, ~á, ~emos,
~éis, ~án
Preterite: hub|e, ~iste, ~o, ~imos,
~isteis, ~ieron
Present subjunctive: hay|a, ~as, ~a,
~amos, ~áis, ~an
Imperfect subjunctive: hub|iera,
~ieras, ~iera, ~iéramos,
~ierais, ~ieran
hub|iese, ~ieses, ~iese,
~iésemos, ~ieseis, ~iesen
Conditional: habr|ía, ~ías, ~ía,
~íamos, ~íais, ~ían

[31] hacer
Present: hago, haces, hace, hacemos,
hacéis, hacen
Future: har|é, ~ás, ~á, ~emos,
~éis, ~án
Preterite: hice, hiciste, hizo, hicimos,
hicisteis, hicieron
Present subjunctive: hag|a, ~as, ~a,
~amos, ~áis, ~an
Imperfect subjunctive: hic|iera,
~ieras, ~iera, ~iéramos,
~ierais, ~ieran
hic|iese, ~ieses, ~iese,
~iésemos, ~ieseis, ~iesen
Conditional: har|ía, ~ías, ~ía,
~íamos, ~íais, ~ían
Past participle: hecho
Imperative: haz, haced

[32] placer
Preterite: plació/plugo
Present subjunctive: plazca
Imperfect subjunctive:
placiera/pluguiera
placiese/pluguiese

[33] poder
Present: puedo, puedes, puede,
podemos, podéis, pueden
Future: podr|é, ~ás, ~á, ~emos,
~éis, ~án
Preterite: pud|e, ~iste, ~o, ~imos,
~isteis, ~ieron
Present subjunctive: pueda, puedas,
pueda, podamos, podáis, puedan
Imperfect subjunctive: pud|iera,
~ieras, ~iera, ~iéramos,
~ierais, ~ieran
pud|iese, ~ieses, ~iese,
~iésemos, ~ieseis, ~iesen
Conditional: podr|ía, ~ías, ~ía,
~íamos, ~íais, ~ían
Past participle: pudiendo

[34] poner
Present: pongo, pones, pone,
ponemos, ponéis, ponen
Future: pondr|é, ~ás, ~á, ~emos,
~éis, ~án
Preterite: pus|e, ~iste, ~o, ~imos,
~isteis, ~ieron
Present subjunctive: pong|a, ~as, ~a,
~amos, ~áis, ~an
Imperfect subjunctive: pus|iera,
~ieras, ~iera, ~iéramos,
~ierais, ~ieran
pus|iese, ~ieses, ~iese,
~iésemos, ~ieseis, ~iesen

Conditional: pondr|ía, ~ías, ~ía,
~íamos, ~íais, ~ían
Past participle: puesto
Imperative: pon, poned

[35] querer
Present: quiero, quieres, quiere,
queremos, queréis, quieren
Future: querr|é, ~ás, ~á, ~emos,
~éis, ~án
Preterite: quis|e, ~iste, ~o, ~imos,
~isteis, ~ieron
Present subjunctive: quiera, quieras,
quiera, queramos, queráis, quieran
Imperfect subjunctive: quis|iera,
~ieras, ~iera, ~iéramos,
~ierais, ~ieran
quis|iese, ~ieses, ~iese,
~iésemos, ~ieseis, ~iesen
Conditional: querr|ía, ~ías, ~ía,
~íamos, ~íais, ~ían
Imperative: quiere, quered

[36] raer
Present: raigo/rayo, raes, rae,
raemos, raéis, raen
Preterite: raí, raíste, rayó, raímos,
raísteis, rayeron
Present subjunctive: raig|a, ~as, ~a,
~amos, ~áis, ~an
ray|a, ~as, ~a, ~amos, ~áis,
~an
Imperfect subjunctive: ray|era,
~eras, ~era, ~éramos, ~erais,
~eran
ray|ese, ~eses, ~ese, ~ésemos,
~eseis, ~esen
Present participle: rayendo
Past participle: raído

[37] roer
Present: roo/roigo/royo, roes, roe,
roemos, roéis, roen
Preterite: roí, roíste, royó, roímos,
roísteis, royeron
Present subjunctive: roa/roiga/roya,
roas, roa, roamos, roáis, roan
Imperfect subjunctive: roy|era,
~eras, ~era, ~éramos, ~erais,
~eran
roy|ese, ~eses, ~ese, ~ésemos,
~eseis, ~esen
Present participle: royendo
Past participle: roído

[38] saber
Present: sé, sabes, sabe, sabemos,
sabéis, saben

Future: sabr|é, ~ás, ~á, ~emos,
~éis, ~án
Preterite: sup|e, ~iste, ~o, ~imos,
~isteis, ~ieron
Present subjunctive: sep|a, ~as, ~a,
~amos, ~áis, ~an
Imperfect subjunctive: sup|iera,
~ieras, ~iera, ~iéramos,
~ierais, ~ieran
sup|iese, ~ieses, ~iese,
~iésemos, ~ieseis, ~iesen
Conditional: sabr|ía, ~ías, ~ía,
~íamos, ~íais, ~ían

[39] ser
Present: soy, eres, es, somos, sois, son
Imperfect: era, eras, era, éramos,
erais, eran
Preterite: fui, fuiste, fue, fuimos,
fuisteis, fueron
Present subjunctive: se|a, ~as, ~a,
~amos, ~áis, ~an
Imperfect subjunctive: fu|era, ~eras,
~era, ~éramos, ~erais, ~eran
fu|ese, ~eses, ~ese, ~ésemos,
~eseis, ~esen
Imperative: sé, sed

[40] tener
Present: tengo, tienes, tiene, tenemos,
tenéis, tienen
Future: tendr|é, ~ás, ~á, ~emos,
~éis, ~án
Preterite: tuv|e, ~iste, ~o, ~imos,
~isteis, ~ieron
Present subjunctive: teng|a, ~as, ~a,
~amos, ~áis, ~an
Imperfect subjunctive: tuv|iera,
~ieras, ~iera, ~iéramos,
~ierais, ~ieran
tuv|iese, ~ieses, ~iese,
~iésemos, ~ieseis, ~iesen
Conditional: tendr|ía, ~ías, ~ía,
~íamos, ~íais, ~ían
Imperative: ten, tened

[41] traer
Present: traigo, traes, trae, traemos,
traéis, traen
Preterite: traj|e, ~iste, ~o, ~imos,
~isteis, ~eron
Present subjunctive: traig|a, ~as, ~a,
~amos, ~áis, ~an
Imperfect subjunctive: traj|era,
~eras, ~era, ~éramos, ~erais,
~eran

traj|ese, ~eses, ~ese, ~ésemos,
~eseis, ~esen
Present participle: trayendo
Past participle: traído

[42] valer
Present: valgo, vales, vale, valemos,
valéis, valen
Future: vald|ré, ~ás, ~á, ~emos,
~éis, ~án
Present subjunctive: valg|a, ~as, ~a,
~amos, ~áis, ~an
Conditional: vald|ría, ~ías, ~ía,
~íamos, ~íais, ~ían
Imperative: val/vale, valed

[43] ver
Present: veo, ves, ve, vemos, veis, ven
Imperfect: ve|ía, ~ías, ~ía, ~íamos,
~íais, ~ían
Preterite: vi, viste, vio, vimos, visteis,
vieron
Present subjunctive: ve|a, ~as, ~a,
~amos, ~áis, ~an
Past participle: visto

[44] yacer
Present: yazco/yazgo/yago, yaces,
yace, yacemos, yacéis, yacen
Present subjunctive:
yazca/yazga/yaga, yazcas,
yazca, yazcamos, yazcáis, yazcan
Imperative: yace/yaz, yaced

[45] asir
Present: asgo, ases, ase, asimos, asís,
asen
Present subjunctive: asg|a, ~as, ~a,
~amos, ~áis, ~an

[46] decir
Present: digo, dices, dice, decimos,
decís, dicen
Future: dir|é, ~ás, ~á, ~emos,
~éis, ~án
Preterite: dij|e, ~iste, ~o, ~imos,
~isteis, ~eron
Present subjunctive: dig|a, ~as, ~a,
~amos, ~áis, ~an
Imperfect subjunctive: dij|era, ~eras,
~era, ~éramos, ~erais, ~eran
dij|ese, ~eses, ~ese, ~ésemos,
~eseis, ~esen
Conditional: dir|ía, ~ías, ~ía,
~íamos, ~íais, ~ían
Present participle: dicho

Imperative: di, decid

[47] reducir
Present: reduzco, reduces, reduce,
reducimos, reducís, reducen
Preterite: reduj|e, ~iste, ~o, ~imos,
~isteis, ~eron
Present subjunctive: reduzc|a, ~as,
~a, ~amos, ~áis, ~an
Imperfect subjunctive: reduj|era,
~eras, ~era, ~éramos, ~erais,
~eran
reduj|ese, ~eses, ~ese,
~ésemos, ~eseis, ~esen

[48] erguir
Present: irgo, irgues, irgue, erguimos,
erguís, irguen
yergo, yergues, yergue, erguimos,
erguís, yerguen
Preterite: erguí, erguiste, irguió,
erguimos, erguisteis, irguieron
Present subjunctive: irg|a, ~as, ~a,
~amos, ~áis, ~an
yerg|a, ~as, ~a, ~amos, ~áis,
~an
Imperfect subjunctive: irgu|iera,
~ieras, ~iera, ~iéramos,
~ierais, ~ieran
irgu|iese, ~ieses, ~iese,
~iésemos, ~ieseis, ~iesen
Present participle: irguiendo
Imperative: irgue/yergue, erguid

[49] ir
Present: voy, vas, va, vamos, vais, van
Imperfect: iba, ibas, iba, íbamos,
ibais, iban
Preterite: fui, fuiste, fue, fuimos,
fuisteis, fueron
Present subjunctive: vay|a, ~as, ~a,
~amos, ~áis, ~an
Imperfect subjunctive: fu|era, ~eras,
~era, ~éramos, ~erais, ~eran
fu|ese, ~eses, ~ese, ~ésemos,
~eseis, ~esen
Present participle: yendo
Imperative: ve, id

[50] oír
Present: oigo, oyes, oye, oímos, oís,
oyen
Preterite: oí, oíste, oyó, oímos, oísteis,
oyeron
Present subjunctive: oig|a, ~as, ~a,
~amos, ~áis, ~an

Imperfect subjunctive: oy|era, ～**eras,**
～**era,** ～**éramos,** ～**erais,** ～**eran**
oy|ese, ～**eses,** ～**ese,** ～**ésemos,**
～**eseis,** ～**esen**
Present participle: oyendo
Past participle: oído
Imperative: oye, oíd

[51] reír
Present: río, ríes, ríe, reímos, reís,
ríen
Preterite: reí, reíste, rió, reímos,
reísteis, rieron
Present subjunctive: ría, rías, ría,
riamos, riáis, rían
Present participle: riendo
Past participle: reído
Imperative: ríe, reíd

[52] salir
Present: salgo, sales, sale, salimos,
salís, salen
Future: saldr|é, ～**ás,** ～**á,** ～**emos,**
～**éis,** ～**án**

Present subjunctive: salg|a, ～**as,** ～**a,**
～**amos,** ～**áis,** ～**an**
Conditional: saldr|ía, ～**ías,** ～**ía,**
～**íamos,** ～**íais,** ～**ían**
Imperative: sal, salid

[53] venir
Present: vengo, vienes, viene,
venimos, venís, vienen
Future: vendr|é, ～**ás,** ～**á,** ～**emos,**
～**éis,** ～**án**
Preterite: vin|e, ～**iste,** ～**o,** ～**imos,**
～**isteis,** ～**ieron**
Present subjunctive: veng|a, ～**as,** ～**a,**
～**amos,** ～**áis,** ～**an**
Imperfect subjunctive: vin|iera,
～**ieras,** ～**iera,** ～**iéramos,**
～**ierais,** ～**ieran**
vin|iese, ～**ieses,** ～**iese,**
～**iésemos,** ～**ieseis,** ～**iesen**
Conditional: vendr|ía, ～**ías,** ～**ía,**
～**íamos,** ～**íais,** ～**ían**
Present participle: viniendo
Imperative: ven, venid

Verbos Irregulares Ingleses

Infinitivo	Pretérito	Participio pasado
arise	arose	arisen
awake	awoke	awoken
be	was	been
bear	bore	borne
beat	beat	beaten
become	became	become
befall	befell	befallen
beget	begot	begotten
begin	began	begun
behold	beheld	beheld
bend	bent	bent
beset	beset	beset
bet	bet, betted	bet, betted
bid	bade, bid	bidden, bid
bind	bound	bound
bite	bit	bitten
bleed	bled	bled
blow	blew	blown
break	broke	broken
breed	bred	bred
bring	brought	brought
broadcast	broadcast(ed)	broadcast
build	built	built
burn	burnt, burned	burnt, burned
burst	burst	burst
buy	bought	bought
cast	cast	cast
catch	caught	caught
choose	chose	chosen
cleave	clove, cleft, cleaved	cloven, cleft, cleaved
cling	clung	clung
clothe	clothed, clad	clothed, clad
come	came	come
cost	cost	cost
creep	crept	crept
crow	crowed, crew	crowed
cut	cut	cut
deal	dealt	dealt
dig	dug	dug
do	did	done
draw	drew	drawn
dream	dreamt, dreamed	dreamt, dreamed
drink	drank	drunk
drive	drove	driven
dwell	dwelt	dwelt
eat	ate	eaten
fall	fell	fallen
feed	fed	fed
feel	felt	felt
fight	fought	fought
find	found	found

Infinitivo	*Pretérito*	*Participio pasado*
flee	fled	fled
fling	flung	flung
fly	flew	flown
forbear	forbore	forborne
forbid	forbad(e)	forbidden
forecast	forecast(ed)	forecast(ed)
foresee	foresaw	foreseen
foretell	foretold	foretold
forget	forgot	forgotten
forgive	forgave	forgiven
forsake	forsook	forsaken
freeze	froze	frozen
gainsay	gainsaid	gainsaid
get	got	got, gotten
give	gave	given
go	went	gone
grind	ground	ground
grow	grew	grown
hang	hung, hanged	hung, hanged
have	had	had
hear	heard	heard
hew	hewed	hewn, hewed
hide	hid	hidden
hit	hit	hit
hold	held	held
hurt	hurt	hurt
inlay	inlaid	inlaid
keep	kept	kept
kneel	knelt	knelt
knit	knitted, knit	knitted, knit
know	knew	known
lay	laid	laid
lead	led	led
lean	leaned, leant	leaned, leant
leap	leaped, leapt	leaped, leapt
learn	learned, learnt	learned, learnt
leave	left	left
lend	lent	lent
let	let	let
lie	lay	lain
light	lit, lighted	lit, lighted
lose	lost	lost
make	made	made
mean	meant	meant
meet	met	met
mislay	mislaid	mislaid
mislead	misled	misled
misspell	misspelled, misspelt	misspelled, misspelt
mistake	mistook	mistaken
misunderstand	misunderstood	misunderstood
mow	mowed	mown
outbid	outbid	outbid
outdo	outdid	outdone
outgrow	outgrew	outgrown
overcome	overcame	overcome

Infinitivo	*Pretérito*	*Participio pasado*
overdo	overdid	overdone
overhang	overhung	overhung
overhear	overheard	overheard
override	overrode	overridden
overrun	overran	overrun
oversee	oversaw	overseen
overshoot	overshot	overshot
oversleep	overslept	overslept
overtake	overtook	overtaken
overthrow	overthrew	overthrown
partake	partook	partaken
pay	paid	paid
prove	proved	proved, proven
put	put	put
quit	quitted, quit	quitted, quit
read /ri:d/	read /red/	read /red/
rebuild	rebuilt	rebuilt
redo	redid	redone
rend	rent	rent
repay	repaid	repaid
rewrite	rewrote	rewritten
rid	rid	rid
ride	rode	ridden
ring	rang	rung
rise	rose	risen
run	ran	run
saw	sawed	sawn, sawed
say	said	said
see	saw	seen
seek	sought	sought
sell	sold	sold
send	sent	sent
set	set	set
sew	sewed	sewn, sewed
shake	shook	shaken
shear	sheared	shorn, sheared
shed	shed	shed
shine	shone	shone
shoe	shod	shod
shoot	shot	shot
show	showed	shown, showed
shrink	shrank	shrunk
shut	shut	shut
sing	sang	sung
sink	sank	sunk
sit	sat	sat
slay	slew	slain
sleep	slept	slept
slide	slid	slid
sling	slung	slung
slit	slit	slit
smell	smelled, smelt	smelled, smelt
smite	smote	smitten
sow	sowed	sown, sowed
speak	spoke	spoken

Infinitivo	*Pretérito*	*Participio pasado*
speed	speeded, sped	speeded, sped
spell	spelled, spelt	spelled, spelt
spend	spent	spent
spill	spilled, spilt	spilled, spilt
spin	spun	spun
spit	spat	spat
split	split	split
spoil	spoiled, spoilt	spoiled, spoilt
spread	spread	spread
spring	sprang	sprung
stand	stood	stood
steal	stole	stolen
stick	stuck	stuck
sting	stung	stung
stink	stank, stunk	stunk
strew	strewed	strewn, strewed
stride	strode	stridden
strike	struck	struck
string	strung	strung
strive	strove	striven
swear	swore	sworn
sweep	swept	swept
swell	swelled	swollen, swelled
swim	swam	swum
swing	swung	swung
take	took	taken
teach	taught	taught
tear	tore	torn
tell	told	told
think	thought	thought
thrive	thrived, throve	thrived, thriven
throw	threw	thrown
thrust	thrust	thrust
tread	trod	trodden, trod
unbend	unbent	unbent
undergo	underwent	undergone
understand	understood	understood
undertake	undertook	undertaken
undo	undid	undone
upset	upset	upset
wake	woke, waked	woken, waked
waylay	waylaid	waylaid
wear	wore	worn
weave	wove	woven
weep	wept	wept
win	won	won
wind	wound	wound
withdraw	withdrew	withdrawn
withhold	withheld	withheld
withstand	withstood	withstood
wring	wrung	wrung
write	wrote	written